谨以此书献给

新疆维吾尔自治区成立五十周年

新疆维吾尔自治区统计局·编

Compiled by Statistics Bureau of Xinjiang Uygur Autonomous Region

新疆统计年鉴

XINJIANG STATISTICAL YEARBOOK

2005

中国统计出版社

China Statistics Press

(京)新登字 041 号

图书在版编目(CIP)数据

新疆统计年鉴. 2005 / 新疆维吾尔自治区统计局编
——北京：中国统计出版社，2005.7
ISBN 7-5037-4658-0

Ⅰ.新…
Ⅱ.新…
Ⅲ.统计资料 - 新疆 -2005- 年鉴
Ⅳ.C832.45

中国版本图书馆 CIP 数据核字 (2005) 第 052382 号

新疆统计年鉴 -2005

作　　者 / 新疆维吾尔自治区统计局
责任编辑 / 蔡启新　阿米娜·依不拉音
E-mail　/ yearbook@stats.gov.cn
责任校对 / 仲　玲
装帧设计 / 黄永中
出版发行 / 中国统计出版社
通信地址 / 北京市西城区三里河月坛南街 75 号　中国统计出版社
邮　　编 / 100826
电　　话 / （010）63262295
正文印刷 / 新疆统计印刷厂
彩色印刷 / 新疆新华印刷三厂
经　　销 / 新疆统计信息咨询服务中心总发行
开　　本 / 890×1240 毫米　1/16 开本
字　　数 / 160 万字
印　　张 / 47.25 印张　　　彩插 6.25 印张
印　　数 / 1-3500 册
版　　别 / 2005 年 7 月第 1 版
版　　次 / 2005 年 7 月第 1 次印刷
书　　号 / ISBN 7-5037-4658-0 / F·2058
定　　价 / 258.00 元(含光盘)

《新疆统计年鉴－2005》编辑委员会

NAME LIST OF EDITORIAL BOARD

数字新疆

Digital Xinjiang

新疆生产总值及指数

Gross Production Value in Xinjiang And Indice

新疆生产总值（亿元）
Gross Production Value in Xinjiang (100 million yuan)

新疆生产总值指数（%）
Indice For Gross Production Value in Xinjiang (%)

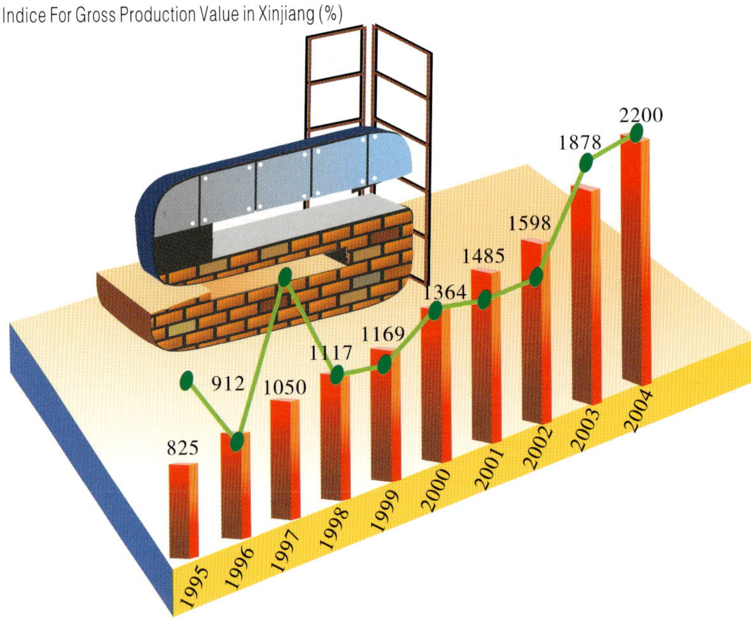

新疆人均生产总值（元）

Per Capita Gross Production Value in Xinjiang (yuan)

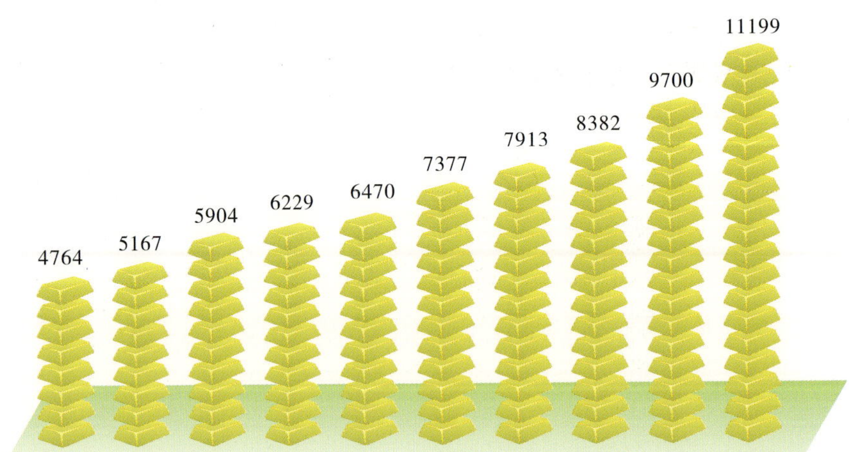

新疆生产总值构成（%）
Composition of Gross Production Value in Xinjiang(%)

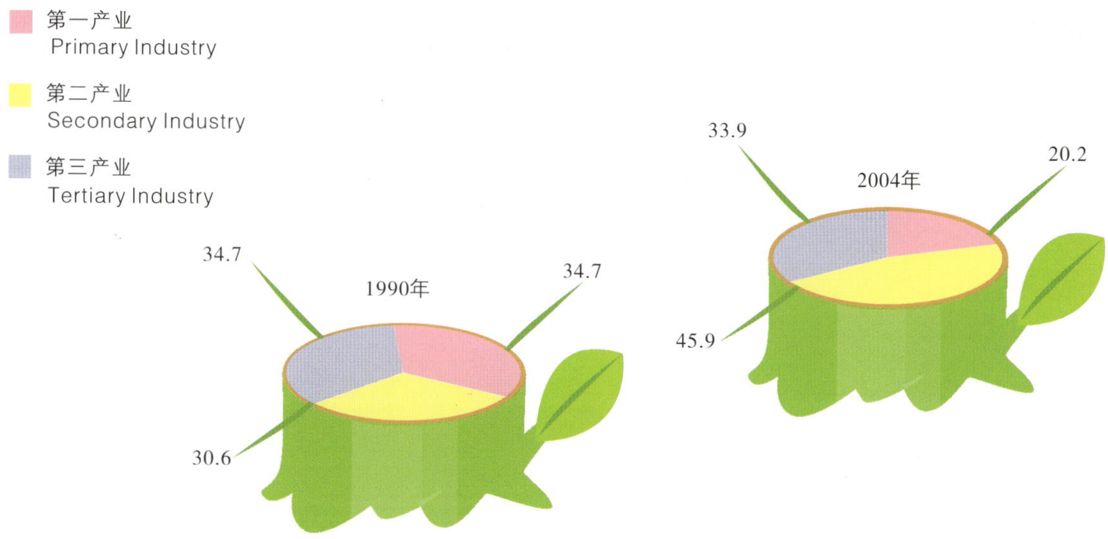

第三产业构成（%）
Composition of Tertiary Industry(%)

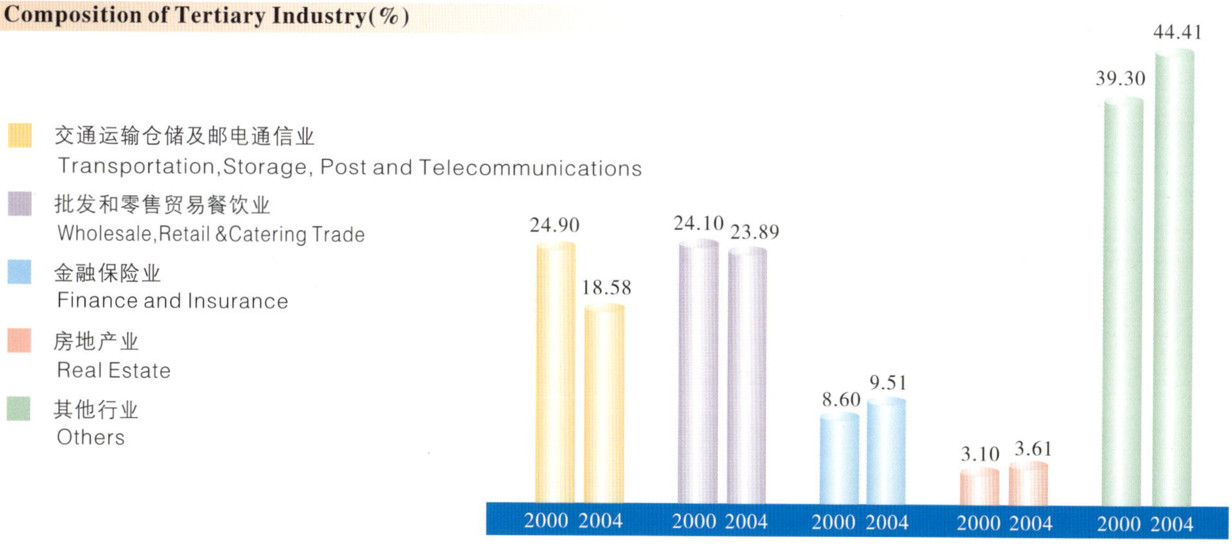

城镇人口与乡村人口（万人）
Urban and Rural Population (10 000 persons)

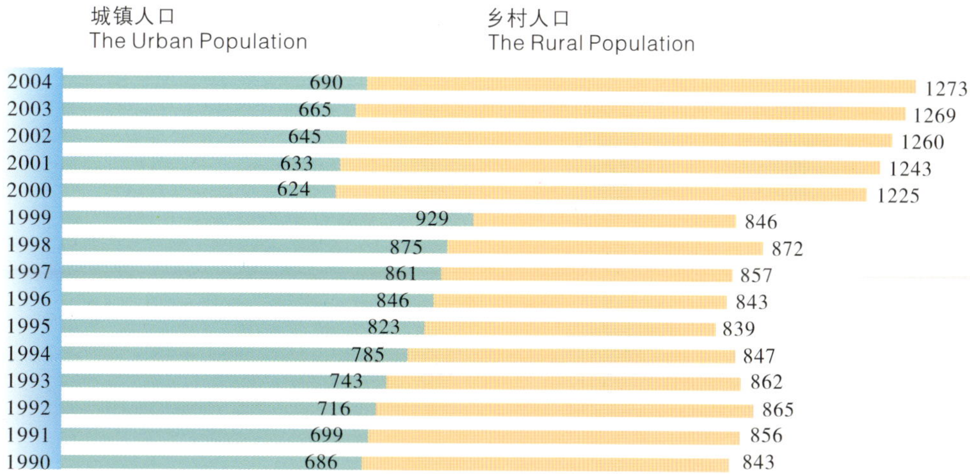

数字新疆

Digital Xinjiang

三次产业从业人员构成(%)

Composition of Employed Persons by Type of Industry(%)

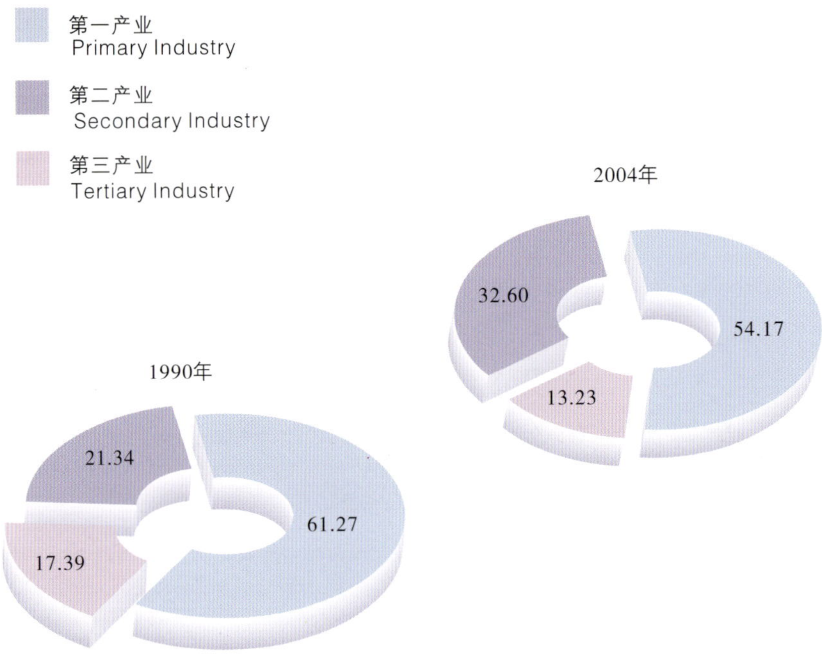

在岗职工工资总额(亿元)

Total Wages of Staff and Workers (100 million yuan)

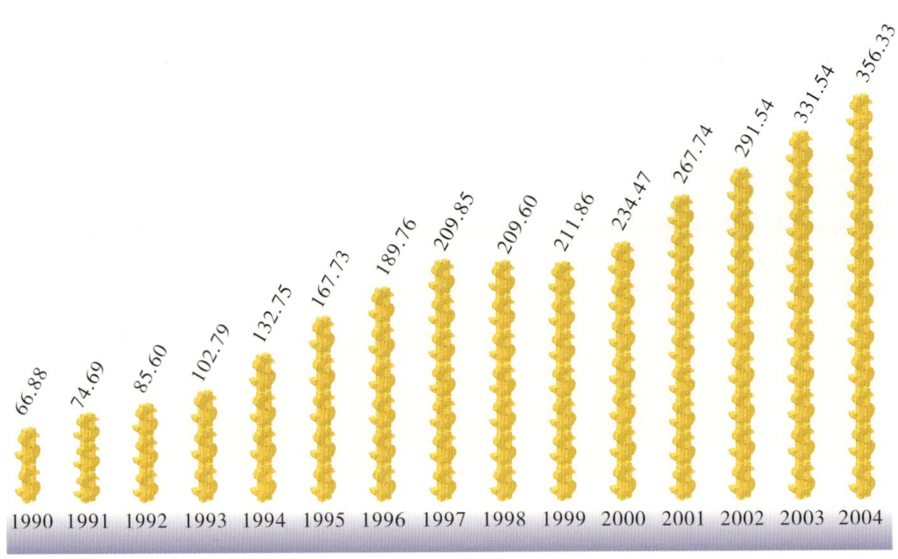

全社会固定资产投资（亿元）

Total Investment in Fixed Assets(100 million yuan)

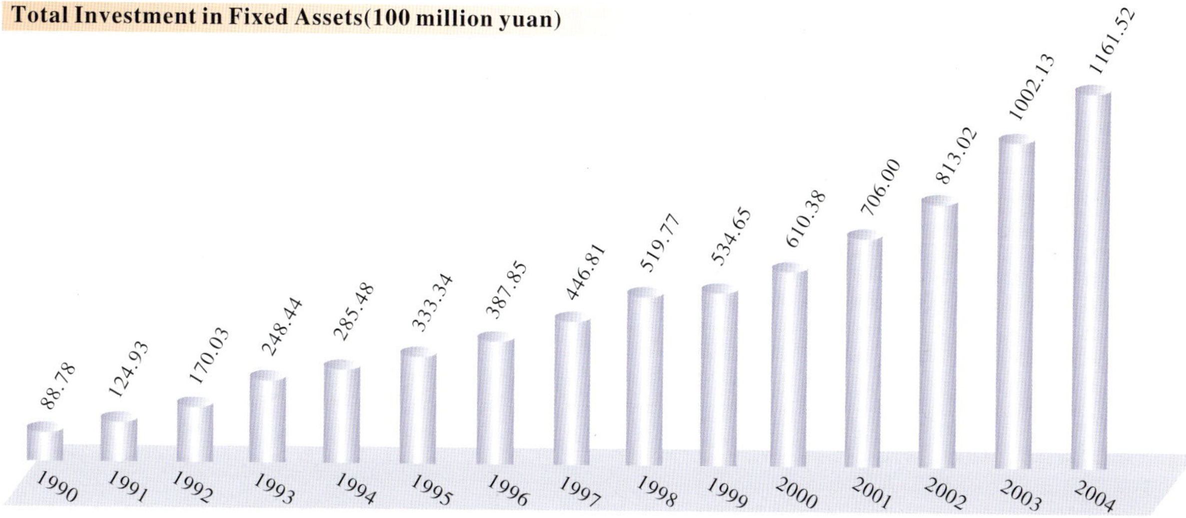

地方财政一般预算收入和支出（亿元）

Local Financial Government Intrabudgetary Ordinary Revenue and Expenditure(100 million yuan)

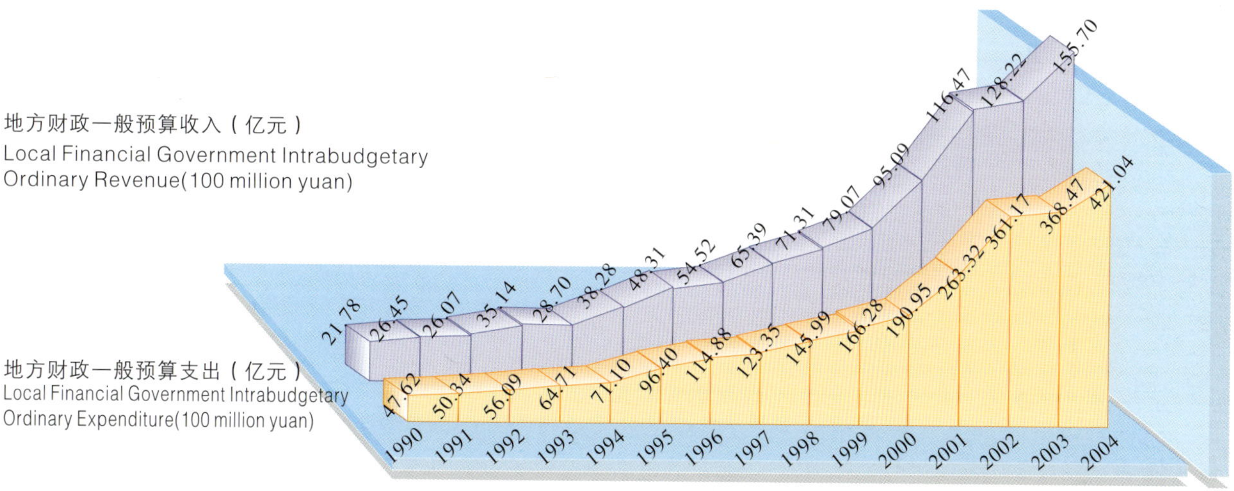

城乡居民储蓄存款年末余额(亿元)

Balance of Saving Deposits in Urban and Rural Areas (100 million yuan)

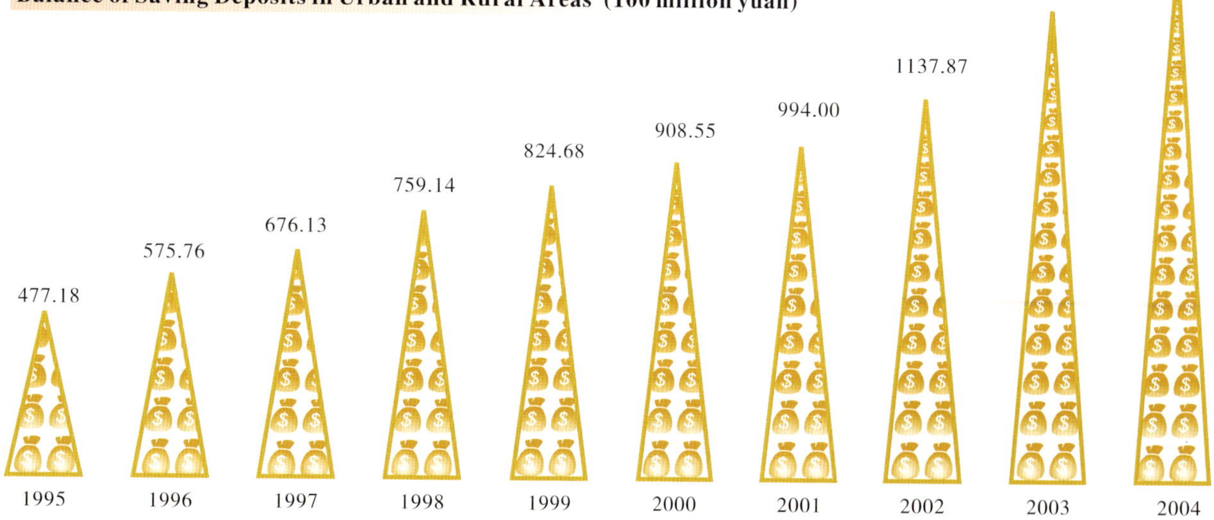

数字新疆

Digital Xinjiang

城镇居民家庭人均年可支配收入(元)

Per Capita Annual Disposable Income of Urban Households (yuan)

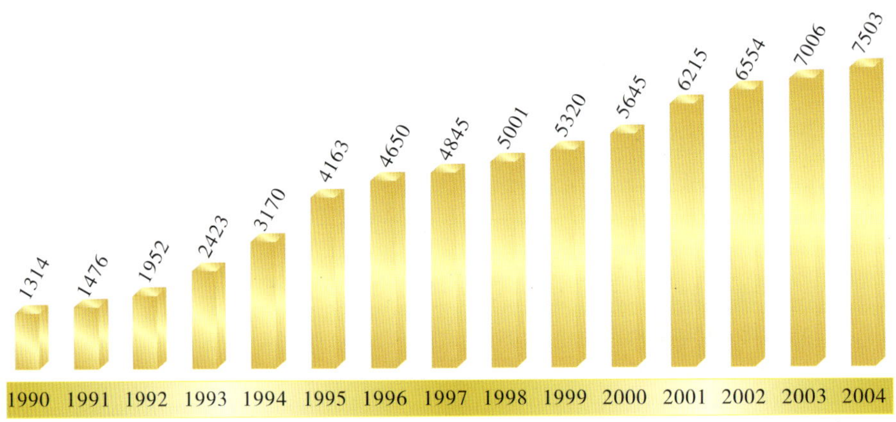

农村居民家庭人均纯收入(元)

Per Capita Annual Net Income of Rural Households (yuan)

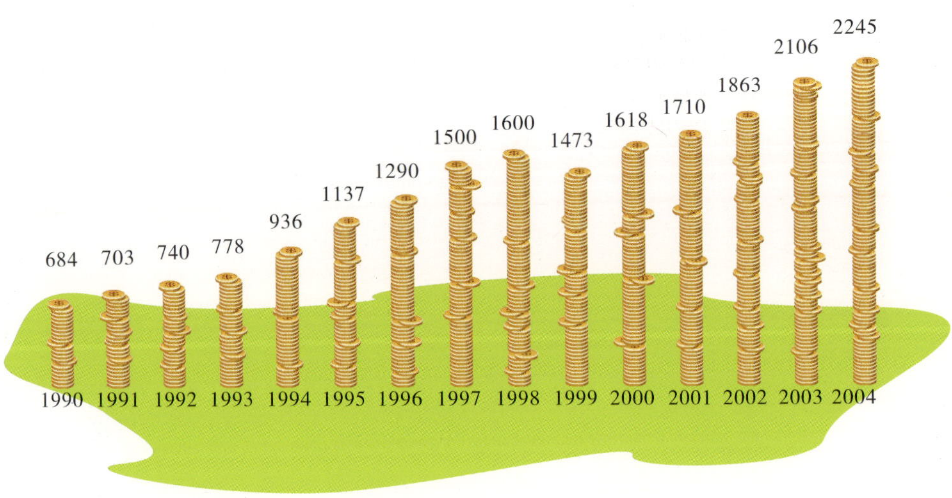

农林牧渔业总产值（亿元）

Gross Output Value of Farming, Forestry, Animal Husbandry and Fishery (100 million yuan)

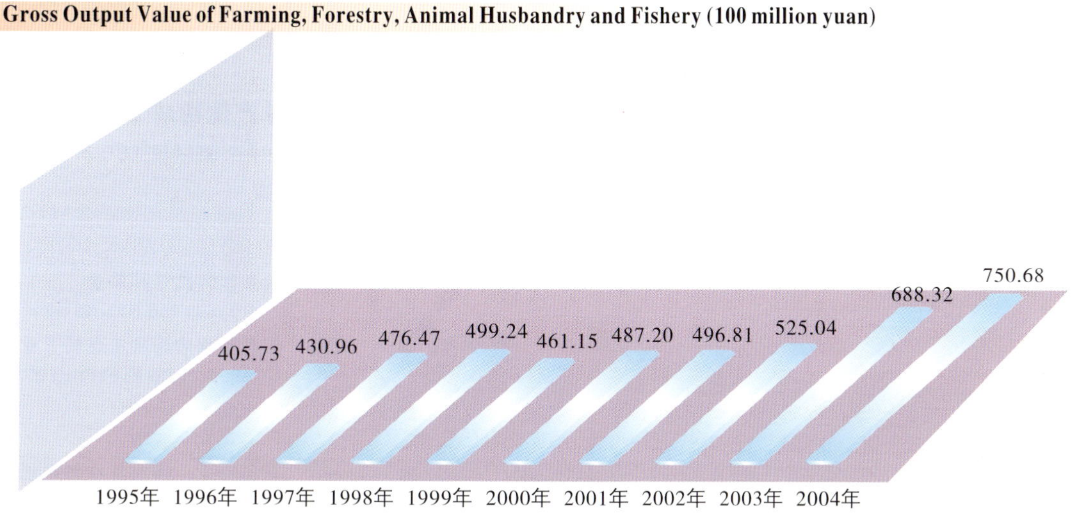

2004年农林牧渔业总产值构成（%）

Composition of Gross Output Value of Farming, Forestry, Animal Husbandry and Fishery(2004)(%)

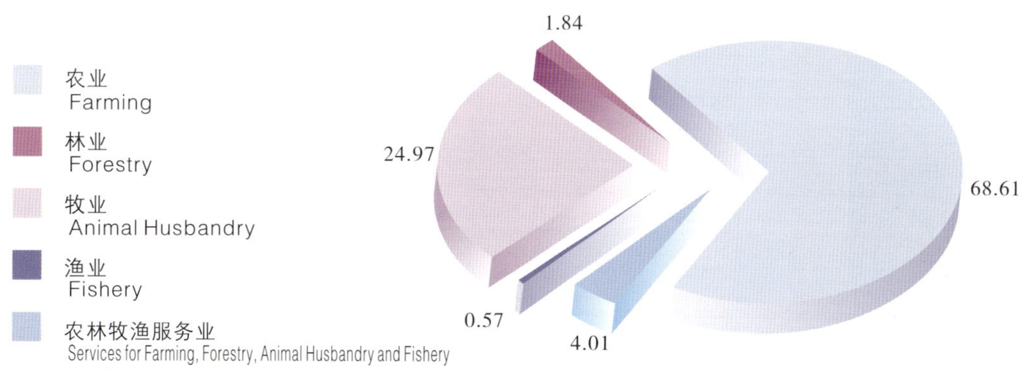

工业增加值及增长速度

Value Added of Industry and Growth Rate

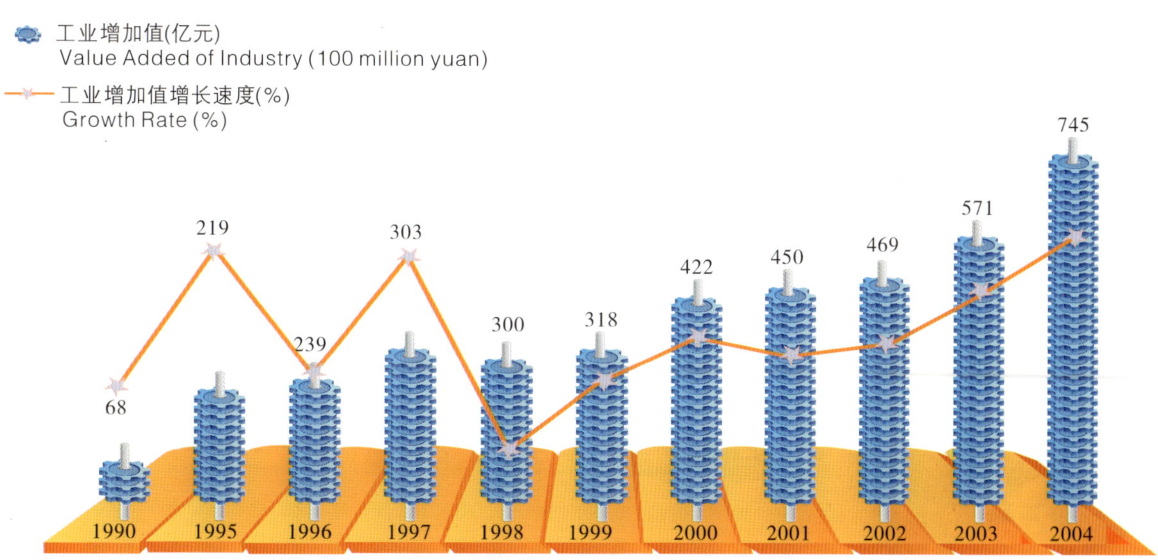

数字新疆

Digital Xinjiang

进出口总额（亿美元）

Total Imports and Exports (USD 100 million)

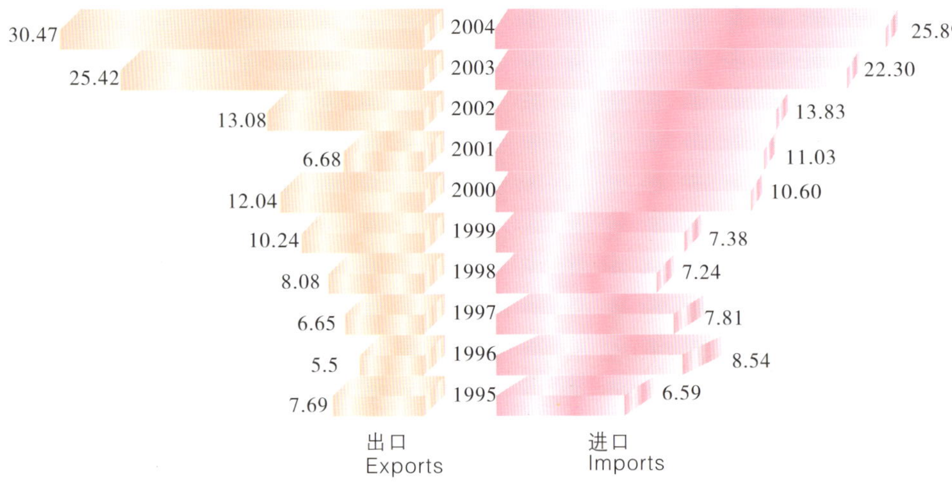

旅游外汇收入（万美元）

Foreign Exchange Earnings from Tourism (USD 10 000)

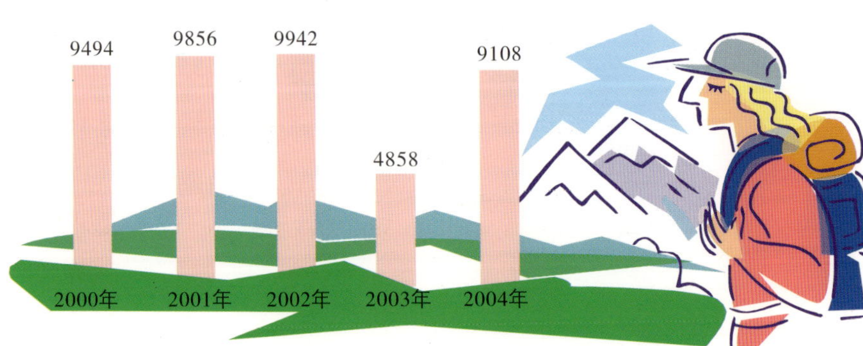

实际利用外商直接投资（万美元）

Amount of Foreign Direct Investment Actually Used (USD 10 000)

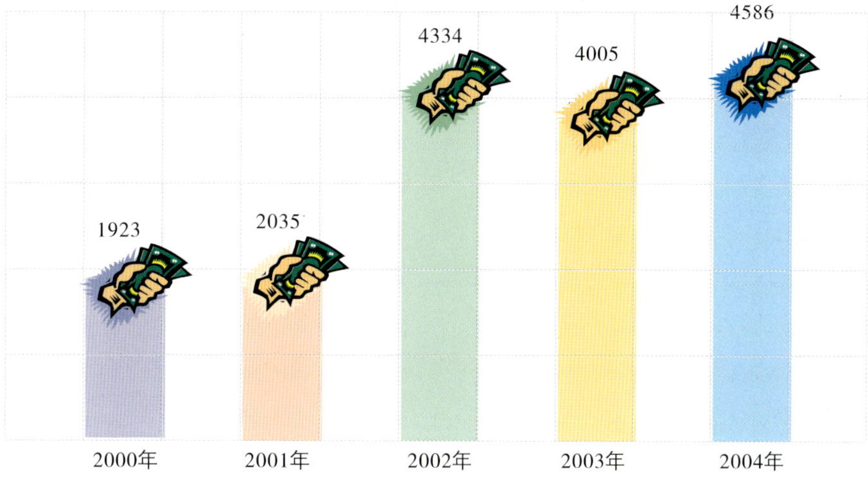

入境旅游人数（万人次）

Total Number of International Tourists Inbound (10 000 persons)

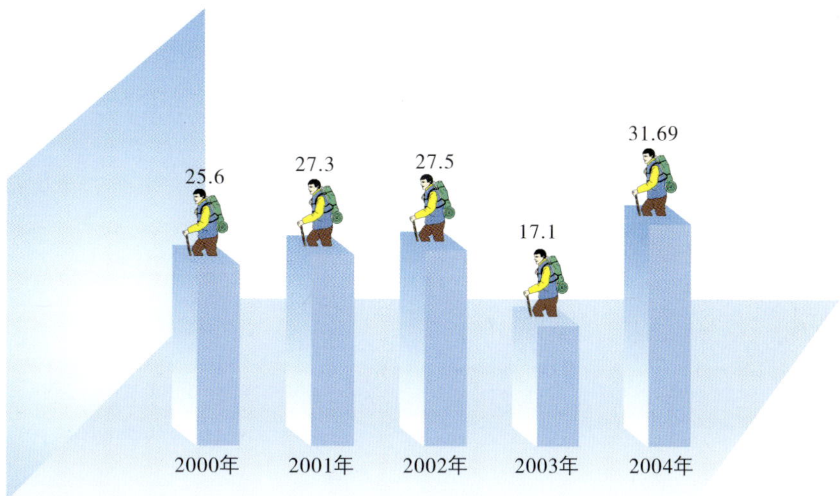

每万人拥有大学生数（人）

Number of University Students per 10 000 Persons (person)

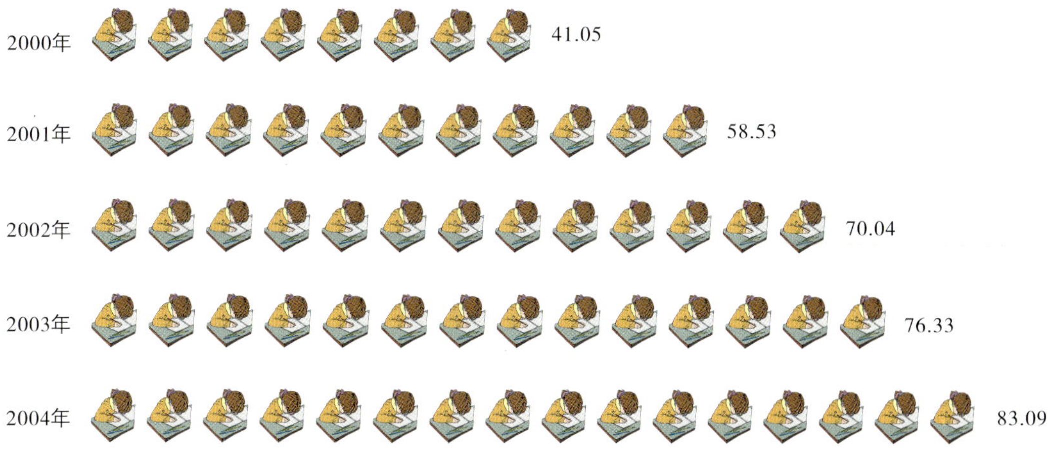

数字新疆

Digital Xinjiang

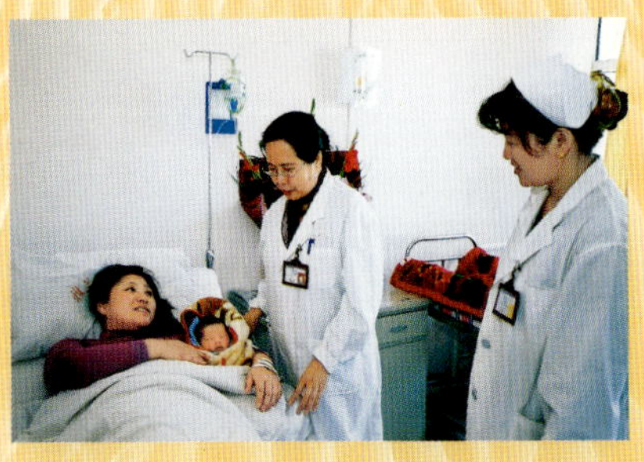

电视覆盖率（%）

Viewer Rate (%)

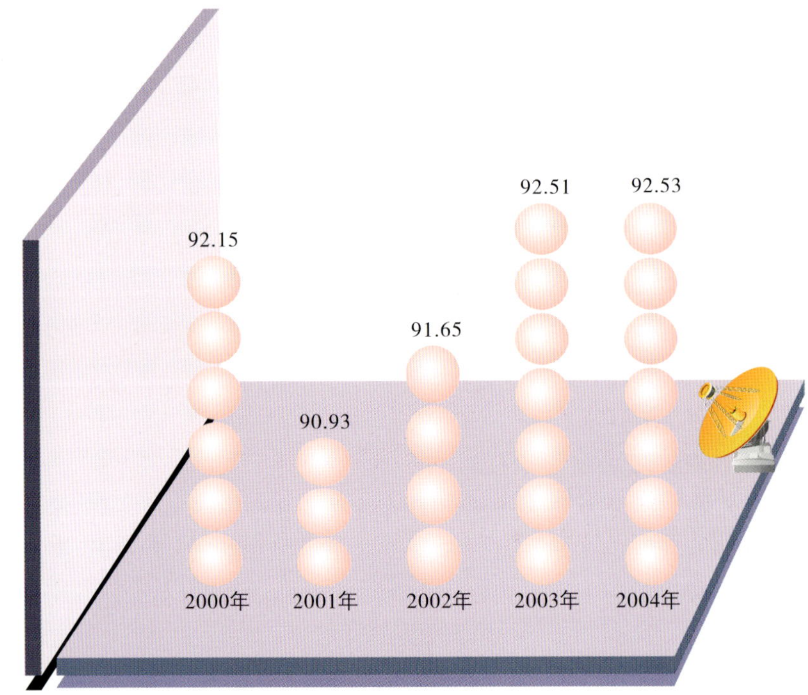

广播覆盖率（%）

Listener Rate (%)

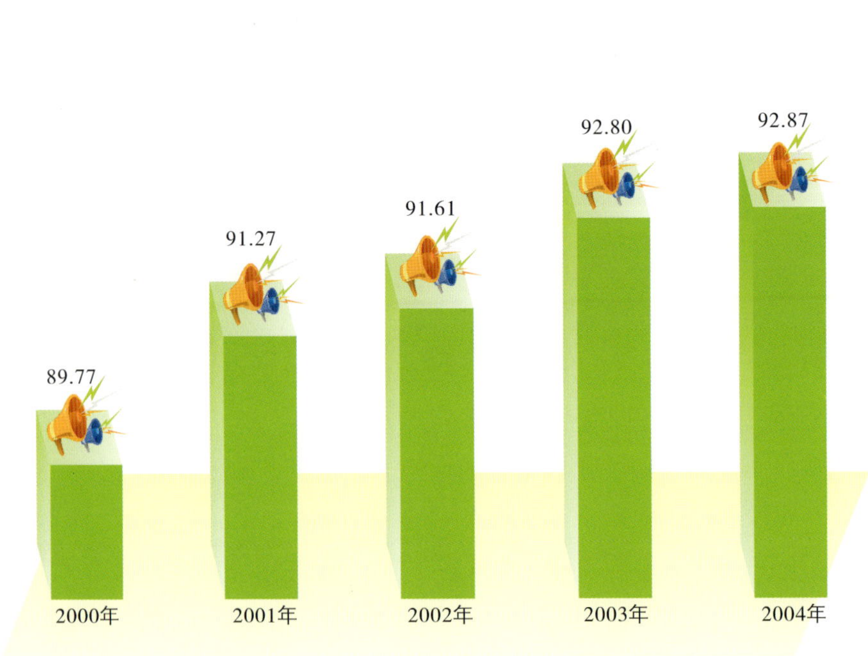

卫生技术人员数（万人）

Number of Medical Personnel (10 000 persons)

环境污染治理投资总额（亿元）

Total Investment in Environment pollution Harnessing Projects(100 million yuan)

环境污染治理投资总额占新疆生产总值比重（%）

Investment in Environment Pollution Harnessing Projects as Percent of GDP(%)

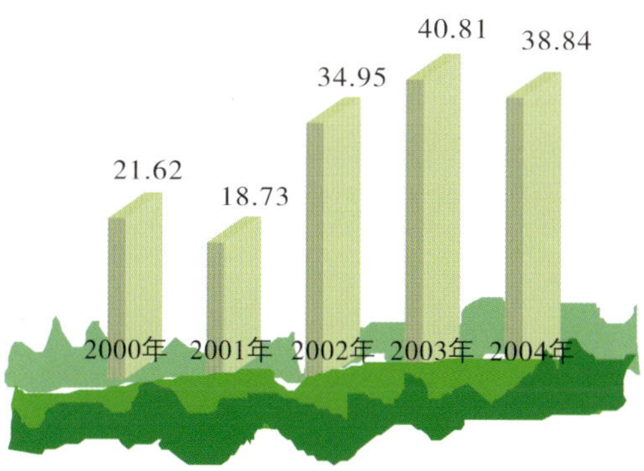

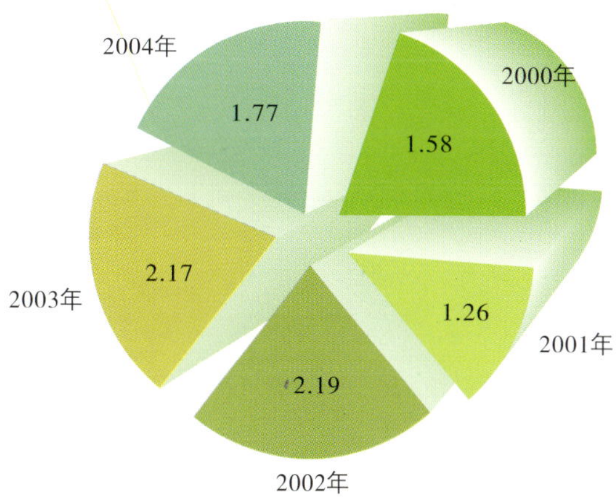

城市人均公共绿地面积(平方米)

Per Capita Public Green Areas (sq.m)

《新疆统计年鉴——2005》特邀编委

（排名不分先后）

自治区劳动和社会保障厅　艾拉提·艾山
自治区审计厅　朱登云
自治区国土资源厅　哈尼巴提·沙布开
自治区司法厅　哈斯木·马木提
自治区卫生厅　买买提明·牙生
自治区供销合作社联合社　马德
自治区高级人民法院　王浪涛
中国人民武装警察部队新疆总队　潘昌杰
自治区公路管理局　甫拉提·伊敏诺夫
自治区通信管理局　黄文玉
自治区粮食局　阿不都克里木·阿西木
自治区旅游局　乃依木·牙森
自治区邮政局　阿不来提·艾吾拉
自治区妇女联合会　热孜万·艾拜
自治区残疾人联合会　刘林亭
自治区红十字会　阿不都热衣木·阿不都拉
自治区文学艺术界联合会　刘宾
自治区党校（新疆行政学院）　牟振江
自治区机械电子行业管理办公室　张启曾
自治区建筑材料行业管理办公室　吕志坚
新疆储备物资管理局　罗歆京
中国民航新疆管理局空中交通管理局　曹琼
自治区监狱管理局　王爱国　张爱国
自治区道路运输管理局　艾尔肯·阿不都热衣木
自治区招生委员会办公室　刘廷胜
乌鲁木齐邮区中心局　肖建新
克孜勒苏柯尔克孜自治州　买买提艾山·托乎达力
巴音郭楞蒙古自治州　巴代
博乐市　巴图
阿拉尔市　王平海
图木舒克市　刘德峰
新疆生产建设兵团农五师　张永乐
新疆生产建设兵团农十师　何建明

新疆生产建设兵团农十四师　何玮
伊宁边境经济合作区管委会　吴奉军
新疆乌鲁木齐矿业(集团)有限责任公司　姚伟
新疆机场(集团)有限责任公司　段子新
新疆八一钢铁股份有限公司　沈东新
美克投资集团有限公司　冯东明
中国石油塔里木油田公司　孙龙德
中国石化西部新区勘探指挥部　李丕龙
新疆金纺纺织股份有限公司　王毅民
新疆天宏纸业股份有限公司　王世超
新疆送变电工程公司　王修江
中国移动新疆分公司　白志刚
中国联通新疆分公司　王金森
自治区房地产协会　藏小军　陈代元
新疆铁路房地产开发总公司　崔鹏林
新疆金谷房地产开发有限公司　马英武
新疆金成房地产开发有限公司　卢连平
新疆金元房地产开发有限公司　朱留根
新疆徕远房地产开发有限公司　张全勇
阿克苏新农房地产有限责任公司　涂昭荣
新疆煤田地质局综合地质勘查队　敬益武
中国华融资产管理公司乌鲁木齐办事处　袁肇绩
乌鲁木齐市公共交通总公司　陆建春
自治区图书馆　张君超
新疆科学技术出版社　王跃平
新疆科技政策研究所　刘理才
伊犁师范学院　赵嘉麒
乌鲁木齐职业大学　陆计明
和田师范专科学校　阿布来提·库尔班
新疆大学旅游学院职业培训中心　海米提·依米提
喀什师范学校　海仁沙·瓦依提
中共乌鲁木齐市水磨沟区委党校　沈智敏

编者说明

一、《新疆统计年鉴—2005》(中英文对照)，是新疆维吾尔自治区统计局以中英文对照形式全面反映新疆经济和社会发展情况的资料性年刊。

这部《年鉴》的出版将为各级领导干部了解新疆区情、掌握新疆经济运行情况、宏观指导经济提供详细、丰富的资料。

二、全书内容分为：特载（新疆维吾尔自治区 2004 年国民经济和社会发展统计公报）；行政区划和自然资源；综合；国民经济核算；人口、就业人员和职工工资；固定资产投资；财政、金融、保险；物价指数；人民生活；城市概况；环境保护；农业； 工业；建筑业；运输和邮电；批发零售贸易和餐饮业；能源生产和消费；对外经济贸易和旅游；教育、科技和文化；体育、卫生及其他；企业集团和企业景气指数；各地、州、市主要经济指标排序；附录（各省、市、区主要经济指标排序）等，各篇末均附有《主要统计指标解释》。

三、资料中所使用的计算单位均采用国家法定计量单位。

四、本《年鉴》总量指标计算所采用的价格均为现行价格。

五、本《年鉴》伊犁哈萨克自治州的数据包括伊犁州直属县（市）、塔城地区和阿勒泰地区。

六、本《年鉴》人口数据中全区总人口为人口变动情况抽样调查数据，分地区人口为公安年报数据。

七、本《年鉴》使用符号说明：

“#”表示其中项；

“...”表示不足小数位的数据；

“空”表示没有或未掌握该指标数据。

八、本《年鉴》在编辑翻译过程中得到自治区内外许多单位和同志们的大力支持，在此深表谢意。由于我们水平有限，加之时间仓促，错误和不足之处不少，敬请各级领导、各界人士和统计战线的同仁不吝批评指正。

Editor's Explanatory Notes

Ⅰ. Xinjiang Statistical Yearbook-2005 (in both Chinese and English) is the annual data of comprehensive information on Xinjiang's economy and social development in both Chinese and English by Statistical Bureau of Xinjiang Uygur Autonomous Region. The publication of the yearbook will provide the leading officials and heads at all levels with detailed and varied information about Xinjiang's situation and Xinjiang's economic operation as well as macro -instruction on economy.

Ⅱ. The yearbook comprises such sections as: Special Article (Statistical Communique on National Economy and Social Development of Xinjiang Uygur Autonomous Region in the year 2004); divisions of administrative areas and natural resoueces; general survey; calculation of nationl economy, population, employment and staff wages; investment in fixed assets;government finance,banking and insurance; price indices; people's livelihood; general survey of cities; environment protections;agriculture;industry; construction; transportation, postal and telecommunication services;wholesale and retail trade and catering trade; production and consumption of energy;foreign trade and economic cooperation and tourism;education,science and technology, culture;sports,public health and others; enterprises group and enterprises climate indices;ranking of main economic indicators by regions, prefectures and cities in Xinjiang; addenda (ranking of main economic indicators by province, munipality and autonomous region),etc.Each section is equipped with Explanatory Notes of Main Statistical Indicators at the end.

Ⅲ. The national legal metering units are adopted as units of computation in the yearbook.

Ⅳ. The computation of all the indicators in the *Yearbook* is equipped with current prices.

Ⅴ. The data about Ili Kazak Autonomous Prefecture in the present Xinjiang Statistical Yearbook covers counties (cities) direct under Ili Prefecture, Tacheng Prefecture and Altay Prefecture.

VI. The data for the total population of Xinjiang is based on the data of sampled survey in population variation and the population by prefectures is based on data from the annual report of the public security.

VII. Description of signs or symbols in the yearbook:

"# "stands for interim item; "..." for data with insufficient decimal place; "blank" for absence of data indicators or ignorance of them.

Ⅷ. In the course of compilation and translation, the yearbook has received great support from many units and comrades in and out of Xinjiang, we acknowledge their help to the book. Mistakes and faults are inevitable to take place for inadequate proficiency and limited time. Leaders, personnel from all walks of life and colleagues from statistical sector are welcome to make their critical comments and suggestions.

目　录 CONTENTS

第 一 篇　行政区划和自然资源
CHAPTER 1 DIVISIONS OF ADMINISTRATIVE AREAS AND NATURAL RESOURCES

第 二 篇　综　合
CHAPTER 2 GENERAL SURVEY

第 三 篇 国民经济核算

CHAPTER 3 NATIONAL ACCOUNTS

第 四 篇 人口、就业人员和职工工资

CHAPTER 4 POPULATION, EMPLOYMENT AND WAGES

目　录

第 五 篇 固定资产投资

CHAPTER 5 INVESTMENT IN FIXED ASSETS

第 六 篇　财政、金融、保险

CHAPTER 6 GOVERNMENT FINANCE, BANKING AND INSURANCE

第 七 篇　物价指数

CHAPTER 7 PRICE INDICES

第 八 篇 人民生活

CHAPTER 8 PEOPLE'S LIVELIHOOD

第九篇 城市概况

CHAPTER 9 GENERAL SURVEY OF CITIES

第 十 篇 环境保护

CHAPTER 10 ENVIORNMENT PROTECTIONS

第十一篇 农 业

CHAPTER 11 AGRICULTURE

第十二篇 工 业

CHAPTER 12 INDUSTRY

第 十三 篇 建筑业

CHAPTER 13 CONSTRUCTION

第十四篇 运输和邮电

CHAPTER 14 TRANSPORTATION, POSTAL AND TELECOMMUNICATIONS SERVICES

第十五篇 批发零售贸易和餐饮业

CHAPTER 15 WHOLESALE AND RETAIL TRADE AND CATERING TRADE

第 十六 篇 能源生产和消费

CHAPTER 16 PRODUCTION AND CONSUMPTION OF ENERGY

第 十七 篇 对外经济贸易和旅游

CHAPTER 17 FOREIGN TRADE AND ECONOMIC COOPERATION AND TOURISM

第十八篇　教育、科技和文化

CHAPTER 18 EDUCATION, SCIENCE AND CULTURE

第十九篇 体育、卫生及其他

CHAPTER 19 SPORTS, PUBLIC HEALTH AND OTHERS

第 二十 篇 企业集团及企业景气指数

CHAPTER 20 ENTERPRISES GROUP AND ENTERPRISES CLIMATE INDEX

第 二十一 篇　各地州市主要经济指标排序

CHAPTER 21 RANKING OF MAIN ECONOMIC INDICATORS BY REGION OF XINJIANG

附录：　各省市区主要经济指标排序

APPENDIX: RANKING OF MAIN ECONOMIC INDICATORS BY REGION

特　　载

SPECIAL ARTICLE

新疆维吾尔自治区
2004年国民经济和社会发展
统 计 公 报

2004年在自治区党委、人民政府的正确领导下，全区各族人民坚持以邓小平理论和“三个代表”重要思想为指导，深入贯彻党的十六大和十六届三中、四中全会精神，全面落实科学发展观，认真贯彻中央宏观调控的一系列政策和措施，开拓创新，扎实工作，国民经济保持较快发展，各项社会事业全面进步，人民生活水平稳步提高。

一、综　合

初步核算，新疆生产总值2200.15亿元，比上年增长11.1%。分三次产业看，第一产业增加值444.70亿元，增长5.1%；第二产业增加值1010.07亿元，增长14.3%，其中，工业增加值745亿元，增长14.5%，建筑业增加值265.07亿元，增长13.9%；第三产业增加值745.38亿元，增长10.4%。新疆人均生产总值11199元，增长9.5%。三次产业比例由上年的22.0:42.4:35.6调整为20.2:45.9:33.9。

2004年，企业家信心指数在一季度即达到125.6，创历史最好水平，随后的三个季度，分别达到124.5、125.2和123.4；企业景气指数继2003年之后又上一个新台阶，全年四个季度分别为115.7、121.1、126.9和120.0。

全年居民消费价格总水平上涨2.7%（见表1），其中服务业价格上涨1.0%。商品零售价格总水平上涨0.7%，工业品出厂价格上涨16.4%，原材料、燃料、动力购进价格上涨18.2%。固定资产投资价格上涨4.5%。农业生产资料价格上涨7.3%。农产品价格指数上涨0.8%。

表 1：2004 年居民消费价格比上年上涨情况

指　　标	增减（%）
居民消费价格总水平	2.7
其中：城市	2.1
农村	4.5
食　品	5.8
其中：粮食	16.3
肉禽	8.8
蛋类	14.1
水产品	15.5
烟　酒	0.3
衣　着	-0.6
家庭设备用品及服务	-1.6
医疗保健及个人用品	1.8
交通和通信	-0.6
娱乐教育文化用品及服务	-1.4
居　住	8.3
其中：水、电、燃料	13.2
租房	11.5
建房及装饰材料	7.5

全区年末就业人员744..49万人，比上年增长3.2%。其中城镇就业人员349.43万人，增长3.1%。据劳动和社会保障部门统计，全年实现就业再就业36.96万人，其中国有单位安置2.55万人，集体单位安置2.90万人，私营、个体和三资企业安置16.23万人，其他单位安置15.28万人。有13.27万名下岗失业人员实现了再就业。年末国有企业下岗职工1.88万

人。年末城镇登记失业人数10.87万人，城镇登记失业率为 3.8%。

二、农　业

全区完成农林牧渔业总产值750.68亿元，比上年增长6.4%。其中，农业产值515.00亿元，增长4.5%；林业产值13.82亿元，增长0.7%；畜牧业产值187.47亿元，增长12.0%；渔业产值4.30亿元，增长8.2%。粮食播种面积137.86万公顷，增长5.5%；棉花播种面积112.76万公顷，增长8.7%；油料播种面积21.55万公顷，下降4.8%；甜菜播种面积5.99万公顷，下降11.0%；蔬菜播种面积18.56万公顷，增长13.3%；水果面积(含果用瓜)45.82万公顷，增长 12.5%。

全年粮食产量828.53万吨，增长3.4%；棉花产量175.25万吨，增长9.5%；油料产量44.54万吨，下降11.2%；甜菜产量344.21万吨，下降9.8%；蔬菜、水果在扩大优质品种的基础上平稳增长（见表2）。

表 2：2004 年主要农产品产量

单位：万吨

产品名称	绝 对 数	比上年增长%
粮　食	828.53	3.4
#夏　粮	354.00	1.1
秋　粮	474.53	5.1
油　料	44.54	-11.2
#油菜籽	12.16	-21.2
棉　花	175.25	9.5
甜　菜	344.21	-9.8
水　果	450.28	10.4
蔬　菜	919.13	20.8

年末牲畜存栏头数为5206.37万头(只)，比上年增长3.6%；牲畜出栏3437.59万头(只)，增长7.4%；肉类总产量128.13万吨，增长11.4%；绵羊毛产量8.49万吨，增长8.3%；牛奶产量133.32万吨，增长18.0%；禽蛋产量24.99万吨，增长5.8%。水产品产量7.33万吨，增长8.9%。

年末农业机械总动力1046.47万千瓦，比上年增长7.6%。拥有大中型拖拉机9.29万台，增长21.8%；小型拖拉机34.06万台，增长9.7%。化肥施用量（折纯）99.17万吨，增长9.3%。农村用电量32.63亿千瓦小时，增长8.9%。全年新增农田有效灌溉面积10.08万公顷，新增节水灌溉面积13.71万公顷。

三、工业和建筑业

全年完成工业增加值 745.00亿元，比上年增长14.5 %。其中规模以上工业企业增加值669.00亿元，增长14.4%。在规模以上工业增加值中，重工业增加值607.08亿元，占90.7%；轻工业61.92亿元，占9.3%。国有及国有控股工业企业增加值585.08亿元，占87.5%。

主要能源、原材料产品产量增长较快，原油加工量增长 7.6%，原煤增长 7.7%，天然气增长 14.3%，发电量增长 13.5%，粗钢增长 22.1%，钢材增长 17.4%（主要工业产品产量见表 3）。

规模以上工业企业产品出口交货值 31.65 亿元，比上年增长 1.6 %。工业产品销售率为 97.8%，下降 0.4 个百分点。其中，轻工业产品销售率 91.1%，下降 4.6 个百分点；重工业产品销售率 99.0%，上升 0.2 个百分点。

规模以上工业企业经济效益综合指数为 249.1，比上年上升 76.4 点。其中，总资产贡献率上升 3.8 个百分点，资产保值增值率下降 0.9 个百分点，资产负债率下降 0.3 个百分点，流动资产周转率加快 0.4 次，成本费用利润率上升 2.5 个百分点，全员劳动生产率提高 9.3 万元/人·年。工业企业实现利润 208.49 亿元，增长 49.2%。

表 3：2004 年主要工业产品产量

产品名称	单　位	绝对数	比上年增长%
原　煤	万吨	3749.4	7.7
原　油	万吨	2253.02	5.2
原油加工量	万吨	1220.18	7.6
天然气	亿立方米	57.48	14.3
发电量	亿千瓦小时	266.30	13.5
粗　钢	万吨	249.13	22.1
钢　材	万吨	238.52	17.4
水　泥	万吨	1213	7.4
纱	万吨	29.14	-0.5
机制糖	万吨	37.26	-18.0
化肥(折 100%)	万吨	86.98	-1.8
变压器	万千伏安	1135.75	-3.2
乙　烯	万吨	25.37	7.5
机制纸及纸板	万吨	26.31	12.7
罐　头	万吨	66.41	39.9

全年资质等级以上建筑企业完成增加值 69.31 亿元，增长 3.1%。实现利税总额 17.43 亿元，增长 2.7%。房屋建筑施工面积 2812.30 万平方米，增长 3.4%，房屋建筑竣工面积 1483.35 万平方米，增长 2.2%。

四、固定资产投资

全社会固定资产投资1161.52亿元，比上年增长15.9%。其中：基本建设投资759.24亿元，增长17.2%；更新改造投资138.65亿元，增长8.8%；房地产开发投资112.56亿元，增长9.8%；其他投资151.07亿元，增长21.3%。按隶属关系分，地方项目投资746.69亿元，增长18.7%；中央项目投资414.83亿元，增长11.2%。按城乡分，城镇投资1060.80亿元，增长15.3%；农村投资100.72亿元，增长24.7%。其中，农户投资54.38亿元，增长13.1%，非农户投资46.34亿元，增长41.7%。从资金来源看，自主投资能力不断增强。在总投资中，自筹资金667.11亿元，增长31.0%。

主要生产能力继续增加（见表4）：

表 4：2004 年固定资产投资新增主要生产能力

指　　标	单 位	绝对数
原煤开采	万吨／年	496
天然原油	万吨／年	110
石油加工	万吨／年	462
生铁	万吨／年	156
炼钢	万吨／年	183
钢材	万吨／年	122
水泥	万吨／年	178
棉纺锭	万锭	42
平板玻璃	万重量箱/年	293
发电机组装机容量	万千瓦	31
新建公路	公里	1423
改建公路	公里	5857
新建微波电路	路	240
程控交换机安装能力	万线/年	572

在投资中，第一产业投资127.01亿元，增长19.9%；第二产业投资442.15亿元，增长28.2%，其中，石油和天然气开采业增长23.0%，石油加工及炼焦业增长99.5%，纺织业增长48.7%，黑色金属冶炼及压延加工业增长2.2倍，有色金属冶炼及压延加工业增长20.2%；第三产业投资592.36亿元，增长7.4%，其中交通运输、仓储及邮政业增长30.4%。

重点项目建设得到加强。大中型建设项目完成投资264.57亿元，增长52.0%。新建、改建公路、石油加工、原煤开采等建设均有较快增长。

五、国内贸易

全年社会消费品零售总额563.65亿元，比上年增长14.5%。分城乡看，城市消费品零售额382.67亿元，增长16.5%；农村消费品零售额180.98亿元，增长8.6%。分行业看，餐饮业零售额78.82亿元，增长29.6%；批发零售贸易业零售额448.29亿元，增长12.4%；其他零售额36.54亿元，增长2.5%。

六、对外经济

全年进出口总额56.36亿美元，比上年增长18.2%。其中，出口总额30.47亿美元，增长19.9%；进口总额25.89亿美元，增长16.1%。在出口总额中，一般贸易5.02亿美元，下降29.3%；加工贸易2.66亿美元，增长36.8%；边境小额贸易22.38亿美元，增长39.6%。在进口总额中，一般贸易10.15亿美元，增长40.1%；加工贸易0.52亿美元，增长67.3%；边境小额贸易14.71亿美元，增长2.5%。全年机电产品出口3.77亿美元，增长1.6%；高新技术产品出口0.38亿美元，增长35.5%。

全年新签外商直接投资合同项目74个，增长13.8%，合同资金2.58亿美元，增长59.7%；实际利用外商直接投资0.46亿美元，增长14.5%；对外承包工程合同金额1.02亿美元，完成营业额0.86亿美元。

七、交通、邮电和旅游

2004年末，铁路营运里程2999公里；公路通车里程8.68万公里，比上年增长0.6%；民航通航里程11.18万公里。各种交通工具完成货物周转量947.24亿吨公里，增长13.2%。其中，铁路548.50亿吨公里，增长15.5%；公路 361亿吨公里，增长11.1%；民航 0.74 亿吨公里，增长15.6%；管道37亿吨公里，增长1.6%。完成旅客周转量 423.80亿人公里，增长23.9%。其中，铁路121.90亿人公里，增长14.9%；公路249亿人公里，增长27.7%；民航52.90亿人公里，增长29.3%。

全年完成邮电业务总量153.18亿元，比上年增长33.8%。其中，电信业务总量145.70亿元，增长35.8%；邮政业务总量7.48亿元，增长3.9%。年末固定电话用户516.70万户，普及率26.3%；移动电话用户489.70万户，普及率24.9%；互联网用户78.05万户，增长28.4%。年末本地电话局用交换机总容量447.0万门，增长2.5%。

全年接待国内游客 1241.58 万人次，增长 22.7 %；国内旅游收入108.96 亿元，增长 22.9%。接待境外游客31.69万人次，增长85.9%，其中港、澳、台同胞4.59万人次，增长122.7%；国际旅游外汇收入0.91亿美元，增长87.5%。

八、财政、金融和保险业

全年地方财政收入完成191.28亿元，比上年增长21.3 %，其中地方财政一般预算收入155.70亿元，增长21.4%；地方财政一般预算支出421.04亿元，增长14.3%。

年末金融机构各项存款余额2959.78亿元，比年初增加293.69亿元，其中，企业存款余额832.50亿元，增加50.25亿元；城乡居民储蓄存款余额1534.67亿元，增加162.85亿元。各项贷款余额2214.66亿元，比年初增加134.66亿元，其中，短期贷款增加95.08亿元；中长期贷款增加88.77亿元。

全区上市公司27家，总市值403.21亿元，总股本83.62亿股，累计募集资金107.43亿元。

全区保费收入68.13亿元，比上年增长9.6%；其中人身险保费收入48.09亿元，增长11.7%；财产险保费收入20.04亿元，增长4.8%。各项赔款和给付总额18.34亿元，其中人身险给付7.70亿元，增长8.4%；财产险赔款10.64亿元，增长2.8%。

九、教育和科学技术

全区普通高等学校28所，本专科招生5.32万人，比上年增长18.9%；在校学生16.82万人，增长11.2%，其中少数民族学生7.03万人，增长7.6%。研究生培养单位11个，招生2336人，增长40.4%；在校学生5120人，增长41.1%，其中少数民族学生498人，增长50.0%。普通中等专业学校78所，在校学生7.13万人，下降0.3%；职业高中及其他机构在校学生1.79万人，增长17.2%；初级职业中学及附设班在校学生4.36万人，增长45.1%。普通高中498所，招生13.83万人，增长9.6%；在校学生35.91万人，增长13.9%；普通初中在校学生115.88万人，增长2.2%；小学在校学生221.81万人，下降3.1%。

小学学龄儿童入学率97.8%，小学毕业生升学率95.3%；初中学龄儿童入学率86.3%，普通初中学生辍学率3.2%，初中毕业升入普通高中升学率41.1%。

成人高等本、专科在校学生8.46万人，比上年下降3.6%；成人中等专业学校在校学生0.71万人，下降12.3%。全年扫除青壮年文盲4.79万人。

2004年，全区安排科技攻关计划项目50项 ，比上年增长19.0%。共受理专利1492件，授权专利792件。签订技术合同1619项，增长6.8%；成交金额13.34亿元，增长10.8%。

十、文化、卫生和体育

全区共有艺术表演团体109个，文化馆、艺术馆108个，公共图书馆92个，博物馆25个，档案馆135个，已开放各类档案42.33万卷。广播电台6座，电视台10座，中短波广播发射台和转播台40座，一千瓦以上电视发射台和转播台64座。全区广播人口覆盖率92.9%，电视人口覆盖率92.5%。有线电视用户130.27万户。拍摄故事片1部，译制少数民族语故事片75部；拍摄电视剧5部，译制电视剧18部。出版各种报纸3.39亿份，其中少数民族文字占38.0%；各类杂志1450万册，其中少数民族文字占35.0%；图书8250万册，其中少数民族文字占40.0%。

全区共有卫生机构9087个，其中医院、卫生院1525个，妇幼保健机构85个；全区拥有病床7.81万张，其中医院、卫生院拥有床位7.40万张。卫生技术人员9.98万人。乡镇卫生院836个，卫生技术人员1.45万人，拥有床位1.28万张。

全区运动健儿在国际、洲际比赛中获冠军5个，获第二名3个，获第三名5个；在全国比赛中，获冠军15个，获亚军15个，第三名19个。有3人达到国际级运动健将，4人达到国家级运动健将，有1人平全国记录。

十一、资源与环境

据国土资源厅统计，全年投入国土资源调查和地质勘查的资金83.76亿元，其中：石油天然气勘查79.89亿元，国土资源调查和非油气矿产地质勘查3.87亿元。地质勘查工作的矿种有30多个，主要矿种为：煤、石油、天然气、铀、铁、铜、镍、铅、锌、金、银、红柱石、钾盐、菱镁矿、膨润土、地下水等。

新发现石油天然气区块3个，天然气田1处；新发现有进一步工作价值的矿产地10处，其中：铜矿2处，铅锌矿1处，钨矿2处，金矿3处，膨润土矿1处，地下水源地1处。在若羌县发现的白干湖钨锡矿，是目前我区预测钨资源量最大的一处钨矿产地。

新增查明矿产资源储量的矿种主要有：石油地质储量4.37亿吨，天然气地质储量563.98亿立方米，煤资源量49.80亿吨，铁矿石资源量894.00万吨，钒矿（五氧化二钒）资源量24.85万吨，铜金属资源量55.95万吨，铅金属资源量47.25万吨，锌金属资源量97.09万吨，金金属资源量22.34吨，银金属资源量312.36吨。

据环保部门统计，全年二氧化硫排放量控制在48.03万吨，比上年增长45.6%；烟尘排放量控制在25.91万吨，增长27.1%；工业粉尘排放量控制在16.77万吨，增长53.4%；工业固体废物排放量控制在102.8

万吨，增长16.6%；化学需氧量排放量控制在26.17万吨，增长14.4%。

在监测的16个城市建成区中，有4个城市空气质量达到二级标准；有5个城市达到三级标准。建成环境噪声达标区40个，达标面积315.20平方公里。建成烟尘控制区58个，面积达351.90平方公里。

在监测的20条主要河流的56个断面中，有40%为优良水质，50%受到轻度或中度污染，10%受到重度污染。与上年相比，有15%的河流水质有所好转，55%的河流水质无明显变化，30%的河流水质有所下降。

全区已建成各类自然保护区26个，其中国家级自然保护区7个。自然保护区总面积20.42万平方公里，占全区国土面积的12.3%；已批准国家级生态示范区8个，生态示范区总面积11.06万平方公里；国家级生态功能保护区试点1个。

十二、人　口

据2004年人口变动情况抽样调查资料推算：全区年末总人口1963.11万人，比上年增加29.16万人，增长1.5%。其中，城镇人口690.11万人，增长3.8%，城镇化率为35.15%；乡村人口1273万人，增长0.3%。男性人口1008.02万人，占51.3%；女性人口955.09万人，占48.7%。人口出生率为16.0‰，死亡率为5.1‰，人口自然增长率为10.9‰。

十三、人民生活和社会保障

2004年，全区城镇居民人均可支配收入7503元，扣除价格因素，实际增长4.9%；农村居民人均纯收入2245元，实际增长3.1%。年末城镇居民人均住房使用面积18.82平方米，增长5.1%；农村居民人均居住面积19.1平方米，增长2.6%。在岗职工平均货币工资14484元，实际增长7.1%。城镇居民恩格尔系数36.1%，比上年下降0.1个百分点；农村居民恩格尔系数45.2%，下降0.3个百分点。

据劳动和社会保障部门统计，全区有138.58万职工参加了失业保险，比上年增长2.6%；有173.76万人参加了基本养老保险，增长9.9%，其中离退休人员42.76万人，增长12.5%；有195.97万职工参加了基本医疗保险，增长11.3%。

据民政部门统计，各种城镇社区综合服务中心150个。城市居民得到最低生活保障救济人数58.84万人，国家抚恤、补助各类优抚对象3.58万人。全区有各类社会福利院496个，床位13438张，收养人数10356人。社会销售福利彩票6.44亿元，筹集社会福利资金2.25亿元，接受社会捐赠0.16亿元。

注：①新疆生产总值、各产业增加值及农林牧渔业总产值指标绝对数按现价计算，增长速度按可比价计算。

②规模以上工业是指国有及年产品销售收入500万元以上的非国有工业企业。

③企业家信心指数和企业景气指数大于100表示景气，小于100表示不景气。

④粮食产量中不包括薯类；水果产量中含果用瓜产量。

Statistical Communique on National Economic & Social Development of Xinjiang Uygur Autonomous Region for the Year 2004

In 2004, under the wise leadership of C.P.C Xinjiang Party Committee and the people's government, the people in different nationalities carefully implemented the important thought "Three Represents" and the spirit of the Sixteenth National Party Congress and the third, the fourth plenary sessions of the Sixteenth National Party Congress, as well as scientific development view and a series of policies and measures on macro-control issued by the central Party committee. In addition, they, blazing their own way and doing solid work, maintain quicker growth in national economy, realize all-round progress in all sectors of social life and steady improvement in the people's living standard.

I General Survey

According to the initial estimate, GDP in Xinjiang amounted to 2200.15 hundred million RMBY, 11. 1% of increase compared with that in the previous year. Judging by three industries, the added value for the first industry came to 444.70 hundred million RMBY, a rise of 5.1%; the added value for the second industry amounted to 1010.07 hundred million RMBY, a rise of 14.3%, of which that for industry was 745 hundred million RMBY, a rise of 14.5%; that for building sector was 265.07 hundred million RMBY, a rise of 13.9%. The added value of the tertiary industry was 745.38 hundred million RMBY, a rise of 10.4%. The Per-capital GDP in Xinjiang was 11,199 RMBY, a rise of 9.5%. The percentages taken up by three industrial sectors have been readjusted to 20.2, 45.9 and 33.9 from 22.0, 42,4 and 35.6 in the previous year.

Table 1: Rise of Residents' Consumption Price for 2004

Items	Increase and Decrease (%)
Overall level of residents' consumption price	2.7
Including: Urban	2.1
Rural	4.5
Foodstuff	5.8
Including: Grain	16.3
Meat	8.8
Egg	14.1
Fishery product	15.5
Tobacco and Wine	0.3
Clothing	-0.6
Household Appliances and Service	-1.6
Medical Care and Personal Supply	1.8
Traffic & Telecommunication	-0.6
Entertainment, Education and Cultural Commodities and Service	-1.4
Housing	8.3
Including: Water, Electricity, Fuel,	13.2
Renting	11.5
House Building and Decorative Material	7.5

In 2004, the index of confidence held by entrepreneurs came up to 125.6 during the first quarter, creating a new record high. The indices in the subsequent three quarters came up to 124.5, 125.2 and 123.4. The prospect index of enterprises came up to a new height following the year 2003. The indices for the fourth quarter came up to 115.7, 121.1, 126.9 and 120.0.

The overall level of consumption price for residents a year was 2.7% higher (shown in Table 1), Of which 1.0 % up for service sector and 0.7% up for the overall level of commodity retail price. The ex-works price for industrial products grew by 16.4%. The purchase price for raw material, fuel and power rose by 18.2%. The price of investment in fixed asset grew by 4.5%, the price of farming materials by 7.3% and the price index of farm produces by 0.8%.

At the end of the year, on-the—job staff workers numbered 7,444,900, a rise of 3.2% against that of the previous year, including the employed urban population of 3,494,300, rise of 3.1%. In light of the statistics of labor and social security department, the employed and reemployed figures numbered 369,600, including 25,500 employed by the state-owned units, 29,000 employed by the collective-owned in urban and town areas, 162,300 employed by private, individual and joint-venture in three forms and 152,800 employed by units in other forms. 132,700 laid-offs were reemployed. At the end of the year, SOEs laid-offs numbered 1.88 million and the urban registered unemployment numbered 109,700, with the rate of unemployment being 3.8%.

II. Agriculture

The gross output value of agriculture, forestry, animal husbandry and fishery for a whole year came to 750.68 hundred million RMB, a rise of 6.4% as opposed to that in the previous year. The output value of agriculture was 515 hundred million RMB, a rise of 4.5%; that of forestry was 13.82 hundred million RMB, a rise of 0.7%; that of animal husbandry was 187.47 hundred million RMB, a rise of 12%; that of fishery was 4.3 hundred million RMB, a rise of 8.2 %; the sown area of grain was 1,378,600 hectares, an increase of 5.5%; the sown area of cotton 1,127,600 hectares, a rise of 8.7%; the sown area for oil-bearing material 215500 hectares, a drop of 4.8%; the sown area of beet 59,900 hectares, a drop of 11.0%; the sown area of vegetable 185,600 hectares, a rise of 13.3%; the sown area of fruit and melon 458,200 hectares, a rise of 12.5%.

The grain output for a whole year reached 8,285,300 tons, a rise of 3.4 %; the cotton output 1,752,500 tons, a rise of 9.5%; oil-bearing output 445,400 tons, a drop of 11.2%; the beet output 3,442,100 tons, a fall of 9.8%; the vegetable, fruit and melons enjoy steady increase on the basis of greater variety of superior strains. (Shown in table 2).

Table 2：Farm crops output for the year 2004

Unit: 10 000 tons

Names of products	Absolute number	% Increase against that last year
Grain	828.53	3.4
Summer grain	354.00	1.1
Autumn grain	474.53	5.1
Oil-bearing Crop	44.54	-11.2
# Rape seed	12.16	-21.2
Cotton	175.25	9.5
Beet	344.21	-9.8
Fruit	450.28	10.4
Vegetable	919.13	20.8

The year-end domesticated animals in stock numbered 52,063,700 head, a rise of 3.6% as against that in the previous year. The domesticated animals out of stock 1,281,300 head, a rise of 11.4%; the output of cotton yarn 84,900 tons, a rise of 8.3%; milk output was 1,333,200 tons, a rise of 18.0%; poultry and egg output was 249,900 tons, a rise of 5.8%; the fishery output 73,300 tons, a rise of 8.9%.

The total power of the year-end farming machinery was 10,464,700 kilowatts, a rise of 7.6% as against that in the previous year. The large and medium tractors numbered 92,900 sets, a rise of 21. 8%; small tractors numbered 340,660 sets, a rise of 9.7%; chemical fertilizer consumed (net) came to 991,700 tons, a rise of 9.3%; rural electric consumption 32.63 hundred million kilowatts, a rise of 8.9%; the year-end efficient irrigated area 100,800 hectares, with the added water-conservation irrigated area comin up to 137,100 hectares.

III. Industry and Architecture

The industrial added value reached 745 hundred million RMB, a rise of 14.5% as against that in the previous year. Of which, the added value for industry at considerable scale was 669 hundred million RMB, a rise of 14.4% and the added value for heavy industry 607.08 hundred million RMB, a rise of 90.7% of the added value for industry at considerable scale; light industry 61.92 hundred million, 9.3%; the added value for state-owned or state holding industrial enterprises came up to 585.08 hundred million RMB Yuan, 87.5%.

Major energy, raw material products gained rapid growth in output. The processing volume of crude oil grew by 7.6%; raw coal by 7.7%; natural gas by 14.3%; electric generation by 13.5%, coarse iron by 22.1% and rolled steel by 17.4%. (Main industrial product output shown in table 3)

Table 3 : Main Industrial Product Output for year 2004

Name of products	Unit	Absolute Number	% increase as against last year
Raw coal	10 000 ton	3749.4	7.7
Crude oil	10 000 ton	2253.02	5.2
Crude oil processing volume	10 000 ton	1220.18	7.6
Natural gas	100 million cubic meters	57.48	14.3
Electric generation	100 million KWH	266.30	13.5
Coarse iron	10 000 ton	249.13	22.1
Rolled steel	10 000ton	238.52	17.4
Cement	10 000 ton	1213	7.4
Cotton yarn	10 000 ton	29.14	-0.5
Machine-made sugar	10 000 ton	37.26	-18.0
Chemical fertilizer(100%)	10 000 ton	86.98	-1.8
Transformer	10 000KVA	1135.75	-3.2
Ethane	10 000 ton	25.37	7.5
Machine-madepaper and paper board	10 000 ton	26.31	12.7
Canned food	10 000 ton	66.41	39.9

The exports of industrial enterprises at considerable scale valued at 31.65 hundred million RMB Yuan, an increase of 1.6% as against that in the previous year. The sales rate of industrial products was 97.8%, a drop of 0.4 percent point. The sales rate of light industrial products was 91.1%, a drop of 4.6 percent point; the sales rate of heavy industrial products was 99.0%, up by 0.2%.

The general index for the economic efficiency of industrial enterprises at a considerable scale was 249.1, a rise of 76.4% as opposed to that in the previous year. Of which, the contribution rate of the total asset rose by 3.8%, the added value rate of asset at guaranteed value dropped by 0.9%, asset-liability rate dropped by 0.3%, the turnover rate of circulating asset quickened by 0.4%, the profit rate for cost expense rose by 2.5%, the productivity for the whole labor force rose to 93,000 RMB/person a year. The profit for industrial enterprise came to 208.49 hundred million RMB, a rise of 49.2%.

The added value of building enterprises with certain qualification for a year was 69.31 hundred million, a rise of 3.1%; the completed profit came up to 17.43 hundred million RMB Yuan, an increase of 2.7%. The floor space of house building under construction was 28,123,000 square meters, an increase of 3.4%; the completed floor space of house building was 14,833,500 square meters, an increase of 2.2%.

IV. Investment in Fixed Asset

The investment in fixed asset in the whole community grew rapidly, a rise of 15.9%, which included capital construction investment 759.24 hundred million RMB Yuan, a rise of 17.2%; the investment in renewal and reconstruction amounted to 138.65 hundred million RMB, a rise of 8.8%; the investment in real estate development was 112.56 hundred million RMB Yuan, a rise of 9.8%; other investment 151.05 hundred million RMB, a rise of 21.3%. Classified by subordination, the investment in the local project was 746.69

hundred million RMB, a rise of 18.7% and the investment in the central project 414.83 hundred million RMB, a rise of 11.2%. Classified by urban and rural areas, the urban investment was 1060.80 hundred million RMB Yuan, a rise of 15.3%; rural investment was 100.72 hundred million RMB Yuan, a rise of 24.7%. Of which, rural household investment was 54.38 hundred million RMB Yuan, a rise of 13.1%; non-rural household investment was 46.34 hundred million RMB Yuan. Classified by sources of funds, self-investment capability has been constantly enhanced. Of the total investment, self-raised funds was 667.11 hundred million RMB Yuan, a rise of 31%.

Increased production capacity (shown in table 4)

items	Unit	Absolute number
Raw coal extraction	10 000 ton / year	496
Natural crude oil	10 000 ton / year	110
Oil processing	10 000 ton / year	462
Pig iron	10 000 ton / year	156
Steel making	10 000 ton / year	183
Rolled steel	10 000 ton / year	122
Cement	10 000 ton / year	178
Cotton weaving spindle	10 000 spindles	42
Plate glass	10 000 cases/year	293
Installing volume of generating unit	10 000KW	31
New-constructed highway	Kilometer	1423
Reconstructed highway	Kilometer	5857
New –built micro-wave circuit	Route	240
Installing capacity of program exchange	10 000 lines/year	572

Classified by industry category, the investment in the first industry was 127.01 hundred million RMB Yuan, a rise of 19.9%; the investment in the second industry was 442.15 hundred million RMB, a rise of 28.2%. Of which the oil and natural gas industry went up by 23.0%; oil processing and coke-making industry grew by 99.5%; the textile industry grew by 48.7%, ferrous metal smeltering and rolling processing grew 2.2 folds, ferrous metal smeltering and rolling sector grew by 20.2%; the investment in tertiary industry was 592.36 hundred million RMB Yuan, a rise of 7.4%, of which traffic and transportation as well as postal service grew by 30.4%.

The construction on the key projects has been intensified. The completed investment in large and medium-size construction came up to 264.57 hundred million RMB Yuan, a rise of 52.0%. Quicker growth has been registered in newly-built, reformed highway, oil processing and raw coal extraction..

V. Domestic Trade

The total retails sum of consumers' goods in society for a year numbered 563.65 hundred million RMB, a rise of 14.5% compared with that of the previous year. Classified by urban and rural areas, the retails sum of urban consumers' goods came up to 382.67 hundred million RMB, a rise of 16.5% and the retails sum of rural consumers' goods to 180.98 hundred million RMB, a rise of 8.6% Classified by trades, the retails for catering service amounted to 78.82 hundred million RMB, a rise of 29.6%; the retail sum of wholesale and retail trade to 448.29 hundred million RMB, a rise of 12.4%; the sum of other retails to 36.54 hundred million RMB, a rise of 2.5%.

VI. Foreign Trade

The export and import volume through customhouse for a year amounted to 56.36 hundred million USD, a rise of 18.2% compared with that of the previous year. Of which the total sum of export was 30.47 hundred million USD, a rise of 19.9% and the total sum of import was 25.89 hundred million USD, a rise of 16.1%. Of the total export volume, the general trade jumped to 5.02 hundred million USD, a rise of 29.3%; the processing trade to 2.66 hundred million USD, a rise of 36.8%; small sum of frontier trade amounted to 22.38 hundred million USD, rising by 39.6%. Of total import sum, the general trade reached 10.15

hundred million USD, growing by 40.1%; processing trade came up to 0.52 hundred million USD, a rise of 67.3%; small sum of frontier trade came up to 14.71 hundred million USD, a rise of 2.5%. The export of electromechanical products amounted to 3.77 hundred million USD, a rise of 1.6% times and the export of new and high-tech products amounted to 0.38 hundred million USD, a rise of 35.5%.

The contract items for direct investment newly signed with foreign businessmen amounted to 74 USD for a year, a rise of 13.8%; the actual direct investment made by foreign business came up to 0.46 hundred million USD, a rise of 14.5%; the contract volume for external undertaken projects to 1.02 hundred million USD and completed business volume to 0.86 hundred million USD.

VII. Communication, Post &Telecommunication and Tourism

By the end of 2004, the business mileage for railway was 2999 kilometers. The mileage for available for road traffic was 86,800 kilometers, a rise of 0.6% as against that in the previous year; the mileage of available for navigation of civil aviation was 111,800 kilometers, a rise of 6.8%. The turnover volume of cargo completed by various transportation means for a year was 947.24 hundred million ton/kilometers, a rise of 13.2%. Of which railway 548.50 hundred million, a rise of 15.5%; highway 361 hundred million tons/kilometers, a rise of 11.1%; civil aviation 0.74 hundred million tons/kilometers, a rise of 15.6%; pipe 37 hundred million tons/kilometers, a rise of 1.6%. The completed turnover of passengers was 423.80 hundred million persons/kilometers, a rise of 23.9%. Of which the railway was 121.90 hundred million persons/kilometers, a rise of 27.7%; the highway 249 hundred million persons/kilometers, a rise of 14.9% and civil aviation 52.90 hundred million persons/ kilometers, a rise of 29.3%.

The total completed volume of post and telecommunication for a year amounted to 153.18 hundred million RMB, a rise of 33.8% as against that of the previous year. Of which the total telecommunication business volume was 145.70 hundred million RMB, a rise of 35.8%; the total postal-service business volume was 7.48 hundred million RMB, a rise of 3.9%. The year-end popularization rate for stationary telephones was 516.70 hundred million, popularization rate of 26.3%. mobile telephopne subscribers numbered 489.70 hundred million, a rate of popularization 24.9% and inter-net subscribers 780,500, a rise of 28.4%. The total volume of the year-end local telephone exchange switchboard was 447.0 lines, a rise of 2.5%.

The home tourists received for a year numbered 12,415,800 men/times, a rise of 22.7%; the income of domestic tourism numbered 108.96 hundred million RMB, a rise of 22.9%. International tourists received came up to 31.69, a drop of 85.9%. Of which compatriots from Hong Kong, Macao and Taiwan came up to 45,900 men/times, a rise of 122.7%; foreign exchange income of international tourism came up to 0.91 hundred million USD, a rise of 87.5%.

VIII. Finance, Banking and Insurance

The general budgetary income of the local finance for a year was 191.28 hundred million RMB, a rise of 21.3%; general budgetary income of the local finance was 155.70 hundred million RMB, a rise of 2.1.4%; the general budgetary expenditure of the local finance was 421.04 hundred million RMB, a rise of 14.3%.

The year-end deposit balance in various items in financial institutions was 2959.69 hundred million RMB, an increase of 293.69 hundred million RMB as against that early in the year. Of which the deposit balance of the enterprises was 832.50 hundred million RMB, a rise of 50.25 hundred million RMB; the deposit balance of the urban and rural residents amounted to

1534.67 hundred million RMB, a rise of 162.85 hundred million RMB as against that in the early year. The balance of various loan amounted to 2214.66 hundred million RMB, an increase of 134.66 hundred million RMB compared with that early in the year, of which short-term loan went up to 95.08 hundred million RMB and mid or long-term loan went up to 88.77 hundred million RMB.

Xinjiang has 27 companies listed in stock market, with the total value of 403.21 hundred million RMB, the total stock capital of 83.62 hundred million shares and accumulative raised funds of 107.43 hundred million RMB.

The income from insurance premium in the region was 68.13 hundred million RMB, 9.6% higher than that in the previous year; the income from life incurance was 48.09 hundred million RMB Yuan, rise of 11.7%; the income from insurance premium of property was 20.04 hundred million RMB, a rise of 4.8%. The payment for various indemnities came to 18.34 hundred million RMB, including the reparation for life insurance amounted to 7.70 hundred million RMB, a rise of 8.4%; the reparation for property insurance to 10.64 hundred million RMB, a rise of 2.8%.

IX. Scientific Technology and Education

Xinjiang owned 26 ordinary institutions of higher education and enrollment for both junior and senior college students numbered 53,200, 18.9% higher than that in the previous year. The registered students totaled up to 168,200, an increase of 11.2%, including 70,300 students with ethnic minority background, an increase of 7.6%. There are eleven postgraduates-cultivating institutions, with enrollment of 2336, an increase of 40.4%; the enrolled postgraduates numbered 5120, an increase of 41.1%, including 498 with ethnic minority background, a rise of 50.0%. The ordinary secondary technical schools numbered 78, with the enrollment of 71,300, a drop of 0.3%; the total enrollment in vocational secondary schools was 17,900, a rise of 17.2%. The vocationary secondary schools and its attached class numbered 43,600, a rise of 45.1%. The ordinary high schools numbered 498, with the enrollment of 138,300, a rise of 9.6%; the registered students numbered 359,100, an increase of 13.9%; the total enrollment for ordinary secondary schools numbered 1,158,800, a rise of 2.2% and the total enrollment for elementary schools numbered 2,218,100, a drop of 3.1%.

The admission rate for school-age children hit 97.8% in elementary schools, the total enrollment for elementary school graduates came up to 95.3%, the enrollment rate of secondary school for school-age was 86.3%, the rate of the secondary school drop-outs came to 3.2%.The enrollment of high schools for junior middle school students was 41.1%.

The total enrollment for three-year and four-year programs was 84,600, a drop of 3.6% as against that of the previous year; the total enrollment for adult technical secondary schools was 7,100, a drop of 12.3%. The anti- illiteracy among the young and prime for a year was 47,900.

In 2004, Xinjiang assigned 50 brainstorming projects, a rise of 19.0% as against that in the previous year. The handled patents numbered 1492 and authorized patents 792. The technical contract signed numbered 1619, a rise of 6.8% and the sum of transaction amounted to 13.24 hundred million RMB, a rise of 10.8%.

X. Culture, Health and Sports

The region had 109 art troupes, 108 cultural palaces and art palaces, 92 public libraries, 25 museums, 135 archives and 423,300 volumes of various files open to the public. 6 radio stations, 10 TV stations, 40 medium and short-wave radio transmission and relay stations, 64 launching and transmitting stations with over one KW or higher. The radio coverage rate among population was 92.9%, TV coverage rate among population was 92.5% and cable TV subscribers numbered 1,302,700 households. The produced 1 film, dubbed 75 feature films in ethnic minority languages, produced 5 TV plays and dubbed 18 TV plays; published 3.39 hundred million various newspapers, of which 38% in ethnic- minority languages; various journals 14.50 million copies, of which 35.0% was the ones in ethnic-minority languages; books numbered 8250 copies, of which 40.0% in ethnic minority languages.

The region had 9087 medical institutions altogether, including 1525 hospitals and public health centers, 85 health centers for women and children. The regions had sick beds 78,100, including 74,000 beds in hospitals and public health centers. The region had 99,,800 medical technical staff, 836 township public health centers, with 14,500 medical technical staff and 12,800 sick beds.

The athletes won five championships, three runner-ups and five who have come to the third place in international or inter-continental matches. In the national matches, 15 have won championships, 15 runner-ups and 19 who have come to the third place. Three are up to international-level sportsmen, four up to national-level sportsmen and one equals to national record.

XI. Environment and Resources

In line with the statistics of the Bureau of State Land Resources, the funds put into the state land-reources census and geological survey a year was 83.76 hundred million RMB, including 79.89 hundred million RMB Yuan for oil and natural gas survey and 3.87 hundred million RMB Yuan for state land-resources survey and non-oil and natural gas ore geological survey. There are more than 30 kinds of ore for geological survey, mainly including: coal, oil, natural gas, uranium, steel, copper, nickel, lead, zinc, gold, silver, andalusite, lithium, baudisserite, bentonite and underground water etc.

There are three new-discovered natural gas sections, one natural gas section; ten new-discovered sections of mineral resources worth further prospecting, including 2 copper mines, 1 zinc and lead mine, 2 tungstern mines, 3 gold mines, 1 benotonite mine and 1underground water resource. The Baigan Lake Tunstern and Tin Ore Mine discovered in Ruoqiang County is a tungstern producer with with the largest reserve of tunstern ore in Xinjiang at present.

The new-added proven mineral resources has the following ores including: 4.37 hundred million tons of oil reserve, 563.98 hundred million cubic meters of natural gas reserve, 49.80 hundred million tons of coal resources, 8.94 million tons of iron ore, 248,500 tons of vitriol ore, 559,500 tons of copper, 472,500 tons of lead resources, 970,900 tons of zinc, 22.34 tons of gold and 312.36 tons of silver.

According to the institution of environment protection, the total discharge volume of sulphur dioxide was kept within 480,300 tons, 45.6% higher than that in the previous year; the discharge volume of smog was within 259,100 tons, a rise of 27.1%, the discharge volume of industrial dust was within 167,700 tons, 53.4% higher than that in the previous year. The discharge of solid wastes was within was within 1,028,00 tons, a rise of 16.6%; the discharge rate of chemical-needed oxygen in waste- water was within 261,700 tons, a rise of 14.4%.

Of 16 urban built areas under monitor, there were 4 cities whose air quality reached Class II, there were five cities whose air quality reached Class III. There were 40 noise-control sections, with the area of 351.20 square kilometers.

Twenty-six various kinds of nature reserves were set up in Xinjiang, of which 7 were nature reserves at state-level, with the total area of 204,200 square kilometers, taking up 12.3% of the total land area. There were 8 authorized eco-exemplary areas at state-level, covering 110,600 square kilometers; there was 1 pilot eco-reserve at state level.

XII. Population

Based on the calculation of sampled survey in the population variation dated 2004, the population had reached 19,631,100 persons, 291,600 more than that of the previous year, a rise of 1.5%. The urban population was 6,901,100 persons, a rise of 3.8%; the rate of urbanization was 35.15%, rural population was 12,730,000 persons, a rise of 0.3%.The male population numbered 10,080,200, accounting for 51.3%; the female population numbered 9,550,900, taking up 48.7%. The birth rate was 16.0% and the mortality rate was 5.1% as well as the natural growth rate of population was 10.9%.

XIII. People's Life and Social Security

In 2004, the per-capital disposal income of residents in the urban areas was 7503 RMB Yuan, 4.9% higher than that of the previous year after the price factor has been deducted; the per-capital net income of rural dwellers was 2245 RMB, a rise of 3.1%. The year-end per-capita floor space for the urban residents was 18.82 square meters, a rise of 5.1%; the per-capita floor space for rural residents was 19.1 square meters, an increase of 2.6%. The average currency salary for on-the-job staff was 14,484 RMB Yuan, an actual increase of 7.1%. The Engle coefficient for urban residents was 36.1%, a drop of 0.1 percent as against that in the previous year; the Engle coefficient for rural residents was 45.2%, a drop of 0.3 percent.

According to the statistics of labor and social security department, there were 1,385,800 staff and workers who joined in the insurance of unemployment, 2.6% higher than that in the previous year, 1,737,600 staff who joined in the social overall arrangement for basic endowment insurance, a rise of 9.9%; 427,600 retired people who joined in the social overall arrangement for the basic endowment insurance, a rise of 12.5%. There were 1,959,700 staff and workers who joined in the basic medical insurance, a rise of 11.3%.

According to the civil affairs department, there were 150 community service establishments. The urban dwellers relieved by social security as minimum secured allowance numbered 588,400 persons. The persons subsidized and pensioned by the state numbered 35,800 persons. There were 496 various social welfare institutes, with 13, 438 beds and 10,356 adopted persons. The sale for welfare lottery in society amounted to 6.44 hundred million RMB, raised social welfare funds to 2.25 hundred million RMB and money donated from community to 16000000RMB.

Note: 1) The XJGPV (Xinjiang gross production value), added values in different industrial sectors and the total output value of agriculture, forest, animal husbandry and fishery are calculated on current price in terms of the absolute number for quota, whose speed is calculated on comparable price. The statistical scope of industrial economic efficiency covers both state-owned industry with independent accounting and non non-state-owned industry with annual sale income of exceeding 5 million RMB.

2) Xinjiang per-capital gross production value is calculated on permanent population.

3) The current communiqué contains the statistical figures in the annual report.

第一篇
CHAPTER 1

行政区划和自然资源

DIVISIONS OF ADMINISTRATIVE AREAS AND NATURAL RESOURCES

1-1 行 政 区 划

Division of Administrative Areas in Xinjiang Uygur Autonomous Region

单位：个 (2004 年) (unit)

区划名称	Region	市、地、州数 Region 合计 Total	地级市 Cities at Prefecture	地区 Administrative Office	自治州 Autonomous Prefecture	市数 City 合计 Total	区辖市 City under the Autonomous region	地州辖市 City under the prefecture	市辖区数 Districts under City Administration
总　计	**Total**	**14**	**2**	**7**	**5**	**20**	**4**	**16**	**11**
乌鲁木齐市	Urumqi City	1	1						7
克拉玛依市	Karamay City	1	1						4
石河子市	Shi Hezi City					1	1		
阿拉尔市	Alar City					1	1		
图木舒克市	Tumxuk City					1	1		
五家渠市	Wujiaqu City					1	1		
吐鲁番地区	Turpan Administrative Offices	1		1		1		1	
哈密地区	Hami [Kumul] Administrative Offices	1		1		1		1	
昌吉回族自治州	Changji Hui Autonomous Prefecture	1			1	3		3	
伊犁哈萨克自治州	Ili Kazak Autonomous Prefecture	3		2	1	5		5	
伊犁州直属县(市)	Counties (Cities) Direct Under Ili Prefecture	1			1	2		2	
塔城地区	Tacheng [Tarbagatai] Administrative Offices	1		1		2		2	
阿勒泰地区	Altay Administrative Offices	1		1		1		1	
博尔塔拉自治州	Bortala Mongol Autonomous Prefecture	1			1	1		1	
巴音郭楞自治州	Bayangol Mongol Autonomous Prefecture	1			1	1		1	
阿克苏地区	Aksu Administrative Offices	1		1		1		1	
克孜勒苏自治州	Kizilsu Kirgiz Autonomous Prefecture	1			1	1		1	
喀什地区	Kashgar [Kaxgar] Administrative Offices	1		1		1		1	
和田地区	Hotan Administrative Offices	1		1		1		1	

区划名称	Region	县数 Number of Counties 合计 Total	县 County	自治县 Autonomous County	乡镇数 Number of Townships and Towns 合计 Total	办事处 Urban Subdistrict Office	镇 Town	乡 Township	民族乡 National Township
总　计	**Total**	**68**	**62**	**6**	**994**	**138**	**229**	**584**	**43**
乌鲁木齐市	Urumqi City	1	1		73	54	3	16	
克拉玛依市	Karamay City				14	12		2	
石河子市	Shi Hezi City				7	5	1	1	
阿拉尔市	Alar City				1			1	
图木舒克市	Tumxuk City								
五家渠市	Wujiaqu City								
吐鲁番地区	Turpan Administrative Offices	2	2		28	2	10	15	1
哈密地区	Hami [Kumul] Administrative Offices	2	1	1	42	5	10	24	3
昌吉回族自治州	Changji Hui Autonomous Prefecture	5	4	1	89	12	41	23	13
伊犁哈萨克自治州	Ili Kazak Autonomous Prefecture	19	17	2	241	24	59	141	17
伊犁州直属县(市)	Counties (Cities) Direct Under Ili Prefecture	8	7	1	110	13	19	68	10
塔城地区	Tacheng [Tarbagatai] Administrative Offices	5	4	1	74	8	27	34	5
阿勒泰地区	Altay Administrative Offices	6	6		57	3	13	39	2
博尔塔拉自治州	Bortala Mongol Autonomous Prefecture	2	2		20	4	7	9	
巴音郭楞自治州	Bayangol Mongol Autonomous Prefecture	8	7	1	90	5	23	61	1
阿克苏地区	Aksu Administrative Offices	8	8		88	5	31	50	2
克孜勒苏自治州	Kizilsu Kirgiz Autonomous Prefecture	3	3		39	2	5	31	1
喀什地区	Kashgar [Kaxgar] Administrative Offices	11	10	1	172	4	28	137	3
和田地区	Hotan Administrative Offices	7	7		90	4	11	73	2

1-2　县级以上行政区划

Divisions of Administrative Areas at and above County Level

(2004 年)

<table>
<tr><th colspan="2">地、州、市名称
Name of Administratice Offices,
Autonomous Prefectures, Cities</th><th>市　县（市辖区名称）
Cities and Counties (names of districts under cities)</th></tr>
<tr><td colspan="2">乌鲁木齐市
Urumqi City</td><td>天山区、沙依巴克区、新市区、水磨沟区、头屯河区、达坂城区、东山区、乌鲁木齐县
Tianshan District, Shayibak District, Xinshi District, Shui Mogou District, Tou Tunhe District, Da Bancheng District, Dongshan District, Urumqi County</td></tr>
<tr><td colspan="2">克拉玛依市
Karamay City</td><td>克拉玛依区、独山子区、白碱滩区、乌尔禾区
Karamay District, Dushanzi District, Bai Jiantan District, Urhe District</td></tr>
<tr><td colspan="2">石河子市
Shi Hezi City</td><td></td></tr>
<tr><td colspan="2">阿拉尔市
Alar City</td><td></td></tr>
<tr><td colspan="2">图木舒克市
Tumxuk City</td><td></td></tr>
<tr><td colspan="2">五家渠市
Wujiaqu City</td><td></td></tr>
<tr><td colspan="2">吐鲁番地区
Turpan Administrative Offices</td><td>吐鲁番市、鄯善县、托克逊县
Turpan City, Shanshan [Piqan] County, Toksun County</td></tr>
<tr><td colspan="2">哈密地区
Hami [Kumul] Administrative Offices</td><td>哈密市、巴里坤哈萨克自治县、伊吾县
Hami [Kumul] City, Barkol Kazak Autonomous County, Yiwu County</td></tr>
<tr><td colspan="2">昌吉回族自治州
Changji Hui Autonomous Prefecture</td><td>昌吉市、阜康市、米泉市、呼图壁县、玛纳斯县、奇台县、吉木萨尔县、木垒哈萨克自治县
Changji City, Fukang City, Miquan City, Hutubi County, Manas County, Qitai County, Jimsar County, Mori Kazak Autonomous County</td></tr>
<tr><td rowspan="3">伊犁哈萨克自治州
Ili Kazak Autonomous Prefecture</td><td>伊犁州直属县(市)
Counties (Cities) Direct Under Ili Prefecture</td><td>伊宁市、奎屯市、伊宁县、察布查尔锡伯自治县、霍城县、巩留县、新源县、昭苏县、特克斯县、尼勒克县
Yining [Gulja] City, Kuytun City , Yining [Gulja] County, Qapqal Xibe AutonomousCounty, Huocheng [Korgas] County, Gongliu [Tokkuztara] County, Xinyuan [Kunes] County, Zhaosu [Mongulkure] County, Tekes County, Nilka County</td></tr>
<tr><td>塔城地区
Tacheng [Tarbagatai] Administrative Office</td><td>塔城市、乌苏市、额敏县、沙湾县、托里县、裕民县、和布克赛尔蒙古自治县
Tacheng [Qoqek] City, Usu City, Emin [Dorbiljin] County, Shawan County, Toli County, Yumin [Qagantokay] County, Hoboksar Mongol Autonomous County</td></tr>
<tr><td>阿勒泰地区
Altay Administrative Offices</td><td>阿勒泰市、布尔津县、富蕴县、福海县、哈巴河县、青河县、吉木乃县
Altay City, Burqin County, Fuyun [Koktokay] County, Fuhai [Burultokay] County, Habahe [Kaba] County, Qinghe [Qinggil] County, Jeminay county</td></tr>
<tr><td colspan="2">博尔塔拉蒙古自治州
Bortala Mongol Autonomous Prefecture</td><td>博乐市、精河县、温泉县
Bole [Bortala] City, Jinghe [Jing] County, Wenquan [Arxang] County</td></tr>
<tr><td colspan="2">巴音郭楞蒙古自治州
Bayangol Mongol Autonomous Prefecture</td><td>库尔勒市、轮台县、尉犁县、若羌县、且末县、焉耆回族自治县、和静县、和硕县、博湖县
Korla City, Luntai [Bugur] County, Yuli [Lopnur] County, Ruoqiang [Qarkilik] County, Qiemo [Qarqan] County, Yanqi Hui Autonomous County, Hejing County, Bohu [Bagrax] County</td></tr>
<tr><td colspan="2">阿克苏地区
Aksu Administrative Offices</td><td>阿克苏市、温宿县、库车县、沙雅县、新和县、拜城县、乌什县、阿瓦提县、柯坪县
Aksu City, Wensu [Onsu] County, Kuqa County, Xayar County, Xinhe [Toksu] County, Baicheng [Bay] County, Wushi [Uqturpan] County, Awat County, Kalpin County</td></tr>
<tr><td colspan="2">克孜勒苏柯尔克孜自治州
Kizilsu Kirgiz Autonomous Prefecture</td><td>阿图什市、阿克陶县、阿合奇县、乌恰县
Artux City, Akto County, Akqi County, Wuqia [Ulugqat] County</td></tr>
<tr><td colspan="2">喀什地区
Kashgar [Kaxgar] Administrative Offices</td><td>喀什市、疏附县、疏勒县、英吉沙县、泽普县、莎车县、叶城县、麦盖提县、岳普湖县、伽师县、巴楚县、塔什库尔干塔吉克自治县
Kashgar [Kaxgar] City, Shufu County, Shule County, Yengisar County, Zepu [Poskam] County, Shache [Yarkant] County, Yecheng [Kagilik] County, Makit County, Yopurga County, Jiashi [Payzawat] County, Bachu [Maralbexi] County, Taxkorgan Tajik Aotonomous County</td></tr>
<tr><td colspan="2">和田地区
Hotan Administrative Offices</td><td>和田市、和田县、墨玉县、皮山县、洛浦县、策勒县、于田县、民丰县
Hotan City, Hotan County, Moyu [Karakax] County, Pishan [Guma] County, Lop County, Qira County, Yutian [Keriya] County, Minfeng [niya] County</td></tr>
</table>

1-3 自 然 资 源
Natural Resources

指 标	Item	2004
自然状况	**State of the Nature**	
经纬度	**Langitude and latitude**	
东 经	East Longitude	73°40′ ~96°23′
北 纬	North Latitude	34°25′ ~49°10′
气 候	**Climate**	
年平均气温(摄氏度)	**Annual Average Temperature (℃)**	**10.4**
北 疆	North Xinjiang	8.3
南 疆	South Xinjiang	13.2
东 疆	East Xinjiang	13.0
年平均降水量(毫米)	**Annual Average Precipitation (mm)**	**188.1**
北 疆	North Xinjiang	285.1
南 疆	South Xinjiang	79.1
东 疆	East Xinjiang	24.0
平均日照时数(小时)	**Average Sunny Hours (hour)**	**2817.7**
北 疆	North Xinjiang	2712.5
南 疆	South Xinjiang	2881.3
东 疆	East Xinjiang	3132.3
自然资源	**Natural Resources**	
土地资源	**Land resources**	
土地总面积(万平方公里)	Total Land Area (10 000 sq. kilometers)	166.49
农用地(万公顷)	Land for farm use (10 000 hectares)	6304.58
耕地面积	Area of Cultivated Land	402.55
园地面积	Garden Area	33.59
林地面积	Woodland Area	675.94
牧草地面积	Pastureland Area	5121.58
其他农用地	Other Land for Agriculture	70.92
建设用地(万公顷)	Land for Cconstruction (10 000 hectare)	121.05
未利用地(万公顷)	Land yet to be Uused (10 000 hectare)	10223.35
林木资源	**Forest resources**	
活立木总蓄积量(万立方米)	Total Standing Stock Volume (10 000 cubic meters)	31419.68
林地蓄积量(万立方米)	Woodland Stock Volume (10 000 cubic meters)	28039.68

1-3 续表 Continued

指　　标	Item	2004
有林地面积(万公顷)	Woodland Area (10 000 hectares)	180.73
灌木林地面积(万公顷)	Bush Woodland Area (10 000 hectares)	704.90
四旁树(万株)	Surrounding Woods (10 000)	23067
森林覆盖率(%)	Forest-coverage (%)	2.94
水资源(亿立方米)	**Water Resources (100 million cu.m)**	
水资源总量	Annual Runoff of Water Resources	855.4
地表水水资源量	Surface Water	809.2
地下水水资源量	Underground Water Volume	502.6
重复计算量	Volume of Repeated Computation	456.4
主要矿产资源保有储量	**Reserve of Main Mineral Resources**	
铁矿(万吨)	Iron ore (10 000 tons)	77853
铬矿(万吨)	Chromium ore (10 000 tons)	170
铜矿(吨)	Copper ore (ton)	2298873
铅矿(吨)	Lead ore (ton)	659276
锌矿(吨)	Zin ore (ton)	1387577
铝矿(万吨)	Aluminium ore (10 000 tons)	57
镍矿(吨)	Nickle ore (ton)	972771
煤(万吨)	Coal (10 000 tons)	9816428
耐火粘土(万吨)	Fire-proof Clay (10 000 tons)	703
钠硝石(万吨)	Nitratite (10 000 tons)	6188
芒硝(万吨)	Mirabilitum (10 000 tons)	182139
盐矿(万吨)	Salt Mine (10 000 tons)	597862
石棉(万吨)	Asbest (10 000 ton)	849
云母(吨)	Mica (ton)	50297
蛭石(万吨)	Roseite (10 000 tons)	1771
水泥用灰岩(万吨)	Limestone Used for Cement (10 000 tons)	166078
澎润土(万吨)	Bentonite (10 000 ton)	52079
饰面用花岗岩(万立方米)	Granite as Veneer (10 000 cubic meter)	10670

注：1.本表资料中土地资源和矿产资源由国土资源厅提供、林木资源由林业局提供、水资源由水利厅提供。
2. 主要矿产资源保有储量为 2003 年数据。

Note: a) The land resources and mineral resources listed in the table are given by the bureau of national-land resources: forest resources by the bureau of forest and water resources by the bureau of water conservancy.
b) Main ore- resources reserve is based on the data in 2003.

1-4 主要山脉基本情况
Main Mountain Ranges

山脉名称	Mountain Range	山峰高程(米) Height of Mountain Peak (m)	雪线高程(米) Height of Snow Line (m)	冰川面积(平方公里) Glacier Area (sq.km)	冰川储量(亿立方米) Glacier Storage (hundred million cudic meters)	冰川年融水量(亿立方米) Annual Glacier Melting Water Volume (Hundred million cudic meters)
合　计	**Total**			**23020**	**21349**	**198.50**
天　山	Tianshan Mountains	7435	3600-4400	9548	10106	96.20
阿尔泰山	Altay Mountains	4374	3000-3200	290	164	3.64
喀喇昆仑山及昆仑山	Karakorum Mountain and Kunlun Mountains	8611	5100-5400	3265	14365	79.09
帕米尔	Pamirs	7579	5500-5700	2258	2487	16.25

1-5 主要湖泊基本情况
Major Lakes

(2004 年)

湖泊名称	Lakes	湖水面积(平方公里) Lake Area (Sq. kilometers)	湖面高程(米) Height of Lake Surface (m)	水质类型 Water Type
博斯腾湖	The Bosten Lake [Bagrax]	972	1048	微咸 slight salty
乌伦古湖	The Ulunggur Lake	736	468	盐 salt
塞里木湖	The Sayram Lake	454	2073	咸 alkaline
艾比湖	The Aybi Lake [Eynur]	898	189	盐 salt

1-6 主要河流基本情况
Major Rivers

(2004 年)

河流名称	Names of Rivers	流域面积(平方公里) Drainage Area (sq.km)	河长(公里) Length (km)	年径流量(亿立方米) Annual Flow (100 million cu.m)
玛纳斯河	Manas River	5156	190	12.40
开都河	Kaidu River	19022	530	34.92
渭干河	Ugan River	16660	256	25.37
克孜河	Kizil River	15710	233	24.41
乌伦古河	Ulunggur River	32040	821	9.06
塔里木河	Tarim River	194210	2437	29.48

1-7 主要城市平均气温

Monthly Average Temperature of Major Cities

单位：摄氏度 (2004 年) (℃)

城 市	City	一月 Jan.	二月 Feb.	三月 Mar.	四月 Apr.	五月 May	六月 June	七月 July
乌鲁木齐市	Urumqi City	-12.6	-6.9	0.4	13.3	18.0	22.5	24.5
克拉玛依市	Karamay City	-15.3	-9.1	2.3	15.3	21.5	26.1	28.0
石河子市	Shi Hezi City	-16.0	-8.8	2.1	14.6	20.2	24.5	25.3
阜康市	Fukang City	-16.5	-10.4	0.7	15.0	20.2	24.7	26.1
米泉市	Miquan City	-13.6	-8.0	1.6	15.2	20.4	25.0	26.7
伊宁市	Yining [Gulja] City	-5.8	-1.1	6.3	14.1	18.7	22.0	23.0
塔城市	Tacheng [Qoqek] City	-10.0	-4.1	0.9	11.5	17.8	21.8	23.4
阿勒泰市	Altay City	-15.7	-11.5	-4.3	9.3	17.8	20.7	22.1
博乐市	Bole City	-16.0	-9.3	1.2	13.1	19.1	22.5	24.1
库尔勒市	Korla City	-6.4	0.1	8.5	18.3	20.8	26.6	29.0
阿克苏市	Aksu City	-5.6	-0.2	7.6	16.9	19.5	23.6	24.8
阿图什市	Artux City	-3.7	2.8	11.0	18.4	20.5	25.3	27.0
喀什市	Kashgar [Kaxgar] City	-4.5	2.6	11.2	17.8	19.9	24.7	26.1
和田市	Hotan City	-3.4	3.4	12.2	18.5	20.6	24.8	26.9
吐鲁番市	Turpan City	-7.1	1.2	11.2	22.6	25.8	31.3	33.8
哈密市	Hami [Kumul] City	-11.3	-3.7	5.0	17.3	21.4	26.0	27.9

城 市	City	八月 Aug.	九月 Sept.	十月 Oct.	十一月 Nov.	十二月 Dec.	全年平均 Annual Average
乌鲁木齐市	Urumqi City	21.8	16.1	7.6	-1.6	-8.4	7.9
克拉玛依市	Karamay City	25.3	19.2	9.7	-0.1	-8.9	9.5
石河子市	Shi Hezi City	22.6	16.9	7.4	-0.8	-9.0	8.3
阜康市	Fukang City	23.1	17.2	7.9	-1.7	-10.1	8.0
米泉市	Miquan City	24.1	18.1	8.9	-0.9	-7.9	9.1
伊宁市	Yining [Gulja] City	22.1	17.8	8.9	4.9	-4.2	10.6
塔城市	Tacheng [Qoqek] City	22.0	15.6	8.2	0.8	-7.2	8.4
阿勒泰市	Altay City	19.7	13.2	6.5	-4.5	-12.2	5.1
博乐市	Bole City	21.7	16.7	7.3	-1.0	-9.0	7.5
库尔勒市	Korla City	25.7	20.4	11.0	3.1	-3.2	12.8
阿克苏市	Aksu City	23.0	19.2	11.1	3.0	-2.7	11.7
阿图什市	Artux City	25.1	21.7	13.0	6.5	-1.2	13.9
喀什市	Kashgar [Kaxgar] City	24.4	20.8	12.8	6.2	-0.7	13.4
和田市	Hotan City	24.8	21.6	13.3	7.2	-0.3	14.1
吐鲁番市	Turpan City	29.8	24.1	11.9	3.1	-2.5	15.4
哈密市	Hami [Kumul] City	24.2	17.6	8.3	0.2	-6.1	10.6

1-8 主要城市降水量

Monthly Precipitation of Major Cities

单位：毫米 (2004 年) (Milli meter)

城 市	City	一月 Jan.	二月 Feb.	三月 Mar.	四月 Apr.	五月 May	六月 June	七月 July
乌鲁木齐市	Urumqi City	9.6	37.6	24.3	23.1	36.5	6.4	59.6
克拉玛依市	Karamay City	11.1	3.3	3.9	2.7	8.1	4.5	86.5
石河子市	Shi Hezi City	12.5	22.7	31.9	25.7	46.3	1.5	62.4
阜康市	Fukang City	7.2	25.1	19.6	19.3	46.9	9.4	52.8
米泉市	Miquan City	9.2	26.2	20.5	24.6	36.0	10.5	70.3
伊宁市	Yining [Gulja] City	20.7	20.6	40.5	8.8	32.7	30.0	152.7
塔城市	Tacheng [Qoqek] City	11.8	21.7	36.1	17.7	16.2	14.8	37.5
阿勒泰市	Altay City	7.8	5.5	11.0	23.7	14.0	13.5	24.6
博乐市	Bole City	8.1	21.8	4.8	17.1	18.6	16.9	73.9
库尔勒市	Korla City	3.5	0	3.8	1.8	11.7	5.2	1.4
阿克苏市	Aksu City	3.7		10.8	3.4	11.6	6.0	32.9
阿图什市	Artux City	3.7	0.1	10.7	2.8	46.2	5.2	11.8
喀什市	Kashgar [Kaxgar] City	7.2	1.4	7.2	0.8	42.2	6.3	8.0
和田市	Hotan City	1.3	0.2	9.0	5.6	14.0	7.2	0
吐鲁番市	Turpan City	2.1		1.0		0.6	0.8	2.7
哈密市	Hami [Kumul] City	6.5		3.8		1.4	2.7	6.6

城 市	City	八月 Aug.	九月 Sept.	十月 Oct.	十一月 Nov.	十二月 Dec.	全 年 Annual Total
乌鲁木齐市	Urumqi City	26.8	14.3	14.8	17.2	44.0	314.2
克拉玛依市	Karamay City	11.1	13.3	5.3	12.4	16.5	178.7
石河子市	Shi Hezi City	11.0	21.0	14.2	27.0	32.2	308.4
阜康市	Fukang City	13.3	16.9	10.0	14.0	18.8	253.3
米泉市	Miquan City	18.6	13.0	16.5	15.7	30.6	291.7
伊宁市	Yining [Gulja] City	4.7	9.7	21.3	114.8	39.8	496.3
塔城市	Tacheng [Qoqek] City	15.6	19.6	6.1	50.1	24.8	272.0
阿勒泰市	Altay City	18.3	17.7	0.5	42.7	40.5	219.8
博乐市	Bole City	8.0	21.2	8.3	8.7	24.4	231.8
库尔勒市	Korla City	3.3	2.7	0		2.8	36.2
阿克苏市	Aksu City	4.6	8.1	0	3.1	4.4	88.6
阿图什市	Artux City	22.7	3.1	14.4	1.7	3.0	125.4
喀什市	Kashgar [Kaxgar] City	15.3	0.9	12.7	1.1	1.7	104.8
和田市	Hotan City	3.0	0			0	40.3
吐鲁番市	Turpan City	1.1	0			2.2	10.5
哈密市	Hami [Kumul] City	5.6	5.4	5.3		0.2	37.5

1-9 主要城市日照时数

Monthly Sunshine Hours of Major Cities

单位：小时 (2004 年) (hour)

城　市	City	一月 Jan.	二月 Feb.	三月 Mar.	四月 Apr.	五月 May	六月 June	七月 July
乌鲁木齐市	Urumqi City	89.1	145.4	153.3	258.5	284.0	309.7	320.8
克拉玛依市	Karamay City	135.4	123.3	183.5	262.6	319.8	321.7	298.2
石河子市	Shi Hezi City	103.2	123.3	189.3	284.9	341.9	365.4	352.6
阜康市	Fukang City	69.8	127.4	175.3	277.8	305.0	350.8	339.1
米泉市	Miquan City	52.6	90.4	169.9	284.1	294.9	347.7	337.2
伊宁市	Yining [Gulja] City	160.8	181.5	186.7	260.5	329.4	344.1	326.3
塔城市	Tacheng [Qoqek] City	166.0	176.3	170.2	252.1	309.7	336.5	301.6
阿勒泰市	Altay City	192.6	198.6	227.6	248.7	342.2	358.2	330.9
博乐市	Bole City	152.2	102.0	172.7	247.5	313.6	331.7	328.3
库尔勒市	Korla City	175.5	222.9	217.3	276.6	300.7	314.6	322.2
阿克苏市	Aksu City	169.9	206.6	157.3	263.1	279.3	319.9	296.9
阿图什市	Artux City	111.7	198.0	192.2	247.1	264.0	276.9	276.7
喀什市	Kashgar [Kaxgar] City	119.0	210.2	201.7	264.5	277.9	318.9	313.5
和田市	Hotan City	161.9	235.6	191.1	243.1	298.6	251.2	270.2
吐鲁番市	Turpan City	129.1	197.2	202.4	263.9	303.3	324.7	332.0
哈密市	Hami [Kumul] City	215.5	244.9	278.0	325.5	368.6	345.2	361.5

城　市	City	八月 Aug.	九月 Sept.	十月 Oct.	十一月 Nov.	十二月 Dec.	全　年 Annual Total
乌鲁木齐市	Urumqi City	292.8	266.1	223.7	95.0	57.3	2495.7
克拉玛依市	Karamay City	287.7	266.0	227.2	64.1	65.8	2555.3
石河子市	Shi Hezi City	327.2	294.6	245.5	78.8	98.7	2805.4
阜康市	Fukang City	309.8	269.0	222.2	99.1	57.5	2602.8
米泉市	Miquan City	305.7	270.0	230.6	51.7	49.1	2483.9
伊宁市	Yining [Gulja] City	355.7	303.3	250.1	168.7	125.2	2992.3
塔城市	Tacheng [Qoqek] City	319.5	288.1	217.9	105.4	122.7	2766.0
阿勒泰市	Altay City	349.3	290.1	263.7	150.5	114.4	3066.8
博乐市	Bole City	321.8	283.8	227.8	66.0	97.2	2644.6
库尔勒市	Korla City	292.5	285.6	256.7	228.2	141.7	3034.5
阿克苏市	Aksu City	291.9	282.8	264.9	198.1	154.7	2885.4
阿图什市	Artux City	327.5	256.1	207.2	181.7	148.7	2687.8
喀什市	Kashgar [Kaxgar] City	340.0	274.3	224.7	204.3	169.0	2918.0
和田市	Hotan City	239.3	271.7	272.8	237.6	207.8	2880.9
吐鲁番市	Turpan City	310.4	266.1	224.5	167.1	62.0	2782.7
哈密市	Hami [Kumul] City	326.1	319.9	272.5	227.3	196.8	3481.8

主要统计指标解释

行政区划 指国家对行政区域的划分.根据宪法规定,我国的行政区域划分如下: (1)全国分为省、自治区、直辖市; (2)省、自治区分为自治州、县、自治县、市; (3)自治州分为县、自治县、市; (4)县、自治县分为乡、民族乡、镇; (5)直辖市和较大的市分为区、县; (6)国家在必要时设立的特别行政区。

国土 指一个主权国家管辖下的领土、领海和领空。

气候 指地球与大气之间长期能量交换与质量交换所形成的一种自然环境状态，它是多种因素综合作用的结果。气候既是人类生活和生产的环境要素之一，又是供给人类生活和生产的重要资源。气温、降水、湿度等气象要素的多年平均值是用来描述一个地区气候状况的主要参数，而各种气象要素某年、某月的平均值(或总量)则可以反映出该时期天气气候状况的重要特征。

自然资源 指人类可以直接从自然界获得，并用于生产和生活的物质资源。自然资源一般可以分成可再生资源和非再生资源两大类。可再生资源指在较短时间内可以再生、可以循环利用的资源，包括土地资源、水资源、气候资源、生物资源和海洋资源等。非再生资源指在使用后不能再生的资源，包括矿产资源和地热能源。

土地资源 土地指陆地的表层部分，它主要由岩石、岩石的风化物和土壤构成。土地资源按利用类型可以分为农用地、建筑用地和未利用地。农用地包括耕地、园地、林地、牧草地和水面。建筑用地包括居民点及工矿用地、交通用地和水利设施用地。未利用地指农用地和建筑用地以外的土地，包括滩涂、荒漠、戈壁、冰川和石山等。

耕地面积 指种植各种农作物的土地面积，包括灌溉水田、望天田、水浇地、旱地、菜地等。

林业用地面积 指生长乔木、竹类、灌木、沿海红树林等林木的土地面积，包括有林地、灌木林、疏林地、未成林造林地、迹地、苗圃等。

草地面积 指牧区和农区用于放牧牲畜或割草，植被盖度在5%以上的草原、草坡、草山等面积。包括天然的和人工种植或改良的草地面积。

森林资源 指森林、林木、林地以及依托森林、林木、林地生存的野生动物、植物和微生物。林木指树木和竹子。森林指以乔木为主体的植物群落，是集生的乔木及与共同作用的植物、动物、微生物和土壤、气候等的总体。

活立木总蓄积量 指一定范围内土地上全部树木蓄积的总量，包括森林蓄积、疏林蓄积、散生木蓄积和四旁树蓄积。

森林面积 指由乔木树种构成，郁闭度0.2以上(含0.2)的林地或冠幅宽度10米以上的林带的面积，即有林地面积。森林面积包括天然起源和人工起源的针叶林面积、阔叶林面积、针阔混交林面积和竹林面积，不包括灌木林地面积和疏林地面积。

森林蓄积量 指一定森林面积上存在着的林木树干部分的总材积。它是反映一个国家或地区森林资源总规模和水平的基本指标之一，也是反映森林资源的丰富程度、衡量森林生态环境优劣的重要依据。

森林覆盖率 指一个国家或地区森林面积占土地面积的百分比。在计算森林覆盖率时，森林面积包括郁闭度0. 2以上的乔木林地面积和竹林地面积，国家特别规定的灌木林地面积、农田林网以及四旁(村旁、路旁、水旁、宅旁)林木的覆盖面积。森林覆盖率是反映森林资源的丰富程度和生态平衡状况的重要指标。计算公式为:

森林覆盖率(%)=森林面积／土地总面积 × 100%

水资源 水在自然界中以固体、液体和气态三种聚集状态存在，分布于海洋、陆地(包括土壤)以及大气之中，通过水循环形成水资源。水资源包括经人类控制并直接可供灌溉、发电、给水、航运、养殖等用途的地表水和地下水，以及江河、湖泊、井、泉、潮汐、港湾和养殖水域等。水资源是发展国民经济不可缺少的重要自然资源。

地表水和地下水 陆地上的水因空间分布不同，可以分为地表水和地下水。地表水指分别存在于河流、湖泊、沼泽、冰川和冰盖等水体中水分的总称，又称陆地水。地下水指储存在地面以下饱和岩土孔隙、裂隙及溶洞中的水。

内陆水域总面积 指江、河、湖泊、池塘、塘堰、水库等各种流水或蓄水的水面占地面积。

径流 指大气降水扣除损耗外，从地表和地下向流域出口断面汇集的水流。径流可分为地表径流、地下径流和壤中流。地表径流指沿地表向河流、湖泊、沼泽、海洋等汇集的水流；地下径流指沿潜水层或隔水层间的含水层，向河流、湖泊、沼泽、海洋等汇集的地下水水流。

径流量 指在一定时段内通过河流某一过水断面的水量，用以反映一个国家或地区水资源的丰歉程度。计算公式为:

径流量=降水量-蒸发量

矿产资源 矿产指由地质作用形成，富集于地壳中或出露于地表达到工农业利用要求的有用矿物。矿产是一种重要的自然资源，是社会发展的重要物质基础。从某种意义上讲，一个国家对矿产资源开发利用的广度和深度，可以作为这个国家经济发展水平的标志。

矿产保有储量 指探明的矿产储量(包括工业储量和远景储量)，扣除已开采部分和地下损失量后的年末实有储量，是反映国家矿产资源现状的重要指标。

流域 每条河流都有自己的干流和支流，干支流共同组成这条河流的水系。每条河流都有自己的集水区域，这个集水区域就称为该河流的流域。

外流河 指直接或间接流入海洋的河流。供给外流河河水的区域称为外流区域。

内陆河 指在陆地内部干燥地区，河水沿途消失于沙漠或注入内陆湖泊的河流。供给内陆河河水的区域称为内陆区域。

气温 指空气的温度，我国一般以摄氏度(℃)为单位表示。气象观测的温度表是放在离地面约1.5米处通风良好的百叶箱里测量的，因此，通常说的气温指的是离地面1.5米处百叶箱中的温度。其统计计算方法为:

月平均气温 是将全月各日的平均气温相加，除以该月的天数而得。

年平均气温 是将12个月的月平均气温累加后除以12而得。

相对湿度 指空气中实际水气压与当时气温下的饱合水气压之比。其统计方法与气温相同。

降水量 指从天空降落到地面的液态或固态(经融化后)水，未经蒸发、渗透、流失而在地面上积聚的深度。其统计计算方法为:

月降水量 是将全月各日的降水量累加而得。

年降水量 是将12个月的月降水量累加而得。

日照时数 指太阳实际照射地面的时间。其统计方法与降水量相同。

Explanatory Notes on Main Statistical Indicators

Administrative Division refers to the division of administrative areas by the state. The Constitution of the People's Republic of China stipulates that the administrative areas in China are divided as: 1) The whole Country is divided into provinces, autonomous regions and municipalities directly under the central government; 2) Provinces and autonomous regions are divided into autonomous prefectures, counties, autonomous counties and cities; 3) Autonomous prefectures are divided into counties, autonomous counties and cities; 4) Counties and autonomous counties are divided into townships, nationality townships and towns; 5) Municipalities and large cities are divided into districts and counties, 6) The state shall, when necessary, establish special administrative regions.

Territory refers to territorial land, sea and air space under the administration of a sovereign state.

Climate refers to the natural environmental status formed by the long-time exchange of energy and mass between the earth and the air, and is the results of interaction of many factors. Climate is both one of the environment factors and the important resources for the living and production activities of the human being. The average values across several years of meteorological factors such as temperature, rainfall and humidity are used as important parameters to describe the climate of a region, while the average values (or total values) of a given year or month of meteorological factors reflect the key characteristics of climate for that period of time.

Natural Resources refer to material resources that could be obtained from the nature by human being and used for production and living. Natural resources in general can be classified as renewable resources and non-renewable resources. Renewable resources refer to resources that could be renewed and recycled during a relatively short period of time, including land resource, water resource, climate resource, biology resource and marine resource. Non-renewable resources include resources that could not be renewed, such as minerals and geothermal resource.

Land Resource Land refers to the surface of the earth, consisting of mainly rocks and its whethering and earth. Land resource can be classified, by its utilization, as land for agriculture, land for construction and unused land. Land for agriculture includes cultivated land, plantation land, forestland, grassland and waters. Land for construction includes land for residential purpose, for manufacturing and mining, for transportation and for water-conservancy projects. Unused land refers to land other than land for agriculture and construction, including beaches, deserts, Gobi, glaciers and rock mountains.

Area of Cultivated Land refers to land for the cultivation of various farm crops, including irrigated land, manual-watered land, dry land and vegetable land.

Area of Afforestated Land refer to land for trees bamboo, bushes and mangrove, including forest-cover land, bush-covered land, sparse forest land, land planned for afforestation and nurseries of young trees.

Area of Grassland refers to areas of grassland, grass-slopes and grass-covered hills with a vegetation-covering rate of over 5% that are used for animal husbandry or harvesting of grass. It includes natural, cultivated and improved grassland areas.

Forest Resource refers to forests, trees, forestland and wild animals, plants and microorganism that live on forest and trees. Trees include trees and bamboo. Forest refers to the population of clusters of trees and other plants, animals and microorganism as well as the earth and climate that have interactions with the trees.

Total Standing Stock Volume refers to the total stock volume of trees growing in land，including trees in forest， tress in sparse forest, scattered trees and trees planted by the side of farm houses and along the roads, rivers and fields.

Forest Area refers to the area of forest land where trees and bamboo grow with canopy density above 0.2，including land of natural woods and planted woods, but excluding bush land and thin forest land. It reflects the total areas of afforestation.

Stock Volume of Forest refers to total stock volume of wood growing in forest area，which shows the total size and level of forest resources of a Country or a region. It is also an important indicator illustrating the richness of forest resource and the status of forest ecological environment.

Forest Coverage Rate refers to the ratio of area of afforested land to total land area. This indicator shows the forest resources and afforestation progress of a Country or a region. According to regulations of the government， in addition to afforested land，the area of bush forest, the area of forest land inside farm land and the area of trees planted by the side of farm houses and along the roads, rivers and fields should also be included in the area of afforested land in the calculation of the forest coverage-rate. The formula for calculating forest coverage rate is as follows：

Forestry coverage rate (%)= (Area of Afforested Land/Area of Total Land)×100%

Water Resource Water exists in the nature in solid, liquid and gaseous states, is distributed in the ocean, land (including earth) and air, and constitutes the water resource through the circulation of water. Water resource includes the surface water and underground water that is controlled by the human being for irrigation, power-generation, water supply, navigation and cultivation. It also includes rivers, lakes, wells, springs, tides, gulf and water area for cultivation. Water resource as an important natural resource is indispensable for the development of the national economy.

Surface Water and Underground Water. Water on earth can be divided into surface water and underground water accordingo its distribution. Surface water refers to moisture exists in rivers, lakes, swamps, glaciers, icecaps and so on. It is also called land water. The underground water refers to water deposited underground in the cranny and the hole of saturated rock soil and in the water-eroded cave.

Inland Water Area refers to water area of rivers，lakes，ponds，reservoir，etc.

Runoff refers to the water gathered at the way out of the cross section of drainage area either from the surface or underground after deducting the wastage of the precipitation. Runoff can be divided into surface runoff, underground runoff and within soil runoff. Surface runoff refers to water flow to the rivers, lakes, swamps, and seas on the surface of the earth. Underground runoff refers to water flow to rivers, lakes, swamps, and seas through the water-bearing stratum of confined layer or unconfined layer.

Volume of Runoff refers to the total volume of water running through a certain cross section of a river during a certain period of time, reflecting the water resource condition in a Country or a region. The formula for calculating volume or runoff is as follows：

Runoff =Precipitation-Evaporation

Mineral Resources refer to useful minerals that can be used for industrial or agricultural purposes enriched in lithosphere or on earth due to the geological process.

Ensured Mineral Reserves refer to the actual mineral reserves, which equal to the proven mineral reserves (including industrial reserves and prospective reserves) minus extracted parts and underground losses. This indicator shows the current condition of the mineral resources of a Country.

Drainage Area Each river has its own main stream and branches to form the water system of the river. Each river has its own catchment area, which is also called as the drainage area of the river.

Out-flowing Rivers refer to rivers directly or indirectly flowing into the sea. The area providing water to the out-flowing rivers is called as out-flowing area.

Inland Rivers refer to rivers in inland dry areas that die away in desert on the way or infuse into inland lakes. The area providing water to the inland rivers is called as inland area.

Temperature refers to the air temperature. China uses centigrade as the unit. The thermometry used for weather observation is put in a breezy shutter, which is 1.5 meters high from the ground. Therefore, the commonly used temperature refers to the temperature in the breezy shutter 1.5 meters away from the ground. The calculation method is as follows:

Monthly average temperature is the summation of average daily temperature of one month divided by the actual days of that particular month.

Annual average temperature is the summation of monthly average of a year divided by 12 months.

Relative Humidity refers to the ratio of actual water vapor pressure to the saturation water vapor pressure under the current temperature. The calculation method is the same as that of temperature.

Volume of Precipitation refers to the deepness of liquid state or solid state (thawed) water falling from the sky to the ground that has not been evaporated, infiltrated or run off. The calculation method is as follows:

Monthly precipitation is the summation of daily precipitation of a month.

Annual precipitation is the summation of 12 months precipitation of a year.

Sunshine Hours refer to the actual hours of sun irradiating the earth. The calculation method is the same as that of the precipitation.

第二篇

CHAPTER 2

综合

GENERAL SURVEY

2-1 各部门机构数
Institutions in Various Sectors

部门	Sector	机构数 Grassroots Units		2004年比上年增长(%)
		2003	2004	Increase Rate % In 2004 Against 2003
农村基层单位(个)	**Rural Grassroots Units (unit)**			
基层组织	Basic Units			
乡政府	Township Governments	632	629	-0.5
镇政府	Town Governments	167	168	0.6
村民委员会	Village Committees	9445	9026	-4.4
乡村户数(户)	Numbers of Rural Households (household)	2147607	2195841	2.2
乡镇企业	Township Enterprises	354640	368553	3.9
国营农场	State-owned Farms	518	509	-1.7
国有及规模以上非国有工业企业(个)	**State-owned and Non-state-owned above Certain scale Industrial Enterprises (unit)**	**1254**	**1430**	**14.0**
内资企业	Domestic Funded Enterprises	1209	1367	13.1
国有企业	State-owned Industry	460	384	-16.5
集体企业	Collective-owned Industry	57	46	-19.3
股份合作企业	Cooperative Enterprises	15	9	-40.0
联营企业	Joint Ownership Enterprises	7	8	14.3
有限责任公司	Limited Liability Corporations	445	571	28.3
股份有限公司	Share Holding Enterprises	34	41	20.6
私营企业	Private Enterprises	187	308	64.7
港澳台商投资企业	Enterprises with Funds from Hong Kong, Macao and Taiwan	10	17	70.0
外商投资企业	Foreign Funded Enterprises	35	46	31.4
建筑业企业（个）	**Construction Enterprises and Units (unit)**	**776**	**932**	**20.1**
国有企业	State-owned Enterprise	112	105	-6.3
城镇集体企业	Urban Collective enterprise	77	51	-33.8
邮电业（个）	**Establishments of Postal and Telecommunication Services (unit)**			
邮政局及电信营业网点	Business Outlets of Post-office and Telecommunication	2905	1344	-53.7
卫生事业（个）	**Health Care (unit)**	**9434**	**9087**	**-3.7**
#医院、卫生院	Hospitals, Clinics	1471	1525	3.7
疗养院	Sanatoriums	7	6	-14.3
门诊部、所	Out-patient Department, Clinics	316	286	-9.5
专科防治所、站	Specialized Prevention & Treatment Stations	17	12	-29.4
卫生防疫站	Sanitation and Antiepidemic Stations	207	193	-6.8
妇幼保健所、站	Maternity and Childcare Centers	88	85	-3.4
社会福利（个）	**Social Welfare Establishments (unit)**			
社会福利事业单位	Social Welfare Institutions	948	966	1.9
#收养性福利事业单位	Adopting Social Welfare Institutions	508	496	-2.4
社会福利企业	Social Welfare Enterprises	159	161	1.3
社区服务单位	Community Services Units	126	146	15.9

2-1 续表 Continued

部 门	Sector	机构数 Grassroots Units 2003	2004	2004年比上年增长(%) Increase Rate % in 2004 Against 2003
教育事业(所)	**Education (unit)**			
普通高等学校	Regular Institutions of Higher Education	26	28	7.7
普通中等学校	Secondary Schools	2154	2186	1.5
#普通中学	Regular Secondary Schools	1932	1965	1.7
小 学	Primary Schools	5832	5451	-6.5
幼儿园	Kindergartens	909	977	7.5
艺术事业(个)	**Art Institutions (unit)**			
#艺术表演团体	Art Performance Troupes	88	109	23.9
艺术表演场所	Art Show Centers	26	30	15.4
#剧场、影剧院	Theaters	26	29	11.5
公共图书馆（个）	**Public Libraries (unit)**	**84**	**92**	**9.5**
群众文化事业(个)	**Mass Cultural Establishments (unit)**	**1014**	**1240**	**22.3**
群众艺术馆	Mass Art Centers	15	16	6.7
文化馆	Cultural Centers	91	92	1.1
文化站	Cultural Stations	908	1132	24.7
#乡镇文化站	Township Cultural Centers	834	994	19.2
艺术教育事业(个)	**Arts Education Establishments (unit)**	**3**	**3**	**持平**
其他文化事业(个)	**Other Cultural Establishments (unit)**	**1545**	**12**	**-99.2**
艺术创作机构	Art Creation Institutions	5	7	40.0
艺术研究机构	Art Research Institutions	1	2	1倍
文化艺术经纪与代理业	Brokers and Agents for Cultural and Arts Activities	2		
出版、发行事业(个)	**Publishing and Distribution Establishments (unit)**	**112**	**108**	**-3.6**
图书、电子音像出版社	Books, Electronic, Audio and Video Publishing House	12	10	-16.7
国家定点书刊印刷厂	Printing Houses	4	4	持平
书 店	Book Stores	96	96	持平
文物事业(个)	**Cultural Relic Establishments (unit)**	**102**	**107**	**4.9**
博物馆	Museums	23	25	8.7
文物机构	Cultural Relic Agencies	78	81	-20.6
文物商店	Antique Shops	1	1	持平
广播电视台站（座）	**Broadcasting and Television Stations (unit)**			
广播电台	Radio Stations	6	6	持平
电视台	Television Stations	16	10	-37.5
县级广播电视台	Number of Wire Broadcasting and Television Stations in County Level	24	24	持平
金融、保险业(个)	**Banking and Insurance (unit)**	**4063**	**4050**	**-0.3**
银行系统合计	Sub-total of Banking System	3675	3659	-0.4
保险系统合计	Sub-total of Insurance System	388	391	0.8

2-2 平均每天主要社会经济活动

Selected Indicators on Average Daily Social and Economic Activities

指 标	Item	1985	1990	1995	2000	2004
每天创造的财富	**Daily Production**					
新疆生产总值(万元)	Gross Domestic Product (10 000 yuan)	3068.49	7506.85	22602.74	37369.86	60278.08
第一产业	Primary Industry	1178.08	2602.74	6602.74	7890.41	12183.56
第二产业	Secondary Industry	1095.89	2301.37	8301.37	16082.19	27673.15
#工 业	Industry	786.71	1863.01	6000.00	11561.64	20410.96
建筑业	Construction	219.18	438.36	2301.37	4520.55	7262.19
第三产业	Tertiary Industry	794.52	2602.74	7726.03	13397.26	20421.37
#交通运输仓储和邮电通信业	Transport, Storage, Post & Telecommunication Services	136.99	547.95	1506.85	3342.47	3794.25
批发和零售贸易餐饮业	Wholesale and Retail Trade & Catering Services	246.58	767.12	2082.19	3232.88	4878.08
地方财政一般预算收入(万元)	Government Revenue (10 000 yuan)	231.95	591.32	1048.82	2165.55	4265.75
地方财政一般预算支出(万元)	Government Expenditures (10 000 yuan)	783.65	1304.68	2641.15	5231.59	11535.34
粮食(吨)	Grain (ton)	13606.85	18544.93	20004.38	22153.42	22699.45
棉花(吨)	Cotton (ton)	514.52	1284.38	2561.64	4109.59	4801.37
油料(吨)	Oil-bearing Crops (ton)	938.36	1067.40	1353.70	1647.67	1220.27
肉类(吨)	Meat (ton)	503.29	834.52	1435.07	2465.75	3510.41
水产品(吨)	Aquatic Products (ton)	24.54	63.61	121.73	164.56	200.81
布(万米)	Cloth (10 000 m)	57.95	82.24	83.45	76.88	38.33
原煤(吨)	Coal (ton)	43841.64	57534.25	74540.80	76682.06	102723.29
发电量(万千瓦小时)	ElectriCity (10 000 kwh)	1044.11	1912.05	3299.45	5013.23	7295.89
原油(吨)	Crude Oil (ton)	13671.23	19041.10	34735.07	50641.88	61726.58
钢(吨)	Steel (ton)	542.19	999.73	1933.97	3005.36	6825.48
成品钢材(吨)	Steel Products (ton)	458.36	780.27	1823.29	3596.09	6534.79
水泥(吨)	Cement (ton)	5508.22	7808.22	13421.37	24538.90	33232.60
每天消费量	**Daily National Consumption**					
最终消费(万元)	Final Consumption Expenditure (10 000 yuan)	2405.45	5155.33	11950.85	20768.59	31528.99
居民消费	Resident Consumption	1870.13	3904.61	8555.61	13429.32	18178.51
农村居民	Peasants Consumption	703.55	1450.37	3065.78	4382.78	6095.51
城镇居民	City and Town Residents	1166.85	2454.24	5489.83	9046.54	12083.00
政府消费	Government Consumption Expenditure	353.04	1250.72	3395.24	7339.26	13350.49
能源消费量(万吨标准煤)	Energy Consumption (10 000 tons of SCE)	3.87	5.27	7.49	9.09	13.11
社会消费品零售总额(万元)	Total Retail Sales of Consumer Goods (10 000 yuan)	1572.17	2857.65	6949.25	10260.27	15443.84
每天其他经济活动	**Other Daily Economic Activities**					
资本形成总额(万元)	Gross Capital Formation (10 000 yuan)	1600.79	3867.58	12978.30	16934.87	37326.11
固定资产形成	Fixed Capital Formation	1281.66	2506.73	10353.61	17756.79	33959.00
存货增加	Increase in Stock	319.13	1360.85	2624.68	-821.92	3367.12
城镇新建住宅面积(万平方米)	Residential Buildings Completed in Urban Areas (10 000 sq.m)	0.97	1.05	1.55	3.64	4.29
农民个人新建住宅面积(万平方米)	Private Residential Buildings Completed in Rural Areas (10 000 sq.m)	1.17	1.60	1.35	1.43	1.95
货运量(万吨)	Freight Volume (10 000 tons)	29.26	38.14	69.61	90.66	106.54
客运量(万人)	Passenger Volume (10 000 persons)	10.21	26.31	48.04	63.54	81.59
邮电业务总量(万元)	Business Volume of Postal and Telecommunications (10 000 yuan)	12.90	47.59	247.19	1295.89	4196.71
进出口总额(万美元)	Total Value of Imports and Exports (USD 10 000)	79.99	112.40	391.23	620.27	1544.01
出口总额	Total Exports	49.40	91.86	210.63	329.88	834.68
进口总额	Total Imports	30.62	20.53	180.60	290.39	709.33
实际利用外资额(万美元)	Foreign Capital Actually Used (USD 10 000)	1.42	20.90	149.86	5.27	12.56
国际旅游人数(人)	Number of Tourists from Abroad (person)	63.65	218.72	557.75	701.59	868.22
居民新增储蓄额(万元)	Outstanding Amount of Savings Deposit (10 000 yuan)	151.34	977.36	3547.12	2297.55	4461.64
每天人口变动和婚姻	**Daily Population Changes and Marriages**					
出 生(人)	Birth (person)	765.10	839.42	852.84	782.00	854.15
死 亡(人)	Death (person)	232.37	229.72	291.05	238.00	271.73
结 婚(对)	Marriages (couple)	436.13	433.79	455.79	445.28	504.12
离 婚(对)	Divorces (couple)	104.31	151.59	146.58	161.64	182.66

2-3 国民经济和社会发展总量与速度指标

指 标	Item	1985
人口与就业	**Population and Employment**	
人口(万人)	**Population (10 000 persons)**	
年底总人口	Population at the Year-end	1361.14
城镇人口	Urban	582.24
乡村人口	Rural	778.90
男性人口	Male	696.81
女性人口	Female	664.33
就业(万人)	**Employment (10 000 persons)**	
就业人员数	Employment	565.81
#职工人数	Staff and Workers	267.56
城镇登记失业人数	Registered Unemployed in Urban Areas	4.04
宏观经济	**Macroeconomic Indicator**	
国民核算(亿元)	**National Accounting (100 million yuan)**	
新疆生产总值	Gross Domestic Product	112
第一产业	Primary Industry	43
第二产业	Secondary Industry	40
第三产业	Tertiary Industry	29
支出法新疆生产总值	Gross Domestic Expenditure	
#最终消费	End Consumption	87.79
居民消费	Resident Consumption	68.26
政府消费	Public Consumption	19.53
资本形成总额	Total of Capital Formation	58.43
固定资本形成	Fixed Assets	46.78
存货增加	Increase in Stock	11.65
固定资产投资(亿元)	**Investment in Fixed Assets (100 million yuan)**	
全社会固定资产投资总额	Total Investment in Fixed Assets	44.48
国有单位	State-Owned Units	39.41
集体单位	Collective-Owned Units	2.10
私营个体经济	Individuals Economy	2.97
财政(亿元)	**Public Finance (100 million yuan)**	
地方财政一般预算收入	Local Financial Governments Intrabudgetary Ordinary Revenue	8.47
各项税收	Various Taxes	9.00
地方财政一般预算支出	Local Financial Governments Intrabudgetary Ordinary Expenditures	28.60
#基本建设支出	Expenditure in Capital Construction	5.33
企业挖潜改造支出	Expenditure in Potential-tapping and Reform for Enterprise	0.86
支援农业生产支出	Expenditure in Support of Farm Production	1.33
城市维护费	Expenditure in City Maintenance	0.56
文教卫生支出	Expenditure in Cultural, Education and Hygeian	7.49
行政管理费支出	Expenditure in Administrative Expense	3.99
物价总指数(上年=100)	**Price Indices (preceding year=100)**	
商品零售价格总指数	General Retail Price Index	108.1
居民消费价格总指数	General Consumer Price Index	107.8
利用外资(万美元)	**Utilization of Foreign Capital (USD 10 000)**	
签订利用外资协议额	Amount of Foreign Capital for Utilization through Signed Contracts or Agreements	4804
实际利用外资额	Amount of Foreign Capital Actually Utilized	518
能源生产与消费(万吨标准煤)	**Production and Consumption of Energy (10 000 tons of SCE)**	
能源生产总量	Total Energy Production	2092.47
能源消费总量	Total Energy Consumption	1410.84

注：2000 年城镇人口和乡村人口按“五普”口径计算，其余年份按公安年报口径计算。

The Total Amount of National Economy and Social Development and Speed Indicators

总量指标 Aggregate				速度指标(%) Indices and Growth Rates							
				指数(2004 年为以下各年) Index (2004 as percentuge of the followingyears)				平均增长速度 Average Annual Growth Rate			
1990	1995	2000	2004	1985	1990	1995	2000	1986-1990	1991-1995	1996-2000	1996-2004
1529.16	1661.35	1849.41	1963.11	144.23	128.38	118.16	106.15	2.4	1.7	2.2	1.9
685.96	822.53	624.18	690.11	118.53	100.60	83.90	110.56	3.3	3.7	-5.4	-1.9
843.20	838.82	1225.23	1273.00	163.44	150.97	151.76	103.90	1.6	-0.1	7.9	4.7
785.06	848.12	957.07	1008.02	144.66	128.40	118.85	105.32	1.3	2.6	2.4	1.9
744.10	813.23	892.34	955.09	143.77	128.36	117.44	107.03	2.3	1.8	1.9	1.8
617.70	676.00	693.85	744.49	131.58	120.53	110.13	107.30	1.8	1.8	0.5	1.1
300.53	311.93	255.75	235.97	88.19	78.52	75.65	92.27	2.4	0.7	-3.9	-3.1
9.60	10.24	11.00	10.87	269.06	113.23	106.15	98.82	18.9	1.3	1.4	0.7
274	825	1364	2200	577.5	364.3	211.3	143.9	9.7	11.5	8.0	8.7
95	240	288	445	328.8	224.7	162.5	122.7	7.9	6.7	5.8	5.5
84	303	587	1010	660.0	450.3	229.5	150.2	7.9	14.4	8.9	9.7
95	282	489	745	866.5	436.4	228.3	148.4	14.7	13.8	9.0	9.6
188.17	436.21	758.05	1150.81								
142.52	312.28	490.17	663.52								
45.65	123.93	267.88	487.29								
141.17	473.71	618.12	1362.40								
91.50	377.91	648.12	1239.50								
49.67	95.80	-30.00	122.90								
88.78	333.34	610.38	1161.52	2611.33	1308.31	348.45	190.29	14.8	30.3	12.9	14.9
75.45	263.28	460.26	759.95	1928.32	1007.22	288.65	165.11	13.9	28.4	11.8	12.5
4.70	22.90	12.45	8.64	411.43	183.83	37.73	69.40	17.5	37.3	-11.5	-10.3
8.63	27.80	63.85	158.73	5344.44	1839.28	570.97	248.60	23.8	26.4	18.1	21.4
21.78	38.28	79.07	155.70	1838.25	714.88	406.74	196.91	20.8	11.9	15.6	16.9
20.45	32.04	64.53	123.18	1368.67	602.35	384.46	190.89	17.8	9.4	15.0	16.1
47.62	96.40	190.95	421.04	1472.17	884.17	436.76	220.50	10.7	15.1	14.6	17.8
4.95	6.74	22.84	62.28	1168.48	1258.18	924.04	272.68	-1.5	6.4	27.6	28.0
1.23	2.53	2.17	2.55	296.51	207.32	100.79	117.51	7.4	15.5	-3.0	0.1
2.87	2.84	2.43	4.66	350.38	162.37	164.08	191.77	16.6	-0.2	-3.1	5.7
1.22	3.79	7.65	14.02	2503.57	1149.18	369.92	183.27	16.9	25.4	15.1	15.6
12.12	29.94	47.12	91.39	1220.16	754.04	305.24	193.95	10.1	19.8	9.5	13.2
5.83	15.78	22.07	48.78	1222.56	836.71	309.13	221.02	7.9	22.0	6.9	13.4
104.1	116.7	98.3	100.7								
105.0	119.7	99.4	102.7								
4463	42039	9212	25786	536.76	577.77	61.34	279.92	-1.5	56.6	-26.2	-5.3
7629	54699	1923	4586	885.33	60.11	8.38	238.48	71.2	48.3	-48.8	-24.1
2801.57	4266.06	5419.77	7112.95	339.93	253.89	166.73	131.24	6.0	8.8	4.9	5.8
1924.38	2733.04	3316.03	4784.83	339.15	248.64	175.07	144.29	6.4	7.3	3.9	6.4

Note: The urban and rural population in the year 2000 is calculated on the 5th National population census and others are calculated on the annals of public security.

2-3 续表 1

指 标	Item	1985
产 业	**Industry**	
农 业	**Agriculture**	
耕地面积(千公顷)	Cultivated Areas (1 000 hectares)	3082.52
农林牧渔业劳动力(万人)	Labor Force of Farming, Forestry, Animal Husbandry and Fishery (10 000 persons)	237.55
农林牧渔业总产值(亿元)	Gross Output Value of Farming, Forestry, Animal Husbandry and Fishery (100 million yuan)	56.57
主要农产品产量(万吨)	Output of Major Farm Products (10 000 tons)	
粮 食	Grain	496.65
棉 花	Cotton	18.78
油 料	Oil-bearing Crops	34.25
甜 菜	Beet Roots	40.69
水 果	Fruits	49.25
肉 类	Meat	18.37
水产品	Aquatic Products	0.90
工 业	**Industry**	
主要工业产品产量	Output of Major Industrial Products	
纱(万吨)	Yarn (10 000 tons)	3.91
布(亿米)	Cloth (100 million meter)	2.11
毛线(吨)	Knitting Wool (ton)	2396
呢绒(万米)	Woolen Goods (10 000 meter)	680
原盐(万吨)	Crude Salt (10 000 tons)	35.09
机制纸及纸板(万吨)	Machine-Made Paper and Paperboards (10 000 tons)	4.15
糖(万吨)	Sugar (10 000 tons)	7.18
原煤(万吨)	Crude Coal (10 000 tons)	1600.22
原油(万吨)	Crude Oil (10 000 tons)	499.00
发电量(亿千瓦小时)	ElectriCity (100 million kwh)	38.11
钢(万吨)	Steel (10 000 tons)	19.79
成品钢材(万吨)	Steel Products (10 000 tons)	16.73
水泥(万吨)	Cement (10 000 tons)	201.05
国有及限额以上非国有工业企业主要指标	Principal Financial Indicators of Industrial Enterprises of State Ownership and Non-state-owned Above Designated Size	
工业总产值(亿元)	Gross industrial Output Value (100 million yuan)	
固定资产原值(亿元)	Original Value of Fixed Assets (100 million yuan)	103.80
固定资产净值年平均余额(亿元)	Annual Average Balance of Net Value of Fixed Assets (100 million yuan)	
利润总额(亿元)	Profits (100 million yuan)	6.26
建筑业	**Construction**	
建筑业企业人数(万人)	Number of Employed Persons (10 000 persons)	25.85
建筑业总产值(亿元)	Gross Output Value (100 million yuan)	17.52
施工房屋面积(万平方米)	Floor Space of Buildings under Construction (10 000 sq.m)	582.20
竣工房屋面积(万平方米)	Floor Space of Buildings Completed (10 000 sq.m)	305.40
交通运输	**Transportation**	
货运量(万吨)	Freight Traffic (10 000 tons)	10681
铁 路	Railways	1278
公 路	Highways	8847
管 道	Pipelines	556
空 运	Civil Aviation	0.11
客运量(万人)	Passenger Traffic Volume (10 000 persons)	3728
铁 路	Railways	320
公 路	Highways	3399
空 运	Civil Aviation	9

Continued

总量指标 Aggregate				速度指标(%) Indices and Growth Rates							
				指数(2004 年为以下各年) Index (2004 as percentuge of the following years)				平均增长速度 Average Annual Growth Rate			
1990	1995	2000	2004	1985	1990	1995	2000	1986-1990	1991-1995	1996-2000	1996-2004
3086.89	3128.26	3416.52	3362.32	109.08	108.92	107.48	98.41	0.03	0.3	1.8	0.8
250.93	283.56	314.45	339.41	142.88	135.26	119.70	107.94	1.1	2.5	2.1	2.0
144.65	405.73	487.20	750.68	387.10	240.14	173.35	124.39	10.0	6.7	6.9	6.3
676.89	730.16	808.60	828.53	166.82	122.40	113.47	102.46	6.4	1.5	2.1	1.4
46.88	93.50	150.00	175.25	933.17	373.83	187.43	116.83	20.1	14.8	9.9	7.2
38.96	49.41	60.14	44.54	130.04	114.32	90.14	74.06	2.6	4.9	4.0	-1.1
224.37	288.14	292.65	344.21	845.93	153.41	119.46	117.62	40.7	5.1	0.3	2.0
79.88	114.43	151.87	264.22	536.49	330.77	230.90	173.98	10.2	7.5	5.8	9.7
30.46	52.38	90.00	128.13	697.50	420.65	244.62	142.37	10.6	11.5	11.4	10.4
2.32	4.44	6.01	7.33	814.44	315.95	165.09	121.96	20.9	13.9	6.2	5.7
10.19	24.47	33.43	29.14	745.27	285.97	119.08	87.17	21.1	19.1	6.4	2.0
3.00	3.05	2.81	1.40	66.35	46.67	45.90	49.82	6.9	0.3	-1.6	-8.3
2179	2286	1184	980	40.90	44.97	42.87	82.77	-2.0	1.0	-12.3	-9.0
1230	1262	754	206	30.28	16.74	16.32	27.31	12.6	0.5	-9.8	-18.2
159.00	25.98	31.78	87.32	248.85	54.92	336.10	274.76	35.3	-30.4	4.1	14.4
9.09	18.04	17.65	26.31	633.98	289.44	145.84	149.07	17.0	14.7	-0.4	4.3
16.84	30.18	30.76	37.26	518.94	221.26	123.46	121.13	16.6	12.4	0.4	2.4
2100.00	2720.74	2798.90	3749.40	234.31	178.54	137.81	133.96	5.6	5.3	0.6	3.6
695.00	1267.83	1848.43	2253.02	451.51	324.18	177.71	121.89	6.9	12.8	7.8	6.6
69.79	120.43	182.98	266.30	698.77	381.57	221.12	145.54	12.9	11.5	8.7	9.2
36.49	70.59	109.70	249.13	1258.87	682.73	352.93	227.10	-1.7	14.1	9.2	15.0
28.48	66.55	131.26	238.52	1425.70	837.50	358.41	181.72	11.2	18.5	14.6	15.2
285.00	489.88	895.67	1212.99	603.33	425.61	247.61	135.43	7.2	11.4	12.8	10.6
174.24	510.55	852.01	1571.84		694.12	355.67	200.68		10.2	5.8	15.1
233.86	809.27	1387.56	2311.41	2226.79	988.37	285.62	166.58	17.6	28.2	11.4	12.4
	492.72	891.27	1393.91			282.90	156.40			12.6	12.2
3.13	-1.18	90.49	226.32	3615.34	7230.67		250.10	-12.9			
22.86	35.33	26.16	33.22	128.51	145.32	94.03	126.99	-2.4	9.1	-5.8	-0.7
27.39	107.01	234.95	344.00	1963.47	1255.93	321.47	146.41	9.3	31.3	17.0	13.9
578.05	837.83	2241.48	2812.30	483.05	486.52	335.66	125.47	-0.1	7.7	21.8	14.4
282.88	364.95	1261.42	1483.35	485.71	524.37	406.45	117.59	-1.5	5.2	28.2	16.9
13920	25406	33091	38886	364.06	279.36	153.06	117.51	5.4	12.8	5.4	4.8
1691	2733	4199	5083	397.72	300.66	185.99	121.05	5.8	10.1	9.0	7.1
11551	21754	27048	31700	358.31	274.44	145.72	117.20	5.5	13.5	4.5	4.3
677	917	1840	2100	377.70	310.19	229.01	114.13	4.0	6.3	14.9	9.6
0.87	2.00	3.50	2.50	2272.73	287.36	125.00	71.43	51.2	18.1	11.8	2.5
9602	17533	23191	29782	798.87	310.16	169.86	128.42	20.8	12.8	5.8	6.1
388	672	1147	1023	319.69	263.66	152.23	89.19	3.9	11.6	11.3	4.8
9161	16739	21877	28473	837.69	310.81	170.10	130.15	21.9	12.8	5.5	6.1
53	122	167	286	3177.78	539.62	234.43	171.26	42.6	18.1	6.5	9.9

2-3 续表 2

指 标	Item	1985
邮电通信业	**Post and Telecommunication Services**	
邮电业务总量(亿元)	Total Business Revenue (100 million yuan)	0.47
函 件(万件)	Number of Letters Delivered (10 000 pieces)	7032.6
报刊期发数(万份)	Number of Newspapers and Magazines Distributed (10 000 copies)	578.9
局用交换机容量(万门)	CapaCity of Office Telephone Exchanges (10 000 lines)	
电话机(万部)	Number of Telephone Sets (10 000 units)	4.72
移动电话用户(万户)	Number of Mobile Telephone Subscribers (10 000 subscribers)	
国内商业	**Domestic Trade**	
社会消费品零售总额(亿元)	Total Retail Sales of Consumer Goods (100 million yuan)	57.38
对外经济贸易	**Foreign Trade**	
进出口总额(万美元)	Total Exports and Imports (USD 10 000)	29197
出口额	Exports	18020
进口额	Imports	11177
国际旅游	**International Tourism**	
来华旅游人数(万人)	Number of Tourists from Abroad (10 000 persons)	2.32
旅游外汇收入(万美元)	Foreign Exchange Earnings from Tourism (USD 10 000)	558
金 融	**Finance and Insurance**	
金融机构各项存款(亿元)	Deposits of National Banking System (100 million yuan)	
金融机构各项贷款(亿元)	Loans of National Banking System (100 million yuan)	
教育、科技、文化	**Education, Science and Technology and Culture**	
教 育	**Education**	
专任教师数(人)	Full-time Teachers (person)	
普通高等学校	Institutions of Higher Education	5473
中等学校	Secondary Schools	69185
小 学	Primary Schools	98294
在校学生数(万人)	Students Enrollment (10 000 persons)	
普通高等学校	Institutions of Higher Education	2.65
中等学校	Secondary Schools	105.43
小 学	Primary Schools	196.63
科 技	**Science and Technology**	
科学家、工程师数(人)	Number of Scientists and Engineers (persons)	
研究与发展经费支出(万元)	Expenditures on Research and Development (10 000 yuan)	
技术市场成交额(万元)	Volume of Transaction in Technical Markets (10 000 yuan)	
文 化	**Culture**	
出版数量	Publications	
图 书(万册 · 张)	Number of Books Published (10 000 copies)	4976
杂 志(万册)	Number of Magazines Issued (10 000 copies)	538
报 纸(万份)	Number of Newspapers Issued (10 000 copies)	11329
电视节目制作时间(小时)	Time for TV Programs Production (hour)	

Continued

总量指标	Aggregate			速度指标(%)				Indices and Growth Rates			
				指数(2004 年为以下各年) Index (2004 as percentuge of the following years)				平均增长速度 Average Annual Growth Rate			
1990	1995	2000	2004	1985	1990	1995	2000	1986-1990	1991-1995	1996-2000	1996-2004
1.74	9.02	47.30	153.18	32591.49	8803.45	1698.23	323.85	29.9	39.0	39.3	37.0
7380.5	9041.8	7148.0	4756.7	67.64	64.45	52.61	66.55	1.0	4.1	-4.6	-6.9
805.7	478.1	534.5	633.4	109.41	78.61	132.48	118.50	6.8	-9.9	2.3	3.2
	85.80	241.67	447.00			520.98	184.96			23.0	20.1
8.94	44.62	191.03	516.70	10947.03	5779.64	1158.00	270.48			33.8	31.3
	2.69	78.00	489.70			18204.46	627.82			96.1	78.3
104.30	253.65	374.50	563.70	982.40	540.46	222.24	150.52	12.7	19.5	8.1	9.3
41025	142798	226399	563563	1930.21	1373.71	394.66	248.92	7.0	28.3	9.7	16.5
33530	76880	120408	304658	1690.67	908.61	396.28	253.02	13.2	18.1	9.4	16.5
7495	65918	105991	258905	2316.41	3454.37	392.77	244.27	-7.7	54.5	10.0	16.4
7.98	20.36	25.61	31.69	1365.95	397.12	155.65	123.74	28.0	20.6	4.7	5.0
1212	5268	9494	9108	1632.31	751.51	172.90	95.94	16.8	34.2	12.5	6.3
223.17	838.42	1863.48	2959.78		1326.24	353.02	158.83		30.3	17.3	15.0
234.54	843.38	1403.13	2214.66		944.26	262.59	157.84		29.2	10.7	11.3
7002	7687	7924	12239	223.63	174.79	159.22	154.45	5.1	1.9	0.6	5.3
78596	76584	89211	106839	154.43	135.93	139.51	119.76	2.6	-0.5	3.1	3.8
95060	106001	131259	134915	137.26	141.93	127.28	102.79	-0.7	2.2	4.4	2.7
3.13	4.49	7.29	16.82	634.72	537.38	374.61	230.73	3.4	7.5	10.2	15.8
101.52	91.26	131.18	167.70	159.06	165.19	183.76	127.84	-0.8	-2.1	7.5	7.0
185.72	230.13	247.74	221.81	112.81	119.43	96.38	89.53	-1.1	4.4	1.5	-0.4
	15677	16018	16575			105.73	103.48	9.6	0.8	-5.1	0.6
		32381	60135				185.71				
	20074	66168	133371			664.40	201.56			26.9	23.4
4794	5653	7287	8250	165.80	172.09	145.94	113.22	-0.7	3.4	5.2	4.3
667	972	1125	1450	269.77	217.39	149.24	128.93	4.4	7.8	3.0	4.5
14048	18700	29486	33910	299.33	241.39	181.34	115.00	4.4	5.9	9.5	6.8
3699	9764	29261	50387		1362.18	516.05	172.20		21.4	24.5	20.0

2-3 续表 3

指 标	Item	1985
家庭、生活、环境	**Family, People's Livelihood and Environment**	
家 庭	**Family**	
家庭总户数(万户)	Total Number of Households (10 000 households)	309.63
城镇居民平均每户家庭人口(人)	Average Household Size in Urban Areas (person)	4.67
农村居民平均每户家庭人口(人)	Average Household Size in Rural Areas (person)	5.22
婚 姻	**Marriages and Divorces**	
结婚数(万对)	Number of Marriages (10 000 couples)	15.89
离婚数 (万对)	Number of Divorces (10 000 couples)	5.56
居 住	**Housing**	
城镇居民人均使用面积(平方米)	Per capita Gross Floor Space of Urban Residents (sq.m)	10.70
城镇居民人均建筑面积(平方米)	Per capita Gross Living Space in Urban Areas (sq.m)	14.27
农村居民人均居住面积(平方米)	Per capita Net Floor Space of Rural Residents (sq.m)	12.72
生 活	**People's Livelihood**	
城镇居民人均可支配收入(元)	Per Capita Annual Disposable Income of Urban Households (yuan)	734.82
农村居民人均纯收入(元)	Per Capita Net Income of Rural Residents (yuan)	394.30
城乡储蓄存款余额(亿元)	Balance of Saving Deposits in Urban and Rural Areas (100 million yuan)	33.51
工 资	**Wages and Welfare**	
工资总额 (亿元)	Total Wages (100 million yuan)	33.91
职工平均工资(元)	Average Wage of Staff and Workers (yuan)	1277
离休、退休、退职费(亿元)	Pensions for Retired Staff and Workers (100 million yuan)	
卫 生	**Health Care**	
医院、卫生院(个)	Number of Hospitals (unit)	947
医生(人)	Number of Doctors (person)	25721
医院、卫生院床位数(张)	Number of Hospital Beds (unit)	55298
市政建设	**Civic Construction**	
自来水供应量(亿吨)	Volume of Tapping Water Supply (100 million tons)	0.85
下水道长度(公里)	Length of Sewer Pipelines (km)	352
城市煤气、液化石油气和天然气供气量(亿立方米)	Volume of Coal Gas and Natural Gas Supply in Urban Areas (100 million cu.m)	
年末营运车辆(辆)	Year-end Operating Vehicles (vehicle)	611
铺装道路长度(公里)	Length of Paved Roads (km)	779
园林绿地面积 (公顷)	Public Green Areas (hectare)	4287
环境、灾害	**Environment and Disaster**	
工业污染治理项目年完成投资额(万元)	Investment Completed in Pollution Treatment Projects (10 000 yuan)	3624
环境污染与破坏事故次数(次)	Number of Pollution Accidents (time)	2
环境污染直接经济损失(万元)	Direct Economic Loss Arisen from Environment Pollution (10 000 yuan)	
环境污染事故赔罚款金额(万元)	Amount of Reparations and Fines (10 000 yuan)	2.4
火灾发生数(起)	Number of Fire Disasters (time)	
火灾损失(万元)	Fire Loss (10 000 yuan)	
交通事故发生数(起)	Number of Traffic Accidents (time)	
交通事故损失(万元)	Loss of Traffic Accidents (10 000 yuan)	

Continued

总量指标	Aggregate			速度指标(%)				Indices and Growth Rates			
				指数(2004 年为以下各年) Index (2004 as percentuge of the followingyears)				平均增长速度 Average Annual Growth Rate			
1990	1995	2000	2004	1985	1990	1995	2000	1986-1990	1991-1995	1996-2000	1996-2004
356.67	408.55	481.91	554.65	179.13	155.51	135.76	115.09	1.9	3.8	-3.6	3.5
4.07	3.44	3.18	3.04	65.10	74.69	88.37	95.60	-2.7	-3.3	-1.6	-1.4
5.37	5.62	5.33	5.11	97.89	95.16	90.93	95.87	0.6	0.9	-1.1	-1.1
15.84	16.64	16.25	18.40	115.80	116.16	110.58	113.23	-0.1	2.9	-2.3	1.1
5.65	5.35	5.90	6.67	119.96	118.05	124.67	113.05	0.3	7.1	8.2	2.5
13.55	16.57	20.06	18.82	175.89	138.89	113.58	93.82	4.8	4.1	3.9	1.4
18.07	22.09	26.75	24.44	171.27	135.25	110.64	91.36	4.8	4.1	3.9	1.1
13.78	16.12	17.25	19.10	150.16	138.61	118.49	110.72	1.6	3.2	1.4	1.9
1313.54	4163.44	5644.86	7503.42	983.67	550.28	193.29	142.57	12.3	23.3	6.3	7.6
683.47	1136.45	1618.08	2244.93	569.31	327.94	197.28	138.67	11.7	10.7	7.3	7.8
128.42	477.18	908.55	1534.67	4579.74	1195.04	321.61	168.91	30.8	30.0	13.7	13.9
66.88	167.73	234.47	356.33	1050.81	532.79	212.44	151.97	14.5	20.2	6.9	8.7
2272	5348	8717	14484	1134.22	637.50	270.83	166.16	12.21	18.7	10.3	11.7
9.43	33.15	75.99	109.83		1164.69	331.31	144.53		28.6	18.0	14.2
1049	1292	1352	1525	161.03	145.38	118.03	112.80	2.1	4.3	0.9	1.9
33686	39636	45402	43053	167.38	127.81	108.62	94.83	5.5	3.3	2.8	0.9
60707	66696	65916	74022	133.86	121.93	110.98	112.30	1.9	1.9	-0.2	1.2
1.57	3.10	5.00	6.60	776.47	420.38	212.90	132.00	13.1	14.6	10.0	8.8
533	1557	2008	2940	835.23	551.59	188.82	146.41	8.7	23.9	5.2	7.3
	151712	249403	245938			162.11	98.61			10.5	5.5
788	3324	5678	7438	1217.35	943.91	223.77	131.00	5.2	33.4	11.3	9.4
970	2403	2809	3706	475.74	382.06	154.22	131.93	4.5	19.9	3.2	4.9
6397	13481	19124	22339	521.09	349.21	165.71	116.81	8.3	16.1	7.2	5.8
5138	23934	22311	29622	817.40	576.54	123.77	93.22	7.2	36.0	-1.4	2.4
11	14	9	13	650.00	118.18	92.86	144.44	40.6	4.9	-8.5	-0.8
		15.95	111.20				697.18				
8.0	89.0	26.7	102.4	4266.67	1280.00	115.06	383.52	27.2	61.9	-21.4	1.6
		3050	4338				142.23				
		2329	2432				104.42				
		10048	8374				83.34				
		4443	2974				66.94				

2-4 国民经济和社会发展结构指标

Structural Indicators on National Economic and Social Development

单位: % (%)

指 标	Item	1985	1990	1995	2000	2004
人口与就业	**Population and Employment**					
人 口	**Population**					
城乡结构	Urban and Rural Structure	100	100	100	100	100
城 镇	Urban	42.8	44.9	49.5	33.8	35.2
乡 村	Rural	57.2	55.1	51.0	66.2	64.8
性别结构	Gender Structure	100	100	100	100	100
男	Male	51.2	51.3	51.1	51.8	51.3
女	Female	48.8	48.7	49.0	48.2	48.7
就 业	**Employment**					
产业结构	Industrial Structure	100	100	100	100	100
第一产业	First Industry	64.2	61.3	57.4	55.9	54.2
第二产业	Secondary Industry	15.8	17.4	18.4	14.1	13.2
第三产业	Tertiary Industry	20.0	21.3	24.2	30.0	32.6
宏观经济	**Macro Economy**					
国民核算	**National Accounting**					
新疆生产总值产业结构	GDP Industrial Structure	100	100	100	100	100
第一产业	Primary Industry	38.2	34.5	29.2	21.1	20.2
第二产业	Secondary Industry	36.1	30.5	36.7	43.0	45.9
第三产业	Tertiary Industry	25.7	35.0	34.1	35.9	33.9
投 资	**Investment**					
全社会固定资产投资结构	Structure of Total Investment in Fixed Assets	100	100.0	100	100	100
基本建设	Capital Construction	59.8	50.7	54.7	64.3	65.4
更新改造	Innovation	13.7	17.2	18.8	12.7	11.9
房地产开发	Real Estate Development		1.1	5.1	9.4	9.7
其他投资	Other Investment	26.5	31.0	21.4	13.6	13.0
资金来源结构	Structure of Funded Sources	100	100	100	100	100
国家预算内资金	State Budgetary Appropriation	26.4	11.9	2.9	8.3	15.8
国内贷款	Domestic Loans	16.2	33.2	24.6	22.1	13.5
利用外资	Foreign Investment	1.7	4.6	9.2	1.6	0.8
自筹和其他投资	Fundraising and Other Investment	55.7	50.3	63.3	68.0	69.9
财 政	**Government Finance**					
地方一般预算收入结构	Structure of Government Revenue	100	100	100	100	100
各项税收	Various Taxes	140.2	93.9	83.7	81.6	79.1
专项收入	Income form Special Item	0.6	2.2	3.7	5.1	6.9
其他各项收入	Other Revenue	-40.8	3.9	12.6	13.3	14.0
地方一般预算支出结构	Structure of Government Expenditures	100	100	100	100	100
基本建设支出	Expenditure in Capital Construction	18.6	10.4	7.0	12.0	14.8
企业挖潜改造支出	Expenditure in Potential-tapping and Reform for Enterprise	3.0	2.6	2.6	1.1	0.6
支援农业生产支出	Expenditure in Support of Farm Production	2.0	2.6	3.9	1.3	1.1
城市维护费	Expenditure in City Maintenance	4.7	6.0	3.0	4.0	3.3
文教卫生支出	Expenditure in Cultural, Education and Hygeian	26.2	25.5	31.6	24.7	21.7
行政管理费支出	Expenditure in Administrative Expense	14.0	12.2	16.4	11.6	11.6
其他各项支出	Other Expense	31.5	40.7	35.5	45.3	46.9
能源生产与消费	**Energy Production and Consumption**					
能源生产总量结构	Structure of Total Energy Production	100	100	100	100	100
原 煤	Coal	60.0	58.8	50..1	40.6	41.4
原 油	Petroleum Crude Oil	34.1	35.8	43.5	48.7	45.3
天然气	Natural Gas	3.5	2.4	3.6	7.9	10.7
水风电	Water, Wind and Electricity	2.4	3.0	2.8	2.8	2.6
能源消费总量结构	Structure of Total Energy Consumption	100	100	100	100	100
煤 炭	Coal	72.0	69.6	66.2	63.6	61.0
石 油	Petroleum Oil	19.3	22.5	23.8	23.3	20.1
天然气	Natural Gas	5.1	3.5	5.6	8.6	15.0
水风电	Water, Wind and Electricity	3.6	4.4	4.4	4.5	3.9

2-4 续表 1 Continued

单位: % (%)

指 标	Item	1985	1990	1995	2000	2004
产 业	**Industrial**					
农 业	**Agriculture**					
农林牧渔业产值结构	Structure of Gross Output Value of AgricultureForestry,Animal Husbandry, Fishery	100	100	100	100	100
农 业	Farming	75.9	76.4	77.6	74.0	68.6
林 业	Forestry	4.6	2.6	1.4	1.7	1.8
牧 业	Animal Husbandry	19.2	20.4	20.3	23.5	25.0
渔 业	Fishery	0.3	0.6	0.7	0.8	0.6
农林牧渔服务业	Agricultural, Forestry, Animal Husbandry, Fishery and Their Services					4.0
工 业	**Industry**					
工业总产值规模结构	Structure of Gross Output Value of Industry	100	100	100	100	100
大型企业	Large Enterprises	28.7	27.5	46.9	53.7	58.9
中型企业	Medium-sized Enterprises	15.4	17.4	13.4	10.1	18.7
小型企业	Small Enterprises	55.9	55.1	39.7	36.2	22.4
建筑业	**Construction**					
建筑业总产值结构	Structure of Gross Output Value of Construction			100	100	100
土木工程建筑业	Civil Engineering Construction			89.1	91.5	87.8
线路管理设备安装业	Line and Equipment Installation			10.3	7.8	9.1
建筑物装修装饰业	Building Decoration			0.6	0.7	1.4
其他建筑业	Other Building Sector					1.7
交通运输业	**Transportation**					
货运量结构按运输方式分	By Means of Transportation	100	100	100	100	100
铁 路	Railways	12.0	12.1	10.8	12.7	13.1
公 路	Highways	82.8	83.0	85.6	81.7	81.5
民用航空	Civil Aviation	…	…	…	…	…
管道输油(气)	Pipelines	5.2	4.9	3.6	5.6	5.4
国内商业	**Domestic Trade**					
社会消费品零售总额结构	Composition of Retail Sales of Consumer Goods	100	100	100	100	100
市	Cities	42.8	54.8	57.5	62.4	67.9
县	Counties	18.6	23.3	19.7	17.4	15.5
县以下	Below Counties	38.6	21.9	22.8	20.2	16.6
对外经济贸易	**Foreign Trade**					
出口商品结构	Structure of Exports	100	100	100	100	100
初级产品	Primary Goods	72.8	59.6	50.3	29.9	12.4
工业制成品	Manufactured Goods	27.2	40.4	49.7	70.1	87.6
进口商品结构	Structure of Imports	100	100	100	100	100
初级产品	Primary Goods	1.4	2.4	41.7	43.9	27.2
工业制成品	Manufactured Goods	98.6	97.6	58.3	56.1	72.8
国际旅游	**International Tourism**					
来华旅游人数结构	Structure of Tourists	100	100	100	100	100
外国人	Foreigners	68.9	80.4	91.1	81.4	85.5
港澳台同胞	Compatriots form Hong Kong, Macao and Taiwan	31.1	19.6	8.9	18.6	14.5
金融保险业	**Finance and Insurance**					
金融机构资金来源结构	Structure of Sources of Funds in State Banks				100	100
各项存款	Various Deposits				122.8	118.6
金融债券	Treasury Bonds				…	-1.7
所有者权益	Owner's Right and Interest				0.1	1.5
其 他	Others				-22.9	-18.4
金融机构资金运用结构	Structure of Fund Uses in State Banks				100	100
各项贷款	Loans				92.5	88.7
有价证券及投资	Securities and Investment				4.4	4.7
应收及预付款	Payable and Pre-payment					1.5
委托投资	Proxy Investment				1.6	0.4
库存现金	Cash in Stock				1.1	0.9
其 他	Others				0.4	3.8
教育、科技、文化	**Education, Science and Culture**					
教 育	**Education**					
在校学生结构	Structure of Student Enrollment	100	100	100	100	100
大学生	College and University Students	0.9	1.1	1.5	2.0	4.1
中学生	Secondary School Students	32.4	31.4	24.2	30.8	41.2
小学生	Primary School Students	66.7	67.5	74.3	67.2	54.7

2-4 续表 2 Continued

单位: % (%)

指 标	Item	1985	1990	1995	2000	2004
专任教师结构	Full-time Teachers by Type	100	100	100	100	100
大 学	College and Universities	3.2	3.9	4.0	3.5	4.8
中 学	Secondary Schools	40.0	43.5	40.3	39.1	42.0
小 学	Primary Schools	56.8	52.6	55.7	57.4	53.2
科 技	**Science and Technology**					
科技经费筹集额结构	Structure of Funding for Scientific and Technological Income			100	100	100
政府资金	Government Fund			20.9	25.6	19.5
企业资金	Enterprises Fund			57.2	58.2	71.0
银行贷款	Loans from Banks			5.8	5.7	3.1
其 他	Others			16.1	10.5	6.4
科技经费内部支出结构	Structure of Internal Expenditures on Scientific and Technological Activities			100	100	100
劳务费	Service Fees			27.5	34.3	34.7
固定资产购建	Purchases of Fixed Assets			28.7	28.5	17.3
研究与发展经费支出	Research and Development Expenses				23.9	44.2
其 他	Others			43.8	13.3	3.8
生活、环境	**Family, People's Livelihood and Environment**					
生 活	**People's Livelihood**					
城市居民消费结构	Consumption Structure of Urban Residents	100	100	100	100	100
食品类	Food	46.8	47.8	44.8	36.4	36.1
衣着类	Clothing	17.8	15.6	17.7	13.1	13.3
家庭设备、用品及其他	Articles for Daily Use and Others	31.9	32.0	31.9	42.7	40.8
居 住	Residence	3.5	4.6	5.6	7.8	9.8
农村居民消费结构	Consumption Structure of Rural Residents	100	100	100	100	100
食品类	Food	57.9	53.7	50.1	50.0	45.2
衣着类	Clothing	16.2	15.2	12.7	9.2	8.2
家庭设备、用品及其他	Articles for Daily Use and Others	14.5	17.4	24.3	27.0	28.6
居 住	Residence	11.4	13.7	12.9	13.8	18.0
福 利	**Social Welfare**					
离退休退职人员结构	Structure of Retired and Resigned Persons		100	100	100	100
离休人员	Retired Veterans		11.9	10.2	6.3	4.4
退休人员	Retired Persons		82.8	86.1	90.2	92.3
退职人员	Resigned Persons		5.3	3.7	3.5	3.3
离退休退职人员保险福利费结构	Structure of Insurance Contribution and Welfare Funds of Retired and Resigned Persons		100	100	100	100.0
离休金	Pensions for Retired Veterans		14.0	10.3	9.0	8.5
退休金	Pensions for Retired Persons		64.2	72.5	76.9	81.3
退职生活费	Resignation Allowances for Living Expenses		1.4	1.3	1.6	1.6
医疗卫生费	Expenses for Medical Care		8.2	10.0	9.2	4.2
其 他	Others		12.2	5.9	3.3	4.4
卫 生	**Health Care**					
医生结构	Doctors by Types	100	100	100	100	100
中 医	Doctors of Traditional Chinese Medicine	8.5	9.2	9.8	8.9	3.5
执业医师(西医师)	(Doctors of Western Medicine)	43.3	64.9	66.0	68.0	75.5
执业助理医师(西医士)	(Paramedics of Western Medicine)	48.2	25.9	24.2	23.1	21.0
医院床位结构	Hospital Beds by Area	100	100	100	100	100
市医院	Hospitals at City Level				58.3	71.8
县医院	Hospitals at County Level				41.7	28.2
环境、灾害	**Environment and Disasters**					
工业治理污染资金使用结构	Uses of Funds Inindustrial Pollution Treatment	100	100	100	100	100
治理废水	Waste Water Treatment	46.6	55.3	54.5	38.2	41.6
治理废气	Waste Gas Treatment	37.8	32.4	29.7	40.9	44.3
治理固体废物	Solid Wastes Treatment	4.6	10.6	14.0	1.6	9.3
治理噪声	Noise Abatement	1.7	0.9	0.5	18.4	0.3
其 他	Others	9.3	0.8	1.3	0.9	4.5
火灾事故损失额结构	Structure of Fire Losses Converted into Cash				100	100
特 大	Extraordinarily Serious Fires				15.7	…
重 大	Serious Fires				14.3	0.1
一 般	Ordinary Fires				70.0	99.9
交通事故损失额结构	Structure of Losses of Traffic Accidents Converted into Cash				100	100
特 大	Extraordinarily Serious Accidents				21.2	29.1
重 大	Serious Accidents				22.4	60.5
一 般	Ordinary Accidents				56.4	10.4

2-5 国民经济和社会发展比例和效益指标

Indicators on Proportions and Efficiency in National Economic and Social Development

指 标	Item	1985	1990	1995	2000	2004
人口与就业	**Population and Employment**					
人 口	**Population**					
出生率(‰)	Birth Rate (‰)	19.80	26.41	18.90	17.57	16.00
死亡率(‰)	Death Rate (‰)	6.39	7.81	6.45	5.4	5.09
自然增长率(‰)	Natural Growth Rate (‰)	13.41	18.60	12.45	12.17	10.91
就 业	**Employment**					
就业者负担人口	Dependency Ratio	1.41	1.48	1.46	1.67	1.64
三次产业从业者比例(以第一产业为 100)	Employment Ratio by Type of Industry (Employment in primary industry=100)					
第一产业	Primary Industry	100	100	100	100	100
第二产业	Secondary Industry	24.7	28.4	32.0	25.2	24.4
第三产业	Tertiary Industry	31.1	34.8	41.9	53.6	60.2
城镇失业率(%)	Unemployment Rate in Urban Areas (%)	1.9	3.8	3.9	3.8	3.8
宏观经济	**Macro Economy**					
国民核算	**National Accounting**					
三次产业增加值比例(以第一产业为 100)	Ratio of Value-added by Type of Industry (Value added in primary industry=100)					
第一产业	Primary Industry	100	100	100	100	100
第二产业	Secondary Industry	93.0	88.4	125.7	203.8	227.1
第三产业	Tertiary Industry	67.4	100.4	117.0	169.8	167.6
全社会劳动生产率(元/人)	Overall Labor Productivity (yuan/person)	1979	4436	12373	19651	30021
第一产业	Primary Industry	1184	2510	6216	7445	11110
第二产业	Secondary Industry	4462	7820	24733	58079	104034
第三产业	Tertiary Industry	2568	7207	17832	23716	31646
人均生产总值(元)	Per capita GDP (yuan)	820	1799	4764	7377	11199
固定资产投资	**Investment in Fixed Assets**					
全社会固定资产投资相当于新疆生产总值比例(%)	Proportion of Investment in Fixed Assets to GDP (%)	39.70	32.40	40.40	44.75	52.79
全社会房屋建筑面积竣工率(%)	Rate of Total Floor Space of Buildings Completed in Construction (%)	79.5	76.8	67.5	58.7	80.8
基本建设固定资产交付使用率(%)	Rate of Fixed Assets Completed in Capital Construction and Put Into Use (%)	66.0	77.2	80.1	122.6	86.3
基本建设项目建成投产率(%)	Rate of Projects Completed in Capital Construction and Put Into Use (%)	59.9	59.9	66.7	72.5	66.3
财 政	**Finance**					
地方财政一般预算收入相当于新疆生产总值比例(%)	GDP Percentage of Local Financial Revenue (%)	7.5	7.9	4.6	5.8	7.1
地方财政一般预算支出相当于新疆生产总值比例(%)	GDP Percentage of Local Financial Expenditure (%)	25.5	17.4	11.7	14.0	19.1
预算外资金收入相当于地方财政一般预算收入比例(%)	Proportion of Extra-budgetary Receipt to Local Government Revenue (%)	139.6	99.8	85.3	66.8	31.6
利用外资	**Utilization of Foreign Capital**					
实际利用外资额相当于签订利用外资额比例(%)	Proportion of Foreign Capital Actually Used to Total Amount of Foreign Capital for Utilization by Signed Contracts or Agreements (%)		80.94	72.23	20.87	17.78
能源生产与消费	**Production and Consumption of Energy**					
能源生产弹性系数	ElastiCity Ratio of Energy Production	0.69	0.50	0.87	0.40	0.61
能源消费弹性系数	ElastiCity Ratio of Energy Consumption	0.80	0.79	0.54	0.38	1.59
每万元新疆生产总值消耗的能源 (吨)	Energy Consumption per 10 000 yuan GDP (ton)	12.60	7.02	3.21	2.43	2.17

2-5 续表 1 Continued

指　　标	Item	1985	1990	1995	2000	2004
产　业	**Industries**					
农 业	**Agriculture**					
农业从业者人均农产品产量（公斤）	Output of Farm Products per Agricultural Laborer (kg)					
粮　食	Grain	2090.7	2514.5	2575.0	2571.5	2441.2
棉　花	Cotton	79.1	237.6	329.7	477.0	516.3
油　料	Oil-bearing Crops	144.2	144.7	174.3	191.3	131.2
肉　类	Meat	77.3	113.2	184.7	286.2	377.5
水产品	Aquatic Products	3.8	8.6	15.7	19.1	21.6
每公顷播种面积农产品产量（公斤）	Output of Farm Crops per Hectare of Sown Area (kg)					
粮　食	Grain	2685	3705	4583	5595	6010
棉　花	Cotton	750	1080	1259	1485	1554
油　料	Oil-bearing Crops	1185	1440	1611	1935	2067
工业企业效益	**Economic Efficiency of Industry**					
总资产贡献率（%）	Ratio of Total Assets to Industrial Output Value (%)				11.24	16.30
资产负债率（%）	Assets-Liability Ratio (%)			71.39	62.71	53.30
成本费用利润率（%）	Ratio of Profits to Industrial Cost (%)	13.1	2.60	-0.25	12.83	17.40
流动资产周转次数（次/年）	Number of Times of Annual of Turnover Circulating Funds (times/year)	2.9	1.50	1.21	1.55	2.20
全员劳动生产率（按增加值计算）(元/人.年)	Overall Labor Productivity(yuan/person-year) (in terms of value-added per employee)			12289	35645	148745
建筑业	**Construction**					
技术装备率（元/人）	Value of Machinery per Laborer (yuan/person)	1332	2511	4211	8582	11389
产值利税率（%）	Ratio of Per-tax Profits to Gross Output Value (%)			3.44	0.82	5.07
全员劳动生产率(按总产值计算)(元/人)	Overall Labor Productivity (yuan/person) (in terms of gross output value per employee)		12014	34668	74994	107150
交通运输业	**Transportation**					
客运量弹性系数	ElastiCity of Passenger Traffic	0.12	0.85	0.23	0.23	0.94
货运量弹性系数	ElastiCity of Freight Traffic	0.25		0.51	0.39	0.34
铁路网密度（公里/万平方公里）	Railway Density (km/10 000 sq.km)	9.48	9.48	12.24	18.08	18.01
公路网密度（公里/万平方公里）	Highway Density (km/10 000 sq.km)	134	153	182	208	522
铁路货运密度(吨/公里)	Railway Freight Traffic Density (ton/km)	646	895	1182	1179	1795
公路货运密度（吨/公里）	Highway Freight Traffic Density (ton/km)	27.55	42.51	72.52	191.09	151.28
邮电通信业	**Post and Communication Services**					
邮电业务总量弹性系数	ElastiCity of Postal and Telecommunication Services	0.93	7.18	6.77	4.43	3.05
固定电话普及率(部/百人)	Access to Telephones, National (set/100 persons)	0.34	0.58	4.01	15.00	26.30
移动电话普及率(部/百人)	(set/100 persons)					24.90
国内商业	**Domestic Trade**					
批零和餐饮业人均消费品零售额(元)	Per capita Retail Sales of Consumer Goods (yuan)	424.2	527.9	1131.9	1547.8	2705.1
对外经济贸易	**Foreign Trade**					
进出口总额相当于新疆生产总值比例(%)	Proportion of Total Imports & Exports to GDP (%)	7.66	7.16	14.45	13.74	21.20
国际旅游	**International Tourism**					
每一来华游客花费(美元)	Expenditure per International Tourist in China (USD)	240	152	259	371	287

2-5 续表 2 Continued

指　　标	Item	1985	1990	1995	2000	2004
金融保险	**Finance and Insurance**					
金融机构存款相当于新疆生产总值比例(%)	Bank Deposits as Percentage of GDP (%)		81.45	101.63	136.62	134.53
金融机构贷款相当于新疆生产总值比例(%)	Bank Loans as Percentage of GDP (%)		85.60	102.23	102.87	100.66
金融机构现金支出相当于收入比例(%)	Proportion of Cash Outlay to Cash Receipt in Bank (%)		105.71	104.59	101.65	100.41
教育、科技、文化	**Education, Science and Technology and Culture**					
教 育	**Education**					
学龄儿童入学率(%)	Rate of School-age Children Enrollment (%)	95.40	97.50	97.03	97.03	97.79
小学升学率(%)	Rate of Graduates of Primary Schools Entering Junior Secondary Schools (%)	85.60	82.17	84.10	92.01	95.33
初中升学率 (%)	Rate of Graduates of Junior Secondary Schools Entering Senior Secondary Schools (%)	47.03	39.12	34.00	30.30	41.14
学校教师负担系数(%)	Student-teacher Ratio (in percentage) (%)					
高等学校	Colleges and Universities	4.84	4.47	5.78	9.34	13.74
中等学校	Secondary Schools	15.68	13.12	11.91	14.92	16.08
小学学校	Primary Schools	20	19.54	20.77	18.87	16.44
科 技	**Science and Technology**					
研究与开发经费支出相当于新疆生产总值比例(%)	R&D Expenditures as Percentage of GDP (%)			0.39	0.23	0.27
文 化	**Culture**					
每百万人有艺术表演团体 (个)	Number of Troupes per Million Persons(unit)	7.79	6.21	5.24	4.76	5.59
每百万人有公共图书馆 (个)	Number of Public Libraries per Million Persons(unit)	4.26	4.05	3.97	4.33	4.72
每百万人有博物馆 (个)	Number of Museums per Million Persons(unit)	0.22	0.52	0.72	1.24	1.28
家庭、生活、环境	**Family, People's Livelihood and Environment**					
家 庭	**Family**					
负担少儿系数 (%)	Dependency Ratio of Children (%)		52.43	46.65	40.06	36.79
负担老年系数 (%)	Dependency Ratio of the Aged (%)		6.20	6.81	6.86	6.70
婚 姻	**Marriages and Divorces**					
离婚率 (‰)	Divorce Rate (‰)			6.4	6.4	6.7
生 活	**People's Livelihood**					
城镇与农村居民收入增长率比例 (以农村居民收入指数为 1)(1978=100)	Proportion of Growth Rate of Annual Income of Urban Residents to the Growth Rate of Annual Net Income of Rural Residents (1978=100)	0.59	0.68	1.40	1.37	1.25
福 利	**Welfare**					
离退休退职费相当于工资总额比例(%)	Pensions for Retired Veterans, Retired and Resigned Persons as Percentage of Total Wages (%)		14.1	19.76	32.41	30.82
离退休退职相当于在职人数比例(%)	Proportion of the Number of Workers Who Have Retired or Resigned to the Number of Employed Ones (%)		17.83	24.80	39.23	45.02
卫 生	**Health Care**					
每万人医院数(个)	Number of Hospitals per 10 000 Persons (unit)	0.70	0.69	0.78	0.73	0.78
每万人医生数(人)	Number of Doctors per 10 000 Persons (unit)	19.00	22.03	23.86	24.59	21.9
每万人医院、卫生院床位数 (张)	Number of Hospital Beds per 10 000 Persons (unit)	40.6	40.5	40.1	35.7	37.7
医院病床使用率(%)	Utilization Rate of Hospital Beds (%)		77.2	66.8	66.31	73.65
市政建设	**City Construction**					
城市自来水普及率(%)	Percentage of Households with Access to Tap Water (%)	62.0	80.9	97.1	98.8	98.1
城市用气普及率(%)	Percentage of Households with Access to Tap Gas (%)	36.0	49.8	81.0	92.8	87.3
每万人园林绿地面积(公顷)	Public Green Areas per 10 000 Persons (hectare)	21.3	21.6	41.5	53.4	44.5
环境、灾害	**Environment and Disasters**					
平均每起火灾损失(元)	Average Loss of per Fire Disaster (yuan)				7635	5607
平均每起交通事故损失(元)	Average Loss of per Traffic Accident (yuan)				4775	3552
平均每起环境污染事故直接经济损失(元)	Average Loss per Pollution Accident (yuan)				17722	85538

2-6 人均主要工农业产品产量

Per capita Output of Major Industrial and Agricultural Products

年 份 Year	粮 食 (公斤) Grain (kg)	棉 花 (公斤) Cotton (kg)	油 料 (公斤) Oil-bearing Crops (kg)	甜 菜 (公斤) Sugar Crops (kg)	水 果 (公斤) Fruits (kg)	猪牛羊肉 (公斤) Pork, Beef and Mutton (kg)	水产品 (公斤) Aquatic Products (kg)
1978	303.0	4.5	8.5	13.4	11.4	7.9	0.5
1980	304.1	6.2	13.9	30.3	12.3	9.4	0.5
1985	367.2	13.9	25.3	30.1	36.4	12.8	0.7
1990	453.8	31.4	26.1	150.4	53.6	18.6	1.6
1991	436.2	41.5	26.3	166.6	52.6	19.3	1.6
1992	450.5	42.6	22.7	209.9	58.6	20.6	1.7
1993	452.2	42.7	23.2	148.7	62.7	21.4	1.8
1994	411.5	54.5	31.4	184.8	66.4	23.3	2.2
1995	443.3	56.8	30.0	174.9	69.4	27.9	2.7
1996	488.4	56.1	18.5	211.6	69.2	31.4	2.9
1997	484.4	67.5	17.6	228.2	72.6	32.7	3.1
1998	479.0	80.8	21.7	296.1	70.1	37.7	3.1
1999	476.3	79.9	34.3	201.1	77.5	39.9	3.2
2000	446.2	82.8	33.2	161.5	83.8	42.4	3.3
2001	427.3	84.3	22.9	244.3	82.8	44.5	3.3
2002	463.3	79.3	23.5	246.9	104.8	46.9	3.4
2003	417.6	83.4	26.1	198.8	113.7	50.4	3.5
2004	425.2	89.9	22.9	176.7	135.6	55.2	3.8

年 份 Year	布 (米) Cloth (m)	机制纸及纸板 (公斤) Machine-made Paper and Paperboard (kg)	纱 (公斤) Yarn (kg)	原 煤 (公斤) Coal (kg)	原 油 (公斤) Crude Oil (kg)	发 电 量 (千瓦小时) ElectriCity (kwh)	钢 (公斤) Steel (kg)	水 泥 (公斤) Cement (kg)
1978	13	1.6	2.29	884	289	173	7	64
1980	13	1.9	2.46	895	308	186	8	72
1985	16	3.1	2.89	1183	369	282	15	149
1990	20	6.1	6.83	1408	466	468	23	191
1991	18	6.6	8.81	1358	490	510	26	211
1992	15	7.5	9.10	1395	526	549	30	237
1993	15	8.5	7.87	1490	664	596	33	261
1994	17	9.0	12.20	1613	708	650	40	276
1995	18	11.0	14.86	1652	770	731	43	297
1996	16	10.1	12.45	1782	870	812	52	336
1997	18	9.5	14.51	1773	956	884	57	369
1998	15	9.7	12.72	1689	940	910	62	421
1999	16	10.2	16.71	1577	988	961	60	458
2000	15	9.7	18.45	1546	1021	1011	61	495
2001	14	10.4	16.25	1514	1045	1061	72	527
2002	11	12.0	16.72	1639	1077	1123	93	545
2003	8	12.2	15.25	1814	1116	1222	106	588
2004	7	13.5	14.95	1924	1156	1367	128	623

2-7 人均国民经济主要指标

Per Capita Main Indicators on National Economy

指 标	Item	1990	1995	2000	2004
新疆生产总值(元)	Gross Domestic Product (yuan)	1799	4764	7377	11199
工农业总产值(元)	Gross Output Value of Industry and Agriculture (yuan)	2444	6066	8544	12865
工业总产值	Gross Industrial Output Value	1474	3603	5856	9013
农林牧渔业总产值	Gross Output Value of Agriculture, Forestry, Animal Husbandry and Fishery	970	2463	2688	3852
固定资产投资总额(元)	Total Investment in Fixed Assets (yuan)	595	2024	3368	5961
国有基本建设投资额(元)	Investment in Capital Construction of State-Owned Units(yuan)	332	1054	2068	2724
地方财政一般预算收入(元)	Local Governments Revenue (yuan)	146	232	436	799
地方财政一般预算支出(元)	Local Governments Expenditures (yuan)	319	585	1054	2161
耕地面积(公顷)	Cultivated Area (hectare)	0.20	0.19	0.18	0.17
粮食产量(公斤)	Grain Yield (kg)	453.8	443.3	446.2	425.2
棉花产量(公斤)	Cotton Yield (kg)	31.4	56.8	82.8	89.9
油料产量(公斤)	Oil-bearing Crops Yield (kg)	26.1	30.0	33.2	22.9
甜菜产量(公斤)	Beet Roots Yield (kg)	150.4	174.9	161.5	176.7
猪牛羊肉产量(公斤)	Pork, Beef and Mutton Yield (kg)	18.6	27.9	42.4	55.2
水产品产量(公斤)	Aquatic Products Yield (kg)	1.6	2.7	3.3	3.8
水果产量(公斤)	Fruits Yield (kg)	53.6	69.4	83.8	135.6
果用瓜产量(公斤)	Fruit Melon Yield (kg)	62.6	41.7	83.3	95.5
布(米)	Cloth (m)	20	18	15	7
机制纸和纸板(公斤)	Machine-made Paper and Paperboard (kg)	6.1	11.0	9.7	13.5
纱(公斤)	Yarn (kg)	6.83	14.86	18.45	14.95
原煤(公斤)	Coal Output (kg)	1408	1652	1546	1924
原油(公斤)	Crude Oil Output (kg)	466	770	1021	1156
发电量(千瓦小时)	Electric Power (kwh)	468	731	1011	1367
水泥(公斤)	Cement (kg)	191	297	495	623
社会消费品零售总额(元)	Total Retail Sales of Consumer Goods (yuan)	699	1540	2067	2893
海关出口总额(美元)	Value of Exports (USD)	23.2	46.7	66.4	156.4
高等学校在校学生数(人/万人)	Students Enrollment in Institions of Higher Education (person/10 000 persons)	20.5	27.0	39.4	85.7
中等专业学校在校学生数(人/万人)	Students Enrollment in Specialized Secondary Schools (person/10 000 persons)	30.0	41.3	56.9	36.6
普通中学在校学生数(人/万人)	Students Enrollment in Regular Secondary Schools (person/10 000 persons)	564	451	613	773
医院床位数(人/万人)	Medical Beds (person/10 000 persons)	40.5	40.1	35.7	39.8
卫生技术人员数(人/万人)	Medical Technical Personnel (person/10 000 persons)	52.2	55.4	53.0	50.8
#医 生	Doctors	22.0	23.9	24.6	21.9
城乡居民储蓄存款余额(元)	Urban and Rural Savings Deposits (yuan)	840	2872	4913	7818

2-8 天山北坡经济带主要经济指标

(2004 年)

指 标	Item	全区合计 total of the whole region	北坡经济带占全区比重(%) ratio of the economic belt	北坡经济带合计 total	乌鲁木齐市 Urumqi City	克拉玛依市 Karamay City
人口与劳动力(万人)	**Population and Labor force (10 000 persons)**					
年末总人口	Year-end Population	1963.11	23.3	458.37	185.96	25.39
#少数民族人口	Population of Ethnic minority	1182.86	8.5	100.97	48.02	6.41
城镇人口	Population of cities and Towns	690.11	63.9	441.30	182.26	25.39
乡村人口	Rural population	1273.00	1.3	17.06	3.70	
从业人员	Employment	744.49	21.0	156.54	86.27	12.33
#职工人数	Staff and Workers	235.97	34.0	80.21	44.81	10.50
综合	**General**					
新疆生产总值(万元)	Xinjiang Gross Production Value (10 000 yuan)	22001500	50.2	11039075	4842599	2962019
第一产业	First Industry	4447000	21.5	955306	70874	8374
第二产业	Second Industry	10100700	57.2	5774634	1868707	2591811
工 业	Industry	7450000	65.3	4861337	1385567	2497548
建筑业	Building Sector	2650700	34.5	913296	483140	94262
第三产业	Tertiary Industry	7453800	57.8	4309135	2903018	361834
#交通运输、仓储、邮电通信业	Communication, Storage and Telecom	1384900	73.5	1017498	719305	110665
批发、零售贸易和餐饮业	Wholesale &Retail and Catering Sectoring	1780500	58.7	1045295	720552	51241
新疆生产总值构成(%)	Composition of Xinjiang Gross Production Value (%)	100		100	100	100
第一产业	First Industry	20.2		8.7	1.5	0.3
第二产业	Second Industry	45.9		52.3	38.6	87.5
工 业	Industry	33.9		44.0	28.6	84.3
建筑业	Building Industry	12.0		8.3	10.0	3.2
第三产业	Tertiary Industry	33.9		39.0	59.9	12.2
#交通运输、仓储、邮电通信业	Communication, Storage and Telecom	6.3		9.2	14.9	3.7
批发、零售贸易和餐饮业	Wholesale &Retail and Catering Sectoring	8.1		9.5	14.9	1.7
财政收入占新疆生产总值比重(%)	Ratio of XGP covered by financial revenue (%)	7.1		7.4	9.6	6.8
财政支出占新疆生产总值比重(%)	Ratio of XGP covered by financial revenue (%)	19.1		7.5	8.1	7.0
固定资产投资(万元)	**Fixed Asset Investment (10 000 yuan)**					
全社会固定资产投资总额	Fixed Asset Value of the Whole Society	11615245	40.3	4685310	2066810	1250936
#基本建设	Capital Construction	7592442	39.8	3019511	1015845	1148828
更新改造	Renewal and Reform	1386532	56.5	783517	498755	12027
财政、金融(万元)	**Finance and Public Money(10 000 yuan)**					
地方财政收入	Local Financial Income	1557040	52.8	821872	463395	202145
#各项税收	Various Tax Incomes	1231878	55.7	686731	394055	169330
地方财政支出	Expenditure of Local Finance	4210446	19.5	823135	393022	206937
#基本建设支出	Expenditure of Capital Construction	622827	17.8	110704	58883	43008
行政管理费支出	Expenditure of Administrative Expense	487805	21.0	102321	50080	20485
社会保障支出	Expenditure of Scoial Securities	208521	10.3	21375	15088	3493
金融机构年末存款余额	Year-end Deposit Balance of Finance	29597800	59.5	17607509	12271700	1846377
金融机构年末贷款余额	Year-end Deposit Balance of Finance	22146600	59.0	13073000	9574500	437897
物价(上年为 100)	**Commodity Price (Preceding year=100)**					
商品零售价格指数	Index of Commodity Retail Price	100.7			101.1	101.7
居民消费价格指数	Index of Price for Residents' Consumption	102.7			100.9	103.7
人民生活	**People's life**					
职工工资总额(万元)	Total Sum of Staff's Salary (10 000 yuan)	3563312	48.2	1716251	953236	247808
职工平均货币工资(元)	Average Staff''s Money Wage (yuan)	14484			19052	19893
农村居民家庭人均纯收入(元)	Annual Per capita Net Income of Rural Residents (yuan)	2244.93			4356	4682
城镇居民家庭人均可支配收入(元)	Annual Per Capital Disposable Income of Urban Residents (yuan)	7503.42				
城乡居民储蓄存款余额(万元)	Balance of Both Urban and Rural Deposit(10 000 yuan)	15346700	52.1	7998859	4884500	988613

Main Economic Indicators for Economic Belt on the Northern Slope of the Tianshan Mountains

石河子市 Shi Hezi City	奎屯市 Kuitun City	乌苏市 Usu City	沙湾县 Shawan County	昌吉市 Changji City	阜康市 Fukang City	米泉市 Miquan City	呼图壁县 Hu Tubi County	玛纳斯县 Manas County	农六师 XJPCC No.6 Division	农七师 XJPCC No.7 Division	农八师 XJPCC No.8 Division	农十二师 XJPCC No.12 Division	建工师 XJPCC architectu-ral engineer Division
64.29	29.91	21.03	20.30	39.35	15.85	18.64	20.72	16.93					
3.42	1.55	7.65	6.38	8.74	4.3	6.77	4.64	3.09					
64.29	29.91	21.03	17.38	39.35	15.85	18.64	17.12	10.08					
			2.92				3.6	6.84					
12.12	5.68	2.99	1.44	7.49	6.06	8.9	6.34	6.92					
7.38	3.33	2.96	1.37	4.34	1.31	1.56	1.27	1.38					
446120	188826	339255	471116	537641	297403	255176	271061	427859					
42235	11835	147415	188423	109321	40323	43415	121281	171810					
188681	94909	92103	138754	251922	193513	141571	67028	145635					
141894	74389	48105	91399	195641	162959	114136	45515	104184					
46787	20520	43998	47355	56281	30554	27435	21513	41451					
215204	82082	99737	143939	176398	63567	70190	82752	110414					
40790	12559	15928	21619	33605	16794	10758	12032	23443					
39971	26367	29944	48633	40813	17429	25271	20289	24785					
100	100	100	100	100	100	100	100	100					
9.5	6.3	43.5	40	20.3	13.5	17	44.7	40.2					
42.3	50.3	27.1	29.5	46.9	65.1	55.5	24.8	34					
31.8	39.4	14.2	19.4	36.4	54.8	44.7	16.8	24.4					
10.5	10.9	13	10.1	10.5	10.3	10.8	7.9	9.7					
48.2	43.4	29.4	30.5	32.8	21.4	27.5	30.5	25.8					
9.1	6.7	4.7	4.6	6.3	5.6	4.2	4.4	5.5					
9	14	8.8	10.3	7.6	5.9	9.9	7.5	5.8					
7.3	10.3	3.2	2.2	5.2	7.1	5.5	3.4	2.7					
10.8	11.6	7.1	5.0	5.8	7.1	7.7	5.8	4.1					
262875	112612	118889	122860	296352	101295	114156	116362	122163					
186707	77614	96110	78037	146390	55456	58853	83390	72281					
43053	12408	3342	38794	61160	39254	32524	22272	19928					
32345	19382	10706	10186	27923	21157	13926	9344	11363					
25309	16533	4745	6623	21771	18947	11572	7806	10040					
48100	21911	24248	23602	31409	21210	19689	15592	17415					
4257	320	490	129	690	260	500	1457	710					
6612	2383	4344	3673	4472	3001	2994	2214	2063					
681	51	673	790	80	330	107	31	51					
1142100	553657	178776	192220	667669	168458	220547	182947	183058					
829700	385459	146787	173531	839190	127009	151293	171668	235966					
102.7	102.2	104.3		103.0									
102.8	102.7	104.7		103.3									
111938	37275	66326	72638	83343	22513	25553	30413	65208					
13234	14328	9975	10819	17012	11184	12734	9388	12368					
5146		5011	5778	5156	4832	4845	5510	6706					
781696	268055	137164		382889	111909	165326	141751	136956					

2-8 续表 1

指 标	item	全区合计 Total of The Whole Region	北坡经济带占全区比重(%) Ratio of The Economic Belt	北坡经济带合计 Total	乌鲁木齐市 Urumqi City	克拉玛依市 Karamay City
农 业	**Agriculture**					
农林牧渔业总产值(万元)	Value of Farm, Forestry, Herding and Fishery (10 000 yuan)	7506792	14.5	1084962	87789	22776
农 业	Farming	5150018	12.7	655187	36461	9543
林 业	Forestry	138204	14.0	19308	845	2788
牧 业	Animal Husbandry	1874660	19.1	358226	45193	4841
渔 业	Fishery	42985	33.7	14503	1873	371
主要农产品产量(万吨)	Main Rural Products Output (10 000 tons)					
粮 食	Grain	828.53	7.0	57.84	4.02	0.27
棉 花	Cotton	175.25	14.8	25.96	0.01	0.58
油 料	Oil-bearing Crops	44.54	4.7	2.10	0.23	0.03
甜 菜	Beet	344.21	4.8	16.66	0.10	
水 果	Fruit	264.22	4.9	12.86		0.63
肉 类	Meat	128.13	16.6	21.24	1.76	0.38
工 业	**Industry**					
工业总产值(亿元)	Total Value of Industrial Products (100 million yuan)	1656.02	71.9	1190.54	450.66	535.16
轻工业	Light Industry	250.81	59.8	150.04	62.42	1.36
重工业	Heavy Industry	1405.21	74.0	1040.50	388.24	533.81
国有工业	State-owned Industry	193.76	68.9	133.57	36.06	68.77
集体工业	Collective-owned industry	16.43	65.0	10.68	5.96	1.07
其他工业	Other Industrial Sectors	1445.83	72.4	1046.29	408.65	465.32
主要工业产品产量	Output of Main Industrial Products					
纱(吨)	Cotton Yarn (ton)	291386	60.3	175632	40421	
布(万米)	Cloth (10 000 m)	13989	71.1	9948	1612	
毛线(吨)	Woolen Yarn (ton)	980	63.4	621	454	
呢绒(万米)	Woolen Goods (10 000 m)	206	100.0	206	18	
原盐(吨)	Crude Salt (ton)	873219	14.4	125777	125667	110
糖(吨)	Sugar (ton)	372605	5.9	22004		
原煤(吨)	Crude Coal (ton)	37493992	49.1	18416425	8940845	72787
原油(吨)	Crude Oil (ton)	22530197	65.4	14735166	3581680	11153486
发电量(万千瓦小时)	Volume of Electric Generation (10 000 kwh)	2662976	67.1	1786161	886844	227031
钢(吨)	Copper (ton)	2491278	99.3	2475045	2278428	
成品钢材(吨)	Finished Steel Material (ton)	2385191	98.9	2359131	2264038	
水泥(万吨)	Cement (10 000 tons)	1213	41.8	507	268	
运输邮电业	**Traffic and Telecommunication Sector**					
公路客运量(万人)	Highway Passenger Volume (10 000 persons)	28473	61.2	17429	1750	3840
公路货运量(万吨)	Highway Cargo Volume (10 000 tons)	31700	33.7	10693	6926	770
公路货物周转量(万吨公里)	Turnover of Highway Cargo (10 000 tons-km)	3610000	29.5	1064650	684400	84059
邮电业务总量(万元)	Volume of Postal-Telecommunication (10 000 yuan)	1531835	36.1	552340	431400	18946
国内贸易	**Domestic Trade**					
社会消费品零售总额(亿元)	Retail Volume of Social Commodities (100 million yuan)	563.65	55.2	311.36	190.97	16.96
教育、文化、卫生	**Education, Culture and Health**					
在校学生数(人)	Number of Registered Students (person)					
高等学校	Institutions of Higher Education	168247	84.8	142696	103378	4399
中等专业学校	Specialized Secondary School	71324	49.9	35557	29991	858
普通中学	Ordinary Middle School	1517948	16.1	244958	116429	19825
小 学	Elementary School	2218109	14.1	312940	148338	24043
毕业生数(人)	Number of Graduates (person)					
高等学校	Institutions of Higher Education	31013	80.5	24973	20523	460
中等专业学校	Specialized Secondary School	24758	41.6	10295	9236	62
普通中学	Ordinary Middle School	420583	13.4	56185	31877	5585
小 学	Elementary School	417588	11.3	46995	23134	3526
医院床位数(张)	Number of Sick Beds (unit)	74022	38.3	28361	15576	1572
卫生技术人员数(人)	Number of Hygiene Technicians (person)	99788	36.7	36598	20947	2290

Continued

石河子市 Shi Hezi City	奎屯市 Kuitun City	乌苏市 Usu City	沙湾县 Shawan County	昌吉市 Changji City	阜康市 Fukang City	米泉市 Miquan City	呼图壁县 Hu Tubi County	玛纳斯县 Manas County	农六师 XPCG No.6 Division	农七师 XPCG No.7 Division	农八师 XPCG No.8 Division	农十二师 XPCG No.12 Division	建工师 XPCG architectu-ral engineer Division
71892	2869	131739	183418	163264	58707	62439	137923	162146	298084	282095	411267	56390	
53786	1385	102393	136285	86253	28516	28348	72596	99621	206677	222703	324222	34584	
457	494	1414	1644	4501	1556	645	1898	3066	3632	2921	4138	1833	
13876	211	24058	42205	64464	27974	32419	57580	45405	52409	36643	55278	18250	
1858	6	752	427	5755	183	882	1665	731	908	704	1967	390	
1.50	0.06	7.8	14.82	8.31	5.13	6.01	5.29	4.63	16.60	5.39	13.18	0.67	
2.86	0.07	5.72	5.11	2.08	0.33	0.12	3.74	5.34	10.05	12.02	20.33	0.12	
0.05	0.12	0.38	0.42	0.25	0.26	0.1	0.1	0.16	1.23		0.11	0.07	
0.01	0.03		4.77	4.71		0.44	5.95	0.65	2.7	3.83	0.18	1.67	
0.62		0.26	0.40	4.01	0.50	0.59	0.50	5.35	1.10	1.55	1.42	3.57	
0.80	0.01	2.00	3.19	3.55	1.86	2.80	2.30	2.59	3.41	1.84	3.21	0.91	
41.06	19.38	6.41	8.52	49.20	15.70	37.78	12.24	14.42					
21.06	13.41	3.33	5.04	19.96	1.30	5.21	9.64	7.32					
20.01	5.97	3.08	3.48	29.24	14.41	32.57	2.59	7.10					
7.52	9.62	0.21	1.23	3.98	4.51	0.18	0.32	1.18					
0.10		0.08	0.21	0.02	0.02	1.31	1.62	0.30					
33.44	9.76	6.12	7.08	45.21	11.17	36.30	10.30	12.94					
39967	26309	13971	8423	6212			32369	7960					
4272	1183	710	641			356	352	823					
167													
101				86									
	7218			14786									
	72724	1265132	921508	1265057	1458710	2365403	1418214	636045					
136236	33183	14782	8775	31820	47728.0	2383		397379					
	68372		56000			72245							
			54000			41093							
		5	73	100	42	19							
3972	392	455.8	640	3972	472	1411	310	214					
546	283	128.8	420	514	565	420	55	65					
51254	70656	21476	33780	82000	4593	8633	5270	18529					
16435	22627	7162	3804	30900	6668	3914	3976	6508					
14.01	6.27	2.92	2.24	22.84	4.27	5.62	4.35	4.31	8.29	6.10	17.58	4.44	0.19
19875				15044									
945	493		77	1177	2016								
12529	13353	15458	15308	13260	6155	14241	9336	9064	20419	12911	29021	5381	3312
12565	14434	20608	18051	24110	10146	16289	12572	11784	29712	20584	42689	7371	7039
1902				2088									
	120		120	329	428								
3265	826	26	2562	3786	1848	2996	2557	857	5375	3396	7401	1422	847
2011	2056	51	3016	4410	1946	3051	2435	1359	5665	3680	7774	1382	1030
3909	1445	380	560	2627	552	599	760	381	1486	1429	3929	248	80
5131	1485	818	676	2805	302	699	752	693	1965	1750	4932	229	132

主要统计指标解释

可比价格 指计算各种总量指标所采用的扣除了价格变动因素的价格，可进行不同时期总量指标的对比。按可比价格计算总量指标有两种方法：一种是直接用产品产量乘某一年的不变价格计算；另一种是用价格指数进行缩减。

不变价格 指以同类产品某年的平均价格作为固定价格，用于计算各年的产品价值。按不变价格计算的产品价值消除了价格变动因素，不同时期对比可以反映生产的发展速度。新中国成立后，随着工农业产品价格水平的变化，国家统计局先后五次制定了全国统一的工业产品不变价格和农业产品不变价格。从 1952 年到 1957 年使用 1952 年工(农)业产品不变价格，从 1957 年到 1970 年使用 1957 年不变价格，从 1971 年到 1980 年使用 1970 年不变价格，从 1981 年到 1990 年使用 1980 年不变价格，从 1991 年开始使用 1990 年不变价格。

平均增长速度 我国计算平均增长速度有两种方法：一种是习惯上经常使用的"水平法"，又称几何平均法，是以间隔期最后一年的水平同基期水平对比来计算平均每年增长(或下降)速度；另一种是"累计法"，又称代数平均法或方程法，是以间隔期内各年水平的总和同基期水平对比来计算平均每年增长(或下降)速度。在一般正常情况下，两种方法计算的平均每年增长速度比较接近；但在经济发展不平衡、出现大起大落时，两种方法计算的结果差别较大。

本《年鉴》内所列的平均增长速度，除固定资产投资用"累计法"计算外，其余均用"水平法"计算。从某年到某年平均增长速度的年份，均不包括基期年在内。如建国四十三年的平均增长速度是以 1949 年为基期计算的，则写为 1950-1992 年平均增长速度，其余类推。

企业(单位)登记注册类型 是以在工商行政管理机关登记注册的各类企业为划分对象，以工商行政管理部门对企业登记注册的类型为依据，将企业登记注册类型分为内资企业、港澳台商投资企业和外商投资企业三大类。内资企业包括国有企业、集体企业、股份合作企业、联营企业、有限责任公司、股份有限公司、私营公司和其他企业；港澳台商投资企业和外商投资企业分别包括合资经营企业、合作经营企业、独资经营企业和股份有限公司。对不在工商行政管理部门进行登记注册的行政机关、事业单位和社会团体，主要按其经费来源和管理方式进行划分。

国有企业 指企业全部资产归国家所有，并按《中华人民共和国企业法人登记管理条例》规定登记注册的非公司制的经济组织。不包括有限责任公司中的国有独资公司。

集体企业 指企业资产归集体所有，并按《中华人民共和国企业法人登记管理条例》规定登记注册的经济组织。

股份合作企业 指以合作制为基础，由企业职工共同出资入股，吸收一定比例的社会资产投资组建，实行自主经营，自负盈亏，共同劳动，民主管理，按劳分配与按股分红相结合的一种集体经济组织。

联营企业 指两个及两个以上相同或不同所有制性质的企业法人或事业单位法人，按自愿、平等、互利的原则，共同投资组成的经济组织。联营企业包括国有联营企业、集体联营企业、国有与集体联营企业和其他联营企业。

有限责任公司 指根据《中华人民共和国公司登记管理条例》规定登记注册，由两个以上、五十个以下的股东共同出资，每个股东以其所认缴的出资额对公司承担有限责任，公司以其全部资产对其债务承担责任的经济组织。有限责任公司包括国有独资公司以及其他有限责任公司。

股份有限公司 指根据《中华人民共和国公司登记管理条例》规定登记注册，其全部注册资本由等额股份构成并通过发行股票筹集资本，股东以其认购的股份对公司承担有限责任，公司以其全部资产对其债务承担责任的经济组织。

私营企业 指由自然人投资设立或由自然人控股，以雇佣劳动为基础的营利性经济组织。包括按照《公司法》、《合伙企业法》、《私营企业暂行条例》规定登记注册的私营有限责任公司、私营股份有限公司、私营合伙企业和私营独资企业。

其他内资企业 指上述企业之外的其他内资经济组织。

与港澳台商合资经营企业 指港澳台地区投资者与内地企业依照《中华人民共和国中外合资经营企业法》及有关法律的规定，按合同规定的比例投资设立、分享利润和分担风险的企业。

与港澳台商合作经营企业 指港澳台地区投资者与内地企业依照《中华人民共和国中外合作经营企业法》及有关法律的规定，依照合作合同的约定进行投资或提供条件设立、分配利润和分担风险的企业。

港澳台商独资经营企业 指依照《中华人民共和国外资企业法》及有关法律的规定，在内地由港澳台地区投资者全额投资设立的企业。

港澳台商投资股份有限公司 指根据国家有关规定，经外经贸部依法批准设立，其中港、澳、台商的股本占公司注册资本的比例达 25% 以上的股份有限公司。凡其中港、澳、台商的股本占公司注册资本的比例小于 25%的，属于内资企业中的股份有限公司。

中外合资经营企业 指外国企业或外国人与中国内地企业依照《中华人民共和国中外合资经营企业法》及有关法律的规定，按合同规定的比例投资设立、分享利润和分担风险的企业。

中外合作经营企业 指外国企业或外国人与中国内地企业依照《中华人民共和国中外合作经营企业法》及有关法律的规定，依照合作合同的约定进行投资或提供条件设立、分配利润和分担风险的企业。

外资企业 指依照《中华人民共和国外资企业法》及有关法律的规定，在中国内地由外国投资者全额投资设立的企业。

外商投资股份有限公司 指根据国家有关规定，经外经贸部依法批准设立，其中外资的股本占公司注册资本的比例达 25% 以上的股份有限公司。凡其中外资股本占公司注册资本的比例小于 25%的，属于内资企业中的股份有限公司。

行政机关、事业单位和社会团体 参照企业登记注册类型，主要按其经费来源和管理方式划分。具体规定如下：

(1)行政机关：包括国家机关和政党机关，原则上均列为"国有"。但有特殊规定的，如供销社等，则列为"集体"。

(2)事业单位：包括经国家机构编制部门和有关业务主管部门批准成立的各类事业单位，不包括实行企业化管理的事业单位。事业单位的划分办法如下：

①由国家财政预算拨款或列入财政预算外资金管理以及经费主要来源于国有主管部门或国有上级单位的事业单位，列为"国有"。

②经费主要来源于集体单位的事业单位，列为"集体"。

③公民个人(或个人合伙)开办的事业单位，列为"私营"。

④上述以外的其他事业单位，如果其经费来源不明确，按管理方式进行归类。

(3)社会团体：包括经民政部门批准成立以及未纳入社会团体管理条例范围的工会、妇联等各类社会团体。社会团体的划分办法如下：

①未纳入民政部社会团体管理条例范围的工会、妇联、共青团、青联、工商联、科协、侨联等社会团体，国家拨款设立的基金会或基金管理组织以及经费主要来源于国有业务主管部门或国有上级单位的社会团体，列为"国有"。

②经费主要来源于集体单位的社会团体，列为"集体"。

③公民个人(或个人合伙)开办的社会团体，划为"私营"。

④上述以外的其他社会团体，如果其经费来源不明确，改按管理方式进行归类。

Explanatory Notes on Main Statistical Indicators

Comparable Prices refer to prices that are used to remove the factors of price change in calculating economic aggregates, so as to facilitate comparison of aggregates over time. Two methods are used for calculating economic aggregates at comparable prices: 1.Multiplying the output of products by their constant prices of certain year; 2.Deflation of data at current prices by relevant price index.

Constant Price refers to the average price of a given product in certain year, which is used for comparison of output value over time.As the output value at constant prices removes the factor of price changes,it reflects the trend of production development over time.Since 1949,with the changes in general price level,the State Statistical Bureau has issued nationally unified constant prices five times:the 1952 constant prices for 1949-1957;the 1957 constant prices for 1957-1971; the 1970 constant prices for 1971-1981; the 1980 constant prices for 1981-1990;and the 1990 constant prices have been used since 1991.

Average Annual Growth Rate Two methods for calculating average annual growth rate are applied in China,one is often called level approachor the method of calculating geometric average,which is derived by comparing the level of the last year of the interval with that of the beginning year;the other is calledaccumulative approach or algebraic average or equation method,which is derived by the summation of the actual figure of each year in the interval divided by the figure in the base year.

Usually the results calculated by the two methods are fairly close, but they differed sharply when uneven economic development occurred with striking fluctuations in growth.

The average annual growth rates listed in this statistical yearbook are calculated by level approach except for the growth rate of investment in fixed assets. The base years are not listed when the years are listed for average annual growth rates. For instance,the average annual growth rate of 43 years since 1949 is listed as average annual growth rate of 1950-1992 without listing the base year 1949.And the analogy of this is also the same for the rest of the years.

Registration Status of Enterprises Enterprises are classified into 3 categories, namely domestic-funded enterprises, enterprises with investment from Hong Kong, Macau and Taiwan, and enterprises with foreign investment, in the light of the registration status of an enterprise in industrial and commercial administration agencies. Domestic-funded enterprises include state-owned enterprises, collective-owned enterprises, cooperative enterprises, joint ownership enterprises, limited liability corporations, share-holding corporations Ltd., private enterprises and other enterprises. Included in the enterprises with investment from Hong Kong, Macau and Taiwan and enterprises with foreign investment are joint-venture enterprises, cooperative enterprises, sole investment enterprises and share-holding corporations Ltd. For government agencies, institutions and social organizations which are not requested to be registered in industrial and commercial administration agencies, they are classified mainly by their sources of funds and way of management.

State-owned Enterprises refer to non-corporation economic units where the entire assets are owned by the state and which have registered in accordance with the Regulation of the Peoples Republic of China on the Management of Registration of Corporate Enterprises. Excluded from this category are sole state-funded corporations in the limited liability corporations.

Collective-owned Enterprises refer to economic units where the assets are owned collectively and which have registered in accordance with the Regulation of the Peoples Republic of China on the Management of Registration of Corporate Enterprises.

Cooperative Enterprises refer to a form of collective economic units (enterprises) where capitals come mainly from employees as their shares, with certain proportion of capital from the outside, where production is organized on the basis of independent operation, independent accounting for profits and losses, joint work, democratic management, and a distribution system that integrates remuneration according to work with dividend according to capital share.

Joint Ownership Enterprises refer to economic units established by two or more corporate enterprises or corporate institutions of the same or different ownership, through joint investment on the basis of equality, voluntary participation and mutual benefits. They include state joint ownership enterprises, collective joint ownership enterprises, joint state-collective enterprises, other joint ownership enterprises.

Limited Liability Corporations refer to economic units established with investment from 2-50 investors and registered in accordance with the Regulation of the Peoples Republic of China on the Management of Registration of Corporations, each investor bearing limited liability to the corporation depending on its share of investment, and the corporation bearing liability to its debt to the maximum of its total assets. Limited liability corporations include exclusive state-funded limited liability corporations and other limited liability corporations.

Share-holding Corporations Ltd. refer to economic units registered in accordance with the Regulation of the Peoples Republic of China on the Management of Registration of Corporations, with total registered capitals divided into equal shares and raised through issuing stocks. Each investor bears limited liability to the corporation depending on the holding of shares, and the corporation bears liability to its debt to the maximum of its total assets.

Private Enterprises refer to profit-making economic units invested and established by natural persons, or controlled by natural persons using employed labour. Included in this category are private limited liability corporations, private share-holding corporations Ltd., private partnership enterprises and private-funded enterprises registered in accordance with the Corporation Law, Partnership Enterprises Law and Interim Regulations on Private Enterprises .

Other Domestic-funded Enterprises refer to domestic-funded economic units other than those mentioned above.

Joint-venture Enterprises with Funds from Hong Kong, Macau and Taiwan refer to enterprises jointly established by investors from Hong Kong, Macau and Taiwan with enterprises in the mainland of China in accordance with the Law of the Peoples Republic of China on Sino-foreign Joint Venture Enterprises and other relevant laws, where the share of investment, profits and risks is stipulated in the contract.

Cooperative Enterprises with Funds from Hong Kong Macau and Taiwan , established by investors from Hong Kong, Macau and Taiwan with enterprises in the mainland of China in accordance with the Law of the Peoples Republic of China on Sino-foreign Cooperative Enterprises and other relevant laws, where the investment or provision of facilities, and the share of profits and risks is stipulated in the cooperative contract.

Enterprises with Sole (exclusive) Investment from Hong Kong, Macau and Taiwan refer to enterprises established in the mainland of China with exclusive investment from investors from Hong Kong, Macau and Taiwan in accordance with the Law of the Peoples Republic of China on Foreign-Funded Enterprises and other relevant laws.

Share-holding Corporations Ltd. with Investment from Hong Kong, Macau and Taiwan refer to share-holding corporations Ltd. established with the approval from the Ministry of Foreign Trade and Economic Relations in line with relevant state regulations, where the share of investment from Hong Kong, Macau or Taiwan businessmen exceeds 25% of the total registered capital of the corporation. In case the share of investment from Hong Kong, Macau or Taiwan is less than 25% of the total registered capital, the enterprise is to be classified as domestic-funded share-holding corporation Ltd.

Joint-venture Enterprises with Foreign Investment refer to enterprises jointly established by foreign enterprises or foreigners with enterprises in the mainland of China in accordance with the Law of the Peoples Republic of China on Sino-foreign Joint Venture Enterprises and other relevant laws, where the share of investment, profits and risks is stipulated in the contract.

Cooperation Enterprises with Foreign Investment refer to enterprises jointly established by foreign enterprises or foreigners with enterprises in the mainland of China in accordance with the Law of the Peoples Republic of China on Sino-foreign Cooperative Enterprises and other relevant laws, where the investment or provision of facilities, and the share of profits and risks is stipulated in the cooperative contract.

Enterprises with Sole (exclusive) Foreign Investment refer to enterprises established in the mainland of China with exclusive investment from foreign investors in accordance with the Law of the Peoples Republic of China on Foreign-Funded Enterprises and other relevant laws.

Share-holding Corporations Ltd. with Foreign Investment refer to share-holding corporations Ltd. established with the approval from the Ministry of Foreign Trade and Economic Relations in line with relevant state regulations, where the share of investment from foreign investors exceeds 25% of the total registered capital of the corporation. In case the share of foreign investment is less than 25% of the total registered capital, the enterprise is to be classified as domestic-funded share-holding corporation Ltd.

Government Agencies, Institutions and Social Organizations are classified into following categories by source of funds and way of management taking reference of the registration status of enterprises:

(1) Government agencies: include state and party agencies, classified in principle as “state-owned”. There are exceptions, such as supply and marketing cooperatives which are classified as “collective”.

(2) Institutions: include institutions of various types established with the approval by organization and staffing departments of the government, but exclude institutions where enterprise management system is introduced. Institutions are further classified as follows:

(a) Institutions whose main budget is listed in the government budget appropriations or extra-budget funds, or allocated from the budget of their competent government agencies. Such institutions are classified as “state-owned”.

(b) Institutions whose budget mainly comes from collective units. Such institutions are classified as “collective”.

(c) Institutions other than those mentioned above whose source of budget is not clear. Such institutions are classified by way of management.

(3) Social organizations: include social organizations established with the approval from the Ministry of Civil Affairs, and organizations that are not covered by social organization management regulations such as trade unions, women’s federations etc.. Social organizations are further classified as follows:

(a) Social organizations that are not covered by social organization management regulations of the Ministry of Civil Affairs such as trade unions, women’s federations, communist youth leagues, youth associations, industrial and commerce associations, scientists associations, overseas Chinese associations, etc., foundations and fund management organizations established with funds from the state, and social organizations whose funds mainly come from the budget of their competent government agencies. Such institutions are classified as “state-owned”.

(b) Social organizations whose budget mainly comes from collective units. Such institutions are classified as “collective”.

(c) Social organizations established by individual or a group of citizens, which are classified as “private”.

(d) Social organizations other than those mentioned above whose source of budget is not clear. Such organizations are classified by way of management.

第三篇

CHAPTER 3

国民经济核算

NATIONAL ACCOUNTS

3-1 新疆生产总值

Gross Domestic Product in Xinjiang

单位：亿元 (100 million yuan)

年 份 Year	新疆生产总值 Gross Domestic Product	第一产业 Primary Industry	第二产业 Secondary Industry	工 业 Industry	建筑业 Construction	第三产业 Tertiary Industry	#运输、仓储及邮电业 Transportation Storage, Post and Telecommunications	#批发和零售贸易、餐饮业 Wholesale, Retail & Catering Trade	人均新疆生产总值(元/人) Per Capita GDP (yuan/person)
1978	39	14	18	14	4	7	1	2	313
1979	46	17	21	17	4	8	2	2	359
1980	53	22	21	17	4	10	2	3	410
1981	59	25	22	18	4	12	2	3	450
1982	65	28	23	18	5	14	3	4	488
1983	79	33	29	23	6	17	3	5	583
1984	90	37	32	26	6	21	4	6	661
1985	112	43	40	32	8	29	5	9	820
1986	129	46	46	37	9	37	6	10	924
1987	149	56	51	41	10	42	8	12	1053
1988	193	72	66	54	12	55	12	16	1347
1989	217	78	74	60	14	65	13	18	1493
1990	274	95	84	68	16	95	20	28	1799
1991	336	112	108	84	24	116	23	37	2101
1992	402	115	147	106	41	140	28	40	2477
1993	506	128	217	156	61	161	32	44	3019
1994	674	188	265	190	75	221	42	59	3953
1995	825	240	303	219	84	282	55	76	4764
1996	912	249	337	239	98	326	67	90	5167
1997	1050	280	413	303	110	357	76	98	5904
1998	1117	291	431	300	131	395	92	103	6229
1999	1169	269	461	318	143	439	109	109	6470
2000	1364	288	587	422	165	489	122	118	7377
2001	1485	288	630	450	180	567	119	128	7913
2002	1598	305	668	469	199	625	131	135	8382
2003	1878	413	797	571	226	668	121	156	9700
2004	2200	445	1010	745	265	745	138	178	11199

注：本表绝对数按当年价格计算。
Note: Data in value terms in this table are calculated at current prices.

3-2 新疆生产总值构成

Composition of Gross Domestic Product in Xinjiang

单位：% (%)

年 份 Year	新疆生产总值构成 Composition of Gross Domestic Product	第一产业 Primary Industry	第二产业 Secondary Industry	工 业 Industry	建筑业 Construction	第三产业 Tertiary Industry	#运输、仓储及邮电业 Transportation Storage, Post and Telecommunications	#批发和零售贸易、餐饮业 Wholesale, Retail & Catering Trade
1978	100.0	35.9	46.2	35.9	10.3	17.9	2.6	5.1
1979	100.0	37.0	45.7	37.0	8.7	17.3	4.3	4.3
1980	100.0	41.5	39.6	32.1	7.5	18.9	3.8	5.7
1981	100.0	42.4	37.3	30.5	6.8	20.3	3.4	5.1
1982	100.0	43.1	35.4	27.7	7.7	21.5	4.6	6.2
1983	100.0	41.8	36.7	29.1	7.6	21.5	3.8	6.3
1984	100.0	41.1	35.6	28.9	6.7	23.3	4.4	6.7
1985	100.0	38.4	35.7	28.6	7.1	25.9	4.5	8.0
1986	100.0	35.7	35.7	28.7	7.0	28.6	4.7	7.8
1987	100.0	37.6	34.2	27.5	6.7	28.2	5.4	8.1
1988	100.0	37.3	34.2	28.0	6.2	28.5	6.2	8.3
1989	100.0	35.9	34.1	27.6	6.5	30.0	6.0	8.3
1990	100.0	34.7	30.6	24.8	5.8	34.7	7.3	10.2
1991	100.0	33.3	32.1	25.0	7.1	34.6	6.8	11.0
1992	100.0	28.6	36.6	26.4	10.2	34.8	7.0	10.0
1993	100.0	25.3	42.9	30.8	12.1	31.8	6.3	8.7
1994	100.0	27.9	39.3	28.2	11.1	32.8	6.2	8.8
1995	100.0	29.1	36.7	26.5	10.2	34.2	6.7	9.2
1996	100.0	27.3	37.0	26.3	10.7	35.7	7.3	9.9
1997	100.0	26.7	39.3	28.8	10.5	34.0	7.2	9.3
1998	100.0	26.1	38.6	26.9	11.7	35.3	8.2	9.2
1999	100.0	23.0	39.4	27.2	12.2	37.6	9.3	9.3
2000	100.0	21.1	43.0	30.9	12.1	35.9	8.9	8.7
2001	100.0	19.4	42.4	30.3	12.1	38.2	8.0	8.6
2002	100.0	19.1	41.8	29.3	12.5	39.1	8.2	8.4
2003	100.0	22.0	42.4	30.4	12.0	35.6	6.4	8.3
2004	100.0	20.2	45.9	33.9	12.0	33.9	6.3	8.1

注：本表按当年价格计算。

Note: Data in value terms in this table are calculated at current prices.

3-3 新疆生产总值指数

Indice for Gross Domestic Product in Xinjiang

(上年=100) (Preceding year=100)

年 份 Year	新疆生产总值 Gross Domestic Product	第一产业 Primary Industry	第二产业 Secondary Industry	工 业 Industry	建筑业 Construction	第三产业 Tertiary Industry	#运输、仓储及邮电业 Transportation Storage, Post and Telecommunications	#批发和零售贸易、餐饮业 Wholesale, Retail & Catering Trade	人均新疆生产总值 Per Capita GDP
1979	112.3	109.9	111.6	111.3	112.6	120.7	121.9	117.2	110.2
1980	107.2	106.0	104.4	108.4	93.1	116.6	115.8	125.5	105.0
1981	108.5	115.3	99.4	99.1	100.2	113.4	119.4	117.9	106.6
1982	109.8	111.2	104.2	104.7	102.8	117.1	119.1	119.8	108.5
1983	113.4	112.1	111.8	112.4	110.0	118.7	113.0	108.8	112.5
1984	114.0	113.5	114.6	115.1	112.8	114.1	100.2	109.2	113.2
1985	116.9	112.9	116.7	116.1	119.0	125.0	100.2	126.6	115.9
1986	111.5	108.3	109.1	111.0	102.6	120.7	124.9	110.0	109.2
1987	109.7	110.7	104.8	108.6	91.3	114.7	119.1	111.1	108.7
1988	109.6	103.3	114.9	113.6	120.3	112.9	118.8	114.7	108.0
1989	105.9	101.8	104.5	106.9	94.5	113.5	112.7	107.6	104.1
1990	111.7	116.0	106.8	106.4	108.5	112.0	106.7	104.4	106.8
1991	114.4	111.2	117.0	113.1	134.9	115.7	129.0	104.7	109.0
1992	113.1	105.5	119.4	112.6	145.4	115.7	125.7	112.6	111.3
1993	110.3	101.1	114.0	111.3	122.1	116.7	115.4	122.4	106.9
1994	110.9	111.2	110.2	111.1	107.9	111.2	107.0	106.5	109.0
1995	109.0	104.9	111.7	113.6	106.6	110.0	116.6	109.9	107.2
1996	106.4	103.5	108.2	107.2	111.1	107.1	110.2	110.6	104.4
1997	111.0	110.8	113.2	113.0	113.7	108.7	116.7	106.7	110.2
1998	107.3	107.2	106.7	103.2	116.7	108.1	114.6	105.8	106.5
1999	107.1	102.7	107.3	106.5	109.3	110.9	111.9	108.9	106.3
2000	108.2	104.8	109.0	109.0	108.9	110.3	111.6	110.5	107.0
2001	108.1	102.8	108.7	108.0	110.6	110.6	106.8	105.9	106.5
2002	108.1	105.0	107.8	107.7	107.9	110.0	111.5	111.3	106.4
2003	110.8	108.2	112.1	111.2	114.5	110.5	112.3	111.9	109.1
2004	111.1	105.1	114.3	114.5	113.9	110.4	112.3	113.6	109.5

注：本表按可比价计算。

Note: Data in this table are calculated at comparable prices.

3-4 新疆生产总值指数

Indice for Gross Domestic Product in Xinjiang

(1978=100)

年 份 Year	新疆生产总值 Gross Domestic Product	第一产业 Primary Industry	第二产业 Secondary Industry	工 业 Industry	建筑业 Construction	第三产业 Tertiary Industry	#运输、仓储及邮电业 Transportation Storage, Post and Telecommunications	#批发和零售贸易、餐饮业 Wholesale, Retail & Catering Trade	人均新疆生产总值 Per Capita GDP
1978	100.0	100.0	100.0	100.0	100.0	100.0	100.0	100.0	100.0
1979	112.3	109.9	111.6	111.3	112.6	120.7	121.9	117.2	110.2
1980	120.4	116.5	116.6	120.7	104.8	140.8	141.1	147.1	115.7
1981	130.6	134.2	115.8	119.6	105.0	159.6	169.5	173.4	123.3
1982	143.3	149.3	120.7	125.2	107.9	186.9	200.7	207.7	133.8
1983	162.5	167.5	135.0	140.7	118.7	221.8	226.8	225.9	150.5
1984	185.3	190.2	154.7	161.9	133.9	253.0	227.2	246.7	170.3
1985	216.5	214.6	180.6	188.0	159.3	316.2	227.7	312.2	197.5
1986	241.3	232.5	197.0	208.7	163.4	381.7	284.4	343.6	215.6
1987	264.7	257.4	206.5	226.5	149.2	437.7	338.7	381.7	234.3
1988	290.1	265.9	237.2	257.4	179.5	494.1	402.5	437.6	253.0
1989	307.2	270.7	247.8	275.2	169.6	560.6	453.6	470.8	263.3
1990	343.2	314.0	264.7	292.8	184.1	627.9	484.0	491.7	281.3
1991	392.6	349.2	309.7	331.2	248.3	726.7	624.2	514.9	306.5
1992	444.1	368.4	369.9	372.9	361.0	840.7	784.5	580.0	341.3
1993	489.9	372.3	421.7	415.0	440.8	981.3	905.1	709.8	364.9
1994	543.1	414.1	464.9	461.0	475.9	1091.4	968.2	755.9	397.8
1995	591.7	434.2	519.4	523.7	507.2	1200.0	1128.5	830.9	426.3
1996	629.5	449.4	562.0	561.4	563.6	1285.3	1243.7	919.2	444.9
1997	698.8	498.0	636.0	634.4	640.8	1396.7	1451.4	981.0	490.5
1998	749.8	533.8	678.9	654.7	748.0	1509.4	1663.3	1037.7	522.2
1999	803.0	548.4	728.4	697.2	817.6	1673.4	1860.8	1129.9	555.1
2000	868.8	574.9	793.7	760.0	890.0	1846.1	2075.8	1248.3	594.0
2001	939.5	590.9	862.9	820.8	984.1	2041.8	2217.1	1321.9	632.6
2002	1015.6	620.4	930.2	884.0	1061.8	2246.0	2472.1	1471.3	673.1
2003	1125.3	671.3	1042.8	983.0	1215.8	2481.8	2776.2	1646.4	734.4
2004	1250.2	705.5	1191.9	1125.5	1384.8	2739.9	3117.7	1870.3	804.2

注：本表按可比价计算。
Note: Data in this table are calculated at comparable prices.

3-5 第三产业增加值、构成和指数

Added Value, Composition and Indice of Tertiary Industry

行业	Sectors	第三产业增加值(亿元) Added Value of the Tertiary Industry (100 million yuan)			构成(%) Composition (%)
		1998	2000	2004	1998
总计	**Total**	**394.89**	**489.34**	**745.38**	**100.00**
交通运输仓储及邮电通信业	Transport, Storage, Post and Telecommunication Services	92.03	121.79	138.49	23.30
批发和零售贸易餐饮业	Wholesale and Retail Trade and Catering Services	103.34	118.08	178.05	26.20
金融保险业	Finance and Insurance	50.21	42.23	70.87	12.70
房地产业	Real Estate	8.94	15.00	26.92	2.30
其他服务行业	Other Sectors	140.37	192.24	331.05	35.50

行业	Sectors	构成(%) Composition (%)		指数(上年=100) Indices (preceding year=100)		
		2000	2004	1998	2000	2004
总计	**Total**	**100**	**100**	**108.1**	**110.3**	**110.4**
交通运输仓储及邮电通信业	Transport, Storage, Post and Telecommunication Services	24.90	18.58	114.6	111.6	112.3
批发和零售贸易餐饮业	Wholesale and Retail Trade and Catering Services	24.10	23.89	105.8	110.5	113.6
金融保险业	Finance and Insurance	8.60	9.51	100.6	80.0	104.5
房地产业	Real Estate	3.10	3.61	120.3	138.1	104.6
其他服务行业	Other Sectors	39.30	44.41	107.3	117.4	109.1

3-6 新疆生产总值项目结构

Structure of Gross Domestic Product by Industrial Sectors in Xinjiang

(2003 年)

指 标	Item	新疆生产总值 Gross Production Value	劳动者报酬 Compensation of Laborers	固定资产折旧 Depreciation of Fixed Assets	生产税净额 Net Taxes on Production	营业盈余 Operating Surplus
新疆生产总值(亿元)	**Gross Domestic Product (100 million yuan)**	**1877.61**	**973.30**	**317.78**	**312.05**	**274.48**
第一产业	Primary Industry	412.90	294.15	18.96	9.95	89.84
第二产业	Secondary Industry	796.83	282.92	149.49	247.27	117.15
工 业	Industry	571.00	140.41	129.23	207.17	94.19
建筑业	Construction	225.83	142.51	20.26	40.10	22.96
第三产业	Tertiary Industry	667.88	396.23	149.33	54.83	67.49
农林牧渔服务业	Farming, Forestry, Animal Husbandry and Fishery Services	13.33	9.49	1.28	0.32	2.24
地质勘探业、水利管理业	Geological Prospecting and Water Conservancy	13.43	7.34	6.05	0.04	
交通运输、仓储、邮电通讯业	Transportaion, Storage, Postal and Telecommunications services	121.25	68.77	62.53	11.45	-21.5
交通运输业和仓储业	Transportation and Storage	78.45	53.59	33.11	8.65	-16.90
邮电通讯业	Post and Telecommunications	42.80	15.18	29.42	2.80	-4.60
批发和零售贸易、餐饮业	Wholesale, Retail Trade and Catering Services	155.60	69.67	19.32	26.02	40.59
批发和零售贸易业	Wholesale and Retail Trade	116.78	51.76	16.47	22.08	26.47
餐饮业	Catering Services	38.82	17.91	2.85	3.94	14.12
金融保险业	Banking and Insurance	65.43	24.08	6.07	5.83	29.45
金融业	Banking	55.73	18.02	5.03	5.20	27.48
保险业	Insurance	9.70	6.06	1.04	0.63	1.97
房地产业	Real Estate Trade	24.67	2.81	14.64	3.17	4.05
房地产管理业	Real Estate Management	0.90	0.78	0.03	0.03	0.06
房地产开发业	Real Estate Development	9.82	2.03	0.66	3.14	3.99
城市居民自有住房	Urban Residents Owner-occupier	2.35		2.35		
农村居民自有住房	Rural Residents Owner-occupier	11.60		11.60		
社会服务业	Social Services	58.18	25.16	18.08	6.97	7.97
卫生、体育、社会福利事业	Health Care, Sports and Social Welfare	26.04	18.75	2.37	0.23	4.69
教育、文艺、广播电影电视业	Education, Culture, Arts, Radio, Film and Television	72.80	65.21	6.82	0.77	
科学研究和综合技术服务业	Scientific Research and Polytechnical Services	6.11	5.11	0.98	0.02	
国家政党机关、社会团体	Governments, Parties and Social Organizations	103.48	94.00	9.48		
其 他	Others	7.56	5.84	1.71	0.01	

注：1.本表按当年价格计算；2.2004 年项目结构仍用 2003 年数。

Note: a) Data in value terms in this table are calculated at current prices; b) Items for 2004 remain the same as those for 2003.

3-7 支出法新疆生产总值

Gross Domestic Product by Expenditure in Xinjiang

单位：万元 (10 000 yuan)

年 份 Year	支出法新疆生产总值 Gross Domestic Product by Expenditure	最终消费 Final Consumption Expenditure	资本形成总额 Gross Capital Formation	货物和服务净出口 Net Export of Goods and Services	最终消费率（消费率）(%) Final Consumption Rate (%)	资本形成率（投资率）(%) Capital Formation Rate (%)
1978	390667	321378	184279	-114990	82.3	47.2
1980	532441	445646	231515	-144720	83.7	43.5
1985	1122379	877988	584289	-339898	78.2	52.1
1986	1290398	1037162	602593	-349357	80.4	46.7
1987	1485104	1173098	699416	-387410	79.0	47.1
1988	1927224	1428627	983051	-484454	74.1	51.0
1989	2174169	1566708	1178441	-570980	72.1	54.2
1990	2740056	1881697	1411667	-553308	68.7	51.5
1991	3359147	2211130	1691482	-543465	65.8	50.4
1992	4023096	2484290	2492589	-953783	61.8	62.0
1993	5056294	3007549	3561561	-1512816	59.5	70.4
1994	6736754	3752048	4875542	-1890836	55.7	72.4
1995	8251152	4362060	4737079	-847987	52.9	57.4
1996	9121450	5460982	4569575	-909107	59.9	50.1
1997	10501384	6037807	5649193	-1185616	57.5	53.8
1998	11166710	6352944	6858461	-2044695	56.9	61.4
1999	11685534	6615128	5815889	-745483	56.6	49.8
2000	13643646	7580534	6181229	-118117	55.6	45.3
2001	14854843	8546011	7714187	-1405355	57.5	51.9
2002	15982812	9489173	8642721	-2149082	59.4	56.3
2003	18776064	10304880	11192144	-2720960	54.9	59.6
2004	22001500	11508083	13624031	-3130614	52.3	61.9

3-8 资本形成总额及其构成

Gross Capital Formation and Its Composition

年 份	Year	资本形成总额 (万元) Gross Capital Formation (10 000 yuan)	固定资本形成 Gross Fixed Capital Formation	存货增加 Increase in Inventories	以资本形成总额为 100 Gross Capital Formation=100 固定资本形成 (%) Gross Fixed Capital Formation (%)	存货增加 (%) Increase in Inventories (%)
	1965	77254	60254	17000	78.0	22.0
	1970	81025	50730	30295	62.6	37.4
	1975	126544	75336	51208	59.5	40.5
	1980	231515	181385	50130	78.3	21.7
	1985	584289	467807	116482	80.1	19.9
	1986	602593	519416	83177	86.2	13.8
	1987	699416	557763	141653	79.7	20.3
	1988	983051	756935	226116	77.0	23.0
	1989	1178441	867326	311115	73.6	26.4
	1990	1411667	914955	496712	64.8	35.2
	1991	1691482	1247717	443765	73.8	26.2
	1992	2492589	1811739	680850	72.7	27.3
	1993	3561561	2648981	912580	74.4	25.6
	1994	4875542	3769512	1106030	77.3	22.7
	1995	4737079	3779069	958010	79.8	20.2
	1996	4569575	4228684	340891	92.5	7.5
	1997	5649193	4614059	1035134	81.7	18.3
	1998	6858461	5437824	1420637	79.3	20.7
	1999	5815889	5517222	298667	94.9	5.1
	2000	6181229	6481229	-300000		
	2001	7714187	7201155	513032	93.3	6.7
	2002	8642721	8567008	75713	99.1	0.9
	2003	11192144	10792366	399778	96.4	3.6
	2004	13624031	12395034	1228997	91.0	9.0
"一五" 时期	"First Five-Year Plan" Period	162638	143262	19376	88.1	11.9
"二五" 时期	"Second Five-Year Plan" Period	363925	266883	97042	73.3	26.7
	1963—1965	193986	143430	50556	73.9	26.1
"三五" 时期	"Third Five-Year Plan" Period	306461	209622	96839	68.4	31.6
"四五" 时期	"Fourth Five-Year Plan" Period	516970	321276	195694	62.1	37.9
"五五" 时期	"Fifth Five-Year Plan" Period	877599	624988	252611	71.2	28.8
"六五" 时期	"Sixth Five-Year Plan" Period	1913818	1584755	329063	82.8	17.2
"七五" 时期	"Seventh Five-Year Plan" Period	4875168	3616395	1258773	74.2	25.8
"八五" 时期	"Eighth Five-Year Plan" Period	17358253	13257018	4101235	76.4	23.6
"九五" 时期	"Ninth Five-Year Plan" Period	29074347	26279018	2795329	90.4	9.6

注：本表按当年价格计算。
Note: Data in value terms in this table are calculated at current prices.

3-9 最终消费及其构成

End Consumption Expenditure and Its Composition

单位：% (%)

年份	Year	最终消费(万元) Final Consumption Expenditure (10 000yuan)	居民消费 Household Consumption	农村居民 Agricultural Household	城镇居民 Non-agricultural Household	政府消费 Government Consumption	最终消费=100 Final Consumption Expenditure=100: 居民消费 Household Consumption	最终消费=100 Final Consumption Expenditure=100: 政府消费 Government Consumption	居民消费=100 Houshold Consumption=100: 农村居民 Agricultural Household	居民消费=100 Houshold Consumption=100: 城镇居民 Non-agricultural Household
	1965	176244	159408	84552	74856	16836	90.4	9.6	53.0	47.0
	1970	201773	186247	70854	115393	15526	92.3	7.7	38.0	62.0
	1975	260614	226751	73366	153385	33863	87.0	13.0	32.4	67.6
	1980	445646	375264	130117	245147	70382	84.2	15.8	34.7	65.3
	1985	877888	682599	256797	425902	195289	77.7	22.3	37.6	62.4
	1986	1037162	774739	282342	492397	262423	74.7	25.3	36.4	63.6
	1987	1173098	895943	330213	565730	277155	76.4	23.6	36.9	63.1
	1988	1428627	1103830	413085	690745	324797	77.3	22.7	37.4	62.6
	1989	1566708	1264177	485515	778662	302531	80.7	19.3	38.4	61.6
	1990	1881697	1425183	529386	895797	456514	75.7	24.3	37.1	62.9
	1991	2211130	1700913	623811	1077102	510217	76.9	23.1	36.7	63.3
	1992	2484290	1860621	682821	1177800	623669	74.9	25.1	36.7	63.3
	1993	3007549	2286150	819639	1466511	721399	76.0	24.0	35.9	64.1
	1994	3752048	2810553	1096179	1714374	941495	74.9	25.1	39.0	61.0
	1995	4362060	3122797	1119008	2003789	1239263	71.6	28.4	35.8	64.2
	1996	5460982	3898104	1607425	2290679	1562878	71.4	28.6	41.2	58.8
	1997	6037807	4286395	1694095	2592299	1751412	71.0	29.0	39.5	60.5
	1998	6352944	4501990	1800718	2701273	1850954	70.9	29.1	40.0	60.0
	1999	6615128	4466843	1606548	2860295	2148285	67.5	32.5	36.0	64.0
	2000	7580534	4901703	1599716	3301987	2678831	64.7	35.3	32.6	67.4
	2001	8546011	5410865	1759959	3650906	3135146	63.3	36.7	32.5	67.5
	2002	9489173	6006703	1908516	4098187	3482470	63.3	36.7	31.8	68.2
	2003	10304880	6101523	1978950	4122573	4203357	59.2	40.8	32.4	67.6
	2004	11508083	6635155	2224861	4410294	4872928	57.7	42.3	33.5	66.5
"一五"时期	"First Five-Year Plan" Period	453281	409774	228447	181327	43507	90.4	9.6	55.7	44.3
"二五"时期	"Second Five-Year Plan" Period	760816	687024	342607	344417	73792	90.3	9.7	49.9	50.1
	1963-1965	502397	456636	239004	217632	45761	90.9	9.1	52.3	47.7
"三五"时期	"Third Five-Year Plan" Period	950680	879458	346357	533101	71222	92.5	7.5	39.4	60.6
"四五"时期	"Forth Five-Year Plan" Period	1193047	1055945	361778	694167	137102	88.5	11.5	34.3	65.7
"五五"时期	"Fifth Five-Year Plan" Period	1722272	1455719	494484	961235	266553	84.5	15.5	34.0	66.0
"六五"时期	"Sixth Five-Year Plan" Period	3243168	2620398	979632	1640766	622770	80.8	19.2	37.4	62.6
"七五"时期	"Seventh Five-Year Plan" Period	7087292	5463872	2040541	3423331	1623420	77.1	22.9	37.3	62.7
"八五"时期	"Eighth Five-Year Plan" Period	15817077	11781034	4341458	7439576	4036043	74.5	25.5	36.9	63.1
"九五"时期	"Ninth Five-Year Plan" Period	32047395	22055035	8308502	13746533	9992360	68.8	31.2	37.7	62.3

注：本表按当年价格计算。

Note: Data in value terms in this table are calculated at current prices.

3-10 各地、州、市、县(市)地区生产总值

单位：万元 (2004 年)

地 区	Region	地区生产总值 Gross Domestic Product	第一产业 Primary Industry
乌鲁木齐市	**Urumqi City**	**4842599**	**70874**
乌鲁木齐县	Urumqi County	68146	28419
克拉玛依市	**Karamay City**	**2962019**	**8374**
石河子市	**Shihezi City**	**446120**	**42235**
阿拉尔市	**Alar City**	**190188**	**115833**
吐鲁番地区	**Turpan Administrative Offices**	**972095**	**109903**
吐鲁番市	Turpan City	205606	48496
鄯善县	Shanshan [Piqan] County	679654	39934
托克逊县	Toksun County	85483	20403
哈密地区	**Hami [Kumul] Administrative Offices**	**523636**	**93097**
哈密市	Hami [Kumul] City	451416	60146
巴里坤哈萨克自治县	Barkol Kazak Autonomous County	59892	24020
伊吾县	Yiwu [Araturuk] County	23330	9311
昌吉回族自治州	**Changji Hui Autonomous Prefecture**	**2119163**	**643207**
昌吉市	Changji City	537641	109321
阜康市	Fukang City	297403	40323
米泉市	Miquan City	255176	43415
呼图壁县	Hutubi County	271061	121281
玛纳斯县	Manas County	427859	171810
奇台县	Qitai County	154598	79156
吉木萨尔县	Jimsar County	99962	46688
木垒哈萨克自治县	Mori Kazak Autonomous County	55805	26718
伊犁哈萨克自治州	**Ili Kazak Autonomous Prefecture**	**3190201**	**1052106**
伊犁州直属县(市)	**Counties (Cities) Direct Under Ili Prefecture**	**1368108**	**406024**
伊宁市	Yining [Gulja] City	280206	27562
奎屯市	Kuytun City	188826	11835
伊宁县	Yining [Gulja] County	167872	66188
察布查尔锡伯自治县	Qapqal Xibe Autonomous County	72186	33917
霍城县	Huocheng [Korgas] County	176697	79693
巩留县	Gongliu [Tokkuztara] County	73211	29492
新源县	Xinyuan [Kunes] County	215007	69581
昭苏县	Zhaosu [Mongolkure] County	81694	39796
特克斯县	Tekes County	55763	26108
尼勒克县	Nilka County	66909	24422
塔城地区	**Tacheng [Tarbagatai] Administrative Offices**	**1296213**	**479174**
塔城市	Tacheng [Qoqek] City	165659	41342
乌苏市	Usu City	339255	147415
额敏县	Emin [Dorbiljin] County	172621	62410
沙湾县	Shawan County	471116	188423
托里县	Toli County	54055	12254
裕民县	Yumin [Qagantokay] County	36514	16994
和布克赛尔蒙古自治县	Hoboksar Mongol Autonomous County	59959	18437
阿勒泰地区	**Altay Administrative Offices**	**525880**	**166908**
阿勒泰市	Altay City	155379	38739
布尔津县	Burqin County	61254	17565
富蕴县	Fuyun [Koktokay] County	115664	29501
福海县	Fuhai [Buruitokay] County	92655	35242
哈巴河县	Habahe [Kaba] County	51653	21707
青河县	Qinghe [Qinggil] County	35278	14812
吉木乃县	Jeminay County	21070	7531

Gross Domestic Product by Prefecture, Autonomous Prefecture, City and County

(10 000 yuan)

第二产业 Secondary Industry	工 业 Industry	建筑业 Construction	第三产业 Tertiary Industry	#运输、仓储及邮电业 Transportation, Post and Telecommunications	#批发和零售贸易餐饮业 Wholesale, Retail & Catering Trade	人均地区生产总值(元) Per Capita GDP (Yuan)
1868707	**1385567**	**483140**	**2903018**	**719305**	**720552**	**22820**
8855	5514	3341	30872	3401	5138	8270
2591811	**2497548**	**94262**	**361834**	**110665**	**51241**	**66674**
188681	**141894**	**46787**	**215204**	**40790**	**39971**	**15016**
27653	**16723**	**10930**	**46702**	**4266**	**6502**	**12007**
643555	**528705**	**114850**	**218637**	**46867**	**68637**	**16887**
59514	35705	23809	97596	20429	27711	8013
571751	484131	87620	67969	28466	10198	32288
35130	17170	17960	29950	5163	10584	7871
190362	**133421**	**56941**	**240177**	**102461**	**41278**	**9965**
165788	117963	47825	225482	100883	37117	11174
17136	11142	5994	18736	2583	4110	5930
7278	3802	3476	6741	539	993	11380
880995	**649300**	**231695**	**594961**	**109220**	**158324**	**12910**
251922	195641	56281	176398	33605	40813	13454
193513	162959	30554	63567	16794	17429	19274
141571	114136	27435	70190	10758	25271	13544
67028	45515	21513	82752	12032	20289	12895
145635	104184	41451	110414	23443	24785	16418
26882	17080	9802	48560	8732	10238	7593
23420	14509	8911	29854	3601	8074	8316
10997	4147	6850	18090	2239	3764	7145
1009560	**611128**	**398432**	**1128535**	**183156**	**289365**	**7544**
486416	**320416**	**166000**	**475668**	**76168**	**108323**	**5754**
109600	56540	53060	143044	29071	35001	6573
94909	74389	20520	82082	12559	26367	13663
60463	40683	19780	41221	4067	11666	4672
16389	7797	8592	21880	3741	2584	4343
44674	32384	12290	52330	11374	9387	4895
24720	9320	15400	18999	5156	2353	4536
76582	63335	13247	68844	12947	20734	7232
15973	10501	5472	25925	3871	5392	5187
10942	5956	4986	18713	3125	4275	3559
20974	5231	15743	21513	2506	3580	4270
340624	**208173**	**132451**	**476415**	**78807**	**141958**	**9992**
35071	15913	19158	89246	15674	25409	10471
92103	48105	43998	99737	15928	29944	10572
38751	23613	15138	71460	11515	16111	8631
138754	91399	47355	143939	21619	48633	11410
20395	11135	9260	21406	3678	3957	17907
5702	2995	2707	13818	2521	673	6968
22192	15013	7179	19330	4688	2924	10142
182520	**82539**	**99981**	**176452**	**28181**	**39084**	**9492**
31374	18249	13125	85266	13840	15513	8793
22918	7630	15288	20771	1457	6702	9848
58785	36366	22419	27370	6024	6635	14368
28163	7550	20613	29250	3896	5669	12959
15207	6775	8432	14739	2603	2250	6961
6901	2016	4885	13565	864	3704	6521
5461	1765	3696	8078	631	1173	6072

3-10 续表 1

单位：万元

地区	Region	地区生产总值 Gross Domestic Product	第一产业 Primary Industry
博尔塔拉蒙古自治州	**Bortala Mongolian Autonomous Prefecture**	**386626**	**157060**
博乐市	Bole [Bortala] City	231301	82856
精河县	Jinghe [Jing] County	101064	49035
温泉县	Wenquan [Araxang] County	45067	22438
巴音郭楞蒙古自治州	**Bayangol Mongol ian Autonomous Prefecture**	**2294733**	**403318**
库尔勒市	Korla City	1739828	117649
轮台县	Luntai [Bugur] County	104244	38207
尉犁县	Yuli [Lopnur] County	126402	71940
若羌县	Ruoqiang [Qarkilik] County	31490	10103
且末县	Qiemo [Qarqan] County	36059	16504
焉耆回族自治县	Yanqi Hui Autonomous County	118579	37630
和静县	Hejing County	144014	61778
和硕县	Hoxud County	66866	28305
博湖县	Bohu [Bagrax] County	50790	20874
阿克苏地区	**Aksu Administrative Offices**	**1535741**	**580375**
阿克苏市	Aksu City	438105	93670
温宿县	Wensu [Onsu] County	121544	63291
库车县	Kuqa County	290135	67579
沙雅县	Xayar County	115686	55616
新和县	Xinhe [Toksu] County	67890	41306
拜城县	Baicheng [Bay] County	110960	36370
乌什县	Wushi [Uxturpan] County	56500	29979
阿瓦提县	Awat County	131580	72020
柯坪县	Kalpin County	13153	4711
克孜勒苏柯尔克孜自治州	**Kizilsu Kirgiz Autonomous Prefecture**	**143312**	**43185**
阿图什市	Artux City	71421	19878
阿克陶县	Akto County	38411	15148
阿合奇县	Akqi County	13054	4025
乌恰县	Wuqia [Ulugqat] County	18681	4490
喀什地区	**Kashgar [Kaxgar] Administrative Offices**	**1195550**	**528772**
喀什市	Kashgar [Kaxgar] City	241015	13603
疏附县	Shufu County	91068	53308
疏勒县	Shule County	75272	41623
英吉沙县	Yengisar County	60498	35910
泽普县	Zepu [Poskam] County	73008	28674
莎车县	Shache [Yarkant] County	144222	84548
叶城县	Yecheng [Kagilik] County	93300	60212
麦盖提县	Makit County	61700	40290
岳普湖县	Yopurga County	43778	20003
伽师县	Jiashi [Payzawat] County	99582	61402
巴楚县	Bachu [Maralbexi] County	118603	60534
塔什库尔干塔吉克自治县	Taxkorgan Tajik Autonomous County	17185	3118
和田地区	**Hotan Administrative Offices**	**429831**	**197609**
和田市	Hotan City	74042	8379
和田县	Hotan County	65673	37669
墨玉县	Moyu [Karakax] County	83873	46759
皮山县	Pishan [Guma] County	44823	23350
洛浦县	Lop County	58046	26919
策勒县	Qira County	33932	15229
于田县	Yutian [Keriya] County	53954	30926
民丰县	Minfeng [Niya] County	15488	7048

Continued

(10 000 yuan)

第二产业 Secondary Industry	工　业 Industry	建筑业 Construction	第三产业 Tertiary Industry	#交通运输、仓储及邮电业 Transportation, Post and Telecommunications	#批发和零售贸易餐饮业 Wholesale, Retail & Catering Trade	人均地区生产总值(元) Per Capita GDP (Yuan)
79195	**36817**	**42378**	**150371**	**33687**	**19039**	**8554**
54002	25754	28248	94443	19430	13095	9490
12793	5153	7640	39236	12606	3760	9784
7070	3659	3411	15559	2305	1597	6687
1450017	**1072406**	**377611**	**441398**	**95203**	**90948**	**19620**
1323255	978800	344455	298924	81038	55359	39265
45638	39307	6331	20399	840	5178	10659
20814	11042	9772	33648	4777	7460	11470
9294	6636	2658	12093	2091	1931	13343
5289	1635	3654	14266	640	2524	6206
49152	33570	15582	31797	3496	7629	9547
37153	27133	10020	45083	13111	6735	7979
12898	8324	4574	25663	2327	4433	8821
12224	7724	4500	17692	2234	3545	8926
373415	**211673**	**161742**	**581951**	**58479**	**151547**	**6771**
115164	61980	53184	229271	23594	76321	10325
23500	11992	11508	34753	5323	5278	5500
108888	68700	40188	113668	12327	25636	6430
14317	6300	8017	45753	2129	15089	5504
8873	2882	5991	17711	1787	2656	4708
43903	30016	13887	30687	3211	7499	5299
7376	3222	4154	19145	1541	2582	2986
21801	8995	12806	37759	3942	9021	6055
1940	863	1077	6502	359	963	3073
28926	**9168**	**19758**	**71201**	**4954**	**3750**	**3054**
14796	5218	9578	36747	2623	2139	3336
6840	1560	5280	16423	1233	899	2261
2168	192	1976	6861	498	650	3538
4615	2081	2534	9576	655	717	4115
220993	**78435**	**142558**	**445785**	**55068**	**110789**	**3497**
70709	46708	24001	156703	20371	54846	6799
11892	3246	8646	25868	1561	1975	2547
8030	5500	2530	25619	1358	5123	2578
8465	2238	6227	16123	482	2639	2612
13332	6460	6872	31002	2297	8518	4086
14046	8204	5842	45628	2266	5216	2164
7107	2996	4111	25981	1950	5941	2439
6245	1712	4533	15165	468	2991	3387
6208	1739	4469	17567	1147	3068	3099
7264	1000	6264	30916	5702	3884	3076
17169	4071	13098	40900	3995	15137	4282
8092	172	7920	5975	12	706	5069
75710	**22156**	**53554**	**156512**	**16468**	**13361**	**2445**
27053	10186	16867	38610	4931	6387	4095
10196	3165	7031	17808	498	465	2368
10610	1224	9386	26504	1885	3798	2024
6133	2161	3972	15340	767	948	1982
9854	4456	5398	21273	823	2799	2385
3875	445	3430	14828	1239	1240	2475
4776	576	4200	18252	1497	3360	2399
3850	1800	2050	4590	554	165	4451

3-11 各地、州、市、县(市)地区生产总值构成

单位：% (2004 年)

地 区	Region	地区生产总值 Gross Domestic Product	第一产业 Primary Industry
乌鲁木齐市	**Urumqi City**	**100**	**1.5**
乌鲁木齐县	Urumqi County	100	41.7
克拉玛依市	**Karamay City**	**100**	**0.3**
石河子市	**Shihezi City**	**100**	**9.5**
阿拉尔市	**Alar City**	**100**	**60.9**
吐鲁番地区	**Turpan Administrative Offices**	**100**	**11.3**
吐鲁番市	Turpan City	100	23.6
鄯善县	Shanshan [Piqan] County	100	5.9
托克逊县	Toksun County	100	23.9
哈密地区	**Hami [Kumul] Administrative Offices**	**100**	**17.8**
哈密市	Hami [Kumul] City	100	13.3
巴里坤哈萨克自治县	Barkol Kazak Autonomous County	100	40.1
伊吾县	Yiwu [Araturuk] County	100	39.9
昌吉回族自治州	**Changji Hui Autonomous Prefecture**	**100**	**30.4**
昌吉市	Changji City	100	20.3
阜康市	Fukang City	100	13.5
米泉市	Miquan City	100	17.0
呼图壁县	Hutubi County	100	44.7
玛纳斯县	Manas County	100	40.2
奇台县	Qitai County	100	51.2
吉木萨尔县	Jimsar County	100	46.7
木垒哈萨克自治县	Mori Kazak Autonomous County	100	47.9
伊犁哈萨克自治州	**Ili Kazak Autonomous Prefecture**	**100**	**33.0**
伊犁州直属县(市)	**Counties (Cities) Direct Under Ili Prefecture**	**100**	**29.7**
伊宁市	Yining [Gulja] City	100	9.8
奎屯市	Kuytun City	100	6.3
伊宁县	Yining [Gulja] County	100	39.4
察布查尔锡伯自治县	Qapqal Xibe Autonomous County	100	47.0
霍城县	Huocheng [Korgas] County	100	45.1
巩留县	Gongliu [Tokkuztara] County	100	40.2
新源县	Xinyuan [Kunes] County	100	32.4
昭苏县	Zhaosu [Mongolkure] County	100	48.7
特克斯县	Tekes County	100	46.8
尼勒克县	Nilka County	100	36.5
塔城地区	**Tacheng [Tarbagatai] Administrative Offices**	**100**	**37.0**
塔城市	Tacheng [Qoqek] City	100	25.0
乌苏市	Usu City	100	43.5
额敏县	Emin [Dorbiljin] County	100	36.2
沙湾县	Shawan County	100	40.0
托里县	Toli County	100	22.7
裕民县	Yumin [Qagantokay] County	100	46.5
和布克赛尔蒙古自治县	Hoboksar Mongol Autonomous County	100	30.7
阿勒泰地区	**Altay Administrative Offices**	**100**	**31.7**
阿勒泰市	Altay City	100	24.9
布尔津县	Burqin County	100	28.7
富蕴县	Fuyun [Koktokay] County	100	25.5
福海县	Fuhai [Burultokay] County	100	38.0
哈巴河县	Habahe [Kaba] County	100	42.1
青河县	Qinghe [Qinggil] County	100	42.0
吉木乃县	Jeminay County	100	35.7

Composition of Gross Domestic Product by Prefecture, Autonomous Prefecture, City and County

(%)

第二产业 Secondary Industry	工业 Industry	建筑业 Construction	第三产业 Tertiary Industry	#交通运输、仓储及邮电业 Transportation, Storage Post and Telecommunications	#批发和零售贸易餐饮业 Wholesale, Retail & Catering Trade
38.6	**28.6**	**10.0**	**59.9**	**14.9**	**14.9**
13.0	8.1	4.9	45.3	5.0	7.5
87.5	**84.3**	**3.2**	**12.2**	**3.7**	**1.7**
42.3	**31.8**	**10.5**	**48.2**	**9.1**	**9.0**
14.5	**8.8**	**5.7**	**24.6**	**2.2**	**3.4**
66.2	**54.4**	**11.8**	**22.5**	**4.8**	**7.1**
28.9	17.4	11.6	47.5	9.9	13.5
84.1	71.2	12.9	10.0	4.2	1.5
41.1	20.1	21.0	35.0	6.0	12.4
36.4	**25.5**	**10.9**	**45.8**	**19.6**	**7.9**
36.8	26.1	10.6	49.9	22.3	8.2
28.6	18.6	10.0	31.3	4.3	6.9
31.2	16.3	14.9	28.9	2.3	4.3
41.5	**30.6**	**10.9**	**28.1**	**5.2**	**7.5**
46.9	36.4	10.5	32.8	6.3	7.6
65.1	54.8	10.3	21.4	5.6	5.9
55.5	44.7	10.8	27.5	4.2	9.9
24.8	16.8	7.9	30.5	4.4	7.5
34.0	24.4	9.7	25.8	5.5	5.8
17.4	11.0	6.3	31.4	5.6	6.6
23.4	14.5	8.9	29.9	3.6	8.1
19.7	7.4	12.3	32.4	4.0	6.7
31.6	**19.2**	**12.5**	**35.4**	**5.7**	**9.1**
35.5	**23.4**	**12.1**	**34.8**	**5.6**	**7.9**
39.1	20.2	18.9	51.1	10.4	12.5
50.3	39.4	10.9	43.4	6.7	14.0
36.0	24.2	11.8	24.6	2.4	6.9
22.7	10.8	11.9	30.3	5.2	3.6
25.3	18.3	7.0	29.6	6.4	5.3
33.8	12.7	21.0	26.0	7.0	3.2
35.6	29.5	6.2	32.0	6.0	9.6
19.6	12.9	6.7	31.7	4.7	6.6
19.6	10.7	8.9	33.6	5.6	7.7
31.3	7.8	23.5	32.2	3.7	5.4
26.3	**16.1**	**10.2**	**36.7**	**6.1**	**11.0**
21.2	9.6	11.6	53.8	9.5	15.3
27.1	14.2	13.0	29.4	4.7	8.8
22.4	13.7	8.8	41.4	6.7	9.3
29.5	19.4	10.1	30.5	4.6	10.3
37.7	20.6	17.1	39.6	6.8	7.3
15.7	8.2	7.4	37.8	6.9	1.8
37.1	25.0	12.0	32.2	7.8	4.9
34.7	**15.7**	**19.0**	**33.6**	**5.4**	**7.4**
20.2	11.7	8.4	54.9	8.9	10.0
37.4	12.5	25.0	33.9	2.4	10.9
50.8	31.4	19.4	23.7	5.2	5.7
30.4	8.1	22.2	31.6	4.2	6.1
29.4	13.1	16.3	28.5	5.0	4.4
19.5	5.7	13.8	38.5	2.4	10.5
25.9	8.4	17.5	38.4	3.0	5.6

3-11 续表 1

单位：%

地　　区	Region	地区生产总值 Gross Domestic Product	第一产业 Primary Industry
博尔塔拉蒙古自治州	**Bortala Mongolian Autonomous Prefecture**	**100**	**40.6**
博乐市	Bole [Bortala] City	100	35.8
精河县	Jinghe [Jing] County	100	48.5
温泉县	Wenquan [Araxang] County	100	49.8
巴音郭楞蒙古自治州	**Bayangol Mongol ian Autonomous Prefecture**	**100**	**17.6**
库尔勒市	Korla City	100	6.8
轮台县	Luntai [Bugur] County	100	36.7
尉犁县	Yuli [Lopnur] County	100	56.9
若羌县	Ruoqiang [Qarkilik] County	100	32.1
且末县	Qiemo [Qarqan] County	100	45.8
焉耆回族自治县	Yanqi Hui Autonomous County	100	31.7
和静县	Hejing County	100	42.9
和硕县	Hoxud County	100	42.3
博湖县	Bohu [Bagrax] County	100	41.1
阿克苏地区	**Aksu Administrative Offices**	**100**	**37.8**
阿克苏市	Aksu City	100	21.4
温宿县	Wensu [Onsu] County	100	52.1
库车县	Kuqa County	100	23.3
沙雅县	Xayar County	100	48.1
新和县	Xinhe [Toksu] County	100	60.8
拜城县	Baicheng [Bay] County	100	32.8
乌什县	Wushi [Uxturpan] County	100	53.1
阿瓦提县	Awat County	100	54.7
柯坪县	Kalpin County	100	35.8
克孜勒苏柯尔克孜自治州	**Kizilsu Kirgiz Autonomous Prefecture**	**100**	**30.1**
阿图什市	Artux City	100	27.8
阿克陶县	Akto County	100	39.4
阿合奇县	Akqi County	100	30.8
乌恰县	Wuqia [Ulugqat] County	100	24.0
喀什地区	**Kashgar [Kaxgar] Administrative Offices**	**100**	**44.2**
喀什市	Kashgar [Kaxgar] City	100	5.7
疏附县	Shufu County	100	58.5
疏勒县	Shule County	100	55.3
英吉沙县	Yengisar County	100	59.4
泽普县	Zepu [Poskam] County	100	39.3
莎车县	Shache [Yarkant] County	100	58.6
叶城县	Yecheng [Kagilik] County	100	64.5
麦盖提县	Makit County	100	65.3
岳普湖县	Yopurga County	100	45.7
伽师县	Jiashi [Payzawat] County	100	61.7
巴楚县	Bachu [Maralbexi] County	100	51.0
塔什库尔干塔吉克自治县	Taxkorgan Tajik Autonomous County	100	18.1
和田地区	**Hotan Administrative Offices**	**100**	**46.0**
和田市	Hotan City	100	11.3
和田县	Hotan County	100	57.4
墨玉县	Moyu [Karakax] County	100	55.7
皮山县	Pishan [Guma] County	100	52.1
洛浦县	Lop County	100	46.4
策勒县	Qira County	100	44.9
于田县	Yutian [Keriya] County	100	57.3
民丰县	Minfeng [Niya] County	100	45.5

Continued

(%)

第二产业 Secondary Industry	工业 Industry	建筑业 Construction	第三产业 Tertiary Industry	#运输、仓储及邮电业 Transportation, Storage Post and Telecommunications	#批发和零售贸易餐饮业 Wholesale, Retail & Catering Trade
20.5	**9.5**	**11.0**	**38.9**	**8.7**	**4.9**
23.3	11.1	12.2	40.9	8.4	5.7
12.7	5.1	7.6	38.8	12.5	3.7
15.7	8.1	7.6	34.5	5.1	3.5
63.2	**46.7**	**16.5**	**19.2**	**4.1**	**4.0**
76.0	56.3	19.8	17.2	4.7	3.2
43.7	37.7	6.1	19.6	0.8	5.0
16.5	8.7	7.7	26.6	3.8	5.9
29.5	21.1	8.4	38.4	6.6	6.1
14.7	4.5	10.1	39.5	1.8	7.0
41.5	28.3	13.1	26.8	2.9	6.4
25.8	18.8	7.0	31.3	9.1	4.7
19.3	12.4	6.8	38.4	3.5	6.6
24.1	15.2	8.9	34.8	4.4	7.0
24.3	**13.8**	**10.5**	**37.9**	**3.8**	**9.9**
26.3	14.1	12.1	52.3	5.4	17.4
19.3	9.9	9.5	28.6	4.4	4.3
37.5	23.7	13.9	39.2	4.2	8.8
12.4	5.4	6.9	39.5	1.8	13.0
13.1	4.2	8.8	26.1	2.6	3.9
39.6	27.1	12.5	27.6	2.9	6.8
13.0	5.7	7.4	33.9	2.7	4.6
16.6	6.8	9.7	28.7	3.0	6.9
14.8	6.6	8.2	49.4	2.7	7.3
20.2	**6.4**	**13.8**	**49.7**	**3.5**	**2.6**
20.7	7.3	13.4	51.5	3.7	3.0
17.8	4.1	13.7	42.8	3.2	2.3
16.6	1.5	15.1	52.6	3.8	5.0
24.7	11.1	13.6	51.3	3.5	3.8
18.5	**6.6**	**11.9**	**37.3**	**4.6**	**9.3**
29.3	19.4	10.0	65.0	8.5	22.8
13.1	3.6	9.5	28.4	1.7	2.2
10.7	7.3	3.4	34.0	1.8	6.8
14.0	3.7	10.3	26.6	0.8	4.4
18.3	8.8	9.4	42.4	3.1	11.7
9.8	5.7	4.1	31.6	1.6	3.6
7.6	3.2	4.4	27.9	2.1	6.4
10.1	2.8	7.3	24.6	0.8	4.8
14.2	4.0	10.2	40.1	2.6	7.0
7.3	1.0	6.3	31.0	5.7	3.9
14.5	3.4	11.0	34.5	3.4	12.8
47.1	1.0	46.1	34.8	0.1	4.1
17.6	**5.2**	**12.5**	**36.4**	**3.8**	**3.1**
36.6	13.8	22.8	52.1	6.7	8.6
15.5	4.8	10.7	27.1	0.8	0.7
12.7	1.5	11.2	31.6	2.2	4.5
13.7	4.8	8.9	34.2	1.7	2.1
17.0	7.7	9.3	36.6	1.4	4.8
11.4	1.3	10.1	43.7	3.7	3.7
8.9	1.1	7.8	33.8	2.8	6.2
24.9	11.6	13.2	29.6	3.6	1.1

3-12 各地、州、市、县(市)地区生产总值指数

单位：% (2004 年)

地区	Region	地区生产总值 Gross Domestic Product	第一产业 Primary Industry
乌鲁木齐市	**Urumqi City**	**112.5**	**110.9**
乌鲁木齐县	Urumqi County	111.3	113.0
克拉玛依市	**Karamay City**	**108.3**	**118.2**
石河子市	**Shihezi City**	**112.6**	**105.6**
阿拉尔市	**Alar City**	**110.9**	**112.2**
吐鲁番地区	**Turpan Administrative Offices**	**112.8**	**110.5**
吐鲁番市	Turpan City	111.6	114.3
鄯善县	Shanshan [Piqan] County	109.6	109.3
托克逊县	Toksun County	109.5	108.1
哈密地区	**Hami [Kumul] Administrative Offices**	**108.5**	**106.5**
哈密市	Hami [Kumul] City	108.5	106.6
巴里坤哈萨克自治县	Barkol Kazak Autonomous County	108.2	105.6
伊吾县	Yiwu [Araturuk] County	120.1	127.2
昌吉回族自治州	**Changji Hui Autonomous Prefecture**	**114.0**	**108.5**
昌吉市	Changji City	113.3	109.4
阜康市	Fukang City	109.8	106.4
米泉市	Miquan City	113.9	107.4
呼图壁县	Hutubi County	117.6	111.1
玛纳斯县	Manas County	116.6	107.0
奇台县	Qitai County	111.7	109.9
吉木萨尔县	Jimsar County	107.5	107.4
木垒哈萨克自治县	Mori Kazak Autonomous County	109.7	100.3
伊犁哈萨克自治州	**Ili Kazak Autonomous Prefecture**	**112.9**	**107.2**
伊犁州直属县(市)	**Counties (Cities) Direct Under Ili Prefecture**	**113.8**	**106.7**
伊宁市	Yining [Gulja] City	113.6	104.7
奎屯市	Kuytun City	114.4	106.7
伊宁县	Yining [Gulja] County	111.8	105.8
察布查尔锡伯自治县	Qapqal Xibe Autonomous County	111.1	107.9
霍城县	Huocheng [Korgas] County	113.4	107.2
巩留县	Gongliu [Tokkuztara] County	111.1	107.4
新源县	Xinyuan [Kunes] County	115.3	106.3
昭苏县	Zhaosu [Mongolkure] County	113.1	106.8
特克斯县	Tekes County	109.5	105.8
尼勒克县	Nilka County	115.4	107.9
塔城地区	**Tacheng [Tarbagatai] Administrative Offices**	**111.7**	**107.4**
塔城市	Tacheng [Qoqek] City	109.0	107.2
乌苏市	Usu City	111.3	104.1
额敏县	Emin [Dorbiljin] County	110.3	103.3
沙湾县	Shawan County	112.5	107.6
托里县	Toli County	117.2	109.7
裕民县	Yumin [Qagantokay] County	112.7	104.9
和布克赛尔蒙古自治县	Hoboksar Mongol Autonomous County	119.4	126.0
阿勒泰地区	**Altay Administrative Offices**	**113.3**	**108.0**
阿勒泰市	Altay City	110.4	107.6
布尔津县	Burqin County	114.8	106.0
富蕴县	Fuyun [Koktokay] County	126.7	108.9
福海县	Fuhai [Burultokay] County	110.6	105.9
哈巴河县	Habahe [Kaba] County	109.9	109.7
青河县	Qinghe [Qinggil] County	112.4	115.7
吉木乃县	Jeminay County	110.2	105.6

Indices of Gross Domestic Product by Prefecture, Autonomous Prefecture, City and County

(%)

第二产业 Secondary Industry	工业 Industry	建筑业 Construction	第三产业 Tertiary Industry	#运输、仓储及邮电业 Transportation, Storage Post and Telecommunications	#批发和零售贸易餐饮业 Wholesale, Retail & Catering Trade
111.6	**115.2**	**103.6**	**113.0**	**112.7**	**116.9**
97.4	89.4	119.0	114.0	109.1	105.9
107.8	**108.7**	**92.1**	**111.0**	**113.4**	**136.4**
112.3	**114.9**	**105.0**	**114.2**	**116.8**	**114.4**
114.9	**117.9**	**110.9**	**105.8**	**126.8**	**102.3**
114.5	**112.4**	**124.6**	**109.5**	**111.4**	**109.6**
108.5	109.2	107.6	112.3	111.8	109.5
109.6	112.2	98.1	109.9	113.7	98.7
109.6	105.1	113.6	110.2	108.9	110.3
103.5	**113.0**	**85.2**	**113.4**	**105.0**	**114.0**
102.3	113.7	81.3	113.7	109.3	114.0
106.8	106.5	107.4	112.8	124.8	112.2
128.1	153.8	114.7	107.9	138.6	112.4
119.1	**116.4**	**127.4**	**113.0**	**113.3**	**114.4**
114.0	114.5	112.4	114.7	118.6	111.0
109.9	109.5	111.7	111.7	117.0	109.5
117.8	117.7	118.1	110.6	110.7	113.5
126.4	126.6	126.1	120.4	107.9	110.2
137.0	139.1	132.0	110.4	114.3	113.1
109.9	107.1	115.3	115.2	125.8	114.1
103.9	107.9	97.7	110.8	111.4	113.0
132.7	104.6	160.9	113.9	111.6	111.3
119.1	**117.0**	**122.5**	**113.3**	**114.9**	**112.0**
121.0	**115.8**	**132.5**	**113.3**	**111.2**	**112.6**
113.9	108.3	120.8	115.3	124.7	111.8
121.4	127.3	106.6	109.3	118.2	104.9
118.7	109.9	147.7	112.6	108.9	111.8
116.9	114.0	119.6	111.8	109.0	107.4
125.5	124.0	130.0	113.5	114.8	118.5
113.7	111.2	115.3	114.0	111.3	112.4
121.6	114.3	180.0	118.2	124.8	105.9
140.6	157.5	121.0	109.9	142.8	108.1
115.9	117.8	113.7	111.7	111.6	105.7
129.9	105.3	140.2	112.4	107.2	107.9
116.0	**119.2**	**111.2**	**114.1**	**117.5**	**110.7**
107.1	116.3	100.8	110.8	127.5	102.6
125.0	120.4	130.3	110.7	112.1	111.2
113.3	119.1	104.9	115.0	115.1	110.2
123.3	122.7	124.7	109.7	108.0	117.8
128.5	133.4	123.2	111.9	113.3	119.8
129.3	118.4	143.1	116.1	107.1	109.9
114.1	111.8	119.0	119.9	125.8	137.8
120.4	**115.7**	**124.5**	**111.3**	**118.2**	**115.1**
104.4	124.5	85.0	114.1	114.4	116.5
119.1	117.2	120.0	117.8	83.5	136.5
146.6	131.0	175.4	115.4	156.0	122.0
113.9	109.9	115.5	112.3	123.3	116.5
108.3	99.3	116.5	111.8	136.7	117.0
108.5	96.1	114.4	111.3	106.9	114.9
115.1	103.2	121.4	111.5	104.1	101.5

3-12 续表 1

单位：%

地区	Region	地区生产总值 Gross Domestic Product	第一产业 Primary Industry
博尔塔拉蒙古自治州	**Bortala Mongolian Autonomous Prefecture**	**110.1**	**107.6**
博乐市	Bole [Bortala] City	112.2	108.7
精河县	Jinghe [Jing] County	108.7	106.6
温泉县	Wenquan [Araxang] County	107.5	109.8
巴音郭楞蒙古自治州	**Bayangol Mongol ian Autonomous Prefecture**	**113.0**	**111.5**
库尔勒市	Korla City	113.0	108.6
轮台县	Luntai [Bugur] County	131.7	107.1
尉犁县	Yuli [Lopnur] County	111.1	113.9
若羌县	Ruoqiang [Qarkilik] County	110.2	107.6
且末县	Qiemo [Qarqan] County	108.9	107.2
焉耆回族自治县	Yanqi Hui Autonomous County	115.0	111.9
和静县	Hejing County	116.1	107.7
和硕县	Hoxud County	112.8	107.5
博湖县	Bohu [Bagrax] County	113.6	123.5
阿克苏地区	**Aksu Administrative Offices**	**113.1**	**106.8**
阿克苏市	Aksu City	113.8	101.7
温宿县	Wensu [Onsu] County	111.4	109.7
库车县	Kuqa County	116.4	104.3
沙雅县	Xayar County	111.5	106.4
新和县	Xinhe [Toksu] County	111.2	107.5
拜城县	Baicheng [Bay] County	114.8	108.6
乌什县	Wushi [Uxturpan] County	109.5	104.3
阿瓦提县	Awat County	111.3	105.8
柯坪县	Kalpin County	116.4	104.2
克孜勒苏柯尔克孜自治州	**Kizilsu Kirgiz Autonomous Prefecture**	**111.2**	**106.7**
阿图什市	Artux City	114.8	109.5
阿克陶县	Akto County	109.3	105.2
阿合奇县	Akqi County	105.7	108.4
乌恰县	Wuqia [Ulugqat] County	109.0	105.7
喀什地区	**Kashgar [Kaxgar] Administrative Offices**	**112.7**	**106.1**
喀什市	Kashgar [Kaxgar] City	124.1	101.8
疏附县	Shufu County	113.1	111.6
疏勒县	Shule County	114.8	109.4
英吉沙县	Yengisar County	111.4	131.0
泽普县	Zepu [Poskam] County	114.1	105.6
莎车县	Shache [Yarkant] County	114.4	108.6
叶城县	Yecheng [Kagilik] County	111.5	110.3
麦盖提县	Makit County	108.4	102.7
岳普湖县	Yopurga County	108.6	95.5
伽师县	Jiashi [Payzawat] County	109.4	107.6
巴楚县	Bachu [Maralbexi] County	110.9	105.1
塔什库尔干塔吉克自治县	Taxkorgan Tajik Autonomous County	116.6	112.9
和田地区	**Hotan Administrative Offices**	**112.0**	**107.1**
和田市	Hotan City	123.3	126.2
和田县	Hotan County	110.3	102.7
墨玉县	Moyu [Karakax] County	113.2	110.4
皮山县	Pishan [Guma] County	111.1	108.8
洛浦县	Lop County	108.7	99.4
策勒县	Qira County	108.5	100.4
于田县	Yutian [Keriya] County	111.4	108.6
民丰县	Minfeng [Niya] County	117.0	109.4

Continued

(%)

第二产业 Secondary Industry	工业 Industry	建筑业 Construction	第三产业 Tertiary Industry	#运输、仓储及邮电业 Transportation, Storage Post and Telecommunications	#批发和零售贸易餐饮业 Wholesale, Retail & Catering Trade
106.8	**105.5**	**107.8**	**114.1**	**113.6**	**116.4**
114.7	112.9	116.4	113.6	120.9	112.1
104.0	111.0	99.6	112.7	114.2	103.7
89.4	104.9	76.6	114.5	109.8	111.9
113.9	**111.8**	**119.7**	**111.7**	**107.3**	**107.7**
113.7	109.5	126.2	111.6	110.7	111.3
184.2	187.6	168.4	110.4	103.8	101.7
100.7	86.2	122.9	112.5	109.9	125.0
100.8	103.9	94.4	120.2	101.8	122.6
108.5	120.4	104.2	111.3	97.6	124.8
116.3	126.0	101.2	117.0	175.5	108.6
149.2	140.4	180.4	107.7	136.0	101.6
121.0	120.2	122.4	114.4	119.1	105.2
113.4	110.7	118.2	103.8	102.8	104.7
119.5	**117.0**	**122.8**	**116.1**	**113.1**	**124.2**
113.0	117.7	108.1	119.9	109.4	132.2
113.1	110.0	116.2	113.5	97.7	115.7
127.7	117.1	150.9	114.5	125.2	126.0
119.6	100.4	142.6	116.6	116.5	116.4
135.0	151.4	130.4	110.6	106.7	113.7
128.9	125.6	135.3	107.5	112.5	115.6
109.3	118.5	103.4	119.3	93.2	106.2
112.8	102.1	121.5	121.8	119.7	113.0
144.9	196.5	117.2	119.0	121.4	113.2
117.8	**119.7**	**117.0**	**111.7**	**111.0**	**117.8**
138.7	160.4	129.0	109.9	102.2	113.5
118.0	106.3	122.7	109.6	110.3	110.9
95.9	118.3	93.3	107.6	111.4	117.3
114.8	91.5	146.3	108.1	104.1	109.4
122.4	**131.2**	**117.0**	**116.9**	**119.2**	**118.6**
132.5	140.7	119.0	122.8	122.6	120.8
110.3	104.3	112.7	117.7	135.1	104.1
109.9	93.8	174.8	126.7	187.4	90.9
92.5	124.0	84.7	91.0	107.5	91.7
131.4	134.5	128.6	116.0	113.5	126.8
127.5	104.7	185.3	122.7	122.2	124.8
108.9	110.7	107.6	115.1	77.5	102.1
139.4	101.3	162.4	115.6	104.3	115.4
113.3	121.4	110.5	122.1	120.9	142.6
109.4	106.2	110.2	113.1	123.7	113.6
106.4	167.0	95.7	123.0	130.8	149.1
127.8	109.9	128.2	105.9		155.6
135.5	**107.9**	**150.1**	**109.6**	**148.3**	**170.1**
143.6	147.5	142.1	113.4	103.0	112.1
137.0	129.6	140.1	115.2	149.6	98.7
136.1	96.4	143.4	110.9	164.8	159.5
128.2	103.2	152.7	109.3	117.4	114.1
108.6	99.1	117.4	121.5	145.8	117.9
111.2	119.1	110.3	117.1	164.1	68.6
89.5	128.2	86.1	125.6	147.9	145.7
151.7	163.2	142.8	107.7	105.8	

3-13 投入产出基本流量表(中间使用部分)

单位：千元 (2002 年)

部门	Sector	农业 Agriculture	煤炭开采和洗选业 Coal Mining And Dressing
总投入合计	**Total input**	**56938617.17**	**3818198.71**
中间投入合计	**Total Intermediate Input**	**30873587.93**	**1130869.99**
农　业	Agriculture	14311921.92	19694.80
煤炭开采和洗选业	Coal Mining and Dressing	49201.24	13304.14
石油和天然气开采业	Extraction of Petroleum and Natural Gas		499.86
金属矿采选业	Mining and Dressing of Metals		
非金属矿采选业	Mining and Dressing of Nonmetal Minerals	10342.18	2006.52
食品制造及烟草加工业	Food Production and Tobacco Processing	3128321.61	4.49
纺织业	Textile Industry	72076.36	15701.13
服装皮革羽绒及其制品业	Leather, Furs, Down, Garments and Other Fiber Products	78.88	38.50
木材加工及家具制造业	Timber Processing and Furniture Manufacturing	2027.42	17889.43
造纸印刷及文教用品制造业	Paper-making , Printing and Cultural, Educational Goods	16433.31	7521.09
石油加工、炼焦及核燃料加工业	Oil Processing, Coking and Nuclear Fuel Processing	1150553.70	30004.08
化学工业	Raw Chemical Materials and Chemical Products	2898781.64	100556.25
非金属矿物制品业	Nonmetal Mineral Products	4224.27	17895.17
金属冶炼及压延加工业	Smelting and Pressing of Metals	6548.27	40397.44
金属制品业	Metal Products	235428.89	19733.87
通用、专用设备制造业	General, Special Purpose Equipment Production	528662.37	88186.02
交通运输设备制造业	Transport and Communication Equipment	4939.07	13701.22
电气、机械及器材制造业	Electric Equipment and Machinery	9578.41	44452.44
通信设备、计算机及其他电子设备制造业	Telecom, Equipment, Computer and Other Electronic Equipment	4199.19	4070.09
仪器仪表及文化办公用机械制造业	Equipment, Meter, Culture and Office Machinery	48771.98	15836.81
其他制造业	Other Manufacturing	1469.90	109742.95
废品废料	Waste material and scrape substances	-628662.68	
电力、热力的生产和供应业	Electric and Thermal Power Production and Supply	864836.69	131588.60

Input and output table (intermediate use)

(1 000 yuan)

石油和天然气开采业 Extraction of Petroleum and Natural Gas	金属矿采选业 Mining and Dressing of Metals	非金属矿采选业 Mining and Dressing of Nonmetal Minerals	食品制造及烟草加工业 Food Production And Tobacco Processing	纺织业 Textile Industry	服装皮革羽绒及其制品业 Leather, Furs, Down, Garments And Other Fiber Products	木材加工及家具制造业 Timber Processing and Furniture Manufacturing	造纸印刷及文教用品制造业 Papermaking , Printing and Cultural, Educational Goods
28279126.12	**978231.91**	**633769.16**	**24940789.11**	**5943395.82**	**168617.85**	**1280912.67**	**2071534.03**
8098105.90	**872590.12**	**261970.00**	**21351277.20**	**4422699.63**	**122613.47**	**874863.84**	**1061214.39**
141.06	46.81	2.29	13940314.52	1805785.77	4596.02	195227.57	93578.67
754.98	5550.58	8803.27	63777.68	13352.16	448.96	4281.68	23782.81
2027291.08			264.47	9.08			2468.65
	279040.40	1100.44	91.27		2.63		
89.36	6549.66	8436.26	7391.26	254.87	4.66	26.63	467.92
	8.24		1058305.45	3851.22	12.45		3514.36
45546.93	1637.29	2537.01	98079.22	356629.07	759.28	15577.60	3054.61
			9.82	255.45	37124.89	561.91	17.90
2945.45	536.02	139.31	75292.23	1693.98	29.82	151537.05	1616.27
34845.24	1454.45	1085.70	253571.20	38952.25	658.56	27998.57	338977.82
47163.45	42006.26	36799.09	47526.98	14397.76	201.36	3641.83	4861.56
142492.06	23763.51	27488.95	357435.33	93309.35	21379.65	88706.28	124824.17
12293.50	7043.31	1949.88	222987.99	10282.99	221.14	11008.84	4869.68
113856.06	12259.31	2606.49	16827.42	4344.62	68.50	4672.96	10961.05
15523.78	3407.48	8143.47	111674.81	19836.54	1794.92	19944.70	6190.88
251252.47	67843.97	17677.30	93814.86	82236.18	509.06	7975.45	22887.55
15136.81	6734.58	1916.20	18871.21	5519.89	51.73	813.52	5747.00
54159.50	5506.31	1480.06	29798.58	16967.27	331.11	2489.53	6875.72
7600.97	2943.05	231.50	8619.30	7774.11	28.46	421.48	1111.40
68656.40	1641.42	423.93	14166.55	4688.97	126.42	686.60	3602.52
7958.73	2068.77	1873.04	10864.75	4103.57	68.62	234.23	9699.45
		2430.23	17950.98	2854.45		4910.29	36288.21
655225.37	47740.49	31004.06	468784.17	408443.80	1456.88	35728.28	47171.42

3-13 续表 1

单位：千元

部　　门	Sector	农　业 Agriculture	煤炭开采和洗选业 Coal Mining And Dressing
燃气生产和供应业	Gas Production and Supply	0.80	21.33
水的生产和供应业	Production and Supply of Tapping Water	18013.10	1826.92
建筑业	Construction	1987.07	2257.10
交通运输及仓储业	Transportation and Storage	2148568.99	121412.22
邮政业	Post Service	24426.29	483.32
信息传输、计算机服务和软件业	Information Transmission, Computer Servcie and Software Industries	17706.64	10224.72
批发和零售贸易业	Wholesale and Retail Trade	1421611.96	78030.99
住宿和餐饮业	Hotel and Catering	123480.93	28921.40
金融保险业	Banking and Insurance	453589.42	91640.39
房地产业	Real Estate	1738.56	495.97
租赁和商务服务业	Leasing and Commercial Service	2667127.70	41945.33
旅游业	Tourism	8.38	521.42
科学研究事业	Scientific Research	832.62	4209.62
综合技术服务业	Polytechnical Services	1140.15	4131.17
其他社会服务业	Other Social Service	796004.55	1395.77
教育事业	Education	44794.35	12644.48
卫生、社会保障和社会福利业	Health, Social Security and Social Welfare	23184.10	27655.26
文化、体育和娱乐业	Culture, Sports and Recreation	21205.36	10227.68
公共管理和社会组织	Public Management and Social Organization	388432.34	
中间投入合计	Total Intermediate Input	30873587.93	1130869.99
增加值合计	**Total Added Value**	**26065029.24**	**2687328.72**
固定资产折旧	Depreciation of Fixed Assets	1457799.16	417355.62
劳动者报酬	Payment for Laborers	18000556.92	1488153.91
生产税净额	Net Taxes on Production	583466.09	234163.44
营业盈余	Operating Surplus	6023207.07	547655.75

Continued

(1 000 yuan)

石油和天然气开采业 Extraction of Petroleum and Natural Gas	金属矿采选业 Mining and Dressing of Metals	非金属矿采选业 Mining and Dressing of Nonmetal Minerals	食品制造及烟草加工业 Food Production And Tobacco Processing	纺织业 Textile Industry	服装皮革羽绒及其制品业 Leather, Furs, Down, Garments And Other Fiber Products	木材加工及家具制造业 Timber Processing and Furniture Manufacturing	造纸印刷及文教用品制造业 Paper-making , Printing and Cultural, Educational Goods
			3424.59	5118.89	72.63		3017.60
684712.12	3447.00	901.46	36636.25	12907.77	79.86	1007.89	4943.01
4037.21	126.35	12.21	1442.75	1045.03	4.65	106.73	309.27
314165.99	310543.39	75903.49	2002003.87	306830.60	5141.48	159294.89	117220.73
2671.26	144.88	236.82	4501.08	1465.12	12.55	515.44	650.53
29287.16	1994.06	1993.81	40596.51	9558.62	322.34	4221.30	5351.13
90211.99	13326.57	12300.50	1172880.23	981205.89	26712.16	103135.24	120378.86
59084.13	3486.94	3582.67	84494.70	22343.93	883.40	4328.52	11199.07
414037.75	13285.29	3992.93	675653.45	118094.50	18068.68	17078.19	26912.33
482.25	56.91	35.65	9717.23	8772.09	291.79	2548.30	2846.91
27529.80	3750.72	1936.49	337271.32	36241.44	378.84	2782.79	7224.10
240.10	40.24	50.92	2387.24	486.83	13.96	30.08	103.15
89719.50	762.91	440.75	10070.05	4328.37	99.84	353.91	805.61
2819578.11	1047.05	21.52	8201.81	2606.70	115.97	179.23	279.34
25115.36	354.02	410.70	12531.06	1941.53	51.16	284.75	929.00
6036.90	1199.09	690.86	8376.94	6264.46	191.51	1141.72	1908.57
17527.06	290.76	2089.79	4705.74	3418.59	9.36	81.31	1099.19
10736.01	952.03	1240.95	19962.33	4525.92	288.17	1328.55	3466.37
8098105.90	872590.12	261970.00	21351277.20	4422699.63	122613.47	874863.84	1061214.39
20181020.22	**105641.79**	**371799.16**	**3589511.91**	**1520696.19**	**46004.38**	**406048.83**	**1010319.64**
5984665.57	46256.91	16993.51	803012.05	389913.47	4338.37	43356.30	124234.21
2001786.36	177363.00	126003.49	1245682.65	922693.92	15247.81	132993.70	272030.82
2951024.78	41336.22	54752.40	788162.97	317818.82	11744.81	77971.22	146084.55
9243543.51	-159314.34	174049.76	752654.24	-109730.02	14673.39	151727.61	467970.06

3-13 续表 2

单位：千元

部门	Sector	石油加工、炼焦及核燃料加工业 Oil Processing, Coking and Nuclear Fuel Processing	化学工业 Raw Chemical Materials and Chemical Products
总投入合计	**Total input**	**22968434.43**	**13450727.39**
中间投入合计	**Total Intermediate Input**	**19843642.52**	**9779153.43**
农 业	Agriculture	561.52	180282.34
煤炭开采和洗选业	Coal Mining and Dressing	22268.94	100023.47
石油和天然气开采业	Extraction of Petroleum and Natural Gas	14803690.88	2019504.60
金属矿采选业	Mining and Dressing of Metals	292.72	97735.66
非金属矿采选业	Mining and Dressing of Nonmetal Minerals	1100.61	72500.09
食品制造及烟草加工业	Food Production and Tobacco Processing	130.17	15010.50
纺织业	Textile Industry	12124.58	88353.86
服装皮革羽绒及其制品业	Leather, Furs, Down, Garments and Other Fiber Products	0.79	26.84
木材加工及家具制造业	Timber Processing and Furniture Manufacturing	4873.97	12157.87
造纸印刷及文教用品制造业	Papermaking , Printing and Cultural, Educational Goods	11538.44	66163.99
石油加工、炼焦及核燃料加工业	Oil Processing, Coking and Nuclear Fuel Processing	1726305.86	485683.86
化学工业	Raw Chemical Materials and Chemical Products	511037.52	3289782.30
非金属矿物制品业	Nonmetal Mineral Products	31052.31	143782.44
金属冶炼及压延加工业	Smelting and Pressing of Metals	31713.02	35149.43
金属制品业	Metal Products	53785.32	50519.82
通用、专用设备制造业	Ordinary, Special Purpose Equipment Production	357689.64	334019.41
交通运输设备制造业	Transport and Communication Equipment	10795.04	24724.79
电气、机械及器材制造业	Electric Equipment and Machinery	59185.41	75117.43
通信设备、计算机及其他电子设备制造业	Telecom, Equipment, Computer and Other Electronic Equipment	26387.00	19954.69
仪器仪表及文化办公用机械制造业	Equipment, Meter, Culture and Office Machinery	51052.12	124857.34
其他制造业	Other Production	4052.85	9233.67
废品废料	Waste Material and Scrape Substances	6204.04	13369.77
电力、热力的生产和供应业	Electric and Thermal Power Production and Supply	110588.90	573578.38

Continued

(1 000 yuan)

非金属矿物制品业 Nonmetal Mineral Products	金属冶炼及压延加工业 Smelting and Pressing of Metals	金属制品业 Metal Products	通用、专用设备制造业 Ordinary, Special Purpose Equipment Production	交通运输设备制造业 Transport and Communication Equipment	电气、机械及器材制造业 Electric Equipment and Machinery	通信设备、计算机及其他电子设备制造业 Telecom, Equipment, Computer and Other Electronic Equipment	仪器仪表及文化办公用机械制造业 Equipment, Meter, Culture And Office Machinery
8067995.80	**6930042.06**	**2361982.66**	**1953096.72**	**2078952.67**	**2327427.65**	**22970.31**	**106616.83**
5013036.54	**4736929.39**	**1701226.22**	**1313177.40**	**1635466.45**	**1670481.86**	**19189.93**	**76088.85**
3178.39	378.75	17.10	0.50			0.08	
156646.95	149326.51	11189.46	1104.56	791.43	1580.54	5.62	21.97
25.37	2569.67	8589.53		3.62			
13962.46	600536.07	24933.54	206.01				
258404.22	60360.48	515.22	482.49	4.03	20.23	0.04	1430.46
2.12	12.33	931.30	51.49	18.05	19.49		
67210.61	11178.82	6680.87	8815.11	3644.99	2713.31	52.66	228.58
42.63	15.51	3.38	135.28	8.34		0.95	1.24
22428.14	2691.13	3857.78	2639.51	1590.44	5161.21	18.91	1914.44
41048.80	7178.17	16114.76	6057.66	4385.76	17200.29	120.65	13595.78
170669.29	161450.12	25109.42	13598.20	18052.66	29835.96	369.12	275.64
790501.49	104989.72	130935.69	45142.77	85128.16	49272.68	2053.69	1018.42
502332.45	104943.78	15327.09	28616.64	3731.10	15777.55	9.92	30.29
88874.70	1061601.90	772985.96	280453.18	176658.05	580695.28	330.18	9262.16
119668.92	28988.30	83940.04	57711.07	13785.03	38402.80	929.48	584.63
144812.81	210890.56	27261.76	258427.28	26757.74	119033.13	136.11	1980.18
27631.12	64815.75	3792.99	18609.04	959434.74	2013.39	57.42	137.89
33334.28	41185.50	20010.04	52251.76	14488.10	193781.79	5549.03	1061.09
3486.48	3991.25	1932.52	8846.18	1664.33	6069.70	1136.79	1668.32
7452.81	17792.17	2646.03	10714.24	5053.02	13231.99	140.47	4607.03
8671.66	16318.31	8450.13	4163.23	1361.45	1627.20	38.41	101.87
61442.02	131562.55	59025.53	36980.55	15902.26	617.93		
500019.41	440750.59	58181.30	63922.48	20216.89	31477.01	296.42	1853.45

3-13 续表 3

单位：千元

部　　门	Sector	石油加工、炼焦及核燃料加工业 Oil Processing, Coking and Nuclear Fuel Processing	化学工业 Raw Chemical Materials and Chemical Products
燃气生产和供应业	Gas Production and Supply	2726.50	1407.27
水的生产和供应业	Production and Supply of Tap Water	35662.96	51048.19
建筑业	Construction	16806.50	35389.23
交通运输及仓储业	Transportation and Storage	1207075.18	899177.55
邮政业	Post Service	1037.51	2680.33
信息传输、计算机服务和软件业	Information Transmission, Computer Servcie and Software Industries	23455.77	31341.46
批发和零售贸易业	Wholesale and Retail Trade	245924.44	397578.97
住宿和餐饮业	Hotel and Catering	47284.57	64410.58
金融保险业	Banking and Insurance	203731.74	241693.67
房地产业	Real Estate	19547.02	7702.49
租赁和商务服务业	Leasing and Commercial Service	43978.51	87190.76
旅游业	Tourism	240.36	1810.22
科学研究事业	Scientific Research	65967.50	39028.45
综合技术服务业	Polytechnical Services	51491.79	38416.61
其他社会服务业	Other Social Service	15502.93	14655.10
教育事业	Education	4264.26	8201.25
卫生、社会保障和社会福利业	Health, Social Security and Social Welfare	14003.74	10652.86
文化、体育和娱乐业	Culture, Sports and Recreation	8509.59	15235.89
公共管理和社会组织	Public Management and Social Organization		
中间投入合计	Total Intermediate Input	19843642.52	9779153.43
增加值合计	**Total Value-added**	**3124791.91**	**3671573.96**
固定资产折旧	Depreciation of Fixed Assets	744242.15	1022198.83
劳动者报酬	Payment for Laborers	1218340.83	1491704.95
生产税净额	Net Taxes on Production	1739591.14	966458.75
营业盈余	Operating Surplus	-577382.21	191211.43

Continued

(1 000 yuan)

非金属矿物制 品 业 Nonmetal Mineral Products	金属冶炼及压延加工业 Smelting and Pressing of Metals	金属制品业 Metal Products	通用、专用设备制造业 Ordinary, Special Purpose Equipment Production	交通运输设备制造业 Transport and Communication Equipment	电气、机械及器材制造业 Electric Equipment and Machinery	通信设备、计算机及其他电子设备制造业 Telecom, Equipment, Computer and Other Electronic Equipment	仪器仪表及文化办公用机械制造业 Equipment, Meter, Culture And Office Machinery
54700.16	104891.60	3394.22	423.83	2916.91	1760.97		
12903.42	10448.08	3075.20	3904.38	1859.12	855.17	54.05	251.16
736.58	3590.01	467.76	755.20	310.03	132.71	0.58	3.34
1387041.95	933857.16	241185.04	196187.06	112970.97	303180.79	2580.66	13445.97
1098.72	565.11	278.61	734.45	488.29	1315.01	14.31	24.78
18638.64	9192.62	5081.27	11113.07	7610.17	7631.06	303.05	2253.10
204913.01	224920.17	116008.43	86809.85	104019.11	165539.16	1595.18	7151.94
28574.61	17600.40	10167.90	27829.92	16261.01	19459.27	653.78	5641.05
190992.55	113070.38	16986.04	34483.06	13069.26	36077.79	798.32	37.65
4472.36	735.90	2806.23	7591.26	2618.42	1357.76	127.47	552.17
39944.30	19741.36	10517.73	20524.40	6314.20	11753.31	1420.44	5077.95
624.41	621.25	166.59	683.85	345.25	738.63	9.43	0.04
3443.97	3502.68	731.96	3461.90	5014.24	2750.32	35.93	27.87
22819.62	56412.58	1806.73	1819.04	394.59	770.66	3.73	611.94
4497.21	2927.08	589.58	7942.62	1431.43	2764.44	64.79	143.70
5890.06	6975.71	1595.54	2996.41	2640.69	1422.05	69.72	479.52
476.74	564.01	527.92	980.62	573.88	3.62		
9421.10	3785.35	3408.03	6007.25	3948.69	4437.66	212.54	613.23
5013036.54	4736929.39	1701226.22	1313177.40	1635466.45	1670481.86	19189.93	76088.85
3054959.26	**2193112.67**	**660756.44**	**639919.32**	**443486.22**	**656945.79**	**3780.38**	**30527.98**
535089.47	410797.99	79519.72	88225.06	52951.09	76099.94	4456.84	2503.06
893761.86	853173.97	375258.27	544768.38	278852.57	190979.81	10400.59	82517.57
610137.73	373802.34	130620.01	146786.13	95402.49	38095.88	1745.33	14124.93
1015970.20	555338.37	75358.44	-139860.25	16280.07	351770.16	-12822.38	-68617.58

3-13 续表 4

单位：千元

部　　门	Sector	其他制造业 Other Production	废品废料 Waste Material and Scrape Substances	电力、热力的生产和供应业 Electric and Thermal Power Production And Supply
总投入合计	**Total input**	**74991.95**		**11818967.94**
中间投入合计	**Total Intermediate Input**	**31199.26**		**6638753.79**
农　业	Agriculture	2473.80		2.65
煤炭开采和洗选业	Coal Mining and Dressing	2346.63		2503324.43
石油和天然气开采业	Extraction of Petroleum and Natural Gas			10696.41
金属矿采选业	Mining and Dressing of Metals			4.18
非金属矿采选业	Mining and Dressing of Nonmetal Minerals	0.73		828.69
食品制造及烟草加工业	Food Production and Tobacco Processing			1445.83
纺织业	Textile Industry	447.98		15569.92
服装皮革羽绒及其制品业	Leather, Furs, Down, Garments and Other Fiber Products			212.70
木材加工及家具制造业	Timber Processing and Furniture Manufacturing	5.45		3244.36
造纸印刷及文教用品制造业	Papermaking , Printing and Cultural, Educational Goods	55.29		16301.07
石油加工、炼焦及核燃料加工业	Oil Processing, Coking and Nuclear Fuel Processing	2208.88		54053.40
化学工业	Raw Chemical Materials and Chemical Products	316.62		42594.39
非金属矿物制品业	Nonmetal Mineral Products	437.29		12039.26
金属冶炼及压延加工业	Smelting and Pressing of Metals	125.22		8892.41
金属制品业	Metal Products	127.60		19244.62
通用、专用设备制造业	Ordinary, Special Purpose Equipment Production	561.73		119455.01
交通运输设备制造业	Transport and Communication Equipment	1757.24		28999.97
电气、机械及器材制造业	Electric Equipment and Machinery	192.64		94858.86
通信设备、计算机及其他电子设备制造业	Telecom, Equipment, Computer and Other Electronic Equipment	20.24		13989.47
仪器仪表及文化办公用机械制造业	Equipment, Meter, Culture and Office Machinery	90.98		43873.09
其他制造业	Other Manufacturing	32.33		2932.29
废品废料	Waste Materials and Scrpae Substances	6777.60		
电力、热力的生产和供应业	Electric and Thermal Power Production and Supply	3342.50		1077694.86

Continued

(1 000 yuan)

燃气生产和供应业 Gas Production And Supply	水的生产和供应业 Production And Supply of Tap Water	建筑业 Construction	交通运输及仓储业 Transportation and Storage	邮政业 Post Service	信息传输、计算机服务和软件业 Information Transmission, Computer Servcie and Software Industries	批发和零售贸易业 Wholesale and Retail Trade	住宿和餐饮业 Hotel and Catering
1727514.28	**1660070.73**	**59924424.16**	**26348525.11**	**704960.05**	**6420099.98**	**28850921.27**	**8340353.36**
1044915.00	**754297.76**	**40961717.99**	**14069249.13**	**324150.42**	**3046244.59**	**17237527.40**	**4426502.96**
		214093.95	143686.36			751.00	428133.31
36758.58	829.59	308569.18	72271.14	2072.39			25566.15
2915.69							896.18
649.70	137.18	1144432.39	8289.06				
			76306.61			12177.23	1357731.83
3823.92	2214.58	52098.94	32447.94	2262.46	5345.56	78297.55	31055.44
			5258.09				
1837.65	1346.26	378434.19	8723.12	2808.09	17546.41	88664.45	22899.39
2875.29	4247.87	262009.88	88348.91	13230.24	22585.67	88224.59	37632.61
442534.58	8163.65	2544081.20	5016648.51	36169.89	6984.19	2474.57	80974.73
8916.70	8640.26	1650707.16	566834.64	2136.59	36616.96	54467.98	72928.11
7089.61	3444.81	5486302.95	81470.71	4452.84	2022.39	5533.69	36804.95
2122.84	4908.81	7685191.49	44735.26			342.18	517.94
1216.41	5446.48	1697244.06	66374.36	438.76	6214.52	62733.37	25493.51
29311.01	16131.23	1029831.44	418028.51	17531.71	35366.26	47376.64	19483.35
10364.95	13418.44	488754.18	1887911.73	2353.95	20038.14	908494.28	2258.22
15858.21	16205.70	645094.81	77053.14	7803.46	248685.44	192295.03	12808.84
713.27	2001.76	24149.09	33918.71	256.92	387870.22	175149.80	3446.26
13510.63	8596.12	188699.78	20219.30	10496.64	412013.96	8407.62	124.00
590.56	1336.38	29767.54	12637.83		1885.12	12457.62	1670.08
-172648.67	222700.81		20415.18				
175056.98	245406.79	610879.45	314500.76	15695.59	144732.79	386121.13	347374.80

3-13 续表 5

单位：千元

部　　门	Sector	其他制造业 Other Production	废品废料 Waste Materials and Scrpae Substances	电力、热力的生产和供应业 Electric and Thermal Power Production and Supply
燃气生产和供应业	Gas Production and Supply			79684.37
水的生产和供应业	Production and Supply of Tapping Water	70.03		130241.42
建筑业	Construction	8.83		1856.80
交通运输及仓储业	Transportation and Storage	4304.57		1222590.00
邮政业	Post Service	68.75		2773.27
信息传输、计算机服务和软件业	Information Transmission, Computer Servcie and Software Industries	339.35		26448.10
批发和零售贸易业	Wholesale and Retail Trade	2711.63		46755.20
住宿和餐饮业	Hotel and Catering	545.45		31093.13
金融保险业	Banking and Insurance	796.95		912989.61
房地产业	Real Estate	58.94		1921.80
租赁和商务服务业	Leasing and Commercial Service	555.42		18319.04
旅游业	Tourism	0.98		61.35
科学研究事业	Scientific Research	15.75		10035.57
综合技术服务业	Polytechnical Services	96.11		4255.83
其他社会服务业	Other Social Service	37.67		53219.97
教育事业	Education	61.25		15230.98
卫生、社会保障和社会福利业	Health, Social Security and Social Welfare			1247.75
文化、体育和娱乐业	Culture, Sports and Recreation	206.83		9771.73
公共管理和社会组织	Public Management and Social Organization			
中间投入合计	Total Intermediate Input	31199.26		6638753.79
增加值合计	**Total Value-added**	**43792.69**		**5180214.15**
固定资产折旧	Depreciation of Fixed Assets	5658.96		2285280.49
劳动者报酬	Payment for Laborers	15544.22		1868261.22
生产税净额	Net Taxes on Production	8035.68		841138.83
营业盈余	Operating Surplus	14553.83		185533.61

Continued

(1 000 yuan)

燃气生产和供应业 Gas Production and Supply	水的生产和供应业 Production and Supply of Tap Water	建筑业 Construction	交通运输及仓储业 Transportation and Storage	邮政业 Postal Service	信息传输、计算机服务和软件业 Information Transmission, Computer Servcie and Software Industries	批发和零售贸易业 Wholesale and Retail Trade	住宿和餐饮业 Hotel and Catering
287170.60	3383.17		185162.66	2703.61			79504.23
2256.94	29036.70	94057.70	25712.76	5465.13	51920.61	41651.16	55045.37
4708.88	345.56		79484.43	8913.40	274604.63	150897.71	97282.61
148116.66	35428.13	10433918.82	1112650.67	26675.36	143286.54	1986787.24	382674.19
385.56	488.87	4964.20	2147.87	2220.91	8256.45	32583.33	1121.24
5358.20	6595.44	103557.34	184525.50	17562.66	361163.45	302568.23	56294.44
2839.64	67694.65	2167045.65	723513.50	100142.85	370028.20	217336.63	243505.95
7470.99	10416.61	368158.13	271213.23	9342.25	109165.68	918438.70	31724.05
-18951.41	18105.66	322265.69	835888.91	1914.86	60035.84	3617470.76	291802.18
783.00	94.17	2504.74	6000.90	6251.88	130201.75	385533.09	467527.49
4968.70	5422.45	2514879.41	703242.81	16933.27	56148.49	6252116.41	152477.20
54.15	58.05		853.77				
1192.17	2126.47	196128.58	271.92				
9048.87	1181.80	75704.34	475890.30	15.20		393439.31	3107.94
1150.58	1975.32	56762.71	133288.15	4749.11	118044.39	250909.16	19900.71
2625.95	2821.98	52318.11	49847.58		2551.01	128096.66	7900.07
			142379.69				13664.68
2237.61	3946.01	79110.86	10944.44		12886.80	435730.28	14611.12
			130150.17	3550.40	43.12		559.79
1044915.00	754297.76	40961717.99	14069249.13	324150.42	3046244.59	17237527.40	4426502.96
682599.28	**905772.97**	**18962706.17**	**12279275.98**	**380809.63**	**3373855.39**	**11613393.87**	**3913850.40**
191997.96	337382.89	2914152.43	4209745.99	91599.89	2696715.03	1606396.88	407317.86
347171.72	511218.52	12698974.04	6513510.62	415049.09	550255.75	5415504.33	1442186.65
92185.30	121825.29	3411778.17	1802723.33	34397.17	51779.07	2076927.14	430895.67
51244.30	-64653.73	-62198.46	-246703.96	-160236.52	75105.54	2514565.52	1633450.22

3-13 续表 6

单位：千元

部 门	Sector	金融保险业 Banking and Insurance	房地产业 Real Estate	租赁和商务服务业 Leasing and Commercial Service
总投入合计	**Total input**	**8444099.95**	**4033090.02**	**15849214.21**
中间投入合计	**Total Intermediate Input**	**2939402.84**	**1312400.94**	**5629714.88**
农 业	Agriculture		4382.25	
煤炭开采和洗选业	Coal Mining and Dressing			
石油和天然气开采业	Extraction of Petroleum and Natural Gas			
金属矿采选业	Mining and Dressing of Metals			
非金属矿采选业	Mining and Dressing of Nonmetal Minerals			
食品制造及烟草加工业	Food Production and Tobacco Processing		592.84	
纺织业	Textile Industry	20889.03	2817.30	9973.65
服装皮革羽绒及其制品业	Leather, Furs, Down, Garments and Other Fiber Products			
木材加工及家具制造业	Timber Processing and Furniture Manufacturing	31968.56	5296.15	11450.49
造纸印刷及文教用品制造业	Paper-making , Printing and Cultural, Educational Goods	236896.27	12768.08	184192.43
石油加工、炼焦及核燃料加工业	Oil Processing, Coking and Nuclear Fuel Processing	73606.66	7930.23	178618.17
化学工业	Raw Chemical Materials and Chemical Products	59599.38	1988.08	317578.10
非金属矿物制品业	Nonmetal Mineral Products		3146.19	71413.17
金属冶炼及压延加工业	Smelting and Pressing of Metals			40050.22
金属制品业	Metal Products	9075.89	17350.83	6339.27
通用、专用设备制造业	Ordinary, Special Purpose Equipment Production	18153.94	112.48	71.79
交通运输设备制造业	Transport and Communication Equipment	27800.36	5827.48	189163.07
电气、机械及器材制造业	Electric Equipment and Machinery	17324.79	7487.79	29185.00
通信设备、计算机及其他电子设备制造业	Telecom, Equipment, Computer and Other Electronic Equipment	21170.81	2108.43	16495.35
仪器仪表及文化办公用机械制造业	Equipment, Meter, Culture and Office Machinery	9756.45	1879.62	117551.34
其他制造业	Other Manufacturing	9650.70	295.17	109191.47
废品废料	Waste Maetrials and Scrpae Substances			7948.36
电力、热力的生产和供应业	Electric and Thermal Power Production and Supply	53233.05	12787.56	259157.08

Continued

(1 000 yuan)

旅游业 Tourism	科学研究事业 Scientific Research	综合技术服务业 Polytechnical Services	其他社会服务业 Other Social Service	教育事业 Education	卫生、社会保障和社会福利业 Health, Social Security and Social Welfare	文化、体育和娱乐业 Culture, Sports and Recreation	公共管理和社会组织 Public Management and Social Organization	中间使用合计 Total Intermediate Use
409569.99	**681759.99**	**2356995.06**	**3394390.02**	**11938230.01**	**8914107.57**	**2331870.65**	**16315994.20**	**405791589.57**
270925.61	**209047.47**	**830674.86**	**1358193.11**	**4891334.27**	**5420705.49**	**1081230.24**	**5932339.31**	**233198712.36**
						36039.15		31385290.58
						2720.83		3580675.87
								18879425.09
								1017905.38
	34.61	240.58	35.95	1553.83	62.18	89.60	410.01	1587151.70
		1479.75				21478.64		5681406.00
780.78	7.37	3259.48	73762.04	2475.09	28.01	337.37	1341.72	1151838.02
		126.19				72.02		43991.31
86.26	989.83	14179.75	60073.06	44153.06	271031.35	3589.19	11911.62	1291279.07
4594.37	6485.25	82279.08	18847.15	294026.30	30413.26	92401.39	152399.90	2555717.39
15349.89	11325.20	87291.09	40227.18	50458.58	36503.49	52862.76	480926.86	13237899.91
389.00	12949.20	35235.52	175536.75	234744.60	2774100.26	21088.31	313569.02	15279537.26
	1176.25	8141.34	24970.40	52624.05	2110.05	4921.68	14052.94	6960534.91
	78.29	534.79	190.28	3460.71	139.31	198.85	961.11	11042715.69
16.52	408.94	2864.04	1011.34	18290.63	44849.81	1053.14	4890.56	2880679.41
	2988.63	5028.83	1500.62	21832.71	304598.70	13318.01	2469.75	4745206.20
12195.60	5878.15	17185.91	42564.50	442425.99	188205.07	38769.76	238495.40	5758305.79
	2482.39	10361.01	9004.41	153659.83	145405.78	9001.56	68511.92	2430883.97
268.49	3333.04	12901.99	11290.36	238797.18	121242.80	14225.28	128698.43	1324184.71
278.75	2193.17	4141.84	8217.45	154308.98	148382.57	18292.66	109019.40	1676203.17
543.01	5.26	933.38	34082.37	706.45	19.76	22505.77	1943.59	445289.47
			5418.36					-148512.23
6263.63	6280.56	29328.95	67583.21	455987.56	66559.23	131790.80	445179.92	9347821.79

3-13 续表 7

单位：千元

部门	Sector	金融保险业 Banking and Insurance	房地产业 Real Estate	租赁和商务服务业 Leasing and Commercial Service
燃气生产和供应业	Gas Production and Supply		75.79	622346.27
水的生产和供应业	Production and Supply of Tap Water	9848.99	1029.42	6945.30
建筑业	Construction	58868.21	4809.73	216971.28
交通运输及仓储业	Transportation and Storage	216028.45	57476.50	594876.71
邮政业	Post Service	21676.71	250.53	7398.66
信息传输、计算机服务和软件业	Information Transmission, Computer Servcie and Software Industries	217397.16	24903.09	221252.17
批发和零售贸易业	Wholesale and Retail Trade	112376.32	15725.29	175641.63
住宿和餐饮业	Hotel and Catering	481697.22	101326.62	244832.02
金融保险业	Banking and Insurance	-33819.67	895631.98	328642.92
房地产业	Real Estate	217164.99	25176.77	
租赁和商务服务业	Leasing and Commercial Service	761523.58	15717.32	1302293.43
旅游业	Tourism		1334.32	4229.95
科学研究事业	Scientific Research			62668.52
综合技术服务业	Polytechnical Services		17.95	47327.45
其他社会服务业	Other Social Service	27136.93	1277.55	137032.22
教育事业	Education	23567.12	4714.37	25543.98
卫生、社会保障和社会福利业	Health, Social Security and Social Welfare	7837.30	2641.78	1299.14
文化、体育和娱乐业	Culture, Sports and Recreation	216106.53	71741.75	2867.64
公共管理和社会组织	Public Management and Social Organization	12867.11	1779.70	79166.63
中间投入合计	Total Intermediate Input	2939402.84	1312400.94	5629714.88
增加值合计	**Total Value-added**	**5504697.11**	**2720689.08**	**10219499.33**
固定资产折旧	Depreciation of Fixed Assets	636857.30	508457.05	4025834.48
劳动者报酬	Payment for Laborers	2568788.78	1596582.59	3106360.00
生产税净额	Net Taxes on Production	804400.72	236490.47	1271995.80
营业盈余	Operating Surplus	1494650.31	379158.97	1815309.05

Continued

(1 000 yuan)

旅游业 Tourism	科学研究事业 Scientific Research	综合技术服务业 Polytechnical Services	其他社会服务业 Other Social Service	教育事业 Education	卫生、社会保障和社会福利业 Health, Social Security and Social Welfare	文化、体育和娱乐业 Culture, Sports and Recreation	公共管理和社会组织 Public Management and Social Organization	中间使用合计 Total Intermediate Use
		51.26	7207.89			697.92		1451865.07
345.70	1521.91	4080.94	17251.92	65907.90	12822.16	22204.07	127241.85	1589195.09
2959.77	3460.06	13307.95	8430.43	222157.97	7253.44	13023.51	104555.19	1343420.70
116028.49	12532.20	77933.94	130659.68	214909.18	240299.46	89973.74	591226.15	28696164.66
1419.83	394.41	4216.49	722.08	2514.09	941.49	1596.80	33756.36	173242.31
11753.12	8226.60	51634.96	36987.57	269512.65	36191.39	34726.56	537960.80	2752835.28
4291.41	5235.07	45339.47	125875.01	170661.93	666023.11	58978.65	137768.76	11033745.20
35582.01	12949.15	82594.08	27897.80	151328.35	39286.01	46987.50	1363543.82	4925281.58
21418.00	3046.10	24064.64	7062.80	99200.22	13990.71	96188.27	47887.78	10228926.19
3481.92		273.78	113700.27			2527.73		1437699.96
17252.48	3088.21	51784.51	219690.27	61376.98	6494.92	30034.04	229107.94	15796078.37
1278.87								16993.79
	61110.84	14154.41	36219.56	382341.51	20686.32	144518.93	136171.21	1303229.76
912.87	4366.67	73846.06	218.39	427.33	1627.21	15.44	754.79	4104102.20
168.87	5438.80	17256.79	15642.73	363906.49	42390.56	22877.26	193379.81	2356082.56
1287.35	1655.86	9445.07	8564.97	79469.37	31943.15	6979.05	75484.50	647892.47
379.42	15287.25	17008.07	16592.22	345798.74	150226.80	10609.23	191478.01	1024294.63
4803.88	12510.93	24374.29	7746.85	265109.28	15490.00	13522.44	118482.59	1451714.56
6795.32	1607.27	3794.63	3407.24	27206.73	1387.13	1012.33	48757.61	710517.52
270925.61	209047.47	830674.86	1358193.11	4891334.27	5420705.49	1081230.24	5932339.31	233198712.36
138644.38	**472712.52**	**1526320.20**	**2036196.91**	**7046895.74**	**3493402.08**	**1250640.41**	**10383654.89**	**172592877.21**
50008.73	85619.15	335168.01	268538.40	392369.87	336353.00	502227.73	808498.25	35000189.67
126559.67	385882.26	1141123.96	1520792.52	6606612.37	2413824.83	1020892.26	9546045.59	90133412.37
22568.97	1206.84	52545.57	167698.53	47842.24	1487.22	182827.91	28984.88	21013024.83
-60492.99	4.27	-2517.34	79167.46	71.26	741737.04	-455307.49	126.17	26446250.34

3-14 投入产出基本流量表(最终使用部分)

单位：千元 (2002 年)

投入 Input \ 产出 Output	最终使用 Final Use 最终消费 Final Consumption Expenditure 居民最终消费 Household Consumption Expenditure 农村居民 Agricultrual Households	城镇居民 Non-agricultural Households	小计 Subtotal	政府消费 Government Consumption Expenditure	合计 Total Consumption
合计 Total	**22905952.69**	**47157482.81**	**70063435.50**	**37464527.84**	**107527963.34**
农业 Agriculture	2160687.99	1682658.03	3843346.02	3503302.44	7346648.46
煤炭采选业 Coal Mining and Dressing	111681.83	20433.50	132115.33		132115.33
石油和天然气开采业 Extraction of Petroleum and Natural Gas					
金属矿采选业 Mining and Dressing of Metals					
非金属矿采选业 Mining and Dressing of Nonmetal Minerals					
食品制造及烟草加工业 Food Production and Tobacco Processing	6182568.07	9131657.41	15314225.48		15314225.48
纺织业 Textile Industry	431004.23	1196452.52	1627456.75		1627456.75
服装皮革羽绒及其他纤维制品制造业 Leather, Furs, Down, Garments and Other Fiber Products	108082.74	493398.46	601481.20		601481.20
木材加工及家俱制造业 Timber Processing and Furniture Manufacturing	114835.95	325819.84	440655.79		440655.79
造纸印刷及文教用品制造业 Papermaking, Printing and Cultural, Educational Goods	43583.27	605798.44	649381.71		649381.71
石油加工及炼焦业 Petroleum Processing and Coking	18769.27	20285.93	39055.20		39055.20
化学工业 Raw Chemical Materials and Chemical Products	359037.02	1277991.31	1637028.33		1637028.33
非金属矿物制品业 Nonmetal Mineral Products	552661.21	262565.91	815227.12		815227.12
金属冶炼及压延加工业 Smelting and Pressing of Metals	40267.94	77602.22	117870.16		117870.16
金属制品业 Metal Products	29067.12	135657.31	164724.43		164724.43
通用、专用设备制造业 Ordinary, Special Purpose Equipment Production	122982.26	59997.09	182979.35		182979.35
交通运输设备制造业 Transport and Communication Equipment	130941.10	177175.44	308116.54		308116.54
电气、机械及器材制造业 Electric Equipment and Machinery	33909.42	352184.32	386093.74		386093.74
通信设备、计算机及其他电子设备制造业 Telecom, Equipment, Computer and Other Electronic Equipment	107282.65	720885.33	828167.98		828167.98
仪器仪表及文化办公用机械制造业 Equipment, Meter, Culture and Office Machinery	59731.27	82383.35	142114.62		142114.62
其他制造业 Other Production	44707.26	158427.12	203134.38		203134.38

Input-Output Table for Final Part of use

(1000 yuan)

最终使用 Final Use					调进(含进口) Import	其他 Other	总产出 Total Output
资本形成总额 Capital Formation			调出(含出口) Export	最终使用合计 Total of Final Use			
固定资本形成总额 Gross Fixed Capital Formaiton	存货增加 Changes in Inventories	合计 Total					
86251395.75	**2425995.13**	**88677390.88**	**76510511.31**	**272715865.53**	**100981329.01**	**928340.69**	**404933248.88**
2620741.89	1820887.36	4441629.25	14038722.29	25827000.00	273673.41		56938617.17
	58881.16	58881.16	54920.81	245917.30	8394.46		3818198.71
	-142003.29	-142003.29	9775301.71	9633298.42	233597.39		28279126.12
	29567.10	29567.10	182525.40	212092.50	251765.97		978231.91
	87664.53	87664.53	75983.98	163648.51	1117031.05		633769.16
	473249.42	473249.42	7351154.76	23138629.66	3879246.55		24940789.11
	-297928.54	-297928.54	6382412.93	7711941.14	2920383.34		5943395.82
	-20677.28	-20677.28	182834.85	763638.77	639012.23		168617.85
191440.62	39822.24	231262.86	376726.94	1048645.59	1059011.99		1280912.67
	76233.73	76233.73	560504.45	1286119.89	1770303.25		2071534.03
	73133.55	73133.55	9909669.64	10021858.39	291323.87		22968434.43
	46670.73	46670.73	5402169.44	7085868.50	8914678.37		13450727.39
432019.18	1075450.35	1507469.53	74070.65	2396767.30	1289306.41		8067995.80
	671992.74	671992.74	8249095.94	9038958.84	13151632.47		6930042.06
216006.41	163107.71	379114.12	433897.47	977736.02	1496432.77		2361982.66
10319419.57	81276.05	10400695.62	397813.68	10981488.65	13773598.13		1953096.72
2261771.70	167407.76	2429179.46	109492.75	2846788.75	6526141.87		2078952.67
1849194.17	162996.73	2012190.90	1288775.20	3687059.84	3790516.16		2327427.65
4434161.37	11105.91	4445267.28	162921.70	5436356.96	6737571.36		22970.31
1063558.08	17436.27	1080994.35	64855.24	1287964.21	2931183.12		32984.26
1210250.56	189906.69	1400157.25	38877.83	1642169.46	1938834.41		148624.52

3-14 续表 1

单位：千元

投入 Input \ 产出 Output	最终使用 Final Use				
	最终消费 Final Consumption Expenditure				
	居民最终消费 Household Consumption Expenditure			政府消费 Government Consumption Expenditure	合 计 Total Consumption
	农村居民 Agricultrual Households	城镇居民 Non-agricultural Households	小 计 Subtotal		
废品废料 Waste Materials and Scrape Substances					
电力、热力的生产和供应业 Electric and Thermal Power Production and Supply	269676.63	1113668.53	1383345.16		1383345.16
燃气生产和供应业 Gas Production and Supply	8733.24	426376.27	435109.51		435109.51
水的生产和供应业 Production and Supply of Tap Water	25412.00	45463.64	70875.64		70875.64
建筑业 Construction	297453.39	154574.45	452027.84		452027.84
交通运输及仓储业 Transportation and Storage	1861924.94	3782462.09	5644387.03		5644387.03
邮政业 Post Service	54176.90	38689.39	92866.29		92866.29
信息传输、计算机服务和软件业 Information Transmission, Computer Servcie and Software Industries	126412.76	1762165.36	1888578.12		1888578.12
批发和零售贸易业 Wholesale and Retail Trade	5311257.16	11585671.45	16896928.61	1738578.47	18635507.08
住宿和餐饮业 Hotel and Catering	590131.26	2539715.63	3129846.89		3129846.89
金融保险业 Banking and Insurance	286199.67	1429831.33	1716031.00		1716031.00
房地产业 Real Estate	1131863.87	365126.37	1496990.24		1496990.24
租赁和商务服务业 Leasing and Commercial Service					
旅游业 Tourism		305586.27	305586.27		305586.27
科学研究事业 Scientific Research				682586.62	682586.62
综合技术服务业 Polytechnical Services				1605193.17	1605193.17
其他社会服务业 Other Social Service	515170.59	549509.25	1064679.84	1263348.81	2328028.65
教育事业 Education	1097413.12	2966031.46	4063444.58	7239387.34	11302831.92
卫生、社会保障和社会福利业 Health, Social Security and Social Welfare	666236.75	2287894.78	2954131.53	4906469.01	7860600.54
文化、体育和娱乐业 Culture, Sports and Recreation	12089.81	986451.58	998541.39	968235.03	1966776.42
公共管理和社会组织 Public Management and Social Organization		36891.43	36891.43	15557426.95	15594318.38

Continued

(1000 yuan)

最终使用 Final Use					调进(含进口) Import	其他 Other	总产出 Total Output
资本形成总额 Capital Formation			调出(含出口) Export	最终使用合计 Total of Final Use			
固定资本形成总额 Gross Fixed Capital Formaiton	存货增加 Changes in Inventories	合计 Total					
	17047.85	17047.85	951033.83	968081.68	819569.45		
				1383345.16		1087800.99	10731166.95
				435109.51		-159460.30	1886974.58
				70875.64			1660070.73
58128975.62		58128975.62		58581003.46			59924424.16
874105.57	-786822.88	87282.69	4003693.46	9735363.18	12083002.73		26348525.11
			438851.45	531717.74			704960.05
			1783410.81	3671988.93	4724.23		6420099.98
2379191.11	-1590410.76	788780.35	2774769.48	22199056.91	4381880.84		28850921.27
			305599.68	3435446.57	20374.79		8340353.36
				1716031.00	3500857.24		8444099.95
198028.90		198028.90	900370.92	2595390.06			4033090.02
			71620.38	71620.38	18484.54		15849214.21
			86989.93	392576.20			409569.99
10257.00		10257.00		692843.62	1314313.39		681759.99
62274.00		62274.00		1667467.17	3414574.31		2356995.06
				2328028.65	1289721.19		3394390.02
				11302831.92	12494.38		11938230.01
			29212.40	7889812.94			8914107.57
			40967.95	2007744.37	1127588.28		2331870.65
			11263.36	15605581.74	105.06		16315994.20

3-15 投入产出完全消耗系数表

(2002 年)

部门	Sector	农业 Agriculture	煤炭采选业 Coal Mining and Dressing	石油和天然气开采业 Extraction of Petroleum and Natural Gas
农业	Agriculture	0.404430	0.017394	0.004620
煤炭采选业	Coal Mining and Dressing	0.012983	0.017761	0.009456
石油和天然气开采业	Extraction of Petroleum and Natural Gas	0.062674	0.032169	0.092261
金属矿采选业	Mining and Dressing of Metals	0.003074	0.004828	0.001747
非金属矿采选业	Mining and Dressing of Nonmetal Minerals	0.001358	0.001844	0.000392
食品制造及烟草加工业	Food Production and Tobacco Processing	0.083478	0.004281	0.002320
纺织业	Textile Industry	0.003529	0.003543	0.001184
服装皮革羽绒及其制品业	Leather, Furs, Down, Garments and Other Fiber Products	0.001642	0.003686	0.002266
木材加工及家具制造业	Timber Processing and Furniture Manufacturing	0.001933	0.007078	0.001535
造纸印刷及文教用品制造业	Papermaking , Printing and Cultural, Educational Goods	0.007457	0.010376	0.008774
石油加工、炼焦及核燃料加工业	Oil Processing, Coking and Nuclear Fuel Processing	0.063607	0.033284	0.017453
化学工业	Raw Chemical Materials and Chemical Products	0.113767	0.054359	0.017606
非金属矿物制品业	Nonmetal Mineral Products	0.004844	0.008410	0.002419
金属冶炼及压延加工业	Smelting and Pressing of Metals	0.014512	0.033917	0.012566
金属制品业	Metal Products	0.009330	0.008964	0.002366
通用、专用设备制造业	Ordinary, Special Purpose Equipment Production	0.025919	0.036980	0.015860
交通运输设备制造业	Transport and Communication Equipment	0.023325	0.024510	0.010688
电气、机械及器材制造业	Electric Equipment and Machinery	0.005583	0.018281	0.005833
通信设备、计算机及其他电子设备制造业	Telecom, Equipment, Computer and Other Electronic Equipment	0.002305	0.003392	0.002089
仪器仪表及文化办公用机械制造业	Equipment, Meter, Culture and Office Machinery	0.005534	0.007961	0.004973
其他制造业	Other Manufacturing	0.001847	0.030087	0.001032
废品废料	Waste Materials and Scrape Substances	-0.013807	0.003408	0.004516
电力、热力的生产和供应业	Electric and Thermal Power Production and Supply	0.044631	0.055235	0.040309
燃气生产和供应业	Gas Production and Supply	0.006501	0.003691	0.001747
水的生产和供应业	Production and Supply of Tap Water	0.004078	0.003036	0.028101
建筑业	Construction	0.003405	0.002774	0.001924
交通运输及仓储业	Transportation and Storage	0.104472	0.078085	0.036060
邮政业	Post Service	0.000973	0.000451	0.000469
信息传输、计算机服务和软件业	Information Transmission, Computer Servcie and Software Industries	0.006820	0.007824	0.006228
批发和零售贸易业	Wholesale and Retail Trade	0.056866	0.040151	0.014697
住宿和餐饮业	Hotel and Catering	0.013858	0.016897	0.010531
金融保险业	Banking and Insurance	0.036372	0.043354	0.026666
房地产业	Real Estate	0.003841	0.003498	0.001918
租赁和商务服务业	Leasing and Commercial Service	0.097717	0.033231	0.012998
旅游业	Tourism	0.000078	0.000193	0.000033
科学研究事业	Scientific Research	0.002259	0.002704	0.005212
综合技术服务业	Polytechnical Services	0.010427	0.007431	0.113771
其他社会服务业	Other Social Service	0.022881	0.002945	0.003025
教育事业	Education	0.002401	0.004461	0.001221
卫生、社会保障和社会福利业	Health, Social Security and Social Welfare	0.002003	0.008445	0.002079
文化、体育和娱乐业	Culture, Sports and Recreation	0.003458	0.005525	0.003096
公共管理和社会组织	Public Management and Social Organization	0.010734	0.000782	0.000524

Total Input Coefficients of Input-Output Table

金属矿采选业 Mining and Dressing of Metals	非金属矿采选业 Mining and Dressing of Nonmetal Minerals	食品制造及烟草加工业 Food Production and Tobacco Processing	纺织业 Textile Industry	服装皮革羽绒及其他纤维制品制造业 Leather, Furs, Down, Garments and Other Fiber Products	木材加工及家俱制造业 Timber Processing and Furniture Manufacturing	造纸印刷及文教用品制造业 Papermaking , Printing and Cultural, Educational Goods
0.017141	0.010241	0.828647	0.470854	0.162183	0.261158	0.087097
0.038817	0.032901	0.019175	0.029132	0.024390	0.022400	0.027506
0.154251	0.089856	0.064850	0.050618	0.056553	0.072521	0.049209
0.409316	0.007097	0.003640	0.003539	0.004296	0.005537	0.004266
0.011827	0.014693	0.001925	0.001199	0.001765	0.001937	0.001615
0.007517	0.003953	0.096150	0.032490	0.016015	0.019472	0.010785
0.003455	0.005046	0.006769	0.053291	0.249287	0.016323	0.002795
0.004911	0.002125	0.002444	0.002776	0.119296	0.003311	0.002237
0.003520	0.001741	0.005753	0.002830	0.003215	0.136261	0.002654
0.014023	0.007777	0.021710	0.017462	0.018525	0.037987	0.202134
0.199231	0.110107	0.069549	0.054655	0.049527	0.069291	0.041050
0.096903	0.081796	0.101315	0.077072	0.135970	0.149456	0.117823
0.019856	0.007545	0.014985	0.006183	0.015325	0.015908	0.007053
0.073482	0.028965	0.019574	0.021297	0.021843	0.029805	0.024171
0.015602	0.017732	0.012529	0.010111	0.014066	0.024032	0.007592
0.141998	0.047231	0.027098	0.035124	0.026011	0.028220	0.028204
0.106476	0.036585	0.037468	0.039976	0.042542	0.044603	0.032234
0.024033	0.009434	0.008409	0.012129	0.011850	0.010522	0.010500
0.009209	0.002779	0.003396	0.005282	0.005064	0.003793	0.003195
0.009985	0.004778	0.006186	0.006213	0.006869	0.006180	0.006413
0.006003	0.004838	0.002630	0.003139	0.003521	0.002360	0.007329
0.007157	0.007011	-0.005873	-0.002210	0.001095	0.004917	0.022384
0.118926	0.076328	0.060521	0.113738	0.066603	0.068576	0.052475
0.010476	0.004320	0.007746	0.008773	0.007975	0.006655	0.006407
0.012948	0.005967	0.005923	0.006751	0.007607	0.005630	0.006194
0.005478	0.002531	0.004345	0.005004	0.006052	0.004322	0.003144
0.562507	0.178056	0.178682	0.143321	0.139697	0.223379	0.121399
0.000867	0.000700	0.001069	0.001090	0.001867	0.001106	0.000802
0.015532	0.008822	0.010529	0.011529	0.015526	0.012480	0.009231
0.069308	0.042396	0.096708	0.209512	0.266139	0.129431	0.091667
0.026666	0.015417	0.020399	0.023466	0.033104	0.020061	0.017863
0.072345	0.032750	0.069438	0.075907	0.131541	0.058656	0.044920
0.006237	0.003200	0.005937	0.008855	0.011337	0.007784	0.005823
0.054755	0.026539	0.098276	0.097702	0.097553	0.064237	0.042773
0.000209	0.000148	0.000184	0.000149	0.000564	0.000114	0.000124
0.004794	0.002769	0.002863	0.003234	0.003417	0.002747	0.002305
0.031079	0.014346	0.013032	0.012544	0.014111	0.015047	0.009885
0.007595	0.003811	0.016359	0.012244	0.008547	0.008430	0.004846
0.004701	0.002467	0.002805	0.003828	0.004035	0.003235	0.002597
0.004994	0.005236	0.002452	0.002583	0.002052	0.002348	0.002100
0.006877	0.004715	0.005746	0.007499	0.011349	0.006252	0.005719
0.003385	0.001186	0.007220	0.004604	0.002572	0.003367	0.001525

3-15 续表 1

部 门	Sector	石油加工、炼焦及核燃料加工业 Oil Processing, Coking and Nuclear Fuel Processing	化学工业 Raw Chemical Materials and Chemical Products	非金属矿物制品业 Nonmetal Mineral Products
农 业	Agriculture	0.007163	0.038928	0.017920
煤炭采选业	Coal Mining and Dressing	0.011831	0.032400	0.048211
石油和天然气开采业	Extraction of Petroleum and Natural Gas	0.782142	0.286865	0.097232
金属矿采选业	Mining and Dressing of Metals	0.003188	0.017749	0.010002
非金属矿采选业	Mining and Dressing of Nonmetal Minerals	0.000867	0.008716	0.036475
食品制造及烟草加工业	Food Production and Tobacco Processing	0.003349	0.007967	0.005342
纺织业	Textile Industry	0.001597	0.009301	0.010555
服装皮革羽绒及其制品业	Leather, Furs, Down, Garments and Other Fiber Products	0.002703	0.003770	0.003425
木材加工及家具制造业	Timber Processing and Furniture Manufacturing	0.001938	0.003316	0.005348
造纸印刷及文教用品制造业	Papermaking , Printing and Cultural, Educational Goods	0.009346	0.016180	0.015111
石油加工、炼焦及核燃料加工业	Oil Processing, Coking and Nuclear Fuel Processing	0.114046	0.097340	0.100009
化学工业	Raw Chemical Materials and Chemical Products	0.052976	0.354674	0.170202
非金属矿物制品业	Nonmetal Mineral Products	0.005172	0.019801	0.072829
金属冶炼及压延加工业	Smelting and Pressing of Metals	0.020762	0.030850	0.043282
金属制品业	Metal Products	0.006230	0.010677	0.022301
通用、专用设备制造业	Ordinary, Special Purpose Equipment Production	0.035838	0.055597	0.044593
交通运输设备制造业	Transport and Communication Equipment	0.022108	0.036343	0.052478
电气、机械及器材制造业	Electric Equipment and Machinery	0.010173	0.016972	0.013998
通信设备、计算机及其他电子设备制造业	Telecom, Equipment, Computer and Other Electronic Equipment	0.003825	0.005366	0.003659
仪器仪表及文化办公用机械制造业	Equipment, Meter, Culture and Office Machinery	0.007842	0.018934	0.006959
其他制造业	Other Manufacuring	0.001464	0.003102	0.003927
废品废料	Waste Materials and Scrape Substances	0.004769	0.005357	0.011148
电力、热力的生产和供应业	Electric and Thermal Power Production and Supply	0.042721	0.093081	0.107284
燃气生产和供应业	Gas Production and Supply	0.003186	0.005491	0.015033
水的生产和供应业	Production and Supply of Tapping Water	0.022589	0.014811	0.007486
建筑业	Construction	0.003302	0.006725	0.003846
交通运输及仓储业	Transportation and Storage	0.103724	0.160537	0.267448
邮政业	Post Service	0.000532	0.000792	0.000657
信息传输、计算机服务和软件业	Information Transmission, Computer Servcie and Software Industries	0.008121	0.011306	0.010895
批发和零售贸易业	Wholesale and Retail Trade	0.031315	0.066416	0.060819
住宿和餐饮业	Hotel and Catering	0.014231	0.020597	0.018541
金融保险业	Banking and Insurance	0.038294	0.058589	0.062959
房地产业	Real Estate	0.003818	0.005360	0.005157
租赁和商务服务业	Leasing and Commercial Service	0.022540	0.043233	0.040899
旅游业	Tourism	0.000065	0.000254	0.000180
科学研究事业	Scientific Research	0.007752	0.007157	0.003115
综合技术服务业	Polytechnical Services	0.086207	0.038775	0.020657
其他社会服务业	Other Social Service	0.004192	0.005953	0.005107
教育事业	Education	0.001627	0.002612	0.002801
卫生、社会保障和社会福利业	Health, Social Security and Social Welfare	0.002902	0.003272	0.002832
文化、体育和娱乐业	Culture, Sports and Recreation	0.003993	0.006007	0.005560
公共管理和社会组织	Public Management and Social Organization	0.000908	0.001475	0.001814

Continued

金属冶炼及压延加工业 Smelting and Pressing of Metals	金属制品业 Metal Products	通用、专用设备制造业 Ordinary, Special Purpose Equipment Production	交通运输设备制造业 Transport and Communication Equipment	电气、机械及器材制造业 Electric Equipment and Machinery	通信设备、计算机及其他电子设备制造业 Telecom, Equipment, Computer and Other Electronic Equipment	仪器仪表及文化办公用机械制造业 Equipment, Meter, Culture and Office Machinery
0.011456	0.014207	0.015427	0.014449	0.014297	0.022122	0.014161
0.056199	0.036594	0.026967	0.021030	0.026963	0.021390	0.011224
0.090655	0.088341	0.065444	0.072875	0.080102	0.098081	0.030511
0.148443	0.068710	0.030694	0.026882	0.045139	0.020018	0.003640
0.013251	0.006053	0.004152	0.003278	0.004834	0.003070	0.000746
0.005014	0.005859	0.007409	0.006978	0.006682	0.011803	0.008815
0.002540	0.004276	0.005571	0.003899	0.002967	0.003482	0.001767
0.004122	0.003953	0.004792	0.003323	0.003299	0.005387	0.003999
0.002781	0.004177	0.004055	0.003695	0.005124	0.004498	0.002395
0.010419	0.017519	0.013442	0.011341	0.019117	0.021815	0.022432
0.114877	0.093823	0.076595	0.078329	0.097904	0.100528	0.036741
0.062875	0.116187	0.073431	0.112694	0.072640	0.172405	0.030059
0.025840	0.019623	0.026642	0.011824	0.019511	0.011766	0.004111
0.216709	0.429146	0.239845	0.209579	0.362270	0.143510	0.025930
0.012302	0.044565	0.041834	0.019012	0.027326	0.055602	0.011770
0.072828	0.051704	0.180326	0.052065	0.096677	0.049557	0.029258
0.071803	0.056602	0.066251	0.900992	0.059568	0.060001	0.030160
0.018710	0.021583	0.044769	0.024381	0.104393	0.289477	0.027977
0.004546	0.004664	0.009288	0.005499	0.007277	0.058220	0.026919
0.008951	0.007857	0.013053	0.011037	0.013447	0.017526	0.161041
0.005998	0.007108	0.005218	0.003608	0.003953	0.005169	0.003775
0.024504	0.036156	0.029219	0.020281	0.010442	0.006490	0.002612
0.121699	0.089123	0.085398	0.061594	0.071846	0.066170	0.042188
0.028179	0.015361	0.010791	0.012378	0.013981	0.012854	0.003813
0.007773	0.007323	0.007244	0.006531	0.005917	0.008935	0.006009
0.004335	0.004250	0.004654	0.004604	0.004603	0.006984	0.003870
0.287828	0.255697	0.229221	0.202794	0.280496	0.265531	0.109304
0.000643	0.000675	0.000989	0.000990	0.001236	0.001575	0.001009
0.010768	0.011360	0.015883	0.015832	0.013953	0.028035	0.037939
0.072216	0.095424	0.090972	0.127728	0.122119	0.135979	0.039034
0.019194	0.020814	0.032470	0.030551	0.027734	0.054182	0.043416
0.060873	0.054177	0.062565	0.054568	0.065465	0.092531	0.023247
0.004929	0.006216	0.010468	0.008373	0.006952	0.015023	0.005883
0.042223	0.048122	0.055054	0.054410	0.057458	0.130491	0.028658
0.000210	0.000204	0.000517	0.000415	0.000483	0.000657	0.000064
0.003262	0.003089	0.004819	0.007525	0.004164	0.006178	0.002923
0.027346	0.020908	0.016621	0.016444	0.019920	0.020296	0.028625
0.003343	0.005089	0.009390	0.006090	0.006727	0.009969	0.006670
0.003538	0.003207	0.003982	0.004544	0.003304	0.006081	0.002311
0.003003	0.002757	0.002891	0.002708	0.002622	0.002822	0.001377
0.005353	0.006306	0.008533	0.008725	0.007739	0.017127	0.017321
0.001887	0.001756	0.001694	0.001542	0.001955	0.002371	0.000902

3-15 续表 2

部 门	Sector	其他制造业 Other Production	电力、热力的生产和供应业 Electric and Thermal Power Production And Supply
农 业	Agriculture	0.049946	0.010452
煤炭采选业	Coal Mining and Dressing	0.035936	0.241768
石油和天然气开采业	Extraction of Petroleum and Natural Gas	0.058624	0.041975
金属矿采选业	Mining and Dressing of Metals	0.012690	0.003173
非金属矿采选业	Mining and Dressing of Nonmetal Minerals	0.011570	0.001005
食品制造及烟草加工业	Food Production and Tobacco Processing	0.012385	0.004348
纺织业	Textile Industry	0.004154	0.002033
服装皮革羽绒及其制品业	Leather, Furs, Down, Garments and Other Fiber Products	0.004452	0.003306
木材加工及家具制造业	Timber Processing and Furniture Manufacturing	0.016534	0.003177
造纸印刷及文教用品制造业	Papermaking , Printing and Cultural, Educational Goods	0.114696	0.010327
石油加工、炼焦及核燃料加工业	Oil Processing, Coking and Nuclear Fuel Processing	0.072115	0.051096
化学工业	Raw Chemical Materials and Chemical Products	0.050928	0.032727
非金属矿物制品业	Nonmetal Mineral Products	0.009359	0.005479
金属冶炼及压延加工业	Smelting and Pressing of Metals	0.098755	0.022457
金属制品业	Metal Products	0.009560	0.006478
通用、专用设备制造业	Ordinary, Special Purpose Equipment Production	0.035381	0.029498
交通运输设备制造业	Transport and Communication Equipment	0.061592	0.034593
电气、机械及器材制造业	Electric Equipment and Machinery	0.016945	0.018102
通信设备、计算机及其他电子设备制造业	Telecom, Equipment, Computer and Other Electronic Equipment	0.011283	0.003989
仪器仪表及文化办公用机械制造业	Equipment, Meter, Culture and Office Machinery	0.007482	0.008968
其他制造业	Other Manufacturing	0.003524	0.008141
废品废料	Waste Materials and Scrape Substances	0.050860	0.002849
电力、热力的生产和供应业	Electric and Thermal Power Production and Supply	0.067884	0.127563
燃气生产和供应业	Gas Production and Supply	0.008929	0.012806
水的生产和供应业	Production and Supply of Tap Water	0.006053	0.015000
建筑业	Construction	0.004735	0.003207
交通运输及仓储业	Transportation and Storage	0.192851	0.163484
邮政业	Post Service	0.001046	0.000759
信息传输、计算机服务和软件业	Information Transmission, Computer Servcie and Software Industries	0.020635	0.010286
批发和零售贸易业	Wholesale and Retail Trade	0.101104	0.029210
住宿和餐饮业	Hotel and Catering	0.050173	0.017474
金融保险业	Banking and Insurance	0.045661	0.108378
房地产业	Real Estate	0.010697	0.005272
租赁和商务服务业	Leasing and Commercial Service	0.082911	0.031144
旅游业	Tourism	0.000106	0.000090
科学研究事业	Scientific Research	0.002603	0.002850
综合技术服务业	Polytechnical Services	0.013562	0.009330
其他社会服务业	Other Social Service	0.005806	0.007940
教育事业	Education	0.005519	0.003494
卫生、社会保障和社会福利业	Health, Social Security and Social Welfare	0.002180	0.003386
文化、体育和娱乐业	Culture, Sports and Recreation	0.007344	0.005868
公共管理和社会组织	Public Management and Social Organization	0.001848	0.001253

Continued

燃气生产和供应业 Gas Production and Supply	水的生产和供应业 Production and Supply of Tapping Water	建筑业 Construction	交通运输及仓储业 Transportation and Storage	邮政业 Post Service	信息传输、计算机服务和软件业 Information Transmission, Computer Servcie and Software Industries	批发和零售贸易业 Wholesale and Retail Trade	住宿和餐饮业 Hotel and Catering
0.009419	0.006258	0.019252	0.020116	0.012360	0.012261	0.017790	0.214930
0.062716	0.039779	0.027360	0.014020	0.015402	0.013232	0.010804	0.021241
0.273984	0.022331	0.105351	0.179500	0.065107	0.030731	0.035578	0.044142
0.003964	0.002675	0.025168	0.004840	0.003214	0.005598	0.003147	0.002471
0.001599	0.000684	0.025441	0.001496	0.001197	0.001925	0.000944	0.001246
0.004138	0.003221	0.006048	0.008880	0.006153	0.007029	0.011176	0.186018
0.002425	0.001233	0.003001	0.002303	0.002106	0.001545	0.002698	0.004447
0.004466	0.002457	0.003183	0.002642	0.005210	0.003017	0.003749	0.003575
0.003262	0.002146	0.009489	0.002470	0.006616	0.005672	0.005947	0.005498
0.009461	0.007630	0.014774	0.012141	0.029401	0.012593	0.017927	0.014792
0.381125	0.026944	0.130552	0.243643	0.087049	0.035068	0.043403	0.051837
0.043042	0.020951	0.088903	0.063132	0.028002	0.038630	0.032839	0.048656
0.010261	0.004711	0.106220	0.008106	0.011772	0.008783	0.005590	0.010708
0.027932	0.019396	0.192851	0.033403	0.023167	0.041465	0.022269	0.015008
0.006583	0.006323	0.037548	0.007832	0.005525	0.009994	0.006397	0.008363
0.046419	0.020758	0.049145	0.036099	0.040398	0.022529	0.013158	0.015934
0.045815	0.031700	0.069789	0.157449	0.035321	0.031477	0.088889	0.025291
0.021475	0.016750	0.022145	0.011680	0.020844	0.069828	0.015864	0.007848
0.003802	0.003384	0.003937	0.004697	0.005343	0.071437	0.010181	0.003135
0.016448	0.009137	0.009524	0.006354	0.022864	0.082777	0.006950	0.004308
0.003216	0.002647	0.003477	0.002164	0.001859	0.002245	0.003631	0.002009
-0.116219	0.137856	0.007420	0.003590	0.002920	0.003277	0.001274	-0.000889
0.162449	0.178398	0.060780	0.040159	0.047765	0.049948	0.040003	0.072335
0.204477	0.006441	0.011935	0.013823	0.010641	0.005190	0.015523	0.016777
0.011986	0.021215	0.007324	0.007782	0.011848	0.011890	0.004803	0.010259
0.006101	0.002238	0.004393	0.006722	0.017531	0.048429	0.012959	0.015161
0.185102	0.069495	0.298017	0.110679	0.099676	0.099359	0.129326	0.117089
0.000669	0.000620	0.000612	0.000602	0.003715	0.001875	0.001919	0.000711
0.010836	0.008874	0.011230	0.015273	0.034468	0.069124	0.024051	0.014516
0.029926	0.055866	0.077612	0.057378	0.166845	0.091884	0.036153	0.062117
0.016799	0.014740	0.022227	0.024464	0.028883	0.034219	0.052943	0.018340
0.024519	0.039939	0.047392	0.059294	0.043198	0.045476	0.155156	0.079039
0.003714	0.003292	0.004781	0.005273	0.015526	0.027755	0.022376	0.061319
0.025377	0.026215	0.084888	0.058820	0.078981	0.052186	0.270988	0.063796
0.000113	0.000080	0.000125	0.000121	0.000075	0.000108	0.000127	0.000090
0.004667	0.002751	0.006449	0.003423	0.002055	0.002218	0.004046	0.001922
0.040519	0.005908	0.022056	0.041596	0.012349	0.008875	0.022269	0.008984
0.004870	0.004005	0.006071	0.009020	0.011507	0.023247	0.014581	0.008712
0.003540	0.002929	0.003176	0.003582	0.001849	0.002177	0.006503	0.002629
0.002625	0.001087	0.002831	0.007354	0.001301	0.001237	0.001853	0.003179
0.004709	0.005325	0.005733	0.004701	0.005313	0.007907	0.021594	0.006979
0.001246	0.000616	0.002182	0.006131	0.006164	0.000992	0.002467	0.002629

3-15 续表 3

部门	Sector	金融保险业 Banking and Insurance	房地产业 Real Estate	租赁和商务服务业 Leasing and Commercial Service
农 业	Agriculture	0.020425	0.013948	0.009850
煤炭采选业	Coal Mining and Dressing	0.007218	0.004254	0.011483
石油和天然气开采业	Extraction of Petroleum and Natural Gas	0.027001	0.014340	0.044049
金属矿采选业	Mining and Dressing of Metals	0.001715	0.001162	0.002634
非金属矿采选业	Mining and Dressing of Nonmetal Minerals	0.000700	0.000376	0.001224
食品制造及烟草加工业	Food Production and Tobacco Processing	0.013055	0.008634	0.005301
纺织业	Textile Industry	0.001507	0.000821	0.001180
服装皮革羽绒及其制品业	Leather, Furs, Down, Garments and Other Fiber Products	0.003745	0.001892	0.001919
木材加工及家具制造业	Timber Processing and Furniture Manufacturing	0.005707	0.003217	0.002376
造纸印刷及文教用品制造业	Paper-making , Printing and Cultural, Educational Goods	0.040113	0.014973	0.020525
石油加工、炼焦及核燃料加工业	Oil Processing, Coking and Nuclear Fuel Processing	0.032030	0.017490	0.052475
化学工业	Raw Chemical Materials and Chemical Products	0.028714	0.013137	0.045922
非金属矿物制品业	Nonmetal Mineral Products	0.003760	0.002699	0.009398
金属冶炼及压延加工业	Smelting and Pressing of Metals	0.011152	0.007657	0.017229
金属制品业	Metal Products	0.003928	0.006224	0.003412
通用、专用设备制造业	Ordinary, Special Purpose Equipment Production	0.009694	0.004758	0.009977
交通运输设备制造业	Transport and Communication Equipment	0.022638	0.013543	0.041317
电气、机械及器材制造业	Electric Equipment and Machinery	0.008230	0.005585	0.007934
通信设备、计算机及其他电子设备制造业	Telecom, Equipment, Computer and Other Electronic Equipment	0.006087	0.002908	0.003967
仪器仪表及文化办公用机械制造业	Equipment, Meter, Culture and Office Machinery	0.006498	0.003298	0.013382
其他制造业	Other Production	0.002957	0.001213	0.008585
废品废料	Waste Materials and Scrpae Substances	0.001283	0.000759	-0.002604
电力、热力的生产和供应业	Electric and Thermal Power Production and Supply	0.025165	0.015289	0.039867
燃气生产和供应业	Gas Production and Supply	0.007399	0.002950	0.054079
水的生产和供应业	Production and Supply of Tap Water	0.003896	0.002092	0.003353
建筑业	Construction	0.011808	0.005045	0.017640
交通运输及仓储业	Transportation and Storage	0.063997	0.041145	0.083931
邮政业	Post Service	0.002894	0.000804	0.000823
信息传输、计算机服务和软件业	Information Transmission, Computer Servcie and Software Industries	0.033039	0.015570	0.020935
批发和零售贸易业	Wholesale and Retail Trade	0.033065	0.017635	0.029193
住宿和餐饮业	Hotel and Catering	0.066367	0.042682	0.025503
金融保险业	Banking and Insurance	0.021225	0.234866	0.038295
房地产业	Real Estate	0.031857	0.015602	0.004001
租赁和商务服务业	Leasing and Commercial Service	0.116255	0.036309	0.108134
旅游业	Tourism	0.000069	0.000362	0.000331
科学研究事业	Scientific Research	0.003231	0.002286	0.006193
综合技术服务业	Polytechnical Services	0.005347	0.002914	0.011049
其他社会服务业	Other Social Service	0.006866	0.002927	0.011877
教育事业	Education	0.003880	0.002386	0.002801
卫生、社会保障和社会福利业	Health, Social Security and Social Welfare	0.002048	0.001579	0.001314
文化、体育和娱乐业	Culture, Sports and Recreation	0.028319	0.025018	0.002884
公共管理和社会组织	Public Management and Social Organization	0.002679	0.001332	0.006159

Continued

旅游业 Tourism	科学研究事业 Scientific Research	综合技术服务业 Polytechnical Services	其他社会服务业 Other Social Service	教育事业 Education	卫生、社会保障和社会福利业 Health, Social Security and Social Welfare	文化、体育和娱乐业 Culture, Sports and Recreation	公共管理和社会组织 Public Management And Social Organization
0.030132	0.010227	0.017643	0.017156	0.012760	0.025739	0.043670	0.023511
0.013317	0.006819	0.008902	0.011767	0.016239	0.017084	0.021462	0.012749
0.095558	0.034497	0.052688	0.045267	0.033493	0.112986	0.045203	0.048714
0.003373	0.002065	0.002224	0.002792	0.004204	0.009405	0.002714	0.002406
0.001112	0.000822	0.000987	0.001354	0.001621	0.003400	0.001038	0.000897
0.021256	0.005733	0.009858	0.004887	0.005522	0.006156	0.018434	0.017551
0.002070	0.000858	0.001465	0.007404	0.001461	0.004259	0.001395	0.001209
0.004027	0.000913	0.002758	0.024812	0.002102	0.002333	0.001545	0.001464
0.002648	0.003771	0.008709	0.021834	0.007418	0.037403	0.003977	0.002927
0.024404	0.017113	0.048567	0.014464	0.036675	0.014663	0.055994	0.016707
0.128340	0.037571	0.065325	0.043269	0.032636	0.057753	0.055110	0.058252
0.039025	0.051558	0.044531	0.093498	0.065992	0.449711	0.041704	0.050430
0.005986	0.004903	0.007319	0.012020	0.010326	0.009904	0.006294	0.004891
0.023720	0.012160	0.013864	0.014399	0.028024	0.037832	0.018156	0.014996
0.005304	0.003395	0.004553	0.004090	0.007002	0.013752	0.004550	0.003949
0.018345	0.013709	0.012139	0.011518	0.016167	0.066583	0.018678	0.010709
0.113082	0.030537	0.031346	0.044843	0.089683	0.071323	0.053193	0.045010
0.009550	0.010481	0.012122	0.009630	0.027644	0.033023	0.013001	0.013538
0.005936	0.008350	0.009341	0.006495	0.025712	0.018955	0.010263	0.012614
0.007912	0.007897	0.006858	0.007620	0.021226	0.028432	0.014078	0.013526
0.003354	0.001031	0.001791	0.011689	0.002044	0.002107	0.011560	0.001454
0.002465	0.001668	0.002122	0.003770	0.003474	0.004369	0.003823	0.002407
0.047376	0.025234	0.031978	0.043445	0.064511	0.053830	0.083898	0.050931
0.009495	0.002309	0.004138	0.009015	0.003901	0.005076	0.004984	0.004391
0.006620	0.004952	0.005118	0.008315	0.009241	0.008143	0.013548	0.011742
0.014285	0.007915	0.009452	0.006336	0.022288	0.005290	0.009477	0.010918
0.357730	0.051853	0.076063	0.089109	0.076957	0.126467	0.094042	0.081949
0.004136	0.000876	0.002180	0.000615	0.000622	0.000712	0.001193	0.002406
0.041878	0.017911	0.029031	0.018023	0.030760	0.013439	0.023400	0.040396
0.048385	0.025006	0.041148	0.063613	0.044083	0.118519	0.051097	0.031653
0.106716	0.027405	0.044932	0.019912	0.024252	0.021136	0.033680	0.092575
0.091539	0.018879	0.030410	0.034818	0.032149	0.044078	0.067779	0.025341
0.019330	0.003423	0.005357	0.037680	0.005167	0.005536	0.006897	0.008035
0.086062	0.019680	0.045709	0.097237	0.031116	0.047288	0.044134	0.035858
0.003222	0.000038	0.000050	0.000090	0.000073	0.000147	0.000060	0.000052
0.003535	0.101130	0.009141	0.013801	0.038978	0.006336	0.070349	0.011377
0.020784	0.012814	0.040643	0.008513	0.007022	0.018604	0.008611	0.008067
0.006661	0.011073	0.010724	0.008215	0.034449	0.009667	0.014249	0.015446
0.005405	0.003557	0.005235	0.003923	0.008247	0.005741	0.004629	0.005802
0.004287	0.026036	0.008913	0.006421	0.031770	0.019170	0.007568	0.013488
0.017098	0.022185	0.013465	0.006158	0.026374	0.007216	0.011098	0.010120
0.019350	0.003120	0.002522	0.002196	0.003141	0.001347	0.001749	0.003881

3-16 资金流量表(实物交易)

单位：亿元 (2002 年)

交易项目 Transaction \ 机构部门 Institutional Sector		非金融企业部门 Non-financial Enterprises		金融机构部门 Financial Institutions	
		使 用 Utilization	来 源 Source	使 用 Utilization	来 源 Source
净出口	**Net Exports**				
增加值	**Value Added**		**1179.08**		**65.43**
劳动者报酬	**Payment of Laborers**	**494.74**		**24.08**	
工资及工资性收入	Wages and Related Income	469.08		20.74	
单位社会保险付款	Employer's Contribution of Social Securities	25.66		3.34	
生产税净额	**Taxes on Production, Net**	**201.32**		**5.83**	
生产税	Taxes on Production	209.24		5.83	
生产补贴	Subsidies to Production	7.92			
财产收入	**Income from Properties**	**38.99**	**14.01**	**39.62**	**39.50**
利 息	Interest	36.87	12.25	39.50	39.50
红 利	Dividend	2.12	1.70		
土地租金	Rent on Land Use				
其 他	Others		0.06	0.12	
初次分配总收入	**Total Income from Primary Distribution**		**458.04**		**35.40**
经常转移	**Current Transfer**	**23.98**	**50.33**	**23.30**	**0.96**
收入税	Taxes on Income	18.80		1.04	
来自省外款项	Capital out of the region				
社会保险付款	Payment to Social Security				
社会补助	Allowances	5.18		1.59	
其 他	Others		50.33	20.67	0.96
可支配总收入	**Total Disposable Income**		**484.39**		**13.06**
最终消费	**Final Consumption Expenditure**				
居民消费	Household Consumption				
政府消费	Government Consumption				
总储蓄	**Savings**		**484.39**		**13.06**
资本转移	**Capital Transfer**		**224.65**		
投资性补助	Investment Allowances		60.65		
其 他	Others		164.00		
资本形成总额	**Gross Capital Formation**	**934.43**		**4.11**	
固定资本形成总额	Gross Fixed Capital Formation	921.58		4.11	
存货增加	Increase in Inventories	12.85			
其他非金融资产获得减处置	**Minus Items from Other Non-finanical Capital**				
净金融投资	**Net Financial Investment**	**-225.39**		**8.95**	
统计误差	**Statistical Discrepancy**				

Table of Funds Flow (Transaction in kind)

(100 million yuan)

政府部门 Government Organs		住户部门 Households		省内合计 Total		国内省外 Other Parts than Xinjiang		总 计 Total	
使 用 Utilization	来 源 Source	使 用 Utilization	来 源 Source	使 用 Utilization	来 源 Source	使 用 Utilization	来 源 Source	使 用 Utilization	来 源 Source
							279.20		**279.20**
	235.86		**397.24**		**1877.61**				**1877.61**
196.91		**257.56**	**938.09**	**973.29**	**938.09**		**35.20**	**973.29**	**973.29**
174.76		257.56	886.94	922.14	886.94		35.20	922.14	922.14
22.15			51.15	51.15	51.15			51.15	51.15
2.33	**101.93**	**20.29**		**229.77**	**101.93**		**127.84**	**229.77**	**229.77**
2.33	109.85	20.29		237.69	109.85		127.84	237.69	237.69
	7.92			7.92	7.92			7.92	7.92
0.74	**2.96**	**2.63**	**25.12**	**81.98**	**81.59**	**0.60**	**0.99**	**82.58**	**82.58**
0.74	2.96	2.63	24.89	79.74	79.60	0.60	0.74	80.34	80.34
			0.17	2.12	1.87		0.25	2.12	2.12
			0.06	0.12	0.12			0.12	0.12
	140.77		**1079.97**		**1714.18**		**163.43**		**1877.61**
68.69	**484.54**	**32.04**	**87.37**	**148.01**	**623.20**	**490.68**	**15.49**	**638.69**	**638.69**
	20.30	15.95		35.79	20.30		15.49	35.79	35.79
	16.09	16.09		16.09	16.09			16.09	16.09
51.77			51.77	51.77	51.77			51.77	51.77
16.92			23.69	23.69	23.69			23.69	23.69
	448.15		11.91	20.67	511.35	490.68		511.35	511.35
	556.62		**1135.30**		**2189.37**		**-311.76**		**1877.61**
420.33		**617.26**		**1037.59**				**1037.59**	
		617.26		617.26				617.26	
420.33				420.33				420.33	
	136.29		**518.04**		**1151.78**		**-32.56**		**1119.22**
87.63	**26.98**			**87.63**	**251.63**	**164.00**		**251.63**	**251.63**
87.63	26.98			87.63	87.63			87.63	87.63
					164.00	164.00		164.00	164.00
93.70		**86.98**		**1119.22**				**1119.22**	
93.70		59.85		1079.24				1079.24	
		27.13		39.98				39.98	
-18.06		**431.06**		**196.56**		**-196.56**			

3-17 居民消费水平及指数

Household Consumption and Its Indices

年 份 Year	居民消费水平(元) Household Consumption (Yuan)	农村居民 Agricultural Households	城镇居民 Non-agricultural Households	居民消费水平指数(%)(1952 年=100) Index of Residents' Consumption Level (%)(1952=100)	农村居民 Agricultural Households
1978	217	131	323	193.1	167.5
1980	289	186	410	239.8	220.9
1985	499	347	678	357.1	362.6
1990	936	662	1239	405.2	406.1
1991	1064	710	1381	424.2	435.6
1992	1146	742	1482	428.6	455.2
1993	1365	791	1756	452.8	484.7
1994	1649	823	2407	418.2	470.6
1995	1803	976	3426	456.7	489.0
1996	2221	1386	3851	530.7	620.0
1997	2410	1444	4283	514.8	622.5
1998	2499	1518	4389	532.3	672.9
1999	2447	1335	4570	530.7	625.8
2000	2650	1308	5274	549.3	594.5
2001	2882	1427	5668	572.3	622.4
2002	3150	1525	6257	627.8	657.9
2003	3152	1565	6143	634.1	683.6
2004	3377	1751	6358	663.3	719.8

年 份 Year	城镇居民 Non-agricultural Households	居民消费水平指数(%)(上年=100) Index of Residents' Consumption Level (%)(Preceding Year=100)	农村居民 Agricultural Households	城镇居民 Non-agriculturatl Households
1978	127.0	102.8	102.2	104.7
1980	143.8	111.7	111.1	111.1
1985	202.4	111.3	109.4	112.8
1990	227.8	103.5	102.6	103.1
1991	232.2	104.7	107.3	101.9
1992	229.4	101.0	104.5	98.8
1993	239.5	105.7	106.5	104.4
1994	213.8	92.4	97.1	89.3
1995	238.8	109.2	103.9	111.7
1996	241.9	110.3	126.8	101.3
1997	249.4	102.2	100.4	103.1
1998	249.7	103.4	108.1	100.1
1999	259.7	99.7	93.0	104.0
2000	285.1	103.5	95.0	109.8
2001	293.4	104.2	104.7	102.9
2002	327.1	109.7	105.7	111.5
2003	323.8	101.0	103.9	99.0
2004	333.2	104.6	105.3	102.9

主要统计指标解释

国内生产总值(GDP) 指一个国家(或地区)所有常住单位在一定时期内生产活动的最终成果。国内生产总值有三种表现形态，即价值形态、收入形态和产品形态。从价值形态看，它是所有常住单位在一定时期内生产的全部货物和服务价值超过同期中间投入的全部非固定资产货物和服务价值的差额，即所有常住单位的增加值之和；从收入形态看，它是所有常住单位在一定时期内创造并分配给常住单位和非常住单位的初次收入分配之和；从产品形态看，它是所有常住单位在一定时期内最终使用的货物和服务价值与货物和服务净出口价值之和。在实际核算中，国内生产总值有三种计算方法，即生产法、收入法和支出法。三种方法分别从不同的方面反映国内生产总值及其构成。

三次产业 是根据社会生产活动历史发展的顺序对产业结构的划分，产品直接取自自然界的部门称为第一产业，对初级产品进行再加工的部门称为第二产业，为生产和消费提供各种服务的部门称为第三产业。它是世界上较为通用的产业结构分类，但各国的划分不尽一致。

我国的三次产业划分是：

第一产业：农业(包括种植业，林业，牧业，渔业和农、林、牧、渔服务业)。

第二产业：工业(包括采掘业，制造业，电力、煤气及水的生产和供应业)和建筑业。

第三产业：除第一、第二产业以外的其他各业。由于第三产业包括的行业多、范围广，根据我国的实际情况，第三产业可分为两大部分：一是流通部门，二是服务部门。具体又可分为四个层次：

第一层次：流通部门，包括交通运输、仓储及邮电通信业，批发和零售贸易、餐饮业。

第二层次：为生产和生活服务的部门，包括金融、保险业，地质勘查业、水利管理业，房地产业，社会服务业，交通运输辅助业，综合技术服务业等。

第三层次：为提高科学文化水平和居民素质服务的部门，包括教育、文化艺术及广播电影电视业，卫生、体育和社会福利业，科学研究业等。

第四层次：为社会公共需要服务的部门，包括国家机关、政党机关和社会团体以及军队、警察等。

支出法国内生产总值 指一个国家(或地区)所有常住单位在一定时期内用于最终消费、资本形成总额，以及货物和服务的净出口总额，它反映本期生产的国内生产总值的使用及构成。

最终消费 指常住单位在一定时期内对于货物和服务的全部最终消费支出，也就是常住单位为满足物质、文化和精神生活的需要，从本国经济领土和国外购买的货物和服务的支出；不包括非常住单位在本国经济领土内的消费支出。最终消费分为居民消费和政府消费。

居民消费 指常住住户对货物和服务的全部最终消费支出。居民消费按市场价格计算，即按居民支付的购买者价格计算。购买者价格是购买者取得货物所支付的价格，包括购买者支付的运输和商业费用。居民消费除了直接以货币形式购买货物和服务的消费之外，还包括以其他方式获得的货物和服务的消费支出，即所谓的虚拟消费支出。居民虚拟消费支出包括以下几种类型：单位以实物报酬及实物转移的形式提供给劳动者的货物和服务；住户生产并由本住户消费了的货物和服务，其中的服务仅指住户的自有住房服务；金融机构提供的金融媒介服务；保险公司提供的保险服务。

政府消费 指政府部门为全社会提供公共服务的消费支出和免费或以较低价格向住户提供的货物和服务的净支出。前者等于政府服务的产出价值减去政府单位所获得的经营收入的价值，政府服务的产出价值等于它的经常性业务支出加上固定资产折旧；后者等于政府部门免费或以较低价格向住户提供的货物和服务的市场价值减去向住户收取的价值。

资本形成总额 指常住单位在一定时期内获得的减去处置的固定资产加存货的变动，包括固定资本形成总额和存货增加。

固定资本形成总额 指常住单位购置、转入和自产自用的固定资产，扣除固定资产的销售和转出后的价值，分有形固定资产形成总额和无形固定资产形成总额。有形固定资产形成总额包括一定时期内完成的建筑工程、安装工程和设备工器具购置(减处置)价值，以及土地改良、新增役、种、奶、毛、娱乐用牲畜和新增经济林木价值。无形固定资产形成总额包括矿藏的勘探、计算机软件、娱乐和文学艺术品原件等获得减处置。

存货增加 指常住单位存货实物量变动的市场价值，即期末价值减期初价值的差额。存货增加可以是正值，也可以是负值；正值表示存货上升，负值表示存货下降。它包括生产单位购进的原材料、燃料和储备物资等存货，以及生产单位生产的产成品、在制品等存货等。

货物和服务净出口 指货物和服务出口减货物和服务进口的差额。出口包括常住单位向非常住单位出售或无偿转让的各种货物和服务的价值；进口包括常住单位从非常住单位购买或无偿得到的各种货物和服务的价值。由于服务活动的提供与使用同时发生，因此服务的进出口业务并不发生出入境现象，一般把常住单位从国外得到的服务作为进口，非常住单位从本国得到的服务作为出口。货物的出口和进口都按离岸价格计算。

劳动者报酬 指劳动者因从事生产活动所获得的全部报酬。包括劳动者获得的各种形式的工资、奖金和津贴，既包括货币形式的，也包括实物形式的；还包括劳动者所享受的公费医疗和医药卫生费、上下班交通补贴和单位支付的社会保险费等。对于个体经济来说，其所有者所获得的劳动报酬和经营利润不易区分，这两部分统一作为劳动者报酬处理。

生产税净额 指生产税减生产补贴后的余额。生产税指政府对生产单位生产、销售和从事经营活动以及因从事生产活动使用某些生产要素(如固定资产、土地、劳动力)所征收的各种税、附加费和规费。生产补贴与生产税相反，指政府对生产单位的单方面收入转移，因此视为负生产税，包括政策亏损补贴、粮食系统价格补贴、外贸企业出口退税收入等。

固定资产折旧 指一定时期内为弥补固定资产损耗按照核定的固定资产折旧率提取的固定资产折旧，或按国民经济核算统一规定的折旧率虚拟计算的固定资产折旧。它反映了固定资产在当期生产中的转移价值。各类企业和企业化管理的事业单位的固定资产折旧是指实际计提并计入成本费中的折旧费；不计提折旧的政府机关、非企业化管理的事业单位和居民住房的固定资产折旧是按照统一规定的折旧率和固定资产原值计算的虚拟折旧。原则上，固定资产折旧应按固定资产的重置价值计算，但是目前我国尚不具备对全社会固定资产进行重估价的基础，所以暂时只能采用上述办法。

营业盈余 指常住单位创造的增加值扣除劳动者报酬、生产税净额和固定资产折旧后的余额。它相当于企业的营业利润加上生产补贴，但要扣除从利润中开支的工资和福利等。

直接消耗系数 指某一个部门生产单位总产出需要直接消耗各部门产品和服务的数量，也称为投入系数。它反映该部门与其他部门之间直接的技术经济联系和直接依赖关系。

完全消耗系数 指增加某一个部门单位总产出需要完全消耗各部门产品和服务的数量。完全消耗系数等于直接消耗系数和全部间接消耗系数之和，它是全面揭示国民经济各部门之间技术经济的全部联系和相互依赖关系的主要指标。

机构单位　指能以自己的名义拥有资产、发生负债、从事经济活动并与其他实体进行交易的经济实体。根据机构单位在生产、消费、融资活动中所起的不同作用，资金流量核算将常住单位区分为如下四类机构单位：非金融企业、金融机构、政府单位、住户和国外。

机构部门　将相同性质的机构单位归并在一起，就形成机构部门。资金流量核算中区分了如下几类机构部门：非金融企业部门、金融机构部门、政府部门、住户部门。

非金融企业与非金融企业部门　非金融企业指主要从事市场货物生产和提供非金融市场服务的常住企业，它主要包括各类法人企业。所有非金融企业归并在一起，就形成非金融企业部门。

金融机构与金融机构部门　金融机构指主要从事金融中介以及与金融中介密切相关的辅助金融活动的常住单位，它主要包括中央银行、商业银行和政策性银行、非银行信贷机构和保险公司。所有金融机构归并在一起，就形成金融机构部门。

政府单位与政府部门　政府单位指在我国境内通过政治程序建立的、在一特定区域内对其他机构单位拥有立法、司法和行政权的法律实体及其附属单位。政府单位的主要职能是利用征税和其他方式获得的资金向社会和公众提供公共服务。通过转移支付，对社会收入和财产进行再分配。它主要包括各种行政单位和事业单位。所有政府单位归并在一起，就形成政府部门。

住户与住户部门　住户指共享同一生活设施、部分或全部收入和财产集中使用、共同消费住房、食品和其他消费品与消费服务的常住个人或个人群体。所有住户归并在一起，就形成住户部门。

非常住单位与国外部门　所有不具有常住性的机构单位都是非常住单位。将所有与我国常住单位发生交易的非常住单位归并在一起，就形成国外部门。

初次分配总收入　初次分配指以劳动者报酬、固定资产折旧、生产税及财产收入等形式对增加值进行的分配。初次分配形成的收入余额为初次分配总收入。

经常转移　指部门间以实物和资金方式实现的单方面转让。包括社会保险付款、社会补助、侨汇、无偿捐赠、赔偿等。

可支配总收入　指各机构部门在初次分配总收入基础上通过经常转移后所获得的收入。这部分收入用于最终消费和储蓄。

总储蓄　指可支配总收入扣除最终消费后的余额。

资本转移　指一个部门无偿地向另一个部门支付用于资本形成的资金，是一种不从对方获取任何对应物作为回报的交易。资本转移具有不同于经常转移的两个特征，一是转移的目的是用于投资，而不是用于消费；二是资产所有权的转移，而不仅仅是使用权的转移。资本转移包括投资性补助和其他资产转移，根据我国目前的实际情况，投资性补助是指财政投资性拨款，即财政拨款中用于基本建设、更新改造和其他固定资产投资的部分。

净金融投资　从实物交易角度看，它是指总储蓄加资本转移收入减资本转移支出减资本形成总额后的余额。从金融交易角度看，它是金融资产的增加额减金融负债的增加额之后的余额。

通货　指以现金形式存在于市场流通领域中的货币，包括辅币和纸币。

存款　指以各种形式存在的所有存款，包括活期存款、定期存款、住户储蓄存款、财政存款、外汇存款和其他存款。

贷款　指金融机构向非金融部门提供的各种形式的所有贷款，包括短期贷款、中长期贷款、财政贷款、外汇贷款和其他贷款。

证券　包括债券和股票。

保险准备金　指对人寿保险准备金和养恤基金的净权益、保险费预付款和未结索赔准备金。

结算资金　指银行的汇兑在途资金。

金融机构往来　指各机构之间的资金往来，包括同业存放款和同业拆借款。

准备金　指各金融机构在中央银行的存款及缴存中央银行的法定准备金。

中央银行贷款　指中央银行向各金融机构的贷款。

经常项目　包括货物、服务、收益及经常性转移。

货物　指通过我国海关进出口的货物，以海关进出口统计资料为基础，并根据国际收支统计口径的要求，出口、进口都以商品所有权变化为原则进行调整。出口和进口金额均按离岸价格统计。

服务　包括运输、旅游、通讯、建筑、保险、国际金融服务、计算机和信息服务、专有权力使用费和特许费、各种商业服务、个人文化娱乐服务以及政府服务。

收益　包括职工报酬和投资收益。投资收益包括直接投资、证券投资和其它投资的收益和支出以及直接投资收益的再投资。

资本项目　包括移民转移、债务减免等资本性转移。

金融项目　包括直接投资、证券投资和其它投资。

直接投资　指外国、港澳台地区在我国和我国在外国、港澳台地区以独资、合资、合作及合作勘探开发方式进行的投资。

证券投资　指外国、港澳台地区购买(或我国买回)我国(包括地方政府和企业)发行的股票、债券等有价证券和我国(政府、企业、私人)买卖外国、港澳台地区发行的股票、债券等有价证券。

其它投资　包括外国提供给我国和我国提供给外国的贸易信贷、贷款、货币和存款以及其它资产。

储备资产增减额　指我国在黄金储备、外汇储备、在国际货币基金组织的储备头寸、特别提款权、使用基金信贷等方面本年末与上年末余额之间的差额。储备资产增加用负号表示。

Explanatory Notes on Main Statistical Indicators

Gross Domestic Product (GDP) refers to the final products of all resident units in a country (or a region) during a certain period of time. Gross domestic product is expressed in three different forms, i.e. value, income, and products respectively. The form of value refers to the total value of all products and services produced by all resident units during a certain period of time minus total value of intimidate input of materials and services of the nature of non-fixed assets or the summation of the value-added of all resident units; the form of income includes all the income created by all resident units and distributed primarily to all resident and non-resident units;the form of products refers to the value of all final goods and services for final use by all resident units plus the value of net exports of goods and services during a given period of time.In the practice of national accounting,gross domestic product is calculated with three approaches, i.e.production approach, income approach, and expenditure approach, which reflect gross domestic product and its composition from different aspects.

Three Industries Industry structure has been classified according to the historical sequence of development. Primary industry refers to extraction of natural resources; secondary industry involves processing of primary products; and tertiary industry provides services of various kinds for production and consumption. The above classification is universal although it varies to some extent form country to country. Industry in China comprises:

Primary industry: agriculture (including farming, forestry, animal husbandry and fishery).

Secondary industry: industry (including mining and quarrying, manufacturing, production and supply of electriCity, water and gas) and construction.

Tertiary industry: all other industries not included in primary or secondary industry.

Due to the fact that tertiary industry involves in a large variety of industries in China, it is divided into two sectors: circulation sector and service sector and further into four levels:

The first level: circulation sector, including transportation, storage, postal and telecommunications, wholesale and retail trade, and catering trade.

The second level: service sector providing services for production and consumption, including banking, insurance, geological survey, water conservancy management, real estates, service for residents, service for agriculture, forestry, animal husbandry, fishery, subsidiary services for transportation and communications, comprehensive technical services, etc.

The third level: service sector for upgrading scientific, educational and cultural level of the people, including education, culture and arts, broadcasting, movies, television, public health, sports, social welfare and scientific research, etc. The fourth level: sector providing services for public needs, including government agencies, political parties, social organizations, military and police service.

GDP Calculated with Expenditure Approach refers to total expenditure on final consumption, total capital formation and net export of goods and services by resident units of a country in a certain period of time. It reflects the composition of GDP by its use.

Final Consumption refers to the total expenditure of resident units on final consumption of goods and services in a certain period, namely the expenditure of the resident units for purchases of goods and services from domestic economic territory and abroad to meet the requirements of material, cultural and spiritual life. It excludes the expenditure of non-resident units on consumption in the economic territory of the country. The final consumption is classified into household consumption and government consumption.

Household consumption refers to the total expenditure of resident households on the final consumption of goods and services. The household consumption is calculated at market prices, namely the purchaser's prices that the households pay; the purchasers prices of goods are the prices the households pay when they obtain the goods, including the transport and commercial expenses paid by the households. In addition to the consumption of goods and services bought by the households directly with money, the expenditure on goods and services obtained by the households in other ways, i.e. the so-called imputed expenditure on consumption is also included in the household consumption. The imputation expenditure of the households on consumption includes the following types: (a) the goods and services provided to the households by the units in the form of payment in kind and transfer in kind; (b) the goods and services produced and consumed by the households themselves, in which the services refer only to the services provided by the residential buildings owned by the households; (c) the services of financial intermediary provided by the financial institutions; (d) the insurance services provided by the insurance companies.

Government Consumption refers to the expenditure on the consumption of the public services provided by the government to the whole society and the net expenditure on the goods and services provided by the government to the households at free charge or lower prices. The former equals to the output value of the government services minus the value of operating income obtained by the government departments. (The output value of the government services equals to its current operating expenditure plus depreciation of fixed assets). The latter equals to the market value of the goods and services provided by the government free of charge or at low prices to the households minus the value received by the government from the households.

Total Capital Formation refers to the fixed assets acquired minus those disposed and the change in inventory, including the total fixed assets formation and the increase in inventory.

Total Fixed Capital Formation refers to the value of fixed assets purchased, transferred in by the resident units and those produced and used by themselves deducting the value of fixed assets sold and transferred out. It can be classified into total tangible assets formation and total intangible assets formation. The total tangible assets formation include the value of the construction projects, installation projects completed and the equipment, apparatus and instruments purchased as well as the value of land improved, the value of draught animals, breeding stock, milk, wool and recreational animals and the newly increased economic forest in a certain period. The total intangible assets formation includes the prospecting of minerals, the acquisition of computer software, the originals of recreational works and works of literature and arts minus the disposal of them.

Increase in Inventory refers to the market value of the change in inventory, i.e.the difference of value between the beginning and the end of the period.The increase in inventory can be positive or negative.A positive value indicates the increase in inventory while a negative value indicates the decrease in stock.The inventory includes the raw materials, fuels and reserve materials purchased by the production units as well as the inventory of finished products, semi-finished products, work-in-progress, etc.

Net Export of Goods and Services refers to the difference of the exports of goods and services minus the imports of goods and services.The imports include the value of various goods and services sold or gratuitously transferred by the resident units to the non-resident units.The imports include the value of various goods and services purchased or gratuitously acquired by the resident units from the non-resident units.Because the provision of services and the use of them happen simultaneously, the import and export of services do not appear to have the phenomena of crossing the border of the country.The acquisition of services by the resident units from abroad is usually treated as import while the acquisition of services by non-resident units in this country is usually treated as export.The export and import of goods are calculated at FOB.

Labourers Remuneration refers to the whole payment of various forms earned by the labourers from the productive activities they are engaged in.It includes wages, bonuses and allowances the labourers earned in monetary form and in kind.It also includes the free medical services provided to the labourers and the medicine expenses, traffic subsidies and social insurance fee paid by the labourers working units for them.As the individual economy is concerned, since the labourers remuneration is not easily distinguished from the operating profit, both are treated as labourers remuneration.

Net Taxes on Production refers to the residual of the taxes on production minus the subsidies on production.The taxes on production refers to the various taxes, extra charges and fees levied on the production units on their production, sale and business activities as well as on some factors of production, such as fixed assets, land and labour force, used in the production activities they are engaged in.In contrast to the taxes on production, the subsidies on production refer to the unilateral transfer of part of the government's revenue to the production units and is therefore regarded as negative taxes on production.They include subsidies on the loss due to implementation of government policies, price subsidies to the grain institutions, foreign trade corporations receipts from drawback, etc.

Depreciation of Fixed Assets refers to the depreciation of fixed assets of a given period, drawn in accordance with the stipulated depreciation rate for the purpose of compensating the wear loss of the fixed assets or the depreciation of fixed assets calculated in a fictitious way in accordance with the stipulated unified depreciation rate in the national economic accounting system. It reflects the value of transfer of the fixed assets in the production of the current period. The depreciation of fixed assets in various enterprises and institutions managed as enterprises refers to the depreciation expenses actually drawn and calculated as part of theterprises which do not draw the depreciation expenses, as well as for the houses of residents, the depreciation of fixed assets is the imputed depreciation, which is calculated in accordance with the stipulated unified depreciation rate. In principle, the depreciation of fixed assets should be calculated on the basis of the re-purchased value of the fixed assets. However, there is no actual condition to re-evaluate all the fixed assets in China. Therefore, the above-mentioned methods are temporarily adopted at present.

Operating Surplus refers to the balance of the value added created by the resident units deducting the labourers remuneration, net taxes on production and the depreciation of fixed assets. It is equivalent to the business profit of the enterprises plus subsidies on production, but the wages and welfare expenses paid from the profits should be deducted.

Direct Input Coefficient refers to the volume of products and services of all sectors consumed directly by a certain sector's productive units, which are needed for their total output. It is also named as technical coefficient. It represents the direct technical economical ties and direct interdependence between the sector and other sectors.

Total Input Coefficient refers to the volume of products and services of all sectors needed for a certain sectors productive units to increase their total output. Total input coefficient is equal to the sum of direct input coefficient and total indirect input coefficient. It is a major indicator to disclose the technical economical ties and interdependence between sectors of the national economy.

Institutional Units refer to economic entities that are in a position to own assets and incur liabilities in their own name, and to engage in economic activities and conduct transactions with other entities. Depending on their different role in production, consumption and financing, 4 groups of resident institutional units are identified in the flow of fund tables, namely, non-financial corporations, financial institutions, governments, households and the rest of the world.

Institutional Sectors refer groups of institutional units that are classified by .their nature. Following groups (or institutional sectors) are identified in the flow of fund accounts: the sector of non-financial corporations, the sector of financial institutions, the sector of governments and the sector of households.

Non-Financial Corporations and the Sector of Non-Financial Corporations Non-financial corporations refer to resident corporations that are engaged in the production of goods and the provision of non financial services in the market, mainly covering corporate enterprises of various types.All non-financial corporations make up the sector of non-financial corporations.

Financial Institutions and the Sector of Financial Institutions Financial institutions refer to resident institutions that are engaged in the financial services or auxiliary financial activities, mainly covering central banks, commercial banks, policy-related banks, non-banking credit institutions and insurance companies.All financial institutions make up the sector of financial institutions.

Government Units and the Sector of Governments Government units refer to legal entities and their auxiliary units within the territory of China that are established through political process and are empowered with legislative, administrative or judicial rights over other institutional units in a given region.The main function of government units is to acquire funds through taxation or other means, to provide public services to the society and households, and to conduct redistribution of income and properties of the society through transfer payment.Government units cover mainly administrative and institutional units of various types.All government units make up the sector of governments.

Households and the Sector of Households Households refer to resident individuals or groups of resident individuals who share common living facilities, pool together entire or part of their income and properties at their common disposal, and share their housing, food and other consumer goods and services.All households make up the sector of households.

Non-resident Units and the Sector of the Rest of the World Non-resident units refer to of units that are of a non-resident nature.All non-resident units that have transactions with resident units make up the sector the rest of the world.

Total Income of Primary Distribution Primary distribution refers to the distribution of value-added in the form of compensation for labours, depreciation of fixed assets, production taxes and property income.The sum of income obtained through primary distribution is called the total income of primary distribution.

Current Transfers refers to one-way transfers with physical and fund form in sectors. include payment to social securities, social allowances remittance from overseas Chinese, grants, donations and reparations and so on.

Total Disposable Income refers to income received by institutional sectors on the basis of total income of primary distribution and through current transfers.This is the income that is used for final consumption and savings.

Total Savings is the difference between total disposable income and the final consumption.

Capital Transfer refers to the free payment from one sector to another sector for capital formation, and is a transaction that seeks no return from the recipient. The capital transfer differs from the current transfer in 2 aspects.Firstly, the objective of the transfer is investment rather than consumption.Secondly, capital transfer features the transfer of the ownership of the capital rather than the utilization right of the capital.Capital transfer in cludes investment subsidies and other capital transfers.Under the current situation in China, investment subsidies refer to investment allocations from government finance, i.e.the financial allocations that are used for capital construction, updating and transformation projects and other investment in fixed assets.

Net Financial Investment refers to total savings plus the net income from capital transfer minus the gross capital formation from the point of view of physical transaction.In terms of monetary transaction, it is the increased value of financial assets minus the increase of the financial liabilities.

Currency in Circulation refers to currency that is in circulation in the market, including notes and fractional currency.

Savings Deposit refers to deposits of all types, including current deposit, fixed deposit, household savings deposit, government deposit, foreign exchange deposit and other deposits.

Loans refer to loans of all forms provided by financial institutions to non-financial sectors, including short-term loans, medium and long-term loans, government loans, foreign exchange loans and other loans.

Securities include bonds and stocks.

Insurance Reserve Funds refer to reserve fund for life insurance, the net pension fund, advance payment of premium and non-claimed reserves.

Settlement Fund refers to bank fund that is in the process of remittance.

Transactions Between Financial Institutions refer to flow of capital between financial institutions, including inter-bank deposits and loans.

Reserve Funds refer to savings of financial institutions in the central bank and designated reserves to the central bank.

Loans from the Central Bank refer to loans from the central bank to financial institutions.

Current Account includes goods, services, earnings and current transfers.

Goods refer to imported or exported goods through Chinese customs.Figures in the Yearbook are based on customs statistics, adjusted in line with the concepts and definitions of the balance of payment statistics and with the change in the ownership of commodities.Statistics on both exports and imports are valued at f.o.b.prices.

Services include transportation, tourism, communications, construction, insurance, international financial services, computer and information service, royalty for patent, trademarks and other special rights, commercial services, personal cultural and recreational services and government services.

Earnings include compensation of employees and earnings from investment (including earnings from and expenses on direct investment, security investment and other investment, as well as reinvestment of earnings from direct investment).

Capital Account includes capital transfers such as immigration transfer, reduction or exemption of debts, etc..

Financial Account includes direct investment, security investment and other investments.

Direct Investment refers to investment, made in forms of exclusive investment, joint investment, contracted operation and cooperative development, by foreign investors or investors from Hong Kong, Macao and Taiwan in China, or by Chinese investors in foreign countries or in Hong Kong, Macao and Taiwan.

Security Investment refers to the purchase of stocks and securities issued by central and local governments and enterprises in China by institutions or individuals of foreign countries or from Hong Kong, Macao and Taiwan (and the re-purchase by Chinese institutions), and the purchase and selling of stocks and securities issued in foreign countries and in Hong Kong, Macao and Taiwan by Chinese governments, enterprises and individuals.

Other Investment includes trade credits, loans, currency, savings and other assets, provided by foreign countries to China and by China to foreign countries.

Reserve Assets, Net Increase refers to the net balance between the end of the reference year and the end of the previous year, in the gold reserve, foreign exchange reserve, reserve and special drawing rights in the International Monetary Fund, and the use of the Fund's credits.The increase in the reserve assets is expressed as a negative figure.

第四篇

CHAPTER 4

人口、就业人员和职工工资

POPULATION EMPLOYMENT AND WAGES

4-1 人口数及构成
Population and Its Composition

单位：万人 (10 000 persons)

年份 Year	年末总人口 Total Population (Year-end)	按性别分 By Sex				按城乡分 By Residence			
		男 Male		女 Female		城镇人口 Urban		乡村人口 Rural	
		人口数 Population	比重 Proportion	人口数 Population	比重 Proportion	人口数 Population	比重 Proportion	人口数 Population	比重 Proportion
1978	1233.01	630.18	51.11	602.83	48.89	321.40	26.07	911.61	73.93
1980	1283.24	654.90	51.03	628.34	48.97	372.74	29.05	910.50	70.95
1985	1361.14	696.81	51.19	664.33	48.81	582.24	42.78	778.90	57.22
1990	1529.16	785.06	51.34	744.10	48.66	685.96	44.86	843.20	55.14
1991	1554.57	798.14	51.34	756.43	48.66	698.79	44.95	855.78	55.05
1992	1580.63	811.45	51.34	769.18	48.66	715.64	45.28	864.99	54.72
1993	1605.26	824.48	51.36	780.78	48.64	743.04	46.29	862.22	53.71
1994	1632.70	838.46	51.35	794.24	48.65	785.43	48.11	847.27	51.89
1995	1661.35	848.12	51.05	813.23	48.95	822.53	49.51	838.82	50.49
1996	1689.29	869.59	51.48	819.70	48.52	846.17	50.09	843.12	49.91
1997	1718.08	883.03	51.40	835.05	48.60	860.76	50.10	857.32	49.90
1998	1747.35	897.90	51.39	849.45	48.61	875.42	50.10	871.93	49.90
1999	1775.00	910.98	51.32	864.02	48.68	929.00	52.34	846.00	47.66
2000	1849.41	957.07	51.75	892.34	48.25	624.18	33.75	1225.23	66.25
2001	1876.19	954.23	50.86	921.96	49.14	633.21	33.75	1242.98	66.25
2002	1905.19	975.46	51.20	929.73	48.80	644.72	33.84	1260.47	66.16
2003	1933.95	994.24	51.41	939.71	48.59	665.11	34.39	1268.84	65.61
2004	1963.11	1008.02	51.30	955.09	48.70	690.11	35.15	1273.00	64.85

4-2 人口出生率、死亡率、自然增长率
Birth Rate, Death Rate and Natural Growth Rate of Population

单位：‰ (‰)

年份 Year	出生率 Birth Rate	死亡率 Death Rate	自然增长率 Natural Growth Rate	年份 Year	出生率 Birth Rate	死亡率 Death Rate	自然增长率 Natural Growth Rate
1978	22.55	7.69	14.86	1994	20.82	7.43	13.39
1979	22.54	8.33	14.21	1995	18.90	6.45	12.45
1980	21.28	7.62	13.66	1996	19.45	6.60	12.85
1985	19.80	6.39	13.41	1997	19.66	6.55	13.11
1986	20.54	6.13	14.41	1998	19.74	6.93	12.81
1987	21.03	5.96	15.07	1999	18.76	6.96	11.80
1988	19.72	5.99	13.73	2000	17.57	5.40	12.17
1989	21.15	5.77	15.38	2001	16.82	5.69	11.13
1990	26.41	7.81	18.60	2002	16.30	5.43	10.87
1991	24.45	7.86	16.59	2003	16.01	5.23	10.78
1992	22.80	7.84	14.96	2004	16.00	5.09	10.91
1993	21.53	7.68	13.85				

4-3　新疆人口普查基本情况

Basic Statistics on National Population Census in Xinjiang

单位：万人　　(10 000 persons)

指　标	Items	第二次普查 (1964 年) 1964 Census	第三次普查 (1982 年) 1982 Census	第四次普查 (1990 年) 1990 Census	第五次普查 (2000 年) 2000 Census
总人口	**Total Population**	**727.01**	**1308.15**	**1515.69**	**1845.95**
男	Male	389.47	673.22	782.32	955.22
女	Female	337.53	634.93	733.37	890.73
总户数(万户)	**Total Number of Households (10000 households)**	**178.00**	**293.79**	**337.41**	**491.66**
家　庭　户	Family Households		292.70	334.89	479.38
集　体　户	Non-family Households		1.09	2.52	12.28
各年龄组人口	**Population by Age**				
0-5　岁	Age 0-5	121.86	186.70	218.85	165.12
6-14 岁	Age 6-14	146.77	330.85	282.12	338.18
15-64 岁	Age 15-64	428.73	742.42	955.49	1256.40
65 岁及以上	Population Aged 65 and Over	29.65	48.18	59.23	86.25
民族人口	**Nationality Population**				
汉 族	Han Nationality	232.12	528.40	569.54	748.99
少数民族	Minority Nationalities	494.89	779.75	946.15	1096.96
各种文化程度人口	**Population by Educational Level**				
大专及以上	College and Above	4.10	8.37	27.98	94.65
高中和中专	Senior Secondary School and Specialized Secondary School	15.51	84.28	157.42	224.79
初 中	Junior Secondary School	50.37	228.63	313.51	508.59
小 学	Primary School	197.34	442.57	552.55	699.78
不识字或识字很少	Illiterate and Semi-iliterate	249.03	265.39	198.11	103.68

注：不识字或识字很少除 1964 年包含 12-14 岁人口外，其他均为 15 岁及以上人口。
Note:Illiterate or semi-illiterate population refers to the population aged above 15 except for the population aged between 12 and 14 in 1964

4-4　婚姻登记情况

Number of Marriages Registry

指　标	Item	1995	2000	2004
登记结婚(对)	**Registered Marriages (couple)**	**166363**	**162527**	**184004**
初婚(人)	First Marriage (person)	249428	250461	282773
再婚(人)	Remarriage (person)	83298	74593	85235
#男	Male	46996	38484	43724
#再婚中恢复结婚(对)	Resumed Marriages (couple)	5194	3954	3897
登记离婚(对)	**Registered Divorces (couple)**	**53500**	**59000**	**66671**
民政部门批准	Approved by the Civil Administration	26759	26003	40280
法院调判	Mediated by the court	26741	32997	26391
海外及华侨港澳台同胞婚姻登记结婚(对)	**Marriages and Divorces of Overseas Chinese from Hong Kong, Macao and Taiwan Registered Marriages (couple)**	**136**	**172**	**223**
国内公民(人)	Citizen (person)	136	172	223
港澳台同胞(人)	Compatriots of Hong Kong, Macao and Taiwan (person)	70	78	64
华侨(人)	Overseas Chinese (person)	33	34	6
外国人(人)	Foreigner (person)	26	60	153
登记离婚(对)	**Registered Divorces (couple)**	**1**	**6**	

4-5 各地、州、市、县(市)户数、人口数、土地面积

Household, Population, Land Area in Prefecture, City and County

(2004 年)

地 区	Region	户数(万户) Household Total Households (10 000 Households)	年末人口(万人) Year-end Population (10 000 Persons)	#男 Male	平均每户人口(人) Average Persons Per Household (person)	土地面积(平方公里) Land Area (sq.km)
总 计	**Total**	**554.65**	**1963.11**	**1008.02**	**3.54**	**1664897.17**
乌鲁木齐市	**Urumqi City**	**58.00**	**185.96**	**96.34**	**3.21**	**11383.91**
克拉玛依市	**Karamay City**	**8.93**	**25.39**	**13.18**	**2.84**	**8654.08**
石河子市	**Shi Hezi City**	**22.86**	**64.29**	**32.96**	**2.81**	**459.94**
吐鲁番地区	**Turpan Administrative Offices**	**16.28**	**57.97**	**29.47**	**3.56**	**67562.91**
吐鲁番市	Turpan City	7.15	25.82	13.09	3.61	13589.21
鄯善县	Shanshan [Piqan] County	6.11	21.20	10.80	3.47	38281.50
托克逊县	Toksun County	3.02	10.95	5.57	3.62	15692.20
哈密地区	**Hami [Kumul] Administrative Offices**	**16.73**	**52.60**	**26.93**	**3.14**	**142094.88**
哈密市	Hami [Kumul] City	13.14	40.44	20.70	3.08	85587.23
巴里坤哈萨克自治县	Barkol Kazak Autonomous County	2.92	10.09	5.16	3.45	36988.55
伊吾县	Yiwu [Araturuk] County	0.67	2.07	1.07	3.07	19519.10
昌吉回族自治州	**Changji Hui Autonomous Prefecture**	**50.47**	**156.44**	**80.45**	**3.10**	**77638.97**
昌吉市	Changji City	13.12	39.35	20.29	3.00	8215.96
阜康市	Fukang City	5.49	15.85	8.15	2.89	8534.97
米泉市	Miquan City	6.22	18.64	9.58	3.00	3788.38
呼图壁县	Hutubi County	6.94	20.72	10.61	2.99	9421.03
玛纳斯县	Manas County	5.32	16.93	8.60	3.18	9597.27
奇台县	Qitai County	6.82	22.89	11.82	3.36	16638.12
吉木萨尔县	Jimsar County	3.94	13.36	6.91	3.39	8144.59
木垒哈萨克自治县	Mori Kazak Autonomous County	2.61	8.70	4.49	3.33	13298.66
伊犁哈萨克自治州	**Ili Kazak Autonomous Prefecture**	**117.24**	**414.58**	**211.66**	**3.54**	**268778.72**
伊犁州直属县(市)	**Counties (Cities) Direct Under Ili Prefecture**	**70.52**	**255.65**	**130.35**	**3.63**	**56381.53**
伊宁市	Yining [Gulja] City	12.36	43.03	21.67	3.48	524.94
奎屯市	Kuytun City	10.26	29.91	15.31	2.91	1109.89
伊宁县	Yining [Gulja] County	8.61	36.27	18.79	4.22	4681.90
察布查尔锡伯自治县	Qapqal Xibe Autonomous County	4.82	16.76	8.66	3.48	4471.95
霍城县	Huocheng [Korgas] County	10.35	36.44	18.44	3.52	5429.83
巩留县	Gongliu [Tokkuztara] County	4.26	16.22	8.26	3.81	4326.90
新源县	Xinyuan [Kunes] County	7.73	29.76	15.07	3.85	6813.74
昭苏县	Zhaosu [Mongolkure] County	4.41	15.89	8.09	3.60	11127.91
特克斯县	Tekes County	3.79	15.69	8.02	4.14	7764.10
尼勒克县	Nilka County	3.94	15.67	8.04	3.98	10130.37
塔城地区	**Tacheng [Tarbagatai] Administrative Offices**	**29.27**	**96.63**	**49.43**	**3.30**	**94698.18**
塔城市	Tacheng [Qoqek] City	4.88	15.95	8.05	3.27	3991.25
乌苏市	Usu City	6.32	21.03	10.96	3.33	14299.86
额敏县	Emin [Dorbiljin] County	6.61	20.12	10.23	3.04	9448.37
沙湾县	Shawan County	6.13	20.30	10.35	3.31	12676.58
托里县	Toli County	2.34	8.91	4.49	3.81	19977.34
裕民县	Yumin [Qagantokay] County	1.56	5.34	2.74	3.42	6112.13
和布克赛尔蒙古自治县	Hoboksar Mongol Autonomous County	1.42	4.99	2.62	3.51	28192.65
阿勒泰地区	**Altay Administrative Offices**	**17.45**	**62.30**	**31.87**	**3.57**	**117699.01**
阿勒泰市	Altay City	6.81	22.63	11.60	3.32	10829.06
布尔津县	Burqin County	1.76	6.59	3.36	3.74	10357.35
富蕴县	Fuyun [Koktokay] County	2.21	8.58	4.41	3.87	32186.11
福海县	Fuhai [Burultokay] County	1.99	7.16	3.68	3.59	33250.74
哈巴河县	Habahe [Kaba] County	2.15	7.97	4.06	3.71	8166.58
青河县	Qinghe [Qinggil] County	1.32	5.62	2.86	4.27	15756.87
吉木乃县	Jemnay County	1.21	3.76	1.90	3.11	7152.30

注：1、全区总计中“户数、年末人口、男”均根据2003年人口变动调查数据推算，各地州市此部分数据为2004年公安年报数据。因此，各地州市此部分数据合计不等于全区总计。2、全疆各地州市土地面积为国土资源厅2002年数据。

Note: a) Households, Year-end population and Male in the census are calculated on the data of surveyed population variation for the year 2003. The data in this part come from the annual data of public security for the year 2004 in prefectures and cities. Therefore, the total of data in this part is not equal to the total in this region. b) The land area of different prefectures and cities is from the date dated 2002 in the bureau of state land.

4-5 续表 Continued

地　区	Region	户数(万户) Household Total Households (10 000 Households)	年末人口(万人) Year-end Population (10 000 Persons)	#男 Male	平均每户人口(人) Average Persons Per Household (person)	土地面积(平方公里) Land Area (sq.km)
博尔塔拉蒙古自治州	**Bortala Mongol Autonomous Prefecture**	**15.09**	**45.20**	**23.32**	**3.00**	**24934.33**
博乐市	Bole [Bortala] City	8.50	24.56	12.61	2.89	7877.34
精河县	Jinghe [Jing] County	4.39	13.30	6.95	3.03	11175.25
温泉县	Wenquan [Araxang] County	2.20	7.34	3.76	3.34	5881.74
巴音郭楞蒙古自治州	**Bayangol Mongol Autonomous Prefecture**	**37.21**	**114.85**	**59.75**	**3.09**	**470954.25**
库尔勒市	Korla City	14.50	42.23	22.13	2.91	7215.90
轮台县	Luntai [Bugur] County	2.73	9.69	4.94	3.55	14156.61
尉犁县	Yuli [Lopnur] County	3.67	11.11	5.93	3.03	59234.48
若羌县	Ruoqiang [Qarkilik] County	1.10	3.16	1.71	2.87	198793.52
且末县	Qiemo [Qarqan] County	1.66	5.81	2.97	3.50	137831.05
焉耆回族自治县	Yanji Hui Autonomous County	3.80	12.47	6.45	3.28	2440.74
和静县	Hejing County	5.77	17.94	9.24	3.11	34886.74
和硕县	Hoxud County	2.24	6.75	3.42	3.01	12816.49
博湖县	Bohu [Bagrax] County	1.74	5.69	2.96	3.27	3578.73
阿克苏地区	**Aksu Administrative Offices**	**58.33**	**222.77**	**115.68**	**3.82**	**131340.91**
阿克苏市	Aksu City	17.20	56.87	30.27	3.31	18183.61
温宿县	Wensu [Onsu] County	6.03	22.74	11.73	3.77	14202.46
库车县	Kuqa County	9.80	41.41	21.24	4.22	14602.95
沙雅县	Xayar County	5.51	21.32	11.07	3.87	31955.15
新和县	Xinhe [Toksu] County	3.80	14.55	7.39	3.83	5817.83
拜城县	Baicheng [Bay] County	5.11	20.94	10.82	4.10	15553.70
乌什县	Wushi [Uxturpan] County	4.81	19.13	9.84	3.97	9082.00
阿瓦提县	Awat County	5.07	21.54	11.13	4.25	13233.57
柯坪县	Kalpin County	1.00	4.29	2.20	4.27	8709.65
克孜勒苏柯尔克孜自治州	**Kizilsu Kirgiz Autonomous Prefecture**	**10.95**	**46.81**	**23.95**	**4.27**	**72468.09**
阿图什市	Artux City	4.89	21.13	10.79	4.32	16151.17
阿克陶县	Akto County	3.92	17.46	8.97	4.45	24539.86
阿合奇县	Akqi County	0.83	3.60	1.83	4.31	12737.09
乌恰县	Wuqia [Ulugqat] County	1.31	4.62	2.36	3.54	19039.96
喀什地区	**Kashgar [Kaxgar] Administrative Offices**	**87.54**	**361.54**	**184.33**	**4.13**	**139479.61**
喀什市	Kashgar [Kaxgar] City	10.69	35.45	18.13	3.31	199.38
疏附县	Shufu County	8.57	37.03	18.99	4.32	3323.12
疏勒县	Shule County	7.47	30.28	15.33	4.05	2485.31
英吉沙县	Yengisar County	5.14	23.30	11.91	4.53	3223.88
泽普县	Zepu [Poskam] County	4.81	17.27	8.75	3.59	826.90
莎车县	Shache [Yarkant] County	14.69	66.67	34.18	4.54	9066.86
叶城县	Yecheng [Kagilik] County	9.28	38.25	19.45	4.12	29359.29
麦盖提县	Makit County	5.21	21.77	11.11	4.18	10276.57
岳普湖县	Yopurga County	3.61	14.13	7.15	3.92	2700.48
伽师县	Jiashi [Payzawat] County	7.37	33.80	17.22	4.59	6668.59
巴楚县	Bachu [Maralbexi] County	9.93	40.21	20.36	4.05	20804.80
塔什库尔干塔吉克自治县	Taxkorgan Tajik Autonomous County	0.76	3.39	1.76	4.45	50544.44
和田地区	**Hotan Administrative Offices**	**44.41**	**177.21**	**90.73**	**3.99**	**249146.58**
和田市	Hotan City	5.45	19.25	9.67	3.53	495.84
和田县	Hotan County	6.39	27.83	14.31	4.35	40876.80
墨玉县	Moyu [Karakax] County	10.77	43.61	22.21	4.05	25624.02
皮山县	Pishan [Guma] County	5.57	22.51	11.62	4.04	39819.75
洛浦县	Lop County	6.05	24.33	12.54	4.03	14286.97
策勒县	Qira County	3.83	13.71	7.00	3.58	31342.58
于田县	Yutian [Keriya] County	5.41	22.49	11.60	4.16	39126.14
民丰县	Minfeng [Niya] County	0.95	3.48	1.78	3.64	57574.49

4-6 各地、州、市、县(市)按城镇、乡村和农业、非农业分人口数

Population of Urban and Rural, Agriculture and Non-Agriculture by Prefecture, Autonomous Prefecture, City and County

单位：万人　　(2004 年)　　(10 000 persons)

地区	Region	城镇人口 Urban Population	#非农业人口 Non-agri-Cultural Population	乡村人口 Rural Population	农业人口 Agricul-Tural Population	非农业人口 Non-agri-Cultural Population
总　计	**Total**	**690.11**	**640.38**	**1273.00**	**1243.24**	**719.87**
乌鲁木齐市	**Urumqi City**	**182.26**	**145.81**	**3.70**	**39.70**	**146.26**
市辖区	Districts Under Municipality	177.56	145.29		32.27	145.29
乌鲁木齐县	Urumqi County	4.70	0.52	3.70	7.43	0.97
克拉玛依市	**Karamay City**	**25.39**	**24.35**		**1.03**	**24.35**
石河子市	**Shi Hezi City**	**64.29**	**36.73**		**27.56**	**36.73**
吐鲁番地区	**Turpan Administrative Offices**	**41.44**	**14.20**	**16.52**	**42.25**	**15.72**
吐鲁番市	Turpan City	25.82	7.91	0.00	17.91	7.91
鄯善县	Shanshan [Piqan] County	13.47	4.36	7.73	16.18	5.02
托克逊县	Toksun County	2.16	1.93	8.79	8.16	2.79
哈密地区	**Hami [Kumul] Administrative Offices**	**45.93**	**25.03**	**6.67**	**26.75**	**25.85**
哈密市	Hami [Kumul] City	40.44	23.10		17.34	23.10
巴里坤哈萨克自治县	Barkol Kazak Autonomous County	4.76	1.50	5.34	7.93	2.16
伊吾县	Yiwu [Araturuk] County	0.73	0.43	1.34	1.47	0.60
昌吉回族自治州	**Changji Hui Autonomous Prefecture**	**123.93**	**58.80**	**32.51**	**93.23**	**63.21**
昌吉市	Changji City	39.35	23.21		16.14	23.21
阜康市	Fukang City	15.85	7.68		8.17	7.68
米泉市	Miquan City	18.64	7.40		11.24	7.40
呼图壁县	Hutubi County	17.12	6.60	3.60	12.74	7.98
玛纳斯县	Manas County	10.08	3.96	6.84	11.78	5.15
奇台县	Qitai County	12.32	4.96	10.57	16.94	5.95
吉木萨尔县	Jimsar County	6.67	3.21	6.68	9.65	3.70
木垒哈萨克自治县	Mori Kazak Autonomous County	3.88	1.79	4.82	6.56	2.14
伊犁哈萨克自治州	**Ili Kazak Autonomous Prefecture**	**228.32**	**129.45**	**186.26**	**260.69**	**153.89**
伊犁州直属县(市)	**Counties (Cities) Direct Under Ili Prefecture**	**126.66**	**68.06**	**128.99**	**173.02**	**82.63**
伊宁市	Yining [Gulja] City	43.03	28.00		15.03	28.00
奎屯市	Kuytun City	29.91	16.54		13.37	16.54

注：①全区城镇、乡村人口按“五普”口径计算，各地、州、市城镇人口为公安年报中市人口+县辖镇人口。②各地、州、市农业人口数均含未落常住户口人员。

Note: a) The Total urban and rural population in Xinjiang is calculated on the 5th National population census, the urban population of different prefectures is calculated on the annals of public security in cities and townships under counties. b) The figure of rural population refers to resident population in rural areas.

4-6 续表 1 Continued

单位：万人　　　　(10 000 persons)

地　　区	Region	城镇人口 City/town Population	#非农业人口 Non-agri-cultural Population	乡村人口 Rural Population	农业人口 Agricul-tural Population	非农业人口 Non-agri-cultural Population
伊宁县	Yining [Gulja] County	5.01	2.63	31.26	31.14	5.13
察布查尔锡伯自治县	Qapqal Xibe Autonomous County	3.17	1.85	13.59	12.85	3.91
霍城县	Huocheng [Korgas] County	17.40	5.08	19.04	28.36	8.08
巩留县	Gongliu [Tokkuztara] County	2.81	2.12	13.41	13.04	3.18
新源县	Xinyuan [Kunes] County	16.19	4.76	13.57	24.14	5.62
昭苏县	Zhaosu [Mongolkure] County	2.49	2.07	13.40	11.80	4.09
特克斯县	Tekes County	3.54	2.55	12.15	11.80	3.89
尼勒克县	Nilka County	3.10	2.45	12.57	11.48	4.19
塔城地区	**Tacheng [Tarbagatai] Administrative Offices**	**67.43**	**38.34**	**29.19**	**53.29**	**43.34**
塔城市	Tacheng [Qoqek] City	15.95	7.64		8.31	7.64
乌苏市	Usu City	21.03	7.73		13.30	7.73
额敏县	Emin [Dorbiljin] County	5.48	5.34	14.64	12.42	7.70
沙湾县	Shawan County	17.38	11.56	2.92	7.71	12.59
托里县	Toli County	3.98	3.01	4.93	5.55	3.36
裕民县	Yumin [Qagantokay] County	1.28	1.27	4.06	3.42	1.92
和布克赛尔蒙古自治县	Hoboksar Mongol Autonomous County	2.34	1.79	2.65	2.59	2.40
阿勒泰地区	**Altay Administrative Offices**	**34.22**	**23.04**	**28.08**	**34.38**	**27.92**
阿勒泰市	Altay City	22.63	12.45		10.18	12.45
布尔津县	Burqin County	1.85	1.80	4.74	4.17	2.42
富蕴县	Fuyun [Koktokay] County	2.78	2.50	5.80	5.01	3.57
福海县	Fuhai [Burultokay] County	2.37	2.37	4.79	3.66	3.50
哈巴河县	Habahe [Kaba] County	1.87	1.76	6.10	5.34	2.62
青河县	Qinghe [Qinggil] County	1.47	1.11	4.16	3.89	1.73
吉木乃县	Jemnay County	1.25	1.06	2.51	2.14	1.62
博尔塔拉蒙古自治州	**Bortala Mongol Autonomous Prefecture**	**31.50**	**12.34**	**13.70**	**31.30**	**13.90**
博乐市	Bole [Bortala] City	24.56	9.41		15.15	9.41
精河县	Jinghe [Jing] County	4.54	1.78	8.76	10.70	2.60
温泉县	Wenquan [Araxang] County	2.40	1.16	4.95	5.45	1.89
巴音郭楞蒙古自治州	**Bayangol Mongol Autonomous Prefecture**	**71.31**	**38.97**	**43.53**	**68.71**	**46.14**
库尔勒市	Korla City	42.23	24.75		17.48	24.75
轮台县	Luntai [Bugur] County	4.33	1.94	5.37	7.17	2.53
尉犁县	Yuli [Lopnur] County	2.03	1.17	9.07	8.65	2.46
若羌县	Ruoqiang [Qarkilik] County	0.74	0.60	2.42	2.36	0.80
且末县	Qiemo [Qarqan] County	1.75	1.46	4.06	3.82	1.99
焉耆回族自治县	Yanji Hui Autonomous County	7.25	3.46	5.22	8.20	4.27
和静县	Hejing County	9.01	3.11	8.93	12.13	5.82
和硕县	Hoxud County	1.65	1.54	5.09	4.42	2.33
博湖县	Bohu [Bagrax] County	2.33	0.93	3.36	4.48	1.21

4-6 续表 2 Continued

单位：万人 (10 000 persons)

地区	Region	城镇人口 City/town Population	#非农业人口 Non-agri-cultural Population	乡村人口 Rural Population	农业人口 Agricul-tural Population	非农业人口 Non-agri-cultural Population
阿克苏地区	**Aksu Administrative Offices**	**139.99**	**54.45**	**82.77**	**162.98**	**59.78**
阿克苏市	Aksu City	56.87	26.48		30.38	26.48
温宿县	Wensu [Onsu] County	11.79	3.74	10.94	18.01	4.72
库车县	Kuqa County	29.41	9.38	12.00	31.08	10.32
沙雅县	Xayar County	14.77	4.14	6.55	16.93	4.39
新和县	Xinhe [Toksu] County	4.32	2.00	10.23	11.95	2.60
拜城县	Baicheng [Bay] County	9.29	3.15	11.65	17.17	3.77
乌什县	Wushi [Uxturpan] County	2.59	2.05	16.53	16.29	2.84
阿瓦提县	Awat County	9.98	2.72	11.56	17.83	3.71
柯坪县	Kalpin County	0.97	0.80	3.31	3.34	0.95
克孜勒苏柯尔克孜自治州	**Kizilsu Kirgiz Autonomous Prefecture**	**26.54**	**9.93**	**20.27**	**35.17**	**11.64**
阿图什市	Artux City	21.13	6.32		14.81	6.32
阿克陶县	Akto County	3.15	1.35	14.31	15.36	2.10
阿合奇县	Akqi County	0.71	0.71	2.89	2.56	1.04
乌恰县	Wuqia [Ulugqat] County	1.55	1.55	3.07	2.45	2.18
喀什地区	**Kashgar [Kaxgar] Administrative Offices**	**112.69**	**58.86**	**248.85**	**278.12**	**83.42**
喀什市	Kashgar [Kaxgar] City	35.45	23.83		11.62	23.83
疏附县	Shufu County	2.76	1.78	34.27	33.86	3.16
疏勒县	Shule County	8.38	2.69	21.90	26.47	3.81
英吉沙县	Yengisar County	2.49	2.44	20.82	19.95	3.36
泽普县	Zepu [Poskam] County	5.04	4.31	12.23	11.88	5.38
莎车县	Shache [Yarkant] County	26.92	7.23	39.75	56.23	10.44
叶城县	Yecheng [Kagilik] County	9.98	6.01	28.27	31.40	6.85
麦盖提县	Makit County	2.87	2.78	18.90	17.81	3.95
岳普湖县	Yopurga County	3.59	1.45	10.54	12.11	2.02
伽师县	Jiashi [Payzawat] County	3.84	1.65	29.96	30.90	2.91
巴楚县	Bachu [Maralbexi] County	10.39	3.94	29.82	23.52	16.69
塔什库尔干塔吉克自治县	Taxkorgan Tajik Autonomous County	1.00	0.74	2.40	2.37	1.02
和田地区	**Hotan Administrative Offices**	**48.31**	**19.22**	**128.89**	**151.98**	**25.23**
和田市	Hotan City	19.25	10.45		8.80	10.45
和田县	Hotan County	5.06	0.28	22.77	26.59	1.23
墨玉县	Moyu [Karakax] County	5.11	1.70	38.50	40.69	2.92
皮山县	Pishan [Guma] County	4.55	1.84	17.97	19.30	3.22
洛浦县	Lop County	5.00	1.57	19.33	21.87	2.46
策勒县	Qira County	2.36	1.05	11.35	12.01	1.70
于田县	Yutian [Keriya] County	5.98	1.70	16.51	20.19	2.30
民丰县	Minfeng [Niya] County	1.01	0.62	2.47	2.53	0.94

4-7　各地、州、市、县(市)民族人口数

单位：人　　　　　　　　　　　　　　　　　　　　　　　　　　　　(2004 年)

地　区	Region	合　计 Total	#少数民族 Minority Natlonalities	维吾尔族 Uygur	汉　族 Han	哈萨克族 Kazak
总　计	**Total**	**19631100**	**11828649**	**8976741**	**7802451**	**1381622**
乌鲁木齐市	**Urumqi City**	**1859559**	**480174**	**231853**	**1379385**	**52324**
克拉玛依市	**Karamay City**	**253864**	**64075**	**39711**	**189789**	**10817**
石河子市	**Shi Hezi City**	**642855**	**34207**	**7187**	**608648**	**3621**
吐鲁番地区	**Turpan Administrative Offices**	**579668**	**444186**	**404865**	**135482**	**252**
吐鲁番市	Turpan City	258209	202575	182088	55634	29
鄯善县	Shanshan [Piqan] County	211986	149630	138672	62356	34
托克逊县	Toksun County	109473	91981	84105	17492	189
哈密地区	**Hami [Kumul] Administrative Offices**	**526000**	**165486**	**97205**	**360514**	**47143**
哈密市	Hami [Kumul] City	404400	117326	88290	287074	10558
巴里坤哈萨克自治县	Barkol Kazak Autonomous County	100900	34607	173	66293	32627
伊吾县	Yiwu [Araturuk] County	20700	13553	8742	7147	3958
昌吉回族自治州	**Changji Hui Autonomous Prefecture**	**1564386**	**397201**	**62614**	**1167185**	**129564**
昌吉市	Changji City	393529	87364	10866	306165	17858
阜康市	Fukang City	158543	42952	9177	115591	12941
米泉市	Miquan City	186396	67744	4980	118652	3663
呼图壁县	Hutubi County	207177	46391	5608	160786	23580
玛纳斯县	Manas County	169275	30907	5175	138368	17710
奇台县	Qitai County	228918	54825	15900	174093	22411
吉木萨尔县	Jimsar County	133564	39150	6562	94414	10093
木垒哈萨克自治县	Mori Kazak Autonomous County	86984	27868	4346	59116	21308
伊犁哈萨克自治州	**Ili Kazak Autonomous Prefecture**	**4145796**	**2278035**	**654922**	**1867761**	**1065273**
伊犁州直属县(市)	**Counties (Cities) Direct Under Ili Prefecture**	**2556489**	**1520361**	**602405**	**1036128**	**517989**
伊宁市	Yining [Gulja] City	430258	277628	210228	152630	19853
奎屯市	Kuytun City	299147	15454	1187	283693	5288
伊宁县	Yining [Gulja] County	362731	291612	161926	71119	43941
察布查尔锡伯自治县	Qapqal Xibe Autonomous County	167607	106960	43000	60647	33683
霍城县	Huocheng [Korgas] County	364429	196861	72286	167568	29774
巩留县	Gongliu [Tokkuztara] County	162198	112520	37167	49678	49681
新源县	Xinyuan [Kunes] County	297613	178909	27781	118704	129355
昭苏县	Zhaosu [Mongolkure] County	158932	110679	15517	48253	73764

Population of Major Nationalities by Prefecture, Autonomous Prefecture, City and County

(Person)

回　族 Hui	柯尔克孜族 Kirgiz	蒙古族 Mongolian	锡伯族 Xibo	俄罗斯族 Russion	塔吉克族 Tajik	乌孜别克族 Uzbek	塔塔尔族 Tatar	满　族 Manchu	达斡尔族 Daur	其　它 Others
876305	**171213**	**169608**	**40762**	**11306**	**43445**	**14197**	**4732**	**24099**	**6688**	**107930**
161276	**1378**	**7713**	**4288**	**3057**	**202**	**1688**	**881**	**8911**	**456**	**6147**
6113	**124**	**2139**	**808**	**570**	**22**	**238**	**80**	**1000**	**109**	**2344**
16083	**60**	**957**	**215**	**241**	**15**	**14**	**4**	**975**	**22**	**4813**
37641		**153**	**36**	**61**		**13**	**1**	**331**	**4**	**829**
19593		88	27	48		9		163	4	526
10457		54	9	13		4	1	136		250
7591		11						32		53
15711	**16**	**2308**	**161**	**110**		**5**	**31**	**1683**	**9**	**1104**
14614	16	926	155	95		5	3	1642	8	1014
289		1373	6	15			28	32	1	63
808		9						9		27
181976	**162**	**6918**	**628**	**765**	**9**	**2372**	**961**	**3457**	**74**	**7701**
52395	84	1466	359	306	7	163	107	1320	28	2405
18781	12	368	75	106	0	30	49	193	8	1212
57104	22	631	41	81	1	6	5	280	22	908
15116	2	278	34	91			19	180	3	1480
6977	31	98	34	96		19	9	173	13	572
11955	4	1690	60	61		594	495	1128		527
18850	6	2371	17	15	1	481	195	133		426
798	1	16	8	9		1079	82	50		171
344532	**17219**	**69814**	**33094**	**5500**	**159**	**5908**	**2611**	**4836**	**5839**	**68328**
255478	**15063**	**30223**	**31167**	**1513**	**132**	**5293**	**959**	**3742**	**440**	**55957**
32456	549	1160	4119	713	65	3445	421	1885	52	2682
6114	24	992	278	101	3	22	5	422	40	978
58753	349	179	196	60	14	320	37	348	5	25484
7151	357	347	20481	137		60	6	87	8	1643
72434	314	642	3098	216	11	155	109	336	301	17185
19373	419	566	1501	103		252	92	272	7	3087
18653	345	141	432	89	5	435	103	166		1404
4382	3533	12365	77	36	19	221	163	86		516

4-7 续表 1

单位：人

地　　区	Region	合　计 Total	#少数民族 Minority Natlonalities	维吾尔族 Uygur	汉　族 Han	哈萨克族 Kazak
特克斯县	Tekes County	156885	117508	15841	39377	63108
尼勒克县	Nilka County	156689	112230	17472	44459	69542
塔城地区	**Tacheng [Tarbagatai] Administrative Offices**	**966281**	**404121**	**42231**	**562160**	**237336**
塔城市	Tacheng [Qoqek] City	159475	57123	5022	102352	23916
乌苏市	Usu City	210255	76475	18174	133780	21417
额敏县	Emin [Dorbiljin] County	201214	89932	7739	111282	67409
沙湾县	Shawan County	203002	63788	8731	139214	34180
托里县	Toli County	89103	63796	1146	25307	60632
裕民县	Yumin [Qagantokay] County	53356	20218	204	33138	15932
和布克赛尔蒙古自治县	Hoboksar Mongol Autonomous County	49876	32789	1215	17087	13850
阿勒泰地区	**Altay Administrative Offices**	**623026**	**353553**	**10286**	**269473**	**309948**
阿勒泰市	Altay City	226317	87594	5030	138723	71245
布尔津县	Burqin County	65896	44911	1148	20985	36743
富蕴县	Fuyun [Koktokay] County	85769	64246	2016	21523	59597
福海县	Fuhai [Burultokay] County	71569	31829	811	39740	27875
哈巴河县	Habahe [Kaba] County	79669	53807	369	25862	47367
青河县	Qinghe [Qinggil] County	56228	46795	609	9433	43900
吉木乃县	Jemnay County	37578	24371	303	13207	23221
博尔塔拉蒙古自治州	**Bortala Mongol Autonomous Prefecture**	**451975**	**146666**	**56947**	**305309**	**42688**
博乐市	Bole [Bortala] City	245586	77600	37871	167986	17580
精河县	Jinghe [Jing] County	132989	39794	16002	93195	12351
温泉县	Wenquan [Araxang] County	73400	29272	3074	44128	12757
巴音郭楞蒙古自治州	**Bayangol Mongol Autonomous Prefecture**	**1148467**	**486934**	**370669**	**661533**	**2066**
库尔勒市	Korla City	422272	129320	108985	292952	960
轮台县	Luntai [Bugur] County	96941	81375	80901	15566	8
尉犁县	Yuli [Lopnur] County	111055	30703	29800	80352	16
若羌县	Ruoqiang [Qarkilik] County	31635	12709	11597	18926	7
且末县	Qiemo [Qarqan] County	58065	42911	42686	15154	
焉耆回族自治县	Yanji Hui Autonomous County	124689	68504	36580	56185	34
和静县	Hejing County	179428	81180	42413	98248	965
和硕县	Hoxud County	67458	21212	9251	46246	29
博湖县	Bohu [Bagrax] County	56924	19020	8456	37904	47
阿克苏地区	**Aksu Administrative Offices**	**2227673**	**1648610**	**1618740**	**579063**	**315**
阿克苏市	Aksu City	568663	227476	217308	341187	179
温宿县	Wensu [Onsu] County	227367	173974	169012	53393	3
库车县	Kuqa County	414060	365952	363055	48108	44

Continued

(Person)

回　族 Hui	柯尔克孜族 Kirgiz	蒙古族 Mongolian	锡伯族 Xibe	俄罗斯族 Russion	塔吉克族 Tajik	乌孜别克族 Uzbek	塔塔尔族 Tatar	满　族 Manchu	达斡尔族 Daur	其　它 Others
21552	8571	5917	280	1		214	19	62	6	1937
14610	602	7914	705	57	15	169	4	78	21	1041
67847	**2061**	**33678**	**1843**	**3535**	**25**	**375**	**495**	**739**	**5389**	**8567**
11079	1702	1718	1410	2437	21	155	262	250	5250	3901
27531	4	8149	163	154	1	38	11	127	28	678
5942	285	5755	81	570		124	57	107	51	1812
18975	13	438	29	110	3	20	41	147	14	1087
1000	20	636	72	10		19	64	56	7	134
2862	6	112	38	214			12	21	22	795
458	31	16870	50	40		19	48	31	17	160
21207	**95**	**5913**	**84**	**452**	**2**	**240**	**1157**	**355**	**10**	**3804**
6480	37	2647	48	215	1	177	369	202	2	1141
3972	6	1623	8	139	1	3	355	41	1	871
1819	13	285	11	44		16	94	44	7	300
2385	1	235	8	35			42	28		409
4856	6	372	4			5	68	3		757
1055	6	732	4	11		25	208	11		234
640	26	19	1	8		14	21	26		92
16214	**81**	**26989**	**390**	**166**	**5**	**145**	**14**	**353**	**24**	**2650**
8528	29	11906	283	138	5	83	9	260	9	899
5177	20	4904	54	26		30	3	62		1165
2509	32	10179	53	2		32	2	31	15	586
59280	**141**	**48083**	**170**	**319**	**3**	**104**	**1**	**1043**	**13**	**5042**
11016	8	5611	149	281	3	62	1	764	7	1473
326		35	7	5				22		71
544		23		4		14		18	6	278
747	1	15						8		334
165		14	2			4		7		33
28090	42	3012		2		19		73		652
6558	79	29778	11	18		5		95		1258
5981	0	5436	1	9				37		468
5853	11	4159						19		475
13562	**9536**	**796**	**94**	**137**	**32**	**145**	**1**	**491**	**3**	**4758**
5441	246	580	63	84	13	44		343	1	3174
761	3649	23	1	2				9	1	513
2340	131	62	14	20	1	30		72		183

4-7 续表 2

单位：人

地　　区	Region	合　计 Total	#少数民族 Minority Natlonalities	维吾尔族 Uygur	汉　族 Han	哈萨克族 Kazak
沙雅县	Xayar County	213174	179773	178161	33401	45
新和县	Xinhe [Toksu] County	145486	136173	135788	9313	10
拜城县	Baicheng [Bay] County	209385	181502	179420	27883	10
乌什县	Wushi [Uxturpan] County	191257	178675	172619	12582	3
阿瓦提县	Awat County	215430	163539	161890	51891	21
柯坪县	Kalpin County	42851	41546	41487	1305	
克孜勒苏柯尔克孜自治州	**Kizilsu Kirgiz Autonomous Prefecture**	**468097**	**436608**	**297273**	**31489**	**140**
阿图什市	Artux City	211265	192227	167823	19038	75
阿克陶县	Akto County	174603	169602	120429	5001	27
阿合奇县	Akqi County	36002	33275	1101	2727	24
乌恰县	Wuqia [Ulugqat] County	46227	41504	7920	4723	14
喀什地区	**Kashgar [Kaxgar] Administrative Offices**	**3615397**	**3305909**	**3252470**	**309488**	**941**
喀什市	Kashgar [Kaxgar] City	354479	283545	280525	70934	43
疏附县	Shufu County	370250	364538	363654	5712	41
疏勒县	Shule County	302832	283131	282169	19701	
英吉沙县	Yengisar County	233029	229000	228281	4029	2
泽普县	Zepu [Poskam] County	172657	138781	134150	33876	4
莎车县	Shache [Yarkant] County	666658	641508	635516	25150	54
叶城县	Yecheng [Kagilik] County	382490	359094	354399	23396	21
麦盖提县	Makit County	217666	170313	169713	47353	3
岳普湖县	Yopurga County	141261	133198	133062	8063	1
伽师县	Jiashi [Payzawat] County	338036	331315	331201	6721	7
巴楚县	Bachu [Maralbexi] County	402096	339119	337820	62977	6
塔什库尔干塔吉克自治县	Taxkorgan Tajik Autonomous County	33943	32367	1980	1576	759
和田地区	**Hotan Administrative Offices**	**1772067**	**1714425**	**1710673**	**57642**	**65**
和田市	Hotan City	192473	158530	157483	33943	23
和田县	Hotan County	278275	276787	276538	1488	
墨玉县	Moyu [Karakax] County	436082	430582	430450	5500	
皮山县	Pishan [Guma] County	225148	222012	220117	3136	
洛浦县	Lop County	243324	239370	239266	3954	24
策勒县	Qira County	137122	134856	134793	2266	
于田县	Yutian [Keriya] County	224882	221321	221103	3561	18
民丰县	Minfeng [Niya] County	34761	30967	30923	3794	

Continued

(Person)

回　族 Hui	柯尔克孜族 Kirgiz	蒙古族 Mongolian	锡伯族 Xibe	俄罗斯族 Russian	塔吉克族 Tajik	乌孜别克族 Uzbek	塔塔尔族 Tatar	满　族 Manchu	达斡尔族 Daur	其　它 Others
1211	7	38	7	14	18	3		30	1	238
286	4	6	2	11				10		56
872	1085	18	2					16		79
1523	4342	14	2	1		54	1	7		109
1121	29	53	3	5		14		4		399
7	43	2								7
590	**134126**	**47**	**14**	**3**	**4085**	**95**	**23**	**39**		**173**
224	23904	35	4	3	24	4	0	28		103
247	44744	10	1		4061	40	23			20
75	32057	2	1							15
44	33421		8			51		11		35
5198	**4193**	**370**	**79**	**153**	**37192**	**3150**	**21**	**442**	**7**	**1693**
1214	220	87	34	48	148	625	16	180	4	401
93	631	10	2		4	18		10		75
256	566	41	1	2		6		15		75
44	590	2		1	19	11	2	20		28
763	102	44	8	15	3264	51	2	33		345
870	981	58	26	7	2428	1446		47	3	72
696	1034	19	5	9	1844	889		29		149
407	1	17		1		26		21		124
60		17			3			6		49
19		16			2	16		27		27
759	17	51	1	8	2	62	1	51		341
17	51	8	2	62	29478			3		7
1376	**904**	**79**	**6**	**8**	**890**	**49**	**13**	**77**		**285**
744	24	34	3	8	5	20	6	45		135
244								3		2
82		3	2			5		8		32
86	877	4			885	4				39
38		17	1					6		18
40		1				7		1		14
134	2	13				1		14		36
8	1	7				12	7			9

4-8　主要年份分民族人口数
Population by Nationality in Main Years

单位：万人　　(10 000 Persons)

年 份 Year	维吾尔族 Uygur	汉 族 Han	哈萨克族 Kazak	回 族 Hui	柯尔克孜族 Kirgiz	蒙古族 Mongolian	锡伯族 Xibo
1978	555.53	512.90	82.10	53.12	10.40	10.74	2.55
1980	576.46	531.03	87.68	56.56	10.89	11.32	2.59
1985	629.44	534.92	98.72	59.96	12.35	12.33	2.93
1990	724.95	574.66	113.92	68.89	14.44	14.28	3.42
1991	736.28	584.21	116.13	70.37	14.69	14.47	3.51
1992	747.41	594.00	118.20	72.18	15.09	14.76	3.58
1993	758.95	603.67	119.64	73.23	15.42	14.92	3.68
1994	769.73	616.48	121.70	74.04	15.62	15.20	3.74
1995	780.00	631.81	123.77	74.76	15.78	15.28	3.82
1996	791.60	643.28	125.70	76.02	16.05	15.54	3.89
1997	802.00	660.13	127.08	77.06	16.27	15.75	3.90
1998	813.95	674.11	128.70	78.20	16.41	15.91	3.95
1999	825.03	687.15	130.45	79.26	16.64	16.13	4.00
2000	852.33	725.08	131.87	83.93	16.47	16.20	4.05
2001	860.56	742.20	131.92	84.42	17.01	16.19	4.13
2002	869.23	759.57	133.35	85.46	17.13	16.38	4.10
2003	882.35	771.10	135.21	86.67	17.37	16.69	4.03
2004	897.67	780.25	138.16	87.63	17.12	16.96	4.08

年 份 Year	俄罗斯族 Russian	塔吉克族 Tajik	乌孜别克族 Uzbek	塔塔尔族 Tatar	满 族 Manchu	达斡尔族 Daur	其他民族 Others
1978	0.06	2.28	0.77	0.31	0.42	0.41	1.42
1980	0.06	2.41	0.79	0.31	0.50	0.40	2.24
1985	0.43	2.89	0.93	0.33	0.95	0.48	4.49
1990	0.75	3.44	1.14	0.40	1.66	0.56	6.65
1991	0.80	3.45	1.17	0.44	1.75	0.55	6.75
1992	0.85	3.60	1.21	0.42	1.84	0.57	6.92
1993	0.86	3.61	1.28	0.44	1.89	0.58	7.09
1994	0.86	3.68	1.29	0.43	1.93	0.59	7.41
1995	0.90	3.82	1.33	0.47	1.99	0.62	7.00
1996	0.92	3.89	1.35	0.47	2.05	0.63	7.90
1997	0.92	3.90	1.35	0.46	2.06	0.63	6.56
1998	0.93	3.96	1.37	0.47	2.09	0.64	6.66
1999	0.94	4.01	1.39	0.48	2.12	0.65	6.75
2000	1.09	4.09	1.36	0.48	2.31	0.66	9.48
2001	1.08	4.12	1.37	0.47	2.30	0.67	9.75
2002	1.12	4.07	1.39	0.48	2.35	0.67	9.89
2003	1.11	4.09	1.46	0.49	2.39	0.67	10.32
2004	1.13	4.35	1.42	0.47	2.41	0.67	10.79

4-9 各地、州、市、县(市)人口自然变动情况

Statistics on Population Natural Changes by Prefecture, Autonomous Prefecture, City and County

单位： (2004 年) (‰)

地　区	Region	出生率 Birth Rate	#少数民族 Minority Natlonalities	死亡率 Death Rate	#少数民族 Minority Natlonalities	自然增长率 Natural Growth Rate	#少数民族 Minority Natlonalities
总　计	**Total**	**16.00**	**20.20**	**5.09**	**5.91**	**10.91**	**14.29**
乌鲁木齐市	**Urumqi City**	**7.96**	**11.53**	**5.37**	**6.98**	**2.59**	**4.55**
克拉玛依市	**Karamay City**	**7.04**	**9.95**	**2.99**	**3.88**	**4.05**	**6.07**
石河子市	**Shi Hezi City**	**6.33**	**11.79**	**4.10**	**4.34**	**2.23**	**7.45**
吐鲁番地区	**Turpan Administrative Offices**	**13.54**	**15.41**	**3.13**	**3.34**	**10.41**	**12.06**
吐鲁番市	Turpan City	14.38	16.08	3.52	3.61	10.86	12.48
鄯善县	Shanshan [Piqan] County	11.33	13.29	2.25	2.35	9.09	10.94
托克逊县	Toksun County	15.86	17.36	3.94	4.38	11.92	12.98
哈密地区	**Hami [Kumul] Administrative Offices**	**9.85**	**15.60**	**3.93**	**4.56**	**5.81**	**11.04**
哈密市	Hami [Kumul] City	9.51	15.25	3.86	4.69	5.65	10.56
巴里坤哈萨克自治县	Barkol Kazak Autonomous County	10.59	17.69	4.38	4.35	5.65	13.34
伊吾县	Yiwu [Araturuk] County	12.89	13.70	3.08	3.98	9.81	9.72
昌吉回族自治州	**Changji Hui Autonomous Prefecture**	**10.38**	**15.68**	**3.42**	**3.28**	**6.96**	**12.39**
昌吉市	Changji City	10.05	14.80	2.97	3.17	7.07	11.63
阜康市	Fukang City	9.74	14.72	3.72	3.55	6.02	11.17
米泉市	Miquan City	11.32	16.10	4.01	3.82	7.31	12.28
呼图壁县	Hutubi County	9.29	13.26	2.69	2.30	6.60	10.95
玛纳斯县	Manas County	10.98	14.90	3.15	2.61	7.83	12.29
奇台县	Qitai County	9.26	15.98	3.45	3.28	5.81	12.70
吉木萨尔县	Jimsar County	11.90	15.74	3.25	2.54	8.65	13.20
木垒哈萨克自治县	Mori Kazak Autonomous County	13.12	23.09	6.05	5.33	7.06	17.76
伊犁哈萨克自治州	**Ili Kazak Autonomous Prefecture**	**14.57**	**18.81**	**3.58**	**4.17**	**10.99**	**14.64**
伊犁州直属县(市)	**Counties (Cities) Direct Under Ili Prefecture**	**15.73**	**19.77**	**3.44**	**3.71**	**12.29**	**16.06**
伊宁市	Yining [Gulja] City	17.55	22.32	3.29	3.67	14.26	18.65
奎屯市	Kuytun City	7.14	10.10	3.37	2.70	3.77	7.40
伊宁县	Yining [Gulja] County	22.09	23.95	2.87	2.83	19.22	21.12
察布查尔锡伯自治县	Qapqal Xibe Autonomous County	13.93	14.51	3.83	4.10	10.10	10.41
霍城县	Huocheng [Korgas] County	13.41	17.18	2.31	2.37	11.10	14.81
巩留县	Gongliu [Tokkuztara] County	14.95	15.72	2.16	2.21	12.79	13.51
新源县	Xinyuan [Kunes] County	17.73	22.27	7.07	8.73	10.66	13.54
昭苏县	Zhaosu [Mongolkure] County	17.53	20.86	3.60	3.92	13.93	16.94
特克斯县	Tekes County	13.73	14.93	2.31	2.49	11.42	12.45
尼勒克县	Nilka County	16.24	17.16	2.91	2.82	13.34	14.34

注:喀什地区莎车县出生率、少数民族出生率有所调整。

Note: Slight shift is made in birth rate and birth rate for ethnic minorities in Shache County in Kashgar prefecture

4-9 续表 1 Continued

单位：‰ (‰)

地　　区	Region	出生率 Birth Rate	#少数民族 Minority Natlonalities	死亡率 Death Rate	#少数民族 Minority Natlonalities	自然增长率 Natural Growth Rate	#少数民族 Minority Natlonalities
塔城地区	**Tacheng [Tarbagatai] Administrative Offices**	**11.31**	**14.36**	**3.20**	**4.31**	**8.11**	**10.05**
塔城市	Tacheng [Qoqek] City	11.00	14.81	4.84	6.81	6.16	7.99
乌苏市	Usu City	11.88	13.40	1.54	2.01	10.34	11.39
额敏县	Emin [Dorbiljin] County	11.64	15.81	3.47	4.28	8.16	11.53
沙湾县	Shawan County	10.89	16.19	2.19	2.47	8.70	13.72
托里县	Toli County	11.42	12.84	4.50	5.15	6.92	7.69
裕民县	Yumin [Qagantokay] County	11.29	14.18	3.54	5.73	7.75	8.44
和布克赛尔蒙古自治县	Hoboksar Mongol Autonomous County	10.08	11.32	5.31	6.46	4.77	4.86
阿勒泰地区	**Altay Administrative Offices**	**14.86**	**19.81**	**4.75**	**6.01**	**10.11**	**13.81**
阿勒泰市	Altay City	12.08	19.22	5.08	7.37	7.00	11.85
布尔津县	Burqin County	17.01	20.59	5.05	6.30	11.96	14.29
富蕴县	Fuyun [Koktokay] County	18.67	21.36	5.24	6.14	13.43	15.22
福海县	Fuhai [Burultokay] County	15.21	23.47	3.59	5.18	11.62	18.29
哈巴河县	Ha Bahe [Kaba] County	13.71	16.18	5.17	6.25	8.54	9.93
青河县	Qinghe [Qinggil] County	18.61	20.39	4.08	4.34	14.53	16.05
吉木乃县	Jeminay County	15.42	18.65	3.40	3.94	12.02	14.71
博尔塔拉蒙古自治州	**Bortala Mongol Autonomous Prefecture**	**12.71**	**18.59**	**3.02**	**4.16**	**9.68**	**14.42**
博乐市	Bole [Bortala] City	11.88	17.26	2.10	2.44	9.78	14.82
精河县	Jinghe [Jing] County	14.57	22.56	3.44	4.69	11.13	17.87
温泉县	Wenquan [Araxang] County	12.13	16.72	5.34	7.96	6.79	8.76
巴音郭楞蒙古自治州	**Bayangol Mongol Autonomous Prefecture**	**11.29**	**15.53**	**3.96**	**5.10**	**7.33**	**10.43**
库尔勒市	Korla City	10.92	17.88	3.12	4.37	7.80	13.51
轮台县	Luntai [Bugur] County	14.12	14.65	3.98	4.30	10.14	10.35
尉犁县	Yuli [Lopnur] County	14.13	14.39	4.91	6.03	9.23	8.37
若羌县	Ruoqiang [Qarkilik] County	12.21	16.07	3.34	3.64	8.87	12.43
且末县	Qiemo [Qarqan] County	12.42	13.61	4.27	5.21	8.14	8.39
焉耆回族自治县	Yanji Hui Autonomous County	16.31	17.91	5.32	5.58	10.99	12.32
和静县	Hejing County	9.60	12.99	4.84	6.27	4.76	6.72
和硕县	Hoxud County	9.60	14.25	3.64	6.70	5.96	7.55
博湖县	Bohu [Bagrax] County	8.92	13.11	3.01	4.05	5.91	9.05
阿克苏地区	**Aksu Administrative Offices**	**13.91**	**15.72**	**3.68**	**4.12**	**10.23**	**11.61**
阿克苏市	Aksu City	9.89	12.67	3.00	3.59	6.89	9.08
温宿县	Wensu [Onsu] County	13.40	15.12	3.71	3.76	9.69	11.36
库车县	Kuqa County	14.20	14.96	4.01	4.25	10.18	10.72

4-9 续表 2 Continued

单位：‰ (‰)

地　　区	Region	出生率 Birth Rate	#少数民族 Minority Natlonalities	死亡率 Death Rate	#少数民族 Minority Natlonalities	自然增长率 Natural Growth Rate	#少数民族 Minority Natlonalities
沙雅县	Xayar County	19.19	19.58	2.69	2.92	16.27	16.65
新和县	Xinhe [Toksu] County	17.67	18.27	5.13	5.40	12.27	12.87
拜城县	Baicheng [Bay] County	13.58	14.91	5.09	5.60	7.99	9.31
乌什县	Wushi [Uxturpan] County	20.23	20.38	5.71	5.69	14.54	14.69
阿瓦提县	Awat County	9.64	9.62	1.39	1.51	8.12	8.11
柯坪县	Kalpin County	24.30	24.77	5.20	5.31	18.99	19.46
克孜勒苏柯尔克孜自治州	**Kizilsu Kirgiz Autonomous Prefecture**	**12.78**	**13.07**	**5.22**	**5.40**	**7.37**	**7.67**
阿图什市	Artux City	10.92	11.13	5.85	6.10	4.82	5.03
阿克陶县	Akto County	14.07	14.34	3.99	4.08	9.99	10.26
阿合奇县	Akqi County	16.69	17.05	8.18	8.72	7.97	8.33
乌恰县	Wuqia [Ulugqat] County	13.26	13.67	4.75	4.97	8.29	8.71
喀什地区	**Kashgar [Kaxgar] Administrative Offices**	**17.21**	**17.97**	**6.19**	**6.49**	**10.72**	**11.48**
喀什市	Kashgar [Kaxgar] City	16.35	18.76	6.22	6.88	9.47	11.88
疏附县	Shufu County	16.59	16.54	7.76	7.89	8.71	8.65
疏勒县	Shule County	13.24	13.69	6.78	6.88	6.37	6.81
英吉沙县	Yengisar County	18.75	18.84	6.40	6.50	12.25	12.34
泽普县	Zepu [Poskam] County	13.08	11.86	5.14	5.12	7.96	6.74
莎车县	Shache [Yarkant] County	18.34	18.93	9.05	9.28	9.06	9.65
叶城县	Yecheng [Kagilik] County	17.30	17.47	4.07	4.20	13.10	13.27
麦盖提县	Makit County	9.82	9.09	3.83	4.09	5.73	5.00
岳普湖县	Yopurga County	15.80	16.22	6.51	6.57	9.23	9.65
伽师县	Jiashi [Payzawat] County	16.68	16.83	5.64	5.71	10.97	11.12
巴楚县	Bachu [Maralbexi] County	25.65	29.80	3.84	4.32	21.33	25.48
塔什库尔干塔吉克自治县	Taxkorgan Tajik Autonomous County	14.54	14.73	3.40	3.54	11.00	11.19
和田地区	**Hotan Administrative Offices**	**18.28**	**18.59**	**5.81**	**5.91**	**12.37**	**12.67**
和田市	Hotan City	14.59	15.67	3.70	3.91	10.68	11.75
和田县	Hotan County	24.87	24.93	4.23	4.25	20.62	20.69
墨玉县	Moyu [Karakax] County	16.96	17.09	5.30	5.29	11.66	11.80
皮山县	Pishan [Guma] County	21.65	21.83	7.29	7.37	14.28	14.47
洛浦县	Lop County	13.69	13.79	6.94	7.02	6.67	6.77
策勒县	Qira County	18.79	18.89	7.30	7.37	11.42	11.51
于田县	Yutian [Keriya] County	17.44	17.57	6.92	7.00	10.44	10.57
民丰县	Minfeng [Niya] County	16.11	17.06	5.94	6.45	9.65	10.60

4-10 各地、州、市计划生育及领证情况

Family Planning and Certificate Receiving by Prefecture, Autonomous Prefecture and City

(2004 年)

地　区	Region	计划生育率 (%) Family Planning Rate (%)	领证率 (%) Coverage of One-child Certificate (%)	领取计划生育证人数 (人) Number of Persons Receiving Certificatesof Honor (person)	领取独生子女证人数 (人) Number of Married Couples with One-child Certificate (person)	已婚育龄妇女人数 (人) Number of Married Bearing-age Women
总　计	**Total**	**99.67**	**20.64**	**176934**	**538036**	**3463581**
乌鲁木齐市	Urumqi City	99.85	56.10	36198	115249	269967
克拉玛依市	Karamay City	99.94	61.21	3379	33815	60768
石河子市	Shi Hezi City	99.80	45.09	959	49230	111313
吐鲁番地区	Turpan Administrative Offices	99.99	18.69	7039	11313	98203
哈密地区	Hami [Kumul] Administrative Offices	99.85	32.88	5910	29598	107994
昌吉回族自治州	Changji Hui Autonomous Prefecture	99.68	23.68	8668	68096	324217
伊犁哈萨克自治州	Ili Kazak Autonomous Prefecture	99.63	19.99	48026	103424	757549
伊犁州直属县(市)	Counties (Cities) Direct Under Ili Prefecture	99.70	19.67	30917	60458	464591
塔城地区	Tacheng [Tarbagatai] Administrative Offices	99.53	19.52	8373	26391	178100
阿勒泰地区	Altay Administrative Offices	99.44	22.04	8736	16575	114858
博尔塔拉蒙古自治州	Bortala Mongol Autonomous Prefecture	99.62	22.64	4616	16255	92187
巴音郭楞蒙古自治州	Bayangol Mongol Autonomous Prefecture	99.73	25.50	13521	43282	222790
阿克苏地区	Aksu Administrative Offices	99.62	11.87	14277	33768	404900
克孜勒苏柯尔克孜自治州	Kizilsu Kirgiz Autonomous Prefecture	99.69	8.20	3868	2437	76871
喀什地区	Kashgar [Kaxgar] Administrative Offices	99.64	7.99	23007	26047	613573
和田地区	Hotan Administrative Offices	99.61	4.02	7466	5522	323249

4-11 各年龄组人口性别构成

Composition of Gender for Population at Different Age Groups

单位：%　　(2004 年)　　(%)

年龄组 Age Group	合 计 Total	男 Male	女 Female	性别比 (女性=100) Sex Ratio (Female=100)	年龄组 Age Group	合 计 Total	男 Male	女 Female	性别比 (女性=100) Gender Ratio (Female=100)
合计 Total	**100**	**50.87**	**49.13**	**103.56**	45-49	5.54	2.69	2.85	94.35
0-4	5.96	3.11	2.85	109.43	50-54	5.26	2.59	2.68	96.66
5-9	6.80	3.43	3.36	102.05	55-59	4.02	1.88	2.14	87.81
10-14	9.31	4.66	4.65	100.33	60-64	4.29	2.16	2.13	101.32
15-19	10.04	5.28	4.77	110.73	65-69	2.92	1.62	1.30	124.80
20-24	8.17	4.14	4.03	102.73	70-74	1.85	1.11	0.74	148.80
25-29	8.41	4.21	4.21	100.00	75-79	0.83	0.49	0.33	148.46
30-34	9.92	5.06	4.86	104.32	80-84	0.45	0.27	0.18	151.43
35-39	9.08	4.45	4.63	96.03	85-89	0.10	0.06	0.05	127.78
40-44	6.93	3.61	3.32	108.86	90 岁及以上 90 and over	0.12	0.05	0.05	79.17

注：表 4-10 根据自治区计生委计划生育统计年报计算，表 4-11 根据 2003 年人口变动调查数据计算。

Note: In table 4-10,data are calculated on the family planning statistic annals of Family Planning Commission in Xinjiang Uygur Autonomous Region. In table 4-11,statistics are based on population variation for the year 2003.

4-12 新疆生产建设兵团人口情况

Population of Xinjiang Production and Construction Corps

单位：人 (Person)

年 份 Year	总人口 Total Population	男 Male	女 Famale	农业人口 Agricultural Population	非农业人口 Non-Agricultural Population
1978	2119835	1090674	1029161		
1980	2200755	1127050	1073705		
1985	2222350	1142630	1079720	1182415	1039935
1990	2143528	1110475	1033053	1132435	1044093
1991	2168428	1123511	1044917	1145227	1023201
1992	2181926	1137548	1044378	1166600	1015326
1993	2197596	1150144	1047452	1143626	1053970
1994	2223957	1159806	1064151	1178247	1045710
1995	2287896	1194166	1093730	1230151	1057745
1996	2343308	1228103	1115205	1277226	1066082
1997	2383983	1252879	1131104	1283523	1100460
1998	2407148	1272600	1134548	1300587	1106561
1999	2420902	1276704	1144198	1360733	1060169
2000	2427920	1272719	1155201	1379913	1048007
2001	2453575	1289954	1163621	1325998	1127577
2002	2501189	1311750	1189439	1355526	1145663
2003	2542170	1330666	1211504	1377224	1164946
2004	2563837	1341213	1222624	1413197	1150640

年 份 Year	出生人口 Birth Population	死亡人口 Death Population	出生率(‰) Birth Rate (‰)	死亡率(‰) Death Rate (‰)	自然增长率(‰) Natural Growth Rate (‰)
1978	32749	6203	16.56	3.14	13.42
1980	26972	7162	12.27	3.26	9.01
1985	16893	7977	7.55	3.57	3.98
1990	24589	9305	11.48	4.35	7.13
1991	21840	8291	10.13	3.85	6.28
1992	21329	9014	9.81	4.14	5.67
1993	21721	9385	9.90	4.30	5.60
1994	22747	10249	10.30	4.60	5.70
1995	22519	10044	9.98	4.45	5.53
1996	21965	10093	9.49	4.36	5.13
1997	20877	9721	8.83	4.11	4.72
1998	20919	10480	8.70	4.40	4.30
1999	20565	9716	8.50	4.00	4.50
2000	22674	12525	9.40	5.20	4.20
2001	19061	9014	7.80	3.70	4.10
2002	18179	9842	7.37	3.99	3.38
2003	17218	9914	6.84	3.94	2.90
2004	15860	9864	6.21	3.86	2.35

4-13 按县、市分列的团场户数、人口数

Household and Population of Regiment Farms by City and County

(2004 年)

团 场	Regiment Farm	户数(户) Nember of Households (household)	人口数(人) Population (person)	团 场	Regiment Farm	户数(户) Nember of Households (household)	人口数(人) Population (person)
总 计	**Total**	**610986**	**1902071**	105 团	No.105 Regiment Farm	3149	9603
乌鲁木齐市	**Urumqi City**	**17616**	**57276**	106 团	No.106 Regiment Farm	1915	5981
市辖区	Areas under Municipality	15550	51005	111 团	No.111 Regiment Farm	1544	4342
104 团	No.104 Regiment Farm	5751	18057	芳草湖农场	Fang Caohu Farm	16828	53852
养禽场	Poultry Farm	865	3723	玛纳斯县	Manas County	46045	126883
三坪农场	Sanping Farm	3820	11687	147 团	No.147 Regiment Farm	7568	19857
五一农场	May Ist Farm	2959	10271	148 团	No.148 Regiment Farm	12948	32665
头屯河农场	Tou Tunhe Farm	2155	7267	149 团	No.149 Regiment Farm	7677	21070
乌鲁木齐县	Urumqi County	2066	6271	150 团	No.150 Regiment Farm	5959	19571
西山农场	Xishan Farm	2066	6271	新湖农场	Xinhu Farm	11893	33720
克拉玛依市	**Karamay City**	**6941**	**18435**	奇台县	Qitai County	11223	36412
136 团	No.136 Regiment Farm	4334	10720	108 团	No.108 Regiment Farm	1711	5703
137 团	No.137 Regiment Farm	2607	7715	109 团	No.109 Regiment Farm	1649	4875
石河子市	**Shi Hezi City**	**22762**	**65784**	110 团	No.110 Regiment Farm	1938	5448
152 团	No.152 Regiment Farm	3957	11362	奇台农场	Qitai Farm	5145	17151
石河子总场	General Shihezi Farm	18805	54422	北塔山牧场	Bei Tashan Ranch	780	3235
吐鲁番地区	**Turpan Administrative Offices**	**1729**	**5588**	阜康市	Fukang City	8294	24236
吐鲁番市	Turpan City	1729	5588	222 团	No.222 Regiment Farm	4497	12106
221 团	No.221 Regiment Farm	1729	5588	土墩子农场	Tu Dunzi Farm	1671	5113
哈密地区	**Hami [Kumul] Administrative Offices**	**21098**	**69956**	六运湖农场	Liu Yunhu Farm	2126	7017
哈密市	Hami [Kumul] City	16604	54097	吉木萨尔县	Jimsar County	4707	16695
红星一场	Red Star No.1 Farm	2521	7701	107 团	No.107 Regiment Farm	1270	4006
红星二场	Red Star No.2 Farm	2296	7174	红旗农场	Red Flag Farm	3437	12689
红星三场	Red Star No.3 Farm	1146	2866	**伊犁哈萨克自治州**	**Ili Kazak Autonomous Prefecture**	**221774**	**669002**
红星四场	Red Star No.4 Farm	1273	4982	**伊犁州直属县(市)**	**Counties (Cities) Direct Under Ili Prefecture**	**65715**	**207446**
黄田农场	Huangtian Farm	2597	8778	伊宁市	Yining [Gulja] City	623	1932
火箭农场	Huojian Farm	3023	9699	良繁场	Fine Breeding Farm	623	1932
柳树泉农场	Liu Shuquan Farm	2913	9773	奎屯市	Kuytun City	5220	19350
红星二牧场	Red Star No.2 Ranch	835	3124	131 团	No.131 Regiment Farm	5220	19350
巴里坤哈萨克自治县	Barkol Kazak Autonomous County	3827	13213	伊宁县	Yining [Gulja] County	4184	12307
红星一牧场	Red Star No.1 Ranch	1362	4463	70 团	No.70 Regiment Farm	3379	9927
红山农场	Hongshan Farm	2465	8750	拜什墩农场	Bai Shidun Farm	805	2380
伊吾县	Yiwu [Araturuk] County	667	2646	察布查尔锡伯自治县	Qapqal Xibe Autonomous County	8202	23647
淖毛湖农场	Zhuo Maohu Farm	667	2646	67 团	No.67 Regiment Farm	2219	7528
昌吉回族自治州	**Changji Hui Autonomous Prefecture**	**119858**	**353093**	68 团	No.68 Regiment Farm	3195	8689
昌吉市	Changji City	19525	57261	69 团	No.69 Regiment Farm	2788	7430
101 团	No.101 Regiment Farm	6608	18171	霍城县	Huocheng [Korgas] County	26398	84751
103 团	No.103 Regiment Farm	6606	18428	61 团	No.61 Regiment Farm	4055	12820
共青团农场	Communist League Farm	2629	9388	62 团	No.62 Regiment Farm	5246	17479
军户农场	Junhu Farm	3682	11274	63 团	No.63 Regiment Farm	3200	9793
米泉市	Miquan City	6628	17828	64 团	No.64 Regiment Farm	6280	21527
102 团	No.102 Regiment Farm	6628	17828	65 团	No.65 Regiment Farm	2371	7754
呼图壁县	Hutubi County	23436	73778	66 团	No.66 Regiment Farm	5246	15378

4-13 续表 1 Continued

团 场	Regiment Farm	户数(户) Nember of Households (household)	人口数(人) Popula-Tion (person)	团 场	Regiment Farm	户数(户) Nember of Households (household)	人口数(人) Popula-Tion (person)
巩留县	Gongliu [Tokkuztara] County	1946	6110	141 团	No.141 Regiment Farm	3212	10026
73 团	No.73 Regiment Farm	1946	6110	142 团	No.142 Regiment Farm	11986	33678
新源县	Xinyuan [Kunes] County	7994	23535	143 团	No.143 Regiment Farm	11471	34911
71 团	No.71 Regiment Farm	4469	13293	144 团	No.144 Regiment Farm	5192	12538
72 团	No.72 Regiment Farm	3525	10242	151 团	No.151 Regiment Farm	2058	6135
昭苏县	Zhaosu [Mongolkure] County	8264	26317	托里县	Toli County	1186	4096
74 团	No.74 Regiment Farm	1219	3712	170 团	No.170 Regiment Farm	1186	4096
75 团	No.75 Regiment Farm	1233	3745	裕民县	Yumin [Qagantokay] County	1697	5299
76 团	No.76 Regiment Farm	3470	10826	161 团	No.161 Regiment Farm	1697	5299
77 团	No.77 Regiment Farm	2342	8034	和布克赛尔蒙古自治县	Hoboksar Mongol Autonomous County	2905	9346
特克斯县	Tekes County	1315	4579	184 团	No.184 Regiment Farm	2905	9346
78 团	No.78 Regiment Farm	1315	4579	**阿勒泰地区**	**Altay Administrative Offices**	**16777**	**51479**
尼勒克县	Nilka County	1569	4918	阿勒泰市	Altay City	5186	15653
79 团	No.79 Regiment Farm	1569	4918	181 团	No.181 Regiment Farm	3915	11745
塔城地区	**Tacheng [Tarbagatai] Administrative Offices**	**139282**	**410077**	189 团	No.189 Regiment Farm	1271	3908
塔城市	Tacheng City	5185	15310	福海县	Fuhai [Burultokay] County	8686	25919
162 团	No.162 Regiment Farm	1501	4544	182 团	No.182 Regiment Farm	1634	5466
163 团	No.163 Regiment Farm	1711	4785	183 团	No.183 Regiment Farm	2285	6006
164 团	No.164 Regiment Farm	1973	5981	187 团	No.187 Regiment Farm	1885	5934
额敏县	Emin [Dorbiljin] County	9985	32553	188 团	No.188 Regiment Farm	1685	5305
165 团	No.165 Regiment Farm	1535	5089	190 团	No.190 Regiment Farm	1197	3208
166 团	No.166 Regiment Farm	2317	8049	哈巴河县	Habahe [Kaba] County	1207	4126
167 团	No.167 Regiment Farm	1972	6180	185 团	No.185 Regiment Farm	1207	4126
168 团	No.168 Regiment Farm	1871	6025	青河县	Qinghe [Qinggil] County	631	2330
169 团	No.169 Regiment Farm	1276	3940	青河农场	Qinghe Farm	631	2330
团结农场	Tuanjie Farm	1014	3270	吉木乃县	Jeminay County	1067	3451
乌苏市	Usu City	50054	153941	186 团	No.186 Regiment Farm	1067	3451
123 团	No.123 Regiment Farm	6165	20359	**博尔塔拉蒙古自治州**	**Bortala Mongol Autonomous Prefecture**	**28190**	**91713**
124 团	No.124 Regiment Farm	5890	21972	博乐市	Bole [Bortala] City	16745	56206
125 团	No.125 Regiment Farm	7929	20866	81 团	No.81 Regiment Farm	3248	11043
126 团	No.126 Regiment Farm	4398	15396	84 团	No.84 Regiment Farm	2567	8457
127 团	No.127 Regiment Farm	5465	16387	85 团	No.85 Regiment Farm	1578	4958
128 团	No.128 Regiment Farm	6767	19167	86 团	No.86 Regiment Farm	2618	8636
129 团	No.129 Regiment Farm	5848	16093	89 团	No.89 Regiment Farm	3938	13380
130 团	No.130 Regiment Farm	7592	23701	90 团	No.90 Regiment Farm	2796	9732
沙湾县	Shawan County	68270	189532	精河县	Jinghe [Jing] County	8102	25443
121 团	No.121 Regiment Farm	8097	21049	82 团	No.82 Regiment Farm	1934	6506
122 团	No.122 Regiment Farm	7261	20120	83 团	No.83 Regiment Farm	5038	14951
132 团	No.132 Regiment Farm	4471	13280	91 团	No.91 Regiment Farm	1130	3986
133 团	No.133 Regiment Farm	5718	16042	温泉县	Wenquan [Araxang] County	3343	10064
134 团	No.134 Regiment Farm	5930	13754	87 团	No.87 Regiment Farm	1736	5593
135 团	No.135 Regiment Farm	2874	7999	88 团	No.88 Regiment Farm	1607	4471

4-13 续表 2 Continued

团 场	Regiment Farm	户数(户) Nember of House-holds (house-hold)	人口数(人) Popula-Tion (person)	团 场	Regiment Farm	户数(户) Nember of House-holds (house-hold)	人口数(人) Popula-Tion (person)
巴音郭楞蒙古自治州	**Bayangol Mongol Autonomous Prefecture**	**52044**	**152753**	乌什县	Wushi [Uxturpan] County	2665	7468
库尔勒市	Korla City	11431	34505	4 团	No.4 Regiment Farm	2665	7468
28 团	No.28 Regiment Farm	2898	8781	阿瓦提县	Awat County	5206	13922
29 团	No.29 Regiment Farm	5031	14647	3 团	No.3 Regiment Farm	5206	13922
30 团	No.30 Regiment Farm	3502	11077	**克孜勒苏柯尔克孜自治州**	**Kizilsu Kirgiz Autonomous Prefecture**	**1052**	**4245**
尉犁县	Yuli [Lopnur] County	15446	42725	阿图什市	Artux City	721	3279
31 团	No.31 Regiment Farm	3424	9873	红旗农场	Red Flag Farm	721	3279
32 团	No.32 Regiment Farm	2652	8052	乌恰县	Wuqia [Ulugqat] County	331	966
33 团	No.33 Regiment Farm	3012	7862	托云牧场	Tuoyun Ranch	331	966
34 团	No.34 Regiment Farm	2794	8495	**喀什地区**	**Kashgar [Kaxgar] Administrative Offices**	**44012**	**173719**
35 团	No.35 Regiment Farm	3564	8443	疏勒县	Shule County	2015	6032
若羌县	Ruoqiang [Qarkilik] County	2269	6773	41 团	No.41 Regiment Farm	2015	6032
36 团	No.36 Regiment Farm	2269	6773	英吉莎县	Yengisar County	352	1528
焉耆回族自治县	Yanji Hui Autonomous County	4033	12793	东风农场	Dong Feng Farm	352	1528
27 团	No.27 Regiment Farm	4033	12793	莎车县	Shache [Yarkant] County	102	404
和静县	Hejing County	13128	38286	莎车农场	Shache Farm	102	404
21 团	No.21 Regiment Farm	4211	11226	叶城县	Yecheng [Kagilik] County	410	1456
22 团	No.22 Regiment Farm	4272	11791	叶城牧场	Yechen Ranch	410	1456
23 团	No.23 Regiment Farm	2506	7298	麦盖提县	Makit County	8351	26883
223 团	No.223 Regiment Farm	2139	7971	43 团	No.43 Regiment Farm	3608	11657
和硕县	Hoxud County	3901	11888	45 团	No.45 Regiment Farm	3800	11972
24 团	No.24 Regiment Farm	3297	10052	46 团	No.46 Regiment Farm	943	3254
26 团	No.26 Regiment Farm	604	1836	岳普湖县	Yopurga County	1689	4724
博湖县	Bohu [Bagrax] County	1836	5783	42 团	No.42 Regiment Farm	1689	4724
25 团	No.25 Regiment Farm	1836	5783	伽师县	Jiashi [Payzawat] County	2868	10835
阿克苏地区	**Aksu Administrative Offices**	**65759**	**212314**	伽师总场	General Jiashi Farm	2868	10835
阿克苏市	Aksu City	49662	163302	巴楚县	Bachu [Maralbexi] County	28225	121857
1 团	No.1 Regiment Farm	6683	21083	44 团	No.44 Regiment Farm	2234	9529
2 团	No.2 Regiment Farm	3889	10489	48 团	No.48 Regiment Farm	2179	7298
7 团	No.7 Regiment Farm	3665	12585	49 团	No.49 Regiment Farm	4808	15977
8 团	No.8 Regiment Farm	3992	9744	50 团	No.50 Regiment Farm	3950	17382
9 团	No.9 Regiment Farm	5494	19874	51 团	No.51 Regiment Farm	7721	38254
10 团	No.10 Regiment Farm	3960	12390	52 团	No.52 Regiment Farm	3872	17136
11 团	No.11 Regiment Farm	3360	12189	53 团	No.53 Regiment Farm	3461	16281
12 团	No.12 Regiment Farm	5592	18106	**和田地区**	**Hotan Administrative Offices**	**8151**	**28193**
13 团	No.13 Regiment Farm	3957	13124	墨玉县	Moyu [Karakax] County	2333	7117
14 团	No.14 Regiment Farm	3037	11304	47 团	No.47 Regiment Farm	1450	4124
15 团	No.15 Regiment Farm	2492	9804	224 团	No.224 Regiment Farm	883	2993
16 团	No.16 Regiment Farm	3541	12610	皮山县	Pishan [Guma] County	5088	18858
温宿县	Wensu [Onsu] County	8226	27622	皮山农场	Pishan Farm	5088	18858
5 团	No.5 Regiment Farm	5248	17987	策勒县	Qira County	730	2218
6 团	No.6 Regiment Farm	2978	9635	一牧场	No.1Ranch	730	2218

4-14 就业基本情况
Employment

项 目	Item	1995	2000	2004
就业人员合计(万人)	**Total Number of Employed Persons (10 000 persons)**	**676.00**	**693.85**	**744.49**
第一产业	Primary Industry	388.16	388.11	403.31
第二产业	Secondary Industry	124.21	97.63	98.49
第三产业	Tertiary Industry	163.63	208.11	242.69
就业人员构成(合计=100)	**Composition of Employed Persons (total=100)**			
第一产业	Primary Industry	57.42	55.94	54.17
第二产业	Secondary Industry	18.37	14.07	13.23
第三产业	Tertiary Industry	24.21	29.99	32.60
按城乡分就业人员(万人)	**Number of Employed Persons by Urban and Rural Areas (10 000 persons)**		**693.85**	**744.49**
城镇就业人员	Urban Employed Persons		296.44	349.43
#国有单位	#State-Owned Units		150.69	188.18
城镇集体单位	Urban Collective-owned Units		71.42	6.86
股份合作单位	Joint-Stock Units		1.35	0.82
联营单位	Joint -Run Units		0.27	0.33
有限责任公司	Limited Liability Corporations		10.76	34.96
股份有限公司	Share-holding Corporations Ltd		5.66	9.70
私营企业	Private Enterprises		14.08	50.75
港澳台商投资单位	Units With Funds From Hong Kong, Macao&Taiwan		0.80	0.66
外商投资单位	Foreign Funded Units		0.48	0.84
个 体	Self-employed Individuals		40.93	55.17
乡村就业人员	Rural Employed Persons		397.41	395.06
#乡镇企业	Township And Village Enterprises		80.64	93.35
私营企业	Private Enterprises		5.24	6.50
个 体	Self-employed Individuals		19.82	19.01
在岗职工人数(万人)	**Number of Staff and Workers (10 000 persons)**	**311.93**	**255.75**	**235.97**
国有单位	State-owned Units	278.49	219.41	182.80
城镇集体单位	Urban Collective-owned Units	29.95	15.28	6.43
其他单位	Units of Other Types of Ownership	3.49	21.06	46.74
城镇单位女性就业人员(万人)	**Number of Female Employment in Urban Units (10 000 persons)**		**107.89**	**101.77**
城镇登记失业人数(万人)	**Number of Reggistered Unemployed Persons in Urban Areas (10 000 persons)**	**10.24**	**11.00**	**10.87**
城镇登记失业率(%)	**Registered Unemployment Rate in Urban Areas (%)**	**3.90**	**3.80**	**3.80**

4-15　城镇失业人数及失业率

Number of Urban Unemployed Persons and Unemployment Rate

单位：万人　　　　(10 000 persons)

年　份 Year	城镇登记失业人数 Unemployment	#失业青年 Youth	失业青年占城镇失业人数(%) Unemployed Youth as Percentage of Urban Unemployees (%)	城镇登记失业率(%) Unemployment Rate (%)
1979	12.16			7.4
1980	13.55			7.5
1985	4.04	3.55	87.9	1.9
1990	9.60	7.32	76.3	3.8
1991	9.95	7.76	78.0	3.8
1992	9.81	7.66	78.1	3.7
1993	9.50	7.53	79.3	3.6
1994	10.00	6.95	69.5	3.8
1995	10.24	6.80	66.4	3.9
1996	9.81	6.51	66.3	3.8
1997	10.20	5.92	58.0	3.8
1998	11.06	5.72	51.7	3.9
1999	10.30			3.7
2000	11.00			3.8
2001	12.07			3.7
2002	12.68			3.6
2003	12.75			3.8
2004	10.87			3.8

4-16 按三次产业分的就业人员

Number of Employed Persons by Industrial Sectors

单位：万人 (10 000 persons)

年 份 Year	经济活动人口 Economically Active Population	就业人员合计 Total	第一产业 Primary Industry	第二产业 Secondary Industry
1978		491.25	353.99	70.42
1980	519.90	506.35	354.49	75.12
1985	569.85	565.81	363.24	89.64
1990	627.30	617.70	378.47	107.42
1991	648.44	638.49	388.88	110.57
1992	656.75	646.94	386.07	111.81
1993	665.48	655.98	387.51	123.01
1994	667.54	657.54	384.08	120.80
1995	686.24	676.00	388.16	124.21
1996	693.81	684.00	390.98	119.39
1997	725.60	715.40	421.30	105.40
1998	691.98	680.92	387.80	106.22
1999	704.64	694.34	385.57	104.51
2000	704.85	693.85	388.11	97.63
2001	697.45	685.38	388.19	92.19
2002	714.17	701.49	391.84	95.82
2003	734.02	721.27	397.20	95.69
2004	755.36	744.49	403.31	98.49

年 份 Year	第三产业 Tertiary Industry	构成(合计=100) Composition in Percentage (total=100) 第一产业 Primary Industry	第二产业 Secondary Industry	第三产业 Tertiary Industry
1978	66.84	72.06	14.33	13.61
1980	76.74	70.01	14.84	15.15
1985	112.93	64.20	15.84	19.96
1990	131.81	61.27	17.39	21.34
1991	139.04	60.90	17.32	21.78
1992	149.06	59.68	17.28	23.04
1993	145.46	59.07	18.75	22.18
1994	152.66	58.41	18.37	23.22
1995	163.63	57.42	18.37	24.21
1996	173.63	57.16	17.45	25.39
1997	188.70	58.89	14.73	26.38
1998	186.90	56.95	15.60	27.45
1999	204.26	55.53	15.05	29.42
2000	208.11	55.94	14.07	29.99
2001	205.00	56.64	13.45	29.91
2002	213.83	55.86	13.66	30.48
2003	228.38	55.07	13.27	31.66
2004	242.69	54.17	13.23	32.60

4-17 按城乡分的年底就业人员数

单位：万人

年 份 Year	地 区 Region	总 计 Total	城 镇 Urban Area	国有单位 State-owned Units	集体单位 Collective-owned Units	股份合作单位 Joint-Stock Units
	2000	693.85	296.44	150.69	71.42	1.35
	2001	685.38	319.92	201.1	12.03	0.93
	2002	701.49	327.37	193.57	9.68	0.77
	2003	721.27	339.00	188.89	8.02	0.64
	2004	744.49	349.43	188.18	6.86	0.82
乌鲁木齐市	Urumqi City	98.25	90.78	33.69	1.61	0.15
克拉玛依市	Karamay City	17.24	17.10	7.54	0.85	0.03
石河子市	Shi Hezi City	12.36	11.24	4.61	0.05	0.02
吐鲁番地区	Turpan Administrative Offices	30.51	9.59	5.63	0.19	0.05
哈密地区	Hami [Kumul] Administrative Offices	19.34	9.83	5.77	0.09	0.01
昌吉回族自治州	Changji Hui Autonomous Prefecture	70.26	30.75	15.90	0.61	0.03
伊犁哈萨克自治州	Ili Kazak Autonomous Prefecture	165.78	71.05	48.80	0.69	0.16
伊犁州直属县(市)	Counties (Cities) Direct Under Ili Prefecture	92.07	33.73	19.76	0.35	0.13
塔城地区	Tacheng [Tarbagatai] Administrative Offices	51.20	25.08	19.70	0.25	0.02
阿勒泰地区	Altay Administrative Offices	22.51	12.24	9.34	0.09	0.01
博尔塔拉蒙古自治州	Bortala Mongol Autonomous Prefecture	19.90	11.66	7.88	0.17	0.01
巴音郭楞蒙古自治州	Bayangol Mongol Autonomous Prefecture	45.54	27.51	16.10	0.41	0.08
阿克苏地区	Aksu Administrative Offices	79.01	27.15	16.56	0.72	0.20
克孜勒苏柯尔克孜自治州	Kizilsu Kirgiz Autonomous Prefecture	15.11	4.69	3.32	0.08	0.01
喀什地区	Kashgar [Kaxgar] Administrative Offices	108.09	26.04	15.12	1.11	0.07
和田地区	Hotan Administrative Offices	63.10	12.04	7.26	0.28	…

Number of Employed Persons at the Year-end By Residence in Urban and Rural Areas

(10 000 persons)

联营单位 Joint -Run Units	有限责任公司 Limited	股份有限公司 Share Holding Corporations Ltd	私营企业 Private Enterprises	港澳台商投资单位 Units With Funds from Hong Kong Macao and Taiwan	外商投资单位 Foreign Funded Units	个　体 Self-employed individuals	乡 村 Rural Area	#乡镇企业 Township and Village Enterprises	#私营企业 Private Enterprises	#个　体 Self-employed individuals
0.27	10.76	5.66	14.08	0.80	0.48	40.93	397.41	80.64	5.24	19.82
0.41	26.54	9.01	23.16	0.96	0.55	45.23	365.37	82.44	4.93	19.1
0.43	33.35	7.81	34.44	1.06	0.65	45.61	373.41	86.67	4.26	20.01
0.27	34.26	10.09	42.35	0.64	0.73	51.98	382.27	88.09	6.82	18.68
0.33	34.96	9.70	50.75	0.66	0.84	55.17	395.06	93.35	6.50	19.01
0.20	11.76	2.23	27.60	0.48	0.50	12.53	7.47	5.77	1.25	0.24
0.02	2.00	2.79	1.14	0.04	…	2.69	0.14	0.14		
	1.44	1.16	1.48	0.03	0.05	2.40	1.12	0.73	0.09	0.84
0.01	0.54	0.47	1.28	0.04	0.09	1.29	20.92	4.28	0.15	2.51
0.03	1.65	0.13	0.47	0.01	0.11	1.55	9.51	2.25	0.16	0.49
0.02	3.81	0.79	4.69	...	0.02	4.83	39.51	12.79	1.16	1.86
0.03	5.09	0.82	5.15	0.05	0.05	9.63	94.73	23.40	1.28	4.10
0.02	3.20	0.62	3.42	0.02	0.05	5.74	58.34	12.07	0.43	2.12
…	1.37	0.05	1.13	0.03		2.52	26.12	6.64	0.72	1.40
0.01	0.52	0.15	0.60	...	...	1.37	10.27	4.69	0.13	0.58
...	0.80	0.02	1.47			1.31	8.24	2.30	0.18	0.64
0.01	2.56	0.33	2.37	0.01	0.02	5.60	18.03	6.50	1.02	1.13
0.01	2.08	0.62	2.15			4.80	51.86	9.33	0.60	1.59
	0.12	0.13	0.21			0.77	10.42	2.41	0.14	0.16
...	2.83	0.21	1.74			4.96	82.05	13.31	0.29	3.03
	0.28		1.00			2.81	51.06	10.14	0.18	2.42

4-18　分行业年底单位就业人员（按经济类型分）

Number of Employed Persons at the Year-end by Sectors

单位：万人　　(2004 年)　　(10 000 persons)

项　目	Item	合 计 Total	国有单位 State-owned Units	城镇集体 Urban Collective-owned Units	其他单位 Units of Other Types of Ownership
总　计	**Total**	**243.51**	**188.18**	**6.86**	**48.47**
农林牧渔业	Farming, Forestry, Animal Husbandry and Fishery	62.53	61.92	0.19	0.42
采 矿 业	Ore Mining	15.38	9.29	0.12	5.97
制 造 业	Manufacturing	25.82	5.50	1.54	18.78
电力、燃气及水的生产和供应业	Power, Gas and Water Production and Supply	5.54	2.44	0.04	3.06
建 筑 业	Construction	15.73	5.17	1.20	9.36
交通运输、仓储和邮政业	Transportation, Logistics and Post Industries	11.56	9.89	0.16	1.51
信息传输、计算机服务和软件业	Information Transmission, Computer Servcie and Software Industries	1.68	1.06	…	0.62
批发和零售业	Retail and Wholesale Industries	7.94	2.58	1.72	3.64
住宿和餐饮业	Hotel and Eateries	2.76	1.52	0.17	1.07
金融业	Financial Industry	6.73	4.63	0.87	1.23
房地产业	Real Estate Industry	2.35	0.99	0.10	1.26
租赁和商务服务业	Leasing and Business Service Industries	3.61	2.26	0.48	0.87
科学研究、技术服务和地质勘查业	Scientific Research, Technology Service and Geological Prospecting	4.60	4.27	0.01	0.32
水利、环境和公共设施管理业	Water Conservancy, Environment and Public Facility Management	4.20	4.04	0.08	0.08
居民服务和其他服务业	Residents' Service and Other Service Trade	0.38	0.30	0.02	0.06
教 育	Education	31.06	30.90	0.02	0.14
卫生、社会保障和社会福利业	Health, Social Security and Welfare Sector	10.50	10.34	0.13	0.03
文化、体育和娱乐业	Culture, Sports and Entertainment	2.38	2.33	…	0.05
公共管理和社会组织	Public Administration and Social Organizations	28.76	28.75	0.01	

4-19 分行业年底单位在岗职工人数

Number of Staff and Workers at the Year-end by Sectors

单位：万人 (2004 年) (10 000 persons)

项 目	Item	合 计 Total	国有单位 State-owned Units	城镇集体 Urban Collective-owned Units	其他单位 Units of Other Types of Ownership
总 计	**Total**	**235.97**	**182.80**	**6.43**	**46.74**
按企、事业、机关分	**Grouped by Enterprises, Institutions and Agencies**				
企 业	Enterprises	150.25	97.36	6.18	46.71
事 业	Institutions	58.33	58.06	0.24	0.03
机 关	Agencies & Organizations	27.39	27.38	0.01	
按国民经济行业分组	**Grouped by Sector**				
农林牧渔业	**Farming, Forestry, Animal Husbandry and Fishery**	**62.04**	**61.43**	**0.19**	**0.42**
农 业	Farming	49.33	49.13	0.07	0.13
林 业	Forestry	0.69	0.69	...	...
畜 牧 业	Animal Husbandry	8.46	8.31	0.01	0.14
渔 业	Fishery	0.05	0.04		0.01
农林牧渔服务业	Farming, forestry, stock-breeding and fishing	3.51	3.26	0.11	0.14
采 矿 业	**Ore Mining**	**13.78**	**7.85**	**0.10**	**5.83**
煤炭开采和洗选业	Coal Mining and Dressing	4.02	0.90	0.06	3.06
石油和天然气开采业	Petroleum and Natural Gas Extraction	8.70	6.44	0.01	2.25
黑色金属矿采选业	Ferrous Metals Mining and Dressing	0.24	0.01	0.01	0.22
有色金属矿采选业	Nonferrous Metals Mining and Dressing	0.39	0.29	...	0.10
非金属矿采选业	Nonmetal Minerals Mining and Dressing	0.42	0.21	0.02	0.19
其他采矿业	Other Ore Extraction	0.01		...	0.01
制 造 业	**Manufacturing**	**25.38**	**5.35**	**1.51**	**18.52**
农副食品加工业	Farming, Non-staple Food Processing	1.97	0.47	0.02	1.48
食品制造业	Food Manufacturing	0.89	0.22	0.02	0.65
饮料制造业	Beverage Manufacturing	1.21	0.10	0.01	1.10
烟草制品业	Tobacco Processing	0.07	0.07		...
纺织业	Textile Industry	5.64	0.81	0.34	4.49
纺织服装、鞋、帽制造业	Textile, Garment, Shoe and Hat Manufacturing	0.18	0.12	0.01	0.05
皮革、毛皮、羽毛(绒)及其制品业	Leather, Furs, Down and Related Products	0.10	...	...	0.10
木材加工及木、竹、藤、棕、草制品业	Timber Processing, Bamboo, Cane, Palm And Grass Products	0.15	0.02	...	0.13
家具制造业	Furniture Manufacturing	0.19	0.02	...	0.17
造纸及纸制品业	Papermaking and Paper Products	0.84	0.11	0.04	0.69
印刷业和记录媒介的复制	Printing and Record Medium Reproduction	0.60	0.36	0.05	0.19
石油加工、炼焦及核燃料加工业	Oil processing, Refining and Nuclear-fuel processing	2.52	1.11	0.11	1.30
化学原料及化学制品制造业	Raw Chemical Materials and Chemical Products	1.73	0.06	0.08	1.59
医药制造业	Medical and Pharmaceutical Products	0.28	0.10	...	0.18

4-19 续表 1 Continued

单位：万人 (10 000 persons)

项目	Item	合计 Total	国有单位 State-owned Units	城镇集体 Urban Collective-Owned Units	其他单位 Units of Other Types of Ownership
化学纤维制造业	Chemical Fiber	0.11	0.02		0.09
橡胶制品业	Rubber Products	0.17	0.01	...	0.16
塑料制品业	Plastic Products	0.89	0.04	0.12	0.73
非金属矿物制品业	Nonmetal Mineral Products	3.14	0.78	0.23	2.13
黑色金属冶炼及压延加工业	Smelting and Pressing of Ferrous Metals	1.60	...	0.04	1.56
有色金属冶炼及压延加工业	Smelting and Pressing of Nonferrous Metals	0.61	0.28	0.04	0.29
金属制品业	Metal Products	0.41	0.05	0.17	0.19
通用设备制造业	Manufacturing of Equipment for General Purpose	0.52	0.13	0.09	0.30
专用设备制造业	Special Purpose Equipment	0.46	0.25	0.05	0.16
交通运输设备制造业	Traffic and Transport Equipment	0.49	0.16	0.04	0.29
电气机械及器材制造业	Electric Equipment and Apparatus Manufacturing	0.49	0.05	0.02	0.42
通信设备、计算机及其他电子设备制造业	Telecommunication Equipment, Computer and Other Electronic Equipment Manufactiring	0.02			0.02
仪器仪表及文化、办公用机械制造业	Instruments, Meters, Cultural and Office Machinery	0.02	0.01		0.01
工艺品及其他制造业	Art and Handicraft Manufacturing	0.05	...	0.02	0.03
废弃资源和废旧材料回收加工业	Recycling and Processing of Deserted Resources and Old Material	0.03		0.01	0.02
电力、燃气及水的生产和供应业	**Power, Gas and Water Production and Supply**	**5.49**	**2.42**	**0.04**	**3.03**
电力、热力的生产和供应业	Electric Power, Thermal Power Production and Supply	4.71	1.78	0.03	2.90
燃气生产和供应业	Gas Production and Supply	0.16	0.12	0.01	0.03
水的生产和供应业	Water Production and Supply	0.62	0.52		0.10
建筑业	**Construction**	**14.70**	**4.89**	**0.94**	**8.87**
房屋和土木工程建筑业	House and Civil Engineering	12.94	4.59	0.68	7.67
建筑安装业	Building and Installing	1.17	0.21	0.24	0.72
建筑装饰业	Building and Decorating	0.08	0.01	0.01	0.06
其他建筑业	Other Building Sector	0.51	0.08	0.01	0.42
交通运输、仓储和邮政业	**Transportation, Logistics and Post Industries**	**10.53**	**8.88**	**0.16**	**1.49**
铁路运输业	Railway Transportation	3.47	3.47		
道路运输业	Road Transportation	3.31	2.68	0.03	0.60
城市公共交通业	Urban Public Transportation	1.41	0.92	0.03	0.46
航空运输业	Air Transportation	0.59	0.38		0.21
管道运输业	Pipe Transportation	0.06	0.01		0.05
装卸搬运和其他运输服务业	Loading and Discharging; Other Transportation Service	0.27	0.15	0.10	0.02
仓储业	Wherehousing	0.24	0.21	...	0.03
邮政业	Postal Service	1.18	1.06		0.12

4-19 续表 2 Continued

单位：万人 (10 000 persons)

项 目	Item	合 计 Total	国有单位 State-owned Units	城镇集体 Urban Collective-owned Units	其他单位 Units of Other Types of Ownership
信息传输、计算机服务和软件业	**Information Transmission, Computer Servcie And Software Industries**	**1.60**	**1.00**	**...**	**0.60**
电信和其他信息传输服务业	Telecommunication and Other I.T Transmission Service	1.52	0.98	...	0.54
计算机服务业	Computer Service	0.03	0.01		0.02
软件业	Software	0.05	0.01		0.04
批发和零售业	**Retail and Wholesale Industries**	**7.71**	**2.50**	**1.62**	**3.59**
批发业	Wholesale Trade	5.11	1.61	1.45	2.05
零售业	Retail Trade	2.60	0.89	0.17	1.54
住宿和餐饮业	**Hotel and Eateries**	**2.61**	**1.37**	**0.17**	**1.07**
住宿业	Hotel	2.05	1.16	0.15	0.74
餐饮业	Catering Trade	0.56	0.21	0.02	0.33
金融业	**Financial Industry**	**5.75**	**4.26**	**0.86**	**0.63**
银行业	Banking	3.87	2.77	0.86	0.24
证券业	Stock Exchange	0.07	0.01		0.06
保险业	Insurance	1.78	1.47		0.31
其他金融活动	Other Finance Activity	0.03	0.01	...	0.02
房地产业	**Real Estate Industry**	**2.21**	**0.87**	**0.10**	**1.24**
房地产开发经营	Real Estate Development and Management	0.82	0.16	0.04	0.62
物业管理	Real Estate Management	1.08	0.54	0.04	0.50
房地产中介服务	Broker's Service for Real Estate	0.04	0.02		0.02
租赁和商务服务业	**Leasing and Business Service Industries**	**3.48**	**2.18**	**0.48**	**0.82**
租赁业	Leasing Service	0.05	0.03	...	0.02
商务服务业	Commercial Service	3.43	2.15	0.48	0.80
科学研究、技术服务和地质勘查业	**Scientific Research, Technology Service and Geological Prospecting**	**4.43**	**4.13**	**0.01**	**0.29**
研究与试验发展	Research and Experiment Development	0.65	0.64	...	0.01
自然科学研究与试验发展	Natural Science Research and Expeirment Development	0.17	0.17		...
工程和技术研究与试验发展	Engineering and Technology Research as well as Expeirment Development	0.14	0.13		0.01
农业科学研究与试验发展	Agricultural Scientific Research and Experiment Development	0.26	0.26	...	...
医学研究与试验发展	Medical Research and Experiment Development	...	...		
社会人文科学研究与试验发展	Social and Humanity Scientific Research And Experiment Development	0.08	0.08		
专业技术服务业	Professional Technique Service	1.84	1.68	0.01	0.15
#气象服务	Meterological Service	0.26	0.26		
地震服务	Earthquake Service	0.04	0.04		
测绘服务	Surveying Service	0.11	0.11		

4-19 续表 3 Continued

单位：万人 (10 000 persons)

项　　目	Item	合 计 Total	国有单位 State-owned Units	城镇集体 Urban Collective-owned Units	其他单位 Units of Other Types of Ownership
技术检测	Technical Inspection and Survey	0.32	0.31	...	0.01
环境监测	Environment Monitoring	0.09	0.09		
工程技术与规化管理	Engineering Technology and Modern Management	0.98	0.83	0.01	0.14
科技交流和推广服务业	Science and Technology Communication and Diffusion Service	0.85	0.80	...	0.05
地质勘查业	Geological Survey	1.09	1.01		0.08
水利、环境和公共设施管理业	**Water Conservancy, Environment and Public Facility Management**	**4.10**	**3.94**	**0.08**	**0.08**
水利管理业	Water Conservance Management	2.17	2.15		0.02
环境管理业	Environment Management	1.00	0.92	0.08	...
公共设施管理业	Management of Public Management	0.93	0.87		0.06
居民服务和其他服务业	**Community Service and Other Service**	**0.38**	**0.30**	**0.02**	**0.06**
居民服务业	Community Service	0.33	0.28	0.01	0.04
其他服务业	Other Service	0.05	0.02	0.01	0.02
教　育	**Education**	**30.63**	**30.49**	**0.01**	**0.13**
#初等教育	Primary Education	13.84	13.80	...	0.04
中等教育	Secondary Education	13.03	12.99		0.04
高等教育	Higher Education	2.39	2.39		...
卫生、社会保障和社会福利业	**Health, Social Security and Welfare Sector**	**10.32**	**10.17**	**0.13**	**0.02**
卫　生	Health Care	9.94	9.79	0.13	0.02
社会保障业	Social Insurance	0.17	0.17		
社会福利业	Social Welfare	0.21	0.21	...	
文化、体育和娱乐业	**Culture, Sports and Entertainment**	**2.33**	**2.28**	**...**	**0.05**
新闻出版业	Press and Publication	0.43	0.40		0.03
广播、电影、电视和音像业	Radio, Film, TV and Audio and Video	0.95	0.95	...	
文化艺术业	Art and Culture	0.83	0.83		
体　育	Sports	0.08	0.08	...	
娱乐业	Entertainment	0.04	0.02	...	0.02
公共管理和社会组织	**Public Administration and Social Organizations**	**28.50**	**28.49**	**0.01**	
#中国共产党机关	C.P.C Organ	1.65	1.65		
国家机构	State Organs	26.36	26.35	0.01	
人民政协和民主党派	C.P..P.C.C and Democratic League	0.20	0.20		
群众团体、社会团体和宗教组织	Mass Groups, Social Groups and Religious Organizations	0.29	0.29		

4-20 分行业离开本单位仍保留劳动关系的职工人数

Number of Staff and Workers Who Have Left Their Working Units While Keeping Their Labour Contract/Employment Relation Unchanged by Sector

单位：人 (2004 年) (person)

项目	Item	合计 Total	国有单位 State-owned Units	城镇集体单位 Urban Collective-owned Units	其他单位 Units of Other Types of Ownership
总计	**Total**	**112888**	**84830**	**3121**	**24937**
按企、事业、机关分	**Grouped by Enterprises, Institutions and Agencies**				
企业	Enterprises	104171	76131	3105	24935
事业	Institutions	7000	6984	14	2
机关	Agencies & Organizations	1717	1715	2	
按国民经济行业分	**Sector**				
农林牧渔业	Farming, Forestry, Animal Husbandry and Fishery	26181	26098	58	25
采矿业	Fishery	18345	14484		3861
制造业	Manufacturing	20909	10229	529	10151
电力、燃气及水的生产和供应业	Power, Gas and Water Production and Supply	2828	991	11	1826
建筑业	Construction	9315	5173	132	4010
交通运输、仓储和邮政业	Transportation, Wherehousing and Post Service	9633	8350	27	1256
信息传输、计算机服务和软件业	Information Transmission, Computer Servcie and Software Industries	1726	1178		548
批发和零售业	Retail and Wholesale	7049	3180	1617	2252
住宿和餐饮业	Hotel and Catering	1245	1012	137	96
金融业	Financial Sector	3258	2793	396	69
房地产业	Real Estate	1589	1171	103	315
租赁和商务服务业	Leasing and Business Service Industries	1978	1548	73	357
科学研究、技术服务和地质勘查业	Scientific Research, Technology Service and Geological Prospecting	3233	3100		133
水利、环境和公共设施管理业	Water Conservancy, Environment and Public Facility Management	479	461		18
居民服务和其他服务业	Community Service and Other Service Industries	176	132	28	16
教育	Education	1850	1844	2	4
卫生、社会保障和社会福利业	Health, Social Security and Welfare Industries	1002	994	8	
文化、体育和娱乐业	Culture, Sports and Entertainment	227	227		
公共管理和社会组织	Public Administration and Social Organizations	1865	1865		
按地区分	**By Region**				
乌鲁木齐市	Urumqi City	33621	22264	884	10473
克拉玛依市	Karamay City	15987	14452	65	1470
石河子市	Shi Hezi City	5084	3828	7	1249
吐鲁番地区	Turpan Administrative Offices	1290	887	105	298
哈密地区	Hami [Kumul] Administrative Offices	3801	2332	128	1341
昌吉回族自治州	Changji Hui Autonomous Prefecture	10157	8478	229	1450
伊犁哈萨克自治州	Ili Kazak Autonomous Prefecture	22736	18513	675	3548
伊犁州直属县(市)	Counties (Cities) Direct Under Ili Prefecture	10750	7481	501	2768
塔城地区	Tacheng [Tarbagatai] Administrative Offices	8129	7343	129	657
阿勒泰地区	Altay Administrative Offices	3857	3689	45	123
博尔塔拉蒙古自治州	Bortala Mongol Autonomous Prefecture	2001	1728	33	240
巴音郭楞蒙古自治州	Bayangol Mongol Autonomous Prefecture	7105	5085	225	1795
阿克苏地区	Aksu Administrative Offices	6440	5257	233	950
克孜勒苏柯尔克孜自治州	Kizilsu Kirgiz Autonomous Prefecture	107	107		
喀什地区	Kashgar [Kaxgar] Administrative Offices	3028	1429	526	1073
和田地区	Hotan Administrative Offices	1531	470	11	1050

4-21 各地、州、市分行业年底单位在岗职工人数

Number of Staff and Workers at the Year-end by Sector and by Prefecture, Autonomous Prefecture and City

单位：万人 (2004 年) (10 000 persons)

地 区	Region	合 计 Total	农林牧渔业 Farming, Forestry, Animal Husbandry and Fishery	采 矿 业 Fishery	制 造 业 Manufacturing	电力、燃气及水的生产和供应业 Power, Gas and Water Production and Supply
总 计	**Total**	**235.97**	**62.04**	**13.78**	**25.38**	**5.49**
乌鲁木齐市	Urumqi City	48.46	1.40	1.58	9.05	0.98
克拉玛依市	Karamay City	11.43	0.87	4.73	2.02	
石河子市	Shi Hezi City	7.33	1.29		1.69	0.42
吐鲁番地区	Turpan Administrative Offices	6.92	0.43	2.28	0.46	0.22
哈密地区	Hami [Kumul] Administrative Offices	7.58	1.95	1.18	0.59	0.21
昌吉回族自治州	Changji Hui Autonomous Prefecture	20.97	7.54	0.38	3.03	0.53
伊犁哈萨克自治州	Ili Kazak Autonomous Prefecture	55.54	25.53	1.14	3.47	1.21
伊犁州直属县(市)	Counties (Cities) Direct Under Ili Prefecture	24.22	8.03	0.12	2.40	0.65
塔城地区	Tacheng [Tarbagatai] Administrative Offices	21.19	12.81	0.68	0.76	0.31
阿勒泰地区	Altay Administrative Offices	10.13	4.69	0.34	0.31	0.25
博尔塔拉蒙古自治州	Bortala Mongol Autonomous Prefecture	8.69	4.69	0.02	0.58	0.23
巴音郭楞蒙古自治州	Bayangol Mongol Autonomous Prefecture	19.31	6.61	1.75	1.78	0.35
阿克苏地区	Aksu Administrative Offices	19.59	6.76	0.41	1.37	0.40
克孜勒苏柯尔克孜自治州	Kizilsu Kirgiz Autonomous Prefecture	3.37	0.30	0.12	0.07	0.04
喀什地区	Kashgar [Kaxgar] Administrative Offices	18.61	3.60	0.02	0.94	0.68
和田地区	Hotan Administrative Offices	8.17	1.07	0.17	0.33	0.22

地 区	Region	建 筑 业 Construction	交通运输、仓储和邮政业 Transportation, Logistics and Post Industries	信息传输、计算机服务和软件业 Information Transmission, Computer Servcie and Software Industries	批发和零售业 Retail and Wholesale Industries	住宿和餐饮业 Hotel and Eateries
总 计	**Total**	**14.70**	**10.53**	**1.60**	**7.71**	**2.61**
乌鲁木齐市	Urumqi City	6.11	6.40	0.43	2.36	1.39
克拉玛依市	Karamay City	1.33	0.15	0.02	0.23	0.06
石河子市	Shi Hezi City	1.09	0.29	0.08	0.08	0.07
吐鲁番地区	Turpan Administrative Offices	0.06	0.17	0.05	0.21	0.08
哈密地区	Hami [Kumul] Administrative Offices	0.17	0.12	0.08	0.15	0.04
昌吉回族自治州	Changji Hui Autonomous Prefecture	0.86	0.46	0.14	0.38	0.05
伊犁哈萨克自治州	Ili Kazak Autonomous Prefecture	1.26	1.15	0.36	1.07	0.38
伊犁州直属县(市)	Counties (Cities) Direct Under Ili Prefecture	0.88	0.64	0.22	0.66	0.27
塔城地区	Tacheng [Tarbagatai] Administrative Offices	0.18	0.25	0.06	0.26	0.05
阿勒泰地区	Altay Administrative Offices	0.20	0.26	0.08	0.15	0.06
博尔塔拉蒙古自治州	Bortala Mongol Autonomous Prefecture	0.16	0.11	0.04	0.23	0.05
巴音郭楞蒙古自治州	Bayangol Mongol Autonomous Prefecture	0.91	0.52	0.11	0.65	0.24
阿克苏地区	Aksu Administrative Offices	1.10	0.31	0.08	0.90	0.08
克孜勒苏柯尔克孜自治州	Kizilsu Kirgiz Autonomous Prefecture	0.03	0.12	0.02	0.08	0.01
喀什地区	Kashgar [Kaxgar] Administrative Offices	1.21	0.51	0.12	1.15	0.12
和田地区	Hotan Administrative Offices	0.41	0.22	0.07	0.22	0.04

4-21 续表 Continued

单位：万人 (10 000 persons)

地 区	Region	金融业 Financial Industry	房地产业 Real Estate Industry	租赁和商务服务业 Leasing and Business Service Industries	科学研究、技术服务和地质勘查业 Scientific Research, Technology Service and Geological Prospecting	水利、环境和公共设施管理业 Water Conservancy, Environment and Public Facility Management Industries
总 计	**Total**	**5.75**	**2.21**	**3.48**	**4.43**	**4.10**
乌鲁木齐市	Urumqi City	2.35	1.24	1.72	1.74	0.52
克拉玛依市	Karamay City	0.14	0.04	0.10	0.07	0.04
石河子市	Shi Hezi City	0.17	0.04	0.38	0.12	0.22
吐鲁番地区	Turpan Administrative Offices	0.16	0.03	0.03	0.26	0.08
哈密地区	Hami [Kumul] Administrative Offices	0.14	0.05	0.02	0.21	0.15
昌吉回族自治州	Changji Hui Autonomous Prefecture	0.41	0.14	0.28	0.38	0.47
伊犁哈萨克自治州	Ili Kazak Autonomous Prefecture	0.87	0.27	0.29	0.58	0.91
伊犁州直属县(市)	Counties (Cities) Direct Under Ili Prefecture	0.44	0.20	0.20	0.27	0.46
塔城地区	Tacheng [Tarbagatai] Administrative Offices	0.24	0.05	0.07	0.16	0.36
阿勒泰地区	Altay Administrative Offices	0.19	0.02	0.02	0.15	0.09
博尔塔拉蒙古自治州	Bortala Mongol Autonomous Prefecture	0.12	0.05	0.03	0.08	0.15
巴音郭楞蒙古自治州	Bayangol Mongol Autonomous Prefecture	0.35	0.15	0.24	0.32	0.41
阿克苏地区	Aksu Administrative Offices	0.35	0.07	0.21	0.20	0.48
克孜勒苏柯尔克孜自治州	Kizilsu Kirgiz Autonomous Prefecture	0.08	0.01	0.05	0.18	0.06
喀什地区	Kashgar [Kaxgar] Administrative Offices	0.42	0.11	0.09	0.22	0.46
和田地区	Hotan Administrative Offices	0.19	0.01	0.04	0.07	0.15

地 区	Region	居民服务和其他服务业 Community Service and Other Service Industries	教 育 Education	卫生、社会保障和社会福利业 Health, Social Security and Welfare Industries	文化、体育和娱乐业 Culture, Sports and Entertainment	公共管理和社会组织 Public Administration and Social Organizations
总 计	**Total**	**0.38**	**30.63**	**10.32**	**2.33**	**28.50**
乌鲁木齐市	Urumqi City	0.07	3.83	1.79	0.86	4.64
克拉玛依市	Karamay City	…	0.52	0.28	0.02	0.81
石河子市	Shi Hezi City	…	0.63	0.31	0.03	0.42
吐鲁番地区	Turpan Administrative Offices	…	1.02	0.29	0.04	1.05
哈密地区	Hami [Kumul] Administrative Offices	0.17	0.92	0.38	0.06	0.99
昌吉回族自治州	Changji Hui Autonomous Prefecture	0.02	2.73	0.89	0.10	2.18
伊犁哈萨克自治州	Ili Kazak Autonomous Prefecture	0.03	7.61	2.42	0.50	6.49
伊犁州直属县(市)	Counties (Cities) Direct Under Ili Prefecture	0.02	4.05	1.24	0.25	3.22
塔城地区	Tacheng [Tarbagatai] Administrative Offices	0.01	2.28	0.76	0.11	1.79
阿勒泰地区	Altay Administrative Offices	…	1.28	0.42	0.14	1.48
博尔塔拉蒙古自治州	Bortala Mongol Autonomous Prefecture	0.01	0.76	0.33	0.05	1.00
巴音郭楞蒙古自治州	Bayangol Mongol Autonomous Prefecture	0.02	2.02	0.75	0.11	2.02
阿克苏地区	Aksu Administrative Offices	0.01	2.86	0.89	0.13	2.98
克孜勒苏柯尔克孜自治州	Kizilsu Kirgiz Autonomous Prefecture	0.02	0.94	0.28	0.09	0.87
喀什地区	Kashgar [Kaxgar] Administrative Offices	0.02	4.64	1.07	0.23	3.00
和田地区	Hotan Administrative Offices	0.01	2.15	0.64	0.11	2.05

4-22　各地、州、市国有单位分行业年底在岗职工人数

Number of Staff and Workers in State-owned Units at the Year-end by Sector in by Prefecture, Autonomous Prefecture and City

单位：万人　　(2004 年)　　(10 000 persons)

地　区	Region	合计 Total	农林牧渔业 Farming, Forestry, Animal Husbandry and Fishery	采矿业 Fishery	制造业 Manufacturing	电力、燃气及水的生产和供应业 Power, Gas and Water Production and Supply
总　计	**Total**	**182.80**	**61.43**	**7.85**	**5.35**	**2.42**
乌鲁木齐市	Urumqi City	31.65	1.33	0.07	2.66	0.41
克拉玛依市	Karamay City	6.09	0.84	3.21	0.07	
石河子市	Shi Hezi City	4.58	1.29		0.26	0.04
吐鲁番地区	Turpan Administrative Offices	5.56	0.42	1.77	0.06	0.19
哈密地区	Hami [Kumul] Administrative Offices	5.65	1.95	0.11	0.06	0.21
昌吉回族自治州	Changji Hui Autonomous Prefecture	15.84	7.39	0.12	0.57	0.18
伊犁哈萨克自治州	Ili Kazak Autonomous Prefecture	48.48	25.48	0.56	0.48	0.60
伊犁州直属县(市)	Counties (Cities) Direct Under Ili Prefecture	19.68	8.02	0.05	0.23	0.36
塔城地区	Tacheng [Tarbagatai] Administrative Offices	19.53	12.81	0.27	0.19	0.09
阿勒泰地区	Altay Administrative Offices	9.27	4.65	0.24	0.06	0.15
博尔塔拉蒙古自治州	Bortala Mongol Autonomous Prefecture	7.72	4.60		0.10	0.20
巴音郭楞蒙古自治州	Bayangol Mongol Autonomous Prefecture	15.96	6.50	1.65	0.55	0.05
阿克苏地区	Aksu Administrative Offices	16.24	6.72	0.19	0.19	0.21
克孜勒苏柯尔克孜自治州	Kizilsu Kirgiz Autonomous Prefecture	3.19	0.29	0.10	0.05	0.04
喀什地区	Kashgar [Kaxgar] Administrative Offices	14.63	3.55	0.01	0.16	0.13
和田地区	Hotan Administrative Offices	7.21	1.07	0.06	0.14	0.16

地　区	Region	建筑业 Construction	交通运输、仓储和邮政业 Transportation, Logistics and Post Industries	信息传输、计算机服务和软件业 Information Transmission, Computer Servcie and Software Industries	批发和零售业 Retail and Wholesale Industries	住宿和餐饮业 Hotel and Eateries
总　计	**Total**	**4.89**	**8.88**	**1.00**	**2.50**	**1.37**
乌鲁木齐市	Urumqi City	2.86	5.68	0.27	0.81	0.72
克拉玛依市	Karamay City	0.01	0.08	0.01	0.06	0.01
石河子市	Shi Hezi City	0.55	0.21	0.06	0.03	0.03
吐鲁番地区	Turpan Administrative Offices	…	0.14	0.06	0.05	0.02
哈密地区	Hami [Kumul] Administrative Offices	0.05	0.12	0.05	0.07	0.03
昌吉回族自治州	Changji Hui Autonomous Prefecture	0.05	0.28	0.08	0.11	0.02
伊犁哈萨克自治州	Ili Kazak Autonomous Prefecture	0.44	0.92	0.18	0.38	0.22
伊犁州直属县(市)	Counties (Cities) Direct Under Ili Prefecture	0.37	0.48	0.04	0.19	0.13
塔城地区	Tacheng [Tarbagatai] Administrative Offices	0.04	0.23	0.06	0.10	0.04
阿勒泰地区	Altay Administrative Offices	0.03	0.21	0.08	0.09	0.05
博尔塔拉蒙古自治州	Bortala Mongol Autonomous Prefecture	0.06	0.09	0.02	0.10	0.04
巴音郭楞蒙古自治州	Bayangol Mongol Autonomous Prefecture	0.33	0.44	0.08	0.26	0.13
阿克苏地区	Aksu Administrative Offices	0.46	0.24	0.06	0.17	0.05
克孜勒苏柯尔克孜自治州	Kizilsu Kirgiz Autonomous Prefecture	0.01	0.10	0.02	0.05	0.01
喀什地区	Kashgar [Kaxgar] Administrative Offices	0.03	0.38	0.04	0.31	0.06
和田地区	Hotan Administrative Offices	0.04	0.20	0.07	0.10	0.03

4-22 续表 Continued

单位：万人 (10 000 persons)

地　区	Region	金融业 Financial Industry	房地产业 Real Estate Industry	租赁和商务服务业 Leasing and Business Service Industries	科学研究、技术服务和地质勘查业 Scientific Research, Technology Service and Geological Prospecting	水利、环境和公共设施管理业 Water Conservancy, Environment and Public Facility Management Industries
总　计	**Total**	**4.26**	**0.87**	**2.18**	**4.13**	**3.94**
乌鲁木齐市	Urumqi City	2.02	0.54	1.31	1.60	0.44
克拉玛依市	Karamay City	0.13	…	0.02	0.01	0.03
石河子市	Shi Hezi City	0.15	0.02	0.22	0.12	0.21
吐鲁番地区	Turpan Administrative Offices	0.10	0.02	0.01	0.26	0.06
哈密地区	Hami [Kumul] Administrative Offices	0.10	0.01	0.02	0.21	0.15
昌吉回族自治州	Changji Hui Autonomous Prefecture	0.24	0.02	0.07	0.35	0.45
伊犁哈萨克自治州	Ili Kazak Autonomous Prefecture	0.51	0.11	0.16	0.55	0.91
伊犁州直属县(市)	Counties (Cities) Direct Under Ili Prefecture	0.21	0.08	0.10	0.25	0.46
塔城地区	Tacheng [Tarbagatai] Administrative Offices	0.17	0.02	0.04	0.16	0.36
阿勒泰地区	Altay Administrative Offices	0.13	0.01	0.02	0.14	0.09
博尔塔拉蒙古自治州	Bortala Mongol Autonomous Prefecture	0.10	0.02	0.01	0.07	0.15
巴音郭楞蒙古自治州	Bayangol Mongol Autonomous Prefecture	0.22	0.05	0.10	0.31	0.39
阿克苏地区	Aksu Administrative Offices	0.24	0.03	0.16	0.18	0.48
克孜勒苏柯尔克孜自治州	Kizilsu Kirgiz Autonomous Prefecture	0.06	…	0.03	0.18	0.06
喀什地区	Kashgar [Kaxgar] Administrative Offices	0.26	0.04	0.05	0.22	0.46
和田地区	Hotan Administrative Offices	0.13	0.01	0.02	0.07	0.15

地　区	Region	居民服务和其他服务业 Community Service and Other Service Industries	教　育 Education	卫生、社会保障和社会福利业 Health, Social Security and Welfare Industries	文化、体育和娱乐业 Culture, Sports and Entertainment	公共管理和社会组织 Public Administration and Social Organizations
总　计	**Total**	**0.30**	**30.49**	**10.17**	**2.28**	**28.49**
乌鲁木齐市	Urumqi City	0.02	3.77	1.67	0.83	4.64
克拉玛依市	Karamay City	...	0.52	0.28	0.01	0.80
石河子市	Shi Hezi City	...	0.63	0.31	0.03	0.42
吐鲁番地区	Turpan Administrative Offices	...	1.02	0.29	0.04	1.05
哈密地区	Hami [Kumul] Administrative Offices	0.17	0.92	0.37	0.06	0.99
昌吉回族自治州	Changji Hui Autonomous Prefecture	0.01	2.73	0.89	0.10	2.18
伊犁哈萨克自治州	Ili Kazak Autonomous Prefecture	0.03	7.55	2.41	0.50	6.49
伊犁州直属县(市)	Counties (Cities) Direct Under Ili Prefecture	0.02	3.99	1.23	0.25	3.22
塔城地区	Tacheng [Tarbagatai] Administrative Offices	0.01	2.28	0.76	0.11	1.79
阿勒泰地区	Altay Administrative Offices	...	1.28	0.42	0.14	1.48
博尔塔拉蒙古自治州	Bortala Mongol Autonomous Prefecture	0.01	0.76	0.33	0.06	1.00
巴音郭楞蒙古自治州	Bayangol Mongol Autonomous Prefecture	0.01	2.00	0.75	0.11	2.03
阿克苏地区	Aksu Administrative Offices	0.01	2.86	0.88	0.13	2.98
克孜勒苏柯尔克孜自治州	Kizilsu Kirgiz Autonomous Prefecture	0.02	0.94	0.28	0.08	0.87
喀什地区	Kashgar [Kaxgar] Administrative Offices	0.01	4.64	1.07	0.22	2.99
和田地区	Hotan Administrative Offices	0.01	2.15	0.64	0.11	2.05

4-23　各地、州、市城镇集体单位分行业年底在岗职工人数

Number of Staff & Workers in Urban Collective-owned Units at the Year-end by Sector and by Prefecture, Autonomous Prefecture and City

单位：万人　　(2004 年)　　(10 000 persons)

地　区	Region	合计 Total	农林牧渔业 Farming, Forestry, Animal Husbandry and Fishery	采矿业 Fishery	制造业 Manufacturing	电力、燃气及水的生产和供应业 Power, Gas and Water Production and Supply
总　计	**Total**	**6.43**	**0.19**	**0.10**	**1.51**	**0.04**
乌鲁木齐市	Urumqi City	1.57	...	0.02	0.42	0.01
克拉玛依市	Karamay City	0.81	0.03	0.01	0.32	
石河子市	Shi Hezi City	0.05			0.01	
吐鲁番地区	Turpan Administrative Offices	0.19	...		0.05	0.01
哈密地区	Hami [Kumul] Administrative Offices	0.09		...	0.01	...
昌吉回族自治州	Changji Hui Autonomous Prefecture	0.61	...	0.02	0.28	0.01
伊犁哈萨克自治州	Ili Kazak Autonomous Prefecture	0.69	0.01	0.02	0.17	...
伊犁州直属县(市)	Counties (Cities) Direct Under Ili Prefecture	0.35	...	...	0.07	...
塔城地区	Tacheng [Tarbagatai] Administrative Offices	0.25	0.01	0.01	0.08	
阿勒泰地区	Altay Administrative Offices	0.09		0.01	0.02	
博尔塔拉蒙古自治州	Bortala Mongol Autonomous Prefecture	0.17	0.03		...	0.01
巴音郭楞蒙古自治州	Bayangol Mongol Autonomous Prefecture	0.39	0.06	0.01	0.03	
阿克苏地区	Aksu Administrative Offices	0.49		0.01	0.06	...
克孜勒苏柯尔克孜自治州	Kizilsu Kirgiz Autonomous Prefecture	0.06	0.01	...	0.01	...
喀什地区	Kashgar [Kaxgar] Administrative Offices	1.04	0.05	...	0.13	
和田地区	Hotan Administrative Offices	0.27		...	0.02	

地　区	Region	建筑业 Construction	交通运输、仓储和邮政业 Transportation, Logistics and Post Industries	信息传输、计算机服务和软件业 Information Transmission, Computer Servcie and Software Industries	批发和零售业 Retail and Wholesale Industries	住宿和餐饮业 Hotel and Eateries
总　计	**Total**	**0.94**	**0.16**	**...**	**1.62**	**0.17**
乌鲁木齐市	Urumqi City	0.24	0.14		0.23	0.07
克拉玛依市	Karamay City	0.29	0.01		0.06	0.02
石河子市	Shi Hezi City	0.02	...		...	...
吐鲁番地区	Turpan Administrative Offices				0.05	0.01
哈密地区	Hami [Kumul] Administrative Offices	0.02			0.01	...
昌吉回族自治州	Changji Hui Autonomous Prefecture	0.03	0.01	...	0.02	...
伊犁哈萨克自治州	Ili Kazak Autonomous Prefecture	0.04	...		0.16	0.03
伊犁州直属县(市)	Counties (Cities) Direct Under Ili Prefecture	0.03	...		0.09	0.02
塔城地区	Tacheng [Tarbagatai] Administrative Offices	...			0.06	0.01
阿勒泰地区	Altay Administrative Offices	0.01			0.01	
博尔塔拉蒙古自治州	Bortala Mongol Autonomous Prefecture	0.04			0.05	0.01
巴音郭楞蒙古自治州	Bayangol Mongol Autonomous Prefecture	...	...		0.17	0.02
阿克苏地区	Aksu Administrative Offices	0.10			0.19	...
克孜勒苏柯尔克孜自治州	Kizilsu Kirgiz Autonomous Prefecture				0.03	
喀什地区	Kashgar [Kaxgar] Administrative Offices	0.06	...		0.59	0.01
和田地区	Hotan Administrative Offices	0.10			0.06	

4-23 续表 Continued

单位：万人 (10 000 persons)

地　区	Region	金融业 Financial Industry	房地产业 Real Estate	租赁和商务服务业 Leasing and Business Service	科学研究、技术服务和地质勘查业 Scientific Research, Technology Service and Geological Prospecting	水利、环境和公共设施管理业 Water Conservancy, Environment and Public Facility Management
总　计	**Total**	**0.86**	**0.10**	**0.48**	**0.01**	**0.08**
乌鲁木齐市	Urumqi City	0.04	0.05	0.11	0.01	0.08
克拉玛依市	Karamay City	0.01	0.02	0.04	...	
石河子市	Shi Hezi City	0.02		...		
吐鲁番地区	Turpan Administrative Offices	0.06	...	0.01		
哈密地区	Hami [Kumul] Administrative Offices	0.03	0.01	...		
昌吉回族自治州	Changji Hui Autonomous Prefecture	0.13	...	0.11	...	
伊犁哈萨克自治州	Ili Kazak Autonomous Prefecture	0.18	0.01	0.07	...	
伊犁州直属县(市)	Counties (Cities) Direct Under Ili Prefecture	0.08	0.01	0.05		
塔城地区	Tacheng [Tarbagatai] Administrative Offices	0.06		0.02		
阿勒泰地区	Altay Administrative Offices	0.04	...	...	...	
博尔塔拉蒙古自治州	Bortala Mongol Autonomous Prefecture	0.02	...	0.01		
巴音郭楞蒙古自治州	Bayangol Mongol Autonomous Prefecture	0.06	0.01	0.03		
阿克苏地区	Aksu Administrative Offices	0.09		0.04	...	
克孜勒苏柯尔克孜自治州	Kizilsu Kirgiz Autonomous Prefecture	0.01		...		
喀什地区	Kashgar [Kaxgar] Administrative Offices	0.14	...	0.05		...
和田地区	Hotan Administrative Offices	0.07	...	0.01		

地　区	Region	居民服务和其他服务业 Community Service and Other Service Industries	教　育 Education	卫生、社会保障和社会福利业 Health, Social Security and Welfare Industries	文化、体育和娱乐业 Culture, Sports and Entertainment	公共管理和社会组织 Public Administration and Social Organizations
总　计	**Total**	**0.02**	**0.01**	**0.13**	**...**	**0.01**
乌鲁木齐市	Urumqi City	0.02	0.01	0.12		
克拉玛依市	Karamay City	...				
石河子市	Shi Hezi City	...				
吐鲁番地区	Turpan Administrative Offices					
哈密地区	Hami [Kumul] Administrative Offices			0.01		...
昌吉回族自治州	Changji Hui Autonomous Prefecture	...				
伊犁哈萨克自治州	Ili Kazak Autonomous Prefecture	...		...	...	...
伊犁州直属县(市)	Counties (Cities) Direct Under Ili Prefecture			...		
塔城地区	Tacheng [Tarbagatai] Administrative Offices	...				...
阿勒泰地区	Altay Administrative Offices				...	
博尔塔拉蒙古自治州	Bortala Mongol Autonomous Prefecture	...				
巴音郭楞蒙古自治州	Bayangol Mongol Autonomous Prefecture	...		...		
阿克苏地区	Aksu Administrative Offices			...		
克孜勒苏柯尔克孜自治州	Kizilsu Kirgiz Autonomous Prefecture				...	
喀什地区	Kashgar [Kaxgar] Administrative Offices		...		...	0.01
和田地区	Hotan Administrative Offices			...		

4-24　其他单位分行业年底职工人数

Number of Staff and Workers in Units of Other Types of Ownership at the Year-end by Sector

单位：万人　(10 000 persons)

项　　目	Item	2003	2004
总　计	**Total**	**46.37**	**46.74**
按登记注册类型分组	**Grouped by Registration Status**		
股份合作单位	Cooperative Units	0.63	0.82
联营单位	Joint Ownership Units	0.27	0.32
有限责任公司	Limited Liability Corporations	33.34	34.01
股份有限公司	Share-holding Corporations Ltd.	9.66	9.00
其他	Others	1.11	1.14
港澳台商投资单位	Units with Funds form Hong Kong, Macao and Taiwan	0.64	0.62
外商投资单位	Foreign Funded Unit	0.72	0.83
按国民经济行业分组	**Grouped by Economic Sector**		
农林牧渔业	Farming, Forestry, Animal Husbandry and Fishery	0.54	0.42
采 矿 业	Fishery	6.72	5.83
制 造 业	Manufacturing	18.17	18.52
电力、燃气及水的生产和供应业	Power, Gas and Water Production and Supply	3.05	3.03
建 筑 业	Construction	8.81	8.87
交通运输、仓储和邮政业	Transportation, Logistics and Post Industries	1.39	1.49
信息传输、计算机服务和软件业	Information Transmission, Computer Servcie and Software Industries	0.47	0.60
批发和零售业	Retail and Wholesale Sectors	3.33	3.59
住宿和餐饮业	Hotel and Catering	1.07	1.07
金融业	Financial Service	0.53	0.63
房地产业	Real Estate	1.04	1.24
租赁和商务服务业	Leasing and Business Service Industries	0.68	0.82
科学研究、技术服务和地质勘查业	Scientific Research, Technology Service and Geological Prospecting	0.23	0.29
水利、环境和公共设施管理业	Water Conservancy, Environment and Public Facility Management	0.08	0.08
居民服务和其他服务业	Community Service and Other Service	0.05	0.06
教　育	Education	0.14	0.13
卫生、社会保障和社会福利业	Health, Social Security and Welfare	0.02	0.02
文化、体育和娱乐业	Culture, Sports and Entertainment	0.05	0.05
公共管理和社会组织	Public Administration and Social Organizations		

4-25 分行业城镇单位年底女性就业人员

Number of Female Employed in Urban Units at the Year-end by Sectors

单位：万人 (2004 年) (10 000 persons)

项 目	Item	合 计 Total	国有单位 State-owned Units	城镇集体 Urban Collective-owned Units	其他单位 Units of Other Types of Ownership
总 计	**Total**	**101.77**	**81.51**	**2.49**	**17.77**
农林牧渔业	Farming, Forestry, Animal Husbandry and Fishery	26.78	26.58	0.07	0.13
采 矿 业	Fishery	4.88	2.99	0.02	1.87
制 造 业	Manufacturing	10.96	2.38	0.71	7.87
电力、燃气及水的生产和供应业	Power, Gas and Water Production and Supply	2.01	0.87	0.01	1.13
建 筑 业	Construction	3.21	1.21	0.18	1.82
交通运输、仓储和邮政业	Transportation, Logistics and Post Industries	3.78	3.14	0.09	0.55
信息传输、计算机服务和软件业	Information Transmission, Computer Servcie and Software Industries	0.70	0.41	…	0.29
批发和零售业	Retail and Wholesale	3.34	1.11	0.64	1.59
住宿和餐饮业	Hotel and Catering	1.59	0.91	0.11	0.57
金融业	Finance	3.42	2.29	0.33	0.80
房地产业	Real Estate	0.98	0.43	0.04	0.51
租赁和商务服务业	Leasing and Business Service	1.30	0.83	0.12	0.35
科学研究、技术服务和地质勘查业	Scientific Research, Technology Service and Geological Prospecting	1.59	1.48	…	0.11
水利、环境和公共设施管理业	Water Conservancy, Environment and Public Facility Management Industries	1.65	1.57	0.05	0.03
居民服务和其他服务业	Community Service and Other Service Sector	0.14	0.09	0.02	0.03
教 育	Education	17.97	17.88	0.01	0.08
卫生、社会保障和社会福利业	Health, Social Security and Welfare	6.90	6.79	0.09	0.02
文化、体育和娱乐业	Culture, Sports and Entertainment	1.07	1.05	…	0.02
公共管理和社会组织	Public Administration and Social Organizations	9.50	9.50	…	

4-26　女性就业人员占全部就业人员比重
Proportion of Female Employment to Total

单位：%　(2004 年)　(%)

项　目	Item	合 计 Total	国有单位 State-owned Units	城镇集体 Urban Collective-owned Units	其他单位 Units of Other Types of Ownership
总　计	**Total**	**41.79**	**43.31**	**36.29**	**36.67**
农林牧渔业	Farming, Forestry, Animal Husbandry and Fishery	42.82	42.92	35.55	30.81
采 矿 业	Fishery	31.72	32.23	15.27	31.26
制 造 业	Manufacturing	42.45	43.20	46.04	41.93
电力、燃气及水的生产和供应业	Power, Gas and Water Production and Supply	36.35	35.81	34.43	36.81
建 筑 业	Construction	20.38	23.34	14.95	19.43
交通运输、仓储和邮政业	Transportation, Logistics and Post Industries	32.65	31.74	54.06	36.35
信息传输、计算机服务和软件业	Information Transmission, Computer Servcie and Software Industries	41.56	38.66	25.00	46.54
批发和零售业	Retail and Wholesale	42.17	42.96	37.51	43.81
住宿和餐饮业	Hotel and Catering	57.67	59.91	61.23	53.90
金融业	Finance	50.81	49.51	38.03	64.68
房地产业	Real Estate	41.65	43.92	36.83	40.32
租赁和商务服务业	Leasing and Business Service	36.17	36.64	26.21	40.45
科学研究、技术服务和地质勘查业	Scientific Research, Technology Service and Geological Prospecting	34.50	34.67	27.78	32.58
水利、环境和公共设施管理业	Water Conservancy, Environment and Public Facility Management	39.22	38.81	61.28	36.97
居民服务和其他服务业	Community Service and Other Service	37.10	31.75	60.54	54.59
教　育	Education	57.87	57.85	72.22	61.02
卫生、社会保障和社会福利业	Health, Social Security and Welfare	65.68	65.63	67.40	75.00
文化、体育和娱乐业	Culture, Sports and Entertainment	45.02	45.10	27.78	41.39
公共管理和社会组织	Public Administration and Social Organizations	33.03	33.03	34.52	

注：本表以本类型从业人员为 100。
Note: Total Number of Employment in this table is based on 100

4-27 单位在岗职工工资总额及构成
Total Wages of Staff and Workers and Its Composition

年 份 Year	地 区 Region	绝对数(万元) Absolute Figure (10 000yuan) 合 计 Total	国有单位 State-owned Units	城镇集体单位 Urban Collective-owned Units	其他单位 Units of Other Types of Ownership	构成(总计=100) composition in percentage(total=100) 国有单位 State-owned Units	城镇集体单位 Urban Collective-owned Units	其他单位 Units of Other Types of ownership
	1978	159409.4	148278.4	11131.0		93.0	7.0	
	1980	212445.6	196710.8	15734.8		92.6	7.4	
	1985	339109.5	304999.3	33788.8	321.4	89.9	10.0	0.1
	1990	668808.3	601299.6	65858.5	1650.2	90.0	9.8	0.2
	1991	746909.6	666971.4	78025.9	1912.3	89.3	10.4	0.3
	1992	856020.4	763348.0	89407.8	3264.6	89.2	10.4	0.4
	1993	1027934.4	905289.2	115638.5	7006.7	88.1	11.2	0.7
	1994	1327539.0	1200161.2	114011.4	13366.4	90.4	8.6	1.0
	1995	1677257.2	1521669.7	135989.5	19598.0	90.7	8.1	1.2
	1996	1897561.1	1719503.9	148059.2	29998.0	90.6	7.8	1.6
	1997	2098467.2	1898581.5	163747.5	36138.2	90.5	7.8	1.7
	1998	2095963.4	1852330.3	147334.4	96298.7	88.4	7.0	4.6
	1999	2118609.1	1857721.8	137261.0	123626.3	87.7	6.5	5.8
	2000	2344694.3	2007822.9	125510.0	211361.4	85.6	5.4	9.0
	2001	2677430.9	2092155.0	105860.5	479415.4	78.1	4.0	17.9
	2002	2915397.5	2211411.3	93604.5	610381.7	75.9	3.2	20.9
	2003	3315399.0	2497369.3	77459.5	740570.2	75.3	2.3	22.4
	2004	3563311.8	2691462.0	78223.8	793626.0	75.5	2.2	22.3
乌鲁木齐市	Urumqi City	953235.7	637967.1	22689.4	292579.2	66.9	2.4	30.7
克拉玛依市	Karamay City	247807.8	123978.9	12023.5	111805.4	50.0	4.9	45.1
石河子市	Shi Hezi City	111937.9	67830.2	1142.0	42965.7	60.6	1.0	38.4
吐鲁番地区	Turpan Administrative Offices	124707.1	98900.3	2386.8	23420.0	79.3	1.9	18.8
哈密地区	Hami [Kumul] Administrative Offices	108071.6	76966.6	1353.9	29751.1	71.2	1.3	27.5
昌吉回族自治州	Changji Hui Autonomous Prefecture	265686.0	193463.0	5900.0	66323.0	72.8	2.2	25.0
伊犁哈萨克自治州	Ili Kazak Autonomous Prefecture	642110.1	551041.1	8235.7	82833.3	85.8	1.3	12.9
伊犁州直属县(市)	Counties (Cities) Direct Under Ili Prefecture	280520.9	223307.0	4985.2	52228.7	79.6	1.8	18.6
塔城地区	Tacheng [Tarbagatai] Administrative Offices	234769.4	212904.5	2253.9	19611.0	90.7	0.9	8.4
阿勒泰地区	Altay Administrative Offices	126819.8	114829.6	996.6	10993.6	90.5	0.8	8.7
博尔塔拉蒙古自治州	Bortala Mongol Autonomous Prefecture	105215.7	94529.5	2158.9	8527.3	89.8	2.1	8.1
巴音郭楞蒙古自治州	Bayangol Mongol Autonomous Prefecture	281682.3	224483.7	4333.8	52864.8	79.7	1.5	18.8
阿克苏地区	Aksu Administrative Offices	288334.6	248340.8	4642.0	35351.8	86.1	1.6	12.3
克孜勒苏柯尔克孜自治州	Kizilsu Kirgiz Autonomous Prefecture	53492.7	51851.6	632.6	1008.5	96.9	1.2	1.9
喀什地区	Kashgar [Kaxgar] Administrative Offices	260453.0	211596.6	10274.3	38582.1	81.3	3.9	14.8
和田地区	Hotan Administrative Offices	120577.3	110512.6	2450.9	7613.8	91.7	2.0	6.3

4-28 在岗职工工资总额指数
Indices of Total Wages of Staff and Workers

年 份 Year	指数(上年=100) Index (Preceding year=100)				指数(1978=100) Index (1978=100)			
	合 计 Total	国有单位 State-owned Units	城镇集体单位 Urban Collective-owned Units	其他单位 Units of Other Types of Ownership	合 计 Total	国有单位 State-owned Units	城镇集体单位 Urban Collective-owned Units	其他单位 Units of Other Types of Ownership
1978	114.2	114.5	109.6		100.0	100.0	100.0	
1980	120.5	120.1	125.2		133.3	132.7	141.4	
1985	117.4	117.5	116.0	167.5	212.7	205.7	303.6	100.0
1990	116.6	116.3	126.9	132.6	419.6	405.5	591.7	513.4
1991	111.7	110.9	118.5	115.9	468.5	449.8	701.0	595.0
1992	114.6	114.4	114.6	170.7	537.0	514.8	803.2	1015.7
1993	120.1	118.6	129.3	214.6	644.8	610.5	1038.9	2180.1
1994	129.1	132.6	98.6	190.8	832.8	809.4	1024.3	4158.8
1995	126.3	126.8	119.3	146.6	1052.2	1026.2	1221.7	6097.7
1996	113.1	113.0	108.8	153.1	1190.4	1159.6	1330.2	9333.5
1997	110.6	110.4	110.6	120.5	1316.4	1280.4	1471.1	11244.0
1998	99.9	97.6	90.0	266.5	1314.8	1249.2	1323.6	29962.3
1999	101.1	100.3	93.2	128.4	1329.0	1252.9	1233.1	38464.9
2000	110.7	108.1	91.4	171.0	1470.9	1354.1	1127.6	65762.7
2001	114.2	104.2	84.3	226.8	1679.6	1411.0	951.0	149164.7
2002	108.9	105.7	88.4	127.3	1828.9	1491.4	840.9	189913.4
2003	113.7	112.9	82.8	121.3	2079.8	1684.2	695.9	230420.0
2004	107.5	107.8	101.0	107.2	2235.3	1815.1	702.8	246927.8

注：2000 年起职工工资总额指数由在岗职工数计算而得。
Note: The indice of total sum of wages for the staff workers fom the year 2000 are calculated on the basis of on-the-job staff.

4-29 在岗职工工资情况
Wages of Full-Employed Staff and Workers

年 份 Year	在岗职工工资总额(万元) Total Wages (10 000 yuan)	国有单位 State-owned Units	城镇单位 Urban Collective-owned Units	其他单位 Units of Other Types of Ownership	在岗职工平均工资(元) Average Money Wage (yuan)	国有单位 State-owned Units	城镇单位 Urban Collective-owned Units	其他单位 Units of Other Types of Ownership
1999	2118609	1857722	137261	123626	7611	7614	6815	8681
2000	2344694	2007823	125510	211361	8717	8731	7489	9498
2001	2677431	2092155	105861	479415	10278	10145	8197	11594
2002	2915398	2211411	93605	610382	11605	11435	9353	12767
2003	3315399	2497369	77460	740570	13255	13199	9966	13937
2004	3563312	2691462	78224	793626	14484	14477	11594	14870

4-30 各地、州、市分行业单位在岗职工工资总额

Total Wages of Staff and Workers by Sector and by Prefecture, Autonomous Prefecture and City

单位：万元 (2004 年) (10 000 yuan)

地 区	Region	合 计 Total	农林牧渔业 Farming, Forestry, Animal Husbandry and Fishery	采 矿 业 Fishery	制 造 业 Manufacturing	电力、燃气及水的生产和供应业 Power, Gas and Water Production and Supply
总 计	**Total**	**3563311.8**	**605282.0**	**294960.2**	**348884.6**	**110530.3**
乌鲁木齐市	Urumqi City	953235.7	13497.5	33617.6	157425.1	31576.2
克拉玛依市	Karamay City	247807.8	9884.5	108856.6	44233.7	
石河子市	Shi Hezi City	111937.9	17335.8		18148.0	5626.3
吐鲁番地区	Turpan Administrative Offices	124707.1	3558.2	58043.4	4538.6	5371.8
哈密地区	Hami [Kumul] Administrative Offices	108071.6	17987.7	21558.4	5692.2	5307.1
昌吉回族自治州	Changji Hui Autonomous Prefecture	265686.0	71618.0	5015.5	29092.9	12430.9
伊犁哈萨克自治州	Ili Kazak Autonomous Prefecture	642110.1	201790.6	15241.9	38284.7	20072.7
伊犁州直属县(市)	Counties (Cities) Direct Under Ili Prefecture	280520.9	51952.5	1092.7	27676.8	10625.3
塔城地区	Tacheng [Tarbagatai] Administrative Offices	234769.4	112693.0	8500.8	7816.8	5387.3
阿勒泰地区	Altay Administrative Offices	126819.8	37145.1	5648.4	2791.1	4060.1
博尔塔拉蒙古自治州	Bortala Mongol Autonomous Prefecture	105215.7	45739.5	281.6	5151.4	3611.1
巴音郭楞蒙古自治州	Bayangol Mongol Autonomous Prefecture	281682.3	60453.1	42833.7	20612.3	6618.9
阿克苏地区	Aksu Administrative Offices	288334.6	109825.0	6661.5	15218.3	7790.0
克孜勒苏柯尔克孜自治州	Kizilsu Kirgiz Autonomous Prefecture	53492.7	3888.1	607.0	511.6	506.5
喀什地区	Kashgar [Kaxgar] Administrative Offices	260453.0	41413.0	153.8	7623.8	8380.6
和田地区	Hotan Administrative Offices	120577.3	8291.0	2089.2	2352.0	3238.2

地 区	Region	建 筑 业 Construction	交通运输、仓储和邮政业 Transportation, Warehouses and Post Service	信息传输、计算机服务和软件业 Information Transmission, Computer Service and Software Industries	批发和零售业 Retail and Wholesale Sector	住宿和餐饮业 Hotel and Catering
总 计	**Total**	**283485.7**	**213542.8**	**37273.9**	**109320.9**	**30310.4**
乌鲁木齐市	Urumqi City	108395.2	160520.1	15370.0	45075.4	18410.7
克拉玛依市	Karamay City	31973.2	2281.5	247.5	3840.3	709.5
石河子市	Shi Hezi City	25530.0	3865.7	1370.4	1690.9	643.9
吐鲁番地区	Turpan Administrative Offices	1525.1	1869.6	834.4	2759.5	754.2
哈密地区	Hami [Kumul] Administrative Offices	3313.4	1542.5	2103.3	1708.0	420.7
昌吉回族自治州	Changji Hui Autonomous Prefecture	23046.0	5013.8	2609.5	4776.8	539.7
伊犁哈萨克自治州	Ili Kazak Autonomous Prefecture	24656.0	15674.6	7269.6	12449.7	3762.1
伊犁州直属县(市)	Counties (Cities) Direct Under Ili Prefecture	16002.8	8004.6	4750.9	7214.8	2475.3
塔城地区	Tacheng [Tarbagatai] Administrative Offices	4416.8	3740.7	1128.0	3303.6	408.6
阿勒泰地区	Altay Administrative Offices	4236.4	3929.3	1390.7	1931.3	878.2
博尔塔拉蒙古自治州	Bortala Mongol Autonomous Prefecture	3016.6	1536.5	964.0	2942.2	501.7
巴音郭楞蒙古自治州	Bayangol Mongol Autonomous Prefecture	24354.5	6901.0	1860.0	8712.7	2323.6
阿克苏地区	Aksu Administrative Offices	12588.8	3532.6	1215.1	9283.7	694.2
克孜勒苏柯尔克孜自治州	Kizilsu Kirgiz Autonomous Prefecture	331.9	1869.5	334.9	785.9	100.3
喀什地区	Kashgar [Kaxgar] Administrative Offices	19961.8	6081.3	2040.3	12565.4	1072.3
和田地区	Hotan Administrative Offices	4793.2	2854.1	1054.9	2730.4	377.5

4-30 续表 Continued

单位：万元 (10 000 yuan)

地　区	Region	金融业 Financial Industry	房地产业 Real Estate Industry	租赁和商务服务业 Leasing and Business Service Industries	科学研究、技术服务和地质勘查业 Scientific Research, Technology Service and Geological Prospecting	水利、环境和公共设施管理业 Water Conservancy, Environment and Public Facility Management Industries
总　计	**Total**	**133540.6**	**30825.6**	**46279.3**	**79128.8**	**54529.8**
乌鲁木齐市	Urumqi City	67084.6	20166.0	25641.1	33937.6	8204.9
克拉玛依市	Karamay City	3152.7	747.4	1832.2	1573.3	604.6
石河子市	Shi Hezi City	3645.0	547.7	5585.1	2187.2	2867.4
吐鲁番地区	Turpan Administrative Offices	2854.0	282.6	215.9	5868.2	972.2
哈密地区	Hami [Kumul] Administrative Offices	3123.8	422.5	322.8	3224.0	1401.3
昌吉回族自治州	Changji Hui Autonomous Prefecture	7822.9	1500.6	2550.1	5512.2	5173.4
伊犁哈萨克自治州	Ili Kazak Autonomous Prefecture	17996.0	2686.3	3081.5	9090.6	10360.0
伊犁州直属县(市)	Counties (Cities) Direct Under Ili Prefecture	9766.7	1898.0	2057.4	4289.5	4910.2
塔城地区	Tacheng [Tarbagatai] Administrative Offices	4644.6	616.4	745.4	2259.1	4349.4
阿勒泰地区	Altay Administrative Offices	3584.7	171.9	278.7	2542.0	1100.4
博尔塔拉蒙古自治州	Bortala Mongol Autonomous Prefecture	2811.8	525.7	345.8	1327.7	1894.3
巴音郭楞蒙古自治州	Bayangol Mongol Autonomous Prefecture	7662.7	1804.6	2929.6	5769.0	5157.5
阿克苏地区	Aksu Administrative Offices	5948.5	838.5	1807.0	3066.2	8785.4
克孜勒苏柯尔克孜自治州	Kizilsu Kirgiz Autonomous Prefecture	1577.3	108.6	532.4	2967.8	940.3
喀什地区	Kashgar [Kaxgar] Administrative Offices	6066.8	1069.4	969.8	3378.5	6252.9
和田地区	Hotan Administrative Offices	3794.5	125.7	466.0	1226.5	1915.6

地　区	Region	居民服务和其他服务业 Community Service and Other Service Industries	教　育 Education	卫生、社会保障和社会福利业 Health, Social Security and Welfare Industries	文化、体育和娱乐业 Culture, Sports and Entertainment	公共管理和社会组织 Public Administration and Social Organizations
总　计	**Total**	**4843.0**	**496464.7**	**169727.6**	**38394.5**	**475987.1**
乌鲁木齐市	Urumqi City	789.3	70109.6	32957.4	16801.4	93656.0
克拉玛依市	Karamay City	68.5	11939.2	6201.2	333.2	19328.7
石河子市	Shi Hezi City	56.0	10053.9	5121.4	439.0	7224.2
吐鲁番地区	Turpan Administrative Offices	21.8	15819.0	4234.1	465.2	14719.3
哈密地区	Hami [Kumul] Administrative Offices	2483.3	14685.0	5814.0	866.2	16095.4
昌吉回族自治州	Changji Hui Autonomous Prefecture	224.7	41945.5	13277.0	1377.5	32159.0
伊犁哈萨克自治州	Ili Kazak Autonomous Prefecture	279.3	115785.9	35529.2	7285.0	100814.4
伊犁州直属县(市)	Counties (Cities) Direct Under Ili Prefecture	168.5	58167.7	17876.4	3558.5	48032.3
塔城地区	Tacheng [Tarbagatai] Administrative Offices	83.5	34840.1	10669.2	1519.4	27646.7
阿勒泰地区	Altay Administrative Offices	27.3	22778.1	6983.6	2207.1	25135.4
博尔塔拉蒙古自治州	Bortala Mongol Autonomous Prefecture	92.0	12239.1	5019.9	830.2	16384.6
巴音郭楞蒙古自治州	Bayangol Mongol Autonomous Prefecture	199.7	33915.8	12972.9	1787.8	34812.9
阿克苏地区	Aksu Administrative Offices	104.6	42452.9	14424.3	1729.9	42368.1
克孜勒苏柯尔克孜自治州	Kizilsu Kirgiz Autonomous Prefecture	287.7	16931.7	5144.3	1402.6	14664.3
喀什地区	Kashgar [Kaxgar] Administrative Offices	128.7	72687.3	18094.1	3336.7	49176.5
和田地区	Hotan Administrative Offices	107.4	37899.8	10937.8	1739.8	34583.7

4-31 各地、州、市国有单位分行业在岗职工工资总额

Total Wages of Staff and Workers in State-Owned Units by Sector and by Prefecture, Autonomous Prefecture and City

单位：万元 (2004 年) (10 000 yuan)

地 区	Region	合 计 Total	农林牧渔业 Farming, Forestry, Animal Husbandry and Fishery	采 矿 业 Fishery	制 造 业 Manufacturing	电力、燃气及水的生产和供应业 Power, Gas and Water Production and Supply
总 计	**Total**	**2691462.0**	**599307.3**	**168838.2**	**72859.1**	**48671.4**
乌鲁木齐市	Urumqi City	637967.1	12562.6	1024.5	46847.7	13214.3
克拉玛依市	Karamay City	123978.9	9412.4	68805.5	1191.4	
石河子市	Shi Hezi City	67830.2	17288.9		2635.3	554.0
吐鲁番地区	Turpan Administrative Offices	98900.3	3542.0	42141.8	505.9	5026.3
哈密地区	Hami [Kumul] Administrative Offices	76966.6	17982.2	1482.0	707.2	5304.5
昌吉回族自治州	Changji Hui Autonomous Prefecture	193463.0	70004.6	1638.6	4848.7	4004.2
伊犁哈萨克自治州	Ili Kazak Autonomous Prefecture	551041.1	201352.5	8345.9	6357.4	8274.0
伊犁州直属县(市)	Counties (Cities) Direct Under Ili Prefecture	223307.0	51891.3	475.7	3665.2	4850.9
塔城地区	Tacheng [Tarbagatai] Administrative Offices	212904.5	112637.3	3698.7	2179.3	1375.1
阿勒泰地区	Altay Administrative Offices	114829.6	36823.9	4171.5	512.9	2048.0
博尔塔拉蒙古自治州	Bortala Mongol Autonomous Prefecture	94529.5	44780.4		1071.6	3287.9
巴音郭楞蒙古自治州	Bayangol Mongol Autonomous Prefecture	224483.7	59736.1	41188.2	4581.5	616.1
阿克苏地区	Aksu Administrative Offices	248340.8	109468.7	2490.2	1866.6	4148.9
克孜勒苏柯尔克孜自治州	Kizilsu Kirgiz Autonomous Prefecture	51851.6	3820.0	521.7	395.5	453.3
喀什地区	Kashgar [Kaxgar] Administrative Offices	211596.6	41065.9	98.9	1012.9	1494.3
和田地区	Hotan Administrative Offices	110512.6	8291.0	1100.9	837.4	2293.6

地 区	Region	建 筑 业 Construction	交通运输、仓储和邮政业 Transportation, Whereheousing and Post Service	信息传输、计算机服务和软件业 Information Transmission, Computer Servcie and Software Industries	批发和零售业 Retail and Wholesale Industries	住宿和餐饮业 Hotel and Catering
总 计	**Total**	**73014.4**	**192734.5**	**24007.2**	**39915.7**	**16881.2**
乌鲁木齐市	Urumqi City	42425.2	148717.7	10799.0	17052.9	10157.1
克拉玛依市	Karamay City	109.0	1260.8	101.9	1005.9	254.6
石河子市	Shi Hezi City	7197.8	2896.1	1106.7	505.1	327.4
吐鲁番地区	Turpan Administrative Offices	33.5	1619.7	834.4	742.9	225.0
哈密地区	Hami [Kumul] Administrative Offices	407.6	1536.1	1423.6	887.9	290.9
昌吉回族自治州	Changji Hui Autonomous Prefecture	589.5	3630.1	1438.2	1614.5	262.3
伊犁哈萨克自治州	Ili Kazak Autonomous Prefecture	10104.7	13546.8	3174.0	4682.9	2107.1
伊犁州直属县(市)	Counties (Cities) Direct Under Ili Prefecture	8493.9	6418.7	730.1	2164.7	1305.5
塔城地区	Tacheng [Tarbagatai] Administrative Offices	742.0	3614.6	1094.0	1375.0	302.6
阿勒泰地区	Altay Administrative Offices	868.8	3513.5	1349.9	1143.2	499.0
博尔塔拉蒙古自治州	Bortala Mongol Autonomous Prefecture	1089.0	1391.1	797.4	1322.3	421.2
巴音郭楞蒙古自治州	Bayangol Mongol Autonomous Prefecture	4416.3	5862.0	1393.7	4627.0	1373.3
阿克苏地区	Aksu Administrative Offices	5759.7	2957.3	892.1	2037.9	489.1
克孜勒苏柯尔克孜自治州	Kizilsu Kirgiz Autonomous Prefecture	126.1	1648.0	334.9	494.9	100.3
喀什地区	Kashgar [Kaxgar] Administrative Offices	247.6	4971.1	656.4	3412.7	531.3
和田地区	Hotan Administrative Offices	508.4	2697.7	1054.9	1528.8	341.6

4-31 续表 Continued

单位：万元 (10 000 yuan)

地　区	Region	金融业 Financial Industry	房地产业 Real Estate Industry	租赁和商务服务业 Leasing and Business Service Industries	科学研究、技术服务和地质勘查业 Scientific Research, Technology Service and Geological Prospecting	水利、环境和公共设施管理业 Water Conservancy, Environment and Public Facility Management Industries
总　计	**Total**	**104761.9**	**14432.7**	**30070.1**	**73413.6**	**53044.3**
乌鲁木齐市	Urumqi City	55810.3	10773.4	19513.6	31199.8	7620.0
克拉玛依市	Karamay City	2867.8	36.8	614.4	132.8	498.4
石河子市	Shi Hezi City	3390.8	296.1	3797.3	2073.8	2867.4
吐鲁番地区	Turpan Administrative Offices	2139.0	142.8	86.0	5868.2	733.4
哈密地区	Hami [Kumul] Administrative Offices	2245.3	145.0	189.2	3203.5	1387.9
昌吉回族自治州	Changji Hui Autonomous Prefecture	5708.7	265.8	553.1	5087.6	4956.5
伊犁哈萨克自治州	Ili Kazak Autonomous Prefecture	12263.6	1236.3	1850.1	8606.3	10255.3
伊犁州直属县(市)	Counties (Cities) Direct Under Ili Prefecture	5578.2	835.8	1131.5	3906.6	4814.7
塔城地区	Tacheng [Tarbagatai] Administrative Offices	3746.2	292.2	527.3	2259.1	4349.4
阿勒泰地区	Altay Administrative Offices	2939.2	108.3	191.3	2440.6	1091.2
博尔塔拉蒙古自治州	Bortala Mongol Autonomous Prefecture	2487.3	223.0	120.3	1089.1	1894.3
巴音郭楞蒙古自治州	Bayangol Mongol Autonomous Prefecture	5098.4	479.4	1000.7	5698.8	4946.6
阿克苏地区	Aksu Administrative Offices	4106.5	291.0	1199.2	2896.5	8785.4
克孜勒苏柯尔克孜自治州	Kizilsu Kirgiz Autonomous Prefecture	1316.5	27.0	292.3	2952.2	940.3
喀什地区	Kashgar [Kaxgar] Administrative Offices	4294.5	452.8	500.8	3378.5	6243.2
和田地区	Hotan Administrative Offices	3033.2	63.3	353.1	1226.5	1915.6

地　区	Region	居民服务和其他服务业 Community Service and Other Service Industries	教　育 Education	卫生、社会保障和社会福利业 Health, Social Security and Welfare	文化、体育和娱乐业 Culture, Sports and Entertainment	公共管理和社会组织 Public Administration and Social Organizations
总　计	**Total**	**4117.9**	**494576.6**	**167179.3**	**37773.9**	**475862.7**
乌鲁木齐市	Urumqi City	289.8	69203.3	30701.6	16398.3	93656.0
克拉玛依市	Karamay City	50.2	11903.9	6201.2	203.2	19328.7
石河子市	Shi Hezi City	55.0	10053.9	5121.4	439.0	7224.2
吐鲁番地区	Turpan Administrative Offices	21.8	15819.0	4234.1	465.2	14719.3
哈密地区	Hami [Kumul] Administrative Offices	2483.3	14630.2	5729.7	866.2	16064.3
昌吉回族自治州	Changji Hui Autonomous Prefecture	116.6	41930.5	13277.0	1377.5	32159.0
伊犁哈萨克自治州	Ili Kazak Autonomous Prefecture	249.9	115141.5	35452.3	7264.0	100776.5
伊犁州直属县(市)	Counties (Cities) Direct Under Ili Prefecture	148.4	57523.3	17799.5	3540.7	48032.3
塔城地区	Tacheng [Tarbagatai] Administrative Offices	74.2	34840.1	10669.2	1519.4	27608.8
阿勒泰地区	Altay Administrative Offices	27.3	22778.1	6983.6	2203.9	25135.4
博尔塔拉蒙古自治州	Bortala Mongol Autonomous Prefecture	80.8	12239.1	5019.9	830.2	16384.6
巴音郭楞蒙古自治州	Bayangol Mongol Autonomous Prefecture	169.5	33730.8	12964.6	1787.8	34812.9
阿克苏地区	Aksu Administrative Offices	97.6	42452.9	14303.2	1729.9	42368.1
克孜勒苏柯尔克孜自治州	Kizilsu Kirgiz Autonomous Prefecture	287.7	16931.7	5144.3	1400.6	14664.3
喀什地区	Kashgar [Kaxgar] Administrative Offices	108.3	72640.0	18094.1	3272.2	49121.1
和田地区	Hotan Administrative Offices	107.4	37899.8	10935.9	1739.8	34583.7

4-32 各地、州、市城镇集体单位分行业在岗职工工资总额

Total Wages of Staff and Workers in Urban Collective-Owned Units by Sector and by Prefecture, Autonomous Prefecture and City

单位：万元　　(2004 年)　　(10 000 yuan)

地　区	Region	合 计 Total	农林牧渔业 Farming, Forestry, Animal Husbandry and Fishery	采 矿 业 Fishery	制 造 业 Manufacturing	电力、燃气及水的生产和供应业 Power, Gas and Water Production and Supply
总　计	**Total**	**78223.8**	**1573.9**	**1155.5**	**16922.3**	**510.6**
乌鲁木齐市	Urumqi City	22689.4	13.9	210.6	5780.0	80.0
克拉玛依市	Karamay City	12023.5	472.1	309.7	4385.8	
石河子市	Shi Hezi City	1142.0			40.6	
吐鲁番地区	Turpan Administrative Offices	2386.8	5.4		761.1	212.4
哈密地区	Hami [Kumul] Administrative Offices	1353.9		3.6	95.3	2.6
昌吉回族自治州	Changji Hui Autonomous Prefecture	5900.0	24.0	186.7	2473.0	56.0
伊犁哈萨克自治州	Ili Kazak Autonomous Prefecture	8235.7	42.7	147.4	1293.9	17.9
伊犁州直属县(市)	Counties (Cities) Direct Under Ili Prefecture	4985.2	5.9	2.6	797.0	17.9
塔城地区	Tacheng [Tarbagatai] Administrative Offices	2253.9	36.8	82.6	393.3	
阿勒泰地区	Altay Administrative Offices	996.6		62.2	103.6	
博尔塔拉蒙古自治州	Bortala Mongol Autonomous Prefecture	2158.9	185.4		57.5	92.2
巴音郭楞蒙古自治州	Bayangol Mongol Autonomous Prefecture	4333.8	419.6	35.4	296.0	
阿克苏地区	Aksu Administrative Offices	4642.0		184.3	591.4	43.9
克孜勒苏柯尔克孜自治州	Kizilsu Kirgiz Autonomous Prefecture	632.6	63.7		29.9	5.6
喀什地区	Kashgar [Kaxgar] Administrative Offices	10274.3	347.1	54.9	986.0	
和田地区	Hotan Administrative Offices	2450.9		22.9	131.8	

地　区	Region	建 筑 业 Construction	交通运输、仓储和邮政业 Transportation, Logistics and Post Industries	信息传输、计算机服务和软件业 Information Transmission, Computer Servcie and Software Industries	批发和零售业 Retail and Wholesale Industries	住宿和餐饮业 Hotel and Catering Trade
总　计	**Total**	**13849.4**	**2473.0**	**3.9**	**17700.8**	**1930.8**
乌鲁木齐市	Urumqi City	3763.3	2188.0		3280.9	1068.8
克拉玛依市	Karamay City	4557.2	188.7		894.1	234.1
石河子市	Shi Hezi City	806.8	2.0		82.1	33.0
吐鲁番地区	Turpan Administrative Offices	4557.2			666.3	35.3
哈密地区	Hami [Kumul] Administrative Offices	239.2			71.6	20.4
昌吉回族自治州	Changji Hui Autonomous Prefecture	403.3	53.3	3.9	162.7	34.5
伊犁哈萨克自治州	Ili Kazak Autonomous Prefecture	1082.2	15.1		1785.5	195.7
伊犁州直属县(市)	Counties (Cities) Direct Under Ili Prefecture	687.4	15.1		1104.4	162.5
塔城地区	Tacheng [Tarbagatai] Administrative Offices	104.0			608.9	33.2
阿勒泰地区	Altay Administrative Offices	290.8			72.2	
博尔塔拉蒙古自治州	Bortala Mongol Autonomous Prefecture	891.0			405.3	53.0
巴音郭楞蒙古自治州	Bayangol Mongol Autonomous Prefecture	5.8	1.9		1865.5	173.7
阿克苏地区	Aksu Administrative Offices	846.8			1313.3	6.0
克孜勒苏柯尔克孜自治州	Kizilsu Kirgiz Autonomous Prefecture				234.9	
喀什地区	Kashgar [Kaxgar] Administrative Offices	373.3	24.0		6379.5	76.3
和田地区	Hotan Administrative Offices	880.5			559.1	

4-32 续表 Continued

单位：万元 (10 000 yuan)

地 区	Region	金融业 Financial Industry	房地产业 Real Estate Industry	租赁和商务服务业 Leasing and Business Service Industries	科学研究、技术服务和地质勘查业 Scientific Research, Technology Service and Geological Prospecting	水利、环境和公共设施管理业 Water Conservancy, Environment and Public Facility Management Industries
总 计	**Total**	**12633.5**	**1009.7**	**4903.7**	**179.6**	**573.9**
乌鲁木齐市	Urumqi City	1113.3	515.5	1595.9	38.5	564.2
克拉玛依市	Karamay City	284.9	210.8	411.1	73.0	
石河子市	Shi Hezi City	168.1		8.4		
吐鲁番地区	Turpan Administrative Offices	661.2	6.8	38.3		
哈密地区	Hami [Kumul] Administrative Offices	723.7	40.2	41.9		
昌吉回族自治州	Changji Hui Autonomous Prefecture	1439.4	6.0	984.5	55.2	
伊犁哈萨克自治州	Ili Kazak Autonomous Prefecture	2908.4	110.9	562.0	8.5	
伊犁州直属县(市)	Counties (Cities) Direct Under Ili Prefecture	1660.5	105.6	402.3		
塔城地区	Tacheng [Tarbagatai] Administrative Offices	833.7		123.1		
阿勒泰地区	Altay Administrative Offices	414.2	5.3	36.6	8.5	
博尔塔拉蒙古自治州	Bortala Mongol Autonomous Prefecture	321.8	31.6	109.9		
巴音郭楞蒙古自治州	Bayangol Mongol Autonomous Prefecture	1211.7	78.9	224.5		
阿克苏地区	Aksu Administrative Offices	1232.2		397.2	4.4	
克孜勒苏柯尔克孜自治州	Kizilsu Kirgiz Autonomous Prefecture	260.8		35.7		
喀什地区	Kashgar [Kaxgar] Administrative Offices	1546.7	7.8	402.1		9.7
和田地区	Hotan Administrative Offices	761.3	1.2	92.2		

地 区	Region	居民服务和其他服务业 Community Service and Other Service Industries	教 育 Education	卫生、社会保障和社会福利业 Health, Social Security and Welfare Industries	文化、体育和娱乐业 Culture, Sports and Entertainment	公共管理和社会组织 Public Administration and Social Organizations
总 计	**Total**	**180.9**	**234.3**	**2251.5**	**12.1**	**124.4**
乌鲁木齐市	Urumqi City	133.4	229.7	2113.4		
克拉玛依市	Karamay City	2.0				
石河子市	Shi Hezi City	1.0				
吐鲁番地区	Turpan Administrative Offices					
哈密地区	Hami [Kumul] Administrative Offices			84.3		31.1
昌吉回族自治州	Changji Hui Autonomous Prefecture	17.5				
伊犁哈萨克自治州	Ili Kazak Autonomous Prefecture	0.4		24.0	3.2	37.9
伊犁州直属县(市)	Counties (Cities) Direct Under Ili Prefecture			24.0		
塔城地区	Tacheng [Tarbagatai] Administrative Offices	0.4				37.9
阿勒泰地区	Altay Administrative Offices				3.2	
博尔塔拉蒙古自治州	Bortala Mongol Autonomous Prefecture	11.2				
巴音郭楞蒙古自治州	Bayangol Mongol Autonomous Prefecture	15.4		5.4		
阿克苏地区	Aksu Administrative Offices			22.5		
克孜勒苏柯尔克孜自治州	Kizilsu Kirgiz Autonomous Prefecture				2.0	
喀什地区	Kashgar [Kaxgar] Administrative Offices		4.6		6.9	55.4
和田地区	Hotan Administrative Offices			1.9		

4-33 其他单位分行业在岗职工工资总额

Total Wages of Staff and Workers in Units of Other Types of Ownership by Sector

单位：万元 (10 000yuan)

项　　目	Item	2003	2004
总　计	**Total**	**740570.2**	**793626.0**
按登记注册类型分组	**Grouped by Registration Status**		
股份合作单位	Cooperative Units	6291.7	11262.0
联营单位	Joint Ownership Units	3170.4	4368.8
有限责任公司	Limited Liability Corporations	499606.5	547196.5
股份有限公司	Share-holding Corporations Ltd.	204187.6	197840.4
其他	Others	9809.4	10881.8
港澳台商投资单位	Units with Funds form Hong Kong, Macao and Taiwan	7694.1	8354.8
外商投资单位	Foreign Funded	9810.5	13721.7
按国民经济行业分组	**Grouped by Economic Sector**		
农、林、牧、渔业	Farming, Forestry, Animal Husbandry and Fishery	4819.7	4400.8
采 矿 业	Fishery	141868.9	124966.5
制 造 业	Manufacturing	229811.5	259103.2
电力、燃气及水的生产和供应业	Power, Gas and Water Production and Supply	55140.2	61348.3
建 筑 业	Construction	186673.9	196621.9
交通运输、仓储和邮政业	Transportation, Logistics and Post Industries	13790.9	18335.3
信息传输、计算机服务和软件业	Information Transmission, Computer Servcie and Software Industries	8295.4	13262.8
批发和零售业	Retail and Wholesale Industries	48268.4	51704.4
住宿和餐饮业	Hotel and Eateries	10885.9	11498.4
金融业	Financial Industry	11454.7	16145.2
房地产业	Real Estate Industry	12565.9	15383.2
租赁和商务服务业	Leasing and Business Service Industries	9162.4	11305.5
科学研究、技术服务和地质勘查业	Scientific Research, Technology Service and Geological Prospecting	4021.9	5535.6
水利、环境和公共设施管理业	Water Conservancy, Environment and Public Facility Management Industries	863.5	911.6
居民服务和其他服务业	Community Service and Other Service Industries	391.7	544.2
教　育	Education	1960.3	1653.8
卫生、社会保障和社会福利业	Health, Social Security and Welfare Industries	200.7	296.8
文化、体育和娱乐业	Culture, Sports and Entertainment	394.3	608.5
公共管理和社会组织	Public Administration and Social Organizations		

4-34 在岗职工平均货币工资

Average Money Wage of Staff and Workers

单位：元 (yuan)

年 份 Year	全部职工 Full Employees	国有单位 State-owned Units	城镇集体单位 Urban Collective-owned Units	其他单位 Units of Other Types of Ownership
1978	717	726	614	
1980	882	904	676	
1985	1277	1310	1038	1707
1990	2272	2345	1765	2498
1991	2455	2510	2060	2683
1992	2742	2801	2317	3286
1993	3239	3286	2889	3689
1994	4252	4322	3586	4940
1995	5348	5431	4509	5973
1996	5987	6067	5111	6626
1997	6644	6709	5849	7428
1998	7121	7167	6239	7847
1999	7611	7614	6815	8681
2000	8717	8731	7489	9498
2001	10278	10145	8197	11594
2002	11605	11435	9353	12767
2003	13255	13199	9966	13937
2004	14484	14477	11594	14870

4-35 在岗职工平均工资指数

Indices of Average Wage of Staff and Workers

(上年=100) (Preceding year=100)

年 份 Year	货币工资 Average Money Wage				实际工资 Average Real Wage			
	合 计 Total	国有单位 State-owned Units	城镇集体单位 Urban Collective-owned Units	其他单位 Units of Other Types of Ownership	合 计 Total	国有单位 State-owned Units	城镇集体单位 Urban Collective-owned Units	其他单位 Units of Other Types of Ownership
1978		105.2				103.9		
1980	114.5	115.3	108.3		109.3	110.0	103.4	
1985	115.7	116.0	112.5	124.6	105.9	106.0	102.7	113.7
1990	113.2	113.3	113.6	96.5	108.3	108.4	108.7	92.3
1991	108.1	107.0	116.7	103.7	98.9	97.9	106.8	98.3
1992	111.7	111.6	112.5	107.4	102.2	102.1	102.9	112.1
1993	118.1	117.3	124.7	112.3	104.0	103.3	109.8	98.7
1994	131.3	131.5	124.1	133.9	103.4	103.6	97.8	105.5
1995	125.8	125.7	125.8	120.9	105.7	105.6	105.7	101.6
1996	111.9	111.7	113.4	110.9	101.3	101.1	102.6	100.4
1997	111.0	110.6	114.4	112.1	107.0	106.6	110.4	108.1
1998	103.4	103.1	102.1	102.6	103.2	102.8	101.9	102.4
1999	106.3	105.6	109.2	109.8	109.1	108.4	112.1	112.7
2000	114.5	114.7	109.9	109.4	115.2	115.4	110.6	110.1
2001	117.9	116.2	109.5	122.1	113.4	111.7	105.3	117.4
2002	112.9	112.7	114.1	110.1	113.6	113.4	114.8	110.8
2003	114.2	115.4	106.6	109.2	113.6	114.8	106.1	108.7
2004	109.3	109.7	116.3	106.7	107.0	107.4	113.9	104.5

4-36 各地、州、市分行业单位在岗职工平均工资

Average Wage of Staff and Workers by Sector and by Prefecture, Autonomous Prefecture, City and County

单位：元 (2004 年) (yuan)

地 区	Region	合 计 Total	农林牧渔业 Farming, Forestry, Animal Husbandry and Fishery	采 矿 业 Fishery	制 造 业 Manufacturing	电力、燃气及水的生产和供应业 Power, Gas and Water Production and Supply
总 计	**Total**	**14484**	**9300**	**21576**	**13518**	**20402**
乌鲁木齐市	Urumqi City	19052	9736	21441	17080	32260
克拉玛依市	Karamay City	19893	10537	22565	21420	
石河子市	Shi Hezi City	13234	12996		11081	15970
吐鲁番地区	Turpan Administrative Offices	17849	8727	25159	9634	25137
哈密地区	Hami [Kumul] Administrative Offices	14220	9190	18357	9631	25105
昌吉回族自治州	Changji Hui Autonomous Prefecture	11880	9187	12551	9482	23952
伊犁哈萨克自治州	Ili Kazak Autonomous Prefecture	11138	7561	13499	10808	16706
伊犁州直属县(市)	Counties (Cities) Direct Under Ili Prefecture	11354	6397	9387	11384	16644
塔城地区	Tacheng [Tarbagatai] Administrative Offices	10550	8266	12629	9921	17261
阿勒泰地区	Altay Administrative Offices	11863	7529	16633	8633	16176
博尔塔拉蒙古自治州	Bortala Mongol Autonomous Prefecture	11799	9476	10277	8813	15360
巴音郭楞蒙古自治州	Bayangol Mongol Autonomous Prefecture	13938	9170	26220	10860	19496
阿克苏地区	Aksu Administrative Offices	13940	13685	21317	11121	18282
克孜勒苏柯尔克孜自治州	Kizilsu Kirgiz Autonomous Prefecture	16012	13122	5325	7693	11779
喀什地区	Kashgar [Kaxgar] Administrative Offices	13565	10930	8314	7961	12361
和田地区	Hotan Administrative Offices	14843	7905	12841	6881	14766

地 区	Region	建 筑 业 Construction	交通运输、仓储和邮政业 Transportation, Waherehousing and Post Industries	信息传输、计算机服务和软件业 Information Transmission, Computer Servcie and Software Industries	批发和零售业 Retail and Wholesale Industries	住宿和餐饮业 Hotel and Catering
总 计	**Total**	**12705**	**20266**	**24032**	**14103**	**11405**
乌鲁木齐市	Urumqi City	13859	24957	37857	18486	13114
克拉玛依市	Karamay City	14793	15778	15184	16314	11518
石河子市	Shi Hezi City	10789	12822	17821	18893	9525
吐鲁番地区	Turpan Administrative Offices	12892	11182	15452	13468	9357
哈密地区	Hami [Kumul] Administrative Offices	12115	12582	25619	11886	9561
昌吉回族自治州	Changji Hui Autonomous Prefecture	11677	10845	19920	12524	9519
伊犁哈萨克自治州	Ili Kazak Autonomous Prefecture	11304	13675	20323	11988	9243
伊犁州直属县(市)	Counties (Cities) Direct Under Ili Prefecture	12221	12610	21914	11373	9074
塔城地区	Tacheng [Tarbagatai] Administrative Offices	10496	14675	17848	13042	7666
阿勒泰地区	Altay Administrative Offices	9393	15319	17898	12807	10855
博尔塔拉蒙古自治州	Bortala Mongol Autonomous Prefecture	12696	13905	25104	13117	9430
巴音郭楞蒙古自治州	Bayangol Mongol Autonomous Prefecture	12952	13421	17902	13384	9858
阿克苏地区	Aksu Administrative Offices	11578	11647	15170	10617	8667
克孜勒苏柯尔克孜自治州	Kizilsu Kirgiz Autonomous Prefecture	12431	15249	17000	9446	9833
喀什地区	Kashgar [Kaxgar] Administrative Offices	11590	12197	16414	10841	8732
和田地区	Hotan Administrative Offices	10330	13482	17408	11996	11038

4-36 续表 Continued

单位：元 (yuan)

地区	Region	金融业 Financial Industry	房地产业 Real Estate Industry	租赁和商务服务业 Leasing and Business Service Industries	科学研究、技术服务和地质勘查业 Scientific Research, Technology Service and Geological Prospecting	水利、环境和公共设施管理业 Water Conservancy, Environment and Public Facility Management Industries
总 计	**Total**	**24416**	**14060**	**13502**	**17777**	**13094**
乌鲁木齐市	Urumqi City	32513	16513	15327	19644	15351
克拉玛依市	Karamay City	22747	16796	18285	19304	14126
石河子市	Shi Hezi City	20375	13040	19494	17710	13075
吐鲁番地区	Turpan Administrative Offices	17029	9235	9949	22020	11756
哈密地区	Hami [Kumul] Administrative Offices	20784	9494	13563	15087	9827
昌吉回族自治州	Changji Hui Autonomous Prefecture	18859	11291	9505	14536	10569
伊犁哈萨克自治州	Ili Kazak Autonomous Prefecture	21409	10360	7622	15343	11412
伊犁州直属县(市)	Counties (Cities) Direct Under Ili Prefecture	22766	9948	6813	15163	10686
塔城地区	Tacheng [Tarbagatai] Administrative Offices	20452	11763	9630	14528	12384
阿勒泰地区	Altay Administrative Offices	19429	10677	11193	16496	11333
博尔塔拉蒙古自治州	Bortala Mongol Autonomous Prefecture	23393	9975	11048	17310	12528
巴音郭楞蒙古自治州	Bayangol Mongol Autonomous Prefecture	21781	11167	12393	18297	12779
阿克苏地区	Aksu Administrative Offices	16847	10403	8946	15580	16898
克孜勒苏柯尔克孜自治州	Kizilsu Kirgiz Autonomous Prefecture	20727	19053	11280	16077	15777
喀什地区	Kashgar [Kaxgar] Administrative Offices	14563	10263	10284	15378	13543
和田地区	Hotan Administrative Offices	19213	9898	12073	16642	12822

地区	Region	居民服务和其他服务业 Community Service and Other Service Industries	教育 Education	卫生、社会保障和社会福利业 Health, Social Security and Welfare Industries	文化、体育和娱乐业 Culture, Sports and Entertainment	公共管理和社会组织 Public Administration and Social Organizations
总 计	**Total**	**14269**	**16403**	**16537**	**16510**	**16802**
乌鲁木齐市	Urumqi City	12087	18427	18438	19469	20178
克拉玛依市	Karamay City	14891	23273	22403	19485	24427
石河子市	Shi Hezi City	16970	16035	16574	15848	17391
吐鲁番地区	Turpan Administrative Offices	7032	15503	14466	13484	14123
哈密地区	Hami [Kumul] Administrative Offices	18193	16659	16626	13837	16181
昌吉回族自治州	Changji Hui Autonomous Prefecture	11348	15438	15074	13956	14787
伊犁哈萨克自治州	Ili Kazak Autonomous Prefecture	10011	15400	14685	14486	15545
伊犁州直属县(市)	Counties (Cities) Direct Under Ili Prefecture	9684	14670	14567	14155	14979
塔城地区	Tacheng [Tarbagatai] Administrative Offices	9176	15421	13871	13901	15445
阿勒泰地区	Altay Administrative Offices	19500	17596	16506	15521	16886
博尔塔拉蒙古自治州	Bortala Mongol Autonomous Prefecture	11948	16196	15398	14413	16375
巴音郭楞蒙古自治州	Bayangol Mongol Autonomous Prefecture	11411	16918	17451	15320	17319
阿克苏地区	Aksu Administrative Offices	10460	14951	16289	13806	14542
克孜勒苏柯尔克孜自治州	Kizilsu Kirgiz Autonomous Prefecture	14385	18020	18191	16899	17052
喀什地区	Kashgar [Kaxgar] Administrative Offices	7800	16026	16939	14382	16492
和田地区	Hotan Administrative Offices	14917	17967	17050	16649	17135

4-37 各地、州、市国有单位分行业在岗职工平均工资

Average Wage of Staff and Workers in State-owned Units by Sector and by Prefecture, Autonomous Prefecture, City and County

单位：元 (2004 年) (yuan)

地区	Region	合计 Total	农林牧渔业 Farming, Forestry, Animal Husbandry and Fishery	采矿业 Fishery	制造业 Manufacturing	电力、燃气及水的生产和供应业 Power, Gas and Water Production and Supply
总计	**Total**	**14477**	**9300**	**21701**	**13467**	**20039**
乌鲁木齐市	Urumqi City	20137	9521	14034	17329	32364
克拉玛依市	Karamay City	19899	10374	20833	16410	
石河子市	Shi Hezi City	14247	13013		9990	14853
吐鲁番地区	Turpan Administrative Offices	17777	8731	23506	8707	26566
哈密地区	Hami [Kumul] Administrative Offices	13811	9190	12853	11050	25140
昌吉回族自治州	Changji Hui Autonomous Prefecture	12039	9191	13724	8548	22445
伊犁哈萨克自治州	Ili Kazak Autonomous Prefecture	11016	7560	14989	12927	13925
伊犁州直属县(市)	Counties (Cities) Direct Under Ili Prefecture	11132	6395	9113	16652	13769
塔城地区	Tacheng [Tarbagatai] Administrative Offices	10454	8268	14347	10631	14676
阿勒泰地区	Altay Administrative Offices	11971	7524	16902	7690	13819
博尔塔拉蒙古自治州	Bortala Mongol Autonomous Prefecture	12043	9467		10846	16382
巴音郭楞蒙古自治州	Bayangol Mongol Autonomous Prefecture	14222	9210	26868	8330	13025
阿克苏地区	Aksu Administrative Offices	14263	13707	19826	10228	17875
克孜勒苏柯尔克孜自治州	Kizilsu Kirgiz Autonomous Prefecture	16356	13282	5610	8415	12805
喀什地区	Kashgar [Kaxgar] Administrative Offices	14402	10985	8174	6206	11286
和田地区	Hotan Administrative Offices	15563	7905	19520	5673	14114

地区	Region	建筑业 Construction	交通运输、仓储和邮政业 Transportation, and Post Service	信息传输、计算机服务和软件业 Information Transmission, Computer Servcie and Software Industries	批发和零售业 Retail and Wholesale Service	住宿和餐饮业 Hotel and Catering
总计	**Total**	**12564**	**21658**	**24917**	**15889**	**12086**
乌鲁木齐市	Urumqi City	13411	26056	40967	20708	14039
克拉玛依市	Karamay City	16515	16524	17877	16069	15913
石河子市	Shi Hezi City	9786	13552	18758	15884	9275
吐鲁番地区	Turpan Administrative Offices	7128	11910	15452	15069	10563
哈密地区	Hami [Kumul] Administrative Offices	8301	12622	27324	12849	10031
昌吉回族自治州	Changji Hui Autonomous Prefecture	9680	12796	20115	14480	10206
伊犁哈萨克自治州	Ili Kazak Autonomous Prefecture	12376	14625	17852	12072	9539
伊犁州直属县(市)	Counties (Cities) Direct Under Ili Prefecture	12698	13496	17851	11417	9488
塔城地区	Tacheng [Tarbagatai] Administrative Offices	9195	14844	17934	12911	9060
阿勒泰地区	Altay Administrative Offices	12987	16957	17785	12453	10000
博尔塔拉蒙古自治州	Bortala Mongol Autonomous Prefecture	15125	15121	33225	13817	10149
巴音郭楞蒙古自治州	Bayangol Mongol Autonomous Prefecture	12955	13764	17356	17997	10556
阿克苏地区	Aksu Administrative Offices	11861	12600	15706	12016	9534
克孜勒苏柯尔克孜自治州	Kizilsu Kirgiz Autonomous Prefecture	14835	15518	17000	10059	9833
喀什地区	Kashgar [Kaxgar] Administrative Offices	8971	13155	17094	11041	8501
和田地区	Hotan Administrative Offices	12678	13687	17408	15958	11580

4-37 续表 Continued

单位：元 (yuan)

地　区	Region	金融业 Financial Industry	房地产业 Real Estate Industry	租赁和商务服务业 Leasing and Business Service Industries	科学研究、技术服务和地质勘查业 Scientific Research, Technology Service and Geological Prospecting	水利、环境和公共设施管理业 Water Conservancy, Environment and Public Facility Management Industries
总　计	**Total**	**26196**	**16677**	**13936**	**17749**	**13244**
乌鲁木齐市	Urumqi City	32281	19862	15283	19610	16870
克拉玛依市	Karamay City	21875	16727	33211	24145	14616
石河子市	Shi Hezi City	21584	14658	23571	17862	13075
吐鲁番地区	Turpan Administrative Offices	20179	9038	11622	22020	11531
哈密地区	Hami [Kumul] Administrative Offices	20656	9667	11975	15097	9822
昌吉回族自治州	Changji Hui Autonomous Prefecture	22835	12903	8330	14704	10514
伊犁哈萨克自治州	Ili Kazak Autonomous Prefecture	24227	11098	7210	15195	11457
伊犁州直属县(市)	Counties (Cities) Direct Under Ili Prefecture	25789	9891	5680	14792	10745
塔城地区	Tacheng [Tarbagatai] Administrative Offices	23326	14832	12988	14528	12384
阿勒泰地区	Altay Administrative Offices	22732	15042	11387	16625	11390
博尔塔拉蒙古自治州	Bortala Mongol Autonomous Prefecture	24873	11320	10741	16304	12528
巴音郭楞蒙古自治州	Bayangol Mongol Autonomous Prefecture	22167	10135	10737	18515	12759
阿克苏地区	Aksu Administrative Offices	17089	10738	7797	15854	16898
克孜勒苏柯尔克孜自治州	Kizilsu Kirgiz Autonomous Prefecture	23260	15882	10256	16239	15777
喀什地区	Kashgar [Kaxgar] Administrative Offices	16894	12508	11104	15378	13546
和田地区	Hotan Administrative Offices	23314	10914	15090	16642	12822

地　区	Region	居民服务和其他服务业 Community Service and Other Service Industries	教　育 Education	卫生、社会保障和社会福利业 Health, Social Security and Welfare Industries	文化、体育和娱乐业 Culture, Sports and Entertainment	公共管理和社会组织 Public Administration and Social Organizations
总　计	**Total**	**15628**	**16418**	**16533**	**16589**	**16802**
乌鲁木齐市	Urumqi City	18818	18468	18452	19613	20178
克拉玛依市	Karamay City	18593	23323	22403	25086	24427
石河子市	Shi Hezi City	18333	16035	16574	15848	17391
吐鲁番地区	Turpan Administrative Offices	7032	15503	14466	13484	14123
哈密地区	Hami [Kumul] Administrative Offices	18193	16661	16739	13837	16191
昌吉回族自治州	Changji Hui Autonomous Prefecture	11431	15440	15074	13956	14787
伊犁哈萨克自治州	Ili Kazak Autonomous Prefecture	10544	15430	14706	14540	15545
伊犁州直属县(市)	Counties (Cities) Direct Under Ili Prefecture	10451	14718	14609	14243	14979
塔城地区	Tacheng [Tarbagatai] Administrative Offices	9160	15421	13871	13901	15443
阿勒泰地区	Altay Administrative Offices	19500	17596	16506	15553	16886
博尔塔拉蒙古自治州	Bortala Mongol Autonomous Prefecture	13695	16196	15398	14413	16375
巴音郭楞蒙古自治州	Bayangol Mongol Autonomous Prefecture	13038	16980	17477	15320	17319
阿克苏地区	Aksu Administrative Offices	10725	14951	16333	13806	14542
克孜勒苏柯尔克孜自治州	Kizilsu Kirgiz Autonomous Prefecture	14385	18020	18191	16936	17052
喀什地区	Kashgar [Kaxgar] Administrative Offices	7905	16028	16939	14674	16494
和田地区	Hotan Administrative Offices	14917	17967	17061	16649	17135

4-38 各地、州、市城镇集体单位分行业在岗职工平均工资

Average Wage of Staff and Workers in Urban Collevtive-Owned Units by Sector in Prefecture, Autonomous Prefecture, City and County

单位：元　　(2004 年)　　(yuan)

地　区	Region	合计 Total	农林牧渔业 Farming, Forestry, Animal Husbandry and Fishery	采矿业 Fishery	制造业 Manufacturing	电力、燃气及水的生产和供应业 Power, Gas and Water Production and Supply
总　计	**Total**	**11594**	**8002**	**11743**	**10706**	**12274**
乌鲁木齐市	Urumqi City	13950	4484	8526	13133	13333
克拉玛依市	Karamay City	12982	15328	28413	12112	
石河子市	Shi Hezi City	11594			5639	
吐鲁番地区	Turpan Administrative Offices	12271	27000		13077	13882
哈密地区	Hami [Kumul] Administrative Offices	15195		3600	12063	6500
昌吉回族自治州	Changji Hui Autonomous Prefecture	9710	7273	10792	8620	10182
伊犁哈萨克自治州	Ili Kazak Autonomous Prefecture	10966	5338	7190	8148	9944
伊犁州直属县(市)	Counties (Cities) Direct Under Ili Prefecture	12819	6556	6500	11069	9944
塔城地区	Tacheng [Tarbagatai] Administrative Offices	9218	5183	6883	5717	
阿勒泰地区	Altay Administrative Offices	8474		7679	5756	
博尔塔拉蒙古自治州	Bortala Mongol Autonomous Prefecture	9266	5812		7012	12630
巴音郭楞蒙古自治州	Bayangol Mongol Autonomous Prefecture	11081	6890	8634	7532	
阿克苏地区	Aksu Administrative Offices	10505		23038	10637	9146
克孜勒苏柯尔克孜自治州	Kizilsu Kirgiz Autonomous Prefecture	9777	8063		5750	11200
喀什地区	Kashgar [Kaxgar] Administrative Offices	9677	6860	8578	7515	
和田地区	Hotan Administrative Offices	9380		5089	6623	

地　区	Region	建筑业 Construction	交通运输、仓储和邮政业 Transportation, Warehouises and Post Industries	信息传输、计算机服务和软件业 Information Transmission, Computer Servcie and Software Industries	批发和零售业 Retail and Wholesale Industries	住宿和餐饮业 Hotel and Catering
总　计	**Total**	**11541**	**15485**	**9750**	**10964**	**11378**
乌鲁木齐市	Urumqi City	12968	15752		14913	15054
克拉玛依市	Karamay City	12606	19255		15103	9039
石河子市	Shi Hezi City	12909	3333		13459	8250
吐鲁番地区	Turpan Administrative Offices				12667	6537
哈密地区	Hami [Kumul] Administrative Offices	13215			8950	9273
昌吉回族自治州	Changji Hui Autonomous Prefecture	13180	8328	9750	10993	9079
伊犁哈萨克自治州	Ili Kazak Autonomous Prefecture	9493	9438		10967	8328
伊犁州直属县(市)	Counties (Cities) Direct Under Ili Prefecture	10543	9438		12057	8880
塔城地区	Tacheng [Tarbagatai] Administrative Offices	10196			9982	6385
阿勒泰地区	Altay Administrative Offices	7534			7078	
博尔塔拉蒙古自治州	Bortala Mongol Autonomous Prefecture	9399			8204	8154
巴音郭楞蒙古自治州	Bayangol Mongol Autonomous Prefecture	5800	4750		10871	10722
阿克苏地区	Aksu Administrative Offices	11382			7492	6000
克孜勒苏柯尔克孜自治州	Kizilsu Kirgiz Autonomous Prefecture				8700	
喀什地区	Kashgar [Kaxgar] Administrative Offices	5673	12000		10641	7480
和田地区	Hotan Administrative Offices	10109			8198	

4-38 续表 Continued

单位：元　　　　　　　　　　　　　　　　　　　　　　　　　　　　　　　　(yuan)

地　　区	Region	金融业 Financial Industry	房地产业 Real Estate Industry	租赁和商务服务业 Leasing and Business Service Industries	科学研究、技术服务和地质勘查业 Scientific Research, Technology Service and Geological Prospecting	水利、环境和公共设施管理业 Water Conservancy, Environment and Public Facility Management Industries
总　计	**Total**	**14919**	**10606**	**10358**	**13606**	**6965**
乌鲁木齐市	Urumqi City	26762	10922	14011	9625	6914
克拉玛依市	Karamay City	37987	14438	10151	22813	
石河子市	Shi Hezi City	10188		6462		
吐鲁番地区	Turpan Administrative Offices	11499	8500	8511		
哈密地区	Hami [Kumul] Administrative Offices	21038	7882	19952		
昌吉回族自治州	Changji Hui Autonomous Prefecture	12096	7500	8743	11500	
伊犁哈萨克自治州	Ili Kazak Autonomous Prefecture	16725	9090	8228	14167	
伊犁州直属县(市)	Counties (Cities) Direct Under Ili Prefecture	21649	9429	8560		
塔城地区	Tacheng [Tarbagatai] Administrative Offices	13735		7157		
阿勒泰地区	Altay Administrative Offices	11348	5300	8927	14167	
博尔塔拉蒙古自治州	Bortala Mongol Autonomous Prefecture	16090	7707	12211		
巴音郭楞蒙古自治州	Bayangol Mongol Autonomous Prefecture	19831	8576	9354		
阿克苏地区	Aksu Administrative Offices	14600		11252	7333	
克孜勒苏柯尔克孜自治州	Kizilsu Kirgiz Autonomous Prefecture	13374		10818		
喀什地区	Kashgar [Kaxgar] Administrative Offices	10741	9750	8876		12125
和田地区	Hotan Administrative Offices	11295	3000	6932		

地　　区	Region	居民服务和其他服务业 Community Service and Other Service Industries	教　育 Education	卫生、社会保障和社会福利业 Health, Social Security and Welfare Industries	文化、体育和娱乐业 Culture, Sports and Entertainment	公共管理和社会组织 Public Administration and Social Organizations
总　计	**Total**	**8453**	**16856**	**17453**	**6722**	**14810**
乌鲁木齐市	Urumqi City	8719	17015	18314		
克拉玛依市	Karamay City	10000				
石河子市	Shi Hezi City	3333				
吐鲁番地区	Turpan Administrative Offices					
哈密地区	Hami [Kumul] Administrative Offices			11392		12440
昌吉回族自治州	Changji Hui Autonomous Prefecture	12500				
伊犁哈萨克自治州	Ili Kazak Autonomous Prefecture	4000		10909	6400	17227
伊犁州直属县(市)	Counties (Cities) Direct Under Ili Prefecture			10909		
塔城地区	Tacheng [Tarbagatai] Administrative Offices	4000				17227
阿勒泰地区	Altay Administrative Offices				6400	
博尔塔拉蒙古自治州	Bortala Mongol Autonomous Prefecture	6222				
巴音郭楞蒙古自治州	Bayangol Mongol Autonomous Prefecture	6696		5400		
阿克苏地区	Aksu Administrative Offices			9000		
克孜勒苏柯尔克孜自治州	Kizilsu Kirgiz Autonomous Prefecture				6667	
喀什地区	Kashgar [Kaxgar] Administrative Offices		11500		6900	14973
和田地区	Hotan Administrative Offices			3800		

4-39 各地、州、市、县(市)在岗职工平均货币工资
Average Money Wages of Fully Employed Staff and Workers by Prefecture, Autonomous Prefecture, City and County

单位：元 (2004 年) (yuan)

地 区	Region	合 计 Total	国有单位 State-owned Units	城镇集体单位 Urban Collective-owned Units	其他单位 Units of Other Types of Ownership
总 计	**Total**	**14484**	**14477**	**11594**	**14870**
乌鲁木齐市	**Urumqi City**	**19052**	**20137**	**13950**	**17493**
乌鲁木齐县	Urumqi County	19469	19469		
克拉玛依市	**Karamay City**	**19893**	**19899**	**12982**	**21094**
石河子市	**Shi Hezi City**	**13234**	**14247**	**11594**	**11938**
吐鲁番地区	**Turpan Administrative Offices**	**17849**	**17777**	**12271**	**19059**
吐鲁番市	Turpan City	14383	15219	11535	11527
鄯善县	Shanshan [Piqan] County	21470	20169	13350	28719
托克逊县	Toksun County	12580	14333	13947	6624
哈密地区	**Hami [Kumul] Administrative Offices**	**14220**	**13811**	**15195**	**15351**
哈密市	Hami [Kumul] City	15077	14883	15679	15470
巴里坤哈萨克自治县	Barkol Kazak Autonomous County	9763	9787	15880	6679
伊吾县	Yiwu [Araturuk] County	14888	15027	13255	10182
昌吉回族自治州	**Changji Hui Autonomous Prefecture**	**11880**	**12039**	**9710**	**11663**
昌吉市	Changji City	17012	19790	11975	12840
阜康市	Fukang City	11184	11652	10585	10072
米泉市	Miquan City	12734	13909	9233	12050
呼图壁县	Hutubi County	9388	9108	10352	10374
玛纳斯县	Manas County	12368	12029	8782	16466
奇台县	Qitai County	11423	11878	9309	9726
吉木萨尔县	Jimsar County	12942	14086	16649	9423
木垒哈萨克自治县	Mori Kazak Autonomous County	13901	15734	11717	7090
伊犁哈萨克自治州	**Ili Kazak Autonomous Prefecture**	**11138**	**11016**	**10966**	**12041**
伊犁州直属县(市)	**Counties (Cities) Direct Under Ili Prefecture**	**11354**	**11132**	**12819**	**12267**
伊宁市	Yining [Gulja] City	13621	14033	11747	12779
奎屯市	Kuytun City	14328	14505	20047	13112
伊宁县	Yining [Gulja] County	8178	7637	9714	11663
察布查尔锡伯自治县	Qapqal Xibe Autonomous County	9362	9432	8529	8261
霍城县	Huocheng [Korgas] County	8930	8787	13920	10037
巩留县	Gongliu [Tokkuztara] County	11791	12274	10143	
新源县	Xinyuan [Kunes] County	11390	10390	15654	14594
昭苏县	Zhaosu [Mongolkure] County	10286	10364	9824	9230
特克斯县	Tekes County	12130	12313	10192	10879
尼勒克县	Nilka County	11431	11880	7527	7930
塔城地区	**Tacheng [Tarbagatai] Administrative Offices**	**10550**	**10454**	**9218**	**11948**
塔城市	Tacheng [Qoqek] City	12781	12675	11390	13604
乌苏市	Usu City	9975	9813	8382	11922
额敏县	Emin [Dorbiljin] County	8820	8652	10120	11516
沙湾县	Shawan County	10819	10841	9353	10753
托里县	Toli County	14042	14051	12326	11000
裕民县	Yumin [Qagantokay] County	10091	10131	8241	8474
和布克赛尔蒙古自治县	Hoboksar Mongol Autonomous County	10172	9860	5827	11473
阿勒泰地区	**Altay Administrative Offices**	**11863**	**11971**	**8474**	**11215**
阿勒泰市	Altay City	12296	12259	10311	12682
布尔津县	Burqin County	11590	11896	7367	9807
富蕴县	Fuyun [Koktokay] County	11253	11453	7650	8082
福海县	Fuhai [Burultokay] County	10865	10920	12663	9670
哈巴河县	Habahe [Kaba] County	12888	13226	12607	11464
青河县	Qinghe [Qinggil] County	13075	13964	2652	1663
吉木乃县	Jeminay County	10858	10880	9210	11040

4-39 续表 Continued

单位：元 (yuan)

地区	Region	合计 Total	国有单位 State-owned Units	城镇集体单位 Urban Collective-owned Units	其他单位 Units of Other Types of Ownership
博尔塔拉蒙古自治州	**Bortala Mongol Autonomous Prefecture**	**11799**	**12043**	**9266**	**10210**
博乐市	Bole [Bortala] City	13318	13723	9209	10820
精河县	Jinghe [Jing] County	10218	10456	9001	8551
温泉县	Wenquan [Araxang] County	8578	8532	17750	8818
巴音郭楞蒙古自治州	**Bayangol Mongol Autonomous Prefecture**	**13938**	**14222**	**11081**	**13104**
库尔勒市	Korla City	15452	16688	10372	13243
轮台县	Luntai [Bugur] County	14973	14893	10550	17565
尉犁县	Yuli [Lopnur] County	12884	13005	9793	9193
若羌县	Ruoqiang [Qarkilik] County	14662	14654	13536	20300
且末县	Qiemo [Qarqan] County	17880	18322	18118	9045
焉耆回族自治县	Yanji Hui Autonomous County	12820	12858	11822	12623
和静县	Hejing County	10033	9969	11052	10925
和硕县	Hoxud County	9602	9728	11549	7731
博湖县	Bohu [Bagrax] County	12418	12423	13938	12066
阿克苏地区	**Aksu Administrative Offices**	**13940**	**14263**	**10505**	**12490**
阿克苏市	Aksu City	14648	15021	11075	12588
温宿县	Wensu [Onsu] County	10579	10636	9543	9997
库车县	Kuqa County	12721	13160	9703	12062
沙雅县	Xayar County	13491	14351	13593	10059
新和县	Xinhe [Toksu] County	13339	14103	10941	9997
拜城县	Baicheng [Bay] County	15893	15027	11998	19175
乌什县	Wushi [Uxturpan] County	14124	14539	9828	11164
阿瓦提县	Awat County	14405	15209	8443	9723
柯坪县	Kalpin County	15695	15975	7410	12410
克孜勒苏柯尔克孜自治州	**Kizilsu Kirgiz Autonomous Prefecture**	**16012**	**16356**	**9777**	**9514**
阿图什市	Artux City	16759	17167	8777	10112
阿克陶县	Akto County	15491	16063	11491	8621
阿合奇县	Akqi County	15739	15846	8783	
乌恰县	Wuqia [Ulugqat] County	14265	14299	10025	
喀什地区	**Kashgar [Kaxgar] Administrative Offices**	**13565**	**14402**	**9677**	**11195**
喀什市	Kashgar [Kaxgar] City	13137	15368	9261	11274
疏附县	Shufu County	14081	14458	7968	5226
疏勒县	Shule County	13806	14682	7581	11144
英吉沙县	Yengisar County	15102	15648	10589	12280
泽普县	Zepu [Poskam] County	13405	14963	8075	9028
莎车县	Shache [Yarkant] County	14593	15288	9384	8247
叶城县	Yecheng [Kagilik] County	13138	14130	7117	4755
麦盖提县	Makit County	12710	12812	9788	17067
岳普湖县	Yopurga County	13900	14353	8425	
伽师县	Jiashi [Payzawat] County	14513	15452	7188	7486
巴楚县	Bachu [Maralbexi] County	12879	12619	17671	13577
塔什库尔干塔吉克自治县	Taxkorgan Tajik Autonomous County	19618	20275	7719	
和田地区	**Hotan Administrative Offices**	**14843**	**15563**	**9380**	**10005**
和田市	Hotan City	15228	16618	10720	10352
和田县	Hotan County	16376	16542	10949	
墨玉县	Moyu [Karakax] County	14556	14977	6361	
皮山县	Pishan [Guma] County	12102	12523	10714	9202
洛浦县	Lop County	15695	16888	13000	9709
策勒县	Qira County	15284	15501	11784	
于田县	Yutian [Keriya] County	15617	15820	9040	9125
民丰县	Minfeng [Niya] County	16365	16975	5877	

4-40 其他单位分行业在岗职工平均工资

Average Wage of Staff and Workers in Units of Other Types of Ownership by Sector

单位：元 (yuan)

登记注册类型及行业	Registration Status and Sector	2003	2004
总　计	**Total**	**13937**	**14870**
按登记注册类型分组	**Grouped by Registration Status**		
股份合作单位	Cooperative Units	9371	13318
联营单位	Joint Ownership Units	10839	12793
有限责任公司	Limited Liability Corporations	12434	13529
股份有限公司	Share-holding Corporations Ltd.	21496	21825
其　他	Others	8782	9196
港澳台商投资单位	Units with Funds form Hong Kong, Macao and Taiwan	11946	13241
外商投资单位	Foreign Funded	13439	15998
按国民经济行业分组	**Grouped by Economic Sector**		
农、林、牧、渔业	Farming, Forestry, Animal Husbandry and Fishery	8814	9885
采 矿 业	Fishery	21209	21574
制 造 业	Manufacturing	12790	13769
电力、燃气及水的生产和供应业	Power, Gas and Water Production and Supply	17718	20815
建 筑 业	Construction	11782	12849
交通运输、仓储和邮政业	Transportation, Logistics and Post Industries	9862	12402
信息传输、计算机服务和软件业	Information Transmission, Computer Servcie and Software Industries	18361	22590
批发和零售业	Retail and Wholesale Industries	14629	14264
住宿和餐饮业	Hotel and Eateries	10259	10538
金融业	Financial Industry	22307	25899
房地产业	Real Estate Industry	12094	12487
租赁和商务服务业	Leasing and Business Service Industries	14221	14198
科学研究、技术服务和地质勘查业	Scientific Research, Technology Service and Geological Prospecting	16984	18336
水利、环境和公共设施管理业	Water Conservancy, Environment and Public Facility Management Industries	10944	11839
居民服务和其他服务业	Community Service and Other Service Industries	8822	9985
教　育	Education	14246	12800
卫生、社会保障和社会福利业	Health, Social Security and Welfare Industries	9790	13075
文化、体育和娱乐业	Culture, Sports and Entertainment	7950	13030
公共管理和社会组织	Public Administration and Social Organizations		

主要统计指标解释

人口数　指一定时点、一定地区范围内的有生命的个人的总和。

年度统计的年末人口数指每年 12 月 31 日 24 时的人口数。

其定义有两种口径：

第一种口径(按行政建制)

市人口：市管辖区域内的全部人口(含市辖镇，不含市辖区县)；

镇人口：县辖镇的全部人口(不含市辖镇)；

县人口：县辖乡人口。

第二种口径(按常住人口划分)

市人口：设区的市的区人口和不设区的市所辖的街道人口；

镇人口：不设区的市所辖镇的居民委员会人口和县辖镇的居民委员会人口；

县人口：除上述两种人口以外的全部人口。

1952-1980 年数据为第一种口径的数据，1982 年以后的数据为第二种口径的数据。

出生率(又称粗出生率)　指在一定时期内(通常为一年)平均每千人所出生的人数的比率，一般用千分率表示。计算公式为：

出生率＝年出生人数／年平均人数×1000‰

式中：出生人数指活产婴儿，即胎儿脱离母体时(不管怀孕月数)，有过呼吸或其他生命现象。年平均人数指年初、年底人口数的平均数，也可用年中人口数代替。

死亡率(又称粗死亡率)　指在一定时期内(通常为一年)一定地区的死亡人数与同期平均人数(或期中人数)之比，一般用千分率表示。计算公式为：

死亡率＝年死亡人数／年平均人数×1000‰

人口自然增长率　指在一定时期内(通常为一年)人口自然增加数(出生人数减死亡人数)与该时期内平均人数(或期中人数)之比，一般用千分率表示。计算公式为：

人口自然增长率＝(本年出生人数－本年死亡人数)／年平均人数×1000‰＝人口出生率－人口死亡率

在业人口(又称就业人口)　指十五周岁及十五周岁以上人口中从事一定的社会劳动并取得劳动报酬或经营收入的人口。

不在业人口　指十五周岁及十五周岁以上人口中未从事社会劳动的人口，包括在校学生、料理家务、待升学、市镇待业、离退休、退职、丧失劳动能力等非在业人口。

经济活动人口　指在 16 岁以上，有劳动能力，参加或要求参加社会经济活动的人口；包括从业人员和失业人员。从业人员指从事一定社会劳动并取得劳动报酬或经营收入的人员，包括全部职工、再就业的离退休人员、私营业主、个体户主、私营和个体从业人员、乡镇企业从业人员、农村从业人员、其他从业人员(包括民办教师、宗教职业者、现役军人等)。这一指标反映了一定时期内全部劳动力资源的实际利用情况，是研究我国基本国情国力的重要指标。

各单位的从业人员　指在各级国家机关、政党机关、社会团体及企业、事业单位中工作，取得工资或其他形式的劳动报酬的全部人员。包括在岗职工、再就业的离退休人员、民办教师以及在各单位中工作的外方人员和港澳台方人员、兼职人员、借用的外单位人员和第二职业者。不包括离开本单位仍保留劳动关系的职工。各单位的从业人员反映了各单位实际参加生产或工作的全部劳动力。

城镇私营和个体从业人员　城镇私营从业人员指在工商管理部门注册登记，其经营地址设在县城关镇(含城关镇)以上的私营企业从业人员；包括私营企业投资者和雇工。城镇个体从业人员指在工商管理部门注册登记，并持有城镇户口或在城镇长期居住，经批准从事个体工商经营的从业人员；包括个体经营者和在个体工商户劳动的家庭帮工和雇工。

城镇登记失业人员　指有非农业户口，在一定的劳动年龄内，有劳动能力，无业而要求就业，并在当地就业服务机构进行求职登记的人员。

城镇登记失业率　指城镇登记失业人数同城镇从业人数与城镇登记失业人数之和的比。计算公式为：

城镇登记失业率=城镇登记失业人数／(城镇从业人数+城镇登记失业人数)×100%

职工　指在国有经济、城镇集体经济、联营经济、股份制经济、外商和港、澳、台投资经济、其他经济单位及其附属机构工作，并由其支付工资的各类人员，不包括返聘的离退休人员、民办教师、在国有经济单位工作的外方人员和港、澳、台人员(1998 年以后的数据均为在岗职工数据，其他相关指标如职工工资总额，职工平均工资等指标也从 1998 年按此口径进行了相应调整)。

国有单位职工　指在国有经济单位及其附属机构工作，并由其支付工资的各类人员。

城镇集体单位职工　指在城镇集体经济单位及其管理部门工作，并由其支付工资的各类人员。

其他单位职工　指在联营经济、股份制经济、外商投资经济、港、澳、台投资经济单位工作，并由其支付工资的各类人员。

在岗职工　指在本单位工作并由单位支付工资的人员，以及有工作岗位，但由于学习、病伤产假等原因暂未工作，仍由单位支付工资的人员。

职工工资总额　指各单位在一定时期内直接支付给本单位全部职工的劳动报酬总额。工资总额的计算原则应以直接支付给职工的全部劳动报酬为根据。各单位支付给职工的劳动报酬以及其他根据有关规定支付的工资，不论是计入成本的还是不计入成本的，不论是按国家规定列入计征奖金税项目的，还是未列入计征奖金税项目的，不论是以货币形式支付的还是以实物形式支付的，均包括在工资总额内。

奖金　指支付给职工的超额劳动报酬和增收节支的劳动报酬。

津贴和补贴　指为了补偿职工特殊或额外的劳动消耗和因其他特殊原因支付给职工的津贴，以及为了保证职工工资水平不受物价影响支付给职工的物价补贴。

职工平均工资　指企业、事业、机关单位的职工在一定时期内平均每人所得的货币工资额。它表明一定时期职工工资收入的高低程度，是反映职工工资水平的主要指标。计算公式为：

职工平均工资＝报告期实际支付的全部职工工资总额／报告期全部职工平均人数

职工平均工资指数　指报告期职工平均工资与基期职工平均工资的比率，是反映不同时期职工货币工资水平变动情况的相对数。计算公式为：

职工平均工资指数＝报告期职工平均工资／基期职工平均工资

职工平均实际工资指数　职工平均实际工资指扣除物价变动因素后的职工平均工资。职工平均实际工资指数是反映实际工资变动情况的相对数，表明职工实际工资水平提高或降低的程度。计算公式为：

职工平均实际工资指数＝报告期职工平均工资指数／报告期城镇居民消费价格指数×100%

Explanatory Notes on Main Statistical Indicators

Total Population refers to the total number of people alive at a certain point of time within a given area.

The annual statistics on total population is taken at midnight,the 3lst of December.

Urban Population and Rural Population There are two definitions.The first definition (according to the administrative organizational system):

City population: Total population under the jurisdiction of City (including population of the town under the jurisdiction of City. excluding the population of counties under the jurisdiction of City).

Town population: Total population of town under the jurisdiction of County (excluding the population of town under the jurisdiction of City).

County population: Total population of country under the jurisdiction of County).

The second definition (classified by the permanent population):

City population: Total population of districts under the jurisdiction of City with district establishment and the population of street under the jurisdiction of City without district establishment.

Town population: Total resident-committees population of towns under the jurisdiction of City without district establishment and the resident-committees population of towns under the jurisdiction of County.

County population: Total population except City population and town population.

Data from 1952 to 1980 are the figures according to the first definition. Data since 1982 are the figure according to the second definition.

Birth Rate or (Crude Birth Rate) refers to the ratio of the number of births to the average population during a certain period of time(usually a year) which is often expressed in‰. The following formula is used:

Number of births refers to live births i.e. the births when babies had showed any vital phenomena regardless of the length of pregnancy.

Annual Average Number of Population is the average of the number of population at the beginning of the year and that at the end of the year. Sometimes it is substituted for with the mid year population.

Death Rate(or Crude Death Rate) refers to the ratio of the number of deaths to the average population (or mid year population) during a certain period of time (usually a year) which is often expressed in‰. The following formula is used:

Death Rate umber of Deaths

Number of Deaths/ Annual Average Number of Population

Natural Growth Rate of Population refers to the ratio of natural increase in population(number of births minus number of deaths)in a certain period of time(usually a year)to the average population(or mid year population)of the same period which is often expressed in‰. The following formulas are applied:

Natural Growth of Population

Number of Births-Number of Deaths / Average Number of Population

Natural Growth Rate of Population=Birth Rate-Death Rate

Employed Population refers to population aged 15 or over engaging in social labour which generates income.

Unemployed Population refers to population aged 15 or over not engaging in any social labour which generates income, including students enrolled in schools, house wives students waiting for entering schools with higher level, urban job seekers, retirees, job quitters, disabled, etc.

Economically Active Population refers to the population aged 16 and over who are capable to work, are participating in or willing to participate in economic activities, including employed persons and unemployed persons.

Persons Employed in Various Units refer to all the persons working in government agencies of various levels, political and party organizations, social organizations, enterprises and institutions, and receiving wages or other forms of payment. They include fully-employed staff and workers, re-employed retirees, teachers in schools run by the local people, foreigners and Chinese compatriots from Hong Kong, Macao, and Taiwan working in various units, part-time employees, employees of other units working temporarily at current posts, and employees holding the second job, but exclude staff and workers who have left their working units while keeping their labour contract (employment relation) unchanged. This indicator reflects the total number of laborers actually engaged in production or other operations in various units.

Persons Employed in Private Enterprises and Self-Employed Individuals in Urban Areas Persons employed in private enterprises refer to the persons employed in the private enterprises which have been registered at the departments of industrial and commercial administration and are situated at a County town (i.e. a town where the County government is located) for business operation or at urban areas with the level higher than a County town. The self-employed individuals in urban areas refer to persons who hold the certificates of residence in urban areas or have resided in the urban areas for a long time and have been registered at the departments of industrial and commercial administration and approved to be engaged in individual industrial or commercial business, including self-employed persons as well as helpers and hired labourers who work in the individual households engaged in industrial or commercial business.

Registered Urban Unemployed Persons The registered unemployed persons in urban areas refer to the persons who are registered as permanent residents in the urban areas engaged in non-agricultural activities, aged within the range of working age, capable to labour, unemployed but desirous to be employed and have been registered at the local employment service agencies to apply for a job.

Registered Urban Unemployment Rate Registered unemployment rate in urban areas refers to the ratio of the number of the registered unemployed persons to the sum of the number of employed persons and the registered unemployed persons . The formula is as follows:

Registered urban unemployment rate = number of registered urban unemployed persons/(number of urban employed persons + number of registered urban unemployed persons) ×100%

Staff and Workers refer to the persons who work in(and receive payment therefrom)enterprises and institutions of state ownership， collective ownership， joint ownership， share holding， foreign ownership， and ownership by entrepreneurs from Hong Kong， Macao， and Taiwan， and other types of ownership and their affiliated units，excluding the retired persons invited to work in the units again, teachers in the schools run by the local people and foreigners and persons coming from Hong Kong, Macao and Taiwan and working in the state-owned economic units. (Number of staff and workers in this yearbook include only fully employed staff and workers, excluding those who have left their working units while keeping their labour contract/employment relation unchanged).

Fully Employed Staff and Workers refer to persons who work in, and receive wages from their working units, as well as persons who have their work posts, but are temporarily absent from work for reasons of study or on sick, injury or maternal leave and still receive wages from their working units.

Staff and Workers in State-owned Economic Units refer to the persons who work in the state-owned economic units or their attached units and are listed in their payrolls.

Staff and Workers of Collective Owned Units in Urban Areas refer to the persons who work in collective owned units in urban areas and their administration departments and receive payment therefrom.

Staff and Workers in Units of Other types of Ownership refer to those who work in(and receive payment therefrom)enterprises and institutions of joint ownership， share holding， foreign ownership， and ownership by entrepreneurs from Hong Kong， Macao， and Taiwan.

Total Wages of Staff and Workers refer to the total remuneration payment to staff and workers in various units during a certain period of time. The calculation of total wages is based on the total remuneration payment to the staff and workers. Therefore， all the wages and salaries and other payments to staff and workers are included in the total wages regardless of their sources， category， and forms (in kind or cash). (Total wages of staff and workers in this yearbook include only total wages of fully employed staff and workers, excluding the living allowances distributed to those who have left their working units while keeping their labour contract/employment relation unchanged).

Bonus refers to remuneration payment to workers for extra work and for increasing earnings and practicing economy.

Subsidies and Allowances refer to subsidies paid to staff and workers for compensating special or extra labour and allowances paid to staff and workers to offset the impact of inflation on real wages.

Average Wage of Staff and Workers refers to the average wage in money terms per person during a certain period of time for staff and workers in enterprises, institutions, and government agencies, which reflects the general level of wage income during a certain period of time and is calculated as follows:

Average Wage of Staff and Workers =Total Wages of Staff and Workers in Reference Period/Average Number of Staff and Workers in Reference Period

Index of Average Wage of Staff and Worker refers to the ratio of average wage of staff and workers at the report time to that at the reference time. It reflects the relative changing degree of average wage in money terms at the various of time, which is calculated as following:

Index of Average Wage of Staff and Worker = average wage of staff and workers at the report time/average wage of staff and workers at the reference time

Index of Average Real Wage of Staff and Worker refers to the average wage which has removed the factor of price change. Index of average real wage of staff and worker reflects the relative changing degree of average real wage, and indicates the degree of the rising or declining degree of real wage of staff and worker, which is calculated as following:

Index of Average Real Wage of Staff and Worker = Index of Average Wage of Staff and Worker at the Report Time/Urban Consumer Prices Index at the Report Time

第五篇
CHAPTER 5

固定资产投资

INVESTMENT IN FIXED ASSETS

5-1 全社会固定资产投资(按管理渠道分)

Total Investment in Fixed Assets in Different Periods (Classified by Administrative Functions)

单位：万元 (10 000 yuan)

年 份 Year	地 区 Region	合 计 Total	基本建设 Capital Construction	更新改造 Renewal and Reform	房地产开发 Real Estate Development	其它投资 Other Investment
1978		129999	129577			422
1980		204652	172316	20601		11735
1985		444758	265826	61135		117797
1990		887775	479986	152712	9456	245621
1991		1249325	735670	181360	16886	315409
1992		1700326	1054876	217891	23941	403618
1993		2484352	1448448	373873	53616	608415
1994		2854786	1689075	431957	86244	647510
1995		3333404	1822429	626739	171238	712998
1996		3878472	2128807	685795	156232	907638
1997		4468148	2559573	739121	169906	999548
1998		5197673	3320951	760914	148577	967231
1999		5346468	3327447	610884	234481	1173656
2000		6103843	3927483	775381	574347	826632
2001		7059970	4002602	1081795	979184	996389
2002		8130223	5036907	1153469	877060	1062787
2003		10021256	6476406	1274279	1024908	1245663
2004		11615245	7592442	1386532	1125577	1510694
乌鲁木齐市	Urumqi City	2066810	1015845	498755	453420	98790
克拉玛依市	Karamay City	1250936	1148828	12027	88877	1204
石河子市	Shihezi City	262875	186707	43053	30599	2516
吐鲁番地区	Turpan Administrative Offices	426121	359380	55569	4876	6296
哈密地区	Hami [Kumul] Administrative Offices	188604	129950	33030	20783	4841
昌吉回族自治州	Changji Hui Autonomous Prefecture	829589	481333	181350	102802	64104
伊犁哈萨克自治州	Ili Kazak Autonomous Prefecture	1318709	986534	166213	123144	42818
伊犁州直属县(市)	Counties (Cities) Direct Under Ili Prefecture	639878	448649	67666	99503	24060
塔城地区	Tacheng [Tarbagatai] Administrative Offices	410719	298815	81850	16675	13379
阿勒泰地区	Altay Administrative Offices	268112	239070	16697	6966	5379
博尔塔拉蒙古自治州	Bortala Mongol Autonomous Prefecture	158681	105008	13535	20511	19627
巴音郭楞蒙古自治州	Bayangol Mongol Autonomous Prefecture	1586819	1288439	125186	138713	34481
阿克苏地区	Aksu Administrative Offices	688063	437100	128152	93835	28976
克孜勒苏柯尔克孜自治州	Kizilsu Kirgiz Autonomous Prefecture	76658	58283		12421	5954
喀什地区	Kashgar [Kaxgar] Administrative Offices	614033	482521	34833	28282	68397
和田地区	Hotan Administrative Offices	204771	184308	6528	7314	6621
跨地区投资	Trans-regional Investment	816507	728206	88301		

注：分地区投资额未包括农村投资和兵团工矿区私人建房投资（以下同）。

Note：Investment sum by prefectures excludes rural investment and investment in private-constructed houses in mining areas under XJPCC (the same as the below)

5-2　全社会固定资产投资

单位：万元　　　　(2004 年)

项　目	Item	总　计 Total	基本建设 Capital Construction
投资总额	**Total Investment**	**11615245**	**7592442**
#住 宅	Residence	1420033	488459
按资金来源分	**Grouped by Source of Funds**		
国家预算内资金	State Budgetary Appropriation	1831272	1506327
国内贷款	Domestic Loans	1570440	1174787
债　券	Bonds	47066	45346
利用外资	Foreign Investment	88619	65423
自筹资金	Fund Raising	6671142	4105698
其他资金来源	Others	1406706	694861
按构成分	**Grouped by Use of Funds**		
建筑工程	Construction	7133323	5016992
安装工程	Installation	806705	516345
设备工器具购置	Purchase of Equipment and Instruments	2304931	1166599
其他费用	Other Expenses	1370286	892506
按登记注册类型分	**Grouped by Ownership**		
内 资	Domestic Fund	11436117	7481488
国 有	State-owned	5307264	4172422
集 体	Collective	69012	14124
股份合作	Share Cooperative	16540	6097
国有联营	State Joint Ownership	2310	2310
集体联营	Collective Joint Ownership	882	
国有与集体联营	Joint State-collective	2345	1155
其他联营	Other Joint Ownership	4282	
国有独资公司	State-funded Corporations	301909	64739
其他有限责任公司	Other Limited Liability Corporations	1674732	694134
股份有限公司	Share-holding Corporations Ltd	2437309	2290747
私营个体	Private	1587304	219537
#个体户	Self-employment	58881	8891
个体合伙	Individual Partenership	7740	6505
其 他	Others	32228	16223
港澳台商投资	Enterprises With Investment from Hong Kong,Macao and Taiwan	122622	68510
合资经营	Joint-venture	71731	21450
合作经营	Cooperative		
独资经营	Sole Proprietor	10333	6502
股份有限	Joint-stock	40558	40558
外商投资	Enterprises With Foreign Investment	56506	42444
合资经营	Joint-venture	46282	33006
合作经营	Cooperative		
独资经营	Sole Proprietor	10224	9438
股份有限	Share-holding		
按隶属关系分	**By Administrative Relationship**		
中 央	Central Government	4148308	3432234
自治区	Autonomous	1595938	1306819
地、州、市	Region, Prefectures, City	729304	578133
县(市)	Counties (City)	1798121	1432832
其 他	Others	3343574	842424
房屋施工面积(万平方米)	**Floor Space of Buildings (10 000 sq.m)**	**5290.77**	**2422.53**
#住 宅	Residential Buildings	2999.85	1164.08
房屋竣工面积(万平方米)	**Floor Space of Buildings Completed (10 000 sq.m)**	**4273.02**	**1463.09**
#住 宅	Residential Buildings	2298.56	849.73

Total Investment in Fixed Assets

(10 000 yuan)

更新改造 Renovation and Transformation	其他投资 Other Investment	房地产开发 Real Estate Development	农村非农户投资 Investment of Non-peasant Households in Rural Areas	城乡个人 Individuals in Both Towns and Rural areas	城镇私人建房 Private-built Houses in Cities and Towns	农村个人投资 Individual's Investment In Rural Areas
1386532	**384625**	**1125577**	**463358**	**662711**	**118872**	**543839**
6476	19219	599276	15226	291377	91985	199392
41345	44229	2120	237251			
177074	32197	116231	35537	34614		34614
794	926					
3170	7624		12402			
1107174	206694	505722	123816	622038	118872	503166
56975	92955	501504	54352	6059		6059
413216	170865	837484	365867	328899	118872	210027
196370	18524	70023	5443			
732509	147892	19926	57105	180900		180900
44437	47344	198144	34943	152912		152912
1377759	376652	1074149	463358	662711	118872	543839
614337	108811	29897	381797			
25913	10678	3762	14535			
4259	4352		1832			
882						
1190						
140			4142			
225054		12116				
293512	55269	621648	10169			
115732	22378	8452				
96285	166400	398274	44097	662711	118872	543839
10458	39532					
116	1119					
455	8764		6786			
630	3800	49682				
630		49651				
	3800	31				
8143	4173	1746				
8143	3387	1746				
	786					
629142	15612	71320				
239046	3765	46308				
43217	32250	75704				
164965	93039	107285				
310162	239959	824960	463358	662711	118872	543839
117.88	**175.69**	**1333.03**	**240.93**	**1000.71**	**223**	**777.71**
6.97	41.73	863.19	23.42	900.46	179.28	721.18
75.15	**68.55**	**704.25**	**968.88**	**993.1**	**223**	**770.1**
4.8	20.3	511.61	22.18	889.94	179.28	710.66

5-3 全社会固定资产投资(按登记注册类型分)

Total Investment in Fixed Assets (classified by registration)

单位：万元 (10 000 yuan)

年 份 Year	地 区 Region	合 计 Total	国有经济 State-owned Economy	集体经济 Collective Economy	股份制经济 Stock Economy	私营个体经济 Private and Individuals Economy	其他经济 Other Economy
1978		129577	129577				
1985		444758	394075	20962		29721	
1990		887775	754469	46966		86340	
1991		1249325	1095603	53861		99861	
1992		1700326	1526267	63682		110377	
1993		2484352	2137627	85670	3731	136014	121310
1994		2854786	2401622	139087	28600	204657	80820
1995		3333404	2632775	228951	64695	277981	129002
1996		3878472	3118118	221641	98490	346949	93274
1997		4468148	3632454	212601	126912	420005	76176
1998		5197673	4345893	214143	119361	437207	81069
1999		5346468	4291067	172851	194894	532104	155552
2000		6103843	4602642	124466	548224	638511	190000
2001		7059970	4955062	107561	1084893	820956	91498
2002		8130223	5623113	78573	1219111	966931	242495
2003		10021256	6712609	93639	1734211	1284477	196320
2004		11615245	7599491	86434	2124033	1587304	217983
乌鲁木齐市	Urumqi City	2066810	1154733	5879	525160	269397	111641
克拉玛依市	Karamay City	1250936	1027308	3500	208978	8730	2420
石河子市	Shihezi City	262875	129154	540	72276	46339	14566
吐鲁番地区	Turpan Administrative Offices	426121	358190	5197	43815	18919	
哈密地区	Hami [Kumul] Administrative Offices	188604	118857	1188	44635	18530	5394
昌吉回族自治州	Changji Hui Autonomous Prefecture	829589	371624	22305	255101	149024	31535
伊犁哈萨克自治州	Ili Kazak Autonomous Prefecture	1318709	874534	10692	325167	96702	11614
伊犁州直属县(市)	Counties (Cities) Direct Under Ili Prefecture	639878	411400	2714	155871	62176	7717
塔城地区	Tacheng [Tarbagatai] Administrative Offices	410719	267149	7248	113828	22309	185
阿勒泰地区	Altay Administrative Offices	268112	195985	730	55468	12217	3712
博尔塔拉蒙古自治州	Bortala Mongol Autonomous Prefecture	158681	117116	2716	18058	18268	2523
巴音郭楞蒙古自治州	Bayangol Mongol Autonomous Prefecture	1586819	1208198	6801	200209	164071	7540
阿克苏地区	Aksu Administrative Offices	688063	402090	860	230221	41670	13222
克孜勒苏柯尔克孜自治州	Kizilsu Kirgiz Autonomous Prefecture	76658	47925	200	23956	4577	
喀什地区	Kashgar [Kaxgar] Administrative Offices	614033	432546	6871	141606	30353	2657
和田地区	Hotan Administrative Offices	204771	158912	3318	24682	13916	3943
跨地区投资	Trans-regional Investment	816507	816507				

注：①1998 年起国有经济包括国有单位以及国有独资公司、纯国有联营和中国石油天然气公司新疆分公司的投资额。②股份制经济包括股份有限公司和其他有限责任公司的投资额，但扣除了中石油股份的投资额,以下同。③各地区按经济类型分的投资中不包括农村投资。

Note: a) From the year 1998, the state-owned economy includes the investment sum of state-owned units and state-owned sole-funded company, state-owned joint-operated and China Petroleum Company. b) Stock economic right includes investment sum from stock limited company and other Limited Liability Corporations,but with investment sum from petroleum share deducted, the same as below. c) Investment classified by economic types in different regions excludes rural investment.

5-4 全社会固定资产投资(按资金来源分)

Total Investment in Fixed Assets (classified by fiancial sources)

单位：万元 (10 000 yuan)

年份 Year	地区 Region	合计 Total	国家预算内资金 Capital within National Budget	国内贷款 Home Loan	债券 Bonds	利用外资 Foreign Capital Available	自筹及其他资金 Self-raised and Other Capital
	1978	129577	102693				26884
	1985	444758	117439	72227		7708	247384
	1990	887775	105423	294985		40927	446440
	1991	1249325	90362	192434		94916	871613
	1992	1700326	129147	328782		265876	976521
	1993	2484352	90270	444118		445543	1504421
	1994	2854786	81544	650076		531902	1591264
	1995	3333404	98004	818914		307619	2108867
	1996	3878472	128725	756412		324532	2668803
	1997	4468148	269106	749345		109629	3340068
	1998	5197673	384195	1116497		133936	3563045
	1999	5346468	512364	1097949	12376	93895	3629884
	2000	6103843	506867	1346175	19429	99942	4131430
	2001	7059970	545176	1321317	8340	64834	5120303
	2002	8130223	1323660	1607535	30504	62992	5105532
	2003	10021256	1626261	1896104	21586	95287	6382018
	2004	11490824	1799593	1555105	46095	87388	8002643
乌鲁木齐市	Urumqi City	2081701	233628	388652		11175	1448246
克拉玛依市	Karamay City	1250222	95819	59778			1094625
石河子市	Shihezi City	262871	11927	97222		3319	150403
吐鲁番地区	Turpan Administrative Offices	443441	27504	40497	400	691	374349
哈密地区	Hami [Kumul] Administrative Offices	165387	30404	26220	230	1811	106722
昌吉回族自治州	Changji Hui Autonomous Prefecture	770353	97845	79459	795	17779	574475
伊犁哈萨克自治州	Ili Kazak Autonomous Prefecture	1298418	295124	182765	32440	6732	781357
伊犁州直属县(市)	Counties (Cities) Direct Under Ili Prefecture	661225	139952	96100	32440	5181	387552
塔城地区	Tacheng [Tarbagatai] Administrative Offices	404696	74042	30092		90	300472
阿勒泰地区	Altay Administrative Offices	232497	81130	56573		1461	93333
博尔塔拉蒙古自治州	Bortala Mongol Autonomous Prefecture	154714	33192	4223			117299
巴音郭楞蒙古自治州	Bayangol Mongol Autonomous Prefecture	1529583	159082	150102		9734	1210665
阿克苏地区	Aksu Administrative Offices	817381	130231	101183	11390	6954	567623
克孜勒苏柯尔克孜自治州	Kizilsu Kirgiz Autonomous Prefecture	77502	38519	776		210	37997
喀什地区	Kashgar [Kaxgar] Administrative Offices	569927	174371	53432	360	1839	339925
和田地区	Hotan Administrative Offices	223661	113222	12387	480	792	96780
跨地区投资	Trans-regional Investment	780005	121474	288258		13950	356323

注：1.各地区资金来源中不包括农村投资的资金来源；2.2004 年资金来源是按实际到位资金数额统计，往年是按投资工作量进行的调整数。
Note: Sources of Capital from defferent regions excludes rural investment.

5-5　全社会固定资产投资(按隶属关系和构成分)

Total Investment in Fixed Assets (classified by subordination and composition)

单位：万元　　(10 000 yuan)

年　份 Year	合　计 Total	按隶属关系分 Classification on Surbordination	
		中　央 Central	地　方 Local
1978	129577	64568	65009
1980	204652	126859	77793
1985	444758	202869	241889
1990	887775	516603	371172
1991	1249325	809478	439847
1992	1700326	1136274	564052
1993	2484352	1518645	965707
1994	2854786	1780723	1074063
1995	3333404	1819621	1513783
1996	3878472	2072722	1805750
1997	4468148	2398515	2069633
1998	5197673	2705328	2492345
1999	5346468	2638879	2707589
2000	6103843	2922259	3181584
2001	7059970	3264641	3795329
2002	8130223	3157268	4972955
2003	10021256	3729989	6291267
2004	11615245	4148308	7466937

年　份 Year	按构成分 Classification on Compostion			
	建筑工程 Construction Works	安装工程 Installation Works	设备工具器具购置 Purchase of Equipment, Tools and Apparatuses	其他费用 Other Expenses
1978	86667		35686	7224
1980	163329		29743	11580
1985	323395		93254	28109
1990	571461		274647	41667
1991	818294		348725	82306
1992	1173109		369373	157844
1993	1816980		442715	224657
1994	1922505		653691	278590
1995	2145762		810995	376647
1996	2245924	278445	929463	424640
1997	2725428	310687	988070	443963
1998	3435120	278895	920992	562666
1999	3245779	344130	1039617	716942
2000	3833328	416759	1254077	599679
2001	4232768	454765	1616907	755530
2002	4815707	593242	1787899	933375
2003	6075091	690459	2030335	1225371
2004	7133323	806705	2304931	1370286

5-6 按行业分的全社会固定资产投资和新增固定资产

Total Investment and Newly - Fixed Assets by Sectors

单位：万元　　(2004 年)　　(10 000 yuan)

行　业	Sector	全社会固定资产投资额 Total Investment in Fixed Assets	新　增 固定资产 Newly Increased Fixed Assets
总　计	**Total**	**11615245**	**9914933**
农、林、牧、渔业	**Farming, Forestry, Animal Husbandry and Fishery**	**1270107**	**685397**
农　业	Farming	264172	256070
林　业	Forestry	95275	76699
畜牧业	Animal Husbandry	107709	90580
渔　业	Fishery	4482	3326
农、林、牧、渔服务业	Agricultural Services	285547	258722
采矿业	**Mining and Quarrying**	**2381041**	**2108572**
煤炭开采和洗选业	Coal Mining and Dressing	130160	81382
石油和天然气开采业	Petroleum and Natural Gas Extraction	2168397	1986304
#天然原油和天然气开采	Crude oil and Natural Gas Extraction	2045120	1865886
黑色金属矿采选业	Black Ferrous Metal Mining and Dressing	35849	13853
#铁矿采选	Iron Ore Extraction and Dressing	33152	13056
有色金属矿采选业	Nonferrous Matals Mining and Dressing	34097	7989
#常用有色金属矿采选	Common Non-ferrous Metal Extracting and Dressing	25458	6309
非金属矿采选业	Nonmetal Minerals mining and Dressing	10482	19044
#土砂石开采	Earth and Gravel Extracting	7736	16837
化学矿采选	Chemical Ore Extracting	920	560
采　盐	Salt Extracting	88	
制造业	**Manufacturing**	**1508283**	**1378566**
农副食品加工业	Farming and Non-staple Food Processing	150228	95941
#制　糖	Sugar Processing	2713	1513
食品制造业	Food Production	75940	56394
#液体乳及乳制品制造	Liquid Milk and Dairy Products	18997	11484
饮料制造业	Beverage Production	47162	44224
烟草加工业	Tobacco	11371	
纺织业	Textile Industry	161321	105707
#棉、化纤纺织及印染精加工	Cotton, Chemical Fiber Textile, Dyeing and Printing, Dressing	146353	94906
毛纺织和染整精加工	Wool Textile, Dyeing and Dressing	2700	1366
麻纺织	Flax Textile	7071	5680
纺织服装、鞋、帽制造业	Garment, Shoe and Hat	4404	240
皮革、毛皮、羽绒及其制品业	Leather, Furs, Down and Related Products	700	700
木材加工及竹、藤、棕、草制品业	Timber Processing, Bamboo, Cane, Palm Fiber And Straw Products	18739	14399
家具制造业	Furniture Manufacturing	3194	1834
造纸及纸制品业	Papermaking and Paper Products	24195	17409
印刷业、记录媒介的复制	Printing and Record Medium Reproduction	2594	1348
石油加工及炼焦业	Petroleum Processing and Coking	331113	587172
#精炼石油产品的制造	Oil Products Production	246071	526258
炼　焦	Coking	85042	60914
化学原料及化学制品制造业	Raw chemical Materials and Chemical Products	170693	74032
#基础化学原料制造	Basic Chemical Material Production	47220	34777
肥料制造	Fertilizer Manufacturing	26819	4515
医药制造业	Medical and Pharmaceutical Products	28851	30057
#中药饮片加工	Chinese Herbs and Tablet Processing	3232	782
中成药制造	Chinese Herbs and Patent Medicine Production	3415	5367
化学纤维制造业	Chemical Fiber Manufacturing	27152	9700

注：①该表大类包括农村投资，中类未包括。②新增固定资产总计包括农村，大类未包括。

Note: a) The major category contains rural investment while sub-category excludes it. b) New-added fixed asset includes rural areas and major .categories.

5-6 续表 1 Continued

单位：万元 (10 000 yuan)

行 业	Sector	全社会固定资产投资额 Total Investment in Fixed Assets	新增固定资产 Newly Increased Fixed Assets
橡胶制品业	Rubber Products	5231	190
塑料制品业	Plastic Products	31004	12620
非金属矿物制品业	Nonmetal Mineral Products	114193	79018
#水泥、石灰和石膏的制造	Cememt, Lime and Gypsum	64569	38439
黑色金属冶炼及压延加工业	Smelting and Pressing of Ferrous Metals	198927	196819
#钢压延加工	Steel Rolling	102700	104536
有色金属冶炼及压延加工业	Non-ferrous Metal Smeltering and rolling process	26177	11631
#常用有色金属冶炼	Common Non-ferrous Metal Smeltering	20072	11416
金属制品业	Metal Products	24476	16885
通用设备制造业	Ordinary Equipment Production	8388	7698
专用设备制造业	Euqipment for Special Purposes	8245	2525
交通运输设备制造业	Traffic, Transport and Equipment Manufacturing	4370	2591
#汽车制造	Car Manufacturing	4185	2406
电气机械及器材制造业	Electric Machinery and Apparatus Manufacturing	12963	7986
工艺品及其他制造业	Art and Handicraft and Others	1851	1446
电力、煤气及水的生产和供应业	**Electric Power, Gas and Water Production and Supply**	**532190**	**361652**
电力、热力的生产和供应业	Electric and Thermal Power Production and Supply	390158	301113
电力生产	Electric Power Production	196836	155447
电力供应	Electric Power Supply	95503	87711
热力生产和供应	Thermal Power Production and Supply	97819	57955
燃气生产和供应业	Gas Production and Supply	70205	24067
水的生产和供应业	Water Production and Supply	68546	36472
#自来水的生产和供应	Running Water Production and Supply	47272	18725
污水处理及其再生利用	Tap Water Production and Supply	20223	17366
建筑业	**Construction**	**87657**	**41533**
房屋和土木工程建筑业	House and Civil Works Construction	39826	40133
建筑安装业	Construction and Installation	3908	1299
交通运输、仓储及邮政业	**Transportation, Storage, Postal and Telecommunications Services**	**1534459**	**1076871**
铁路运输业	Railway Transport	212194	139662
道路运输业	Road Transport	1114823	882319
城市公共交通业	Urban Public Traffic	7689	7689
航空运输业	Air Transportation	57809	24404
管道运输业	Pipeline Transport	35762	1040
装卸搬运和其他运输服务业	Loading, Discharging and Other Transport Service	473	423
仓储业	Storage	15404	16391
邮政业	Post Service	3922	4943
信息传输、计算机服务和软件业	**Information Transmission, Computer and Software**	**362985**	**317643**
电信和其他信息传输服务业	Telecommunication and Other Message Transmission	357090	315643
#电 信	Telecommunication	331933	302799
批发和零售业	**Wholesal&Retail Trade**	**258382**	**216366**
批发业	Wholesale Trade	126440	106618
零售业	Retail Trade	127490	109748
住宿和餐饮业	**Horel and Catering**	**87052**	**70629**
住宿业	Hotel	68835	59397
#旅游饭店	Tourist Restaurant	57111	38004
餐饮业	Catering Service	11291	11232
金融业	**Finance**	**53981**	**54421**
银行业	Banking Service	35290	37403

5-6 续表 2 Continued

单位：万元 (10 000 yuan)

行 业	Sector	全社会固定资产投资额 Total Investment in Fixed Assets	新增固定资产 Newly Increased Fixed Assets
证券业	Stock Exchange	391	391
保险业	Insurance	16461	16461
其他金融活动	Other Financial Activities	166	166
房地产业	**Real Estate management**	**1325431**	**1013746**
#房地产开发与经营业	Real Estate Development and Operation	1303862	1004532
物业管理	Real Estate Management	7772	8712
租赁和商务服务业	**Leasing and Commercial Service**	**80664**	**15069**
租赁业	Leasing Service	300	300
商务服务业	Commercial Service	31187	14769
#旅行社	Travel Service	1196	1181
科学研究、技术服务和地质勘查业	**Scientific Research, Technical Service and Geological Survey**	**55766**	**48216**
研究与试验发展	Research and Experiment Development	9135	6503
专业技术服务业	Specialized Technical Service	22508	26710
科技交流和推广服务业	Scientific Exchange and Difussion	3008	2738
地质勘查业	Geological Survey	20156	12265
水利、环境和公共设施管理业	**Water Conservancy, Environment and Public Works**	**1147825**	**751568**
水利管理业	Water Conservancy Management	472009	215856
环境管理业	Environment Management	38496	10228
公共设施管理业	Public Works Management	479238	525484
市政公共设施管理	Management Over Civil Works	428016	486763
城市绿化管理	Urban Greening Management	20161	19440
游览景区管理	Scenic-Spot Management	31061	19281
居民服务和其他服务业	**Resident Service and Other Service**	**53326**	**11089**
教 育	**Education**	**244292**	**240784**
#初等教育	Elementary Education	36669	38321
中等教育	Secondary Education	101778	106440
高等教育	Higher Education	74091	74533
卫生、社会保障和社会福利业	**Health, Social Insurance and Social Welfare**	**118291**	**95772**
卫 生	Health Care	108520	92762
#医 院	Hospital	86519	74173
专科疾病防治活动	Control Over Special Diseases	202	187
疾病预防控制及防疫活动	Disease Prevention and Control	15540	12206
社会保障业	Social Security	474	474
社会福利业	Social Welfare	3079	2536
文化、体育和娱乐业	**Culture, Sport and Recreation**	**62605**	**32589**
新闻出版业	News and Press	2609	2609
广播、电视、电影和音像业	Radio, TV, Film and Audio & Video	14698	13493
文化艺术业	Art and Culture	23830	13536
体 育	Sports	8356	978
娱乐业	Recreational	7528	1973
公共管理和社会组织	**Public Management and Social Organization**	**450706**	**382857**
中国共产党机关	C.P.C Organizations	17755	20286
国家机构	State Organs	385521	341449
人民政协和民主党派	C.P.P.C.C and Democratic Parties	3994	16144
群众团体、社会团体和宗教组织	Mass Group, Social Groups and Religious Organization	1936	891
基层群众自治组织	Grass-root Mass Organizations	5050	4087
国际组织	**International Organizations**	**202**	**202**

5-7　全社会固定资产投资新增固定资产

Total Investment in Fixed Assets in Newly Increased Fixed Assets

单位：万元　　(10 000 yuan)

年份 Year	地区 Region	合计 Total	基本建设 Capital Construction	更新改造 Renewal and Reform	房地产开发 Real Estate Development	其他投资 Other Investment
	1978	68503	68503			
	1985	300610	175362	47963		77285
	1990	766178	370692	144094	7573	243819
	1991	909679	445046	175849	14390	274394
	1992	1181669	677120	172007	18997	313545
	1993	1741816	904770	306347	33749	496950
	1994	2112180	1160192	404659	50819	496510
	1995	2664392	1460481	571695	92175	540041
	1996	2894822	1481199	582377	106198	725048
	1997	3747436	2128903	713105	113272	792156
	1998	3991426	2522232	652196	101681	715317
	1999	4226624	2693366	597432	159174	776652
	2000	6585973	4813694	737741	345181	689357
	2001	6122085	3600498	919095	643624	958868
	2002	6408842	3676834	928669	824462	978877
	2003	7752524	4491348	1071988	998808	1190380
	2004	9914933	6552613	1074250	860334	1427736
乌鲁木齐市	Urumqi City	1970919	1086553	464307	335592	84467
克拉玛依市	Karamay City	1096759	1032708	5247	57600	1204
石河子市	Shihezi City	158824	112168	18629	25511	2516
吐鲁番地区	Turpan Administrative Offices	396144	336083	50308	3356	6397
哈密地区	Hami [Kumul] Administrative Offices	147437	109063	16148	16704	5522
昌吉回族自治州	Changji Hui Autonomous Prefecture	652766	350560	159880	75827	66499
伊犁哈萨克自治州	Ili Kazak Autonomous Prefecture	950580	662430	125646	94036	68468
伊犁州直属县(市)	Counties (Cities) Direct Under Ili Prefecture	442038	295365	43538	68374	34761
塔城地区	Tacheng [Tarbagatai] Administrative Offices	358835	246743	71099	15149	25844
阿勒泰地区	Altay Administrative Offices	149707	120322	11009	10513	7863
博尔塔拉蒙古自治州	Bortala Mongol Autonomous Prefecture	147369	92094	13291	25217	16767
巴音郭楞蒙古自治州	Bayangol Mongol Autonomous Prefecture	1739292	1474444	108852	120875	35121
阿克苏地区	Aksu Administrative Offices	495872	373456	20925	64499	36992
克孜勒苏柯尔克孜自治州	Kizilsu Kirgiz Autonomous Prefecture	106704	88435		12421	5848
喀什地区	Kashgar [Kaxgar] Administrative Offices	504400	379113	35384	27939	61964
和田地区	Hotan Administrative Offices	174844	145386	4606	757	24095
跨地区投资	Trans-regional Investment	361147	310120	51027		

注：①全疆其他投资新增固定资产包括城镇工矿区私人建房和农村投资新增固定资产。②各地区全社会新增固定资产投资中不包括农村新增固定资产。

Note: a) Other new-added investment in fixed asset for whole society includes private-built houses in industry and mining areas in cities and towns,and new-added fixed asset in rural areas. b) New-added investment in fixed asset for whole society in different regions excludes rural new-added fixed asset.

5-8 全社会房屋施工面积、竣工面积

Total Floor Space Under Construction and Completed Floor Space of Houses in Whole Community

单位：万平方米 (10 000 sq.m)

年 份 Year	地 区 Region	施工面积 Area of Construction	#住 宅 Flat	竣工面积 Area of Completion	#住 宅 Flat	房屋建筑面积竣工率(%) Completion Rate of Area for House Structure (%)	#住 宅 Flat
	1985	1670.30	945.76	1327.69	816.26	79.50	86.30
	1990	1740.94	1074.98	1337.06	912.57	76.80	84.90
	1991	1863.86	1156.56	1426.10	962.96	76.50	83.30
	1992	1942.40	1119.34	1364.86	884.28	70.30	79.00
	1993	2355.61	1380.46	1681.61	937.28	71.40	67.90
	1994	2278.65	1254.54	1745.12	1080.08	76.60	86.10
	1995	2420.38	1368.84	1634.33	1064.14	67.50	77.70
	1996	2952.02	1901.01	2095.58	1441.22	71.00	75.80
	1997	2574.79	1732.19	1903.96	1393.11	73.90	80.40
	1998	2946.76	2057.08	2148.75	1604.68	72.90	78.00
	1999	3439.11	2470.41	2618.98	2020.89	76.20	81.80
	2000	4485.77	2509.17	2633.23	1881.88	58.70	75.00
	2001	4940.70	3282.51	3386.60	2411.78	68.50	73.50
	2002	3986.81	2358.04	2706.44	1790.82	67.90	75.90
	2003	5004.13	2863.92	3599.74	2347.04	71.90	82.00
	2004	5290.77	2999.85	4273.02	2298.56	80.76	76.62
乌鲁木齐市	Urumqi City	1064.40	439.07	457.32	255.72	42.97	58.24
克拉玛依市	Karamay City	149.28	98.13	73.94	47.68	49.53	48.59
石河子市	Shihezi City	119.68	56.72	55.58	39.80	46.44	70.17
吐鲁番地区	Turpan Administrative Offices	53.28	24.12	26.42	13.63	49.59	56.51
哈密地区	Hami [Kumul] Administrative Offices	119.47	56.60	72.64	31.62	60.80	55.87
昌吉回族自治州	Changji Hui Autonomous Prefecture	405.42	215.06	252.83	139.22	62.36	64.74
伊犁哈萨克自治州	Ili Kazak Autonomous Prefecture	594.10	310.89	447.97	270.22	75.40	86.92
伊犁州直属县(市)	Counties (Cities) Direct Under Ili Prefecture	339.90	174.93	255.67	151.90	75.22	86.83
塔城地区	Tacheng [Tarbagatai] Administrative Offices	162.66	89.40	131.79	78.29	81.02	87.57
阿勒泰地区	Altay Administrative Offices	91.54	46.56	60.51	40.03	66.10	85.98
博尔塔拉蒙古自治州	Bortala Mongol Autonomous Prefecture	100.28	48.01	73.72	36.21	73.51	75.42
巴音郭楞蒙古自治州	Bayangol Mongol Autonomous Prefecture	390.79	168.17	226.47	123.66	57.95	73.53
阿克苏地区	Aksu Administrative Offices	327.72	158.92	233.01	123.52	71.10	77.72
克孜勒苏柯尔克孜自治州	Kizilsu Kirgiz Autonomous Prefecture	92.28	82.74	89.95	77.69	97.48	93.90
喀什地区	Kashgar [Kaxgar] Administrative Offices	574.77	415.23	429.95	345.93	74.80	83.31
和田地区	Hotan Administrative Offices	270.49	181.41	88.06	60.65	32.56	33.43
跨地区投资	Trans-regional Investment	5.53		5.53		100.00	

注：分地区房屋施工面积、竣工面积未包括农村。
Note: Floor space under construction and completed floor space by sectors exclude those in rural areas.

5-9　按经济类型分的基本建设投资

Investment in Capital Construction by Registration

单位：万元　　　　(10 000 yuan)

年 份 Year	地 区 Region	合 计 Total	国有经济 State-owned Economy	集体经济 Collective Economy	股份经济 Stock Economy	外商港澳台经济 Economy of Hongkong, Macao and Taiwan Compatriots	其他经济 Other Economy
	1978	129577	129577				
	1985	265826	265826				
	1990	479986	479986				
	1991	735670	735670				
	1992	1054876	1054876				
	1993	1448448	1448448				
	1994	1689075	1655439		10880	10564	12192
	1995	1822429	1735234		15670	53638	17887
	1996	2128807	2079380		15273	27640	6514
	1997	2559573	2513917		9672	9879	26105
	1998	3320951	3297672	132	11883	3815	7449
	1999	3327447	3259985		41620	6199	19643
	2000	3927483	3746947		43347	15386	121803
	2001	4002602	3649261	2255	111065	23482	216539
	2002	5036907	4491758	10903	419961	77911	36374
	2003	6476406	5607947	25421	684499	62817	95722
	2004	7592442	6227479	20221	996873	110954	236915
乌鲁木齐市	Urumqi City	1015845	770013	85	190832	53323	1592
克拉玛依市	Karamay City	1148828	1023095		122008	1125	2600
石河子市	Shihezi City	186707	115657		38389	14566	18095
吐鲁番地区	Turpan Administrative Offices	359380	310237	800	35175		13168
哈密地区	Hami [Kumul] Administrative Offices	129950	87072	738	34261	1147	6732
昌吉回族自治州	Changji Hui Autonomous Prefecture	481333	296117	4416	92053	22344	66403
伊犁哈萨克自治州	Ili Kazak Autonomous Prefecture	986534	778428	5869	161176	6269	34792
伊犁州直属县(市)	Counties (Cities) Direct Under Ili Prefecture	448649	348147	615	71288	5237	23362
塔城地区	Tacheng [Tarbagatai] Administrative Offices	298815	245313	4524	45410		3568
阿勒泰地区	Altay Administrative Offices	239070	184968	730	44478	1032	7862
博尔塔拉蒙古自治州	Bortala Mongol Autonomous Prefecture	105008	86812	2105	12749		3342
巴音郭楞蒙古自治州	Bayangol Mongol Autonomous Prefecture	1288439	1134577	3055	81752	207	68848
阿克苏地区	Aksu Administrative Offices	437100	294957	860	126614	9002	5667
克孜勒苏柯尔克孜自治州	Kizilsu Kirgiz Autonomous Prefecture	58283	41971	200	11535		4577
喀什地区	Kashgar [Kaxgar] Administrative Offices	482521	406469	522	74059	1471	
和田地区	Hotan Administrative Offices	184308	153868	1571	16270	1500	11099
跨地区投资	Trans-regional Investment	728206	728206				

5-10 按构成分的基本建设投资

Investment in Capital Construction by Use of Funds

单位：万元 (10 000 yuan)

年 份 Year	地 区 Region	合 计 Total	建筑安装工程 Works of Construction and Installation	设备工具器具购置 Purchase of Equipment, Tools and Devices	其他费用 Other Expenses
	1978	129577	86667	35686	7224
	1985	265826	199879	40570	25377
	1990	479986	326169	120770	33047
	1991	735670	514192	169300	52178
	1992	1054876	751167	192599	111110
	1993	1448448	1031392	229628	187428
	1994	1689075	1114001	355647	219427
	1995	1822429	1222215	361701	238513
	1996	2128807	1447482	400056	281269
	1997	2559573	1857733	427821	274019
	1998	3320951	2525720	422991	372240
	1999	3327447	2532825	443525	351097
	2000	3927483	2965788	626985	334710
	2001	4002602	2985281	625150	392171
	2002	5036907	3685209	787344	564354
	2003	6476406	4818664	898369	759373
	2004	7592442	5533337	1166599	892506
乌鲁木齐市	Urumqi City	1015845	631607	284337	99901
克拉玛依市	Karamay City	1148828	953244	86984	108600
石河子市	Shihezi City	186707	103682	65705	17320
吐鲁番地区	Turpan Administrative Offices	359380	250760	45428	63192
哈密地区	Hami [Kumul] Administrative Offices	129950	95595	20806	13549
昌吉回族自治州	Changji Hui Autonomous Prefecture	481333	336309	85874	59150
伊犁哈萨克自治州	Ili Kazak Autonomous Prefecture	986534	655238	156098	175198
伊犁州直属县(市)	Counties (Cities) Direct Under Ili Prefecture	448649	276388	91881	80380
塔城地区	Tacheng [Tarbagatai] Administrative Offices	298815	199104	44595	55116
阿勒泰地区	Altay Administrative Offices	239070	179746	19622	39702
博尔塔拉蒙古自治州	Bortala Mongol Autonomous Prefecture	105008	69961	18858	16189
巴音郭楞蒙古自治州	Bayangol Mongol Autonomous Prefecture	1288439	867565	226773	194101
阿克苏地区	Aksu Administrative Offices	437100	311413	90904	34783
克孜勒苏柯尔克孜自治州	Kizilsu Kirgiz Autonomous Prefecture	58283	48817	7532	1934
喀什地区	Kashgar [Kaxgar] Administrative Offices	482521	386422	63988	32111
和田地区	Hotan Administrative Offices	184308	163640	1649	19019
跨地区投资	Trans-regional Investment	728206	659084	11663	57459

5-11 基本建设投资资金来源

Sources of Funds for Capital Construiction Investment

单位：万元 (10 000 yuan)

年份 Year / 地区	Region	合计 Total	国家预算内资金 Capital within National Budget	国内贷款 Domestic Loan	债券 Bonds	利用外资 Foreign Capital Available	自筹资金 Self-raised Funds	其他资金 Other Funds
	1978	129577	102693				26884	
	1985	265826	110460	47031		7708	93745	6882
	1990	479986	97941	226258		36360	101136	18291
	1991	735670	84056	117432		73272	439242	21668
	1992	1054876	115154	226999		260940	280969	170814
	1993	1448448	79293	251746		405184	349574	362651
	1994	1689075	70342	343540		471515	676334	127344
	1995	1822429	78364	541261		244205	770887	187712
	1996	2128807	99774	424511		262384	1085381	256757
	1997	2559573	243362	494887		89612	1511773	219939
	1998	3320951	353248	934451		114669	1546828	371755
	1999	3327447	450376	895593	12376	69486	1395196	504420
	2000	3927483	448423	994081	19349	89293	1947006	429331
	2001	4002602	451625	843534	8298	51100	2148464	499581
	2002	5036907	1153321	1102201	28468	54145	2182921	515851
	2003	6476406	1434709	1278368	19440	85785	2999790	658314
	2004	7425669	1473240	1148982	44350	63986	4015513	679598
乌鲁木齐市	Urumqi City	956058	221031	247661		10324	419206	57836
克拉玛依市	Karamay City	1129321	93765	48428			978836	8292
石河子市	Shihezi City	186837	11583	73046		3319	89995	8894
吐鲁番地区	Turpan Administrative Offices	376786	26795	39497	400	691	83441	225962
哈密地区	Hami [Kumul] Administrative Offices	108711	27436	22293	230	1311	45958	11483
昌吉回族自治州	Changji Hui Autonomous Prefecture	428522	81148	25913		16779	259498	45184
伊犁哈萨克自治州	Ili Kazak Autonomous Prefecture	948459	277670	156126	32440	6732	365018	110473
伊犁州直属县(市)	Counties (Cities) Direct Under Ili Prefecture	451210	129553	81993	32440	5181	152629	49414
塔城地区	Tacheng [Tarbagatai] Administrative Offices	291889	68897	20972		90	161956	39974
阿勒泰地区	Altay Administrative Offices	205360	79220	53161		1461	50433	21085
博尔塔拉蒙古自治州	Bortala Mongol Autonomous Prefecture	98980	28968	2802			53874	13336
巴音郭楞蒙古自治州	Bayangol Mongol Autonomous Prefecture	1240973	149481	116349		4385	924591	46167
阿克苏地区	Aksu Administrative Offices	541400	115962	69594	10690	3654	304901	36599
克孜勒苏柯尔克孜自治州	Kizilsu Kirgiz Autonomous Prefecture	60227	33620	776		210	22001	3620
喀什地区	Kashgar [Kaxgar] Administrative Offices	454068	172665	45852	360	1839	161714	71638
和田地区	Hotan Administrative Offices	203623	111642	12387	230	792	38458	40114
跨地区投资	Trans-regional Investment	691704	121474	288258		13950	268022	

5-12 分行业基本建设主要指标

Main Indicators of Capital Construction by Sectors

(2004 年)

行 业	Sector	基本建设投资额(万元) Investment in Capital Construction (10 000 yuan)	#地 方 Local	施工项目个数(个) Number of Projects under Construction (unit)	竣工项目个数(个) Number of Projects Completed (unit)	本年新增固定资产(万元) Newly Increased Fixed Assets (10 000 yuan)
总 计	**Total**	**7592442**	**4160208**	**4889**	**3243**	**6552613**
农、林、牧、渔业	**Farming, Forestry, Animal Husbandry and Fishery**	**599324**	**288149**	**987**	**804**	**540137**
农 业	Farming	201990	56762	332	293	195156
林 业	Forestry	83176	63539	190	154	64026
畜牧业	Animal Husbandry	88042	56550	128	86	76440
渔 业	Fishery	1022	660	4	3	796
农、林、牧、渔服务业	Agricultural Services	225094	110638	333	268	203719
采矿业	**Mining and Quarrying**	**2215005**	**85261**	**82**	**44**	**1987179**
煤炭开采和洗选业	Coal Mining and Dressing	38557	34060	23	11	26315
石油和天然气开采业	Petroleum and Natural Gas Extraction	2127933	4847	11	8	1945840
#天然原油和天然气开采	Crude Oil and Natural Gas Extraction	2004656	4747	6	4	1825422
黑色金属矿采选业	Black Ferrous Metal Mining and Dressing	15491	15491	16	7	3746
#铁矿采选	Iron Ore Extracting and Dressing	13991	13991	15	7	3746
有色金属矿采选业	Nonferrous Matals Mining and Dressing	29206	27136	20	8	7639
#常用有色金属矿采选	Common Nonferrous Metal Extracting and Dressing	24090	22020	12	4	6009
非金属矿采选业	Nonmetal Minerals mining and Dressing	3818	3727	12	10	3639
#土砂石开采	Earth and Gravel Extraction	2808	2808	6	6	2808
化学矿采选	Extraction of Chemical Ore	560	560	1	1	560
采 盐	Salt Extraction	88	88	1		
制造业	**Manufacturing**	**780224**	**569747**	**410**	**219**	**846525**
农副食品加工业	Farm and Non-staple Food Processing	103980	76027	82	47	62166
食品制造业	Food Production	41375	32352	35	24	26356
#液体乳及乳制品制造	Liquid Milk and Dairy Products	10811	10811	11	8	5520
饮料制造业	Beverage Production	24559	22590	21	12	23835
纺织业	Textile Industry	104538	103256	30	11	52242
#棉、化纤纺织及印染精加工	Cotton, Chemical Fiber, Dyeing and Printing, Dressing	98765	97483	23	9	47779
麻纺织	Flax Textitle	573	573	2	1	263
皮革、毛皮、羽绒及其制品业	Leather, Furs, Down and Related Products	700	700	1	1	700
木材加工及竹、藤、棕、草制品业	Timber Processing,Bamboo,Cane,Palm Fiber and Straw Products	10645	10498	16	11	7129
家具制造业	Furniture Manufacturing	1450	1450	2	2	1330
造纸及纸制品业	Papermaking and Paper Products	17244	13467	16	7	11607
印刷业、记录媒介的复制	Printing and Record Medium Reproduction	865	865	3		85
石油加工及炼焦业	Petroleum Processing and Coking	177305	57834	26	9	503467
#精炼石油产品的制造	Refined Oil Products	134483	23174	18	6	469294
炼 焦	Coking	42822	34660	8	3	34173

5-12 续表 1 Continued

行业	Sector	基本建设投资额（万元）Investment in Capital Construction (10 000 yuan)	#地方 Local	施工项目个数（个）Number of Projects under Construction (unit)	竣工项目个数（个）Number of Projects Completed (unit)	本年新增固定资产（万元）Newly Increased Fixed Assets (10 000 yuan)
化学原料及化学制品制造业	Raw chemical Materials and Chemical Products	92700	60027	29	14	24945
#基础化学原料制造	Basic Chemical Material	10695	10695	7	4	2360
肥料制造	Fertilizer Production	23634	20865	9	4	3573
医药制造业	Medical and Pharmaceutical Products	8914	8794	14	4	4252
#中药饮片加工	Herb Tablets Processing	1098	1098	3	1	148
中成药制造	Herbs and Patent Medicine	422	422	1		
橡胶制品业	Rubber Products	4941	4941	1		
塑料制品业	Plastic Products	20041	20041	24	14	6149
非金属矿物制品业	Nonmetal Mineral Products	55285	41343	33	20	38506
#水泥、石灰和石膏的制造	Cement, Lime and Gypsum	23732	10040	4	2	14170
黑色金属冶炼及压延加工业	Smelting and Pressing of Ferrous Metals	67161	67161	22	14	59500
#钢压延加工	Steel Rolling and Processing	10462	10462	4	2	9828
有色金属冶炼及压延加工业	Non-ferrous Metal Smeltering and rolling process	2631	2631	4	2	915
#常用有色金属冶炼	Common Nonferrous Metal Smeltering	2416	2416	3	1	700
金属制品业	Metal Products	20584	20584	19	12	15153
通用设备制造业	Ordinary Equipment Production	5960	5960	11	8	5390
专用设备制造业	Euqipment for Special Purposes	6154	6154	7	3	554
交通运输设备制造业	Traffic, Transport and Equipment Manufacturing	1809	1689	4	3	440
#汽车制造	Truck Production	1624	1624	2	1	255
电气机械及器材制造业	Electric Machinery and Apparatus Manufacturing	5670	5670	6	1	1000
电力、煤气及水的生产和供应业	**Electric Power, Gas and Water Production and Supply**	**454895**	**305467**	**240**	**135**	**288182**
电力、蒸汽、热水的生产和供应业	Electric power, Steam and Hot Water Production and Supply	325542	184922	139	84	235354
电力生产	Electric Power Production	165718	93570	40	19	107346
电力供应	Electric Power Supply	85951	30009	51	32	81688
热力生产和供应	Thermal Power Production and Supply	73873	61343	48	33	46320
燃气生产和供应业	Gas Production and Supply	70205	70205	17	6	24067
水的生产和供应业	Water Production and Supply	59148	50340	84	45	28761
#自来水的生产和供应	Running-water Production and Supply	42593	34345	69	35	14833
污水处理及其再生利用	Tap Water Production and Supply	16174	15614	14	9	13547
建筑业	**Construction**	**31871**	**17076**	**63**	**39**	**29941**
房屋和土木工程建筑业	House and Civil Works Construction	28154	14935	57	36	28920
建筑安装业	Construction and Installation	3309	1733	4	2	920

5-12 续表 2 Continued

行 业	Sector	基本建设投资额（万元）Investment in Capital Construction (10 000 yuan)	#地 方 Local	施工项目个数（个）Number of Projects under Construction (unit)	竣工项目个数（个）Number of Projects Completed (unit)	本年新增固定资产（万元）Newly Increased Fixed Assets (10 000 yuan)
交通运输、仓储及邮政业	**Transportation, Storage, Postal and Telecommunications Services**	**1231985**	**1049211**	**485**	**305**	**942837**
铁路运输业	Railway Transport	75308		11	9	63334
道路运输业	Road Transport	1050198	955881	425	264	836003
城市公共交通业	Urban Public Traffic	1541	376	2	2	1541
航空运输业	Air Transport	52453	44898	11	4	22308
管道运输业	Pipeline Transport	35762	35762	3	1	1040
仓储业	Storage	13367	11339	20	15	14284
邮政业	Post Service	3156	905	11	9	4177
信息传输、计算机服务和软件业	**Message Transmission, Computer Service and Software**	**142432**	**12014**	**75**	**51**	**146598**
电信和其他信息传输服务业	Telecom. And Other Message Transmission	142432	12014	75	51	146598
#电 信	Telecommunication	129685	5578	58	40	135828
批发和零售业	**Wholesal&Retail Trade**	**181975**	**166020**	**211**	**144**	**153758**
批发业	Wholesale Trade	76299	72114	77	50	57935
零售业	Retail Trade	105676	93906	134	94	95823
住宿和餐饮业	**Hotel and Catering**	**64825**	**59614**	**81**	**52**	**57888**
住宿业	Hotel	57464	52562	60	37	50688
#旅游饭店	Tourist Restaurant	48892	48730	42	24	31912
金融业	**Finance**	**47169**	**13856**	**62**	**45**	**49282**
银行业	Banking	30542	13690	58	41	32655
保险业	Insurance	16461		3	3	16461
其他金融活动	Other Financial Activities	166	166	1	1	166
房地产业	**Real Estate management**	**52407**	**44937**	**55**	**32**	**28154**
#房地产开发与经营业	Real Estate Development and Operation	43585	37457	44	24	18940
物业管理	Real Estate Management	7772	6430	8	6	8712
租赁和商务服务业	**Leasing and Commercial Service**	**30127**	**22985**	**29**	**19**	**13709**
租赁业	Leasing Service					
商务服务业	Commercial Service	30127	22985	29	19	13709
#旅行社	Travel Service	215	215	1	1	200
科学研究、技术服务和地质勘查业	**Scientific Research, Technical Service and Geological Survey**	**47454**	**30509**	**73**	**41**	**42480**
研究与试验发展	Research and Experiment Development	8732	3277	9	5	6100
专业技术服务业	Professional and Technical Service	18119	9175	36	19	22321
科技交流和推广服务业	Scientific Exchnage and Difussion	2945	2945	9	5	2675

5-12 续表 3 Continued

行 业	Sector	基本建设投资额（万元） Investment in Capital Construction (10 000 yuan)	#地 方 Local	施工项目个数（个） Number of Projects under Construction (unit)	竣工项目个数（个） Number of Projects Completed (unit)	本年新增固定资产（万元） Newly Increased Fixed Assets (10 000 yuan)
地质勘查业	Geological Survey	17658	15112	19	12	11384
水利、环境和公共设施管理业	**Water Conservancy, Environment and Public Works**	**953610**	**838949**	**603**	**348**	**720833**
水利管理业	Water Conservancy Management	462875	406811	265	153	206633
环境管理业	Environment Management	29523	29243	29	9	4337
公共设施管理业	Public Works Management	461212	402895	309	186	509863
市政公共设施管理	Civil Works Management	414695	359017	225	143	474619
城市绿化管理	Urban Tree-planting Management	18711	17892	34	22	18008
游览景区管理	Scenic-spot Management	27806	25986	50	21	17236
居民服务和其他服务业	**Community Service and Others**	**7366**	**4866**	**13**	**8**	**10080**
教 育	**Education**	**219357**	**182950**	**424**	**288**	**228413**
#初等教育	Elementary Education	34737	27406	107	74	36479
中等教育	Secondary Education	93777	79440	219	147	97055
高等教育	Higher Education	73505	60693	35	25	73947
卫生、社会保障和社会福利业	**Health, Social Security and Welfare**	**93700**	**75213**	**247**	**160**	**78087**
卫 生	Health	90221	72126	224	146	75151
#医 院	Hospital	68305	52362	119	76	56647
专科疾病防治活动	Prevention and Control of Special Diseases	202	187	3	1	187
疾病预防控制及防疫活动	Diseases Prevention and Control; Epidemic Disease Prevention	15540	13531	84	56	12206
社会保障业	Social Security	400	400	1	1	400
社会福利业	Social Welfare	3079	2687	22	13	2536
文化、体育和娱乐业	**Culture, Sports and Recreation**	**51846**	**48947**	**117**	**76**	**30334**
新闻出版业	News and Press	2410	2215	2	2	2410
广播、电视、电影和音像业	Radio, TV, Film and Audio & Video	14161	14061	27	18	12956
文化艺术业	Art and Culture	22751	20147	76	49	13384
体 育	Sports	8356	8356	6	3	978
娱乐业	Recreation	4168	4168	6	4	606
公共管理和社会组织	**Public Management and Social Organization**	**386668**	**344235**	**631**	**432**	**357994**
中国共产党机关	C.P.C Organization	17690	17690	26	22	20221
国家机构	State Organs	359966	317658	587	399	318619
人民政协和民主党派	C.P.P.C.C and Democratic Parties	3994	3994	1	1	16144
群众团体、社会团体和宗教组织	Masses Group, Social Groups and Religious Organization	1936	1811	8	6	891
基层群众自治组织	Grass-root Masses Organization	3082	3082	9	4	2119
国际组织	International Organization	202	202	1	1	202

5-13 各地、州、市、县(市)基本建设投资和新增固定资产

Investment and Newly Increased Fixed Assets in Capital Construction by Prefecture, Autonomous Prefecture, City and County

单位：万元 (2004 年) (10 000 yuan)

地区 Region	投资总额 Total Investment	第一产业 Primary Industry	第二产业 Secondary Industry	第三产业 Tertiary Industry	住宅 Residence	新增固定资产 Newly Increased Fixed Assets	房屋建筑面积(万平方米) Floor Space of Buildings (10 000sq.m) 施工面积 Floor Space Under Construction	竣工面积 Floor Space Completed
总计 Total	**7592442**	**483920**	**3426283**	**3193780**	**488459**	**6552613**	**2422.53**	**1463.09**
按隶属关系分 By administrative relationship								
中央 Central government	3432234	202723	2489030	558548	181933	3489740	584.51	447.59
地方 Local	4160208	281197	937253	2635232	306526	3062873	1838.02	1015.50
按区域分 Grouped by Region								
乌鲁木齐市 Urumqi City	**1015845**	**7378**	**189548**	**750354**	**68565**	**1086553**	**434.24**	**165.02**
乌鲁木齐县 Urumqi County	19520	2220	350	14280	2670	58425	6.58	6.58
克拉玛依市 Karamay City	**1148828**	**8191**	**937084**	**191453**	**12100**	**1032708**	**46.37**	**27.69**
石河子市 Shihezi City	**186707**	**4262**	**122601**	**47956**	**11888**	**112168**	**68.22**	**27.08**
吐鲁番地区 Turpan Administrative Offices	**359380**	**28945**	**264058**	**60432**	**5945**	**336083**	**34.06**	**12.42**
吐鲁番市 Turpan City	66206	18567	8318	37104	2217	49720	13.17	1.43
鄯善县 Shanshan [Piqan] County	265601	7931	238940	16129	2601	258790	15.55	10.99
托克逊县 Toksun County	27573	2447	16800	7199	1127	27573	5.33	
哈密地区 Hami [Kumul] Administrative Offices	**129950**	**27852**	**28135**	**63607**	**10356**	**109063**	**77.19**	**51.27**
哈密市 Hami [Kumul] City	101427	22849	24436	45597	8545	98931	63.60	46.19
巴里坤哈萨克自治县 Barkol Kazak Autonomous County	19308	3705	2300	12245	1058	8064	5.50	3.19
伊吾县 Yiwu [Araturuk] County	9215	1298	1399	5765	753	2068	8.08	1.90
昌吉回族自治州 Changji Hui Autonomous Prefecture	**481333**	**53896**	**160187**	**223471**	**43779**	**350560**	**191.94**	**134.81**
昌吉市 Changji City	146390	9600	58137	67814	10839	108559	63.65	45.18
阜康市 Fukang City	55456	7298	23940	19324	4894	21240	14.86	8.04
米泉市 Miquan City	58853	519	38511	18466	1357	37403	25.14	14.13
呼图壁县 Hutubi County	83390	5851	12098	61687	3754	88367	15.77	10.90
玛纳斯县 Manas County	72281	22358	20528	18769	10626	48727	32.68	27.42
奇台县 Qitai County	30844	4756	3580	15728	6780	24880	20.57	16.57
吉木萨尔县 Jimsar County	19063	1953	2433	12223	2454	13726	10.92	10.18
木垒哈萨克自治县 Mori Kazak Autonomous County	15056	1561	960	9460	3075	7658	8.35	2.40

5-13 续表 1 Continued

单位：万元 (10 000 yuan)

地区 Region	投资总额 Total Investment	第一产业 Primary Industry	第二产业 Secondary Industry	第三产业 Tertiary Industry	住宅 Residence	新增固定资产 Newly Increased Fixed Assets	房屋建筑面积(万平方米) Floor Space of Buildings (10 000sq.m) 施工面积 Floor Space Under Construction	竣工面积 Floor Space Completed
伊犁哈萨克自治州 Ili Kazak Autonomous Prefecture	**986534**	**164617**	**257041**	**484796**	**80080**	**662430**	**353.41**	**253.26**
伊犁州直属县(市) Counties (Cities) Direct Under Ili Prefecture	**448649**	**41663**	**156151**	**214856**	**35979**	**295365**	**181.48**	**131.76**
伊宁市 Yining [Gulja] City	73778	498	20153	46650	6477	53154	33.78	22.97
奎屯市 Kuytun City	77614	7549	41315	24461	4289	74550	26.66	16.27
伊宁县 Yining [Gulja] County	28197	2386	9867	15370	574	17029	10.17	6.70
察布查尔锡伯自治县 Qapqal Xibe Autonomous County	30854	6557	6920	14298	3079	21518	19.04	10.51
霍城县 Huocheng [Korgas] County	43436	3924	13494	18861	7157	44106	33.74	30.67
巩留县 Gongliu [Tokkuztara] County	63226	4378	3600	54240	1008	17667	9.45	8.85
新源县 Xinyuan [Kunes] County	25180	5676	2824	13048	3632	13995	15.11	7.94
昭苏县 Zhaosu [Mongolkure] County	25808	2050	3618	13692	6448	17983	19.50	16.69
特克斯县 Tekes County	15483	5358	1684	6935	1506	15583	5.72	5.72
尼勒克县 Nilka County	65073	3287	52676	7301	1809	19780	8.31	5.45
塔城地区 Tacheng [Tarbagatai] Administrative Offices	**298815**	**90237**	**65985**	**113224**	**29369**	**246743**	**103.38**	**80.23**
塔城市 Tacheng [Qoqek] City	49779	4648	8547	34054	2530	30618	10.76	4.88
乌苏市 Usu City	96110	35416	31938	23330	5426	91277	29.42	20.55
额敏县 Emin Ciunty	30423	9336	1327	13223	6537	31639	16.33	15.09
沙湾县 Shawan County	78037	32069	7001	27014	11953	72963	35.19	33.41
托里县 Toli County	22047	2030	13821	5206	990	4424	3.15	1.92
裕民县 Yumin [Qagantokay] County	5721	1811	383	2627	900	3242	1.88	1.70
和布克赛尔蒙古自治县 Hoboksar Mongol Autonomous County	16698	4927	2968	7770	1033	12580	6.65	2.68
阿勒泰地区 Altay Administrative Offices	**239070**	**32717**	**34905**	**156716**	**14732**	**120322**	**68.55**	**41.27**
阿勒泰市 Altay City	88855	5052	5303	74084	4416	51974	19.20	12.11
布尔津县 Burqin County	43268	2856	680	37051	2681	13210	20.92	6.58
富蕴县 Fuyun [Koktokay] County	25516	2284	8435	14706	91	14798	3.38	1.88
福海县 Fuhai [Burultokay] County	20745	7855	3356	4478	5056	13173	13.57	11.86
哈巴河县 Habahe [Kaba] County	32521	6860	14427	10505	729	9294	3.59	2.52

5-13 续表 2 Continued

单位：万元 (10 000 yuan)

地　区 Region	投资总额 Total Investment	第一产业 Primary Industry	第二产业 Secondary Industry	第三产业 Tertiary Industry	住宅 Residence	新增固定资产 Newly Increased Fixed Assets	房屋建筑面积(万平方米) Floor Space of Buildings (10 000sq.m) 施工面积 Floor Space Under Construction	竣工面积 Floor Space Completed
青河县 Qinghe [Qinggil] County	15573	5401	2400	6900	872	12076	4.19	3.69
吉木乃县 Jeminay County	12592	2409	304	8992	887	5797	3.69	2.63
博尔塔拉蒙古自治州 Bortala Mongol Autonomous Prefecture	**105008**	**18717**	**18972**	**51739**	**15580**	**92094**	**61.67**	**46.44**
博乐市 Bole [Bortala] City	79039	12405	17692	38527	10415	71028	43.46	35.58
精河县 Jinghe [Jing] County	14943	4752	980	6118	3093	9433	12.97	5.65
温泉县 Wenquan [Araxang] County	11026	1560	300	7094	2072	11633	5.24	5.20
巴音郭楞蒙古自治州 Bayangol Mongol Autonomous Prefecture	**1288439**	**42710**	**840872**	**365088**	**39769**	**1474444**	**197.32**	**113.33**
库尔勒市 Korla City	1055579	15739	757452	256515	25873	1324781	111.18	66.30
轮台县 Luntai [Bugur] County	26791	3123	19340	4101	227	14125	16.89	2.31
尉犁县 Yuli [Lopnur] County	30032	10790	932	14128	4182	31443	9.64	8.83
若羌县 Ruoqiang [Qarkilik] County	37244	1442	1990	32329	1483	6559	5.47	3.66
且末县 Qiemo [Qarqan] County	30033	589	4181	24529	734	3780	10.74	0.97
焉耆回族自治县 Yanqi Hui Autonomous County	38283	2665	21606	10681	3331	36102	13.76	8.35
和静县 Hejing County	43991	3146	30179	8591	2075	34170	15.95	14.53
和硕县 Hoxud County	12309	2073	4672	4540	1024	11435	7.32	5.09
博湖县 Bohu [Bagrax] County	14177	3143	520	9674	840	12049	6.37	3.30
阿克苏地区 Aksu Administrative Offices	**437100**	**71899**	**146365**	**184323**	**34513**	**373456**	**193.61**	**142.18**
阿克苏市 Aksu City	216398	41820	66303	92938	15337	225453	107.44	84.71
温宿县 Wensu [Onsu] County	34134	4684	2448	21825	5177	33828	16.91	12.96
库车县 Kuqa County	93483	3470	55344	31769	2900	39276	16.34	8.91
沙雅县 Xayar County	23451	8220	1130	8311	5790	11015	21.59	15.50
新和县 Xinhe [Toksu] County	6305	2530	435	3260	80	6435	3.35	2.44
拜城县 Baicheng [Bay] County	17735	3380	3970	9187	1198	15807	9.62	3.66
乌什县 Wushi [Uxturpan] County	13950	1349	355	9563	2683	13950	8.57	7.12
阿瓦提县 Awat County	27937	5873	15500	5805	759	25149	5.45	5.45
柯坪县 Kalpin County	3707	573	880	1665	589	2543	4.34	1.43

5-13 续表 3 Continued

单位：万元 (10 000 yuan)

地 区 Region	投资总额 Total Investment	第一产业 Primary Industry	第二产业 Secondary Industry	第三产业 Tertiary Industry	住宅 Residence	新增固定资产 Newly Increased Fixed Assets	房屋建筑面积(万平方米) Floor Space of Buildings (10 000sq.m) 施工面积 Floor Space Under Construction	 竣工面积 Floor Space Completed
克孜勒苏柯尔克孜自治州 Kizilsu Kirgiz Autonomous Prefecture	**58283**	**14047**	**4919**	**20818**	**18499**	**88435**	**77.85**	**75.61**
阿图什市 Artux City	27491	8453	666	12462	5910	57572	38.36	36.99
阿克陶县 Akto County	18550	3174	4253	3239	7884	19180	26.68	25.96
阿合奇县 Akqi County	4894	550		2423	1921	5935	5.89	5.73
乌恰县 Wuqia [Ulugqat] County	7348	1870		2694	2784	5748	6.92	6.92
喀什地区 Kashgar [Kaxgar] Administrative Offices	**482521**	**24152**	**74960**	**272972**	**110437**	**379113**	**447.65**	**357.41**
喀什市 Kashgar [Kaxgar] City	176628	3380	49190	103858	20200	100537	82.55	38.56
疏附县 Shufu County	26397	3721	7494	11826	3356	23584	17.63	17.63
疏勒县 Shule County	9710	647	2821	2325	3917	8710	21.55	21.55
英吉沙县 Yengisar County	13058	170	135	7919	4834	13959	32.31	23.62
泽普县 Zepu [Poskam] County	23385		3535	8570	11280	20478	51.87	50.96
莎车县 Shache [Yarkant] County	40383			24853	15530	27374	65.34	63.07
叶城县 Yecheng [Kagilik] County	31388	396	1523	20596	8873	26045	37.00	9.95
麦盖提县 Makit County	50372	3291	3312	32385	11384	40484	32.96	27.71
岳普湖县 Yopurga County	18379	592	300	12244	5243	18379	23.96	23.96
伽师县 Jiashi [Payzawat] County	22548	2800		12113	7635	31020	7.06	7.06
巴楚县 Bachu [Maralbexi] County	60243	9155	6650	27243	17195	62657	74.09	72.01
塔什库尔干塔吉克自治县 Taxkorgan Tajik Autonomous County	10030			9040	990	5886	1.33	1.33
和田地区 Hotan Administrative Offices	**184308**	**17254**	**14653**	**117597**	**34804**	**145386**	**238.90**	**56.48**
和田市 Hotan City	53141	488	5429	33242	13982	31697	84.73	20.69
和田县 Hotan County	16445	122	7091	6987	2245	21991	5.84	4.49
墨玉县 Moyu [Karakax] County	53969	16267	766	28647	8289	41646	89.78	10.48
皮山县 Pishan [Guma] County	17256	205	734	12096	4221	14220	38.94	6.66
洛浦县 Lop County	14525		353	10906	3266	8362	5.72	5.24
策勒县 Qira County	19285	172	100	17679	1334	19249	4.99	4.60
于田县 Yutian [Keriya] County	6925			6270	655	5612	4.20	3.33
民丰县 Minfeng [Niya] County	2762		180	1770	812	2609	4.71	1.00
跨地区投资 Trans-regional Investment	**728206**		**366888**	**359174**	**2144**	**310120**	**0.09**	**0.09**

5-14 基本建设、更新改造投资项目个数

Investment Items for both Capital construction and Innovation Projects

单位：个 (unit)

年 份 Year	基本建设 Capital Construction				更新改造 Innovation			
	施工项目 Number of Projects under Construction	#本年新开工 Started This Year	全部建成投产项目 Number of Projects Completed and Put into Use	投产率(%) Rate of Projects Completed& Put into Use(%)	施工项目 Number of Projects under Construction	#本年新开工 Started This Year	全部建成投产项目 Number of Projects Completed and Put into Use	投产率(%) Rate of Projects Completed& Put into Use(%)
1978	1765		414	23.5				
1980	1879		633	33.7				
1985	2928		1755	59.9	1392		926	66.5
1990	2441	1518	1457	59.9	1990	1443	1486	74.7
1991	2669	1705	1554	58.2	2261	1804	1670	73.9
1992	3064	2032	1804	58.9	2547	1950	1795	70.5
1993	3241	2188	1975	60.9	2321	1597	1572	67.7
1994	3140	2058	1892	60.3	1848	1421	1449	78.4
1995	2897	1977	1932	66.7	2106	1735	1714	81.4
1996	3063	2140	2138	69.8	2294	2000	1873	81.6
1997	2621	1841	1757	67.0	2807	2501	2264	80.7
1998	3159	2354	1993	63.1	1830	1586	1510	82.5
1999	3294	2209	2293	69.6	1327	1121	1110	83.6
2000	3060	2192	2219	72.5	1273	1114	1031	81.0
2001	2957	2125	2027	68.5	1395	1277	1188	85.2
2002	3238	2488	2181	67.4	1297	1096	1049	80.9
2003	4177	3312	2765	66.2	1305	1152	1013	77.6
2004	4889	3845	3243	66.3	1188	1034	845	71.1

5-15 基本建设房屋施工面积、竣工面积

Floor Space of Construction and Completion for Capital Construction

单位：万平方米 (10 000 sq.m)

年 份 Year	施工面积 Floor Space of Construction	#住 宅 Flat	竣工面积 Completed Floor Space	#住 宅 Flat	房屋建筑面积竣工率(%) Ratio of Completed Area (%)	#住 宅 Flat
1978	457.00	179.00	273.00	125.00	59.7	69.8
1980	728.00	350.00	432.00	238.00	59.3	68.0
1985	846.60	325.00	487.70	209.73	57.6	64.5
1990	610.90	259.50	347.80	153.70	56.9	59.2
1991	681.35	299.87	384.76	177.20	56.5	59.1
1992	794.64	331.80	393.96	191.06	49.6	57.6
1993	902.94	353.14	451.91	219.76	50.0	62.2
1994	895.90	363.16	537.86	250.06	60.0	68.9
1995	903.06	364.39	509.16	242.95	56.4	66.7
1996	923.75	488.24	574.38	321.99	62.2	65.9
1997	1000.25	517.33	599.25	333.99	59.9	64.6
1998	1328.18	803.45	791.63	501.82	59.6	62.5
1999	1717.61	1170.97	1213.68	927.53	70.7	79.2
2000	1541.06	957.90	1100.06	760.85	71.4	79.4
2001	1440.49	822.10	987.57	652.74	68.6	79.4
2002	1410.48	604.52	863.20	451.95	61.2	74.8
2003	1912.40	833.47	1287.68	678.57	67.3	81.4
2004	2422.53	1164.08	1463.09	849.73	60.4	73.0

5-16 各地、州、市分行业基本建设投资

单位：万元　　　　(2004 年)

行业 Sector	合计 Total	乌鲁木齐市 Urumqi City	克拉玛依市 Karamay City	石河子市 Shihezi City	吐鲁番地区 Turpan Administrative Offices	哈密地区 Hami [Kumul] Administrative Offices	昌吉回族自治州 Changji Hui Autonomous Prefecture
总计 Total	**7592442**	**1015845**	**1148828**	**186707**	**359380**	**129950**	**481333**
农、林、牧、渔业 Farming, Forestry, Animal Husbandry and Fishery	599324	8362	10966	9624	29326	32755	71638
采矿业 Mining and Quarrying	2215005	12536	829339	1634	216175	8038	12732
制造业 Manufacturing	780224	109165	106165	68503	34013	5689	114519
电力、煤气及水的生产和供应业 Electric Power, Gas and Water Production and Supply	454895	84961	650	52464	16127	14082	35013
建筑业 Construction	31871	7070	3600	2546	480	1035	1557
交通运输、仓储及邮政业 Transportation, Storage, Postal and Telecommunications Services	1231985	92274	103989	31241	17477	25566	68804
信息传输、计算机服务和软件业 Message Transmission, Computer and Software Service	142432	96920	3930	2700	7859	3273	4001
批发和零售业 Wholesal&Retail Trade	181975	93456	12325	1062	2110	2631	16274
住宿和餐饮业 Hotel and Catering Service	64825	18232	3500		170	530	3900
金融业 Finance	47169	29327	3076		265	970	233
房地产业 Real Estate management	52407	8278	8000				4548
租赁和商务服务业 Leasing and Commercial Service	30127	411		1500	932	444	1229
科学研究、技术服务和地质勘查业 Scientific Research, Technical Service and Geological Survey	47454	22994			132	1126	4048
水利、环境和公共设施管理业 Water Conservancy, Environment and Public Works	953610	192291	42595	2268	21483	14144	95867
居民服务和其他服务业 Community Service and Others	7366	3070					2600
教育 Education	219357	79210	11944	7321	1112	6357	20669
卫生、社会保障和社会福利业 Health, Social Security and Welfare	93700	33546	305	1660	1629	2626	4260
文化、体育和娱乐业 Culture, Sports and Creation	51846	16357		2400	4062	407	3016
公共管理和社会组织 Public Management and Social Organization	386668	107385	8444	1784	6028	10277	16425

Investment in Capital Construction by Sectors in Prefecture, Autonomous Prefecture and City

(10 000 yuan)

伊犁哈萨克自治州 Ili Kazak Autonomous Prefecture	伊犁州直属县(市) Counties (Cities) Direct Under Ili Prefecture	塔城地区 Tacheng [Tarbagatai] Administrative Offices	阿勒泰地区 Altay Administrative Offices	博尔塔拉蒙古自治州 Bortala Mongol Autonomous Prefecture	巴音郭楞蒙古自治州 Bayangol Mongol Autonomous Prefecture	阿克苏地区 Aksu Administrative Offices	克孜勒苏柯尔克孜自治州 Kizilsu Kirgiz Autonomous Prefecture	喀什地区 Kashgar [Kaxgar] Administrative Offices	和田地区 Hotan Administrative Offices	跨地区投资 Trans-regional Investment
986534	**448649**	**298815**	**239070**	**105008**	**1288439**	**437100**	**58283**	**482521**	**184308**	**728206**
207008	57921	107693	41394	25889	51500	86723	14047	29901	21585	
30854	742	9172	20940		722001	8716	3425		2667	366888
105600	71142	29068	5390	12773	87092	124393	764	5667	5881	
121680	84478	28557	8645	6089	33611	13126	770	68978	7344	
3463	2463	598	402	1028	1972	3484		4308	1328	
186399	48006	42827	95566	15080	214417	74844	10065	124024	46487	221318
5294	2404	269	2621	789	2907	8404		6165	190	
13093	8311	2265	2517	3466	10883	13998	812	6293	5572	
30256	8793	2261	19202	200	3937	942	450	170	2538	
3527	1292	1995	240	548	170	2099	206	5988	760	
2355	140	2215		1290	10922	631		4706	11677	
225	80		145	420	19599	681		2136	2550	
14155	4397	78	9680	1962	1066	1110	115	713	33	
166634	103528	47191	15915	20942	79379	53496	3831	85030	35650	140000
846	45		801	730	120					
33640	20612	8255	4773	6659	15375	17613	1524	13298	4635	
17822	10175	5645	2002	1551	6559	6567	890	10899	5386	
7999	1753	3252	2994	450	3941	1196	453	8262	3303	
35684	22367	7474	5843	5142	22988	19077	20931	105983	26520	

5-17 基本建设大中型及更新改造限额以上项目一览表

单位：万元　　　　　　　　(2004 年)

项目名称 Project	建设地址 Seat of Construction Projects	开工时间 Starting Date	投产时间 Date of Putting into Operation	计划总投资 Total Invest-memt Planned
基本建设大中型项目 **Large and Medium Projects in Capital Construction**				
中油股份新疆油田公司 Karamay Oil Refinery, China Petroleum & Natural Gas Ltd.,Co.	克拉玛依市 Karamay City	200404	200412	583748
中油公司吐哈油田分公司 Turpan-Hami Sub-company, China Petroleum & Natural Gas Ltd.,Co.	鄯善县 Shanshan County	200402	200412	159963
中油公司塔里木油田分公司 Tarim Oil-field Sub-company, China Petroleum & Natural Gas Ltd.,Co.	库尔勒市 Korla City	200402	200412	694460
中国石油化工股份有限公司西北分公司 Northwest Sub-company, China Petro-chemical Ltd. Co.		200101		1024822
新疆石油管理局低效油田开发 Low-Efficiency Oil-field Development under XJ Oil Administration	克拉玛依市 Karamay City	200404	200412	151000
哈密市大明实业有限公司天湖铁矿 1 号矿体二期工程 No. 1 Mine at the Second-phase project under Tianhu Iron Mine, Hami mUnicipal Daming Industrial Ltd. Co.	哈密市 Hami [Kumul] City	200406		8642
新疆阿舍勒铜业股份有限公司 XJ Ashle Copper Industrial Ltd. Co.	哈巴河县 Habahe [Kaba] County	200204		54800
中油股份克拉玛依石化公司 Karamay Petro-chemical Company under China National Petroleum Stock Ltd. Co.	克拉玛依市 Karamay City	200403	200412	47300
中油股份独山子石化公司 Du Shanzi Petro-chemical Company under China Oil Stock Ltd. Co.	克拉玛依市 Karamay City	200404	200409	20618
新疆广汇实业股份有限公司 LNG 项目 LNG Project under Xinjiang Guanghui Industrial Ltd. Co.	鄯善县 Shanshan County	200208	200411	68530
阿克苏天山多浪水泥有限责任公司 Aksu Tianshan Duolang Cement Ltd. Co.	喀什市 Kashgar City	200401	200406	4000
青松建化股份有限公司 Baisong Chemical-building Ltd. Co.	库车县 Kuqa County	200311		14522
新疆天基钢铁有限公司 Xinjiang Tianji Steel and Iron Ltd. Co.	奎屯市 Kuytun City	200306	200412	16000
新疆吐鲁番发电有限责任公司 Xinjiang Turpan Electric Generation Ltd. Co.	托克逊县 Toksun County	200207		120000
哈密天光发电有限责任公司 Hami Tianguang Electric Generation Ltd. Co.	哈密市 Hami [Kumul] City	200107	200404	97772
国电新疆开都河流域水电开发有限公司 State Electricity Xinjiang Kaidu River Valley Hydropower Development Ltd. Co.	和静县 Hejing County			172890
新疆吉林台水梯级开发有限责任公司 Xinjiang-Jilin Taishui Step-up Development Ltd. Co	尼勒克县 Nilka County	200106		228604
新疆乌鲁木齐天然气工程指挥部 Xinjiang Urumqi Natural Gas Project Head-office	乌鲁木齐市 Urumqi City	200101	200412	55562
新疆广汇液化天然气发展有限公司哈密分公司 Hami Sub-company, Xinjiang Guanghui Liquefied Natural Gas Development Ltd. Co.	哈密市 Hami [Kumul] City	200405		5001

List of Large and Medium-sized Projects of Capital Construction and Quota for Innovation and Reform

(10 000yuan)

自开始建设至本年底止累计完成投资 Accumula-tive Investment Actually Made	#本年完成投资 Investment Made in the Year	自开始建设至本年底累计新增固定资产 Accumulative New-added Fixed Assets form It's Start to the Year-end	#本年新增固定资产 Newly-Increased Fixed Assets in the Year	建设规模和新增生产能力 Construction Scale and Newly-Added Production CapaCity				
				生产能力(或效益)名称 Name of Production Capal City (or Efficiency)	计量单位 Metering Unit	建设规模 Scale of construction Projects	累计新增 Accumula-tive Newly-Increased Production CapaCity	#本 年 In the Present year
711248	711248	711248	711248	天然原油开采 Natural Crude Oil Prospecting	万吨/年 10 000 tons/year	201.83	201.83	201.83
				天然气开采 Natural Gas Prospecting	亿立方米/年 100 millionu.m/year	1.32	1.32	1.32
210665	210665	210665	210665	天然原油开采 Natural Crude Oil Prospecting	万吨/年 10 000 tons/year	30	28	28
				天然气开采 Natural Gas Prospecting	亿立方米/年 100 millioncum/year	3	3	3
694460	694460	694460	694460	天然原油开采 Natural Crude Oil Prospecting	万吨/年 10 000 tons/year	77	77	77
				天然气开采 Natural Gas Prospecting	亿立方米/年 100 millioncum/year	66	66	66
1013452	366888	757300	186586	天然原油开采 Natural Crude Oil Prospecting	万吨/年 10 000 tons/year	438	438	144
				天然气开采 Natural Gas Prospecting	亿立方米/年 100 millioncum/year	6		
151000	118000	118000	118000	天然原油开采 Natural Crude Oil Prospecting	万吨/年 10 000 tons/year	11.48	11.48	11.48
1379	1379	780	780	铁矿开采(原矿) Iron Ore Prospecting	万吨/年 10 000 tons/year	60		
40801	13112			铜采矿(原矿) Copper Mining	万吨/年 10 000 tons/year	132		
				铜选矿:(1)处理原矿 CopperDressing(1)CrudeOreProcessing	万吨/年 10 000 tons/year	132		
				(2)铜含量 Copper Content	万吨/年 10 000 tons/year	25000		
56048	56048	56048	56048	石油加工：蒸馏设备能力处理 Oil Processing: Treatment by Distillary Equipment	万吨/年 10 000 tons/year	150	150	150
36471	36471	36471	36471	加氢精制设备能力处理 Teatment by hydrogen-adding Refining Equipment	万吨/年 10 000 tons/year	60	60	60
67189	14115	67189	14115	液化天然气 Liquefied Natural Gas	标准立方米/日 Standard Cubic Meter/Day			
4000	4000	4000	4000	水 泥 Cement	万吨/年 100 00 tons /year	24	24	24
13663	12442	8800	8800	水 泥 Cement	万吨/年 100 00 tons /year	30		
16000	4897	16000	4897	炼 钢 Steel Making	万吨/年 100 00 tons /year	30	30	30
24241	10946	24241	10946	火力发电 Thermal-Power	万千瓦 10 000 kw/year	50		
90516	9928	90516	33392	火力发电 Thermal-Power	万千瓦 10 000 kw/year	27	27	13.5
6083	6083	150	150	水力发电 Water-Power	万千瓦 10 000 kw/year	30		
160626	52250	160626	626	水力发电 Water-Power	万千瓦 10 000 kw/year	46		
61487	12344	61487	12344		万立方米／日 10 000 cum/ Day			
900	900			城市天然气储气能力 Urban Natural Gas Storing Cpacity	公里 kilometer	2		

5-17 续表 1

单位：万元

项目名称 Project	建设地址 Seat of Construction Projects	开工时间 Starting Date	投产时间 Date of Putting into Operation	计划总投资 Total Invest-memt Planned
新建精伊霍铁路 Jinghe-Yili-Huocheng Railway under Construction		200411		600000
S306 八盘水磨——阿合奇公路 S306 Bapan Waterwill-Akqi Highway	阿合奇县 Akqi County	200207	200410	34402
S303 巴里坤——木垒公路 Balikon-Mori Highway	巴里坤县 Barkol Kazak County	200205	200409	53792
奎屯-赛里木湖公路 Kuytun-sayram Lake Highway		200206		305537
新疆库尔勒机场建设指挥部 Xinjiang Korla Airport	库尔勒市 Korla City	200310		44000
恰甫其海水利枢纽工程办公室 Qapuqi Water Diversion Pivotal Works Office	巩留县 Gongliu County	200206		189045
新疆水利厅引额济乌工程 Xinjiang Water Conservancy Department,Works of Diverting the water of the Ertix River to Urumqi		200109		441990
更新改造限额以上项目 Renovation and Transformation				
乌鲁木齐矿业（集团）有限责任公司 Urumqi Mining Industrial (group) Ltd. Co.	乌鲁木齐市 Urumqi City	200407		16027
新疆哈密煤业集团 150 万吨矿井技改 Coal Pit Technical Reform, Hami Coal Industrial Group	昌吉市 Changji City	200306		15968
新疆钢铁雅满苏矿业有限责任公司 2×60 万吨球团项目 2×600,000 –tons pillets Xinjiang Steel and Iron Ya Mansu Mining Ltd. Co.	哈密市 Hami [Kumul] City	200407		12000
新疆麦趣尔乳品生产线三期工程 3rd Projects of Production Line, Maiquer Dairy Products Production Line	昌吉市 Changji City	200305		18600
新疆新欧奶业发展有限公司 2000 吨奶酪及干酪素技改 2000 tons cheese and dried cheese innovation in Xinjiang Xinou Dairy Development Ltd. Co.	昌吉市 Changji City	200406		15086
新疆呼图壁县天山棉纺厂引进 36 台气流纺机技术改造项目 36 sets of jet-loom technical innovation introduced by XJ Hu Bubi County Tianshan Cotton Mill	呼图壁县 Hutubi County	200204	200406	24000
新疆呼图壁县天山棉纺厂引进十万锭数字化紧密纺项目 100,000 –spindle digital tight weaving project introduced by XJ Hu Tubi County Tianshan	呼图壁县 Hutubi County	200308		47000
新棉集团喀什纺织有限责任公司 7 万锭棉纱扩建 70,000 spindles cotton –yarn enlargement by Xinjiang Cotton Group, Kashgar Textile Ltd. Co	喀什市 Kashgar [Kaxgar] City	200310		25000
新疆新星事业集团公司塔里木石油化工分公司塔化沥青二期扩建 Bitumen Phase- II Enlargement Tarim Petro-chemical Sub-company under Xinxing Group	库车县 Kuqa County	200308		106256
新疆八一钢铁集团有限责任公司 42 孔焦炉工程 Xinjiang Iron & Steel Corporation,42 holes Coking Oven Works	乌鲁木齐市 Urumqi City	200211	200412	9346

Continued

(10 000yuan)

自开始建设至本年底止累计完成投资 Accumulative Investment Actually Made	#本年完成投资 Investment Made in the Year	自开始建设至本年底累计新增固定资产 Accumulative New-added Fixed Assets form It's Start to the Year-end	#本年新增固定资产 Newly-Increased Fixed Assets in the Year	建设规模和新增生产能力 Construction Scale and Newly-Added Production CapaCity				
				生产能力(或效益)名称 Name of Prodction CapaCity	计量单位 Metering Unit	建设规模 Scale of constrac-tion Projects	累计新增 Accumula-tive Newly-Increased Production	#本年 Current year
20000	20000			新建铁路主线正线交付运营里程 Milage in service for new-built railway trunk line	公里 kilometer	302		
34400	4384	34400	34400	改建公路 Rebuilt Highway	公里 kilometer	259	259	259
51065	4043	51065	4328	改建公路 Rebuilt Highway	公里 kilometer	316	316	316
				二级公路 Second class Highway	公里 kilometer	316	316	316
180243	78305			新建公路 New-built Highway	公里 kilometer	303		
				#高速公路 Express Highway	公里 kilometer	18		
				一级公路 First class Highway	公里 kilometer	229		
				二级公路 Second class Highway	公里 kilometer	56		
23759	20000			民航机场跑道 Run-way for Civil Aviation Airport	条 Lane	1		
				民航机场跑道 Run-way for Civil Aviation Airport	米 Meter	2800		
113592	42753			水库容量(总库容) Reservoir Volume	亿立方米 100 millioncum	17.7		
390000	140000	2324		水库容量(总库容) Reservoir Volume	亿立方米 100 millioncum	2		
				城市自来水供水能力 Urban Tapping Water Supply Capacity	万吨/日 10 000 tons/Day	305		
4508	4508	154	154	原煤开采 Raw Coal Mining	万吨/年 10 000 tons/year	45		
				城市供热能力：蒸汽 CapaCity of City Thermal System:Vapor	吨/小时 ton/hours	63.45		
				热 水 Hot Water	兆瓦/小时 megawatt / hour	46		
7992	5963	3500	3500	原煤开采 Crude coal Mining	万吨/年 10 000 tons/year	150		
5118	5118			铁矿石成品矿 Iron Ore Product Mine	万吨/年 10 000 tons/year	60		
7210	2200			其他乳制品 Other Dairy Products	万吨/年 10 000 tons/year	100000		
1500	1500	1500	1500	其他乳制品 Other Dairy Products	万吨/年 10 000 tons/year	2000		
24000	10000	24000	23658	棉纺锭 Cotton Spindle	锭 Spindle	100000	100000	100000
6039	3829	6039	6039	棉纺锭 Cotton Spindle	锭 Spindle	100000		
20550	8400			棉纺锭 Cotton Spindle	锭 Spindle	70000		
69619	57619			焦 炭 Coke	万吨/年 10 000 tons/year			
9346	3266	9346	9346	焦 炭 Coke	万吨/年 10 000 tons/year	26	26	26

5-17 续表 2

单位：万元

项 目 名 称　　Project	建设地址 Seat of Construction Projects	开工时间 Starting Date	投产时间 Date of Putting into Operation	计划总投资 Total Invest-memt Planned
新疆八一钢铁集团有限责任公司新建 4 号焦炉 No. 4 Coking Furnance, Xinjiang August 1st Steel and Iron Group Co.	乌鲁木齐市 Urumqi City	200406	200412	9871
伊犁金志焦化有限责任公司 Yili Jinrui Coking Ltd. Co	尼勒克县 Nilka County	200406	200412	7500
新疆中泰化学股份有限公司五万吨/年聚氯乙烯专用树脂技术改造续建 50,000 tons/year Polyvinyl Chloride Special Rosin Technical Transformation XJ Zhongtai Chemical Stock Ltd. Co.	乌鲁木齐市 Urumqi City	200301	200412	27158
新疆八一钢铁集团有限责任公司新建 2 万立方米制氧机 Oxygen-making Machine with volume of 20,000 cubic meters, XJ August 1st Steel and Iron Group Ltd. Co.	乌鲁木齐市 Urumqi City	200406		28000
新疆制药厂 GMP 重点技术改造 GMP Key Technical Reform under Xinjiang Pharmaceutical Factory	乌鲁木齐市 Urumqi City	200204	200412	12648
青松建化股份有限公司 1000 吨/日生产线 1000 tons/ daily production line of Usun Chemical Building Stock Ltd. Co	库车县 Kuqa County	200401		14500
新疆兵团四师伊力特集团公司和什托洛盖水泥厂扩建 XJPCC No. 4 Division Ilite Group Co and Shituogailuo Cement Factory	和布克赛尔县 Hoboksar County	200304	200406	14000
乌鲁木齐柏青实业有限责任公司玻璃制品厂 Glass Products Factory, Urumqi Bobai Industrial Company	乌鲁木齐市 Urumqi City	200306		14000
新疆八一钢铁集团有限责任公司新建 380 立方米高炉 Newly-built 380 Cubic Meters of Furnace, Xinjiang Steel and Iron Corporation	乌鲁木齐市 Urumqi City	200311	200412	10000
新疆八一钢铁集团有限责任公司新建 5 号 380 立方米高炉 XJ August 1st Steel and Iron Group Ltd. Co. New-built No.5 380-meter Furnance	乌鲁木齐市 Urumqi City	200405	200411	9500
新疆八一钢铁集团有限责任公司八钢转炉工程升级改造 Upgrading Innovation on August 1st revolving furnance project of XJ August 1st Steel and Iron Group Ltd. Co	乌鲁木齐市 Urumqi City	200407	200412	9501
新疆八一钢铁集团有限责任公司板带工程 Iron Plate Works, Xinjiang Steel and Iron Corporation	乌鲁木齐市 Urumqi City	200308		245000
新疆八一钢铁集团有限责任公司新建棒材厂 New Constructed Bar Material Plant, XJ August 1st Steel and Iron Group Ltd. Co.	乌鲁木齐市 Urumqi City	200406		12000
新疆众和股份有限公司电子铝箔、精铝二期扩建 Aluminium Phase II Enlargement for electronic aluminium foil and refined aluminium, Xinjiang Joint World Ltd. Co	乌鲁木齐市 Urumqi City	200109		9166
新疆众和股份有限公司高压电极箔二期扩建工程 Phase II Enlargement Works on High-Voltage Electro-Foil of Xinjiang Joint World Stock Ltd. Co	乌鲁木齐市 Urumqi City	200302		14000
新疆众和股份有限公司精铝三期改造 Refined aluminium Phase III Reconstruction of XJ Joint World Stock Ltd. Co.	乌鲁木齐市 Urumqi City	200410		9238
新疆特变电工股份有限公司大型智能化变压器技术改造 Transformation of Large-size Intelligent Transformer,Xinjiang Toban Electric Engineering	昌吉市 Changji City	200204	200412	6280
新疆八一钢铁集团有限责任公司热电联产供热工程 Thermal Works by ThermoelectriCity Linking Production,Xinjiang Iron & Steel Corporation	乌鲁木齐市 Urumqi City	200210	200412	22668
新疆华电昌吉热电有限公司热电二期工程 XJ Huadian Changji Thermal Electricity Ltd. Co Phase II Project	昌吉市 Changji City	200405		98996
新疆风能公司达坂城风电场 Dabancheng Wind Power Plant, Xinjiang Wind Energy Co.	乌鲁木齐市 Urumqi City	200206		16311
昌吉电信局数据交换传输等工程 Data Exchange Transmission Project of Changji Telecommunication Bureau	昌吉市 Changji City	200403	200412	8408

Continued

(10 000yuan)

自开始建设至本年底止累计完成投资 Accumulative Investment Actually Made	#本年完成投资 Investment Made in the Year	自开始建设至本年底累计新增固定资产 Accumulative New-added Fixed Assets form It's Start to the year-end	#本年新增固定资产 Newly-Increased Fixed Assets in the Year	建设规模和新增生产能力 Construction Scale and Newly-Added Production CapaCity				
				生产能力(或效益)名称 Name of Production CapaCity	计量单位 Metering Unit	建设规模 Scale of constraction Projects	累计新增 Accumulative Newly-Increased Production CapaCity	#本 年 In the Present year
9871	9871	9871	9871	焦 炭 Coke	万吨/年 10 000 tons/year	27	27	27
6000	6000	6000	6000	焦 炭 Coke	万吨/年 10 000 tons/year	20	20	20
27158	6650	27158	6650	烧 碱 Caustic Soda	吨/年 tons/year	60000	60000	30000
				塑料树脂及共聚物 Plastic Rosin and Polyaster	吨/年 tons/year	60000	60000	10000
1921	1921							
13900	4693	13900	13900		吨/年 tons/year	150	150	150
					吨/年 tons/year	1000	1000	1000
14500	14500	14500		水 泥 Cement	万吨/年 100 00 tons /year	36	36	36
14000	2750	14000	14000	水 泥 Cement	万吨/年 100 00 tons /year	30	30	30
569	399							
10062	6745	10062	10062	生 铁 Pig Iron	万吨/年 10 000 tons/year	46	46	46
9597	9597	9597	9597	生 铁 Pig Iron	万吨/年 10 000 tons/year	46	46	46
9501	9501	9501	9501	炼 钢 Steel Making	万吨/年 100 00 tons /year	80	80	80
				转炉钢 Revolving Furnance	万吨/年 100 00 tons /year	80	80	80
74988	63988	74988	74988	冷加工钢材 Cold-Processed Steel Material	万吨/年 10 000 tons/year	75	75	75
11817	11817			热轧钢材 Hot-Rolled Steel Material	万吨/年 10 000 tons/year	60		
				型 材 Section Bar	万吨/年 10 000 tons/year	60		
10502	1900	7363	1900	铝加工 Aluminium Processing	吨/年 tons /year	9000	8000	8000
13147	4815	9978	4816	铝加工 Aluminium Processing	吨/年 tons /year	949		
4961	4961	4561						
6280	767	4962	767	大中型变压器 Large & Medium Type Transformer	万千伏安 10 000 kev	400	400	150
22668		22668	22668	火力发电 Thermal Power Generation	万千瓦 10 000 kw	5	5	5
				城市供热能力：蒸汽 CapaCity of City Thermal System:Vapor	吨/小时 ton/hours	260	260	260
				热 水 Hot Water	兆瓦/小时 megawatt / hour	203	203	203
5569	5569			火力发电 Thermal Power Generation	万千瓦 10 000 kw	25		
12177	4782	10990	5574	其他发电 Others Generation	万千瓦 10 000 kw	2.28	2.28	2.28
8449	8449	7479	7479	程控交换机(指安装能力) Program exchange switchboard (Installing capacity)	万线／年 10 000 lines/year	3.44	3.44	3.44

5-18 基本建设投资效果指标
Investment Result of capital Construction

指 标	Item	1990	1995	2000	2004
建设周期(年)	Construction Cycle (year)	4.2	3.7	4.5	2.4
计划总投资(万元)	Total Planned Investment (10 000 yuan)	2014004	6684819	17588605	18264049
本年完成投资(万元)	Completed Invetsment for the Current Year (10 000 yuan)	479986	1822429	3927483	7592442
建设项目投产率(%)	Ratio of Operation for Construction Items (%)	59.9	66.7	72.5	66.3
#大中型项目	Large and Medium-size Projects	16.7	16.7	33.3	50.0
施工项目个数(个)	Number of Construction Projects (unit)	2430	2897	3060	4889
#大中型项目	Large and Medium –size Projects	24	30	24	26
竣工项目个数(个)	Number of Completed Projects (unit)	1456	1932	2219	3243
#大中型项目个数	Number of Large and Medium-size Projects	4	5	8	13
本年新增固定资产(万元)	New-added Fixed Asset for the Current Year (10 000 yuan)	370692	1460481	4813694	6552613
固定资产交付使用率(%)	Ratio of Fixed Asset Put in Use (%)	77.2	80.1	122.6	86.3
未完工程投资(万元)	Invetsment in Unfinished Works (10 000 yuan)	298778	1051687	1405192	2658878
未完工程占用率(%)	Ratio of Unfinished Works (%)	62.2	49.4	35.8	35.0
施工面积(万平方米)	Construction Area (10 000 Square Meters)	610.88	903.06	1541.06	2422.53
#住 宅	Flat	259.59	364.08	957.90	1164.08
竣工面积(万平方米)	Completed Area (10 000 Square Meters)	347.80	509.16	1100.06	1463.09
#住宅	Flat	153.70	242.95	760.85	849.73
房屋面积竣工率(%)	Completed Ratio of Flat Floor Space (%)	56.9	56.4	71.4	60.4
#住 宅	Flat	59.2	66.7	79.4	73.0

5-19 基本建设在建项目计划总投资及完成情况
Total Planned Investment in Capital Works under Construction and its Completion

单位：万元 (10 000 yuan)

指 标	Item	2003	2004
计划总投资	Planned total Investment	14365086	18264049
自开始建设至本年底累计完成投资	Accumulated Investment from the Start of Construction to the Year-end	10336716	12188413
#本年完成投资	Investment Completed at the end of a Year	6476406	7592442
自开始建设至本年底累计新增固定资产	New-added Fixed Asset Accumulated from start of Construction to the Year-end	5614132	8485441
自开始建设至本年底未完工程完成投资	Investment Completetd in Unfinished Works from the Start of Construction to the Year-end	4076288	2658878
全部建成尚需投资	Investment yet to be made for whole-completetd works	4028370	6075636
未完工程占用率(%)	Ratio of Occupancy by Unfinished Works (%)	62.9	35.0
建设周期(年)	Construction Cycle (year)	2.2	1.5

5-20 基本建设大中型项目计划总投资及完成情况
Total Planned Investment and its Completion for Large and Medium-size of Capital Construction Items

单位：万元 (10 000 yuan)

指 标	Item	2003	2004
计划总投资	Total Planned Investment	4217949	5197000
自开始建设至本年底累计完成投资	Investment Accumulated from the Start of Construction to the Year-end	3322756	4173288
#本年完成投资	Investment made by the Current Year	1740427	2645661
自开始建设至本年底累计新增固定资产	New-added Fixed Asset from the Start of Construction to the Year-end	1322981	3105770
自开始建设至本年底未完工程完成投资	Investment made in Unfinished Project from the Start of Construction to the Year-end	1931107	495454
全部建成尚需投资	Invetsment yet to be made in full-completion	895193	1023712
未完工程占用率(%)	Ratio of Occupancy by Unfinished Works (%)	111.0	18.7
建设周期(年)	Construction Cycle (year)	2.4	1.2

5-21 按登记注册类型分的更新改造投资

Investment in Renewal and Reform by Registration

单位：万元 (10 000 yuan)

年 份 Year	地 区 Region	合 计 Total	国有经济 State-owned Units	集体经济 Collective-owned Units	股份经济 Share Holding Economic Units	其他经济 Other Types of Ownership
	1980	20601	20601			
	1985	61135	61135			
	1990	152712	152712			
	1991	181360	181360			
	1992	217891	217891			
	1993	373873	373873			
	1994	431957	423096	141	4705	4015
	1995	626739	610942		2531	13266
	1996	685795	670822		6542	8431
	1997	739121	711812		22187	5122
	1998	760914	690845		43797	26272
	1999	610884	503713		50082	57089
	2000	775381	565581		130029	79771
	2001	1081795	831320	520	107361	142594
	2002	1153469	711342	14225	383521	44381
	2003	1274279	681336	27109	445832	120002
	2004	1386532	839391	31054	409244	106843
乌鲁木齐市	Urumqi City	498755	352456		113860	32439
克拉玛依市	Karamay City	12027	3939	3500	4588	
石河子市	Shihezi City	43053	12753		26167	4133
吐鲁番地区	Turpan Administrative Offices	55569	44702	4397	4800	1670
哈密地区	Hami [Kumul] Administrative Offices	33030	28971	450	3079	530
昌吉回族自治州	Changji Hui Autonomous Prefecture	181350	59298	17209	75158	29685
伊犁哈萨克自治州	Ili Kazak Autonomous Prefecture	166213	60448	2956	89255	13554
伊犁州直属县(市)	Counties (Cities) Direct Under Ili Prefecture	67666	36993	232	26508	3933
塔城地区	Tacheng [Tarbagatai] Administrative Offices	81850	15990	2724	54484	8652
阿勒泰地区	Altay Administrative Offices	16697	7465		8263	969
博尔塔拉蒙古自治州	Bortala Mongol Autonomous Prefecture	13535	11068		2000	467
巴音郭楞蒙古自治州	Bayangol Mongol Autonomous Prefecture	125186	61811	2430	44789	16156
阿克苏地区	Aksu Administrative Offices	128152	88828		33800	5524
克孜勒苏柯尔克孜自治州	Kizilsu Kirgiz Autonomous Prefecture					
喀什地区	Kashgar [Kaxgar] Administrative Offices	34833	24278		10555	
和田地区	Hotan Administrative Offices	6528	2538	112	1193	2685
跨地区投资	Trans-regional Investment	88301	88301			

5-22 按构成分的更新改造投资

Investment in Innovation and Reform by Composition

单位：万元 (10 000 yuan)

年 份 Year	地 区 Region	合 计 Total	建筑工程 Construction	安装工程 Installation	设备工器具购置 Purchase of Equipment and Instruments	其他费用 Other Expense
	1980	20601	12444		7934	223
	1985	61135	33298		26725	1112
	1990	152712	60295	18825	69643	3949
	1991	181360	76725	10967	89676	3992
	1992	217891	103919	13278	95753	4941
	1993	373873	174937	39264	152309	7363
	1994	431957	188681	51133	174034	18109
	1995	626739	244886	70854	283255	27744
	1996	685795	267886	76125	317325	24459
	1997	739121	289479	74542	333961	41139
	1998	760914	348517	61455	325631	25311
	1999	610884	199764	61039	319117	30964
	2000	775381	265394	75350	421833	12804
	2001	1081795	283545	84207	665646	48397
	2002	1153469	323746	103552	679640	46531
	2003	1274279	363916	136472	709316	64575
	2004	1386532	413216	196370	732509	44437
乌鲁木齐市	Urumqi City	498755	102328	103598	278419	14410
克拉玛依市	Karamay City	12027	11999		28	
石河子市	Shi Hezi City	43053	12864	4259	22873	3057
吐鲁番地区	Turpan Administrative Offices	55569	13165	2644	38030	1730
哈密地区	Hami [Kumul] Administrative Offices	33030	17599	2421	12833	177
昌吉回族自治州	Changji Hui Autonomous Prefecture	181350	60597	22814	88376	9563
伊犁哈萨克自治州	Ili Kazak Autonomous Prefecture	166213	57347	12676	89063	7127
伊犁州直属县(市)	Counties (Cities) Direct Under Ili Prefecture	67666	25512	3508	36762	1884
塔城地区	Tacheng [Tarbagatai] Administrative Offices	81850	25501	7591	43632	5126
阿勒泰地区	Altay Administrative Offices	16697	6334	1577	8669	117
博尔塔拉蒙古自治州	Bortala Mongol Autonomous Prefecture	13535	4229	1095	7646	565
巴音郭楞蒙古自治州	Bayangol Mongol Autonomous Prefecture	125186	47779	7391	66063	3953
阿克苏地区	Aksu Administrative Offices	128152	33265	24302	68386	2199
克孜勒苏柯尔克孜自治州	Kizilsu Kirgiz Autonomous Prefecture					
喀什地区	Kashgar [Kaxgar] Administrative Offices	34833	8992	2757	22210	874
和田地区	Hotan Administrative Offices	6528			6192	336
跨地区投资	Trans-regional Investment	88301	43052	12413	32390	446

5-23 按资金来源分的更新改造投资

Sources of Funds for Investment in Renewal and Reform

单位：万元 (10 000 yuan)

年 份 Year	地 区 Region	合 计 Total	国家预算内资金 Funds within State Budget	国内贷款 Domestic Loan	利用外资 Foreign Capital Applied	自筹资金 Self-raised Funds	其他资金 Other Funds
	1980	20601					
	1985	61135	3201	19798		37588	548
	1990	152712	3181	41623	4441	97471	5996
	1991	181360	3614	46797	118	126544	4287
	1992	217891	5453	61248	4884	135949	10357
	1993	373873	3312	104208	5202	237714	23437
	1994	431957	5372	129102	7395	262325	27763
	1995	626739	10568	122467	41848	402318	49538
	1996	685795	6006	160800	42584	439885	36520
	1997	739121	9354	143800	3137	551203	31627
	1998	760914	11345	115357	16401	564156	53655
	1999	610884	16130	113965	16710	415611	48468
	2000	775381	27354	190600	8291	497088	52048
	2001	1081795	31924	306927	9868	698408	34668
	2002	1153469	58304	259882	2251	750718	82314
	2003	1274279	46770	370598	2359	796794	57758
	2004	1388869	41415	177372	3175	1109040	57867
乌鲁木齐市	Urumqi City	500252	6277	67548	851	414881	10695
克拉玛依市	Karamay City	12027				12027	
石河子市	Shi Hezi City	43065		20956		21569	540
吐鲁番地区	Turpan Administrative Offices	55957	72	800		54685	400
哈密地区	Hami [Kumul] Administrative Offices	29961	2608			20031	7322
昌吉回族自治州	Changji Hui Autonomous Prefecture	169060	12728	36461		105220	14651
伊犁哈萨克自治州	Ili Kazak Autonomous Prefecture	169508	3940	12633		144089	8846
伊犁州直属县(市)	Counties (Cities) Direct Under Ili Prefecture	67215	1517	1996		60756	2946
塔城地区	Tacheng [Tarbagatai] Administrative Offices	86746	2043	7225		72303	5175
阿勒泰地区	Altay Administrative Offices	15547	380	3412		11030	725
博尔塔拉蒙古自治州	Bortala Mongol Autonomous Prefecture	12135	960	891		9156	1128
巴音郭楞蒙古自治州	Bayangol Mongol Autonomous Prefecture	126379	3459	21511	2324	96949	2136
阿克苏地区	Aksu Administrative Offices	152763	9550	16535		120712	5966
克孜勒苏柯尔克孜自治州	Kizilsu Kirgiz Autonomous Prefecture						
喀什地区	Kashgar [Kaxgar] Administrative Offices	22903	1706	37		20327	833
和田地区	Hotan Administrative Offices	6558	115			1093	5350
跨地区投资	Trans-regional Investment	88301				88301	

5-24 分行业更新改造投资主要指标

Main Indicators of Investment in Innovation by Sector

(2004 年)

行业	Sector	投资额(万元) Investment (10 000 yuan)	#地方 Local	施工项目个数(个) Number of Projects under Construction (unit)	竣工项目个数(个) Number of Projects Completed (unit)	本年新增固定资产(万元) Newly Increased Fixed Assets (10 000 yuan)
总计	**Total**	**1386532**	**757390**	**1188**	**845**	**1074250**
农、林、牧、渔业	**Farming, Forestry, Animal Husbandry and Fishery**	**80780**	**33014**	**223**	**202**	**70973**
农业	Farming	25733	8459	97	95	25393
林业	Forestry	282	160	2	1	242
畜牧业	Animal Husbandry	10810	5355	24	23	5727
农、林、牧、渔服务业	Agricultural Services	43955	19040	100	83	39611
采矿业	**Mining and Quarrying**	**156822**	**105756**	**116**	**45**	**116485**
煤炭开采和洗选业	Coal Mining and Dressing	90284	80768	90	33	54148
石油和天然气开采业	Petroleum and Natural Gas Extraction	40464		1		40464
#天然原油和天然气开采	Crude Oil and Natural Gas Extraction	40464		1		40464
黑色金属矿采选业	Black Ferrous Metal Mining and Dressing	20248	20248	8	2	9997
#铁矿采选	Iron Ore Extraction	19051	19051	6	1	9200
有色金属矿采选业	Nonferrous Matals Mining and Dressing	2741	2173	6	1	50
#常用有色金属矿采选	Common Nonferrous Metal Extraction	868	300	2		
非金属矿采选业	Nonmetal Minerals mining and Dressing	3085	2567	11	9	11826
#土砂石开采	Earth, Sand and Stone Extraction	2207	2207	4	3	11308
化学矿采选	Chemical Ore Mining and Dressing	360	360	1		
采盐	Salt Mining					
制造业	**Manufacturing**	**621953**	**490581**	**351**	**236**	**469383**
农副食品加工业	Farm and Non-Staple Food Processing	21550	20869	34	21	11583
#制糖	Sugar Processing	1547	1340	3	1	347
食品制造业	Food Production	33493	23317	27	21	28686
#液体乳及乳制品制造	Liquid Milk and Dairy Products Production	8186	7956	11	8	5964
饮料制造业	Beverage Production	16095	15666	16	10	15132
烟草加工业	Tobacco	11371	11371	11		
纺织业	Textile Industry	47049	47049	19	6	44293
#棉、化纤纺织及印染精加工	Cotton, Chemical textitle, Dyeing and Printing	38376	38376	12	5	38035
毛纺织和染整精加工	Woolen Textitle, Dyeing and Printing, Dressing	1500	1500	1		166
麻纺织	Flax Textitle	6498	6498	4		5417
木材加工及竹、藤、棕、草制品业	Timber Processing,Bamboo,Cane,Palm Fiber and Straw Products	3762	3762	3	2	4280
家具制造业	Furniture Manufacturing	74	74	1	1	74
造纸及纸制品业	Papermaking and Paper Products	5075	4450	9	5	3950
印刷业、记录媒介的复制	Printing and Record Medium Reproduction	1030	1030			1030
石油加工及炼焦业	Petroleum Processing and Coking	151276	91428	78	65	81325
#精炼石油产品的制造	Refined Oil Products	109056	49208	68	60	54584
炼焦	Coking	42220	42220	10	5	26741
化学原料及化学制品制造业	Raw chemical Materials and Chemical Products	74303	35596	29	16	44249
#基础化学原料制造	Basic Chemical Material	36125	25205	14	4	32017
肥料制造	Fertilizer Manufacturing	3185	3113	3	3	942

5-24 续表 1 Continued

行 业	Sector	投资额(万元) Investment (10 000 yuan)	#地 方 Local	施工项目个数(个) Number of Projects under Construction (unit)	竣工项目个数(个) Number of Projects Completed (unit)	本年新增固定资产(万元) Newly Increased Fixed Assets (10 000 yuan)
医药制造业	Medical and Pharmaceutical Products	17000	16540	11	7	25325
#中药饮片加工	Herb Tablet Processing	1734	1500	2	1	234
中成药制造	Herbs and Patent Medicine	2913	2913	5	3	5287
化学纤维制造业	Chemical Fiber Manufacturing	12382	12382	3	2	9700
橡胶制品业	Rubber Products	50	50	1	1	50
塑料制品业	Plastic Products	6007	5787	12	9	4454
非金属矿物制品业	Nonmetal Mineral Products	53764	34069	37	21	36566
#水泥、石灰和石膏的制造	Cement, Lime and Gypsum	39277	20086	13	8	23384
黑色金属冶炼及压延加工业	Smelting and Pressing of Ferrous Metals	131186	131186	32	30	136819
#钢压延加工	Steel Rolling and Processing	91658	91658	21	19	94208
有色金属冶炼及压延加工业	Non-ferrous Metal Smeltering and rolling process	23546	23546	7	1	10716
#常用有色金属冶炼	Common Nonferrous Metal Smeltering	17656	17656	6	1	10716
金属制品业	Metal Products	1346	1346	5	4	696
通用设备制造业	Ordinary Equipment Production	1590	1590	4	4	1470
专用设备制造业	Euqipment for Special Purposes	481	481	2	2	481
交通运输设备制造业	Traffic, Transport and Equipment Manufacturing	2363	2232	2	2	1953
#汽车制造	Truck Manufacturing	2363	2232	2	2	1953
电气机械及器材制造业	Electric Machinery and Apparatus Manufacturing	6942	6542	7	5	6333
工艺品及其他制造业	Art and Handicraft and Others	218	218	1	1	218
电力、煤气及水的生产和供应业	**Electric Power, Gas and Water Production and Supply**	**61523**	**35863**	**173**	**90**	**69883**
电力、蒸汽、热水的生产和供应业	Electric power, Steam and Hot Water Production and Supply	54172	29338	164	86	64019
电力生产	Electric Power Production	30143	23559	87	63	47126
电力供应	Electric Power Supply	8662	1230	56	9	5313
热力生产和供应	Thermal Power Production and Supply	15367	4549	21	14	11580
燃气生产和供应业	Gas Production and Supply					
水的生产和供应业	Water Production and Supply	7351	6525	9	4	5864
#自来水的生产和供应	Running Water Production and Supply	3531	3055	6	3	2944
污水处理及其再生利用	Tap Water Production and Supply	3150	2800	2	1	2920
建筑业	**Construction**	**11032**	**2899**	**3**	**2**	**10876**
房屋和土木工程建筑业	House and Civil Works Construction	10653	2899	3	2	10497
建筑安装业	Construction and Installation	379				379
交通运输、仓储及邮政业	**Transportation, Storage, Postal and Telecommunications Services**	**161178**	**19527**	**67**	**43**	**96295**
铁路运输业	Railway Transport	136886		47	33	76328
道路运输业	Road Transport	11596	9661	6	5	10531
城市公共交通业	Urban Public Transport	4985	4985	1	1	4985
航空运输业	Air Transportation	5356	3260	9		2096
仓储业	Storage	1589	855	4	4	1589

5-24 续表 2 Continued

行　　业	Sector	投资额（万元）Investment (10 000 yuan)	#地 方 Local	施工项目个数（个）Number of Projects under Construction (unit)	竣工项目个数（个）Number of Projects Completed (unit)	本年新增固定资产（万元）Newly Increased Fixed Assets (10 000 yuan)
邮政业		766	766			766
信息传输、计算机服务和软件业	**Message Transmission, Computer and Software**	**214301**	**11030**	**136**	**131**	**169038**
电信和其他信息传输服务业	Telecom. and Other Message Transmission	212301	9030	135	131	167038
#电　信	Telecommunication	200241		131	128	164964
批发和零售业	**Wholesal&Retail Trade**	**19977**	**19580**	**20**	**14**	**16352**
批发业	Wholesale Trade	13970	13743	7	4	12649
零售业	Retail Trade	6007	5837	13	10	3703
住宿和餐饮业	Hotel and Catering	8560	5728	17	12	6900
住宿业	Hotel	6819	3987	13	9	5159
#旅游饭店	Tourist Resraurant	4903	2522	8	5	3498
金融业	**Finance**	**4810**	**960**			**4810**
银行业	Banking	4419	569			4419
证券业	Stock Exchange	391	391			391
保险业	Insurance					
其他金融活动	Other Financial Activities					
房地产业	**Real Estate management**	**278**	**278**	**1**	**1**	**278**
#房地产开发与经营业	Real Estate Development and Operation	278	278	1	1	278
物业管理	Real Estate Management					
租赁和商务服务业	**Leasing and Commercial Service**	**1060**				**1060**
#商务服务业	Commercial Service	1060				1060
科学研究、技术服务和地质勘查业	**Scientific Research, Technical Service and Geological Survey**	**5198**	**4702**	**3**	**1**	**5198**
研究与试验发展	**Research and Experimental Development**	**57**				**57**
专业技术服务业	Special Technical Service	4319	3943	2		4319
科技交流和推广服务业	Scientific Communication and diffusion	63				63
地质勘查业	Geological Survey	759	759	1	1	759
水利、环境和公共设施管理业	**Water Conservancy, Environment and Public Works Management**	**25621**	**18005**	**47**	**43**	**24439**
水利管理业	Water Conservancy Management	7819	3293	27	27	8013
环境管理业	Environment Management	5950	5950	1		5731
公共设施管理业	Public Works Management	11852	8762	19	16	10695
市政公共设施管理	Civil Works Management	11442	8587	12	9	10265
游览景区管理	Scenic Spot Management	410	175	7	7	430
居民服务和其他服务业	**Community Service and Other Service**	**136**	**136**	**2**	**1**	**103**
教　育	**Education**	**2682**	**556**	**13**	**12**	**2582**
#初等教育	Elementary Education	1432	52	6	6	1432
中等教育	Secondary Education	406	270	4	3	306
高等教育	Higher Education	286	104	2	2	286

5-24 续表 3 Continued

行　　业	Sector	投资额（万元） Investment (10 000 yuan)	#地 方 Local	施工项目个数（个） Number of Projects under Construction (unit)	竣工项目个数（个） Number of Projects Completed (unit)	本年新增固定资产（万元） Newly Increased Fixed Assets (10 000 yuan)
卫生、社会保障和社会福利业	**Health, Social Security and Social Welfare**	**5135**	**3652**	**7**	**4**	**4758**
卫 生	Health Care	5135	3652	7	4	4758
#医 院	Hospital	5135	3652	7	4	4758
文化、体育和娱乐业	**Culture, Sports and Recreation**	**788**	**666**	**3**	**3**	**788**
新闻出版业	**Press and Publishing**	**199**	**199**			**199**
广播、电视、电影和音像业	Radio, TV, Film and Video and Audio	437	367	2	2	437
文化艺术业	Cultural and Art	152	100	1	1	152
公共管理和社会组织	**Public Management and Social Organization**	**4698**	**4457**	**6**	**5**	**4049**
国家机构	State Organs	2989	2748	2	1	2340
基层群众自治组织	Mass Autonomous Organization at Grass Root	1709	1709	4	4	1709

5-25 按建设性质分的更新改造投资
Investment in Innovation and Reform by Nature of Construction

单位：万元　　(10 000 yuan)

年 份 Year	合 计 Total	新 建 New Construction	扩 建 Expansion	改 建 Reconstruction	其 他 Others
1985	61135	794	26010	29388	4943
1990	152712	3194	42753	96940	9825
1991	181360	2957	57854	107341	13208
1992	217891	2519	65939	134013	15420
1993	373873	8575	131043	213539	20716
1994	431957	12895	187215	203603	28244
1995	626739	41464	264956	303689	16630
1996	685795	56557	232580	370857	25801
1997	739121	1769	271932	431351	34069
1998	760914	19675	234055	447661	59523
1999	610884	31858	254066	263185	61775
2000	775381	100871	194116	416123	64271
2001	1081795	133746	424503	449727	73819
2002	1153469	128944	474334	453370	96821
2003	1274279	155287	658756	373516	86720
2004	1386532	105671	545195	642529	93137

5-26 各地、州、市分行业更新改造投资

单位：万元 (2004 年)

行 业 Sector	总 计 Total	乌鲁木齐市 Urumqi City	克拉玛依市 Karamay City	石河子市 Shihezi City	吐鲁番地区 Turpan Administrative Offices	哈密地区 Hami [Kumul] Administrative Offices	昌吉回族自治州 Changji Hui Autonomous Prefecture	伊犁哈萨克自治州 Ili Kazak Autonomous Prefecture
合 计 Total	**1386532**	**498755**	**12027**	**43053**	**55569**	**33030**	**181350**	**166213**
农、林、牧、渔业 Farming,Forestry,Animal Husbandry and Fishrey	80780	5663	196	1178	1820	1177	22877	14588
采矿业 Mining and Quarrying	156822	9376			48639	10325	39676	32626
制造业 Manufac-turing	621953	258236	6888	38470	1989	3436	68739	85689
电力、煤气及水的生产和供应业 Production and Supply of Electric Power, Gas and Water	61523	11258					30695	11324
建筑业 Construction	11032	9371		745			247	394
交通运输仓储及邮政业 Transporta-tion, Storage, Postal and Telecommun ications Services	161178	30761		1045		15042		4287
信息传输、计算机服务和软件业 Message Transmission, Computer and Software	214301	139789			2905	130	10449	13153
批发和零售业 Wholesale & Retail Trade	19977	11101	1200		150	50		1606
住宿和餐饮业 Hotel and Catering	8560	4460		1442				551
金融业 Banking	4810	4485						325
房地产业 Real Estate	278	278						
租赁和商务服务业 Leasing and Commercial Service	1060	981						
科学研究、技术服务和地质勘查业 Scientific Research, Technical Service and Geological Survey	5198	1256	3743					
水利、环境和公共设施管理业 Water Conservancy, Environment and Public Works Management	25621	6436		173		2328	7346	219
居民服务和其他服务业 Community Service and Other Service	136	103						33
教 育 Education	2682	404				100	182	50
卫生、社会保障和社会福利业 Health, Social Security and Social Welfare	5135	578			66		895	1071
文化、体育和娱乐业 Culture, Sports and Recreation	788	232				122	70	297
公共管理和社会组织 Public Management and Social Organization	4698	3987				320	174	

Investment in Innovation and Reform by Nature of Construction in Prefectures and Cities

(10 000 yuan)

伊犁哈萨克自治州直属县(市) Counties (Cities) Direct Under Ili Prefecture	塔城地区 Tacheng [Tarbagatai] Administrative Offices	阿勒泰地区 Altay Administrative Offices	博尔塔拉蒙古自治州 Bortala Mongol Autonomous Prefecture	巴音郭楞蒙古自治州 Bayinggol Mongol Autonomous Prefecture	阿克苏地区 Aksu Administrative Offices	克孜勒苏柯尔克孜自治州 Kizilsu Kirgiz Autonomous Prefecture	喀什地区 Kashgar Administrative Offices	和田地区 Hotan Administrative Offices	跨地区投资 Trans-regional Investment
67666	**81850**	**16697**	**13535**	**125186**	**128152**		**34833**	**6528**	**88301**
3679	10479	430	5888	16742	7826		2762	63	
6052	13433	13141		11031	4414			735	
39358	43205	3126	2235	39810	103011		9220	4230	
5015	6309		2545	5036	284		381		
394				165	110				
3432	855		103	20288	150		954	247	88301
7875	5278		2034	21722	8314		15805	0	
120	1486			5395			227	248	
451	100			2107					
	325								
			79						
				91	108				
219			514	1462	3373		3770		
	33								
	50			138	428		1380		
1071			137	1049			334	1005	
	297				67				
				150	67				

5-27 各地、州、市、县(市)更新改造投资和新增固定资产

Investment in Innvoation and Newly Increased Fixed Assets by Prefecture, Autonomous Prefecture, City and County

单位：万元　　(2004 年)　　(10 000 yuan)

地　区	Region	投资总额 Total Investment	第一产业 Primary Industry	第二产业 Secondary Industry	第三产业 Tertiary Industry	住宅 Residence	新增固定资产 Newly Increased Fixed Assets	本年施工房屋面积(万平方米)Floor Space of Buildings(10 000sq.m) 施工面积 Floor Space Under Construction	竣工面积 Floor Space Completed
总　计	**Total**	**1386532**	**78800**	**847321**	**453935**	**6476**	**1074250**	**117.88**	**75.15**
按隶属关系分	**By Administrative Relationship**								
中　央	Central Government	629142	45916	213674	364693	4859	433210	39.90	31.44
地　方	Local	757390	32884	633647	89242	1617	641040	77.98	43.71
按区域分	**Grouped by Region**								
乌鲁木齐市	**Urumqi City**	**498755**	**5663**	**288135**	**204851**	**106**	**464307**	**34.65**	**21.35**
乌鲁木齐县	Urumqi County	1021			1021		1021		
克拉玛依市	**Karamay City**	**12027**	**196**	**6888**	**4943**		**5247**	**0.58**	**0.06**
石河子市	**Shi Hezi City**	**43053**	**1178**	**38915**	**2660**	**300**	**18629**	**5.76**	**0.92**
吐鲁番地区	**Turpan Administrative Offices**	**55569**	**1820**	**48102**	**3112**	**2535**	**50308**	**3.42**	**1.35**
吐鲁番市	Turpan City	5355	160	2290	2896	9	2253	0.46	
鄯善县	Shanshan [Piqan] County	43090		40378	216	2496	40931	2.79	1.35
托克逊县	Toksun County	7124	1660	5434		30	7124	0.17	
哈密地区	**Hami [Kumul] Administrative Offices**	**33030**	**1177**	**13761**	**18092**		**16148**	**2.11**	**0.59**
哈密市	Hami [Kumul] City	30648	1177	11821	17650		15066	2.02	0.59
巴里坤哈萨克自治县	Barkol Kazak Autonomous County	2382		1940	442		1082	0.09	
昌吉回族自治州	**Changji Hui Autonomous Prefecture**	**181350**	**22806**	**139207**	**19116**	**221**	**159880**	**21.76**	**14.32**
昌吉市	Changji City	61160	5069	43004	13087		47111	6.85	5.02
阜康市	Fukang City	39254	976	38148		130	25980	2.46	2.37
米泉市	Miquan City	32524	320	28210	3974	20	26510	3.32	3.32
呼图壁县	Hutubi County	22272	5527	15217	1497	31	38032	5.74	0.41
玛纳斯县	Manas County	19928	10383	9505		40	18305	2.99	2.92
奇台县	Qitai County	2477	276	1643	558		2157	0.28	0.28
吉木萨尔县	Jimsar County	3235	255	2980			1285		
木垒哈萨克自治县	Mori Kazak Autonomous County	500		500			500	0.12	

5-27 续表 1 Continued

单位：万元 (10 000 yuan)

地 区	Region	投资总额 Total Investment	第一产业 Primary Industry	第二产业 Secondary Industry	第三产业 Tertiary Industry	住宅 Residence	新增固定资产 Newly Increased Fixed Assets	本年施工房屋面积(万平方米)Floor Space of Buildings(10 000sq.m) 施工面积 Floor Space Under Construction	竣工面积 Floor Space Completed
伊犁哈萨克自治州	**Ili Kazak Autonomous Prefecture**	**166213**	**14501**	**129316**	**21562**	**834**	**125646**	**22.8**	**16.19**
伊犁州直属县(市)	**Counties (Cities) Direct Under Ili Prefecture**	**67666**	**3652**	**50581**	**13168**	**265**	**43538**	**7.96**	**4.45**
伊宁市	Yining [Gulja] City	14083		2319	11764		14083	0.04	0.04
奎屯市	Kuytun City	12408		12408			1037	2.30	
伊宁县	Yining [Gulja] County	12020	93	11889		38	5251	1.62	1.14
察布查尔锡伯自治县	Qapqal Xibe Autonomous County	3086	2171	510	405		3124	1.67	1.20
霍城县	Huocheng [Korgas] County	3128	430	2123	548	27	3128	0.65	0.65
巩留县	Gongliu [Tokkuztara] County	1200	463	737			463	0.25	0.25
新源县	Xinyuan [Kunes] County	3007		3007			2407	0.08	0.03
昭苏县	Zhaosu [Mongolkure] County	5210	379	4380	451		3310	1.14	1.14
特克斯县	Tekes County	180		180			180		
尼勒克县	Nilka County	13344	116	13028		200	10555	0.21	
塔城地区	**Tacheng [Tarbagatai] Administrative Offices**	**81850**	**10419**	**62468**	**8394**	**569**	**71099**	**13.44**	**11.34**
塔城市	Tacheng [Qoqek] City	8988	1024	2292	5642	30	8649	0.12	0.12
额敏县	Usu City	15758	440	15258		60	10778	0.17	0.17
乌苏市	Emin [Dorbiljin] County	3342	1103	2137	102		3892	0.52	0.23
沙湾县	Shawan County	38794	7053	29599	1726	416	26940	8.64	7.94
托里县	Toli County	3124	55	2976	93		485	0.39	0.15
裕民县	Yumin [Qagantokay] County	1814	604	1110	100		1014		
和布克赛尔蒙古自治县	Hoboksar Mongol Autonomous County	10030	140	9096	731	63	19341	3.60	2.72
阿勒泰地区	**Altay Administrative Offices**	**16697**	**430**	**16267**			**11009**	**1.40**	**0.40**
阿勒泰市	Altay City	580		580			580	0.35	0.35
布尔津县	Burqin County	367		367				0.99	0.00
富蕴县	Fuyun [Koktokay] County	12868		12868			9000		
福海县	Fuhai [Burultokay] County	1770	430	1340			490		
青河县	Qinghe [Qinggil] County	939		939			939	0.06	0.06
吉木乃县	Jemnay County	173		173					
博尔塔拉蒙古自治州	**Bortala Mongol Autonomous Prefecture**	**13535**	**4663**	**4780**	**2867**	**1225**	**13291**	**2.94**	**2.88**
博乐市	Bole [Bortala] City	10898	3376	4323	2730	469	10662	1.98	1.92
精河县	Jinghe [Jing] County	2114	1287	407	137	283	2106	0.39	0.39
温泉县	Wenquan [Araxang] County	523		50		473	523	0.57	0.57

5-27 续表 2 Continued

单位：万元 (10 000 yuan)

地区	Region	投资总额 Total Investment	第一产业 Primary Industry	第二产业 Secondary Industry	第三产业 Tertiary Industry	住宅 Residence	新增固定资产 Newly Increased Fixed Assets	本年施工房屋面积(万平方米)Floor Space of Buildings(10 000sq.m) 施工面积 Floor Space Under Construction	竣工面积 Floor Space Completed
巴音郭楞蒙古自治州	**Bayangol Mongol Autonomous Prefecture**	**125186**	**16576**	**55832**	**52397**	**381**	**108852**	**6.93**	**5.05**
库尔勒市	Korla City	80288	8566	23619	48065	38	65863	0.94	0.36
轮台县	Luntai [Bugur] County	16705		16568		137	12216	2.18	2.18
尉犁县	Yuli [Lopnur] County	4042	3176	780	86		4042	0.45	0.45
若羌县	Ruoqiang [Qarkilik] County	2166	587	1325	181	73	1186	0.96	0.56
且末县	Qiemo [Qarqan] County	230		230			150		
焉耆回族自治县	Yanqi Hui Autonomous County	10999	872	9128	999		18536	0.06	0.06
和静县	Hejing County	1047	787	250		10	2197	0.19	0.19
和硕县	Hoxud County	9476	2445	3842	3066	123	4429	2.09	1.19
博湖县	Bohu [Bagrax] County	233	143	90			233	0.06	0.06
阿克苏地区	**Aksu Administrative Offices**	**128152**	**7826**	**107819**	**12079**	**428**	**20925**	**6.45**	**4.45**
阿克苏市	Aksu City	24656	4899	9709	9620	428	11222	2.61	2.45
温宿县	Wensu [Onsu] County	2861	741	2120			1661	2.00	2.00
库车县	Kuqa County	76369		76369				1.58	
拜城县	Baicheng County	19621		19621			3397	0.25	
乌什县	Wushi [Uxturpan] County	431	431				431		
阿瓦提县	Awat County	4214	1755		2459		4214		
克孜勒苏柯尔克孜自治州	**Kizilsu Kirgiz Autonomous Prefecture**								
喀什地区	**Kashgar [Kaxgar] Administrative Offices**	**34833**	**2331**	**9601**	**22455**	**446**	**35384**	**5.06**	**2.56**
喀什市	Kashgar [Kaxgar] City	26540		9220	17320		27091	2.88	0.38
英吉沙县	Yengisar	381		381			381		
麦盖提县	Makit County	190			175	15	190	0.02	0.02
巴楚县	Bachu [Maralbexi] County	7722	2331		4960	431	7722	2.16	2.16
和田地区	**Hotan Administrative Offices**	**6528**	**63**	**4965**	**1500**		**4606**		
和田市	Hotan City	2781		2332	449		981		
和田县	Hotan County	1365		1365			1365		
墨玉县	Moyu [Karakax] County	150		150			150		
皮山县	Pishan [Guma] County	250		250			180		
洛浦县	Lop County	742		180	562		742		
策勒县	Qira County	789		300	489		789		
于田县	Yutian County	115	63	52			63		
民丰县	Mingfeng County	336		336			336		
跨地区投资	**Trans-regional Investment**	**88301**			**88301**		**51027**	**5.43**	**5.43**

5-28 更新改造投资效果主要指标

Main Indicators of Investment Result from Renewal and Reform

指　标	Item	1990	1995	2000	2004
建设周期(年)	Construction Cycle (year)	2.8	1.6	1.1	1.6
计划总投资(万元)	Total Planned Investment (10 000 yuan)	433376	988247	877088	2817892
本年完成投资(万元)	Investment Completed for the Current Year (10 000 yuan)	152712	626739	775381	1386532
#限额以上项目	Projects above Quota		143149	107155	282078
建设项目投产率(%)	Ratio of Operation for Construction Items (%)	74.7	81.4	81.0	71.1
#限额以上项目	Items above Quota		37.0	60.0	41.9
施工项目个数(个)	Construction Items (unit)	1990	2106	1273	1188
#限额以上项目	Item above Quota		27	20	31
竣工项目个数(个)	Completetd Items (unit)	1486	1714	1031	845
#限额以上项目	Items above Quota		10	12	13
本年新增固定资产(万元)	Additional Fixed Capital for the Current Year(10 000yuan)	144094	571695	737741	1074250
固定资产交付使用率(%)	Ratio of Application for Fixed Assets (%)	94.4	91.2	95.2	77.5
未完工程投资额(万元)	Sum of Investment for incompleted Works (10 000 yuan)	62011	153781	158548	409795
未完工程占用率(%)	Ratio of Coverage for incomplete Works (%)	40.6	24.5	20.5	29.6
施工面积(万平方米)	Construction Area (10 000 Sq. Meters)	190.20	250.11	165.40	117.88
#住 宅	Residence	70.80	122.46	84.20	6.97
竣工面积(万平方米)	Completed Floor Space (10 000 Sq. Meters)	122.95	185.45	120.90	75.15
#住 宅	Residence	45.84	95.41	62.80	4.8
房屋面积竣工率(%)	Rate of Completed House (%)	64.6	74.1	73.1	63.7
#住 宅	Residence	64.7	77.9	74.6	68.9

5-29 房地产开发企业基本情况

Basic Condition of Real Estate Development Enterprises

指 标	Item	2000	2003	2004
企业单位数(个)	**Number of Enterprises (unit)**	**209**	**492**	**709**
#亏损企业	Including: Lost Enterprises	101	225	395
从业人员数(人)	**Number of Persons Engaged in the Sector (person)**	**10311**	**14036**	**15434**
从业人员劳动报酬(万元)	**Work Pay for Employees (10 000 yuan)**	**10706**	**34741**	**23379**
主要财务指标（万元)	**Main Financial Indices (10 000 yuan)**			
实收资本合计	Total of Actual Capital	200762	593611	826114
#国家资本	State Capital	21344	19327	48411
年末资产负债情况	Situation of Year-end Liabilities			
资产总计	Total of Asset	1332444	3470803	3817473
固定资产累计折旧	Accumulated Depreciation of Fixed Assets	15027	45509	54373
#本年折旧	Depreciation for the Current Year	4450	11293	15041
负债总计	Total of Liabilities	1081934	2371870	2608758
所有者权益合计	Total of Owner's Right and Interest	250510	1098933	1208714
损益情况	Situation of Profit and Loss			
经营收入总计	Total of Business Income	342400	1075181	1029175
土地转让收入	Income of Land Transfer		1153	2650
商品房销售收入	Sales Income of Commercial Flat	319460	1054213	1006345
房屋出租收入	Income of Renting House	2558	11414	14176
其他收入	Other Income	20382	8401	6004
经营成本	Business Cost	272611	859503	816509
销售费用	Sales Expanses	9711	21287	24910
经营税金及附加	Business Tax and Addition	17697	53591	56396
其他业务利润	Other Business Profit	2167	2151	9462
管理费用及财务费用	Expanses for both Management and Finance	34988	71364	99672
投资收益及营业外收入	Investment earnings and Extra-business Income	2395	8076	7965
营业外支出	Extra-business Expenditure	2060	3175	4108
利润总额	Total Profit	9895	76488	45007

注：2004 年房地产数据为经济普查数据（以下同），因此企业个数包括了没有开发量的企业数，而往年未包括。
Note: Data from real estate in 2004 come from economic census (the same as below), so the figure of enterprises include enterprises yet to be developed while the previous years fail to contain those

5-30 房地产投资主要指标
Main Indicators of Real Estate Investment

指 标	Item	2000	2003	2004
本年购置土地面积(万平方米)	**Land Area Purchased for the Current Year (10 000 Sq. Meter)**	**496.02**	**664.27**	**699.53**
#完成开发土地面积	Land Area Completed for Development	248.21	382.4	398.24
房地产开发投资额(万元)	**Sum of Investment for Real-Estate Development (10 000 yuan)**	**574347**	**1024908**	**1125577**
#商品房建设投资	Investment in Commercial Flat	510144	856318	937618
土地开发投资	Investment in Land Development	34057	85631	78840
按中央和地方分	Classified by Central and Local			
中央企业	Central Enterprises	50536	28954	71320
地方企业	Local Enterprises	523811	995954	1054257
按经济类型分	Classified by Economic Ownership			
国有单位	State-owned Enterprises	126304	63834	42013
集体单位	Collective Enterprises	13618	16790	3762
私营及个体	Private-owned and Self-employed	131935	331769	398274
其他单位	Other Enterprises	302490	612515	681528
按投资构成分	Classified by Field of Investment			
建筑工程	Construction Works	419216	771530	837484
安装工程	Works of Installation	7568	41965	70023
设备工器具购置	Purchase of Equipment and Devices	21845	24216	19926
其他费用	Other Expenses	125718	187197	198144
#土地购置费	Expenses of Land Purchase	73811	132948	134936
按工程用途分	Classified by Purpose of Works			
住 宅	Residence	500381	547770	599276
办公楼	Office Building	13171	81497	77843
商业营业用房	Houses for Commercial and Business Purpose	42601	286896	390566
其 他	Others	18194	108745	57892
本年资金来源小计 (万元)	**Sub-total of Capital Sources for the Current Year (10 000 yuan)**	**701332**	**1117659**	**1215850**
国家预算内资金	Capital within State Budget			2290
国内贷款	Domestic Loan	113823	208348	125553
债 券	Bonds			
利用外资	Foreign Capital Applied	600		
自筹资金	Self-raised Funds	232768	448441	546282
其它资金	Other Funds	354141	460870	541725

5-31 商品房建筑、销售情况

Condition of Construction and Sales for Commodity Flat

单位：万平方米、万元 (10 000 sq.m; 10 000 yuan)

指 标	Item	2000	2003	2004
商品房屋建筑面积	**Floor Space of Commercial Houses**			
施工面积	**Floor Space of Construction**	**771.86**	**1382.14**	**1333.03**
住 宅	Residence	665.30	962.89	863.19
办公楼	Office Building	28.06	88.17	90.49
商业营业用房	Houses for Commerce and Business	74.20	298.51	357.53
其 他	Others	4.31	32.57	21.82
#新开工面积	Including: Area of Newly-constructed Area	453.63	782.78	771.48
住 宅	Residence	397.77	557.28	550.66
办公楼	Office Building	10.17	32.88	32.85
商业营业用房	Houses for Gommerce and Business	43.00	175.73	178.42
其 他	Others	2.69	16.89	9.55
竣工面积	**Completed Area**	**330.11**	**791.14**	**704.26**
住 宅	Residence	298.79	626.50	511.62
办公楼	Office Building	7.12	26.99	28.53
商业营业用房	Houses for Commerce and Business	23.07	126.42	156.54
其 他	Others	1.13	11.23	7.57
商品房屋销售建筑面积	**Floor Space of Sales and Construction for Commercial Houses**	**262.52**	**587.02**	**635.53**
住 宅	Residence	250.95	516.48	538.33
办公楼	Office Building	1.46	15.30	13.63
商业营业用房	Houses for Commerce and Business	9.82	53.44	81.27
其 他	Others	0.28	1.80	2.30
销售给个人	Including: Sold to Individuals	233.85	557.85	615.9
#住 宅	Residence	222.35	496.25	530.35
商品房空置面积	**Floor-space of Idle Commercial Houses**	**69.75**	**422.11**	**400.41**
住 宅	Residence	58.92	313.93	248.38
办公楼	Office Buildings	3.75	13.21	16.10
商业营业用房	Houses of Commerce and Business	6.35	84.81	125.31
其 他	Others	0.73	10.16	10.62
#商品房空置一年以上(含一年)	Including: Idle for over a year (including a year)	13.18	168.81	173.83
商品房竣工价值	**Value of Completed Commercial Flat**	**329195**	**910871**	**779224**
住 宅	Residence	288955	641200	487702
办公楼	Office Building	7804	55109	55919
商业营业用房	Houses for both Commerce and Business	30445	197770	226341
其 他	Others	1991	16792	9262
商品房屋销售额	**Sales Sum of Commercial Houses**	**373801**	**1066640**	**1106143**
住 宅	Residence	333166	768012	784408
办公楼	Office Building	4842	70174	35971
商业营业用房	Houses for Commerce and Business	35153	224579	281856
其 他	Others	640	3875	3908
#销售给个人	Including: Sold to Individuals	331269	996107	1055926
#住 宅	Residence	299621	732352	774286

5-32 各地、州、市房地产开发情况

Condition of Real-Estate Development by Prefecture, Autonomous Prefecture and City

(2004 年)

地　区	Region	企业个数（个）Number of Enterprise (unit)	本年完成投资（万元）Investment Made for the Current Year (10 000 yuan)	#商品房建设投资 Construction and Investment for Commercial Flat	#土地开发投资额 Investment Sum of Land Development
总　计	**Total**	**709**	**1125577**	**937618**	**78840**
乌鲁木齐市	Urumqi City	238	453420	391110	36715
克拉玛依市	Karamay City	22	88877	68407	8613
石河子市	Shihezi City	37	30599	24040	819
吐鲁番地区	Turpan Administrative Offices	8	4876	2890	382
哈密地区	Hami [Kumul] Administrative Offices	24	20783	13536	2843
昌吉回族自治州	Changji Hui Autonomous Prefecture	72	102802	74497	7013
伊犁哈萨克自治州	Ili Kazak Autonomous Prefecture	110	123144	109147	8672
伊犁州直属县(市)	Counties (Cities) Direct Under Ili Prefecture	77	99503	89161	6298
塔城地区	Tacheng [Tarbagatai] Administrative Offices	22	16675	13904	2350
阿勒泰地区	Altay Administrative Offices	11	6966	6082	24
博尔塔拉蒙古自治州	Bortala Mongol Autonomous Prefecture	38	20511	17523	
巴音郭楞蒙古自治州	Bayangol Mongol Autonomous Prefecture	62	138713	121288	7211
阿克苏地区	Aksu Administrative Offices	52	93835	80785	5127
克孜勒苏柯尔克孜自治州	Kizilsu Kirgiz Autonomous Prefecture	5	12421	12121	300
喀什地区	Kashgar [Kaxgar] Administrative Offices	31	28282	21514	695
和田地区	Hotan Administrative Offices	10	7314	760	450

地　区	Region	本年完成开发土地面积（平方米）Area of Land Developed for the Current Year (sq.m)	待开发的土地面积（平方米）Area of Land to be Developed (sq.m)	本年购置土地面积（平方米）Area of Land Purchased for the Current Year (sq.m)
总　计	**Total**	**398.24**	**404.62**	**699.52**
乌鲁木齐市	Urumqi City	101.49	199.01	245.66
克拉玛依市	Karamay City	65.35	43.82	42.27
石河子市	Shihezi City	10.66	23.68	25.09
吐鲁番地区	Turpan Administrative Offices	5.00	1.45	3.13
哈密地区	Hami [Kumul] Administrative Offices	6.53	6.53	15.88
昌吉回族自治州	Changji Hui Autonomous Prefecture	42.84	31.94	75.29
伊犁哈萨克自治州	Ili Kazak Autonomous Prefecture	39.21	39.16	100.94
伊犁州直属县(市)	Counties (Cities) Direct Under Ili Prefecture	32.58	38.61	84.45
塔城地区	Tacheng [Tarbagatai] Administrative Offices	5.49	0.55	13.42
阿勒泰地区	Altay Administrative Offices	1.14		3.08
博尔塔拉蒙古自治州	Bortala Mongol Autonomous Prefecture			11.96
巴音郭楞蒙古自治州	Bayangol Mongol Autonomous Prefecture	63.47	33.34	122.09
阿克苏地区	Aksu Administrative Offices	34.69	7.13	50.76
克孜勒苏柯尔克孜自治州	Kizilsu Kirgiz Autonomous Prefecture	12.00	18.00	
喀什地区	Kashgar [Kaxgar] Administrative Offices	16.88	0.56	5.79
和田地区	Hotan Administrative Offices	0.12		0.66

5-33 按工程用途分的房地产投资额及新增固定资产

Sum of Investment and New-Added Fixed Assets Classified by Purpose of Works

单位：万元 (2004 年) (10 000 yuan)

地 区	Region	本年完成投资 Investment Made for the Current Year	住宅 Residence	#别墅、高档公寓 Villa and High-grade Apartment	#经济适用房 Economic Houses
总 计	**Total**	**1125577**	**599276**	**29585**	**207447**
乌鲁木齐市	Urumqi City	453420	221759	18425	89495
克拉玛依市	Karamay City	88877	63007		49109
石河子市	Shihezi City	30599	17106	156	557
吐鲁番地区	Turpan Administrative Offices	4876	2832		800
哈密地区	Hami [Kumul] Administrative Offices	20783	12829		240
昌吉回族自治州	Changji Hui Autonomous Prefecture	102802	50115		1527
伊犁哈萨克自治州	Ili Kazak Autonomous Prefecture	123144	78486		14982
伊犁州直属县(市)	Counties (Cities) Direct Under Ili Prefecture	99503	63544		4765
塔城地区	Tacheng [Tarbagatai] Administrative Offices	16675	11121		6729
阿勒泰地区	Altay Administrative Offices	6966	3821		3488
博尔塔拉蒙古自治州	Bortala Mongol Autonomous Prefecture	20511	15601		3672
巴音郭楞蒙古自治州	Bayangol Mongol Autonomous Prefecture	138713	71623	8200	18137
阿克苏地区	Aksu Administrative Offices	93835	36376	2804	18118
克孜勒苏柯尔克孜自治州	Kizilsu Kirgiz Autonomous Prefecture	12421	10837		5700
喀什地区	Kashgar [Kaxgar] Administrative Offices	28282	11687		4490
和田地区	Hotan Administrative Offices	7314	7018		620

地 区	Region	办公楼 Office	商业营业用房 Houses for Commerce and Business	其 他 Others	本年新增固定资产 Added Fixed Asset for the Current Year
总 计	**Total**	**77843**	**390566**	**57892**	**860334**
乌鲁木齐市	Urumqi City	46878	158559	26224	335592
克拉玛依市	Karamay City	578	24183	1109	57600
石河子市	Shihezi City	1242	11981	270	25511
吐鲁番地区	Turpan Administrative Offices	120	1792	132	3356
哈密地区	Hami [Kumul] Administrative Offices	540	3653	3761	16704
昌吉回族自治州	Changji Hui Autonomous Prefecture	7453	37891	7343	75827
伊犁哈萨克自治州	Ili Kazak Autonomous Prefecture	3442	32598	8618	94036
伊犁州直属县(市)	Counties (Cities) Direct Under Ili Prefecture	3102	26507	6350	68374
塔城地区	Tacheng [Tarbagatai] Administrative Offices	80	3760	1714	15149
阿勒泰地区	Altay Administrative Offices	260	2331	554	10513
博尔塔拉蒙古自治州	Bortala Mongol Autonomous Prefecture		4597	313	25217
巴音郭楞蒙古自治州	Bayangol Mongol Autonomous Prefecture	9244	56776	1070	120875
阿克苏地区	Aksu Administrative Offices	7451	41058	8950	64499
克孜勒苏柯尔克孜自治州	Kizilsu Kirgiz Autonomous Prefecture		1584		12421
喀什地区	Kashgar [Kaxgar] Administrative Offices	837	15758		27939
和田地区	Hotan Administrative Offices	58	136	102	757

5-34 房地产业房屋施工面积、竣工面积

Investment in Capital Construction by Registration

单位：万平方米 (10 000 sq.m)

年份 地区 Year Region	施工面积 Area of Construction	#住宅 Flat	竣工面积 Area of Completion	#住宅 Flat	房屋销售面积 Completion Rate of Area for House Structure	#住宅 Flat	房屋空置面积 Floor space at idle	#住宅 Flat
1995	273.73	164.54	101.96	78.77	53.15	47.93		
1996	224.90	150.80	81.19	64.51	45.60	41.29	33.20	27.41
1997	222.20	144.50	93.56	73.32	55.43	52.48	36.33	25.58
1998	252.61	188.38	94.28	79.92	83.27	75.97	27.20	20.33
1999	343.37	295.61	159.99	143.92	127.48	120.44	63.01	49.00
2000	771.86	665.30	330.11	298.79	262.52	250.95	69.75	58.92
2001	1433.54	1207.89	633.25	559.91	419.87	381.67	200.46	169.78
2002	1246.89	946.11	727.21	616.12	506.66	455.68	353.23	285.87
2003	1382.14	962.89	791.14	626.50	587.02	516.48	422.11	313.93
2004	1333.03	863.19	704.25	511.62	635.53	538.33	400.41	248.38
乌鲁木齐市 Urumqi City	496.07	309.45	242.01	173.89	273.87	234.74	187.35	114.80
克拉玛依市 Karamay City	101.67	85.20	45.54	39.31	51.55	47.65	4.81	3.01
石河子市 Shihezi City	42.48	30.97	24.36	16.73	22.99	20.74	14.59	8.44
吐鲁番地区 Turpan Administrative Offices	7.82	5.30	4.65	2.63	3.32	2.15	1.16	0.38
哈密地区 Hami [Kumul] Administrative Offices	34.22	29.15	16.43	13.06	13.36	12.55	4.54	2.43
昌吉回族自治州 Changji Hui Autonomous Prefecture	134.90	91.41	65.95	43.83	54.98	45.06	38.02	26.18
伊犁哈萨克自治州 Ili Kazak Autonomous Prefecture	137.14	100.11	98.75	81.27	67.62	58.86	46.32	33.82
伊犁州直属县(市) Counties (Cities) Direct Under Ili Prefecture	100.44	69.68	69.86	57.76	46.67	39.76	36.91	28.14
塔城地区 Tacheng [Tarbagatai] Administrative Offices	22.25	18.02	16.64	13.06	11.88	10.79	5.63	2.77
阿勒泰地区 Altay Administrative Offices	14.45	12.40	12.25	10.45	9.07	8.31	3.78	2.91
博尔塔拉蒙古自治州 Bortala Mongol Autonomous Prefecture	31.34	20.39	20.06	12.34	14.90	11.45	4.65	3.04
巴音郭楞蒙古自治州 Bayangol Mongol Autonomous Prefecture	170.46	92.37	93.84	62.13	66.97	51.11	55.32	27.23
阿克苏地区 Aksu Administrative Offices	96.46	55.30	55.78	36.09	39.47	29.65	29.95	17.61
克孜勒苏柯尔克孜自治州 Kizilsu Kirgiz Autonomous Prefecture	15.69	14.44	11.59	10.44	3.44	3.24	8.15	7.20
喀什地区 Kashgar [Kaxgar] Administrative Offices	64.31	28.75	24.80	19.52	23.05	21.14	5.19	3.99
和田地区 Hotan Administrative Offices	0.47	0.37	0.47	0.37			0.36	0.26

5-35 按行业和地、州、市分的其他固定资产投资

Other Investment in Fixed Assets Classified by Sector and by Prefecture, Autonomous Prefecture and City

单位:万元、个 (2004 年) (10 000 yuan、unit)

指 标	Indicator	固定资产投资额 Sum of Investm-Ent for Fixed Asset	施工项目个数 Number of Construct-ion Items	#本年新开工 Operation for the Current Year	竣工项目个数 Number of Complete-td Items	本年新增固定资产 Added Fixed Asset for the Current Year
总 计	**Total**	**384625**	**457**	**372**	**317**	**297473**
农、林、牧、渔业	Farming,Forestry, Animal Husbandry and Fishrey	77081	141	134	126	74287
采矿业	Mining and Quarrying	7158	9	9	4	4908
制造业	Manufac-turing	91605	103	80	61	62658
电力、煤气及水的生产和供应业	Production and Supply of Electric Power, Gas and Water	12491	13	11	7	3587
建筑业	Construction	1239	2	2	0	716
交通运输仓储及邮政业	Transporta-tion, Storage, Postal and Telecommun ications Services	54913	33	21	21	37739
信息传输、计算机服务和软件业	Message Transmission, Computer and Software	2357	5	5	4	2007
批发和零售业	Wholesale & Retail Trade	51978	54	37	34	46256
住宿和餐饮业	Hotel and Catering	6741	16	13	12	5841
金融业	Banking	329	2	2	2	329
房地产业	Real Estate	15550	15	12	9	6108
租赁和商务服务业	Leasing and Commercial Service	300	1	1	1	300
科学研究、技术服务和地质勘查业	Scientific Research, Technical Service and Geological Survey	2155	3	2	2	538
水利、环境和公共设施管理业	Water Conservancy, Environment and Public Works Management	10512	28	17	15	6296
居民服务和其他服务业	Community Service and Other Service	906	1	1	1	906
教 育	Education	8795	4	3	1	9789
卫生、社会保障和社会福利业	Health, Social Security and Social Welfare	13238	7	6	4	12927
文化、体育和娱乐业	Culture, Sports and Recreation	4387	8	4	3	1467
公共管理和社会组织	Public Management and Social Organization	22890	12	12	10	20814
按地区分	**Classified by Prefecture**					
乌鲁木齐市	Urumqi City	98790	78	49	39	71830
克拉玛依市	Karamay City	1204	2	2	1	1204
石河子市	Shihezi City	2516	6	5	6	2516
吐鲁番地区	Turpan Administrative Offices	6296	5	5	4	4559
哈密地区	Hami [Kumul] Administrative Offices	4841	8	8	4	3878
昌吉回族自治州	Changji Hui Autonomous Prefecture	64104	77	72	65	52539
伊犁哈萨克自治州	Ili Kazak Autonomous Prefecture	42818	59	47	45	31677
伊犁州直属县(市)	Counties (Cities) Direct Under Ili Prefecture	24060	36	26	29	14792
塔城地区	Tacheng [Tarbagatai] Administrative Offices	13379	10	9	5	11848
阿勒泰地区	Altay Administrative Offices	5379	13	12	11	5037
博尔塔拉蒙古自治州	Bortala Mongol Autonomous Prefecture	19627	10	9	8	14244
巴音郭楞蒙古自治州	Bayangol Mongol Autonomous Prefecture	34481	51	31	28	31932
阿克苏地区	Aksu Administrative Offices	28976	46	45	38	26678
克孜勒苏柯尔克孜自治州	Kizilsu Kirgiz Autonomous Prefecture	5954	7	7	6	4354
喀什地区	Kashgar [Kaxgar] Administrative Offices	68397	91	75	57	46111
和田地区	Hotan Administrative Offices	6621	17	17	16	5951

5-36 主要新增生产能力

Newly Increased Production Capacity Through Investment in Fixed Assets

(2004 年)

项 目	Item	合 计 Total	基本建设 Investment in Capital Construction	更新改造 Investment in Innovation	其他投资 Others
原煤开采(万吨/年)	Coal Mining (10 000 tons/year)	495.75	288.00	207.75	
天然原油(万吨/年)	Petroleum Extractin (10 000 tons/year)	462.31	462.31		
天然气开采(亿立方米/年)	Natural Gas Extraction (100 million cubic meters/year)	70.32	70.32		
石油加工:	Oil Processing				
蒸馏设备(万吨/年)	Distilling Equipment (10 000 tons/year)	192.4	160	32.4	
焦化设备能力(万吨/年)	Coking Equipment Capacity (10 000 tons/year)	110		110	
加氢精制设备能力(处理万吨/年)	Oxygen-adding Refining Equipment Capacity (10 000 tons/ year)	95	65	30	
铁矿石原矿开采(万吨/年)	Iron-Ore Mining (10 000 tons/year)	1			1
铁矿选矿处理量(万吨/年)	Iron-ore Dressing (10 000 tons/year)	72.03	12.03	60	
铁矿石成品矿(万吨/年)	Iron-ore Products Mine (10 000 tons/year)	28.8	28.8	0	
生铁(万吨/年)	Pig-iron (10 000 tons/ year)	156.6	64.6	92	
炼钢(万吨/年)	Iron Making (10 000 tons/ year)	183	90	93	
转炉钢(万吨/年)	Revolving Furnance Steel (10 000 tons/year)	110	30	80	
铁合金(万吨/年)	Steel Alloy (10 000 tons/year)	7	5	2	
钢 材	Steel Material	122.25	13	97.25	12
热轧钢材(万吨/年)	Hot-rolled Material (10 000 tons/year)	42	10	20	12
冷加工钢材(万吨/年)	Cold-rolled steel (10 000 tons/year)	80.25	3	77.25	
挤压钢材	Extruded Material				
线材(万吨/年)	Wire-Rod (10 000 tons/Year)	20		20	
无缝钢管(万吨/年)	Seamless Iron Tube (10 000 tons/year)	0.75		0.75	
焊接钢管(万吨/年)	Welded Steel Pipe (10 000 tons/year)	1.5		1.5	
铜采矿(原矿)(万吨/年)	Copper Ore Mining (10 000 tons/year)	2	2		
铜选矿	Copper Ore Dressing				
铜含量(吨/年)	Crude Ore Dressing(ton/Year)	1500	1500		
铜冶炼(吨/年)	Iron Smeltering (ton/year)	18000		18000	
其中:电解铜(吨/年)	Including: Electro-analytical copper (tons/year)	18000		18000	
铅锌采矿(原矿)(万吨/年)	Lead and Zinc Extraction (10 000 tons/year)	0.2	0.2		
铅锌选矿:处理原矿(万吨/年)	Laed and Zinc Dressing: (Raw Ore Treatment (10 000 tons/year)	32.8	32.8		
铅含量(吨/年)	Lead Content (ton/year)	1200	1200		
锌含量(吨/年)	Zinc Content (ton/year)	2800	2800		
铅冶炼(吨/年)	Lead Smeltering (ton/year)	4000			4000
锌冶炼(吨/年)	Zinc Smeltering (ton/year)	2000			2000

5-36 续表 1 Continued

项　　目	Item	合　计 Total	基本建设 Investment in Capital Construction	更新改造 Investment in Innovation	其他投资 Others
镍选矿：处理原矿(万吨/年)	Nickle Dressing: Raw Ore Treatment (10 000 tons/year)	27	27		
镍含量(吨/年)	Nickle Content (ton/year)	19000	19000		
铝加工(吨/年)	Aluminium Processing (ton/year)	8000		8000	
金采矿(原矿)(万吨/年)	Gold Prospecting (Raw Ore) (10 000 tons/year)	2.5	2.5		
金选矿：处理原矿(吨/年)	Gold ore Dressing: Crude Ore Dressing (ton/year)	30003.5	3.5		30000
金含量(公斤/年)	Gold Content (Kilo/year)	85.75	37.75		48
原料云母(吨/年)	Material mica (ton/year)	60	60		
发电机组装机容量(万千瓦)	Capacity of Generating Setes (10 000 kw/year)	30.87	22.84	8.03	
水力发电	Hydropower	1.79	1.64	0.15	
火力发电	Thermal Power	24.34	18.74	5.6	
其他发电	Other	4.74	2.46	2.28	
输电线路长度(11 万伏及以上)(公里)	Transmission Line (110 000V)(kilometer)	793.8	733.8	60	
变电设备能力(11 万伏及以上)(万仟伏安)	Power Equipment (110 000V)(10 000 kilovotampere)	135.51	116.71	18.8	
水泥(万吨/年)	Cement (10 000 tons/year)	178	56	122	
平板玻璃(万重量箱/年)	Plate Glass (10 000 weight case/year)	292.74	41.74	251	
木材(万立方米/年)	Timber (10 000 cubic meters/year)	1			1
锯　材(万立方米/年)	Sawn Material (10 000 cubic meter/year)	16	6		10
胶合板(万立方米/年)	Plywood (10 000 cu.m/year)	0.7	0.7		
纤维板(万立方米/年)	Fiber Board (10 000 cubic meter/year)	10.6	4.6	6	
刨花板(万立方米/年)	Plane Board (10 000 cubic meter/year)	0.1	0.1		
烧碱(吨/年)	Caustic Soda (ton/year)	129000		129000	
纯碱(吨/年)	Caustic Soda (tons/year)	20000		20000	
电石(吨/年)	Calcium carbide (tons/ year)	200000		200000	
农用氮、磷、钾化学肥料(吨/年)	Farm-use Nitrogen, Phosphorus and Potassium Fertilizer (ton/year)	60000	50000	10000	
磷肥(吨/年)	Phosphorous fertilizer (ton/year)	20000	20000		
钾肥(吨/年)	Potash fertilizer	40000	30000	10000	
精甲醇(吨/年)	Refined methanol (ton/year)	90000	90000		
油　漆(吨/年)	Paint (ton/year)	13000	3000		10000
塑料树脂及共聚物(吨/年)	Plastic Resin and Copolyment (ton/year)	95250	10000	85250	
化学原料药(吨/年)	Medcine with Chemical Ingredients (ton/year)	239.5	77.5	162	
中成药(吨/年)	Chinese Patent Medicine (ton/year)	2864	754	2110	

5-36 续表 2 Continued

项　目	Item	合　计 Total	基本建设 Investment in Capital Construction	更新改造 Investment in Innovation	其他投资 Others
大中型变压器(万千伏安)	Large & Medium Type Transformer (10 000 kev)	150		150	
化学纤维(吨 / 年)	Chemical Fiber (ton/year)	6500		6500	
棉纺锭(锭)	Cotton Spindle (Spindle)	414500	215000	175000	24500
食用植物油:	Edible Vegetable Oil				
日处理原料：吨	Raw Materials Processing (ton/day)	3796	1646	1150	1000
日精练油：吨	Oil Refining (ton/day)	962.3	386.7	423.6	152
乳制品(吨 / 年)	Dairy Products (ton/ year)	42025	9000	33025	
奶　粉(吨 / 年)	Milk Powder (ton/year)	8400	8000	400	
其他乳制品(吨 / 年)	Other Dairy Products (ton/year)	33625	1000	32625	
酒(万吨/年)	Liquors (10 000 tons/year)	9.14		9.1	0.04
啤酒(万吨/年)	Beer (10 000 tons/year)	9		9	0
白酒(万吨/年)	Liquor (10 000 tons/year)	0.12		0.1	0.02
其他酒(万吨/年)	Other (10 000 tons/year)	0.02			0.02
机制纸浆(万吨 / 年)	Machine-made pulp (10 000 tons/year)	1.6	1.6		
机制纸(万吨 / 年)	Machine-made Paper (10 000 tons/ year)	5.05	4.55	0.3	0.2
机制纸板(万吨/年)	Machine-made Paperboard (10 000 tons/year)	1		1	
移动通信基站设备(个/年)	Mobile Communicating Base Station Equipment (unit/year)	619	619		
程控交换机(万线/年)	Program-Controlled Telephone Exchange (10 000 lines/year)	572.3	558.9	13.4	
新建公路(公里)	Length of New Highways (km)	1422.86	1264.86		158
二级公路(公里)	Second-Class Highway (kilometers)	110	110		
改建公路(公里)	Length of Reconstructed Highways (km)	5856.59	5214.09	26.5	616
#一级公路	First Class Highway	311.89	311.89		
二级公路	Second Class highway	1623.76	1623.76		
新建独立公路桥梁(延长米)	New-Built Separate Highway and Bridge (Extended Length)	683	683		
(座)	(unit)	5	5		
新(扩)建客、货运站(个)	Number of newly-Built or Expanded Passenger and Freight Stations	6	5	1	
(平方米)	(sq.m)	36765	35396	1369	
长途电缆线路长度(公里)	Long-Distance Cable (km)	8388.4	8220.4	168	
新建微波电路(路)	New-built Micro-wave electric circuit	240	240		
耕地面积(万公顷)	Tilled land Area (10 000 hectares)	0.49	0.46		0.03
造林面积(万公顷)	Afforested Area (10 000 hectares)	14.41	13.18	0.03	1.2
水库容量(亿立方米)	Reservoir Capacity (100 million cu.m)	0.89	0.64		0.25

5-36 续表 3 Continued

项　目	Item	合　计 Total	基本建设 Investment in Capital Construction	更新改造 Investment in Innovation	其他投资 Others
有效灌溉面积(万公顷)	Effective Irrigated Area (10 000 hectares)	21.26	19.76	0.4	1.1
除涝面积(万亩)	Anti-flood area (10 000 mu)	12.7			12.7
商业石油库(万立方米)	Commercial Oil Tank (10 000 Cubic Meters)	0.09	0.09		
商业冷藏库(万吨)	Commercial Freezers (10 000 tons)	0.75	0.75		
水产冷藏库(万吨)	Fishery Cold-Storage Warehouse (10 000 tons)	1	1		
粮食仓库(万公斤)	Grain Storehouses (10 000 kg)	3830	2820	1010	
(平方米)	(sq.m)	15049	10788	4261	
高等院校:学生席位(个)	Number of Student Seat of University and College (unit)	21081	21081		
建筑面积(平方米)	Floor Space (sq.m)	114806	114806		
中等学校:学生席位(个)	Number of Student Seat of Regular Secondary School (unit)	94627	91027		3600
建筑面积(平方米)	(sq.m)Flloor Space	466713	454906		11807
小 学 校:学生席位(个)	Number of Student Seat of Primary School (unit)	70710	66710	3700	300
建筑面积(平方米)	(sq.m)Floor Space	245123	226590	13133	5400
其他院校:学生席位(个)	Number of Student Seat of Other School (unit)	19792	19792		
建筑面积(平方米)	(sq.m) Floor Space	81853	81853		
公共图书馆:藏书量(万册)	Book Collection (10 000 copies)	68	68		
阅览室座席(个)	Seats in Reading Room(unit)	490	490		
建筑面积(平方米)	Floor Space (sq.m)	8646	8646		
医院病床(张)	Sick Beds (unit)	4353	4303		50
宾馆、旅馆、招待所客房数(间)	Number of Rooms in Guest Houses, Hotels and Hostels	1500	1342	64	94
(平方米)	(sq.m)	146797	136369	1958	8470
城市自来水供水能力(万吨/日)	Capacity of City Tap Water Supply (10 000 tons/day)	27.62	20.52	1.1	6
城市自来水管道长度(公里)	Length of City Tap Water Pipe (km)	531.85	372.45	64.4	95
城市天然气储气能力(万立方米/日)	Urban Natural Gas Storing Capacity (10 000 cubic meters/day)	0.08	0.08		
城市液化石油气储气能力(吨)	Capacity of City Liquefied Petroleum Gas Storage(ton)	350	350		
城市供热能力:蒸汽(吨/小时)	City Heat-Supply Capacitys (ton/hour)	1662.36	1199.46	402.9	60
热水(兆瓦/小时)	Hot Water (MW/hour)	1358.4	1005.1	309.8	43.5
城市公共交通车辆购置(辆)	Purchase of City Communiting Vehicles (unit)	227		170	57
城市道路扩建长度(公里)	Length of City Road Extended (km)	387.24	387.24		
城市道路扩建面积(万平方米)	Area of City Road Extended (10 000 sq.m)	427.04	427.04		
城市排水管道铺设长度(公里)	Length of Sewer Pipelines (km)	274.9	200.7	74.2	
城市污水处理能力(万吨/日)	Disposal Capacity of Sewer (10 000 tons/day)	18.04	12.79	5.25	
城市永久性桥梁(座)	City Permanent Bridge (unit)	1	1		
城市防洪堤长度(公里)	Length of City Embarkment (km)	18	18		

5-37 各地、州、市城镇和工矿区私人建房

Building Construction by Individuals in Cities and Towns as well as in Industrial Mining Areas by Prefecture, Autonomous Prefecture and City

(2004 年)

地 区	Region	建房户数（户） Number of Households with Buildings Construction (household)	竣工房屋建筑面积（平方米） Floor Space of Residential Buildings (sq.m)	#住 宅 Residence	竣工房屋价 值（万元） Value of Buildings Completed (10 000 yuan)	#住 宅 Residence
总 计	**Total**	**14543**	**2230045**	**1792770**	**118872**	**91985**
乌鲁木齐市	Urumqi City	1003	192430	191570	12637	11837
克拉玛依市	Karamay City					
石河子市	Shihezi City					
吐鲁番地区	Turpan Administrative Offices	297	58358	48282	1838	1562
哈密地区	Hami [Kumul] Administrative Offices	233	41732	41732	1644	1644
昌吉回族自治州	Changji Hui Autonomous Prefecture	880	238166	154499	13960	8176
伊犁哈萨克自治州	Ili Kazak Autonomous Prefecture	4618	689860	475004	36791	24754
伊犁州直属县(市)	Counties (Cities) Direct Under Ili Prefecture	2619	404082	254495	19969	11472
塔城地区	Tacheng [Tarbagatai] Administrative Offices	1572	231074	174113	13996	10907
阿勒泰地区	Altay Administrative Offices	427	54704	46396	2826	2375
博尔塔拉蒙古自治州	Bortala Mongol Autonomous Prefecture	228	43220	32475	2523	1776
巴音郭楞蒙古自治州	Bayangol Mongol Autonomous Prefecture	401	72401	47678	3189	1578
阿克苏地区	Aksu Administrative Offices	2260	246237	243237	10314	10239
克孜勒苏柯尔克孜自治州	Kizilsu Kirgiz Autonomous Prefecture	230	27428	20398	1494	1052
喀什地区	Kashgar [Kaxgar] Administrative Offices	2363	302449	259135	15853	12581
和田地区	Hotan Administrative Offices	2018	311149	277045	18144	16636
新疆生产建设兵团	Xinjiang Production & Construction Group	12	6615	1715	485	150
在总计中:	**Grand total**					
#农业户建房	Peasant Households	5694	873364	764294	47927	42002
市	Cities	5821	1006058	880070	61810	52698
#农业户建房	Peasant Households	2478	449411	422618	31370	28520
县 城	County Seat	4740	666389	497141	34486	24134
#农业户建房	Peasant Households	679	74623	55744	3114	2455
镇	Towns	3845	522507	387582	21169	14055
#农业户建房	Farmer Households	2482	332960	271872	12923	10595
工矿区	Industry and Mining Areas	137	35091	27977	1407	1098
#农业户建房	Farmer Households	55	16370	14060	520	432

5-38　城镇及工矿区私人建房

Buildings Construction by Individuals in Cities and Towns as well as in Industrial Mining Areas

年　份 Year	建房户数 (户) Number of Households with Buildings Construction (household)	竣工房屋建筑面积 (万平方米) Floor Space of Residential Buildings (10 000 sq.m)	#住　宅 Residence	竣工房屋价值 (万元) Value of Buildings Completed (10 000 yuan)	#住　宅 Residence
1985	12577	93.17	82.28	4926	4477
1990	8875	88.09	76.75	10698	8890
1991	6412	68.74	53.36	7637	6923
1992	8370	85.03	73.30	14709	11925
1993	17762	190.32	179.31	29210	25414
1994	10466	121.25	103.77	34171	27885
1995	13496	160.51	123.06	52330	37374
1996	13311	163.27	138.90	59513	48050
1997	13481	143.24	123.67	56774	47141
1998	13135	151.45	129.16	60390	50028
1999	12479	166.49	130.15	67566	49840
2000	14876	208.37	175.10	88500	69927
2001	18305	271.55	224.23	127503	91892
2002	14186	199.62	146.97	98992	72309
2003	24374	254.91	200.53	117648	85691
2004	14543	223.00	179.28	118872	91985

5-39　农村私人固定资产投资和建房

Individual Investment in Fixed Assets and Building Construction in Rural Areas

年　份 Year	投资总额 (万元) Total Investment (10 000 yuan)	#住　宅 Residential Buildings	竣工房屋建筑面积 (万平方米) Floor Space of Buildings Completed (10 000 sq.m)	#住　宅 Residential Buildings
1985	24795	11410	488.17	426.24
1990	75649	26071	642.80	585.80
1991	92224	36103	676.36	610.37
1992	95668	35492	575.41	483.69
1993	106804	32665	718.57	574.57
1994	170266	48237	661.56	545.63
1995	205900	60095	554.52	493.87
1996	270594	76240	947.08	754.16
1997	349958	157087	736.79	701.28
1998	351477	132234	801.47	720.42
1999	348127	96584	1198.00	682.00
2000	363489	111596	611.22	522.86
2001	380177	158852	974.26	844.44
2002	403308	78612	671.08	567.32
2003	480830	122303	917.39	773.81
2004	543839	199392	770.10	710.66

5-40 农村非农户固定资产投资情况

Investment in Fixed Assets of Non-Peasant Households in Rural Areas

单位：万元、万平方米　　(2004 年) (抽样调查 Sampled Survey)　　(10 000 yuan, 10 000 sq.m)

指　　标	Item	合　计 Total 数　量 Amount	构　成(%) Composition(%)
新增固定资产原值	**Investment in Fixed Assets**	**462287**	
固定资产投资完成额	**Completed Investment in Fixed Assets**	**463359**	**100**
按投资来源分	By Source of Fund		
国内资金	State Appropriation	237251	51.20
国家贷款	Domestic Loans	35537	7.67
利用外资	Application of Foreign Capital	12402	2.68
自筹资金	Self-raising Capital	123816	26.72
其他资金	Other Funds	54352	11.73
按投资构成分	By Use of Fund		
建筑工程	Construction Works	365867	78.96
水　利	Water Conservancy	164037	35.40
房　屋	Building	74838	16.15
#住　宅	Residential Building	15227	3.29
安装工程	Installation Works	5443	1.17
设备工器具购置	Purchase of Equipment and Instruments	57105	12.32
#生产设备	Production Equipment	38785	8.37
其　他	Others	34944	7.54
按投资方向分	By Sector of Investment		
农、林、牧、渔业	Farming, Forestry, AnimalHusbandryand Fishery	138425	29.87
采矿业	Fishery	2056	0.44
制造业	Manufacturing	9321	2.01
电力煤气及水的生产及供应业	Production and Supply of Power and Gas	3281	0.71
建筑业	Construction	7043	1.52
交通运输仓储和邮政业	Transportation, Logistics and Post Industries	68086	14.69
信息传输、计算机服务和软件业	Information Transmission, Computer Servcie and Software Industries	3388	0.73
批发和零售业	Retail and Wholesale Sectors	2975	0.64
住宿和餐饮业	Hotel and Catering	867	0.19
金融业	Financial Service	1673	0.36
房地产业	Real Estate	10142	2.19
租赁和商务服务业	Leasing and Business Service Industries	705	0.15
科学研究、技术服务和地质勘查业	Scientific Research, Technology Service and Geological Prospecting	959	0.21
水利、环境和公共设施管理业	Water Conservancy, Environment and Public Facility Management	156991	33.88
居民服务和其他服务业	Community Service and Other Service	5739	1.24
教　育	Education	13458	2.90
卫生、社会保障和社会福利业	Health, Social Security and Welfare	6218	1.34
文化、体育和娱乐业	Culture, Sports and Entertainment	672	0.14
公共管理和社会组织	Public Administration and Social Organizations	31360	6.77
按具体投资项目分	By Project of Investment		
房　屋	Building	74838	16.15
#住　宅	Residential Building	15227	3.29
道　路	Roads	116779	25.20
桥　梁	Bridges	5674	1.22
设　备	Equipment	57105	12.32
水　利	Water Conservancy	164037	35.40
其　他	Others	44925	9.70
本年施工房屋面积	**Floor Space of Buildings Under Construction**	**241**	
#住　宅	Residence	23	
当年新开工	Newly-opened Ones this Year	76	
本年竣工房屋面积	**Floor Space of Completed Building**	**969**	
#住　宅	Residential Building	22	
本年竣工房屋投资完成额	**Investment of Buildings Completed**	**61780**	
#住　宅	Residential Building	14404	
调查乡、镇、村个数(个)	**Number of Townships, Town and Village Surveyed (unit)**	**190**	
调查乡、镇、村人口(万人)	**Population in Townships, Town and Rural Areas (10 000 person)**	**145**	

5-40 续表 Continued

单位：万元、万平方米　　(10 000 yuan, 10 000 sq.m)

指　　标	Item	乡　镇 Township and Town Governments		村 Village	
		数　量 Amount	构成(%) Composition (%)	数　量 Amount	构成(%) Composition (%)
新增固定资产原值	**Investment in Fixed Assets**	**343069**		**119219**	
固定资产投资完成额	**Completed Investment in Fixed Assets**	**344140**	**100**	**119219**	**100**
按投资来源分	By Source of Fund				
国内资金	State Appropriation	208345	60.54	28906	24.25
国家贷款	Domestic Loans	35372	10.28	165	0.14
利用外资	Application of Foreign Capital	520	0.15	11882	9.97
自筹资金	Self-raising Capital	96839	28.14	26977	22.63
其他资金	Other Funds	3065	0.89	51288	43.02
按投资构成分	By Use of Fund				
建筑工程	Construction Works	259871	75.51	105997	88.91
水　利	Water Conservancy	159048	46.22	4989	4.18
房　屋	Building	50767	14.75	24072	20.19
#住　宅	Residential Building	13687	3.98	1540	1.29
安装工程	Installation Works	4768	1.39	675	0.57
设备工器具购置	Purchase of Equipment and Instruments	53372	15.51	3732	3.13
#生产设备	Production Equipment	37055	10.77	1729	1.45
其　他	Others	26129	7.59	8815	7.39
按投资方向分	By Sector of Investment				
农、林、牧、渔业	Farming, Forestry, AnimalHusbandryand Fishery	89240	25.93	49185	41.26
采矿业	Fishery	1472	0.43	584	0.49
制造业	Manufacturing	9259	2.69	62	0.05
电力煤气及水的生产及供应业	Production and Supply of Power and Gas	3065	0.89	216	0.18
建筑业	Construction	4748	1.38	2295	1.92
交通运输仓储和邮政业	Transportation, Logistics and Post Industries	16122	4.68	51964	43.59
信息传输、计算机服务和软件业	Information Transmission, Computer Servcie and Software Industries	3388	0.98		
批发和零售业	Retail and Wholesale Sectors	2772	0.81	203	0.17
住宿和餐饮业	Hotel and Catering	867	0.25		
金融业	Financial Service	1673	0.49		
房地产业	Real Estate	10142	2.95		
租赁和商务服务业	Leasing and Business Service Industries	705	0.20		
科学研究、技术服务和地质勘查业	Scientific Research, Technology Service and Geological Prospecting	959	0.28		
水利、环境和公共设施管理业	Water Conservancy, Environment and Public Facility Management	155222	45.10	1769	1.48
居民服务和其他服务业	Community Service and Other Service	5734	1.67	514	0.43
教　育	Education	12944	3.76	514	0.43
卫生、社会保障和社会福利业	Health, Social Security and Welfare	4912	1.43	1306	1.10
文化、体育和娱乐业	Culture, Sports and Entertainment	600	0.17	72	0.06
公共管理和社会组织	Public Administration and Social Organizations	20318	5.90	11042	9.26
按具体投资项目分	By Project of Investment				
房　屋	Building	50767	14.75	24072	20.19
#住　宅	Residential Building	13687	3.98	1540	1.29
道　路	Roads	47342	13.76	69437	58.24
桥　梁	Bridges	80	0.02	5594	4.69
设　备	Equipment	53372	15.51	3732	3.13
水　利	Water Conservancy	159048	46.22	4989	4.18
其　他	Others	33531	9.74	11395	9.56
本年施工房屋面积	**Floor Space of Buildings Under Construction**	**212**		**29**	
#住　宅	Residence	212		2	
当年新开工	Newly-opened Ones this Year	61		16	
本年竣工房屋面积	**Floor Space of Completed Building**	**949**		**20**	
#住　宅	Residential Building	21		2	
本年竣工房屋投资完成额	**Investment of Buildings Completed**	**51034**		**10746**	
#住　宅	Residential Building	13680		724	
调查乡、镇、村个数(个)	**Number of Townships, Town and Village Surveyed (unit)**	**80**		**110**	
调查乡、镇、村人口(万人)	**Population in Townships, Town and Rural Areas (10 000 person)**	**131**		**14**	

5-41 农户固定资产投资情况

Investment in Fixed Assets of Peasant Households in Rural Areas

单位:万元 (2004 年) (抽样调查 Sampled Survey) (10 000 yuan)

指 标	Item	2003	2004
新增固定资产原值	**Investment in Added Fixed Assets**	**480829.96**	**549103.80**
固定资产投资完成额	**Complete Investment in Fixed Assets**	**480829.96**	**543839.50**
按投资来源分	By Source of Fund		
国内贷款	Domestic Loans	41486.38	34614.17
自筹资金	Self-raising Capital	410506.73	503166.30
其他资金	Others	28836.85	6059.08
按投资构成分	By Use of Fund		
建筑工程	Construction	138110.28	210026.60
#水 利	Water Conservancy	1074.28	1112.45
房 屋	Building	136000.22	208914.20
#住 宅	Residence	122303.18	199392.30
安装工程	Installation	3003.41	
设备工、器具购置	Purchase of Equipment And Instruments	214274.95	180900.10
#生产设备	Production of Equipment	135817.11	109392.40
其 它	Others	125441.32	152912.80
按投资方向分	By Sector of Funds		
农、林、牧、渔业	Farming, Forestry, AnimalHusbandryand Fishery	334653.14	374496.70
采矿业	Fishery		
制造业	Manufacturing	3096.89	5180.63
电力煤气及水的生产及供应业	Production and Supply of Power and Gas	182.82	
建筑业	Construction	58084.42	36472.24
交通运输仓储和邮政业	Transportation, Logistics and Post Industries	24567.03	18296.59
信息传输、计算机服务和软件业	Information Transmission, Computer Servcie and Software Industries		506.90
批发和零售业	Retail and Wholesale Sectors		1476.60
住宿和餐饮业	Hotel and Catering	20685.38	6059.08
金融业	Financial Service		
房地产业	Real Estate		2605.40
租赁和商务服务业	Leasing and Business Service Industries		48472.61
科学研究、技术服务和地质勘查业	Scientific Research, Technology Service and Geological Prospecting		
水利、环境和公共设施管理业	Water Conservancy, Environment and Public Facility Management	925.43	1090.63
居民服务和其他服务业	Community Service and Other Service	29239.36	39179.32
教 育	Education		
卫生、社会保障和社会福利业	Health, Social Security and Welfare	1982.98	
文化、体育和娱乐业	Culture, Sports and Entertainment	4537.45	4913.18
公共管理和社会组织	Public Administration and Social Organizations	2875.06	5089.62
按具体投资项目分	By Project of Investment		
房 屋	Building	136000.22	208914.20
#住 宅	Residence	114929.82	199392.30
道 路	Roads		
桥 梁	Bridges	3003.41	
设 备	Equipment	214274.95	180900.10
水 利	Water Conservancy	1074.28	1112.45
其 他	Others	126477.10	152912.80
调查户总人口(人)	**Total Number of Households (person)**	**7922**	**7922**

主要统计指标解释

全社会固定资产投资 以货币形式表现的在一定时期内全社会建造和购置固定资产的工作量以及与此有关的费用的总称。该指标是反映固定资产投资规模、结构和发展速度的综合性指标，又是观察工程进度和考核投资效果的重要依据。全社会固定资产投资按登记注册类型可分为国有、集体、个体、联营、股份制、外商、港澳台商、其他等。按照管理渠道，可分为基本建设、更新改造、房地产开发投资和其他固定资产投资四个部分。

基本建设投资 基本建设指企业、事业、行政单位以扩大生产能力(或新增工程效益)为主要目的的新建、扩建工程及有关工作。其综合范围为总投资50 万元以上(含50 万元，下同)的基本建设项目。具体包括:(1)列入中央和各级地方本年基本建设计划的建设项目，以及虽未列入本年基本建设计划，但使用以前年度基建计划内结转投资(包括利用基建库存设备材料)在本年继续施工的建设项目;(2)本年基本建设计划内投资与更新改造计划内投资结合安排的新建项目和新增生产能力(或工程效益)达到大中型项目标准的扩建项目，以及为改变生产力布局而进行的全厂性迁建项目;(3)国有经济中既未列入基建计划，也未列入更新改造计划的总投资在50 万元以上的新建、扩建、恢复项目和为改变生产力布局而进行的全厂性迁建项目，以及行政、事业单位增建业务用房和行政单位增建生活福利设施的项目。

更新改造投资 更新改造一般是指企业、事业单位对原有设施进行技术改造(包括固定资产更新)以及相应配套的辅助性生产、生活福利设施等工程和有关的工作。其综合范围为总投资50 万元以上的更新改造单位(或项目)。具体包括:(1)列入中央和各级地方本年更新改造计划的投资单位(或项目)以及虽未列入本年更新改造计划，但使用上年更新改造计划内结转的投资在本年继续施工的单位(或项目);(2)本年更新改造计划内投资与基本建设计划内投资结合安排的对企、事业单位原有设施进行技术改造或更新的项目和增建主要生产车间、分厂等其新增生产能力(或工程效益)未达到大中型项目标准的项目，以及由于城市环境保护和安全生产的需要而进行的迁建工程;(3)国有经济中既未列入基建计划也未列入更新改造计划，总投资在50 万元以上的属于改建或更新改造性质的项目，以及由于城市环境保护和安全生产的需要而进行的迁建工程。

房地产开发投资 指各种登记注册类型的房地产开发公司、商品房建设公司及其他房地产开发法人单位和附属于其他法人单位实际从事房地产开发或经营活动的单位统一开发的包括统代建、拆迁还建的住宅、厂房、仓库、饭店、宾馆、度假村、写字楼、办公楼等房屋建筑物和配套的服务设施，土地开发工程(如道路、给水、排水、供电、供热、通讯、平整场地等基础设施工程)的投资;不包括单纯的土地交易活动。

其他固定资产投资 指全社会固定资产投资中未列入基本建设、更新改造和房地产开发投资的总投资在50 万元以上的城镇范围内建造和购置固定资产的活动，以及城镇私人建房和农村企业、事业、行政单位和农村个人固定资产投资活动。具体包括:(1)国有单位未纳入基本建设计划和更新改造计划管理,计划总投资(或实际需要总投资)在50 万元以上的以下工程:①用油田维护费和石油开发基金进行的油田维护和开发工程;②煤炭、铁矿、森工等采掘采伐业用维简费进行的开拓延伸工程;③交通部门用公路养路费对原有公路、桥梁进行改建的工程;④商业部门用简易建筑费建造的仓库工程。(2)城镇集体固定资产投资:指所有隶属直辖市、省辖市、县级市和县城所在地城关镇区域范围内的集体经济单位(乡镇企业局管理的除外)建造和购置固定资产其计划总投资(或实际需要总投资)在50 万元及50 万元以上,未列入基本建设和更新改造计划的单位(项目)投资。(3)除上述以外的其他各种登记注册类型的企、事业单位(包括城镇私营企、事业单位和个体户)建造和购置固定资产总投资在50 万元及50 万元以上、未列入基本建设计划和更新改造计划的单位(项目)。其中个体经营户只统计50 万元以上非建房投资。(4)城镇和工矿区私人建房投资:包括市、县城、城关镇、工矿区所辖范围内的全部私人建房，不论其房主是否系本地的常住户口均应包括。(5)农村投资:包括农村区域范围内进行固定资产投资活动的企业、事业、行政单位及农村个人投资。

固定资产投资的资金来源 根据固定资产投资的资金来源不同，分为国家预算内资金、国内贷款、利用外资、自筹资金和其他资金来源。(1)国家预算内资金:分为财政拨款和财政安排的贷款两部分。包括中央财政的基本建设基金(分经营性基金和非经营性基金两部分)、专项支出(如煤代油专项等)、收回再贷、贴息资金，财政安排的挖潜改造和新产品试制支出、城建支出、商业部门简易建筑支出、不发达地区发展基金等资金中用于固定资产投资的资金;地方财政中由国家统筹安排的资金等。(2)国内贷款:指报告期固定资产投资单位向银行及非银行金融机构借入的用于固定资产投资的各种国内借款，包括银行利用自有资金及吸收的存款发放的贷款、上级主管部门拨入的国内贷款、国家专项贷款(包括煤代油贷款、劳改煤矿专项贷款等)、地方财政专项资金安排的贷款、国内储备贷款、周转贷款等。(3)利用外资:指报告期收到的用于固定资产建造和购置的国外资金(包括设备、材料、技术在内)。包括对外借款(外国政府、国际金融组织贷款、出口信贷、外国银行商业贷款、对外发行债券和股票)、外商直接投资及外商其他投资。不包括我国自有外汇资金(国家外汇、地方外汇、留成外汇、调剂外汇和中国银行自有资金发行的外汇贷款等)。计算利用外资时，需要折算成人民币，折算中所使用的外汇汇率按现汇计算，即按使用外汇时的汇率计算。(4)自筹资金:指固定资产投资单位报告期收到的，由各地区、各部门及企、事业单位筹集用于固定资产投资的预算外资金，包括中央各部门、各级地方和企、事业单位的自筹资金。(5)其他资金来源:指在报告期收到的除以上各种资金之外其他用于固定资产投资的资金，包括企业或金融机构通过发行各种债券筹集到的资金、群众集资、个人资金、无偿捐赠的资金及其他单位拨入的资金等。

固定资产投资按国民经济行业分 建设项目归哪个行业，按其建成投产后的主要产品或主要用途及社会经济活动性质来确定。基本建设按建设项目划分国民经济行业，更新改造、其他固定资产投资根据整个企业、事业单位所属的行业来划分。一般情况下，一个建设项目或一个企业、事业单位只能属于一种国民经济行业。为了更准确地反映国民经济各行业之间的比例关系，联合企业(总厂)所属分厂属于不同行业的，原则上按分厂划分行业。

固定资产投资按建设性质分 建设项目的性质一般分为新建、扩建、改建、迁建、恢复。房地产开发单位、农村投资、城镇工矿区私人建房投资不划分建设性质。基本建设按建设项目划分建设性质，更新改造、国有经济中其他固定资产投资及城镇集体投资等按整个企业、事业单位的建设情况确定建设性质。(1)新建:一般指从无到有“平地起家”开始建设的企业、事业和行政单位或独立的工程。现有企业、事业、行政单位一般不属于新建。但如有的单位原有基础很小，经过建设后新增的固定资产价值超过该企、事业、行政单位原有固定资产价值(原值)三倍以上的也应作为新建。(2)扩建:指在厂内或其他地点，为扩大原有产品的生产能力(或效益)或增加新的产品生产能力，而增建主要的生产车间(或主要工程)、分厂、独立的生产线。行政、事业单位在原单位增建业务用房(如学校增建教学用房、医院增建门诊部、病房等)也作为扩建。现有企、事业单位为扩大原有主要产品生产能力或增加新的产品生产能力，增建一个或几个主要生产车间(或主要工程)、分厂，同时进行一些更新改造工程的，也应作为扩建。(3)改建:指对原有设施进行技术改造或更新(包括相应配套的辅助性生产、生活福利设施)，没有增建主要生产车间、分厂等。现有企、事业单位为适应市场变化的需要，而改变企业的主要产品种类(如军工企业转产民品等)，或原有产品生产作业线由于各工序(车间)之间能力不平衡，为填平补齐充分发挥原有生产能力而增建不增加本企业主要产品设计能力的车间，也应作为改建。

固定资产投资按构成分 固定资产投资活动按其工作内容和实现方式分为建筑安装工程，设备、工具、器具购置，其他费用三个部分。(1)

建筑安装工程(建筑安装工作量):指各种房屋、建筑物的建造工程和各种设备、装置的安装工程。包括各种房屋建造工程，各种用途设备基础和各种工业窑炉的砌筑工程及金属结构工程;为施工而进行的各种准备工作和临时工程以及完工后的清理工作等;铁路、道路的铺设，矿井的开凿及石油管道的架设等;水利工程;防空地下建筑等特殊工程;列入房屋工程预算内的暖气、卫生、通风、照明、煤气等设备的价值及装设油饰工程;列入建筑工程预算内的各种管道(蒸汽、压缩空气、石油、给排水等管道)、电力、电讯电缆导线等的敷设工程;以及各种机械设备的安装工程;为测定安装工程质量，对设备进行的试运工作;房地产开发单位进行的商品房屋开发建设工程、土地开发工程。在安装工程中，不包括被安装设备本身的价值。(2)设备、工具、器具购置:指建设单位或企、事业单位购置或自制的，达到固定资产标准的设备、工具、器具的价值。新建单位及扩建单位的新建车间，按照设计或计划要求购置或自制的全部设备、工具、器具，不论是否达到固定资产标准均计入“设备、工具、器具购置”中。(3)其他费用:指在固定资产建造和购置过程中发生的，除上述几项内容以外的各种应分摊计入固定资产的费用。

基本建设项目按大中小型划分 基本建设划分大中小型项目原则上应按照上级批准的设计任务书或初步设计所确定的总规模或总投资划分，没有正式批准设计任务书或初步设计的，按国家或省、自治区、直辖市年度基本建设投资计划中所列的总规模或总投资划分。上述两条均不具备的，按本年计划施工工程的建设总规模或总投资划分。生产单一产品的工业项目，按产品的设计能力划分;生产多种产品的工业项目，按其主要产品的设计能力划分。品种繁多，难以按生产能力划分的，按全部计划总投资划分。划分标准以国家颁发的《大中小型建设项目划分标准》为依据。国家曾在1953年、1962 年、1972 年、1977 年和1979 年先后五次修订《大中小型建设项目划分标准》，因此各历史时期的大中型项目数不完全可比。

施工项目 指报告期内进行过建筑或安装施工活动的项目。凡是报告期内施过工的建设项目，不论施工时间长短，均作为施工项目统计。施工项目个数可以反映一定时期固定资产投资的实际规模，与同期建成投产的建设项目个数相比，可以从建设速度的角度反映固定资产投资的效果。根据建设项目施工活动的不同性质，施工项目又分为:本年正式施工项目、本年收尾项目和以前年度全部停缓建项目。

全部建成投产项目 工业项目指设计文件规定形成生产能力的主体工程及其相应配套的辅助设施全部建成，经负荷试运转，证明具备生产设计规定合格产品的条件，并经过验收鉴定合格或达到竣工验收标准，与生产性工程配套的生活福利设施可以满足近期正常生产的需要，正式移交生产的建设项目。非工业项目指设计文件规定的主体工程和相应的配套工程全部建成，能够发挥设计规定的全部效益，经验收鉴定合格或达到竣工验收标准，正式移交使用的建设项目。新增生产能力(或工程效益)指通过固定资产投资活动而增加的设计能力(或工程效益)，该指标是以实物形态表现的反映固定资产投资成果的指标，也是考核投资经济效果的重要依据之一。

新增生产能力(或工程效益) 一般有以下几种表现形式:(1)用产品数量表示，以工程在单位时间内(一般是一年)所能生产的产品数量(即年产量)表示。如原煤开采用万吨/年表示，化学农药用吨/年表示，拖拉机制造用台/年表示等。某些化工产品由于含量差别较大，按其设计含量计算折合量表示，如硫酸、纯碱、烧碱等。(2)用单位时间内所能处理的原料数量表示，以工程每天(或小时)所能处理原料的数量表示。如机制糖工程日处理原料吨，食用植物油日处理原料吨，城市污水处理能力用万吨/日表示等。(3)用新增加的主要设备的数量或容量表示，如新增棉布织机、丝织机等台数，毛纺锭等锭数，发电厂新增发电机组容量用千瓦表示等。(4)以节约的原材料、燃料、动力实物量表示，适用于反映更新改造节约项目的效益。(5)用建筑物容积、容量、面积、长度表示，是非工业项目或工程新增效益的一种表现形式。如铁路里程、公路里程、水库容量、仓库容量、房屋建筑面积、学校学生席位、医院病床、灌区灌溉面积等。根据工程的特点，有时需要用两种或两种以上的复合计量单位表示新增生产能力(或工程效益)，如新增内燃机生产能力同时用年产台数、千瓦数表示等。为了规范新增生产能力(或工程效益)的名称和计算单位，国家统计局制订了《新增生产能力(或工程效益)目录》和《节约原材料、燃料、动力目录》，各固定资产投资单位在统计新增生产能力(或工程效益)时，必须按目录中规定的名称和计量单位填报。

房屋建筑面积 指房屋建筑物勒脚以上外墙外围的水平截面面积，包括房屋建筑物的有效面积和结构面积。该指标是从实物形态上反映建设规模和建设成果的重要指标之一，也是检查工程形象进度、计算工程造价、分析投资效果、研究施工任务和建筑材料之间平衡情况的重要依据。

住宅建筑面积 指施工和竣工房屋建筑面积中供居住用的房屋建筑面积。

施工面积 指报告期内施工的全部房屋建筑面积。包括本期新开工的面积和上期开工跨入本期继续施工的房屋面积，以及上期已停建在本期恢复施工的房屋面积。本期竣工和本期施工后又停缓建的房屋，其建筑面积仍计入本期房屋施工面积中。

竣工面积 指在报告期内房屋建筑按照设计要求已经全部完工，达到住人和使用条件，经验收鉴定合格(或达到竣工验收标准)，正式移交使用单位的各栋房屋建筑面积的总和。

房屋建筑面积竣工率 指一定时期内房屋竣工面积占同期房屋施工面积的比率。该指标从房屋建筑施工速度的角度反映投资效果的指标。

新增固定资产 指报告期内已经完成建造和购置过程，并已交付生产或使用单位的固定资产价值。该指标是表示固定资产投资成果的价值指标，也是反映建设进度，计算固定资产投资效果的重要指标。

建设项目投产率 指一定时期内全部建成投产项目个数与同期施工项目个数的比率。该指标是从建设单位建设速度的角度反映投资效果的指标。

固定资产交付使用率 指一定时期新增固定资产与同期完成投资额的比率。该指标是反映固定资产动用速度，衡量建设过程中宏观投资效果的综合指标。由于新增固定资产是较长时期内形成的结果，而投资额则是当年完成的，因此，该指标一般适宜于反映较长时期内固定资产的动用情况。

竣工房屋住宅套数 指报告期内按照设计要求全部完工，经验收合格，达到居住和使用条件并正式交付使用的成套住宅数量。包括独立厨房、独立卫生间、若干卧室、室内走廊等设施在内的供一户居住和使用的房屋。该指标可以反映住宅建设的产业化程度和城市化进程以及人民居住水平提高的情况。

别墅、高档公寓 指建筑造价和销售价格明显高于一般商品住宅的商品住宅。别墅一般指地处郊区，独立成栋的商品住宅;高档公寓一般指地处市内高尚社区，高层或多层的商品住宅。别墅、高档公寓的确定标准:一是经有房地产投资计划审批权的主管部门审批建设的别墅、高档公寓开发项目;二是销售价格高于当地同等地段商品住宅平均销售价格一倍以上的别墅、公寓开发项目。该指标可以分析房地产投资结构，反映高收入家庭商品住宅的供求平衡情况。

经济适用房 指根据国家经济适用房计划安排建设的政策性住宅。经济是指房屋建筑造价和销售价格低于一般商品住宅;适用是指适合中低收入家庭购买使用。经济适用房主要是由国家统一下达投资计划，房地产公司开发，对外销售;用地一般采用行政划拨或招标投标方式，免收土地出让金;对各种经批准的收费减半征收，开发利润不超过3%;销售价格实行政府指导价。该指标可以分析房地产投资结构，反映中低收入家庭商品住宅的供求平衡情况。

Explanatory Notes on Main Statistical Indicators

Total Investment in Fixed Assets in the Whole Country refers to the volume of activities in construction and purchases of fixed assets and related fees, expressed in monetary terms. It is a comprehensive indicator which shows the size, structure and growth of the investment in fixed assets, providing basis for observing the progress of const ruction projects and evaluating results of investment. Total investment in fixed assets in the whole country includes, by type of ownership, the investment by the state-owned units, collective units, individuals, joint ownership units, share-holding units, as well as investment by businessmen from foreign countries and from Hong Kong, Mac au and Taiwan, and by other units. According to China's current management system, the investment in fixed assets is classified into the following four parts: investment in capital construction, investment in innovation, investment in real estates development and other investment in fixed assets.

Investment in Capital Construction Capital construction refers to the new construction projects or extension projects and the related activities of the enterprises, institutions or administrative units mainly for the purpose of expanding production capaCity (or improving project efficiency), covering only projects each with a total investment of 500,000 RMB yuan and over. It includes: (1) projects listed in t he capital construct ion plan of the current year of the central government and the local governments at various levels as well as the projects, though not listed in the capital construction plan of the current year, but Continued to be constructed in this year, using the investment listed in the plan of capital construction of previous years and carried forward to this year (also using the equipment and materials kept in stock of the capital construction); (2) new construction projects arranged both in the plan of capital const ruction and the plan of innovation; extension projects with the newly increased production capaCity (or project efficiency) up to the standard of a large and medium-sized project; and the projects of moving the whole factory to a new site so as to improve t he distribution of productive forces; (3) new construction projects, extension projects or restoration projects with the total investment of 500,000 RMB yuan and over by the state-owned units, though listed neither in the plan of capital construction nor in the plan of innovation; the projects in the state-owned units of moving the whole factory to a new site so as to improve the distribution of productive forces; and the projects of building additional business houses by the administrative units and institutions and building welfare facilities by the administrative units.

Investment in Innovation Innovation refers in general to the technological innovation of the original facilities (including renewal of fixed assets) by the enterprises and institutions as well as the corresponding supplementary projects for production or welfare facilities and the related activities, covering only projects each with a total investment of 500,000 RMB yuan and over. It includes: (1) projects listed in the innovation plan of the current year of the central government and the local governments at various levels as well as the projects, though not listed in the innovation plan of the current year, but Continued to be constructed in this year , using the investment listed in the plan of innovation of previous years and carried forward to this year; (2)projects of technological innovation or renewal of t he original facilities, arranged both in the plan of innovation and in the plan of capital construction; extension projects (main workshops or a branch of the factory) with the newly increased production capaCity (or project efficiency) not up to the standard of a large and medium-sized project; and the projects of moving the whole factory to a new site so as to meet the requirements of urban environmental protection or safe production; (3) projects of reconstruction or technological innovation wit h the total investment of 500,000 RMB yuan and over by the state-owned units, though listed neither in the plan of capital construction nor in the plan of innovation; the projects in the state-owned units of moving the whole factory to a new site so as to meet the requirements of urban environmental protection or safe production.

Investment in Real Estate Development It includes the investment by the real estate development companies, commercial buildings construction companies and other real estate development units of various types of ownership in the construction of house buildings, such as residential buildings, factory buildings, warehouses, hotels, guesthouses, holiday villages, off ice buildings, and the complementary ser vice facilities and land development projects, such as roads, water supply, water drainage, power supply, heating, telecommunications, land leveling and other projects of infrastructure. It excludes the activities in simple land transact ions.

Other Investment in Fixed Assets refers to the construction and purchases of fixed assets with an investment of over 500,000 yuan which are not listed in the investment in capital construction, investment in innovation and investment in realest ate development, as well as urban private housing projects and investment in fixed assets by enterprises, institutions and individuals in rural areas. It includes: 1) The following projects of the state-owned units with the tot al planned (or actually needed) investment of over 500, 000 yuan, which are not included in the plan of capital construction and the plan of innovation: (1) projects of oil fields maintenance and exploitation with the oil fields maintenance funds and petroleum development funds; (2) opening and extending projects with the maintenance funds in coal, ore and other mining enterprises and logging enterprises; (3) project of reconstruction of the original highways and bridges with the highway maintenance funds in the department of communication; (4) projects of construction of warehouses with the funds of simple construction in the commercial department.

2) The investment in fixed assets by urban collective units: refer to projects of construction and purchases of fixed assets with the planned total investment of 500,000 yuan and over by all collective unit s in areas under the jurisdiction of cities and County towns (excluding investment by collective unit s under township enterprise administration off ices).

3) The projects of const ruction and purchases of fixed as-sets by the enterprises, institutions (including urban private enterprises or institutions) or individuals other than those mentioned above with total investment of 500, 000 yuan and over, which are not included in the plan of capital construction and the plan of innovation. For individual investment, only the investment in non-housing projects is to be included.

4) The private investment in housing construction in the urban areas and in industrial and mining areas: including all private housing construction under t he jurisdiction of cities, County towns and industrial and mining areas, no matter whether the owner of the house is registered as the permanent resident in the locality or not.

5) The investment in rural areas: including investment in fixed assets by enterprises, institutions and individuals in the rural areas.

Sources of Funds for Investment in Fixed Assets include fund from state budget, domestic loans, foreign investment, self-raised funds, and others depending on the source of investment.

(1) Fund from stat e budget consists of budgetary appropriation and loans from state budget. More specifically, it includes, from the budget of the central government, capital construction fund (operation fund and non-operational fund), special expenses (e.g. expenses on substituting petroleum with coal), loans from repayment, discount fund, expenses on innovation and trial production of new products, expenses on urban construction, expenses on temporary construction by trade departments, development fund for less developed areas, as well as local budgetary fund transfer red from the central budget.

(2) Domestic loans refer to loans of various forms borrowed by investing units from banks and non-bank financial institutions during the reference period for the purpose of investment in fixed assets, including loans issued by banks from their self owned funds and deposit, loans

appropriated by higher responsible authorities, special loans by government (including loan for substituting petroleum with coal, special loan for reform-through-labour coal mines), loans arranged by local government from special funds, domestic reserve loan, and working loan, etc..

(3) Foreign Investment refers to foreign funds received during the reference period for the construct ion and purchase of investment in fixed assets (covering equipment, materials and technology) , including foreign borrowings (loans from foreign governments and international financial institutions, export credit, commercial loans from foreign banks, issue of bonds and stocks overseas) , foreign direct investment and other foreign investment. Excluded in this category are capitals in foreign exchanges owned by China (foreign exchanges owned by the central and local governments, foreign exchanges retained by enterprises, foreign exchanges by enterprises through regulating mechanism, loans in foreign exchanges issued by the Bank of China with its own fund, etc.). In calculating the utilization of foreign capitals, foreign currencies are converted into Chinese Renminbi applying the current exchange rate when the foreign capitals are actually used.

(4) Self-raised funds refer to extra-budgetary funds for in-vestment in fixed assets received by investing units from central government ministries, local governments, enterprises and institutions, including their self-raised funds.

(5) Others refer to funds for investment in fixed assets received from the sources other than those listed above, including capitals raised through issuing bonds by enterprises or financial institutions, funds raised from individuals and through donations, and funds transferred from other units.

Investment in Fixed Assets by Sector The classification of construction projects by sector is determined by the major products or the purpose of the projects when they are put into production or use, and by the nature of their social economic activities. The investment in capital construction is classified into different sectors of the national economy by the nature of construction projects, while investment in innovation and other investment are classified according to the sector to which the whole enterprise or institution belongs. In general, one project or one enterprise or institution can only be classified into one sector. In order to reflect more accurately the relation among various sectors, the branch factories of an integrated complex are classified into different sectors according to the economic activities of the branch factories.

Investment in Fixed Assets by Type of Construction The const ruction projects in general can be classified, by t he type of construct ion, into new construction, expansion, reconstruction, moving and restoration. However, investment by type of construction is not applied to investment by real-estate development units, investment in rural areas and investment in housing by urban individuals. In capital construct ion, the type of construction is determined by the nature of the project. In in-vestment in innovation, in other investment by state-owned units and investment by collective-owned units, the type of construction is determined by the condition of the whole enterprise or institutions.

(1) New construction in general refers to newly constructed enterprises, institutions, administrative agencies or independent projects from scratch. Construction in the existing enterprises, institutions or agencies is not considered as new construction. In case the assets of the existing unit is quite small, and the value of newly added fixed asset s exceeds the original value of assets by three times, the expansion will be considered as new construction.

(2) Expansion refers to const ruction of new major production workshop, branch factory or independent production line within a factory or in other locations, for the purpose of increasing the production capaCity (or improving efficiency) of the original products. Newly constructed houses for the operation of institutions and administrative organizations (such as the newly constructed buildings for teaching in schools, buildings for clinics or wards in hospitals, etc.) are also classified as expansion. Also included in t he expansion are investments by existing enterprises or institutions in building major production line(s) or branch factory (ies) along with some work on innovation, for the purpose of exp ending the production capaCity of original products or producing new products.

(3) Reconstruction refers to innovation or technical transformation of the existing facilities (including auxiliary production equipment and welfare facilities), without building major new workshops or branch factories. Also considered as reconstruction is the construction of new work shops by the existing enterprises or institutions for improving the existing production capaCity (improving or changing the variety of products to meet the market demand), rather than increasing the designed capaCity of the main products.

Investment in Fixed Assets by Structure By their contents, investment activities are classified into 3 categories, i.e. construction and installation, purchase of equipment and instrument, and other expenses.

(1) Construction and installation (work volume of construction and installation) refers to the construction of various houses and buildings and installation of various kinds of equipment and instruments. They include construction of various houses; equipment foundations, industrial kilns and stoves, and met al structure work; preparation works for project construction, and clearing up works post project construction; pavement of railways and roads, drilling of mines and putting up of oil pipes; construction of projects of water conservancy; construction of under-ground air-raid shelters and construction of other special projects; value of equipment for heating, sanitation, ventilation, lighting, gas, painting, etc. that are covered by the budget of housing projects; laying out of various pipelines (for steam, compressed air, petroleum, tap water and sewage) and lines for electric power and for communications; installation of various machinery equipment, testing operation for pre-testing the quality of installation projects, and land and other development work conducted by real estate developers for commercial housing. The value of equipment installed is not included in the value of installation projects.

(2) Purchase of equipment and instrument s refers to the tot al value of equipment, tools, and instruments purchased or self-produced which come up to standards for fixed assets by the construction units or investing enterprises or institutions. Equipment, tools and instruments purchased or self-produced for new workshops by newly established or expanded units are categorized as "purchase of equipment and instruments" no matter whether they come up to the standards for fixed assets.

(3) Other expenses refer to expenses occurring during the construct ion or purchase of fixed assets other than those mentioned above.

Capital Construction Project s by Size The classification of size of capital construction projects should be determined according to the total scale or tot al investment set in the approved construct ion plan by higher responsible authorities or in the tentative design, otherwise according to the total scale or tot al investment set in the current capital construction plan of the state, provinces, autonomous regions, and municipalities directly under central government. Industrial projects which pro-duce unitary products are classified according to its design capaCity of products; project s which produce multi- products are classified by the design capaCity of the major product or by the total planned investment. Standards for the Classification of Construction Project s into large, medium-sized and small ones issued by the government are the base for size division of construction projects, which was revised five times in 1958, 1962, 1972, 1977, and 1979 respectively and therefore, data on projects by size are not entirely comparable from year to year.

Projects under Construction refer to projects with construction and installation activities undertaken in the reference period. All projects that have construction activities undertaken during the reference period are reported as projects under construction irrespective of the length of construction work. The number of projects under construction can reflect the actual size of investment in fixed assets during a given period, and when compared with the number of projects completed and put into use during the same period, it demonstrates the results of investment in fixed assets. Depending on the nature of const ruction activities, projects under construction can also be classified into projects under construct ion in current y ear, winding-up projects in current year and stopped or suspended projects in previous years (with preservation work in current year).

Projects Completed and Put into Use Industrial projects refer to the major projects and accessory facilities completed which result in forming production capaCity and have been checked and accepted while the living and welfare facilities have been completed and can ensure normal production and formally put into production. Non-industrial projects refer to the major project s and accessory facilities completed which possess the designed capaCity and have been checked, accepted and formally put into production.

Newly Increased Production CapaCity (or Project Efficiency) refers to the increase of designed capaCity (or project efficiency) through investment in fixed assets, which reflects the accomplishment of investment in fixed assets in kind and serves as important basis for evaluating the economic efficiency of in-vestment.

The newly increased product ion capaCity (project efficiency) are usually expressed in one of the following forms:

(1) output of products, i.e. the output that the project can produce during a given period (usually a year). For instance, the capaCity in coal mining is expressed in 10, 000 tons/year , the capaCity in producing chemical pesticides expressed in ton/year, the capaCity in producing tractors in tractor/year, etc. For some chemical products where the effective contents differ significantly, the production capaCity is expressed as the designed effective content equivalent, such as in the case of sulphuric acid, soda ash, caustic soda, etc;

(2) raw materials processing capaCity, i.e. the volume of raw materials that could be processed by the project per day (or per hour), such as tons of materials processed per day by a sugar refining project or edible vegetable oil project, or tons of urban sewage processed per day;

(3) number or capaCity of major equipment increased, such as number of cotton or silk looms increased, wool spindles in-creased, or capaCity (in kilowatt s) of power generators increased;

(4) saved raw materials, fuels or power, which are mainly used for the efficiency of innovation and transformation projects; and

(5) physical measures (volume, capaCity, area, and length) of construction, which is typical for non industrial projects, for instance, the length of new railways or highways, the capaCity of reservoirs, the floor space of housing projects, capaCity f or new students in schools or beds in hospitals, areas under new irrigation project, etc. Features of projects sometimes call for combined use of two or more measurement to reflect the increased production capaCity (or project efficiency), for instance, the new capaCity for the production of internal combustion engines are expressed in set s per year and kilowatts per year simultaneously. To standardize the nomenclature and unit of measurement for new production capaCity (or project efficiency), the National Bureau of Statistics has developed Nomenclature for New Production CapaCity (Project Efficiency) and Nomenclature for Saving Raw Materials, Fuels and Power. All reporting units with investment activities are required to follow these two nomenclatures in reporting statistics on new production capaCity (project efficiency).

Floor Space of Buildings under Construction and Completed refers to total floor space of the horizontal section of outer walls above the plinth of the building, including the effective area and the area occupied by the structure. This indicator is one of the important indicators in physical terms to reflect the scale and accomplishment of the construction industry, and important basis for monitoring the pr ogress, calculating the cost, analyzing the efficiency and studying the sup ply of building materials in relation with the construction projects.

Floor Space of Residential Buildings refers to the floor space of the residential buildings among the total space of buildings under construction or completed.

Floor Space under Construction refers to total floor space of all buildings under construct ion during the reference period, including floor space of newly start ed buildings during the reference period, floor space of construction extended from the previous period to the current period, and floor space of construction suspended during the previous period and resumed in the current period. Floor space of const ruction completed in the current period, and floor space of const ruction started and then suspended in the current period are also included in the floor space under const ruction of the current year.

Floor Space of Buildings Completed refers to the floor space of all buildings completed in the reference period, which have been appraised and accepted (or come up to the designed standards) and have been transferred to the owners for use.

Completion Rate of Floor Space of Buildings refers to the ratio of the floor space of buildings completed in certain period of time to the floor space of buildings under const ruction in the same period. This indicator reflects the investment result from the perspective of t he speed of construction.

Newly Increased Fixed Assets refer to the newly in-creased value of fixed assets, constructed or purchased, that have been transfer red to the investors. This is an indicator that demonstrates the results of investment in fixed assets in monetary terms, and an important indicator to reflect the speed of construct ion and to calculate the efficiency of investment.

Rate of Construction Projects Completed and Put into Use refers to the ratio of the number of construction projects completed and put into use in certain period of time to the number of projects under construction in the same period. This reflects the investment efficiency from the perspective of the speed of projects construction.

Rate of Projects of Fixed Assets Completed and Put into Operation refers to the ratio of the newly increased fixed assets to the total investment made in the same period. This is a comprehensive indicator reflecting the speed of the employment of fixed assets and the investment efficiency at the macro-level. As the newly increase fixed assets is the result of a long period while the investment is completed in the current year, this indicator is expected to be used to reflect the employment of fixed assets over a long period of time.

Number of Flats in Completed Residential Buildings refers to total number of flats completed during the reference period, appraised and accepted as meeting the standards for living, and transfer red for use. A flat includes separate kitchen and bathroom, several bedrooms and corridor, suitable for one household. This indicator reflects the degree of industrialization of the residential building construction, the process of urbanization and the improvement of the living standard of people.

Villas, High-Grade Apartments refers to commercial houses whose const ruction costs and marketing pr ices are significantly higher than ordinary housing. Villas are independent structures generally located in the suburbs; high-grade apartments are multi-story buildings located in elegant urban neighborhoods. Criteria for villas and high-grade apartments include: 1) projects for the construction of villas or high-grade apartments have to be approved by competent departments in charge of real estate development and investment plans, and 2) pr ices f or projects on villas or high- grade apartments are higher by over 100% com-pared with the aver age prices of ordinary commercial housing projects in similar location. This indicator helps to analyze the investment structure of the real estate industry and the demand and supply of housing for high-income households.

Economically Affordable Housing refers to housing constructed according to the state plan for economically affordable housing. Houses of this category featured in low cost in construct ion and low prices, and therefore are affordable to mid-income or low-income households. Economically affordable housing projects are developed by real estate companies under the state investment plan, with the land provided through government allocation or tendering procedures. Developers are exempted from land utilization fees and enjoy another 50% exemption of all other legitimate fees, while their profits are limited to less than 3%, and the completed houses are sold under the government guided prices. This indicator helps to analyze the investment structure of the real estate industry and the demand and supply of housing for mid or low income households.

第六篇

CHAPTER 6

财政、金融、保险

GOVERNMENT FINANCE BANKING AND INSURANCE

6-1 地方财政一般预算收支及增长速度
The General Budget Income&Expenses and Increasing Speed of Local Finance

年 份 Year	地方财政一般预算收入(万元) Total Revenue (10 000 yuan)	地方财政一般预算支出(万元) Total Expenditure (10 000 yuan)	收支差额(万元) Balance (10 000 yuan)	指数(上年=100) Indices (Precding year=100) 地方财政一般预算收入 Total Revenue	地方财政一般预算支出 Total Expenditure
1978	71416	170169	-98753	196.5	153.3
1980	40309	162159	-121850	73.4	95.4
1985	84663	286031	-201368	117.2	122.6
1990	217784	476210	-258426	118.9	114.2
1991	264491	503401	-238910	121.5	105.7
1992	260737	560931	-300194	107.4	111.4
1993	351346	647111	-295765	134.8	115.4
1994	286989	710962	-423973	127.7	109.9
1995	382818	964021	-581203	133.4	135.6
1996	483051	1148790	-665739	126.2	119.2
1997	545248	1233534	-688286	112.9	107.4
1998	653928	1459933	-806005	119.9	118.4
1999	713110	1662788	-949678	109.1	113.9
2000	790724	1909529	-1118805	110.9	114.8
2001	950933	2633232	-1682299	120.3	137.9
2002	1164724	3611729	-2447005	122.5	137.2
2003	1282218	3684676	-2402458	110.1	102.0
2004	1557040	4210446	-2653406	121.4	114.3

6-2 地方财政一般预算收入占新疆生产总值的比重
General Budget Income of Local Finance

年 份 Year	地方财政一般预算收入(亿元) General Budgetary Revenue in Local Finance (100 million yuan)	新疆生产总值(亿元) Gross Domestic Product in Xinjiang (100 million yuan)	地方财政一般预算收入占新疆生产总值的比重(%) Percentage of Budgetary Revenue to Xinjiang Gross Production Value (%)
1978	7.14	39.07	18.3
1980	4.03	53.24	7.6
1985	8.47	112.24	7.5
1990	21.78	274.01	7.9
1991	26.45	335.91	7.9
1992	26.07	402.31	6.5
1993	35.13	505.63	6.9
1994	28.70	673.68	4.3
1995	38.28	825.12	4.6
1996	48.31	912.15	5.3
1997	54.52	1050.14	5.2
1998	65.39	1116.67	5.9
1999	71.31	1168.55	6.1
2000	79.07	1364.36	5.8
2001	95.09	1485.48	6.4
2002	116.47	1598.28	7.3
2003	128.22	1877.61	6.8
2004	155.70	2200.15	7.1

6-3 财政收支情况

Statistics on Total Government Revenue and Expenditures

单位：万元 (10 000 yuan)

项　　目	Item	2003	2004
收入合计	**Total Revenue**	**3641483**	**4369088**
地方财政一般预算收入	General Budgetary Income in Local Financial	1282218	1557040
各项税收	Various Taxes	1052621	1231878
工商税收	Industrial and Commercial Tax	926274	1077689
农牧业税	Agriculture and Animal Husbandry	74045	91160
企业所得税	Income Tax of Enterprises	52302	63029
专项收入	Income from Special Items	66712	107814
其他各项收入	Other Revenue	162885	217348
中央补助收入	Income from the Central Subsidy	2318365	2827132
#定额补助	Quota Subsidy	193723	193723
国债转贷收入	Income from State Bond-Turned Loan	45100	6380
国债转贷资金上年结余	Balance of the Previous Year from State Bond-Turned Capital	5712	2300
调入资金	Transfer of Funds	14330	25730
上年结余收入	Income of Balance in the Previous Year	-24242	-57876
支出合计	**Total Expenditures**	**3641483**	**4369088**
地方财政一般预算支出	Local Financial Government Intrabudgetary Ordinary Expenditure	3684676	4210446
基本建设支出	Expenditure for Capital Construction	639934	622827
企业挖潜改造支出	Technical Updates and Transformation of Enterprises	27812	25516
农林水气等部门事业费支出	Expenditure for Operating Expenses of Departments of Agriculture, Forestry, Water Conservansy and Meteorology	231983	338104
工业交通等部门事业费支出	Expenditure for Operating Expenses of Departments of Industry, Commerce &Transportation	31476	36800
城市维护费支出	Expenditure for City Maintenance	96583	140191
文教卫生事业费支出	Operating Expenses of Culture, Education &Health Care	799383	913914
行政管理费支出	Expenditure For Government Administration	381102	487805
行政事业单位离退休支出	Expenditures for Retirement in Executive Institutions	328174	361586
公检法司支出	Expenditures for Public Security, Procuratorate, Law Court and Justice	218775	260148
其他各项支出	Other Various Expenditures	886261	1023555
上解中央支出	Division of Central Expenditure	21204	22659
增设预算周转金	Addition of Budgetary Turn-overs	700	2940
国债转贷收入安排的支出	Expenditure of State Bond Turned-Loan Income	48512	2300
国债转贷收入的结余	Balance of State Bond Turned-Loan Income	2300	6380
凋出资金	Output Capital		192
年终滚存结余	Accumulated Balance at the End of a Year	-115909	124171

6-4 各地、州、市、县(市)地方财政一般预算收支

Government Revenue and Expenditures by Prefecture, Autonomous Prefecture, City and County

单位：万元 (2004 年) (10 000 yuan)

地　　区	Region	收 入 Revenue	支 出 Expenditures
总 计	**Total**	**1557040**	**4210446**
自治区本级	Autonomous regional Level	203275	1556085
乌鲁木齐市	**Urumqi City**	**463395**	**393022**
#乌鲁木齐县	Urumqi County	4987	20575
市本级	City Level	338526	240995
克拉玛依市	**Karamay City**	**202145**	**206937**
市本级	City Level	157497	133010
石河子市	**Shihezi City**	**32345**	**48100**
吐鲁番地区	**Turpan Administrative Offices**	**50296**	**81277**
吐鲁番市	Turpan City	12051	23922
鄯善县	Shanshan [Piqan] County	24364	26518
托克逊县	Toksun County	4362	14233
地区本级	Regional Level	9519	16604
哈密地区	**Hami [Kumul] Administrative Offices**	**29749**	**75752**
哈密市	Hami [Kumul] City	18916	31802
巴里坤县	Barkol Kazak Autonomous County	1709	15192
伊吾县	Yiwu [Araturuk] County	1096	8949
地区本级	Region Level	8028	19809
昌吉回族自治州	**Chahgji Hui Autonomous Prefecture**	**100499**	**193226**
昌吉市	Changji City	27923	31409
阜康市	Fukang City	21157	21210
米泉市	Miquan City	13926	19689
呼图壁县	Hutubi County	9344	15592
玛纳斯县	Manas County	11363	17415
奇台县	Qitai County	4363	18824
吉木萨尔县	Jimsar County	6932	15084
木垒哈萨克自治县	Mori Kazak Autonomous County	1276	13757
州本级	Autonomous Prefecture Level	4215	40246
伊犁哈萨克自治州	**Ili Kazak Autonomous Prefecture**	**154917**	**548273**
州本级	Autonomous Prefecture Level	11106	93674
伊犁州直属县(市)	**Counties (Cities) Direct Under Ili Prefecture**	**75248**	**267542**
伊宁市	Yining [Gulja] City	22926	39800
奎屯市	Kuytun City	19382	21911
伊宁县	Yining [Gulja] County	4913	27359
察布查尔县	Qapqal Xibe Autonomous County	2653	18539
霍城县	Huocheng [Korgas] County	4452	20590
巩留县	Gongliu [Tokkuztara] County	2940	16971
新源县	Xinyuan [Kunes] County	6417	24990
昭苏县	Zhaosu [Mongolkure] County	2111	14465
特克斯县	Tekes County	1661	15768
尼勒克县	Nilka County	2757	16027
州直属县(市)本级	Counties (Cities) Direct under the Prefecture	5036	51122
塔城地区	**Tacheng [Tarbagatai] Administrative Office**	**57557**	**159280**
塔城市	Tacheng [Qoqek] City	7275	18872
乌苏市	Usu City	10706	24248

6-4 续表 1 Continued

单位：万元 (10 000 yuan)

地　　区	Region	收 入 Revenue	支 出 Expenditures
额敏县	Emin [Dorbiljin] County	4986	18935
沙湾县	Shawan County	10186	23602
托里县	Toli County	2097	14385
裕民县	Yumin [Qagantokay] County	1351	11114
和布克赛尔蒙古自治县	Hoboksar Mongol Autonomous County	16879	25520
地区本级	Prefecture Level	4077	22604
阿勒泰地区	**Altay Administrative Offices**	**22112**	**121451**
阿勒泰市	Altay City	4622	24723
布尔津县	Burqin County	2651	12184
富蕴县	Fuyun [Koktokay] County	4928	17007
福海县	Fuhai [Burultokay] County	4286	13457
哈巴河县	Habahe [Kaba] County	2211	13687
青河县	Qinghe [Qinggil] County	711	10622
吉木乃县	Jeminay County	710	9823
地区本级	Prefecture	1993	19948
博尔塔拉蒙古自治州	**Bortala Mongol Autonomous Prefecture**	**23643**	**72631**
博乐市	Bole [Bortala] City	9589	22808
精河县	Jinghe [Jing] County	4549	18066
温泉县	Wenquan [Araxang] County	1292	11888
州本级	Autonomous Prefecture Level	8213	19869
巴音郭楞蒙古自治州	**Bayangol Mongol Autonomous Prefecture**	**106904**	**202238**
库尔勒市	Korla City	49353	45951
轮台县	Luntai [Bugur] County	16629	19480
尉犁县	Yuli [Lopnur] County	5059	13660
若羌县	Ruoqiang [Qarkilik] County	1722	8528
且末县	Qiemo [Qarqan] County	11530	15103
焉耆回族自治县	Yanqi Hui Autonomous County	6299	15976
和静县	Hejing County	5292	18003
和硕县	Hoxud County	3062	10074
博湖县	Bohu [Bagrax] County	2533	9398
州本级	Autonomous Prefecture Level	5425	46065
阿克苏地区	**Aksu Administrative Offices**	**98295**	**259597**
阿克苏市	Aksu City	26414	35680
温宿县	Wensu [Onsu] County	5410	22411
库车县	Kuqa County	29516	47951
沙雅县	Xayar County	13270	29337
新和县	Xinhe [Toksu] County	2272	14566
拜城县	Baicheng [Bay] County	5752	24371
乌什县	Wushi [Uxturpan] County	1318	15916
阿瓦提县	Awat County	4014	20112
柯坪县	Kalpin County	461	9052
地区本级	Prefecture Level	9868	40201
克孜勒苏柯尔克孜自治州	**Kizilsu Kirgiz Autonomous Prefecture**	**6750**	**87532**
阿图什市	Artux City	3105	24301
阿克陶县	Akto County	1337	17255
阿合奇县	Akqi County	547	8835
乌恰县	Wuqia [Ulugqat] County	859	11422
州本级	Autonomous Prefecture	902	25719
喀什地区	**Kashgar [Kaxgar] Administrative Offices**	**57064**	**293124**
喀什市	Kashgar [Kaxgar] City	16650	32095
疏附县	Shufu County	2575	22690

6-4 续表 2 Continued

单位：万元 (10 000 yuan)

地 区	Region	收 入 Revenue	支 出 Expenditures
疏勒县	Shule County	2959	19421
英吉沙县	Yengisar County	1395	15864
泽普县	Zepu [Poskam] County	8306	19353
莎车县	Shache [Yarkant] County	6442	39837
叶城县	Yecheng [Kagilik] County	4540	25558
麦盖提县	Makit County	2970	17587
岳普湖县	Yopurga County	1317	14309
伽师县	Jiashi [Payzawat] County	2188	20617
巴楚县	Bachu [Maralbexi] County	3495	23114
塔什库尔干塔吉克自治县	Taxkorgan Tajik Autonomous County	536	10531
地区本级	Prefecture Level	3691	32148
和田地区	**Hotan Administrative Offices**	**19956**	**178839**
和田市	Hotan City	6539	20337
和田县	Hotan County	1865	19814
墨玉县	Moyu [Karakax] County	2591	31012
皮山县	Pishan [Guma] County	1657	17991
洛浦县	Lop County	1907	22078
策勒县	Qira County	1222	14951
于田县	Yutian [Keriya] County	1440	18551
民丰县	Minfeng [Niya] County	1491	9469
地区本级	Prefecture Level	1244	24636
阿拉尔市	**Alar City**	**3044**	**4731**
图木舒克市	**Tumxuk City**	**3289**	**7289**
五家渠市	**Wujiaqu City**	**1474**	**1793**

6-5 地方财政用于农业和教育等事业的支出

Local Government Expenditure for Agriculture, Education etc.

单位：万元 (10 000 yuan)

项 目	Item	1985	1990	1995	2000	2004
财政用于农业的支出合计	**Total Expenditure for Agriculture**	**35129**	**56234**	**93730**	**128198**	**338104**
农、林、水利、气象等部门事业费	Expenditure for Operating Expenses of Agriculture, Forestry, Water Conservancy and Meteorology	21859	27368	56103	84748	338104
支援农业生产支出	Expenditure for Supporting Agricultural Production	13270	28866	28431	24314	
农业综合开发支出	Expenditure for Comprehensive Development of Agriculture			9196	19136	
财政用于教育的支出	**Expenditure for Operating Expenses of Education**	**45641**	**74937**	**187832**	**313538**	**613943**
财政用于科学事业支出	**Expenditure for Operating Expenses in Science**	**3533**	**7878**	**13766**	**22037**	**46622**
科技三项费	Expenditure for Science and Technology Promotion	2303	3206	4759	11624	26181
科学事业费	Expenditure for Operating Expenses of Science	1230	4672	9007	10413	20441
抚恤和社会福利救济支出	**Expenditure for Pensions and Relief Funds for Social Welfare**	**4338**	**5834**	**12354**	**28517**	**94260**
价格补贴支出	**Expenditure for Price Subsidies**	**22371**	**78220**	**70929**	**59652**	**87954**
支援不发达地区支出	**Expenditure for Supporting Underdeveloped Areas**	**5855**	**6767**	**7031**	**57662**	**67006**

6-6 国家银行各项存款和各项贷款余额

单位：亿元

年 份 Year	各项存款 Deposits	企业存款 Deposits of Enterprises	财政存款 Treasury Deposits	城镇储蓄存款 Urban and Town Savings Deposits	农业存款 Agricultural Deposits	其他存款 Other Deposits
1978	32.07	6.86	13.52	6.42	5.28	
1979	33.44	7.03	13.10	7.21	6.09	
1980	38.56	9.60	12.73	9.52	6.71	
1981	45.59	12.21	13.32	12.29	7.71	0.05
1982	53.47	15.23	14.41	15.30	8.44	0.10
1983	61.94	17.95	15.36	19.01	9.38	0.24
1984	73.63	23.35	15.06	24.31	9.87	1.04
1985	82.96	29.87	13.48	29.55	9.14	0.92
1986	102.75	38.15	11.34	40.37	11.91	0.98
1987	124.93	44.13	12.69	53.25	13.51	1.36
1988	141.10	47.41	11.13	66.25	14.59	1.72
1989	167.03	52.76	14.13	83.33	15.49	1.32
1990	221.80	71.23	14.00	114.13	21.82	0.62
1991	282.21	92.78	17.25	145.01	26.67	0.51
1992	336.58	119.51	14.12	175.62	26.59	0.74
1993	397.39	129.98	16.75	220.45	29.33	0.89
1994	555.60	192.19	17.76	306.66	38.50	0.48
1995	714.64	245.67	20.54	418.10	23.53	6.80
1996	890.63	326.57	21.27	514.68	27.37	0.74
1997	1069.57	401.39	13.15	594.85	30.43	29.74
1998	1189.01	421.52	13.94	667.60	42.69	43.27
1999	1364.59	500.65	13.10	732.28	51.37	67.19
2000	1601.77	648.39	12.46	800.62	57.60	82.71
2001	1679.51	606.00	29.86	859.51	63.43	120.71
2002	1845.56	576.03	17.05	971.04	76.55	204.89
2003	2139.97	604.11	18.38	1152.65	86.60	278.23
2004	2333.50	634.64	41.17	1270.66	96.47	97.06

Balance of Deposits and Loans at State Bank

(100 million yuan)

各项贷款 Loans	工业贷款 Industrial Loans	商业贷款 Commercial Loans	农业贷款 Agricultural Loans	其他贷款 Other Loans
18.26	5.11	12.15	1.00	
21.19	6.48	12.21	2.49	
24.74	5.65	16.09	2.26	0.74
28.84	5.05	19.48	2.46	1.85
32.86	5.23	21.37	3.65	2.61
38.85	6.27	24.03	3.47	5.07
52.02	8.91	27.47	6.49	9.14
72.68	12.78	35.82	7.38	16.70
93.18	18.21	40.43	10.07	24.46
111.14	21.33	44.52	12.61	32.67
139.43	26.80	54.73	14.97	42.93
173.02	36.55	68.48	17.46	50.54
233.72	46.82	100.17	18.66	68.06
299.59	60.39	134.28	22.58	82.34
380.26	75.06	165.36	29.76	110.08
467.81	98.65	191.17	23.93	154.05
573.92	122.29	222.22	28.44	200.97
767.06	153.15	314.96	34.90	264.05
937.94	196.10	381.37	44.48	315.99
1125.96	236.53	437.98	37.62	413.83
1218.43	255.52	478.40	65.91	418.61
1276.73	267.61	464.59	71.12	473.40
1286.64	240.39	384.69	61.02	600.54
1415.71	285.26	401.99	67.62	660.84
1567.16	290.83	365.44	72.08	838.81
1777.91	294.77	372.11	70.01	1041.02
1842.23	276.82	431.83	85.96	1047.62

6-7　金融机构和人员数

Number of Financial Institutions and Staff

单位：个、人　　　　(2004 年)　　　　(unit, person)

项　目	Item	合　计 Total		自治区级 Level of Autonomous Region		地区级 Prefectural Level	
		机　构 Institutions	人　员 Employees	机　构 Institutions	人　员 Employees	机　构 Institutions	人　员 Employees
总　计	**Total**	**3582**	**44117**	**14**	**2710**	**97**	**8675**
人民银行	**The People's Bank of China**	**77**	**3192**	**1**	**345**	**14**	**1412**
政策性银行	**Policy Bank**	**86**	**1853**	**2**	**143**	**16**	**451**
农业发展银行	The Bank of Agricultural Development	85	1798	1	88	16	451
国家开发银行	The Bank of State Development	1	55	1	55		
国有独资商业银行	**State Sole-funded Commercial Bank**	**1637**	**25400**	**5**	**1768**	**57**	**6128**
工商银行	Industrial and Commercial Bank	379	7912	1	374	14	2685
农业银行	Agricultural Bank	544	7409	1	243	14	1251
农业银行兵团分行	Agricultural Bank, XPCG Branch	307	2958	1	179	3	246
中国银行	Bank of China	183	2642	1	481	13	809
建设银行	Bank of Construction	224	4479	1	491	13	1137
其他商业银行	**Other Commercial Bank**	**34**	**800**	**2**	**259**	**1**	**90**
交通银行	Bank of Communication	24	475	1	201		
招商银行	Merchants Bank	8	220	1	58		
华夏银行	Hua Xia Bank	2	105			1	90
城市商业银行	**City Commercial Bank**	**70**	**1037**			**1**	**279**
乌鲁木齐市商业银行	Urumqi Commercial Bank	70	1037			1	279
城市信用社	**City Credit Cooperative**	**29**	**515**			**1**	**49**
农村信用社	**Rural Credit Cooperative**	**1041**	**8518**				
乌鲁木齐县联社	Urumqi United Credit Coopertive	67	399				
资产管理公司	**Assets Management Company**	**3**	**123**	**3**	**123**		
信达公司	Xinda Firm	1	37	1	37		
华融公司	Huarong Firm	1	49	1	49		
长城公司	Great Wall Firm	1	37	1	37		
信托投资公司	**Trust and Investment Company**	**2**	**53**			**2**	**53**
金新信托公司	Jinxin Trust Company	1				1	
国际信托公司	International Trust Company	1	53			1	53
金融租赁公司	**Financial Leasing Company**	**1**	**63**			**1**	**63**
邮政储汇	**Postal Remittence**	**602**	**2563**	**1**	**72**	**4**	**150**

项　目	Item	县级 County Level		营业网点 Business Outlets	
		机　构 Institutions	人　员 Employees	机　构 Institutions	人　员 Employees
总　计	**Total**	**826**	**15709**	**2645**	**17023**
人民银行	**The People's Bank of China**	**62**	**1435**		
政策性银行	**Policy Bank**	**68**	**1259**		
农业发展银行	The Bank of Agricultural Development	68	1259		
国家开发银行	The Bank of State Development				
国有独资商业银行	**State Sole-funded Commercial Bank**	**243**	**6870**	**1332**	**10634**
工商银行	Industrial and Commercial Bank	63	2105	301	2748
农业银行	Agricultural Bank	90	2694	439	3221
农业银行兵团分行	Agricultural Bank, XPCG Branch	31	880	272	1653
中国银行	Bank of China	21	314	148	1038
建设银行	Bank of Construction	38	877	172	1974
其他商业银行	**Other Commercial Bank**			**31**	**451**
交通银行	Bank of Communication			23	274
招商银行	Merchants Bank			7	162
华夏银行	Hua Xia Bank			1	18
城市商业银行	**City Commercial Bank**			**69**	**758**
乌鲁木齐市商业银行	Urumqi Commercial Bank			69	758
城市信用社	**City Credit Cooperative**	**9**	**342**	**19**	**124**
农村信用社	**Rural Credit Cooperative**	**398**	**5392**	**643**	**3126**
乌鲁木齐县联社	Urumqi United Credit Coopertive	1	40	66	359
资产管理公司	**Assets Management Company**				
信达公司	Xinda Firm				
华融公司	Huarong Firm				
长城公司	Great Wall Firm				
信托投资公司	**Trust and Investment Company**				
金新信托公司	Jinxin Trust Company				
国际信托公司	International Trust Company				
金融租赁公司	**Financial Leasing Company**				
邮政储汇	**Postal Remittence**	**46**	**411**	**551**	**1930**

6-8 金融机构信贷资金平衡表

Credit Funds Balance Sheet of Financial Institutions by Sources

单位：亿元 (100 million yuan)

项　　目	Item	2003	2004
资金来源合计	**All Sources**	**2374.25**	**2495.96**
各项存款	Deposits	2661.65	2959.78
企业存款	Deposits of Enterprises	763.49	832.50
#活期存款	Current Deposits	579.50	616.16
定期存款	Fixed-term Deposits	183.99	216.34
财政存款	Treasury Deposits	18.87	44.73
机关团体存款	Deposits of Government Agencies and Organizations	156.95	210.87
城乡居民储蓄存款	Urban and Rural Savings Deposits	1371.59	1534.67
#活期存款	Demand Deposits	491.66	543.05
定期存款	Time Deposits	879.93	991.62
农业存款	Agricultural Deposits	131.49	151.32
信托存款	Trusted Deposits	47.22	48.23
委托存款	Commission Deposits	10.85	12.20
其他存款	Others	161.19	125.26
金融债券	Financial Bonds	-15.19	-42.03
应付及暂收款	Payable and Temporary Collection	43.45	45.11
各项准备	Various Preparations	10.25	34.72
所有者权益	Owner's Right and Interest	43.60	37.53
其　他	Others	-369.51	-558.58
资金运用合计	**All Uses**	**2374.25**	**2495.96**
各项贷款	Loans	2099.09	2214.66
短期贷款	Short-term Loans	1074.98	1155.10
工业贷款	Industrial Loans	319.51	309.38
商业贷款	Commercial Loans	411.22	471.42
#农副产品贷款	Agricultural and Sideline Products Loans	224.79	314.73
建筑业贷款	Construction Loans	27.62	20.56
农业贷款	Agricultural Loans	123.03	149.20
乡镇企业贷款	Loans to Township Enterprises	21.79	22.31
三资企业贷款	Loans to Sino-foreign Joint Venture and Cooperative Enterprises and Foreign-funded Enterprises	10.15	7.97
私营企业及个体贷款	Loans to Private Enterprises and Individuals	12.10	16.86
其他短期贷款	Other Short-term Loans	149.56	157.40
中期流动资金贷款	Medium-term Working Capital Loans	125.22	106.59
中长期贷款	Medium-term & Long-term Loans	798.24	883.16
基本建设贷款	Capital Construction	368.00	419.11
技术改造贷款	Technical Innovation	33.33	35.87
其他中长期贷款	Other Medium-term & Long-term Loans	396.91	428.18
信托贷款	Credit Loans	5.16	2.97
其他贷款	Other Loans	95.49	66.87
有价证券及投资	Securities & Investment	112.74	118.00
同业往来	Dealings in the Same Trade		9.57
应付及预付款	Payable and Temporary Collection	40.19	36.66
委托投资	Trusted Investment	14.00	9.92
外汇占款	Money in Form of Foreign Exchange	-0.07	0.10
库存现金	Inventory Cash	17.44	21.94
其　他	Others	90.86	85.11

6-9 国家银行信贷资金平衡表

Credit Funds Balance Sheet of State Banks

单位：亿元 (100 million yuan)

项　　目	Item	2003	2004
资金来源合计	**All Sources**	**1845.39**	**1909.57**
各项存款	Deposits	2139.97	2333.50
企业存款	Deposits of Enterprises	604.11	634.64
#活期存款	Demand Deposits	462.08	483.14
定期存款	Time Deposits	142.03	151.50
财政存款	Treasury Deposits	18.38	41.17
机关团体存款	Deposits of Government Agencies and Organizations	149.11	193.50
城镇居民储蓄存款	Urban and Rural Savings Deposits	1152.65	1270.66
#活期存款	Demand Deposits	394.69	431.95
定期存款	Time Deposits	757.96	838.71
农业存款	Agricultural Deposits	86.60	96.47
其他存款	Other Deposits	129.12	97.06
应付及暂收款	Payable and Temporary Collection	27.31	29.41
同业往来	Dealing in the Same Trade	49.26	25.72
各项准备	Various Preparations	6.52	29.41
所有者权益	Owner's Right and Interest	-3.96	-13.53
其　他	Others	-373.71	-494.94
资金运用合计	**Total of Capital Application**	**1845.39**	**1909.57**
各项贷款	Loans	1777.91	1842.23
短期贷款	Short-term Loans	868.67	911.23
工业贷款	Industrial Loans	294.77	276.82
商业贷款	Commercial Loans	372.11	431.83
#农副产品贷款	Agricultural and Sideline Products Loans	224.79	314.73
建筑业贷款	Construction Loans	24.54	15.58
农业贷款	Agricultural Loans	70.01	85.96
乡镇企业贷款	Loans to Township Enterprises	10.91	11.03
三资企业贷款	Loans to Sino-foreign Joint Venture and Cooperative Enterprises and Foreign-funded Enterprises	10.15	7.77
私营企业及个体贷款	Loans to Private Enterprises and Individuals	6.24	3.41
其他短期贷款	Other Short-term Loans	79.94	78.83
中期流动资金贷款	Medium-term Working Capital Loans	114.29	95.25
中长期贷款	Medium-term & Long-term Loans	745.60	805.57
基本建设贷款	Capital Construction	357.33	399.01
技术改造贷款	Technical Innovation	32.53	31.93
其他中长期贷款	Other Medium-term & Long-term Loans	355.74	374.63
其他贷款	Other Loans	49.35	30.18
有价证券及投资	Securities & Investment	18.49	20.13
应收及预付款	Payable and Pre-payment	26.61	21.56
同业往来	Dealings in the Same Trade	10.84	10.47
金银占款	Money in forms of Gold and Silver		
外汇占款	Money in Forms of Foreign Exchange	-0.24	0.01
库存现金	Others	11.78	15.17

6-10 金融机构现金收支表
Cash Income of Financial Institutions

单位：亿元 (100 million yuan)

项　目	Item	2003	2004	2004 年比 2003 年增减(%) Increase Ratein 2004over 2003
收入合计	**Total Income**	**6686.35**	**7937.21**	**18.71**
商品销售收入	Income from Commodity Sales	569.74	617.29	8.35
服务业收入	Income from Service Trade	352.07	425.75	20.93
税款收入	Income from Taxes	24.66	26.18	6.06
城乡个体经营收入	Income from Urban and Rural Individual Business	209.76	214.86	2.43
储蓄存款收入	Income from Savings Deposits	4760.29	5603.69	17.72
其他金融机构收入	Income from Other Financial Institutions	37.01	41.48	12.08
居民归还贷款收入	Income from Repayment of Loans by Residents	110.24	134.92	22.39
汇兑收入	Income from Remittances	224.20	267.54	19.33
有价证券收入	Income from Securities	58.28	79.47	36.36
其他收入	Other Income	340.10	526.03	54.67
#兑换外币收入	Income from Exchange of Foreign Currencies	10.12	14.48	33.83
支出合计	**Total**	**6767.75**	**7969.36**	**17.75**
工资性支出	Wages	555.22	578.30	4.16
国家工资及奖金支出	Wages and Bonuses to the Staff and Workers From Government	269.96	267.71	-0.83
国家对个人及其他支出	Other Payments to Individuals From Government	176.87	180.57	2.09
部队存款支出	Expenditure from Arming Umit's Deposit	40.52	44.58	10.02
其他单位工资性支出	Other Wages Expenditure	67.87	85.44	25.89
农副产品采购支出	Purchases of Agricultural and Sideline Products	270.14	308.61	14.24
工矿及其他产品采购支出	Expenditure for Purchases of Industrial and Mineral Products	57.02	52.63	-7.70
行政事业管理费支出	Government and Enterprises Overhead	273.83	302.02	10.29
城乡个体经营支出	Expenditure for Individual Business	317.94	309.11	-2.78
储蓄存款支出	Expenditure for Savings Deposits	4665.74	5550.60	18.97
其他现金机构支出	Expenditure for Other Financial Institutions	80.43	69.79	-13.23
居民提取贷款支出	Expenditure for Loans withdrawn by Residents	102.84	113.65	10.51
汇兑支出	Expenditure for Remittances	51.55	43.16	-16.28
有价证券支出	Expenditure for Securities	29.68	25.42	-14.35
其他支出	Other Expenditures	363.36	616.07	69.55
兑换外币支出	Expenditure to Cash Foreign Currency	33.33	48.18	44.55
投放(+)、回笼(-)	Monetary Issues (+) Cash Withdrawn (-)	81.40	32.15	-60.50
附：代发工资	Payment for Salary	152.48	176.86	15.99

6-11 保险机构
Number of Insurance Institutions

(2004 年)

项　目	Item	机构数(个) Number of Institution (unit)	总公司 General Corpora-tion	自治区分公司 Xinjiang Branch Company	地区级中心支公司 Branch Company at Prefecture Level	县级支公司 Branch Company at County Level
总　计	**Total**	**391**	**1**	**10**	**79**	**301**
中国人民财产保险公司新疆分公司	The People's Insurance Corporation of China	103		1	16	86
中国人寿保险公司新疆分公司	The Life Insurance Corporation of China	80		1	16	63
中华联合财产保险公司	The Property Insurance Corporation, XPCG	160	1		15	144
中国平安财产保险公司	The Ping An Insurance Corporation, Property Insurance Company	9		1	6	2
中国平安人寿保险公司	The Ping An Insurance Corporation, Life Insurance Company	14		1	9	4
中国太平洋财产保险公司	The Pacific Insurance Corporation, Property Insurance Company	4		1	2	1
中国太平洋人寿保险公司	The Pacific Insurance Corporation, Life Insurance Company	7		1	5	1
永安财产保险公司	Yong An Property Insurance Corporation	9		1	8	
新华人寿保险公司	Xin Hua Life Insurance Corporation	3		1	2	
天安财产保险公司	Tian An Property Insurance Corporation	1		1		
泰康人寿保险公司	Tai Kang Life Insurance Corporation	1		1		

6-12　国内保险业务情况

Conditions of Domestic Insurance Service

年　份 Year	承保额(亿元) Amount Insured (100 million yuan)		保费(万元) Premium (10 000 yuan)		赔款及给付(万元) Claim and Payment (10 000 yuan)	
	财产险 Property Insurance	人身险 Life Insruance	财产险 Property Insurance	人身险 Life Insruance	财产险 Property Insurance	人身险 Life Insruance
1980	4		93			
1985	70	2	3969	108	1475	19
1990	241	41	10385	5277	4702	836
1991	306	60	14466	7216	5672	1105
1992	348	83	19065	11201	9662	1803
1993	495	91	23824	14406	16845	2559
1994	511	95	34788	16841	17663	2749
1995	613	168	45906	20576	23761	4113
1996	1123	363	57470	29088	33745	8013
1997	1060	705	68661	59921	34254	20591
1998	1228	847	77542	97226	41525	23219
1999	1283	1217	112583	133300	65695	23668
2000	1612	1711	124931	157235	59935	37204
2001	2112	1371	141724	199840	74304	43749
2002	2283	3524	164764	352540	78359	50246
2003	5588	1362	191155	430634	103584	71011
2004	6401	1662	200387	480920	106468	76963

6-13　保险事业发展情况

Statistics on Development of Insurance

(2004 年)

项　　目	Item	承保额(亿元) Amount Insured (100 million yuan)	保费(万元) Premium (10 000 yuan)	赔款及给付(万元) Claim and Payment (10 000 yuan)
总　计	**Total**	**8063**	**681307**	**183431**
中国人民财产保险公司新疆分公司	The People's Insurance Corporation of China	2021	109756	57125
中国人寿保险公司新疆分公司	The Life Insurance Corporation of China	154	308451	55137
中华联合财产保险公司	The Property Insurance Corporation, XPCG	3720	89888	49043
中国平安财产保险公司	Ping An Insurance Corporation (Property Insurance)	56	6000	3219
中国平安人寿保险公司	Ping An Insurance Corporation (Life Insurance)	953	75931	8872
中国太平洋财产保险公司	The Pacific Insurance Corporation, Property Insurance Company	362	8363	3566
中国太平洋人寿保险公司	The Pacific Insurance Corporation, Life Insurance Company	423	48416	3762
永安财产保险公司	Yong An Property Insurance Corporation	106	7694	2300
新华人寿保险公司	Xinhua Life Insurance Corporation	126	11528	195
天安财产保险公司	TianAn Property Insurance Corporation	136	1231	176
泰康人寿保险公司	Tai Kang Life Insurance Corporation	6	14049	33

6-14 各地区保险业务情况

Conditions of Insurance Service by Region

(2004 年)

地 区	Region	全部业务(万元) All Insurance Business (10 000 yuan)		财产保险公司业务(万元) Property Insurance Business(10 000 yuan)		人身保险业务(万元) Life Insurance Business (10 000 yuan)	
		保费收入 Premium Income	同比增长(%) Increase Rate as to the Same Period in Preceding year	保费收入 Premium Income	同比增长(%) Increase Rate as to the Same Period in Preceding year	保费收入 Premium Income	同比增长(%) Increase Rate as to the Same Period in Preceding year
总 计	**Total**	**681307**	**9.57**	**200387**	**-2.82**	**480920**	**15.72**
乌鲁木齐市	Urumqi City	210770	6.35	51842	-8.04	158928	12.06
克拉玛依市	Karamay City	49486	8.76	15496	4.15	33989	11.00
石河子市	Shihezi City	33746	24.19	12512	-4.25	21234	50.55
吐鲁番地区	Turpan Administrative Offices	17759	4.05	7634	-3.55	10125	10.63
哈密地区	Hami [Kumul] Administrative Offices	22163	9.52	3941	-13.27	18222	16.12
昌吉回族自治州	Changji Hui Autonomous Prefecture	74905	11.85	18036	1.86	56869	15.43
伊犁州直属县(市)	Counties (Cities) Direct Under Ili Prefecture	62997	3.11	18503	-7.54	44494	8.29
塔城地区	Tacheng [Tarbagatai] Administrative Offices	27485	10.76	5678	-11.16	21807	18.37
阿勒泰地区	Altay Administrative Offices	18446	17.96	4416	22.70	14030	16.54
博尔塔拉蒙古自治州	Bortala Mongol Autonomous Prefecture	15850	11.38	5962	-11.62	9888	32.10
巴音郭楞蒙古自治州	Bayangol Mongol Autonomous Prefecture	59589	6.67	19906	-0.99	39683	10.98
阿克苏地区	Aksu Administrative Offices	37977	17.71	15706	3.13	22271	30.74
克孜勒苏柯尔克孜自治州	Kizilsu Kirgiz Autonomous Prefecture	3161	11.97	914	-9.24	2247	23.79
喀什地区	Kashgar [Kaxgar] Administrative Offices	37852	17.67	15783	7.60	22069	26.12
和田地区	Hotan Administrative Offices	9121	17.60	4059	2.53	5062	33.34

地 区	Region	保险密度(元) Insurance Density(yuan)			保险深度(%) Insurance Depth(%)		
		全部业务 All Insurance Business	财产保险 Property Insurance	人身保险 Life Insurance	全部业务 All Insurance Business	财产保险 Property Insurance	人身保险 Life Insurance
总 计	**Total**	**349.65**	**102.84**	**246.81**	**3.10**	**0.91**	**2.19**
乌鲁木齐市	Urumqi City	1147.08	282.14	864.94	4.35	1.07	3.28
克拉玛依市	Karamay City	1921.79	601.79	1319.96	1.67	0.52	1.15
石河子市	Shihezi City	533.28	197.72	335.56	7.56	2.80	4.76
吐鲁番地区	Turpan Administrative Offices	308.48	132.60	175.87	1.83	0.79	1.04
哈密地区	Hami [Kumul] Administrative Offices	421.79	75.00	346.79	4.23	0.75	3.48
昌吉回族自治州	Changji Hui Autonomous Prefecture	482.06	116.07	365.99	3.53	0.85	2.68
伊犁州直属县(市)	Counties (Cities) Direct Under Ili Prefecture	248.32	72.94	175.39	4.60	1.35	3.25
塔城地区	Tacheng [Tarbagatai] Administrative Offices	286.35	59.16	227.19	2.12	0.44	1.68
阿勒泰地区	Altay Administrative Offices	298.55	71.47	227.08	3.51	0.84	2.67
博尔塔拉蒙古自治州	Bortala Mongol Autonomous Prefecture	355.54	133.74	221.80	4.10	1.54	2.56
巴音郭楞蒙古自治州	Bayangol Mongol Autonomous Prefecture	523.86	175.00	348.86	2.60	0.87	1.73
阿克苏地区	Aksu Administrative Offices	171.80	71.05	100.75	2.47	1.02	1.45
克孜勒苏柯尔克孜自治州	Kizilsu Kirgiz Autonomous Prefecture	68.24	19.73	48.51	2.21	0.65	1.57
喀什地区	Kashgar [Kaxgar] Administrative Offices	106.38	44.36	62.02	3.17	1.32	1.85
和田地区	Hotan Administrative Offices	51.88	23.09	28.79	2.12	0.94	1.18

6-15 保险业务经济技术指标

Main Economic and Technological Indicators of Insurance Company

(2004 年)

项 目	Item	保 费（万元）Premium (10 000 yuan)	赔款及给付（万元）Claim and Payment (10 000 yuan)
财产保险业务	**Property Insurance Corporation**	**200387**	**106468**
企业财产险	Insurance of Enterprise Property	24407	8417
家庭财产险	Insurance of Family Property	1335	981
机动车辆险	Insurance of Mobile Vehicles	122987	69641
工程保险	Engineering Insurance	2279	1656
责任保险	Insurance of Liability	4461	1965
保证保险	Insurance of Guaranty	5861	2558
货物运输险	Insurance of Cargo Transportation	5195	1216
特殊风险保险	Special insurance against risk	4735	873
农业保险	Insurance of Agriculture	24942	16473
其他险	Other Insurance	4185	2689
人寿保险业务	**Life Insurance Corporation**	**480920**	**76963**
寿 险	Life Insurance	390322	40448
健康险	Health-care Insurance	66215	29682
人身意外伤害险	Insurance of People's Accidental Harm	24383	6833

6-16 新疆辖区证券、期货经营机构和人员数

Operators and Staff of Securities and Futures in Xinjiang

单位：个、人 (2004 年) (unit, person)

公司名称	Name of Enterprise	机构数 Number of Institutution	人员 Staff	营业部数量 Number of Business Department	人员 Staff	服务部数量 Number of Service Department	人员 Staff
总 计	**Total**		**793**	**31**	**572**	**19**	**65**
新疆辖区证券机构	**Stock Instituions in the Territory of Xinjiang**	**2**	**678**	**19**	**328**		**61**
新疆证券股份有限公司	Xinjiang Securities Stock Limited Company	1	392	15	207	12	26
宏源证券股份有限公司	Hongyuan Securities Stock Limited Company	1	286	4	121	4	35
异地证券公司乌鲁木齐营业部	**Urumqi Business Department, Yidi Stock Company**			**12**	**244**	**3**	**14**
金元证券公司	Jinyuan Securities Company			1	17		
平安证券有限责任公司	Pin'An Securities Liability Ltd. Co.			1	16		
中国银河证券有限责任公司	China Yinhe Securities Liability Ltd. Co.			1	31		
湘财证券有限责任公司	Xiangcai Securities Liability Ltd. Co.			1	18	1	4
大鹏证券有限责任公司	Dapeng Securities Liability Ltd. Co.			1	24		
光大证券有限责任公司	Everbright Securities Liability Ltd. Co.			1	17		
国泰君安证券股份有限公司	Jun"an Securities Stock Ltd. Co.			1	16		
申银万国股份有限公司	Shenyin Universal Stock Ltd. Co.			1	14		
海通证券公司	Haitong Securities Company			1	12		
德恒证券公司	Deheng Securities Company			2	55	2	10
民族证券公司	Nationality Securities Company			1	24		
新疆期货经纪公司	**Xinjiang Futures Broker's Company**	**4**	**115**				
新疆汇和期货经纪有限公司	Huihe Futures	1	26				
新疆璐通过期货经纪有限公司	Lutong Futures	1	20				
新疆新兴期货经纪有限公司	Xinxing Futures	1	31				
新天期货经纪有限公司	Suntime Futures	1	38				

6-17 上市公司基本情况表

Basic Condition of Listed Companies

公司名称 Names of Businesses		上市时间 Listed Time	上市交易所 Listing Stock Exchange	发行时股本(万股) Total Capital Stock (10 000 share)		发行募集资金(万元) Floated Raised Funds (10 000 yuan)	2004年末股本(万股) Stock Capital by 2004 (10 000 share)		2004年累计募集资金(万元) Capital Raised by 2004 (10 000 yuan)
				总股本 Total Stock Capital	流通股本 Circulating Capital Stock		总股本 Total Stock Capital	流通股本 Circulating Stock Capital	
总　计	**Total**			**403215**	**125785**	**725288**	**836206**	**325107**	**1074286**
宏源信托	Hongyuan Trust	1994	深交所 SZSE	17500	4500	10550	60875	24246	76971
新疆众和	Xijiang Zhonghe	1996	上交所 SHSE	7953	2025	9450	10340	2925	9450
百花村	Bai Huacun	1996	上交所 SHSE	6128	2700	10800	9480	4650	19500
汇通水利	Huitong Water Conservancy	1996	深交所 SZSE	5000	1250	7062	23318	9596	17270
友好集团	Youhao Group	1996	上交所 SHSE	10700	2700	10607	31149	17131	51157
新疆屯河	Xinjiang Tunhe	1997	上交所 SHSE	7000	1750	9400	80560	40629	44400
啤酒花	Hop	1997	上交所 SHSE	8000	3000	11523	36792	17412	24877
新疆天业	Xinjiang Tianye	1997	上交所 SHSE	6300	2430	16896	22680	9720	43482
特变电工	Toban Electric Engineering	1997	上交所 SHSE	8168	3000	14820	29861	16954	86230
新天国际	Suntime International	1997	上交所 SHSE	8600	2700	24071	47036	17846	32887
天山纺织	Tianshan Textile	1998	深交所 SZSE	18782	4230	20783	36346	10998	40571
天山股份	Tianshan Stock	1999	上交所 SHSE	12946	4500	26394	20802	9360	44044
新农开发	Xinnong Development	1999	上交所 SHSE	29400	9000	32905	32100	11700	63420
伊力特	Yilite	1999	上交所 SHSE	22050	7500	45375	44100	15000	45375
新中基	Xin Zhongji	2000	上交所 SHSE	12459	4500	21011	12459	4500	21011
广汇股份	Guanghui Stock	2000	上交所 SHSE	35378	5000	31652	86606	24480	31652
国际实业	Industry International	2000	深交所 SZSE	17179	7000	39837	17179	7000	39837
美克股份	Markor Stock	2000	上交所 SHSE	9208	4000	50923	19889	8640	50923
天利高科	Tianli High-Tech	2000	上交所 SHSE	17000	6000	42653	35700	12600	42653
新疆天宏	Xinjinag Tianhong	2001	上交所 SHSE	8016	3000	16633	8016	3000	16633
香梨股份	Fragrant Pear Stock	2001	上交所 SHSE	16050	5000	23141	16050	5000	23141
天富热电	Tianfu Thermoelectricity	2002	上交所 SHSE	16909	6000	42000	25363	9000	42000
八一钢铁	August 1st Steel	2002	上交所 SHSE	40943	13000	95940	58958	18720	95940
冠农股份	Guannong Stock	2003	上交所 SHSE	12000	4000	21610	18000	6000	21610
青松建化	Qubgsibg Cement	2003	上交所 SHSE	18493	6000	24265	18493	6000	24265
新疆城建	Xinjiang Urban Construction	2003	上交所 SHSE	16054	6000	33546	16054	6000	33546
新赛股份	Xinsai Stock	2003	上交所 SHSE	15000	5000	31441	18000	6000	31441

主要统计指标解释

财政收入 指国家财政参与社会产品分配所取得的收入，是实现国家职能的财力保证。财政收入所包括的内容几经变化，目前主要包括：

(1)各项税收：包括增值税、营业税、消费税、土地增值税、城市维护建设税、资源税、城市土地使用税、印花税、个人所得税、企业所得税、关税、农牧业税和耕地占用税等。

(2)专项收入：包括征收排污费收入、征收城市水资源费收入、教育费附加收入等。

(3)其他收入：包括基本建设贷款归还收入、基本建设收入、捐赠收入等。

(4)国有企业计划亏损补贴：这项为负收入，冲减财政收入。

财政支出 国家财政将筹集起来的资金进行分配使用，以满足经济建设和各项事业的需要，主要包括：

(1)基本建设支出：指按国家有关规定，属于基本建设范围内的基本建设有偿使用、拨款、资本金支出以及经国家批准对专项和政策性基建投资贷款，在部门的基建投资额中统筹支付的贴息支出。

(2)企业挖潜改造资金：指国家预算内拨给的用于企业挖潜、革新和改造方面的资金。包括各部门企业挖潜改造资金和企业挖潜改造贷款资金，为农业服务的县办"五小"企业技术改造补助，挖潜改造贷款利息支出。

(3)地质勘探费用：指国家预算用于地质勘探单位的勘探工作费用，包括地质勘探管理机构及其事业单位经费、地质勘探经费。

(4)科技三项费用：指国家预算用于科技支出的费用，包括新产品试制费、中间试验费、重要科学研究补助费。

(5)支援农村生产支出：指国家财政支援农村集体(户)各项生产的支出。包括对农村举办的小型农田水利和打井、喷灌等的补助费，对农村水土保持措施的补助费，对农村举办的小水电站的补助费，特大抗旱的补助费，农村开荒补助费，扶持乡镇企业资金，农村农技推广和植保补助费，农村草场和畜禽保护补助费，农村造林和林木保护补助费，农村水产补助费，发展粮食生产专项资金。

(6)农林水利气象等部门的事业费用：指国家财政用于农垦、农场、农业、畜牧、农机、林业、森工、水利、水产、气象、乡镇企业的技术推广、良种推广(示范)、动植物(畜禽、森林)保护、水质监测、勘探设计、资源调查、干部训练等项费用，园艺特产场补助费，中等专业学校经费，飞播牧草试验补助费，营林机构、气象机构经费，渔政费以及农业管理事业费等。

(7)工业交通商业等部门的事业费：指国家预算支付给工交商各部门用于事业发展的经费，包括勘探设计费、中等专业学校经费、技术学校经费、干部训练费。

(8)文教科学卫生事业费：指国家预算用于文化、出版、文物、教育、卫生、中医、公费医疗、体育、档案、地震、海洋、通讯、电影电视、计划生育、党政群干部训练、自然科学、社会科学、科协等项事业的经费支出和高技术研究专项经费。主要包括工资、补助工资、福利费、离退休费、助学金、公务费、设备购置费、修缮费、业务费、差额补助费。

(9)抚恤和社会福利救济费：指国家预算用于抚恤和社会福利救济事业的经费。包括由民政部门开支的烈士家属和牺牲病残人员家属的一次性、定期抚恤金，革命伤残人员的抚恤金，各种伤残补助费，烈军属、复员退伍军人生活补助费，退伍军人安置费，优抚事业单位经费，烈士纪念建筑物管理、维修费，自然灾害救济事业费和特大自然灾害灾后重建补助费等。

(10)国防支出：指国家预算用于国防建设和保卫国家安全的支出，包括国防费、国防科研事业费、民兵建设以及专项工程支出等。

(11)行政管理费：包括行政管理支出，党派团体补助支出，外交支出，公安安全支出，司法支出，法院支出，检察院支出和公检法办案费用补助。

(12)价格补贴支出：指经国家批准，由国家财政拨给的政策性补贴支出。主要包括粮食加价款，粮、棉、油差价补贴，棉花收购价外奖励款，副食品风险基金，市镇居民的肉食价格补贴，平抑市价肉食、蔬菜价差补贴等以及经国家批准的教材课本、报刊新闻纸等价格补贴。

地方财政收入 属于地方财政的收入包括营业税，地方企业所得税，个人所得税，城镇土地使用税，固定资产投资方向调节税，城镇维护建设税，房产税，车船使用税，印花税，屠宰税，农牧业税，农业特产税，耕地占用税，契税，增值税25%部分，证券交易税(印花税)50%部分和除海洋石油资源税以外的其他资源税。

地方财政支出 地方财政支出主要包括地方行政管理和各项事业费，地方统筹的基本建设、技术改造支出，支援农村生产支出，城市维护和建设经费，价格补贴支出等。

预算外资金收支 预算外资金指国家机关、事业单位和社会团体为履行或代行政府职能，依据国家法律、法规和具有法律效力的规章而收取、提取和安排使用的未纳入国家预算管理的各种财政性资金。其范围主要包括：法律、法规规定的行政事业性收费、基金和附加收入等；国务院或省级人民政府及其财政、计划(物价)部门审批的行政事业性收费；国务院及财政部审批建立的基金、附加收入等；主管部门所属单位集中上缴资金；用于乡镇政府开支的乡自筹和乡统筹资金；其他未纳入预算管理的财政性资金。社会保障基金在国家财政尚未建立社会保障预算制度以前，先按预算外资金管理制度进行管理，专款专用。财政部门在银行开设统一的专户，用于预算外资金收入和支出管理。部门和单位的预算外收入必须上缴同级财政专户，支出由同级财政按预算外资金收支计划和单位财务收支计划统筹安排，从财政专户中拨付，实行收支两条线管理。

信贷资金 指金融机构以信用方式积聚和分配的货币资金。金融机构信贷资金的来源有各项存款、对国际金融机构负债、流通中货币、银行自有资金及当年结益等；信贷资金的运用有各项贷款、黄金占款、外汇占款、财政借款及在国际金融机构中的资产等。

存款 指企业、机关、团体或居民根据资金必须收回的原则，把货币资金存入银行或其他信用机构保管并取得一定利息的一种信用活动形式。根据存款对象的不同可划分为企业存款、财政存款、机关团体存款、基本建设存款、城镇储蓄存款、农村存款等科目。它是银行信贷资金的主要来源。

贷款 指银行或其他信用机构根据资金必须归还的原则，按一定利率，为企业、个人等提供资金的一种信用活动形式。我国银行贷款分为流动资金贷款、固定资产贷款、城乡个体工商户贷款以及农业贷款等科目。

中资保险公司 指中国公民、法人或其他组织出资(含外资参股)设立的保险公司。

保险金额 指保险人承担赔偿或者给付保险金责任的最高限额。

保费 指投保人为取得保险人在约定范围内所承担赔偿责任而支付给保险人的费用。

赔款 指保险人根据保险合同的规定，向被保险人支付的赔偿保险责任损失的金额。

给付 包括死伤医疗给付和满期给付。死伤医疗给付是指保险人根据人寿保险及长期健康保险合同的规定，因被保险人在保险期内发生保险责任范围内的保险事故支付给被保险人(或受益人)的金额。满期给付是指被保险人生存期满，保险人按人寿保险合同规定支付给被保险人的满期保险金额。

Explanatory Notes on Main Statistical Indicators

Government Revenue refers to the revenue of the government finance by means of participating in the distribution of the social products, which is the financial resources for ensuring the government to function. The contents of government revenue have been changed several times. Now it includes the following main items:

(1) Various tax revenues, including value added tax, business tax, consumption tax, land value added tax, tax on City maintenance and construction, resources tax, tax on use of urban land, stamp tax, personal income tax, enterprise income tax, tariff, tax on agriculture and animal husbandry and tax on occupancy of cultivated land, etc.

(2) Special revenues, including revenue collected from imposing fee on sewage treatment, revenue collected from imposing fee on urban water resources, and extra-charges for education, etc.

(3) Other revenues, including revenue from the repayment of capital construction loan, revenue from capital construction projects, and donations and grants.

(4) Planned subsidies for the losses of the state-owned enterprises. This is an item of negative revenue, used to eat up part of the government revenue.

Government Expenditure refers to the distribution and use of the funds the government finance has raised, so as to meet the needs of economic construction and various causes. It includes the following main items:

(1) Expenditure for capital construction: It refers to the non-gratuitous use and appropriation of funds for capital construction in the range of capital construction, outlay of capital as well as the loans on capital construction approved by the government for special purpose or policy purpose and the expenditure with discount paid in an overall way within the amount of the funds appropriated to the departments for capital construction.

(2) Innovation funds of the enterprises: They refer to the funds appropriated from the government budget for the enterprises to tap the latent power, upgrade the technology and carry out innovation, including the innovation fund of the departments, loan of the enterprises for innovation, subsidies on the innovation of the small fertilizer plant, small cement plant, small coal mines, small machinery plant and small steel plant, the expenditure of interest for the loan for innovation.

(3) Geological prospecting expenses: They refer to the expenses appropriated from the government budget to the geological prospecting units for the expenditure of the prospecting work, including the expenditures of the administrative agencies for geological prospecting and their institutional units as well as the geological prospecting expenditure.

(4) expenditures for science and technology promotion: They refer to the expenses appropriated from the government budget for the scientific and technological expenditure, including new products development expenditure, expenditure for intermediate trial and subsidies on important scientific researches.

(5) Expenditure for supporting rural production: It refers to the expenditures appropriated from the government budget for supporting the various expenditures of the rural collective units or households for production, including the subsidies to the small water conservancy projects and well drilling, sprinkling irrigation projects run by the villages; subsidies on the rural water and soil conserving measures; subsidies to the small power stations run by the villages; subsidies to the expenditure for fighting against particularly severe draughts; subsidies on the rural waste land exclamation; fund for supporting the township enterprises; subsidies to the expenditure for popularization of the agricultural technologies and plant protection in the rural areas; subsidies to the expenditure for the protection of grasslands and cattle and fowls; subsidies on afforestation and forest protection in rural areas; subsidies on the rural aquatic products industry; special fund for developing grain production.

(6) Operating expenses of the departments of farming, forestry, water conservancy and meteorology etc.: They refer to the expenses appropriated from the government budget for the expenditures of agricultural exclamation, farms, agriculture, animal husbandry, agricultural machinery, forestry, timber industry, water conservancy, aquatic products industry, meteorology, technology popularization in township enterprises, popularization (demonstration) of improved varieties, plant (cattle and fowls, forest) protection, water quality monitoring, prospecting and designing, resources investigation, cadres training, subsidies to horticulture gardens, expenditure of specialized secondary schools, subsidies on the experiments of sowing herbage seeds by flights, expenditures of afforestation agencies and meteorology agencies, expenses for fishery administration and operating expenses for agricultural administration, etc.

(7) Operating expenses of the departments of industry, transport and commerce: They refer to the expenses appropriated from the government budget to the departments of industry, transport and commerce for the expenditure of business development, including expenses for prospecting and designing, expenditures of specialized secondary schools, expenditures of the technical training schools and expenditures for cadres training, etc.

(8) Operating expenses of the departments of culture, eduation, science and public health: They refer to the expenses appropriated from the government budget for the expenditures of the causes of culture, publication, cultural relics, education, public health, traditional Chinese medical science, free medical services, sports, archives, earthquake, ocean, communications, broadcasting, film and television, family planning; expenditure for training of cadres of government, party and mass organization; expenditures for natural sciences, social sciences, associations for science and technology and the special expenditure for the high-tech researches. They include mainly wages, extra wages, welfare funds, pension for the retirees, stipend, expenses for official business, expenses for equipment purchases, expenses for repairs, business expenses and subsidies to the units which are unable to support their expenditures by their own earnings.

(9) Pension for the disabled or for the families of the bereaved and relief funds for social welfare: They refer to the funds appropriated from the government budget for the expenditures of pension for the disabled or for the families of the bereaved and relief funds for social welfare, including the lump-sum or regular pension paid by the departments of civil affairs to the members of martyrs families and families of those who died for the public

interest, pension to the revolutionary disabled, subsidies for permanent disability of various kinds, subsidies to the military martyrs dependents and the demobilized servicemen, expenditure for settling down the demobilized servicemen, operating expenses of the consoling institutions, expenses for management and repair of the commemorative buildings for the martyrs, the expenses managed by the departments of civil affairs for the retirees and those who have quitted their work, expenses for social relief in rural and urban areas, operating expenses for providing relief to the areas of natural calamity and subsidies on the reconstruction after the particularly severe natural calamities, etc.

(10) Expenditures for national defence: They refer to the funds appropriated from the government budget for the expenditures for building up national defence and safeguarding national security, including expenses of national defence, expenses of scientific researches on national defence, expenses for building up peoples militia and expenditure for special projects, etc.

(11) Administrative expenses: They include expenditure for administration, subsidies to the parties and mass organizations, diplomatic expenditure, expenditure for public security, judicial expenditure, law court expenditure, procuratorial expenditure and subsidies to the expenses for treating the cases by the public security departments, procuratorial organs and law courts.

(12) Expenditure for price subsidies: It refers to the expenditure appropriated, with the approval of the government, from the government budget for the policy subsidies to price adjustment, including the fund for the increase of grain prices, the subsidies to the difference between the selling prices and purchasing prices of grains, cotton and edible oil, awards in addition to the purchasing prices of cotton, risk fund for non-staple food, subsidies on the prices of meat and meat products, subsidies on the price difference for curbing the high market prices of meat, meat products and vegetables and the subsidies approved by the government on the prices of textbooks and newsprint of newspapers and periodicals.

revenue of the local governments The revenue of the local governments includes business tax, income tax of the enterprises subordinate to the local government, personal income tax, tax on the use of urban land, tax on the adjustment of the investment in fixed assets, tax on town maintenance and construction, tax on real estates, tax on the use of vehicles and ships, stamp tax, slaughter tax, tax on agriculture and animal husbandry, tax on special agricultural products, tax on the occupancy of cultivated land, contract tax, 25% of the value added tax, 50% of the tax on stock dealing (stamp tax) and tax on resources other than the ocean petroleum resources.

expenditure of the local governments The expenditure of the local governments includes mainly the administrative expenses and various operating expenses at the vel of local governments, the expenditure for capital construction and technological innovation with the funds raised by the local government, expenditure for supporting rural production, expenditure for City maintenance and construction and expenditure for price subsidies, etc.

Extra-budgetary revenue and expenditure Extra-budgetary fund refers to financial fund of various types not covered by the regular government budgetary management, which is collected, allocated or arranged by government agencies, institutions and social organizations while performing duties delegated to them or on behalf of the government in accordance with laws, rules and regulations. It mainly covers following items: administrative and institutional fees, funds and extra charges that are stipulated by laws and regulations; administrative and institutional fees approved by the State Council and provincial governments and their financial and planning (price management) departments; funds and extra charges established by the State Council and the Ministry of Finance; funds turned over to competent departments by their subordinate institutions; self-raised and collected funds by township governments for their own expenditure; and other financial funds that are not covered in budgetary management. Social security funds are treated as extra-budget fund and managed for its exclusive use, given the circumstance that separate government budgetary system for social security is yet to be designed. Special accounts are opened by the financial departments in banks for the management of revenue and expenditure of extra-budgetary fund. Extra-budgetary revenue and expenditure is managed separately, namely, revenue of institutions and departments must enter into the special accounts of the financial departments at the same administrative level, and their extra-budgetary expenditure is arranged in line with the extra-budget plans and appropriated from these accounts.

redit Funds refer to the funds issued as loans by banking institutions. The sources of credit funds of the banking institutions included deposits, liabilities to international financial institutions, currency in circulation, self-owned funds and current retained profits, etc. The credit funds can be used in forms of loans, gold, foreign exchange, government debt and assets in the international financial institutions.

Deposit is a form of credit by which enterprises, institutions, organizations or households can put money into banks and other credit institutions for safekeeping and interest earning under the principle of free withdrawal. According to different depositors, deposits are divided into enterprise deposits,treasury deposits, deposits of government agencies and organizations,capital construction deposits, urban savings deposits, rural deposits and other deposits. Deposits are major sources of the credit funds of banks.

Loan is a form of credit by which banks and other credit institutions provide funds at certain interest rate to enterprises and individuals in the light of the principle of unconditional repayment. Loans from Chinese banks include circulating capital loans, fixed assets loans, loans to urban and rural individuals engaged in industrial and commercial business and agricultural loans.

Insurance Companies Funded with Chinese Capital refer to insurance companies established with capitals from Chinese citizens, corporate institutions or other organizations (including companies with shares from foreign capital).

Amount Insured refers to the maximum that the insurant will get for the claim of the case insured.

Premium is the fee paid by the insurant to the insurer to obtain the obligation of compensation from the insurance within the agreed terms.

Settled Claim is the compensation paid by the insurer to the insurant in accordance with the insurance contract.

Payment includes payment for death, injury or medical treatment and mature payment. Payment for death, injury or medical treatment refers to the money paid to the insurant (or the beneficiary) in accordance with the life or health insurance contract when the insurant encounters accidents within the insured period covered in the contract. Mature payment refers to the mature payment to the insurant in accordance with the life insurance contract at the end of the insured period.

第七篇
CHAPTER 7

物 价 指 数

PRICE INDICES

7-1 各种物价指数
Price Indices

年 份 Year	居民消费价格指数 Consumers' Price Index	城市居民消费价格指数 Urban Areas	农村居民消费价格指数 Rural Areas	商品零售价格指数 Retail Price Indices for Commodities
上年=100 Preceding year=100				
1978	101.2	101.4	100.3	101.4
1980	102.8	104.1	102.0	104.2
1985	107.8	109.5	106.4	108.1
1990	105.0	104.5	105.9	104.1
1991	108.6	109.3	107.9	108.0
1992	108.6	109.3	107.6	108.1
1993	113.0	113.6	110.8	112.6
1994	126.7	127.7	125.6	125.7
1995	119.7	118.4	122.5	116.7
1996	110.5	110.4	110.6	108.8
1997	103.7	103.5	103.9	101.8
1998	100.2	99.9	100.8	99.7
1999	97.4	97.7	96.8	96.2
2000	99.4	100.1	97.6	98.3
2001	104.0	104.0	103.8	102.5
2002	99.4	98.9	100.9	97.9
2003	100.4	100.5	100.2	99.2
2004	102.7	102.1	104.5	100.7
1978 年=100 Year 1978 =100				
1978	100.0	100.0	100.0	100.0
1980	105.1	106.6	103.8	107.8
1985	120.9	125.6	117.9	124.2
1990	194.3	206.0	184.0	197.6
1991	211.0	225.2	198.6	213.4
1992	229.1	246.1	213.7	230.7
1993	258.9	279.6	236.7	259.8
1994	328.1	357.0	297.3	326.5
1995	392.7	422.7	364.2	381.0
1996	433.9	466.7	402.9	414.6
1997	450.0	483.0	418.6	422.0
1998	450.9	482.5	421.9	420.8
1999	439.2	471.4	408.4	404.8
2000	436.5	471.9	398.6	397.9
2001	454.0	490.8	413.8	407.8
2002	451.3	485.4	417.5	399.3
2003	453.1	487.8	418.3	396.1
2004	465.3	498.1	437.1	398.9

7-2 居民消费价格分类指数

Consumer Price Indices by Category

(上年=100)　　(2004 年)　　(Preceding year=100)

项　目	Item	全　区 Province	城　市 Urban Areas	农　村 Rural Areas
居民消费价格指数	**Consumers' Price Index**	**102.7**	**102.1**	**104.5**
食　品	**Food**	**105.8**	**104.7**	**109.3**
粮　食	Grain	116.3	115.5	118.8
大　米	Rice	130.2	129.8	130.7
面　粉	Flour	112.1	111.9	112.5
粮食制品	Grain Products	104.5	103.9	108.4
其　它	Others	113.3	110.9	134.3
淀粉及薯类	Starches and Tubers	102.8	104.4	99.0
干豆类及豆制品	Bean and Its Products	118.2	118.9	115.0
油　脂	Oil or Fat	106.1	105.5	107.8
肉禽及其制品	Meat, Poultry and Their Products	108.8	108.5	109.7
蛋	Eggs	114.1	113.9	115.1
水产品	Aquatic Products	115.5	116.5	112.2
菜	Vegetables	100.3	95.0	118.5
鲜　菜	Fresh Vegetables	100.2	94.7	119.5
干菜及菜制品	Dried Vegetables and Vegetable Products	100.9	100.9	100.8
调味品	Flavoring	99.0	98.9	99.1
糖	Carbohydrate Products	100.4	100.1	101.3
食　糖	Sugar	99.9	99.4	101.2
糖　果	Candy	99.6	98.7	102.4
巧克力制品	Chocolate Goods	100.4	100.1	101.9
糖制小食品	Carbohydrate	102.1	103.1	98.5
茶及饮料	Tea and Beverages	99.3	99.4	98.9
干鲜瓜果	Dried and Fresh Melons and Fruits	104.8	104.5	105.6
鲜　果	Fresh Fruits	104.2	104.1	104.7
干(坚)果及瓜果制品	Dried(nut)Fruits and Melon and Fruits Products	107.2	106.5	109.2
糕点饼干面包	Cake, Cookie, Bread	99.7	99.0	102.0
奶及奶制品	Milk and Its Products	100.6	101.0	98.8
在外用膳食品	Catering Trade	101.2	100.6	103.5
主　食	Staple Food	101.6	100.9	104.2
炒　菜	Fried Dishes	100.9	100.4	103.1
地方小吃	Local Snack	101.0	100.6	102.6
其他食品及食品加工服务	Other Food and Food Processing	99.2	97.9	102.5
烟酒及用品	**Tobacco, Liquor and Articles**	**100.3**	**100.1**	**100.9**
烟　草	Tobacco	98.4	97.5	100.8
酒	Liquor	102.2	102.7	101.2
吸烟饮酒用品	Articles	100.5	100.8	99.1
衣　着	**Clothing**	**99.4**	**99.1**	**100.6**
服　装	Garments	100.0	99.8	100.6
衣着材料	Clothing Material	101.4	101.1	101.9
棉　布	Cotton Cloth	104.3	101.8	106.8
棉花化纤混纺布	Blend Cloth	100.9	100.3	101.9

7-2 续表 Continued

(上年=100) (Preceding year=100)

项　　目	Item	全　区 Province	城　市 Urban Areas	农　村 Rural Areas
化纤布	Chemical Fiber Cloth	100.4	100.1	100.8
毛织品	Woolen Fabric	101.1	101.4	99.7
丝织品	Silk	100.3	99.3	102.6
毛　线	Wool	100.3	101.2	98.4
其　它	The Others	102.6	102.3	103.4
鞋袜帽	Footwear and Hats	97.3	96.6	100.0
鞋	Shoes	97.4	96.6	100.3
袜　子	Socks and Stockings	96.6	96.0	99.3
帽　子	Hats	99.7	100.1	98.8
衣着加工服务	Clothing Processing	100.1	99.8	101.6
家庭设备及用品	**Household Facilities and Articles**	**98.4**	**98.2**	**98.8**
耐用消费品	Durable Consumer Goods	97.4	97.4	97.6
家　具	Furniture	97.8	97.0	99.7
家庭设备	Household Facilities	97.3	97.6	95.5
室内装饰品	Interior Decorations	97.4	97.0	98.3
床上用品	Bed Articles	100.7	100.2	101.6
家庭日用杂品	Daily Use Household Articles	99.0	98.8	99.7
家庭服务及加工维修服务	Household Service	100.2	100.0	100.5
医疗保健和个人用品	**Medicine and Personal Articles**	**101.8**	**101.4**	**102.8**
医疗保健	Medicine	102.6	102.2	103.5
医疗器具及用品	Medical Appliances and Articles	100.1	101.3	97.7
中药材及中成药	Traditional Chinese Medicine	99.8	99.9	98.6
西　药	Western Medicine	98.7	100.3	94.6
保健器具及用品	Constitutional Appliances and Articles	100.2	100.6	97.8
医疗保健服务	Medical and Health Service	110.9	107.0	124.1
个人用品及服务	Personal Articles and Services	100.3	100.0	101.2
交通和通讯	**Transportation and Communication**	**99.4**	**99.2**	**99.8**
交　通	Transportation	101.0	100.7	101.8
通　讯	Communication	97.7	97.9	96.8
娱乐教育文化用品及服务	**Recreation, Education, Culture Articles and Services**	**98.6**	**98.2**	**99.9**
文娱用耐用消费品	Durable Consumer Goods for Recreationl Use	94.8	94.3	96.7
教　育	Education	100.7	101.0	99.9
文化娱乐用品	Cultural and Recreational Articles	101.4	101.5	100.8
文化娱乐	Culture and Recreation	99.0	99.1	97.7
书报杂志	Newspapers and Magazines	100.3	99.7	104.0
文娱费	Recreation	104.2	104.5	101.2
旅游及外出	Touristry and Outside	89.9	86.8	104.1
居　住	**Residence**	**108.3**	**108.3**	**108.1**
建房及装修材料	Builing and handling Materials	107.5	106.7	108.9
租　房	Tenancy	111.5	113.0	101.9
自有住房	Housing	100.8	100.5	101.4
水、电、燃料	Water, ElectriCity and Fuels	113.2	113.9	111.0
服务项目价格指数	**Services**	**101.0**	**100.5**	**102.6**

7-3 各市县居民消费价格分类指数

(上年=100) (2004 年)

项目	Item	乌鲁木齐市 Urumqi City	喀什市 Kashgar [Kaxgar] City	伊宁市 Yining [Gulja] City	和田市 Hotan City	克拉玛依市 Karamay City	哈密市 Hami [Kumul] City
居民消费价格指数	**Consumers' Price Index**	**100.9**	**101.6**	**104.0**	**103.0**	**103.7**	**102.2**
食 品	**Food**	**102.1**	**105.0**	**108.3**	**108.3**	**105.2**	**108.1**
粮 食	Grain	114.2	115.6	116.2	112.9	113.5	115.1
大 米	Rice	130.1	127.0	123.7	124.4	128.7	123.6
面 粉	Flour	109.1	112.0	115.6	108.0	110.7	109.4
粮食制品	Grain Products	101.2	115.5	104.6	98.0	99.8	115.1
其 它	The Others	107.7	100.0	112.8	115.4	108.8	118.8
淀粉及薯类	Starches and Tubers	101.6	93.4	106.1	101.8	103.1	116.3
干豆类及豆制品	Bean and Its Products	123.2	115.7	123.3	101.2	110.1	121.9
油 脂	Oil or Fat	105.0	104.1	108.1	112.5	116.0	108.4
肉禽及其制品	Meal, Poultry and Their Products	107.5	109.4	110.5	116.3	107.8	107.6
蛋	Eggs	116.2	110.9	116.9	110.6	115.1	108.2
水产品	Aquatic Products	118.2	122.3	129.3	99.7	121.2	117.2
菜	Vegetables	83.0	84.8	103.8	107.4	98.0	106.7
鲜 菜	Fresh Vegetables	82.1	84.5	103.5	108.3	98.2	107.0
干菜及菜制品	Dried Vegetables and Vegetable Products	101.2	94.7	106.9	99.9	95.5	99.7
调味品	Flavoring	100.7	99.1	101.2	100.4	100.5	97.3
糖	Carbohydrate Products	100.2	101.6	96.5	100.0	99.1	100.4
食 糖	Sugar	104.6	106.3	88.8	100.0	96.6	104.2
糖 果	Candy	98.5	100.0	99.3	100.0	96.2	98.2
巧克力制品	Chocolate Goods	99.3	100.0	98.0	100.0	102.8	100.0
糖制小食品	Carbohydrate	104.2	95.4	100.4	100.0	100.8	100.0
茶及饮料	Tea and Beverages	100.2	93.2	89.9	97.6	102.2	96.2
干鲜瓜果	Dried and Fresh Melons and Fruits	103.7	110.5	98.7	103.8	97.7	108.6
鲜 果	Fresh Fruits	103.8	122.5	96.7	104.5	96.9	107.6
干(坚)果及瓜果制品	Dried(nut)Fruits and Melon and Fruits Products	104.5	91.2	105.3	102.1	101.5	109.9
糕点饼干面包	Cake, Cookie, Bread	99.4	101.1	93.9	100.0	98.7	100.0
奶及奶制品	Milk and Its Products	100.5	93.7	105.8	100.0	102.8	99.9
在外用膳食品	Catering Trade	99.8	100.5	102.8	100.0	103.3	101.3
主 食	Staple Food	100.0	100.0	100.0	100.0	105.2	101.7
炒 菜	Fried Dishes	100.0	98.3	106.3	100.0	100.3	98.9
地方小吃	Local Snack	98.7	103.0	100.0	100.0	105.1	104.2
其他食品及食品加工服务	Other Food and Food Processing	97.5	91.4	105.1	100.0	97.6	94.9
烟酒及用品	**Tobacco, Liquor and Articles**	**99.1**	**96.3**	**102.6**	**101.2**	**102.6**	**100.4**
烟 草	Tobacco	96.6	97.4	102.0	105.7	95.2	99.7
酒	Liquor	102.4	94.4	102.5	96.8	108.8	101.3
吸烟饮酒用品	Articles	100.0	100.0	106.1	100.0	99.3	99.3
衣 着	**Clothing**	**99.5**	**100.1**	**98.3**	**99.6**	**99.7**	**97.3**
服 装	Garments	101.7	100.1	97.7	100.0	99.9	97.4
衣着材料	Clothing Material	101.9	100.0	100.7	99.9	99.3	99.1
棉 布	Cotton Cloth	103.3	100.0	103.9	100.0	98.1	96.8
棉花化纤混纺布	Blend Cloth	100.0	100.0	100.0	97.9	100.2	101.6

Consumer Price Indices by Category in Cities and Counties

(Preceding year=100)

昌吉市 Changji City	库尔勒市 Korla City	阿克苏市 Aksu City	焉耆回族自治县 Yanqi Hui Autonomous County	塔城市 Tacheng [Qoqek] City	阿勒泰市 Altay City	乌苏市 Usu City	博乐市 Bole [Bortala] City	吐鲁番市 Turpan City	库车县 Kuqa County	阿图什市 Artux City	莎车县 Shache [Yarkant] County	奎屯市 Kuytun City	石河子市 Shihezi City
103.3	**103.9**	**102.2**	**103.2**	**100.7**	**103.2**	**104.7**	**102.8**	**104.7**	**107.0**	**103.3**	**106.4**	**102.7**	**102.8**
110.4	**108.4**	**105.9**	**107.9**	**105.9**	**109.7**	**108.6**	**104.3**	**110.2**	**114.2**	**107.5**	**113.2**	**103.9**	**107.7**
117.7	118.7	117.9	117.5	122.7	116.4	118.6	116.2	111.8	120.4	114.3	115.3	119.3	118.3
127.9	130.2	131.9	124.6	133.4	133.4	125.0	127.4	121.1	132.3	130.5	136.1	137.0	129.0
113.9	117.4	110.3	113.4	129.0	110.6	115.9	114.0	104.3	109.5	109.6	95.5	106.4	115.1
109.4	105.1	111.3	112.1	110.1	98.1	113.1	101.2	106.8	111.7	102.6	109.9	120.2	102.0
109.3	0.0	101.1	121.1	0.0	105.9	109.2	109.1	116.1	121.1	124.6	184.9	100.3	123.5
102.9	116.6	100.9	95.0	84.6	100.0	88.6	103.9	122.5	125.7	112.4	76.6	100.2	109.1
110.8	119.4	106.9	116.1	118.0	116.0	116.1	112.0	105.7	120.6	127.1	128.5	119.6	129.0
109.5	104.3	108.4	105.4	106.6	101.5	108.2	101.1	107.8	118.8	106.5	115.0	109.6	106.1
106.2	106.7	107.4	109.0	108.5	110.1	103.8	104.2	112.9	111.4	114.0	113.2	102.0	116.2
114.0	123.6	114.4	119.9	129.5	123.2	105.3	127.5	124.3	106.4	106.1	109.7	109.9	108.1
125.3	120.7	126.6	105.4	111.6	113.2	114.8	136.3	122.0	112.7	106.4	108.2	122.5	116.1
115.4	103.8	95.3	110.1	90.7	110.9	123.9	86.3	102.3	116.8	99.8	133.9	96.0	99.2
115.8	103.5	95.1	112.0	86.9	111.3	127.5	84.1	102.7	120.1	99.0	136.4	95.8	99.9
103.6	100.3	99.2	95.2	97.7	102.8	105.7	97.5	91.9	101.5	119.2	98.7	106.2	97.4
98.9	100.9	101.4	96.0	85.3	99.1	99.9	100.8	98.9	104.0	103.7	99.3	104.2	105.5
104.0	101.0	102.1	100.4	93.4	100.8	100.0	99.7	98.8	112.8	103.8	96.2	103.1	97.6
96.1	102.0	103.4	98.0	78.4	101.4	100.0	95.2	91.8	118.1	108.9	96.3	91.2	101.7
109.1	99.7	102.2	102.8	106.6	99.9	100.0	105.1	103.0	109.2	100.0	94.8	110.4	97.4
98.6	100.1	100.0	99.0	99.9	100.4	100.0	101.8	95.7	128.7	101.8	47.5	115.5	97.0
100.0	105.2	102.0	99.4	84.0	97.6	100.0	94.5	100.0	100.0	100.0	133.6	100.0	95.7
100.0	101.3	97.7	96.1	92.1	98.5	100.0	105.3	97.7	103.8	99.9	119.1	100.1	99.7
104.1	116.4	103.0	106.8	112.9	112.6	99.2	93.4	120.5	117.8	101.7	107.9	93.3	96.7
107.2	114.0	94.0	105.0	112.4	113.8	97.1	91.4	127.2	122.4	100.8	108.5	90.7	91.2
95.9	123.3	120.8	110.9	114.6	108.6	105.9	102.8	99.3	111.8	104.4	107.3	99.1	119.7
103.9	98.3	100.0	99.7	102.5	99.9	99.5	107.5	98.3	101.8	103.5	95.3	108.1	102.8
103.1	98.9	100.0	99.2	95.6	103.5	100.0	95.6	95.5	102.6	100.0	99.1	103.2	100.0
103.2	100.9	100.0	101.8	105.4	101.0	100.4	107.6	102.0	112.6	105.0	99.9	93.5	103.5
101.5	102.5	100.0	103.4	108.1	100.0	100.0	105.4	100.0	105.8	112.5	101.2	104.3	104.4
104.2	99.8	100.0	100.8	102.9	102.3	100.0	112.4	104.5	118.9	100.6	97.9	91.6	104.1
104.4	100.0	100.0	102.6	105.7	100.0	106.3	101.3	100.0	109.1	100.0	100.0	100.0	100.0
98.4	100.3	98.4	105.0	85.0	97.7	114.2	96.4	100.4	100.0	100.0	94.9	102.0	100.0
101.2	**100.8**	**99.6**	**99.1**	**95.4**	**100.8**	**100.0**	**100.7**	**103.3**	**103.4**	**103.9**	**114.5**	**101.7**	**101.0**
98.7	97.8	97.8	100.4	88.1	98.0	100.0	100.0	102.3	105.8	109.6	102.2	103.8	102.5
103.8	102.6	101.7	97.2	105.8	105.4	100.0	101.9	104.3	99.8	99.0	124.9	99.6	100.5
96.0	104.7	100.0	99.8	91.1	94.7	100.0	98.2	100.0	98.7	94.7	90.3	100.0	97.7
99.4	**99.6**	**100.9**	**98.5**	**102.1**	**97.6**	**100.3**	**106.6**	**102.9**	**99.9**	**96.6**	**103.6**	**101.0**	**99.1**
97.8	98.6	99.5	97.6	102.8	96.5	100.1	109.5	105.3	99.6	95.8	103.6	101.1	98.8
103.8	101.5	99.7	100.0	98.7	106.6	101.7	103.5	100.4	100.0	95.4	99.3	100.9	99.9
108.8	103.0	100.0	100.0	100.0	112.7	111.0	112.4	104.4	100.0	110.8	114.4	101.4	100.0
100.0	101.4	100.0	100.0	100.0	116.5	100.0	102.4	100.0	100.0	86.8	100.0	100.0	99.1

7-3 续表

(上年=100)

项 目	Item	乌鲁木齐市 Urumqi City	喀什市 Kashgar [Kaxgar] City	伊宁市 Yining [Gulja] City	和田市 Hotan City	克拉玛依市 Karamay City	哈密市 Hami [Kumul] City
化纤布	Chemical Fiber Cloth	100.0	100.0	100.0	96.7	99.7	100.0
毛织品	Woolen Fabric	100.0	100.0	116.6	101.4	99.5	96.9
丝织品	Silk	100.0	100.0	100.7	100.0	98.0	100.0
毛 线	Wool	105.3	100.0	84.3	104.0	100.1	100.0
其 它	The Others	100.3	100.0	100.0	100.0	99.6	
鞋袜帽	Footwear and Hats	93.7	100.0	99.6	98.9	99.0	95.9
鞋	Shoes	93.8	100.0	99.3	98.7	98.9	95.3
袜 子	Socks and Stockings	91.5	100.0	101.5	100.0	98.3	97.1
帽 子	Hats	100.0	100.0	100.0	100.0	101.5	100.0
衣着加工服务	Clothing Processing	100.0	100.6	93.9	100.0	100.2	100.0
家庭设备及用品	**Household Facilities and Articles**	**98.1**	**95.5**	**95.8**	**99.9**	**98.1**	**96.0**
耐用消费品	Durable Consumer Goods	97.9	96.0	94.7	99.6	97.8	92.4
家 具	Furniture	97.0	95.5	89.2	100.0	98.6	95.4
家庭设备	Household Facilities	98.5	96.4	96.9	99.5	97.2	91.3
室内装饰品	Interior Decorations	92.1	98.8	98.6	100.0	99.9	98.2
床上用品	Bed Articles	101.0	99.2	96.4	100.7	96.2	96.7
家庭日用杂品	Daily Use Household Articles	100.6	90.8	95.7	100.0	97.8	97.8
家庭服务及加工维修服务	Household Service	97.5	105.1	100.0	100.0	100.0	106.0
医疗保健和个人用品	**Medicine and Personal Articles**	**100.6**	**98.1**	**102.3**	**93.7**	**100.6**	**98.1**
医疗保健	Medicine	101.8	96.3	103.2	89.3	99.1	96.4
医疗器具及用品	Medical Appliances and Articles	100.0	104.1	103.2	95.0	112.1	92.2
中药材及中成药	Traditional Chinese Medicine	98.6	93.2	104.7	88.1	102.0	94.7
西 药	Western Medicine	102.9	95.5	96.5	88.6	96.8	95.0
保健器具及用品	Constitutional Appliances and Articles	103.7	100.7	96.8	84.6	96.1	98.5
医疗保健服务	Medical and Health Service	101.8	102.6	125.5	100.0	100.0	103.7
个人用品及服务	Personal Articles and Services	98.1	100.9	101.2	101.7	101.9	100.1
交通和通讯	**Transportation and Communication**	**100.1**	**99.7**	**99.0**	**100.4**	**98.6**	**97.6**
交 通	Transportation	101.4	101.9	101.2	101.3	100.2	98.2
通 讯	Communication	99.1	96.9	97.2	100.0	97.1	96.5
娱乐教育文化用品及服务	**Recreation, Education, Culture Articles and Services**	**96.8**	**99.7**	**101.9**	**99.7**	**99.2**	**97.7**
文娱用耐用消费品	Durable Consumer Goods for Recreationl Use	93.0	92.1	92.2	99.0	95.4	95.9
教 育	Education	100.1	104.1	108.2	100.0	100.8	101.4
文化娱乐用品	Cultural and Recreational Articles	101.3	97.7	99.5	100.0	100.2	98.2
文化娱乐	Culture and Recreation	99.6	94.3	96.9	100.0	98.5	96.9
书报杂志	Newspapers and Magazines	101.5	100.8	102.1	100.0	100.0	100.0
文娱费	Recreation	103.1	100.7	100.0	100.0	106.2	97.9
旅游及外出	Touristry and Outside	87.1	95.9	100.0	100.0	104.2	90.8
居 住	**Residence**	**107.9**	**103.2**	**107.3**	**102.4**	**118.4**	**101.8**
建房及装修材料	Builing and handling Materials	106.6	100.4	101.2	100.0	100.5	95.8
租 房	Tenancy	127.1	100.0	100.0	100.0	106.6	100.0
自有住房	Housing	100.7	98.3	101.5	100.1	100.2	103.6
水、电、燃料	Water, ElectriCity and Fuels	108.0	106.7	113.4	104.8	131.6	106.1
服务项目价格指数	**Services**	**99.6**	**100.6**	**104.5**	**100.3**	**101.5**	**100.4**

Continued

(Preceding year=100)

昌吉市 Changji City	库尔勒市 Korla City	阿克苏市 Aksu City	焉耆回族自治县 Yanqi Hui Autonomous County	塔城市 Tacheng [Qoqek] City	阿勒泰市 Altay City	乌苏市 Usu City	博乐市 Bole [Bortala] City	吐鲁番市 Turpan City	库车县 Kuqa County	阿图什市 Artux City	莎车县 Shache [Yarkant] County	奎屯市 Kuytun City	石河子市 Shihezi City
103.3	98.6	100.0	100.0	100.0	104.9	101.1	100.9	101.5	100.0	96.5	100.0	104.5	100.0
100.2	103.2	100.0	100.0	110.7	103.7	100.0	95.5	100.0	100.0	91.8	89.4	100.0	100.0
100.0	100.0	100.0	100.0	100.0	106.9	100.0	102.2	102.1	100.0	92.2	100.0	100.0	100.0
104.5	100.4	98.2	100.0	87.6	101.2	100.0	98.5	97.0	100.0	96.0	100.0	100.0	100.0
126.3		100.0	100.0			100.0	120.0	101.8	100.0	100.0	107.1	100.0	100.0
100.9	101.1	104.4	100.0	100.3	96.9	100.0	100.9	98.7	100.2	97.7	105.2	101.2	98.9
100.4	101.7	105.5	100.0	100.2	96.7	100.0	105.2	99.3	100.2	97.8	105.2	103.3	98.8
103.8	94.3	101.5	100.0	101.0	100.0	100.0	95.1	94.7	100.0	97.6	106.5	93.6	100.1
100.0	94.6	100.0	100.0	100.0	100.0	100.0	87.4	100.0	100.0	96.5	97.9	99.5	93.4
100.0	101.0	100.0	96.8	100.0	98.7	100.0	115.1	100.0	100.0	109.6	101.9	97.4	100.0
98.7	**99.0**	**95.8**	**99.8**	**90.4**	**102.2**	**100.1**	**100.0**	**97.1**	**99.5**	**91.5**	**101.1**	**99.7**	**99.9**
97.4	98.7	93.4	99.6	87.3	99.5	100.0	100.1	94.5	98.6	89.0	100.2	99.8	96.7
99.4	99.5	89.9	101.3	86.6	101.7	100.0	96.0	92.9	97.4	92.7	104.4	99.3	94.9
96.5	98.4	96.3	98.7	87.5	98.0	100.0	103.0	95.2	99.8	85.7	97.6	100.0	97.5
96.9	98.5	100.0	100.0	90.9	102.7	100.0	102.4	99.4	100.0	99.3	94.3	99.2	99.4
101.4	102.0	100.0	100.0	100.0	108.3	100.0	105.2	101.7	100.0	88.0	94.6	99.8	98.8
100.0	98.9	96.2	99.9	95.4	102.8	100.3	96.2	98.0	100.0	92.3	110.0	100.8	105.2
103.3	100.0	101.9	100.0	98.6	100.6	100.0	103.4	100.0	100.9	101.8	103.4	98.6	100.0
98.6	**103.9**	**103.8**	**99.1**	**96.9**	**100.2**	**111.5**	**100.4**	**97.7**	**106.4**	**99.7**	**98.8**	**110.6**	**98.6**
97.1	104.9	106.5	99.1	95.9	98.5	122.1	95.3	96.6	110.1	101.9	97.2	106.7	95.3
100.0	100.6	94.3	100.0	76.0	96.7	100.0	97.6	105.4	103.1	97.1	101.5	101.3	107.2
101.7	103.3	101.5	96.1	95.8	95.2	106.6	97.3	105.3	98.3	100.0	92.9	100.7	89.5
92.1	99.8	97.4	100.2	88.5	94.6	100.7	89.2	89.3	95.5	96.3	100.6	102.1	88.3
100.8	100.1	80.4	96.7	94.6	94.4	99.9	94.9	96.3	98.4	99.1	100.2	100.0	98.7
101.4	126.1	127.7	100.0	102.5	107.1	165.4	104.3	101.5	125.3	122.8	95.6	123.1	98.1
100.1	102.9	101.2	99.1	99.0	103.6	100.5	106.3	100.6	100.9	95.8	100.9	115.0	101.9
97.3	**100.5**	**94.9**	**99.9**	**101.4**	**98.6**	**100.9**	**101.6**	**96.5**	**102.6**	**102.6**	**96.3**	**100.4**	**97.5**
100.4	102.0	101.4	103.0	103.2	100.0	101.9	109.4	100.8	106.5	108.0	101.5	100.5	98.8
93.8	99.3	89.6	97.9	98.7	97.3	100.0	95.4	93.8	98.6	97.3	92.1	99.3	95.8
98.1	**100.3**	**98.1**	**100.7**	**94.5**	**99.2**	**100.1**	**100.1**	**99.2**	**100.4**	**99.7**	**97.6**	**101.0**	**99.8**
93.4	99.7	91.0	99.3	88.7	95.1	100.0	96.7	93.2	99.2	91.5	95.5	99.9	99.3
101.9	100.2	99.8	100.8	98.7	100.0	100.2	101.1	99.0	100.6	102.0	98.0	105.5	100.0
100.5	102.5	100.2	100.6	102.2	98.6	99.9	100.9	96.8	101.6	102.2	101.1	101.4	100.2
99.5	100.4	99.2	100.0	97.6	97.1	99.9	100.7	93.6	99.9	93.6	99.2	101.1	100.3
99.1	100.7	100.0	104.3	104.4	100.0	100.0	104.3	100.5	100.0	108.8	99.4	101.8	100.0
103.6	109.0	101.4	100.0	105.0	100.0	100.0	98.5	100.0	107.5	106.4	104.3	101.6	100.2
97.8	100.2	100.1	104.6	75.8	107.5	100.0	102.9	126.3	123.0	100.0	98.7	101.6	100.0
102.6	**106.3**	**105.5**	**107.5**	**101.4**	**102.7**	**104.3**	**102.0**	**108.6**	**103.2**	**107.5**	**112.8**	**102.9**	**105.1**
103.1	101.9	103.6	100.9	100.4	98.8	100.0	98.6	101.2	101.5	99.0	110.4	100.0	99.1
100.0	109.8	100.0	100.0	105.6	106.9	100.0	101.4	100.0	100.0	131.0	101.4	100.0	112.8
105.3	100.2	99.3	111.0	99.5	100.3	100.3	97.1	101.1	100.0	107.4		101.6	100.2
102.5	110.7	114.7	109.2	102.5	107.4	110.6	107.7	117.3	107.0	110.7	115.9	110.4	109.3
100.7	**101.8**	**100.3**	**101.7**	**99.5**	**102.1**	**105.8**	**103.5**	**101.9**	**105.1**	**106.4**	**98.0**	**110.4**	**100.0**

7-4 商品零售价格分类指数

Retail Price Indices by Category of Commodities

(上年=100) (2004 年) (Preceding year=100)

项目	Item	全区 Province	城市 Urban Areas	农村 Rural Areas
商品零售价格指数	**General Retail Price Index**	**100.7**	**99.4**	**103.2**
食品类	**Food**	**103.3**	**100.1**	**109.0**
粮 食	Grain	115.2	112.9	118.1
油 脂	Oil or Fat	108.6	108.4	109.2
肉禽及其制品	Meat, Poultry and Their Products	108.5	108.8	108.1
猪 肉	Pork	129.1	131.0	126.1
牛 肉	Beef	104.6	105.0	104.2
羊 肉	Lamb	102.5	104.5	99.8
鸡	Chicken	107.2	104.5	112.6
鲜 蛋	Fresh Egg	110.7	106.4	117.6
水产品	Aquatic Products	122.5	123.8	119.8
鲜 果	Fresh Fruits	91.5	85.1	102.9
糕 点	Cake	99.8	99.4	100.9
饮料、烟酒	**Beverage, Tobacco and Wine**	**98.7**	**97.9**	**100.1**
茶及饮料	Tea and Drinks	98.3	98.0	98.8
#饮 料	Beverage	97.8	98.1	96.9
烟 草	Tobacco	96.3	94.9	98.7
酒	Liquor	101.6	101.2	102.3
服装鞋帽	**Garments, Shoes and Hats**	**99.1**	**98.2**	**101.1**
服 装	Garments	99.7	99.0	101.4
鞋袜帽	Shoes, Stocks and Hats	97.8	96.1	100.7
#鞋	Shoes	97.9	95.9	101.4
纺织品类	**Textiles**	**100.3**	**100.8**	**99.6**
棉 布	Cotton Cloth	104.4	101.6	106.8
棉花化纤混纺布	Blend Cloth	100.4	100.2	100.5
化纤布	Chemical Fiber Cloth	100.2	99.9	100.6
毛织品	Woolen Fabric	99.7	100.2	98.8
毛 线	Wool	98.6	99.8	97.1
家用电器及音响器材	**Electric Household Appliance and Sound Apparatus**	**95.2**	**95.1**	**95.3**
家庭设备	Household Facilities	95.8	96.2	95.0
文娱用耐用消费品	Durable Consuming Goods for Entertainment	94.3	93.4	95.4
音响器材类	Sound Apparatus	97.5	96.9	98.6

7-4 续表 Continued

(上年=100) (Preceding year=100)

项　目	Item	全　区 Province	城　市 Urban Areas	农　村 Rural Areas
文化办公用品	**Cultural and Office Goods**	**96.1**	**95.5**	**98.0**
日用品	**Articles for Daily Use**	**98.9**	**98.8**	**99.1**
日用百货	Merchandiles for Daily Use	98.9	99.0	98.7
日用杂品	Sundries for Daily Use	100.0	99.3	101.2
洗涤用品	Washing and Cleaning Goods	99.1	100.3	95.6
其他日用品	Other Daily-use Goods	98.1	97.1	100.1
体育娱乐用品	**Sports and Entertainment Goods**	**98.4**	**98.3**	**98.5**
体育用品	Sports Goods	97.7	97.2	98.2
娱乐用品	Recreational Goods	98.9	99.0	98.8
交通、通信用品	**Traffic and Telecommunication Goods**	**92.5**	**90.7**	**95.3**
交通运输机械	Traffic and Transport Machinery	96.4	94.5	98.8
通讯器材类	Telecommunication Apparatus	89.1	88.0	91.2
家　具	**Furniture**	**97.5**	**97.4**	**97.8**
化妆品类	**Cosmetics**	**100.9**	**101.7**	**99.2**
金银珠宝类	**Gold and Silver Jewls**	**107.5**	**105.8**	**111.5**
中西药品及医疗保健用品类	**Chinese and Western Medicine, Medical-care and Healthy Goods**	**99.9**	**102.3**	**95.0**
医疗器具及用品	Medical-care Apparatus and Goods	103.8	107.7	98.9
中药材及中成药	Chinese Herbs and Patent Medicine	103.1	105.9	97.2
西　药	Western Medicine	97.0	99.5	91.8
保健器具及用品	Healthy Devices and Goods	97.3	97.3	97.5
书报杂志及电子出版物类	**Books, Magazines and Electronic Publications**	**99.9**	**99.7**	**100.3**
教材及参考书	Texts and Reference Books	103.6	106.9	98.8
书报杂志	Newspapers and Magazines	102.1	100.5	106.1
电子音像制品	Electronic Audio and Video Products	94.6	94.2	95.8
燃料类	**Fuel**	**108.4**	**108.2**	**108.7**
煤炭及制品类	Coal and Its Products	102.2	95.5	106.7
石油及制品类	Oil and its Products	111.5	111.9	110.9
建筑器材及五金电料类	**Building Apparatus and Hardwares**	**101.4**	**101.2**	**101.8**
建筑装璜材料	Building Decoration Materials	100.8	100.4	101.4
五金电料类	Hardwares and Electrical Apparatus	103.0	103.0	102.7

7-5 各市县商品零售价格分类指数

(上年=100) (2004 年)

项目	Item	乌鲁木齐市 Urumqi City	喀什市 Kashgar [Kaxgar] City	伊宁市 Yining [Gulja] City	和田市 Hotan City	克拉玛依市 Karamay City	哈密市 Hami [Kumul] City
商品零售价格指数	**General Retail Price Index**	**101.1**	**100.9**	**103.3**	**102.9**	**101.7**	**101.3**
食品类	**Food**	**102.0**	**105.4**	**108.7**	**109.1**	**105.3**	**108.0**
粮　食	Grain	115.2	116.6	116.0	114.4	113.5	115.2
油　脂	Oil or Fat	105.0	104.2	108.1	111.2	115.9	108.4
肉禽及其制品	Meat, Poultry and Their Products	107.5	109.4	110.5	115.8	107.8	107.7
猪　肉	Pork	127.9	124.3	139.4	102.0	123.6	130.1
牛　肉	Beef	105.7	106.5	104.4	124.2	102.8	104.9
羊　肉	Lamb	99.7	106.9	100.1	122.5	98.1	94.8
鸡	Chicken	110.4	108.0	115.3	113.0	107.3	109.0
鲜　蛋	Fresh Egg	116.8	110.4	117.4	111.3	115.8	107.8
水产品	Aquatic Products	118.3	120.6	129.3	99.7	121.2	117.4
鲜　果	Fresh Fruits	103.8	122.5	97.0	104.5	96.9	107.6
糕　点	Cake	98.1	100.0	94.2	100.0	100.5	100.0
饮料、烟酒	**Beverage, Tobacco and Wine**	**99.1**	**96.1**	**98.6**	**100.6**	**102.2**	**99.5**
茶及饮料	Tea and Drinks	100.2	94.1	91.5	98.4	102.4	96.1
#饮　料	Beverage	101.1	92.6	88.6	96.9	98.6	94.6
烟　草	Tobacco	96.6	97.4	102.0	105.7	95.1	99.6
酒	Liquor	102.4	94.4	101.7	97.2	107.9	100.6
服装鞋帽	**Garments, Shoes and Hats**	**99.1**	**100.0**	**98.6**	**99.6**	**99.7**	**96.8**
服　装	Garments	101.7	100.1	97.7	99.9	100.1	97.4
鞋袜帽	Shoes, Stocks and Hats	93.7	100.0	99.6	99.0	98.7	95.8
#鞋	Shoes	93.8	100.0	99.3	98.5	98.5	95.2
纺织品类	**Textiles**	**101.3**	**99.8**	**99.0**	**100.1**	**97.8**	**98.1**
棉　布	Cotton Cloth	103.3	100.0	103.9	100.0	98.1	96.8
棉花化纤混纺布	Blend Cloth	100.0	100.0	100.0	97.9	100.1	101.6
化纤布	Chemical Fiber Cloth	100.0	100.0	100.0	96.7	99.7	100.0
毛织品	Woolen Fabric	100.0	100.0	116.6	101.4	99.5	96.9
毛　线	Wool	105.3	100.0	84.3	104.0	99.8	100.0
家用电器及音响器材	**Electric Household Appliance and Sound Apparatus**	**96.2**	**93.2**	**95.2**	**99.2**	**95.6**	**93.4**
家庭设备	Household Facilities	98.5	95.4	97.8	99.3	96.9	91.0
文娱用耐用消费品	Recreational and Durable Goods	93.0	90.4	88.6	98.9	94.3	95.7
音响器材类	Sound Apparatus	98.8	100.0	90.0	100.0	94.5	96.6

Retail Price Indices by Category of Commoditles in Cities and Counties

(Preceding year=100)

昌吉市 Changji City	库尔勒市 Korla City	阿克苏市 Aksu City	焉耆回族自治县 Yanqi Hui Autonomous County	塔城市 Tacheng [Qoqek] City	阿勒泰市 Altay City	乌苏市 Usu City	博乐市 Bole [Bortala] City	吐鲁番市 Turpan City	库车县 Kuqa County	阿图什市 Artux City	莎车县 Shache [Yarkant] County	奎屯市 Kuytun City	石河子市 Shihezi City
103.0	**104.3**	**101.8**	**103.2**	**100.4**	**103.7**	**104.3**	**102.2**	**103.0**	**105.1**	**102.6**	**105.4**	**102.2**	**102.7**
110.5	**109.2**	**106.0**	**107.3**	**106.4**	**109.7**	**109.6**	**104.7**	**110.3**	**114.4**	**108.8**	**112.6**	**105.0**	**108.2**
117.4	120.4	117.6	117.5	122.2	120.1	118.5	114.6	111.9	120.7	116.6	124.7	116.8	119.2
109.6	105.8	108.4	106.0	107.0	101.5	107.8	100.7	108.8	118.8	115.5	114.4	112.1	106.1
106.1	107.6	107.4	108.1	108.5	110.0	104.5	104.3	112.7	110.2	111.8	108.6	102.8	116.0
123.6	131.1	111.9	135.2	142.3	132.6	112.0	131.6	131.5	114.7	100.0	116.0	102.1	124.2
102.3	105.8	116.3	106.4	100.0	103.7	102.2	107.4	106.2	108.7	120.0	115.8	100.9	120.3
98.9	102.6	110.5	102.2	93.7	96.4	95.5	94.1	100.8	110.2	113.0	110.2	97.2	96.0
105.5	106.8	98.1	111.6	115.4	105.9	98.9	107.2	125.9	115.1	116.4	127.1	103.3	119.4
116.5	122.5	114.9	119.8	130.5	125.8	105.6	135.6	125.0	105.4	106.6	111.4	110.5	109.8
125.3	111.7	126.6	105.7	111.7	115.5	115.2	128.0	122.3	112.7	108.7	104.4	120.8	116.4
107.2	114.0	94.0	105.0	112.4	113.8	97.1	91.4	127.2	122.4	100.8	110.1	90.7	91.2
100.0	100.0	100.0	99.4	98.5	100.0	97.2	105.9	99.2	102.6	100.0	119.9	117.6	103.4
100.7	**101.0**	**99.4**	**98.5**	**96.3**	**101.5**	**100.0**	**102.2**	**101.2**	**103.6**	**102.4**	**124.8**	**101.5**	**100.5**
100.0	102.1	95.5	95.7	92.3	98.8	100.0	106.8	98.8	104.0	100.0	148.2	100.1	99.8
100.3	99.9	94.3	96.7	92.1	100.0	100.0	96.5	95.2	101.7	100.0	101.2	100.1	99.7
99.0	98.4	98.2	100.4	88.1	98.8	100.0	100.0	102.3	106.0	104.9	102.3	103.3	101.3
103.7	103.4	101.7	97.5	105.8	105.2	100.0	101.0	104.3	99.8	100.5	127.7	99.5	100.1
99.1	**100.2**	**101.4**	**98.2**	**102.3**	**97.3**	**100.1**	**103.5**	**103.0**	**99.8**	**97.4**	**103.6**	**101.5**	**98.6**
97.9	100.1	99.5	97.2	103.0	96.3	100.3	108.5	105.4	99.6	97.0	103.9	101.9	99.0
101.0	100.3	104.4	100.0	100.3	98.2	100.0	99.5	98.7	100.2	97.0	104.4	101.2	97.4
100.4	102.1	105.5	100.0	100.2	96.5	100.0	104.4	99.3	100.2	97.1	105.5	103.2	98.6
102.2	**101.5**	**99.8**	**100.0**	**99.3**	**107.1**	**101.0**	**105.0**	**101.0**	**100.0**	**93.6**	**98.0**	**100.6**	**99.0**
108.8	103.0	100.0	100.0	100.0	112.7	111.0	112.4	104.4	100.0	110.8	114.4	101.4	100.0
100.0	101.4	100.0	100.0	100.0	116.5	100.0	102.4	100.0	100.0	86.8	100.0	100.0	99.1
103.3	98.6	100.0	100.0	100.0	104.9	101.1	100.9	101.5	100.0	96.5	100.0	104.5	100.0
100.2	103.2	100.0	100.0	110.7	103.7	100.0	95.5	100.0	100.0	91.8	89.4	100.0	100.0
104.5	100.4	98.2	100.0	87.6	101.2	100.0	98.5	97.0	100.0	96.0	100.0	100.0	100.0
95.9	**98.7**	**93.9**	**99.3**	**80.9**	**97.7**	**100.0**	**99.6**	**93.2**	**99.6**	**88.0**	**95.7**	**100.0**	**98.5**
96.9	98.7	95.9	100.1	83.3	99.2	100.0	102.0	94.8	99.8	86.1	96.9	100.1	97.9
92.2	99.0	90.9	99.3	83.7	95.4	100.0	97.4	90.9	98.9	90.3	94.2	99.8	99.4
97.9	96.0	100.0	95.1	68.1	100.0		98.3		100.0		100.0	100.0	100.0

7-5 续表

(上年=100)

项目	Item	乌鲁木齐市 Urumqi City	喀什市 Kashgar [Kaxgar] City	伊宁市 Yining [Gulja] City	和田市 Hotan City	克拉玛依市 Karamay City	哈密市 Hami [Kumul] City
文化办公用品	**Cultural and Office Goods**	**97.0**	**93.8**	**95.5**	**99.9**	**95.8**	**95.2**
日用品	**Articles for Daily Use**	**97.8**	**96.0**	**99.2**	**100.0**	**98.0**	**97.8**
日用百货	Daily Merchandiles	98.1	101.3	100.9	100.1	98.0	97.7
日用杂品	Sundries for Daily Use	97.4	100.0	101.3	100.0	98.1	96.5
洗涤用品	Washing and Cleaning Goods	98.7	89.1	97.2	100.0	96.6	98.0
其他日用品	Other Daily Goods	95.2	100.0	98.4	100.1	99.8	99.3
体育娱乐用品	**Sports and Creational Goods**	**94.6**	**95.8**	**100.4**	**100.7**	**98.8**	**98.3**
体育用品	Sports Goods	93.1	92.6	100.0	100.3	96.3	97.6
娱乐用品	Recreational Goods	95.9	99.2	100.7	101.2	100.5	100.0
交通、通信用品	**Traffic and Telecommunication Goods**	**92.9**	**90.8**	**89.8**	**99.1**	**94.9**	**93.0**
交通运输机械	Traffic and Transport Machinery	92.7	93.2	94.7	97.8	96.6	92.3
通讯器材类	Telecommunication Apparatus	93.1	87.4	85.3	99.4	93.2	94.1
家具	**Furniture**	**98.3**	**95.5**	**89.2**	**100.0**	**98.6**	**95.4**
化妆品类	**Cosmetic Products**	**98.9**	**99.8**	**95.0**	**100.1**	**97.2**	**94.2**
金银珠宝类	**Gold and Silver Jewls**	**109.7**	**106.2**	**111.8**	**103.3**	**107.7**	**108.1**
中西药品及医疗保健用品类	**Chinese and Western Medicine, Medical-care and Healthy Goods**	**101.7**	**95.6**	**99.4**	**87.9**	**100.7**	**95.1**
医疗器具及用品	Medical-care Apparatus and Goods	100.0	104.1	103.2	95.0	112.1	92.2
中药材及中成药	Chinese Herbs and Patent Medicine	98.8	92.9	104.7	88.1	102.0	94.7
西药	Western Medicine	103.4	95.5	96.5	88.2	96.8	94.9
保健器具及用品	Healthy Apparatus and Goods	103.7	100.4	96.8	84.8	96.1	98.5
书报杂志及电子出版物类	**Newspapers, Magazines and Electronic Publications**	**99.9**	**104.2**	**100.5**	**100.6**	**101.3**	**99.8**
教材及参考书	Texts and Reference Books	101.3	110.0	99.3	100.0	102.0	100.4
书报杂志	Newspapers and Magazines	101.5	100.9	102.1	100.0	100.0	100.0
电子音像制品	Electronic Audio and Video Products	92.8	98.7	100.0	101.6	101.4	97.4
燃料类	**Fuels**	**109.9**	**111.5**	**114.8**	**105.2**	**118.7**	**109.5**
煤炭及制品类	Coal and its Products	91.7	103.4	111.4	103.8	103.7	107.2
石油及制品类	Oil and its Products	113.1	115.2	115.1	107.3	125.6	111.1
建筑器材及五金电料类	**Building Apparatus, Hardware and Electrical Apparatus**	**103.3**	**102.6**	**100.4**	**100.0**	**101.4**	**95.9**
建筑装璜材料	Building Decoration Materials	103.0	101.0	101.2	100.0	100.2	95.8
五金电料类	Hardware and Electrical Apparatus	104.0	108.5	97.4	100.0	103.1	96.0

Continued

(Preceding year=100)

昌吉市 Changji City	库尔勒市 Korla City	阿克苏市 Aksu City	焉耆回族自治县 Yanqi Hui Autonomous County	塔城市 Tacheng [Qoqek] City	阿勒泰市 Altay City	乌苏市 Usu City	博乐市 Bole [Bortala] City	吐鲁番市 Turpan City	库车县 Kuqa County	阿图什市 Artux City	莎车县 Shache [Yarkant] County	奎屯市 Kuytun City	石河子市 Shihezi City
98.6	**99.8**	**95.1**	**100.6**	**99.6**	**96.1**	**100.0**	**94.8**	**95.3**	**99.9**	**95.7**	**99.8**	**100.2**	**90.8**
98.8	**100.1**	**96.8**	**99.8**	**92.9**	**99.6**	**100.1**	**98.2**	**94.6**	**100.0**	**97.2**	**102.6**	**100.3**	**102.3**
98.5	98.9	98.1	101.5	82.9	100.3	100.0	97.1	93.3	100.0	96.7	97.3	100.6	100.7
98.1	103.4	100.3	100.0	100.0	106.7	100.3	98.1	98.4	100.0	93.1	116.5	99.2	109.3
100.4	100.1	90.3	98.3	90.0	90.6	100.0	90.6	92.4	100.0	97.9	99.2	101.1	99.4
99.3	99.7	99.4	100.0	96.2	99.9	100.0	105.6	98.6	100.0	97.9	100.1	100.4	98.5
97.9	**100.2**	**99.3**	**100.0**	**97.0**	**99.7**	**100.0**	**99.6**	**93.1**	**99.8**	**98.4**	**100.0**	**102.4**	**100.1**
100.0	100.0	99.9	100.0	99.6	100.5	100.0	99.7	90.7	99.6	100.0	100.0	105.7	100.4
95.2	100.5	99.0	100.0	96.7	99.2	100.0	99.6	96.7	100.0	96.5	100.0	100.0	99.7
91.2	**98.6**	**95.6**	**94.6**	**97.4**	**93.5**	**100.0**	**88.4**	**83.1**	**98.6**	**94.3**	**93.9**	**99.4**	**92.5**
95.7	100.0	97.4	97.8	101.0	95.2	100.0	98.8	96.1	100.0	99.4	97.8	99.9	93.7
86.0	95.6	92.7	93.1	90.6	91.8	100.0	80.0	74.5	96.8	89.9	91.6	98.8	90.5
100.1	**100.1**	**90.0**	**101.2**	**86.8**	**102.0**	**100.0**	**95.8**	**92.9**	**96.8**	**93.4**	**103.4**	**99.2**	**93.8**
100.1	**105.7**	**98.4**	**98.1**	**101.2**	**96.9**	**100.0**	**99.6**	**91.8**	**100.0**	**104.4**	**100.0**	**101.1**	**99.1**
109.9	**102.9**	**98.9**	**112.0**	**106.6**	**117.3**	**119.5**	**118.8**	**116.0**	**100.0**	**111.5**	**102.6**	**106.0**	**103.6**
97.3	**101.3**	**95.9**	**98.4**	**91.1**	**95.0**	**101.9**	**94.7**	**97.1**	**99.5**	**97.4**	**99.0**	**100.7**	**93.0**
100.0	100.6	94.3	100.0	76.0	96.7	100.0	97.6	105.4	103.1	97.1	101.5	101.3	107.2
102.3	103.5	103.2	95.6	95.5	94.5	106.1	97.5	105.3	98.6	100.0	93.5	100.9	89.5
92.2	99.4	97.4	100.7	87.7	95.1	100.1	89.5	89.3	95.5	94.5	101.1	100.7	88.4
101.1	100.2	80.4	96.5	94.6	94.3	99.9	95.5	96.3	98.4	99.1	104.0	100.0	98.7
99.8	**101.0**	**98.3**	**101.4**	**101.1**	**98.7**	**100.2**	**101.9**	**95.9**	**100.0**	**108.8**	**99.5**	**100.5**	**100.0**
100.5	101.5	100.0	99.2	98.6	100.4	100.8	100.1	94.9	100.0	100.0	100.0	101.6	100.0
99.2	101.2	100.0	105.8	104.4	100.0	100.0	106.2	100.5	100.0	114.5	99.5	103.1	100.0
99.3	100.0	97.0	100.0	96.2	95.0	100.0	98.7	85.9	100.0	89.3	99.3	97.4	100.0
104.7	**112.0**	**119.3**	**109.3**	**110.6**	**107.2**	**106.3**	**111.7**	**111.2**	**106.2**	**117.7**	**106.5**	**98.2**	**118.3**
100.1	108.7	93.9	109.2	111.9	102.1	100.0	113.4	103.0	100.2	107.8	117.4	84.6	134.5
107.2	113.0	127.2	110.0	111.1	111.1	110.4	111.2	115.6	114.1	119.3	100.5	104.0	111.2
101.8	**100.8**	**102.4**	**99.4**	**100.4**	**105.7**	**100.0**	**103.8**	**98.5**	**102.2**	**99.0**	**108.2**	**99.7**	**99.4**
103.1	101.2	103.6	100.9	100.4	99.8	100.0	100.9	101.2	103.2	98.2	111.8	99.7	98.2
98.8	100.0	97.7	95.7	98.6	115.9	100.0	109.6	93.1	100.0	100.0	99.3	100.0	101.2

7-6 农业生产资料价格分类指数

Indices of Agricultural Means Production by Category

(上年=100) (Preceding year=100)

项 目	Item	1995	2000	2003	2004
农业生产资料价格指数	**General Index**	**126.6**	**97.9**	**101.1**	**107.3**
小农具	Small Fram Tools	124.0	99.1	105.4	108.3
饲料类	Forage	161.3	93.5	100.6	116.4
产品畜	Animals for Products	137.1	94.4	105.9	111.1
役 畜	Animals for Labor Force	148.0	99.7	104.2	103.9
半机械化农具	Semi-mechanized Farm Toowls	109.4	97.8	98.8	102.0
机械化农具	Mechanized Farm Mchinery	122.3	97.7	97.6	99.9
化学肥料	Chemical Fertilizer	130.4	92.8	102.9	109.7
农业及农药械	Pesticide & Its Appliances	103.9	98.5	97.6	100.7
农机用油	Oil for Farm Machinery	126.9	110.3	101.4	112.8
其他农业生产资料	Others	116.0	98.4	98.8	102.8

7-7 各市县农业生产资料价格指数

Price Indices of Agricultural Means of Production by Category in Cities and Counties

(上年=100) (2004 年) (Preceding year=100)

项 目	Item	塔城市 Kashgar [Kaxgar] City	阿勒泰市 Altay City	乌苏市 Usu City	博乐市 Bole [Bortala] City	吐鲁番市 Turpan City	库车县 Kuqa County	阿图什市 Artux City	莎车县 Shache [Yarkant] County	焉耆回族自治县 Yanqi Hui Autonomous County
总指数	**General Index**	**107.8**	**109.0**	**111.2**	**109.3**	**109.3**	**103.6**	**99.1**	**106.0**	**107.8**
小农具	Small Farm Tools	100.0	100.4	104.2	104.9	124.1	100.0	110.5	101.8	111.9
饲料类	Forage	105.0	112.0	129.6	115.3	111.9	104.9	121.3	126.4	115.9
产品畜	Animal for Products	133.5	117.2	104.5	99.6	130.8	99.4	106.4	106.5	143.2
役 畜	Animal for Labor Force	103.4	101.4	100.6	117.5	114.1	99.5	101.8	106.6	107.1
半机械化农具	Semi-mechanized Farm Tools	96.1	106.3	100.0	100.9	100.0	101.5	100.0	102.3	101.2
机械化农具	Mechanized Farm Machinery	106.6	106.5	100.0	100.2	101.6	102.0	100.0	90.9	100.0
化学肥料	Chemical Fertilizer	112.2	114.1	120.8	110.8	114.8	105.1	88.2	108.9	110.4
农药及农药械	Pesticide and Its Appliances	100.2	105.3	99.3	100.1	96.5	101.0	98.7	104.8	96.7
农用机油	Oil for Farm Machinery	102.9	111.5	134.4	107.0	115.6	108.5	106.6	100.0	111.2
其他农业生产资料	Others	114.4	102.3	99.1	125.3	100.4	99.5	99.6	99.7	103.0

7-8 建筑安装工程价格指数
Price Indices of Agricultural Means Production by Category

(上年=100) (Preceding year=100)

项 目	Item	1995	2000	2004
建筑安装工程价格总指数	**General Index**	**105.1**	**105.5**	**105.8**
直接费用价格指数	Price Indices of Direct Expenditures	105.2	105.5	105.8
#人工费	Labour Cost	120.1	108.2	103.0
材料费	Material cost	102.3	104.9	107.7
机械费用费	Usage in Machinary		104.4	101.2
间接费用价格指数	Price Indices of Indirect Expenditures	104.8	105.3	

7-9 房屋销售价格指数
Selling Price Indices of Houses

(上年=100) (2004 年) (Preceding year=100)

项 目	Item	一季度 First Quarter	二季度 Second Quarter	三季度 Third Quarter	四季度 Fourth Quarter
房屋销售价格指数	**Selling Price Indices of Houses**	**100.3**	**101.0**	**101.0**	**100.4**
商品房	Commercial Houses	100.4	101.3	100.9	100.5
住 宅	Residential Buildings	100.1	101.3	101.0	100.2
经济适用房	Economical Houses	99.7	102.2	101.9	100.1
普通住宅	General Residential Buildings	100.8	101.4	100.8	100.1
多层住宅	Multilayer Buildings	101.6	102.0	103.6	101.7
高层住宅	High-rise Apartment Buildings	99.3	99.1	96.5	98.1
豪华住宅	Luxury Residential Buildings	94.4	98.3	100.8	101.3
非住宅	Non-Residential Buildings	101.6	101.3	100.7	101.7
写字楼	Office Buildings	105.0	100.1	101.0	100.0
商业用房	Houses for Business Purpose	101.2	101.4	100.6	102.3

7-10　工业品出厂价格分类指数

Ex-Factory Price Indices of Industrial Products By Category

(上年=100)　　(preceding year=100)

项　　目	Item	1995	2000	2004
全部工业品	**Total Industrial Products**	**117.2**	**129.4**	**116.4**
轻工业	Light Industry	125.1	97.3	106.6
以农产品为原料	Using Farm Produces as Raw Materials	126.9	97.1	108.3
以非农产品为原料	Using Non-farm Produces as Raw Materials	113.2	103.5	103.4
重工业	Heavy Industry	110.0	141.8	119.9
采　掘	Mining and Quarrying	113.7	164.2	130.0
原　料	Raw Materials	108.2	114.3	110.3
加　工	Manufacturing	112.8	98.6	121.6
生产资料	Means of Production	112.2	138.0	117.7
采　掘	Mining and Quarrying	113.7	164.0	129.8
原　料	Raw Materials	111.2	113.7	110.3
加　工	Manufacturing	114.0	97.7	112.1
生活资料	Consumer Goods	124.6	96.6	105.9
食　品	Food	130.0	93.0	107.2
衣　着	Clothing	121.7	100.3	101.9
一般日用品	Articles for Daily Use	122.6	98.1	99.6
耐用消费品	Durable Consumer Goods	101.5	99.7	99.7
按工业部门分	**Division of Industrial Setors**			
冶金工业	Metallurgical Industry	100.8	103.9	127.6
电力工业	Power Industry	120.2	104.8	102.9
煤炭及炼焦工业	Coal and Coking Industry	113.2	98.2	112.5
石油工业	Petroleum Industry	101.1	162.2	123.0
化学工业	Chemical Industry	133.3	102.6	108.5
机械工业	Machine Buiding Industry	105.5	97.4	101.9
建筑材料工业	Buiding Materials Industry	101.5	98.4	99.0
森林工业	Timber Industry	88.1	99.7	99.5
食品工业	Food Industry	130.0	92.2	108.3
纺织工业	Textile Industry	119.9	101.8	111.0
缝纫工业	Tailoring Industry		101.7	102.0
皮革工业	Leather Industry	123.6	95.7	99.7
造纸工业	Paper Industry	149.2	98.4	99.2
文教艺术用品工业	Cultural, Educational and Handicraft Articles	108.5	98.2	99.7
其他工业	Other Industry	157.1	98.8	104.2

7-11 原材料、燃料、动力购进价格分类指数

Purchasing Price Indices of Raw Material, Fuels and Power Purchased by Category of Commodities

(上年=100) (Preceding year=100)

项目	Iterm	1995	2000	2004
全部原材料价格指数	**Total of Raw Material**	**116.9**	**115.2**	**118.2**
燃料、动力类	Fuels and Power	117.0	137.9	120.6
黑色金属材料类	Material of Black Metal	96.1	100.5	127.8
#钢　材	Rolled Steel	96.1	104.8	125.4
其　他	Other	96.5	95.5	130.7
有色金属材料和电线类	Material of Coloured Metal	125.1	112.2	115.5
化工原料类	Material of Chemistry	125.4	104.4	106.6
木材及纸浆类	Wood and Paper Pulp	100.9	100.5	103.9
建筑材料及非金属矿类	Building Material and Non-metal Ore	95.5	100.4	100.1
其他工业原材料及半成品类	Other Industrial Raw Material and Semi-finished Category	103.2	111.4	112.0
农副产品类	Agricultural and Side-line Produces	152.0	97.2	121.1
纺织原料类	Textile Raw Material	125.1	95.2	117.9

7-12 固定资产投资价格指数

Price Indices of Investment in Fixed Assets

(上年=100) (preceding year=100)

项目	Item	1995	2000	2004
固定资产投资	**Investment in Fixed Assets**	**106.2**	**103.6**	**104.5**
建筑安装工程	**Construction and Installtion**	**105.1**	**105.5**	**105.8**
直接工程费	Expenses of Direct Project	105.2	105.5	105.8
人工费	Manpower Expenses	120.1	108.2	103.0
材料费	Material Expenses	102.3	104.9	107.7
#钢　材	Rolled Steel	96.3	108.3	113.2
木　材	Timber	106.8	102.2	104.8
水　泥	Cement	109.7	100.6	101.1
地方材料	Material Local	103.4	102.8	102.1
化工材料	Material Chemical		107.4	105.1
电　料	Electrical Wire		99.2	103.3
其他材料	Other Material	92.8	102.9	101.8
机械使用费	Expenses of Machine Use		104.4	101.2
间接费用	Indirect Expense	104.8	105.3	
设备工器具	**Purchase of Equipment,Tools and Instruments**	**112.7**	**97.4**	**101.9**
其他费用	**Others**	**125.0**	**103.2**	**100.7**

主要统计指标解释

商品零售价格指数 是反映城乡商品零售价格变动趋势的一种经济指数。零售物价的调整变动直接影响到城乡居民的生活支出和国家的财政收入，影响居民购买力和市场供需平衡，影响消费与积累的比例。因此，计算零售价格指数，可以从一个侧面对上述经济活动进行观察和分析。

居民消费价格指数 是反映一定时期内城乡居民所购买的生活消费品价格和服务项目价格变动趋势和程度的相对数，是对城市居民消费价格指数和农村居民消费价格指数进行综合汇总计算的结果。利用居民消费价格指数，可以观察和分析消费品的零售价格和服务价格变动对城乡居民实际生活费支出的影响程度。

城市居民消费价格指数 是反映城市居民家庭所购买的生活消费品价格和服务项目价格变动趋势和程度的相对数。城市居民消费价格指数可以观察和分析消费品的零售价格和服务项目价格变动对职工货币工资的影响，作为研究职工生活和确定工资政策的依据。

农村居民消费价格指数 是反映农村居民家庭所购买的生活消费品价格和服务项目价格变动趋势和程度的相对数。农村居民消费价格指数可以观察农村消费品的零售价格和服务项目价格变动对农村居民生活消费支出的影响，直接反映农民生活水平的实际变化情况，为分析和研究农村居民生活问题提供依据。

农产品收购价格指数 是反映国有商业、集体商业、个体商业、外贸部门、国家机关、社会团体等各种经济类型的商业企业和有关部门收购农产品价格的变动趋势和程度的相对数。农产品收购价格指数可以观察和研究农产品收购价格总水平的变化情况，以及对农民货币收入的影响，作为制订和检查农产品价格政策的依据。

农村工业品零售价格指数 是反映农村市场工业品零售价格水平变动趋势和程度的相对数。通过农村工业品零售价格指数，可以观察工业品零售价格变动对农民货币支出的影响。

工业品出厂价格指数 是反映全部工业产品出厂价格总水平的变动趋势和程度的相对数，包括工业企业售给本企业以外所有单位的各种产品和直接售给居民用于生活消费的产品。通过工业品出厂价格指数能观察出厂价格变动对工业总产值的影响。

固定资产投资价格指数 是反映固定资产投资额价格变动趋势和程度的相对数。固定资产投资额是由建筑安装工程投资完成额、设备、工器具购置投资完成额和其他费用投资完成额三部分组成的。编制固定资产投资价格指数应首先分别编制上述三部分投资的价格指数，然后采用加权算术平均法求出固定资产投资价格总指数。

编制固定资产投资价格指数可以准确地反映固定资产投资中涉及的各类商品和取费项目价格变动趋势和变动幅度，消除按现价计算的固定资产投资指标中的价格变动因素，真实地反映固定资产投资的规模、速度、结构和效益，为国家科学地制定、检查固定资产投资计划并提高宏观调控水平，为完善国民经济核算体系提供科学的、可靠的依据。

Explanatory Notes on Main Statistical Indicators

Retail Price Index reflects the general change in retail prices of commodities. The change and adjustment in retail prices directly affect the living expenditure of urban and rural residents, government revenue, purchasing power of residents and the equilibrium of market supply and demand,and the ratio of consumption to accumulation. Therefore, the calculation of retail price index is useful to analyze the changes of the above economic activities.

Consumer Price Index reflects the trend and degree of changes in prices of consumer goods and services purchased by urban and rural residents,and is a composite index derived from the urban consumer price index and the rural consumer price index. Consumer price index can be used to analyze the impact of consumer price change on actual expenditure for living cost of urban and rural residents.

Urban Consumer Price Index reflects the trend and degree of changes in prices of consumer goods and services purchased by urban households. It can be used to observe and analyze the impact of price changes in consumer goods and services on money wages of staff and workers, and provide basis for policymaking concerning the living cost and wages of staff and workers.

Rural Consumer Price Index reflects the trend and degree of changes in prices of consumer goods and services purchased by rural households. It can be used to observe the impact of change in retail prices of consumer goods and service prices in rural areas on living expenditure of rural households, and to show the changes in the living standard of peasants. It provides basis for analysis and research on condition of life in rural areas.

Index of Purchasing Prices of Farm Products reflects the trend and degree of changes in purchasing prices of farm products purchased by state-owned, collective-owned,and individual commercial enterprises,foreign trade sectors,government agencies,social organizations and other units of various types of ownership. It is used to observe the impact of change in purchasing prices of farm products on the cash income of peasants, and serves as basis for the formulation and supervision of pricing policies for farm products.

Retail Price Index of Rural Industrial Products reflects the trend and degree of changes in prices of industrial products in rural market and can be used to observe the impact of the price change on farmers money expenditure.

Ex-factory Price Index of Industrial Products reflects the trend and degree of changes in general ex-factory prices of all industrial products,including sales of industrial products by an industrial enterprise to all units outside the enterprise, as well as sales of consumer goods to residents. It can be used to analyze the impact of ex-factory prices on gross industrial output value.

Price Index of Investment in Fixed Assets reflects the trend and degree of changes in prices of investment in fixed assets. The investment in fixed assets consists of three components, namely the investment in construction and installation, the investment in purchases of equipment and instrument,and the investment in other items. Price index of investment in fixed assets is calculated as the weighted arithmetic mean of the price indices of the three components of investment in fixed assets. Removing the factor of price change in the aggregates of investment at current prices, this indicator shows the changes in the prices of commodities and fees involved in the investment of fixed assets, and can be used to observe the actual size, growth, structure,and efficiency of investment in fixed assets and provides reliable and scientific data for government planning, management, decision making, and further improving the current national accounting system..

第八篇

CHAPTER 8

人民生活

PEOPLE'S LIVELIHOOD

8-1 人民物质文化生活情况
People's Material and Cultural Life

项　　目	Item	1985	1990	1995	2000	2004
就 业	**Employment**					
每一农村劳动力负担人数(人)	Number of Dependents Per Rural Laborer (person)	2.00	1.94	1.84	1.74	1.62
每一城镇就业者负担人数(人)	Number of Dependents Per Urban Employee (person)	2.17	1.98	1.87	2.11	1.88
城镇登记失业率(%)	Urban Registered Unemployment Rate (%)	1.9	3.8	3.9	3.8	3.8
收 入	**Income of Rural and Urban Residents**					
农村居民家庭人均纯收入(元)	Annual Per capita Net Income of Rural Residents (yuan)	394.3	683.47	1136.45	1618.08	2244.93
农村居民家庭人均纯收入指数 (1978=100)	Index of Annual Per capita Net Income of Rural Residents (1978=100)	331.1	574.8	955.5	1359.3	1885.0
城镇居民家庭人均可支配收入(元)	Annual Per capita Disposable Income of Urban Residents (yuan)	734.82	1313.54	4163.44	5644.86	7503.42
城镇居民家庭人均可支配收入指数 (1978=100)	Index of Annual Per capita Disposable Income Urban Residents (1978=100)	230.35	411.77	1172.25	1589.36	2265.88
职工年平均工资(元)	Annual Average Wages of Staff and Workers (yuan)	1277	2272	5348	8717	14844
消费水平 (元)	**Annual Per capita Consumption (yuan)**					
全区居民	All Residents	499	936	1803	2650	3377
农村居民	Rural Residents	347	662	976	1308	1751
城镇居民	Urban Residents	678	1239	3426	5274	6358
储 蓄	**Savings**					
城乡居民年底储蓄存款余额(亿元)	Balance of Savings Deposit of Rural and Urban Residents (Year-end) (100 million yuan)	33.51	128.42	477.18	908.55	1534.67
平均每人储蓄存款余额(元)	Per capita Balance of Saving Deposit (yuan)	246	840	2872	4913	7818
住房面积 (平方米)	**Per capita Floor Space of Residential Buildings (sq.m)**					
农村居民人均住房面积	Per-capital Living Space in Rural Areas (Net)	12.75	14.04	16.12	17.25	19.10
城镇居民人均使用面积	Per-capital Using Space in Urban Areas (Gross)	10.70	13.55	16.57	20.06	18.82
交 通	**Traffic**					
城镇每百户拥有摩托车(辆)	Number of Motorcycle per 100 Households in Urban Areas (unit)	1.22	3.22	6.33	8.53	19.10
城镇每万人拥有营运车辆(辆)	Number of Public Transportation Vehicles (unit)	2.3	3.5	10.8	13.8	13.1
城镇公用事业	**Public Utilities in Urban Areas**					
用水普及率 (%)	Percentage of Population with Access to Tap Water (%)	62.0	80.9	97.1	98.8	98.1
用气普及率 (%)	Rate of Access to Gas (%)	36.0	49.8	81.0	92.8	87.3
每万人拥有园林绿地 (公顷)	Green Area per 10 000 Persons (hectare)	21.3	21.6	41.5	53.4	44.5
文 化	**Culture**					
城镇每百户拥有彩色电视机(台)	Number of Color TV Sets per 100 Households in Urban Areas (sets)	35.10	67.80	85.50	102.57	111.95
农村每百户拥有电视机(台)	Number of TV Sets per 100 Households in Rural Areas (sets)	10.00	33.95	69.42	91.20	103.74
广播综合人口覆盖率 (%)	Broadcast Covering Rate of Population (%)		70.00	78.41	89.77	92.87
电视综合人口覆盖率 (%)	TV Covering Rate of Population (%)		65.00	80.48	92.15	92.53
教 育	**Education**					
学龄儿童入学率(%)	Enrollment Ratio of School-Age Children (%)	95.40	97.50	97.03	97.03	97.79
每万人口中在校大学生数(人)	Number of University Students per 10 000 Persons (person)	19.50	20.50	26.80	41.10	83.09
卫 生	**Public Health**					
每万人有医院、卫生院病床(张)	Number of Hospital Beds per 10 000 Persons (unit)	40.6	40.5	40.1	35.7	37.7
每万人有医生数(人)	Number of Doctors per 10 000 Persons (person)	19.0	22.0	23.9	24.6	21.9

注：2002 年以后的人均拥有指标按城镇全社会人口计算。以前按非农业人口计算。
Note: Per Capita Ownership is calculated on the total population in cities for the year 2002.Prior to 2002, it was based on non-agricultural Population.

8-2　城乡居民储蓄存款年底余额和年增加额

Savings Deposit in Urban and Rural Areas (Year-end)

单位: 亿元　　(100 million yuan)

年 份 Year	年底余额 Outstanding Amount			年增加额 Increased Amount		
	总 计 Total	定 期 Fixed Deposits	活 期 Current Deposits	总 计 Total	定 期 Fixed Deposits	活 期 Current Deposits
1978	7.00					
1980	10.74	9.48	1.26	2.74		
1985	33.51	28.72	4.79	5.52	4.88	0.64
1990	128.42	108.15	20.27	35.67	28.72	6.96
1991	162.22	135.16	27.05	33.80	27.02	6.78
1992	193.80	162.69	31.12	31.59	27.52	4.06
1993	244.12	199.14	44.99	50.32	36.45	13.87
1994	347.71	274.72	72.99	103.59	75.58	28.01
1995	477.18	382.61	94.57	129.47	107.90	21.57
1996	575.79	556.70	19.09	98.61	174.09	-75.48
1997	676.13	543.77	132.36	100.34	-12.93	113.27
1998	759.14	597.17	161.97	83.01	53.40	29.61
1999	824.68	631.18	193.50	65.54	34.01	31.53
2000	908.55	653.58	254.97	83.86	22.50	61.36
2001	994.00	722.85	271.15	85.46	39.32	48.59
2002	1137.87	760.32	377.55	143.85	68.39	75.46
2003	1371.59	879.93	491.66	233.81	119.59	114.23
2004	1534.67	991.62	543.05	162.85	111.61	51.24

8-3　城乡居民家庭人均收入及指数

Per Capita Annual Income of Urban and Rural Households and the Related Index

年份 Year	农村居民家庭人均纯收入(元) Per capita Annual Net Income of Rural Households (yuan)		城镇居民家庭人均年可支配收入(元) Per capita Annual Disposable Income of Urban Households (yuan)		农村居民家庭恩格尔系数 (%) Engle Coefficient of Rural Households (%)	城镇居民家庭恩格尔系数 (%) Engle Coefficient of Urban Households (%)
	绝对数（元） Value (yuan)	指数(1978=100) Index	绝对数（元） Value (yuan)	指数(1978=100) Index		
1978	119	100.0	319	100.0		
1980	201	168.9	427	133.9	60.8	57.3
1985	394	331.1	735	230.4	57.9	46.8
1990	684	574.8	1314	411.8	53.7	47.8
1991	703	590.8	1476	462.6	53.7	48.2
1992	740	621.8	1952	549.6	54.8	49.1
1993	778	653.8	2423	682.2	52.2	49.5
1994	936	786.6	3170	892.6	50.5	46.2
1995	1137	955.5	4163	1172.3	50.1	44.8
1996	1290	1084.1	4650	1309.2	45.8	44.3
1997	1500	1260.5	4845	1364.1	48.0	43.3
1998	1600	1344.5	5001	1408.0	49.2	44.3
1999	1473	1238.0	5320	1497.8	53.5	38.6
2000	1618	1359.3	5645	1589.4	50.0	36.4
2001	1710	1437.0	6215	1749.9	50.4	34.8
2002	1863	1564.9	6554	1979.1	49.0	33.9
2003	2106	1768.3	7006	2115.7	45.5	35.9
2004	2245	1885.0	7503	2265.9	45.2	36.1

注: 1992 年以前人均年可支配收入为人均年生活费收入。

Note: Per Capita disposal income before the year 1992 is Per Capita Annual income as Life Expense.

8-4 城镇居民家庭生活基本情况

Basic Living Conditions of Urban Households

(抽样调查 Sampled Survey)

项　　目	Item	1985	1990	1995	2000	2004
调查户数（户）	**Number of Households Surveyed (household)**	**490**	**590**	**590**	**790**	**1060**
平均每户家庭人口(人)	**Average Household Size (person)**	**4.60**	**3.92**	**3.37**	**3.15**	**3.04**
平均每户就业人口(人)	**Average Number of Employed Persons Per Household (person)**	**2.14**	**1.86**	**1.85**	**1.55**	**1.62**
平均每户就业面（%）	**Percentage of Employment per Household (%)**	**46.52**	**47.45**	**54.9**	**49.21**	**53.29**
平均每一就业者负担人数(包括就业者本人)(人)	**Number of Persons Supported by Each Employee (including the employee himself or herself) (person)**	**2.15**	**1.98**	**1.87**	**2.11**	**1.88**
平均每人全部年收入(元)	**Per capita Annual Income (yuan)**	**797.26**	**1432.38**	**4183.81**	**5686.52**	**8201.82**
#可支配收入	Disposable Income	734.82	1313.54	4163.44	5644.86	7503.42
工薪收入	Salaried Income	692.47	1166.64	3509.20	4128.29	6394.40
工资及补贴收入	Salary & subsidy	684.84	1146.15	3468.37	4027.36	6245.29
其他劳动收入	Part-time Income	7.63	20.49	40.83	100.93	149.11
经营净收入	Net Income of Management	49.14	21.75	85.43	230.29	371.83
财产性收入	Property Income		8.81	54.94	38.03	62.95
转移性收入	Transfer Income	43.88	235.18	501.71	1243.55	1372.63
平均每人消费性支出(元)	**Per Capita Annual Living Expenditures for Consumption (yuan)**	**650.81**	**1104.42**	**3186.75**	**4422.92**	**5773.61**
食　品	Food	304.67	527.74	1428.47	1609.17	2083.13
衣　着	Clothing	115.64	172.17	562.41	577.40	766.73
家庭设备用品及服务	Household Facilities, Articles and Service	70.90	121.51	248.07	410.88	292.14
医疗保健	Medicine and Medical Service	7.11	27.39	133.84	330.54	375.18
交通通讯	Transport, Post and Communication Services	8.39	17.88	175.95	331.03	615.19
娱乐教育文化服务	Recreation, Education and Cultural Services	99.06	123.95	290.78	600.34	840.59
居　住	Residence	23.01	51.22	179.06	343.25	566.99
杂项商品与服务	Miscellaneous Commodities and Service	22.03	62.56	168.17	220.31	233.66
平均每人消费性支出构成(人均消费支出=100)	**Composition of Per Capita Annual Living Expenditures for Consumption (%)**	**100**	**100**	**100**	**100**	**100**
食　品	Food	46.82	47.78	44.83	36.38	36.08
衣　着	Clothing	17.77	15.59	17.65	13.05	13.28
家庭设备用品及服务	Household Facilities, Articles and Service	10.89	11.01	7.78	9.29	5.06
医疗保健	Medicine and Medical Service	1.09	2.48	4.20	7.48	6.50
交通通讯	Transport, Post and Communication Services	1.29	1.62	5.52	7.48	10.65
娱乐教育文化服务	Recreation, Education and Cultural Services	15.22	11.22	9.12	13.58	14.56
居　住	Residence	3.54	4.64	5.62	7.76	9.82
杂项商品与服务	Miscellaneous Commodities and Service	3.38	5.66	5.28	4.98	4.05

8-5　城镇居民家庭基本情况
Basic Conditions of Urban Households

(2004 年) (抽样调查　Sampled Survey)

项　　目	Item	全　区 Whole Region	最低收入户 Lowest Income Households	#困难户 Poor Households	低收入户 Low Income Households
调查户数(户)	Number of Households Surveyed (household)	1060	105	53	106
比重(%)	Proportion (%)		9.88	4.95	10.02
平均每户家庭人口(人)	Average Household Size (person)	3.04	3.79	4.12	3.17
平均每户就业人口(人)	Average Number of Employees per Household (person)	1.62	1.29	1.30	1.52
平均每户就业面(%)	Percentage of Employed Persons per Household (%)	53.29	34.04	31.55	47.95
平均每一就业者负担人数(包括就业者本人)(人)	Number of Persons Supported by Each Employee (Including the employee himself or herself) (person)	1.88	2.93	3.17	2.08
平均每人全部年收入(元)	Per capita Annual Income (yuan)	8201.82	2314.49	1614.84	4401.54
平均每人可支配收入(元)	Per capita Disposable Income (yuan)	7503.42	2152.55	1525.81	3900.66
平均每人消费性支出(元)	Per capita Annual Living Expenditure (yuan)	5773.61	2284.84	1698.95	3578.70

项　　目	Item	中等偏下户 Lower Middle Income Households	中等收入户 Middle Income Households	中等偏上户 Upper Middle Income Households	高收入户 High Income Households	最高收入户 Highest Income Households
调查户数(户)	Number of Households Surveyed (household)	211	213	213	105	107
比重(%)	Proportion (%)	19.93	20.10	20.05	9.94	10.08
平均每户家庭人口(人)	Average Household Size (person)	3.17	3.05	2.93	2.66	2.47
平均每户就业人口(人)	Average Number of Employees per Household (person)	1.70	1.70	1.74	1.62	1.35
平均每户就业面(%)	Percentage of Employed Persons per Household (%)	53.63	55.74	59.39	60.90	54.66
平均每一就业者负担人数(包括就业者本人)(人)	Number of Persons Supported by Each Employee (Including the employee himself or herself) (person)	1.86	1.80	1.68	1.65	1.84
平均每人全部年收入(元)	Per capita Annual Income (yuan)	5953.59	7841.95	10446.27	13256.45	18190.80
平均每人可支配收入(元)	Per Capita Disposable Income (yuan)	5433.73	7139.05	9505.17	12125.04	17066.24
平均每人消费性支出(元)	Per Capita Annual Living Expenditure (yuan)	4512.65	6196.24	6671.54	9208.33	10329.98

8-6 城镇居民家庭平均每人全年消费性支出
Per Capita Annual Living Expenditure of Urban Households

(2004 年) (抽样调查 Sampled Survey)

项 目	Item	总平均 Total Average	最低收入户 Lowest Income Households	#困难户 Poor Households	低收入户 Low Income Households
消费性支出(元)	**Total Living Expenditures (yuan)**	**5773.61**	**2284.84**	**1698.95**	**3578.70**
食 品	Food	2083.13	1095.90	868.63	1475.36
#粮 食	Grain	209.72	202.62	185.44	204.47
肉禽及其制品	Meat, Poultry and Related Products	411.29	284.72	236.70	301.96
蛋 类	Eggs	44.69	31.03	26.15	33.86
水产品	Aquatic Products	54.98	18.41	7.20	31.93
奶及奶制品	Milk and Dairy Products	117.28	37.60	18.13	71.90
衣 着	Clothing	766.73	223.10	175.89	428.52
#服 装	Garments	536.28	133.55	105.47	288.55
家庭设备用品及服务	Household Facilities, Articles and Services	292.14	65.38	58.04	125.12
#耐用消费品	Durable Consumer Goods	130.42	3.01	2.61	22.67
医疗保健	Medicine and Medical Services	375.18	169.15	95.39	225.05
交通通讯	Transport, Post and Communication Services	615.19	157.81	116.07	294.41
娱乐教育文化服务	Recreation, Education and Cultural Services	840.59	266.39	196.75	594.84
#文化娱乐用品	Amusement & Culture Goods	183.75	18.42	9.55	49.13
居 住	Residence	566.99	236.79	160.27	332.27
#住 房	Housing	113.99	23.65	23.04	54.27
杂项商品与服务	Miscellaneous Commodities and Services	233.66	70.32	27.91	103.13

项 目	Item	中等偏下户 Lower Middle Income Households	中等收入户 Middle Income Households	中等偏上户 Upper Middle Income Households	高收入户 High Income Households	最高收入户 Highest Income Households
消费性支出(元)	**Total Living Expenditures (yuan)**	**4512.65**	**6196.24**	**6671.54**	**9208.33**	**10329.98**
食 品	Food	1888.12	2153.51	2325.20	2930.14	3152.42
#粮 食	Grain	208.25	229.56	193.06	214.29	219.29
肉禽及其制品	Meat, Poultry and Related Products	389.68	439.95	452.49	486.63	537.46
蛋 类	Eggs	42.28	50.42	46.90	49.51	59.95
水产品	Aquatic Products	47.89	62.44	59.34	82.34	99.23
奶及奶制品	Milk and Dairy Products	98.35	124.92	140.07	180.94	199.02
衣 着	Clothing	553.72	798.80	940.12	1371.97	1441.82
#服 装	Garments	360.50	560.19	662.26	995.83	1083.52
家庭设备用品及服务	Household Facilities, Articles and Services	189.34	422.44	296.67	571.11	492.06
#耐用消费品	Durable Consumer Goods	72.56	230.79	125.88	298.69	194.12
医疗保健	Medicine and Medical Services	245.97	356.13	363.13	673.91	1049.16
交通通讯	Transport, Post and Communication Services	448.75	651.43	794.74	1025.43	1186.75
娱乐教育文化服务	Recreation, Education and Cultural Services	559.39	975.03	1045.77	1179.51	1571.82
#文化娱乐用品	Amusement & Culture Goods	80.86	270.87	271.77	267.95	354.08
居 住	Residence	466.61	648.87	613.15	965.80	885.80
#住 房	Housing	87.68	153.10	72.06	283.77	230.64
杂项商品与服务	Miscellaneous Commodities and Services	160.74	190.03	292.76	490.46	550.14

8-7 城镇居民家庭平均每人全年消费性支出构成
Composition of Per Capita Annual Living Expenditure of Urban Households

(2004 年) (抽样调查 Sampled Survey)

项 目	Item	总平均 Total Average	最低收入户 Lowest Income Households	#困难户 Poor Households	低收入户 Low Income Households
消费性支出(%)	**Total Living Expenditures (%)**	**100**	**100**	**100**	**100**
食 品	Food	36.08	47.96	51.13	41.23
衣 着	Clothing	13.28	9.76	10.35	11.97
家庭设备用品及服务	Household Facilities, Articles and Services	5.06	2.86	3.42	3.50
医疗保健	Medicine and Medical Services	6.50	7.40	5.61	6.29
交通通讯	Transport, Post and Communication Services	10.65	6.92	6.83	8.23
娱乐教育文化服务	Recreation, Education and Cultural Services	14.56	11.66	11.58	16.62
居 住	Residence	9.82	10.36	9.43	9.28
杂项商品与服务	Miscellaneous Commodities and Services	4.05	3.08	1.65	2.88

项 目	Item	中等偏下户 Lower Middle Income Households	中等收入户 Middle Income Households	中等偏上户 Upper Middle Income Households	高收入户 High Income Households	最高收入户 Highest Income Households
消费性支出(%)	**Total Living Expenditures (%)**	**100**	**100**	**100**	**100**	**100**
食 品	Food	41.84	34.76	34.85	31.82	30.52
衣 着	Clothing	12.27	12.89	14.09	14.90	13.96
家庭设备用品及服务	Household Facilities, Articles and Services	4.20	6.82	4.45	6.20	4.76
医疗保健	Medicine and Medical Services	5.45	5.75	5.44	7.32	10.16
交通通讯	Transport, Post and Communication Services	9.94	10.51	11.81	11.14	11.47
娱乐教育文化服务	Recreation, Education and Cultural Services	12.40	15.74	15.78	12.81	15.22
居 住	Residence	10.34	10.47	9.19	10.49	8.58
杂项商品与服务	Miscellaneous Commodities and Services	3.56	3.06	4.39	5.32	5.33

8-8 城镇居民家庭年人均购买的主要商品数量
Per Capita Annual Purchases of Major Commodities in Urban Households

(抽样调查 Sampled Survey)

项　目	Item	1985	1990	1995	2000	2004
粮食(千克)	Grain (kg)	127.20	139.73	95.97	81.91	71.32
鲜菜(千克)	Fresh Vegetables (kg)	128.30	132.96	113.41	90.56	97.59
食用植物油(千克)	Edible Vegetable Oil (kg)	8.70	10.09	9.01	9.69	9.57
猪肉(千克)	Pork (kg)	5.50	5.56	6.34	5.17	7.05
牛肉(千克)	Beef (kg)	12.30	13.51	2.95	3.62	2.85
羊肉(千克)	Mutton(kg)			10.43	13.06	9.42
家禽(千克)	Poultry (kg)	1.50	2.12	4.65	6.11	6.23
鲜蛋(千克)	Fresh Eggs (kg)	4.10	4.46	5.11	7.39	7.21
水产品(千克)	Aquatic Products (kg)	3.50	3.73	4.89	4.35	4.74
鲜乳品(千克)	Fresh Dairy Products (kg)	9.40	12.7	12.98	18.44	29.20
鲜瓜果(千克)	Fresh Fruits & Melons(kg)	64.30	59.47	43.54	64.31	65.49
酒(千克)	Liquor (kg)	4.80	3.48	3.72	3.21	4.22
鞋(双)	Shoes(pair)	1.40	2.25	2.87	2.82	2.89
服装(件)	Clothes(piece)	1.50	2.12	5.84	6.36	7.43
液化石油气(千克)	Liquefied Petrolum Gas (kg)	12.34	11.40	21.62	24.77	18.36
天然气(立方米)	Natural Gas (cum)			0.08	1.93	19.43
煤炭(千克)	Coal (kg)	267.38	90.10	180.46	123.78	103.17

8-9 城镇居民家庭平均每百户年底耐用消费品拥有量
Number of Durable Consumer Goods Owned Per-100 Urban Households at Year-end by Level of Income

项　目	Item	1985	1990	1995	2000	2004
摩托车(辆)	Motorcycle (unit)	1.22	3.22	6.33	8.53	19.10
家用汽车(辆)	Automobil (unit)				0.82	0.79
冰柜(台)	Freezer (set)			0.69	3.20	3.75
家用电脑(台)	Computer (set)				5.68	17.84
组合音响(套)	Hi-Fi Stereo Component System (set)		0.51	7.38	17.53	18.29
摄相机(架)	Video Camera (set)				1.02	1.16
钢琴(架)	Piano (set)			1.20	1.38	2.51
其他中高档乐器(件)	Other Medium and High Grade Musical Instrument (piece)	5.71	11.53	11.84	9.09	12.24
微波炉(台)	Oven (set)				5.39	14.29
空调器(台)	Air Conditioner (set)	0.20	0.17	0.93	2.78	6.15
取暖器(台)	Electric Heater (set)			1.67		7.58
电炊具(件)	Electric Cooking Appliances (piece)	5.92	39.83	72.57	82.07	76.99
淋浴热水器(台)	Shower (set)			32.46	47.91	61.46
排油烟机(台)	Smoke Absorber (set)			38.06	64.75	75.98
消毒碗柜(台)	Disinfectant Machine (set)					4.23
洗碗机(台)	Dishwasher (set)					0.14
饮水机(台)	Clean water Fountain (set)					26.82
吸尘器(台)	Dust Catcher (set)			15.64	17.43	16.59
健身器材(台)	Healthy Equipment (set)				2.35	2.72
普通电话(部)	Telephone (set)				71.69	91.69
移动电话(部)	Hand Telephone (set)				4.81	87.13
传真机(部)	Fax (set)					0.14
洗衣机(台)	Washing Machine (set)	52.24	79.66	92.10	95.48	91.46
电冰箱(台)	Refrigerator (set)	8.57	32.20	60.36	81.76	83.52
彩色电视机(台)	Color TV Set (set)	35.10	67.80	85.50	102.57	111.95
影碟机(台)	Video Disc Player (set)				33.56	56.19
照相机(架)	Camera (set)	8.16	20.00	37.15	33.71	40.33

8-10 按收入等级分的城镇居民家庭平均每人全年购买商品数量

Composition of Per Capita Annual Living Expenditure of Urban Households

(2004 年) (抽样调查 Sampled Survey)

项 目	Item	总 平 均 Total Average	最低收入户 Lowest Income Households	#困难户 Poor Households	低收入户 Low Income Households
粮食(千克)	Grain (kg)	71.32	89.34	88.72	74.57
食用植物油(千克)	Edible Vegetable Oil (kg)	9.57	11.98	11.08	10.69
食用动物油(千克)	Edible Animal Oil (kg)	0.03	0.05	0.07	0.03
猪 肉(千克)	Pork (kg)	7.05	3.51	1.39	6.18
牛 肉(千克)	Beef (kg)	2.85	1.82	1.08	2.11
羊 肉(千克)	Mutton (kg)	9.42	9.63	9.71	7.28
家 禽(千克)	Poultry (kg)	6.23	2.86	1.74	4.50
鲜 蛋(千克)	Fresh Eggs (kg)	7.21	5.38	4.55	5.77
鱼 (千克)	Fish (kg)	4.05	1.74	0.86	3.07
虾 (千克)	Shrimp (kg)	0.48	0.17	0.10	0.17
鲜 菜(千克)	Fresh Vegetables (kg)	97.59	78.55	70.24	98.17
白 酒(千克)	Liquor (kg)	1.44	0.34	0.12	1.15
果 酒(千克)	Fruit Wine (kg)	0.42	0.08	0.06	0.15
啤 酒(千克)	Beer (kg)	2.27	0.46	0.25	1.43
其他酒(千克)	Other Liquor (kg)	0.08	0.02		0.10
鲜瓜果(千克)	Fresh Melons & Fruits (kg)	65.49	47.11	26.30	50.13
糕 点(千克)	Cake (kg)	3.30	1.60	0.92	2.16
鲜乳品(千克)	Fresh Dairy Products (kg)	29.20	13.27	6.54	21.00
奶 粉(千克)	Milk Powder (kg)	0.13	0.08	0.03	0.05
酸 奶(千克)	Sour Milk (kg)	1.94	0.33	0.25	1.43
男士服装(件)	Men's Clothing (piece)	2.54	1.35	1.05	1.85
女士服装(件)	Women's Clothing (piece)	3.57	1.55	1.59	2.49
儿童服装(件)	Children's Clothing (piece)	1.32	1.12	1.18	1.21

8-10 续表 Continued

项　　目	Item	中等偏下户 Lower Middle Income Households	中等收入户 Middle Income Households	中等偏上户 Upper Middle Income Households	高收入户 High Income Households	最高收入户 Highest Income Households
粮食(千克)	Grain (kg)	72.24	76.48	61.09	62.56	62.60
食用植物油(千克)	Edible Vegetable Oil (kg)	9.37	10.27	8.00	9.02	8.22
食用动物油(千克)	Edible Animal Oil (kg)	0.05	0.02	0.03	0.02	0.02
猪　肉(千克)	Pork (kg)	6.72	7.29	8.47	7.91	8.82
牛　肉(千克)	Beef (kg)	3.22	2.80	2.84	3.82	3.33
羊　肉(千克)	Mutton (kg)	9.11	10.43	9.33	9.05	11.16
家　禽(千克)	Poultry (kg)	5.82	6.79	7.61	7.40	8.00
鲜　蛋(千克)	Fresh Eggs (kg)	6.87	8.26	7.41	7.48	9.20
鱼　　(千克)	Fish (kg)	3.68	4.83	4.07	5.33	6.28
虾　　(千克)	Shrimp (kg)	0.42	0.50	0.53	0.84	0.90
鲜　菜(千克)	Fresh Vegetables (kg)	93.70	99.84	94.87	108.09	126.08
白　酒(千克)	Liquor (kg)	1.73	1.80	1.38	1.45	1.74
果　酒(千克)	Fruit Wine (kg)	0.31	0.45	0.57	0.65	0.96
啤　酒(千克)	Beer (kg)	3.33	2.04	2.66	2.20	2.36
其他酒(千克)	Other Liquor (kg)	0.04	0.09	0.09	0.08	0.19
鲜瓜果(千克)	Fresh Melons & Fruits (kg)	62.05	67.51	70.90	77.82	88.69
糕　点(千克)	Cake (kg)	3.00	3.69	3.87	4.79	4.00
鲜乳品(千克)	Fresh Dairy Products (kg)	26.76	32.31	33.84	37.01	40.95
奶　粉(千克)	Milk Powder (kg)	0.07	0.19	0.22	0.12	0.13
酸　奶(千克)	Sour Milk (kg)	1.14	2.05	2.30	3.52	4.46
男士服装(件)	Men's Clothing (piece)	2.20	2.82	2.69	3.47	4.05
女士服装(件)	Women's Clothing (piece)	2.85	3.80	4.24	5.49	5.56
儿童服装(件)	Children's Clothing (piece)	1.13	1.45	1.51	1.61	1.19

8-11 按收入等级分城镇居民家庭平均每百户年底耐用消费品拥有量

Number of Durable Consumer Goods Owned Per-100 Urban Households at Year-end by Level of Income

(2004 年) (抽样调查 Sampled Survey)

项目	Item	总平均 Total Average	最低收入户 Lowest Income Households	#困难户 Poor Households	低收入户 Low Income Households
组合家具(套)	Composite Furniture (set)	70.11	56.70	63.90	63.06
摩托车(辆)	Motorcycle(unit)	19.10	15.81	24.94	9.12
自行车(辆)	Bicycle(unit)	133.58	126.00	109.60	134.32
家用汽车(辆)	Automobile(unit)	0.79			
洗衣机(台)	Washing Machine (set)	91.46	70.44	60.52	76.74
电风扇(台)	Electric Fan (set)	57.77	40.61	29.15	58.78
电冰箱(台)	Refrigerator (set)	83.52	47.72	32.76	72.69
冰　柜(台)	Freezer (set)	3.75	4.47	2.85	1.17
彩色电视机(台)	Color TV (set)	111.95	97.97	88.27	100.66
影碟机(台)	Video Disc Player (set)	56.19	22.32	18.08	35.54
录放像机(台)	Video-recorder (set)	16.26	13.66	4.99	10.10
家用电脑(台)	Household Computer (set)	17.84	2.59	3.54	2.88
组合音响(套)	Hi-Fi Stereo Sound System (set)	18.29	0.49		11.24
录音机(台)	Tape Recorder (set)	59.80	46.68	51.13	49.65
摄相机(架)	Video Camera (set)	1.16			0.72
照相机(架)	Camera (set)	40.33	16.38	6.29	22.19
钢　琴(架)	Piano (set)	2.51			0.02
中高档乐器(件)	Other Medium and High Grade Musical Instrument (piece)	12.24	0.91		9.01
微波炉(台)	Microwave Oven (set)	14.29			2.15
空调器(台)	Air Conditioner (set)	6.15			0.00
电炊具(台)	Electric Cooking Appliances (set)	76.99	41.84	15.40	48.07
淋浴热水器(台)	Shower (set)	61.46	18.58	15.01	30.01
排油烟机(台)	Smoke Exhauster (set)	75.98	24.68	8.05	65.08
吸尘器(台)	Dust Vaccum Cleaner (set)	16.59	1.35		5.85
健身器材(件)	Body-building Apparatus (piece)	2.72			0.76
移动电话(部)	Mobile Phone (set)	87.13	17.61	14.38	41.27

8-11 续表 Continued

项目	Item	中等偏下户 Lower Middle Income Households	中等收入户 Middle Income Households	中等偏上户 Upper Middle Income Households	高收入户 High Income Households	最高收入户 Highest Income Households
组合家具(套)	Composite Furniture (set)	72.72	70.90	77.59	77.36	56.73
摩托车(辆)	Motorcycle(unit)	17.44	26.72	22.36	13.05	18.95
自行车(辆)	Bicycle(unit)	150.95	134.33	133.81	136.92	90.73
家用汽车(辆)	Automobile(unit)	0.53	0.91	0.50	0.38	3.96
洗衣机(台)	Washing Machine (set)	92.26	93.41	98.85	95.39	99.57
电风扇(台)	Electric Fan (set)	63.43	57.02	57.34	54.99	64.45
电冰箱(台)	Refrigerator (set)	85.20	84.29	89.49	94.13	97.95
冰　柜(台)	Freezer (set)	3.66	4.67	3.62	3.18	5.10
彩色电视机(台)	Color TV (set)	106.64	113.56	117.19	119.27	127.22
影碟机(台)	Video Disc Player (set)	50.65	63.43	69.53	65.24	67.17
录放像机(台)	Video-recorder (set)	11.90	21.61	18.88	13.20	21.35
家用电脑(台)	Household Computer (set)	15.29	19.72	22.29	21.20	36.99
组合音响(套)	Hi-Fi Stereo Compound System (set)	17.84	21.20	25.05	15.96	23.76
录音机(台)	Tape Recorder (set)	60.86	47.71	72.35	76.20	60.80
摄相机(架)	Pickup Camera (set)		0.18	2.80	2.62	2.43
照相机(架)	Camera (set)	31.49	37.38	55.58	51.41	63.75
钢　琴(架)	Piano (set)	0.32	4.72	4.12	1.53	5.32
中高档乐器(件)	Other Medium and High- Grade Musical Instrument (piece)	15.04	12.13	15.51	13.92	10.21
微波炉(台)	Microwave Oven (set)	6.03	13.36	20.58	26.25	36.48
空调器(台)	Air Conditioner (set)	1.63	8.20	10.16	7.58	14.33
电炊具(台)	Electric Cooking Appliances (set)	78.49	72.77	96.75	85.06	92.52
淋浴热水器(台)	Shower Heater (set)	51.22	63.91	80.18	84.68	87.77
排油烟机(台)	Smoke Exhauster (set)	75.13	76.97	87.22	92.70	91.83
吸尘器(台)	Vaccum Cleaner (set)	13.07	15.87	22.97	23.29	31.04
健身器材(件)	Body-building Apparatus (piece)	1.79	1.45	2.82	7.94	6.90
移动电话(部)	Mobile Telephone (set)	75.12	87.79	121.20	117.81	118.53

8-12　城镇家庭基本情况表

Basic Condition of Urban Familiy

(2004 年 6 月) (抽样调查 Sampled Survey)

地　区 Region	人　均总收入(元/人) Total Per-capita Income (yuan/person)	#工　薪收　入 Salary Income	人　均总支出(元/人) Total Per-capita Expenditure (yuan/person)	家　庭人口数(人/户) Number of Familiy Members (person/household)	#常　住人口数 Resident Population	基尼系数 Guini Coefficient	人均住房面积(平方米/人) Per-capita Floor Space (Sq.eter/man)
总　计 Total	**5622.66**	**4166.12**	**4648.69**	**3.31**	**3.21**	**0.3951**	**25.25**
乌鲁木齐市 Urumqi City	**8369.25**	**5107.81**	**7269.26**	**2.64**	**2.61**	**0.3236**	**25.72**
克拉玛依市 Karamay City	**11032.45**	**8114.68**	**7594.01**	**2.73**	**2.61**	**0.2656**	**24.41**
石河子市 Shihezi City	**6504.07**	**3669.68**	**4589.99**	**2.79**	**2.70**	**0.2960**	**22.75**
吐鲁番地区 Turpan Administrative Offices	**5546.23**	**4613.24**	**4935.61**	**3.38**	**3.29**	**0.3612**	**32.94**
吐鲁番市 Turpan City	5388.72	4763.57	4052.18	3.40	3.37	0.3052	33.93
鄯善县 Shanshan [Piqan] County	7239.41	5717.94	6603.57	3.35	3.21	0.3859	31.29
托克逊县 Toksun County	4182.65	3479.46	4359.40	3.38	3.29	0.3426	33.43
哈密地区 Hami [Kumul] Administrative Offices	**6143.07**	**5715.97**	**4710.27**	**3.16**	**2.99**	**0.2833**	**25.27**
哈密市 Hami [Kumul] City	5744.50	5094.61	4278.22	2.82	2.71	0.3325	27.25
巴里坤哈萨克自治县 Barkol Kazak Autonomous County	4898.93	4453.82	3965.38	3.65	3.43	0.2886	23.71
伊吾县 Yiwu [Araturuk] County	7996.12	7789.67	5903.92	2.98	2.82	0.1891	25.45
昌吉回族自治州 Changji Hui Autonomous Prefecture	**5683.88**	**3751.18**	**5065.02**	**3.12**	**2.94**	**0.3641**	**30.30**
昌吉市 Changji City	6488.60	5199.24	5714.80	2.73	2.54	0.3127	25.52
阜康市 Fukang City	5604.91	3651.96	5232.09	3.12	2.97	0.3724	33.92
米泉市 Miquan City	7211.67	3448.50	6732.30	3.08	2.94	0.3651	28.93
呼图壁县 Hutubi County	5177.92	3850.17	4915.76	3.30	3.09	0.3688	25.29
玛纳斯县 Manas County	6486.43	4317.60	4794.30	2.92	2.75	0.3036	33.08
奇台县 Qitai County	3532.43	1968.43	2908.52	3.32	3.24	0.4672	25.39
吉木萨尔县 Jimsar County	5279.40	4068.54	4635.69	3.03	2.92	0.3540	39.37
木垒哈萨克自治县 Mori Kazak Autonomous County	6015.23	3778.46	5624.80	3.47	3.12	0.3074	30.31
伊犁哈萨克自治州 Ili Kazak Autonomous Prefecture	**5749.83**	**3888.05**	**4623.42**	**3.29**	**3.20**	**0.3399**	**25.41**
伊宁市 **Yining [Gulja] City**	7141.24	4383.13	5591.52	3.13	3.06	0.3150	25.48
奎屯市 Kuytun City	6239.30	3646.34	5168.26	2.74	2.65	0.3108	26.20
察布查尔锡伯自治县 Qapqal Xibe Autonomous County	5224.40	4664.38	4314.51	3.49	3.44	0.3149	27.59
特克斯县 Tekes County	3722.75	2602.36	2724.61	3.95	3.76	0.3894	22.78

8-12 续表 1 Continued

地　区 Region	人均总收入(元/人) Total Per-capita Income (yuan/person)	#工薪收入 Salary Income	人均总支出(元/人) Total Per-capita Expenditure (yuan/person)	家庭人口数(人/户) Number of Familiy Members (person/household)	#常住人口数 Resident Population	基尼系数 Guini Coefficient	人均住房面积(平方米/人) Per-capita Floor Space (Sq. eter/man)
塔城地区 Tacheng [Tarbagatai] Administrative Offices	**5405.16**	**3980.41**	**4235.59**	**3.21**	**3.10**	**0.3861**	**26.71**
塔城市 Tacheng [Qoqek] City	6067.77	3643.08	5236.04	3.06	2.95	0.3756	26.82
乌苏市 Usu City	4742.63	4160.16	3731.93	3.04	2.93	0.3939	26.43
额敏县 Emin Ciunty	4719.12	3724.96	3275.71	3.39	3.26	0.4062	27.93
沙湾县 Shawan County	5579.47	3449.14	4024.25	2.98	2.96	0.3521	26.93
托里县 Toli County	4289.04	2693.17	3422.43	3.50	3.33	0.4044	26.12
裕民县 Yumin [Qagantokay] County	5934.69	5244.98	5954.90	3.13	2.97	0.3292	25.22
和布克赛尔蒙古自治县 Hoboksar Mongol Autonomous County	6609.34	5171.23	4376.50	3.42	3.30	0.4017	27.30
阿勒泰地区 Altay Administrative Offices	**6297.91**	**4218.53**	**5391.66**	**3.16**	**3.05**	**0.3509**	**25.98**
阿勒泰市 Altay City	7112.83	4229.70	6255.75	2.88	2.80	0.3396	24.68
福海县 Fuhai [Burultokay] County	5767.05	4270.94	5108.58	3.24	3.08	0.3536	24.99
哈巴河县 Habahe [Kaba] County	6093.60	4166.40	4939.11	3.36	3.28	0.3550	28.08
博尔塔拉蒙古自治州 Bortala Mongol Autonomous Prefecture	**7066.70**	**5891.42**	**5344.47**	**3.04**	**2.95**	**0.2928**	**26.67**
博乐市 Bole [Bortala] City	8510.96	8211.67	5815.00	2.95	2.88	0.3212	26.68
精河县 Jinghe [Jing] County	6928.07	4792.01	5838.30	2.85	2.76	0.2448	30.53
温泉县 Wenquan [Araxang] County	6075.24	5075.50	4546.12	3.35	3.23	0.3167	22.97
巴音郭楞蒙古自治州 Bayangol Mongol Autonomous Prefecture	**7219.96**	**5158.88**	**5874.95**	**3.04**	**2.97**	**0.2587**	**26.63**
库尔勒市 Korla City	7279.92	5933.81	6301.45	2.82	2.75	0.2637	25.80
轮台县 Luntai [Bugur] County	6769.11	4164.60	5111.64	3.27	3.24	0.2663	26.00
且末县 Qiemo [Qarqan] County	7516.86	5557.11	5116.14	3.12	3.09	0.2650	28.31
焉耆回族自治县 Yanqi Hui Autonomous County	7292.24	4412.02	6651.11	3.17	3.02	0.2521	27.12
阿克苏地区 Aksu Administrative Offices	**3982.49**	**2777.07**	**3339.98**	**3.54**	**3.45**	**0.4710**	**26.99**
阿克苏市 Aksu City	4683.08	2344.52	3515.79	3.16	3.08	0.5760	33.18
温宿县 Wensu [Onsu] County	3182.66	2012.75	2356.60	3.68	3.34	0.4909	23.20
库车县 Kuqa County	3968.54	3660.49	3466.18	3.64	3.54	0.4183	29.24
沙雅县 Xayar County	3934.80	2533.36	4791.44	3.73	3.67	0.4511	29.80
新和县 Xinhe [Toksu] County	4357.06	3699.30	3377.25	3.22	3.17	0.4506	24.03

8-12 续表 2 Continued

地　区 Region	人　均 总收入 (元/人) Total Per-capita Income (yuan/person)	#工　薪 收　入 Salary Income	人　均 总支出 (元/人) Total Per-capita Expenditure (yuan/person)	家　庭 人口数 (人/户) Number of Familiy Members (person/household)	#常　住 人口数 Resident Population	基尼系数 Guini Coefficient	人均住 房面积 (平方米/人) Per-capita Floor Space (Sq. eter/man)
拜城县 Baicheng [Bay] County	3181.72	2203.53	2452.47	3.70	3.69	0.4291	22.89
乌什县 Wushi [Uxturpan] County	2823.91	1848.45	2189.13	3.67	3.66	0.4771	19.83
阿瓦提县 Awat County	5038.70	3231.07	3949.12	3.66	3.63	0.3798	26.25
柯坪县 Kalpin County	5533.31	5102.22	5614.29	3.82	3.80	0.2578	24.22
克孜勒苏柯尔克孜自治州 Kizilsu Kirgiz Autonomous Prefecture	**5506.93**	**5114.88**	**4230.38**	**3.82**	**3.71**	**0.3437**	**21.60**
阿图什市 Artux City	7088.89	6546.02	5200.45	3.61	3.41	0.3305	21.41
阿克陶县 Akto County	5198.68	4772.19	4325.62	3.93	3.80	0.3092	23.95
阿合奇县 Akqi County	4650.33	4345.12	3470.24	4.12	4.04	0.3686	19.83
乌恰县 Wuqia [Ulugqat] County	5216.64	4923.41	4025.31	3.62	3.58	0.3358	21.39
喀什地区 Kashgar [Kaxgar] Administrative Offices	**3596.17**	**2706.03**	**3160.16**	**3.93**	**3.84**	**0.4680**	**19.71**
喀什市 Kashgar [Kaxgar] City	3969.79	1970.54	3949.21	4.09	4.06	0.4505	20.50
疏附县 Shufu County	4510.06	3595.56	3815.26	3.71	3.60	0.3520	19.52
疏勒县 Shule County	3732.88	2652.35	5269.14	3.64	3.41	0.4595	21.08
英吉沙县 Yengisar County	4271.76	3129.43	4106.49	3.74	3.73	0.4386	22.78
泽普县 Zepu [Poskam] County	4200.96	3889.74	3252.07	3.66	3.53	0.4013	25.04
叶城县 Yecheng [Kagilik] County	3508.28	2383.15	2970.37	4.02	4.01	0.3943	16.97
麦盖提县 Makit County	3163.43	2191.54	2959.19	4.01	3.89	0.4711	18.74
岳普湖县 Yopurga County	5489.09	4300.34	4259.42	3.54	3.40	0.4197	19.47
伽师县 Jiashi [Payzawat] County	6268.38	5899.66	3686.31	3.45	3.30	0.2784	20.50
和田地区 Hotan Administrative Offices	**5483.09**	**4868.24**	**4861.16**	**3.46**	**3.33**	**0.3537**	**25.50**
和田市 Hotan City	6466.59	5964.88	4282.34	3.29	3.20	0.3397	23.58
墨玉县 Moyu [Karakax] County	5526.72	5113.53	6210.38	3.59	3.45	0.2993	21.85
皮山县 Pishan [Guma] County	6613.46	6163.99	5629.86	3.29	3.16	0.2165	23.05
洛浦县 Lop County	5451.25	4758.54	3670.04	3.56	3.44	0.3819	29.31
策勒县 Qira County	3978.19	3499.84	4123.90	3.57	3.41	0.4643	28.06
于田县 Yutian [Keriya] County	4569.12	3792.30	5471.60	3.35	3.22	0.3332	24.81
民丰县 Minfeng [Niya] County	5831.61	4854.84	4771.83	3.53	3.41	0.3881	27.41

8-13 农村居民家庭基本情况
Basic Conditions of Rural Households

(抽样调查 Sampled Survey)

项 目	Item	1990	1995	2000	2004
调查户数(户)	**Number of Household Surveyed(household)**	**1240**	**1550**	**1500**	**1550**
调查户人口(人)	**Number of Residents Surveyed (person)**	**6659**	**8711**	**7999**	**7922**
平均每户常住人口	Average Number of Permanent Residents per Household	5.37	5.62	5.33	5.11
平均每户整半劳动力	Average Number of Laborers per Household	2.76	3.06	3.06	3.15
平均每个劳动力负担人口(含本人)	Average Number of Persons Supported by a Laborer (Including oneself)	1.94	1.84	1.74	1.62
户均经营耕地面积(亩)	Per Household Area of Cultivated Land Managed(mu)	21.80	25.68	22.39	21.26
平均每人经营耕地面积(亩)	Per capita Area of Cultivated Land Managed(mu)	4.06	4.57	4.20	4.16
年内每户新建房屋面积(平方米)	Space of Rooms per Household Newly Built Within the Year (sq.m)	4.18	2.49	2.03	3.72
年底人均居住面积(平方米)	Per Capita Net Living Rooms Space in Rural Area (sq.m)	14.04	16.12	17.25	19.10
平均每人年收入(元)	**Per Capita Annual Income(yuan)**				
总收入	Total Revenue	1112.01	2414.59	3129.35	3777.91
工资性收入	Wages Income	56.53	64.47	104.58	138.23
家庭经营收入	Household Business Income	1034.69	2238.71	2926.75	3485.40
财产性收入	Property Income		65.30	40.43	81.08
转移性收入	Transfer Income	20.79	46.11	57.60	73.20
#现金收入	Cash Income	830.88	1876.61	2444.30	2945.19
工资性收入	Wages Income	55.50	64.41	104.46	138.23
家庭经营收入	Household Business Income	750.34	1700.93	2245.31	2660.93
财产性收入	Property Income		59.19	37.87	72.90
转移性收入	Transfer Income	25.04	52.08	56.67	73.13
平均每人年支出(元)	**Per capita Annual Expenditure(yuan)**				
总支出	Total Expenditure	971.46	2363.45	2819.77	3419.60
家庭经营费用支出	Expenditure for Household Business	325.97	1035.08	1198.23	1311.53
购置生产性固定资产	Purchasing Productive Fixed Assets	57.71	144.33	115.19	238.51
税费支出	Expenditure for Tax	62.07	173.36	177.24	63.45
生活消费支出	Expenditure for Consumption	506.82	941.58	1236.45	1689.91
转移性和财产性支出	Expenditure for Transfer and Property	18.89	69.10	92.66	116.20
#现金支出	Cash Expenditure	716.73	2009.15	2353.45	2904.92
家庭经营费用支出	Expenditure for Household Business	236.36	940.40	1100.43	1204.95
购置生产性固定资产	Purchasing Productive Fixed Assets	57.71	144.33	115.19	238.51
税费支出	Expenditure for Tax	58.19	172.55	177.22	63.33
生活消费支出	Expenditure for Consumption	333.88	682.13	871.37	1283.90
转移性和财产性支出	Expenditure for Transfer and Property	30.59	69.74	89.24	114.23
平均每人年纯收入(元)	**Per capita Annual Net Income (yuan)**	**683.47**	**1136.45**	**1618.08**	**2244.93**
工资性收入	Wages Income	56.53	64.47	104.58	138.23
家庭经营纯收入	Household Business Income	612.70	967.59	1451.33	1970.36
财产性收入	Property Income		65.30	40.43	81.08
转移性收入	Transfer Income	14.24	39.09	21.74	55.26

8-14　农村居民家庭人均年总收入、纯收入和构成

Per Capita Annual Gross and Net Income and It's Composition of Rural Households

单位：元　　(抽样调查 Sampled Survey)　　(yuan)

项　　目	Item	2003	2004	构成(%) Composition 2003	构成(%) Composition 2004
全年总收入	**Annual Gross Income**	**3564.11**	**3777.91**	**100**	**100**
工资性收入	Wages Income	140.27	138.23	3.94	3.66
家庭经营收入	Household business operation	3319.61	3485.40	93.14	92.26
转移性收入	Transfer Income	45.32	81.08	1.27	2.14
财产性收入	Property Income	58.91	73.20	1.65	1.94
全年总支出	**Annual Gross Expenditure**	**3082.75**	**3419.60**	**100**	**100**
#家庭经营费用支出	Expenditure for Household Business	1209.87	1311.53	39.25	38.35
生活消费支出	Expenditure for Consumption	1465.31	1689.91	47.53	49.42
全年纯收入	**Annual Net Income**	**2106.19**	**2244.93**	**100**	**100**
基本纯收入	Basic Net Income	2015.30	2108.59	95.68	93.93
转移性纯收入	Transfer Net Income	31.98	55.26	1.52	2.46
财产性纯收入	Property Net Income	58.91	81.08	2.80	3.61

8-15　农村居民家庭平均每人总收入和纯收入

Per Capita Annual Gross and Net Income of Rural Households

单位：元　　(抽样调查 Sampled Survey)　　(yuan)

项　　目	Item	1985	1990	1995	2000	2004
总 收 入	**Gross Income**	**588.07**	**1112.01**	**2414.59**	**3129.35**	**3777.91**
基本收入	Basic Income	569.74	1091.22	2303.18	3031.33	3623.63
工资性收入	WagesIncome	39.63	56.53	64.47	104.58	138.23
#集体组织劳动报酬	Income From collective organization			35.49	55.73	
家庭经营收入	Income From Household Business Operation	530.11	1034.69	2238.71	2926.75	3485.40
转移性和财产性收入	Transfer Income and Property Income	18.33	20.79	111.41	98.02	154.28
纯收入	**Net Income**	**394.30**	**683.47**	**1136.45**	**1618.08**	**2244.93**
按收入来源分	By source					
基本收入	Basic Income	382.70	669.23	1032.06	1555.91	2108.59
工资性收入	WagesIncome	39.63	56.53	64.47	104.58	138.23
家庭经营纯收入	Income From Household Business Operation	343.07	612.70	967.59	1451.33	1970.36
农业收入	Agriculture	279.81	541.84	724.06	1109.39	1386.38
林业收入	Forestry	4.79	8.80	27.69	22.51	34.55
牧业收入	Animal Husbandry	34.75	25.39	113.88	171.18	372.88
渔业收入	Fishery	-0.20		3.49		
工业收入	Industry	1.23	1.05	0.73	6.35	13.17
建筑业收入	Construction	3.86	2.51	4.33	4.31	10.49
运输业收入	Transportation	8.35	12.29	12.09	26.48	23.24
批发和零售贸易、餐饮业收入	Wholesale &Retail Trade and Catering Services	6.15	14.13	15.93	23.80	54.85
服务业收入	Services Trade	2.53	4.17	23.80	15.01	20.14
其他收入	Others	1.80	2.52	41.59	72.30	54.66
转移性和财产性收入	Transfer Income and Property Income	11.60	14.24	104.39	62.17	136.34
按收入性质分	Grouped by Type of Income					
生产性纯收入	Productive Income	382.70	669.23	1032.06	1555.91	2108.59
第一产业收入	Primary Industry	319.15	576.03	869.12	1303.08	1793.81
第二产业收入	Secondary Industry	5.09	3.56	5.06	10.66	23.66
第三产业收入	Tertiary Industry	58.46	89.64	157.88	242.17	291.12
非生产性纯收入	Nonproductive Incom	11.60	14.24	104.39	62.17	136.34

8-16 主要年份农村居民家庭人均主要消费品消费量

Per Capita Consumption of Major Consumer Goods of Rural Households in Main Years

单位:公斤 (抽样调查 Sampled Survey) (kg)

项 目	Item	1985	1990	1995	2000	2004
粮食(原粮)	Grain(Unprocessed)	218.95	249.71	206.68	244.83	232.19
#小 麦	Wheat	166.27	201.37	162.52	199.83	189.78
稻 谷	Rice	13.81	13.39	8.44	15.19	18.53
豆类及豆制品	Soybeans and Related Products			0.10	0.50	0.35
#大 豆	Soybean			0.09	0.04	0.06
蔬 菜	Fresh Vegetable	101.35	121.56	64.02	89.24	68.33
食 油	Edible Oil	5.61	7.87	6.38	9.64	8.94
#植物油	Vegetable Oil	4.90	7.41	6.14	9.56	8.83
肉禽及制品	Meats,Poultry and Related Products		9.02	8.11	12.41	13.44
#猪 肉	Pork	2.23	2.25	1.58	1.95	0.89
牛 肉	Beef	6.55	6.77	2.09	1.95	2.04
羊 肉	Mutton			3.22	7.03	8.77
家 禽	Poultry	0.46	0.90	1.00	1.36	1.55
蛋及制品	Eggs and Related Products	1.24	1.77	0.80	1.20	1.02
食 糖	Sugar	0.89	0.63	0.51	0.42	0.38
酒	Liquor	0.78	1.04	0.92	1.12	0.99
糖 果	Candy	0.42	0.36	0.52	0.42	
糕 点	Cake	0.21	0.22	0.24	0.21	
水果及制品	Fruits and Related Products	27.60	41.94	21.78	46.89	34.24
茶 叶	Tea	0.63	5.96	0.56	0.37	0.33

8-17 主要年份农村居民家庭平均每百户耐用消费品拥有量

Number of Durable Consumer Goods Owned by Per-100 Rural Households in Main Years

(抽样调查 Sampled Survey)

项 目	Item	1985	1990	1995	2000	2004
洗衣机(台)	Washing Machine (set)	2.10	12.58	16.39	20.87	27.23
电风扇(台)	Electric Fan (set)	0.78	3.47	7.10	11.60	17.29
电冰箱(台)	Refrigerator (set)		0.40	2.26	9.93	15.87
空调机(台)	Air Conditioner (set)					0.06
抽油烟机(台)	Vaccum Cleaner (set)			0.13	1.13	1.55
自行车(辆)	Bicycle(unit)	68.55	111.21	151.29	136.60	122.19
摩托车(辆)	Motorcycle(unit)	0.31	1.37	4.90	18.33	33.48
电话机(部)	Telephone (set)				15.07	28.19
移动电话(部)	Mobile Telephone (set)				0.33	13.87
组合音响(台)	Hi-Fi Stereo Compound System (set)				8.27	3.16
寻呼机(台)	Beep-pager (set)				1.60	1.42
黑白电视机(台)	Black and White TV (set)	10.00	28.79	55.03	59.33	52.39
彩色电视机(台)	Color TV (set)	0.73	5.16	14.39	31.87	51.35
录放像机(台)	Video-recorder (set)			0.58	1.40	9.42
收录机(台)	Radio Cassette Player (set)	2.29	31.77	48.97	54.87	60.39
照像机(架)	Camera (set)		0.73	1.16	2.20	2.32

8-18 农村居民人均生活消费支出及构成
Per -Capita Annual Living Expendture and Its Composition of Rural Households

单位：元　　(抽样调查 Sampled Survey)　　(yuan)

项　　目	Item	2003	2004	构成(%) Composition(%)	
				2003	2004
生活消费支出	**Expenditure for Consumption**	**1465.31**	**1689.91**	**100**	**100**
食 品	Food	667.11	763.43	45.53	45.18
#主 食	Staple Food	224.99	275.00	15.35	16.27
副 食	Non-Staple Food	387.30	424.64	26.43	25.13
衣 着	Clothing	135.65	138.88	9.25	8.22
居 住	Residence	254.63	304.81	17.38	18.04
家庭设备、用品及服务	Household Facilities, Articles and Services	50.92	56.03	3.48	3.31
医疗保健	Medicines and Medical Services	116.48	141.97	7.95	8.40
交通和通讯	Transportation and Communications	99.04	131.59	6.76	7.79
文教娱乐用品及服务	Cultural, Education and Recreation	112.93	126.92	7.71	7.51
其他商品和服务	Other Commodities and Services	28.55	26.28	1.94	1.55

8-19 农村居民家庭平均每百户耐用消费品拥有量
Number of Durable Consumer Goods Owned by Per100 Rural Households

(抽样调查 Sampled Survey)

项　　目	Item	2003	2004
自行车(辆)	Bicycle(unit)	120.06	122.19
黑白电视机(台)	Black and White TV (set)	53.55	52.39
彩色电视机(台)	Color TV (set)	45.68	51.35
录音机(台)	Tape Recorder (set)	58.52	60.39
照像机(架)	Camera (set)	2.45	2.32
电风扇(台)	Electric Fan (set)	16.06	17.29
洗衣机(台)	Washing Machine (set)	24.90	27.23
电冰箱(台)	Refrigerator (set)	14.19	15.87
摩托车(辆)	Motorcycle(unit)	27.48	33.48
大型家具(件)	Big Furniture (piece)	215.23	228.32

8-20 农村居民家庭人均商品性和自给性生活消费品支出

Per-Capita Self-Sufficiency and Consumption on Commodity Goods of Living Expenditure in Rural Households

(抽样调查 Sampled Survey)

项 目	Item	2003			2004		
		合 计 Total	货币性 In Money	实物性 In Kind	合 计 Total	货币性 In Money	实物性 In Kind
生活消费支出合计(元/人)	**Expenditure for Consumption (yuan/person)**	**1465.31**	**1108.04**	**357.27**	**1689.91**	**1283.90**	**406.01**
食 品	Food	667.11	331.60	335.51	763.43	384.25	379.18
衣 着	Clothing	135.65	125.23	10.42	138.88	134.81	4.07
居 住	Residence	254.63	244.27	10.36	304.81	283.78	21.03
家庭设备、用品及服务	Household Facilities, Articles and Services	50.92	49.94	0.98	56.03	54.30	1.73
医疗保健	Medical Care and Medical Services	116.48	116.48		141.97	141.97	
交通和通讯	Transportation and Communications	99.04	99.04		131.59	131.59	
文教娱乐用品及服务	Cultural, Education and Recreational Articles and Services	112.93	112.93		126.92	126.92	
其他商品和服务	Other Commodities and Services	28.55	28.55		26.28	26.28	
生活消费支出构成(%)	**Living Expendture and It's Composition (%)**	**100**	**100**	**100**	**100**	**100**	**100**
食 品	Food	45.53	29.93	93.91	45.18	29.93	93.39
衣 着	Clothing	9.25	11.30	2.92	8.22	10.50	1.00
居 住	Residence	17.38	22.05	2.90	18.04	22.10	5.18
家庭设备、用品及服务	Household Facilities, Articles and Services	3.48	4.51	0.27	3.31	4.23	0.43
医疗保健	Medical Care and Medical Services	7.95	10.51		8.40	11.06	
交通和通讯	Transportation and Communications	6.76	8.94		7.79	10.25	
文教娱乐用品及服务	Cultural, Education and Recreational Articles and Services	7.71	10.19		7.51	9.89	
其他商品和服务	Other Commodities and Services	1.94	2.58		1.55	2.05	
生活消费支出中货币性和实物性比重(%)	**Percentage of Expenditure for Consumption in Money and Kind (%)**	**100**	**75.62**	**24.38**	**100**	**75.97**	**24.03**
食 品	Food	100	49.71	50.29	100	50.33	49.67
衣 着	Clothing	100	92.32	7.68	100	97.07	2.93
居 住	Residence	100	95.93	4.07	100	93.10	6.90
家庭设备、用品及服务	Household Facilities, Articles and Services	100	98.08	1.92	100	96.91	3.09
医疗保健	Medical Care and Medical Services	100	100		100	100	
交通和通讯	Transportation and Communications	100	100		100	100	
文教娱乐用品及服务	Cultural, Education and Recreational Articles and Services	100	100		100	100	
其他商品和服务	Other Commodities and Services	100	100		100	100	

8-21　农村居民家庭人均纯收入分组

Rural Households Grouped by Per Capita Annual Net Income

(2004 年) (抽样调查 Sampled Survey)

项　目	Item	合 计 Total	0-400 元 0-400 yuan	400-600 元 400-600 yuan	600-800 元 600-800 yuan	800-1000 元 800-1000 yuan	1000-1200 元 1000-1200 yuan
调查户数(户)	**Number of household Surveyed (household)**	**1550**	**27**	**43**	**106**	**121**	**101**
构成(%)	Percentage (%)	100	1.74	2.77	6.84	7.81	6.52
常住人口(人)	**Number of Permanent Residents in the Households Surveyed (person)**	**7922**	**151**	**262**	**645**	**723**	**538**
构成(%)	Percentage (%)	100	1.91	3.31	8.14	9.13	6.79
人均纯收入(元)	**Per Capita Net Income (yuan)**	**2244.93**	**318.89**	**502.82**	**704.08**	**887.01**	**1096.20**

项　目	Item	1200-1500 元 1200-1500 yuan	1500-1700 元 1500-1700 yuan	1700-2000 元 1700-2000 yuan	2000-2500 元 2000-2500 yuan	2500-3000 元 2500-3000 yuan
调查户数(户)	**Number of household Surveyed (household)**	**156**	**110**	**138**	**184**	**157**
构成(%)	Percentage (%)	10.06	7.10	8.90	11.87	10.13
常住人口(人)	**Number of Permanent Residents in the Households Surveyed (person)**	**842**	**575**	**723**	**890**	**785**
构成(%)	Percentage (%)	10.63	7.26	9.13	11.23	9.91
人均纯收入(元)	**Per Capita Net Income (yuan)**	**1335.45**	**1581.37**	**1850.84**	**2227.77**	**2749.21**

项　目	Item	3000-3500 元 3000-3500 yuan	3500-4000 元 3500-4000 yuan	4000-4500 元 4000-4500 yuan	4500-5000 元 4500-5000 yuan	5000 元以上 over 5000 yuan
调查户数(户)	**Number of household Surveyed (household)**	**86**	**91**	**66**	**36**	**128**
构成(%)	Percentage (%)	5.55	5.87	4.26	2.32	8.26
常住人口(人)	**Number of Permanent Residents in the Households Surveyed (person)**	**407**	**403**	**285**	**166**	**527**
构成(%)	Percentage (%)	5.14	5.09	3.60	2.10	6.65
人均纯收入(元)	**Per Capita Net Income (yuan)**	**3227.3**	**3746.36**	**4246.46**	**4714.94**	**7257.53**

8-22 分地区农村居民家庭人均总收入和纯收入

Per Capita Annual Gross and Net Income by Region

单位：元 (2004 年) (抽样调查 Sampled Survey) (yuan)

项目 Item	自治区 Autonomous Region	昌吉州 Changji Hui Autonomous Prefecture	伊犁州直属县(市) Counties (Cities) Direct Under Ili Prefecture	塔城地区 Tacheng [Tarbagatai] Administrative Office
调查县、市 Number of County and City Surveyed	**30**	**4**	**5**	**4**
调查户数(户) Number of Household Surveyed (household)	**1550**	**155**	**240**	**145**
常住人口(人) Number of Permanent ResidentsIn the Households Surveyed (person)	**7922**	**593**	**1237**	**730**
总收入 Annual Gross Income	**3777.91**	**7842.22**	**4101.02**	**6405.70**
工资性收入 Wages Income	138.23	439.17	236.36	310.50
在非企业组织中劳动得到的 From Non-enterprise Organization	55.90	106.45	59.59	173.95
在本地企业中劳动得到的 From Local Enterprise	53.36	198.10	168.20	108.33
常住人口外出从业得到的 Out of Migrant Workers	28.97	134.62	8.57	28.22
家庭经营收入 Income From Household opertation	3485.40	7152.33	3728.27	5874.56
农业收入 Agriculture	2575.87	5264.86	2598.56	4249.26
#种植业收入 Farming	2501.97	5142.53	2460.61	4218.01
林业收入 Forestry	38.12	3.07	11.87	1.77
牧业收入 Animal Husbandry	619.08	1282.60	827.17	1488.78
渔业收入 Fishery		174.60		
工业收入 Industry	20.35	15.09	38.78	3.25
建筑业收入 Construction	15.91	9.77	78.20	
交通、运输和邮电业收入 Transportation, Postal and Telecommunications Services	52.61	224.82	58.23	43.01
批发和零售贸易、餐饮业收入 Wholesale, Retail Sail and Catering Trades	76.15	50.96	78.07	76.24
社会服务业收入 Social Sservices	23.53	49.54	12.75	7.31
文教卫生业收入 Cultural, Education, Medicines and Medical Services	3.39	2.86	18.91	
其他家庭经营收入 Others	60.39	74.16	5.73	4.94
财产性收入 Property Income	81.08	76.76	55.90	105.48
#利 息 Interest	1.02	9.02		1.02
租 金 Rent	13.66	11.47	2.73	26.03
转移性收入 Transfer Income	73.20	173.96	80.49	115.16
可支配收入 Disposable Income	2146.77	3949.51	2407.35	2330.22
全年家庭纯收入 Annual Net Income	2244.93	4328.43	2576.34	2902.79

8-22 续表 Continued

单位：元 (yuan)

项　　目　　Item	阿勒泰地区 Altay Adminis trative Office	巴音郭楞蒙古自治州 Bayangol Mongol Autonomous Prefecture	阿克苏地区 Aksu Adminis-trative Office	喀什地区 Kashgar [Kaxgar] Adminis-trative Office	和田地区 Hotan Adminis-trative Office
调查县、市 Number of County and City Surveyed	**4**	**6**	**5**	**6**	**4**
调查户数(户) Number of Household Surveyed (household)	**130**	**250**	**255**	**330**	**225**
常住人口(人) Number of Permanent ResidentsIn the Households Surveyed (person)	**707**	**1235**	**1316**	**1750**	**1130**
总收入 Annual Gross Income	**4403.50**	**6462.38**	**4610.33**	**2492.91**	**1773.61**
工资性收入 Wages Income	269.14	225.47	62.38	36.94	85.15
在非企业组织中劳动得到的 From Non-enterprise Organization	151.75	99.89	33.45	18.51	16.66
在本地企业中劳动得到的 From Local Enterprise	49.50	108.34	28.93	18.43	4.14
常住人口外出从业得到的 Out of Migrant Workers	67.89	17.25			64.35
家庭经营收入 Income From Household opertation	3995.21	5999.55	4425.69	2404.57	1647.73
农业收入 Agriculture	1879.92	4599.26	3366.82	1711.89	907.89
#种植业收入 Farming	1879.92	4465.75	3228.39	1687.51	891.51
林业收入 Forestry		61.33	42.11	49.40	58.70
牧业收入 Animal Husbandry	1665.77	1193.02	742.75	533.02	357.42
渔业收入 Fishery				1.14	
工业收入 Industry	12.73	5.36	3.95	4.94	69.33
建筑业收入 Construction	27.51	14.43	0.92	5.37	7.58
交通、运输和邮电业收入 Transportation, Postal and Telecommunications Services	53.68	62.95	34.72	16.46	6.33
批发和零售贸易、餐饮业收入 Wholesale, Retail Sail and Catering Trades	127.28	30.10	178.92	31.09	19.73
社会服务业收入 Social Services	44.55	5.28	33.14	12.62	13.46
文教卫生业收入 Cultural, Education, Medicines and Medical Services					
其他家庭经营收入 Others	183.77	27.82	22.36	38.64	207.29
财产性收入 Property Income	35.96	153.48	68.90	13.95	5.61
#利　息 Interest	9.64	9.42	0.35		
租　金 Rent		18.95	0.76	0.06	
转移性收入 Transfer Income	103.19	83.88	53.36	37.45	35.12
可支配收入 Disposable Income	7144.58	3453.82	2849.28	1577.15	1124.67
全年家庭纯收入 Annual Net Income	2830.99	3623.70	2919.71	1589.25	1133.01

8-23 分地区农村居民家庭平均每人总支出

Per Capita Total Expenditure of Rural Household by Region

单位：元 (2004 年)(抽样调查 Sampled Survey) (yuan)

项 目 Item	自治区 Autonomous Region	昌吉州 Changji Hui Autonomous Prefecture	伊犁州直属县(市) Counties (Cities) Direct Under Ili Prefecture	塔城地区 Tacheng [Tarbagatai] Administrative Office
全年总支出 Annual Total Expenditure	**3419.60**	**6314.29**	**3286.50**	**6109.34**
家庭经营费用支出 Expenditure for Household Business	**1311.53**	**3231.28**	**1318.04**	**2935.33**
农业生产 Agriculture	1052.80	2385.68	977.98	2417.07
#种植业 Farming	631.06	1024.94	684.55	1135.38
林业生产 Forestry	3.33	1.30	7.37	17.32
牧业生产 Animal Husbandry	194.43	502.19	250.14	468.49
渔业生产 Fishery		137.67	0.01	
工业生产 Industry	6.09		3.62	3.00
建筑业生产 Construction	4.72	6.48	22.22	
交通、运输和邮电业 Transportation, Postal and Telecommunications Services	22.50	81.73	30.20	10.06
批发和零售贸易、餐饮业 Wholesale, Retail Sale and Catering Trades	18.49	14.84	13.09	16.15
社会服务业支出 Social Services	1.58	29.80	1.24	1.83
其他经营支出 Others	7.59	71.59	12.17	1.41
购置生产用固定资产支出 Expenditure for Productive Fixed Assets	**238.51**	**111.78**	**89.68**	**463.16**
税费支出 Taxes and Fee	**63.45**	**125.72**	**46.42**	**167.13**
生活消费支出 Expenditure for Consumption	**1689.91**	**2646.15**	**1640.99**	**2326.56**
食 品 Food	763.43	1103.98	704.88	1176.33
#主 食 Staple Food	275.00	306.08	240.04	281.28
副 食 Non-Staple Food	343.13	584.75	361.03	692.30
其他食品 Other Food	81.51	88.12	71.53	96.58
衣 着 Clothing	138.88	212.52	161.62	246.64
居 住 Residence	304.81	265.60	264.26	245.07
家庭设备、用品及服务 Household Facilities, Articles and Services	56.03	107.43	49.28	85.99
医疗保健 Medicines and Medical Services	141.97	219.70	142.66	164.40
交通和通讯 Transportation and Communications	131.59	196.79	151.71	170.34
文化教育娱乐用品及服务 Cultural, Education and Recreational Articles and Services	126.92	470.33	137.63	212.54
其他商品和服务 Other Commodities and Services	26.28	69.80	28.95	25.25
附：生产用固定资产折旧 Depreciation Charge for productive Fixed Assets	140.05	249.06	137.84	267.76

8-23 续表 Continued

单位：元 (yuan)

项 目 Item	阿勒泰地区 Altay Adminis-trative Office	巴音郭楞蒙古自治州 Bayangol Mongol Autonomous Prefecture	阿克苏地区 Aksu Adminis-Trative Office	喀什地区 Kashgar [Kaxgar] Adminis-trative Office	和田地区 Hotan Adminis-trative Office
全年总支出 Annual Total Expenditure	**3236.61**	**5779.92**	**3852.23**	**2085.01**	**1591.85**
家庭经营费用支出 Expenditure for Household Business	**1251.91**	**2521.39**	**1371.49**	**796.48**	**566.61**
农业生产 Agriculture	629.21	1885.53	1119.15	642.35	353.51
#种植业 Farming	396.89	1041.46	755.55	447.16	246.61
林业生产 Forestry		3.52	8.27	1.50	1.26
牧业生产 Animal Husbandry	492.11	612.87	141.65	145.87	135.34
渔业生产 Fishery		0.04	0.01		
工业生产 Industry	3.39	0.72		0.32	27.63
建筑业生产 Construction	1.98	3.02	0.98	0.64	0.85
交通、运输和邮电业 Transportation, Postal and Telecommunications Services	41.60	13.67	7.49	0.46	2.66
批发和零售贸易、餐饮业 Wholesale, Retail Sale and Catering Trades	43.58	1.25	91.61	0.38	1.33
社会服务业支出 Social Services	1.56	0.19	0.38	1.28	
其他经营支出 Others	38.48	0.58	1.95	3.68	44.03
购置生产用固定资产支出 Expenditure for Productive Fixed Assets	**144.28**	**353.36**	**413.76**	**163.29**	**83.59**
税费支出 Taxes and Fee	**86.31**	**93.49**	**109.87**	**38.98**	**34.40**
生活消费支出 Expenditure for Consumption	**1655.42**	**2633.13**	**1887.01**	**1071.59**	**881.33**
食 品 Food	969.10	1115.98	826.21	564.45	484.73
#主 食 Staple Food	293.45	247.94	278.58	233.33	222.22
副 食 Non-Staple Food	621.82	655.54	374.84	250.85	173.06
其他食品 Other Food	28.75	108.22	123.29	40.42	50.27
衣 着 Clothing	206.19	232.25	157.27	119.29	90.47
居 住 Residence	155.31	304.68	324.61	227.08	126.40
家庭设备、用品及服务 Household Facilities, Articles and Services	75.48	95.30	53.98	25.51	32.94
医疗保健 Medicines and Medical Services	38.95	228.78	249.93	58.55	68.28
交通和通讯 Transportation and Communications	81.61	294.60	157.17	52.67	56.83
文化教育娱乐用品及服务 Cultural, Education and Recreational Articles and Services	109.71	324.91	92.32	14.14	11.43
其他商品和服务 Other Commodities and Services	19.07	36.63	25.52	9.90	10.25
附：生产用固定资产折旧 Depreciation Charge for productive Fixed Assets	207.48	215.43	209.59	65.71	22.05

8-24 分地区农村居民家庭人均现金收支

Per Capita Income and Expenditure in Cash of Rural Household by Region

单位：元 (2004 年)(抽样调查 Sampled Survey) (yuan)

项 目	Item	自治区 Autonomous Region	昌吉州 Changji Hui Autonomous Prefecture	伊犁州直属县(市) Counties (Cities) Direct Under Ili Prefecture	塔城地区 Tacheng Administrative Office
期内现金收入	**Annual Total Income In Cash**	**2945.19**	**6225.89**	**3243.21**	**5268.42**
工资性收入	Wages Income	138.23	439.17	235.31	252.09
在非企业组织中劳动得到的	From Non-enterprise Organization	55.90	106.45	59.11	134.22
在本地企业中劳动得到的	From Local Enterprise	53.36	198.10	167.63	97.04
常住人口外出从业得到的	Out of Migrant Workers	28.97	134.62	8.57	20.83
其 他	Others				
家庭经营收入	Income of Household Operation	2660.93	5573.54	2897.71	4804.68
出售产品的收入	From Products Sales	2408.66	5135.37	2608.24	4669.94
出售农业产品收入	Agriculture	1847.19	3920.93	1852.99	3189.76
#种植业	Farming	1773.52	3901.72	1720.89	3131.11
出售林业产品收入	Forestry	32.77	3.07	11.57	1.77
出售牧业产品收入	Animal Husbandry	528.64	1036.95	742.48	1478.41
出售渔业产品收入	Fishery		174.42		
出售工业产品的收入	Industrial	0.06		1.20	
出售其他产品的收入	Others				
工业加工费	Industry	20.29	15.09	37.58	3.25
建 筑 业	Construction	15.91	20.73	78.20	
交通运输	Transportation	52.61	224.82	58.23	43.01
批发和零售贸易、餐饮业	Wholesale, Retail Sale and Catering Trades	76.15	50.96	78.07	76.24
社会服务业	Social Services	23.53	49.54	12.75	7.31
文教卫生业	Culture, Education, Medicines and Medical Services	3.39	2.86	18.91	
其他家庭经营收入	Others	60.39	74.17	5.73	4.93
财产性收入	Property Income	72.90	40.59	29.70	96.49
#利 息	Interest	1.02	9.02		1.02
租 金	Rent	13.66	11.47	2.73	26.03
转移性收入	Transfer Income	73.13	172.59	80.49	115.16
非收入所得	**Non-income Gain**	**842.25**	**1159.68**	**381.36**	**1680.29**
从银行信用社得到的贷款	Credit	351.36	517.28	170.45	1069.59
借入款	Borrowed Money	171.40	83.25	98.00	331.82
收回借出款	Recall Loaned Money	42.85	173.55	11.96	28.73
从银行信用社取回存款	Take Deposit back	141.23	315.85	35.84	222.78
出售财产所得款	Sold Property	58.78	11.41	27.35	7.31
期内现金支出	**Annual Expenditure in Cash**	**2904.92**	**5655.73**	**2831.66**	**5388.47**
生产费用支出	Producing Expenditure	1443.57	3222.85	1276.61	3130.48
家庭经营费用支出	Expenditure for Household Business	1204.95	3091.10	1186.93	2667.31
农业生产支出	Agriculture	995.66	2357.55	919.03	2264.97
林业生产支出	Forestry	3.33	1.30	7.37	21.07
牧业生产支出	Animal Husbandry	145.00	425.11	177.98	348.80
渔业生产支出	Fishery		137.67	0.01	

8-24 续表 1Continued

单位：元 (yuan)

项　　目	Item	自治区 Autonomous Region	昌吉州 Changji Hui Autonomous Prefecture	伊犁州直属县(市) Counties (Cities) Direct Under Ili Prefecture	塔城地区 Tacheng Administrative Office
工业生产支出	Industry	6.09		3.62	3.00
建筑业生产支出	Construction	4.72	6.48	22.22	
交通运输支出	Transportation	22.50	81.73	30.20	10.06
批发和零售贸易、餐饮业	Wholesale, Retail Sale and Catering Trades	18.49	14.84	13.09	16.15
社会服务业支出	Social Services	1.58	29.80	1.24	1.84
文教卫生业	Cultural, Education, Medicines and Medical Services	...	16.53	...	1.40
其他经营支出	Others	7.58	20.09	12.17	0.02
购置生产性固定资产支出	Expenditure for Productive Fixed Assets	238.62	131.75	89.68	463.17
税费支出	Taxes and Fee	63.33	101.55	46.42	167.13
生活消费支出	Expenditure for Consumption	1283.90	2132.35	1317.25	1876.46
财产性支出	Expenditure for Property	38.33	43.43	64.67	153.75
转移性支出	Expenditure for Transfer	75.79	155.55	126.71	60.65
非消费性现金付出	**Expenditure for Non-Consumption**	**809.91**	**1528.49**	**319.82**	**1292.96**
归还银行信用社贷款	Loan Returned to Bank	261.03	613.59	140.86	444.90
借出款	Lending Money	17.03	15.01	3.29	39.45
归还借款	Return Borrowed Money	177.93	208.93	55.72	135.92
存入银行信用社	Deposit	274.93	555.23	33.95	593.29
期末金融资产余额	**Balance of Financial Assets in Year-end**	**1502.87**	**3916.93**	**1818.68**	**2276.66**
银行存款	Deposit	824.98	3330.61	442.17	1980.96
手存现金	Cash	677.89	287.84	1376.51	295.70
期末债务余额	**Balance of Debt in Year-end**	**287.67**	**367.62**	**126.72**	**750.27**
银行、信用社贷款	Loan from Bank and Credit Cooperatives	196.85	258.01	89.98	408.63
乡村集体组织、企业借(欠)款	Borrowed Money from Collective Units and Enterprises	5.46	5.06		15.75
个人借(欠)款	Borrowed Money from Individual	83.98	104.55	44.02	325.89
生活消费支出的现金	**Expenditure for Consumption**	**1283.90**	**2132.35**	**1317.25**	**1876.46**
食　品	Food	384.25	659.38	397.43	726.23
#主　食	Staple Food	74.66	138.51	99.55	191.35
副　食	Non-Staple Food	211.22	303.90	219.11	286.78
衣　着	Clothing	134.81	203.25	160.93	246.64
居　住	Residence	283.78	256.04	250.44	245.07
家庭设备、用品及服务	Household Facilities，Articles and Services	54.32	107.26	48.12	85.99
医疗保健	Medicines and Medical Services	141.97	189.70	142.66	164.40
交通和通讯	Transportation and Communications	131.59	192.15	151.71	170.34
文化教育、娱乐用品及服务	Cultural，Education and Recreational Articles and Services	126.92	457.43	137.63	212.54
文化教育、娱乐用品	Cultural，Education and Recreational Articles	20.97	42.60	19.85	15.99
文化教育、娱乐服务	Cultural，Education and Recreational Services	89.62	402.07	109.50	194.28
#学杂费	Tuition	80.90	383.03	98.78	186.11
技术培训费	Charge for Training	3.60	1.50	3.29	4.88
其他商品和服务	Other Commodities and Services	26.26	67.14	28.33	25.25
商品性支出	Commodities	13.50	25.17	13.16	15.05
服务支出	Services	12.76	41.97	15.17	10.20

8-24 续表 2 Continued

单位：元 (yuan)

项 目	Item	阿勒泰地区 Altay Administrative Office	巴音郭楞蒙古自治州 Bayangol Mongol Autonomous Prefecture	阿克苏地区 Aksu Administrative Office	喀什地区 Kashgar [Kaxgar] Administrative Office	和田地区 Hotan Administrative Office
期内现金收入	**Annual Total Income In Cash**	**3484.71**	**5968.56**	**3508.49**	**1707.02**	**1167.35**
工资性收入	Wages Income	269.14	225.47	62.38	36.94	85.15
在非企业组织中劳动得到的	From Non-enterprise Organization	151.75	99.89	33.45	18.51	16.66
在本地企业中劳动得到的	From Local Enterprise	49.50	108.34	28.93	18.43	4.14
常住人口外出从业得到的	Out of Migrant Workers	67.89	17.24			64.35
其 他	Others					
家庭经营收入	Income of Household Operation	3112.97	5572.31	3356.50	1624.56	1042.25
出售产品的收入	From Products Sales	2838.14	5426.36	3082.88	1515.43	718.53
出售农业产品收入	Agriculture	1471.78	4239.93	2614.35	1009.96	370.32
#种植业	Farming	1471.78	4106.42	2475.91	985.58	353.93
出售林业产品收入	Forestry		81.24	41.27	45.51	42.34
出售牧业产品收入	Animal Husbandry	1366.36	1105.19	426.88	458.82	305.87
出售渔业产品收入	Fishery				1.14	
出售工业产品的收入	Industrial			0.38		
出售其他产品的收入	Others					
工业加工费	Industry		5.36	3.57	4.94	69.33
建 筑 业	Construction	27.51	14.43	0.92	5.37	7.58
交通运输	Transportation	54.98	62.95	34.72	16.46	6.33
批发和零售贸易、餐饮业	Wholesale, Retail Sale and Catering Trades	127.34	30.10	178.92	31.09	19.73
社会服务业	Social Services	55.59	5.28	33.14	12.62	13.46
文教卫生业	Culture, Education, Medicines and Medical Services					
其他家庭经营收入	Others	9.41	27.83	22.35	38.65	207.29
财产性收入	Property Income	27.39	86.91	36.24	8.08	4.83
#利 息	Interest	9.64	9.42	0.35		
租 金	Rent		18.95	0.76	0.06	
转移性收入	Transfer Income	75.21	83.87	53.37	37.44	35.12
非收入所得	**Non-income Gain**	**138.22**	**1876.06**	**1255.91**	**340.61**	**199.88**
从银行信用社得到的贷款	Credit	86.99	437.31	585.71	210.78	45.71
借入款	Borrowed Money	5.66	100.75	179.40	46.22	41.76
收回借出款	Recall Loaned Money		25.59	20.47	8.09	15.23
从银行信用社取回存款	Take Deposit back	42.43	1112.53	182.07	30.94	3.27
出售财产所得款	Sold Property		19.98	110.28	21.30	38.66
期内现金支出	**Annual Expenditure in Cash**	**2439.98**	**5273.26**	**3143.05**	**1570.46**	**1210.29**
生产费用支出	Producing Expenditure	1076.79	2754.03	1657.11	840.60	607.55
家庭经营费用支出	Expenditure for Household Business	984.85	2400.37	1243.34	677.23	523.91
农业生产支出	Agriculture	550.84	1874.38	1015.55	559.59	325.83
林业生产支出	Forestry		3.52	8.27	1.50	1.26
牧业生产支出	Animal Husbandry	324.41	503.01	117.10	109.38	120.33
渔业生产支出	Fishery		0.04	0.01		

8-24 续表 3 Continued

单位：元 (yuan)

项　目	Item	阿勒泰地区 Altay Administrative Office	巴音郭楞蒙古自治州 Bayangol Mongol Autonomous Prefecture	阿克苏地区 Aksu Administrative Office	喀什地区 Kashgar [Kaxgar] Administrative Office	和田地区 Hotan Administrative Office
工业生产支出	Industry	8.05	0.72		0.32	27.63
建筑业生产支出	Construction	1.98	3.02	0.98	0.64	0.85
交通运输支出	Transportation	18.80	13.67	7.49	0.46	2.66
批发和零售贸易、餐饮业	Wholesale, Retail Sale and Catering Trades	42.95	1.25	91.61	0.38	1.33
社会服务业支出	Social Services	2.26	0.19	0.38	1.28	
文教卫生业	Cultural, Education, Medicines and Medical Services					0.05
其他经营支出	Others	35.56	0.57	1.95	3.68	43.97
购置生产性固定资产支出	Expenditure for Productive Fixed Assets	91.94	353.66	413.77	163.37	83.64
税费支出	Taxes and Fee	87.97	93.34	109.87	38.98	34.40
生活消费支出	Expenditure for Consumption	1213.73	2247.64	1317.93	676.31	542.46
财产性支出	Expenditure for Property	1.29	94.01	46.27	2.18	1.95
转移性支出	Expenditure for Transfer	60.20	84.24	11.87	12.39	23.93
非消费性现金付出	**Expenditure for Non-Consumption**	**873.20**	**1746.20**	**856.15**	**265.48**	**123.57**
归还银行信用社贷款	Returned Loan to Bank	67.56	315.00	384.07	161.72	61.36
借出款	Lending Money	4.37	12.03	16.35	8.39	4.15
归还借款	Return Borrowed Money	5.66	94.13	166.30	21.48	31.69
存入银行信用社	Deposit	785.01	1250.23	171.50	26.21	22.07
期末金融资产余额	**Balance of Financial Assets in Year-end**	**3329.70**	**3073.60**	**1336.88**	**369.41**	**219.13**
银行存款	Deposit	2397.73	2328.64	833.78	163.99	4.42
手存现金	Cash	931.97	744.96	503.02	205.42	214.70
期末债务余额	**Balance of Debt in Year-end**	**8.20**	**326.03**	**198.33**	**68.29**	**55.26**
银行、信用社贷款	Loan from Bank and Credit Cooperatives	2.12	283.40	142.40	40.74	30.22
乡村集体组织、企业借(欠)款	Borrowed Money from Collective Units and Enterprises			2.28	14.24	0.99
个人借(欠)款	Borrowed Money from Individuals	6.08	42.63	48.64	13.31	20.19
生活消费支出的现金	**Expenditure for Consumption**	**1213.73**	**2247.64**	**1317.93**	**676.31**	**542.46**
食　品	Food	507.87	733.81	340.31	225.11	175.67
#主　食	Staple Food	195.20	127.16	63.68	27.26	19.63
副　食	Non-Staple Food	257.42	430.90	208.37	140.56	103.32
衣　着	Clothing	206.16	229.09	153.62	111.15	89.09
居　住	Residence	155.32	304.68	245.25	183.40	104.27
家庭设备、用品及服务	Household Facilities，Articles and Services	75.48	95.14	53.82	21.39	26.64
医疗保健	Medicines and Medical Services	38.95	228.78	249.93	58.55	68.28
交通和通讯	Transportation and Communications	101.17	294.60	157.17	52.67	56.83
文化教育、娱乐用品及服务	Cultural,Education and Recreational Articles and Services	109.71	324.91	92.32	14.14	11.43
文化教育、娱乐用品	Cultural, Education and Recreational Articles	19.16	41.22	29.29	4.69	2.22
文化教育、娱乐服务	Cultural, Education and Recreational Services	90.36	264.95	49.82	9.08	8.97
#学杂费	Tuition	90.10	252.20	45.04	7.44	8.56
技术培训费	Charge for Training		2.99	2.59	0.29	
其他商品和服务	Other Commodities and Services	19.07	36.63	25.51	9.90	10.25
商品性支出	Commodities Expenditure	12.81	15.68	21.37	2.98	8.44
服务支出	Services Expenditure	6.26	20.95	4.14	6.92	1.81

8-25 农村居民家庭房屋使用情况

Housing Conditions of Rural Households

(抽样调查 Sampled Survey)

项 目	Item	1985	1990	1995	2000	2004
本年新建房屋	**Newly-Built House Within the Year**					
面积(平方米/人)	Per Capita Floor Space of Houses (sq.m/person)	0.93	0.78	0.44	0.38	0.73
价值(元/平方米)	Value of Houses (yuan/sq.m)	19.93	51.25	140.33	169.37	190.34
住房结构	Structure of House (sq.m/person)					
#钢筋混凝土结构	Reinforced Concrete Structure	0.03	0.08	0.05	0.03	
砖木结构	Brick and Wood Structure	0.25	0.44	0.18	0.16	0.52
生活用房面积(平方米 /人)	Per Capita Living Rooms Space (sq.m/person)	0.73	0.55	0.34	0.38	0.50
年末住房情况	**Housing at the End of Year**					
住房面积(平方米/人)	Per capita Floor Space of Houses (sq.m/person)	12.72	14.04	16.12	17.25	19.10
住房价值(元/平方米)	Value of Houses (yuan/sq.m)	15.98	22.16	51.63	120.86	146.00
住房结构(平方米 /人)	Structure of House (sq.m/person)					
#钢筋混凝土结构	Reinforced Concrete Structure	0.05	0.29	0.30	0.53	0.64
砖木结构	Brick and Wood Structure	1.63	3.97	6.71	2.75	4.89

8-26 城乡新建住宅面积和居民住房情况

Floor Space Completed and Housing Conditions of Urban and Rural Residents

年 份 Year	城镇新建住宅面积(万平方米) Floor Space of New Residential Buildings in Urban Areas (10 000 sq.m)	#城镇个人 Constructed by Urban Individuals	农村新建房屋面积(万平方米) Floor Space of Newly-Built Houses in Rural Areas (10 000 sq.m)	城镇人均使用面积(平方米) Per capita Gross Living Space in Urban Areas (sq.m)	城镇人均建筑面积(平方米) Per capita Floor Space in Urban Areas (sq.m)	农村人均居住面积(平方米) Per capita Net Living Space in Rural Areas (sq.m)
1985	353.26	82.28	463.00	10.70	14.27	12.75
1990	381.61	76.75	593.96	13.55	18.07	14.04
1991	336.96	53.36	626.00	14.39	19.19	13.63
1992	398.68	73.30	485.60	15.83	21.11	14.27
1993	360.20	179.31	577.08	16.82	22.43	16.21
1994	530.92	103.77	549.16	16.06	21.41	16.33
1995	567.54	123.06	496.60	16.57	22.09	16.12
1996	683.51	138.90	757.71	17.61	23.48	16.12
1997	673.58	123.67	719.53	13.62	18.16	16.13
1998	874.97	129.16	729.71	18.95	25.27	16.20
1999	1315.89	130.15	705.00	19.76	26.35	16.90
2000	1327.29	175.10	554.59	20.06	26.75	17.25
2001	1517.22	224.23	894.56	20.90	27.47	18.04
2002	1256.72	146.97	534.10	18.17	23.43	18.56
2003	1546.23	200.53	800.81	17.91	23.23	18.62
2004	1565.16	179.28	732.84	18.82	24.44	19.10

8-27 分地区农村居民家庭平均每人粮食收支平衡表

Per Capita Grain Banlance of Debit and Credit by Region

单位：公斤　　(2004 年)(抽样调查 Sampled Survey)　　(kg)

项 目	Item	自治区 Autonomous Region	昌吉州 Changji Hui Autonomous Prefecture	伊犁州直属县(市) Counties (Cities) Direct Under Ili Prefecture	塔城地区 Tacheng [Tarbagatai] Administrative Office
年初粮食结存	**Inventory of Grain at Beginning of year**	**614.83**	**837.36**	**558.08**	**330.99**
粮食收入合计	**Total of Debit**	**900.57**	**1984.19**	**1532.23**	**767.74**
家庭经营生产的	From household Operation	819.97	1768.80	1423.93	600.87
购 入	Purchases	79.64	199.18	108.30	162.55
借 入	Borrowing	0.53			1.64
收回借出粮	Recall Lent Grain	0.25			2.68
其他粮食收入	Others	0.18	16.21		
粮食支出合计	**Total of Expenditure**	**684.47**	**1471.79**	**1197.50**	**726.86**
主食用粮	Staple Food	232.19	219.89	195.89	218.22
其他生活用粮	Grain for Other Living				3.67
出 售	Sales	312.21	1011.95	873.11	298.76
种 籽	Seeds	26.66	37.02	64.11	25.58
饲 料	Fodder	109.63	161.47	64.39	180.63
借 出	Lending				
归还借粮	Return Borrowed Grain				
其他粮食支出	Others	3.78	41.46		
年末粮食结存(实际数)	**Inventory of Grain at Year-end**	**456.20**	**751.10**	**861.70**	**334.98**
#口 粮	Rations	160.58	165.31	184.40	96.49
种 籽	Seeds	17.17	44.32	72.08	29.32
饲 料	Fodder	141.62	263.11	303.21	133.32

项 目	Item	阿勒泰地区 Altay Adminis-trative Office	巴音郭楞蒙古自治州 Bayangol Mongol Autonomous Prefecture	阿克苏地区 Aksu Adminis-trative Office	喀什地区 Kashgar [Kaxgar] Adminis-trative Office	和田地区 Hotan Adminis-trative Office
年初粮食结存	**Inventory of Grain at Beginning of year**	**366.72**	**341.01**	**683.15**	**440.77**	**325.77**
粮食收入合计	**Total of Debit**	**1060.88**	**749.47**	**906.72**	**713.11**	**572.29**
家庭经营生产的	From household Operation	899.36	612.57	835.90	678.28	556.19
购 入	Purchases	161.52	136.90	70.63	34.83	16.10
借 入	Borrowing			0.19		
收回借出粮	Recall lent Grain					
其他粮食收入	Others					
粮食支出合计	**Total of Expenditure**	**1033.12**	**705.22**	**829.21**	**452.48**	**364.57**
主食用粮	Staple Food	209.76	181.89	234.52	208.02	211.79
其他生活用粮	Grain for Other Living					
出 售	Sales	708.41	349.06	416.79	105.75	116.21
种 籽	Seeds	24.40	19.02	16.22	31.44	18.80
饲 料	Fodder	90.55	154.95	150.74	99.03	17.77
借 出	Lending		0.16			
归还借粮	Return Borrowed Grain					
其他粮食支出	Others		0.14	10.94	8.24	
年末粮食结存(实际数)	**Inventory of Grain at Year-end**	**346.99**	**392.55**	**397.24**	**356.90**	**336.08**
#口 粮	Rations	26.63	155.64	193.25	172.40	154.23
种 籽	Seeds	2.84	10.62	6.33	14.93	27.31
饲 料	Fodder	5.63	133.85	117.15	86.57	87.21

8-28 农村居民家庭平均每户饲养畜禽、其他小动物生产情况
Output of Livestock, Poultry and Other Small Animals Per Rural Households

单位：公斤 (抽样调查)(Sampled Surrey) (kg)

年 份 Year	出售自宰猪肉产量 Output of Pork Sold Self-slaugutered	出售自宰羊肉产量 Output of Mutton Sold and Self-slaughtered	羊毛产量 Output of Wool	牛羊奶产量 Output of Cow and Sheep Milk	出售自宰家禽产量 Output of Poultry Sold and Self-slaughtered	禽蛋产量 Output of Poultry and Eggs	蚕茧产量 Output of Silkworm
1980	14.46	20.35	6.16			7.23	
1985	16.76	47.54	10.51	51.53		13.95	0.26
1990	24.97	45.72	15.86	67.16		17.68	1.26
1991	18.23	66.45	11.79	77.31		18.20	2.44
1992	15.73	69.42	9.33	92.63		23.86	1.31
1993	21.97	47.29	9.68	83.19	17.22	32.56	2.10
1994	17.47	41.32	13.77	72.74	14.44	41.86	2.20
1995	23.42	61.41	14.86	66.16	28.86	23.14	1.69
1996	23.10	62.09	7.61	34.93	7.61	8.20	0.89
1997	12.46	73.78	7.37	33.57	9.87	7.97	1.08
1998	10.18	84.42	5.40	42.53	7.39	8.78	1.58
1999	12.91	100.45	4.06	34.92	7.65	13.90	1.38
2000	16.48	94.55	5.49	34.27	13.03	25.26	1.01
2001	13.24	91.54			16.92	35.71	
2002	11.01	110.97			16.09	41.07	
2003	13.16	86.23	4.51	91.91	12.48	37.10	0.66
2004	10.30	105.20	4.09	89.54	12.75	6.03	0.23

8-29 农村居民家庭平均每户饲养畜禽、其他小动物出售量
Quantities of Livestock, Poultry and Other Small Animals Sold Per Rural Households

(抽样调查) (Sampled Surrey)

年 份 Year	猪(头) Pork (head)	牛(头) Cattle (head)	羊(只) Sheep (head)	家禽(只) Poultry (head)	蛋类(公斤) Eggs (kg)	羊毛(公斤) Wool (kg)	牛羊奶(公斤) Milk (kg)
1985	0.10		1.94	3.30	7.68	6.87	5.68
1990	0.22	0.11	1.50	4.15	8.25	9.63	17.47
1991	0.15	0.20	2.58	3.64	5.92	5.77	19.00
1992	0.12	0.18	2.47	3.37	13.51	3.56	19.57
1993	0.23	1.02	3.00	3.68	23.45	4.98	24.30
1994	0.02	0.22	3.21	5.97	33.23	5.58	38.66
1995	0.17	0.22	2.21	11.69	17.28	5.80	26.76
1996	0.24	0.14	2.14	1.98	3.08	3.13	12.43
1997	0.11	0.16	2.74	3.00	3.51	4.16	11.56
1998	0.07	0.15	3.47	2.14	4.30	2.23	18.04
1999	0.08	0.25	3.89	2.70	9.23	1.67	12.75
2000	0.14	0.39	3.81	4.89	21.27	1.82	21.30
2001	0.12	0.37	3.85	7.55	31.60	1.43	39.77
2002	0.11	0.35	4.61	6.64	34.55	1.95	55.33
2003	0.18	0.35	4.14	3.60	33.55	1.81	73.94
2004	0.12	0.32	4.55	4.28	3.01	1.86	77.30

主要统计指标解释

城镇居民家庭全部收入　指被调查城镇居民家庭全部的实际收入，包括经常或固定得到的收入和一次性收入。不包括周转性收入，如提取银行存款、向亲友借款、收回借出款以及其他各种暂收款。

城镇居民家庭可支配收入　指被调查的城镇居民家庭在支付个人所得税、财产税及其他经常性转移支出后所余下的实际收入。

城镇居民家庭消费性支出　指被调查的城镇居民家庭用于日常生活的全部支出，包括购买商品支出和文化生活、服务等非商品性支出。不包括罚没、丢失款和缴纳的各种税款(如个人所得税、牌照税、房产税等)，也不包括个体劳动者生产经营过程中发生的各项费用。

城镇居民家庭购买商品支出　指被调查的城镇居民家庭为自用或赠送亲友而购买商品的全部支出，包括从商店、工厂、饮食业、工作单位食堂、集市以及直接从农民手中购买各种商品的开支。商品支出分为以下八类：食品；衣着；家庭设备用品及服务；医疗保健；交通与通信；娱乐、教育、文化服务；居住；杂项商品和服务。

农村居民家庭纯收入　指农村常住居民家庭总收入中，扣除从事生产和非生产经营费用支出、缴纳税款和上交承包集体任务金额以后剩余的，可直接用于进行生产性、非生产性建设投资、生活消费和积蓄的那一部分收入。农村居民家庭纯收入包括从事生产性和非生产性的经营收入，取自在外人口寄回带回和国家财政救济、各种补贴等非经营性收入；既包括货币收入，又包括自产自用的实物收入。但不包括向银行、信用社和向亲友借款等属于借贷性的收入。

农村居民家庭生活消费支出　指农村常住居民家庭用于日常生活的全部开支，是反映和研究农民家庭实际生活消费水平高低的重要指标。

全国城乡居民储蓄存款余额　指某一时点城乡居民存入银行及农村信用社的储蓄金额，包括城镇居民储蓄存款和农民个人储蓄存款，不包括居民的手存现金和工矿企业、部队、机关、团体等单位存款。

Explanatory Notes on Main Statistical Indicators

Total Income of Urban Households refers to the total actual income of the sample households,including regular or fixed income and occasional income. The income of a circulating nature such as withdrawal from bank deposits, loans borrowed from relatives or friends,repayment of loans received and various temporary collection of money is excluded.

Disposable Income of Urban Households refers to the income of the sample households which can be used for daily expenses,i.e.. total income minus income tax,property tax and other current transfers.

Expenditure for Consumption of Urban Households refers to total expenditure of the sample households for consumption in daily life,including expenditure for various commodities and expenses for non-commodity items such as culture and service, etc. ,but excluding fines and confiscation, loss, tax payments (such as income tax, license tax,real estates tax,etc.) and various expenses by individual laborers for business purposes.

Expenditure for Purchases of Commodities of Urban Households refers to total expenses of the sample households for the purchases of commodities, for their own use or as gifts to relatives and friends, from shops, factories,catering trade, canteens, markets and from the peasants. Such expenditure is classified into eight categories:food, clothing, household appliances and services, health care and medical services, transport and communications, recreation, education and cultural services, housing, miscellaneous goods and services.

Net Income of Rural Households refers to the total income of the permanent residents of the rural households during a year after the deduction of the expenses for productive and non-productive business operation, the payment for taxes and the payment for collective units for their contracted tasks, which can then be spent for investments in productive and non-productive construction, for consumption in daily life and for savings deposit. It is a comprehensive indicator to show the actual level of the income of the peasants household. The net income of the rural households includes not only the income from the productive and non-productive business operation, but also the income from the non-business operation, such as the money remitted or brought back by the members of the household who are in other places, the government relief payment and various subsidies. It includes not only the money income, but also the income in kind. But the income from borrowing from banks, friends and relatives is excluded.

Expenditure of Rural Households for Consumption refers to total expenses of rural households on daily life,including expenses on food, clothing, housing, fuel, articles for daily use,and expenses on cultural life and services. This indicator is used to show the actual consumption level of peasants.

The Savings Deposits of Urban and Rural Residents refers to the total value of savings deposits of urban and rural households in banks and rural credit cooperatives at a given point of time, including the savings deposit of urban residents and the savings deposit of rural residents. The cash in hand by residents and the deposits of organizations such as enterprises, military units, government agencies, institutions, etc. are not included.

第九篇

CHAPTER 9

城市概况

GENERAL SURVEY OF CITIES

9-1 城市公用事业基本情况
Basic Statistics on Urban Public Utilities

项 目	Item	1995	2000	2004
城市及建筑物面积	**Urban Areas and Floor Space of Buildings**			
建成区面积(平方公里)	Developed Areas (sq.m)	435	473	585
征用土地面积(平方公里)	Land Requisited for State Construction Projects (sq. km)	3.6	2.4	7.0
城市人口密度(人/平方公里)	Population Density of Urban Districts (persons/sq.km)	25	26	213
供水、供气及供热	**Water Supply, Gas Supply and Heating**			
自来水年供水量(亿吨)	Annual Supply of Tap Water (100 million tons)	3.1	5.0	6.6
#生活用水量	Water Consumption for Residential use	1.4	2.5	2.8
平均每人生活用水(吨)	Per -Capita Water Consumption for Residential Use (ton)	158.3	165.1	206.3
用水普及率(%)	Percentage of Population with Access to Tap Water (%)	97.1	98.8	98.1
人工煤气供气量(万立方米)	Coal Gas Supply (10 000 cu.m)			54182
#家庭用量	Consumption of Coal Gas for Residential Use			1200
天然气供气量(万立方米)	Natural Gas Supply (10 000 cu.m)	2432	5385	37230
#家庭用量	Consumption of Coal Gas for Residential Use	598	1119	14571
液化石油气供气量(万立方米)	Liquefied Petroleum Gas (10 000 cu.m)	149280	244018	154526
#家庭用量	Consumption of Liquefied Gas for Residential Use	83771	151984	101085
天然气、煤气管道长度(公里)	Length of Gas Pipelines (km)		385	1951
用气普及率(%)	Percentage of Population with Access to Gas (%)	86.2	92.84	87.25
集中供热面积(万平方米)	Heated Area (10 000 sq.m)	2100	5170	10322
#住 宅	Residential Buildings			7073
市政工程	**Municipal Engineering**			
铺装道路长度(公里)	Length of Paved Roads (km)	2403	2809	3706
平均每万人拥有	Length of Paved Roads per 10 000 Population	4.9	4.5	7.4
铺装道路面积(万平方米)	Area of Paved Roads (10 000 sq.m)	2589	3654	5532
平均每人拥有(平方米)	Area of Paved Roads per Population (sq.m)	5.7	5.9	11.0
下水道长度(公里)	Length of Sewer Pipelines (km)	1557	2008	2940
平均每万人拥有	Length of Sewer Pipelines per 10 000 Population	4.8	5.6	5.9
公共交通	**Public Traffic**			
年末运营车辆(辆)	Number of Public Transportation Vehicles (unit)	3324	5678	7438
平均每万人拥有(标台)	Number of Public Transportation Vehicles per 10 000 Population (unit)	10.8	13.8	13.11
出租汽车数量(辆)	Taxi (unit)	11762	22193.0	23008
城市绿化	**Afforestation in Cities**			
园林绿地面积(公顷)	Public Green Areas (hectare)	13481	19124	22339
每万人园林绿地面积(公顷)	Public Green Areas per 10 000 Population (hectare)	41.5	53.4	44.5
公园动物园个数(个)	Number of Parks and Zoos (unit)	55	84	109
公园动物园面积(公顷)	Area of Parks and Zoos (hectare)	1331	1568	2203
环境卫生	**Environmental Sanitation**			
清运生活垃圾(万吨)	Volume of Garbage Disposal (10 000 tons)	198	259	345
清运粪便(万吨)	Volume of Disposal of Excrement and Urine (10 000 tons)	26	16	8.7
每万人有公厕(座)	Number of Public Lavatories per 10 000 Population	3.5	4.7	4.1

注: 人均拥有指标2002年及以前按城市人口中非农业人口计算、2001年按城市人口计算（以下同）。
Note: Per-capita indicators in 2002 and before are computed on non-rural population in urban population while computation is made on urban population for the year 2001.

9-2 各城市主要经济指标

Major Economic Indicators by Cities

单位: 万元 (2004 年) (10 000 yuan)

城市名称	City	年底总人口(万人) Total Population (Year-end) (10 000 persons)	从业人员数(万人) Employment (10 000persons)	在岗职工人数(万人) Number of Fully-employed Staff and Workers (10 000 persons)	新疆生产总值(当年价格) Gross Production (current-year price)	第一产业 Primary Industry	第二产业 Secondary Industry
总 计	**Total**	**699.65**	**138.96**	**134.89**	**13925134**	**1073008**	**7427132**
乌鲁木齐市	Urumqi City	185.96	46.08	46.38	4842599	70874	1868707
克拉玛依市	Karamay City	30.58	12.33	11.46	2962020	10853	2591513
石河子市	Shi Hezi City	32.49	7.41	8.39	446120	49510	187145
吐鲁番市	Turpan City	25.82	2.47	2.40	205606	49655	59514
哈 密 市	Hami [Kumul] City	40.44	7.64	7.31	451416	64020	165671
昌 吉 市	Changji City	39.35	7.49	6.51	537641	114692	251431
阜 康 市	Fukang City	15.85	2.45	2.60	297403	42287	193238
米 泉 市	Miquan City	18.60	1.56	1.99	255176	44576	141099
奎 屯 市	Kuytun City	14.03	3.50	3.33	188814	11835	95526
伊 宁 市	Yining [Gulja] City	43.03	6.22	6.42	280206	28804	109600
塔 城 市	Tacheng [Qoqek] City	15.95	2.46	2.14	165659	41342	35071
乌 苏 市	Usu City	32.44	2.97	3.05	339255	153888	92103
阿勒泰市	Altay City	19.26	6.19	4.09	155379	38739	31374
博 乐 市	Bole [Bortala] City	24.56	5.27	5.23	231301	89838	54002
库尔勒市	Korla City	42.23	11.05	11.60	1739828	122919	1322116
阿克苏市	Aksu City	40.43	4.99	2.99	440233	93647	116514
阿图什市	Artux City	21.12	2.04	1.77	71421	23372	14746
喀 什 市	Kashgar [Kaxgar] City	38.26	4.89	5.29	241015	13603	70709
和 田 市	Hotan City	19.25	1.95	1.94	74042	8554	27053

城市名称	City	第三产业 Tertiary Industry	固定资产投资 Investment in Fixed Assets	工业总产值 Gross industrial Output Value	地方财政收入 Local Governments Revenue	地方财政支出 Local Governments Expenditures
总 计	**Total**	**5424994**	**5999865**	**13394189**	**1008498**	**1210124**
乌鲁木齐市	Urumqi City	2903018	1759856	4182170	463395	393022
克拉玛依市	Karamay City	359654	1124548	5339760	202145	206937
石河子市	Shi Hezi City	209465	264598	427902	32345	48100
吐鲁番市	Turpan City	96437	81528	62622	21570	40526
哈 密 市	Hami [Kumul] City	221725	139580	267920	26944	51611
昌 吉 市	Changji City	171518	266420	432357	30893	34481
阜 康 市	Fukang City	61878	81175	333984	21157	21210
米 泉 市	Miquan City	69501	120481	248904	13926	19689
奎 屯 市	Kuytun City	81453	86005	196653	19382	21911
伊 宁 市	Yining [Gulja] City	141802	160972	117947	22926	39800
塔 城 市	Tacheng [Qoqek] City	89246	47013	24643	11352	41476
乌 苏 市	Usu City	93264	83952	43332	10706	24248
阿勒泰市	Altay City	85266	54096	31395	5056	24723
博 乐 市	Bole [Bortala] City	87461	103624	51476	9589	22808
库尔勒市	Korla City	294793	1177626	1430753	49353	45951
阿克苏市	Aksu City	230072	159732	97954	31944	41435
阿图什市	Artux City	33303	42045	13503	4007	50214
喀 什 市	Kashgar [Kaxgar] City	156703	181742	72489	24025	37009
和 田 市	Hotan City	38435	64872	18425	7783	44973

9-2 续表 Continued

单位: 万元 (10 000 yuan)

城市名称	City	城乡居民储蓄存款余额 Balance of Saving Deposits in Urban and Rural Areas	在岗职工工资总额 Total Wages	铁路客运总量(万人) Total Railway Passenger Traffic (10 000 persons)	公路客运总量(万人) Total Highway Passenger Traffic (10 000 persons)	铁路货运总量(万吨) Total Railway Freight Traffic (10 000 tons)	公路货运总量(万吨) Total Highway Freight Traffic (10 000 tons)
总 计	**Total**	**11105319**	**2217348**	**1585**	**17288**	**6628**	**12252**
乌鲁木齐市	Urumqi City	4884500	870713	1283	1750	5148	6926
克拉玛依市	Karamay City	988613	265528		4012		1005
石河子市	Shi Hezi City	547188	112070	28	572	30	546
吐鲁番市	Turpan City	139346	35292				
哈 密 市	Hami [Kumul] City	609868	114605	83	309	661	482
昌 吉 市	Changji City	382889	82918		4538		890
阜 康 市	Fukang City	111908	37538		938		153
米 泉 市	Miquan City	165326	25397		1485		316
奎 屯 市	Kuytun City	268055	45818	31	392	356	283
伊 宁 市	Yining [Gulja] City	419540	87345		1162		371
塔 城 市	Tacheng [Qoqek] City	122774	30793		217		82
乌 苏 市	Usu City	137164	32482		456		128
阿勒泰市	Altay City	130224	50900		201		218
博 乐 市	Bole [Bortala] City	227988	69155		469		509
库尔勒市	Korla City	704325	187459	75	69	223	104
阿克苏市	Aksu City	716828	38544	38	401	61	74
阿图什市	Artux City	91222	32332	4	185	10	140
喀 什 市	Kashgar [Kaxgar] City	353859	68915	43	95	139	19
和 田 市	Hotan City	103702	29544		37		6

城市名称	City	邮电业务总量 Business Volume of Post and Telecommunications	邮政业务总量 Business Volume of Post	电信业务总量 Business Volume of Telecommunic-Ations	社会消费品零售总额 Total Retail Sales of Consumer Goods	进出口总额(万美元) Imports and Exports (10 000 USD)	#出口额(万美元) Imports (10 000 USD)
总 计	**Total**	**762527**	**50049**	**712478**	**3846247**	**339259**	**170762**
乌鲁木齐市	Urumqi City	451878	20478	431400	2001520	165154	91707
克拉玛依市	Karamay City	18946	3331	15615	168041	6497	2538
石河子市	Shi Hezi City	16135	2099	14036	140080	16343	3709
吐鲁番市	Turpan City	9367	1351	8016	64849	423	217
哈 密 市	Hami [Kumul] City	24320	2411	21909	174490	1403	1351
昌 吉 市	Changji City	34799	2599	32200	146495	24196	16919
阜 康 市	Fukang City	6668	603	6065	63186		
米 泉 市	Miquan City	3927	544	3383	80798		
奎 屯 市	Kuytun City	22627	1795	20832	76209		
伊 宁 市	Yining [Gulja] City	35408	2201	33207	128843	5586	5586
塔 城 市	Tacheng [Qoqek] City	6072	746	5326	42361	51751	31145
乌 苏 市	Usu City	7162	882	6280	38921		
阿勒泰市	Altay City	11152	1240	9912	70315	2118	813
博 乐 市	Bole [Bortala] City	14113	1065	13048	75490	55383	10112
库尔勒市	Korla City	64770	2844	61926	255212	1578	1074
阿克苏市	Aksu City	14599	2687	11912	139851		
阿图什市	Artux City	3380	486	2894	20744	4013	1148
喀 什 市	Kashgar [Kaxgar] City	11537	1629	9908	122378	4814	4443
和 田 市	Hotan City	5667	1058	4609	36464		

9-3 各城市市区设施水平

Level of Urban Public Facilities in Cities

(2004 年)

城市名称 City		城市人口用水普及率(%) Percentage of Population with Access to Tap Water	城市用气普及率(%) Percentage of population with access to gas	每万人拥有公共汽车(标台) Number of public transportation vehicles per 10 000 population (unit)	人均拥有铺装道路面积(平方米) Per-Capital Area of Paved Roads (sq.m)	人均公共绿地面积(平方米) Per-Capital Public Green Areas (sq.m)	水冲公厕比率(%) Ratio of public flush toilets
总 计	**Total**	**98.12**	**87.25**	**13.11**	**11.01**	**6.75**	**70.59**
乌鲁木齐市	Urumqi City	99.99	99.70	19.26	6.71	4.24	60.88
克拉玛依市	Karamay City	100.00	100.00	16.90	22.76	11.00	90.30
石河子市	Shihezi City	100.00	86.50	12.35	17.37	8.51	75.83
吐鲁番市	Turpan City	55.31		5.97	2.23	15.00	100.00
阿拉尔市	Alar City	75.45	68.93	5.65	26.67		100.00
图木舒克市	Tumxuk City	90.25	50.00	1.08	14.12	2.36	22.62
五家渠市	Wujiaqu City	100.00	95.74	14.68	18.19	2.62	100.00
哈密市	Hami [Kumul] City	92.59	78.70	6.74	10.95	7.54	78.43
昌吉市	Changji City	100.00	100.00	11.74	7.45	5.05	100.00
阜康市	Fukang City	82.71	67.67	3.38	9.21	11.13	81.08
米泉市	Miquan City	100.00	99.43	22.43	12.54	5.55	88.06
奎屯市	Kuytun City	100.00	100.00	5.27	13.19	9.19	95.45
伊宁市	Yining [Gulja] City	100.00	100.00	9.29	6.98	7.98	100.00
塔城市	Tacheng [Qoqek] City	71.08	71.08	4.82	11.54	14.53	93.75
乌苏市	Usu City	97.64	97.64	6.64	16.56	7.67	72.94
阿勒泰市	Altay City	93.57	93.57	5.86	8.84	14.43	28.57
博乐市	Bole [Bortala] City	99.15	90.01	8.40	11.06	14.01	100.00
库尔勒市	Korla City	100.00	100.00	11.62	20.73	7.04	100.00
阿克苏市	Aksu City	100.00	100.00	9.68	14.79	8.05	96.63
阿图什市	Artux City	97.66			21.09	9.00	21.48
喀什市	Kashgar [Kaxgar] City	98.93	61.97	4.86	10.10	5.89	76.12
和田市	Hotan City	95.60	82.42	11.54	16.46	12.88	100.00

9-4 城市自来水情况

Basic Statistics on Tapping Water Supply in Cities

指 标	Item	1995	2000	2004
年末水厂生产能力(万吨/日)	Production capacity of tapping water (10 000tons per day)	69	292	360
年末供水管道总长度(公里)	Length of water supply piplines (km)	1032	4448	4089
全年供水总量(亿立方米)	Total annual volume of tap water supply (100 millon.tons)	3.1	5.0	6.6
#生活用水	Water consumption For residential use	1.4	2.5	2.8
生产用水	Water for Production	1.7	2.0	2.2
平均每人日生活用水量(升)	Per-Capitall daily consumption of tap water for residential use (litre)	158.3	165.1	153.5
用水人口(万人)	Number of Residents with Access to Tap Water (10 000 person)	231	418	493

9-5 城市公用交通情况
Basic Statistics on Public Traffic in Cities

指　　标	Item	1995	2000	2004
年末营运车辆(辆)	Number of vehicles for business transportation (unit)	3324	5678	7438
平均每万人拥有(标台)	Number of vehicles for business transportation per 10 000 popuation (unit)	10.8	15.8	14.8
出租汽车(辆)	Number of taxis (unit)	11762	22193	23008
年末营运线路长度(公里)	Length of business transportation routes (km)	3203	1700	2096
运客总数(亿人次)	Number of passengers carried (100 millon person-times)	6.7	9.5	8.5
平均每日运客数(万人次)	Number of passengers carried per day (10 000 person-times)	183.1	260.3	232.1

9-6 城市市政建设情况
Basic Statistics on Municipal Construction in Cities

指　　标	Item	1995	2000	2004
实有道路长度(公里)	Length of paved roads (km)	2403	2809	3706
实有道路面积(万平方米)	Area of paved roads (10 000 sq.m)	2589	3654	5532
城市桥梁(座)	Number of Bridges (unit)	165	253	308
防洪堤长度(公里)	Length of dyke for control of flood (km)	112	130	158
城市下水道总长度(公里)	Length of sewer pipelines (km)	1557	2008	2940
城市污水日处理能力(万吨)	Daily disposal capacity of sewage (10 000 tons)	34	46	116
城市路灯盏数(千盏)	Number of street light (1 000 unit)	28.8	72.9	215.0

注：城市污水日处理能力指污水处理厂处理能力，不包括其他污水处理设施处理量。
Note: The daily treatment capacity in urban area refers to the treatment capacity of a waste- water treatment plant, excluding the volume handled by other polluted-water treatment facility.

9-7 城市园林绿化情况
Basic Statistics on Urban Gardens and Green Areas in Cities

指　　标	Item	1995	2000	2004
城市园林绿地面积(公顷)	Total Area of Parks, Gardens and Green Areas in Cities (hectare)	13481	19124	22339
#公共绿地	Public Green Areas	1576	2281	3391
每万人园林绿地面积(公顷)	Public Green and Garden Areas Per 10 000 Population (hectare)	41.5	53.4	44.5
建成区绿化覆盖率(%)	Green covrage rate in established district (%)	24.2	29.1	31.8
平均每人公共绿地面积(平方米)	Per-Capitall public Green Areas (sq.m)	5.1	6.4	6.8
公园、动物园数(个)	Number of Parks and Zoos	55	84	109
公园、动物园面积(公顷)	Area of Parks and Zoos (hectare)	1331	1568	2203
年游园人数(万人次)	Number of Visitors of Parks and Zoos In the Year (10 000 person-times)	895	686	704

9-8 城市环境卫生情况

Basic Statistics on Urban Environment and Sanitation in Cities

指　　标	Item	1995	2000	2004
从业人员数(人)	Number of Employed Persons (person)	3340	5010	10624
环卫机械数量(辆)	Environmental Sanitation Equipment (unit)	566	767	1058
公共厕所(座)	Number of Public Lavatories (unit)	1147	1684	2030
每万人拥有公共厕所(座)	Number of Public Lavatories Per 10 000 Population (unit)	3.5	4.7	4.0
道路清扫面积(万平方米)	Area under Cleaning Program (10 000 sq.m)	1743	3224	5300
生活垃圾清运量(万吨)	Volum of Garbage Disposal (10 000 tons)	198	259	345
粪便清运量(万吨)	Volum of Excrement and Urine Disposal (10 000 tons)	26	16	9

注：2001 年前从业人员数指标为年末职工数。

Note: The number of employment before the year 2001 refers to the number of employment at the end of the year.

9-9 城市煤气、液化石油气、天然气情况

Basic Statistics on Supply of Gas, Liquefied Petroleum Gas and Natural Gas in Cities

指　　标	Item	2000	2003	2004
人工煤气生产能力(万立方米/日)	Production CapaCity of Coal Gas (10 000 cu.m/day)		624	1205
管道长度(公里)	Length of Gas Pipelines (km)		1437	1951
人工煤气	Coal Gas		61	63
液化石油气	Liquefied Petroleum Gas		13	
天然气	Natural Gas	385	1363	1888
全年供气总量(万立方米)	Total Gas Supply (10 000 cu.m)	249403	235032	245938
人工煤气	Coal Gas		40650	54182
液化石油气	Liquefied Petroleum Gas	244018	171867	154526
天然气	Natural Gas	5385	22515	37230
用气人口(万人)	Population with Access to Gas (10 000 persons)		434.06	
人工煤气	Coal Gas		5.86	5.00
液化石油气	Liquefied Petroleum Gas	305.70	286.24	264.94
天然气	Natural Gas	27.00	141.96	186.34

9-10 城市集中供热情况

Basic Statistics on Heating in Cities by Region

指　　标	Item	2000	2003	2004
供应能力	**Heating CapaCity**			
蒸汽(吨/小时)	Steam (ton/hour)	1638	1396	1487
热水(兆瓦)	Hot Water (1 billion kw)	6145	8951	11077
供热总量	**Volume Supplied**			
蒸汽(吨)	Steam (ton)	554	856	855
热水(万百万千焦)	Hot Water (10 billion joule)	5204	8600	7269
管道长度(公里)	**Length of Pipelines (km)**			
蒸 汽	Steam	250	171	128
热 水	Hot Water	2064	2611	2696
供热面积(万平方米)	**Heated Area (10 000 sq.m)**	**5170**	**8939**	**10321**
#住 宅	Residential Buildings		6715	7073

主要统计指标解释

年末自来水生产能力 指年底城建部门管理的自来水厂和自备水源的社会单位取水、净化、送水、出厂输水干管等环节实际生产能力。

年末供水管道长度 指从送水泵到用户水表之间所有管道的长度。

全年供水总量 指公用自来水厂和自备水源的社会单位全年的供水总量，包括有效供水量及损失水量。

生活用水量 指居民日常生活与公共福利设施的用水量，包括居民、饮食店、旅馆、医院、理发店、浴池、洗衣店、游泳池、商店、学校、机关、部队等单位的用水量。

城市人口用水普及率 指城市用水的非农业人口数(不包括临时人口和流动人口)与城市非农业人口总数之比。计算公式为：

用水普及率＝城市用水的非农业人口数／城市非农业人口数×100%

人工煤气生产能力 指城市煤气厂制气、净化、输送等环节的综合实际生产能力。

输气管道长度 指由压缩机、鼓风机、储气罐的出口到用户煤气表之间的全部管道长度。

全年供气总量 指全年售给各类用户的全部煤气量，包括工业用量、家庭用量和其他用量。

城市用气普及率 指使用煤气(包括人工煤气、液化石油气、天然气)的城市非农业人口数(不包括临时人口和流动人口)与城市非农业人口总数之比。计算公式为：

城市煤气普及率＝城市用气的非农业人口数／城市非农业人口总数×100%

城市供热能力 指热电厂、热力公司和达到标准的集中采暖锅炉房向城市输送的供热源的设计能力，即每小时向城市输送蒸汽、热水的能力。

城市供热总量 指热电厂、热力公司和达到标准的集中采暖锅炉房向城市输送的全部蒸汽、热水量。

城市供热管道长度 指热电厂、热力公司和达到标准的集中采暖锅炉房管理的集中供热热源到用户之间的全部供气、供热水的管道长度。

年底实有铺装道路长度 指除土路外，路面经过铺装宽度在3.5米以上的道路，包括高级、次高级道路和普通道路。

城市桥梁 指城市范围内，修建在河道上的桥梁和道路与道路立交、道路跨越铁路的立交桥及人行天桥。包括永久性桥和半永久性桥，不包括临时性桥、铁路桥、涵洞。

城市下水道总长度 指所有排水总管、干管、支管及暗渠、检查井、连接井进出水口等长度之和。

城市污水日处理能力 指污水处理厂每昼夜处理污水量的设计能力。

年末实有公共汽(电)车 指年底可参加营运的全部车辆数，包括营运车辆数和库存查封未参加营运的车辆。不包括非营运车辆，如架线车、油罐车、工程车、货车及其他专用车辆和借入的客运车辆。

城市园林绿地面积 指城市公共绿地、专用绿地、生产绿地、防护绿地、郊区风景名胜区的全部面积。

公共绿地 指供游览休息的各种公园、动物园、植物园、陵园以及花园、游园和供游览休息用的林荫道绿地、广场绿地，不包括一般栽植的行道树及林荫道的面积。

Explanatory Notes on Main Statistical Indicators

Production CapaCity of Tap Water at the Year-end refers to the actual comprehensive production capaCity of the waterworks administered by the urban construction department and those owned by enterprises or institutions, taking the capaCity of the main links, such as water inflow, purification,conveyance and outflow of the trunk pipelines into account.

Length of Water Supply Pipelines at the Year-end refers to the total length of all the pipelines between the water pumps and the users water meters.

Annual Volume of Water Supply refers to the total volume of water supplied by the public water-works and those owned by individual enterprises and institutions during the whole year, including both the effective water supply and loss during the water supply.

Consumption of Water for Residential Use refers to the water consumption of households for daily life and the water consumption of public welfare facilities,including the consumption of restaurants,hotels,hospitals,barber shops,public bathhouses,laundries,swimming pools, shops, schools, institutions, army units and other units.

Percentage of Urban Population with Access to Tap Water refers to the ratio of the urban non-agricultural population (excluing temporary and mobile population)with access to tap water to the total urban non-agricultural population.The formula is:

Percentage of Population with Access to Tap Water = Urban Non-agricultural Population with Access to Tap Water ÷Urban Non-agricultural Population×100%

Production CapaCity of Gaswork Gas refers to the actual comprehensive production capaCity of the urban gasworks in gas generation,purification and delivery.

Length of Gas Pipelines refers to the total length of pipelines between the outlet of the compressor, blower or gas tank and the gas meters of users.

Volume of Gas Supply refers to the total volume of gas sold to users in a year, including the volume for industrial use, residential use and other uses.

Percentage of Urban Population with Access to Gas refers to the ratio of the urban non-agricultural population with access to gas (including gas, liquefied petroleum gas and natural gas) to the urban non-agricultural population(excluding temporary and mobile population). The formula is:

Percentage of Population with Access to Gas =Urban Non-agricultural Population with Access to Gas÷Urban Non-agricultural Population×100%

Heating CapaCity in Urban Area refers to the capaCity of hourly supply of steam and hot water to cities by thermal power plants,heating corporations and centralized heating boiler rooms which meet certain standard.

Heating Volume in Urban Area refers to the total volume of steam and hot water supplied to cities every year by thermal power plants,heating corporations and centralized heating boiler rooms which meet certain standard.

Length of Heating Pipelines refers to the total length of pipelines for centralized supply of steam and hot water from the thermal power plants,heating corporations and centralized heating boiler rooms which meet certain standard to the users.

Length of Paved Roads at the Year-end refers to the length of roads with a paved surface,and with a width of more than 3-5 meters, including high quality,medium quality and ordinary roads.

Urban Bridges refer to bridges over river courses, great separated junctions and overpasses in urban areas.Permanent bridges and semi-permanent bridges are included.Temporary bridges,railway bridges and culverts are excluded.

Length of Urban Sewage Pipes refers to the total length of general drainage, trunks. branch and blind drainage, inspection wells, connection wells, inlets and outlets, etc.

Daily Disposal CapaCity of Urban Sewage refers to the designed 24 hour capaCity of sewage disposal at the sewage treatment works.

Number of Public Vehicles (Buses and Trolley buses) at the Year-end refers to the total number of operational buses available at the year-end, including the year-end operational vehicles and vehicles in stock.Non-operational vehicles such as stringing cars,tank cars,machine shop cars,trucks and other special vehicles and the borrowed passenger vehicles are excluded.

Area of Urban Gardens and Green Areas refers to the total area of urban public green land,special green land,production green land,protection green land and suburban scenic spots.

Public Green Area refers to green areas of various parks, zoos, botanical gardens, cemeteries, amusement parks, tree-flanked boulevards greenland squares for tourism and relaxing.Areas with trees planted along-side the streets and boulevards are excluded.

第十篇

CHAPTER 10

环境保护

ENVIORNMENT PROTECTIONS

10-1 环境保护基本情况

Basic Statistics on Environmental Protection

项　　目	Item	1999	2000	2001	2002	2003	2004
水环境	**Water**						
水资源总量(亿立方米)	Water Resources (100 million cu.m)		952.40	1024.40	1068.60	920.10	855.40
#地表水	Surface Water		897.76	966.90	1006.00	863.20	809.60
地下水	Underground water		636.29	692.31	724.85	604.30	502.60
人均水资源量(立方米/人)	Per Captia Water Resources (cu.m/person)		5255	5500	5652	4793	4390
供水总量(亿立方米)	Water Supply (100 million cu.m)		479.76	487.34	475.03	494.40	497.06
#地表水	Surface Water		425.49	431.56	421.23	440.70	438.88
地下水	Under Groundwater		54.19	54.40	52.46	53.06	57.52
用水总量(亿立方米)	Water Use (100 million cu.m)		480.00	487.15	475.00	494.40	497.06
#农 业	Agriculture		453.20	463.85	449.23	457.70	459.07
工 业	Industry		10.89	9.64	10.18	8.28	11.59
生 活	Consumption		15.85	13.66	15.52	6.19	6.69
废水排放总量(亿吨)	Waste Water Discharge (100 million tons)	4.55	4.54	4.76	4.89	5.59	6.00
#工业废水排放量	Industry	1.69	1.54	1.68	1.64	1.64	1.93
城镇生活废水排放量	Consumption	2.86	3.00	3.08	3.25	3.95	4.07
工业废水排放达标量(亿吨)	Industrial Waste Water Meeting Discharge Standards (100 million tons)	0.73	0.79	1.01	1.12	0.97	1.12
工业废水排放达标率(%)	Percentage of Industrial Waste Water Meeting Discharge Standards (%)	43.40	51.60	60.40	68.10	59.70	58.10
化学需氧量排放量(万吨)	Discharge Amount of COD (10 000 tons)	22.55	19.71	20.10	20.49	22.88	26.17
#工业化学需氧量排放量	Industry	13.26	10.07	9.52	10.60	12.63	15.12
城镇生活化学需氧量排放量	Consumption	9.29	9.64	10.58	9.89	10.25	11.05
氨氮排放量(万吨)	Ammonia Nitrogen Discharge (10 000 tons)			1.83	1.79	1.91	2.02
#工业氨氮排放量	Industry			0.21	0.21	0.22	0.40
城镇生活氨氮排放量	Consumption			1.62	1.58	1.69	1.62
大气环境	**Atmosphere Environment**						
工业废气排放量(亿标立方米)	Industrial Waste Gas Emission (100 million cu.m)	1838.70	1943.60	2352.80	2512.20	2933.90	3809.50
#燃料燃烧	Fuels Combustion	1210.20	1389.10	1599.00	1930.20	2310.80	2756.30
生产工艺	Process of Industrial Production	628.50	554.50	753.80	582.00	623.10	1053.20
二氧化硫排放量(万吨)	Sulphur Dioxide Emission (10 000 tons)	33.71	31.05	29.99	29.61	32.99	48.03
#工 业	Industry	19.79	18.77	18.89	19.30	22.18	31.46
生 活	Consumption	13.92	12.28	11.10	10.31	10.81	16.57
烟尘排放量(万吨)	Soot Emission (10 000 tons)	24.39	20.47	19.82	19.10	20.38	25.91
#工 业	Industry	12.54	8.40	9.81	9.80	10.69	14.16
生 活	Consumption	11.85	12.07	10.01	9.30	9.69	11.75
工业粉尘排放量(万吨)	Industrial Dust Emission (10 000 tons)	12.04	11.26	9.82	9.37	10.93	16.77
建成城市烟尘控制区数(个)	Number of Soot Control Zones Established (unit)	76	79	63	70	58	58
烟尘控制区面积(万平方公里)	Area of Soot Control Zones (10 000 sq.km)	281.79	292.39	344.80	351.10	351.90	351.90

注：本卷数据由自治区水利厅、环保局、国土资源厅、地震局、林业局和建设厅提供。

Note: Date in volume are offered by Xinjiang Water Conservancy Bureau,Adminstration of Environment Protection,Bureau of State Land Resource,Seismic Bureau,Bureau of Forestry and Bureau of Construction.

10-1 续表 1 Continued

项 目	Item	1999	2000	2001	2002	2003	2004
固体废物	**Solid Wastes**						
工业固体废物产生量(万吨)	Industrial Solid Wastes Produced (10 000 tons)	702.3	718.2	783.6	1008.5	1087.4	1128.6
#危险废物	Hazardous Wastes	56.2	67.1	45.3	23.1	50.7	39.4
工业固体废物综合利用量(万吨)	Industrial Solid Wastes Utilized (10 000 tons)	267.4	291.9	387.4	515.7	540.3	532.3
工业固体废物综合利用率(%)	Ratio of Industrial Solid Wastes Utilized (%)	38.1	41.2	49.4	49.6	48.9	48.3
工业固体废物排放量(万吨)	Industrial Solid Wastes Discharged (10 000 tons)	111.4	92.6	62.5	68.9	88.2	102.8
#危险废物(吨)	Hazardous Wastes (ton)			25			5000
"三废"综合利用产品产值(亿元)	Output Value of Products Made from Waste Gas, WasteWater & Solid Wastes (100 million yuan)	3.8	4.8	3.9	6.6	8.0	7.2
噪 声	**Noise**						
建成城市环境噪声达标区数(个)	Developed Districts of Environmental Noise Meeting National Standard (unit)	54	58	40	40	39	40
城市环境噪声达标区面积(万平方公里)	Area of Urban Environmental Noise Meeting National Standard (10 000 sq.km)	169.5	193.4	268.1	300.3	315.2	315.2
生态环境	**Eco-Environment Protection**						
有林地面积(万公顷)	Woodland Area (10 000 hectares)						180.73
森林覆盖率(%)	Forest Coverage (%)						2.94
当年造林面积(万公顷)	Area of Reforestation of the Year (10 000 hectares)		6.42	10.68	21.69	26.38	17.65
自然保护区数(个)	Number of Nature Reserves (unit)	21	23	26	26	26	26
#国家级	National Level	3	4	5	5	7	7
自然保护区面积(万公顷)	Area of Nature Reserves (10 000 hectares)	1046.4	1594.1	2042.4	2042.4	2042.4	2042.4
自然保护区面积占辖区面积比重(%)	Area of Nature Reserves in Regions (%)	6.3	9.6	12.3	12.3	12.3	12.3
生态示范区数(个)	Number of Demonstration Zones of Ecology (unit)	2	5	7	7	8	8
#国家级	National Level	2	5	7	7	8	8
天然湿地面积(万公顷)	Area of Wetland (10 000 hectares)						1267.85
天然湿地面积占土地总面积比重(%)	Proportion of Natural wetlands in Total area of Territory (%)						76.15
自然灾害	**Natural Disaster**						
发生地质灾害起数(次)	Geological Disaster (unit)		10	12	206	50	98
#滑 坡	Landslide		2	7	201	26	83
崩 塌	Collapse		1	2	1	5	4
泥石流	Mudflow		6	3	3	15	7
发生地震灾害次数(次)	Seismic Disaster (unit)	3	1	1	1	8	
#5.0 级以上	Magnitude above 5 Richter scale	3	1	1	1	8	
森林火灾次数(次)	Forest Fire (unit)		17	41	38	27	27
#重 大	Serious		1		2		
特 大	Extraordinarily Serious						
森林火灾受灾面积 (万公顷)	Fire-Affected Forest Area (10 000 hectares)		852	253	1256	129	140
森林病虫害发生面积(万公顷)	Forest Area Affected by Disease and Pests (10 000 hectares)		15.81	15.12	17.31	17.19	18.15
森林病虫害防治面积(万公顷)	Forest Area Provented and Cured from Disease and Pests (10 000 hectares)		10.81	13.31	14.75	14.62	15.25
森林病虫害防治率(%)	Rate of Prevention and Cure (%)		68.35	88.03	85.21	85.03	84.02

10-1 续表 2 Continued

项　　目	Item	1999	2000	2001	2002	2003	2004
环境污染	**Pollution**						
环境污染与破坏事故次数(次)	PollutionAccidents (unit)	14	9	5	21	7	13
#水污染	Water Pollution	8	3	5	10	4	10
大气污染	Air Pollution	3	3		6		1
固体废物污染	Solid Wastes Pollution	3	1			1	
噪声与振动危害	Noise and Vibration Pollution				4		
其　他	Other		2		1	2	2
污染直接经济损失(万元)	Direct Economic Loss Due to Pollution (10 000 yuan)	11.3	16.0	13.2	29.6	156.2	111.2
污染事故赔款总额(万元)	Reparations for Pollution Incidents (10 000 yuan)	8.4	14.8	13.3	28.1	10.0	87.8
污染事故罚款总额(万元)	Fines to Pollution Incidents (10 000 yuan)	3.2	11.9		32.9	2.0	14.6
环境污染治理投资	**Investment in Pollution Treatment**						
环境污染治理投资总额(亿元)	Investment in Pollution Treatment (100 million yuan)	12.42	21.62	18.73	34.95	40.81	38.84
#城市环境基础设施建设投资	Urban Environmental Infrastructure	7.66	14.79	14.29	30.98	31.27	27.83
工业污染源治理投资	Urban Environmental Infrastructure	1.35	2.23	3.20	1.70	2.65	2.96
建设项目“三同时”环保投资	Urban Environmental Infrastructure	3.41	4.60	1.24	2.27	6.89	8.05
环境污染治理投资总额占新疆生产总值比重(%)	Investment in Pollution Treatment Out of XDP(%)	1.06	1.58	1.26	2.19	2.17	1.77
城市环境基础设施建设投资额(万元)	Investment in Urban Environment Infrastructure (10 000 yuan)	76593	147855	142900	309848	312711	278278
#污水处理	Volume of Waste Water	15276	30407	19806	53236	29903	29723
垃圾处理	Volume of Garbage Disposal	2675	8549	6080	12977	8576	15327
燃　气	Gas Supply	13347	10460	7426	56725	76430	81026
集中供热	Central Heating	23001	78427	54980	101019	108438	92125
园林绿化	Landscape and Greening	22294	20012	24010	48630	44277	60086
当年施工工业污染治理项目数(个)	Investment in Pollution Treatment Projects of the Year, by Source (unit)	108	203	113	129	104	146
当年竣工工业污染治理项目数(个)	Industrial Pollution Treatment Projects Projects under Construction of the Year(unit)	101	198	106	85	94	110
工业污染治理项目年完成投资总额(万元)	Investment Completed in Pollution Treatment Projects (10 000 yuan)	13520.2	22310.9	32008.7	16951.8	26508.8	29622.4
#治理废水	Waste Water	2755.9	8528.2	25917.3	5014.7	9297.7	12334.1
治理废气	WasteGas	9978.3	9116.2	4886.4	8240.8	9514.3	13114.1
治理固体废物	Solid Wastes	435.0	349.0	723.0	2206.0	4865.0	2766.7
治理噪声	Noise Pollution	114.0	4108.5	66.0	261.0	21.0	80.5
治理其他	Other	237.0	209.0	416.0	1229.3	2810.8	1327.0
实际执行“三同时”项目环保投资总额(万元)	Investment in "Three Simultaneity" Projects (10 000 yuan)	34066.8	45986.0	12379.5	22675.1	68920.9	80479.2
#治理废水	New Projects	2200.2	25256.1	3240.8	5258.5	39279.1	45231.4
治理废气	Expansion	31090.7	19361.6	6932.8	10365.0	21240.1	10475.3
治理固体废物	Technical Improvement		1339.1	30.0	224.4	3104.0	7491.4
治理噪声	Noise Pollution			273.4	521.5	886.4	930.9
其　他	Other	775.9	29.2	1902.5	6305.7	4411.3	16350.2

10-2　水资源情况

Water Resource

年 份 Year	地 区 Region	水资源总量(亿立方米) Total Amount Of Water Resource (100 million cu.m)	地表水资源量 Surface Water	地下水资源量 Ground Water	地下水与地下水资源重复量 Duplicated Measurement Between surface Waterand Groundwater	人均水资源量(立方米/人) Per Capita Water Resources (cu/m/person)
	2000	952.40	897.10	636.29	580.99	5255
	2001	1024.40	966.90	692.31	634.81	5500
	2002	1068.60	1006.00	724.85	662.25	5652
	2003	920.10	863.20	604.30	547.40	4793
	2004	855.40	809.20	502.60	456.40	4390
乌鲁木齐市	Urumqi City	10.59	10.24	5.12	4.77	576
克拉玛依市	Karamay City	0.44	0.06	1.15	0.76	172
石河子市	Shihezi City	0.14	0.07	0.89	0.82	23
吐鲁番地区	Turpan Administrative Offices	7.67	5.71	6.36	4.40	1331
哈密地区	Hami [Kumul] Administrative Offices	11.82	9.74	7.44	5.36	2250
昌吉回族自治州	Changji Hui Autonomous Prefecture	33.51	29.51	20.28	16.28	2157
伊犁州直属县(市)	Counties (Cities) Direct Under Ili Prefecture	167.54	164.22	84.29	80.97	6604
塔城地区	Tacheng [Tarbagatai] Administrative Offices	62.31	57.85	37.06	32.60	6492
阿勒泰地区	Altay Administrative Offices	111.31	106.71	44.62	40.02	18016
博尔塔拉蒙古自治州	Bortala Mongol Autonomous Prefecture	30.20	27.94	16.84	14.58	6774
巴音郭楞蒙古自治州	Bayangol Mongol Autonomous Prefecture	121.68	116.32	65.67	60.31	10697
阿克苏地区	Aksu Administrative Offices	77.05	69.77	81.24	73.96	3486
克孜勒苏柯尔克孜自治州	Kizilsu Kirgiz Autonomous Prefecture	67.01	65.94	35.66	34.59	14465
喀什地区	Kashgar [Kaxgar] Administrative Offices	65.67	60.98	55.86	51.17	1846
和田地区	Hotan Administrative Offices	88.37	84.16	40.14	35.93	5027

10-3 供水用水情况

Water Supply and Water Used

年 份 Year	地 区 Region	供水总量（亿立方米） Water Supply (100 million cu.m)	地表水 Surface Water	地下水 Ground Water	其 他 Other	用水总量（亿立方米） Water Used (100 million cu.m)
	2000	479.96	425.49	54.19	0.28	480.00
	2001	487.34	431.56	54.40	1.38	487.15
	2002	475.03	421.23	52.46	1.34	475.00
	2003	494.40	440.70	53.06	0.64	494.40
	2004	497.06	438.88	57.52	0.66	497.06
乌鲁木齐市	Urumqi City	8.37	5.55	2.52	0.30	8.37
克拉玛依市	Karamay City	3.56	3.05	0.42	0.09	3.56
石河子市	Shihezi City	15.93	11.88	4.05		15.93
吐鲁番地区	Turpan Administrative Offices	11.89	7.30	4.57	0.02	11.89
哈密地区	Hami [Kumul] Administrative Offices	10.97	4.38	6.57	0.02	10.97
昌吉回族自治州	Changji Hui Autonomous Prefecture	29.92	16.34	13.41	0.17	29.92
伊犁州直属县(市)	Counties (Cities) Direct Under Ili Prefecture	52.84	50.66	2.18		52.84
塔城地区	Tacheng [Tarbagatai] Administrative Offices	20.58	15.26	5.32		20.58
阿勒泰地区	Altay Administrative Offices	39.63	39.54	0.09		39.63
博尔塔拉蒙古自治州	Bortala Mongol Autonomous Prefecture	13.02	9.92	3.10		13.02
巴音郭楞蒙古自治州	Bayangol Mongol Autonomous Prefecture	40.63	36.89	3.68	0.06	40.63
阿克苏地区	Aksu Administrative Offices	100.08	98.07	2.01		100.08
克孜勒苏柯尔克孜自治州	Kizilsu Kirgiz Autonomous Prefecture	7.68	6.82	0.86		7.68
喀什地区	Kashgar [Kaxgar] Administrative Offices	101.60	95.55	6.05		101.60
和田地区	Hotan Administrative Offices	40.36	37.67	2.69		40.36

年 份 Year	地 区 Region	农 业 Agriculture	生 产 Production	生 活 Consumption	生 态 Ecology	人均用水量（立方米/人） Per Capita Water Used (cu/m/person)
	2000	453.20	10.89	15.85		2649
	2001	463.85	9.64	13.66		2615
	2002	449.33	10.18	15.52		2512
	2003	457.70	8.28	6.19	18.13	2576
	2004	459.07	11.59	6.69	19.71	2551
乌鲁木齐市	Urumqi City	5.17	1.55	1.45	0.20	456
克拉玛依市	Karamay City	1.23	0.95	0.27	1.11	1383
石河子市	Shihezi City	14.10	1.03	0.56	0.24	2517
吐鲁番地区	Turpan Administrative Offices	10.81	0.76	0.12	0.20	2065
哈密地区	Hami [Kumul] Administrative Offices	9.96	0.50	0.22	0.29	2088
昌吉回族自治州	Changji Hui Autonomous Prefecture	27.70	1.70	0.43	0.09	1926
伊犁州直属县(市)	Counties (Cities) Direct Under Ili Prefecture	49.59	1.18	0.85	1.22	2083
塔城地区	Tacheng [Tarbagatai] Administrative Offices	18.69	0.47	0.22	1.20	2144
阿勒泰地区	Altay Administrative Offices	29.65	0.31	0.18	9.49	6414
博尔塔拉蒙古自治州	Bortala Mongol Autonomous Prefecture	12.62	0.27	0.13		2921
巴音郭楞蒙古自治州	Bayangol Mongol Autonomous Prefecture	37.76	0.77	0.50	1.60	3572
阿克苏地区	Aksu Administrative Offices	98.45	0.91	0.64	0.08	4527
克孜勒苏柯尔克孜自治州	Kizilsu Kirgiz Autonomous Prefecture	7.40	0.13	0.11	0.04	1658
喀什地区	Kashgar [Kaxgar] Administrative Offices	99.18	0.64	0.77	1.01	2855
和田地区	Hotan Administrative Offices	36.76	0.42	0.24	2.94	2296

10-4 环保系统机构、人员数

Environmental Protection Agencies and Persons Engaged

年 份 Year	机构数 (个) Number of Agencies (unit)	人员数 (人) Total Number of Staff & Workers (person)	科技人员 ScientificAnd Technical Personnel	监测人员 Monitoring Personal	监察人员 Supervising and Administrative Personnel
2000	208	1965	110	654	416
2001	208	2096	109	636	420
2002	238	2386	99	692	523
2003	275	2588	107	766	671
2004	288	2694	107	763	701

10-5 各地区自然保护基本情况

Basic Situation of Natural Protection by Region

(2004 年)

年 份 Year	自然保护区 Nature Reserves			珍稀濒危动物繁殖场 (个) Number of Farms to Breed Rare or Endangered Animals (unit)	珍稀植物引种栽培场 (个) Cultivating Farms of RarePlants (unit)	已批准国家级生态示范区 (个) Number of Approvedthe ational-level Ecological Demonstration Zones (unit)	已批准国家级生态示范区面积 (万公顷) Area of Demonstration Zone of Ecology (10 000 hectares)
	个 数 (个) Number of Nature Reserves (unit)	面 积 (万公顷) Area of Nature Reserves (10 000hectares)	占辖区面积比重 (%) Percentage of Nature Reserves in the Region (%)				
2000	23	1594.05	9.6	1		5	869.08
2001	26	2042.40	12.3			7	1105.50
2002	26	2042.40	12.3	2		7	1105.50
2003	26	2042.40	12.3	2	1	8	1105.96
2004	26	2042.40	12.3	2	1	8	1105.96

10-6 环境污染与破坏事故情况

Environment Pollution and Destruction Accidents

年 份 Year	环境污染与破坏事故次数(次) Number of Pollution andDestruction Accidents (time)	水污染 Water Pollution	大气污染 Air Pollution	固体废物 Solid Wastes Pollution	噪声与振动危害 Noise and Vibration Pollution	其 他 Others	污染直接经济损失(万元) Direct Economic Losses (10 000yuan)	污染事故赔、罚款总 额(万元) Reparations and Fines on Pollution Accidents (10 000 yuan)
2000	9	3	3	1		2	16.0	26.7
2001	5	5					13.2	13.3
2002	21	10	6		4	1	29.6	61.0
2003	7	4		1		2	156.2	12.0
2004	13	10	1			2	111.2	102.4

10-7 环境污染治理投资

Investment in Environment Pollution Harnessing Projects

项 目	Item	2000	2001	2002	2003	2004
环境污染治理投资总额(亿元)	**Total Investment in Environment Pollution Harnessing Projects (100 million yuan)**	**21.62**	**18.73**	**34.95**	**40.81**	**38.84**
#城市环境基础设施建设投资	Investment in Urban Environment Infrastructure Facilities	14.79	14.29	30.98	31.27	27.83
#污水处理	Volume of Waste Water	3.04	1.98	5.32	2.99	2.97
垃圾处理	Volume of Garbage Disposal	0.85	0.61	1.30	0.86	1.53
燃 气	Gas Supply	1.05	0.74	5.67	7.64	8.10
集中供热	Central Heating	7.84	5.50	1.01	10.84	9.21
园林绿化	Land scape and Greening	2.00	2.40	4.86	4.43	6.01
工业污染源治理投资	Investment in Harnessing Sources of Industrial Pollution	2.23	3.20	1.70	2.65	2.96
建设项目"三同时"环保投资	Investment in Environment Protection Facilities Designed Concurrently with Construction Projects	4.60	1.24	2.27	6.89	8.05
环境污染治理投资总额占新疆生产总值比重(%)	**Investment in Environment Pollution Harnessing Projects as Percent of GDP (%)**	**1.58**	**1.26**	**2.19**	**2.17**	**1.77**

10-8 工业污染治理投资完成情况

Completed Investment in Industrial Pollution Harnessing Projects

年 份 Year	汇总工业企业数（个） Number of Industrial Enterprises (unit)	污染治理项目本年完成投资（万元） Investment Completed in Pollution Hanessing Projects (10 000 yuan)	治理废水 Treatment of Waste Water	治理废气 Treatment of Waste Gas	治理固体废物 Treatment of Solid Waste	治理噪声 Treatment of Noise Pollution	治理其他 Treatment of Other Pollution	本年施工项目数（个） Projects Under Construction (unit)	本年竣工项目数（个） Number of Projects Completed (unit)
2000	154	22310.9	8528.2	9116.2	349.0	4108.5	209.0	203	198
2001	113	32008.7	25917.3	4886.4	723.0	66.0	416.0	113	106
2002	89	16951.8	5014.7	8240.8	2206.0	261.0	1229.3	129	85
2003	83	26508.8	9297.7	9514.3	4865.0	21.0	2810.8	104	94
2004	94	29622.4	12334.1	13114.1	2755.7	91.5	1327.0	146	110

10-9 工业污染治理投资来源

Source of Investment in Industrial Pollution Harnessing Projects

年 份 Year	污染治理项目当年投资来源总额（万元） Source of Current Investment in Pollution Harnessing Projects (10 000 yuan)	国家预算内资金 State Budgetary Appropriations	环保专项资金 Special Funds For Enviromental Protection	其他资金 Other Funds	国内贷款 Domestic Loans	企业自筹 Enterprise Fundraising
2000	22310.9	11415.0	2045.5	88504.0		8850.4
2001	32008.7	20771.2	2016.9	9220.6	3306.9	5913.7
2002	16951.8	1867.8	5297.7	9786.3	6055.8	3730.5
2003	26508.8	2738.9	10611.9	13158.0	2286.2	10871.8
2004	29622.4	2546.0	15038.1	12038.3	161.0	11877.3

10-10 各地区废水排放及处理情况

Discharge and Treatment of Industrial Waste Water by Region

(2004 年)

地区	Region	汇总工业企业数（个） Number ofIndustrial Enterprises (unit)	废水治理设施数（套） Number of Facilities for Treatment of Waste Water (set)	工业废水排放总量（万吨） TotalVolume ofWaste Water Discharged (10 000 tons)	#排入污水处理厂的 Industrial WasteWater Meeting Discharge Standards	工业废水排放达标量（万吨） Industrial WasteWater Meeting Discharge Standards (10 000 tons)
总　计	**Total**	**687**	**451**	**19307.40**	**1458.23**	**11220.83**
乌鲁木齐市	Urumqi City	114	49	4394.56	282.80	3473.21
克拉玛依市	Karamay City	13	27	1808.83	96.20	1776.29
石河子市	Shihezi City	21	23	3554.38		2184.67
吐鲁番地区	Turpan Administrative Offices	39	17	78.63	13.61	65.68
哈密地区	Hami [Kumul] Administrative Offices	37	22	1064.41	579.24	908.35
昌吉回族自治州	Changji Hui Autonomous Prefecture	104	46	1937.33	48.55	698.06
伊犁州直属县(市)	Counties (Cities) Direct Under Ili Prefecture	60	65	778.16	48.39	167.81
塔城地区	Tacheng [Tarbagatai] Administrative Offices	20	28	611.93	0.36	185.51
阿勒泰地区	Altay Administrative Offices	34	22	604.13	0.12	134.27
博尔塔拉蒙古自治州	Bortala Mongol Autonomous Prefecture	37	13	368.94		172.87
巴音郭楞蒙古自治州	Bayangol Mongol Autonomous Prefecture	82	73	3119.48	221.85	1017.68
阿克苏地区	Aksu Administrative Offices	69	39	544.34	22.49	154.72
克孜勒苏柯尔克孜自治州	Kizilsu Kirgiz Autonomous Prefecture	10	6	28.59		26.91
喀什地区	Kashgar [Kaxgar] Administrative Offices	30	6	351.42	137.03	226.85
和田地区	Hotan Administrative Offices	17	15	62.26	7.61	27.96

地区	Region	工业废水中化学需氧量排放量（吨） COD Discharge From Industral WasteWater (ton)	工业废水中氨氮排放量（吨） Ammonia Nitrogen Discharge Form Industrial Waste Water (ton)	生活污水排放量（万吨） Comsumption Waste Water Discharge (10 000 tons)	生活污水中化学需氧量排放量（吨） COD Discharge form Consumption Waste Water (ton)	生活污水中氨氮排放量（吨） Ammonia Nitrogen Discharge from Consumption Waste Water (ton)
总　计	**Total**	**151179.63**	**4043.71**	**40733**	**110565.2**	**16189.0**
乌鲁木齐市	Urumqi City	3288.27	1331.14	11222	10772.1	3167.7
克拉玛依市	Karamay City	2029.49	197.67	1828	1638.7	388.8
石河子市	Shihezi City	67589.23	154.80	2490	7113.1	829.9
吐鲁番地区	Turpan Administrative Offices	174.09	68.01	838	3073.2	479.4
哈密地区	Hami [Kumul] Administrative Offices	951.83	63.16	1534	5862.6	683.9
昌吉回族自治州	Changji Hui Autonomous Prefecture	12910.58	1257.88	2386	10402.9	1339.4
伊犁州直属县(市)	Counties (Cities) Direct Under Ili Prefecture	11657.46	174.32	6230	16013.7	1911.7
塔城地区	Tacheng [Tarbagatai] Administrative Offices	3884.52	61.12	1859	9305.3	1085.5
阿勒泰地区	Altay Administrative Offices	8004.42	42.84	1222	5702.4	632.0
博尔塔拉蒙古自治州	Bortala Mongol Autonomous Prefecture	3041.12	63.70	609	893.0	355.1
巴音郭楞蒙古自治州	Bayangol Mongol Autonomous Prefecture	31300.68	431.96	2446	7332.3	970.6
阿克苏地区	Aksu Administrative Offices	5176.73	112.82	2791	7706.2	1378.2
克孜勒苏柯尔克孜自治州	Kizilsu Kirgiz Autonomous Prefecture	131.53	51.45	510	2547.0	298.0
喀什地区	Kashgar [Kaxgar] Administrative Offices	851.89	30.85	3663	17601.7	2024.6
和田地区	Hotan Administrative Offices	187.79	1.99	1105	4601.0	644.2

10-11　各地区废气排放及处理情况

Emission and Treatment of Industrial Waste Gas by Region

(2004 年)

地　区	Region	工业废气排放总量(亿标立方米) Total Volume of Industrial Waste Gas Emission (100 million cu.m)	燃料燃烧过程中废气排放量 Volume of Waste Gas from Process of Fuel Burning	生产工艺过程中废气排放量 Volume of Waste Gas from Process of Production	废气治理设施数(套) Number of Facilities for Treatment of Waste Gas (set)	工业二氧化硫排放量(吨) Volume of Sulphur Dioxide Emission by Industry (ton)	生活二氧化硫排放量(吨) Volume of Sulphur Dioxide Emission by Consumption (ton)
总　计	**Total**	**3809.47**	**2756.30**	**1053.17**	**2354**	**314624.07**	**165694**
乌鲁木齐市	Urumqi City	983.10	679.47	303.63	467	85327.58	9898
克拉玛依市	Karamay City	483.94	408.81	75.13	164	22970.43	154
石河子市	Shihezi City	128.98	118.45	10.53	75	11186.27	5142
吐鲁番地区	Turpan Administrative Offices	214.07	148.51	65.57	92	20366.12	20660
哈密地区	Hami [Kumul] Administrative Offices	236.24	219.34	16.89	129	40690.05	4581
昌吉回族自治州	Changji Hui Autonomous Prefecture	413.95	352.74	61.21	368	45314.44	13892
伊犁州直属县(市)	Counties (Cities) Direct Under Ili Prefecture	199.11	149.43	49.68	141	15694.59	36137
塔城地区	Tacheng [Tarbagatai] Administrative Offices	145.77	112.60	33.17	44	5683.35	22979
阿勒泰地区	Altay Administrative Offices	118.86	25.66	93.20	98	10400.22	8961
博尔塔拉蒙古自治州	Bortala Mongol Autonomous Prefecture	76.72	51.38	25.35	69	4366.23	3266
巴音郭楞蒙古自治州	Bayangol Mongol Autonomous Prefecture	388.23	182.58	205.65	217	24085.21	6003
阿克苏地区	Aksu Administrative Offices	266.30	182.82	83.48	457	20078.03	5038
克孜勒苏柯尔克孜自治州	Kizilsu Kirgiz Autonomous Prefecture	25.31	7.51	17.81	8	445.53	3608
喀什地区	Kashgar [Kaxgar] Administrative Offices	96.34	86.24	10.10	8	6277.58	16391
和田地区	Hotan Administrative Offices	32.55	30.75	1.80	17	1738.45	8984

地　区	Region	工业二氧化硫去除量(吨) Volume of Industry Sulphur Dioxide Removed (ton)	工业烟尘排放量(吨) Volume of Industrial Soot Emission (ton)	生活烟尘排放量(吨) Volumeof Consumption Soot Emission (ton)	工业烟尘去除量(吨) Volume of Industrial Soot Removed (ton)	工业粉尘排放量(吨) Volume of Industrial Dust Emission (ton)	工业粉尘去除量(吨) Volume of Industrial Dust Romoved (ton)
总　计	**Total**	**48206.80**	**141570.73**	**117556**	**1414875.99**	**167688.46**	**669514.39**
乌鲁木齐市	Urumqi City	42013.92	42873.70	14971	542301.39	11732.07	178146.98
克拉玛依市	Karamay City		3438.61	197	262238.89		
石河子市	Shihezi City	254.15	4054.93	2571	192263.57	3584.67	19763.98
吐鲁番地区	Turpan Administrative Offices	467.85	8072.01	16172	5631.68	7612.12	8092.26
哈密地区	Hami [Kumul] Administrative Offices	183.58	20551.05	1398	104143.23	17615.65	23824.01
昌吉回族自治州	Changji Hui Autonomous Prefecture	1084.53	12172.66	9324	132674.34	13603.75	61838.16
伊犁州直属县(市)	Counties (Cities) Direct Under Ili Prefecture	1941.64	8333.21	31014	35579.73	12713.08	43788.72
塔城地区	Tacheng [Tarbagatai] Administrative Offices	280.00	5154.76	13449	11115.51	25367.02	14303.20
阿勒泰地区	Altay Administrative Offices		1947.32	4484	6624.77	14939.04	34193.82
博尔塔拉蒙古自治州	Bortala Mongol Autonomous Prefecture	488.26	2330.17	2221	12571.42	3016.32	6871.63
巴音郭楞蒙古自治州	Bayangol Mongol Autonomous Prefecture	811.32	13704.97	2563	63071.73	15982.20	83819.34
阿克苏地区	Aksu Administrative Offices	656.90	12368.35	4143	34078.02	9741.46	87302.47
克孜勒苏柯尔克孜自治州	Kizilsu Kirgiz Autonomous Prefecture	24.65	487.01	1920	2604.01	6487.59	24753.57
喀什地区	Kashgar [Kaxgar] Administrative Offices		4661.62	8194	8826.24	17972.69	74619.36
和田地区	Hotan Administrative Offices		1123.36	4935	1151.48	7320.81	8196.91

10-12 各地区工业固体废物产生及处理利用情况

Production, Treatment and Utilization of Industrial Solid Wastes by Region

(2004 年)

地　区	Region	工业固体废物产生量(万吨) Volume of Industrial SolidWastes Produced (10 000 tons)	#危险废物(吨) Hazardous Wastes (ton)	工业固体废物综合利用量(万吨) Volume of Industrial SolidWastes Utilized (10 000 tons)	工业固体废物贮存量(万吨) Volume of Industrial SolidWastes in Stocks (10 000 tons)	工业固体废物处置量(万吨) Volume of Industrial SolidWastes Treated (10 000 tons)
总　计	**Total**	**1128.58**	**394030**	**556.71**	**399.99**	**95.05**
乌鲁木齐市	Urumqi City	310.64	27460	192.72	91.53	45.44
克拉玛依市	Karamay City	28.23	57374	19.64	0.46	8.12
石河子市	Shihezi City	40.27		17.40		22.84
吐鲁番地区	Turpan Administrative Offices	49.06	26000	13.65	5.48	3.69
哈密地区	Hami [Kumul] Administrative Offices	148.11	29000	22.75	110.58	2.14
昌吉回族自治州	Changji Hui Autonomous Prefecture	125.33		88.02	31.55	5.13
伊犁州直属县(市)	Counties (Cities) Direct Under Ili Prefecture	50.08	214338	22.78	26.36	0.09
塔城地区	Tacheng [Tarbagatai] Administrative Offices	15.90		10.79	3.82	
阿勒泰地区	Altay Administrative Offices	89.30	39816	28.16	14.39	
博尔塔拉蒙古自治州	Bortala Mongol Autonomous Prefecture	26.39		20.15	3.64	0.13
巴音郭楞蒙古自治州	Bayangol Mongol Autonomous Prefecture	174.78	42	67.64	99.72	6.64
阿克苏地区	Aksu Administrative Offices	56.71		41.53	12.36	0.04
克孜勒苏柯尔克孜自治州	Kizilsu Kirgiz Autonomous Prefecture	1.17		0.36		0.57
喀什地区	Kashgar [Kaxgar] Administrative Offices	8.97		8.09		
和田地区	Hotan Administrative Offices	3.61		3.03	0.11	0.21

地　区	Region	工业固体废物排放量(万吨) Volume of Industrial SolidWastes Discharged (10 000 tons)	#危险废物(吨) Hazardous Wastes (ton)	"三废"综合利用产品产值(万吨) Output Valueof Products Made FromUtilization of Waste Gas, Water & Solid Wastes (10 000 yuan)	工业固体废物综合利用率(%) Rate of Comprehensive Application of Industrial Solid Wastes (%)
总　计	**Total**	**102.80**	**5000**	**71716.5**	**48.28**
乌鲁木齐市	Urumqi City	0.20		28138.5	58.70
克拉玛依市	Karamay City			2318.5	69.58
石河子市	Shihezi City	0.10		4913.9	43.14
吐鲁番地区	Turpan Administrative Offices	26.82		771.2	27.51
哈密地区	Hami [Kumul] Administrative Offices	12.64		1.3	15.36
昌吉回族自治州	Changji Hui Autonomous Prefecture	6.73		14664.5	66.97
伊犁州直属县(市)	Counties (Cities) Direct Under Ili Prefecture	0.85		5050.2	45.48
塔城地区	Tacheng [Tarbagatai] Administrative Offices	1.29		7719.0	67.85
阿勒泰地区	Altay Administrative Offices	46.76	5000	1530.6	31.53
博尔塔拉蒙古自治州	Bortala Mongol Autonomous Prefecture	2.48		1540.9	76.34
巴音郭楞蒙古自治州	Bayangol Mongol Autonomous Prefecture	0.77		3931.0	38.70
阿克苏地区	Aksu Administrative Offices	2.78		639.4	73.24
克孜勒苏柯尔克孜自治州	Kizilsu Kirgiz Autonomous Prefecture	0.23		51.8	31.03
喀什地区	Kashgar [Kaxgar] Administrative Offices	0.88			90.16
和田地区	Hotan Administrative Offices	0.27		445.7	83.89

10-13 各地区城市生活垃圾清运和处理情况

Collection, Transport and Disposal of Consumption Wastes in Cities by Region

(2004 年)

地 区 Region	生活垃圾清运量（万吨） Wastes Collected and Transported (10 000 tons)	无害化处理厂数（座） Number of Factories for Wastes Treatment (unit)	卫生填埋 Landfill	堆肥 Piling	焚烧 Burning	无害化处理能力（吨/日） Treatment Capacity (ton/day)	卫生填埋 Landfill	堆肥 Piling
总 计 Total	**346**	**19**	**16**	**1**	**2**	**4096**	**4068**	**20**
乌鲁木齐市 Urumqi City	127	2	2			2083	2083	
克拉玛依市 Karamay City	23	5	4		1	423	420	
石河子市 Shihezi City	12							
阿拉尔市 Alar city	2	1	1					
图木舒克市 Tumxuk city								
五家渠市 Wujiaqu city	3							
吐鲁番市 Turpan city	7							
哈密市 Hami [Kumul] city	13							
昌吉市 Changji city	16	1	1			450	450	
阜康市 Fukang city	5							
米泉市 Miquan city	7							
奎屯市 Kuytun city	8	2	1	1		200	200	
伊宁市 Yining [Gulja] city	16							
塔城市 Tacheng [Qoqek] city	7							
乌苏市 Usu city	10	1	1			160	160	
阿勒泰市 Altay city	9	1	1					
博乐市 Bole [Bortala] city	17							
库尔勒市 Korla city	27	3	2		1	700	695	
阿克苏市 Aksu city	10	1	1					
阿图什市 Artux city	1	1	1			80	60	20
喀什市 Kashgar [Kaxgar] city	18	1	1					
和田市 Hotan city	8							

10-13 续表 Continued

地　区 Region	焚　烧 Burning	无害化处理量（万吨） Volume of Wastes Disposed (10 000 tons)	卫　生 填　埋 Landfill	焚　烧 Burning	简　易 处理量（万吨） Volume of Wastes Disposed in a Simple Way (10 000 tons)	粪　便 清运量（万吨） Collection and Transport of Excrement and Urine (10 000 tons)	粪　便 处理量（万吨） Disposal of Excrement and Urine (10 000 tons)	生活垃圾无害化处理率（%） Treatment Rate of Consumption Wastes (%)
总　计 Total	**8**	**123.80**	**123.55**	**0.25**	**184.33**	**8.70**	**3.20**	**35.85**
乌鲁木齐市 Urumqi City		75.00	75.00		25.00	2.70	0.30	59.06
克拉玛依市 Karamay City	3	2.90	2.90		18.70	2.40		12.78
石河子市 Shihezi City					11.50	0.10	0.10	
阿拉尔市 Alar city								
图木舒克市 Tumxuk city					0.07	0.50		
五家渠市 Wujiaqu city					2.40	0.10	0.10	
吐鲁番市 Turpan city					7.00			
哈密市 Hami [Kumul] city					13.00			
昌吉市 Changji city		15.50	15.50					100.00
阜康市 Fukang city					4.00			
米泉市 Miquan city					6.97			
奎屯市 Kuytun city		3.60	3.60		4.50	0.20	0.20	44.44
伊宁市 Yining [Gulja] city					15.60			
塔城市 Tacheng [Qoqek] city					7.00			
乌苏市 Usu city					10.00	2.50	2.30	
阿勒泰市 Altay city					8.50			
博乐市 Bole [Bortala] city					17.30			
库尔勒市 Korla city	5	26.80	26.55	0.25				100.00
阿克苏市 Aksu city					10.00	0.20	0.20	
阿图什市 Artux city					0.09			
喀什市 Kashgar [Kaxgar] city					18.30			
和田市 Hotan city					4.40			

10-14 地质灾害及防治情况

Prevention of Geological Disasters

年份 Year	地区 Region	发生地质灾害起数(次) Geological Disasters (case)	滑坡 Land-slide	崩塌 Collapse	泥石流 Mud-rock Flow	地面塌陷 Land Subside
	2000	10	2	1	6	1
	2001	12	7	2	3	
	2002	206	201	1	3	1
	2003	50	26	5	15	4
	2004	98	83	4	7	4
乌鲁木齐市	Urumqi City	1	1			
克拉玛依市	Karamay City					
石河子市	Shihezi City					
吐鲁番地区	Turpan Administrative Offices					
哈密地区	Hami [Kumul] Administrative Offices					
昌吉回族自治州	Changji Hui Autonomous Prefecture	3	2		1	
伊犁州直属县(市)	Counties (Cities) Direct Under Ili Prefecture	86	77	3	4	2
塔城地区	Tacheng [Tarbagatai] Administrative Offices	4		1	1	2
阿勒泰地区	Altay Administrative Offices					
博尔塔拉蒙古自治州	Bortala Mongol Autonomous Prefecture	1			1	
巴音郭楞蒙古自治州	Bayangol Mongol Autonomous Prefecture					
阿克苏地区	Aksu Administrative Offices					
克孜勒苏柯尔克孜自治州	Kizilsu Kirgiz Autonomous Prefecture					
喀什地区	Kashgar [Kaxgar] Administrative Offices	3	3			
和田地区	Hotan Administrative Offices					

年份 Year	地区 Region	人员伤亡(人) Casualties Casualties (person)	死亡人数 Deaths Deaths	直接经济损失(万元) Direct Economic Loss (10 000 yuan)	地质灾害防治 Projects of prevention of Geological Disasters	
					项目数(个) Projects (unit)	投资(万元) Investment (10 000 yuan)
	2000	8	8	1000.00		
	2001	4	4	1312.00		
	2002	19	14	10775.00	3	140
	2003	27	13	2252.00	6	165
	2004	12	2	609.00	17	375
乌鲁木齐市	Urumqi City	1	1	0.54	2	125
克拉玛依市	Karamay City					
石河子市	Shihezi City					
吐鲁番地区	Turpan Administrative Offices					
哈密地区	Hami [Kumul] Administrative Offices					
昌吉回族自治州	Changji Hui Autonomous Prefecture			50.12	6	120
伊犁州直属县(市)	Counties (Cities) Direct Under Ili Prefecture	11	1	445.54	3	50
塔城地区	Tacheng [Tarbagatai] Administrative Offices			60.30	1	20
阿勒泰地区	Altay Administrative Offices				2	
博尔塔拉蒙古自治州	Bortala Mongol Autonomous Prefecture			25.00	1	20
巴音郭楞蒙古自治州	Bayangol Mongol Autonomous Prefecture					
阿克苏地区	Aksu Administrative Offices					
克孜勒苏柯尔克孜自治州	Kizilsu Kirgiz Autonomous Prefecture				2	40
喀什地区	Kashgar [Kaxgar] Administrative Offices			27.50		
和田地区	Hotan Administrative Offices					

10-15 各地区土地利用情况

Land Use by Region

单位:万公顷 (10 000 hectares)

年份 地区 Year Region	土地调查面积 Area under Land Survey	农用地 Land for Agriculture Use	园地 Garden Land	牧草地 Grazing and Pasture Land	建设用地 Land for Construction	居民点及工矿用地 Land for Living Quarters, Mining and Manufacturing Sites	交通用地 Land for Transport Facilities	水利设施用地 Land for Water Conservancy Facilities
2000	16648.97	6346.21	19.22	5136.05	154.38	88.69	22.3	43.39
2001	16648.97	6295.64	19.68	5135.35	112.11	88.88	5.25	17.98
2002	16648.97	6297.36	22.21	5135.75	118.20	94.63	5.49	18.08
2003	16648.97	6301.54	29.58	5131.49	119.96	96.12	5.76	18.08
2004	16648.97	6304.57	33.59	5121.58	121.05	97.02	5.89	18.14
乌鲁木齐市 Urumqi City	113.84	90.98	0.28	78.48	4.07	3.58	0.32	0.18
克拉玛依市 Karamay City	86.54	36.07	0.03	23.25	6.39	5.82	0.35	0.22
石河子市 Shihezi City	4.60	3.49	0.08	0.61	0.55	0.50	0.05	0.00
吐鲁番地区 Turpan Administrative Offices	675.63	84.20	2.17	72.97	2.66	2.21	0.34	0.11
哈密地区 Hami [Kumul] Administrative Offices	1420.95	443.02	1.36	374.24	18.51	17.90	0.49	0.12
昌吉回族自治州 Changji Hui Autonomous Prefecture	776.39	602.72	0.83	498.20	11.36	9.61	0.69	1.05
伊犁州直属县(市) Counties (Cities) Direct Under Ili Prefecture	563.82	476.06	2.08	360.85	8.97	8.18	0.47	0.32
塔城地区 Tacheng [Tarbagatai] Administrative Offices	946.98	765.18	0.56	643.35	9.81	8.08	0.52	1.21
阿勒泰地区 Altay Administrative Offices	1176.99	1069.66	0.03	963.22	4.35	3.03	0.29	1.03
博尔塔拉蒙古自治州 Bortala Mongol Autonomous Prefecture	249.34	192.59	0.40	159.85	2.11	1.83	0.17	0.11
巴音郭楞蒙古自治州 Bayangol Mongol Autonomous Prefecture	4709.54	970.09	6.89	831.15	10.81	8.60	0.71	1.49
阿克苏地区 Aksu Administrative Offices	1313.41	541.53	5.61	403.81	12.53	7.88	0.38	4.26
克孜勒苏柯尔克孜自治州 Kizilsu Kirgiz Autonomous Prefecture	724.68	324.50	0.62	298.49	1.49	1.16	0.16	0.18
喀什地区 Kashgar [Kaxgar] Administrative Offices	1394.80	302.18	9.68	160.76	18.28	12.80	0.48	5.00
和田地区 Hotan Administrative Offices	2491.46	402.30	2.96	252.34	9.16	5.82	0.47	2.87

10-16　造林面积

Area of Afforestation

单位:公顷　(hectares)

年份　地区 Year　Region	造林总面积 Total area of Afforestation	按造林方式分 By Approach 人工造林 Manua Plantingl	 飞机播种 Airplane Planting	按林种用途分 By Function of Forest 用材林 Timber Forests	 经济林 By-product Forests	 防护林 Protection Forests	 薪炭林 Fuel Forests	 特种用途林 Forests for Special Purpose
2000	64173	63793	200	1605	44564	16512	1012	480
2001	106771	106771		2149	78203	24536	1424	459
2002	216924	216924		3034	78302	134723	706	159
2003	263781	253781	10000	10152	59777	191380	2390	82
2004	176540	176540		3897	73103	96897	2638	5
乌鲁木齐市 Urumqi City	1763	1763			62	1701		
克拉玛依市 Karamay City	182	182				182		
石河子市 Shihezi City	230	230			17	213		
吐鲁番地区 Turpan Administrative Offices	3155	3155			756	2399		
哈密地区 Hami [Kumul] Administrative Offices	3887	3887			328	3559		
昌吉回族自治州 Changji Hui Autonomous Prefecture	23555	23555		106	3160	20289		
伊犁州直属县(市) Counties (Cities) Direct Under Ili Prefecture	12830	12830		2946	1857	8027		
塔城地区 Tacheng [Tarbagatai] Administrative Offices	4155	4155		24	106	4025		
阿勒泰地区 Altay Administrative Offices	17610	17610				17450	160	
博尔塔拉蒙古自治州 Bortala Mongol Autonomous Prefecture	5377	5377			162	5215		
巴音郭楞蒙古自治州 Bayangol Mongol Autonomous Prefecture	13617	13617		186	4412	9018		
阿克苏地区 Aksu Administrative Offices	38093	38093			25372	12716		5
克孜勒苏柯尔克孜自治州 Kizilsu Kirgiz Autonomous Prefecture	6870	6870			2363	3852	655	
喀什地区 Kashgar [Kaxgar] Administrative Offices	32184	32184		633	28191	3231	129	
和田地区 Hotan Administrative Offices	12943	12943		2	6316	4931	1694	
自治区林业局 Xinjiang Forestry Bureau	89	89				89		

10-17 林业重点工程造林面积

Area of Key Afforestation Projects

单位:公顷 (hectares)

年份 Year	地区 Region	造林总面积 Total Area of Afforestation	退耕还林工程 Grain for GreenProjects	三北及长江流域等防护林工程 Protection Forests in North China and Yangtze River Basin
	2001	102317	13173	
	2002	199324	113010	
	2003	235924	175314	
	2004	152967	82838	70129
乌鲁木齐市	Urumqi City	1763	700	1063
克拉玛依市	Karamay City	182		182
吐鲁番地区	Turpan Administrative Offices	3155	2360	795
哈密地区	Hami [Kumul] Administrative Offices	3887	3380	507
昌吉回族自治州	Changji Hui Autonomous Prefecture	23555	16683	6872
伊犁州直属县(市)	Counties (Cities) Direct Under Ili Prefecture	12308	9362	2946
塔城地区	Tacheng [Tarbagatai] Administrative Offices	4155	2416	1739
阿勒泰地区	Altay Administrative Offices	17610	15167	2443
博尔塔拉蒙古自治州	Bortala Mongol Autonomous Prefecture	5377	4514	863
巴音郭楞蒙古自治州	Bayangol Mongol Autonomous Prefecture	13617	6668	6949
阿克苏地区	Aksu Administrative Offices	38093	12323	25770
克孜勒苏柯尔克孜自治州	Kizilsu Kirgiz Autonomous Prefecture	6870	3556	3114
喀什地区	Kashgar [Kaxgar] Administrative Offices	12887	1588	11299
和田地区	Hotan Administrative Offices	9431	4121	5310
自治区林业局	Xinjiang Forestry Bureau	77		77

10-18 各地区天然湿地面积

Area of Wetlands by Region

(2004 年)

地 区 Region	天然湿地面积(百公顷) Area of Natural Wetlands (100 hectares)	河 流 Rivers	湖 泊 Lakes	沼 泽 Marshland	天然湿地面积占土地总面积比重(%) Proportion of Natural Wetlands in Total Area of Territory(%)
总 计 Total	**12678.50**	**4734.16**	**4763.29**	**3181.05**	**0.76**
乌鲁木齐市 Urumqi City	74.74	20.99	39.37	14.38	0.66
克拉玛依市 Karamay City	214.68	23.59	154.58	36.51	2.48
石河子市 Shihezi City	4.92	4.77		0.15	1.07
吐鲁番地区 Turpan Administrative Offices	127.85	5.99	0.19	121.67	0.19
哈密地区 Hami [Kumul] Administrative Offices	179.00	35.73	122.34	20.93	0.13
昌吉回族自治州 Changji Hui Autonomous Prefecture	264.52	50.28	2.58	211.66	0.34
伊犁州直属县(市) Counties (Cities) Direct Under Ili Prefecture	544.02	246.61	6.59	290.82	0.96
塔城地区 Tacheng [Tarbagatai] Administrative Offices	352.88	113.36	5.98	233.54	0.37
阿勒泰地区 Altay Administrative Offices	1353.85	353.78	845.49	154.58	1.15
博尔塔拉蒙古自治州 Bortala Mongol Autonomous Prefecture	1331.27	28.88	1176.41	125.98	5.34
巴音郭楞蒙古自治州 Bayangol Mongol Autonomous Prefecture	4036.34	979.88	2098.19	958.27	0.86
阿克苏地区 Aksu Administrative Offices	1018.49	708.82	68.68	240.99	0.78
克孜勒苏柯尔克孜自治州 Kizilsu Kirgiz Autonomous Prefecture	327.15	94.18	46.61	186.36	0.45
喀什地区 Kashgar [Kaxgar] Administrative Offices	1058.46	556.59	87.85	414.02	0.76
和田地区 Hotan Administrative Offices	1790.33	1510.71	108.43	171.19	0.72

10-19 森林火灾情况
Forest Fires

年份 Year	地区 Region	森林火灾次数(次) Forest Fires (case)	森林火警 Fire Alarms	一般火灾 Ordinary Fires	重大火灾 Major Fires	特大火灾 Severe Fires
	2000	17	13	3	1	
	2001	41	33	8		
	2002	38	34	2	2	
	2003	27	16	9		
	2004	27	17	10		
乌鲁木齐市	Urumqi City					
克拉玛依市	Karamay City					
吐鲁番地区	Turpan Administrative Offices					
哈密地区	Hami [Kumul] Administrative Offices	1	1			
昌吉回族自治州	Changji Hui Autonomous Prefecture	2	2			
伊犁州直属县(市)	Counties (Cities) Direct Under Ili Prefecture	8	4	4		
塔城地区	Tacheng [Tarbagatai] Administrative Offices	1		1		
阿勒泰地区	Altay Administrative Offices	8	7	1		
博尔塔拉蒙古自治州	Bortala Mongol Autonomous Prefecture					
巴音郭楞蒙古自治州	Bayangol Mongol Autonomous Prefecture	1	1			
阿克苏地区	Aksu Administrative Offices	4	1	3		
克孜勒苏柯尔克孜自治州	Kizilsu Kirgiz Autonomous Prefecture					
喀什地区	Kashgar [Kaxgar] Administrative Offices	1		1		
和田地区	Hotan Administrative Offices	1	1			

年份 Year	地区 Region	火场总面积(公顷) Total (hectare)	受灾森林总面积(公顷) Destructed Forest Area (hectare)	天然林 Natural Forest	人工林 Manmade Forest	经济损失(万元) Economic Loss (10 000yuan)
	2000	1667.00	852.00	849.00	3.00	28.00
	2001	287.00	253.00	251.00	2.00	17.00
	2002	4134.58	1256.19	913.65	0.10	317.39
	2003	370.10	129.27	46.71	82.56	43.81
	2004	291.74	139.64	120.29	31.45	451.31
乌鲁木齐市	Urumqi City					
克拉玛依市	Karamay City					
吐鲁番地区	Turpan Administrative Offices					
哈密地区	Hami [Kumul] Administrative Offices	…	…	…		
昌吉回族自治州	Changji Hui Autonomous Prefecture	0.002	0.001	0.001		1.25
伊犁州直属县(市)	Counties (Cities) Direct Under Ili Prefecture	47.00	21.30	12.70	20.70	7.04
塔城地区	Tacheng [Tarbagatai] Administrative Offices	4.67	3.34	3.34		1.00
阿勒泰地区	Altay Administrative Offices	20.40	4.40	4.10	0.30	141.45
博尔塔拉蒙古自治州	Bortala Mongol Autonomous Prefecture					
巴音郭楞蒙古自治州	Bayangol Mongol Autonomous Prefecture	1.00	0.30	0.30		
阿克苏地区	Aksu Administrative Offices	203.77	95.50	85.05	10.45	300.20
克孜勒苏柯尔克孜自治州	Kizilsu Kirgiz Autonomous Prefecture					
喀什地区	Kashgar [Kaxgar] Administrative Offices	14.60	14.60	14.60		
和田地区	Hotan Administrative Offices	0.20	0.20	0.20		0.38

10-20 森林病虫害防治情况

Prevention of Forest Diseases and Pests

年 份 Year	合计 Total			森林病害 Forest Diseases		
	发生面积（公顷） Area of Occurrence (hectare)	防治面积（公顷） Area of Prevention (hectare)	防治率（%） Prevention Rate (%)	发生面积（公顷） Area of Occurrence (hectare)	防治面积（公顷） Area of Prevention (hectare)	防治率（%） Prevention Rate (%)
2000	158073.33	108053.33	68.35	8033.33	3233.33	40.24
2001	151213.33	133120.00	88.03	4213.33	3020.00	71.67
2002	173066.67	147466.67	85.21	4920.00	3613.33	73.44
2003	171907.67	146173.33	85.03	1940.00	1780.00	91.75
2004	181473.33	152466.67	84.02	3286.00	2686.67	81.74

年 份 Year	森林虫害 Forest Pest Plague			森林鼠害 Forest Rat Plague		
	发生面积（公顷） Area of Occurrence (hectare)	防治面积（公顷） Area of Prevention (hectare)	防治率（%） Prevention Rate (%)	发生面积（公顷） Area of Occurrence (hectare)	防治面积（公顷） Area of Prevention (hectare)	防治率（%） Prevention Rate (%)
2000	134660.00	92746.67	68.87	15380.00	12073.33	78.50
2001	133206.67	117686.67	88.34	13793.33	12413.33	89.99
2002	132133.33	118133.33	89.40	36006.67	25693.33	71.36
2003	152426.67	130593.33	85.68	17540.00	13806.67	78.72
2004	165520.00	138140.00	83.46	12666.67	11640.00	91.89

10-21 地震灾害情况

Earthquake Disasters

年 份 Year	地 区 Region	地震次数(次) Number of Earthquakes (case)	5.0-5.9 级 5.0-5.9 Richterscale	6.0-6.9 级 6.0-6.9 Richterscale	7.0 级以上 Over 7.0 Richterscale
	2000	**1**	**1**		
若羌县	Ruoqiang [Qarkilik] County	1	1		
	2001	**1**	**1**		
和静县	Hejing County	1	1		
	2002	**1**	**1**		
乌恰县	Wuqia [Ulugqat] County	1	1		
	2003	**8**	**5**	**2**	**1**
伽师县	Jiashi [Payzawat] County	1	1		
石河子市	Shi Hezi City	2	2		
巴楚县	Bachu [Maralbexi] County	1		1	
伽师县	Jiashi [Payzawat] County				
岳普湖县	Yopurga County	1	1		
阿克陶县	Akto County	1	1		
阿勒泰市	Altay City	1			1
昭苏县	Zhaosu [Mongolkure] County	1		1	

年 份 Year	地 区 Region	人员伤亡(人) Casualties (person)	死亡人数 Deaths	经济损失(万元) Direct Economic Loss (10 000 yuan)	失去住所(户) Homeless (household)	牲畜死亡数(只) Number of dead domestic animals (head)
	2000			**467.10**		**40**
若羌县	Ruoqiang [Qarkilik] County			467.10		40
	2001			**125.00**		**42**
和静县	Hejing County			125.00		42
	2002	**3**	**1**	**3045.85**	**666**	
乌恰县	Wuqia [Ulugqat] County	3	1	3045.85	666	
	2003	**7261**	**279**	**174531.17**	**64220**	**78404**
伽师县	Jiashi [Payzawat] County			3121.79	1738	1119
石河子市	Shi Hezi City			50.00		
巴楚县	Bachu [Maralbexi] County	7179	268	137130.57	49656	62341
伽师县	Jiashi [Payzawat] County					
岳普湖县	Yopurga County	4	1	7720.05	5409	1112
阿克陶县	Akto County			847.37	240	1991
阿勒泰市	Altay City			7635.60	2460	75
昭苏县	Zhaosu [Mongolkure] County	78	10	18025.79	4717	11766

注：2003 年阿勒泰市北 232 公里在俄罗斯边界处发生 7.9 级地震。

Note: In 2003, the earthquake at the ritcher scale of 7.9 happened in the border area of Russia, 232 kilometers north of Altay City.

10-22 林业系统营林固定资产投资资金来源

Source of Investment in Fixed Assets for Silviculture Performance in Forest System

单位:万元 (10 000 yuan)

年 份 Year	地 区 Region	合 计 Source of Funds This Year	上年底结余资金 Unspent Capitals From Last Year	国家预算内资金 State Budgetary Approp-riations	国债资金 National Debts	中央财政专项资金 Central Funds Earmarked for Environment Protection
	2000	22086	255	13748	5325	
	2001	44669	359	23835	11892	7322
	2002	47718	2439	35930	19693	12503
	2003	60179	1338	51933	21954	18979
	2004	58111	2015	42074	17035	22491
乌鲁木齐市	Urumqi City	2892		158	150	8
克拉玛依市	Karamay City	517	50		25	
吐鲁番地区	Turpan Administrative Offices	836		590		
哈密地区	Hami [Kumul] Administrative Offices	2953		767	254	459
昌吉回族自治州	Changji Hui Autonomous Prefecture	7881		5040	2220	2536
伊犁州直属县(市)	Counties (Cities) Direct Under Ili Prefecture	5457		5454	911	4543
塔城地区	Tacheng [Tarbagatai] Administrative Offices	6200		3697	664	2766
阿勒泰地区	Altay Administrative Offices	3609		3609	3017	592
博尔塔拉蒙古自治州	Bortala Mongol Autonomous Prefecture	3424		2188	370	1816
巴音郭楞蒙古自治州	Bayangol Mongol Autonomous Prefecture	3447		3447	3447	
阿克苏地区	Aksu Administrative Offices	2035		2035	733	1302
克孜勒苏柯尔克孜自治州	Kizilsu Kirgiz Autonomous Prefecture	1448		1448	1078	370
喀什地区	Kashgar [Kaxgar] Administrative Offices	1294		1197	499	698
和田地区	Hotan Administrative Offices	3509		3118	800	2198
自治区林业局	Xinjiang Forestry Bureau	12609	1965	9326	2867	5203

年 份 Year	地 区 Region	国内贷款 Domestic Loans	利用外资 Foreign Capitals	自筹资金 Enterprise Fundraising	其他资金 Other Funds
	2000	718		6205	1160
	2001	487		16763	3225
	2002			6131	3218
	2003			3919	2989
	2004		234	12578	1210
乌鲁木齐市	Urumqi City			2654	80
克拉玛依市	Karamay City			467	
吐鲁番地区	Turpan Administrative Offices		234		12
哈密地区	Hami [Kumul] Administrative Offices			2186	
昌吉回族自治州	Changji Hui Autonomous Prefecture			2642	199
伊犁州直属县(市)	Counties (Cities) Direct Under Ili Prefecture			3	
塔城地区	Tacheng [Tarbagatai] Administrative Offices			2436	67
阿勒泰地区	Altay Administrative Offices				
博尔塔拉蒙古自治州	Bortala Mongol Autonomous Prefecture			1236	
巴音郭楞蒙古自治州	Bayangol Mongol Autonomous Prefecture				
阿克苏地区	Aksu Administrative Offices				
克孜勒苏柯尔克孜自治州	Kizilsu Kirgiz Autonomous Prefecture				
喀什地区	Kashgar [Kaxgar] Administrative Offices			45	52
和田地区	Hotan Administrative Offices				391
自治区林业局	Xinjiang Forestry Bureau			909	409

10-23 林业系统营林固定资产投资完成情况

Completed Investment in Fixed Assets for Silviculture Performance in Forest System

年 份 Year	地 区 Region	本年完成投资（万元） Completed InvestmentDuring the Year (10 000 yuan)	国家投资 State Investment	国债资金 National Debt	本年新增固定资产（万元） New Increased Fixed Assets (10 000 yuan)
	2000	23582	11686	5170	4542
	2001	45890	23725	5433	12492
	2002	68861	35835	21369	
	2003	71277	40821	20448	27223
	2004	60631	43475	15748	23047
乌鲁木齐市	Urumqi City	2892	158	25	2576
克拉玛依市	Karamay City	517			517
石河子市	Shi Hezi City	1035			
吐鲁番地区	Turpan Administrative Offices	1626	1626		
哈密地区	Hami [Kumul] Administrative Offices	2953	767	254	2688
昌吉回族自治州	Changji Hui Autonomous Prefecture	9242	5827	2545	6761
伊犁州直属县(市)	Counties (Cities) Direct Under Ili Prefecture	2169	2166	640	
塔城地区	Tacheng [Tarbagatai] Administrative Offices	8059	4587	530	713
阿勒泰地区	Altay Administrative Offices	3609	3609	3017	3609
博尔塔拉蒙古自治州	Bortala Mongol Autonomous Prefecture	4168	2188	370	1776
巴音郭楞蒙古自治州	Bayangol Mongol Autonomous Prefecture	3447	3447	3202	339
阿克苏地区	Aksu Administrative Offices	2035	2035	733	2035
克孜勒苏柯尔克孜自治州	Kizilsu Kirgiz Autonomous Prefecture	1448	1448	1078	
喀什地区	Kashgar [Kaxgar] Administrative Offices	1423	1341	115	127
和田地区	Hotan Administrative Offices	4352	3962	1075	18
自治区林业局	Xinjiang Forestry Bureau	11656	10314	2164	1888

主要统计指标解释

水资源总量　一定区域内的水资源总量指当地降水形成的地表和地下产水量，即地表径流量与降水入渗补给量之和，不包括过境水量。

地表水资源量　指河流、湖泊、冰川等地表水体中由当地降水形成的、可以逐年更新的动态水量，即天然河川径流量。

地下水资源量　指当地降水和地表水对饱水岩土层的补给量。

地表水与地下水资源重复计算量　指地表水和地下水相互转化的部分，即在河川径流量中包括一部分地下水排泄量，地下水补给量中包括一部分来源于地表水的入渗量。

供水总量　指各种水源工程为用户提供的包括输水损失在内的毛供水量。

地表水源供水量　指地表水体工程的取水量，按蓄、引、提、调四种形式统计。从水库、塘坝中引水或提水，均属蓄水工程供水量；从河道或湖泊中自流引水的，无论有闸或无闸，均属引水工程供水量；利用扬水站从河道或湖泊中直接取水的，属提水工程供水量；跨流域调指水资源一级区或独立流域之间的跨流域调配水量，不包括在蓄、引、提水量中。

地下水源供水量　指水井工程的开采量，按浅层谈水、深层承压水和微咸水分别统计。城市地下水源供水量包括自来水厂的开采量和工矿企业自备井的开采量。

其他水源供水量　包括污水处理再利用、集雨工程、海水淡化等水源工程的供水量。

用水总量　指分配给用户的包括输水损失在内的毛用水量。按用户特性分为农业、工业、生活和生态用水四大类。

农业用水　包括农田灌溉和林牧渔业用水。林牧渔业用水指林果地灌溉、草地灌溉和鱼塘补水。

工业用水　按新水取用量计，不包括企业内部的重复利用水量。

生活用水　包括城镇生活用水和农村生活用水。城镇生活用水由居民用水和公共用水(含服务业、商饮业、货运邮电业及建筑业等用水)组成；农村生活用水除居民生活用水外，还包括畜用水在内。

生态用水　仅包括河湖人工补水和城市环境用水。

工业废水排放量　指经过企业厂区所有排放口排到企业外部的工业废水量。包括生产废水、外排的直接冷却水、超标排放的矿井地下水和与工业废水混排的厂区生活污水，不包括外排的间接冷却水(清污不分流的间接冷却水应计算在内)。

直接排入海的　指经企业位于海边的排放口，直接排入海的废水量。直接排放指废水经过工厂的排污口直接排入海，而未经过城市下水道或其他中间体，也不受其他水体的影响。

工业废水排放达标量　指报告期内废水中各项污染物指标都达到国家或地方排放标准的外排工业废水量，包括未经处理外排达标的，经废水处理设施处理后达标排放的，以及经污水处理厂处理后达标排放的。

工业废水排放达标率　指工业废水排放达标量占工业废水排放量的百分率，计算公式为：

工业废水排放达标率=工业废水排放达标量/工业废水排放量×100%

城镇生活污水排放量　指城镇居民每年排放的生活污水。用人均系数法测算。测算公式为：

城镇生活污水排放量=城镇生活污水排放系数×市镇非农业人口×365

城镇生活污水中化学需氧量(COD)产生量　指城镇居民每年排放的生活污水中的 COD 的产生量。用人均系数法测算。测算公式为：

城镇生活污水中 COD 产生量=城镇生活污水中 COD 产生系数×市镇非农业人口×365

化学需氧量(COD)　测量有机和无机物质化学所消耗氧的质量浓度的水污染指数。

工业废气排放量　指报告期内企业厂区内燃料燃烧和生产工艺过程中产生的各种排入大气的含有污染物的气体的总量，以标准状态(273K，101325Pa)计算。测算公式为：

工业废气排放量=燃料燃烧过程中废气排放量+生产工艺过程中废气排放量

生活及其他 SO2 排放量　以生活及其他煤炭消费量和其含硫量为基础，根据以下公式计算：

生活及其他 SO2 排放量=生活及其他煤炭消费量×含硫量×0.8×2

工业 SO2 排放量　指报告期内企业在燃料燃烧和生产工艺过程中排入大气的 SO2 总量，计算公式为：

工业 SO2 排放量=燃料燃烧过程中 SO2 排放量+生产工艺过程中 SO2 排放量

工业烟尘排放量　指企业厂区内燃料燃烧过程中产生的烟气中夹带的颗粒物排放量。

生活及其他烟尘排放量　指除工业生产活动以外的所有社会、经济活动及公共设施的经营活动中燃烧所排放的烟尘纯重量。以生活及其他煤炭消费量为基础进行测算。

工业粉尘排放量　指企业在生产工艺过程中排放的能在空气中悬浮一定时间的固体颗粒物排放量。如钢铁企业的耐火材料粉尘、焦化企业的筛焦系统粉尘、烧结机的粉尘、石灰窑的粉尘、建材企业的水泥粉尘等。不包括电厂排入大气的烟尘。

工业固体废物产生量　指报告期内企业在生产过程中产生的固体状、半固体状和高浓度液体状废弃物的总量，包括危险废物、冶炼废渣、粉煤灰、炉渣、煤矸石、尾矿、放射性废物和其他废物等；不包括矿山开采的剥离废石和掘进废石(煤矸石和呈酸性或碱性的废石除外)。酸性或碱性废石指采掘的废石其流经水、雨淋水的 pH 值小于 4 或 pH 值大于 10.5 者。

危险废物　指列入国家危险废物名录或根据国家规定的危险废物鉴别标准和鉴别方法认定的，具有爆炸性、易燃性、易氧化性、毒性、腐蚀性、易传染疾病等危险特性之一的废物。

工业固体废物综合利用量　指报告期内企业通过回收、加工、循环、交换等方式，从固体废物中提取或者使其转化为可以利用的资源、能源和其他原材料的固体废物量(包括当年利用往年的工业固体废物贮存量)，如用作农业肥料、生产建筑材料、筑路等。综合利用量由原产生固体废物的单位统计。

工业固体废物综合利用率　指工业固体废物综合利用量占工业固体废物产生量(包括综合利用往年贮存量)的百分率。计算公式为：

工业固体废物综合利用率=工业固体废物综合利用量/(工业固体废物产生量+综合利用往年贮存量)×100%

工业固体废物贮存量　指报告期内企业以综合利用或处置为目的，将固体废物暂时贮存或堆存在专设的贮存设施或专设的集中堆存场所内的数量。专设的固体废物贮存场所或贮存设施必须有防扩散、防流失、防渗漏、防止污染大气、水体的措施。

工业固体废物处置量　指报告期内企业将固体废物焚烧或者最终置于符合环境保护规定要求的场所，并不再回取的工业固体废物量(包括当年处置往年的工业固体废物贮存量)。处置方式有填埋(其中危险废物应安全填埋)、焚烧、专业贮存场(库)封场处理、深层灌注、回填矿井及海洋处置(经海洋管理部门同意投海处置)等。

工业固体废物排放量　指报告期内企业将所产生的固体废物排到固体废物污染防治设施、场所以外的数量，不包括矿山开采的剥离废石和掘进废石(煤矸石和呈酸性或碱性的废石除外)。

“三废”综合利用产品产值 指报告期内利用“三废” 作为主要原料生产的产品价值(现行价)；已经销售或准备销售的应计算产品价值，留作生产自用的不应计算产品价值。

生活垃圾清运量 指报告期内收集和运送到垃圾处理厂(场)的生活垃圾数量。生活垃圾指城市日常生活或为城市日常生活提供服务的活动中产生的固体废物以及法律行政规定的视为城市生活垃圾的固体废物。包括：居民生活垃圾、商业垃圾、集市贸易市场垃圾、街道清扫垃圾、公共场所垃圾和机关、学校、厂矿等单位的生活垃圾。

生活垃圾无害化处理率 指报告期生活垃圾无害化处理量与生活垃圾产生量比率。在统计上，由于生活垃圾产生量不易取得，可用清运量代替。计算公式为：

生活垃圾无害化处理率=生活垃圾无害化处理量/生活垃圾产生量×100%

土地调查面积 指行政区域内的土地调查总面积，包括农用地、建设用地和未利用地。

农用地 指直接用于农业生产的土地，包括耕地、园地、林地、牧草地及其他农用地。

人工林面积 指由人工播种、植苗或扦插造林形成的生长稳定，(一般造林3-5年后或飞机播种5-7年后)每公顷保存株数大于或等于造林设计植树株数80%或郁闭度0.20以上(含02.0)的林分面积。

造林总面积 指报告期内在荒山、荒地、沙丘、退耕地等一切可以造林的土地上，采用人工播种、飞机播种、植苗造林、分植造林等方法新植成片乔木林和灌木林，经过检查验收符合《造林技术规程》要求的单位面积株数，并按《中华人民共和国森林法实施条例》规定，成活率达85%以上(含85%，年降雨量在400毫米以下且无浇灌条件的地区造林成活率达70%以上)的总面积。四旁植树如一侧在四行以上，连片面积0.066公顷(一亩)以上，应统计在造林面积内。造林面积，通常按所有制(国有、国有集体合作、集体和个人)、造林方式(人工、飞机播种)、主要林种用途(用材林、经济林、防护林、薪炭林、特种用途林)分组进行统计。

用材林 指以生产木材为主要目的的森林和林木，包括以生产竹材为主要目的的竹林。

速生丰产林 指在凡具备一定条件的宜林地，经过科学规划设计，相对集中连片，采取集约经营方式，以达到高速度、高质量、高标准地提供林木产品的基地上，选用生长快、成材早、材质好、经济价值高的速生优良树种，通过各项技术措施培育，以缩短林木生长周期，提高林木生长量和木材质量，并达到部颁标准(每亩年生长量0.6立方米以上)或省颁标准而营造的森林。

经济林 指以生产果品，食用油料、饮料、调料，工业原料和药材为主要目的的林木。经济林是人们为了取得林木的果实、叶片、皮层、胶液等产品作为工业原料或者供食用所营造的林木，如油茶、油桐、核桃、樟树、花椒、茶、桑、果等。

防护林 指以防护为主要目的的森林、林木和灌木丛。包括水源涵养林，水土保持林，防风固沙林，农田、牧场防护林，护岸林，护路林等。

薪炭林 指以生产燃料为主要目的的林木。

特种用途林 指以国防、环境保护、科学实验等为主要目的的森林和林木。包括国防林、实验林、母树林、环境保护林、风景林，名胜古迹和革命纪念地的林木，自然保护区的森林。

天然林保护工程 是我国林业的“天”字号工程、一号工程,也是投资最大的生态工程。具体包括三个层次:全面停止长江上游、黄河上中游地区天然林采伐；大幅度调减东北、内蒙古等重点国有林区的木材产量；同时保护好其他地区的天然林资源。主要解决这些区域天然林资源的休养生息和恢复发展问题。

退耕还林还草工程 是我国林业建设上涉及面最广、政策性最强、工序最复杂、群众参与度最高的生态建设工程。主要解决重点地区的水土流失问题。

三北和长江流域等重点防护林体系建设工程 三北和长江中下游地区等重点防护林体系建设工程,是我国涵盖面最大、内容最丰富的防护林体系建设工程。具体包括三北防护林四期工程、长江中下游及淮河太湖流域防护林二期工程、沿海防护林二期工程、珠江防护林二期工程、太行山绿化二期工程和平原绿化二期工程。主要解决三北地区的防沙治沙问题和其他区域各不相同的生态问题。

野生动植物保护及自然保护区建设工程 野生动植物保护及自然保护区建设工程,是一个面向未来,着眼长远,具有多项战略意义的生态保护工程,也是呼应国际大气候、树立中国良好国际形象的“外交工程”。主要解决基因保存、生物多样性保护、自然保护、湿地保护等问题。

重点地区速生丰产用材林基地建设工程 重点地区以速生丰产用材林为主的林业产业基地建设工程,是我国林业产业体系建设的骨干工程,也是增强林业实力的“希望工程”。主要解决我国木材和林产品的供应问题。

湿地 指天然或人工、长久或暂时性的沼泽地、泥炭地或水域地带，包括静止或流动、淡水、半咸水、咸水体，低潮时水深不超过6米的水域以及海岸地带地区的珊瑚滩和海草床、滩涂、红树林、河口、河流、淡水沼泽、沼泽森林、湖泊、盐沼及盐湖。

自然保护区 指对有代表性的自然生态系统、珍稀濒危野生动植物物种的天然分布区、水源涵养区、有特殊意义的自然历史遗迹等保护对象所在的陆地、陆地水体或海域，依法划出一定面积进行特殊保护和管理的区域。以县及县以上各级人民政府正式批准建立的自然保护区为准(包括“六五”以前由部门或“革委会”批准且现仍存在的自然保护区)。风景名胜区、文物保护区不计在内。

生态示范区 指省级以上环境保护行政主管部门批准，以省、地、县政府为主按批准的生态示范区建设规划实施的行政区域。包括已经过国家或省级环境保护行政主管部门验收的和正在开展试点工作的。

滑坡 指斜坡上不稳定的岩土体在重力作用下沿一定软面(或滑动带)整体向下滑动的物理地质现象。地表水和地下水的作用以及人为的不合理工程活动对斜坡岩、土体稳定性的破坏，经常是促使滑坡发生的主要因素。在露天采矿、水利、铁路、公路等工程中，滑坡往往造成严重危害。

崩塌 指陡坡上大块的岩土体在重力作用下突然脱离母体崩落的物理地质现象。它可因多裂隙的岩体经强烈的物理风化、雨水渗入或地震而造成，往往毁坏建筑物，堵塞河道或交通路线。

泥石流 指山地突然爆发的包含大量泥沙、石块的特殊洪流，多见于半干旱山地高原地区。其形成条件是地形陡峻，松散堆积物丰富，有特大暴雨或大量冰融水的流出。

地面塌陷 指地表岩、土体在自然或人为因素作用下向下陷落，并在地面形成塌陷坑(洞)的一种动力地质现象。由于其发育的地质条件和作用因素的不同，地面塌陷可分为：岩溶塌陷、非岩溶塌陷。

环境污染与破坏事故 指由于违反环境保护法规的经济、社会活动与行为，以及意外因素的影响或不可抗拒的自然灾害等原因，致使环境受到污染，国家重点保护的野生动植物、自然保护区受到破坏，人体健康受到危害，社会经济和人民财产受到损失，造成不良社会影响的突发性事件。

环境污染治理投资 指在工业污染源治理和城市环境基础设施建设的资金投入中，用于形成固定资产的资金。包括工业新老污染源治理工程投资、建设项目“三同时”环保投资，以及城市环境基础设施建设所投入的资金。

营林固定资产投资 指在报告期内进行的营林基本建设和营林更新改造活动投资。

上年末结余资金 指在上年资金来源中没有形成固定资产投资额而结余的资金。包括尚未用到工程上去的材料价值、未开始安装的需要安装设备价值及结存的现金和银行存款等。

本年完成投资 指从本年1月1日起至本年最后一天止完成的全部投资额。本年完成投资是反映本年的实际投资规模，计算有关投资效果，进行年度国民经济平衡分析的重要指标。

Explanatory Notes on Main Statistical Indicators

Total Water Resources refers to total volume of water resources measured as run-off for surface water from rainfall and recharge for groundwater in a given area, excluding transit water.

Surface Water Resources refers to total renewable resources which exist in rivers, lakes, glaciers and other collectors from rainfall and are measured as run-off of rivers.

Groundwater Resources refers to replenishment of aquifers with rainfall and surface water.

Duplicated Measurement Between Surface Water and Groundwater refers to mutual exchange between surface water and groundwater, i.e. run-off of rivers includes some depletion with groundwater while groundwater includes some replenishment with surface water.

Water Supply refers to gross water supply by supply systems from sources to consumers, including losses during distribution.

Surface Water Supply refers to withdrawals by surface water supply system, broken down with storage, flow, pumping and transfer. Supply from storage projects includes withdrawals from reservoirs； supply from flow includes withdrawals from rivers and lakes with natural flows no matter if there are locks or not; supply from pumping projects includes withdrawals from rivers or lakes with pumping stations; and supply from transfer refers to water supplies transferred from first-level regions of water resources or independent river drainage areas to others, and should not be covered under supplies of storage, flow and pumping.

Groundwater Supply refers to withdrawals from supplying wells, broken down with shallow layer freshwater, deep layer freshwater and slightly brackish water. Groundwater supply for urban areas includes water mining by both waterworks and own wells of enterprises.

Other Water Supply Sources include supplies by waste water treatment, rain collection, seawater desalinization and other water projects.

Water Use refers to gross water use distributed to users, including loss during transportation, broken down with use by agriculture, industry, living consumption and biological protection.

Water Use by Agriculture includes uses of water by irrigation of farming fields and by forestry, animal husbandry and fishing. Water use by forestry, animal husbandry and fishing includes irrigation of forestry and orchards, irrigation of grassland and replenishment of fishing pools.

Water Use by Industry refers to new withdrawals of water, excluding reuse of water within enterprises.

Water Use by Living Consumption includes use of water for living consumption in both urban and rural areas. Urban water use by living consumption is composed of household use and public use (including services, commerce, restaurants, cargo transportation, posts, telecommunication and construction). Rural water use by living consumption includes both households and animals.

Water Use by Biological Protection includes replenishment of rivers and lakes and use for urban environment.

Waste Water Discharged by Industry refers to the volume of waste water discharged by industrial enterprises through all their outlets, including waste water from production process, directly cooled water, groundwater from mining wells which does not meet discharge standards and sewage from households mixed with waste water produced by industrial activities, but excluding indirectly cooled water discharged (It should be included if the discharge is not separated with waste water).

Waste Water Directly Discharged into Sea refers to the volume of waste water directly discharged into sea through outlets of enterprises situated by sea without going through municipal sewerage networks or any other intermediates or being affected by any other water bodies.

Industrial Waste Water Meeting Discharge Standards refers to volume of industrial waste water discharge which, with or without treatment, reaches national or local standards.

Ratio of Industrial Waste Water Meeting Discharge Standards refers to percentage of industrial waste water meeting discharge standards over total industrial waste water discharge. Its calculation formula is:

Ratio=industrial waste water meeting discharge standards/total industrial waste water discharge×100%

Urban Consumption Waste Water Discharge refers to annual discharge of consumption waste water by urban households. Its calculation formula is:

Discharge=discharge of consumption wastewater by urban households × urban nonagricultural population × 365

COD Generated by Urban Consumption Waster Water refers to chemical oxygen demand generated by annual consumption waste water by urban households. Its formula is:

COD Generated=coefficient of COD generated by annual consumption waste water by urban households ×urban non-agricultrual population ×365

Chemical Oxygen Demand (COD) refers to index of water pollution measuring the mass concentration of oxygen consumed by the chemical breakdown of organic and inorganic matter.

Industrial Waste Air Emission refers to discharge into atmosphere of waste air containing pollutants generated from fuel burning and production process in enterprises within a given period of time. It is converted into standard (273K, 101325Pa) with the following formula:

Emission=waste air emission from fuel burning+waste air emission from production process

SO_2 Emission by Consumption and Others is calculated on the basis of consumption of coal by households and others and sulphur content of coal with the following formula:

Emission=consumption of coal by households and others × sulphur content of coal × 0.8 × 2

Industrial SO_2 Emission refers to volume of sulphur dioxide emission from fuel burning and production process in premises of enterprises for a given period of time. Its calculation formula is:

Emission=SO_2 Emission from fuel burning+ SO_2 Emission form production process

Industrial Soot Emission refers to volume of soot in smoke emitted in process of fuel burning in premises of enterprises.

Soot Emission by Consumption and Others refers to net volume of soot emitted by fuel burning from all social and economic activities and operation of public facilities other than industrial activities. It is calculated on the basis of coal consumption by households and others.

Industrial Dust Emission refers to volume of dust emitted by production process of enterprises and suspended in the air for a given period of time, including dust from refractory material of iron and steel works, dust from coke-screening systems and sintering machines of coke plants, dust from lime kilns and dust from cement production in building material enterprises, but excluding soot and dust emitted from power plants.

Industrial Solid Wastes Produced refers to total volume of solid, semi-solid and high concentration liquid residues produced by industrial enterprises from production process in a given period of time, including hazardous wastes, slag, coal ash, gangue, tailings, radioactive residues and other wastes, but excluding stones stripped or dug out in mining (gangue and acid or alkaline stones not included). A stone is acid or alkaline depending on the pH value of the water below 4 or above 10.5 when the stone is in, or soaked by, the water.

Hazardous Wastes refers to those included in the national hazardous wastes catalogue or specified as any one of the following properties in the national hazardous wastes identification standards: explosive, ignitable, oxidizable, toxic, corrosive or liable to cause infectious diseases or lead to other dangers.

Industrial Solid Wastes Utilized refers to volume of solid wastes from which useful materials can be extracted or which can be converted into usable resources, energy or other materials by means of reclamation, processing, recycling and exchange (including utilizing in the year the stocks of industrial solid wastes of the previous year). Examples of such utilizations include fertilizers, building materials and road materials. The information shall be collected by the producing units of the wastes.

Ratio of Industrial Solid Wastes Utilized refers to the percentage of industrial solid wastes utilized over industrial solid wastes produced (including stocks of the previous year). Its calculation formula is:

Ratio=industrial solid wastes utilized/(industrial solid wastes produced+stocks of previous year utilized)×100%

Stocks of Industrial Solid Wastes refers to volume of solid wastes placed in special facilities or special sites for purposes of utilization or disposal. The sites or facilities should take measures against dispersion, loss, seepage, and air and water contamination.

Industrial Solid Wastes Disposed refers to quantity of industrial solid wastes which are burnt or placed ultimately in the sites meeting the requirements for environmental protection and not salvaged or recycled (including disposition in the year of those wastes of previous years). The disposition includes landfill (Safe landfills should be conducted for hazardous wastes), incineration, containment spaces, deep underground disposal, backfill in mining pits and disposal at sea.

Industrial Solid Wastes Discharged refers to volume of industrial solid wastes discharged by producing enterprises to disposal facilities or to other sites. The wastes exclude stones stripped or dug from mining (gangue and acid or alkaline waste stones not included).

Output Value of Products Made from Waste Gas, Waste Water and Solid Wastes refers current value of products with waste gas, waste water and solid wastes as main materials of production. Products sold and ready to sell shall be included while those produced for own use shall not be included.

Consumption Wastes Transported refers to volume of consumption wastes collected and transported to disposal factories or sites. Consumption wastes are solid wastes produced from urban households or from service activities for urban households, and solid wastes regarded by laws and regulations as urban consumption wastes, including those from households, commercial activities, markets, cleaning of streets, public sites, offices, schools, factories, mining units and other sources.

Ratio of Consumption Wastes Treated refers to consumption wastes treated over that produced. In practical statistics, as it is difficult to estimate, the volume of consumption wastes produced is replaced with that transported. Its calculation formula is:

Ratio=consumption wastes treated/consumption wastes produced × 100%

Area under Land Survey refers to the total area of land, under the land survey, within the jurisdiction of the administrative region, including land for agriculture use, land for construction and unused land.

Land for Agriculture Use refers to land directly used for agriculture production, including land for cultivation, gardening, forests, herbage and other agriculture activities.

Cultivated Land at Beginning (End) of the Year refers to total area of cultivated land within the geographic area of statistical survey at the beginning (end) of the year.

Increase of Cultivated Land during the Year refers to the increase of cultivated land during the year as a result of land preparation, reclamation, new development, adjustment of agriculture structure and other reasons.

Decrease of Cultivated Land during the Year refers to the decrease of cultivated land during the year as a result of adjustment of agriculture structure, construction projects, natural disasters, conversion for ecological purpose, and other reasons.

Area of Man-made Forests refer to the area of stable growing forests, planted manually or by airplanes, with a survival rate of 80% or higher of the designed number of trees per hectare, or with a canopy density of or above 0.20 after 3-5 years of manual planting or 5-7 years of airplane planting.

Total Area of Afforestation refers to the total area of land suitable for afforestation, including barren hills, idle land, sand dunes, "grain for green" land, on which acres of arbores or bushes are planted through manual planting, airplane planting, plant seedlings, etc. in accordance with the required density standards of the Technical Procedures of Afforestation, and with a survival rate of over 85% in line with the Implementing Rules of the Forest Law of the People's Republic of China (or a survival rate of 75% in areas with less that 400 mm of annual rainfall and without irrigation facilities). Included in the this category are trees planted alone the roadsides, riversides, or next to houses that occupy an area over 0.066 hectares, or where more than 4 lines of trees are planted. Total area of afforestation is further classified by ownership (state-owned, state-collective, collective or private), by approach of planting (manual, airplane), and by type of forests (timber, by-products, protection, fuel, special use, etc.).

Timber Forests refer to forests which is mainly for the production of timber, including bamboo groves planted to harvest bamboos.

Fast-growing Timber Forests refer to forests intensively planted and managed through scientific planning to produce fast-growing, high quality timber product. In these forest bases, Superior species of trees with shorter growing span, good quality and high economic value are planted and grow under various technological measures so as to meet the standards set by the Ministry of Forest (annual growth of over 0.6 cubic metres per 0.066 hectares of trees) of by the provincial authorities.

By product Forests refer to forests that mainly produce fruits, nuts, edible oil, beverages, indigents, raw materials and medicine materials. By-product forests are planted to harvest the fruits, leaves, bark or liquid of trees, and consume them as food or raw materials for the manufacturing industry, such as tea-oil trees, tung oil trees, walnut trees, camphor trees, tea bushes, mulberry trees, fruit trees, etc.

Protection Forests refer to forests, trees and bushes planted mainly for protection or preservation purpose, including water resource conservation forests, water and soil conservation forests, windbreak and dune-fixing forests, farmland and pasture protection forests, riverside protection forests, roadside protection forests, etc.

Fuel Forests refer to forests planted mainly for fuels.

Forests for Special Purpose refer to forests planted mainly for national defence, environment protection or scientific experiments, including national defence forests, experimental forests, mother-tree forests, environment protection forests, scenery forests, trees in historical or scenic spots, forests in natural reserves.

Project on Preservation of Natural Forests is the Number One ecological project in China's forest industry that involves the largest investment. It consists of 3 components: 1) Complete halt of all cutting and logging activities in the natural forests at the upper stream of Yangtze River and the upper and middle streams of the Yellow River. 2) Significant reduction of timber production of key state forest zones in northeast provinces and in Inner Mongolia. 3) Better protection of natural forests in other regions through rehabilitation programmes.

Projects on Converting Cultivated Land to Forests and Grassland (Grain for Green Projects) aiming at preventing soil erosion in key regions, these projects are ecological construction projects in the development of forest industry that have the widest coverage and most sophisticated procedures, with strong policy implications and most active participation of the people.

Projects on Protection Forests in North China and Yangtze River Basin covering the widest areas in China with a rich variety of contents, these projects aim at solving the problem of sand and dust in northeastern China, northern China and northwestern China and the ecological issues in other areas. More specifically, they include phase IV of project on North China protection forests, phase II of project on protection forests at the middle and lower streams of Yangtze River and at the Huihe River and Taihu Lake valley, phase II of project on coastal protection forests, phase II of project on Pearl River protection forests, phase II project on greenery of Taihang Mountain and phase II projects on greenery of plains.

Projects on Preserving Wild Animals and Plants and on Construction of Nature Reserves aiming at gene preservation and protection of bio-diversity, nature and wetlands, these projects look into the future with strategic perspective and are integrated with international trends.

Projects on Fast-growing Timber Forests Bases in Key Regions these are key projects for the forest industry to strengthen its capacity in supplying more timber and forest by-products.

Wetlands refer to marshland and peat bog, whether natural or man-made, permanent or temporary; water covered areas, whether stagnant or flowing, with fresh or semi-fresh or salty water that is less than 6 metres deep at low tide; as well as coral beach, weed beach, mud beach, mangrove, river outlet, rivers, fresh-water marshland, marshland forests, lakes, salty bog and salt lakes along the coastal areas.

Nature Reserves refer to certain areas of land, waters or sea that are representative in natural ecological systems, or are natural habitats for rare or endangered wild animals or plants, or water conservation zones, or the location of important natural or historic relics, which are demarked by law and put under special protection and management. Nature reserves are designated by the formal approval of governments at and above county level (including those approved by relevant departments or "revolutionary committees" before 1980). Scenic spots and cultural preservation zones are not included.

Ecological Demonstration Zones refer to administrative areas approved by the environment protection agencies of central and provincial governments and established by provincial, prefecture or county governments in line with the approved programme for ecological demonstration zones. They include those evaluated and accepted by the environment protection agencies of central and provincial governments and those under pilot development stage.

Landslides refer to the geological phenomenon of unstable rocks and earth on slopes sliding down along certain soft surface as a result of gravitational force. Role of surface water and underground water, and destruction of the stability of slopes by irrational construction work are usually main factors triggering the landslides. Several damages are often caused by landslides in open mining, in water conservancy projects, and in the construction of railways and highways.

Collapse refers to the geological phenomenon of large mass of rocks or earth suddenly collapsing from the mountain or cliff as a result of gravitational force. Usually caused by weathering of rocks, permeance of rain or earthquakes, collapse often destructs buildings and blocks river course or transport routes.

Mud-rock Flow refers to the sudden rush of flood torrents containing large amount of mud and rocks in mountainous areas. It is found mostly in semi-arid hills or plateaus. High and precipitous topographic features, loose soil mass, heavy rains or melting water contribute to the mud-rock flow.

Land Subside refers to the geological phenomenon of surface rocks or earth subsiding into holes or pits as a result of natural or human factors. Land subside can be classified as karst subside and non-karst subside.

Environment Pollution and Destruction Accidents refer to sudden accidents, due to economic or social activities that are in contrast to environment protection laws or due to unforeseen factors or natural disasters, that lead to the environment pollution, the destruction of protected wild animals, plants or nature reserves, the damage to human health, the economic and property losses, and the negative impact on the society.

Investment in Environment Pollution Harnessing Projects refers to the proportion of investment in fixed assets in the total investment in harnessing industrial pollution and in the construction of urban environment infrastructure facilities. It includes investment in harnessing sources of industrial pollution, investment in environment protection facilities designed concurrently with construction projects, and investment in urban environment infrastructure facilities.

Investment in Fixed Assets for Silviculture Performance refers to the investment in capital construction and updating projects in afforestation during the reference period.

Unspent Capitals from Last Year refer to capitals from the last year that have not been invested in the fixed assets, including value of materials that have not been used yet, the value of equipment yet to be installed, as well as cash in hand and bank deposits.

Completed Investment during the Year reflecting the actual size of investment completed during January 1 and December 31 of the reference year, this indicator is important in estimating investment efficiency and in making annual analysis of the performance of the national economy.

第十一篇

CHAPTER 11

农　业

AGRICULTURE

11-1 农村基层组织情况

Basic Conditions of State Farm, Forestry, Pasture and Fishery

指标	Item	1995	2000	2004
乡镇政府(个)	**Township and Town Governments (unit)**	**798**	**794**	**797**
#镇政府	TownshipGovernments		124	168
村民委员会(个)	Number of Villagers'Committees (unit)	8943	9378	9026
乡村户数(户)	Rural Households (household)	1811804	2008794	2195841
乡村人口(人)	Rural Population (person)	8664329	9131922	9755277
乡村从业人员(人)	**Rural Employed (persons)**	**3124888**	**3540789**	**3950606**
按性别分	Grouped By Gender			
男	Male	1725300	1950559	2176318
女	Female	1399588	1590230	1774288
按行业分	Groped By Sector			
农林牧渔业	Farming, Forestry, Animal Husbandry & Fishery	2835581	3144461	3394061
工　业	Industry	77948	84766	106092
建筑业	Construction	35535	49126	76607
交运仓储和邮政业	Transportation,Storage,Postal and Telecommunications Services			103976
信息传输、计算机服务和软件业	Information transmission, Computer Service and software sector			15132
批发与零售业	Wholesale and Retail Sector		76727	111020
住宿和餐饮业	Hotel and Catering Services		109217	53270
其　他	Others		76492	90448

11-2 国有农林牧渔场基本情况

Basic Conditions of State Farm, Forestry, Pasture and Fishery

指标	Item	2003	2004
场数合计(个)	**Total (unit)**	**518**	**509**
农　场	Number of Farms	301	302
林　场	Number of Forest Farms	47	46
牧　场	Number of Ranch	152	143
渔　场	Number of Fishing Ground	18	18
场内户数(户)	**Number of Households on a Farm (household)**	**761549**	**767313**
#牧业户数	Number of Stock-breeding Household	63131	62921
场内人口(人)	**Population (person)**	**2550613**	**2539576**
#牧业人口	Stock-breeding Population	278028	250921
场内实有从业人员(人)	**Persons Actually Engaged on a Farm (person)**	**986761**	**992626**
男	Male	557413	562028
女	Female	429348	430598
农业从业人员	Persons in Farm	717997	730222
工业从业人员	Persons in Industry		92078
建筑业从业人员	Persons in Construction	57223	54882
交运仓储和邮政业	Transportation,Storage, Postal and Telecommunications Services	34024	31522
信息传输、计算机服务和软件业	Information transmission, Computer Service and software sector		26200
批发与零售业	Wholesale and Retail Sector		429
住宿和餐饮业	Accomodation and Catering Services		40990
其　他	Others		16303

11-3 各地、州、市、县(市)农村基层组织情况

单位：人 (2004 年)

地 区	Region	乡镇数(个) Number of Township and Town Governments (unit)	#镇 town	村民委员会(个) Number of Villagers' Committees (unit)	乡村户数(户) Number of Rural Households (unit)	#牧业户数 Stock-breeding household
总 计	**Total**	**797**	**168**	**9026**	**2195841**	**225895**
一、地 方	**Local Regions**	**795**	**168**	**9001**	**2188830**	**225680**
乌鲁木齐市	**Urumqi City**	**20**	**3**	**110**	**34521**	**3453**
乌鲁木齐县	Urumqi County	10	2	59	15958	2527
市直单位	Direct Under the Municipality	10	1	51	18563	926
克拉玛依市	**Karamay City**	**2**		**6**	**592**	**58**
吐鲁番地区	**TurpanAdministrative Offices**	**23**	**7**	**172**	**88574**	**2899**
吐鲁番市	Turpan City	8	1	60	34607	1391
鄯善县	Shanshan County	9	4	67	34381	425
托克逊县	Toksun County	6	2	45	19586	1083
哈密地区	**Hami Administrative Offices**	**32**	**5**	**183**	**48427**	**12826**
哈密市	Hami City	16	2	108	27701	6583
巴里坤哈萨克自治县	Barkol KazakAutonomous County	10	2	43	19105	5709
伊吾县	Yiwu County	6	1	32	1621	534
昌吉回族自治州	**Changji Hui Autonomous Prefecture**	**73**	**37**	**805**	**177238**	**23928**
昌吉市	Changji City	10	6	89	25643	4692
阜康市	Fukang City	6	3	106	16337	2324
米泉市	Miquan City	6	5	78	23353	2196
呼图壁县	Hutubi County	6	5	52	17988	2898
玛纳斯县	Manas County	11	6	152	22820	3017
奇台县	Qitai County	15	6	102	33130	2927
吉木萨尔县	Jimsar County	9	4	167	21325	1832
木垒哈萨克自治县	Mori Kazak Autonomous County	10	2	59	16642	4042
伊犁哈萨克自治州	**Ili Kazak Autonomous Prefecture**	**209**	**48**	**2009**	**453433**	**70132**
伊犁州直属县(市)	**Counties (Cities) Direct Under Ili Prefecture**	**99**	**20**	**682**	**278683**	**37775**
伊宁市	Yining City	9	1	49	28884	787
奎屯市	Kuytun City	1		4	248	25
伊宁县	Yining County	18	2	129	58503	7330
察布查尔锡伯自治县	Qapqal Xibe Autonomous County	13	2	61	22987	1010
霍城县	Huocheng County	10	5	75	43489	2454
巩留县	Gongliu County	8	1	52	24583	2876
新源县	Xinyuan County	11	6	99	39212	6787
昭苏县	Zhaosu County	10	1	84	19901	4473
特克斯县	Tekes County	8	1	59	19501	6166
尼勒克县	Nilka County	11	1	70	21375	5867
塔城地区	**Tacheng [Tarbagatai] Administrative Offices**	**59**	**18**	**816**	**115465**	**12551**
塔城市	Tacheng [Qoqek] City	6	1	115	16241	1146
乌苏市	Usu City	14	7	155	23955	382
额敏县	Emin [Dorbiljin] County	11		139	18363	1028
沙湾县	Shawan County	12	9	239	33325	1063
托里县	Toli County	5		67	12734	6247
裕民县	Yumin [Qagantokay] County	5		45	6575	1429
和布克赛尔蒙古自治县	Hoboksar Mongol Autonomous County	6	1	56	4272	1256
阿勒泰地区	**Altay Administrative Offices**	**51**	**10**	**511**	**59285**	**19806**
阿勒泰市	Altay City	10	2	98	13443	2741
布尔津县	Burqin County	7	1	63	9593	3732
富蕴县	Fuyun [Koktokay] County	9	3	73	7494	2793
福海县	Fuhai [Burultokay] County	5		65	9131	3053
哈巴河县	Habahe [Kaba] County	7	1	117	8097	2926
青河县	Qinghe [Qinggil] County	7	2	54	7085	3702
吉木乃县	Jeminay County	6	1	41	4442	859

Basic Conditions of Rural Grassroots Units by Prefecture, Autonomous Prefecture, City and County

(person)

乡村人口数 Rural Population	#牧业人口数 Population Engaged in Livestocks	乡村从业人员 Number of Rural Laborers	男 Male	女 Female	农林牧渔业 Farming, Forestry, Animal Husbandry & Fishery	工业 Industry	建筑业 Construction	交通仓储及邮政业 Transport, Storage, Post and Telecommunication Services	信息传输、计算机服务和软件业 Information Transmission, Computer Servcie and Software Industries	批发与零售业 Retail and Wholesale Industries	住宿和餐饮业 Hotel and Eateries	其他 Others
9755277	**1034642**	**3950606**	**2176318**	**1774288**	**3394061**	**106092**	**76607**	**103976**	**15132**	**111020**	**53270**	**90448**
9733473	**1033745**	**3939433**	**2170570**	**1768863**	**3384995**	**105213**	**76566**	**103768**	**15132**	**110731**	**52999**	**90029**
130539	**15308**	**74731**	**40062**	**34669**	**50535**	**3889**	**384**	**4625**	**5059**	**5998**	**1721**	**2520**
65801	10522	37650	20167	17483	30894	411	47	1096	4	957	1721	2520
64738	4786	37081	19895	17186	19641	3478	337	3529	5055	5041		
2099	**269**	**1451**	**932**	**519**	**1330**	**35**	**28**	**22**	**34**	**2**		
395615	**10191**	**209222**	**113149**	**96073**	**180297**	**3887**	**1989**	**10705**	**374**	**7575**	**3627**	**768**
167405	4557	84118	44701	39417	70976	1285	586	4121	270	3874	2577	429
145404	1741	82334	43436	38898	73736	1275	578	3502	76	2493	547	127
82806	3893	42770	25012	17758	35585	1327	825	3082	28	1208	503	212
183844	**56340**	**95084**	**52945**	**42139**	**75776**	**3236**	**2271**	**4759**	**53**	**3606**	**1877**	**3506**
100455	25621	58195	31116	27079	48133	1516	1030	2949	38	1918	847	1764
76809	28583	33215	19707	13508	24453	1650	1144	1698	15	1568	973	1714
6580	2136	3674	2122	1552	3190	70	97	112		120	57	28
723110	**102354**	**395089**	**210816**	**184273**	**324188**	**12894**	**5796**	**14668**	**365**	**11288**	**8693**	**17197**
99634	17019	58619	30950	27669	47986	2338	767	2045	259	2095	824	2305
63251	10012	33240	18098	15142	28329	1308	691	810	16	722	501	863
94170	6189	56716	29134	27582	30977	6025	2099	6750	5	2456	4318	4086
74200	13691	39147	21395	17752	35724	378	92	1204	6	912	516	315
88774	12066	48998	26648	22350	43707	925	328	1070	10	1260	633	1065
143097	15668	72764	39296	33468	62867	569	939	1517		1841	1215	3816
90592	8382	48076	25184	22892	41006	841	664	889	17	1396	597	2666
69392	19327	37529	20111	17418	33592	510	216	383	52	606	89	2081
2123071	**356723**	**947236**	**548262**	**398974**	**799834**	**30433**	**21229**	**29659**	**3347**	**28978**	**13240**	**20516**
1363969	**195363**	**583401**	**342091**	**241310**	**483271**	**21683**	**15076**	**21120**	**2945**	**19027**	**8257**	**12022**
135898	4911	60353	34872	25481	39619	6008	2246	5165	42	3792	1528	1953
1048	210	640	371	269	574					6		60
291238	29149	139515	83085	56430	122586	3361	2097	4172	420	5363	1112	404
110048	7986	39182	24014	15168	32909	2555	1049	954	114	1432	40	129
204775	11806	107721	58392	49329	91538	2430	2137	3209	320	3250	2070	2767
114053	16607	35743	21374	14369	31439	924	653	1100	1545	82		
200518	36685	80047	48276	31771	64291	4000	3135	2534	204	2675	1337	1871
97662	24400	34973	24637	10336	30293	1052	926	800	90	934	437	441
101992	33316	45969	25049	20920	37010	696	1607	1261	210	1185	500	3500
106737	30293	39258	22021	17237	33012	657	1226	1925		308	1233	897
486941	**59320**	**261165**	**143271**	**117894**	**231774**	**5121**	**2206**	**5206**	**342**	**7053**	**3246**	**6217**
61343	4577	36856	19507	17349	29461	776	712	1110	13	1803	888	2093
99999	1793	54085	29549	24536	49495	1322	354	477	86	576	551	1224
79910	5023	40475	22942	17533	35759	824	369	920	10	1454	322	817
138095	4839	79632	42201	37431	72251	1500	271	1453	151	2171	903	932
57714	30190	24808	15002	9806	22143	381	378	594	33	536	109	634
30805	7477	16069	8494	7575	14410	192	82	363	4	327	246	445
19075	5421	9240	5576	3664	8255	126	40	289	45	186	227	72
272161	**102040**	**102670**	**62900**	**39770**	**84789**	**3629**	**3947**	**3333**	**60**	**2898**	**1737**	**2277**
57174	13721	20188	12540	7648	17157	757	509	595	12	604	130	424
45144	18340	18539	10936	7603	16220	363	338	271		405	678	264
36934	14448	13753	8162	5591	10645	624	516	348	25	363	195	1037
36808	14559	15488	8950	6538	11319	732	1855	812		333	63	374
43479	15896	15759	10010	5749	13119	536	490	762	12	605	235	
37785	21162	14513	8315	6198	12237	576	239	536	11	504	300	110
14837	3914	4430	3987	443	4092	41		9		84	136	68

11-3 续表

单位：人

地 区	Region	乡镇数（个） Number of Township and Town Governments (Unit)	#镇 town	村民委员会（个） Number of Villagers' Committees (Unit)	乡村户数（户） Number of Rural Households (unit)	#牧业户数 Stock-Breeding household
博尔塔拉蒙古自治州	**Bortala Mongol Autonomous Prefecture**	**14**	**5**	**257**	**44733**	**4777**
博乐市	Bole [Bortala] City	5	3	134	17414	2080
精河县	Jinghe [Jing] County	4	1	58	18202	1488
温泉县	Wenquan [Araxang] County	5	1	65	9117	1209
巴音郭楞蒙古自治州	**Bayangol Mongol Autonomous Prefecture**	**71**	**10**	**384**	**100676**	**9193**
库尔勒市	Korla City	10	1	57	17273	579
轮台县	Luntai [Bugur] County	9	2	64	16420	679
尉犁县	Yuli [Lopnur] County	7		47	10419	1765
若羌县	Ruoqiang [Qarkilik] County	5		17	3694	209
且末县	Qiemo [Qarqan] County	11		54	7569	762
焉耆回族自治县	Yanji Hui Autonomous County	7	3	46	14019	532
和静县	Hejing County	11	3	54	17416	3612
和硕县	Hoxud County	5		20	5688	602
博湖县	Bohu [Bagrax] County	6	1	25	8178	453
阿克苏地区	**Aksu Administrative Offices**	**73**	**21**	**1125**	**279634**	**17714**
阿克苏市	Aksu City	6	2	121	27890	3949
温宿县	Wensu [Onsu] County	9	4	104	25468	1841
库车县	Kuqa County	13	7	218	59384	2767
沙雅县	Xayar County	7	3	146	36949	1407
新和县	Xinhe [Toksu] County	7	1	112	25340	2300
拜城县	Baicheng [Bay] County	12	2	165	29602	2383
乌什县	Wushi [Uxturpan] County	8		108	36123	1130
阿瓦提县	Awat County	7	2	118	31331	1227
柯坪县	Kalpin County	4		33	7547	710
克孜勒苏柯尔克孜自治州	**Kizilsu Kirgiz Autonomous Prefecture**	**35**	**3**	**223**	**70995**	**18377**
阿图什市	Artux City	7		72	30371	5080
阿克陶县	Akto County	13	2	106	30383	6630
阿合奇县	Akqi County	6	1	22	4961	2621
乌恰县	Wuqia [Ulugqat] County	9		23	5280	4046
喀什地区	**Kashgar [Kaxgar] Administrative Offices**	**157**	**18**	**2354**	**542187**	**41872**
喀什市	Kashgar [Kaxgar] City	4		63	22343	2091
疏附县	Shufu County	16		208	68004	6398
疏勒县	Shule County	14	2	223	53093	2019
英吉沙县	Yengisar County	13		164	44340	352
泽普县	Zepu [Poskam] County	11	1	130	22936	1175
莎车县	Shache [Yarkant] County	28	6	498	105316	8359
叶城县	Yecheng [Kagilik] County	19	2	305	57928	6731
麦盖提县	Makit County	9		129	25168	1608
岳普湖县	Yopurga County	8	1	88	24714	1757
伽师县	Jiashi [Payzawat] County	13	2	296	63015	4119
巴楚县	Bachu [Maralbexi] County	11	3	201	50170	4155
塔什库尔干塔吉克自治县	Taxkorgan Tajik Autonomous County	11	1	49	5160	3108
和田地区	**Hotan Administrative Offices**	**86**	**11**	**1373**	**347820**	**20451**
和田市	Hotan City	4	1	58	19493	4440
和田县	Hotan County	12	1	216	62326	3687
墨玉县	Moyu [Karakax] County	16	1	364	92832	3809
皮山县	Pishan [Guma] County	15	2	169	37272	1229
洛浦县	Lop County	10	2	238	54172	2721
策勒县	Qira County	8	1	125	30116	2844
于田县	Yutian [Keriya] County	15	2	174	46220	691
民丰县	Minfeng [Niya] County	6	1	29	5389	1030
二、生产建设兵团	**Xinjiang Production & Construction Group**	**2**		**25**	**7011**	**215**

Continued

(person)

乡村人口数 Rural Population	#牧业人口数 Population Engaged in Livestocks	乡村从业人员 Number of Rural Laborers	男 Male	女 Female	农林牧渔业 Farming, Forestry, Animal Husbandry & Fishery	工业 Industry	建筑业 Construction	交通仓储及邮政业 Transport, Storage, Post and Telecommunic-ation Services	信息传输、计算机服务和软件业 Information Transmission, Computer Servcie and Software Industries	批发与零售业 Retail and Wholesale Industries	住宿和餐饮业 Accomodation and catering service	其他 Others
189876	**21068**	**82365**	**44813**	**37552**	**66401**	**3018**	**2160**	**2662**	**95**	**3185**	**1861**	**2983**
79206	9440	34085	19258	14827	26267	1313	1013	1473	20	1900	656	1443
67654	5493	30204	16074	14130	25227	1181	639	854		784	875	644
43016	6135	18076	9481	8595	14907	524	508	335	75	501	330	896
406109	**35310**	**180340**	**101927**	**78413**	**150606**	**6211**	**4352**	**4894**	**249**	**7199**	**2719**	**4110**
67184	1741	28782	17137	11645	24829	175	122	838		2363	336	119
61751	1935	24529	13413	11116	21158	440	798	245	33	523	350	982
38522	5529	15501	8947	6554	13391	242	396	501	42	468	13	448
12299	801	5595	3023	2572	5142	70	13	64		194	15	97
35328	3690	12615	7214	5401	10896	444	227	326		350	205	167
58589	2264	28352	17783	10569	21115	2693	1291	1097	54	1068	669	365
75815	14739	38160	19953	18207	32101	1609	1039	980	24	1171	513	723
21217	2590	10561	5620	4941	8230	265	331	219	27	689	442	358
35404	2021	16245	8837	7408	13744	273	135	624	69	373	176	851
1293249	**75082**	**518642**	**285838**	**232804**	**472568**	**9465**	**4982**	**7020**	**432**	**11329**	**5714**	**7132**
130224	14864	47826	26642	21184	44004	803	327	1029	51	910	503	199
119823	7893	36427	21407	15020	33817	316	114	250	26	941	173	790
284778	11778	128765	72826	55939	114045	3205	2081	2746	96	2523	2098	1971
162250	7613	65537	36129	29408	58329	1334	256	264	30	2265	1010	2049
117855	6900	53196	29595	23601	49933	569	263	633	120	1000	280	398
144236	11659	55900	30845	25055	53711	202	193	417	21	696	410	250
155737	5650	47444	25030	22414	42670	1152	586	691	45	1040	600	660
145446	5262	67948	35203	32745	61934	1416	881	796	43	1454	609	815
32900	3463	15599	8161	7438	14125	468	281	194		500	31	
346931	**84629**	**104240**	**61302**	**42938**	**85357**	**4977**	**1903**	**2918**	**48**	**6966**	**1339**	**732**
154101	22733	52337	29764	22573	38183	3732	1286	2292	48	5392	979	425
143586	29397	40409	25430	14979	37282	754	598	294		840	360	281
25968	13992	4870	2678	2192	4632	47	19	69		77		26
23276	18507	6624	3430	3194	5260	444		263		657		
2478154	**202156**	**820469**	**436732**	**383737**	**732891**	**12042**	**19014**	**14704**	**4911**	**14772**	**7643**	**14492**
101962	11758	36644	20606	16038	23732	875	4367	1230		1843	1120	3477
329258	38500	116849	67250	49599	99615	2510	5032	3626	4706	1360		
247693	16000	65881	36749	29132	58313	637	1205	1166	45	2000	60	2455
196200	442	72610	38483	34127	70363	523	464	602		571		87
95188	3268	28266	14411	13855	26550	241	477	306		466		226
480256	36167	179152	90242	88910	158124	4528	3831	3144		2974	1999	4552
281850	38094	73330	38851	34479	67796	689	1227	1124		640	964	890
121582	3898	41443	21939	19504	40419	139	254	262	5	364		
108368	6123	41277	21300	19977	38176	904	244	450	15	500	710	278
284235	16476	89886	47640	42246	83014	505	1217	1950	65	1085	1650	400
207836	15177	66736	34702	32034	58927	466	664	689	50	2765	1070	2105
23726	16253	8395	4559	3836	7862	25	32	155	25	204	70	22
1460876	**74315**	**510564**	**273792**	**236772**	**445212**	**15126**	**12458**	**7132**	**165**	**9833**	**4565**	**16073**
84338	16810	25411	14569	10842	18427	1174	1312	830	77	837	567	2187
258663	12846	93065	50570	42495	78226	4659	2562	1480	16	1857	503	3762
396661	13025	124339	69499	54840	101149	4741	5888	2475	22	3631	936	5497
159497	4971	57029	30674	26355	52192	781	444	513		701	302	2096
217181	8267	81854	42858	38996	73235	2749	1478	1107	15	1233	570	1467
117924	11019	44536	22997	21539	40431	746	644	385		926	494	910
203698	3044	77655	38902	38753	75735	201	52	79	35	521	1012	20
22914	4333	6675	3723	2952	5817	75	78	263		127	181	134
21804	**897**	**11173**	**5748**	**5425**	**9066**	**879**	**41**	**208**		**289**	**271**	**419**

11-4 各地、州、市、县(市)耕地面积

Area Under Cultivation by Prefecture, Autonomous Prefecture, City and County

单位：千公顷 (2004 年) (1 000 hectares)

地 区	Region	年末耕地面积 Cultivated Areas (Year-end)	年内增加的耕地面积 Newly increased Cultivated Areas in Current year	#新开荒地面积 Newly reclaimed Wildland Area
总 计	**Total**	**3362.32**	**108.03**	**44.78**
一、地 方	**Local Regions**	**2322.42**	**91.68**	**44.78**
乌鲁木齐市	**Urumqi City**	**31.52**	**0.15**	**0.08**
乌鲁木齐县	Urumqi County	18.51		
市直单位	Direct Under the Municipality	13.01	0.15	0.08
克拉玛依市	**Karamay City**	**15.48**		
吐鲁番地区	**TurpanAdministrative Offices**	**35.39**	**4.57**	**0.31**
吐鲁番市	Turpan City	11.03	2.45	0.25
鄯善县	Shanshan County	10.57	0.06	0.06
托克逊县	Toksun County	13.79	2.06	
哈密地区	**Hami Administrative Offices**	**53.24**	**7.99**	**1.16**
哈密市	Hami City	19.07	4.94	0.32
巴里坤哈萨克自治县	Barkol KazakAutonomous County	28.38	1.09	0.36
伊吾县	Yiwu County	5.79	1.96	0.48
昌吉回族自治州	**Changji Hui Autonomous Prefecture**	**307.23**	**8.93**	**7.08**
昌吉市	Changji City	45.51	1.01	0.81
阜康市	Fukang City	18.83	1.20	1.01
米泉市	Miquan City	13.76		
呼图壁县	Hutubi County	45.00	2.27	1.50
玛纳斯县	Manas County	49.46	2.99	2.98
奇台县	Qitai County	71.21	0.55	0.13
吉木萨尔县	Jimsar County	31.09	0.08	0.08
木垒哈萨克自治县	Mori Kazak Autonomous County	32.37	0.83	0.57
伊犁哈萨克自治州	**Ili Kazak Autonomous Prefecture**	**702.10**	**27.82**	**20.77**
伊犁州直属县(市)	**Counties (Cities) Direct Under Ili Prefecture**	**279.93**	**8.69**	**3.14**
伊宁市	Yining City	15.80	0.22	0.10
奎屯市	Kuytun City	1.70	0.02	0.02
伊宁县	Yining County	61.91	2.23	1.77
察布查尔锡伯自治县	Qapqal Xibe Autonomous County	30.97	1.83	0.80
霍城县	Huocheng County	32.31	0.97	
巩留县	Gongliu County	26.66	1.90	
新源县	Xinyuan County	37.86	0.45	0.45
昭苏县	Zhaosu County	37.10		
特克斯县	Tekes County	17.43	1.07	
尼勒克县	Nilka County	18.19		
塔城地区	**Tacheng [Tarbagatai] Administrative Offices**	**303.97**	**14.43**	**12.93**
塔城市	Tacheng [Qoqek] City	77.92	4.33	4.30
乌苏市	Usu City	48.67		
额敏县	Emin [Dorbiljin] County	58.13	1.26	
沙湾县	Shawan County	65.10	0.75	0.59
托里县	Toli County	14.45	0.22	0.22
裕民县	Yumin [Qagantokay] County	26.59	0.05	
和布克赛尔蒙古自治县	Hoboksar Mongol Autonomous County	13.11	7.82	7.82
阿勒泰地区	**Altay Administrative Offices**	**118.20**	**4.70**	**4.70**
阿勒泰市	Altay City	19.15	1.23	1.23
布尔津县	Burqin County	19.28	0.37	0.37
富蕴县	Fuyun [Koktokay] County	16.10	0.98	0.98
福海县	Fuhai [Burultokay] County	22.04	1.09	1.09
哈巴河县	Habahe [Kaba] County	19.00	0.15	0.15
青河县	Qinghe [Qinggil] County	11.48	0.88	0.88
吉木乃县	Jeminay County	11.15		

11-4 续表 Continued

单位：千公顷 (1 000 hectares)

地　　区	Region	年末耕地面　　积 Cultivated Areas (Year-end)	年内增加的耕地面积 Newly increased Cultivated Areas in Current year	#新开荒地面积 Newly reclaimed Wildland Area
博尔塔拉蒙古自治州	**Bortala Mongol Autonomous Prefecture**	**72.06**	**1.76**	**1.66**
博乐市	Bole [Bortala] City	27.57	0.10	
精河县	Jinghe [Jing] County	23.68	1.30	1.30
温泉县	Wenquan [Araxang] County	20.81	0.36	0.36
巴音郭楞蒙古自治州	**Bayangol Mongol Autonomous Prefecture**	**167.06**	**20.19**	**6.29**
库尔勒市	Korla City	37.02	5.48	0.08
轮台县	Luntai [Bugur] County	18.10	0.15	
尉犁县	Yuli [Lopnur] County	31.68	5.10	
若羌县	Ruoqiang [Qarkilik] County	3.53	0.41	0.41
且末县	Qiemo [Qarqan] County	10.30	0.15	0.15
焉耆回族自治县	Yanji Hui Autonomous County	21.00	3.75	3.75
和静县	Hejing County	16.70	2.18	1.72
和硕县	Hoxud County	15.93	0.75	0.18
博湖县	Bohu [Bagrax] County	12.80	2.22	
阿克苏地区	**Aksu Administrative Offices**	**336.32**	**11.92**	**2.49**
阿克苏市	Aksu City	39.74	0.57	0.36
温宿县	Wensu [Onsu] County	47.03	2.14	2.04
库车县	Kuqa County	50.06	0.21	0.07
沙雅县	Xayar County	48.42	1.95	
新和县	Xinhe [Toksu] County	33.45	5.57	
拜城县	Baicheng [Bay] County	40.08	0.02	0.02
乌什县	Wushi [Uxturpan] County	24.07		
阿瓦提县	Awat County	46.80	1.46	
柯坪县	Kalpin County	6.67		
克孜勒苏柯尔克孜自治州	**Kizilsu Kirgiz Autonomous Prefecture**	**28.91**	**0.19**	**0.13**
阿图什市	Artux City	8.13	0.12	0.07
阿克陶县	Akto County	16.69	0.06	0.06
阿合奇县	Akqi County	2.13		
乌恰县	Wuqia [Ulugqat] County	1.96	0.01	
喀什地区	**Kashgar [Kaxgar] Administrative Offices**	**402.08**	**5.40**	**3.21**
喀什市	Kashgar [Kaxgar] City	5.05	0.17	
疏附县	Shufu County	37.49	0.39	0.39
疏勒县	Shule County	36.17	0.57	0.57
英吉沙县	Yengisar County	24.48		
泽普县	Zepu [Poskam] County	24.31	0.49	0.22
莎车县	Shache [Yarkant] County	81.35	2.15	1.35
叶城县	Yecheng [Kagilik] County	46.83	0.21	0.18
麦盖提县	Makit County	35.67	0.22	
岳普湖县	Yopurga County	20.01	0.03	0.03
伽师县	Jiashi [Payzawat] County	40.57	0.35	0.30
巴楚县	Bachu [Maralbexi] County	45.43	0.82	0.17
塔什库尔干塔吉克自治县	Taxkorgan Tajik Autonomous County	4.72		
和田地区	**Hotan Administrative Offices**	**171.03**	**2.76**	**1.60**
和田市	Hotan City	4.75		
和田县	Hotan County	26.13	0.02	0.02
墨玉县	Moyu [Karakax] County	34.98	0.40	0.18
皮山县	Pishan [Guma] County	30.05	0.11	0.11
洛浦县	Lop County	25.58	0.04	0.02
策勒县	Qira County	15.83	0.28	0.15
于田县	Yutian [Keriya] County	26.81	0.45	
民丰县	Minfeng [Niya] County	6.90	1.46	1.12
二、生产建设兵团	**Xinjiang Production & Construction Group**	**1039.90**	**16.35**	

11-5 农、林、牧、渔业总产值

Gross Output Value of Farming, Forestry, Animal Husbandry and Fishery

单位：万元 (10 000 yuan)

年份 Year	地区 Region	农林牧渔业总产值 Total	农业产值 Farming	林业产值 Forestry	牧业产值 Animal Husbandry	渔业产值 Fishery	农林牧渔服务业产值 Output Value of Farming, Forestry, Animal Husbandary, Fishery and Service
1978		191184	142460	3397	44990	337	
1980		220135	164187	5394	50148	406	
1985		565699	429519	25906	108598	1676	
1990		1446535	1104742	38152	294963	8678	
1991		1620078	1245437	42356	322413	9872	
1992		1724197	1312184	42221	358244	11548	
1993		1982025	1468176	47737	451759	11353	
1994		3064721	2337813	59772	646907	20229	
1995		4057332	3150055	56381	823351	27545	
1996		4309617	3340735	61940	875560	31382	
1997		4764743	3738602	64913	925923	35305	
1998		4992355	3873616	74394	1008783	35562	
1999		4611503	3409380	75565	1092279	34279	
2000		4872005	3605405	83451	1145142	38007	
2001		4968125	3488409	100847	1340236	38633	
2002		5250446	3627669	110897	1480382	31498	
2003		6883187	4827597	136936	1619823	32065	266766
2004		7506792	5150018	138204	1874660	42985	300925
一、地　方	**Local Regions**	**5590243**	**3441069**	**177750**	**1763826**	**38222**	**169376**
乌鲁木齐市	Urumqi City	87789	36461	845	45193	1873	3416
克拉玛依市	Karamay City	22776	9543	2788	4841	371	5233
吐鲁番地区	Turpan Administrative Offices	182982	136555	1748	40738	215	3726
哈密地区	Hami [Kumul] Administrative Offices	105009	62348	2613	37297	752	1999
昌吉回族自治州	Changji Hui Autonomous Prefecture	843990	431158	17001	372106	9556	14169
伊犁哈萨克自治州	Ili Kazak Autonomous Prefecture	1388266	744099	31393	570645	11218	30911
伊犁州直属县(市)	Counties (Cities) Direct Under Ili Prefecture	603376	298992	14847	268447	5622	15468
塔城地区	Tacheng [Tarbagatai] Administrative Offices	548323	355240	7999	175048	2301	7735
阿勒泰地区	Altay Administrative Offices	236567	89866	8547	127151	3295	7708
博尔塔拉蒙古自治州	Bortala Mongol Autonomous Prefecture	185272	120818	3179	57408	510	3356
巴音郭楞蒙古自治州	Bayangol Mongol Autonomous Prefecture	539000	362830	8899	140886	4220	22165
阿克苏地区	Aksu Administrative Offices	778039	567025	33377	126436	5119	46082
克孜勒苏柯尔克孜自治州	Kizilsu Kirgiz Autonomous Prefecture	96190	51067	1456	33771	146	9749
喀什地区	Kashgar [Kaxgar] Administrative Offices	952840	624649	52844	250233	3359	21755
和田地区	Hotan Administrative Offices	408090	294515	21606	84272	884	6813
二、生产建设兵团	**Xinjiang Production & Construction Group**	**2394489**	**1806076**	**33233**	**350077**	**11861**	**193242**

注：本表按当年价格计算；全区合计不等于各地、州汇总数。

Note : The number in this form is computed by current price. Gross output value of autonomous region is not equal to the sum of output value of every prefecture.

11-6 农、林、牧、渔业总产值指数

Indices of Gross Output Value of Farming, Forestry, Animal Husbandry and Fishery

年 份 Year	农林牧渔业总产值 Total	农业产值 Farming	林业产值 Forestry	牧业产值 Animal Husbandry	渔业产值 Fishery
(上年=100) (preceding year=100)					
1978	113.0	118.6	108.8	105.4	106.7
1980	108.9	108.4	151.2	104.4	112.7
1985	110.9	111.5	131.3	104.6	135.1
1990	115.1	119.2	95.2	102.0	111.3
1991	108.0	109.2	99.6	103.4	105.8
1992	105.6	106.0	96.0	104.8	107.3
1993	102.3	101.6	108.3	104.6	113.8
1994	110.9	111.6	110.4	108.1	119.0
1995	107.1	107.0	88.5	109.0	127.0
1996	104.2	103.3	101.0	107.7	112.3
1997	109.5	109.6	100.5	110.2	108.6
1998	110.8	111.5	105.5	109.0	102.0
1999	104.8	103.9	100.9	108.1	106.3
2000	105.3	104.2	110.3	108.0	116.4
2001	104.5	103.9	116.1	105.8	104.2
2002	105.2	103.9	111.5	108.9	102.1
2003	106.3	105.2	120.7	108.7	101.7
2004	106.4	104.5	100.7	112.0	108.2
(1978=100) (year of 1978=100)					
1978	100.0	100.0	100.0	100.0	100.0
1980	115.9	115.5	158.8	111.1	120.5
1985	188.4	194.3	245.4	160.0	140.9
1990	303.7	322.6	244.4	243.7	442.4
1991	328.0	352.3	243.5	251.9	468.0
1992	346.3	373.4	233.8	264.1	502.1
1993	354.2	379.4	253.2	276.2	571.3
1994	392.8	423.6	279.6	298.5	680.0
1995	420.7	453.3	247.4	325.5	863.7
1996	438.4	468.1	249.8	350.6	970.0
1997	480.2	512.8	251.1	386.4	1053.2
1998	531.8	571.7	265.1	421.1	1073.9
1999	557.1	593.8	267.5	455.3	1141.6
2000	586.3	618.8	295.0	491.9	1328.4
2001	612.9	642.8	342.5	520.6	1384.1
2002	644.8	668.1	381.9	566.9	1413.2
2003	685.4	702.6	460.9	616.0	1437.2
2004	729.3	734.2	464.1	689.9	1555.1

11-7 各地、州、市、县(市)农林牧渔业总产值

Gross Output Value of Farming, Forestry, Animal Husbandry and Fishery by Prefecture, Autonomous Prefecture, City and County

单位：万元 (2004 年) (10 000 yuan)

地 区	Region	农林牧渔业总产值 Total	农业产值 Farming	林业产值 Forestry	牧业产值 Animal Husbandry	渔业产值 Fishery	农林牧渔服务业产值 Output Value of Farming, Forestry, Animal Husbandary, Fishery and Service
总 计	**Total**	**7506792**	**5150018**	**138204**	**1874660**	**42985**	**300925**
一、地 方	**Local Regions**	**5590243**	**3441069**	**177750**	**1763826**	**38222**	**169376**
乌鲁木齐市	**Urumqi City**	**87789**	**36461**	**845**	**45193**	**1873**	**3416**
乌鲁木齐县	Urumqi County	43648	11497	271	30383	469	1028
市直单位	Direct Under the Municipality	44195	25021	574	14808	1404	2388
克拉玛依市	**Karamay City**	**22776**	**9543**	**2788**	**4841**	**371**	**5233**
吐鲁番地区	**Turpan Administrative Offices**	**182982**	**136555**	**1748**	**40738**	**215**	**3726**
吐鲁番市	Turpan City	76295	58513	747	15314	129	1593
鄯善县	Shanshan County	69645	54913	557	13144	31	1000
托克逊县	Toksun County	37037	23129	445	12275	56	1133
哈密地区	**Hami Administrative Offices**	**105009**	**62348**	**2613**	**37297**	**752**	**1999**
哈密市	Hami City	56470	42393	952	11242	627	1257
巴里坤哈萨克自治县	Barkol KazakAutonomous County	33300	12070	820	20054	115	242
伊吾县	Yiwu County	15239	7885	841	6002	10	500
昌吉回族自治州	**Changji Hui Autonomous Prefecture**	**843990**	**431158**	**17001**	**372106**	**9556**	**14169**
昌吉市	Changji City	163264	86253	4501	64464	5755	2291
阜康市	Fukang City	58707	28516	1556	27974	183	478
米泉市	Miquan City	62439	28348	645	32419	882	145
呼图壁县	Hutubi County	137923	72596	1898	57580	1665	4184
玛纳斯县	Manas County	162146	99621	3066	54505	731	4224
奇台县	Qitai County	128622	63704	2363	62444	36	75
吉木萨尔县	Jimsar County	74348	36515	1909	35014	280	630
木垒哈萨克自治县	Mori Kazak Autonomous County	56540	15604	1063	37706	25	2142
伊犁哈萨克自治州	**Ili Kazak Autonomous Prefecture**	**1388266**	**744099**	**31393**	**570645**	**11218**	**30911**
伊犁州直属县(市)	**Counties (Cities) Direct Under Ili Prefecture**	**603376**	**298992**	**14847**	**268447**	**5622**	**15468**
伊宁市	Yining City	49938	27599	521	19204	1196	1418
奎屯市	Kuytun City	2869	1385	494	211	6	773
伊宁县	Yining County	147074	76921	4521	58613	3519	3500
察布查尔锡伯自治县	Qapqal Xibe Autonomous County	46746	26333	2001	16496	262	1655
霍城县	Huocheng County	84885	47676	1951	32249	319	2690
巩留县	Gongliu County	55578	26748	980	27623	139	87
新源县	Xinyuan County	96939	47428	1387	45814	119	2191
昭苏县	Zhaosu County	37954	17153	444	19527	33	798
特克斯县	Tekes County	39158	14747	950	23068	29	365
尼勒克县	Nilka County	42237	13014	1599	25632		1992

注： ①本表按当年价格计算。 ②全区农林牧渔业总产值不等于各地汇总数。

Note: a) The number in this form is computed by current price. b) Gross output value of autonomous region is not equal to the sum of output value of every prefecture.

11-7 续表 1 Continued

单位：万元 (10 000 yuan)

地　区	Region	农林牧渔业总产值 Total	农业产值 Farming	林业产值 Forestry	牧业产值 Animal Husbandry	渔业产值 Fishery	农林牧渔服务业产值 Output Value of Farming, Forestry, Animal Husbandary, Fishery and Service
塔城地区	**Tacheng [Tarbagatai] Administrative Offices**	**548323**	**355240**	**7999**	**175048**	**2301**	**7735**
塔城市	Tacheng [Qoqek] City	72624	46641	1742	22971	761	510
乌苏市	Usu City	131739	102393	1414	24058	752	3122
额敏县	Emin [Dorbiljin] County	84066	37367	1865	44503	331	
沙湾县	Shawan County	183418	136285	1644	42205	427	2858
托里县	Toli County	22712	7511	375	14634		192
裕民县	Yumin [Qagantokay] County	29002	16228	811	11568	21	375
和布克赛尔蒙古自治县	Hoboksar Mongol Autonomous County	24761	8816	148	15111	9	678
阿勒泰地区	**Altay Administrative Offices**	**236567**	**89866**	**8547**	**127151**	**3295**	**7708**
阿勒泰市	Altay City	49265	23696	1114	23287	260	909
布尔津县	Burqin County	30819	12894	1375	15698	164	688
富蕴县	Fuyun [Koktokay] County	44352	12727	774	29668	96	1087
福海县	Fuhai [Burultokay] County	45050	14244	2365	22658	2715	3068
哈巴河县	Habahe [Kaba] County	33235	14538	2014	15873	22	788
青河县	Qinghe [Qinggil] County	21045	7703	562	12091	19	671
吉木乃县	Jeminay County	12801	4064	344	7876	20	497
博尔塔拉蒙古自治州	**Bortala Mongol Autonomous Prefecture**	**185272**	**120818**	**3179**	**57408**	**510**	**3356**
博乐市	Bole [Bortala] City	78155	48409	1913	26221	320	1291
精河县	Jinghe [Jing] County	72957	54287	784	16212	174	1500
温泉县	Wenquan [Araxang] County	34165	18121	482	14981	16	565
巴音郭楞蒙古自治州	**Bayangol Mongol Autonomous Prefecture**	**539000**	**362830**	**8899**	**140886**	**4220**	**22165**
库尔勒市	Korla City	159693	114722	1275	37461	574	5662
轮台县	Luntai [Bugur] County	62223	47862	237	12482	180	1462
尉犁县	Yuli [Lopnur] County	68708	54913	257	7525	81	5931
若羌县	Ruoqiang [Qarkilik] County	11126	6850	627	3277		372
且末县	Qiemo [Qarqan] County	31235	20663	1138	6731	123	2581
焉耆回族自治县	Yanqi Hui Autonomous County	62414	36034	1666	21733	462	2520
和静县	Hejing County	68523	27081	1429	37971	24	2018
和硕县	Hoxud County	42078	31267	1782	7470	386	1174
博湖县	Bohu [Bagrax] County	33000	23439	488	6237	2390	446
阿克苏地区	**Aksu Administrative Offices**	**778039**	**567025**	**33377**	**126436**	**5119**	**46082**
阿克苏市	Aksu City	127827	96069	2684	20041	1381	7652
温宿县	Wensu [Onsu] County	114052	76000	6330	16944	578	14200
库车县	Kuqa County	129615	97849	6212	23840	168	1546

11-7 续表 2 Continued

单位：万元 (10 000 yuan)

地 区	Region	农林牧渔业总产值 Total	农业产值 Farming	林业产值 Forestry	牧业产值 Animal Husbandry	渔业产值 Fishery	农林牧渔服务业产值 Output Value of Farming, Forestry, Animal Husbandary, Fishery and Service
沙雅县	Xayar County	101992	81724	2785	14266	665	2552
新和县	Xinhe [Toksu] County	79922	55743	7557	8812	76	7734
拜城县	Baicheng [Bay] County	65673	41960	3921	16623	2105	1064
乌什县	Wushi [Uxturpan] County	48575	32585	2260	11470	60	2200
阿瓦提县	Awat County	100441	78122	1419	12366	86	8448
柯坪县	Kalpin County	9942	6973	209	2073		686
克孜勒苏柯尔克孜自治州	**Kizilsu Kirgiz Autonomous Prefecture**	**96190**	**51067**	**1456**	**33771**	**146**	**9749**
阿图什市	Artux City	41654	23356	509	12237	141	5411
阿克陶县	Akto County	38734	24082	441	11020	5	3186
阿合奇县	Akqi County	7504	1674	350	4947		532
乌恰县	Wuqia [Ulugqat] County	8298	1955	156	5566		620
喀什地区	**Kashgar [Kaxgar] Administrative Offices**	**952840**	**624649**	**52844**	**250233**	**3359**	**21755**
喀什市	Kashgar [Kaxgar] City	25201	14294	441	10010	346	110
疏附县	Shufu County	114124	69494	2699	37545	321	4066
疏勒县	Shule County	76601	56191	1378	18128	219	685
英吉沙县	Yengisar County	54872	34542	3629	13840	60	2801
泽普县	Zepu [Poskam] County	63680	39216	3966	19193	865	439
莎车县	Shache [Yarkant] County	159907	102641	15898	36650	649	4069
叶城县	Yecheng [Kagilik] County	118858	73391	11105	32975	433	954
麦盖提县	Makit County	79104	51203	1559	22516	79	3747
岳普湖县	Yopurga County	36155	28171	973	6447	45	520
伽师县	Jiashi [Payzawat] County	108543	74892	2967	28746	192	1746
巴楚县	Bachu [Maralbexi] County	110194	79764	8121	19590	149	2570
塔什库尔干塔吉克自治县	Taxkorgan Tajik Autonomous County	5600	850	109	4593		49
和田地区	**Hotan Administrative Offices**	**408090**	**294515**	**21606**	**84272**	**884**	**6813**
和田市	Hotan City	18761	11781	703	5613	414	249
和田县	Hotan County	76117	54908	7602	12289	125	1193
墨玉县	Moyu [Karakax] County	93835	68811	3458	19996	81	1489
皮山县	Pishan [Guma] County	46056	33167	4386	7380	22	1102
洛浦县	Lop County	58223	44451	1328	11428	126	890
策勒县	Qira County	31023	19873	1440	9193	16	501
于田县	Yutian [Keriya] County	65985	47970	2214	14618	77	1106
民丰县	Minfeng [Niya] County	18091	13555	474	3756	23	283
二、生产建设兵团	**Xinjiang Production&Construction Group**	**2394489**	**1806076**	**33233**	**350077**	**11861**	**193242**

11-8 各地、州、市、县(市)农业机械拥有量

Farm Machinery by Prefecture, Autonomous Prefecture, City and County

(2004 年)

地　　区	Region	农业机械总动力(千瓦) Total Power of Agricultural Machinery (kw)	农用大中型拖拉机 Large and Medium Agricultural Tractors		小型拖拉机 Mini-Tractors	
			数量(台) Number (unit)	动力(千瓦) CapaCity (kw)	数量(台) Number (unit)	动力(千瓦) CapaCity (kw)
总　计	**Total**	**10464737**	**92873**	**3273004**	**340625**	**3998783**
一、地 方	**Local Regions**	**8135355**	**72815**	**2250567**	**306760**	**3603496**
乌鲁木齐市	**Urumqi City**	**151915**	**454**	**17902**	**6504**	**71565**
乌鲁木齐县	Urumqi County	82497	384	14595	4155	45313
市直单位	Direct Under the Municipality	69418	70	3307	2349	26252
克拉玛依市	**Karamay City**	**10251**	**80**	**4181**	**225**	**3150**
吐鲁番地区	**Turpan Administrative Offices**	**466085**	**1298**	**40827**	**13054**	**148686**
吐鲁番市	Turpan City	147568	293	6160	3458	38438
鄯善县	Shanshan County	219602	600	21302	6585	77614
托克逊县	Toksun County	98915	405	13365	3011	32634
哈密地区	**Hami Administrative Offices**	**229729**	**1317**	**41523**	**9901**	**116905**
哈密市	Hami City	101736	532	16174	4399	52236
巴里坤哈萨克自治县	Barkol KazakAutonomous County	112989	682	21939	4920	57859
伊吾县	Yiwu County	15004	103	3410	582	6810
昌吉回族自治州	**Changji Hui Autonomous Prefecture**	**1421730**	**8300**	**329560**	**54007**	**623042**
昌吉市	Changji City	192914	1173	50036	6640	79883
阜康市	Fukang City	110993	610	23904	3927	43907
米泉市	Miquan City	114989	394	13605	2221	23286
呼图壁县	Hutubi County	216915	1624	67448	8755	111675
玛纳斯县	Manas County	204000	1794	56192	9364	106819
奇台县	Qitai County	332236	1505	70109	11147	119389
吉木萨尔县	Jimsar County	141763	515	23056	6320	72070
木垒哈萨克自治县	Mori Kazak Autonomous County	107920	685	25210	5633	66013
伊犁哈萨克自治州	**Ili Kazak Autonomous Prefecture**	**2299847**	**23178**	**749705**	**75688**	**908671**
伊犁州直属县(市)	**Counties (Cities) Direct Under Ili Prefecture**	**759192**	**7764**	**286730**	**22895**	**269446**
伊宁市	Yining City	46993	583	18486	1146	12819
奎屯市	Kuytun City	1840	10	910	20	210
伊宁县	Yining County	168449	1861	80261	4290	52027
察布查尔锡伯自治县	Qapqal Xibe Autonomous County	84663	1193	30971	2302	28775
霍城县	Huocheng County	129800	1637	56237	4535	48201
巩留县	Gongliu County	80654	488	21081	3609	43563
新源县	Xinyuan County	76974	631	26438	2263	26393
昭苏县	Zhaosu County	67877	532	17895	1959	26067
特克斯县	Tekes County	44055	487	14617	1239	14539
尼勒克县	Nilka County	57887	342	19834	1532	16852
塔城地区	**Tacheng [Tarbagatai] Administrative Offices**	**1196801**	**11740**	**360245**	**41729**	**505362**
塔城市	Tacheng [Qoqek] City	200417	1299	52670	5103	61120
乌苏市	Usu City	306455	2381	79243	14228	174363
额敏县	Emin [Dorbiljin] County	195000	1536	60846	5902	72790
沙湾县	Shawan County	330581	5396	129940	12449	146965
托里县	Toli County	55717	285	10421	1048	13624
裕民县	Yumin [Qagantokay] County	86429	649	21989	2275	27943
和布克赛尔蒙古自治县	Hoboksar Mongol Autonomous County	22202	194	5136	724	8557
阿勒泰地区	**Altay Administrative Offices**	**343854**	**3674**	**102730**	**11064**	**133863**
阿勒泰市	Altay City	82173	1195	26632	2697	33496
布尔津县	Burqin County	55598	710	19577	2199	26574
富蕴县	Fuyun [Koktokay] County	47519	464	17663	1328	16120
福海县	Fuhai [Burultokay] County	62337	461	12582	1611	18739
哈巴河县	Habahe [Kaba] County	49828	410	13449	1855	22372
青河县	Qinghe [Qinggil] County	31169	277	7816	841	10284
吉木乃县	Jeminay County	15230	157	5011	533	6278

11-8 续表 1 Continued

地 区	Region	农业机械总动力(千瓦) Total Power of Agricultural Machinery (kw)	农用大中型拖拉机 Large and Medium Agricultural Tractors 数量(台) Number (unit)	动力(千瓦) CapaCity (kw)	小型拖拉机 Mini-Tractors 数量(台) Number (unit)	动力(千瓦) CapaCity (kw)
博尔塔拉蒙古自治州	**Bortala Mongol Autonomous Prefecture**	**307856**	**3045**	**91219**	**11943**	**143025**
博乐市	Bole [Bortala] City	125585	1385	37924	4576	54889
精河县	Jinghe [Jing] County	107677	1051	30445	5482	65629
温泉县	Wenquan [Araxang] County	74594	609	22850	1885	22507
巴音郭楞蒙古自治州	**Bayangol Mongol Autonomous Prefecture**	**706589**	**7111**	**211427**	**23968**	**282612**
库尔勒市	Korla City	174606	1545	35535	7186	86232
轮台县	Luntai [Bugur] County	79262	602	16254	3291	41121
尉犁县	Yuli [Lopnur] County	69539	783	25056	1413	15543
若羌县	Ruoqiang [Qarkilik] County	23206	321	7383	467	6094
且末县	Qiemo [Qarqan] County	43589	510	14233	1786	22165
焉耆回族自治县	Yanji Hui Autonomous County	82305	1104	36402	2646	29790
和静县	Hejing County	103629	1149	40462	2450	29531
和硕县	Hoxud County	52289	376	12986	1494	16375
博湖县	Bohu [Bagrax] County	78164	721	23116	3235	35761
阿克苏地区	**Aksu Administrative Offices**	**1017444**	**11629**	**285789**	**48660**	**575893**
阿克苏市	Aksu City	125853	1020	28189	6767	84553
温宿县	Wensu [Onsu] County	184879	2594	74078	7126	81948
库车县	Kuqa County	155350	1482	34143	7741	90957
沙雅县	Xayar County	129017	2237	41959	5356	66950
新和县	Xinhe [Toksu] County	67932	894	16926	3548	43463
拜城县	Baicheng [Bay] County	113253	1109	29689	4845	58177
乌什县	Wushi [Uxturpan] County	69486	786	14051	4042	47898
阿瓦提县	Awat County	150841	1254	40078	8573	94646
柯坪县	Kalpin County	20833	253	6676	662	7301
克孜勒苏柯尔克孜自治州	**Kizilsu Kirgiz Autonomous Prefecture**	**143773**	**2095**	**56245**	**4676**	**52303**
阿图什市	Artux City	59848	813	25029	1430	14429
阿克陶县	Akto County	64957	854	21961	2769	31709
阿合奇县	Akqi County	7827	253	5042	177	2051
乌恰县	Wuqia [Ulugqat] County	11141	175	4213	300	4114
喀什地区	**Kashgar [Kaxgar] Administrative Offices**	**994232**	**10842**	**298376**	**47212**	**548808**
喀什市	Kashgar [Kaxgar] City	24958	223	4086	913	10290
疏附县	Shufu County	131397	1456	29602	6932	80262
疏勒县	Shule County	101121	564	22045	5470	66115
英吉沙县	Yengisar County	55509	615	13364	2851	33288
泽普县	Zepu [Poskam] County	65087	617	17117	4211	46426
莎车县	Shache [Yarkant] County	170525	2210	61418	7598	88636
叶城县	Yecheng [Kagilik] County	103574	342	26045	4987	60136
麦盖提县	Makit County	84408	610	27839	3703	45626
岳普湖县	Yopurga County	48739	1048	20145	1859	21395
伽师县	Jiashi [Payzawat] County	84424	379	14878	5776	62438
巴楚县	Bachu [Maralbexi] County	114410	2682	59146	2614	30709
塔什库尔干塔吉克自治县	Taxkorgan Tajik Autonomous County	10080	96	2691	298	3487
和田地区	**Hotan Administrative Offices**	**385904**	**3466**	**123813**	**10922**	**128836**
和田市	Hotan City	24291	221	6806	648	7419
和田县	Hotan County	75734	651	22353	2008	24222
墨玉县	Moyu [Karakax] County	80218	663	19936	1910	21438
皮山县	Pishan [Guma] County	37623	271	11002	1107	14365
洛浦县	Lop County	67892	645	23665	1918	23783
策勒县	Qira County	34222	332	12625	1434	15869
于田县	Yutian [Keriya] County	52005	486	21296	1485	17064
民丰县	Minfeng [Niya] County	13919	197	6130	412	4676
二、生产建设兵团	**Xinjiang Production & Construction Group**	**2329382**	**20058**	**1022437**	**33865**	**395287**

11-8 续表 2 Continued

地　　区	Region	大中型拖拉机配套农具(部) Number of Large and Medium Tractor Towing Farm Machinery (unit)	小型拖拉机配套农具(部) Number of Small Tractor Towing Farm Machinery (unit)	农用排灌柴油机 Diesel Engines	
				数　量(台) Number (unit)	动　力(千瓦) CapaCity (kw)
总　计	**Total**	**198516**	**453792**	**7676**	**106201**
一、地　方	**Local Regions**	**140439**	**434142**	**6303**	**87440**
乌鲁木齐市	**Urumqi City**	**600**	**2968**		
乌鲁木齐县	Urumqi County	524	2173		
市直单位	Direct Under the Municipality	76	795		
克拉玛依市	**Karamay City**	**223**	**151**	**2**	**40**
吐鲁番地区	**Turpan Administrative Offices**	**2512**	**18379**	**28**	**363**
吐鲁番市	Turpan City	231	3897	4	71
鄯善县	Shanshan County	1411	5812		
托克逊县	Toksun County	870	8670	24	292
哈密地区	**Hami Administrative Offices**	**2474**	**15945**	**14**	**252**
哈密市	Hami City	959	5415		
巴里坤哈萨克自治县	Barkol KazakAutonomous County	1371	10002	14	252
伊吾县	Yiwu County	144	528		
昌吉回族自治州	**Changji Hui Autonomous Prefecture**	**18213**	**47233**	**77**	**1935**
昌吉市	Changji City	2540	7803		
阜康市	Fukang City	1116	2700		
米泉市	Miquan City	1097	1071	5	153
呼图壁县	Hutubi County	4085	10266		
玛纳斯县	Manas County	3879	13773	15	183
奇台县	Qitai County	3152	5783	17	1030
吉木萨尔县	Jimsar County	1266	3422	12	132
木垒哈萨克自治县	Mori Kazak Autonomous County	1078	2415	28	437
伊犁哈萨克自治州	**Ili Kazak Autonomous Prefecture**	**54809**	**110540**	**3363**	**48330**
伊犁州直属县(市)	**Counties (Cities) Direct Under Ili Prefecture**	**19788**	**18291**	**585**	**5839**
伊宁市	Yining City	1601	584	14	149
奎屯市	Kuytun City	20			
伊宁县	Yining County	3600	4348	178	1575
察布查尔锡伯自治县	Qapqal Xibe Autonomous County	3698	3157	91	539
霍城县	Huocheng County	4056	5499	134	1305
巩留县	Gongliu County	1513	1936	48	576
新源县	Xinyuan County	1647	2032	29	382
昭苏县	Zhaosu County	1008	65	14	154
特克斯县	Tekes County	1694	358	5	367
尼勒克县	Nilka County	951	312	72	792
塔城地区	**Tacheng [Tarbagatai] Administrative Offices**	**27645**	**89725**	**1843**	**29499**
塔城市	Tacheng [Qoqek] City	4425	3412	119	2140
乌苏市	Usu City	8507	43380	424	4985
额敏县	Emin [Dorbiljin] County	2766	5973	1020	16952
沙湾县	Shawan County	8515	33461	76	833
托里县	Toli County	899	654	92	2229
裕民县	Yumin [Qagantokay] County	2439	2730	84	2065
和布克赛尔蒙古自治县	Hoboksar Mongol Autonomous County	94	115	28	295
阿勒泰地区	**Altay Administrative Offices**	**7376**	**2524**	**935**	**12992**
阿勒泰市	Altay City	2390	624	33	825
布尔津县	Burqin County	1435	440	83	963
富蕴县	Fuyun [Koktokay] County	928	332	220	3380
福海县	Fuhai [Burultokay] County	935	188	293	3366
哈巴河县	Habahe [Kaba] County	820	320	76	838
青河县	Qinghe [Qinggil] County	554	540	207	3307
吉木乃县	Jeminay County	314	80	23	313

11-8 续表 3 Continued

地 区	Region	大中型拖拉机配套农具(部) Number of Large and Medium Tractor Towing Farm Machinery (unit)	小型拖拉机配套农具(部) Number of Small Tractor Towing Farm Machinery (unit)	农用排灌柴油机 Diesel Engines	
				数 量(台) Number (unit)	动 力(千瓦) CapaCity (kw)
博尔塔拉蒙古自治州	**Bortala Mongol Autonomous Prefecture**	**5184**	**14022**	**8**	**187**
博乐市	Bole [Bortala] City	1379	4323	3	33
精河县	Jinghe [Jing] County	2158	9053		
温泉县	Wenquan [Araxang] County	1647	646	5	154
巴音郭楞蒙古自治州	**Bayangol Mongol Autonomous Prefecture**	**10398**	**45206**	**1890**	**21641**
库尔勒市	Korla City	1981	13173	1394	13798
轮台县	Luntai [Bugur] County	763	5964		
尉犁县	Yuli [Lopnur] County	1375	4950	358	4158
若羌县	Ruoqiang [Qarkilik] County	327	1636	98	2940
且末县	Qiemo [Qarqan] County	1015	2884		
焉耆回族自治县	Yanji Hui Autonomous County	1963	6066	2	22
和静县	Hejing County	1687	5077	32	421
和硕县	Hoxud County	400	1500	6	302
博湖县	Bohu [Bagrax] County	887	3956		
阿克苏地区	**Aksu Administrative Offices**	**22823**	**80456**	**406**	**4898**
阿克苏市	Aksu City	4610	7987	34	424
温宿县	Wensu [Onsu] County	3677	7523	14	102
库车县	Kuqa County	2721	16705	38	509
沙雅县	Xayar County	3244	11248	230	2530
新和县	Xinhe [Toksu] County	1537	7096	10	110
拜城县	Baicheng [Bay] County	2665	11385		
乌什县	Wushi [Uxturpan] County	1084	4566	5	55
阿瓦提县	Awat County	3145	13035	45	705
柯坪县	Kalpin County	140	911	30	463
克孜勒苏柯尔克孜自治州	**Kizilsu Kirgiz Autonomous Prefecture**	**1715**	**5941**	**33**	**575**
阿图什市	Artux City	754	1827	31	560
阿克陶县	Akto County	613	3762		
阿合奇县	Akqi County	240	137	1	11
乌恰县	Wuqia [Ulugqat] County	108	215	1	4
喀什地区	**Kashgar [Kaxgar] Administrative Offices**	**16810**	**81042**	**96**	**1275**
喀什市	Kashgar [Kaxgar] City		1589		
疏附县	Shufu County	1240	18032		
疏勒县	Shule County	1448	3386	12	221
英吉沙县	Yengisar County	1221	3879		
泽普县	Zepu [Poskam] County	1875	9422		
莎车县	Shache [Yarkant] County	2195	15787	14	278
叶城县	Yecheng [Kagilik] County	1029	7210		
麦盖提县	Makit County	1289	1874		
岳普湖县	Yopurga County	2093	3721		
伽师县	Jiashi [Payzawat] County	1289	10784		
巴楚县	Bachu [Maralbexi] County	3033	4594	70	776
塔什库尔干塔吉克自治县	Taxkorgan Tajik Autonomous County	98	764		
和田地区	**Hotan Administrative Offices**	**4678**	**12259**	**386**	**7944**
和田市	Hotan City	281	516	5	60
和田县	Hotan County	674	500	5	70
墨玉县	Moyu [Karakax] County	554	2014	17	204
皮山县	Pishan [Guma] County	767	3060	10	592
洛浦县	Lop County	969	2333	310	5758
策勒县	Qira County	435	1982	20	1051
于田县	Yutian [Keriya] County	829	1560		
民丰县	Minfeng [Niya] County	169	294	19	209
二、生产建设兵团	**Xinjiang Production & Construction Group**	**58077**	**19650**	**1373**	**18761**

11-9 各地、州、市、县(市)农村电气化和农田水利情况
Statistics on Water Conservancy and Electrification in Rural Areas by Prefecture, Autonomous Prefecture, City and County

(2004 年)

地　区	Region	有效灌溉面积(千公顷) Irrigated Area (1000 hectares)	化肥施用量(吨)(折纯) Consumption of Chemical Fertilizer (ton) (100% Purity)	氮 肥 Nitrogenous Fertilizer	磷 肥 Phosphate Fertilizer	钾 肥 Potash Fertilizer
总 计	**Total**	**3106.64**	**991729**	**488669**	**235614**	**36823**
一、地 方	**Local Regions**	**2132.45**	**633775**	**320450**	**174412**	**23855**
乌鲁木齐市	**Urumqi City**	**30.32**	**5349**	**2475**	**1973**	**361**
乌鲁木齐县	Urumqi County	15.91	3596	1665	1380	250
市直单位	Direct Under the Municipality	14.41	1754	810	593	111
克拉玛依市	**Karamay City**	7.56	1080	570	270	20
吐鲁番地区	**Turpan Administrative Offices**	**31.48**	**11073**	**5860**	**949**	**171**
吐鲁番市	Turpan City	11.03	4722	1824	161	63
鄯善县	Shanshan County	10.57	5295	3518	250	108
托克逊县	Toksun County	9.88	1056	518	538	
哈密地区	**Hami Administrative Offices**	**38.60**	**5632**	**2749**	**923**	**233**
哈密市	Hami City	19.73	3606	1786	655	211
巴里坤哈萨克自治县	Barkol KazakAutonomous County	15.39	1462	844		
伊吾县	Yiwu County	3.48	564	119	268	22
昌吉回族自治州	**Changji Hui Autonomous Prefecture**	**265.30**	**81891**	**43457**	**17769**	**2471**
昌吉市	Changji City	43.72	13704	7136	1929	27
阜康市	Fukang City	17.70	4179	2871	624	1
米泉市	Miquan City	13.12	3079	2696	246	5
呼图壁县	Hutubi County	42.27	18659	9979	6203	528
玛纳斯县	Manas County	50.68	20289	8954	3815	1290
奇台县	Qitai County	55.33	11937	5694	3092	
吉木萨尔县	Jimsar County	26.33	7098	4332	838	613
木垒哈萨克自治县	Mori Kazak Autonomous County	16.15	2946	1795	1022	7
伊犁哈萨克自治州	**Ili Kazak Autonomous Prefecture**	**610.36**	**133558**	**62981**	**23915**	**2539**
伊犁州直属县(市)	**Counties (Cities) Direct Under Ili Prefecture**	**230.24**	**51457**	**19099**	**5846**	**1029**
伊宁市	Yining City	15.80	2479	1263		
奎屯市	Kuytun City	1.66	601	237	92	
伊宁县	Yining County	59.22	11903	4153	1275	141
察布查尔锡伯自治县	Qapqal Xibe Autonomous County	22.70	4985	2380	1181	
霍城县	Huocheng County	32.31	10734	3620	1612	642
巩留县	Gongliu County	23.73	4390	2070		
新源县	Xinyuan County	29.86	6503	1916	801	206
昭苏县	Zhaosu County	16.49	4161	1716	132	
特克斯县	Tekes County	13.64	2653	665	206	
尼勒克县	Nilka County	14.83	3048	1079	547	40
塔城地区	**Tacheng [Tarbagatai] Administrative Offices**	**276.14**	**68403**	**34676**	**14071**	**1419**
塔城市	Tacheng [Qoqek] City	72.70	11727	5766	4506	207
乌苏市	Usu City	49.17	15945	8921	1114	556
额敏县	Emin [Dorbiljin] County	51.04	10710	5351	3014	18
沙湾县	Shawan County	63.69	21650	11274	4414	588
托里县	Toli County	13.48	450	278	108	
裕民县	Yumin [Qagantokay] County	17.49	4684	1960	704	
和布克赛尔蒙古自治县	Hoboksar Mongol Autonomous County	8.57	3237	1126	211	50
阿勒泰地区	**Altay Administrative Offices**	**103.98**	**13698**	**9206**	**3997**	**92**
阿勒泰市	Altay City	19.15	3014	1925	1078	6
布尔津县	Burqin County	12.71	2593	1631	962	
富蕴县	Fuyun [Koktokay] County	11.54	650	396	246	1
福海县	Fuhai [Burultokay] County	21.90	2340	1477	816	1
哈巴河县	Habahe [Kaba] County	18.67	2219	1752	384	83
青河县	Qinghe [Qinggil] County	11.48	1908	1565		
吉木乃县	Jeminay County	8.53	974	460	512	1

11-9 续表 1 Continued

地区	Region	有效灌溉面积(千公顷) Irrigated Area(1000 hectares)	化肥施用量(吨)(折纯) Consumption of Chemical Fertilizer (ton) (100% Purity)	氮肥 Nitrogenous Fertilizer	磷肥 Phosphate Fertilizer	钾肥 Potash Fertilizer
博尔塔拉蒙古自治州	**Bortala Mongol Autonomous Prefecture**	**72.06**	**17477**	**8836**	**4393**	**320**
博乐市	Bole [Bortala] City	27.57	6555	2326	2331	73
精河县	Jinghe [Jing] County	23.68	5397	3177	683	197
温泉县	Wenquan [Araxang] County	20.81	5525	3333	1379	50
巴音郭楞蒙古自治州	**Bayangol Mongol Autonomous Prefecture**	**166.01**	**62736**	**32842**	**21342**	**2850**
库尔勒市	Korla City	37.02	13008	7175	4576	622
轮台县	Luntai [Bugur] County	18.10	8154	4626	1435	202
尉犁县	Yuli [Lopnur] County	31.58	15550	4071	9485	1614
若羌县	Ruoqiang [Qarkilik] County	2.58	753	482	148	51
且末县	Qiemo [Qarqan] County	10.30	4129	2845	262	
焉耆回族自治县	Yanji Hui Autonomous County	21.00	6644	5065	1107	125
和静县	Hejing County	16.70	5771	3624	1680	161
和硕县	Hoxud County	15.93	4566	2362	1715	
博湖县	Bohu [Bagrax] County	12.80	4160	2592	934	75
阿克苏地区	**Aksu Administrative Offices**	**323.64**	**125606**	**58290**	**43239**	**5285**
阿克苏市	Aksu City	33.59	22141	8908	9005	991
温宿县	Wensu [Onsu] County	46.62	19252	9598	5118	576
库车县	Kuqa County	50.06	19436	8671	7971	224
沙雅县	Xayar County	45.19	20869	10033	9061	1514
新和县	Xinhe [Toksu] County	33.45	6438	2566	2310	443
拜城县	Baicheng [Bay] County	37.03	10583	3631	3760	1058
乌什县	Wushi [Uxturpan] County	24.07	7769	5285	414	
阿瓦提县	Awat County	46.80	17577	8906	4751	479
柯坪县	Kalpin County	6.83	1541	692	849	
克孜勒苏柯尔克孜自治州	**Kizilsu Kirgiz Autonomous Prefecture**	**31.17**	**9745**	**6253**	**3462**	**7**
阿图什市	Artux City	9.75	4762	2632	2123	7
阿克陶县	Akto County	16.69	4846	3566	1280	
阿合奇县	Akqi County	2.79	40	6	11	
乌恰县	Wuqia [Ulugqat] County	1.94	97	49	48	
喀什地区	**Kashgar [Kaxgar] Administrative Offices**	**395.74**	**133546**	**69646**	**44503**	**7861**
喀什市	Kashgar [Kaxgar] City	3.58	3322	2196	1126	
疏附县	Shufu County	36.46	22202	12815	8644	118
疏勒县	Shule County	36.10	11090	2500	4900	3690
英吉沙县	Yengisar County	24.48	5889	3697		
泽普县	Zepu [Poskam] County	24.31	9632	5545	4040	38
莎车县	Shache [Yarkant] County	77.80	24147	11915	5785	1385
叶城县	Yecheng [Kagilik] County	47.49	13091	7605	3963	620
麦盖提县	Makit County	35.67	10668	8130	2285	12
岳普湖县	Yopurga County	20.17	7174	2993	2667	934
伽师县	Jiashi [Payzawat] County	40.00	12554	7064	4080	260
巴楚县	Bachu [Maralbexi] County	46.47	13777	5186	7013	804
塔什库尔干塔吉克自治县	Taxkorgan Tajik Autonomous County	3.21				
和田地区	**Hotan Administrative Offices**	**160.21**	**46083**	**26491**	**11674**	**1736**
和田市	Hotan City	4.74	1531	950	485	70
和田县	Hotan County	21.81	10245	5816	3564	746
墨玉县	Moyu [Karakax] County	34.81	12116	4511	1495	825
皮山县	Pishan [Guma] County	29.83	6214	3652	1866	19
洛浦县	Lop County	23.68	7435	5050	2385	
策勒县	Qira County	13.70	2892	1915	907	70
于田县	Yutian [Keriya] County	25.74	4338	3822	441	
民丰县	Minfeng [Niya] County	5.90	1312	776	530	6
二、生产建设兵团	**Xinjiang Production & Construction Group**	**72.06**	**357954**	**168219**	**61202**	**12968**

11-9 续表 2 Continued

地　区	Region	乡村及村以下办水电站 Hydro-Power Station Run by Village or Below		农村用电量(万千瓦小时) ElectriCity Consumed in Rural Areas (10 000 kwh)
		站数(个) Station Number	发电量(万千瓦) Generating CapaCity (10 000 kw)	
总　计	**Total**	**130**	**18807.30**	**326299.00**
一、地 方	**Local Regions**	**80**	**5074.87**	**187332.38**
乌鲁木齐市	**Urumqi City**			**8876.71**
乌鲁木齐县	Urumqi County			2995.82
市直单位	Direct Under the Municipality			5880.89
克拉玛依市	**Karamay City**			**292.00**
吐鲁番地区	**Turpan Administrative Offices**	**3**	**34.74**	**23450.00**
吐鲁番市	Turpan City	2	30.94	8236.00
鄯善县	Shanshan County			12046.00
托克逊县	Toksun County	1	3.80	3168.00
哈密地区	**Hami Administrative Offices**	**5**	**373.00**	**10302.00**
哈密市	Hami City			8332.00
巴里坤哈萨克自治县	Barkol KazakAutonomous County	4	92.00	1650.00
伊吾县	Yiwu County	1	281.00	320.00
昌吉回族自治州	**Changji Hui Autonomous Prefecture**	**5**	**120.00**	**54101.32**
昌吉市	Changji City			12149.53
阜康市	Fukang City			3565.00
米泉市	Miquan City			6092.32
呼图壁县	Hutubi County			9331.77
玛纳斯县	Manas County			4305.01
奇台县	Qitai County			14685.30
吉木萨尔县	Jimsar County	5	120.00	908.00
木垒哈萨克自治县	Mori Kazak Autonomous County			3064.39
伊犁哈萨克自治州	**Ili Kazak Autonomous Prefecture**	**24**	**2125.12**	**28960.13**
伊犁州直属县(市)	**Counties (Cities) Direct Under Ili Prefecture**	**19**	**1720.12**	**8380.88**
伊宁市	Yining City			815.70
奎屯市	Kuytun City			56.00
伊宁县	Yining County	2	72.00	2073.00
察布查尔锡伯自治县	Qapqal Xibe Autonomous County			524.00
霍城县	Huocheng County	5	240.00	620.00
巩留县	Gongliu County	2	350.00	740.00
新源县	Xinyuan County	8	1008.00	2440.00
昭苏县	Zhaosu County	2	50.12	463.50
特克斯县	Tekes County			549.70
尼勒克县	Nilka County			98.98
塔城地区	**Tacheng [Tarbagatai] Administrative Offices**			**17286.84**
塔城市	Tacheng [Qoqek] City			2831.40
乌苏市	Usu City			2150.03
额敏县	Emin [Dorbiljin] County			1598.47
沙湾县	Shawan County			6868.48
托里县	Toli County			929.36
裕民县	Yumin [Qagantokay] County			1891.80
和布克赛尔蒙古自治县	Hoboksar Mongol Autonomous County			1017.30
阿勒泰地区	**Altay Administrative Offices**	**5**	**405.00**	**3292.41**
阿勒泰市	Altay City	1	180.00	721.60
布尔津县	Burqin County			420.00
富蕴县	Fuyun [Koktokay] County	2	165.00	597.60
福海县	Fuhai [Burultokay] County			417.00
哈巴河县	Habahe [Kaba] County			386.00
青河县	Qinghe [Qinggil] County	2	60.00	689.00
吉木乃县	Jeminay County			61.21

11-9 续表 3 Continued

地 区	Region	乡村及村以下办水电站 Hydro-Power Station Run by Village or Below 站数(个) Station Number	发电量(万千瓦) Generating CapaCity (10 000 kw)	农村用电量(万千瓦小时) ElectriCity Consumed in Rural Areas (10 000 kwh)
博尔塔拉蒙古自治州	**Bortala Mongol Autonomous Prefecture**	**4**	**1302.00**	**3142.00**
博乐市	Bole [Bortala] City	2	635.00	1522.00
精河县	Jinghe [Jing] County	2	667.00	1120.00
温泉县	Wenquan [Araxang] County			500.00
巴音郭楞蒙古自治州	**Bayangol Mongol Autonomous Prefecture**	**1**	**14.40**	**15599.32**
库尔勒市	Korla City			4574.00
轮台县	Luntai [Bugur] County			950.00
尉犁县	Yuli [Lopnur] County			1932.51
若羌县	Ruoqiang [Qarkilik] County	1	14.40	65.00
且末县	Qiemo [Qarqan] County			289.00
焉耆回族自治县	Yanji Hui Autonomous County			811.00
和静县	Hejing County			902.00
和硕县	Hoxud County			4937.81
博湖县	Bohu [Bagrax] County			1138.00
阿克苏地区	**Aksu Administrative Offices**	**1**	**96.00**	**19964.42**
阿克苏市	Aksu City			2466.47
温宿县	Wensu [Onsu] County	1	96.00	2541.00
库车县	Kuqa County			4291.00
沙雅县	Xayar County			3111.58
新和县	Xinhe [Toksu] County			2180.37
拜城县	Baicheng [Bay] County			1277.00
乌什县	Wushi [Uxturpan] County			897.00
阿瓦提县	Awat County			2611.00
柯坪县	Kalpin County			589.00
克孜勒苏柯尔克孜自治州	**Kizilsu Kirgiz Autonomous Prefecture**	**5**	**217.35**	**1422.64**
阿图什市	Artux City	4	216.00	1063.46
阿克陶县	Akto County	1	1.35	270.00
阿合奇县	Akqi County			17.90
乌恰县	Wuqia [Ulugqat] County			71.28
喀什地区	**Kashgar [Kaxgar] Administrative Offices**	**13**	**78.00**	**11393.00**
喀什市	Kashgar [Kaxgar] City			493.00
疏附县	Shufu County	4	20.00	1910.00
疏勒县	Shule County			680.00
英吉沙县	Yengisar County	3	36.00	400.00
泽普县	Zepu [Poskam] County			507.00
莎车县	Shache [Yarkant] County			1571.00
叶城县	Yecheng [Kagilik] County			847.00
麦盖提县	Makit County			1430.00
岳普湖县	Yopurga County			694.00
伽师县	Jiashi [Payzawat] County			1211.00
巴楚县	Bachu [Maralbexi] County			1630.00
塔什库尔干塔吉克自治县	Taxkorgan Tajik Autonomous County	6	22.00	20.00
和田地区	**Hotan Administrative Offices**	**19**	**714.26**	**9828.84**
和田市	Hotan City			790.00
和田县	Hotan County	4	350.00	2829.00
墨玉县	Moyu [Karakax] County	2	55.00	1852.00
皮山县	Pishan [Guma] County	5	0.95	468.93
洛浦县	Lop County	3	300.14	2036.00
策勒县	Qira County	4	0.07	731.16
于田县	Yutian [Keriya] County			759.00
民丰县	Minfeng [Niya] County	1	8.10	362.75
二、生产建设兵团	**Xinjiang Production & Construction Group**	**50**	**13732.43**	**138966.62**

11-10 灌溉、水库和除涝、治水、治碱情况

Irrigation, Reservoirs, Flood Prevention, Water and Soil Conservation and Improvement of Saline-Alkaline Land

项　目	Item	2000	2003
灌溉面积(千公顷)	Irrigated Areas (1000 hectares)	3388	3518.38
有效灌溉面积	Effective Irrigated Areas	2257	2286.07
林地灌溉面积	Irrigated Wooded-land Areas	426	477.57
果园灌溉面积	Irrigated Orchard Areas	142	211.36
牧草灌溉面积	Irrigated Pasture-land Areas	439	469.05
其他灌溉面积	Other Irrigated Areas	125	74.33
水库(座)	Number of Reservoirs (unit)	373	391
大型水库	Large	6	9
中型水库	Medium-sized	69	81
小型水库	Small	298	301
水库库容量（亿立方米)	CapaCity of Reservoirs (100 million cu.m)	39.25	49.79
大型水库	Large	13.22	20.51
中型水库	Medium-sized	19.88	23.04
小型水库	Small	6.15	6.24
节水灌溉面积（千公顷)	Water-saving Irrigated Areas (1000 hectares)	1265.94	1289.73
除涝面积　（千公顷)	Area with Flood Prevention Measures (1000 hectares)	37.81	36.15
水土流失治理面积(千公顷)	Area of Soil Erosion under Control (1000 hectares)	68.78	117.51
治碱面积　（千公顷)	Improved Area of Saline-Alkaline Land (1000 hectares)	502.85	402.83
堤防长度（公里)	Total Length of Dikes (km)	5129.00	5880.93
堤防保护面积（千公顷)	Area of Land Protected by Dikes (1000 hectares)	1167.00	1185.80

注: ①大型水库库容: 1 亿立方米以上; 中型水库库容: 1 千万至 1 亿立方米;小型水库库容: 10 万至 1 千万立方米。②本表和 11-11，12 表资料由水利厅提供。③本表 2000 年数据不含兵团。

Note: a) The capaCity of the large reservoirs is over 100 million cubic meters, while that of the medium ones is from 10 million to 100 million cubic meters, and that of the small ones is from 100 000 to 10 million cubic meters. b) The data in the table is offered by the Bureau of Water Conservancy, together with table 11-11,12. c) The data in 2000 exclude that for Xinjiang Production & Construction Group.

11-11 各地、州、市水利设施和除涝、治碱面积

Water Conservancy Facilities and Area with Flood Prevention Measures and Improved Area Of Saline-Alkaline Land by Prefecture, Autonomous Prefecture and City

(2003 年)

地 区	Region	水库数 (座) Number of Reservoirs (Unit)	水库总库容量 (万立方米) CapaCity of Reservoirs (10 000 cu.m)	除涝面积 (千公顷) Area with Flood Prevention Measures (1000 hectares)	治碱面积 (千公顷) Improved Area of Saline-alkaline Land (1000 hectares)	水土流失治理面积 (千公顷) Area of Soil Erosion under Control (1000 hectares)
总 计	**Total**	**391**	**497867**	**36.15**	**402.83**	**117.51**
乌鲁木齐市	Urumqi City	15	14926	3.00		8.39
克拉玛依市	Karamay City	6	28410		0.05	3.48
吐鲁番地区	Turpan Administrative Offices	15	8365		5.49	2.51
哈密地区	Hami Administrative Offices	40	10470		8.14	9.75
昌吉回族自治州	Changji HuiAutonomous Prefecture	71	29411		18.31	12.16
伊犁州直属县(市)	Counties (Cities) Direct Under Ili Prefecture	10	1540	13.51	16.21	25.48
塔城地区	Tacheng [Tarbagatai] Administrative Offices	28	14623		16.80	3.10
阿勒泰地区	Altay Administrative Offices	50	92435		1.15	9.34
博尔塔拉蒙古自治州	Bortala Mongol Autonomous Prefecture	3	5405		12.62	5.72
巴音郭楞蒙古自治州	Bayangol Mongol Autonomous Prefecture	10	11001		7.53	3.53
阿克苏地区	Aksu Administrative Offices	12	21550	19.04	102.24	21.54
克孜勒苏柯尔克孜自治州	Kizilsu Kirgiz Autonomous Prefecture	12	9572		17.35	1.09
喀什地区	Kashgar [Kaxgar] Administrative Offices	56	77943		146.66	3.14
和田地区	Hotan Administrative Offices	53	35836		41.58	8.28
其 他	Other	10	136380	0.60	8.70	

11-12 各地、州、市农村改善人畜饮水情况

Improvement of Drinking Water for Human Being and Livestock by Prefecture, Autonomous Prefecture and City

单位:万人、万头 (2003 年) (10 000 persons, 10 000 heads)

地 区	Region	已改善人畜饮水 Improved Drinking Water for Human Being and Livestock		其中：氟病区改水 Reform on Water in Fluorine-Stricken Area	
		受益人数 Beneficial Persons	牲畜头数 Livestock Head	需改善人数 Number of Persons for Improvement	已受益人数 Beneficial Persons
总 计	**Total**	**219.66**	**292.03**	**76.32**	**57.36**
乌鲁木齐市	Urumqi City	2.70	9.12		
克拉玛依市	Karamay City	0.35	4.10		
吐鲁番地区	Turpan Administrative Offices	3.90	13.31		
哈密地区	Hami Administrative Offices	2.90	4.12	0.20	0.20
昌吉回族自治州	Changji HuiAutonomous Prefecture	12.40	39.82	0.20	0.11
伊犁州直属县(市)	Counties (Cities) Direct Under Ili Prefecture	20.00	9.93	0.84	0.84
塔城地区	Tacheng [Tarbagatai] Administrative Offices	20.29	19.38	9.59	9.58
阿勒泰地区	Altay Administrative Offices	2.36	17.44	0.21	0.21
博尔塔拉蒙古自治州	Bortala Mongol Autonomous Prefecture	5.54	8.73	1.14	1.14
巴音郭楞蒙古自治州	Bayangol Mongol Autonomous Prefecture	14.98	38.50	4.40	4.40
阿克苏地区	Aksu Administrative Offices	34.29	26.29	19.75	13.29
克孜勒苏柯尔克孜自治州	Kizilsu Kirgiz Autonomous Prefecture	11.02	15.20	6.00	2.09
喀什地区	Kashgar [Kaxgar] Administrative Offices	27.51	41.82	15.29	8.21
和田地区	Hotan Administrative Offices	38.08	16.09	18.70	17.29
其 他	Other	23.34	28.18		

11-13 主要年份农作物播种面积

Total Sown Areas of Farm Crops in Main Years

单位：千公顷 (1000 hectares)

年份 Year	农作物播种面积 Total Sown Area	粮食作物播种面积 Sown Area of Grain Crops	#谷物 Cereal	#水稻 Rice	#小麦 Wheat	#玉米 Corn	#大麦 Barley	#豆类 Soybeans	薯类 Tubers	棉花 Cotton
1978	3021.67	2310.71	2297.44	105.59	1348.82	621.39	50.01	13.27	23.09	150.42
1980	2993.71	2162.37	2147.60	98.39	1354.83	555.79	23.24	14.77	17.55	181.22
1985	2846.63	1853.04	1844.47	74.50	1278.43	418.43	13.63	8.57	10.56	253.52
1990	2979.51	1826.61	1813.16	84.13	1180.11	442.40	42.92	13.45	10.67	435.22
1991	3036.09	1769.99	1741.17	79.93	1149.87	436.56	35.05	28.82	9.52	546.94
1992	3067.85	1730.26	1701.45	76.20	1126.76	429.84	28.12	28.81	12.09	643.30
1993	2995.10	1697.57	1627.10	67.74	1087.14	397.94	36.84	70.47	11.68	606.35
1994	2993.75	1496.04	1396.25	63.25	850.19	387.89	68.69	99.79	10.36	749.82
1995	3051.44	1593.29	1528.62	73.38	952.58	439.16	41.58	64.67	10.34	742.90
1996	3081.15	1648.83	1604.08	75.87	985.39	467.88	54.72	44.75	11.93	799.26
1997	3191.48	1673.73	1618.33	82.06	1017.43	439.83	59.63	55.40	11.58	883.65
1998	3278.55	1573.43	1512.40	69.06	966.80	428.58	31.55	61.03	12.18	999.26
1999	3379.89	1521.65	1453.53	75.56	888.50	432.91	26.02	68.12	17.34	995.93
2000	3388.76	1445.77	1353.99	78.15	838.99	382.45	33.50	91.78	22.59	1012.39
2001	3404.12	1394.96	1281.38	73.28	744.27	410.29	34.11	113.58	20.77	1129.72
2002	3478.37	1493.96	1386.81	74.96	749.74	501.93	36.45	107.15	20.65	943.97
2003	3470.28	1307.02	1202.61	67.16	626.09	454.14	38.25	104.41	23.89	1037.05
2004	3571.89	1378.61	1273.03	66.77	658.08	505.69	24.53	105.58	24.23	1127.55

年份 Year	#长绒棉 Long-Staple Cotton	油料 Oil Bearing Crops	#油菜 Rapeseeds	#胡麻 Flax	#葵花 Sun-flower	甜菜 Beetroots	蔬菜 Vegetables	果用瓜 Melon	#甜瓜 Musk-melon	苜蓿 Lucerne
1978	29.05	202.13	90.90	65.49	23.68	17.67	55.12	41.95		174.90
1980	38.50	269.39	107.47	81.85	50.08	24.27	46.99	39.54		191.65
1985	26.28	294.78	89.82	81.12	111.39	15.51	54.91	53.69	27.95	132.07
1990	62.69	269.27	117.35	46.04	96.11	66.87	58.07	28.84	15.09	159.34
1991	55.52	272.22	125.85	38.26	103.57	74.19	55.34	29.29	13.72	142.11
1992	16.96	223.38	102.28	32.67	80.53	84.20	58.40	32.70	14.05	132.83
1993	23.83	232.02	99.16	28.70	84.71	59.86	65.04	32.02	16.47	127.71
1994	9.77	317.32	148.27	30.21	123.43	76.84	63.76	29.03	13.37	127.31
1995	8.35	306.70	130.11	26.75	140.10	71.10	71.54	25.15	9.72	120.25
1996	14.68	194.05	85.24	20.19	82.73	87.41	78.95	23.72	8.19	117.20
1997	39.09	176.01	70.44	17.51	81.88	92.21	75.70	29.70	12.09	113.53
1998	10.74	212.14	84.09	16.48	94.11	110.75	82.62	31.90	14.62	115.27
1999	12.92	327.19	107.65	17.95	161.54	78.54	103.73	52.26	22.21	115.51
2000	49.29	310.07	96.23	24.57	157.05	55.75	127.75	55.99	26.01	120.49
2001	67.69	217.64	72.85	17.10	99.76	85.54	125.96	58.19	26.55	165.06
2002	46.30	215.05	70.00	23.84	96.60	85.32	164.21	82.47	48.47	235.11
2003	70.13	226.38	74.48	22.30	100.07	67.31	163.84	62.45	32.82	294.13
2004	70.63	215.47	67.52	13.74	85.55	59.88	185.60	61.29	36.07	301.10

11-14 各地、州、市、县(市)农作物播种面积

单位：千公顷 (2004 年)

地 区	Region	农作物播种面积 Total Sown Area	粮食作物 Sown Area of Grain Crops	薯 类 Tubers
总 计	**Total**	**3571.89**	**1378.61**	**24.23**
一、地 方	**Local Regions**	**2617.96**	**1174.85**	**20.88**
乌鲁木齐市	**Urumqi City**	**29.03**	**10.55**	**2.95**
乌鲁木齐县	Urumqi County	19.02	7.03	2.68
市直单位	Direct Under the Municipality	10.01	3.52	0.27
克拉玛依市	**Karamay City**	**8.40**	**0.95**	
吐鲁番地区	**Turpan Administrative Offices**	**51.20**	**18.90**	
吐鲁番市	Turpan City	16.98	5.01	
鄯善县	Shanshan County	14.16	4.04	
托克逊县	Toksun County	20.06	9.85	
哈密地区	**Hami Administrative Offices**	**41.85**	**16.71**	**0.81**
哈密市	Hami City	19.84	4.50	0.03
巴里坤哈萨克自治县	Barkol KazakAutonomous County	17.66	10.14	0.75
伊吾县	Yiwu County	4.35	2.07	0.03
昌吉回族自治州	**Changji Hui Autonomous Prefecture**	**315.09**	**128.51**	**6.04**
昌吉市	Changji City	49.70	14.00	0.42
阜康市	Fukang City	23.25	9.09	0.32
米泉市	Miquan City	14.66	6.85	0.01
呼图壁县	Hutubi County	42.34	8.33	0.26
玛纳斯县	Manas County	47.33	7.30	0.22
奇台县	Qitai County	77.05	47.98	1.47
吉木萨尔县	Jimsar County	29.85	9.37	2.02
木垒哈萨克自治县	Mori Kazak Autonomous County	30.91	25.59	1.32
伊犁哈萨克自治州	**Ili Kazak Autonomous Prefecture**	**704.78**	**315.12**	**7.38**
伊犁州直属县(市)	**Counties (Cities) Direct Under Ili Prefecture**	**307.89**	**176.86**	**5.41**
伊宁市	Yining City	19.88	11.68	0.10
奎屯市	Kuytun City	1.70	0.20	
伊宁县	Yining County	73.02	52.49	0.23
察布查尔锡伯自治县	Qapqal Xibe Autonomous County	32.59	18.46	0.07
霍城县	Huocheng County	36.60	19.30	0.17
巩留县	Gongliu County	32.45	24.68	0.38
新源县	Xinyuan County	38.96	21.42	2.11
昭苏县	Zhaosu County	37.09	10.66	0.75
特克斯县	Tekes County	17.42	8.48	0.10
尼勒克县	Nilka County	18.18	9.49	1.50
塔城地区	**Tacheng [Tarbagatai] Administrative Offices**	**289.38**	**88.96**	**0.99**
塔城市	Tacheng [Qoqek] City	59.13	27.15	
乌苏市	Usu City	50.36	7.68	0.09
额敏县	Emin [Dorbiljin] County	60.31	18.87	
沙湾县	Shawan County	67.02	16.59	0.72
托里县	Toli County	13.49	6.04	0.06
裕民县	Yumin [Qagantokay] County	30.51	11.69	0.09
和布克赛尔蒙古自治县	Hoboksar Mongol Autonomous County	8.56	0.94	0.03
阿勒泰地区	**Altay Administrative Offices**	**107.51**	**49.30**	**0.98**
阿勒泰市	Altay City	19.15	6.45	0.11
布尔津县	Burqin County	19.20	11.91	0.07
富蕴县	Fuyun [Koktokay] County	15.59	8.39	0.52
福海县	Fuhai [Burultokay] County	14.56	2.67	0.04
哈巴河县	Habahe [Kaba] County	19.00	11.37	0.12
青河县	Qinghe [Qinggil] County	11.48	4.89	0.10
吉木乃县	Jeminay County	8.53	3.62	0.02

Sown Areas of Farm Crops by Prefecture, Autonomous Prefecture, City and County

(1000 hectares)

棉花 Cotton	#长绒棉 Long Staple Cotton	油料 Oil Bearing Crops	甜菜 Beetroots	蔬菜 Vegetables	果用瓜 Melon	#甜瓜 Muskmelon
1127.55	**70.63**	**215.47**	**59.88**	**185.60**	**61.29**	**36.07**
655.48	**35.43**	**158.46**	**40.97**	**128.87**	**50.30**	**29.98**
0.10		**1.09**	**0.02**	**6.39**	**0.20**	
0.01		0.33		4.05	0.08	
0.09		0.76	0.02	2.34	0.12	
5.90		**0.18**		**0.05**	**0.16**	**0.05**
14.15		**0.31**		**3.27**	**4.94**	**4.10**
4.27		0.06		1.68	1.57	0.87
4.86				1.06	3.00	2.97
5.02		0.25		0.53	0.37	0.26
9.03		**1.98**		**1.23**	**2.42**	**2.22**
8.93		1.84		1.05	1.05	0.85
0.02		0.12		0.17	0.12	0.12
0.08		0.02		0.01	1.25	1.25
73.55		**14.99**	**3.79**	**34.41**	**5.37**	**0.60**
15.88		1.51	0.73	10.46	2.68	0.19
3.09		1.27		3.76	0.37	0.09
0.99		1.12	0.08	3.82	0.27	0.02
22.63		0.63	0.82	3.23	0.70	0.15
29.11		0.52	0.10	6.17	0.24	
		4.23	1.88	2.05	0.27	0.03
1.85		4.85	0.16	4.71	0.77	0.09
		0.86	0.02	0.21	0.07	0.03
75.27		**116.98**	**27.79**	**29.12**	**3.20**	**1.20**
6.36		**49.72**	**19.73**	**11.92**	**0.96**	**0.07**
0.06		1.23	0.80	3.32	0.15	
0.74		0.17	0.01	0.01		
0.15		5.69	3.93	3.55	0.40	0.02
3.07		0.88	1.37	0.98	0.10	0.03
2.34		3.68	6.93	2.17	0.12	
		2.51	1.13	0.76	0.11	0.01
		4.34	5.13	0.42	0.07	
		22.47		0.16		
		5.74	0.10	0.27		
		3.01	0.33	0.28	0.01	0.01
68.91	**3.50**	**54.65**	**6.34**	**16.41**	**1.06**	**0.10**
		15.68	0.46	0.77	0.02	0.02
32.80		1.27		4.14	0.19	0.04
0.04		19.42	5.11	0.39	0.03	0.02
32.42		1.22	0.76	10.96	0.82	0.02
0.15		4.20		0.04		
0.01	0.01	12.45	0.01			
3.49	3.49	0.41		0.11		
		12.61	**1.72**	**0.79**	**1.18**	**1.03**
		3.93	0.94	0.21	0.91	0.91
		1.16		0.06	0.02	0.02
		1.33		0.17	0.09	0.06
		2.76	0.75	0.10	0.04	0.02
		1.97		0.15	0.12	0.02
		0.17		0.08		
		1.29	0.03	0.02		

11-14 续表

单位：千公顷

地　区	Region	农作物播种面积 Total Sown Area	粮食作物 Sown Area of Grain Crops	薯类 Tubers
博尔塔拉蒙古自治州	**Bortala Mongol Autonomous Prefecture**	**71.12**	**22.23**	**0.18**
博乐市	Bole [Bortala] City	28.17	10.45	
精河县	Jinghe [Jing] County	22.16	1.65	
温泉县	Wenquan [Araxang] County	20.79	10.13	0.18
巴音郭楞蒙古自治州	**Bayangol Mongol Autonomous Prefecture**	**181.31**	**43.54**	**0.43**
库尔勒市	Korla City	34.52	4.77	0.03
轮台县	Luntai [Bugur] County	21.50	7.46	
尉犁县	Yuli [Lopnur] County	27.73	1.11	
若羌县	Ruoqiang [Qarkilik] County	3.09	1.18	
且末县	Qiemo [Qarqan] County	12.50	3.66	
焉耆回族自治县	Yanji Hui Autonomous County	29.76	11.09	
和静县	Hejing County	20.64	7.21	0.33
和硕县	Hoxud County	15.87	2.43	0.07
博湖县	Bohu [Bagrax] County	15.70	4.63	
阿克苏地区	**Aksu Administrative Offices**	**391.20**	**166.53**	**1.64**
阿克苏市	Aksu City	43.71	13.72	
温宿县	Wensu [Onsu] County	47.32	18.22	0.17
库车县	Kuqa County	65.11	33.09	0.23
沙雅县	Xayar County	60.94	24.48	0.02
新和县	Xinhe [Toksu] County	37.53	13.90	0.01
拜城县	Baicheng [Bay] County	42.63	25.48	1.13
乌什县	Wushi [Uxturpan] County	38.28	21.44	0.08
阿瓦提县	Awat County	47.71	12.85	
柯坪县	Kalpin County	7.97	3.35	
克孜勒苏柯尔克孜自治州	**Kizilsu Kirgiz Autonomous Prefecture**	**43.33**	**29.78**	**0.07**
阿图什市	Artux City	14.32	10.13	0.05
阿克陶县	Akto County	24.17	18.15	
阿合奇县	Akqi County	2.69	0.80	0.01
乌恰县	Wuqia [Ulugqat] County	2.15	0.70	0.01
喀什地区	**Kashgar [Kaxgar] Administrative Offices**	**555.56**	**286.74**	**0.81**
喀什市	Kashgar [Kaxgar] City	11.00	4.00	0.12
疏附县	Shufu County	61.83	39.34	0.04
疏勒县	Shule County	50.83	27.69	
英吉沙县	Yengisar County	26.90	18.93	
泽普县	Zepu [Poskam] County	30.83	13.78	
莎车县	Shache [Yarkant] County	109.38	60.69	0.02
叶城县	Yecheng [Kagilik] County	60.55	35.52	0.60
麦盖提县	Makit County	45.67	15.84	0.02
岳普湖县	Yopurga County	30.34	13.98	
伽师县	Jiashi [Payzawat] County	59.22	29.72	
巴楚县	Bachu [Maralbexi] County	65.25	23.58	
塔什库尔干塔吉克自治县	Taxkorgan Tajik Autonomous County	3.76	3.67	0.01
和田地区	**Hotan Administrative Offices**	**225.09**	**135.29**	**0.57**
和田市	Hotan City	6.70	4.39	
和田县	Hotan County	35.65	25.01	0.05
墨玉县	Moyu [Karakax] County	54.48	35.87	0.01
皮山县	Pishan [Guma] County	28.80	15.51	0.49
洛浦县	Lop County	35.35	22.75	
策勒县	Qira County	20.46	10.57	0.02
于田县	Yutian [Keriya] County	34.47	18.23	
民丰县	Minfeng [Niya] County	9.18	2.96	
二、生产建设兵团	**Xinjiang Production & Construction Group**	**953.93**	**203.76**	**3.35**

Continued

(1000 hectares)

棉花 Cotton	#长绒棉 Long Staple Cotton	油料 Oil Bearing Crops	甜菜 Beetroots	蔬菜 Vegetables	果用瓜 Melon	#甜瓜 Muskmelon
30.15		**5.58**	**1.89**	**1.33**	**0.26**	**0.04**
14.13		0.55	0.75	0.62	0.09	0.01
16.02		0.06		0.26	0.13	0.03
		4.97	1.14	0.45	0.04	
85.31	**1.93**	**3.50**	**3.96**	**14.96**	**1.00**	**0.27**
25.93	1.93			1.06	0.19	0.02
12.06		0.03		0.31	0.10	0.06
25.03				0.10	0.09	0.02
1.47				0.03	0.08	0.07
6.98		0.05		0.22	0.26	
0.50		1.01	2.21	4.16	0.08	0.06
2.19		1.53	0.86	3.40	0.07	0.02
8.11		0.15	0.32	1.54	0.05	
3.04		0.73	0.57	4.14	0.08	0.02
160.67	**29.69**	**9.99**	**3.52**	**12.99**	**7.09**	**1.84**
23.08	5.14	0.12	0.02	3.76	1.45	0.29
24.47		0.38	0.48	1.26	0.44	0.07
27.47		0.73		1.66	0.64	0.23
30.00	6.47	0.26		0.79	0.95	0.29
18.49		0.26		0.54	0.29	0.10
3.33		4.84	1.67	3.04	0.98	0.03
2.40		3.32	1.35	0.75	0.52	0.19
28.00	18.08	0.01		0.91	1.62	0.49
3.43		0.07		0.28	0.21	0.15
6.14		**0.79**		**0.72**	**0.47**	**0.22**
1.37		0.13		0.41	0.21	0.15
4.77		0.17		0.26	0.26	0.07
		0.40		0.02		
		0.09		0.03		
171.88	**0.31**	**2.03**		**16.82**	**20.62**	**15.57**
0.52				3.66	0.16	0.01
9.33		0.33		2.60	2.20	1.00
16.13		0.09		1.21	1.38	0.82
5.77		0.02		0.56	0.33	0.10
11.35		0.12		0.52	0.33	0.09
38.57		0.22		2.31	1.30	0.80
10.68		0.87		3.15	0.29	0.29
24.33		0.10		0.45	0.77	0.53
6.33		0.20		0.43	4.00	3.33
16.47		0.08		0.93	6.53	5.50
32.40	0.31			0.99	3.33	3.10
				0.01		
23.33		**1.04**		**7.58**	**4.57**	**3.87**
		0.02		1.13	0.55	0.33
4.46		0.04		0.91	0.19	0.11
4.99		0.24		1.15	0.20	0.09
3.09		0.24		0.92	0.04	0.03
5.69		0.12		0.80	0.14	0.07
1.87		0.37		0.33	0.10	0.04
2.23				2.24	1.34	1.20
1.00		0.01		0.10	2.01	2.00
472.07	**35.20**	**57.01**	**18.91**	**56.73**	**10.99**	**6.09**

11-15 主要农作物种植结构

Planting Structure of Major Farm Crops

单位：% (%)

项 目	Item	1990	1995	2000	2004
农作物总播种面积	**Total Sown Areas of Farm Crops**	**100**	**100**	**100**	**100**
粮食作物	Grain Crops	61.30	52.21	42.66	38.60
谷 物	Cereal	60.85	50.10	39.95	35.64
稻 谷	Rice	2.82	2.40	2.31	1.87
小 麦	Wheat	39.61	31.22	24.75	18.42
玉 米	Corn	14.85	14.39	11.29	14.16
谷 子	Millet	0.02	0.02	0.04	0.03
高 粱	Jowar	0.72	0.47	0.39	0.30
其它谷物	Other Cereal	2.83	1.59	1.18	0.86
豆 类	Soybeans	0.45	2.12	2.71	2.96
#大 豆	Soja	0.45	0.94	1.85	2.23
杂 豆	Miscellaneous Beans		1.18	0.20	0.11
薯 类	Tubers	0.36	0.34	0.66	0.68
油 料	Oil-bearing Crops	9.04	10.05	9.15	6.03
#花 生	Peanuts	0.01		0.14	0.07
油菜籽	Rapeseeds	3.94	4.26	2.84	1.89
芝 麻	Sesame	0.05		0.02	0.01
胡麻籽	Benne	1.55	0.88	0.72	0.38
向日葵	Helianthus	3.23	4.59	4.63	2.40
棉 花	Cotton	14.61	24.35	29.87	31.57
麻 类	Fiber Crops	0.11	0.14	0.21	0.82
甜 菜	Beetroots	2.24	2.33	1.65	1.68
烟 叶	Tobacco	0.03	0.03	0.08	0.01
药 材	Medicinal Materials	0.04	0.22	0.38	0.55
蔬菜、瓜类	Vegetables and Melon	2.92	3.17	5.42	6.93
#蔬 菜	Vegetables	1.95	2.34	3.77	5.20
其他农作物	Other Farm Crops	9.35	7.16	9.92	13.13
#青饲料	Succulence	0.41	3.94	3.56	10.23

11-16 主要年份农作物产品产量

Total Yield of Major Farm Crops in Main Years

单位：万吨 (10 000 tons)

年份 Year	粮食 Grain Crops	谷物 Cereal	#水稻 Rice	#小麦 Wheat	#玉米 Corn	#大麦 Barley	豆类 Soybeans	薯类 Tubers	棉花 Cotton	#长绒棉 Long-staple Cotton
1978	370.01	367.71	27.39	180.02	134.45	5.01	2.30	22.91	5.50	1.19
1980	386.13	384.16	25.62	213.19	126.43	3.50	1.97	16.03	7.92	1.74
1985	496.65	495.16	30.63	314.52	139.38	1.93	1.49	15.14	18.78	1.40
1990	676.89	673.18	47.27	390.80	209.42	10.51	3.71	22.57	46.88	3.48
1991	672.52	667.82	46.10	382.65	222.25	6.70	4.70	19.81	63.95	3.85
1992	706.27	700.59	43.28	418.62	219.61	7.25	5.68	26.21	66.76	5.65
1993	720.37	703.58	39.12	419.18	219.90	11.44	16.79	23.48	68.00	5.97
1994	666.17	642.89	41.58	337.87	229.49	22.72	23.28	24.95	88.21	1.94
1995	730.16	716.83	48.25	381.21	266.74	12.82	13.33	26.43	93.50	1.13
1996	818.20	808.67	51.49	420.32	312.54	17.39	9.53	32.50	94.04	1.72
1997	825.34	813.07	55.27	437.60	294.31	17.92	12.27	26.73	115.00	3.10
1998	830.00	814.54	49.56	444.00	302.25	11.00	15.46	33.12	140.00	1.39
1999	838.78	821.70	54.14	423.29	323.06	8.00	17.08	46.06	140.75	1.67
2000	808.60	782.93	60.35	405.80	298.22	11.75	25.67	64.01	150.00	6.16
2001	796.00	767.53	56.79	374.14	318.41	11.86	28.47	60.02	157.00	9.71
2002	875.87	849.48	60.62	386.44	379.05	13.78	26.39	62.41	150.00	6.67
2003	801.64	774.62	50.73	335.67	366.25	14.33	27.02	71.80	160.00	10.10
2004	828.53	800.04	51.31	345.94	388.12	8.06	28.49	70.79	175.25	11.22

年份 Year	油料 Oil bearing Crops	#油菜 Rapeseeds	#胡麻 Flax	#葵花 Sunflower	甜菜 Beetroots	蔬菜 Vegetables	果用瓜 Melons	#甜瓜 Muskmelon	苜蓿 Lucerne
1978	10.33	3.30	3.14	2.29	16.37	91.26	44.05		
1980	17.59	5.59	5.17	4.59	38.52	73.44	55.68		
1985	34.25	7.29	8.10	16.90	40.69	111.08	103.18	47.02	49.69
1990	38.96	12.17	6.32	18.17	224.37	187.42	93.38	37.75	89.29
1991	40.49	14.63	5.56	19.16	256.85	172.21	81.68	29.07	76.46
1992	35.62	13.18	5.23	15.93	329.07	193.30	94.17	28.37	75.58
1993	37.02	12.75	4.65	16.65	236.91	191.82	75.49	29.27	73.43
1994	50.76	18.80	4.72	25.05	299.24	210.99	77.12	25.47	77.31
1995	49.41	15.12	3.79	29.06	288.14	269.56	68.75	18.31	82.62
1996	30.95	10.15	3.12	16.91	354.52	301.94	67.16	17.33	75.42
1997	29.95	8.92	2.53	17.69	388.71	295.59	86.78	25.90	70.05
1998	37.52	12.32	2.53	20.82	513.12	321.79	88.32	29.45	67.56
1999	60.46	16.37	2.75	35.69	354.24	406.18	143.49	46.38	69.98
2000	60.14	14.75	3.60	35.47	292.65	527.84	151.03	51.22	76.32
2001	42.64	12.19	2.47	23.31	455.12	486.74	156.87	56.86	103.12
2002	44.37	12.90	3.69	23.26	466.81	674.96	233.40	107.49	149.93
2003	50.13	15.43	3.49	25.80	381.65	761.00	189.32	77.61	249.60
2004	44.54	12.16	2.10	21.90	344.21	919.13	186.06	92.54	273.04

11-17 各地、州、市、县(市)主要农产品产量

单位：吨 (2004 年)

地区	Region	粮食作物 Grain Crops	谷物 Cereal	#水稻 Rice	#小麦 Wheat	#玉米 Corn	豆类 Soy-beans
总　计	**Total**	**8285300**	**8083625**	**533170**	**3499389**	**3890685**	**284933**
一、地 方	**Local Regions**	**7146518**	**6915808**	**359558**	**3011126**	**3429502**	**230710**
乌鲁木齐市	**Urumqi City**	**40228**	**35084**	**3640**	**18162**	**4036**	**5144**
乌鲁木齐县	Urumqi County	25671	24320	3582	11695	39	1351
市直单位	Direct Under the Municipality	14557	10764	58	6467	3997	3793
克拉玛依市	**Karamay City**	**2735**	**2735**		**500**	**2235**	
吐鲁番地区	**Turpan Administrative Offices**	**77905**	**77749**		**35425**	**4293**	**156**
吐鲁番市	Turpan City	21353	21353		8584	1699	
鄯善县	Shanshan County	16130	16130		6851	1406	
托克逊县	Toksun County	40422	40266		19990	1188	156
哈密地区	**Hami Administrative Offices**	**64950**	**63879**		**48434**	**6107**	**1071**
哈密市	Hami City	21047	20777		11988	5482	270
巴里坤哈萨克自治县	Barkol KazakAutonomous County	38775	38276		34836	337	499
伊吾县	Yiwu County	5128	4826		1610	288	302
昌吉回族自治州	**Changji Hui Autonomous Prefecture**	**711675**	**689669**	**53696**	**231108**	**365185**	**22006**
昌吉市	Changji City	83079	81083	1658	24005	54926	1996
阜康市	Fukang City	51346	48760	1131	12920	33789	2586
米泉市	Miquan City	60093	60093	49853	5102	5129	
呼图壁县	Hutubi County	52944	52180	882	23562	27640	764
玛纳斯县	Manas County	46345	46173	172	5474	40527	172
奇台县	Qitai County	278063	273238		127400	111383	4825
吉木萨尔县	Jimsar County	61880	59664		16221	42409	2216
木垒哈萨克自治县	Mori Kazak Autonomous County	77925	68478		16424	49382	9447
伊犁哈萨克自治州	**Ili Kazak Autonomous Prefecture**	**1923627**	**1737254**	**54420**	**643883**	**1028903**	**186373**
伊犁州直属县(市)	**Counties (Cities) Direct Under Ili Prefecture**	**1117903**	**999551**	**47700**	**285708**	**660889**	**118352**
伊宁市	Yining City	88846	86147		17446	68648	2699
奎屯市	Kuytun City	578	578		478	100	
伊宁县	Yining County	396553	363203		48550	313660	33350
察布查尔锡伯自治县	Qapqal Xibe Autonomous County	119030	112777	41246	25994	45537	6253
霍城县	Huocheng County	145107	135897	384	32571	102942	9210
巩留县	Gongliu County	118435	86508	1852	38074	46582	31927
新源县	Xinyuan County	119094	88459	3278	43584	40855	30635
昭苏县	Zhaosu County	34003	34003		32784		
特克斯县	Tekes County	53514	52430		21506	30015	1084
尼勒克县	Nilka County	42743	39549	940	24721	12550	3194
塔城地区	**Tacheng [Tarbagatai] Administrative Offices**	**580442**	**573829**	**6720**	**274791**	**287962**	**6613**
塔城市	Tacheng [Qoqek] City	170528	169795		86949	81732	733
乌苏市	Usu City	77975	77525	6720	10936	59869	450
额敏县	Emin [Dorbiljin] County	86979	86678		66808	18185	301
沙湾县	Shawan County	148204	143310		52572	90083	4894
托里县	Toli County	24338	24262		17008	6352	76
裕民县	Yumin [Qagantokay] County	66808	66769		37758	29011	39
和布克赛尔蒙古自治县	Hoboksar Mongol Autonomous County	5610	5490		2760	2730	120
阿勒泰地区	**Altay Administrative Offices**	**225282**	**163874**		**83384**	**80052**	**61408**
阿勒泰市	Altay City	31253	25544		11303	14241	5709
布尔津县	Burqin County	44994	15863		6399	9464	29131
富蕴县	Fuyun [Koktokay] County	44706	39351		18026	21324	5355
福海县	Fuhai [Burultokay] County	21496	21130		2566	18564	366
哈巴河县	Habahe [Kaba] County	45889	25162		11055	13879	20727
青河县	Qinghe [Qinggil] County	26213	26093		23445	2440	120
吉木乃县	Jeminay County	10731	10731		10590	140	

注：各地州市县粮食、棉花产量合计不等于全区总计数(以下同)。

Total Yield of Major Farm Crops by Prefecture, Autonomous Prefecture, City and County

(ton)

薯类 Tubers	棉花 Cotton	#长绒棉 Longstaple Cotton	油料 Oil Bearing Crops	#油菜 Rapeseeds	#胡麻 Flax	#葵花 Sunflower	甜菜 Beetroots	蔬菜 Vegetables	果用瓜 Melon	#甜瓜 Muskmelon	苜蓿 Lucerne
707877	**1752500**	**112240**	**445404**	**121647**	**21045**	**218968**	**3442102**	**9191313**	**1860576**	**925443**	**2730446**
609170	**1071791**	**48210**	**311458**	**69984**	**19988**	**140236**	**2258030**	**5781771**	**1461540**	**757941**	**2316373**
67621	**105**		**2345**	**130**	**24**	**2023**	**998**	**307793**	**7026**	**252**	**33461**
58577	10		662	109	12	541	140	189476	3434	252	17962
9044	95		1683	21	12	1482	858	118317	3592		15499
	5841		**324**			**324**		2325	**6300**	**1125**	**630**
	18519		**582**			**23**		126085	**135116**	**103025**	**59534**
	5170		55					62423	51570	23955	14729
	6419							48000	73045	72045	6345
	6930		527			23		15662	10501	7025	38460
30602	**14356**		**1883**	**1054**	**396**	**433**		**50852**	**72956**	**64497**	**65827**
1135	14230		1643	874	356	413		46023	34455	25996	9977
28650	20		200	180		20		4557	1049	1049	52070
817	106		40		40			272	37452	37452	3780
192376	**118099**		**39129**	**638**	**205**	**26037**	**207847**	**1761056**	**235912**	**15922**	**198501**
14314	20806		2511			1786	47086	574071	125636	5180	30935
9991	3277		2570			2057		174346	12230	2584	25230
304	1160		994			739	4426	162200	14168	833	10688
7309	37444		1033			768	59526	192799	28766	3282	31782
5536	53370		1592			1592	6519	331141	14925		26368
58818			18521	485		9043	81237	116224	12255	734	40044
80482	2042		11291	71		9722	8612	208894	27009	2877	29785
15622			617	82	205	330	441	1381	923	432	3669
239871	**119955**	**4559**	**212902**	**52308**	**12942**	**81261**	**1507933**	**1361347**	**106111**	**29640**	**494984**
175921	**6773**		**113763**	**36478**	**12852**	**35891**	**1073907**	**468034**	**35651**	**2204**	**50216**
4272	60		3130	1128	102	1180	41575	189297	3556		7581
	736		1148			128	300	120			8000
6116	211		18410	4115	762	8128	212822	105746	14192	1011	3381
2015	3116		4280	23	166	517	84699	27387	4207	927	16639
5100	2650		14894		825	3607	314226	83913	4500		450
8845			6459	1123	730	3203	55725	26363	2926	266	2792
88539			13699	1659	1641	4824	345246	19264	3046		3254
17828			33631	25667	5071	2893		1877			
2976			14074	1761	1162	11151	4350	6075			
40230			4038	1002	2393	260	14964	7992	224		8119
30656	**113182**	**4559**	**68298**	**15830**	**90**	**14529**	**343056**	**859397**	**39451**	**2435**	**200988**
			18503	7960		1302	24643	44480	800	640	33794
3925	57237		3800			3800		231066	7770	995	3592
	120		23378	6379		4682	270370	12375	625	400	103756
21531	51098		4216			3374	47668	568750	30256	400	10875
946	168		5086	1053	90	488		856			15240
3654	9	9	12552	438		120	375				13221
600	4550	4550	763			763		1870			20510
33294			**30841**			**30841**	**90970**	**33916**	**31009**	**25001**	**243780**
3079			10703			10703	55416	13020	20864	20864	40403
3245			3104			3104		4943	644	644	36855
17928			3577			3577		5591	2736	1745	37165
1741			6603			6603	34994	4140	1995	948	55805
3375			4805			4805		3996	4770	800	22120
3750			390			390		1876			39015
176			1659			1659	560	350			12417

Note: Total yield of grain and cotton by prefecture, city and county is not equal to the total sum of the whole region (the same as below).

11-17 续表

单位：吨

地 区	Region	粮食作物 Grain Crops	谷物 Cereal	#水稻 Rice	#小麦 Wheat	#玉米 Corn	豆类 Soy-beans
博尔塔拉蒙古自治州	**Bortala Mongol Autonomous Prefecture**	**201550**	**195074**	**2870**	**45222**	**146722**	**6476**
博乐市	Bole [Bortala] City	106009	101781	2870	13287	85624	4228
精河县	Jinghe [Jing] County	19927	19927		1731	18196	
温泉县	Wenquan [Araxang] County	75614	73366		30204	42902	2248
巴音郭楞蒙古自治州	**Bayangol Mongol Autonomous Prefecture**	**266217**	**265870**	**8672**	**161995**	**94909**	**347**
库尔勒市	Korla City	24666	24625	1926	14891	7808	41
轮台县	Luntai [Bugur] County	44813	44813		23921	20892	
尉犁县	Yuli [Lopnur] County	5989	5989	376	1384	4229	
若羌县	Ruoqiang [Qarkilik] County	7038	7024		3993	3031	14
且末县	Qiemo [Qarqan] County	19082	18910		13810	4806	172
焉耆回族自治县	Yanji Hui Autonomous County	65374	65302	265	48631	16406	72
和静县	Hejing County	51455	51440		34461	16979	15
和硕县	Hoxud County	18700	18667	1229	4217	13221	33
博湖县	Bohu [Bagrax] County	29100	29100	4876	16687	7537	
阿克苏地区	**Aksu Administrative Offices**	**1152211**	**1147334**	**128673**	**507353**	**507653**	**4877**
阿克苏市	Aksu City	92404	91553	18926	48797	23830	851
温宿县	Wensu [Onsu] County	150053	149997	80460	39074	30172	56
库车县	Kuqa County	206203	206203		114240	91963	
沙雅县	Xayar County	166255	165561		72024	93537	694
新和县	Xinhe [Toksu] County	88022	87669	4158	43175	40336	353
拜城县	Baicheng [Bay] County	196845	196367	12575	71000	111900	478
乌什县	Wushi [Uxturpan] County	149111	146696	11816	59400	73008	2415
阿瓦提县	Awat County	82166	82136	738	49249	32149	30
柯坪县	Kalpin County	21152	21152		10394	10758	
克孜勒苏柯尔克孜自治州	**Kizilsu Kirgiz Autonomous Prefecture**	**165418**	**164943**	**4750**	**85076**	**73823**	**475**
阿图什市	Artux City	57126	57126	247	32000	24722	
阿克陶县	Akto County	102650	102650	4503	49859	47694	
阿合奇县	Akqi County	2787	2553		819	1321	234
乌恰县	Wuqia [Ulugqat] County	2855	2614		2398	86	241
喀什地区	**Kashgar [Kaxgar] Administrative Offices**	**1658000**	**1654795**	**55564**	**850890**	**745889**	**3205**
喀什市	Kashgar [Kaxgar] City	32700	32700	3700	13000	16000	
疏附县	Shufu County	203000	203000	17000	126200	59800	
疏勒县	Shule County	147016	147016	2500	84000	60516	
英吉沙县	Yengisar County	121805	121715		57000	64715	90
泽普县	Zepu [Poskam] County	98078	97033	2500	47700	46833	1045
莎车县	Shache [Yarkant] County	344384	344264	26300	179640	137884	120
叶城县	Yecheng [Kagilik] County	224509	224359	3564	99100	121695	150
麦盖提县	Makit County	99279	99279		45300	53979	
岳普湖县	Yopurga County	80600	80600		43000	37600	
伽师县	Jiashi [Payzawat] County	164078	164078		86900	77178	
巴楚县	Bachu [Maralbexi] County	136397	136397		67100	69297	
塔什库尔干塔吉克自治县	Taxkorgan Tajik Autonomous County	6154	4354		1950	392	1800
和田地区	**Hotan Administrative Offices**	**882002**	**881422**	**47273**	**383078**	**449747**	**580**
和田市	Hotan City	33476	33476	1578	14086	17812	
和田县	Hotan County	159251	159251	12207	70492	75686	
墨玉县	Moyu [Karakax] County	227667	227605	15140	101107	111358	62
皮山县	Pishan [Guma] County	108045	107810		41946	65829	235
洛浦县	Lop County	142459	142459	10	69060	73389	
策勒县	Qira County	71314	71031		29820	40788	283
于田县	Yutian [Keriya] County	120153	120153	18088	49085	52980	
民丰县	Minfeng [Niya] County	19637	19637	250	7482	11905	
二、生产建设兵团	**Xinjiang Production & Construction Group**	**1222040**	**1167817**	**173612**	**488263**	**461183**	**54223**

Continued

(ton)

薯 类 Tubers	棉 花 Cotton	#长绒棉 Longstaple Cotton	油 料 Oil Bearing Crops	#油 菜 Rapeseeds	#胡 麻 Flax	#葵 花 Sunflower	甜 菜 Beetroots	蔬 菜 Vegetables	果用瓜 Melon	#甜 瓜 Muskmelon	苜 蓿 Lucerne
5956	**58764**		**14867**		**12**	**14825**	**96994**	**51594**	**9016**	**1580**	**25694**
	27505		1205			1205	37695	15801	2640	720	9229
	31259		148			118		7585	4583	860	5905
5956			13514		12	13502	59299	28208	1793		10560
13564	**144543**	**2754**	**6376**	**1994**		**4382**	**258993**	**956259**	**35081**	**8093**	**107314**
566	43492	2754						94316	9765	626	28910
	21358		29	29				8735	2965	1794	10580
	45107							2189	2632	603	1680
	2990							672	1468	1417	4080
	13259		88	17		71		4950	4662		8738
	475		1994	185		1809	136390	265533	3848	3150	16080
9998	2588		2456	1714		742	57885	152869	3540		14980
3000	12214		230	31		199	21859	99803	2108	170	16461
	3060		1579	18		1561	42859	327192	4093	333	5805
34423	**281692**	**40592**	**17634**	**12382**	**4033**	**1217**	**185265**	**324409**	**188629**	**39435**	**163235**
	47328	6294	219	51	74	94	1050	169317	41575	4179	9335
1780	40460		840	580	260		23340	17842	12576	1260	23000
3803	49028		1012	994	18			35021	14775	4932	12638
600	55000	10291	306	254		50		13088	23543	6198	20341
340	31822		394	338		56		10206	4002	2213	16200
25500	4175		8697	6540	1498	659	90000	46300	26996	675	12384
2400	2700		5976	3625	2183	168	70875	13500	15600	5700	32180
	45972	24007	3			3		14993	46261	11691	36020
	5207		187			187		4142	3301	2587	1137
1148	**8244**		**979**	**232**	**555**	**192**		**14275**	**6595**	**2545**	**29465**
853	2049		233	30	135	68		8128	1890	1225	4965
	6195		124			124		5795	4705	1320	5290
190			420		420			235			8760
105			202	202				117			10450
19753	**263334**	**305**	**11214**	**77**	**1533**	**8065**		**650990**	**546697**	**409017**	**657562**
3600	715							191300	5000	185	10544
965	12500		1500	77	801	622		90520	27500	4366	27295
	28309		595			595		55495	28767	12400	41084
	7900		3500		12	3488		25200	7500	7500	38220
	18860		198		198			14748	7500	1700	48860
410	52500		526		236	198		81200	47900	16602	48203
14049	15000		2084		286	1012		100627	13280	13280	217202
689	35350		511					12000	17250	8000	41350
	9700		300			150		17700	101000	101000	64500
	22500		2000			2000		28000	216000	180744	75000
	60000	305						34155	75000	63240	45200
40								45			104
3856	**38339**		**3223**	**1169**	**288**	**1454**		**174786**	**112101**	**82810**	**480166**
			70	70				43254	16500	2281	13267
1535	7200		68	31	37			20522	4679	2559	37303
377	8029		722	428	162			28430	4635	2325	100745
1289	5563		1849	488		1254		8277	527	322	64132
	9298		60	10	37			19510	5258	1374	77597
655	3035		449	142	52	195		7879	3743	1229	41800
	3414							45125	30120	26100	125480
	1800		5			5		1789	46639	46620	19842
98707	**877760**	**64030**	**133946**	**51663**	**1057**	**78732**	**1184072**	**3409542**	**399036**	**167502**	**414073**

11-18 各地、州、市、县(市)农作物单位面积产量

Yield of Major Farm Crops Per Hectare by Prefecture, Autonomous Prefecture, City and County

单位：公斤/公顷　　(2004 年)　　(kg / hectare)

地 区	Region	粮 食 Sown Area of Grain Crops	#谷 物 Cereal	#水 稻 Rice	#小 麦 Wheat	#玉 米 Corn	棉 花 Cotton	油 料 Oil-Bearing Crops	甜 菜 Beetroots
总 计	**Total**	**6010**	**6350**	**7985**	**5318**	**7694**	**1554**	**2067**	**57483**
一、地 方	**Local Regions**	**6083**	**6361**	**8547**	**5298**	**7749**	**1635**	**1966**	**55114**
乌鲁木齐市	**Urumqi City**	**3813**	**4005**	**9838**	**4137**	**6306**	**1050**	**2151**	**49900**
乌鲁木齐县	Urumqi County	3652	3782	9950	4177	3900	1000	2006	
市直单位	Direct Under the Municipality	4136	4620	5800	4067	6344	1056	2214	42900
克拉玛依市	**Karamay City**	**2879**	**4208**		**1471**	**7210**	**990**	**1800**	
吐鲁番地区	**Turpan Administrative Offices**	**4122**	**4140**		**3897**	**5172**	**1309**	**1877**	
吐鲁番市	Turpan City	4262	4262		3489	6535	1211	917	
鄯善县	Shanshan County	3993	3993		4229	3906	1321		
托克逊县	Toksun County	4104	4138		3990	5657	1380	2108	
哈密地区	**Hami Administrative Offices**	**3887**	**4007**		**4348**	**6786**	**1590**	**951**	
哈密市	Hami City	4677	4701		5235	6768	1594	893	
巴里坤哈萨克自治县	Barkol KazakAutonomous County	3824	3995		4103	8425	1000	1667	
伊吾县	Yiwu County	2477	2488		4472	5760	1325	2000	
昌吉回族自治州	**Changji Hui Autonomous Prefecture**	**5538**	**6085**	**9537**	**4570**	**7899**	**1606**	**2610**	**54841**
昌吉市	Changji City	5934	6461	10363	5715	6953	1310	1663	64501
阜康市	Fukang City	5649	6035	10282	5717	6363	1061	2024	
米泉市	Miquan City	8773	8773	9496	5206	8408	1172	887	55325
呼图壁县	Hutubi County	6356	6514	9800	5259	8226	1655	1640	72593
玛纳斯县	Manas County	6349	6369	8600	5702	6464	1833	3062	65190
奇台县	Qitai County	5795	5935		4800	10098		4378	43211
吉木萨尔县	Jimsar County	6604	6954		5069	8299	1104	2328	53825
木垒哈萨克自治县	Mori Kazak Autonomous County	3045	4288		2066	7437		717	22050
伊犁哈萨克自治州	**Ili Kazak Autonomous Prefecture**	**6104**	**6889**	**8806**	**4411**	**10643**	**1594**	**1820**	**54262**
伊犁州直属县(市)	**Counties (Cities) Direct Under Ili Prefecture**	**6321**	**7311**	**8657**	**4243**	**10606**	**1065**	**2288**	**54430**
伊宁市	Yining City	7607	8135		4767	9935	1000	2545	51969
奎屯市	Kuytun City	2890	2890		2516	10000	995	6753	30000
伊宁县	Yining County	7555	8848		3893	11111	1407	3236	54153
察布查尔锡伯自治县	Qapqal Xibe Autonomous County	6448	6932	8757	4094	8740	1015	4864	61824
霍城县	Huocheng County	7518	8373	9600	5011	10624	1132	4047	45343
巩留县	Gongliu County	4799	6812	8819	4783	10283		2573	49314
新源县	Xinyuan County	5560	7180	7450	5251	11981		3156	67299
昭苏县	Zhaosu County	3190	3190		3180			1497	
特克斯县	Tekes County	6311	6513		4425	10350		2452	43500
尼勒克县	Nilka County	4504	4577	8545	3673	8838		1342	45345
塔城地区	**Tacheng [Tarbagatai] Administrative Offices**	**6525**	**6593**	**10030**	**4643**	**11257**	**1642**	**1250**	**54110**
塔城市	Tacheng [Qoqek] City	6281	6317		4665	10255		1180	53572
乌苏市	Usu City	10153	10255	10030	4714	13100	1745	2992	
额敏县	Emin [Dorbiljin] County	4609	4655		4139	10274	3000	1204	52910
沙湾县	Shawan County	8933	9300		6156	13465	1576	3456	62721
托里县	Toli County	4029	4044		3697	6686	1120	1211	
裕民县	Yumin [Qagantokay] County	5715	5717		4533	8660	900	1008	37500
和布克赛尔蒙古自治县	Hoboksar Mongol Autonomous County	5968	6169		4525	9750	1304	1861	
阿勒泰地区	**Altay Administrative Offices**	**4570**	**5766**		**4283**	**9118**		**2446**	**52890**
阿勒泰市	Altay City	4845	5589		4186	7616		2723	58953
布尔津县	Burqin County	3778	6172		4155	9188		2676	
富蕴县	Fuyun [Koktokay] County	5328	6569		4575	10453		2689	
福海县	Fuhai [Burultokay] County	8051	8352		3830	9981		2392	46659
哈巴河县	Habahe [Kaba] County	4036	5825		4125	9071		2439	
青河县	Qinghe [Qinggil] County	5361	5413		5365	6100		2294	
吉木乃县	Jeminay County	2964	2964		2966	2800		1286	18667

注：个别县(市)油料等作物种植在边角地头，未计面积，故单产偏高。

Note: The oil-bearing crop planted at the edge or margin of fields in small number of counties (cities), whose area is not calculated, thus per-unit output is relatively higher.

11-18 续表 Continued

单位：公斤/公顷 (kg/ hectare)

地区	Region	粮食 Sown Area of Grain Crops	#谷物 Cereal	#水稻 Rice	#小麦 Wheat	#玉米 Corn	棉花 Cotton	油料 Oil-Bearing Crops	甜菜 Beet-roots
博尔塔拉蒙古自治州	**Bortala Mongol Autonomous Prefecture**	**9067**	**9696**	**10250**	**5087**	**13498**	**1949**	**2664**	**51320**
博乐市	Bole [Bortala] City	10144	11172	10250	5606	13254	1947	2191	50260
精河县	Jinghe [Jing] County	12077	12077		5770	13479	1951	2467	
温泉县	Wenquan [Araxang] County	7464	7838		4856	14020		2719	52017
巴音郭楞蒙古自治州	**Bayangol Mongol Autonomous Prefecture**	**6114**	**6133**	**6671**	**5775**	**6833**	**1694**	**1822**	**65402**
库尔勒市	Korla City	5171	5184	9171	5189	4675	1677		
轮台县	Luntai [Bugur] County	6007	6007		5449	6805	1771	967	
尉犁县	Yuli [Lopnur] County	5395	5395	7520	4772	5492	1802		
若羌县	Ruoqiang [Qarkilik] County	5964	6003		5872	6186	2034		
且末县	Qiemo [Qarqan] County	5214	5297		5480	5113	1900	1760	
焉耆回族自治县	Yanji Hui Autonomous County	5895	5910	5300	5755	6434	950	1974	61715
和静县	Hejing County	7137	7144		6490	8984	1182	1605	67308
和硕县	Hoxud County	7695	7746	6145	5777	8933	1506	1533	68309
博湖县	Bohu [Bagrax] County	6285	6285	6172	5938	7317	1007	2163	75191
阿克苏地区	**Aksu Administrative Offices**	**6919**	**6983**	**9250**	**6161**	**7628**	**1753**	**1765**	**52632**
阿克苏市	Aksu City	6735	6707	9099	6621	5674	2051	1825	52500
温宿县	Wensu [Onsu] County	8236	8255	10058	6784	6968	1653	2211	48625
库车县	Kuqa County	6232	6232		6301	6147	1785	1386	
沙雅县	Xayar County	6791	7090		6542	7580	1833	1177	
新和县	Xinhe [Toksu] County	6333	6371	6816	5963	6825	1721	1515	
拜城县	Baicheng [Bay] County	7725	7737	7530	5326	11190	1254	1797	53892
乌什县	Wushi [Uxturpan] County	6955	7063	8321	5940	8775	1125	1800	52500
阿瓦提县	Awat County	6394	6427	5677	6438	6430	1642	300	
柯坪县	Kalpin County	6314	6314		5588	7220	1518	2671	
克孜勒苏柯尔克孜自治州	**Kizilsu Kirgiz Autonomous Prefecture**	**5555**	**5569**	**7661**	**5337**	**5920**	**1343**	**1239**	
阿图什市	Artux City	5639	5639	8233	5298	6196	1496	1792	
阿克陶县	Akto County	5656	5656	7632	5437	5831	1299	729	
阿合奇县	Akqi County	3484	3450		3900	4555		1050	
乌恰县	Wuqia [Ulugqat] County	4079	4357		4612	8600		2244	
喀什地区	**Kashgar [Kaxgar] Administrative Offices**	**5782**	**5804**	**8318**	**5807**	**5706**	**1532**	**5524**	
喀什市	Kashgar [Kaxgar] City	8175	8175	6981	6500	10884	1375		
疏附县	Shufu County	5160	5160	6367	6760	3322	1340	4545	
疏勒县	Shule County	5309	5309	9259	5447	5043	1755	6611	
英吉沙县	Yengisar County	6434	6430		5700	7247	1369	175000	
泽普县	Zepu [Poskam] County	7117	7379	7576	7151	7615	1662	1650	
莎车县	Shache [Yarkant] County	5674	5682	11435	5758	5122	1361	2391	
叶城县	Yecheng [Kagilik] County	6321	6336	6145	5612	7088	1404	2395	
麦盖提县	Makit County	6268	6268		5406	7236	1453	5110	
岳普湖县	Yopurga County	5765	5765		6160	5371	1532	1500	
伽师县	Jiashi [Payzawat] County	5521	5521		5391	5675	1366	25000	
巴楚县	Bachu [Maralbexi] County	5784	5784		5794	5775	1852		
塔什库尔干塔吉克自治县	Taxkorgan Tajik Autonomous County	1677	1517		1054	13067			
和田地区	**Hotan Administrative Offices**	**6519**	**6525**	**6658**	**5891**	**7197**	**1643**	**3099**	
和田市	Hotan City	7626	7626	4782	6613	9229		3500	
和田县	Hotan County	6367	6367	6292	5974	6868	1614	1700	
墨玉县	Moyu [Karakax] County	6347	6349	7279	5913	6680	1609	3008	
皮山县	Pishan [Guma] County	6966	6992		5615	8312	1800	7704	
洛浦县	Lop County	6262	6262	1000	5913	6636	1634	500	
策勒县	Qira County	6747	6784		5757	7982	1623	1214	
于田县	Yutian [Keriya] County	6591	6591	6775	5964	7228	1531		
民丰县	Minfeng [Niya] County	6634	6634	3571	5196	8210	1800	500	
二、生产建设兵团	**Xinjiang Production & Construction Group**	**5997**	**6284**	**7029**	**5438**	**7308**	**1859**	**2350**	**62616**

11-19 各地、州、市林业生产情况

Statistics on Forest Products by Prefecture, Autonomous Prefecture, City

单位:公顷 (2004 年) (hectare)

地 区	Region	当年造林面积 Planting Area in the Current Year	用材林 Timber Forest	经济林 Economic Forest	防护林 Windbreak	薪炭林 Firewood Forest	特种用途林 Forest for Special Purpose
总 计	**Total**	**189782**	**4343**	**48143**	**135195**	**2089**	**12**
一、地 方	**Local Regions**	**151800**	**4276**	**47070**	**98375**	**2074**	**5**
乌鲁木齐市	Urumqi City	1199	15	34	1150		
克拉玛依市	Karamay City	425		71	354		
吐鲁番地区	Turpan Administrative Offices	3539		92	3447		
哈密地区	Hami Administrative Offices	3894			3894		
昌吉回族自治州	Changji Hui Autonomous Prefecture	22271	106		22165		
伊犁哈萨克自治州	Ili Kazak Administrative Prefecture	34470	2970	1857	29483	160	
伊犁州直属县(市)	Counties (Cities) Direct Under Ili Prefecture	12830	2946	1857	8027		
塔城地区	Tacheng [Tarbagatai] Administrative Offices	4049	24		4025		
阿勒泰地区	Altay Administrative Offices	17591			17431	160	
博尔塔拉蒙古自治州	Bortala Mongol Autonomous Prefecture	5403			5403		
巴音郭楞蒙古自治州	Bayangol Mongol Autonomous Prefecture	7751	550		7201		
阿克苏地区	Aksu Administrative Offices	27327		14049	13273		5
克孜勒苏柯尔克孜自治州	Kizilsu Kirgiz Autonomous Prefecture	5044		537	3852	655	
喀什地区	Kashgar [Kaxgar] Administrative Offices	32184	633	28191	3231	129	
和田地区	Hotan Administrative Offices	8293	2	2239	4922	1130	
二、生产建设兵团	**Xinjiang Production & Construction Group**	**37982**	**67**	**1073**	**36820**	**15**	**7**

地 区	Region	迹地更新面积 Renewing Area in Slash	当年零星植树(万株) Fragmentary Planting (10 000)	年末实有育苗面积 Actual Sapling Breeding Area	幼林抚育作业面积 Tending Area of Young Growth	成林抚育面积 Tending Area of Full Growth	核桃产量(吨) Walnut Output (ton)	村及村以下木材采伐量(立方米) Timber Felling out put in Village or Below (cu.m)
总 计	**Total**	**2767**	**4060.36**	**8514**	**1759211**	**873043**	**22310**	**645802**
一、地 方	**Local Regions**	**2192**	**2838.21**	**6608**	**1445803**	**740403**	**22212**	**600775**
乌鲁木齐市	Urumqi City	2	6.00	231	4495	2248		527
克拉玛依市	Karamay City		70.00	8	5267	4700		
吐鲁番地区	Turpan Administrative Offices	26	23.00	47	8210	11018	98	1275
哈密地区	Hami Administrative Offices		5.96	66	48297	7074		2215
昌吉回族自治州	Changji Hui Autonomous Prefecture	214	154.00	1565	158013	53405		21200
伊犁哈萨克自治州	Ili Kazak Administrative Prefecture	862	587.96	917	318031	171983	245	135312
伊犁州直属县(市)	Counties (Cities) Direct Under Ili Prefecture	540	359.00	389	137617	45623	245	99626
塔城地区	Tacheng [Tarbagatai] Administrative Offices		157.00	317	94858	72917		30700
阿勒泰地区	Altay Administrative Offices	322	71.96	211	85556	53443		4986
博尔塔拉蒙古自治州	Bortala Mongol Autonomous Prefecture	9	68.00	70	17516	15555		11227
巴音郭楞蒙古自治州	Bayangol Mongol Autonomous Prefecture	105	246.30	290	47586	25714	3	61934
阿克苏地区	Aksu Administrative Offices	503	513.00	838	303716	145845	2665	72157
克孜勒苏柯尔克孜自治州	Kizilsu Kirgiz Autonomous Prefecture		80.32	460	4321	7344	1	7759
喀什地区	Kashgar [Kaxgar] Administrative Offices	144	332.71	911	428053	250937	8583	242100
和田地区	Hotan Administrative Offices	327	750.96	1205	102298	44580	10617	45069
二、生产建设兵团	**Xinjiang Production & Construction Group**	**575**	**1222.15**	**1906**	**313408**	**132640**	**98**	**45027**

11-20 各地、州、市水果种植面积
Planted Area of Fruits by Prefecture, Autonomous Prefecture, City

单位:公顷 (2004 年) (hectare)

地 区	Region	合 计 Total	苹 果 Apples	梨 Pears	葡 萄 Grapes	#无核葡萄 Seedless Grapes
总 计	**Total**	**396207**	**28942**	**53273**	**92178**	**32692**
一、地 方	**Local Regions**	**337545**	**21125**	**39692**	**74950**	**27351**
乌鲁木齐市	Urumqi City	1004	111	3	640	21
克拉玛依市	Karamay City					
吐鲁番地区	TurpanAdministrative Offices	32463	3	80	27299	22946
哈密地区	Hami Administrative Offices	7458	59	151	3267	2873
昌吉回族自治州	Changji Hui Autonomous Prefecture	12382	1074	2	8382	12
伊犁哈萨克自治州	Ili Kazak Autonomous Prefecture	17005	7937	275	2255	
伊犁州直属县(市)	Counties (Cities) Direct Under Ili Prefecture	15929	7431	260	1836	
塔城地区	Tacheng [Tarbagatai] Administrative Offices	1013	460	15	414	
阿勒泰地区	Altay Administrative Offices	63	46		5	
博尔塔拉蒙古自治州	Bortala MongolAutonomous Prefecture	370	80	1	263	
巴音郭楞蒙古自治州	Bayangol Mongol Autonomous Prefecture	54901	1454	19306	7836	482
阿克苏地区	Aksu Administrative Offices	78711	6388	17444	7841	24
克孜勒苏柯尔克孜自治州	Kizilsu Kirgiz Autonomous Prefecture	12974	161	74	4281	
喀什地区	Kashgar [Kaxgar] Administrative Offices	78891	2615	1913	3772	12
和田地区	Hotan Administrative Offices	41386	1243	443	9114	981
二、生产建设兵团	**Xinjiang Production & Construction Group**	**58662**	**7817**	**13581**	**17228**	**5341**

地 区	Region	桃 Peaches	杏 Apricots	红 枣 Jujubes	石 榴 Pomegraniate	其 它 Others
总 计	**Total**	**10821**	**134857**	**41497**	**11719**	**22920**
一、地 方	**Local Regions**	**8023**	**131166**	**30977**	**11384**	**20228**
乌鲁木齐市	Urumqi City	136	19			95
克拉玛依市	Karamay City					
吐鲁番地区	TurpanAdministrative Offices	21	218	4386	451	5
哈密地区	Hami Administrative Offices	5	1131	2652		193
昌吉回族自治州	Changji Hui Autonomous Prefecture	598	2016			310
伊犁哈萨克自治州直	Ili Kazak Autonomous Prefecture	551	1347	88		4552
伊犁州直属县(市)	Counties (Cities) Direct Under Ili Prefecture	470	1345	88		4499
塔城地区	Tacheng [Tarbagatai] Administrative Offices	71	2			51
阿勒泰地区	Altay Administrative Offices	10				2
博尔塔拉蒙古自治州	Bortala Mongol Autonomous Prefecture	4	2			20
巴音郭楞蒙古自治州	Bayangol Mongol Autonomous Prefecture	543	14495	9986	137	1144
阿克苏地区	Aksu Administrative Offices	1115	27457	9574	1499	7393
克孜勒苏柯尔克孜自治州	Kizilsu Kirgiz Autonomous Prefecture	105	7834	12	167	340
喀什地区	Kashgar [Kaxgar] Administrative Offices	2295	56757	1710	4676	5153
和田地区	Hotan Administrative Offices	2650	19890	2569	4454	1023
二、生产建设兵团	**Xinjiang Production & Construction Group**	**2798**	**3691**	**10520**	**335**	**2692**

11-21 各地、州、市水果产量

Output of Fruits by Prefecture, Autonomous Prefecture, City

单位：吨 (2004 年) (ton)

地 区	Region	合 计 Total	苹 果 Apples	梨 Pears	葡 萄 Grapes	#无核葡萄 Seedless Grapes
总 计	**Total**	**2642218**	**293850**	**285703**	**1241450**	**702406**
一、地 方	**Local Regions**	**2251924**	**183981**	**186426**	**1091239**	**636901**
乌鲁木齐市	Urumqi City	6470	389	6	5169	13
克拉玛依市	Karamay City					
吐鲁番地区	TurpanAdministrative Offices	614668	10	557	610812	569748
哈密地区	Hami Administrative Offices	56496	12	122	53619	49017
昌吉回族自治州	Changji Hui Autonomous Prefecture	117680	6938	1	105642	105
伊犁哈萨克自治州	Ili Kazak Autonomous Prefecture	116622	63774	2754	25253	
伊犁州直属县(市)	Counties (Cities) Direct Under Ili Prefecture	103572	57749	2160	19822	
塔城地区	Tacheng [Tarbagatai] Administrative Offices	12675	5812	594	5312	
阿勒泰地区	Altay Administrative Offices	375	213		119	
博尔塔拉蒙古自治州	Bortala MongolAutonomous Prefecture	4620	1262	3	3320	
巴音郭楞蒙古自治州	Bayangol Mongol Autonomous Prefecture	183711	8027	99987	22741	2213
阿克苏地区	Aksu Administrative Offices	364407	61278	62295	69192	60
克孜勒苏柯尔克孜自治州	Kizilsu Kirgiz Autonomous Prefecture	48293	643	334	31814	
喀什地区	Kashgar [Kaxgar] Administrative Offices	522495	31205	16931	56693	440
和田地区	Hotan Administrative Offices	216462	10443	3436	106984	15305
二、生产建设兵团	**Xinjiang Production & Construction Group**	**390294**	**109869**	**99277**	**150211**	**65505**

地 区	Region	桃 Peachs	杏 Apricots	红 枣 Jujubes	石 榴 Pomegranate	其 它 Other
总 计	**Total**	**49390**	**681883**	**15840**	**36088**	**38014**
一、地 方	**Local Regions**	**32630**	**675290**	**10683**	**36065**	**35610**
乌鲁木齐市	Urumqi City	520	257			129
克拉玛依市	Karamay City					
吐鲁番地区	TurpanAdministrative Offices	300	2116	763	102	8
哈密地区	Hami Administrative Offices	1	1392	1341		9
昌吉回族自治州	Changji Hui Autonomous Prefecture	2098	2616			385
伊犁哈萨克自治州	Ili Kazak Autonomous Prefecture	5670	11200	100		7871
伊犁州直属县(市)	Counties (Cities) Direct Under Ili Prefecture	5362	11180	100		7199
塔城地区	Tacheng [Tarbagatai] Administrative Offices	283	20			654
阿勒泰地区	Altay Administrative Offices	25				18
博尔塔拉蒙古自治州	Bortala MongolAutonomous Prefecture	16	9			10
巴音郭楞蒙古自治州	Bayangol Mongol Autonomous Prefecture	904	49115	1719		1218
阿克苏地区	Aksu Administrative Offices	1994	160728	2194	312	6414
克孜勒苏柯尔克孜自治州	Kizilsu Kirgiz Autonomous Prefecture	201	14201		500	600
喀什地区	Kashgar [Kaxgar] Administrative Offices	13409	355350	2772	29110	17025
和田地区	Hotan Administrative Offices	7517	78306	1794	6041	1941
二、生产建设兵团	**Xinjiang Production & Construction Group**	**16760**	**6593**	**5157**	**23**	**2404**

11-22 牲畜饲养情况
Number of Livestock

单位：万头(只) (10 000 heads)

年 份 Year	大牲畜年底头数 Large Animals (year-end)	牛 Cattle and Buffaloes	马 Horses	驴 Donkeys	骡 Mules	骆驼 Camels	役畜 Draught Animals
1978	446.19	222.39	112.39	96.61	1.61	13.19	148.34
1980	482.55	250.65	106.89	108.88	1.72	14.41	154.86
1985	517.55	293.26	99.54	106.57	2.17	16.05	197.29
1990	575.88	338.22	104.58	112.96	2.69	17.43	209.95
1991	572.18	336.32	102.78	112.85	2.68	17.55	211.95
1992	565.81	332.94	100.45	112.40	2.68	17.34	209.62
1993	563.76	331.62	99.68	112.75	2.65	17.06	214.02
1994	572.01	337.31	100.31	114.96	2.75	16.68	214.53
1995	580.04	343.54	100.47	117.04	2.77	16.22	213.61
1996	589.41	349.78	101.16	119.36	2.76	16.34	215.05
1997	600.12	359.81	100.32	120.74	2.87	16.38	207.15
1998	606.79	364.29	100.26	123.45	2.80	15.99	205.31
1999	615.91	370.52	101.47	124.99	2.78	16.15	189.86
2000	632.93	384.98	102.57	125.94	2.74	16.70	173.37
2001	630.67	386.40	99.38	126.06	2.84	15.99	172.08
2002	654.46	414.13	99.71	122.22	2.59	15.81	169.51
2003	694.53	453.06	99.39	124.02	2.48	15.58	163.72
2004	716.56	482.30	95.78	120.82	2.36	15.30	151.49

年 份 Year	猪年底头数 Hogs	羊年底只数 Sheep and Goats	山羊 Goats	绵羊 Sheep	牲畜出栏头数 Number of Animals for Sale within a Year	#猪 Pork Pig	#牛 Beef Cattle	#羊 Mutton Sheep
1978	103.25	1927.34	349.63	1577.91	460.41	50.75	18.75	382.76
1980	84.62	2105.43	388.89	1716.54	584.09	67.32	24.22	477.81
1985	66.58	2431.91	394.79	2037.12	836.39	49.07	42.33	723.51
1990	89.71	2830.81	449.43	2381.38	1242.89	78.93	70.10	1070.43
1991	91.17	2830.65	460.05	2370.6	1312.91	77.88	77.31	1130.97
1992	99.24	2830.36	458.69	2371.67	1396.03	84.31	81.93	1199.85
1993	108.13	2842.83	448.11	2394.72	1397.04	88.74	82.70	1194.80
1994	121.20	2905.80	458.64	2447.16	1534.34	101.34	90.25	1309.97
1995	135.26	3009.02	471.38	2537.64	1709.93	122.32	101.20	1448.72
1996	138.18	3136.21	498.10	2638.11	1859.28	153.75	116.25	1550.65
1997	145.73	3261.81	514.60	2747.21	2096.67	173.06	125.72	1753.88
1998	169.82	3447.38	528.05	2919.33	2222.27	197.39	140.82	1837.57
1999	188.34	3592.29	555.21	3037.08	2223.89	203.87	145.95	1820.71
2000	201.53	3690.21	586.70	3103.51	2455.99	224.46	154.53	2017.36
2001	208.23	3764.88	601.14	3163.74	2633.83	246.00	179.32	2147.31
2002	219.08	3908.23	626.42	3281.81	2878.39	259.05	188.65	2363.02
2003	227.71	4104.30	657.15	3447.15	3201.99	307.74	202.23	2626.94
2004	223.08	4266.73	669.47	3597.26	3437.59	352.83	220.80	2790.53

注：牲畜出栏数 1999 年以后计算口径与 1998 年以前不同。
Note: The calculating norm of cattles out of stock in the year 1999 was different from that prior to that in 1998.

11-23 各地、州、市、县(市)牲畜年底头数

Number of Livestock by Prefecture, Autonomous Prefecture, City and County

单位：万头(只) (2004 年) (10 000 heads)

地 区	Region	合 计 Total	#牛 Cattle and Buffaloes	#马 Horses	#驴 Donkeys	#猪 Hogs	#山羊 Goats	#绵羊 Sheep
总 计	**Total**	**5206.37**	**482.30**	**95.78**	**120.82**	**223.08**	**669.47**	**3597.26**
一、地 方	**Local Regions**	**4496.43**	**444.76**	**92.47**	**116.81**	**145.99**	**609.94**	**3069.45**
乌鲁木齐市	**Urumqi City**	**54.17**	**4.25**	**1.12**	**0.22**	**1.44**	**14.34**	**32.65**
乌鲁木齐县	Urumqi County	28.08	1.88	0.81	0.14	0.86	3.85	20.51
市直单位	Direct Under the Municipality	26.09	2.37	0.31	0.08	0.58	10.49	12.14
克拉玛依市	**Karamay City**	**9.31**	**0.59**	**0.05**		**3.49**	**1.70**	**3.48**
吐鲁番地区	**Turpan Administrative Offices**	**113.01**	**4.70**	**0.41**	**4.82**	**0.60**	**14.74**	**87.20**
吐鲁番市	Turpan City	37.40	0.85	0.05	1.59	0.16	7.28	27.37
鄯善县	Shanshan County	39.28	0.88	0.19	1.97	0.33	3.14	32.53
托克逊县	Toksun County	36.33	2.97	0.17	1.26	0.11	4.32	27.30
哈密地区	**Hami Administrative Offices**	**116.42**	**6.41**	**1.81**	**2.07**	**3.06**	**23.68**	**78.01**
哈密市	Hami City	42.79	2.07	0.61	0.83	0.70	8.08	29.81
巴里坤哈萨克自治县	Barkol KazakAutonomous County	54.83	3.30	0.82	1.07	2.06	10.53	36.57
伊吾县	Yiwu County	18.80	1.04	0.38	0.17	0.30	5.07	11.63
昌吉回族自治州	**Changji Hui Autonomous Prefecture**	**422.75**	**40.84**	**6.80**	**2.75**	**42.46**	**63.68**	**263.61**
昌吉市	Changji City	55.50	6.61	0.90	0.26	6.21	7.75	33.57
阜康市	Fukang City	36.91	3.13	0.56	0.09	2.32	8.71	21.86
米泉市	Miquan City	22.77	2.96	0.34	0.16	3.50	5.96	9.78
呼图壁县	Hutubi County	57.01	6.74	0.77	0.11	3.85	5.19	40.17
玛纳斯县	Manas County	48.16	3.37	0.56	0.08	5.71	5.53	32.71
奇台县	Qitai County	77.90	7.53	0.59	0.56	12.38	6.12	50.42
吉木萨尔县	Jimsar County	56.04	6.06	1.28	0.44	5.81	5.56	36.76
木垒哈萨克自治县	Mori Kazak Autonomous County	68.46	4.44	1.80	1.05	2.68	18.86	38.34
伊犁哈萨克自治州	**Ili Kazak Autonomous Prefecture**	**1465.50**	**179.91**	**60.43**	**5.12**	**54.44**	**171.16**	**987.02**
伊犁州直属县(市)	**Counties (Cities) Direct Under Ili Prefecture**	**633.14**	**92.96**	**36.22**	**4.24**	**20.75**	**25.83**	**452.51**
伊宁市	Yining City	25.87	6.44	0.72	0.89	1.06	0.86	15.87
奎屯市	Kuytun City	0.66	0.06	0.01		0.07	0.08	0.44
伊宁县	Yining County	81.38	12.11	3.18	1.46	2.21	5.98	56.31
察布查尔锡伯自治县	Qapqal Xibe Autonomous County	43.72	4.36	1.15	0.75	1.56	3.46	32.44
霍城县	Huocheng County	71.08	9.12	1.98	0.56	5.47	2.01	51.87
巩留县	Gongliu County	60.53	10.15	3.34	0.25	2.50	2.35	41.90
新源县	Xinyuan County	105.21	18.29	9.21	0.07	4.38	2.53	70.70
昭苏县	Zhaosu County	92.36	12.00	6.48	0.16	0.68	1.96	71.01
特克斯县	Tekes County	68.21	8.41	3.71	0.04	1.68	2.68	51.67
尼勒克县	Nilka County	84.12	12.02	6.44	0.06	1.14	3.92	60.30
塔城地区	**Tacheng [Tarbagatai] Administrative Offices**	**506.40**	**48.86**	**12.35**	**0.79**	**30.79**	**83.56**	**327.84**
塔城市	Tacheng [Qoqek] City	83.03	8.16	1.38	0.12	2.47	7.75	62.97
乌苏市	Usu City	81.55	5.31	1.85	0.50	12.45	12.23	48.68
额敏县	Emin [Dorbiljin] County	85.02	8.50	2.50	0.01	1.61	11.91	60.19
沙湾县	Shawan County	76.67	8.33	1.12	0.08	12.92	8.46	45.66
托里县	Toli County	67.14	7.28	2.01	0.05	0.22	18.29	38.80
裕民县	Yumin [Qagantokay] County	50.69	5.12	1.37		0.76	6.99	36.15
和布克赛尔蒙古自治县	Hoboksar Mongol Autonomous County	62.30	6.16	2.12	0.03	0.36	17.93	35.39
阿勒泰地区	**Altay Administrative Offices**	**325.96**	**38.09**	**11.86**	**0.09**	**2.90**	**61.77**	**206.67**
阿勒泰市	Altay City	61.34	8.22	2.71	0.03	0.31	7.27	41.85
布尔津县	Burqin County	38.51	6.13	1.37		0.20	4.79	25.76
富蕴县	Fuyun [Koktokay] County	76.00	6.27	2.35	0.05	0.74	15.00	50.32
福海县	Fuhai [Burultokay] County	45.63	3.94	1.00		0.90	6.51	32.60
哈巴河县	Habahe [Kaba] County	42.26	7.62	1.92		0.25	7.37	24.65
青河县	Qinghe [Qinggil] County	38.00	3.70	1.73		0.22	16.00	15.75
吉木乃县	Jeminay County	24.22	2.21	0.78	0.01	0.28	4.83	15.74

11-23 续表 Continued

单位：万头(只) (10 000 heads)

地　区	Region	合 计 Total	#牛 Cattle and Buffaloes	#马 Horses	#驴 Donkeys	#猪 Hogs	#山 羊 Goats	#绵 羊 Sheep
博尔塔拉蒙古自治州	**Bortala Mongol Autonomous Prefecture**	**134.08**	**12.53**	**2.01**	**0.44**	**3.73**	**11.84**	**103.17**
博乐市	Bole [Bortala] City	51.82	5.29	0.57	0.26	2.32	2.88	40.32
精河县	Jinghe [Jing] County	40.51	4.06	0.60	0.04	0.65	4.73	30.36
温泉县	Wenquan [Araxang] County	41.75	3.18	0.84	0.14	0.76	4.23	32.49
巴音郭楞蒙古自治州	**Bayangol Mongol Autonomous Prefecture**	**350.92**	**29.37**	**5.41**	**6.52**	**19.64**	**67.50**	**221.80**
库尔勒市	Korla City	38.12	5.08	0.14	0.31	6.10	4.26	22.21
轮台县	Luntai [Bugur] County	35.52	1.43	0.10	1.69	0.32	14.87	17.09
尉犁县	Yuli [Lopnur] County	34.58	1.68	0.22	0.94	0.47	17.77	13.48
若羌县	Ruoqiang [Qarkilik] County	12.73	0.85	0.13	0.72	0.65	2.53	7.75
且末县	Qiemo [Qarqan] County	35.10	1.84	0.22	1.74	1.07	8.32	21.73
焉耆回族自治县	Yanji Hui Autonomous County	34.24	4.67	0.12	0.25	1.88	2.61	24.70
和静县	Hejing County	112.49	10.34	4.13	0.61	4.84	10.03	82.38
和硕县	Hoxud County	25.61	1.63	0.17	0.07	1.02	5.39	17.18
博湖县	Bohu [Bagrax] County	22.53	1.85	0.18	0.19	3.29	1.72	15.28
阿克苏地区	**Aksu Administrative Offices**	**514.45**	**53.17**	**8.57**	**15.73**	**10.89**	**137.25**	**286.77**
阿克苏市	Aksu City	43.58	6.65	0.59	0.80	5.52	6.10	23.91
温宿县	Wensu [Onsu] County	65.20	6.65	1.79	0.90	0.62	16.27	38.89
库车县	Kuqa County	95.88	11.45	1.41	4.31	0.73	20.87	56.75
沙雅县	Xayar County	67.12	3.77	0.77	2.21	1.19	31.02	27.82
新和县	Xinhe [Toksu] County	33.32	4.01	0.66	1.60	0.09	3.83	22.98
拜城县	Baicheng [Bay] County	83.80	6.95	1.21	3.30	2.20	20.02	49.98
乌什县	Wushi [Uxturpan] County	56.88	7.61	1.82	1.70	0.14	18.89	26.42
阿瓦提县	Awat County	50.17	5.70	0.22	0.32	0.40	10.71	32.81
柯坪县	Kalpin County	18.50	0.38	0.10	0.59		9.54	7.21
克孜勒苏柯尔克孜自治州	**Kizilsu Kirgiz Autonomous Prefecture**	**158.66**	**17.10**	**2.19**	**4.44**	**0.05**	**35.74**	**98.39**
阿图什市	Artux City	44.00	4.63	0.35	1.00	0.02	10.28	27.58
阿克陶县	Akto County	60.29	9.45	0.33	2.86	0.03	9.56	37.88
阿合奇县	Akqi County	25.11	1.91	1.05	0.24		8.08	13.72
乌恰县	Wuqia [Ulugqat] County	29.26	1.11	0.46	0.34		7.82	19.21
喀什地区	**Kashgar [Kaxgar] Administrative Offices**	**730.85**	**75.26**	**2.09**	**43.40**	**5.05**	**42.64**	**562.00**
喀什市	Kashgar [Kaxgar] City	17.96	0.88	0.01	1.14	1.07	0.25	14.61
疏附县	Shufu County	104.59	9.22	0.10	4.57	0.46	3.64	86.52
疏勒县	Shule County	69.00	8.70	0.03	4.58	0.55	0.98	54.13
英吉沙县	Yengisar County	37.10	5.30	0.04	2.88	0.12	0.43	28.31
泽普县	Zepu [Poskam] County	35.66	4.87	0.18	2.14	1.02	1.36	26.07
莎车县	Shache [Yarkant] County	108.24	10.34	0.49	6.90	0.15	3.27	87.07
叶城县	Yecheng [Kagilik] County	111.42	10.57	0.41	6.08	0.69	5.83	87.72
麦盖提县	Makit County	56.10	6.92	0.11	2.27	0.22	4.05	42.52
岳普湖县	Yopurga County	28.46	4.27	0.06	4.84	0.07	2.40	16.82
伽师县	Jiashi [Payzawat] County	88.00	4.95	0.24	6.51	0.25	5.63	70.41
巴楚县	Bachu [Maralbexi] County	56.10	6.62	0.29	0.92	0.45	8.50	39.32
塔什库尔干塔吉克自治县	Taxkorgan Tajik Autonomous County	18.22	2.62	0.13	0.57		6.30	8.50
和田地区	**Hotan Administrative Offices**	**426.31**	**20.63**	**1.58**	**31.30**	**1.14**	**25.67**	**345.35**
和田市	Hotan City	13.15	1.31	0.04	0.98	0.54	0.21	10.07
和田县	Hotan County	75.12	4.54	0.21	5.40	0.08	2.57	62.23
墨玉县	Moyu [Karakax] County	93.76	4.78	0.32	6.76	0.07	1.59	80.22
皮山县	Pishan [Guma] County	45.53	1.60	0.14	3.35	0.06	2.54	37.74
洛浦县	Lop County	52.92	3.91	0.10	4.45	0.09	1.22	43.11
策勒县	Qira County	49.65	1.36	0.24	3.93	0.01	2.97	41.03
于田县	Yutian [Keriya] County	73.22	2.74	0.42	5.63	0.10	7.17	56.96
民丰县	Minfeng [Niya] County	22.96	0.39	0.11	0.80	0.19	7.40	13.99
二、生产建设兵团	**Xinjiang Production & Construction Group**	**709.94**	**37.54**	**3.31**	**4.01**	**77.09**	**59.53**	**527.81**

11-24 主要年份畜产品产量
Output of Livestock Products in Main Years

年份 Year	肉类产量(万吨) Output of meat (10 000 tons)	#牛 Beef	#马 Horse Meat	#骆驼 Camels	#猪 Pork	#羊 Mutton	禽兔肉(万吨) Poultry and Rabbit Meat (10 000 tons)
1978	9.65	1.85			2.48	5.32	
1980	12.70	2.20	0.60	0.05	3.29	6.48	
1985	18.37	4.23	0.86	0.15	3.09	9.97	
1990	30.46	7.08	1.18	0.18	4.93	15.75	1.22
1991	32.94	8.11	1.34	0.23	5.01	16.71	1.42
1992	36.02	8.71	1.57	0.28	5.46	18.08	1.78
1993	38.30	9.32	1.63	0.28	6.18	18.61	2.05
1994	42.81	10.03	1.67	0.33	6.89	20.77	2.91
1995	52.38	13.14	2.05	0.40	8.37	24.48	3.61
1996	60.31	15.18	2.24	0.38	10.43	26.93	4.82
1997	64.40	16.40	2.55	0.38	11.52	27.72	5.38
1998	75.19	19.19	2.82	0.47	13.60	32.49	6.16
1999	81.36	20.61	2.93	0.62	16.02	33.57	6.94
2000	90.00	22.24	3.57	0.63	17.18	37.50	7.76
2001	97.00	23.99	3.55	0.72	18.36	40.48	8.66
2002	105.44	25.90	3.65	0.68	19.70	43.06	10.38
2003	115.00	28.77	3.88	0.69	22.41	45.54	11.46
2004	128.13	30.42	4.34	0.70	24.58	52.65	13.27

年份 Year	羊毛(万吨) Wool (10 000 tons)	#绵羊毛 Sheep Wool	山羊绒(吨) Cashmere (ton)	驼毛(吨) Camel Hair (ton)	牛奶(万吨) Cow Milk (10 000 tons)	羊奶(万吨) Sheep Milk (10 000 tons)	牛皮(万张) Oxhide (10 000 sheets)	羊皮(万张) Sheep Skin (10 000 sheets)	禽蛋(万吨) Poultry Eggs (10 000 tons)
1978	3.08	3.00	324	371	4.50	0.75	17.36	300.05	
1980	3.31	3.21	263	353	5.84	1.44	18.22	338.32	
1985	7.07	3.91	325	530	16.43	3.27	35.72	587.69	4.29
1990	5.09	4.93	607	656	30.81	4.83	56.76	839.69	6.30
1991	5.19	4.96	632	655	33.66	3.83	59.80	864.48	6.71
1992	5.20	5.00	750	747	35.97	3.82	64.66	924.64	7.63
1993	5.28	5.08	642	678	37.03	3.82	68.85	916.55	7.22
1994	5.46	5.24	684	685	40.75	4.08	74.51	1060.64	8.43
1995	5.66	5.45	716	716	45.21	4.60	91.54	1125.72	9.51
1996	5.99	5.77	780	787	48.76	5.46	92.31	1178.39	10.33
1997	6.25	6.01	813	742	54.18	4.60	96.88	1326.69	12.16
1998	6.48	6.22	811	768	59.96	5.06	110.12	1391.77	13.34
1999	6.76	6.50	849	727	64.81	5.62	118.35	1569.50	16.68
2000	6.98	6.67	893	757	72.54	5.69	125.62	1686.03	18.53
2001	7.30	6.99	973	736	81.09	6.76	143.13	1689.24	20.37
2002	7.78	7.44	1034	824	94.87	5.84	139.87	1801.67	22.64
2003	8.21	7.84	1143	793	113.00	6.21	141.57	1692.35	23.62
2004	8.91	8.49	1228	770	133.32	6.41	150.15	1981.82	24.99

11-25 各地、州、市、县(市)总产肉量

Total Output of Meat by Prefecture, Autonomous Prefecture, City and County

单位：吨　　　　(2004 年)　　　　(ton)

地　区	Region	合 计 Total	#牛 Beef	#马 Horse	#骆 驼 Donkeys	#猪 Pork	#山 羊 Goats	#绵 羊 Sheep	#禽 肉 Poultry Meat	#兔肉 Rabbit Meat
总　计	**Total**	**1281300**	**304200**	**43419**	**7026**	**245800**	**73411**	**453089**	**129400**	**3284**
一、地 方	**Local Regions**	**1160583**	**302921**	**42131**	**6882**	**173997**	**64793**	**445318**	**103868**	**1349**
乌鲁木齐市	**Urumqi City**	**17599**	**3899**	**888**	**90**	**2497**	**1569**	**6609**	**1983**	**6**
乌鲁木齐县	Urumqi County	8955	2008	618	25	1256	400	3404	1213	3
市直单位	Direct Under the Municipality	8644	1891	270	65	1241	1169	3204	770	3
克拉玛依市	**Karamay City**	**3817**	**168**	**30**	**18**	**2821**	**86**	**481**	**206**	**7**
吐鲁番地区	**Turpan Administrative Offices**	**40759**	**10893**	**96**	**97**	**493**	**3821**	**24164**	**1086**	**44**
吐鲁番市	Turpan City	22450	4674	6	2	90	2740	14833	40	
鄯善县	Shanshan County	9962	1701	60	75	343	551	6468	740	24
托克逊县	Toksun County	8347	4518	30	20	60	530	2863	306	20
哈密地区	**Hami Administrative Offices**	**25157**	**4977**	**862**	**534**	**3880**	**2965**	**9862**	**1009**	**43**
哈密市	Hami City	12410	2535	230	165	1128	1587	5555	654	40
巴里坤哈萨克自治县	Barkol KazakAutonomous County	9946	2012	442	216	2400	1036	3144	280	3
伊吾县	Yiwu County	2801	430	190	153	352	342	1163	75	
昌吉回族自治州	**Changji Hui Autonomous Prefecture**	**212875**	**41193**	**3210**	**1276**	**58311**	**10029**	**52986**	**43630**	**438**
昌吉市	Changji City	35503	9041	481	39	8352	1562	9830	5674	160
阜康市	Fukang City	18635	3195	290	90	3195	1338	5239	5204	56
米泉市	Miquan City	28004	6670	23	25	7716	990	3297	9201	30
呼图壁县	Hutubi County	23008	5904	361	128	5142	595	6703	4112	35
玛纳斯县	Manas County	25913	2926	351	64	9096	1062	6052	6288	36
奇台县	Qitai County	38132	6240	287	126	15160	750	9430	5790	20
吉木萨尔县	Jimsar County	18924	4143	482	43	4409	1168	3423	4960	42
木垒哈萨克自治县	Mori Kazak Autonomous County	24756	3074	935	761	5241	2564	9012	2401	59
伊犁哈萨克自治州	**Ili Kazak Autonomous Prefecture**	**347716**	**108557**	**29060**	**3234**	**55010**	**18519**	**113465**	**18580**	**248**
伊犁州直属县(市)	**Counties (Cities) Direct Under Ili Prefecture**	**157241**	**60444**	**16538**	**224**	**18125**	**2596**	**49338**	**9016**	**165**
伊宁市	Yining City	10282	5935	529	14	634	112	2345	474	
奎屯市	Kuytun City	126	6	1		52	16	35	16	
伊宁县	Yining County	27209	12984	1862	32	1832	581	7959	1725	
察布查尔锡伯自治县	Qapqal Xibe Autonomous County	9710	2803	637		1448	318	3631	708	7
霍城县	Huocheng County	21311	5889	1365		5075	362	5832	2600	118
巩留县	Gongliu County	17734	7965	2000	15	2378	195	4468	663	
新源县	Xinyuan County	24750	8203	3600	15	4267	219	7412	1007	13
昭苏县	Zhaosu County	15288	6263	1992	13	420	136	6276	158	
特克斯县	Tekes County	12161	3847	1600		1147	252	4676	634	5
尼勒克县	Nilka County	18670	6549	2952	135	872	405	6704	1031	22

11-25 续表 1 Continued

单位：吨 (ton)

地 区	Region	合 计 Total	#牛 Beef	#马 Horse	#骆 驼 Donk-eys	#猪 Pork	#山 羊 Goats	#绵 羊 Sheep	#禽 肉 Poultry Meat	#兔 肉 Rabbit Meat
塔城地区	**Tacheng [Tarbagatai] Administrative Officess**	**113462**	**25069**	**7233**	**1240**	**27347**	**9270**	**34298**	**8730**	**44**
塔城市	Tacheng [Qoqek] City	12445	3215	702	31	1865	763	5267	554	1
乌苏市	Usu City	20007	2384	688	144	7323	1982	6136	1259	15
额敏县	Emin [Dorbiljin] County	25228	5190	2976	504	7284	1663	6604	998	
沙湾县	Shawan County	31863	6942	764	60	9880	1572	7028	5508	28
托里县	Toli County	9487	1968	838	233	103	1837	4473	29	
裕民县	Yumin [Qagantokay] County	6976	2430	705	160	420	398	2562	301	
和布克赛尔蒙古自治县	Hoboksar Mongol Autonomous County	7456	2940	560	108	472	1055	2228	81	
阿勒泰地区	**Altay Administrative Offices**	**77014**	**23044**	**5289**	**1770**	**9538**	**6653**	**29829**	**834**	**40**
阿勒泰市	Altay City	13343	4990	676	456	608	663	5842	90	5
布尔津县	Burqin County	10175	2916	938	203	1035	578	4252	253	
富蕴县	Fuyun [Koktokay] County	16244	3952	804	380	2272	1404	7354	57	17
福海县	Fuhai [Burultokay] County	11885	2619	361	347	2857	871	4627	189	14
哈巴河县	Habahe [Kaba] County	13234	4876	1537	96	2176	1113	3285	150	
青河县	Qinghe [Qinggil] County	7292	2655	493	180	270	1540	2098	53	3
吉木乃县	Jeminay County	4841	1036	480	108	320	484	2371	42	
博尔塔拉蒙古自治州	**Bortala Mongol Autonomous Prefecture**	**25692**	**6125**	**794**	**85**	**5373**	**879**	**10390**	**1894**	**40**
博乐市	Bole [Bortala] City	11423	2398	263	52	2126	226	5341	978	1
精河县	Jinghe [Jing] County	7208	2510	144	13	1153	347	2229	769	36
温泉县	Wenquan [Araxang] County	7061	1217	387	20	2094	306	2820	147	3
巴音郭楞蒙古自治州	**Bayangol Mongol Autonomous Prefecture**	**92762**	**20564**	**1335**	**136**	**27600**	**6322**	**27205**	**7710**	**136**
库尔勒市	Korla City	26350	7249	150		7079	740	5401	5350	35
轮台县	Luntai [Bugur] County	6625	894			533	1504	3370	252	25
尉犁县	Yuli [Lopnur] County	6168	2045	58		492	1405	1522	360	13
若羌县	Ruoqiang [Qarkilik] County	2027	459	44	43	300	172	569	232	11
且末县	Qiemo [Qarqan] County	7160	1206	130	50	782	1108	3304	95	30
焉耆回族自治县	Yanji Hui Autonomous County	12512	3750	3		3936	352	3608	655	4
和静县	Hejing County	24896	3864	888	30	11766	623	7350	162	3
和硕县	Hoxud County	3723	563	27	12	1189	341	1184	396	
博湖县	Bohu [Bagrax] County	3301	534	35	1	1523	77	897	208	15
阿克苏地区	**Aksu Administrative Offices**	**109550**	**36318**	**2967**	**683**	**9808**	**11072**	**41773**	**2058**	**13**
阿克苏市	Aksu City	22733	6023	216		5942	1404	6519	569	
温宿县	Wensu [Onsu] County	10615	3584	544	26	488	1396	4270	140	11
库车县	Kuqa County	27620	11030	768		994	1185	12935	708	

11-25 续表 2 Continued

单位：吨 (ton)

地　区	Region	合 计 Total	#牛 Beef	#马 Horse	#骆 驼 Donkeys	#猪 Pork	#山 羊 Goats	#绵 羊 Sheep	#禽 肉 Poultry Meat	#兔 肉 Rabbit Meat
沙雅县	Xayar County	9383	2779			510	2334	3102	241	
新和县	Xinhe [Toksu] County	5465	1806	257		54	340	2858	150	
拜城县	Baicheng [Bay] County	13100	4250	550	90	1280	1400	4600	80	
乌什县	Wushi [Uxturpan] County	9236	3838	580	176	135	1186	2610	92	
阿瓦提县	Awat County	8798	2865	41		405	957	3804	78	2
柯坪县	Kalpin County	2600	143	11	391		870	1075		
克孜勒苏柯尔克孜自治州	**Kizilsu Kirgiz Autonomous Prefecture**	**23984**	**8526**	**1392**	**457**	**24**	**2706**	**10543**	**333**	**3**
阿图什市	Artux City	7888	3124	84	65	16	826	3703	70	
阿克陶县	Akto County	8352	3433	146	51	8	715	3838	158	3
阿合奇县	Akqi County	3827	1132	770	80		625	1148	72	
乌恰县	Wuqia [Ulugqat] County	3917	837	392	261		540	1854	33	
喀什地区	**Kashgar [Kaxgar] Administrative Offices**	**211752**	**54161**	**1263**	**131**	**7789**	**5141**	**111340**	**23487**	**317**
喀什市	Kashgar [Kaxgar] City	11205	2065			504	11	8174	346	
疏附县	Shufu County	27103	8504	32	26	352	635	15748	1279	6
疏勒县	Shule County	19192	2900	30	35	2192	100	9400	3500	85
英吉沙县	Yengisar County	12500	6227	14	15	40	65	5154	535	
泽普县	Zepu [Poskam] County	12700	2822	30		2826	87	3928	2830	12
莎车县	Shache [Yarkant] County	32304	6090	456	7	136	486	20134	4600	45
叶城县	Yecheng [Kagilik] County	31353	7790	120	48	655	868	15047	5954	110
麦盖提县	Makit County	13209	3050	6		108	167	8810	1060	
岳普湖县	Yopurga County	7150	2478	12		64	290	4020	268	18
伽师县	Jiashi [Payzawat] County	22960	4400	225		80	664	12519	675	
巴楚县	Bachu [Maralbexi] County	18200	6069	160		832	1125	7117	2440	41
塔什库尔干塔吉克自治县	Taxkorgan Tajik Autonomous County	3876	1766	178			643	1289		
和田地区	**Hotan Administrative Offices**	**48920**	**7540**	**234**	**140**	**390**	**1684**	**36501**	**1894**	**54**
和田市	Hotan City	3806	1030	9		235	12	2259	261	0
和田县	Hotan County	6814	1120	27		15	140	5282	225	6
墨玉县	Moyu [Karakax] County	11458	1710	36		15	111	9180	395	11
皮山县	Pishan [Guma] County	4216	340	18	14	15	191	3498	131	9
洛浦县	Lop County	6511	1800	27		35	97	4419	132	1
策勒县	Qira County	5182	480	36	14	5	201	4305	135	6
于田县	Yutian [Keriya] County	8886	910	63	84	45	479	6260	546	18
民丰县	Minfeng [Niya] County	2047	150	18	28	25	453	1299	70	4
二、生产建设兵团	**Xinjiang Production & Construction Group**	**200092**	**21284**	**1288**	**144**	**81077**	**7838**	**62949**	**22522**	**1935**

注:全区总产肉量不等于各地州市汇总数。
Note: The total output of meat in the whole region does not equal to the total number gathered by different administrative offices, autonomous prefectures and cities.

11-26 水产品产量和养殖面积

Output of Aquatic Products and Cultured Area

年 份 地 区 Year Region		水产品产量（吨） Aquatic Products (ton)	养殖产量（吨） Cultured Output (ton)	养殖面积（公顷） Culture Area (hectare)
	1985	8958	3403	32775
	1986	11312	6473	34093
	1987	13485	7559	75199
	1988	18549	10930	79143
	1989	20549	12956	80600
	1990	23217	15401	68838
	1991	25200	17700	57117
	1992	26593	19733	60389
	1993	28831	22216	68519
	1994	35297	27766	68314
	1995	44432	35341	72538
	1996	47890	38876	79006
	1997	52366	42656	75895
	1998	53391	44557	67473
	1999	55840	48068	70524
	2000	60065	50874	69806
	2001	60876	50902	63340
	2002	63906	55159	62629
	2003	67278	57244	67374
	2004	73296	60405	74996
一、地 方	**Local Regions**	**55656**	**44250**	**43155**
乌鲁木齐市	Urumqi City	3152	3054	3151
克拉玛依市	Karamay City	550	277	36
吐鲁番地区	Turpan Administrative Offices	290	290	330
哈密地区	Hami [Kumul] Administrative Offices	793	743	850
昌吉回族自治州	Changji Hui Autonomous Prefecture	12601	12601	3042
伊犁哈萨克自治州	Ili Kazak Autonomous Prefecture	16904	13316	14377
伊犁州直属县(市)	Counties (Cities) Direct Under Ili Prefecture	8698	8583	1004
塔城地区	Tacheng [Tarbagatai] Administrative Offices	2968	2903	1804
阿勒泰地区	Altay Administrative Offices	5238	1830	11569
博尔塔拉蒙古自治州	Bortala Mongol Autonomous Prefecture	772	772	31
巴音郭楞蒙古自治州	Bayangol Mongol Autonomous Prefecture	8551	2263	3368
阿克苏地区	Aksu Administrative Offices	5719	4610	2727
克孜勒苏柯尔克孜自治州	Kizilsu Kirgiz Autonomous Prefecture	160	160	306
喀什地区	Kashgar [Kaxgar] Administrative Offices	5182	5182	11364
和田地区	Hotan Administrative Offices	982	982	3573
二、生产建设兵团	**Xinjiang Production & Construction Group**	**17640**	**16155**	**31841**

11-27 受灾面积情况

Areas Covered by Natural Disaster

单位：公顷 (hectares)

年 份 Year	地 区 Region	受灾面积总数 Areas Covered	#水 灾 Flood	#旱 灾 Drought
	1990	282787	16900	87040
	1991	530933	30733	256000
	1992	511067	35333	72067
	1993	378833	63538	55778
	1994	568782	54413	139366
	1995	665580	49812	210422
	1996	558297	114905	83547
	1997	372060	20200	165400
	1998	535900	74990	22340
	1999	1290799	145633	36696
	2000	932545	49219	461136
	2001	740888	82242	151703
	2002	493400	128345	16634
	2003	440982	80231	21291
	2004	524402	35562	368935
乌鲁木齐市	Urumqi City	23		23
克拉玛依市	Karamay City	275		
石河子市	Shihezi city	1025		
吐鲁番地区	Turpan Administrative Offices	18992	2459	
哈密地区	Hami [Kumul] Administrative Offices	26036		25569
昌吉回族自治州	Changji Hui Autonomous Prefecture	79454	6435	70933
伊犁哈萨克自治州	Ili Kazak Autonomous Prefecture	39877	10320	11349
伊犁州直属县(市)	Counties (Cities) Direct Under Ili Prefecture	11633	2813	
塔城地区	Tacheng [Tarbagatai] Administrative Offices	22132	1395	11349
阿勒泰地区	Altay Administrative Offices	6112	6112	
博尔塔拉蒙古自治州	Bortala Mongol Autonomous Prefecture	12300	5167	7133
巴音郭楞蒙古自治州	Bayangol Mongol Autonomous Prefecture	261736	4145	253101
阿克苏地区	Aksu Administrative Offices	31420	541	
克孜勒苏柯尔克孜自治州	Kizilsu Kirgiz Autonomous Prefecture	2078	1716	135
喀什地区	Kashgar [Kaxgar] Administrative Offices	31694	328	393
和田地区	Hotan Administrative Offices	19492	4451	299

11-28 乡镇企业主要指标

Main Indicators of Township Enterprises

单位：万元 (10 000 yuan)

年 份 Year	地 区 Region	企业个数 (个) Enterprise (unit)	企业人数 (人) Employees of Enterprise (person)	总产值 (万元) Total Output Value (10 000 yuan)	#工业产值 Industrial Output Value
	1985	98826	367753	75179	31389
	1990	144281	464027	222218	73125
	1991	145762	472332	314765	178113
	1992	155711	498132	402139	214462
	1993	202274	600687	553616	285276
	1994	250037	686425	924082	465446
	1995	281130	745291	1319217	639617
	1996	282733	781784	1622442	796908
	1997	43548	355585	1219032	793959
	1998	269048	712490	2457410	1112091
	1999	297147	749205	2736766	1239596
	2000	316524	806368	3022076	1352454
	2001	334694	824499	3316049	1479954
	2002	307963	866661	3629499	1591886
	2003	354640	880874	4119555	1883101
	2004	368553	933473	4562898	2211905
乌鲁木齐市	Urumqi City	20054	57674	381676	159919
克拉玛依市	Karamay City	119	1435	6110	1315
石河子市	Shihezi City	2179	7322	34804	17334
吐鲁番地区	Turpan Administrative Offices	23838	42798	131610	61668
哈密地区	Hami [Kumul] Administrative Offices	9864	22510	69816	28706
昌吉回族自治州	Changji Hui Autonomous Prefecture	48399	127846	1211633	778278
伊犁州直属县(市)	Counties (Cities) Direct Under Ili Prefecture	50586	120694	779436	301836
塔城地区	Tacheng [Tarbagatai] Administrative Offices	24346	66434	533429	334228
阿勒泰地区	Altay Administrative Offices	21764	46883	207209	70275
博尔塔拉蒙古自治州	Bortala Mongol Autonomous Prefecture	7435	22937	141021	75851
巴音郭楞蒙古自治州	Bayangol Mongol Autonomous Prefecture	22318	65026	474216	163414
阿克苏地区	Aksu Administrative Offices	34208	93287	199190	85443
克孜勒苏柯尔克孜自治州	Kizilsu Kirgiz Autonomous Prefecture	12304	24119	21894	6485
喀什地区	Kashgar [Kaxgar] Administrative Offices	50631	133121	233301	86203
和田地区	Hotan Administrative Offices	40508	101387	137553	40950

11-28 续表 Continued

单位：万元 (10 000 yuan)

年 份 Year	地 区 Region	营业收入 Business Income	税后净利润 Post-tax Net Profit	国家税金 National Tax	增加值 Added Value
	1985	105072	9357	3136	
	1990	249906	8614	5206	
	1991	299890	25974	13747	
	1992	374810	34644	16976	
	1993	584089	51880	27354	
	1994	957701	75439	69494	
	1995	1493924	110656	76479	
	1996	1927425	136410	76479	
	1997	1128271	43337	48945	
	1998	2455629	156578	82365	
	1999	2742029	164949	93490	
	2000	3071497	191764	100444	745728
	2001	3377589	211439	108864	807174
	2002	3739524	225723	126732	904892
	2003	4276322	264661	137880	1024772
	2004	4757808	304998	152243	1153561
乌鲁木齐市	Urumqi City	388375	32431	15751	71438
克拉玛依市	Karamay City	5792	386	272	1866
石河子市	Shihezi City	48647	2577	907	8701
吐鲁番地区	Turpan Administrative Offices	144344	13892	5736	38709
哈密地区	Hami [Kumul] Administrative Offices	71603	5433	2498	20059
昌吉回族自治州	Changji Hui Autonomous Prefecture	1314604	77925	45511	333441
伊犁州直属县(市)	Counties (Cities) Direct Under Ili Prefecture	877511	43831	17884	189301
塔城地区	Tacheng [Tarbagatai] Administrative Offices	485741	35660	13561	124180
阿勒泰地区	Altay Administrative Offices	232026	12586	5332	50948
博尔塔拉蒙古自治州	Bortala Mongol Autonomous Prefecture	140755	5062	4742	32708
巴音郭楞蒙古自治州	Bayangol Mongol Autonomous Prefecture	470171	28448	17735	111547
阿克苏地区	Aksu Administrative Offices	197132	13201	6963	59734
克孜勒苏柯尔克孜自治州	Kizilsu Kirgiz Autonomous Prefecture	23075	2168	1057	7913
喀什地区	Kashgar [Kaxgar] Administrative Offices	221962	23112	8783	67010
和田地区	Hotan Administrative Offices	136070	8286	5511	36006

11-29 乡镇企业单位数

Number of Township Enterprises

单位：个 (unit)

年份 Year	地区 Region	合计 Tatal	# 乡办 Township-run	农业 Agricul-ture	工业 Industry	建筑业 Building	交通运输业 Traffic and Transport-ation	商业饮食服务业 Commer-cial and Catering Service
1985		98826	4496	1426	30847	1064	736	1230
1990		144281	4383	1076	32050	4336	70793	66026
1991		145762	4349	1245	31597	3581	42822	66517
1992		155711	4263	1323	35704	4669	45758	68257
1993		202274	4789	1515	47198	6221	60220	87120
1994		250037	4893	2432	52170	6254	70615	118566
1995		281130	4793	1861	52339	7844	79712	139374
1996		282733	4415	1594	55269	7514	81312	126212
1997		43548	5798	1166	11924	2339	7404	19837
1998		269048	5043	1053	50172	5359	71930	130955
1999		297147	4656	1112	52614	5572	79949	157900
2000		316524	4133	994	57501	5868	82507	156605
2001		334694	3625	1557	56780	6205	86575	183577
2002		351963	2801	10142	55727	5391	87141	193562
2003		354640	2158	12745	54818	5746	84934	196397
2004		368553	1761	12366	53492	6143	85698	210854
乌鲁木齐市	Urumqi City	20054	102	7	1116	110	3631	15190
克拉玛依市	Karamay City	119	7	9	11	11	49	39
石河子市	Shihezi City	2179	2	26	180	4	257	1712
吐鲁番地区	Turpan Administrative Offices	23838	69	4	1894	204	8713	13023
哈密地区	Hami [Kumul] Administrative Offices	9864	20	164	520	185	4988	4007
昌吉回族自治州	Changji Hui Autonomous Prefecture	48399	107	28	4827	579	15226	27739
伊犁州直属县(市)	Counties (Cities) Direct Under Ili Prefecture	50586	98	741	6740	944	14743	27418
塔城地区	Tacheng [Tarbagatai] Administrative Offices	24346	47	3072	2757	80	5190	13247
阿勒泰地区	Altay Administrative Offices	21764	57	36	3332	387	7257	10752
博尔塔拉蒙古自治州	Bortala Mongol Autonomous Prefecture	7435	25	29	1297	81	1676	4352
巴音郭楞蒙古自治州	Bayangol Mongol Autonomous Prefecture	22318	37	365	2039	92	4505	15317
阿克苏地区	Aksu Administrative Offices	34208	160	960	5080	548	7012	20608
克孜勒苏柯尔克孜自治州	Kizilsu Kirgiz Autonomous Prefecture	12304	85	14	2894	31	2401	6964
喀什地区	Kashgar [Kaxgar] Administrative Offices	50631	840	5927	7508	1721	6771	28704
和田地区	Hotan Administrative Offices	40508	105	984	13297	1166	3279	21782

11-30 乡镇企业职工人数
Employment in Township Enterprises

单位：人 (person)

年 份 Year	地 区 Region	合 计 Tatal	# 乡办 Township-run	农 业 Agricul-ture	工 业 Industry	建筑业 Building	交 通 运输业 Traffic and Transport-ation	商业饮食 服 务 业 Commer-cial and Catering Service
1985		367753	136869	20689	140301	71200	4828	11553
1990		464027	151240	12722	187441	70905	56779	136180
1991		472332	154191	13469	194962	74193	57688	132020
1992		498132	160984	13580	202914	78678	60016	142944
1993		600687	177797	14768	235053	90167	79423	181276
1994		686425	181993	18149	261828	94893	91905	219650
1995		745291	187277	22023	264030	99598	104259	255381
1996		781784	188135	20018	284083	98214	106499	247310
1997		355585	206712	20223	176847	62830	17016	72777
1998		712490	191148	20127	252639	79703	94792	245987
1999		749205	169677	17169	262187	75185	104113	29055
2000		806368	155304	18670	271976	72606	109000	302649
2001		824499	139757	23662	264818	75161	111013	349845
2002		866661	85195	43567	264717	67743	113547	367087
2003		880874	68993	49853	270680	72806	114203	373332
2004		933473	48674	45356	275201	74305	117454	421157
乌鲁木齐市	Urumqi City	57674	3773	100	16840	2295	4599	33840
克拉玛依市	Karamay City	1435	274	390	326	398	250	71
石河子市	Shihezi City	7322	203	64	2935	183	852	3288
吐鲁番地区	Turpan Administrative Offices	42798	2965	29	11760	660	8973	21376
哈密地区	Hami [Kumul] Administrative Offics	22510	1397	857	4389	1839	7135	8290
昌吉回族自治州	Changji Hui Autonomous Prefecture	127846	7038	1160	45428	6775	18921	55562
伊犁州直属县(市)	Counties (Cities) Direct Under Ili Prefecture	120694	4122	2287	39620	10810	18152	49825
塔城地区	Tacheng [Tarbagatai] Administrative Offices	66434	2959	9560	18972	2269	7521	28112
阿勒泰地区	Altay Administrative Offices	46883	1637	406	13321	6593	9069	17494
博尔塔拉蒙古自治州	Bortala Mongol Autonomous Prefecture	22937	1195	527	8927	2759	2613	8111
巴音郭楞蒙古自治州	Bayangol Mongol Autonomous Prefecture	65026	895	1097	19439	11124	6321	27045
阿克苏地区	Aksu Administrative Offices	93287	5313	7566	19914	8084	12091	45632
克孜勒苏柯尔克孜自治州	Kizilsu Kirgiz Autonomous Prefecture	24119	1413	320	7857	258	2757	12927
喀什地区	Kashgar [Kaxgar] Administrative Offices	133121	12884	17803	30827	11453	12841	60197
和田地区	Hotan Administrative Offices	101387	2606	3190	34646	8805	5359	49387

11-31 乡镇企业总产值

Total Output Value of Township Enterprises

单位：万元 (10 000 yuan)

年份 Year	地区 Region	合计 Total	# 乡办 Township-run	农业 Agriculture	工业 Industry	建筑业 Building	交通运输业 Traffic and Transportation	商业饮食服务业 Commercial and Catering Service
1985		109559	56215	3638	44647	33302	2753	3124
1990		253149	128918	4044	127841	47568	34417	39279
1991		300704	167380	4384	164741	58071	32601	40907
1992		393289	219602	6428	205395	90508	40806	50152
1993		582345	298868	8830	308924	126902	67289	70400
1994		1054688	475066	15783	569628	172561	121761	174955
1995		1649049	662986	23050	841315	240317	224709	319658
1996		2118572	695582	34357	1017275	295262	336898	434780
1997		1219032	827003	280861	793959	210003		175853
1998		2457410	813033	30061	1112091	287278	381719	605770
1999		2736766	803554	29797	1239596	299723	421120	746530
2000		3022076	849462	32475	352454	310890	438741	821747
2001		3316049	876772	36418	1479954	361297	450634	987746
2002		3629499	452871	76770	1591886	392515	470855	1097473
2003		4119555	416400	110199	1883101	470894	492814	1162547
2004		4562898	267391	139119	2211905	478330	516511	1217033
乌鲁木齐市	Urumqi City	381676	46549	1793	159919	10354	33430	176180
克拉玛依市	Karamay City	6110	1119	1980	1315	1059	1518	238
石河子市	Shihezi City	34804	1006	324	17334	1061	3809	12276
吐鲁番地区	Turpan Administrative Offices	131610	12494	683	61668	4328	20246	44685
哈密地区	Hami [Kumul] Administrative Offices	69816	6015	1717	28706	9811	14801	14781
昌吉回族自治州	Changji Hui Autonomous Prefecture	1211633	50718	26536	778278	46592	144450	215777
伊犁州直属县(市)	Counties (Cities) Direct Under Ili Prefecture	779436	20835	12968	301836	44684	103407	316541
塔城地区	Tacheng [Tarbagatai] Administrative Offices	533429	53385	29839	334228	16421	58137	94804
阿勒泰地区	Altay Administrative Offices	207209	5391	1633	70275	33057	46006	56238
博尔塔拉蒙古自治州	Bortala Mongol Autonomous Prefecture	141021	6466	6015	75851	10343	20020	28792
巴音郭楞蒙古自治州	Bayangol Mongol Autonomous Prefecture	474216	4884	3539	163414	238864	17226	51173
阿克苏地区	Aksu Administrative Offices	199190	16269	27127	85443	20686	17796	48138
克孜勒苏柯尔克孜自治州	Kizilsu Kirgiz Autonomous Prefecture	21894	1509	162	6485	134	2854	12259
喀什地区	Kashgar [Kaxgar] Administrative Offices	233301	37169	18374	86203	15419	20517	92788
和田地区	Hotan Administrative Offices	137553	3582	6429	40950	25517	12294	52363

主要统计指标解释

农林牧渔业总产值 指以货币形式表现的农、林、牧、渔业全部产品的总量，它反映一定时期内农业生产总规模和总成果。农林牧渔业总产值的计算方法通常是按农、林、牧、渔业产品及其副产品的产量分别乘以各自单位产品价格求得;少数生产周期较长，当年没有产品或产品产量不易统计的，则采用间接方法匡算其产值；然后将四业产品产值相加即为农林牧渔业总产值。1957年以前的农林牧渔业总产值中包括了厩肥和农民自给性手工业(如农民自制衣服、鞋、袜，自己从事粮食初步加工等)。1958年及以后，林业中增加了村及村以下竹木采伐产值；牧业中取消了厩肥产值；副业中取消了农民自给性手工业产值，增加了村及村以下办的工业产值;渔业中增加了海洋捕捞水产品产值。1980 年及以后，在副业中增加了农民家庭兼营工业商品部分的产值。从1984年起村及村以下工业产值划归工业。从1993年起取消副业，将野生动物的捕猎划入牧业、野生植物采集和农民家庭兼营商品性工业划归农业。1996 年第一次农业普查以后，由于畜牧业产品年报数据与普查数据之间存在一定的差距，国家统计局对畜牧业年报数据与普查数据进行衔接，相应的畜牧业产值进行调整。

粮食产量 指稻谷、小麦、玉米、高粱等谷物及薯类和豆类的全社会产量。包括国有经济经营的、集体统一经营的和农民家庭经营的粮食产量，还包括工矿企业办的农场和其他生产单位的产量。其产量计算方法，豆类按去豆荚后的干豆计算；薯类(包括甘薯和马铃薯，不包括芋头和木薯)1963年以前按每4 公斤鲜薯折1 公斤粮食计算，从1964年开始改为按5 公斤鲜薯折1 公斤粮食计算。城市郊区作为蔬菜的薯类(如马铃薯等)按鲜品计算，并且不作粮食统计。其他粮食一律按脱粒后的原粮计算。1989年以前全国粮食产量数据的取得主要是靠全面报表取得，1989年以后开始使用抽样调查数据。

棉花产量 指春播棉和夏播棉的全社会产量。产量按皮棉计算。3 公斤籽棉折1 公斤皮棉，不包括木棉。

油料产量 指全部油料作物的生产量。包括花生、油菜籽、芝麻、向日葵籽、胡麻籽(亚麻籽)和其他油料。不包括大豆、木本油料和野生油料。花生以带壳干花生计算。

水产品产量 指人工养殖的水产品和天然生长的水产品的捕捞量。包括海水的鱼类、虾蟹类、贝类和藻类以及内陆水域的鱼类、虾蟹类和贝类，不包括淡水生植物。水产品产量是通过各级水产和统计部门逐级上报取得数据。1995年及以前，贝类中牡蛎按鲜肉计算；蚶、蛤、蛏按 5 斤鲜品折 1 斤计算。1996 年以后则统一按鲜品计算。

猪、牛、羊肉产量 指当年出栏并已屠宰、除去头蹄下水后带骨肉(即胴体重) 的重量。其统计范围为全社会。1996年前为各级逐级上报数据。1996 年第一次农业普查以后，由于畜牧业产品年报数据与普查数据之间存在一定的差距，国家统计局对畜牧业年报数据与普查数据进行了衔接。1999 年以后，国家统计局开展了猪、牛、羊、禽等主要畜禽品种的抽样调查，并用抽样数据作为国家定案数据使用。未开展抽样调查的品种，仍使用各级统计部门逐级上报数据。

期初(末)畜禽存栏头(只)数 指报告期初(末)农村各种合作经济组织和国营农场、农民个人、机关、团体、学校、工矿企业、部队等单位以及城镇居民饲养的大牲畜、猪、羊、家禽等畜禽的存栏数。数据上报方式及数据调整情况同猪、牛、羊肉产量。

常用耕地 指耕地总资源中专门种植农作物并经常进行耕种、能够正常收获的土地。包括当年实际耕种的熟地;弃耕、休闲不满三年，随时可以复耕的地；开荒利用三年以上的土地。在统计口径上包括南方小于1 米、北方小于2 米宽的沟、渠、路和田埂。不包括临时种植农作物的坡度在25度以上的陡坡地；在河套、湖畔、库区临时开发的成片或零星土地；也不包括已列为国家和省(区、市)退耕计划但临时耕种的土地。常用耕地是国家需要重点保护的耕地，可以反映我国农业的综合生产能力。

农作物播种面积 指实际播种或移植有农作物的面积。凡是实际种植农作物的面积，不论种植在耕地上还是种植在非耕地上，均包括在农作物播种面积中。在播种季节基本结束后，因遭灾而重新改种和补种的农作物面积，也包括在内。该指标可以反映我国耕地面积的利用情况。目前，农作物播种面积主要包括粮食、棉花、油料、糖料、麻类、烟叶、蔬菜和瓜类、药材和其它农作物九大类。

有效灌溉面积 指具有一定的水源，地块比较平整，灌溉工程或设备已经配套，在一般年景下当年能够进行正常灌溉的耕地面积。在一般情况下，有效灌溉面积应等于灌溉工程或设备已经配备，能够进行正常灌溉的水田和水浇地面积之和。该指标可以反映我国耕地的抗旱能力。

农用化肥施用量 指本年内实际用于农业生产的化肥数量，包括氮肥、磷肥、钾肥和复合肥。化肥施用量要求按折纯量计算数量。折纯量是指把氮肥、磷肥、钾肥分别按含氮、含五氧化二磷、含氧化钾的百分之百成份进行折算后的数量。复合肥按其所含主要成分折算。公式: 折纯量= 实物量 × 某种化肥有效成份含量的百分比

农业机械总动力 指主要用于农、林、牧、渔业的各种动力机械的动力总和。包括耕作机械、排灌机械、收获机械、农用运输机械、植物保护机械、牧业机械、林业机械、渔业机械和其他农业机械〔内燃机按引擎马力折成瓦(特)计算、电动机按功率折成瓦(特)计算〕。不包括专门用于乡、镇、村、组办工业、基本建设、非农业运输、科学试验和教学等非农业生产方面用的动力机械与作业机械。这个指标的统计数据主要来源于农机部门。

乡村从业人员 指乡村人口中劳动年龄在16 周岁以上实际参加生产经营活动并取得实物或货币收入的人员，包括劳动年龄内经常参加劳动的人员，也包括超过劳动年龄但经常参加劳动的人员，但不包括户口在家的在外学生、现役军人和丧失劳动能力的人，也不包括待业人员和家务劳动者。从业人员按从事主业时间最长(时间相同按收入)分为农业从业人员、工业从业人员、建筑从业人员、交运仓储及邮电业从业人员、批零贸易及餐饮业从业人员、其它从业人员。

乡镇企业 指农村集体经济组织或者农民投资为主， 在乡镇(包括所辖村)举办的承担支援农业义务的各类企业。投资为主是指农村集体经济组织或农民投资超过百分之五十，或者虽不足百分之五十，但能起到控股或者实际支配作用。其范围包括乡(镇)办企业、村办企业、联户办企业、户(私营、个体)办企业，以及这些企业之间或者这些企业与国有企业、城镇集体企业、私营企业以及外资(包括我国港澳台地区)等多种经济成分联合投资建立的企业。

Explanatory Notes on Main Statistical Indicators

Gross Output Value of Farming, Forestry, Animal Husbandry and Fishery refers to the total value of products of farming, forestry, animal husbandry and fishery, which reflects the total scale and result of agricultural production during a given period. Gross output value of agriculture is obtained by first multiplying the output of each product or by product by its price, resulting in t he output value of each s ingle item. For a small number of products, annual output of which is not available or difficult to get due to the long production growing process involved, t he output value is estimated through an indirect approach. The sum of out put value of all products of farming, forestry, animal husbandry, and fishery is then equal to the gross output value of agriculture. Prior to 1957, Chinas gross agricultural output value included barnyard manure and handicraft products for self-consumption (clothes, shoes, stockings, and initial grain processing undertaken by peasants). Since 1958, cutting and felling of bamboo and trees by villages and other cooperative organizations under villages have been included in forestry; value of barnyard manure has been excluded from animal husbandry; self consumed handicraft s has been excluded from sideline occupations, while the output value of industries run by villages and cooperative organizations under village had been included inside line occupations and the out put value of fish catches by motor fishing boats has been added to fishery. Since 1980, the value of handicraft products made for sale by individuals in households had been added to sideline occupations. Since 1984, industries run by villages and under villages have been included in the sector of industry. Since 1993, the subdivision of sideline occupations has been canceled, and the hunting of wild animals has been classified into animal husbandry, and the gathering of wild plants and commodity industry run by rural household have been included in farming. The firs t agriculture census of China in 1996 revealed some discrepancy between the production of animal products from the annual reports and that from the census. Efforts were made by NBS to adjust the output value of animal husbandry to make the figures from the annual reports consistent with the census data.

Grain Output refers to the total output of rice, wheat, corn, sorghum, millet and other miscellaneous grains as well as tubers and bean in the whole country including grains produced by state farms, collective units, industrial enterprises and mines. Output of beans refers to dry beans without pods. The output of tubers (sweet potatoes and potatoes, not including taros and cassava) was converted into that of grain at the ratio 4:1, i.e. 4 kilograms of fresh tubers was equivalent to 1 kilogram of grain up to 1963. Since 1964 the ratio for conversion has been 5:1.Tubers supplied as vegetables (such as potatoes) in cities and suburbs are calculated as fresh vegetables and their output is not included in the output of grain. Output of all other grains refers to husked grain. Data on grain production before 1989 were obtained through Comprehensive Statistical Reporting System, since then, sample survey data are used.

Cotton Output refers to t he cot ton product ion in the whole country including cotton sown in spring and in autumn. Output is measured as the weight of ginned cotton. Three kilograms of seed-cotton are equivalent to 1 kilogram of ginned cotton, excluding ceiba.

Output of Oil-bearing Crops refers to the total production of oil-bearing crops of various kinds, including peanuts, (dry, in shell) rapeseeds, sesame, sunflower seeds, flax seeds, and other oil-bearing crops. Soybeans, oil-bearing woody plants, and wild oil-bearing crops are not included.

Output of Aquatic Products refers to catches of both artificially cultured and naturally grown aquatic products, including fish, shrimps, crabs and shellfish in sea and inland water as well as seaweed. Freshwater plants are not included. Data on output of aquatic products are reported by aquatic product and statistical agencies level by level. Before 1995, among the shellfish, the oyster was counted as fresh meat; 5 kilograms of ark shell, clams and frogs are equivalent to 1 kilogram of fresh aquatic product s; t hey are all counted as fresh aquatic product s since1996.

Output of Pork, Beef, and Mutton refers to the meat of slaughtered hogs, cattle, sheep and goats wit h head, feet, and offal taken away. The statistical scope is of the whole society. The first agriculture census of China in 1996 revealed some discrepancy between the production of animal products from the annual reports and that from the census. Efforts were made by NBS to adjust the output value of animal husbandry to make the figures from the annual rep orts consistent with the census data. Since 1999, NBS conducted sample survey for t he major animal husbandry products, such as hogs, cattle, sheep and goats and fowls, and the data from sample surveys are used as national finalized data. Those products, which are not covered by the sample survey, are st ill reported by statistical agencies level by level.

Number of Livestock or Poultry in Stock at Beginning (or End) refers to the total number of large animals, pigs, sheep, fowls, etc. raised by rural cooperative organizations, state farms, rural individuals, government agencies, schools, industrial and mining enterprises, army, and urban residents at the beginning (or end) of the reference period. Data rep or ting system and data adjustment are the same as that in the output of pork, beef and mutton.

Regularly Cultivated Land refers to farmland among the total land resources, which is exclusively used for farming and is under regular cultivation with harvest in normal years. Include dare currently cultivated land, land that has been abandoned or put in idle for less than 3 years and could be re-used for cultivation at any time, and new-claimed land that has been put into cultivation for more than 3 years. According to statistical coverage, it includes the gouges, dykes, roads and ridges of field with 1 meter wide in Southern areas and 2 meters wide in Northern areas. Excluded under this category are steep slope land over 25 degrees under temporary cultivation, land (large or small plots) that is claimed along river bends, lake sides or banks of reservoirs, as well as land that has been designated under the "Green for Grain" programs of the state and provincial governments but is still temporarily under cultivation. The regularly cultivated land is the key protection land of the nation, which reflects the comprehensive productivity of agriculture of China.

Sown Area of Crops refers t o area of land sown or transplanted with crop s regardless of being in cultivated area or no cultivated area. Area of land re-sown due to natural disasters is also included. The indicator can reflect the utilization condition of the cultivated land in China. At p resent, t he sown area of crops mainly include the following 9 categories of crops: grain, cotton, oil-bearing crops, sugar crops, fiber crops, Tobacco, Vegetables and melons, medicinal materials and other farm crops.

. **Irrigated Area** refers to areas that are effectively irrigated, i.e. level land, which has water source and complete sets of irrigation facilities to lift and move adequate water for irrigation purpose under normal conditions. Under normal conditions, irrigated area is the sum of watered fields and irrigated fields where irrigation systems or equipment have been installed for regular irrigation purpose. This indicator can reflect drought resistance capaCity of the cultivated land in China.

Consumption of Chemical Fertilizers in Agriculture refers to the quantity of chemical fertilizers applied in agriculture in the y ear, including nitrogenous fertilizer, phosphate fertilizer, potash fertilizer, and compound fertilizer. The consumption of chemical fertilizers is required in calculation to convert the gross weight into weight containing 100% effective component (e.g. 100% nitrogen content in nitrogenous fertilizer, 100%phosphorous pent oxide contents in phosphate fertilizer, 100%potassium oxide contents in potash fertilizer). Compound fertilizer is converted with it s major component. The formula is:

Volume of effective component = physical quantity X effective component of certain chemical fertilizer (%)

Total Power of Farm Machinery refers to total mechanical power of machinery used in farming, forestry, animal husbandry, and fishery, including ploughing, irrigation and drainage, harvesting, transport, plant protection, stock breeding, forestry and fishery. The power of internal combust ion engines is required to convert horsepower into watts and the power of electric motors is required to be converted into watts. Machinery employed for non-agricultural purposes, such as the machines used in township run and village-run industry, construction, nonagricultural transport, scientific experiments and teaching, is excluded. Data are mainly from agricultural machinery agencies.

Rural Employed Persons refer to rural labor forces aged over 16 years old who are engaged in real production and management activities and receive payment in kind or wages, including those covered within the age frame and regularly participating in production activities, and those who are out of the range of age frame and also participating in product ion activities regularly. Excluding students studying in other places with their permanent residence registered in local areas, servicemen and persons incapable of working; also excluding those who are waiting for jobs and those engaged in household work. Persons employed are classified as rural employed persons; industrial employed

persons; const ruction industry employed persons; transport, storage and telecommunications industries employed persons; whole sales and retail sales trade and catering industry employed persons and others according to the longest period of persons engaged in major activities (or using income indicator when periods are the same).

Township Enterprises refer to collective economic organization in rural areas or various enterprises bearing the responsibilities of supporting the agricultural sector in t own (including related village), which mainly invest ed by farmers. The share of rural economic organizations or farmers should account for over50%, if it were below 50%, it should play the leading role or hold the share. Those enterprises include: township enterprises, village enterprises, joint-household enterprises, household (private, individual) enterprises; and also the joint venture enterprises with various ownership s among above-mentioned enterprises, or with state-owned enterprises, urban collective enterprises, private enterprises and foreign funded (including Hong Kong, Macao and Taiwan) enterprises.

第十二篇

CHAPTER 12

工　　业

INDUSTRY

12-1 工业总产值
Gross Industrial Output Value

单位:亿元 (100 million yuan)

年份 Year	工业总产值 Gross Industrial Output Value	国有工业 State-owned Enterprises	集体工业 Collective owned	城乡个体工业 Urban and Rural Private	其它经济类型工业 Industry of Other Types of Ownership
1978	33.91	30.22	3.69		
1980	40.71	36.20	4.50	0.01	
1985	86.78	73.18	11.93	1.20	0.47
1990	219.92	176.52	36.72	3.39	3.29
1991	280.59	220.71	52.25	4.30	3.33
1992	317.22	248.54	59.55	5.00	4.13
1993	448.41	352.25	80.39	8.59	7.18
1994	590.52	444.44	111.97	20.17	13.94
1995	593.43	461.31	89.24	16.21	26.67
1996	682.24	519.37	94.71	35.58	32.58
1997	771.17	580.48	99.49	46.10	45.10
1998	758.01	501.08	85.49	54.87	116.57
1999	802.09	506.84	74.01	53.61	167.63
2000	1061.29	258.93	72.78	65.59	663.99
2001	1084.22	155.26	53.31	66.21	809.44
2002	1133.38	159.73	46.39	67.36	859.90
2003	1330.15	161.94	35.69	72.13	1060.39
2004	1756.18	224.63	19.14	49.56	1462.85

12-2 工业总产值指数
Indices of Gross Industrial Output Value

(1978=100)

年份 Year	工业总产值 Gross Industrial Output Value	国有工业 State-owned Enterprises	集体工业 Collective owned	城乡个体工业 Urban and Rural Private	其它经济类型工业 Industry of Other Types of Ownership
1978	100.0	100.0	100.0		
1980	117.7	118.0	113.2	(1981=100)	(1981=100)
1985	220.6	199.5	428.2	2288.8	324.1
1990	380.3	326.0	915.9	5070.9	1004.0
1991	439.0	367.3	1171.7	6254.7	1024.5
1992	476.7	392.5	1350.2	6543.0	1154.8
1993	528.0	417.6	1618.2	10260.2	2065.5
1994	585.4	449.9	1780.8	17020.6	3499.9
1995	670.8	506.1	2104.5	14298.8	4924.2
1996	754.0	551.4	2209.3	29430.3	7657.1
1997	837.7	597.7	2306.5	37965.1	10987.9
1998	863.1	530.9	2032.0	39597.6	29065.2
1999	921.0	538.9	1839.0	37197.4	36734.1
2000	1000.4	227.3	1763.6	41359.8	75408.1
2001	1077.8	151.0	1311.5	42542.8	103834.6
2002	1180.9	149.3	1123.1	42975.1	120162.0
2003	1306.7	152.9	837.3	44659.7	139213.8
2004	1567.8	210.4	442.4	41982.4	169384.6

12-3 工业法人单位及工业总产值

Industrial Incorporate Unit and Total Industrial Output Value

单位: 万元 (2004 年) (10 000 yuan)

项 目	Item	企业单位数（个） Number of Enterprises (unit)	工业总产值（当年价格） Gross Industrial Output Value (At Current Prices)
总 计	**Total**	**5798**	**16560208.6**
按登记注册类型分	Grouped by Registry Types		
内资企业	Domestic Enterprises	5692	16175644.2
国有企业	State-owned Enterprises	385	1937594.0
集体企业	Collective-owned Enterprises	546	164289.6
股份合作企业	Share Cooperative Enterprises	71	24740.9
联营企业	Joint-owned Enterprises	48	32356.1
#国有联营企业	State Ownership Joint Enterprises	19	14198.5
集体联营企业	Collective Ownership Joint Enterprises	16	6062.5
国有与集体联营企业	State-collective Joint Enterprises	6	10228.3
有限责任公司	Limited Liability Corporations	1191	3562486.3
#国有独资公司	State-funded Corporations	77	730407.9
股份有限公司	Share-holding Corporations Ltd.	44	9178517.9
私营企业	Private Enterprises	3399	1274834.0
其他企业	Other Enterprises	8	825.4
港、澳、台商投资企业	Enterprises With Investment from Hong Kong, Macau and Taiwan	32	127691.9
外商投资企业	Enterprises With Foreign Investment	74	256872.5
在总计中: 国有控股企业	Of the Total: State-Owned Holding Enterprise	746	12788038.6
按轻、重工业分	**Grouped by Light & Heavy Industry**		
轻工业	Light Industry	2201	2508082.7
以农产品为原料	Using Farm Produces as Raw Materials	1774	2342412.5
以非农产品为原料	Using Non-Farm Produces as Raw Materials	427	165670.2
重工业	Heavy Industry	3597	14052125.9
采掘工业	Mining and Quarrying	670	5879907.5
原料工业	Raw Material Industry	839	6689610.1
加工工业	Manufacturing Industry	2088	1482608.3
按企业规模分	**Grouped by Size of Enterprises**		
大型企业	Large	23	9751820.9
中型企业	Medium	180	3090203.6
小型企业	Small	5595	3718184.1

12-4 按行业分工业法人单位数及工业总产值

Industrial Incorporate Unit and Total Industrial Output Value by Sectors

单位：万元 (2004 年) (10 000 yuan)

行业	Item	企业单位数(个) Number of Enterprises (unit)	工业总产值(当年价格) Gross Industrial Output Value (At Current Prices)
煤炭开采和洗选业	Coal Extracting and Dressing	349	305714.3
石油和天然气开采业	Petroleum and Natural Gas Extraction	29	5333576.2
＃天然原油和天然气开采	Crude Oil and Natural Gas Extraction	5	4406905.1
黑色金属矿采选业	Ferrous Metals Mining and Dressing	45	113325.7
有色金属矿采选业	Nonferrous Metals Mining and Dressing	60	85616.6
非金属矿采选业	Nonmetal Minerals Mining and Dressing	185	41493.4
＃采　盐	Salt Extraction	8	5434.7
其他采矿业	Other Ore Extraction	2	181.3
农副食品加工业	Farm and Non-staple Food Processing	490	706872.8
＃谷物磨制	Grain Grinding	161	135669.9
饲料加工	Fodder Processing	54	151052.9
制　糖	Sugar Making	17	107353.2
食品制造业	Food Manufacturing	239	401185.4
＃罐头制造	Canned Food Production	41	222559.9
饮料制造业	Beverage Production	210	207089.8
＃酒的制造	Wine Production	125	173520.7
烟草制品业	Tobacco Products	4	71375.6
纺织业	Textile Industry	168	611809.1
＃棉、化纤纺织及印染精加工	Cotton and Chemical Fiber, Dyeing and Printing	92	497428.1
毛纺织和染整精加工	Wool Textile, Dyeing and Printing, Dressing	11	17154.2
纺织服装、鞋、帽制造业	Textile Garment, Shoe and Hat	75	12077.0
皮革、毛皮、羽毛(绒)及其制品业	Leather, Fur, Feather (down) and its Products	28	44511.6
＃皮革鞣制加工	Leather Tanning and Processing	10	42409.1
皮革制品制造	Leather Products	13	1269.7
木材加工及木、竹、藤、棕、草制品业	Timber Production, Wood, Bamboo, Cane and Grass	119	53298.6
家具制造业	Furniture Manufacturing	93	78760.7
造纸及纸制品业	Papermaking and Paper Products	139	114434.5

12-4 续表 Continued

单位: 万元 (10 000 yuan)

行 业	Item	企业单位数(个) Number of Enterprises (unit)	工业总产值(当年价格) Gross Industrial Output Value (At Current Prices)
印刷业和记录媒介的复制	Printing and Copying of Medium for Record	291	54758.9
文教体育用品制造业	Cultural, Educational and Sports Goods	7	332.7
石油加工、炼焦及核燃料加工业	Oil Processing, Coking and Nuclear Fuel Processing	86	3553947.2
#炼 焦	Coking	15	37138.4
化学原料及化学制品制造业	Raw Chemical Material and Chemical Products	373	567519.0
#基础化学原料制造	Basic Chemical Material Production	90	186880.6
肥料制造	Fertilizer Production	63	83321.4
医药制造业	Medical and Pharmaceutical Products	60	38197.4
化学纤维制造业	Chemical Fiber	9	43033.0
橡胶制品业	Rubber Products	35	54470.1
塑料制品业	Plastic Products	346	306958.5
非金属矿物制品业	Nonmetal Mineral Products	923	562115.1
#水泥制造	Cement Manufacturing	72	274602.0
黑色金属冶炼及压延加工业	Smelting and Pressing of Ferrous Metals	72	1187956.7
有色金属冶炼及压延加工业	Smelting and Pressing of Nonferrous Metals	29	171905.8
金属制品业	Metal Products	278	160635.1
通用设备制造业	Ordinary Equipment Production	213	102664.6
专用设备制造业	Special Purpose Equipment	123	63241.5
交通运输设备制造业	Transport and Communication Equipment	147	97807.6
电气机械及器材制造业	Electric Equipment and Machinery	123	251538.3
通信设备、计算机及其他电子设备制造业	Telecom. Equipment, Computer and Other Electronic Equipment	4	62354.3
仪器仪表及文化、办公用机械制造业	Equipment, Meter, Culture and Office Machinery	17	7303.3
工艺品及其他制造业	Arts and Handicraft, Other Manufacturing Sector	35	1392.8
废弃资源和废旧材料回收加工业	Recycling and Processing of Deserted Resources and Waste Material	26	4923.6
电力、热力的生产和供应业	Electric and Thermal Power Production and Supply	247	1011683.1
#电力生产和电力供应	Electric Production and Supply	123	897844.8
燃气生产和供应业	Gas Production and Supply	15	37849.2
水的生产和供应业	Water Production and Supply	104	36298.2

12-5 各地、州、市、县(市)工业法人单位数和工业总产值

Industrial Incorporate Unit and Total Industrial Output Value by Prefectures, Cities and Counties

单位: 万元 (2004 年) (10 000 yuan)

行　业	Item	企业单位数(个) Number of Enterprises (unit)	工业总产值(当年价格) Gross Industrial Output Value (At Current Prices)
总　计	**Total**	**5798**	**16560208.6**
乌鲁木齐市	**Urumqi City**	**1386**	**4506589.8**
乌鲁木齐县	Urumqi County	53	7625.9
克拉玛依市	**Karamay City**	**213**	**5351618.2**
石河子市	**Shihezi City**	**258**	**410645.3**
阿拉尔市	**Alar City**	**5**	**4764.4**
图木舒克市	**Tumxuk City**	**7**	**6494.9**
五家渠市	**Wujiaqu City**	**23**	**29841.7**
吐鲁番地区	**Turpan Administrative Offices**	**185**	**983408.3**
吐鲁番市	Turpan City	75	74093.4
鄯善县	Shanshan [Piqan] County	71	881148.1
托克逊县	Toksun County	39	28166.8
哈密地区	**Hami [Kumul] Administrative Offices**	**182**	**319999.8**
哈密市	Hami [Kumul] City	142	294642.1
巴里坤哈萨克自治县	Barkol Kazak Autonomous County	33	16220.0
伊吾县	Yiwu [Araturuk] County	7	9137.7
昌吉回族自治州	**Changji Hui Autonomous Prefecture**	**1019**	**1359448.8**
昌吉市	Changji City	322	492042.3
阜康市	Fukang City	114	157003.3
米泉市	Miquan City	224	377847.2
呼图壁县	Hutubi County	134	122376.4
玛纳斯县	Manas County	84	144153.6
奇台县	Qitai County	46	32631.8
吉木萨尔县	Jimsar County	61	26979.6
木垒哈萨克自治县	Mori Kazak Autonomous County	34	6414.6
伊犁哈萨克自治州	**Ili Kazak Autonomous Prefecture**	**1006**	**1019587.1**
伊犁州直属县(市)	**Counties (Cities) Direct Under Ili Prefecture**	**515**	**616647.6**
伊宁市	Yining [Gulja] City	167	139852.1
奎屯市	Kuytun City	105	193799.9
伊宁县	Yining [Gulja] County	45	66563.0
察布查尔锡伯自治县	Qapqal Xibe Autonomous County	47	15324.0
霍城县	Huocheng [Korgas] County	40	59116.5
巩留县	Gongliu [Tokkuztara] County	58	13995.4
新源县	Xinyuan [Kunes] County	11	99212.2

12-5 续表 1 Continued

单位: 万元 (10 000 yuan)

行 业	Item	企业单位数(个) Number of Enterprises (unit)	工业总产值(当年价格) Gross Industrial Output Value (At Current Prices)
昭苏县	Zhaosu [Mongolkure] County	18	21924.2
特克斯县	Tekes County	7	1292.6
尼勒克县	Nilka County	17	5567.7
塔城地区	**Tacheng [Tarbagatai] Administrative Officess**	**327**	**264948.5**
塔城市	Tacheng [Qoqek] City	25	23716.2
乌苏市	Usu City	59	64094.5
额敏县	Emin [Dorbiljin] County	30	46747.7
沙湾县	Shawan County	107	85244.5
托里县	Toli County	60	19241.3
裕民县	Yumin [Qagantokay] County	14	1962.0
和布克赛尔蒙古自治县	Hoboksar Mongol Autonomous County	32	23942.3
阿勒泰地区	**Altay Administrative Offices**	**164**	**137991.0**
阿勒泰市	Altay City	58	51956.7
布尔津县	Burqin County	19	10400.1
富蕴县	Fuyun [Koktokay] County	23	55744.6
福海县	Fuhai [Burultokay] County	20	8897.5
哈巴河县	Habahe [Kaba] County	17	5758.9
青河县	Qinghe [Qinggil] County	17	2395.0
吉木乃县	Jeminay County	10	2838.2
博尔塔拉蒙古自治州	**Bortala Mongol Autonomous Prefecture**	**109**	**119765.0**
博乐市	Bole [Bortala] City	69	101012.6
精河县	Jinghe [Jing] County	26	14753.0
温泉县	Wenquan [Araxang] County	14	3999.4
巴音郭楞蒙古自治州	**Bayangol Mongol Autonomous Prefecture**	**464**	**1722711.5**
库尔勒市	Korla City	217	1455062.5
轮台县	Luntai [Bugur] County	39	87093.7
尉犁县	Yuli [Lopnur] County	36	39767.7
若羌县	Ruoqiang [Qarkilik] County	14	16808.8
且末县	Qiemo [Qarqan] County	13	2336.7
焉耆回族自治县	Yanji Hui Autonomous County	36	25840.8
和静县	Hejing County	54	55321.2
和硕县	Hoxud County	35	18661.9
博湖县	Bohu [Bagrax] County	20	21818.2
阿克苏地区	**Aksu Administrative Offices**	**401**	**475733.3**
阿克苏市	Aksu City	137	188708.7

12-5 续表 2 Continued

单位: 万元 (10 000 yuan)

行　业	Item	企业单位数（个） Number of Enterprises (unit)	工业总产值（当年价格） Gross Industrial Output Value (At Current Prices)
温宿县	Wensu [Onsu] County	40	15166.9
库车县	Kuqa County	97	187168.5
沙雅县	Xayar County	17	9540.6
新和县	Xinhe [Toksu] County	19	8216.6
拜城县	Baicheng [Bay] County	51	56290.0
乌什县	Wushi [Uxturpan] County	9	476.2
阿瓦提县	Awat County	23	8349.8
柯坪县	Kalpin County	8	1816.0
克孜勒苏柯尔克孜自治州	**Kizilsu Kirgiz Autonomous Prefecture**	**55**	**21027.3**
阿图什市	Artux City	29	14336.0
阿克陶县	Akto County	20	3318.2
阿合奇县	Akqi County	3	139.0
乌恰县	Wuqia [Ulugqat] County	3	3234.1
喀什地区	**Kashgar [Kaxgar] Administrative Offices**	**357**	**177777.7**
喀什市	Kashgar [Kaxgar] City	131	105561.1
疏附县	Shufu County	30	6023.4
疏勒县	Shule County	24	20796.9
英吉沙县	Yengisar County	15	5479.1
泽普县	Zepu [Poskam] County	28	10434.0
莎车县	Shache [Yarkant] County	31	7497.8
叶城县	Yecheng [Kagilik] County	39	6892.6
麦盖提县	Makit County	12	1857.7
岳普湖县	Yopurga County	9	4161.8
伽师县	Jiashi [Payzawat] County	16	2286.8
巴楚县	Bachu [Maralbexi] County	17	6463.3
塔什库尔干塔吉克自治县	Taxkorgan Tajik Autonomous County	5	323.2
和田地区	**Hotan Administrative Offices**	**128**	**50795.5**
和田市	Hotan City	34	29707.9
和田县	Hotan County	19	8631.7
墨玉县	Moyu [Karakax] County	11	965.0
皮山县	Pishan [Guma] County	16	1202.2
洛浦县	Lop County	24	9094.7
策勒县	Qira County	12	419.4
于田县	Yutian [Keriya] County	8	437.2
民丰县	Minfeng [Niya] County	4	337.4

12-6 全部国有及规模以上非国有工业企业主要经济指标

单位: 万元 (2004 年)

项　目	Item	企业单位数(个) Number of Enterprises (unit)	#亏损企业 Loss (unit)	工业总产值(当年价格) Gross Industrial Output Value (At Current Prices)
总　计	**Total**	**1430**	**539**	**15718444.4**
按登记注册类型分	**Grouped by Registry Type**			
内资企业	Domestic Investment	1367	514	15341608.3
国有企业	State-owned	384	205	1715019.5
#中央企业	Central	98	45	1261386.6
地方企业	Iocal Enterprises	286	160	453632.9
#自治区属企业	Autonomous	72	30	253252.0
地区(州、市)属企业	Prefecture or City	53	33	113267.4
县(市)属企业	County or City	154	93	76561.9
集体企业	Collective-owned	46	18	101233.2
#自治区属企业	Autonomous	8	2	28691.5
地区(州、市)属企业	Prefecture or City	5	2	13565.6
县(市)属企业	County or City	13	6	29864.6
镇属企业	Town	3	1	3537.9
乡属企业	Country	2	1	2212.4
股份合作企业	Share Cooperative	9	4	15373.8
联营企业	Joint Owned	8	2	24837.6
#国有联营企业	State Ownership Joint Enterprises	3	1	12069.0
集体联营企业	Collective Joint-operative Enterprises	2		4270.3
国有与集体联营企业	State-collective Joint Enterprises	3	1	8498.3
其他联营企业	Other Joint-operative Enterprises			
有限责任公司	Limited Liability Corporations	571	186	3421179.6
#国有独资公司	State-funded Corporations	46	18	722172.2
其他有限责任公司	Other Limited Liability Corporations	525	168	2699007.4
股份有限公司	Share-holding Corporations Ltd.	41	12	9178255.9
私营企业	Private Enterprises	308	87	885708.7
#私营独资企业	Private-funded Enterprises	24	2	37357.2
私营合伙企业	Private Partnership Enterprises	9	2	23007.8
私营有限责任公司	Private Limited Liability Corporations	269	82	770221.1
私营股份有限公司	Private Stock Ltd. Co.	6	1	55122.6
港、澳、台商投资企业	Enterprises with Funds from Hong Kong, Macao and Taiwan	17	5	124410.6
外商投资企业	Foreign Funded Enterprises	46	20	252425.5
在总计中: 国有控股企业	Of the Total : State-Owned Holding Enterprise	617	281	12535046.5
在总计中:农村工业	Of the Total : Rural Industry	11	5	20728.3
按轻、重工业分	**Grouped by Light & Heavy Industry**			
轻工业	Light Industry	594	248	2305998.5
以农产品为原料	Using Farm Produces as Raw Materials	479	192	2174763.2
以非农产品为原料	Using Non-Farm Produces as Raw Materials	115	56	131235.3
重工业	Heavy Industry	836	291	13412445.9
采掘工业	Mining and Quarrying	138	40	5554139.1
原料工业	Raw Material Industry	360	148	6598274.7
加工工业	Manufacturing Industry	338	103	1260032.1
按企业规模分	**Grouped by Size of Enterprises**			
大型企业	Large	23	4	9751820.9
中型企业	Medium	180	61	3090203.6
小型企业	Small	1227	474	2876419.9

Main Economic Indicators of All State-owned and Non-state-owned Industrial Enterprises above Designated Size

(10 000 yuan)

工业增加值 Added Value of Industry	工业销售产值(当年价) Sales Value of Industry Products (At Current Prices)	出口交货值 Delivery Value of Industry Export	实收资本 Total Capital Hold	资产合计 Total Assets	流动资产合计 Circulating Funds	#产成品 Finished Product	流动资产年平均余额 Annual Average Balance of Circulating Funds	固定资产原价 Original Value of Fixed Assets
6689966.6	**15373639.7**	**316548.2**	**7274478.1**	**24880833.1**	**7670908.8**	**1098278.8**	**7236560.6**	**23114141.3**
6567401.8	15011687.3	225782.1	7092350.3	24331704.8	7403396.7	1074224.2	6967314.7	22789695.7
706066.6	1684407.8	21099.8	1538945.2	4176738.5	1616695.0	88745.6	1524791.3	3178938.1
536568.2	1239581.0	6755.4	1156686.7	2858301.0	1163674.9	58351.2	1091286.4	2147998.8
169498.4	444826.8	14344.4	382258.5	1318437.5	453020.1	30394.4	433504.9	1030939.3
99591.2	252410.5	2535.7	173721.8	608732.4	231911.3	13835.7	210226.4	507514.2
42527.2	111724.5	4135.0	120271.1	394047.8	134095.9	9757.5	137602.8	289271.5
26283.9	71285.2		72673.8	248284.6	62274.3	4918.1	57011.2	218359.9
12435.9	98224.7		30226.6	116448.4	71766.8	14881.0	81244.2	70570.7
6958.8	29694.8		4211.8	21142.9	17998.6	2410.2	17202.1	7638.5
2136.3	14474.4		2056.6	13672.5	8012.2	833.5	8786.5	9844.6
6212.5	26875.6		15968.9	40320.0	20404.9	5232.8	30766.7	28583.6
1329.3	3380.2		1038.5	5015.6	2964.4	398.7	2674.2	2614.2
32.5	2212.4		1155.8	12879.8	7516.6	0.8	7484.2	6647.2
5888.7	14167.5	2491.2	8186.4	23154.6	10903.4	2415.2	10109.6	17896.2
7667.3	20542.4		9713.2	26957.2	11406.0	1323.3	11299.1	16983.9
4288.5	8382.7		1720.1	12704.3	5439.8	80.7	5189.9	8169.5
1358.6	3977.5		5513.8	7638.1	2263.0	959.4	2395.2	5588.7
2020.2	8182.2		2479.3	6614.8	3703.2	283.2	3714.0	3225.7
1107531.1	3279745.6	99560.8	1828810.1	6710655.4	2391335.5	374395.8	2337632.2	4951243.5
280259.2	702345.8	19.7	457368.3	1849505.4	487682.6	51486.9	510141.8	1684430.7
827271.9	2577399.8	99541.1	1371441.8	4861150.0	1903652.9	322908.9	1827490.4	3266812.8
4513846.8	9082861.5	88030.7	3277861.5	12009087.6	2725603.3	491149.2	2472124.9	14058404.5
213965.4	831737.8	14599.6	398607.3	1268663.1	575686.7	101314.1	530113.4	495658.8
11157.4	37202.8		17749.3	49004.9	20046.5	2967.1	18097.1	32002.0
7031.2	23419.1		3711.8	8931.0	5016.2	1178.2	4700.1	3203.2
179420.8	712161.9	14599.6	278348.5	933592.3	455697.6	87426.0	420520.4	418997.3
16356.0	58954.0		98797.7	277134.9	94926.4	9742.8	86795.8	41456.3
39030.6	117281.5	36556.6	75370.5	183105.4	90501.0	10482.1	89464.9	155284.8
83534.2	244670.9	54209.5	106757.3	366022.9	177011.1	13572.5	179781.0	169160.8
5850758.9	12384915.5	118839.2	5971047.0	19682108.1	5354950.7	687182.6	5003834.0	20432898.0
4705.0	20026.3		8223.6	35660.4	19960.1	4513.5	19375.9	18526.7
619174.9	2101158.2	243670.6	1126056.9	4011044.6	1841918.4	432252.5	1825347.3	2335291.2
568521.0	1974352.8	235566.0	1014018.9	3627450.3	1725339.3	417713.8	1703932.7	2045962.0
50653.9	126805.4	8104.6	112038.0	383594.3	116579.1	14538.7	121414.6	289329.2
6070791.7	13272481.5	72877.6	6148421.2	20869788.5	5828990.4	666026.3	5411213.3	20778850.1
4025877.4	5507223.3	3753.1	3493476.1	9783928.9	2077412.8	143788.0	1820554.9	11731509.4
1725895.6	6537330.2	36117.6	1845340.3	8277723.7	2412311.8	323969.3	2338575.1	7839839.2
319018.7	1227928.0	33006.9	809604.8	2808135.9	1339265.8	198269.0	1252083.3	1207501.5
4926891.4	9697644.5	37930.5	4238094.4	13348480.8	3150727.2	392848.4	2881073.6	15563871.2
1015656.3	2958907.2	165784.7	1696584.3	6905729.9	2502123.9	345832.8	2400856.2	4838715.9
747418.9	2717088.0	112833.0	1339799.4	4626622.4	2018057.7	359597.6	1954630.8	2711554.2

12-6 续表

单位: 万元

项 目	Item	固定资产净值年平均余额 Annual Average Balance of Net Value of Fixed Assets	流动负债合计 Liquid Liabilities	长期负债合计 Long-term Liabilities	所有者权益合计 Creditors' Equity
总 计	**Total**	**13939098.1**	**9450307.6**	**3732716.9**	**11614702.1**
按登记注册类型分	**Grouped by Registry Type**				
内资企业	Domestic Investment	13740668.9	9246644.0	3690992.6	11312180.0
国有企业	State-owned	2092947.8	1875739.8	637088.2	1662373.8
#中央企业	Central	1396591.8	1323590.1	392180.5	1142524.4
地方企业	Iocal Enterprises	696356.0	552149.7	244907.7	519849.4
#自治区属企业	Autonomous	329528.9	257334.9	106593.1	244551.3
地区(州、市)属企业	Prefecture or City	205647.7	178743.4	67568.0	146489.9
县(市)属企业	County or City	153134.0	88758.4	66864.4	92630.7
集体企业	Collective-owned	37728.5	62748.9	18561.5	35065.2
#自治区属企业	Autonomous	2910.3	13165.4	164.9	7739.8
地区(州、市)属企业	Prefecture or City	4417.6	6728.1	6101.1	843.3
县(市)属企业	County or City	18874.9	14132.9	11416.6	14770.5
镇属企业	Town	1917.9	3383.1	473.5	1159.0
乡属企业	Township	2959.2	7505.1	212.0	5162.7
股份合作企业	Share Cooperative	10049.6	7192.9	2062.0	13808.4
联营企业	Joint Owned	10601.6	10405.6	2831.1	13720.5
#国有联营企业	State Ownership Joint Enterprises	3851.3	4841.7	2727.8	5134.8
集体联营企业	Collective Ownership Joint Enterprises	4743.9	2731.4	103.3	4803.4
国有与集体联营企业	State-collective and Joint Enterprises	2006.4	2832.5		3782.3
其他联营企业	Other Ownership Joint Enterprises				
有限责任公司	Limited Liability Corporations	3403982.1	3484111.6	818467.3	2339308.9
#国有独资公司	State-funded Corporations	1088167.1	988850.2	278965.8	516081.6
其他有限责任公司	Other Limited Liability Corporations	2315815.0	2495261.4	539501.5	1823227.3
股份有限公司	Share-holding Corporations Ltd.	7812359.8	3248517.9	2114170.1	6636056.4
私营企业	Private Enterprises	372999.5	557927.3	97812.4	611846.8
#私营独资企业	Private-funded Enterprises	22699.9	20681.8	5799.7	22475.2
私营合伙企业	Private Partnership Enterprises	2301.2	2983.1	529.2	5418.7
私营有限责任公司	Private Limited Liability Corporations	322679.8	458791.2	66169.2	407603.6
私营股份有限公司	Private Stock Ltd. Co.	25318.6	75471.2	25314.3	176349.3
港、澳、台商投资企业	Enterprises with Funds from Hong Kong, Macao and Taiwan	83191.1	74242.2	17676.8	90568.2
外商投资企业	Foreign Funded Enterprises	115238.1	129421.4	24047.5	211953.9
在总计中: 国有控股企业	Of the Total: State-Owned Holding Enterprise	12071356.7	6914792.0	3171973.7	9514581.4
在总计中: 农村工业	Of the Total: Rural Industry	11790.4	20844.7	1735.3	12991.9
按轻、重工业分	**Grouped by Light & Heavy Industry**				
轻工业	Light Industry	1542419.3	2108603.8	446050.4	1451522.6
以农产品为原料	Using Farm Produces as Raw Material	1325365.4	1950485.0	396508.4	1275837.9
以非农产品为原料	Using Non-Farm Produces as Raw Material	217053.9	158118.8	49542.0	175684.7
重工业	Heavy Industry	12396678.8	7341703.8	3286666.5	10163179.5
采掘工业	Mining and Quarrying	6534745.3	2591081.1	1762935.3	5428791.5
原料工业	Raw Material Industry	5026257.7	3491428.8	1242126.2	3477336.5
加工工业	Manufacturing Industry	835675.8	1259193.9	281605.0	1257051.5
按企业规模分	**Grouped by Size of Enterprises**				
大型企业	Large	8797491.1	3802564.9	2163589.8	7372281.2
中型企业	Medium	3213919.9	3362182.7	1015810.4	2457875.6
小型企业	Small	1927687.1	2285560.0	553316.7	1784545.3

Continued

(10 000 yuan)

主营业务收入 Income of Major Business	#主营业务成本 Cost of Major Business	主营业务税金及附加 Major Business, Tax and Addition	营业利润 Business Profit	利润总额 Total Profit	亏损企业亏损总额 Lost Business Total Loss	利税总额 Total Profits and Taxes	本年应交增值税 Value Added Taxes Payable	全部从业人员年平均人数(人) Average Number of Staff and Workers (Person)
15834415.5	**11290005.9**	**315383.3**	**2378328.8**	**2263156.6**	**431474.2**	**3494005.3**	**915465.4**	**449761**
15452355.2	11006546.0	311774.8	2337578.4	2221086.1	425831.3	3432647.5	899786.6	438636
2039681.1	1788135.5	41955.7	-71912.6	-101626.6	150910.0	74855.2	134526.1	123207
1546369.5	1372008.4	38621.6	-47085.2	-81038.9	98123.3	61029.5	103446.8	82303
493311.6	416127.1	3334.1	-24827.4	-20587.7	52786.7	13825.7	31079.3	40904
300429.3	260276.6	1931.3	-5786.8	-1575.1	27672.8	20734.6	20378.4	16520
111512.5	96895.4	659.4	-14714.9	-16513.9	18077.6	-9088.5	6766.0	13669
71012.6	50374.3	733.2	-2563.8	-2456.3	5932.1	2031.0	3754.1	9888
106966.4	94641.8	535.7	-384.8	1139.1	2465.8	6560.0	4885.2	6936
31866.0	28076.1	160.7	1099.9	1360.1	47.1	3320.6	1799.8	1403
14727.8	13274.6	47.6	-905.5	-994.1	1115.1	-99.6	846.9	921
25479.8	23139.2	130.3	-461.7	52.3	734.1	1529.4	1346.8	1958
3184.2	2423.0	12.4	102.5	82.8	87.1	290.7	195.5	420
2128.9	1314.0	10.0	-287.4	-176.5	235.0	-128.0	38.5	223
15698.4	12173.2	41.2	1772.3	1669.5	135.8	2359.6	648.9	919
23158.4	16630.0	393.0	628.6	1246.9	149.1	3093.0	1453.1	1097
9753.2	4955.8	305.2	274.8	688.8	113.4	1784.8	790.8	331
4338.8	3735.2	42.1	-61.6	97.4		344.3	204.8	436
9066.4	7939.0	45.7	415.4	460.7	35.7	963.9	457.5	330
3321098.5	2694200.9	28890.8	111384.9	168066.8	139443.8	390070.7	193113.1	183088
706274.5	588733.9	7507.4	-11362.1	28527.7	34440.1	83584.2	47549.1	45218
2614824.0	2105467.0	21383.4	122747.0	139539.1	105003.7	306486.5	145564.0	137870
9099599.2	5672720.2	235314.8	2257635.5	2083901.0	119555.9	2862516.7	543300.9	86386
846153.2	728044.4	4643.6	38454.5	66689.4	13170.9	93192.3	21859.3	37003
37920.9	27894.7	266.6	1822.4	1807.7	29.2	3301.2	1226.9	2436
21087.8	18193.6	199.1	1395.1	1397.7	21.4	2152.9	556.1	464
737943.2	642977.0	4058.0	35055.8	40110.6	11138.6	62738.7	18570.1	30623
49201.3	38979.1	119.9	181.2	23373.4	1981.7	24999.5	1506.2	3480
128401.0	104657.5	97.4	11161.4	11517.7	1312.0	16727.7	5112.6	4814
253659.3	178802.4	3511.1	29589.0	30552.8	4330.9	44630.1	10566.2	6311
12779766.5	8784901.9	292037.3	2256677.2	2084933.2	365370.5	3182621.6	805651.1	301025
20550.0	15991.9	292.0	2029.8	2118.8	871.2	3034.3	623.5	1322
2142891.5	1736946.5	48312.0	26335.4	19140.9	100489.5	146403.8	78950.9	131414
2013940.1	1636421.8	47247.5	27607.6	21826.6	89600.5	142197.8	73123.7	119888
128951.4	100524.7	1064.5	-1272.2	-2685.7	10889.0	4206.0	5827.2	11526
13691524.0	9553059.4	267071.3	2351993.4	2244015.7	330984.7	3347601.5	836514.5	318347
5668509.1	2676697.1	102129.2	2065094.0	1971689.7	74651.0	2550226.2	476407.3	133132
6597467.8	5694586.7	158345.9	232818.7	179396.9	233973.8	649859.0	312116.2	128955
1425547.1	1181775.6	6596.2	54080.7	92929.1	22359.9	147516.3	47991.0	56260
10026531.7	6527052.8	241143.4	2282151.6	2120540.5	166902.4	2999633.6	637949.7	156043
3004933.8	2442254.4	53926.3	13207.4	41980.8	173065.5	276959.2	181052.1	157275
2802950.0	2320698.7	20313.6	82969.8	100635.3	91506.3	217412.5	96463.6	136443

12-7 按行业分的全部国有及规模以上非国有工业企业主要经济指标

单位: 万元 (2004 年)

行 业	Sector	企业单位数(个) Number of Enterprises (unit)	#亏损企业 Loss (unit)	工业总产值(当年价格) Gross Industrial Output Value (At Current Prices)
煤炭开采和洗选业	Coal Extracting and Dressing	69	27	228747.9
石油和天然气开采业	Petroleum and Natural Gas Extraction	14	2	5110995.9
#天然原油和天然气开采	Crude Oil and Natural Gas Extraction	5		4406905.1
黑色金属矿采选业	Ferrous Metals Mining and Dressing	21	3	108864.7
有色金属矿采选业	Nonferrous Metals Mining and Dressing	18	3	77388.0
非金属矿采选业	Nonmetal Minerals Mining and Dressing	16	5	28142.6
#采 盐	Salt Extraction	5	2	4932.4
其他采矿业	Other Ore Extraction			
农副食品加工业	Farm and Non-staple Processing	170	54	653868.3
#谷物磨制	Grain Grinding	38	11	120669.4
饲料加工	Fodder Processing	29	6	147113.7
制 糖	Sugar Making	15	6	107318.8
食品制造业	Food Manufacturing	84	31	379728.5
#罐头制造	Beverage Production	28	16	218684.6
饮料制造业	Beverage Production	36	14	186699.5
#酒的制造	Wine Manufacturing	28	11	160946.1
烟草制品业	Tobacco Products	2	1	71374.3
纺织业	Textile Industry	73	44	595723.2
#棉、化纤纺织及印染精加工	Cotton, Chemical Fiber, Dyeing, Printing and Dressing	56	37	490631.9
毛纺织和染整精加工	Wool Textile, Dyeing and Printing	6	5	16681.9
纺织服装、鞋、帽制造业	Textile Garment, Shoe and Hat	9	5	7293.5
皮革、毛皮、羽毛(绒)及其制品业	Leather, Fur, Feather (down) its Products	6	1	38257.1
#皮革鞣制加工	Leather Tanning and Processing	4		37769.6
皮革制品制造	Leather Products Manufacturing	2	1	487.5
木材加工及木、竹、藤、棕、草制品业	Timber Processing, Wood, Bamboo, Cane, Grass Products	13	5	38321.3
家具制造业	Furniture Manufacturing	9	3	70615.5
造纸及纸制品业	Papermaking and Paper Products	36	13	100314.4
印刷业和记录媒介的复制	Printing and Copying of Medium for Record	49	23	35245.3
文教体育用品制造业	Cultural, Educational and Sports Goods			
石油加工、炼焦及核燃料加工业	Oil Processing, Coking and Nuclear Fuel Processing	43	11	3545412.7
#炼 焦	Coking	7		35813.2
化学原料及化学制品制造业	Raw Chemical Material and Chemical Products	98	22	528105.0
#基础化学原料制造	Basic Chemical Material	25	9	176876.2
肥料制造	Fertilizer Making	19	5	77707.0
医药制造业	Medical and Pharmaceutical Products	15	4	31569.3
化学纤维制造业	Chemical Fiber	4	1	42087.4
橡胶制品业	Rubber Products	4		49285.4
塑料制品业	Plastic Products	68	21	258820.8
非金属矿物制品业	Nonmetal Mineral Products	120	41	479640.2
#水泥制造	Cement Manufacturing	56	24	269970.9
黑色金属冶炼及压延加工业	Smelting and Pressing of Ferrous Metals	37	16	1178679.2
有色金属冶炼及压延加工业	Smelting and Pressing of Nonferrous Metals	18	4	169147.6
金属制品业	Metal Products	52	14	125179.4
通用设备制造业	Ordinary Equipment Production	40	10	76253.9
专用设备制造业	Special Purposes Equipment	27	13	50490.1
交通运输设备制造业	Transport Equipment	20	9	86656.0
电气机械及器材制造业	Electric Equipment and Machinery	38	15	239338.8
通信设备、计算机及其他电子设备制造业	Telecom Equipment, Computer and Other Electronic Equipment	1		61898.4
仪器仪表及文化、办公用机械制造业	Equipment, Meter and Cultural and Office Machinery	3	1	4533.9
工艺品及其他制造业	Art and Handicraft as well as Other Manufacturing Sector			
废弃资源和废旧材料回收加工业	Recycling and Processing of Deserted Resources and Waste Material	2		3212.4
电力、热力的生产和供应业	Electric and Thermal Production and Supply	131	76	987051.8
#电力生产和电力供应	Electric Power Production and Supply	77	50	891241.1
燃气生产和供应业	Gas Production and Supply	9	4	36415.7
水的生产和供应业	Water Production and Supply	75	43	33086.4

Main Indicators on Economic of All State-owned and Non-state-owned Industrial Enterprises by Industry Sector

(10 000 yuan)

工业增加值 Added Value of Industry	工业销售产值（当年价） Sales Value of Industry Products (At Current Prices)	出口交货值 Delivery Value of Industry Export	实收资本 Total Capital Hold	资产合计 Total Assets	流动资产合计 Circulating Funds	#产成品 Finished Product	流动资产年平均余额 Annual Average Balance of Circulating Funds	固定资产原价 Original Value of Fixed Assets
136769.2	224714.4	8.3	267048.1	684846.5	218435.4	17732.9	210095.7	448744.1
3810058.3	5084372.8		3155679.7	8799967.2	1693594.0	108912.8	1459543.9	11137413.3
3474516.0	4391163.0		2442629.6	7222574.7	924767.5	99494.4	748037.8	10038108.1
30136.3	102165.4		35216.6	160217.7	91557.8	5668.0	76710.5	68003.4
37303.6	73300.5		19245.3	85334.8	43728.4	4482.8	43191.1	51722.9
11610.0	22670.2	3744.8	16286.4	53562.7	30097.2	6991.5	31013.7	25625.7
2645.4	4200.9		876.8	4537.8	1814.9	435.2	1844.7	2655.8
114563.4	616061.6	24265.8	192573.7	773974.1	420955.3	112384.5	396071.4	353432.5
21086.0	116007.5		28003.0	89473.8	52313.3	5236.5	49836.1	53275.4
22666.9	147661.1		29887.4	95290.0	46337.0	3772.5	46400.6	47729.8
25049.4	94703.2	458.5	34409.9	177320.7	99199.0	62782.4	82250.6	122014.4
105467.5	292043.8	111826.4	130169.5	675170.6	282978.6	110688.6	259933.5	401172.1
59252.9	143608.9	100617.2	57881.0	439131.0	194396.1	93178.2	172492.8	285475.3
86046.1	174442.6	2579.1	142829.3	510543.8	228892.9	19482.8	228048.4	255031.2
76387.7	149483.7	166.2	120848.4	459001.8	213749.4	14865.3	213798.1	216780.2
50699.0	71329.6		21010.8	89732.2	55391.5	14.1	54650.7	45524.9
121805.0	550195.4	36825.6	388297.9	1043290.5	494599.3	131848.2	526456.7	723240.6
92662.0	457266.4	15609.1	275167.7	749992.7	324738.5	86401.1	351064.8	561898.4
2326.3	18057.9	462.7	56237.3	145207.9	87448.4	27260.3	86840.6	83163.1
2408.5	7617.2	15.0	3369.6	7992.5	5103.0	671.2	5386.6	4497.6
10065.4	33637.3		8186.2	40514.9	23305.9	4497.6	25686.7	17153.9
9804.7	32981.5		7880.0	39466.4	22762.4	4324.4	25171.8	16807.5
260.7	655.8		306.2	1048.5	543.5	173.2	514.9	346.4
8805.4	36924.3	4423.7	14581.2	39319.0	16449.7	3800.3	14948.2	24926.1
16813.8	69926.5	59537.3	33099.5	114556.0	48628.7	4071.0	52403.2	32262.3
39278.5	93304.0		51323.1	250155.3	112395.2	26232.3	108327.0	134368.5
12845.8	35824.0		21981.9	53387.0	19921.7	2125.1	19689.3	51614.6
659181.9	3506913.0	10097.9	549586.4	2466232.5	864259.0	215468.9	799622.8	2757351.3
18162.5	34699.9	2424.2	23005.0	59845.7	20666.6	1256.1	18361.7	32447.8
167776.4	510586.0	20604.1	268954.2	809392.5	348091.9	55044.3	325617.5	469420.1
60779.3	174494.0	7005.8	70048.0	248710.1	103030.7	12532.4	91827.4	156242.2
23756.1	75877.7	423.0	100748.5	179627.9	82432.6	12816.9	65747.3	99608.3
13381.0	32319.7	2319.0	21780.4	72817.3	34838.7	5898.8	38502.5	31128.9
11734.4	35661.8		18415.0	60762.6	21688.6	5007.2	17746.6	28639.0
10269.5	47624.8	632.0	14169.8	80598.9	39664.1	8448.0	42795.0	34318.5
69068.9	252986.4	25762.5	248355.8	768742.4	369345.4	70655.3	353950.7	398387.2
155133.4	474734.8		356081.4	1363556.2	504688.5	34206.8	490168.3	756585.4
96779.1	266562.8		194629.2	859518.4	298588.7	16713.6	298274.1	593967.2
354804.2	1171894.6	4200.4	332445.9	959071.8	376784.0	41439.9	346704.7	589249.3
38198.4	171642.4	2541.2	58231.4	206639.6	84300.0	6852.0	81229.2	144682.6
29447.4	116214.5		43265.7	122554.1	73692.5	14432.7	68202.7	47928.5
24200.7	73376.4	484.7	44384.5	159539.9	85532.3	15409.2	80021.0	58740.0
12746.3	46795.4	239.5	21322.0	134221.4	76129.4	13736.8	74146.1	66000.0
16574.3	85084.8		36984.9	115284.9	73231.9	13249.4	77574.4	40754.5
49930.6	236145.5	1291.5	73143.1	478001.0	259244.6	29143.0	232039.6	112721.0
16134.0	59274.5	5149.4	10339.0	141596.2	41128.4	6144.1	39218.8	113230.7
2048.3	4533.9		1863.0	9200.0	4545.8	154.0	4388.7	6028.3
869.1	3014.8		1306.0	3084.5	1752.7	163.6	1631.9	793.6
435717.4	987130.5		543435.0	3165219.3	534483.5	2331.3	565763.4	3383359.2
402110.9	891152.9		414943.3	2711071.2	436028.2	2303.6	469937.7	2991111.5
10924.4	36917.1		60133.8	149224.8	48050.4	841.2	40059.1	78873.8
17150.2	32259.2		69382.0	232528.4	43422.5	48.6	45021.0	221215.7

12-7 续表

单位: 万元

行 业	Sector	固定资产净值年平均余额 Annual Average Balance of Net Value of Fixed Assets	流动负债合计 Liquid Liabilities	长期负债合计 Long-term Liabilities	所有者权益合计 Creditors' Equity
煤炭开采和洗选业	Coal Extracting and Dressing	278103.5	268601.7	71780.6	343344.3
石油和天然气开采业	Petroleum and Natural Gas Extraction	6160023.7	2169591.6	1662074.0	4968301.6
＃天然原油和天然气开采	Crude Oil and Natural Gas Extraction	5464533.2	1358980.2	1648239.1	4215355.4
黑色金属矿采选业	Ferrous Metals Mining and Dressing	44687.9	78052.7	16646.9	65517.9
有色金属矿采选业	Nonferrous Metals Mining and Dressing	33926.7	44744.9	11126.9	29462.2
非金属矿采选业	Nonmetal Minerals Mining and Dressing	18003.5	30090.2	1306.9	22165.5
＃采 盐	Salt Extraction	1672.1	2688.0	768.9	1080.9
其他采矿业	Other Ore Extraction				
农副食品加工业	Farm and Non-staple Processing	214799.4	427662.8	37225.3	307273.4
＃谷物磨制	Grain Grinding	29874.2	43604.5	5503.1	40317.9
饲料加工	Fodder Processing	32468.0	39134.1	6465.5	49690.4
制 糖	Sugar Making	64282.0	126891.6	11548.0	38577.4
食品制造业	Food Manufacturing	296098.2	457136.3	55300.1	160221.9
＃罐头制造	Beverage Production	215018.3	336075.9	36035.9	64735.4
饮料制造业	Beverage Production	173763.3	238955.9	70653.4	200934.4
＃酒的制造	Wine Manufacturing	143260.3	214689.4	68457.7	175854.6
烟草制品业	Tobacco Products	27090.3	35214.1	17900.0	36618.0
纺织业	Textile Industry	428728.0	567919.6	181196.6	293672.4
＃棉、化纤纺织及印染精加工	Cotton, Chemical Fiber, Dyeing, Printing and Dressing	340029.0	389470.7	139953.5	220466.6
毛纺织和染整精加工	Wool Textile, Dyeing and Printing	47213.1	104799.5	37295.0	2713.4
纺织服装、鞋、帽制造业	Textile Garment, Shoe and Hat	2539.3	5641.0	203.5	2147.4
皮革、毛皮、羽毛(绒)及其制品业	Leather, Fur, Feather (down) its Products	14794.4	24287.6		16227.3
＃皮革鞣制加工	Leather Tanning and Processing	14575.8	23576.4		15890.0
皮革制品制造	Leather Products Manufacturing	218.6	711.2		337.3
木材加工及木、竹、藤、棕、草制品业	Timber Processing, Wood, Bamboo, Cane, Grass Products	18791.8	16111.5	6824.8	16382.6
家具制造业	Furniture Manufacturing	25865.2	13817.4	446.7	100291.9
造纸及纸制品业	Papermaking and Paper Products	87429.1	120492.6	27934.0	101710.6
印刷业和记录媒介的复制	Printing and Copying of Medium for Record	29825.8	22108.2	2298.7	28978.6
文教体育用品制造业	Cultural, Educational and Sports Goods				
石油加工、炼焦及核燃料加工业	Oil Processing, Coking and Nuclear Fuel Processing	1558413.5	647712.9	223287.0	1528959.9
＃炼 焦	Coking	27210.6	26128.6		33117.1
化学原料及化学制品制造业	Raw Chemical Material and Chemical Products	322790.3	339343.9	82356.9	387691.4
＃基础化学原料制造	Basic Chemical Material	108379.0	113236.9	53168.4	82304.8
肥料制造	Fertilizer Making	64503.4	49904.5	11506.7	118216.4
医药制造业	Medical and Pharmaceutical Products	27211.5	42480.0	4106.3	26231.0
化学纤维制造业	Chemical Fiber	25842.8	33363.8	5181.6	22217.2
橡胶制品业	Rubber Products	17731.3	41667.1	10152.7	18775.1
塑料制品业	Plastic Products	276529.7	337349.1	87826.3	343424.1
非金属矿物制品业	Nonmetal Mineral Products	497167.8	600264.1	161304.8	601986.8
＃水泥制造	Cement Manufacturing	380659.2	420597.9	125682.8	313237.4
黑色金属冶炼及压延加工业	Smelting and Pressing of Ferrous Metals	370105.5	391678.6	48393.2	518960.2
有色金属冶炼及压延加工业	Smelting and Pressing of Nonferrous Metals	92123.0	106651.7	24531.1	75238.6
金属制品业	Metal Products	35964.7	67117.4	3404.3	52031.8
通用设备制造业	Ordinary Equipment Production	35822.3	80111.8	4105.8	75249.5
专用设备制造业	Special Purposes Equipment	40898.6	97561.1	10214.7	26395.5
交通运输设备制造业	Transport Equipment	22397.7	81477.3	1459.9	32347.6
电气机械及器材制造业	Electric Equipment and Machinery	79027.5	240550.9	39238.3	198197.3
通信设备、计算机及其他电子设备制造业	Telecom Equipment, Computer and Other Electronic Equipment	78409.9	58881.4	44341.6	38373.2
仪器仪表及文化、办公用机械制造业	Equipment, Meter and Cultural and Office Machinery	4131.1	4501.5	43.4	4655.1
工艺品及其他制造业	Art and Handicraft as well as Other Manufacturing Sector				
废弃资源和废旧材料回收加工业	Recycling and Processing of Deserted Resources and Waste Material	618.7	1423.0		1661.5
电力、热力的生产和供应业	Electric and Thermal Production and Supply	2359553.3	1646106.6	746239.7	772571.8
＃电力生产和电力供应	Electric Power Production and Supply	2065210.9	1468384.8	626361.6	616070.8
燃气生产和供应业	Gas Production and Supply	76037.0	39377.2	40389.8	69457.7
水的生产和供应业	Water Production and Supply	163851.8	72260.1	33221.1	127026.8

Continued

(10 000 yuan)

主营业务收入 Added Value of Industry	#主营业务成本 Cost of Major Business	主营业务税金及附加 Major Business, Tax and Addition	营业利润 Business Profit	利润总额 Total Sum of Profit	亏损企业亏损总额 Lost Enterprise Total Loss	利税总额 Total Profits And Taxes	本年应交增值税 Value Added Taxes Payable	全部从业人员年平均人数(人) Average Number of Staff and Workers (Person)
221153.1	143966.6	2337.8	17612.3	16344.3	4518.3	37611.3	18929.2	40201
5246456.9	2409327.4	96285.6	2018042.8	1924736.9	68753.1	2463574.0	442551.5	80965
4227408.0	1494840.1	86082.5	2042079.5	1987773.6		2447108.1	373252.0	32531
109393.5	67844.8	2479.7	12830.7	13232.9	361.9	22893.7	7181.1	3956
71653.6	45533.6	426.8	14703.1	15337.9	276.8	22158.7	6394.0	4865
19852.0	10024.7	599.3	1905.1	2037.7	740.9	3988.5	1351.5	3145
4228.4	1708.8	331.4	343.4	313.2	99.8	1237.5	592.9	1030
671302.8	576960.9	3481.3	9124.3	12621.3	12683.1	25986.4	9883.8	20785
117260.6	108422.1	84.6	2388.3	2982.4	876.2	3686.3	619.3	2576
150853.0	115252.2	2259.6	3475.2	6387.1	884.8	9152.7	506.0	2129
99294.5	76524.2	950.5	3249.9	3131.3	2745.2	9157.5	5075.7	7084
287834.0	200837.0	1004.8	11692.1	10002.6	11156.0	21092.9	10085.5	10397
146893.4	102283.0	289.2	2541.6	1277.8	8463.0	6770.5	5203.5	3662
155763.8	89350.8	13795.7	13860.2	12180.8	10732.0	38286.3	12309.8	9771
131377.1	74747.6	13768.1	11024.5	10676.8	9211.5	35729.8	11284.9	8440
72167.4	29741.7	26703.1	6650.9	5945.2	406.5	39798.1	7149.8	571
557474.5	524531.3	1575.7	-29219.1	-40142.3	51354.7	-17087.7	21478.9	60320
461074.2	446696.6	1331.1	-33307.4	-31408.2	36630.3	-11879.5	18197.6	47922
16853.5	15647.9	27.5	-4412.9	-4489.4	4540.0	-3790.2	671.7	2937
8093.7	6983.6	32.3	54.7	-21.9	241.7	295.2	284.8	1070
33382.2	29128.4	88.9	1701.2	1724.9	86.9	3271.0	1457.2	828
32724.3	28654.3	83.8	1775.5	1810.9		3290.8	1396.1	686
657.9	474.1	5.1	-74.3	-86.0	86.9	-19.8	61.1	142
34447.2	31030.9	136.7	56.6	784.3	448.3	2267.8	1346.8	2612
72794.9	57630.3	32.3	6748.8	9261.6	31.7	9540.6	246.7	2746
91725.0	74509.8	541.9	3317.5	4946.9	1236.6	12193.2	6704.4	8477
35123.1	26714.1	173.9	688.6	951.5	1001.6	2864.7	1739.3	4009
3507205.6	3062405.4	141991.7	156335.3	49659.9	85145.7	294728.5	103076.9	20586
35238.5	19867.0	103.9	10976.0	10998.0		13781.2	2679.3	1892
541281.8	422199.2	3773.2	39766.9	38821.7	4707.0	71408.7	28813.8	21380
177630.9	128235.1	1487.3	17541.6	14300.0	2094.1	29959.0	14171.7	8336
76204.5	58436.8	382.9	4593.6	5735.7	1588.9	8450.7	2332.1	4255
31317.8	18114.7	251.0	2111.7	3710.3	2203.1	6736.0	2774.7	2043
32133.4	25674.8	68.7	2335.9	2267.3	526.0	3644.4	1308.4	1509
46474.3	39155.0	499.8	224.3	218.6		2516.9	1798.5	2581
436295.4	383266.6	1752.3	16516.4	19557.2	2182.5	30802.6	9493.1	10698
464105.4	369575.2	1741.6	1097.8	30609.2	27549.2	59909.0	27558.2	30418
262880.3	206685.7	1037.0	-13031.1	-8877.0	26885.8	12537.1	20377.1	22072
1192885.9	978470.6	3632.6	159876.4	158416.2	5741.7	231068.2	69019.4	20748
167194.5	143542.4	438.0	5320.6	10060.6	1361.9	17293.4	6794.8	4663
122078.3	107064.7	498.0	3234.2	4052.0	761.7	7637.1	3087.1	6035
73383.6	59719.3	587.9	1833.2	2361.6	1591.2	7307.1	4357.6	6151
55499.4	42550.2	265.3	-1771.8	-1806.1	7218.6	1596.9	3137.7	3890
86491.4	77987.5	302.2	-1898.4	-2071.0	4831.5	970.9	2739.7	5252
249184.5	206009.6	950.3	8200.4	17291.6	2492.6	23695.1	5453.2	5263
56510.6	34972.6	540.5	9295.3	8569.3		14523.8	5414.0	2317
5163.4	2540.2	35.5	1008.6	1073.1	48.2	1260.6	152.0	455
3006.7	2674.1	25.7	56.3	33.7		264.7	205.3	133
1006971.0	939563.9	7963.2	-110347.0	-63206.8	112190.4	32131.6	87375.2	44464
910103.2	859601.6	7393.8	-107664.0	-66925.4	105919.4	23378.7	82910.3	38675
32439.4	22057.5	146.7	-441.6	-621.0	1770.6	1216.2	1690.5	1524
36175.4	28346.5	223.3	-4195.5	-5785.4	7122.2	-3441.1	2121.0	4933

12-8 各地、州、市、县(市)全部国有及规模以上非国有工业企业主要经济指标

单位：万元 (2004 年)

地 区	Region	企业单位数(个) Number of Enterprises (unit)	#亏损企业 Loss	工业总产值(当年价格) Gross Industrial Output Value (At Current Prices)
总 计	**Total**	**1430**	**539**	**15718444.4**
乌鲁木齐市	**Urumqi City**	**332**	**132**	**4355365.2**
乌鲁木齐县	Urumqi County	2	1	1329.9
克拉玛依市	**Karamay City**	**74**	**12**	**5330473.7**
石河子市	**Shihezi City**	**52**	**26**	**388727.0**
阿拉尔市	**Alar City**	**2**	**1**	**4246.0**
图木舒克市	**Tumxuk City**	**5**	**1**	**6288.9**
五家渠市	**Wujiaqu City**	**14**	**4**	**28529.9**
吐鲁番地区	**Turpan Administrative Offices**	**55**	**29**	**745980.2**
吐鲁番市	Turpan City	21	12	68311.7
鄯善县	Shanshan [Piqan] County	22	8	652265.5
托克逊县	Toksun County	12	9	25403.0
哈密地区	**Hami [Kumul] Administrative Offices**	**70**	**24**	**305940.4**
哈密市	Hami [Kumul] City	53	19	283786.2
巴里坤哈萨克自治县	Barkol Kazak Autonomous County	13	2	13313.3
伊吾县	Yiwu [Araturuk] County	4	3	8840.9
昌吉回族自治州	**Changji Hui Autonomous Prefecture**	**240**	**78**	**1224291.1**
昌吉市	Changji City	68	21	455681.9
阜康市	Fukang City	27	10	147168.8
米泉市	Miquan City	74	15	339775.3
呼图壁县	Hutubi County	29	11	99248.4
玛纳斯县	Manas County	23	11	135609.9
奇台县	Qitai County	11	6	28003.2
吉木萨尔县	Jimsar County	5	2	17247.8
木垒哈萨克自治县	Mori Kazak Autonomous County	3	2	1555.8
伊犁哈萨克自治州	**Ili Kazak Autonomous Prefecture**	**247**	**92**	**896854.3**
伊犁州直属县(市)	**Counties (Cities) Direct Under Ili Prefecture**	**126**	**41**	**560395.5**
伊宁市	Yining [Gulja] City	31	15	122701.2
奎屯市	Kuytun City	33	10	186031.4
伊宁县	Yining [Gulja] County	16	3	61496.5
察布查尔锡伯自治县	Qapqal Xibe Autonomous County	5	3	6298.8
霍城县	Huocheng [Korgas] County	18	6	53937.8
巩留县	Gongliu [Tokkuztara] County	3		9627.5
新源县	Xinyuan [Kunes] County	8	2	97365.4
昭苏县	Zhaosu [Mongolkure] County	8	1	20245.6
特克斯县	Tekes County	1		69.5
尼勒克县	Nilka County	3	1	2621.8

Main Economic Indicators of All State-owned and Non-state-owned above Designated Size Industrial Enterprises by Prefecture, Autonomous Prefecture, City and County

(10 000 yuan)

工业增加值 Added Value of Industry	工业销售产值（当年价） Sales Value of Industry Products (At Current Prices)	出口交货值 Delivery Value of Industry Export	实收资本 Total Capital Hold	资产合计 Total Assets	流动资产合计 Circulating Funds	#产成品 Finished Product	流动资产年平均余额 Annual Average Balance of Circulating Funds	固定资产原价 Original Value of Fixed Assets
6689966.6	**15373639.7**	**316548.2**	**7274478.1**	**24880833.1**	**7670908.8**	**1098278.8**	**7236560.6**	**23114141.3**
1323619.8	**4300477.3**	**159087.0**	**2035726.9**	**6774529.7**	**2193754.5**	**285871.5**	**2039790.0**	**5236051.9**
581.9	1124.8		993.8	3328.0	1563.6	1.6	1494.8	2710.2
2651371.8	**5291791.9**	**7673.7**	**2208036.0**	**6632916.6**	**1598022.3**	**154657.6**	**1536425.6**	**8162279.0**
115823.0	**370505.2**	**37063.1**	**213375.6**	**1079145.3**	**501299.3**	**111767.4**	**476607.0**	**569309.5**
147.0	**3644.0**		**2726.8**	**11148.5**	**4096.5**	**1200.6**	**3547.4**	**6265.5**
1849.3	**6886.5**		**13779.2**	**32700.8**	**8438.8**	**707.4**	**8912.6**	**20075.2**
4830.2	**26070.2**	**2160.8**	**13935.6**	**48814.9**	**26287.7**	**8869.2**	**27008.1**	**33536.9**
534595.7	**734772.2**	**2100.6**	**337452.9**	**1067432.4**	**218584.9**	**27460.5**	**190445.7**	**1558984.9**
25371.4	64064.5	2100.6	42706.0	208060.5	90640.9	5963.5	67746.2	165218.7
500849.8	645727.5		281819.0	818450.7	112855.6	14680.3	106901.6	1367734.2
8374.5	24980.2		12927.9	40921.2	15088.4	6816.7	15797.9	26032.0
128039.1	**297613.7**	**11918.7**	**157778.5**	**640822.0**	**244136.3**	**21479.8**	**239014.3**	**485994.8**
118614.6	277345.2	11918.7	152379.9	617216.9	230342.5	18926.2	227234.8	474682.7
5035.9	11611.6		2966.1	17330.3	9305.8	2326.8	8748.5	9212.6
4388.6	8656.9		2432.5	6274.8	4488.0	226.8	3031.0	2099.5
347961.0	**1175311.1**	**36494.4**	**407054.5**	**1929739.5**	**809119.5**	**124646.4**	**797359.6**	**1141882.4**
111881.4	445089.3	22090.6	179993.7	976210.4	449076.9	50452.3	432725.8	427311.6
51459.6	146035.5	4200.1	60742.5	228471.3	83348.6	5910.6	73600.8	152926.4
96451.2	319996.7	423.0	86185.0	294711.4	140069.1	25013.1	135778.1	158226.6
24079.0	97077.8	2085.1	28003.9	116372.0	36128.0	11975.0	53789.8	93195.9
50048.8	123035.0	7695.6	34406.1	232734.3	69733.2	21006.2	68151.1	251847.9
8530.2	27542.0		9158.2	38343.4	14448.5	4169.3	14602.2	29431.4
5794.2	14063.9		6542.3	35134.0	14735.9	5907.3	14974.8	22153.3
-283.4	2470.9		2022.8	7762.7	1579.3	212.6	3737.0	6789.3
325190.7	**852656.8**	**29752.3**	**461088.8**	**1782231.8**	**653349.9**	**119369.2**	**628540.6**	**1283739.3**
216316.7	**533995.4**	**14764.6**	**282125.0**	**1033655.3**	**406462.2**	**72611.0**	**393233.6**	**742774.2**
40504.7	120031.5	803.5	69334.8	286465.6	83356.5	12039.3	92886.2	261591.9
82188.2	179672.9	6741.8	75996.3	319468.8	144300.1	16976.8	131607.3	209566.6
23115.7	60154.8		43442.1	111841.0	35270.2	7629.6	34271.1	102550.2
1003.7	6114.3		3133.9	8022.9	2531.7	681.7	2322.7	5908.3
12910.1	47741.8	3887.1	24402.6	100716.2	45408.5	18428.6	40468.5	71824.1
4564.0	10022.7		5754.3	12880.6	6379.9	441.4	6712.2	7470.0
47309.0	89083.1	1439.0	56368.5	172880.0	76914.2	13884.2	72597.1	73690.6
3712.0	19303.0	1893.2	1955.3	15520.6	9779.0	1697.1	10143.1	6984.0
44.0	69.5		129.2	1136.8	210.7		210.7	505.9
965.3	1801.8		1608.0	4722.8	2311.4	832.3	2014.7	2682.6

12-8 续表 1

单位: 万元

地 区	Region	企业单位数(个) Number of Enterprises (unit)	#亏损企业 Loss	工业总产值(当年价格) Gross Industrial Output Value (At Current Prices)
塔城地区	**Tacheng [Tarbagatai] Administrative Offices**	**77**	**32**	**221186.2**
塔城市	Tacheng [Qoqek] City	7	7	20141.2
乌苏市	Usu City	18	8	50533.2
额敏县	Emin [Dorbiljin] County	14	6	45656.6
沙湾县	Shawan County	22	7	71786.0
托里县	Toli County	3		12884.3
裕民县	Yumin [Qagantokay] County	1		91.7
和布克赛尔蒙古自治县	Hoboksar Mongol Autonomous County	12	4	20093.2
阿勒泰地区	**Altay Administrative Offices**	**44**	**19**	**115272.6**
阿勒泰市	Altay City	20	10	46366.8
布尔津县	Burqin County	3		5555.0
富蕴县	Fuyun [Koktokay] County	11	2	52262.1
福海县	Fuhai [Burultokay] County	5	3	7519.2
哈巴河县	Habahe [Kaba] County	2	1	2582.8
青河县	Qinghe [Qinggil] County	2	2	191.2
吉木乃县	Jeminay County	1	1	795.5
博尔塔拉蒙古自治州	**Bortala Mongol Autonomous Prefecture**	**29**	**11**	**101830.5**
博乐市	Bole [Bortala] City	21	9	87988.9
精河县	Jinghe [Jing] County	7	2	12520.9
温泉县	Wenquan [Araxang] County	1		1320.7
巴音郭楞蒙古自治州	**Bayangol Mongol Autonomous Prefecture**	**118**	**49**	**1678695.3**
库尔勒市	Korla City	58	20	1436404.2
轮台县	Luntai [Bugur] County	9	5	78424.6
尉犁县	Yuli [Lopnur] County	6	3	36333.6
若羌县	Ruoqiang [Qarkilik] County	5	2	15732.9
且末县	Qiemo [Qarqan] County	2	2	1168.6
焉耆回族自治县	Yanji Hui Autonomous County	9	6	22879.5
和静县	Hejing County	14	5	51399.5
和硕县	Hoxud County	10	3	15626.0
博湖县	Bohu [Bagrax] County	5	3	20726.4
阿克苏地区	**Aksu Administrative Offices**	**87**	**23**	**442996.2**
阿克苏市	Aksu City	30	5	180707.9
温宿县	Wensu [Onsu] County	9	3	12390.4
库车县	Kuqa County	23	2	179678.5

Continued

(10 000 yuan)

工业增加值 Added Value of Industry	工业销售产值(当年价) Sales Value of Industry Products (At Current Prices)	出口交货值 Delivery Value of Industry Export	实收资本 Total Capital Hold	资产合计 Total Assets	流动资产合计 Circulating Funds	#产成品 Finished Product	流动资产年平均余额 Annual Average Balance of Circulating Funds	固定资产原价 Original Value of Fixed Assets
68515.5	**208228.3**	**14987.7**	**108296.0**	**514200.4**	**173949.7**	**37289.8**	**162530.2**	**357805.4**
8028.6	19475.3	67.0	10327.0	75418.1	17992.4	2557.8	18048.5	70791.1
16165.2	46962.8	5731.5	9450.5	87698.3	36785.9	7688.5	35692.6	73809.2
13599.0	45043.5	458.5	27373.9	123555.7	36814.2	8488.6	30535.7	52692.0
13469.9	63542.4	8730.7	36122.9	142804.2	53030.2	15548.7	49144.8	100623.3
6769.6	12909.0		7711.7	28669.5	11453.5	1717.3	10738.5	15846.6
35.5	91.7		243.8	435.8	128.1		128.1	307.7
10447.7	20203.6		17066.2	55618.8	17745.4	1288.9	18242.0	43735.5
40358.5	**110433.1**		**70667.8**	**234376.1**	**72938.0**	**9468.4**	**72776.8**	**183159.7**
10798.8	46031.6		23778.9	126372.3	31431.8	3738.8	28909.1	102093.5
2169.9	5644.2		11088.7	18151.5	3034.0	49.9	3621.8	15450.8
23483.7	47816.6		12823.4	58671.8	27256.0	4611.2	29824.0	40227.2
2178.4	7373.0		20855.5	24133.1	6552.2	1062.8	6037.1	21446.1
1351.1	2582.8		1200.0	4360.2	2831.3		2730.7	1738.6
97.9	191.2		164.8	682.6	182.1		200.5	725.0
278.7	793.7		756.5	2004.6	1650.6	5.7	1453.6	1478.5
17686.6	**97710.9**		**36370.5**	**180920.2**	**76174.0**	**26875.5**	**67089.2**	**129299.7**
14651.1	84804.0		29395.4	165826.5	69790.1	24546.8	60001.2	116630.1
2767.9	11727.1		6925.0	14201.6	5631.8	1976.8	6335.9	12545.6
267.6	1179.8		50.1	892.1	752.1	351.9	752.1	124.0
1031353.9	**1595257.8**	**27880.6**	**1047124.4**	**3123534.4**	**871549.1**	**156184.4**	**746091.0**	**3248103.9**
948415.5	1414153.1	4767.0	925632.2	2736693.7	689866.2	105215.1	584507.9	3008103.0
35134.3	48003.7		14180.1	43844.0	20689.8	6583.0	18294.5	24045.4
8106.0	35006.1	6720.2	21122.1	80105.1	31157.5	4246.7	32839.9	62929.0
5460.2	12095.0	109.0	58972.8	77934.0	44510.4	2914.2	31073.4	26407.3
426.3	897.7		901.6	4658.1	626.2		721.9	5679.4
5718.9	12377.3	1602.1	4858.9	42166.0	16006.9	9434.7	12793.6	35391.8
18065.3	44446.6		15462.6	82262.3	41744.1	14781.2	38365.2	45426.8
5324.8	13776.3	4646.2	5527.2	25159.9	13116.3	5924.0	13335.3	13590.0
4702.6	14502.0	10036.1	466.9	30711.3	13831.7	7085.5	14159.3	26531.2
143414.7	**425700.2**	**2417.0**	**206355.2**	**888853.5**	**270801.2**	**41862.4**	**258770.5**	**635288.8**
59624.2	174020.9		102211.6	441257.2	137788.7	17721.8	145145.5	313969.1
5713.8	12101.8		3242.0	19646.0	6311.1	313.3	5540.0	13620.9
51641.8	171601.4	2417.0	57225.7	288840.3	85286.2	20014.3	70883.1	198584.4

12-8 续表 2

单位: 万元

地 区	Region	企业单位数(个) Number of Enterprises (unit)	#亏损企业 Loss	工业总产值(当年价格) Gross Industrial Output Value (At Current Prices)
沙雅县	Xayar County	4	4	5664.2
新和县	Xinhe [Toksu] County	4	2	7304.6
拜城县	Baicheng [Bay] County	10	2	51416.9
乌什县	Wushi [Uxturpan] County			
阿瓦提县	Awat County	3	2	4161.7
柯坪县	Kalpin County	4	3	1672.0
克孜勒苏柯尔克孜自治州	**Kizilsu Kirgiz Autonomous Prefecture**	**17**	**7**	**17641.1**
阿图什市	Artux City	8	2	13274.0
阿克陶县	Akto County	3	2	1024.0
阿合奇县	Akqi County	2	1	109.0
乌恰县	Wuqia [Ulugqat] County	4	2	3234.1
喀什地区	**Kashgar [Kaxgar] Administrative Offices**	**59**	**31**	**146652.6**
喀什市	Kashgar [Kaxgar] City	15	8	96944.4
疏附县	Shufu County	5	5	3747.4
疏勒县	Shule County	9	2	19242.7
英吉沙县	Yengisar County	5	3	3409.2
泽普县	Zepu [Poskam] County	4	2	6627.5
莎车县	Shache [Yarkant] County	5	2	5485.7
叶城县	Yecheng [Kagilik] County	4	1	2317.9
麦盖提县	Makit County	3	3	539.1
岳普湖县	Yopurga County	4	1	3132.8
伽师县	Jiashi [Payzawat] County	1	1	155.5
巴楚县	Bachu [Maralbexi] County	3	2	5005.2
塔什库尔干塔吉克自治县	Taxkorgan Tajik Autonomous County	1	1	45.2
和田地区	**Hotan Administrative Offices**	**29**	**19**	**43932.0**
和田市	Hotan City	11	7	27599.8
和田县	Hotan County	4	3	7579.5
墨玉县	Moyu [Karakax] County	2	1	426.0
皮山县	Pishan [Guma] County	2	2	190.9
洛浦县	Lop County	4	1	7638.2
策勒县	Qira County	1	1	81.6
于田县	Yutian [Keriya] County	3	2	351.5
民丰县	Minfeng [Niya] County	2	2	64.5

Continued

(10 000 yuan)

工业增加值 Added Value of Industry	工业销售产值(当年价) Sales Value of Industry Products (At Current Prices)	出口交货值 Delivery Value of Industry Export	实收资本 Total Capital Hold	资产合计 Total Assets	流动资产合计 Circulating Funds	#产成品 Finished Product	流动资产年平均余额 Annual Average Balance of Circulating Funds	固定资产原价 Original Value of Fixed Assets
1542.4	5546.1		7107.4	20879.0	7719.4	1106.8	5338.5	12436.6
-213.8	6331.7		4362.4	20178.7	5773.2	1252.1	5293.0	3823.4
23420.0	50494.8		26563.9	84574.6	20766.0	1113.7	19524.9	85674.4
911.9	3931.5		2480.0	7863.9	5018.5	339.0	4977.8	3712.6
774.4	1672.0		3162.2	5613.8	2138.1	1.4	2067.7	3467.4
3961.3	**17080.7**		**7846.7**	**37332.2**	**15201.0**	**1612.1**	**15034.1**	**29620.8**
2611.7	12662.8		5118.3	20320.8	10148.9	1161.3	10017.2	10930.2
319.0	1025.4		606.1	7355.7	1286.9		1498.5	8165.9
35.5	101.4		102.5	168.7	58.1	8.0	58.1	128.3
995.1	3291.1		2019.8	9487.0	3707.1	442.8	3460.3	10396.4
43082.9	**137118.8**		**59891.4**	**424571.4**	**110590.1**	**10764.6**	**127363.3**	**382670.3**
33417.4	92417.7		33582.8	339861.1	72741.0	2940.4	88742.5	330786.3
916.3	3512.6		3764.2	8390.8	2249.3	331.4	1932.1	8266.9
3218.2	17530.0		8230.6	23282.1	11074.4	3769.9	11545.8	14052.9
514.0	3527.0		2311.9	6806.9	2803.1	36.7	2638.5	4033.2
1443.4	7006.4		4258.4	8298.4	3215.7	630.8	3912.2	5193.6
1214.8	2678.3		2250.2	15950.0	8935.6	2126.8	9141.2	8693.0
856.8	2255.8		1965.1	4976.9	1545.9	23.1	1605.7	4285.4
161.4	502.5		1098.3	3315.5	977.8	22.3	1289.8	2038.1
872.6	3178.9		592.5	3815.2	2303.1	141.3	2204.4	1365.1
53.8	155.5		50.0	2957.8	92.0		88.7	2892.7
397.3	4308.9		1766.3	6051.6	4016.2	741.9	3626.4	838.9
16.9	45.2		21.1	865.1	636.0		636.0	224.2
17039.6	**41042.4**		**65935.1**	**226139.9**	**69503.7**	**4950.2**	**74561.6**	**191038.4**
10219.8	24920.3		21070.6	156771.7	51154.3	3999.3	57647.5	127695.5
3449.4	7454.1		41254.8	53660.1	12793.7		11942.5	50303.9
135.3	426.0		426.7	1927.2	153.6		231.8	2092.1
45.7	190.9		255.2	434.6	77.4	27.7	56.2	436.1
3030.0	7548.6		1745.4	10630.5	5021.6	918.7	4378.6	7673.7
29.7	81.6		163.8	207.5	62.3		42.8	250.0
114.1	356.4		546.9	1260.4	221.3	4.5	241.3	2132.5
15.6	64.5		471.7	1247.9	19.5		20.9	454.6

12-8 续表 3

单位: 万元

地 区	Region	固定资产净值年平均余额 Annual Average Balance of Net Value of Fixed Assets	流动负债合计 Liquid Liabilities	长期负债合计 Long-term Liabilities	所有者权益合计 Creditors' Equity
总 计	**Total**	**13939098.1**	**9450307.6**	**3732716.9**	**11614702.1**
乌鲁木齐市	**Urumqi City**	**3479252.5**	**2772291.8**	**847609.6**	**3152043.6**
乌鲁木齐县	Urumqi County	1676.8	2447.4	368.5	512.1
克拉玛依市	**Karamay City**	**4604974.7**	**1656941.4**	**970202.9**	**4005722.3**
石河子市	**Shihezi City**	**380568.5**	**567671.2**	**145285.4**	**366149.2**
阿拉尔市	**Alar City**	**4519.8**	**3937.2**	**1600.0**	**5611.3**
图木舒克市	**Tumxuk City**	**14080.0**	**7826.6**	**11434.1**	**13440.0**
五家渠市	**Wujiaqu City**	**19307.0**	**35963.9**	**5220.3**	**7630.7**
吐鲁番地区	**Turpan Administrative Offices**	**721029.9**	**312248.1**	**212909.8**	**542274.3**
吐鲁番市	Turpan City	99718.5	94543.0	21096.7	92420.7
鄯善县	Shanshan [Piqan] County	603560.4	197422.3	184427.7	436600.7
托克逊县	Toksun County	17751.0	20282.8	7385.4	13252.9
哈密地区	**Hami [Kumul] Administrative Offices**	**314858.7**	**287469.2**	**126401.3**	**226439.9**
哈密市	Hami [Kumul] City	307620.2	272974.5	125114.1	218617.5
巴里坤哈萨克自治县	Barkol Kazak Autonomous County	5526.0	12930.6	1202.7	3197.0
伊吾县	Yiwu [Araturuk] County	1712.5	1564.1	84.5	4625.4
昌吉回族自治州	**Changji Hui Autonomous Prefecture**	**777454.3**	**1042311.9**	**228480.9**	**657276.1**
昌吉市	Changji City	313301.5	499651.3	127188.0	349351.8
阜康市	Fukang City	105219.7	114241.9	20964.9	91661.5
米泉市	Miquan City	113397.9	140786.2	21882.5	132042.6
呼图壁县	Hutubi County	52151.2	48082.1	34012.1	34277.8
玛纳斯县	Manas County	151939.9	176570.5	21140.3	35023.5
奇台县	Qitai County	19879.1	28039.5	292.1	9963.6
吉木萨尔县	Jimsar County	16382.6	28026.6	2000.0	5107.4
木垒哈萨克自治县	Mori Kazak Autonomous County	5182.4	6913.8	1001.0	-152.1
伊犁哈萨克自治州	**Ili Kazak Autonomous Prefecture**	**884296.2**	**886826.9**	**279119.6**	**613884.2**
伊犁州直属县(市)	**Counties (Cities) Direct Under Ili Prefecture**	**497972.7**	**440659.7**	**197739.8**	**394933.3**
伊宁市	Yining [Gulja] City	182411.2	161309.4	52841.9	72313.9
奎屯市	Kuytun City	140489.9	102827.3	92313.7	124305.9
伊宁县	Yining [Gulja] County	62461.0	42830.0	24815.4	44195.6
察布查尔锡伯自治县	Qapqal Xibe Autonomous County	4591.2	2588.1	236.2	5198.6
霍城县	Huocheng [Korgas] County	48143.6	57432.8	8824.8	34158.6
巩留县	Gongliu [Tokkuztara] County	5421.2	3013.3		9867.3
新源县	Xinyuan [Kunes] County	47707.5	59445.0	17125.3	96309.5
昭苏县	Zhaosu [Mongolkure] County	4678.1	8795.0	241.5	6484.1
特克斯县	Tekes County	382.2	95.4	851.0	190.4
尼勒克县	Nilka County	1686.8	2323.4	490.0	1909.4

Continued

(10 000 yuan)

主营业务收入 Income of Major Business	#主营业务成本 Cost of Major Business	主营业务税金及附加 Major Business, Tax and Addition	营业利润 Business Profit	利润总额 Total Sum of Profit	亏损企业亏损总额 Lost Enterprise Total Loss	利税总额 Total Profits And Taxes	本年应交增值税 Value Added Taxes Payable	全部从业人员年平均人数(人) Average Number of Staff and Workers (Person)
15834415.5	**11290005.9**	**315383.3**	**2378328.8**	**2263156.6**	**431474.2**	**3494005.3**	**915465.4**	**449761**
4385108.0	**3447570.0**	**77380.7**	**372130.5**	**289289.2**	**181313.0**	**558286.4**	**191616.5**	**107900**
1074.5	861.7	4.1	-282.4	-273.5	300.0	-225.1	44.3	265
5395544.6	**3641575.6**	**138517.5**	**1152142.6**	**1056988.4**	**69174.7**	**1582693.6**	**387187.7**	**84609**
539544.5	**451158.6**	**2489.2**	**9382.4**	**12232.6**	**12780.6**	**31776.8**	**17055.0**	**22197**
5539.0	**5913.4**	**0.1**	**-686.0**	**-685.6**	**838.9**	**-685.5**		**154**
6447.5	**6681.2**	**0.4**	**-1245.7**	**-1089.9**	**1384.2**	**-296.1**	**793.4**	**445**
24726.1	**22092.8**	**64.8**	**-2145.3**	**-2045.8**	**2636.2**	**-540.6**	**1440.4**	**3348**
766367.7	**407375.6**	**12769.0**	**300421.9**	**300473.9**	**16536.0**	**375273.1**	**62030.2**	**13728**
96464.5	97488.4	421.6	-10885.1	-10698.3	12682.8	-4624.3	5652.4	4809
646214.0	290440.1	11926.9	311324.2	311219.6	1407.5	378044.7	54898.2	6646
23689.2	19447.1	420.5	-17.2	-47.4	2445.7	1852.7	1479.6	2273
292157.4	**231972.3**	**2956.8**	**10351.1**	**9182.3**	**9847.4**	**32327.7**	**20188.6**	**24302**
272151.0	221688.1	2656.7	7625.9	6492.8	9705.4	27702.6	18553.1	22253
11332.9	7587.8	84.7	298.8	250.3	49.0	1113.5	778.5	1913
8673.5	2696.4	215.4	2426.4	2439.2	93.0	3511.6	857.0	136
1189641.0	**1011504.7**	**7342.4**	**22925.4**	**36532.8**	**31131.1**	**88223.4**	**44348.2**	**45474**
459658.9	398175.0	3869.5	-7858.6	5886.4	17447.7	20235.9	10480.0	14587
145466.5	108822.1	652.5	20632.4	20562.7	857.2	31347.3	10132.1	7450
313512.1	270575.9	1184.6	13232.9	13922.9	1295.1	24456.2	9348.7	10247
104325.9	93914.7	607.4	-1465.9	-1012.9	2813.7	4024.9	4430.4	4862
120770.8	101340.8	651.0	3110.0	2765.5	2161.8	12159.6	8743.1	5603
28524.7	24307.0	181.8	-1289.1	-1419.0	2064.7	-650.6	586.6	1382
15178.3	11976.8	190.9	-1975.8	-2624.9	2934.9	-1877.7	556.3	1126
2203.8	2392.4	4.7	-1460.5	-1547.9	1556.0	-1472.2	71.0	217
895042.6	**711273.0**	**37668.3**	**4955.6**	**8950.3**	**54836.3**	**103523.6**	**56905.0**	**58140**
558832.1	**437882.2**	**34019.5**	**8470.6**	**12522.2**	**27981.0**	**80547.9**	**34006.2**	**31382**
122262.1	109223.3	1198.1	-8799.7	-8366.1	15174.6	774.1	7942.1	10929
205704.9	153244.6	27161.2	-1188.8	437.3	10395.3	40738.4	13139.9	6011
55158.1	42221.5	111.5	260.2	3394.2	426.0	6781.8	3276.1	4987
6123.4	5813.6	4.7	507.5	-168.2	364.6	-91.2	72.3	273
46544.5	38656.9	417.5	257.8	440.7	994.8	2937.9	2079.7	3254
9950.3	6422.8	35.8	3024.7	3322.0		3934.2	576.4	862
91971.2	62851.6	5062.9	13761.2	13305.1	617.6	24979.1	6611.1	3878
19214.6	18010.5	23.2	623.5	133.8	0.3	382.5	225.5	948
69.5	35.5	0.3	1.3	1.5		6.4	4.6	29
1833.5	1401.9	4.3	22.9	21.9	7.8	104.7	78.5	211

12-8 续表 4

单位: 万元

地　　区	Region	固定资产净值年平均余额 Annual Average Balance of Net Value of Fixed Assets	流动负债合　计 Liquid Liabilities	长期负债合　计 Long-term Liabilities	所有者权益合计 Creditors' Equity
塔城地区	**Tacheng [Tarbagatai] Administrative Offices**	**247774.4**	**314443.5**	**45825.8**	**151863.9**
塔城市	Tacheng [Qoqek] City	49131.8	53349.9	13064.2	8913.2
乌苏市	Usu City	47999.7	66200.1	2551.3	18946.9
额敏县	Emin [Dorbiljin] County	32320.3	52784.7	3056.6	66854.3
沙湾县	Shawan County	71436.1	105709.5	7067.4	30027.3
托里县	Toli County	11244.4	15246.3	3855.0	8461.7
裕民县	Yumin [Qagantokay] County	307.7	192.0		243.8
和布克赛尔蒙古自治县	Hoboksar Mongol Autonomous County	35334.4	20961.0	16231.3	18416.7
阿勒泰地区	**Altay Administrative Offices**	**138549.1**	**131723.7**	**35554.0**	**67087.0**
阿勒泰市	Altay City	84108.8	87615.5	20069.3	18687.3
布尔津县	Burqin County	12502.9	5586.3	1472.6	11092.5
富蕴县	Fuyun [Koktokay] County	23908.0	29663.4	11495.2	17502.1
福海县	Fuhai [Burultokay] County	15681.3	4620.0	1781.2	17731.9
哈巴河县	Habahe [Kaba] County	1536.9	2747.7	500.0	1112.5
青河县	Qinghe [Qinggil] County	426.8	277.0	235.7	169.9
吉木乃县	Jeminay County	384.4	1213.8		790.8
博尔塔拉蒙古自治州	**Bortala Mongol Autonomous Prefecture**	**94640.5**	**94469.6**	**41768.7**	**44681.5**
博乐市	Bole [Bortala] City	86948.9	88281.3	39959.9	37584.9
精河县	Jinghe [Jing] County	7596.5	5412.1	1761.3	7028.2
温泉县	Wenquan [Araxang] County	95.1	776.2	47.5	68.4
巴音郭楞蒙古自治州	**Bayangol Mongol Autonomous Prefecture**	**1781940.7**	**953434.7**	**655900.7**	**1504147.3**
库尔勒市	Korla City	1610990.8	758317.6	616690.6	1351656.9
轮台县	Luntai [Bugur] County	19322.9	20463.0	128.7	23229.6
尉犁县	Yuli [Lopnur] County	44774.8	18774.2	24839.0	36491.9
若羌县	Ruoqiang [Qarkilik] County	20478.9	14757.5	180.0	62996.4
且末县	Qiemo [Qarqan] County	3668.3	2085.3	2820.5	-247.9
焉耆回族自治县	Yanji Hui Autonomous County	20218.9	36570.5	1393.8	4201.7
和静县	Hejing County	35837.5	59559.3	1997.2	20705.7
和硕县	Hoxud County	9098.5	16214.0	3198.1	5747.8
博湖县	Bohu [Bagrax] County	17550.1	26693.3	4652.8	-634.8
阿克苏地区	**Aksu Administrative Offices**	**441277.8**	**359566.6**	**97674.3**	**365925.6**
阿克苏市	Aksu City	219909.6	211837.4	22390.1	207028.3
温宿县	Wensu [Onsu] County	9685.7	12155.0	3634.9	3855.9
库车县	Kuqa County	138760.3	73442.0	66195.0	83619.2

Continued

(10 000 yuan)

主营业务收入 Income of Major Business	#主营业务成本 Cost of Major Business	主营业务税金及附加 Major Business, Tax and Addition	营业利润 Business Profit	利润总额 Total Sum of Profit	亏损企业亏损总额 Lost Enterprises Total Loss	利税总额 Total Profits And Taxes	本年应交增值税 Value Added Taxes Payable	全部从业人员年平均人数(人) Average Number of Staff and Workers (Person)
224254.5	**190563.9**	**2724.4**	**-7807.5**	**-7829.4**	**19982.6**	**9174.3**	**14279.3**	**19636**
16313.9	23072.6	96.5	-10556.9	-11141.7	11141.7	-8316.5	2728.7	1933
54863.4	42589.2	1616.1	2559.2	1847.2	3748.0	7100.9	3637.6	4002
44806.1	36421.9	301.2	2055.8	2681.0	962.5	5216.1	2233.9	2355
77630.4	67515.5	106.8	-78.5	-350.5	2058.1	2755.5	2999.2	5029
12351.4	8028.5	121.4	-15.6	243.2		1340.2	975.6	3016
50.3	192.1	1.2		122.0		123.2		35
18239.0	12744.1	481.2	-1771.5	-1230.6	2072.3	954.9	1704.3	3266
111956.0	**82826.9**	**924.4**	**4292.5**	**4257.5**	**6872.7**	**13801.4**	**8619.5**	**7122**
46018.0	40630.6	232.6	-4384.1	-4460.8	5659.4	-1779.6	2448.6	2956
5644.2	3448.2	13.0	3.0	343.9		884.3	527.4	361
49612.8	29161.5	631.5	9333.8	8964.0	178.9	14506.4	4910.9	2897
7133.9	6974.9	42.5	-723.8	-632.8	701.9	-84.9	505.4	447
2582.9	1799.1	1.7	218.5	220.7	155.0	388.5	166.1	231
174.4	149.5	1.1	-60.5	-82.2	82.2	-70.7	10.4	88
789.8	663.1	2.0	-94.4	-95.3	95.3	-42.6	50.7	142
93886.6	**85028.2**	**490.2**	**-4136.8**	**-3228.5**	**5405.9**	**502.0**	**3240.3**	**7474**
79431.8	71912.9	392.9	-4110.4	-3319.6	5319.2	-335.3	2591.4	6384
13253.8	11945.6	97.3	25.4	89.2	86.7	835.4	648.9	1051
1201.0	1169.7		-51.8	1.9		1.9		39
1615828.3	**733541.0**	**28670.5**	**515647.6**	**510358.5**	**19272.8**	**639007.2**	**99978.2**	**40389**
1417718.1	583478.2	27108.7	498118.1	491806.2	15850.5	613145.2	94230.3	27623
54758.2	38979.0	596.6	12696.1	12974.6	276.5	14630.3	1059.1	632
38411.2	30651.1	138.5	1869.4	1983.4	129.5	3150.5	1028.6	4562
11963.3	7943.0	323.4	919.2	764.3	148.3	1495.7	408.0	1570
766.9	667.8	4.2	-159.8	-141.8	141.8	-130.6	7.0	176
12730.1	10185.6	159.7	-1068.4	-1072.3	1207.3	-68.3	844.3	966
50342.4	39090.5	241.1	3047.5	3982.3	308.6	5799.0	1575.6	3204
14636.1	11811.8	77.5	816.7	787.4	13.3	1528.7	663.8	1225
14502.0	10734.0	20.8	-591.2	-725.6	1197.0	-543.3	161.5	431
425534.6	**331270.0**	**5311.1**	**31282.7**	**37911.5**	**3726.2**	**62149.2**	**18926.6**	**21694**
181792.3	141392.4	911.4	7226.9	14011.6	1129.4	24915.0	9992.0	13220
10921.2	7399.5	499.0	545.2	573.1	106.1	1884.4	812.3	1350
171215.4	134383.3	3336.9	20897.6	20952.3	415.4	28831.4	4542.2	2715

12-8 续表 5

单位: 万元

地 区	Region	固定资产净值年平均余额 Annual Average Balance Of Net Value of Fixed Assets	流动负债合 计 Liquid Liabilities	长期负债合 计 Long-term Liabilities	所有者权益 合 计 Creditors' Equity
沙雅县	Xayar County	8503.6	6813.6	3171.2	10894.2
新和县	Xinhe [Toksu] County	3159.0	5176.3	200.0	14802.4
拜城县	Baicheng [Bay] County	56573.1	42930.5	732.5	40901.5
乌什县	Wushi [Uxturpan] County				
阿瓦提县	Awat County	2057.6	5591.6	343.1	1929.0
柯坪县	Kalpin County	2628.9	1620.2	1007.5	2895.1
克孜勒苏柯尔克孜自治州	**Kizilsu Kirgiz Autonomous Prefecture**	**18756.7**	**26130.7**	**6659.8**	**4541.6**
阿图什市	Artux City	9058.8	12055.3	3021.6	5243.9
阿克陶县	Akto County	5545.2	5897.1	1823.3	-364.7
阿合奇县	Akqi County	110.6	60.4		108.3
乌恰县	Wuqia [Ulugqat] County	4042.1	8117.9	1814.9	-445.9
喀什地区	**Kashgar [Kaxgar] Administrative Offices**	**253378.7**	**298851.8**	**77293.8**	**48416.4**
喀什市	Kashgar [Kaxgar] City	214334.1	244216.1	69563.9	26081.1
疏附县	Shufu County	5938.6	2936.6	2682.2	2771.9
疏勒县	Shule County	10402.7	15252.6	330.9	7698.6
英吉沙县	Yengisar County	2771.9	3119.8	2474.2	1212.9
泽普县	Zepu [Poskam] County	4263.2	3701.8	392.1	4204.5
莎车县	Shache [Yarkant] County	6407.5	16462.1	565.0	-1077.1
叶城县	Yecheng [Kagilik] County	3310.1	2285.7	94.0	2596.9
麦盖提县	Makit County	1292.3	1210.1	884.3	1212.1
岳普湖县	Yopurga County	1148.8	2245.2		1570.0
伽师县	Jiashi [Payzawat] County	2795.9	2091.5		866.3
巴楚县	Bachu [Maralbexi] County	501.8	4486.3	307.2	1258.1
塔什库尔干塔吉克自治县	Taxkorgan Tajik Autonomous County	211.8	844.0		21.1
和田地区	**Hotan Administrative Offices**	**148762.1**	**144366.0**	**25155.7**	**56518.1**
和田市	Hotan City	99908.7	133386.6	11725.9	11559.2
和田县	Hotan County	40388.4	6242.0	8835.0	38583.0
墨玉县	Moyu [Karakax] County	1560.1	299.9	31.0	1596.3
皮山县	Pishan [Guma] County	340.1	247.4		187.2
洛浦县	Lop County	5214.0	3558.8	3357.5	3714.2
策勒县	Qira County	150.7	49.4	4.4	153.7
于田县	Yutian [Keriya] County	1051.0	471.9	501.2	287.3
民丰县	Minfeng [Niya] County	149.1	110.0	700.7	437.2

Continued

(10 000 yuan)

主营业务收入 Income of Major Business	#主营业务成本 Cost of Major Business	主营业务税金及附加 Major Business, Tax and Addition	营业利润 Business Profit	利润总额 Total Profit	亏损企业亏损总额 Lost Enterprise and Total Loss	利税总额 Total Profits And Taxes	本年应交增值税 Value Added Taxes Payable	全部从业人员年平均人数(人) Average Number of Staff and Workers (person)
4997.5	4228.6	36.8	59.0	-131.3	131.3	-30.9	63.6	312
7048.0	6919.6	3.1	-671.4	-626.0	675.7	-585.5	37.4	137
43675.0	31182.2	274.7	3477.2	3620.8	459.0	7317.0	3421.5	3632
3362.5	3522.4	0.2	-346.9	-585.4	585.7	-530.0	55.2	204
2522.7	2242.0	249.0	95.1	96.4	223.6	347.8	2.4	124
16775.1	**15307.5**	**67.2**	**-1181.9**	**-1514.7**	**1905.4**	**-620.4**	**827.1**	**2001**
11957.0	10556.9	40.9	-55.4	52.9	265.1	563.5	469.7	647
1070.8	1721.9	4.8	-1083.9	-1081.9	1086.9	-988.4	88.7	256
80.5	43.2	3.1	-7.6	-7.6	8.4	1.2	5.7	23
3666.8	2985.5	18.4	-35.0	-478.1	545.0	-196.7	263.0	1075
135885.4	**146620.7**	**1308.6**	**-26108.7**	**16450.4**	**8983.6**	**25072.5**	**7313.5**	**12025**
92370.4	107582.5	1069.5	-25095.9	17778.5	5640.6	24710.6	5862.6	7498
3052.4	2989.3	27.3	-134.6	-661.5	661.5	-556.5	77.7	726
17306.2	14964.3	52.2	520.4	868.4	708.1	1414.6	494.0	1316
3712.9	3195.2	18.0	-372.6	-207.2	225.1	28.6	217.8	426
6404.4	6493.5	68.1	-1021.3	-1020.9	1031.4	-759.2	193.6	586
2956.8	2363.7	45.2	47.5	-68.0	263.0	100.6	123.4	701
2145.2	1861.9	14.7	147.5	136.6	24.2	279.9	128.6	286
585.1	660.6	1.2	-200.0	-250.0	250.0	-231.6	17.2	72
2842.4	2460.8	7.4	102.4	-20.7	74.7	63.3	76.6	198
155.5	86.2	1.8	-12.5	-12.5	12.5	-1.2	9.5	31
4308.9	3955.6	2.3	-83.3	-86.0	86.2	26.1	109.8	161
45.2	7.1	0.9	-6.3	-6.3	6.3	-2.7	2.7	24
46387.1	**41121.3**	**346.5**	**-5406.6**	**-6648.8**	**11701.9**	**-2687.6**	**3614.7**	**5881**
29800.9	29832.4	223.4	-7253.9	-7186.4	9679.3	-4622.5	2340.5	3997
7453.5	5188.2	43.4	93.6	-207.6	799.5	414.6	578.8	803
420.9	416.5	3.2	-57.8	-58.7	63.0	-35.9	19.6	132
191.0	151.6	1.6	-1.2	-18.7	18.7	12.8	4.3	28
7978.4	5065.7	60.7	1966.2	1936.3	23.0	2636.8	639.8	728
89.6	40.6	0.6	-4.8	-4.8	4.8	-0.1	4.1	20
371.0	379.2	10.7	-141.8	-136.9	141.6	-101.7	24.5	138
81.8	47.1	2.9	-6.9	-972.0	972.0	-966.0	3.1	35

12-9 全部国有及规模以上非国有工业企业主要经济效益指标

单位: %　　　　(2004 年)

项 目	Item	工业增加值率 Ratio of Value-Added to Gross Industrial Output Value	资金利税率 Ratio of profits and Taxes to Capital	产值利税率 Ratio of profits and Taxes to Industrial Output Value
总 计	**Total**	**36.8**	**16.5**	**22.2**
按登记注册类型分	**Grouped by Registry Type**			
内资企业	Domestic Investment	37.0	16.6	22.4
国有企业	State-owned	35.5	2.1	4.4
#中央企业	Central	36.3	2.5	4.8
地方企业	Iocal Enterprises	32.9	1.2	3.1
#自治区属企业	Autonomous	34.1	3.8	8.2
地区(州、市)属企业	Prefecture or City	33.0	-2.7	-8.0
县(市)属企业	County or City	32.1	1.0	2.7
集体企业	Collective-owned	10.5	5.5	6.5
#自治区属企业	Autonomous	20.4	16.5	11.6
地区(州、市)属企业	Prefecture or City	13.2	-0.8	-0.7
县(市)属企业	County or City	18.6	3.1	5.1
镇属企业	Town	32.6	6.3	8.2
乡属企业	Township	1.5	-1.2	-5.8
股份合作企业	Share Cooperative	31.5	11.7	15.4
联营企业	Joint Owned	27.5	14.1	12.5
#国有联营企业	State Ownership Joint Enterprises	33.0	19.7	14.8
集体联营企业	Collective Ownership Joint Enterprises	27.1	4.8	8.1
国有与集体联营企业	State-collective Joint Enterprises	20.4	16.9	11.3
其他联营企业	Other Ownership Joint Enterprises			
有限责任公司	Limited Liability Corporations	28.2	6.8	11.4
#国有独资公司	State-funded Corporations	33.9	5.2	11.6
其他有限责任公司	Other Limited Liability Corporations	26.7	7.4	11.4
股份有限公司	Share-holding Corporations Ltd.	42.2	27.8	31.2
私营企业	Private Enterprises	21.5	10.3	10.5
#私营独资企业	Private-funded Enterprises	27.6	8.1	8.8
私营合伙企业	Private Partnership Enterprises	26.9	30.8	9.4
私营有限责任公司	Private Limited Liability Corporations	20.6	8.4	8.2
私营股份有限公司	Private Stock Ltd.Co.	27.2	22.3	45.4
港、澳、台商投资企业	Enterprises with Funds from Hong Kong, Macao and Taiwan	27.6	9.7	13.5
外商投资企业	Foreign Funded Enterprises	29.9	15.1	17.7
在总计中: 国有控股企业	Of the Total: State-Owned Holding Enterprise	40.1	18.6	25.4
在总计中: 农村工业	Of the Total: Rural Industry	20.8	9.7	14.6
按轻、重工业分	**Grouped by Light & Heavy Industry**			
轻工业	Light Industry	23.9	4.4	6.4
以农产品为原料	Using Farm Produces as Raw Materials	23.3	4.7	6.5
以非农产品为原料	Using Non-Farm Produces as Raw Materials	34.5	1.2	3.2
重工业	Heavy Industry	38.9	18.8	25.0
采掘工业	Mining and Quarrying	62.6	30.5	45.9
原料工业	Raw Materials Industry	22.3	8.8	9.9
加工工业	Manufacturing Industry	22.3	7.1	11.7
按企业规模分	**Grouped by Size of Enterprises**			
大型企业	Large	43.2	25.7	30.8
中型企业	Medium	28.7	4.9	9.0
小型企业	Small	23.1	5.6	7.6

注：本年度全员劳动生产率是用现价工业增加值计算(以下同)。

Main Indicators on Economic Benefit of All State-owned and Non-state-owned above Designated Size Industrial Enterprises

(%)

总资产贡献率 Ratio of Total Assets to Industrial Output Value	资本保值增值率 Ratio of Capital-Hold and Rise	资产负债率 Assets Liability Ratio	流动资产周转次数(次/年) Number of Times of Annual Turnover Circulating Funds (times/year)	成本费用利润率 Ratio of Profits to Industrial Cost	全员劳动生产率(元/人·年) Overall Labor Productivity (yuan/person-year)	工业经济效益综合指数 Comprehensive Index of Industry Economic Results
16.3	**119.4**	**53.3**	**2.2**	**17.4**	**148744.9**	**249.1**
16.4	118.3	53.5	2.2	17.5	149723.3	250.4
3.0	197.6	60.2	1.3	-4.9	57307.3	86.8
3.7	292.4	60.0	1.4	-5.2	65194.3	105.3
2.0	115.3	60.6	1.1	-3.9	41438.1	65.7
3.9	142.8	59.8	1.4	-0.5	60285.2	100.5
-1.4	84.3	62.8	0.8	-12.6	31112.2	12.3
1.6	102.1	62.7	1.3	-3.6	26581.6	55.3
4.4	49.1	69.9	1.3	1.1	17929.5	64.7
27.3	1210.9	63.4	1.9	4.4	49599.4	302.5
0.2	26.4	93.8	1.7	-6.3	23195.4	27.1
3.3	63.0	63.4	0.8	0.2	31728.8	65.8
12.1	246.8	76.9	1.2	2.7	31650.0	116.4
0.3	125.0	59.9	0.3	-7.3	1457.4	18.8
8.9	140.5	40.4	1.6	11.8	64077.3	158.4
12.1	91.9	49.1	2.1	5.6	69893.4	141.9
10.4	38.6	59.6	1.9	7.5	129561.9	171.2
4.5	100.0	37.1	1.8	2.2	31160.6	98.4
22.5	233.1	42.8	2.4	5.3	61218.2	179.4
8.1	118.2	65.1	1.4	5.2	60491.7	124.7
5.4	58.4	72.1	1.4	4.0	61979.6	105.7
9.5	166.4	62.5	1.4	5.6	60003.8	135.8
26.1	108.4	44.7	3.7	32.5	522520.6	564.2
9.6	119.7	51.8	1.6	8.3	57823.8	140.6
5.5	68.7	54.1	2.1	5.4	45802.1	113.8
25.4	126.4	39.3	4.5	7.2	151534.5	253.2
9.9	165.9	56.3	1.8	5.7	58590.2	139.4
9.5	77.2	36.4	0.6	47.8	47000.0	268.9
11.1	125.3	50.5	1.4	9.8	81077.3	162.4
16.0	233.4	42.1	1.4	14.3	132362.9	234.1
18.2	115.0	51.6	2.6	20.7	194361.2	295.8
6.2	38.6	63.6	1.1	11.2	35590.0	115.1
5.1	110.7	63.8	1.2	0.9	47116.4	91.1
5.4	111.2	64.8	1.2	1.1	47421.0	92.4
2.1	107.4	54.2	1.1	-2.0	43947.5	72.7
18.7	120.8	51.3	2.5	20.5	190697.3	294.4
31.0	133.1	44.5	3.1	59.6	302397.4	540.0
9.5	102.5	58.0	2.8	2.9	133837.0	176.7
7.4	132.9	54.9	1.1	6.7	56704.4	127.8
25.9	123.5	44.7	3.5	28.9	315739.3	425.2
6.0	106.1	64.4	1.3	1.4	64578.4	105.8
6.2	123.9	61.4	1.4	3.7	54778.8	113.8

Note: Productivity for whole staff is computed on current industrial added value(the same as below).

12-10 分行业全部国有及规模以上非国有工业企业主要经济效益指标

单位: %　　　　(2004 年)

行　　业	Sector	工业增加值率 Ratio of Value Added to Gross Industrial Output Value	资金利税率 Ratio of profits and Taxes to Capital	产值利税率 Ratio of profits and Taxes to Industrial Output Value
煤炭开采和洗选业	Coal Extracting and Dressing	53.2	7.7	16.4
石油和天然气开采业	Petroleum and Natural Gas Extraction	64.2	32.3	48.2
#天然原油和天然气开采	Crude Oil and Natural Gas	68.4	39.4	55.5
黑色金属矿采选业	Ferrous Metals Mining and Dressing	24.4	18.9	21.0
有色金属矿采选业	Nonferrous Metals Mining and Dressing	42.5	28.7	28.6
非金属矿采选业	Nonmetal Minerals Mining and Dressing	37.7	8.1	14.2
#采　盐	Salt Extraction	47.1	35.2	25.1
其他采矿业	Other Ore Extraction			
农副食品加工业	Farm and Non-staple Food Processing	16.0	4.3	4.0
#谷物磨制	Grain Grinding	15.7	4.6	3.1
饲料加工	Fodder Processing	15.2	11.6	6.2
制　糖	Sugar Making	20.2	6.3	8.5
食品制造业	Food Manufacturing	25.5	3.8	5.6
#罐头制造	Canned Food Production	25.4	1.8	3.1
饮料制造业	Beverage Production	39.2	9.5	20.5
#酒的制造	Wine Making	40.1	10.0	22.2
烟草制品业	Tobacco Making	60.5	48.7	55.8
纺织业	Textile Industry	17.8	-1.8	-2.9
#棉、化纤纺织及印染精加工	Cotton, Chemical Fiber, Dyeing and Printing and	16.4	-1.7	-2.4
毛纺织和染整精加工	Wool Textile, Dyeing and Printing and Dressing	12.1	-2.8	-22.7
纺织服装、鞋、帽制造业	Garment, Shoe and Hat	30.6	3.7	4.1
皮革、毛皮、羽毛(绒)及其制品业	Leather, Wool, Feather (down) its Products	22.9	8.1	8.6
#皮革鞣制加工	Leather Tanning and Processing	22.6	8.3	8.7
皮革制品制造	Leather Products Making	43.5	-2.7	-4.1
木材加工及木、竹、藤、棕、草制品业	Timber Processing,	20.9	6.7	5.9
家具制造业	Furniture Manufacturing	22.7	12.2	13.5
造纸及纸制品业	Papermaking and Paper Products	34.3	6.2	12.2
印刷业和记录媒介的复制	Printing and Copying of Medium for Record	32.0	5.8	8.1
文教体育用品制造业	Cultural, Educational and Sports Goods			
石油加工、炼焦及核燃料加工业	Oil Processing, Coking and Nuclear Fuel Processing	15.7	12.5	8.3
#炼 焦	Coking	46.2	30.2	38.5
化学原料及化学制品制造业	Raw Chemical Material and Chemical Products Making	27.6	11.0	13.5
#基础化学原料制造	Basic Chemical Material Making	29.5	15.0	16.9
肥料制造	Fertilizer Making	28.7	6.5	10.9
医药制造业	Medical and Pharmaceutical Products	36.3	10.3	21.3
化学纤维制造业	Chemical Fiber	24.7	8.4	8.7
橡胶制品业	Rubber Products	15.5	4.2	5.1
塑料制品业	Plastic Products	24.6	4.9	11.9
非金属矿物制品业	Nonmetal Mineral Products	29.5	6.1	12.5
#水泥制造	Cement Manufacturing	31.9	1.9	4.6
黑色金属冶炼及压延加工业	Smelting and Pressing of Ferrous Metals	25.5	32.2	19.6
有色金属冶炼及压延加工业	Smelting and Pressing of Nonferrous Metals	19.2	10.0	10.2
金属制品业	Metal Products	20.4	7.3	6.1
通用设备制造业	Ordinary Equipment Production	27.3	6.3	9.6
专用设备制造业	Special Purposes Equipment	21.8	1.4	3.2
交通运输设备制造业	Transport Equipment	15.7	1.0	1.1
电气机械及器材制造业	Electric Equipment and Machinery	17.9	7.6	9.9
通信设备、计算机及其他电子设备制造业	Telecom. Equipment, Computer and Other Electronic Equipment	22.7	12.4	23.5
仪器仪表及文化、办公用机械制造业	Equipment, Meter, Cultural and Offiice Machinery	38.1	14.8	27.8
工艺品及其他制造业	Art and Handicraft and Others			
废弃资源和废旧材料回收加工业	Recycling and Processing Deserted Resources and waste Material	23.6	11.8	8.2
电力、热力的生产和供应业	Electric and Thermal Power Production and Supply	39.1	1.1	3.3
#电力生产和电力供应	Power Production and Supply	39.7	0.9	2.6
燃气生产和供应业	Gas Production and Supply	26.2	1.1	3.3
水的生产和供应业	Water Production and Supply	48.3	-1.7	-10.4

Main Indicators on Economic Benefit of All State-owned and Non-state-owned Industrial Enterprises by Branch of Industry

(%)

总资产贡献率 Ratio of Total Assets to Industrial Output Value	资本保值增值率 Ratio of Capital Hold and Rise	资产负债率 Assets Liability Ratio	流动资产周转次数（次/年） Number of Times of Annual Turnover Circulating Funds (times/year)	成本费用利润率 Ratio of Profits to Industrial Cost	全员劳动生产率（元/人·年） Overall Labor Productivity (yuan/person-year)	工业经济效益综合指数 Comprehensive Index of Industry Economic Results
6.3	104.0	49.9	1.1	8.1	34021.3	112.7
33.7	135.9	43.5	3.6	65.4	470580.9	674.0
37.5	115.7	41.6	5.7	104.8	1068063.1	1209.5
17.3	131.3	59.1	1.4	14.7	76178.7	190.3
30.7	124.3	65.5	1.7	27.0	76677.5	262.0
8.8	114.8	58.6	0.6	11.3	36915.7	125.8
16.4	28.4	76.2	2.3	8.9	25683.5	124.9
5.2	172.1	60.3	1.7	2.0	55118.3	114.9
5.0	106.3	54.9	2.4	2.6	81855.6	131.2
13.2	182.5	47.9	3.3	5.1	106467.4	190.3
6.0	107.5	78.2	1.2	3.2	35360.5	89.5
6.3	136.4	75.9	1.1	3.8	101440.3	134.1
5.1	110.0	84.7	0.9	0.9	161804.8	147.5
8.4	91.6	60.6	0.7	9.1	88062.7	146.8
9.0	100.6	61.7	0.6	9.6	90506.8	151.5
50.2	135.4	59.2	1.3	15.3	887898.4	746.2
-0.4	86.0	71.9	1.1	-6.7	20193.1	29.0
-0.4	91.8	70.6	1.3	-6.3	19336.0	33.9
-2.1	16.8	98.1	0.2	-21.3	7920.7	-60.0
4.2	59.1	73.1	1.5	-0.3	22509.4	65.4
11.2	195.4	60.0	1.3	5.4	121562.8	177.8
14.0	136.8	59.7	1.3	5.8	142925.7	189.8
-0.1	2933.0	67.8	1.3	-11.7	18359.2	398.3
9.5	194.2	58.3	2.3	2.3	33711.3	120.4
8.6	110.7	12.5	1.4	13.9	61230.2	159.6
6.2	101.9	59.3	0.9	5.6	46335.4	107.4
5.5	87.3	45.7	1.8	2.7	32042.4	95.0
12.5	107.3	38.0	4.4	1.5	320208.8	306.2
26.7	243.4	44.7	1.9	52.2	95996.3	381.6
9.8	122.0	52.1	1.7	7.8	78473.5	152.8
13.2	90.6	66.9	1.9	9.0	72911.8	157.1
6.8	200.0	34.2	1.2	8.0	55831.0	140.1
9.0	68.9	64.0	0.8	12.6	65496.8	146.0
8.0	77.6	63.4	1.8	7.5	77762.8	141.1
4.5	83.5	64.3	1.1	0.5	39788.8	80.0
6.6	134.6	55.3	1.2	4.7	64562.4	124.4
6.3	100.5	55.9	1.0	6.6	51000.5	115.6
3.5	85.8	63.6	0.9	-3.2	43847.0	65.5
28.9	118.5	45.9	3.4	15.3	171006.5	290.5
8.8	92.6	63.6	2.1	6.3	81918.1	146.9
8.0	136.2	57.5	1.8	3.4	48794.4	117.8
5.3	158.4	52.8	0.9	3.2	39344.3	101.1
1.6	82.3	80.3	0.8	-3.1	32766.8	47.9
1.5	90.4	71.9	1.1	-2.3	31558.1	58.1
7.3	127.0	58.5	1.1	7.2	94871.0	151.0
26.5	3813.3	72.9	1.4	18.2	69633.2	704.1
21.0	177.3	49.4	1.2	24.8	45017.6	220.6
12.4	606.8	46.1	1.8	1.2	65345.9	191.0
3.7	92.5	75.6	1.8	-5.6	97993.3	95.9
3.7	87.0	77.3	1.9	-6.5	103971.8	96.3
1.9	162.2	53.5	0.8	-1.7	71682.4	95.7
-0.8	101.5	45.4	0.8	-14.1	34766.3	13.1

12-11 各地、州、市、县(市)全部国有及规模以上非国有工业企业主要经济效益指标

单位: %　　(2004 年)

地 区	Region	工业增加值率 Ratio of Value Added to Gross Industrial Output Value	资金利税率 Ratio of profits and Taxes to Capital	产值利税率 Ratio of profits And Taxes to Industrial Output Value
总 计	**Total**	**36.8**	**16.5**	**22.2**
乌鲁木齐市	**Urumqi City**	**26.2**	**10.1**	**12.8**
乌鲁木齐县	Urumqi County	41.4	-7.1	-16.9
克拉玛依市	**Karamay City**	**41.9**	**25.8**	**29.7**
石河子市	**Shihezi City**	**27.1**	**3.7**	**8.2**
阿拉尔市	**Alar City**	**3.0**	**-8.5**	**-16.1**
图木舒克市	**Tumxuk City**	**24.2**	**-1.3**	**-4.7**
五家渠市	**Wujiaqu City**	**15.1**	**-1.2**	**-1.9**
吐鲁番地区	**Turpan Administrative Offices**	**61.7**	**41.2**	**50.3**
吐鲁番市	Turpan City	32.2	-2.8	-6.8
鄯善县	Shanshan [Piqan] County	66.0	53.2	58.0
托克逊县	Toksun County	29.0	5.5	7.3
哈密地区	**Hami [Kumul] Administrative Offices**	**36.9**	**5.8**	**10.6**
哈密市	Hami [Kumul] City	36.9	5.2	9.8
巴里坤哈萨克自治县	Barkol Kazak Autonomous County	33.2	7.8	8.4
伊吾县	Yiwu [Araturuk] County	44.2	74.0	39.7
昌吉回族自治州	**Changji Hui Autonomous Prefecture**	**25.2**	**5.6**	**7.2**
昌吉市	Changji City	22.0	2.7	4.4
阜康市	Fukang City	29.5	17.5	21.3
米泉市	Miquan City	25.6	9.8	7.2
呼图壁县	Hutubi County	21.0	3.8	4.1
玛纳斯县	Manas County	32.6	5.5	9.0
奇台县	Qitai County	28.2	-1.9	-2.3
吉木萨尔县	Jimsar County	29.4	-6.0	-10.9
木垒哈萨克自治县	Mori Kazak Autonomous County	-15.5	-16.5	-94.6
伊犁哈萨克自治州	**Ili Kazak Autonomous Prefecture**	**31.6**	**6.8**	**11.5**
伊犁州直属县(市)	**Counties (Cities) Direct Under Ili Prefecture**	**33.7**	**9.0**	**14.4**
伊宁市	Yining [Gulja] City	28.2	0.3	0.6
奎屯市	Kuytun City	38.1	15.0	21.9
伊宁县	Yining [Gulja] County	34.3	7.0	11.0
察布查尔锡伯自治县	Qapqal Xibe Autonomous County	14.2	-1.3	-1.5
霍城县	Huocheng [Korgas] County	21.4	3.3	5.5
巩留县	Gongliu [Tokkuztara] County	41.2	32.4	40.9
新源县	Xinyuan [Kunes] County	42.6	20.8	25.7
昭苏县	Zhaosu [Mongolkure] County	16.6	2.6	1.9
特克斯县	Tekes County	59.4	1.1	9.2
尼勒克县	Nilka County	34.2	2.8	4.0

Main Indicators on Economic Benefit of All State-owned and Non-state-owned above Designated Size Industrial Enterprises by Prefecture, Autonomous Prefecture, City and County

(%)

总资产贡献率 Ratio of Total Assets to Industrial Output Value	资本保值增值率 Ratio of Capital Hold And Rise	资产负债率 Assets Liability Ratio	流动资产周转次数(次/年) Number of Times of Annual Turnover Circulating Funds (times/year)	成本费用利润率 Ratio of Profits to Industrial Cost	全员劳动生产率(元/人·年) Overall Labor Productivity (yuan/person-year)	工业经济效益综合指数 Comprehensive Index of Industry and Economic Results
16.3	**119.4**	**53.3**	**2.2**	**17.4**	**148744.9**	**249.1**
10.3	**115.6**	**53.4**	**2.2**	**7.4**	**122671.0**	**183.6**
-7.8	62.6	84.6	0.7	-21.2	21958.5	-49.8
27.6	**128.4**	**39.6**	**3.5**	**26.5**	**313367.6**	**418.5**
4.6	**93.5**	**66.1**	**1.1**	**2.4**	**52179.6**	**95.9**
-4.5	**119.7**	**49.7**	**1.6**	**-11.0**	**9545.5**	**11.0**
-0.8	**196.2**	**58.9**	**0.7**	**-14.1**	**41557.3**	**30.6**
1.2	**120.0**	**84.4**	**0.9**	**-7.6**	**14427.1**	**24.4**
39.7	**116.4**	**49.2**	**4.0**	**65.8**	**389419.9**	**639.2**
-1.3	123.3	55.6	1.4	-9.9	52758.2	47.6
51.4	113.2	46.7	6.0	96.0	753610.9	1015.1
6.4	263.3	67.6	1.5	-0.2	36843.4	106.5
7.4	**117.7**	**64.6**	**1.2**	**3.3**	**52686.7**	**109.5**
6.8	116.8	64.5	1.2	2.5	53302.8	105.5
8.6	102.1	81.6	1.3	2.3	26324.6	84.6
75.4	221.9	26.3	2.9	40.4	322691.2	572.1
6.1	**100.2**	**65.9**	**1.5**	**3.1**	**76518.7**	**121.0**
3.8	120.2	64.2	1.1	1.3	76699.4	108.9
16.9	161.3	59.9	2.0	16.4	69073.3	201.7
10.7	143.3	55.2	2.3	4.6	94126.3	161.1
5.5	67.1	70.5	1.9	-1.0	49524.9	86.9
4.9	23.2	85.0	1.8	2.4	89325.0	109.6
	134.5	74.0	2.0	-4.8	61723.6	77.8
-1.6	107.2	85.5	1.0	-15.6	51458.3	9.2
-14.1		102.0	0.6	-41.6	-13059.9	-163.9
7.9	**118.6**	**65.6**	**1.4**	**1.0**	**55932.4**	**105.6**
10.1	**111.1**	**61.8**	**1.4**	**2.4**	**68930.2**	**122.8**
2.7	86.6	74.8	1.3	-6.4	37061.7	48.7
15.8	126.9	61.1	1.6	0.2	136729.7	170.5
8.2	115.4	60.5	1.6	6.2	46351.9	123.0
-0.9	364.8	35.2	2.6	-2.7	36765.6	110.4
5.3	119.2	66.1	1.2	1.0	39674.6	87.0
29.9	104.4	23.4	1.5	47.8	52946.6	323.0
15.7	102.6	44.3	1.3	17.6	121993.3	220.3
6.5	919.2	58.2	1.9	0.7	39156.1	204.7
0.3	120.0	83.3	0.3	1.7	15172.4	53.9
3.4	98.1	59.6	0.9	1.2	45748.8	82.1

12-11 续表 1

单位: %

地　区	Region	工业增加值率 Ratio of Value Added to Gross Industrial Output Value	资金利税率 Ratio of profits and Taxes to Capital	产值利税率 Ratio of profits and Taxes to Industrial Output Value
塔城地区	**Tacheng [Tarbagatai] Administrative Offices**	**26.9**	**2.2**	**4.2**
塔城市	Tacheng [Qoqek] City	34.5	-12.4	-41.3
乌苏市	Usu City	28.4	8.5	14.1
额敏县	Emin [Dorbiljin] County	25.8	8.3	11.4
沙湾县	Shawan County	15.9	2.3	3.8
托里县	Toli County	47.4	6.1	10.4
裕民县	Yumin [Qagantokay] County	38.7	28.3	134.4
和布克赛尔蒙古自治县	Hoboksar Mongol Autonomous County	45.6	1.8	4.8
阿勒泰地区	**Altay Administrative Offices**	**30.8**	**6.5**	**12.0**
阿勒泰市	Altay City	20.6	-1.6	-3.8
布尔津县	Burqin County	34.7	5.5	15.9
富蕴县	Fuyun [Koktokay] County	38.9	27.0	27.8
福海县	Fuhai [Burultokay] County	25.6	-0.4	-1.1
哈巴河县	Habahe [Kaba] County	48.8	9.1	15.0
青河县	Qinghe [Qinggil] County	48.6	-11.3	-37.0
吉木乃县	Jeminay County	35.0	-2.3	-5.4
博尔塔拉蒙古自治州	**Bortala Mongol Autonomous Prefecture**	**15.6**	**0.3**	**0.5**
博乐市	Bole [Bortala] City	15.1	-0.2	-0.4
精河县	Jinghe [Jing] County	19.1	6.0	6.7
温泉县	Wenquan [Araxang] County	18.4	0.2	0.1
巴音郭楞蒙古自治州	**Bayangol Mongol Autonomous Prefecture**	**55.2**	**25.3**	**38.1**
库尔勒市	Korla City	59.1	27.9	42.7
轮台县	Luntai [Bugur] County	40.6	38.9	18.7
尉犁县	Yuli [Lopnur] County	21.6	4.1	8.7
若羌县	Ruoqiang [Qarkilik] County	33.4	2.9	9.5
且末县	Qiemo [Qarqan] County	36.5	-3.0	-11.2
焉耆回族自治县	Yanji Hui Autonomous County	23.2	-0.2	-0.3
和静县	Hejing County	30.7	7.8	11.3
和硕县	Hoxud County	30.4	6.8	9.8
博湖县	Bohu [Bagrax] County	22.3	-1.7	-2.6
阿克苏地区	**Aksu Administrative Offices**	**28.6**	**8.9**	**14.0**
阿克苏市	Aksu City	29.1	6.8	13.8
温宿县	Wensu [Onsu] County	43.0	12.4	15.2
库车县	Kuqa County	24.9	13.8	16.1

Continued

(%)

总资产贡献率 Ratio of Total Assets to Industrial Output Value	资本保值增值率 Ratio of Capital Hold and Rise	资产负债率 Assets Liability Ratio	流动资产周转次数（次/年） Number of Times of Annual Turnover Circulating Funds (times/year)	成本费用利润率 Ratio of Profits to Industrial Cost	全员劳动生产率（元/人·年） Overall Labor Productivity (yuan/person-year)	工业经济效益综合指数 Comprehensive Index of Industry Economic Results
3.6	**135.2**	**70.5**	**1.4**	**-3.3**	**34892.8**	**68.6**
-10.1	74.2	88.2	0.9	-39.0	41534.4	-105.3
10.0	80.5	78.4	1.5	3.5	40392.8	101.4
6.4	911.5	45.9	1.5	6.2	57745.2	231.8
4.9	87.7	79.0	1.6	-0.4	26784.5	69.2
5.7	43.3	70.5	1.2	2.0	22445.6	71.2
39.2	220.4	44.1	0.4	60.8	10142.9	367.7
3.2	118.2	66.9	1.0	-5.9	31989.3	52.3
7.8	**134.4**	**71.4**	**1.5**	**4.2**	**56667.4**	**119.3**
1.4	109.5	85.2	1.6	-8.8	36531.8	39.7
7.1	128.4	38.9	1.6	6.6	60108.0	133.0
25.2	89.3	70.2	1.7	25.4	81062.1	241.7
-0.3	438.4	26.5	1.2	-8.1	48733.8	93.8
14.4	187.3	74.5	1.0	9.3	58489.2	153.1
-8.7	83.3	75.1	0.9	-35.2	11125.0	-101.4
-1.5	120.0	60.6	0.5	-10.6	19626.8	16.0
1.7	**118.2**	**75.3**	**1.4**	**-3.4**	**23664.2**	**54.8**
1.1	117.0	77.3	1.3	-4.1	22949.7	49.2
7.4	125.3	50.5	2.1	0.7	26335.9	94.5
2.8	103.8	92.3	1.6	0.2	68615.4	91.3
23.7	**126.3**	**51.5**	**2.2**	**47.5**	**255355.2**	**441.6**
25.5	118.6	50.2	2.4	55.1	343342.7	528.8
41.6	138.3	47.0	3.0	31.3	555922.5	601.1
9.7	639.6	54.4	1.2	5.4	17768.5	171.1
4.1	815.2	19.2	0.4	6.7	34778.3	188.6
0.2		105.3	1.1	-14.6	24221.6	-19.4
3.5	84.5	90.0	1.0	-7.6	59201.9	45.2
8.7	288.3	74.8	1.3	8.3	56383.6	152.3
8.3	126.1	77.2	1.1	5.7	43467.8	109.8
2.4		102.1	1.0	-4.8	109109.1	72.1
9.8	**147.8**	**58.8**	**1.6**	**9.6**	**66108.0**	**155.7**
8.6	145.3	53.1	1.3	8.0	45101.5	130.2
7.3	32.4	80.4	2.0	5.7	42324.4	103.5
15.4	460.2	71.1	2.4	14.0	190209.2	303.5

12-11 续表 2

单位: %

地 区	Region	工业增加值率 Ratio of Value Added to Gross Industrial Output Value	资金利税率 Ratio of profits and Taxes to Capital	产值利税率 Ratio of profits and Taxes to Industrial Output Value
沙雅县	Xayar County	24.9	-0.2	-0.6
新和县	Xinhe [Toksu] County	-2.6	-6.9	-8.0
拜城县	Baicheng [Bay] County	41.9	9.6	14.2
乌什县	Wushi [Uxturpan] County			
阿瓦提县	Awat County	20.0	-7.5	-12.7
柯坪县	Kalpin County	46.3	7.4	20.8
克孜勒苏柯尔克孜自治州	**Kizilsu Kirgiz Autonomous Prefecture**	**20.0**	**-1.8**	**-3.5**
阿图什市	Artux City	17.3	3.0	4.3
阿克陶县	Akto County	28.7	-14.0	-96.5
阿合奇县	Akqi County	31.0	0.7	1.1
乌恰县	Wuqia [Ulugqat] County	28.4	-2.6	-6.1
喀什地区	**Kashgar [Kaxgar] Administrative Offices**	**26.5**	**6.6**	**17.1**
喀什市	Kashgar [Kaxgar] City	30.6	8.2	25.5
疏附县	Shufu County	22.4	-7.1	-14.9
疏勒县	Shule County	15.7	6.5	7.4
英吉沙县	Yengisar County	14.8	0.5	0.8
泽普县	Zepu [Poskam] County	19.2	-9.3	-11.5
莎车县	Shache [Yarkant] County	21.5	0.7	1.8
叶城县	Yecheng [Kagilik] County	35.0	5.7	12.1
麦盖提县	Makit County	28.8	-9.0	-43.0
岳普湖县	Yopurga County	25.2	1.9	2.0
伽师县	Jiashi [Payzawat] County	34.6	0.0	-0.8
巴楚县	Bachu [Maralbexi] County	7.3	0.6	0.5
塔什库尔干塔吉克自治县	Taxkorgan Tajik Autonomous County	35.3	-0.3	-6.0
和田地区	**Hotan Administrative Offices**	**34.5**	**-1.2**	**-6.1**
和田市	Hotan City	31.7	-2.9	-16.8
和田县	Hotan County	41.5	0.8	5.5
墨玉县	Moyu [Karakax] County	31.8	-2.0	-8.4
皮山县	Pishan [Guma] County	23.4	-3.2	-6.7
洛浦县	Lop County	39.4	27.5	34.5
策勒县	Qira County	34.7	-0.1	-0.1
于田县	Yutian [Keriya] County	31.1	-7.9	-28.9
民丰县	Minfeng [Niya] County	23.1	-568.2	-1497.7

Continued

(%)

总资产贡献率 Ratio of Total Assets to Industrial Output Value	资本保值增值率 Ratio of Capital Hold and Rise	资产负债率 Assets Liability Ratio	流动资产周转次数(次/年) Number of Times of Annual Turnover Circulating Funds (times/year)	成本费用利润率 Ratio of Profits to Industrial Cost	全员劳动生产率(元/人·年) Overall Labor Productivity (yuan/person-year)	工业经济效益综合指数 Comprehensive Index of Industry Economic Results
	67.5	47.8	0.9	-2.8	49435.9	62.8
-5.2	1032.3	26.6	1.3	-8.2	-15605.8	124.5
9.0	83.7	51.6	2.2	9.5	64482.4	150.5
-3.1	22.5	75.5	0.7	-15.3	44701.0	-6.4
12.2	5283.0	48.4	1.2	3.8	62451.6	816.9
-0.8	**80.2**	**87.8**	**1.1**	**-8.3**	**19796.6**	**17.8**
5.0	217.3	74.2	1.2	0.4	40366.3	96.9
-11.1		105.0	0.7	-51.4	12460.9	-186.4
0.5	62.2	35.8	1.4	-8.1	15434.8	26.2
-1.7		104.7	1.1	-11.5	9256.7	-16.7
7.3	**49.9**	**88.6**	**1.1**	**9.9**	**35827.8**	**106.1**
9.6	41.8	92.3	1.0	14.8	44568.4	132.0
-6.5	142.6	67.0	1.6	-18.4	12621.2	-16.9
5.7	94.6	66.9	1.5	5.2	24454.4	94.6
1.9	32.6	82.2	1.4	-4.3	12065.7	32.4
-4.8	49.7	49.3	1.6	-13.8	24631.4	2.9
1.0		106.8	0.3	-2.3	17329.5	13.5
2.3	74.2	47.8	1.3	6.6	29958.0	95.6
-3.5	43.6	63.4	0.5	-31.0	22416.7	-76.1
3.2	358.0	58.9	1.3	-0.8	44070.7	116.1
0.4	208.0	70.7	1.8	-7.6	17354.8	50.0
3.5	378.6	79.2	1.2	-2.0	24677.0	94.2
-0.3	11.7	97.6	0.1	-12.5	7041.7	-26.8
0.9	**85.3**	**75.0**	**0.6**	**-12.6**	**28974.0**	**9.2**
-0.3	38.3	92.6	0.5	-19.0	25568.7	-32.0
1.4	108.7	28.1	0.6	-2.8	42956.4	64.1
-0.4	744.2	17.2	1.8	-11.2	10250.0	106.0
-0.1	28.2	56.9	3.4	-9.0	16321.4	38.7
19.0	120.0	65.1	1.8	32.3	41620.9	240.7
	30.3	25.9	2.1	-5.1	14850.0	39.9
-1.4	176.5	77.2	1.5	-30.2	8268.1	-52.2
-31.2	2602.4	65.0	3.9	-1132.9	4457.1	-3921.0

12-12 国有及国有控股工业企业主要经济指标

单位: 万元 (2004 年)

项 目	Item	企业单位数(个) Number of Enterprises (unit)	#亏损企业 Loss	工业总产值(当年价格) Gross Industrial Output Value (At Current Prices)
总 计	**Total**	**617**	**281**	**12535046.5**
按登记注册类型分	**Grouped by Registry Type**			
内资企业	Domestic Investment	606	277	12488035.5
国有企业	State-owned	384	205	1715019.5
#中央企业	Central	98	45	1261386.6
地方企业	Iocal Enterprises	286	160	453632.9
#自治区属企业	Autonomous	72	30	253252.0
地区(州、市)属企业	Prefecture or City	53	33	113267.4
县(市)属企业	County or City	154	93	76561.9
集体企业	Collective-owned			
县(市)属企业	County or City			
联营企业	Joint Owned	7	2	23757.6
#国有联营企业	State Ownership Joint Enterprises	3	1	12069.0
国有与集体联营企业	State-collective Joint Enterprises	3	1	8498.3
其他联营企业	Other Ownership Joint Enterprises			
有限责任公司	Limited Liability Corporations	186	63	1893306.9
#国有独资公司	State-funded Corporations	46	18	722172.2
其他有限责任公司	Other Limited Liability Corporations	140	45	1171134.7
股份有限公司	Share-holding Corporations Ltd.	28	6	8855055.3
私营企业	Private Enterprises			
私营有限责任公司	Private Limited Liability Corporations			
港、澳、台商投资企业	Enterprises with Funds from Hong Kong, Macao and Taiwan	5	2	25340.5
外商投资企业	Foreign Funded Enterprises	6	2	21670.5
在总计中: 国有控股企业	Of the Total : State-Owned Holding Enterprise	617	281	12535046.5
按轻、重工业分	**Grouped by Light & Heavy Industry**			
轻工业	Light Industry	248	121	814028.6
以农产品为原料	Using Farm Produces as Raw Materials	161	75	755385.8
以非农产品为原料	Using Non-Farm Produces as Raw Materials	87	46	58642.8
重工业	Heavy Industry	369	160	11721017.9
采掘工业	Mining and Quarrying	74	28	5405514.6
原料工业	Raw Material Industry	171	86	5759196.3
加工工业	Manufacturing Industry	124	46	556307.0
按企业规模分	**Grouped by Size of Enterprises**			
大型企业	Large	20	4	9607399.1
中型企业	Medium	103	42	2001357.7
小型企业	Small	494	235	926289.7

Main Economic Indicators on Economic Benefit of State-Owned and State-Holding Industrial Enterprises

(10 000 yuan)

工业增加值 Added Value of Industry	工业销售产值(当年价) Sales Value of Industry Products (At Current Prices)	出口交货值 Delivery Value of Industry Export	实收资本 Total Capital Hold	资产合计 Total Assets	流动资产合计 Circulating Funds	#产成品 Finished Product	流动资产年平均余额 Annual Average Balance of Circulating Funds	固定资产原价 Original Value of Fixed Assets
5850758.9	**12384915.5**	**118839.2**	**5971047.0**	**19682108.1**	**5354950.7**	**687182.6**	**5003834.0**	**20432898.0**
5838837.1	12337785.8	116764.3	5945230.2	19599131.5	5301761.7	682118.6	4950872.2	20388705.4
706066.6	1684407.8	21099.8	1538945.2	4176738.5	1616695.0	88745.6	1524791.3	3178938.1
536568.2	1239581.0	6755.4	1156686.7	2858301.0	1163674.9	58351.2	1091286.4	2147998.8
169498.4	444826.8	14344.4	382258.5	1318437.5	453020.1	30394.4	433504.9	1030939.3
99591.2	252410.5	2535.7	173721.8	608732.4	231911.3	13835.7	210226.4	507514.2
42527.2	111724.5	4135.0	120271.1	394047.8	134095.9	9757.5	137602.8	289271.5
26283.9	71285.2		72673.8	248284.6	62274.3	4918.1	57011.2	218359.9
7246.1	19755.2		9628.3	26124.8	10803.4	1118.7	10696.5	16750.5
4288.5	8382.7		1720.1	12704.3	5439.8	80.7	5189.9	8169.5
2020.2	8182.2		2479.3	6614.8	3703.2	283.2	3714.0	3225.7
685013.5	1832426.7	52748.4	1184547.5	4093677.1	1229951.0	170667.0	1196052.2	3520085.2
280259.2	702345.8	19.7	457368.3	1849505.4	487682.6	51486.9	510141.8	1684430.7
404754.3	1130080.9	52728.7	727179.2	2244171.7	742268.4	119180.1	685910.4	1835654.5
4440435.5	8800329.6	42849.1	3212040.7	11301913.8	2443855.7	421477.5	2218928.3	13672575.2
5667.6	25021.0		18996.3	44432.9	25426.1	2170.7	24227.9	28180.0
6254.2	22108.7	2074.9	6820.5	38543.7	27762.9	2893.3	28733.9	16012.6
5850758.9	12384915.5	118839.2	5971047.0	19682108.1	5354950.7	687182.6	5003834.0	20432898.0
254892.8	737535.1	77497.7	570949.4	1787461.2	822994.7	189395.1	804377.7	1140104.5
228476.9	679574.3	75346.2	500258.4	1519464.2	762667.8	183645.1	739533.3	904269.6
26415.9	57960.8	2151.5	70691.0	267997.0	60326.9	5750.0	64844.4	235834.9
5595866.1	11647380.4	41341.5	5400097.6	17894646.9	4531956.0	497787.5	4199456.3	19292793.5
3957630.8	5363841.3	117.3	3445439.8	9575269.6	1981109.6	134025.8	1736329.4	11613415.3
1492692.8	5737866.7	18672.4	1487676.5	6947625.0	1864048.8	258145.5	1814702.4	6962874.0
145542.5	545672.4	22551.8	466981.3	1371752.3	686797.6	105616.2	648424.5	716504.2
4891960.4	9560067.2	26426.0	4192662.0	13102242.4	3066704.8	376527.6	2795141.9	15370088.9
705633.7	1923308.7	79953.3	1150072.0	4621522.9	1538182.8	201581.7	1477401.5	3723681.3
253164.8	901539.6	12459.9	628313.0	1958342.8	750063.1	109073.3	731290.6	1339127.8

12-12 续表

单位: 万元

项 目	Item	固定资产净值年平均余额 Annual Average Balance of Net Value of Fixed Assets	流动负债合计 Liquid Liabilities	长期负债合计 Long-term Liabilities	所有者权益合计 Creditors' Equity
总 计	**Total**	**12071356.7**	**6914792.0**	**3171973.7**	**9514581.4**
按登记注册类型分	**Grouped by Registry Type**				
内资企业	Domestic Investment	12046921.9	6869892.1	3168149.6	9480947.0
国有企业	State-owned	2092947.8	1875739.8	637088.2	1662373.8
#中央企业	Central	1396591.8	1323590.1	392180.5	1142524.4
地方企业	Local Enterprises	696356.0	552149.7	244907.7	519849.4
#自治区属企业	Autonomous	329528.9	257334.9	106593.1	244551.3
地区(州、市)属企业	Prefecture or City	205647.7	178743.4	67568.0	146489.9
县(市)属企业	County or City	153134.0	88758.4	66864.4	92630.7
集体企业	Collective-owned				
县(市)属企业	County or City				
联营企业	Joint Owned	10380.8	9671.3	2828.1	13625.4
#国有联营企业	State Ownership Joint Enterprises	3851.3	4841.7	2727.8	5134.8
国有与集体联营企业	State-collective Joint Enterprises	2006.4	2832.5		3782.3
其他联营企业	Other Ownership Joint Enterprises				
有限责任公司	Limited Liability Corporations	2394392.1	2154060.6	493956.6	1377487.7
#国有独资公司	State-funded Corporations	1088167.1	988850.2	278965.8	516081.6
其他有限责任公司	Other Limited Liability Corporations	1306225.0	1165210.4	214990.8	861406.1
股份有限公司	Share-holding Corporations Ltd.	7549006.8	2829952.9	2034190.8	6427427.0
私营企业	Private Enterprises				
私营有限责任公司	Private Limited Liability Corporations				
港、澳、台商投资企业	Enterprises with Funds from Hong Kong, Macao and Taiwan	16679.6	27650.3	548.1	15616.3
外商投资企业	Foreign Funded Enterprises	7755.2	17249.6	3276.0	18018.1
在总计中: 国有控股企业	Of the Total : State-Owned Holding Enterprise	12071356.7	6914792.0	3171973.7	9514581.4
按轻、重工业分	**Grouped by Light & Heavy Industry**				
轻工业	Light Industry	729873.0	1003424.5	176441.6	604258.9
以农产品为原料	Using Farm Produces as Raw Materials	555945.1	908125.6	138985.8	469265.2
以非农产品为原料	Using Non-Farm Produces as Raw Materials	173927.9	95298.9	37455.8	134993.7
重工业	Heavy Industry	11341483.7	5911367.5	2995532.1	8910322.5
采掘工业	Mining and Quarrying	6454453.9	2483120.4	1750667.2	5340371.2
原料工业	Raw Materials Industry	4398744.6	2798340.9	1110535.2	2972628.3
加工工业	Manufacturing Industry	488285.2	629906.2	134329.7	597323.0
按企业规模分	**Grouped by Size of Enterprises**				
大型企业	Large	8657926.3	3726420.2	2079193.1	7286586.0
中型企业	Medium	2479840.0	2311491.0	749798.7	1490372.5
小型企业	Small	933590.4	876880.8	342981.9	737622.9

Continued

(10 000 yuan)

主营业务收入 Income of Major Business	#主营业务成本 Cost of Major	主营业务税金及附加 Major Business, Tax and Addition	营业利润 Business Profit	利润总额 Total Sum of Profit	亏损企业亏损总额 Lost Enterprise Total Loss	利税总额 Total Profits And Taxes	本年应交增值税 Value Added Taxes Payable	全部从业人员年平均人数(人) Average Number of Staff and Workers (Person)
12779766.5	**8784901.9**	**292037.3**	**2256677.2**	**2084933.2**	**365370.5**	**3182621.6**	**805651.1**	**301025**
12713994.8	8730166.9	291872.8	2251648.1	2079910.9	364293.2	3175218.6	803434.9	299734
2039681.1	1788135.5	41955.7	-71912.6	-101626.6	150910.0	74855.2	134526.1	123207
1546369.5	1372008.4	38621.6	-47085.2	-81038.9	98123.3	61029.5	103446.8	82303
493311.6	416127.1	3334.1	-24827.4	-20587.7	52786.7	13825.7	31079.3	40904
300429.3	260276.6	1931.3	-5786.8	-1575.1	27672.8	20734.6	20378.4	16520
111512.5	96895.4	659.4	-14714.9	-16513.9	18077.6	-9088.5	6766.0	13669
71012.6	50374.3	733.2	-2563.8	-2456.3	5932.1	2031.0	3754.1	9888
22371.3	16029.8	380.2	615.8	1234.1	149.1	3002.4	1388.1	959
9753.2	4955.8	305.2	274.8	688.8	113.4	1784.8	790.8	331
9066.4	7939.0	45.7	415.4	460.7	35.7	963.9	457.5	330
1842211.2	1477566.0	15630.0	72496.2	111654.3	98735.1	262629.3	135345.0	98142
706274.5	588733.9	7507.4	-11362.1	28527.7	34440.1	83584.2	47549.1	45218
1135936.7	888832.1	8122.6	83858.3	83126.6	64295.0	179045.1	87795.9	52924
8808907.1	5447573.0	233906.4	2250529.9	2068712.4	114435.7	2834794.5	532175.7	77352
25254.2	20796.4	1.3	1672.3	1811.5	754.9	2534.9	722.1	669
40517.5	33938.6	163.2	3356.8	3210.8	322.4	4868.1	1494.1	622
12779766.5	8784901.9	292037.3	2256677.2	2084933.2	365370.5	3182621.6	805651.1	301025
746665.3	565790.5	35238.2	560.0	-12544.0	56609.3	60910.2	38216.0	58239
686568.6	521361.2	34684.9	3505.1	-8897.4	48758.7	60220.1	34432.6	50881
60096.7	44429.3	553.3	-2945.1	-3646.6	7850.6	690.1	3783.4	7358
12033101.2	8219111.4	256799.1	2256117.2	2097477.2	308761.2	3121711.4	767435.1	242786
5530345.8	2592364.6	100293.6	2039012.1	1946050.0	73613.1	2513141.3	466797.7	119352
5766001.8	5004368.0	152921.8	197391.7	129378.8	218524.3	559332.8	277032.2	93954
736753.6	622378.8	3583.7	19713.4	22048.4	16623.8	49237.3	23605.2	29480
9895135.8	6424693.9	240336.0	2272289.5	2111326.1	166902.4	2980988.8	629326.7	143487
1969082.0	1607919.6	45609.0	-23239.0	-36333.8	152553.8	146609.0	137333.8	100781
915548.7	752288.4	6092.3	7626.7	9940.9	45914.3	55023.8	38990.6	56757

12-13 分行业国有及国有控股工业企业主要经济指标

单位: 万元 (2004 年)

行 业	Sector	企业单位数(个) Number of Enterp-rises (unit)	#亏损企业 Loss	工业总产值(当年价格) Gross Industrial Output Value (At Current Prices)
煤炭开采和洗选业	Coal Extracting and Dressing	36	18	166824.9
石油和天然气开采业	Petroleum and Natural Gas Extraction	7	1	5078671.1
#天然原油和天然气开采	Crude Oil and Natural Gas Extraction	5		4406905.1
黑色金属矿采选业	Ferrous Metals Mining and Dressing	9	2	90106.6
有色金属矿采选业	Nonferrous Metals Mining and Dressing	9	2	50353.5
非金属矿采选业	Nonmetal Minerals Mining and Dressing	13	5	19558.5
#采 盐	Salt Extraction	5	2	4932.4
其他采矿业	Other Ore Extraction			
农副食品加工业	Farm and Non-staple Processing	39	12	178694.9
#谷物磨制	Grain Grinding	15	6	40034.3
饲料加工	Fodder Processing	6		32132.5
制 糖	Sugar Making	8	2	59392.6
食品制造业	Food Manufacturing	22	8	135156.8
#罐头制造	Beverage Production	7	3	97769.1
饮料制造业	Beverage Production	13	6	67324.7
#酒的制造	Wine Manufacturing	12	6	65765.0
烟草制品业	Tobacco Products	2	1	71374.3
纺织业	Textile Industry	23	18	216262.2
#棉、化纤纺织及印染精加工	Cotton, Chemical Fiber, Dyeing, Printing and Dressing	15	12	163742.0
毛纺织和染整精加工	Wool Textile, Dyeing and Printing	5	5	13880.6
纺织服装、鞋、帽制造业	Textile Garment, Shoe and Hat	8	4	6606.5
皮革、毛皮、羽毛(绒)及其制品业	Leather, Fur, Feather (down) its Products	1	1	45.9
#皮革鞣制加工	Leather Tanning and Processing	1	1	45.9
皮革制品制造	Leather Products Manufacturing			
木材加工及木、竹、藤、棕、草制品业	Timber Processing, Wood, Bamboo, Cane, Grass Products	1	1	2287.5
家具制造业	Furniture Manufacturing	3	2	635.1
造纸及纸制品业	Papermaking and Paper Products	11	3	58325.8
印刷业和记录媒介的复制	Printing and Copying of Medium for Record	39	20	24937.4
文教体育用品制造业	Cultural, Educational and Sports Goods			
石油加工、炼焦及核燃料加工业	Oil Processing, Coking and Nuclear Fuel Processing	11	3	3327481.6
#炼 焦	Coking			
化学原料及化学制品制造业	Raw Chemical Material and Chemical Products	30	6	353414.2
#基础化学原料制造	Basic Chemical Material	7	3	144947.7
肥料制造	Fertilizer Making	6		45916.5
医药制造业	Medical and Pharmaceutical Products	6		13336.2
化学纤维制造业	Chemical Fiber	2	1	6861.0
橡胶制品业	Rubber Products	2		47825.0
塑料制品业	Plastic Products	21	6	169376.6
非金属矿物制品业	Nonmetal Mineral Products	44	17	190831.4
#水泥制造	Cement Manufacturing	22	12	117988.9
黑色金属冶炼及压延加工业	Smelting and Pressing of Ferrous Metals	9	5	1011491.9
有色金属冶炼及压延加工业	Smelting and Pressing of Nonferrous Metals	7	1	85448.3
金属制品业	Metal Products	12	5	17912.8
通用设备制造业	Ordinary Equipment Production	11	2	21952.6
专用设备制造业	Special Purposes Equipment	21	12	35418.1
交通运输设备制造业	Transport Equipment	15	8	74564.2
电气机械及器材制造业	Electric Equipment and Machinery	11	7	33887.4
通信设备、计算机及其他电子设备制造业	Telecom Equipment, Computer and Other Electronic Equipment			
仪器仪表及文化、办公用机械制造业	Equipment, Meter and Cultural and Office Machinery			
工艺品及其他制造业	Art and Handicraft as well as Other Manufacturing Sector			
废弃资源和废旧材料回收加工业	Recycling and Processing of Deserted Resources and Waste Material			
电力、热力的生产和供应业	Electric and Thermal Production and Supply	102	60	920144.9
#电力生产和电力供应	Electric Power Production and Supply	67	45	858105.7
燃气生产和供应业	Gas Production and Supply	4	2	28122.1
水的生产和供应业	Water Production and Supply	73	42	29812.5

Main Economic Indicators of State-Owned or Holding Enterprises With Independent Accounting System by Branch of Industry

(10 000 yuan)

工业增加值 Added Value of Industry	工业销售产值(当年价) Sales Value of Industry Products (At Current Prices)	出口交货值 Delivery Value of Industry Export	实收资本 Total Capital Hold	资产合计 Total Assets	流动资产合计 Circulating Funds	#产成品 Finished Product	流动资产年平均余额 Annual Average Balance of Circulating Funds	固定资产原价 Original Value of Fixed Assets
102190.0	162554.7	8.3	243890.8	588725.6	180497.8	15764.9	176417.7	382095.9
3799728.7	5052048.0		3144000.9	8762376.3	1672480.9	108904.8	1441893.2	11121306.2
3474516.0	4391163.0		2442629.6	7222574.7	924767.5	99494.4	748037.8	10038108.1
22566.4	85031.6		29961.2	126326.4	74309.1	1857.8	62615.6	52019.2
25694.9	49277.5		12860.5	59226.7	32653.7	3067.4	33362.2	35442.5
7450.8	14929.5	109.0	14726.4	38614.6	21168.1	4430.9	22040.7	22551.5
2645.4	4200.9		876.8	4537.8	1814.9	435.2	1844.7	2655.8
31441.7	169358.5	2226.1	59532.3	215122.2	128944.7	50474.2	117085.8	121941.5
6161.9	38355.0		12762.2	29956.5	16649.7	1645.0	15479.5	29027.4
4390.6	32674.8		6588.0	28838.3	12961.7	860.9	13625.1	10105.5
13945.2	52933.7	458.5	24149.9	97391.1	63939.7	40867.2	53231.0	51417.3
36201.0	102133.0	49266.8	59856.9	271816.6	121819.3	39790.3	107492.3	149807.9
25697.5	67157.6	41579.3	43805.5	223253.9	98626.9	35606.0	82538.4	129911.9
34523.5	69202.7		67478.9	192272.2	92125.7	5070.6	92546.3	85092.5
34381.5	67765.4		67277.9	190219.8	91567.3	4948.7	92030.9	84288.7
50699.0	71329.6		21010.8	89732.2	55391.5	14.1	54650.7	45524.9
38656.1	187908.6	24957.0	229619.9	510683.2	263558.2	71530.8	271481.3	349366.0
24287.0	146493.0	5128.5	138506.7	289770.1	133688.2	33870.3	137244.2	226010.4
946.4	14274.5	462.7	53630.3	139159.7	83083.2	25127.7	82534.5	81833.4
2206.4	6897.2	15.0	3319.6	7562.8	4723.9	654.1	5036.6	4434.5
-2.6	45.9		2.3	86.7	39.8	13.3	51.3	35.4
-2.6	45.9		2.3	86.7	39.8	13.3	51.3	35.4
-51.4	2090.2		27.1	6313.1	2267.0	403.8	2173.8	5254.5
271.7	612.5		336.6	1040.6	526.5	145.2	525.6	616.6
28348.8	52829.3		34302.7	173490.9	71269.1	13404.8	67037.9	95477.5
9425.2	25380.8		16131.8	40277.3	13099.4	1233.8	12939.9	43951.1
598318.8	3319226.9	7673.7	477378.7	2235386.6	757296.9	199472.2	704308.0	2638132.4
129693.9	338699.0	4574.5	199564.2	538711.5	195682.9	33582.5	176943.4	348950.6
50592.1	144329.1	4554.8	48751.8	194941.2	74607.1	9019.2	63526.0	123841.0
19187.3	45936.2		90030.2	132332.9	52737.6	1282.3	37197.6	84867.1
6095.3	13005.6	1032.8	11301.2	40729.1	17822.4	3981.0	21227.2	20589.2
660.0	5534.4		6415.0	19761.5	5921.6	897.3	5388.7	10455.4
9864.4	46352.0	632.0	13614.1	78958.7	38722.4	8372.9	41899.3	33664.9
49726.9	161293.0	21660.6	204714.7	603993.9	285511.1	57346.0	273716.8	343991.3
64504.6	189353.7		141317.1	632205.2	231717.1	15612.2	221557.4	385014.9
46832.1	115779.6		105856.7	499007.0	156223.8	8466.9	149887.0	319923.1
317367.1	1012728.3	4200.4	287562.7	796050.1	282491.0	14288.5	267164.0	524123.9
20401.4	86933.3	2243.5	32285.0	96054.7	45975.9	2407.4	43048.9	55629.3
3480.6	18615.4		9722.7	18880.1	12755.5	1892.7	13446.5	8745.0
6017.5	21724.3		4043.9	27636.6	20468.5	3217.7	20448.0	9169.7
8135.6	34547.1	239.5	19291.6	120279.7	69551.3	12438.2	66773.7	58929.3
12408.9	72163.6		23834.9	82815.8	50287.6	11281.8	50859.1	34640.8
7914.9	34555.4		17703.7	53263.2	38771.8	2458.8	35964.5	16630.0
404590.7	920829.1		481811.6	2929465.8	489524.7	2331.3	521790.2	3170076.3
382475.0	858533.0		388108.2	2621729.5	417950.7	2303.6	452053.4	2893395.4
7236.8	28697.8		46081.2	111504.2	38771.2	792.7	31985.3	53889.4
14991.3	29027.0		57346.0	212744.0	38804.1	48.6	39962.1	205347.9

12-13 续表

单位: 万元

行 业	Sector	固定资产净值年平均余额 Annual Average Balance of Net Value of Fixed Assets	流动负债合计 Liquid Liabilities	长期负债合计 Long-term Liabilities	所有者权益合计 Creditors' Equity
煤炭开采和洗选业	Coal Extracting and Dressing	236037.8	220181.3	65210.7	302223.9
石油和天然气开采业	Petroleum and Natural Gas Extraction	6148772.7	2150476.4	1662074.0	4949825.9
＃天然原油和天然气开采	Crude Oil and Natural Gas Extraction	5464533.2	1358980.2	1648239.1	4215355.4
黑色金属矿采选业	Ferrous Metals Mining and Dressing	33206.8	58382.8	12281.1	55662.3
有色金属矿采选业	Nonferrous Metals Mining and Dressing	20691.8	32446.4	9878.5	16901.0
非金属矿采选业	Nonmetal Minerals Mining and Dressing	15744.8	21633.5	1222.9	15758.1
＃采 盐	Salt Extraction	1672.1	2688.0	768.9	1080.9
其他采矿业	Other Ore Extraction				
农副食品加工业	Farm and Non-staple Processing	71731.2	141409.9	9240.0	64167.7
＃谷物磨制	Grain Grinding	13825.9	15384.8	2759.1	11812.6
饲料加工	Fodder Processing	6608.1	10146.4	5226.0	13465.9
制 糖	Sugar Making	29312.2	70838.3	1.0	26248.2
食品制造业	Food Manufacturing	114284.2	163898.1	28925.8	76483.1
＃罐头制造	Beverage Production	100146.4	135287.0	26926.1	58759.5
饮料制造业	Beverage Production	50610.2	102211.4	5141.8	84919.0
＃酒的制造	Wine Manufacturing	50038.4	101572.3	5141.8	83505.7
烟草制品业	Tobacco Products	27090.3	35214.1	17900.0	36618.0
纺织业	Textile Industry	197372.1	351727.8	61580.5	96874.9
＃棉、化纤纺织及印染精加工	Cotton, Chemical Fiber, Dyeing, Printing and Dressing	132291.9	207873.6	23337.4	58459.1
毛纺织和染整精加工	Wool Textile, Dyeing and Printing	46249.6	101393.5	37295.0	71.2
纺织服装、鞋、帽制造业	Textile Garment, Shoe and Hat	2504.3	5250.0	203.5	2109.2
皮革、毛皮、羽毛(绒)及其制品业	Leather, Fur, Feather (down) its Products	35.4	52.5		34.2
＃皮革鞣制加工	Leather Tanning and Processing	35.4	52.5		34.2
皮革制品制造	Leather Products Manufacturing				
木材加工及木、竹、藤、棕、草制品业	Timber Processing, Wood, Bamboo, Cane, Grass Products	3844.6	2599.6	4404.6	-691.1
家具制造业	Furniture Manufacturing	450.1	257.7	3.0	779.9
造纸及纸制品业	Papermaking and Paper Products	60952.2	80198.1	13600.0	79692.8
印刷业和记录媒介的复制	Printing and Copying of Medium for Record	25211.5	18051.1	1985.7	20239.1
文教体育用品制造业	Cultural, Educational and Sports Goods				
石油加工、炼焦及核燃料加工业	Oil Processing, Coking and Nuclear Fuel Processing	1468048.3	527978.5	220636.0	1421188.0
＃炼 焦	Coking				
化学原料及化学制品制造业	Raw Chemical Material and Chemical Products	243641.9	211784.3	58387.2	268539.8
＃基础化学原料制造	Basic Chemical Material	87455.5	91359.1	43787.2	59794.9
肥料制造	Fertilizer Making	56057.7	23031.2	9801.1	99500.4
医药制造业	Medical and Pharmaceutical Products	17416.7	18206.4	2994.5	19528.2
化学纤维制造业	Chemical Fiber	9540.1	10164.1	3150.0	6447.4
橡胶制品业	Rubber Products	17383.1	40965.0	10152.7	17837.0
塑料制品业	Plastic Products	235490.8	263771.2	65166.1	274917.7
非金属矿物制品业	Nonmetal Mineral Products	240478.3	289716.6	84127.1	258361.4
＃水泥制造	Cement Manufacturing	192889.7	223623.4	80218.9	195164.6
黑色金属冶炼及压延加工业	Smelting and Pressing of Ferrous Metals	324353.8	284151.1	44561.4	467297.9
有色金属冶炼及压延加工业	Smelting and Pressing of Nonferrous Metals	29155.5	42749.2	14870.2	38217.1
金属制品业	Metal Products	5296.4	9195.2	892.4	8792.5
通用设备制造业	Ordinary Equipment Production	4532.9	14262.6	530.9	12843.1
专用设备制造业	Special Purposes Equipment	35650.9	87793.0	9999.2	22437.4
交通运输设备制造业	Transport Equipment	17772.8	63540.1	1449.7	17825.9
电气机械及器材制造业	Electric Equipment and Machinery	10853.7	27193.1	3953.9	22116.1
通信设备、计算机及其他电子设备制造业	Telecom Equipment, Computer and Other Electronic Equipment				
仪器仪表及文化、办公用机械制造业	Equipment, Meter and Cultural and Office Machinery				
工艺品及其他制造业	Art and Handicraft as well as Other Manufacturing Sector				
废弃资源和废旧材料回收加工业	Recycling and Processing of Deserted Resources and Waste Material				
电力、热力的生产和供应业	Electric and Thermal Production and Supply	2199173.9	1541214.6	699888.0	688084.7
＃电力生产和电力供应	Electric Power Production and Supply	1999431.9	1430336.0	617183.5	573956.0
燃气生产和供应业	Gas Production and Supply	54101.8	30769.8	26045.5	54688.9
水的生产和供应业	Water Production and Supply	149925.8	67346.5	31516.8	113860.3

Continued

(10 000 yuan)

主营业务收入 Income of Major Business	#主营业务成本 Cost of Major Business	主营业务税金及附加 Major Business, Tax and Addition	营业利润 Business Profit	利润总额 Total Profit	亏损企业亏损总额 Lost Enterprise Total Loss	利税总额 Total Profits And Taxes	本年应交增值税 Value Added Taxes Payable	全部从业人员年平均人数(人) Average Number of Staff and Workers (person)
167966.8	114618.3	1778.1	6169.3	5348.6	4030.3	21092.6	13965.9	31227
5214117.7	2386131.7	95570.5	2013590.3	1920318.9	68372.9	2456770.2	440880.8	79042
4227408.0	1494840.1	86082.5	2042079.5	1987773.6		2447108.1	373252.0	32531
87201.1	53055.0	2028.6	9717.0	10107.0	347.2	18205.1	6069.5	2572
47523.6	30772.6	358.9	8969.5	9658.2	121.8	14628.6	4611.5	3852
13536.6	7787.0	557.5	566.0	617.3	740.9	2444.8	1270.0	2659
4228.4	1708.8	331.4	343.4	313.2	99.8	1237.5	592.9	1030
179775.1	134257.5	512.5	5660.2	6372.2	2624.8	11213.8	4329.1	8125
36587.7	34002.1	34.1	141.4	477.2	709.2	550.0	38.7	920
34588.5	10760.8		1938.7	2133.4		2343.9	210.5	541
58154.6	43633.2	446.8	3694.2	3867.6	352.2	7255.6	2941.2	3908
103348.8	70300.7	406.9	10323.9	8979.6	423.5	14049.7	4663.2	4028
69075.2	45487.8	74.5	7798.9	7778.0	96.0	11029.3	3176.8	1373
60624.0	34653.0	6167.1	6309.1	4591.1	5503.2	16623.9	5865.7	4472
59186.7	33563.4	6158.3	6299.6	4568.7	5503.2	16592.7	5865.7	4358
72167.4	29741.7	26703.1	6650.9	5945.2	406.5	39798.1	7149.8	571
191494.8	189079.1	543.8	-25495.1	-36858.4	37991.5	-29754.6	6560.0	24924
147037.7	151076.4	458.0	-24351.3	-23473.7	23899.0	-17583.7	5432.0	19663
13172.1	12667.3	24.0	-4464.9	-4540.0	4540.0	-4085.2	430.8	2158
7373.6	6279.0	29.5	69.7	-7.1	226.9	187.2	164.8	1010
48.0	34.8	0.5	-79.8	-86.9	86.9	-82.7	3.7	29
48.0	34.8	0.5	-79.8	-86.9	86.9	-82.7	3.7	29
2090.2	1933.8	10.0	-443.4	-180.1	180.1	-44.6	125.5	137
613.0	544.0	4.9	-3.6	27.7	5.3	80.9	48.3	125
51360.8	39354.6	441.9	2617.4	3282.6	215.8	8645.0	4920.5	4808
25228.9	19138.2	124.9	-308.0	-147.5	946.9	1175.4	1198.0	3269
3287049.9	2889350.3	139683.4	128672.8	21828.2	84031.6	257482.5	95970.9	15230
363931.2	274991.5	2494.7	34884.7	31078.2	2088.0	56299.4	22726.5	13109
147174.9	104672.8	1328.9	17506.6	14103.7	1286.2	27765.4	12332.8	5365
47101.2	33135.4	316.3	5407.8	5546.0		7725.8	1863.5	2831
11979.8	7420.9	80.4	665.6	2760.3		3918.5	1077.8	1177
5534.4	5080.8	10.0	-478.8	-480.8	526.0	-338.8	132.0	347
44890.9	37909.9	488.8	200.4	204.9		2383.9	1690.2	2473
344861.2	306000.8	1413.8	11506.4	12095.4	1363.0	21052.5	7543.3	7382
190661.6	152680.8	637.5	-4476.1	-6190.6	22362.4	7498.0	13051.1	15385
114350.3	91152.3	409.5	-11139.1	-14581.2	22298.2	-3402.8	10768.9	12327
1033432.8	833804.8	3093.7	156029.8	154867.1	603.7	221439.7	63478.9	14689
85224.7	70856.3	153.7	5302.2	8456.7	25.1	12017.7	3407.3	2210
19987.6	17391.7	116.4	-13.5	225.8	237.5	1082.6	740.4	1176
22234.3	19850.2	155.0	221.5	135.7	546.9	1921.2	1630.5	1704
41500.8	31298.4	229.0	-2978.1	-3047.8	7205.4	-631.1	2187.7	3264
72912.6	65918.1	282.3	-3345.7	-3526.0	4820.4	-1294.9	1948.8	4491
34781.8	27084.6	148.3	3102.5	3303.0	912.2	5004.7	1553.4	1022
939537.8	884930.9	7495.2	-110873.5	-66930.0	110008.4	24050.0	83484.8	40659
875908.4	833018.5	7143.4	-110156.8	-69730.6	104590.8	17631.2	80218.4	37094
23797.1	16346.2	112.3	-1338.1	-1514.8	1525.0	-129.4	1273.1	1202
32977.6	26304.7	204.1	-4718.3	-6300.5	6890.4	-4168.3	1928.1	4655

12-14 各地、州、市、县(市)国有及国有控股工业企业主要经济指标

单位: 万元 (2004 年)

地 区	Region	企业单位数(个) Number of Enterprises (unit)	#亏损企业 Loss	工业总产值(当年价格) Gross Industrial Output Value (At Current Prices)
总 计	**Total**	**617**	**281**	**12535046.5**
乌鲁木齐市	**Urumqi City**	**162**	**72**	**3685188.8**
乌鲁木齐县	Urumqi County	2	1	1329.9
克拉玛依市	**Karamay City**	**23**	**5**	**5166914.7**
石河子市	**Shihezi City**	**35**	**17**	**288546.9**
阿拉尔市	**Alar City**	**1**		**430.0**
图木舒克市	**Tumxuk City**	**4**	**1**	**5688.9**
五家渠市	**Wujiaqu City**	**9**	**3**	**23266.8**
吐鲁番地区	**Turpan Administrative Offices**	**24**	**15**	**652581.0**
吐鲁番市	Turpan City	11	7	18366.2
鄯善县	Shanshan [Piqan] County	8	4	631599.8
托克逊县	Toksun County	5	4	2615.0
哈密地区	**Hami [Kumul] Administrative Offices**	**39**	**14**	**221490.6**
哈密市	Hami [Kumul] City	30	11	207611.9
巴里坤哈萨克自治县	Barkol Kazak Autonomous County	5		5037.8
伊吾县	Yiwu [Araturuk] County	4	3	8840.9
昌吉回族自治州	**Changji Hui Autonomous Prefecture**	**35**	**15**	**235860.8**
昌吉市	Changji City	11	4	48202.8
阜康市	Fukang City	6	2	49026.5
米泉市	Miquan City	5	2	60539.3
呼图壁县	Hutubi County	4	2	3211.8
玛纳斯县	Manas County	6	2	66503.9
奇台县	Qitai County	2	2	7419.0
吉木萨尔县	Jimsar County			
木垒哈萨克自治县	Mori Kazak Autonomous County	1	1	957.5
伊犁哈萨克自治州	**Ili Kazak Autonomous Prefecture**	**116**	**50**	**452343.3**
伊犁州直属县(市)	**Counties (Cities) Direct Under Ili Prefecture**	**51**	**20**	**270553.4**
伊宁市	Yining [Gulja] City	9	5	42424.7
奎屯市	Kuytun City	17	5	117262.5
伊宁县	Yining [Gulja] County	7	2	41762.9
察布查尔锡伯自治县	Qapqal Xibe Autonomous County	2	2	1128.4
霍城县	Huocheng [Korgas] County	6	4	21204.1
巩留县	Gongliu [Tokkuztara] County	1		179.1
新源县	Xinyuan [Kunes] County	3	1	43274.3
昭苏县	Zhaosu [Mongolkure] County	2		626.1
特克斯县	Tekes County	1		69.5
尼勒克县	Nilka County	3	1	2621.8

Main Economic Indicators of Enterprises With Independent Accounting System by Prefecture, Autonomous Prefecture, City and County

(10 000 yuan)

工业增加值 Added Value of Industry	工业销售产值(当年价) Sales Value of Industry Products (At Current Prices)	出口交货值 Delivery Value of Industry Export	实收资本 Total Capital Hold	资产合计 Total Assets	流动资产合计 Circulating Funds	#产成品 Finished Product	流动资产年平均余额 Annual Average Balance of Circulating Funds	固定资产原价 Original Value of Fixed Assets
5850758.9	**12384915.5**	**118839.2**	**5971047.0**	**19682108.1**	**5354950.7**	**687182.6**	**5003834.0**	**20432898.0**
1163936.6	**3648553.9**	**70046.0**	**1623049.2**	**5327154.4**	**1562518.2**	**197822.1**	**1422737.9**	**4569615.7**
581.9	1124.8		993.8	3328.0	1563.6	1.6	1494.8	2710.2
2614424.0	**5136444.1**	**7673.7**	**2162800.0**	**6445502.1**	**1489303.1**	**148977.3**	**1435922.6**	**8071645.1**
91908.9	**279437.4**	**28434.2**	**184602.4**	**945818.8**	**447579.4**	**88492.5**	**428916.3**	**481851.4**
13.7	**430.0**		**1726.8**	**1904.7**	**110.9**		**94.4**	**2072.5**
1636.3	**6286.5**		**13259.2**	**31602.8**	**7768.8**	**107.4**	**8242.6**	**19647.2**
4040.1	**21355.9**	**507.9**	**11244.8**	**39907.7**	**21491.8**	**7511.0**	**22337.3**	**28263.1**
504404.3	**646367.7**		**295629.8**	**898725.2**	**144072.0**	**14061.0**	**114608.9**	**1430656.3**
8123.4	18085.0		21493.3	125800.3	56597.7	1349.7	32800.2	86768.8
495524.5	625758.4		273415.7	768445.7	84202.6	12198.9	78536.2	1341915.9
756.4	2524.3		720.8	4479.2	3271.7	512.4	3272.5	1971.6
93078.9	**222122.6**		**134612.6**	**536721.3**	**184040.7**	**12765.2**	**182024.3**	**445265.8**
86892.3	209328.3		130606.4	522697.4	175136.8	11232.0	174585.4	439339.1
1798.0	4137.4		1573.7	7749.1	4415.9	1306.4	4407.9	3827.2
4388.6	8656.9		2432.5	6274.8	4488.0	226.8	3031.0	2099.5
97605.1	**231453.8**	**1790.9**	**57152.5**	**342424.3**	**112576.9**	**12390.9**	**121557.3**	**358739.8**
23018.6	48768.6	15.0	10636.0	74937.4	25528.5	1395.4	29364.5	71621.3
18111.2	48794.3	1775.9	18362.7	62510.9	25959.7	1336.5	22655.3	36568.6
20460.8	57450.4		14258.1	56613.1	29017.8	3029.8	32194.0	39156.5
310.3	3147.7		777.1	6178.2	4341.8	916.2	4245.4	3535.3
32454.6	64916.3		10521.4	125181.0	26667.9	5713.0	31843.6	189323.4
2812.9	7419.0		2282.7	13027.9	921.9		1055.6	13797.5
436.7	957.5		314.5	3975.8	139.3		198.9	4737.2
206807.6	**441101.7**	**5510.5**	**317311.8**	**1145119.5**	**373332.3**	**50139.3**	**360844.8**	**921622.9**
140790.8	**260664.7**	**4985.0**	**193357.2**	**710276.5**	**240218.2**	**34510.0**	**230565.3**	**570511.3**
20506.9	41557.5		39588.2	187361.9	32667.8	2615.0	39676.8	203931.4
69419.9	113808.0	4985.0	53245.6	244741.1	108054.1	8883.8	99129.0	174600.1
17699.6	40793.0		36275.5	97629.2	28290.3	5457.1	27778.0	94963.9
278.7	826.3		365.9	2310.7	367.0	152.7	373.2	2069.5
4404.1	18398.2		16495.4	63183.2	27948.1	14589.1	21189.3	51664.7
130.5	172.5		174.3	855.0	350.9		353.2	339.3
26931.2	42611.8		44852.8	107207.3	39587.2	1980.0	39417.2	38047.0
410.6	626.1		622.3	1128.5	430.7		423.2	1706.9
44.0	69.5		129.2	1136.8	210.7		210.7	505.9
965.3	1801.8		1608.0	4722.8	2311.4	832.3	2014.7	2682.6

12-14 续表 1

单位：万元

地 区	Region	企业单位数(个) Number of Enterprises (unit)	#亏损企业 Loss	工业总产值(当年价格) Gross Industrial Output Value (At Current Prices)
塔城地区	**Tacheng [Tarbagatai] Administrative Offices**	**39**	**19**	**95669.3**
塔城市	Tacheng [Qoqek] City	5	5	17383.3
乌苏市	Usu City	4	3	3379.0
额敏县	Emin [Dorbiljin] County	10	5	32576.1
沙湾县	Shawan County	6	3	14903.6
托里县	Toli County	3		12884.3
裕民县	Yumin [Qagantokay] County	1		91.7
和布克赛尔蒙古自治县	Hoboksar Mongol Autonomous County	10	3	14451.3
阿勒泰地区	**Altay Administrative Offices**	**26**	**11**	**86120.6**
阿勒泰市	Altay City	11	6	32989.1
布尔津县	Burqin County	2		2415.8
富蕴县	Fuyun [Koktokay] County	8	2	47330.1
福海县	Fuhai [Burultokay] County	2	1	2088.4
哈巴河县	Habahe [Kaba] County	1		1106.0
青河县	Qinghe [Qinggil] County	2	2	191.2
吉木乃县	Jeminay County			
博尔塔拉蒙古自治州	**Bortala Mongol Autonomous Prefecture**	**20**	**8**	**62186.7**
博乐市	Bole [Bortala] City	15	7	52016.9
精河县	Jinghe [Jing] County	5	1	10169.8
温泉县	Wenquan [Araxang] County			
巴音郭楞蒙古自治州	**Bayangol Mongol Autonomous Prefecture**	**54**	**28**	**1407012.2**
库尔勒市	Korla City	25	12	1363343.3
轮台县	Luntai [Bugur] County	3	2	2902.7
尉犁县	Yuli [Lopnur] County	2	1	1103.6
若羌县	Ruoqiang [Qarkilik] County	5	2	15732.9
且末县	Qiemo [Qarqan] County	2	2	1168.6
焉耆回族自治县	Yanji Hui Autonomous County	4	3	844.6
和静县	Hejing County	7	2	17787.7
和硕县	Hoxud County	4	3	1721.3
博湖县	Bohu [Bagrax] County	2	1	2407.5
阿克苏地区	**Aksu Administrative Offices**	**29**	**9**	**224958.7**
阿克苏市	Aksu City	13		88785.2
温宿县	Wensu [Onsu] County	5	3	4503.1
库车县	Kuqa County	5	1	117808.9

Continued

(10 000 yuan)

工业增加值 Added Value of Industry	工业销售产值(当年价) Sales Value of Industry Products (At Current Prices)	出口交货值 Delivery Value of Industry Export	实收资本 Total Capital Hold	资产合计 Total Assets	流动资产合计 Circulating Funds	#产成品 Finished Product	流动资产年平均余额 Annual Average Balance of Circulating Funds	固定资产原价 Original Value of Fixed Assets
33016.2	**97279.5**	**525.5**	**66669.8**	**237725.7**	**78321.5**	**10865.0**	**75567.3**	**190701.9**
6465.9	17355.5	67.0	9939.3	72640.9	16845.0	2295.0	16787.4	68711.7
973.2	3007.0		686.1	6246.0	2456.6	180.4	1790.8	3706.1
10456.8	32498.9	458.5	22954.8	50825.6	21508.2	4506.4	19835.3	37087.0
-318.3	16200.0		9465.9	36912.0	12501.5	1100.2	12276.0	35166.8
6769.6	12909.0		7711.7	28669.5	11453.5	1717.3	10738.5	15846.6
35.5	91.7		243.8	435.8	128.1		128.1	307.7
8633.5	15217.4		15668.2	41995.9	13428.6	1065.7	14011.2	29876.0
33000.6	**83157.5**		**57284.8**	**197117.3**	**54792.6**	**4764.3**	**54712.2**	**160409.7**
7404.0	32845.1		21224.9	116820.4	26031.7	1486.7	23797.0	96462.8
1264.4	2415.8		8470.1	11195.5	1059.3		1032.6	9323.4
22405.6	44511.0		11231.7	51532.4	23931.8	3277.6	26655.4	36740.1
1028.1	2088.4		16193.3	15827.3	2638.5		2283.6	16955.8
800.6	1106.0			1059.1	949.2		743.1	202.6
97.9	191.2		164.8	682.6	182.1		200.5	725.0
10729.3	**60104.8**		**30822.6**	**140858.9**	**51991.1**	**16785.5**	**49892.0**	**113189.7**
8357.8	50584.4		24815.6	130247.8	48014.0	15588.7	45941.5	102463.9
2371.5	9520.4		6007.0	10611.1	3977.1	1196.8	3950.5	10725.8
940088.3	**1375270.2**	**4876.0**	**928648.6**	**2707279.9**	**705913.8**	**115344.3**	**586919.3**	**2999342.5**
926965.7	1340438.4	4767.0	859664.3	2582640.2	632478.8	99568.7	529622.3	2946207.8
1102.9	2902.7		674.7	2900.3	874.9	87.8	733.3	2211.9
379.8	1064.2		594.1	4442.5	1220.6		1411.1	3579.6
5460.2	12095.0	109.0	58972.8	77934.0	44510.4	2914.2	31073.4	26407.3
426.3	897.7		901.6	4658.1	626.2		721.9	5679.4
86.6	459.7		1224.2	2745.7	920.5	76.3	940.2	2794.5
4987.6	13621.4		5234.3	22403.3	20550.0	11547.3	18124.5	5255.4
652.4	1596.4		1315.7	3066.4	2335.0	693.9	1984.7	1883.0
26.8	2194.7		66.9	6489.4	2397.4	456.1	2307.9	5323.6
84013.9	**213752.8**		**109637.1**	**570593.6**	**124663.4**	**17680.2**	**116082.3**	**457100.3**
41839.6	85828.5		70583.1	312580.3	68466.6	3970.7	73174.3	249344.0
2463.2	4366.7		1396.4	10116.4	1825.3	38.6	1544.4	7681.9
30749.4	109696.1		34041.6	217470.1	50182.9	13669.5	38181.2	155917.2

12-14 续表 2

单位: 万元

地　　区	Region	企业单位数(个) Number of Enterprises (unit)	#亏损企业 Loss	工业总产值(当年价格) Gross Industrial Output Value (At Current Prices)
沙雅县	Xayar County	1	1	182.8
新和县	Xinhe [Toksu] County	1	1	144.0
拜城县	Baicheng [Bay] County	2	1	13467.7
乌什县	Wushi [Uxturpan] County			
阿瓦提县	Awat County			
柯坪县	Kalpin County	2	2	67.0
克孜勒苏柯尔克孜自治州	**Kizilsu Kirgiz Autonomous Prefecture**	**14**	**7**	**5737.3**
阿图什市	Artux City	5	2	1370.2
阿克陶县	Akto County	3	2	1024.0
阿合奇县	Akqi County	2	1	109.0
乌恰县	Wuqia [Ulugqat] County	4	2	3234.1
喀什地区	**Kashgar [Kaxgar] Administrative Offices**	**28**	**20**	**75374.4**
喀什市	Kashgar [Kaxgar] City	7	5	71033.0
疏附县	Shufu County	4	4	1047.1
疏勒县	Shule County			
英吉沙县	Yengisar County	3	2	413.3
泽普县	Zepu [Poskam] County	1		182.3
莎车县	Shache [Yarkant] County	3	1	1063.0
叶城县	Yecheng [Kagilik] County	3	1	455.7
麦盖提县	Makit County	3	3	539.1
岳普湖县	Yopurga County	1	1	134.1
伽师县	Jiashi [Payzawat] County	1	1	155.5
巴楚县	Bachu [Maralbexi] County	1	1	306.1
塔什库尔干塔吉克自治县	Taxkorgan Tajik Autonomous County	1	1	45.2
和田地区	**Hotan Administrative Offices**	**24**	**17**	**27465.4**
和田市	Hotan City	7	5	18289.1
和田县	Hotan County	4	3	7579.5
墨玉县	Moyu [Karakax] County	2	1	426.0
皮山县	Pishan [Guma] County	2	2	190.9
洛浦县	Lop County	3	1	482.3
策勒县	Qira County	1	1	81.6
于田县	Yutian [Keriya] County	3	2	351.5
民丰县	Minfeng [Niya] County	2	2	64.5

Continued

(10 000 yuan)

工业增加值 Added Value of Industry	工业销售产值(当年价) Sales Value of Industry Products (At Current Prices)	出口交货值 Delivery Value of Industry Export	实收资本 Total Capital Hold	资产合计 Total Assets	流动资产合计 Circulating Funds	#产成品 Finished Product	流动资产年平均余额 Annual Average Balance of Circulating Funds	固定资产原价 Original Value of Fixed Assets
107.1	182.8		620.0	1982.6	406.1		246.4	1585.0
5.7	144.0		1497.1	1994.0	588.0		337.9	1268.8
8803.9	13467.7		1392.7	26293.1	3109.5		2512.5	41235.6
45.0	67.0		106.2	157.1	85.0	1.4	85.6	67.8
1874.2	**5795.1**		**4486.7**	**23288.9**	**7179.9**	**590.9**	**7076.2**	**23416.4**
524.6	1377.2		1758.3	6277.5	2127.8	140.1	2059.3	4725.8
319.0	1025.4		606.1	7355.7	1286.9		1498.5	8165.9
35.5	101.4		102.5	168.7	58.1	8.0	58.1	128.3
995.1	3291.1		2019.8	9487.0	3707.1	442.8	3460.3	10396.4
26131.5	**71083.8**		**33419.3**	**322776.4**	**66126.7**	**2051.7**	**83893.9**	**331806.3**
24597.5	66867.7		25991.5	294887.7	59684.8	1958.9	76791.8	307224.6
376.3	1042.5		2581.7	6258.4	1318.2	5.1	1298.9	7002.9
96.3	413.3		1761.9	3865.0	696.9		708.1	3898.6
122.7	182.3		181.4	1200.4	361.7		360.0	1121.7
418.2	1080.9		481.9	5229.5	924.3	65.4	802.0	4148.3
87.0	455.7		322.7	2123.6	595.7		595.1	2120.9
161.4	502.5		1098.3	3315.5	977.8	22.3	1289.8	2038.1
62.0	134.1		442.5	670.9	172.7		196.1	599.8
53.8	155.5		50.0	2957.8	92.0		88.7	2892.7
139.4	204.1		486.3	1402.5	666.6		1127.4	534.5
16.9	45.2		21.1	865.1	636.0		636.0	224.2
10066.2	**25355.2**		**62643.6**	**202429.6**	**56281.7**	**2463.3**	**62683.9**	**178663.0**
6133.4	16305.2		18133.1	141733.4	42691.3	2431.1	49857.9	120706.4
3449.4	7454.1		41254.8	53660.1	12793.7		11942.5	50303.9
135.3	426.0		426.7	1927.2	153.6		231.8	2092.1
45.7	190.9		255.2	434.6	77.4	27.7	56.2	436.1
143.0	476.5		1391.4	1958.5	262.6		290.5	2287.4
29.7	81.6		163.8	207.5	62.3		42.8	250.0
114.1	356.4		546.9	1260.4	221.3	4.5	241.3	2132.5
15.6	64.5		471.7	1247.9	19.5		20.9	454.6

12-14 续表 3

单位: 万元

地 区	Region	固定资产净值年平均余额 Annual Average Balance of Net Value of Fixed Assets	流动负债合计 Liquid Liabilities	长期负债合计 Long-term Liabilities	所有者权益合计 Creditors' Equity
总 计	**Total**	**12071356.7**	**6914792.0**	**3171973.7**	**9514581.4**
乌鲁木齐市	**Urumqi City**	**3015467.7**	**2204154.1**	**647529.0**	**2472961.6**
乌鲁木齐县	Urumqi County	1676.8	2447.4	368.5	512.1
克拉玛依市	**Karamay City**	**4546813.7**	**1560876.8**	**961206.3**	**3923369.0**
石河子市	**Shihezi City**	**321868.2**	**475632.3**	**136077.6**	**334069.5**
阿拉尔市	**Alar City**	**1828.5**	**177.8**		**1726.9**
图木舒克市	**Tumxuk City**	**13712.0**	**7356.6**	**11434.1**	**12812.0**
五家渠市	**Wujiaqu City**	**15831.4**	**31357.5**	**2020.3**	**6529.9**
吐鲁番地区	**Turpan Administrative Offices**	**647130.9**	**230716.7**	**183795.2**	**484213.1**
吐鲁番市	Turpan City	59003.6	58795.6	4721.5	62283.1
鄯善县	Shanshan [Piqan] County	587040.9	168109.6	178280.3	422055.8
托克逊县	Toksun County	1086.4	3811.5	793.4	-125.8
哈密地区	**Hami [Kumul] Administrative Offices**	**285006.3**	**231002.1**	**113673.0**	**191534.6**
哈密市	Hami [Kumul] City	280900.4	224103.9	112953.2	185129.5
巴里坤哈萨克自治县	Barkol Kazak Autonomous County	2393.4	5334.1	635.3	1779.7
伊吾县	Yiwu [Araturuk] County	1712.5	1564.1	84.5	4625.4
昌吉回族自治州	**Changji Hui Autonomous Prefecture**	**220323.1**	**230025.5**	**47934.1**	**64461.8**
昌吉市	Changji City	64314.8	49507.8	20909.3	4520.3
阜康市	Fukang City	18496.3	25014.9	13346.2	24146.9
米泉市	Miquan City	21661.6	26673.8	1720.7	28218.6
呼图壁县	Hutubi County	1555.5	3571.0	1020.2	1587.0
玛纳斯县	Manas County	100806.6	107935.9	10892.7	6352.4
奇台县	Qitai County	10114.0	13178.1	45.0	-195.2
吉木萨尔县	Jimsar County				
木垒哈萨克自治县	Mori Kazak Autonomous County	3374.3	4144.0		-168.2
伊犁哈萨克自治州	**Ili Kazak Autonomous Prefecture**	**637672.9**	**534136.2**	**234171.7**	**374888.1**
伊犁州直属县(市)	**Counties (Cities) Direct Under Ili Prefecture**	**380180.5**	**282732.7**	**162426.0**	**264813.7**
伊宁市	Yining [Gulja] City	146219.0	110876.4	39735.2	36750.0
奎屯市	Kuytun City	114258.9	69117.4	85960.5	89659.4
伊宁县	Yining [Gulja] County	56066.3	38342.6	23454.7	35831.9
察布查尔锡伯自治县	Qapqal Xibe Autonomous County	1826.8	429.3	236.2	1645.2
霍城县	Huocheng [Korgas] County	32469.4	36625.1	8482.5	17775.6
巩留县	Gongliu [Tokkuztara] County	262.3	666.1		188.9
新源县	Xinyuan [Kunes] County	26443.0	23917.1	3166.0	80124.2
昭苏县	Zhaosu [Mongolkure] County	565.8	339.9	49.9	738.7
特克斯县	Tekes County	382.2	95.4	851.0	190.4
尼勒克县	Nilka County	1686.8	2323.4	490.0	1909.4

Continued

(10 000 yuan)

主营业务收入 Incoem of Major Business	#主营业务成本 Cost of Major Business	主营业务税金及附加 Major Business, Tax and Addition	营业利润 Business Profit	利润总额 Total Profit	亏损企业亏损总额 Lost Enterprise Total Loss	利税总额 Total Profits and Taxes	本年应交增值税 Value Added Taxes Payable	全部从业人员年平均人数(人) Average Number of Staff and Workers (person)
12779766.5	**8784901.9**	**292037.3**	**2256677.2**	**2084933.2**	**365370.5**	**3182621.6**	**805651.1**	**301025**
3715612.6	**2903015.1**	**72346.2**	**345117.3**	**230695.4**	**169057.7**	**470142.9**	**167101.3**	**76201**
1074.5	861.7	4.1	-282.4	-273.5	300.0	-225.1	44.3	265
5220575.5	**3499081.3**	**136318.7**	**1139557.2**	**1042197.1**	**69029.6**	**1558623.9**	**380108.1**	**76424**
463024.7	**396793.5**	**2417.4**	**10683.5**	**13522.8**	**7426.6**	**31090.8**	**15150.6**	**18388**
376.6	**181.9**	**0.1**	**153.3**	**153.3**		**153.4**		**34**
5847.5	**6264.2**	**0.4**	**-1245.7**	**-1222.9**	**1384.2**	**-429.1**	**793.4**	**423**
19868.9	**18001.0**	**60.8**	**-2206.0**	**-2138.1**	**2538.2**	**-820.9**	**1256.4**	**3006**
677488.8	**332845.2**	**12298.9**	**299899.3**	**298936.4**	**12189.4**	**368447.2**	**57211.9**	**6810**
50338.2	57319.8	248.6	-10718.1	-11295.1	11421.8	-8510.5	2536.0	1892
624291.2	273515.7	11752.3	310662.8	310254.2	708.4	376421.9	54415.4	4642
2859.4	2009.7	298.0	-45.4	-22.7	59.2	535.8	260.5	276
218257.4	**177751.6**	**2472.4**	**3165.6**	**2360.8**	**6615.4**	**21417.4**	**16584.2**	**19984**
205873.5	172807.7	2211.7	579.0	-229.1	6522.4	17387.7	15405.1	19307
3710.4	2247.5	45.3	160.2	150.7		518.1	322.1	541
8673.5	2696.4	215.4	2426.4	2439.2	93.0	3511.6	857.0	136
240635.6	**212653.4**	**1629.2**	**-556.8**	**-1278.3**	**15020.2**	**16760.3**	**16409.4**	**10043**
48932.6	53285.5	586.6	-11450.6	-11456.5	11822.3	-7793.4	3076.5	2804
47700.1	35286.4	130.1	7657.7	7483.8	38.7	10803.4	3189.5	2530
66518.3	55830.8	333.9	3360.5	3252.5	649.8	6742.2	3155.8	881
3056.8	3205.3	5.5	-522.1	-516.3	532.0	-450.5	60.3	514
66030.7	56375.7	542.2	1999.8	1524.7	410.9	8914.6	6847.7	2837
7439.6	7581.6	26.2	-1230.5	-1199.3	1199.3	-1158.3	14.8	333
957.5	1088.1	4.7	-371.6	-367.2	367.2	-297.7	64.8	144
444743.3	**332180.4**	**33031.4**	**-8757.6**	**-7140.4**	**42181.6**	**63649.7**	**37758.7**	**31336**
266100.9	**187877.9**	**31330.4**	**-3451.7**	**293.0**	**20968.1**	**54414.4**	**22791.0**	**14606**
42274.3	43757.0	364.1	-12671.4	-12283.9	12832.2	-6826.1	5093.7	3831
131678.5	85251.9	26950.3	-229.0	566.9	6773.6	38425.8	10908.6	3268
36263.5	25114.9	85.1	-452.8	2654.7	410.5	5167.6	2427.8	3322
1010.4	877.0	0.6	-7.2	-3.9	3.9	34.3	37.6	77
17053.7	12787.1	316.5	-548.0	-565.5	923.6	296.7	545.7	2098
81.9	28.0	0.6	16.3	0.9		6.4	4.9	28
35193.0	18118.5	3601.8	10411.0	9896.5	16.5	17109.6	3611.3	1653
642.6	506.1	6.8	5.0	3.9		89.0	78.3	89
69.5	35.5	0.3	1.3	1.5		6.4	4.6	29
1833.5	1401.9	4.3	22.9	21.9	7.8	104.7	78.5	211

12-14 续表 4

单位: 万元

地 区	Region	固定资产净值年平均余额 Annual Average Balance of Net Value of Fixed Assets	流动负债合 计 Liquid Liabilities	长期负债合 计 Long-term Liabilities	所有者权益 合 计 Creditors' Equity
塔城地区	**Tacheng [Tarbagatai] Administrative Offices**	**135498.0**	**142099.6**	**39126.8**	**54891.2**
塔城市	Tacheng [Qoqek] City	48077.5	50871.6	13061.2	8617.3
乌苏市	Usu City	2925.6	4867.1	1012.1	366.8
额敏县	Emin [Dorbiljin] County	26138.4	34718.9	2916.6	12789.1
沙湾县	Shawan County	20886.3	22699.0	5409.5	8803.5
托里县	Toli County	11244.4	15246.3	3855.0	8461.7
裕民县	Yumin [Qagantokay] County	307.7	192.0		243.8
和布克赛尔蒙古自治县	Hoboksar Mongol Autonomous County	25918.1	13504.7	12872.4	15609.0
阿勒泰地区	**Altay Administrative Offices**	**121994.4**	**109303.9**	**32618.9**	**55183.2**
阿勒泰市	Altay City	80144.2	80198.6	19802.1	16819.6
布尔津县	Burqin County	7476.1	1248.9	1472.6	8473.9
富蕴县	Fuyun [Koktokay] County	20958.3	26575.5	10095.2	14850.6
福海县	Fuhai [Burultokay] County	12868.1	482.5	513.3	14831.5
哈巴河县	Habahe [Kaba] County	120.9	521.4	500.0	37.7
青河县	Qinghe [Qinggil] County	426.8	277.0	235.7	169.9
吉木乃县	Jeminay County				
博尔塔拉蒙古自治州	**Bortala Mongol Autonomous Prefecture**	**81169.5**	**64039.2**	**40744.3**	**36075.2**
博乐市	Bole [Bortala] City	75154.0	60223.6	39504.9	30519.1
精河县	Jinghe [Jing] County	6015.5	3815.6	1239.4	5556.1
温泉县	Wenquan [Araxang] County				
巴音郭楞蒙古自治州	**Bayangol Mongol Autonomous Prefecture**	**1601393.6**	**751334.3**	**617098.1**	**1328819.2**
库尔勒市	Korla City	1564947.1	704082.4	608583.8	1259946.1
轮台县	Luntai [Bugur] County	1623.2	1409.9	108.7	1381.7
尉犁县	Yuli [Lopnur] County	2011.4	1968.4	119.9	2354.2
若羌县	Ruoqiang [Qarkilik] County	20478.9	14757.5	180.0	62996.4
且末县	Qiemo [Qarqan] County	3668.3	2085.3	2820.5	-247.9
焉耆回族自治县	Yanji Hui Autonomous County	1649.7	1930.3	368.0	447.4
和静县	Hejing County	2383.0	20561.7	57.0	1784.5
和硕县	Hoxud County	761.0	1784.9	455.6	825.9
博湖县	Bohu [Bagrax] County	3871.0	2753.9	4404.6	-669.1
阿克苏地区	**Aksu Administrative Offices**	**314034.5**	**211774.7**	**83113.3**	**210120.1**
阿克苏市	Aksu City	174334.5	142797.0	17506.3	152275.7
温宿县	Wensu [Onsu] County	5267.6	6942.0	1982.0	1192.3
库车县	Kuqa County	109523.3	43312.9	62440.0	46133.1

Continued

(10 000 yuan)

主营业务收入 Income of Major Business	#主营业务成本 Cost of Major Business	主营业务税金及附加 Major Business, Tax and Addition	营业利润 Business Profit	利润总额 Total Profit	亏损企业亏损总额 Lost Enterprise Total Loss	利税总额 Total Profits and Taxes	本年应交增值税 Value Added Taxes Payable	全部从业人员年平均人数(人) Average Number of Staff and Workers (person)
95351.5	**85655.9**	**923.7**	**-9505.7**	**-11183.4**	**15386.5**	**-2427.0**	**7832.7**	**11390**
14347.8	21140.3	92.9	-10514.1	-10973.1	10973.1	-8176.2	2704.0	1767
2409.2	1898.0	10.4	19.2	-374.3	396.2	-210.6	153.3	251
33005.9	27838.7	208.1	1059.5	1700.5	923.7	3665.3	1756.7	1679
20049.5	18505.6	65.0	808.3	-819.4	1183.2	46.0	800.4	1589
12351.4	8028.5	121.4	-15.6	243.2		1340.2	975.6	3016
50.3	192.1	1.2		122.0		123.2		35
13137.4	8052.7	424.7	-863.0	-1082.3	1910.3	785.1	1442.7	3053
83290.9	**58646.6**	**777.3**	**4199.8**	**3750.0**	**5827.0**	**11662.3**	**7135.0**	**5340**
32419.8	29255.5	147.6	-5325.1	-5265.6	5477.5	-3226.6	1891.4	2281
2415.8	1284.3	12.4	220.2	209.5		369.1	147.2	198
45343.3	25941.5	611.1	9030.4	8554.4	178.9	13809.7	4644.2	2586
1831.5	1562.4	3.4	-38.7	-41.8	88.4	237.3	275.7	88
1106.1	453.4	1.7	373.5	375.7		543.5	166.1	99
174.4	149.5	1.1	-60.5	-82.2	82.2	-70.7	10.4	88
66199.8	**60964.9**	**324.2**	**-3019.5**	**-2608.3**	**4424.2**	**268.7**	**2552.8**	**6096**
56643.2	52570.8	229.8	-3084.1	-2736.8	4408.4	-603.1	1903.9	5154
9556.6	8394.1	94.4	64.6	128.5	15.8	871.8	648.9	942
1386029.4	**557063.6**	**27330.5**	**494610.1**	**486008.8**	**16043.5**	**605809.4**	**92470.1**	**28656**
1344726.9	525807.7	26837.4	492075.4	483298.7	15238.7	600976.6	90840.5	24424
2855.7	2035.2	10.9	648.5	654.3	29.6	801.2	136.0	100
1021.5	666.1	2.5	214.2	202.7	58.0	268.2	63.0	198
11963.3	7943.0	323.4	919.2	764.3	148.3	1495.7	408.0	1570
766.9	667.8	4.2	-159.8	-141.8	141.8	-130.6	7.0	176
477.7	504.9	2.2	-223.4	-147.9	159.3	-128.8	16.9	138
20342.0	15998.4	112.6	1578.3	1568.1	74.4	2510.1	829.4	1460
1680.7	1443.9	19.3	-1.3	-10.7	13.3	46.1	37.5	444
2194.7	1996.6	18.0	-441.0	-178.9	180.1	-29.1	131.8	146
213216.2	**162011.9**	**2987.3**	**16113.7**	**21976.0**	**864.9**	**35798.4**	**10835.1**	**10764**
86344.1	59583.6	597.3	4654.9	10382.7		18249.8	7269.8	7936
4323.1	2909.5	32.2	49.6	34.0	106.1	325.9	259.7	817
109645.0	87329.3	2210.4	11766.6	11923.7	393.4	15700.1	1566.0	1284

12-14 续表 5

单位: 万元

地 区	Region	固定资产净值年平均余额 Annual Average Balance of Net Value of Fixed Assets	流动负债合计 Liquid Liabilities	长期负债合计 Long-term Liabilities	所有者权益合计 Creditors' Equity
沙雅县	Xayar County	1147.0	560.2	370.0	1052.4
新和县	Xinhe [Toksu] County	980.1	264.5	200.0	1529.5
拜城县	Baicheng [Bay] County	22750.1	17851.9	615.0	7826.2
乌什县	Wushi [Uxturpan] County				
阿瓦提县	Awat County				
柯坪县	Kalpin County	31.9	46.2		110.9
克孜勒苏柯尔克孜自治州	**Kizilsu Kirgiz Autonomous Prefecture**	**13217.7**	**15475.1**	**6659.8**	**1153.9**
阿图什市	Artux City	3519.8	1399.7	3021.6	1856.2
阿克陶县	Akto County	5545.2	5897.1	1823.3	-364.7
阿合奇县	Akqi County	110.6	60.4		108.3
乌恰县	Wuqia [Ulugqat] County	4042.1	8117.9	1814.9	-445.9
喀什地区	**Kashgar [Kaxgar] Administrative Offices**	**215116.3**	**231360.6**	**66459.5**	**24946.9**
喀什市	Kashgar [Kaxgar] City	196317.6	220483.2	59697.6	14706.9
疏附县	Shufu County	4787.3	1239.9	2682.2	2336.2
疏勒县	Shule County				
英吉沙县	Yengisar County	2906.1	1248.2	1855.2	761.6
泽普县	Zepu [Poskam] County	838.7	391.9	374.0	434.5
莎车县	Shache [Yarkant] County	3779.3	1727.4	565.0	2937.1
叶城县	Yecheng [Kagilik] County	1408.9	1032.3	94.0	997.0
麦盖提县	Makit County	1292.3	1210.1	884.3	1212.1
岳普湖县	Yopurga County	494.2	293.5		377.4
伽师县	Jiashi [Payzawat] County	2795.9	2091.5		866.3
巴楚县	Bachu [Maralbexi] County	284.2	798.6	307.2	296.7
塔什库尔干塔吉克自治县	Taxkorgan Tajik Autonomous County	211.8	844.0		21.1
和田地区	**Hotan Administrative Offices**	**140770.4**	**135372.5**	**20057.4**	**46899.6**
和田市	Hotan City	95401.5	127405.1	9906.1	4322.2
和田县	Hotan County	40388.4	6242.0	8835.0	38583.0
墨玉县	Moyu [Karakax] County	1560.1	299.9	31.0	1596.3
皮山县	Pishan [Guma] County	340.1	247.4		187.2
洛浦县	Lop County	1729.5	546.8	79.0	1332.7
策勒县	Qira County	150.7	49.4	4.4	153.7
于田县	Yutian [Keriya] County	1051.0	471.9	501.2	287.3
民丰县	Minfeng [Niya] County	149.1	110.0	700.7	437.2

Continued

(10 000 yuan)

主营业务收入 Major Business Income	#主营业务成本 Cost of Major Business	主营业务税金及附加 Major Business, Tax and Addition	营业利润 Business Profit	利润总额 Total Profit	亏损企业亏损总额 Lost Enterprise Total Loss	利税总额 Total Profits and Taxes	本年应交增值税 Value Added Taxes Payable	全部从业人员年平均人数(人) Average Number of Staff and Workers (person)
167.4	112.7	6.0	-7.1	-10.9	10.9	13.1	18.0	49
106.4	152.7	2.5	-98.4	-99.1	99.1	-93.2	3.4	27
12508.6	11823.7	137.9	-246.7	-250.5	251.5	1603.2	1715.8	609
121.6	100.4	1.0	-5.2	-3.9	3.9	-0.5	2.4	42
5972.8	**5657.2**	**52.1**	**-1384.9**	**-1749.4**	**1905.4**	**-1225.7**	**471.6**	**1622**
1154.7	906.6	25.8	-258.4	-181.8	265.1	-41.8	114.2	268
1070.8	1721.9	4.8	-1083.9	-1081.9	1086.9	-988.4	88.7	256
80.5	43.2	3.1	-7.6	-7.6	8.4	1.2	5.7	23
3666.8	2985.5	18.4	-35.0	-478.1	545.0	-196.7	263.0	1075
71737.6	**89640.0**	**535.8**	**-26683.2**	**15238.6**	**6046.9**	**20404.0**	**4629.6**	**7065**
67418.1	86477.1	490.6	-26104.2	15972.5	5261.6	20844.4	4381.3	5942
1050.5	778.9	23.9	-134.6	-110.0	110.0	-21.5	64.6	269
493.7	333.7	1.9	-180.1	-182.0	182.0	-155.5	24.6	124
187.6	62.1	1.0	5.5	5.4		19.3	12.9	32
1008.1	580.6	6.6	65.1	-50.4	90.1	22.9	66.7	312
455.6	411.5	6.2	-11.9	-17.9	24.2	15.6	27.3	166
585.1	660.6	1.2	-200.0	-250.0	250.0	-231.6	17.2	72
134.1	102.9	0.7	-69.6	-74.7	74.7	-65.6	8.4	42
155.5	86.2	1.8	-12.5	-12.5	12.5	-1.2	9.5	31
204.1	139.3	1.0	-34.6	-35.5	35.5	-20.1	14.4	51
45.2	7.1	0.9	-6.3	-6.3	6.3	-2.7	2.7	24
30179.8	**30796.7**	**231.9**	**-8769.1**	**-10018.6**	**10642.7**	**-7468.8**	**2317.9**	**4173**
21104.1	24258.2	154.3	-8632.0	-8598.6	8620.1	-6789.5	1654.8	2899
7453.5	5188.2	43.4	93.6	-207.6	799.5	414.6	578.8	803
420.9	416.5	3.2	-57.8	-58.7	63.0	-35.9	19.6	132
191.0	151.6	1.6	-1.2	-18.7	18.7	-12.8	4.3	28
467.9	315.3	15.2	-18.2	-21.3	23.0	22.6	28.7	118
89.6	40.6	0.6	-4.8	-4.8	4.8	-0.1	4.1	20
371.0	379.2	10.7	-141.8	-136.9	141.6	-101.7	24.5	138
81.8	47.1	2.9	-6.9	-972.0	972.0	-966.0	3.1	35

12-15　国有及国有控股工业企业主要经济效益指标

单位: %　　(2004 年)

项　　目	Item	工业增加值率 Ratio of Value Added to Gross Industrial Output Value	资金利税率 Ratio of profits and Taxes to Capital	产值利税率 Ratio of profits and Taxes to Industrial Output Value
总　　计	**Total**	**40.1**	**18.6**	**25.4**
按登记注册类型分	**Grouped by Registry Type**			
内资企业	Domestic Investment	40.2	18.7	25.4
国有企业	State-owned	35.5	2.1	4.4
#中央企业	Central	36.3	2.5	4.8
地方企业	Local Enterprises	32.9	1.2	3.1
#自治区属企业	Autonomous	34.1	3.8	8.2
地区(州、市)属企业	Prefecture or City	33.0	-2.7	-8.0
县(市)属企业	County or City	32.1	1.0	2.7
集体企业	Collective-owned			
县(市)属企业	County or City			
联营企业	Joint Owned	27.1	14.2	12.6
#国有联营企业	State Ownership Joint Enterprises	33.0	19.7	14.8
国有与集体联营企业	State-collective Joint Enterprises	20.4	16.9	11.3
其他联营企业	Other Ownership Joint Enterprises			
有限责任公司	Limited Liability Corporations	31.2	7.3	13.9
#国有独资公司	State-funded Corporations	33.9	5.2	11.6
其他有限责任公司	Other Limited Liability Corporations	29.6	9.0	15.3
股份有限公司	Share-holding Corporations Ltd.	43.0	29.0	32.0
私营企业	Private Enterprises			
私营有限责任公司	Private Limited Liability Corporations			
港、澳、台商投资企业	Enterprises with Funds from Hong Kong, Macao and Taiwan	19.6	6.2	10.0
外商投资企业	Foreign Funded Enterprises	22.2	13.3	22.5
在总计中: 国有控股企业	Of the Total : State-Owned Holding Enterprise	40.1	18.6	25.4
在总计中: 农村工业	Of the Total : Rural Industry	7.9	-3.4	-2.0
按轻、重工业分	**Grouped by Light & Heavy Industry**			
轻工业	Light Industry	27.6	4.0	7.5
以农产品为原料	Using Farm Produces as Raw Materials	26.6	4.7	8.0
以非农产品为原料	Using Non-Farm Produces as Raw Materials	40.6	0.3	1.2
重工业	Heavy Industry	40.9	20.1	26.6
采掘工业	Mining and Quarrying	63.2	30.7	46.5
原料工业	Raw Materials Industry	22.0	9.0	9.7
加工工业	Manufacturing Industry	23.1	4.3	8.9
按企业规模分	**Grouped by Size of Enterprises**			
大型企业	Large	43.5	26.0	31.0
中型企业	Medium	30.8	3.7	7.3
小型企业	Small	24.1	3.3	5.9

Main Indicators on Economic Benefit of State-Owened and Holding Enterprises with Independent Accounting System

(%)

总资产贡献率 Ratio of Total Assets to Industrial Output Value	资本保值增值率 Ratio of Capital Hold and Rise	资产负债率 Assets Liability Ratio	流动资产周转次数(次/年) Number of Times of Annual Turnover Circulating Funds (times/year)	成本费用利润率 Ratio of Profits to Industrial Cost	全员劳动生产率(元/人·年) Overall Labor Productivity (yuan/person-year)	工业经济效益综合指数 Comprehensive Index of Industry Economic Results
18.2	**115.0**	**51.6**	**2.6**	**20.7**	**194361.2**	**295.8**
18.2	115.0	51.6	2.6	20.8	194800.6	296.6
3.0	197.6	60.2	1.3	-4.9	57307.3	86.8
3.7	292.4	60.0	1.4	-5.2	65194.3	105.3
2.0	115.3	60.6	1.1	-3.9	41438.1	65.7
3.9	142.8	59.8	1.4	-0.5	60285.2	100.5
-1.4	84.3	62.8	0.8	-12.6	31112.2	12.3
1.6	102.1	62.7	1.3	-3.6	26581.6	55.3
12.0	91.3	47.8	2.1	5.7	75558.9	145.9
10.4	38.6	59.6	1.9	7.5	129561.9	171.2
22.5	233.1	42.8	2.4	5.3	61218.2	179.4
8.4	98.3	66.3	1.5	6.3	69798.2	133.4
5.4	58.4	72.1	1.4	4.0	61979.6	105.7
12.1	166.3	61.5	1.7	7.8	76478.4	161.7
27.1	107.9	43.0	4.0	33.8	574055.7	604.9
10.2	152.2	64.9	1.0	7.6	84717.5	153.7
10.8	75.5	53.3	1.4	8.4	100549.8	162.7
18.2	115.0	51.6	2.6	20.7	194361.2	295.8
-0.2	3.0	48.6	2.0	-2.3	51368.4	65.6
3.9	80.3	66.1	0.9	-1.8	43766.7	69.5
4.4	76.8	69.0	0.9	-1.4	44904.2	71.1
1.0	95.5	49.6	0.9	-5.6	35900.9	49.7
20.0	118.4	50.2	2.9	22.4	230485.5	331.1
31.2	132.8	44.2	3.2	60.9	331593.2	563.5
9.6	98.3	57.2	3.2	2.4	158874.9	193.2
5.2	124.7	55.7	1.1	3.1	49369.9	104.3
26.0	122.1	44.3	3.5	29.3	340934.1	442.4
5.1	96.3	67.7	1.3	-1.9	70016.5	93.6
3.6	97.4	62.3	1.3	1.1	44605.0	87.7

12-16 分行业国有及国有控股工业企业主要经济效益指标

单位: %　　　　(2004 年)

行　　业	Sector	工业增加值率 Ratio of Value Added to Gross Industrial Output Value	资金利税率 Ratio of profits and Taxes to Capital	产值利税率 Ratio of profits and Taxes toIndustrial Output Value
煤炭开采和洗选业	Coal Extracting and Dressing	54.6	5.1	12.6
石油和天然气开采业	Petroleum and Natural Gas Extraction	64.4	32.4	48.4
＃天然原油和天然气开采	Crude Oil and Natural Gas Extraction	68.4	39.4	55.5
黑色金属矿采选业	Ferrous Metals Mining and Dressing	22.1	19.0	20.2
有色金属矿采选业	Nonferrous Metals Mining and Dressing	44.7	27.1	29.1
非金属矿采选业	Nonmetal Minerals Mining and Dressing	35.1	6.5	12.5
＃采　盐	Salt Extraction	47.1	35.2	25.1
其他采矿业	Other Ore Extraction			
农副食品加工业	Farm and Non-staple Processing	15.8	5.9	6.3
＃谷物磨制	Grain Grinding	13.8	1.9	1.4
饲料加工	Fodder Processing	13.7	11.6	7.3
制　糖	Sugar Making	20.2	8.8	12.2
食品制造业	Food Manufacturing	24.4	6.3	10.4
＃罐头制造	Beverage Production	23.9	6.0	11.3
饮料制造业	Beverage Production	44.1	11.6	24.7
＃酒的制造	Wine Manufacturing	44.9	11.7	25.2
烟草制品业	Tobacco Products	60.5	48.7	55.8
纺织业	Textile Industry	15.5	-6.4	-13.8
＃棉、化纤纺织及印染精加工	Cotton, Chemical Fiber, Dyeing, Printing and Dressing	12.7	-6.5	-10.7
毛纺织和染整精加工	Wool Textile, Dyeing and Printing	6.0	-3.2	-29.4
纺织服装、鞋、帽制造业	Textile Garment, Shoe and Hat	31.3	2.5	2.8
皮革、毛皮、羽毛(绒)及其制品业	Leather, Fur, Feather (down) its Products	-4.9	-95.4	-180.2
＃皮革鞣制加工	Leather Tanning and Processing	-4.9	-95.4	-180.2
皮革制品制造	Leather Products Manufacturing			
木材加工及木、竹、藤、棕、草制品业	Timber Processing, Wood, Bamboo, Cane, Grass Products	-2.3	-0.7	-2.0
家具制造业	Furniture Manufacturing	39.2	8.3	12.7
造纸及纸制品业	Papermaking and Paper Products	42.0	6.8	14.8
印刷业和记录媒介的复制	Printing and Copying of Medium for Record	33.4	3.1	4.7
文教体育用品制造业	Cultural, Educational and Sports Goods			
石油加工、炼焦及核燃料加工业	Oil Processing, Coking and Nuclear Fuel Processing	15.1	11.9	7.7
＃炼　焦	Coking			
化学原料及化学制品制造业	Raw Chemical Material and Chemical Products	31.7	13.4	15.9
＃基础化学原料制造	Basic Chemical Material	29.8	18.4	19.2
肥料制造	Fertilizer Making	38.6	8.3	16.8
医药制造业	Medical and Pharmaceutical Products	39.4	10.1	29.4
化学纤维制造业	Chemical Fiber	8.3	-2.3	-4.9
橡胶制品业	Rubber Products	15.2	4.0	5.0
塑料制品业	Plastic Products	27.6	4.1	12.4
非金属矿物制品业	Nonmetal Mineral Products	30.3	1.6	3.9
＃水泥制造	Cement Manufacturing	34.9	-1.0	-2.9
黑色金属冶炼及压延加工业	Smelting and Pressing of Ferrous Metals	26.5	37.4	21.9
有色金属冶炼及压延加工业	Smelting and Pressing of Nonferrous Metals	19.9	16.6	14.1
金属制品业	Metal Products	16.2	5.8	6.0
通用设备制造业	Ordinary Equipment Production	24.0	7.7	8.8
专用设备制造业	Special Purposes Equipment	19.7	-0.6	-1.8
交通运输设备制造业	Transport Equipment	14.3	-1.9	-1.7
电气机械及器材制造业	Electric Equipment and Machinery	19.8	10.7	14.8
通信设备、计算机及其他电子设备制造业	Telecom Equipment, Computer and Other Electronic Equipment			
仪器仪表及文化、办公用机械制造业	Equipment, Meter and Cultural and Office Machinery			
工艺品及其他制造业	Art and Handicraft as well as Other Manufacturing Sector			
废弃资源和废旧材料回收加工业	Recycling and Processing of Deserted Resources and Waste Material			
电力、热力的生产和供应业	Electric and Thermal Production and Supply	38.9	0.9	2.6
＃电力生产和电力供应	Electric Power Production and Supply	39.3	0.7	2.1
燃气生产和供应业	Gas Production and Supply	22.2	-0.2	-0.5
水的生产和供应业	Water Production and Supply	46.9	-2.2	-14.0

Main Indicators on Economic Benefit of State-Owened and Holding Enterprises with Independent Accounting System by Branch of Industry

(%)

总资产贡献率 Ratio of Total Assets to Industrial Output Value	资本保值增值率 Ratio of Capital Hold and Rise	资产负债率 Assets Liability Ratio	流动资产周转次数(次/年) Number of Times of Annual Turnover Circulating Funds (times/year)	成本费用利润率 Ratio of Profits to Industrial Cost	全员劳动生产率(元/人·年) Overall Labor Productivity (yuan/person-year)	工业经济效益综合指数 Comprehensive Index of Industry Economic Results
4.3	101.0	48.7	1.0	3.4	32724.9	88.6
33.7	135.9	43.5	3.6	65.9	480722.7	682.1
37.5	115.7	41.6	5.7	104.8	1068063.1	1209.5
16.5	124.4	55.9	1.4	14.3	87738.7	193.0
26.7	84.8	71.5	1.4	25.1	66705.4	232.2
7.6	115.8	59.2	0.6	4.7	28021.1	92.7
19.0	33.7	76.2	2.3	8.9	25683.5	130.6
5.6	82.9	70.2	1.5	4.0	38697.5	97.1
2.1	70.1	60.6	2.4	1.3	66977.2	106.8
10.1	92.6	53.3	2.5	15.4	81157.1	189.3
7.1	142.6	73.1	1.1	7.0	35683.7	111.2
8.5	137.9	71.0	1.0	9.6	89873.4	153.3
8.5	129.4	72.7	0.8	12.7	187163.2	220.3
6.7	67.1	55.8	0.7	9.1	77199.2	134.7
6.7	66.7	56.1	0.6	9.3	78892.8	136.5
50.2	135.4	59.2	1.3	15.3	887898.4	746.2
-3.4	48.6	81.0	0.7	-16.3	15509.6	-27.7
-3.2	47.8	79.8	1.1	-13.5	12351.6	-14.2
-2.4	0.5	100.0	0.2	-26.0	4385.5	-84.4
3.1	59.2	72.1	1.5	-0.1	21845.5	63.5
-0.9	120.0	60.6	0.9	-68.0	-896.6	-208.3
-60.9	297.4	60.6	0.9	-68.0	-896.6	-296.7
4.0		111.0	1.0	-7.1	-3751.8	0.2
4.3	40.3	25.1	1.2	4.4	21736.0	79.7
6.2	97.0	54.1	0.8	6.8	58961.7	117.5
3.2	80.9	49.8	2.0	-0.6	28832.1	77.0
11.7	103.3	36.4	4.7	0.7	392855.4	348.0
12.0	121.9	50.2	2.1	9.5	98935.0	179.6
15.2	79.5	69.3	2.3	10.9	94300.3	183.1
8.5	234.7	24.8	1.3	13.3	67775.7	176.7
8.0	65.9	52.1	0.6	23.7	51786.8	175.3
0.2	29.8	67.4	1.0	-7.6	19020.2	18.1
4.4	80.4	64.7	1.1	0.5	39888.4	79.2
6.0	118.7	54.5	1.3	3.6	67362.4	118.9
3.1	96.9	59.1	0.9	-3.1	41926.9	66.1
1.4	87.6	60.9	0.8	-11.6	37991.5	26.1
32.2	115.2	41.3	3.9	17.6	216057.7	336.7
8.5	55.5	60.2	2.0	10.6	92314.0	164.5
7.5	130.8	53.4	1.5	1.1	29596.9	94.3
6.1	120.0	53.5	1.1	0.6	35314.0	87.3
	92.5	81.4	0.6	-6.7	24925.3	27.0
-0.6	79.4	78.5	1.4	-4.6	27630.6	42.6
10.2	102.0	58.5	1.0	10.4	77445.2	154.1
3.6	88.2	76.5	1.8	-6.3	99508.3	93.2
3.6	83.6	78.1	1.9	-7.0	103109.7	93.0
0.5	128.3	51.0	0.7	-5.5	60206.3	67.0
-1.2	91.3	46.5	0.8	-16.4	32204.7	0.9

12-17 各地、州、市、县(市)国有及国有控股工业企业主要经济效益指标

单位: %　　(2004 年)

地 区	Region	工业增加值率 Ratio of Value Added to Gross Industrial Output Value	资金利税率 Ratio of profits and Taxes to Capital	产值利税率 Ratio of profits And Taxes to Industrial Output Value
总 计	**Total**	**40.1**	**18.6**	**25.4**
乌鲁木齐市	**Urumqi City**	**27.2**	**10.6**	**12.8**
乌鲁木齐县	Urumqi County	41.4	-7.1	-16.9
克拉玛依市	**Karamay City**	**42.6**	**26.1**	**30.2**
石河子市	**Shihezi City**	**29.0**	**4.1**	**10.8**
阿拉尔市	**Alar City**	**3.2**	**8.0**	**35.7**
图木舒克市	**Tumxuk City**	**23.2**	**-2.0**	**-7.5**
五家渠市	**Wujiaqu City**	**15.4**	**-2.2**	**-3.5**
吐鲁番地区	**Turpan Administrative Offices**	**66.4**	**48.4**	**56.5**
吐鲁番市	Turpan City	37.9	-9.3	-46.3
鄯善县	Shanshan [Piqan] County	67.4	56.6	59.6
托克逊县	Toksun County	24.3	12.3	20.5
哈密地区	**Hami [Kumul] Administrative Offices**	**36.9**	**4.6**	**9.7**
哈密市	Hami [Kumul] City	36.7	3.8	8.4
巴里坤哈萨克自治县	Barkol Kazak Autonomous County	32.0	7.6	10.3
伊吾县	Yiwu [Araturuk] County	44.2	74.0	39.7
昌吉回族自治州	**Changji Hui Autonomous Prefecture**	**36.0**	**4.9**	**7.1**
昌吉市	Changji City	44.6	-8.3	-16.2
阜康市	Fukang City	30.4	26.3	22.0
米泉市	Miquan City	28.9	12.5	11.1
呼图壁县	Hutubi County	7.9	-7.8	-14.0
玛纳斯县	Manas County	42.2	6.7	13.4
奇台县	Qitai County	37.9	-10.4	-15.6
吉木萨尔县	Jimsar County			
木垒哈萨克自治县	Mori Kazak Autonomous County	41.3	-8.3	-31.1
伊犁哈萨克自治州	**Ili Kazak Autonomous Prefecture**	**39.9**	**6.4**	**14.1**
伊犁州直属县(市)	**Counties (Cities) Direct Under Ili Prefecture**	**45.4**	**8.9**	**20.1**
伊宁市	Yining [Gulja] City	40.2	-3.7	-16.1
奎屯市	Kuytun City	51.0	18.0	32.8
伊宁县	Yining [Gulja] County	39.1	6.2	12.4
察布查尔锡伯自治县	Qapqal Xibe Autonomous County	21.8	1.6	3.0
霍城县	Huocheng [Korgas] County	18.8	0.6	1.4
巩留县	Gongliu [Tokkuztara] County	72.9	1.0	3.6
新源县	Xinyuan [Kunes] County	54.9	26.0	39.5
昭苏县	Zhaosu [Mongolkure] County	57.8	9.0	14.2
特克斯县	Tekes County	59.4	1.1	9.2
尼勒克县	Nilka County	34.2	2.8	4.0

Main Indicators on Economic Benefit of State-Owened and Holding Enterprises with Independent Accounting System by Prefecture, Autonomous Prefecture, City and County

(%)

总资产贡献率 Ratio of Total Assets to Industrial Output Value	资本保值增值率 Ratio of Capital Hold And Rise	资产负债率 Assets Liability Ratio	流动资产周转次数(次/年) Number of Times of Annual Turnover Circulating Funds (times/year)	成本费用利润率 Ratio of Profits to Industrial Cost	全员劳动生产率(元/人·年) Overall Labor Productivity (yuan/person-year)	工业经济效益综合指数 Comprehensive Index of Industry and Economic Results
18.2	**115.0**	**51.6**	**2.6**	**20.7**	**194361.2**	**295.8**
10.6	**112.0**	**53.5**	**2.6**	**7.1**	**152745.6**	**205.4**
-7.8	62.6	84.6	0.7	-21.2	21958.5	-49.8
27.9	**128.5**	**39.1**	**3.6**	**27.2**	**342094.6**	**440.7**
4.8	**88.2**	**64.7**	**1.1**	**3.0**	**49983.1**	**96.8**
4.5	**38.5**	**9.3**	**4.0**	**62.9**	**4029.4**	**318.0**
-1.2	**187.0**	**59.5**	**0.7**	**-16.9**	**38683.2**	**16.5**
0.4	**120.0**	**83.6**	**0.9**	**-9.7**	**13440.1**	**14.7**
46.1	**117.5**	**46.1**	**5.9**	**81.3**	**740681.8**	**941.0**
-6.8	170.8	50.5	1.5	-18.0	42935.5	8.6
54.3	112.6	45.1	8.0	102.5	1067480.6	1254.2
18.0		102.8	0.9	-0.9	27405.8	68.6
6.0	**112.4**	**64.3**	**1.2**	**1.1**	**46576.7**	**94.8**
5.4	112.2	64.5	1.2	-0.1	45005.6	87.8
6.6	53.5	77.0	0.8	4.2	33234.8	81.9
75.4	221.9	26.3	2.9	40.4	322691.2	572.1
5.0	**32.1**	**81.2**	**2.0**	**-0.5**	**97187.2**	**108.9**
-5.3	33.4	94.0	1.7	-19.2	82092.0	3.9
14.7	72.8	61.4	2.1	18.1	71585.8	194.8
12.1	132.4	50.2	2.1	5.2	232245.2	245.7
-6.2	90.3	74.3	0.7	-13.9	6037.0	-20.0
4.5	4.9	94.9	2.1	2.4	114397.6	122.6
-11.5		101.5	7.1	-13.7	84471.5	61.0
-4.9		104.2	4.8	-26.6	30326.4	-18.0
7.4	**104.0**	**67.3**	**1.2**	**-1.7**	**65996.8**	**96.6**
9.5	**101.3**	**62.7**	**1.2**	**0.1**	**96392.4**	**125.8**
-1.1	74.1	80.4	1.1	-22.5	53528.8	-14.8
18.9	122.0	63.4	1.3	0.6	212423.2	219.7
7.8	106.4	63.3	1.3	7.2	53280.0	125.4
2.1	219.7	28.8	2.7	-0.4	36194.8	102.2
1.9	96.5	71.9	0.8	-3.2	20991.9	45.3
0.8	100.2	77.9	0.2	1.0	46607.1	68.7
15.4	96.7	25.3	0.9	42.3	162923.2	334.2
7.9	104.7	34.5	1.5	0.6	46134.8	99.4
0.3	120.0	83.3	0.3	1.7	15172.4	53.9
3.4	98.1	59.6	0.9	1.2	45748.8	82.1

12-17 续表 1

单位: %

地 区	Region	工业增加值率 Ratio of Value Added to Gross Industrial Output Value	资金利税率 Ratio of profits and Taxes to Capital	产值利税率 Ratio of profits and Taxes to Industrial Output Value
塔城地区	**Tacheng [Tarbagatai] Administrative Offices**	**30.3**	**-1.2**	**-2.5**
塔城市	Tacheng [Qoqek] City	32.3	-12.6	-47.0
乌苏市	Usu City	26.1	-4.5	-6.2
额敏县	Emin [Dorbiljin] County	27.5	8.0	11.3
沙湾县	Shawan County	-1.9	0.1	0.3
托里县	Toli County	47.4	6.1	10.4
裕民县	Yumin [Qagantokay] County	38.7	28.3	134.4
和布克赛尔蒙古自治县	Hoboksar Mongol Autonomous County	52.7	2.0	5.4
阿勒泰地区	**Altay Administrative Offices**	**33.5**	**6.6**	**13.5**
阿勒泰市	Altay City	19.9	-3.1	-9.8
布尔津县	Burqin County	49.3	4.3	15.3
富蕴县	Fuyun [Koktokay] County	40.9	29.0	29.2
福海县	Fuhai [Burultokay] County	43.3	1.6	11.4
哈巴河县	Habahe [Kaba] County	61.9	62.9	49.1
青河县	Qinghe [Qinggil] County	48.6	-11.3	-37.0
吉木乃县	Jeminay County			
博尔塔拉蒙古自治州	**Bortala Mongol Autonomous Prefecture**	**15.3**	**0.2**	**0.4**
博乐市	Bole [Bortala] City	14.3	-0.5	-1.2
精河县	Jinghe [Jing] County	20.2	8.8	8.6
温泉县	Wenquan [Araxang] County			
巴音郭楞蒙古自治州	**Bayangol Mongol Autonomous Prefecture**	**59.8**	**27.7**	**43.1**
库尔勒市	Korla City	60.9	28.7	44.1
轮台县	Luntai [Bugur] County	33.0	34.0	27.6
尉犁县	Yuli [Lopnur] County	34.2	7.8	24.3
若羌县	Ruoqiang [Qarkilik] County	33.4	2.9	9.5
且末县	Qiemo [Qarqan] County	36.5	-3.0	-11.2
焉耆回族自治县	Yanji Hui Autonomous County	9.8	-5.0	-15.3
和静县	Hejing County	23.5	12.2	14.1
和硕县	Hoxud County	33.2	1.7	2.7
博湖县	Bohu [Bagrax] County	1.1	-0.5	-1.2
阿克苏地区	**Aksu Administrative Offices**	**32.1**	**8.3**	**15.9**
阿克苏市	Aksu City	40.2	7.4	20.6
温宿县	Wensu [Onsu] County	52.1	4.8	7.2
库车县	Kuqa County	22.6	10.6	13.3

Continued

(%)

总资产贡献率 Ratio of Total Assets to Industrial Output Value	资本保值增值率 Ratio of Capital Hold and Rise	资产负债率 Assets Liability Ratio	流动资产周转次数(次/年) Number of Times of Annual Turnover Circulating Funds (times/year)	成本费用利润率 Ratio of Profits to Industrial Cost	全员劳动生产率(元/人·年) Overall Labor Productivity (yuan/person-year)	工业经济效益综合指数 Comprehensive Index of Industry Economic Results
0.1	**89.8**	**76.9**	**1.3**	**-10.1**	**28987.0**	**24.6**
-20.4	348.4	88.1	0.9	-41.7	36592.5	-101.1
-1.5	4.8	94.1	1.4	-13.2	38772.9	-1.5
9.1	318.1	74.8	1.7	5.2	62279.9	154.5
1.8	49.7	76.2	1.6	-3.9	-2003.2	32.2
5.9	44.1	70.5	1.2	2.0	22445.6	71.7
39.2	220.4	44.1	0.4	60.8	10142.9	367.7
3.4	157.5	62.8	0.9	-7.3	28278.7	51.6
7.8	**146.0**	**72.0**	**1.5**	**5.1**	**61798.9**	**127.3**
0.3	127.1	85.6	1.4	-13.9	32459.5	15.8
3.9	139.1	24.3	2.3	12.0	63858.6	158.6
26.1	78.9	71.2	1.7	27.4	86641.9	253.3
2.6	5333.2	6.3	0.8	-2.3	116829.6	811.8
43.3	12.8	96.4	1.5	51.4	80868.7	354.9
-8.7	83.3	75.1	0.9	-35.2	11125.0	-101.4
1.7	**120.2**	**74.4**	**1.3**	**-3.7**	**17600.6**	**49.7**
1.0	104.4	76.6	1.2	-4.5	16216.1	41.0
14.8	714.0	47.6	2.4	1.4	25175.2	191.8
25.1	**118.2**	**50.6**	**2.4**	**56.2**	**328059.9**	**521.9**
26.2	114.2	50.8	2.5	58.6	379530.7	565.6
33.0	114.8	52.4	3.9	29.8	110290.0	320.3
7.0	117.8	47.0	0.7	19.7	19181.8	147.0
4.1	815.2	19.2	0.4	6.7	34778.3	188.6
0.2		105.3	1.1	-14.6	24221.6	-19.4
-1.1	34.5	83.7	0.5	-19.1	6275.4	-48.7
5.4	33.8	92.0	1.1	8.0	34161.6	89.3
1.7	139.3	73.1	0.9	-0.6	14693.7	57.3
2.7		110.3	1.0	-6.8	1835.6	2.2
8.4	**118.8**	**63.2**	**1.8**	**11.1**	**78050.8**	**162.9**
8.9	145.8	51.3	1.2	12.5	52721.3	151.9
2.4	13.4	88.2	2.8	0.8	30149.3	71.8
11.2	1034.7	78.8	2.9	12.4	239481.3	398.1

12-17 续表 2

单位: %

地　区	Region	工业增加值率 Ratio of Value Added to Gross Industrial Output Value	资金利税率 Ratio of profits and Taxes to Capital	产值利税率 Ratio of profits and Taxes to Industrial Output Value
沙雅县	Xayar County	19.4	0.9	7.2
新和县	Xinhe [Toksu] County	4.0	-7.1	-64.7
拜城县	Baicheng [Bay] County	56.5	6.4	11.9
乌什县	Wushi [Uxturpan] County			
阿瓦提县	Awat County			
柯坪县	Kalpin County	67.2	-0.4	-0.8
克孜勒苏柯尔克孜自治州	**Kizilsu Kirgiz Autonomous Prefecture**	**30.0**	**-6.0**	**-21.4**
阿图什市	Artux City	34.5	-0.8	-3.1
阿克陶县	Akto County	28.7	-14.0	-96.5
阿合奇县	Akqi County	31.0	0.7	1.1
乌恰县	Wuqia [Ulugqat] County	28.4	-2.6	-6.1
喀什地区	**Kashgar [Kaxgar] Administrative Offices**	**30.2**	**6.8**	**27.1**
喀什市	Kashgar [Kaxgar] City	30.0	7.6	29.3
疏附县	Shufu County	35.9	-0.4	-2.1
疏勒县	Shule County			
英吉沙县	Yengisar County	23.3	-4.3	-37.6
泽普县	Zepu [Poskam] County	67.3	1.6	10.6
莎车县	Shache [Yarkant] County	37.1	0.5	2.2
叶城县	Yecheng [Kagilik] County	18.0	0.8	3.4
麦盖提县	Makit County	28.8	-9.0	-43.0
岳普湖县	Yopurga County	43.5	-9.5	-48.9
伽师县	Jiashi [Payzawat] County	34.6	0.0	-0.8
巴楚县	Bachu [Maralbexi] County	43.5	-1.4	-6.6
塔什库尔干塔吉克自治县	Taxkorgan Tajik Autonomous County	35.3	-0.3	-6.0
和田地区	**Hotan Administrative Offices**	**31.6**	**-3.7**	**-27.2**
和田市	Hotan City	27.9	-4.7	-37.1
和田县	Hotan County	41.5	0.8	5.5
墨玉县	Moyu [Karakax] County	31.8	-2.0	-8.4
皮山县	Pishan [Guma] County	23.4	-3.2	-6.7
洛浦县	Lop County	29.7	1.1	4.7
策勒县	Qira County	34.7	-0.1	-0.1
于田县	Yutian [Keriya] County	31.1	-7.9	-28.9
民丰县	Minfeng [Niya] County	23.1	-568.2	-1497.7

Continued

(%)

总资产贡献率 Ratio of Total Assets to Industrial Output Value	资本保值增值率 Ratio of Capital Hold and Rise	资产负债率 Assets Liability Ratio	流动资产周转次数(次/年) Number of Times of Annual Turnover Circulating Funds (times/year)	成本费用利润率 Ratio of Profits to Industrial Cost	全员劳动生产率(元/人·年) Overall Labor Productivity (yuan/person-year)	工业经济效益综合指数 Comprehensive Index of Industry Economic Results
0.2	8.2	46.9	0.7	-4.9	21857.1	28.7
-4.9	106.7	23.3	0.3	-48.0	2111.1	-146.3
3.5	21.0	70.2	5.0	-1.8	144563.2	161.6
-0.4	202.4	29.4	1.4	-3.0	10714.3	60.8
-4.1	**24.7**	**95.1**	**0.8**	**-22.6**	**11554.9**	**-59.1**
0.4	130.0	70.4	0.6	-13.1	19574.6	8.5
-11.1		105.0	0.7	-51.4	12460.9	-186.4
0.5	62.2	35.8	1.4	-8.1	15434.8	26.2
-1.7		104.7	1.1	-11.5	9256.7	-16.7
7.6	**31.2**	**92.3**	**0.9**	**15.1**	**36987.3**	**121.2**
9.3	26.1	95.0	0.9	16.6	41396.0	131.6
1.4	120.2	62.7	0.8	-9.3	13988.9	24.7
-1.7	20.5	80.3	0.7	-27.0	7766.1	-71.4
0.6	7.8	63.8	0.5	2.9	38343.8	66.0
1.3	126.6	43.8	1.3	-5.2	13403.9	46.1
0.4	43.3	53.1	0.8	-3.3	5241.0	30.4
-3.5	43.6	63.4	0.5	-31.0	22416.7	-76.1
-7.1	85.0	43.8	0.7	-38.5	14761.9	-106.2
0.4	208.0	70.7	1.8	-7.6	17354.8	50.0
0.2	89.3	78.8	0.2	-15.0	27333.3	-10.4
-0.3	11.7	97.6	0.1	-12.5	7041.7	-26.8
-1.3	**70.8**	**76.8**	**0.5**	**-25.2**	**24122.2**	**-49.4**
-2.0	14.9	97.0	0.4	-28.3	21157.0	-78.6
1.4	108.7	28.1	0.6	-2.8	42956.4	64.1
-0.4	744.2	17.2	1.8	-11.2	10250.0	106.0
-0.1	28.2	56.9	3.4	-9.0	16321.4	38.7
0.4	509.4	32.0	1.6	-4.2	12118.6	101.4
0.0	30.3	25.9	2.1	-5.1	14850.0	39.9
-1.4	176.5	77.2	1.5	-30.2	8268.1	-52.2
-31.2	2602.4	65.0	3.9	-1132.9	4457.1	-3921.0

12-18 分行业大中型工业企业主要经济指标

单位: 万元 (2004 年)

行业	Sector	企业单位数(个) Number of Enterp-rises (unit)	#亏损企业 Loss	工业总产值(当年价格) Gross Industrial Output Value (At Current Prices)
煤炭开采和洗选业	Coal Extracting and Dressing	10	1	160282.2
石油和天然气开采业	Petroleum and Natural Gas Extraction	6	1	5079747.1
#天然原油和天然气开采	Crude Oil and Natural Gas Extraction	4		4399642.0
黑色金属矿采选业	Ferrous Metals Mining and Dressing	3	1	61622.0
有色金属矿采选业	Nonferrous Metals Mining and Dressing	4		42938.1
非金属矿采选业	Nonmetal Minerals Mining and Dressing	1		7266.1
#采 盐	Salt Extraction			
其他采矿业	Other Ore Extraction			
农副食品加工业	Farm and Non-staple Processing	17	5	174434.4
#谷物磨制	Grain Grinding	1	1	9795.4
饲料加工	Fodder Processing	1		22389.2
制 糖	Sugar Making	11	3	95812.6
食品制造业	Food Manufacturing	6	1	132272.8
#罐头制造	Beverage Production	2	1	99227.5
饮料制造业	Beverage Production	6	2	112088.2
#酒的制造	Wine Manufacturing	6	2	112088.2
烟草制品业	Tobacco Products	1		71289.8
纺织业	Textile Industry	33	18	490030.7
#棉、化纤纺织及印染精加工	Cotton, Chemical Fiber, Dyeing, Printing and Dressing	27	16	413826.5
毛纺织和染整精加工	Wool Textile, Dyeing and Printing	2	1	8589.2
纺织服装、鞋、帽制造业	Textile Garment, Shoe and Hat			
皮革、毛皮、羽毛(绒)及其制品业	Leather, Fur, Feather (down) its Products	1		19759.9
#皮革鞣制加工	Leather Tanning and Processing	1		19759.9
皮革制品制造	Leather Products Manufacturing			
木材加工及木、竹、藤、棕、草制品业	Timber Processing, Wood, Bamboo, Cane, Grass Products			
家具制造业	Furniture Manufacturing	3		66516.1
造纸及纸制品业	Papermaking and Paper Products	4		61084.7
印刷业和记录媒介的复制	Printing and Copying of Medium for Record	1		3823.4
文教体育用品制造业	Cultural, Educational and Sports Goods			
石油加工、炼焦及核燃料加工业	Oil Processing, Coking and Nuclear Fuel Processing	9	2	3203246.7
#炼 焦	Coking	2		17347.6
化学原料及化学制品制造业	Raw Chemical Material and Chemical Products	13	1	362525.6
#基础化学原料制造	Basic Chemical Material	6	1	154245.2
肥料制造	Fertilizer Making	2		42557.7
医药制造业	Medical and Pharmaceutical Products	1		7525.7
化学纤维制造业	Chemical Fiber	1		33848.5
橡胶制品业	Rubber Products	1		43825.0
塑料制品业	Plastic Products	3	2	133470.6
非金属矿物制品业	Nonmetal Mineral Products	21	7	287048.1
#水泥制造	Cement Manufacturing	16	6	191110.4
黑色金属冶炼及压延加工业	Smelting and Pressing of Ferrous Metals	8	2	1048928.3
有色金属冶炼及压延加工业	Smelting and Pressing of Nonferrous Metals	3		87491.9
金属制品业	Metal Products	3		30132.4
通用设备制造业	Ordinary Equipment Production	4		25824.3
专用设备制造业	Special Purposes Equipment	3	1	18821.9
交通运输设备制造业	Transport Equipment	4	2	57937.1
电气机械及器材制造业	Electric Equipment and Machinery	2		138888.4
通信设备、计算机及其他电子设备制造业	Telecom Equipment, Computer and Other Electronic Equipment	1		61898.4
仪器仪表及文化、办公用机械制造业	Equipment, Meter and Cultural and Office Machinery			
工艺品及其他制造业	Art and Handicraft as well as Other Manufacturing Sector			
废弃资源和废旧材料回收加工业	Recycling and Processing of Deserted Resources and Waste Material			
电力、热力的生产和供应业	Electric and Thermal Production and Supply	28	17	782598.9
#电力生产和电力供应	Electric Power Production and Supply	26	16	764758.1
燃气生产和供应业	Gas Production and Supply	1	1	26601.9
水的生产和供应业	Water Production and Supply	1	1	8255.3

Main Indicators of Large-scale and Medium-scale Industrial Enterprises by Industrial Sectors

(10 000 yuan)

工业增加值 Added Value of Industry	工业销售产值(当年价) Sales Value of Industry Products (At Current Prices)	出口交货值 Delivery Value of Industry Export	实收资本 Total Capital Hold	资产合计 Total Assets	流动资产合计 Circulating Funds	#产成品 Finished Product	流动资产年平均余额 Annual Average Balance of Circulating Funds	固定资产原价 Original Value of Fixed Assets
99720.9	158044.5	8.3	212199.8	498104.6	168791.1	12678.6	165927.1	332823.0
3798935.8	5053378.1		3149676.6	8775211.3	1679437.0	108495.3	1447591.9	11124048.8
3470249.8	4384154.0		2441109.4	7217810.8	922419.4	99084.9	745754.2	10033690.3
13066.2	61439.6		27088.2	108121.8	61847.2	833.0	53082.9	46981.3
23353.3	42326.0		11176.5	47992.9	26670.4	3011.4	29535.2	31496.1
2268.3	4009.8	109.0	2999.9	12129.1	8044.6	2375.1	8572.7	7286.5
41554.2	161625.7	12989.1	60498.1	249806.2	138271.7	60416.1	123556.6	160151.1
859.0	9659.9		4493.8	8508.4	3384.1	4.0	2945.7	15629.0
3762.4	22645.7		4800.0	24091.2	10072.7	645.1	10714.6	7759.2
27274.4	85372.1	458.5	28721.0	154639.6	83553.2	52899.8	68232.8	109988.4
34901.4	101091.3	51977.4	59300.0	302328.6	122323.7	39712.6	107906.3	154691.1
25920.7	68408.7	44289.9	33800.0	227007.3	97419.6	37390.6	81722.6	135082.5
56431.1	102837.5	166.2	96682.5	352032.4	153808.1	6877.4	149071.0	160326.1
56431.1	102837.5	166.2	96682.5	352032.4	153808.1	6877.4	149071.0	160326.1
50593.6	71245.1		18142.1	85193.3	54953.9	14.1	54071.4	40914.0
110406.6	452166.4	32363.1	302030.8	827881.5	388056.2	102394.8	412570.1	585941.8
87637.8	385402.6	15609.1	234822.2	639629.6	271456.4	74171.8	290073.9	493411.8
2457.8	9327.2	217.5	13863.0	55169.9	43274.5	12888.1	43572.7	21985.8
4655.4	18007.3		3000.0	20701.9	10564.8	1188.9	13039.9	10100.2
4655.4	18007.3		3000.0	20701.9	10564.8	1188.9	13039.9	10100.2
15767.9	65783.7	59537.3	30750.9	109386.5	45368.2	3369.2	49222.4	29644.2
28733.7	56953.0		25372.8	137596.4	72048.2	13811.3	69076.3	81698.3
2211.2	4009.9		3094.7	9180.6	2082.4	207.1	2500.8	10755.3
581355.1	3194141.1	7673.7	499130.2	2226670.6	711181.4	193366.3	649414.4	2664785.2
6719.8	17741.0		17125.0	40455.4	7909.7	230.5	7997.7	28326.9
131776.8	345367.8	4574.5	189119.2	525686.0	187419.3	31421.2	168745.2	345264.2
53585.3	153629.8	4554.8	55762.9	208113.9	79943.9	9029.7	69070.4	134743.3
18682.5	42310.8		86221.2	124397.5	47573.0	598.7	33005.8	81909.0
3669.8	7282.1	725.5	4093.4	24036.9	8316.4	867.0	11451.8	12567.9
10607.2	29171.9		10000.0	35140.5	14019.1	3251.8	10610.0	14070.9
10053.2	42352.0	632.0	13330.0	76898.5	37420.2	8372.9	40581.4	32409.8
41810.8	126719.4	21593.6	181027.5	549262.1	257371.1	49106.0	246353.0	310407.6
99434.4	288648.1		251415.5	1005891.4	351143.4	13030.2	341257.2	513454.6
71226.8	188278.2		140031.4	658925.8	219333.7	8637.0	220301.8	439452.3
329198.9	1047051.2	4200.4	303633.5	859548.3	316082.6	27094.7	290409.6	542619.3
24341.5	87618.1		38369.0	119633.8	34714.2	2796.9	31372.6	109685.2
8221.7	24518.9		16580.0	33109.6	18107.9	4614.4	14608.9	13454.8
8401.8	24812.6	484.7	10450.5	51188.6	34239.2	5794.3	33771.1	19684.5
2738.8	18503.0	239.5	8849.7	79779.5	44910.9	7175.7	43420.6	41375.4
6191.3	56497.4		18000.0	76425.5	51295.5	10211.7	55933.9	21357.3
27708.0	134219.6	1291.5	34861.5	345002.0	162468.4	17123.5	142387.0	73336.1
16134.0	59274.5	5149.4	10339.0	141596.2	41128.4	6144.1	39218.8	113230.7
345606.0	782598.9		293410.0	2400663.9	399922.5	2157.9	431388.5	2685212.1
340116.1	764758.1		268704.0	2324441.1	376009.2	2157.9	408634.8	2613190.2
7386.3	26601.9		41111.9	94966.4	37839.6	767.7	31097.0	38033.5
5312.5	8255.3		8944.9	73043.8	13003.5		14184.2	74780.2

12-18 续表

单位: 万元

行　　业	Sector	固定资产净值年平均余额 Annual Average Balance of Net Value of Fixed Assets	流动负债合计 Liquid Liabilities	长期负债合计 Long-term Liabilities	所有者权益合计 Creditors' Equity
煤炭开采和洗选业	Coal Extracting and Dressing	194685.9	184429.7	53775.0	258790.4
石油和天然气开采业	Petroleum and Natural Gas Extraction	6152251.5	2156118.9	1662074.0	4957018.4
＃天然原油和天然气开采	Crude Oil and Natural Gas Extraction	5462446.9	1357337.3	1648239.1	4212234.4
黑色金属矿采选业	Ferrous Metals Mining and Dressing	29775.5	50234.5	11075.3	46812.0
有色金属矿采选业	Nonferrous Metals Mining and Dressing	18148.6	26256.0	7019.5	14716.6
非金属矿采选业	Nonmetal Minerals Mining and Dressing	4172.8	7444.4		4684.7
＃采　盐	Salt Extraction				
其他采矿业	Other Ore Extraction				
农副食品加工业	Farm and Non-staple Processing	85802.2	153344.9	25171.2	70986.5
＃谷物磨制	Grain Grinding	6236.0	3872.6	2400.0	2235.8
饲料加工	Fodder Processing	4530.8	7630.3	5060.0	11400.9
制　糖	Sugar Making	58112.9	109608.4	11547.7	33179.9
食品制造业	Food Manufacturing	122884.7	175330.4	31511.7	92977.1
＃罐头制造	Beverage Production	107777.5	144233.8	26766.7	53725.6
饮料制造业	Beverage Production	106302.8	139330.0	60364.5	152337.9
＃酒的制造	Wine Manufacturing	106302.8	139330.0	60364.5	152337.9
烟草制品业	Tobacco Products	23261.4	31858.6	17900.0	35434.6
纺织业	Textile Industry	335040.4	444755.1	131138.3	251886.2
＃棉、化纤纺织及印染精加工	Cotton, Chemical Fiber, Dyeing, Printing and Dressing	291853.1	330686.4	127435.7	181405.6
毛纺织和染整精加工	Wool Textile, Dyeing and Printing	6873.9	46930.8	2.6	8236.5
纺织服装、鞋、帽制造业	Textile Garment, Shoe and Hat				
皮革、毛皮、羽毛(绒)及其制品业	Leather, Fur, Feather (down) its Products	8274.7	11328.7		9373.2
＃皮革鞣制加工	Leather Tanning and Processing	8274.7	11328.7		9373.2
皮革制品制造	Leather Products Manufacturing				
木材加工及木、竹、藤、棕、草制品业	Timber Processing, Wood, Bamboo, Cane, Grass Products				
家具制造业	Furniture Manufacturing	24066.4	11413.7	443.7	97529.1
造纸及纸制品业	Papermaking and Paper Products	45162.0	66631.8	8533.6	62430.9
印刷业和记录媒介的复制	Printing and Copying of Medium for Record	6695.0	4492.4	888.4	3799.8
文教体育用品制造业	Cultural, Educational and Sports Goods				
石油加工、炼焦及核燃料加工业	Oil Processing, Coking and Nuclear Fuel Processing	1493185.9	552156.0	218432.5	1390498.0
＃炼　焦	Coking	23835.2	21325.3		19130.1
化学原料及化学制品制造业	Raw Chemical Material and Chemical Products	239123.1	193812.6	60073.3	271800.0
＃基础化学原料制造	Basic Chemical Material	93790.5	91618.0	46580.4	69915.5
肥料制造	Fertilizer Making	53987.9	18633.9	9588.1	96175.4
医药制造业	Medical and Pharmaceutical Products	11929.6	10821.5	2640.0	10575.4
化学纤维制造业	Chemical Fiber	12190.0	19339.1	2031.6	13769.8
橡胶制品业	Rubber Products	16602.1	39677.4	10152.7	17064.4
塑料制品业	Plastic Products	212870.3	232978.5	63149.2	253095.3
非金属矿物制品业	Nonmetal Mineral Products	326940.8	429558.4	117699.7	458633.2
＃水泥制造	Cement Manufacturing	276133.3	325585.4	87460.1	245880.3
黑色金属冶炼及压延加工业	Smelting and Pressing of Ferrous Metals	340564.0	333232.2	46052.3	480263.8
有色金属冶炼及压延加工业	Smelting and Pressing of Nonferrous Metals	71895.3	57915.4	16252.1	45466.3
金属制品业	Metal Products	8468.5	15260.4		17849.2
通用设备制造业	Ordinary Equipment Production	11466.9	32073.7	1781.0	17333.9
专用设备制造业	Special Purposes Equipment	22574.4	61266.5	8581.3	9931.7
交通运输设备制造业	Transport Equipment	10142.7	58793.8	93.6	17538.1
电气机械及器材制造业	Electric Equipment and Machinery	52189.3	163489.9	32102.2	149409.9
通信设备、计算机及其他电子设备制造业	Telecom Equipment, Computer and Other Electronic Equipment	78409.9	58881.4	44341.6	38373.2
仪器仪表及文化、办公用机械制造业	Equipment, Meter and Cultural and Office Machinery				
工艺品及其他制造业	Art and Handicraft as well as Other Manufacturing Sector				
废弃资源和废旧材料回收加工业	Recycling and Processing of Deserted Resources and Waste Material				
电力、热力的生产和供应业	Electric and Thermal Production and Supply	1851752.9	1388286.3	522628.3	489496.0
＃电力生产和电力供应	Electric Power Production and Supply	1804387.2	1356808.6	511167.3	456211.9
燃气生产和供应业	Gas Production and Supply	39805.2	22406.5	21493.6	51066.3
水的生产和供应业	Water Production and Supply	54776.2	31828.9	2000.0	39214.9

Continued

(10 000 yuan)

主营业务收入 Income of Major Business	#主营业务成本 Cost of Major Business	主营业务税金及附加 Major Business, Tax and Addition	营业利润 Business Profit	利润总额 Total Profit	亏损企业亏损总额 Lost Enterprises Total Loss	利税总额 Total Profits and Taxes	本年应交增值税 Value Added Taxes Payable	全部从业人员年平均人数(人) Average Number of Staff and Workers (person)
160270.5	106160.5	1727.4	10805.2	7471.2	1688.2	23163.8	13965.2	27384
5215570.1	2385803.8	95492.8	2014546.0	1921124.1	68372.9	2457485.4	440868.5	79887
4220399.0	1490471.5	85883.4	2040554.1	1986245.7		2444338.9	372209.8	32426
59673.2	43325.1	1212.2	5213.6	5857.4	333.8	10968.1	3898.5	2224
41067.4	26124.0	293.8	7849.9	8637.8		13182.3	4250.7	3646
3721.6	2339.8	139.8	637.9	558.3		899.7	201.6	913
166988.3	115842.2	868.4	6306.6	6369.7	2508.1	12252.3	5014.2	8537
9353.4	9133.3	13.6	-471.0	-269.8	269.8	-249.1	7.1	333
23183.1	33.9		1965.0	2037.7		2142.2	104.5	345
84774.7	64176.1	836.1	3661.0	3672.3	1650.3	8856.9	4348.5	6023
102359.9	67501.5	263.7	11195.9	10398.5	90.6	15386.0	4723.8	3109
69919.0	44551.7	90.3	7685.8	7657.6	90.6	11153.1	3405.2	1148
86278.6	46886.0	8984.1	9264.8	10423.6	5264.1	27196.7	7789.0	4451
86278.6	46886.0	8984.1	9264.8	10423.6	5264.1	27196.7	7789.0	4451
71245.1	28818.9	26703.1	7004.5	6351.7		40047.8	6993.0	480
452499.9	423648.5	1259.8	-21601.3	-31928.9	41280.9	-12607.0	18062.1	50235
381310.2	368316.9	1111.9	-28601.1	-26710.0	30818.9	-9598.1	16000.0	41512
8487.8	7839.0	3.5	-895.7	-858.9	909.5	-614.5	240.9	1922
18000.8	15684.8	43.9	617.4	585.5		1724.9	1095.5	390
18000.8	15684.8	43.9	617.4	585.5		1724.9	1095.5	390
68621.6	53776.6	17.0	6708.6	9193.6		9334.8	124.2	2242
53744.6	41275.1	379.7	2866.8	3546.1		8208.2	4282.4	4574
4049.5	2730.8	33.4	69.4	66.1		433.6	334.1	566
3173255.8	2792036.0	139567.0	120075.8	13713.6	84395.9	247490.5	94209.9	17861
17741.0	11683.9	32.2	1775.6	1809.2		2558.5	717.1	1424
370133.6	279113.2	3001.1	36669.6	32892.3	1065.7	58180.9	22287.5	13469
156688.0	112710.6	1396.5	18324.9	14901.0	1065.7	29237.9	12940.4	5834
43133.7	30079.2	314.4	5405.6	5462.8		7592.4	1815.2	2594
7248.9	4394.5	60.9	659.1	2475.5		3113.4	577.0	723
25643.5	19879.8	55.6	2736.0	2736.0		3968.0	1176.4	877
41190.9	34768.7	488.4	196.1	202.9		2377.8	1686.5	2382
305910.1	273092.6	1291.6	10743.0	11150.3	469.0	18908.2	6466.3	5542
276362.1	212108.6	811.9	-1784.7	24995.5	22340.4	44094.1	18286.7	17802
184100.9	140750.7	610.2	-9165.5	-7752.9	22310.9	8136.6	15279.3	14897
1048255.6	844891.4	3227.4	156060.9	154915.7	4277.9	224030.4	65887.3	16930
86067.8	69355.9	255.5	5170.2	7689.2		12508.5	4563.8	3025
25830.2	22186.9	75.4	868.7	797.5		1772.1	899.2	1505
25096.0	21047.5	132.6	903.4	1178.9		3443.5	2132.0	1983
22888.4	17241.5	149.3	-3534.5	-3753.7	5926.3	-2528.6	1075.8	1651
56314.9	52552.8	148.6	-3365.7	-3055.7	3161.8	-1618.2	1288.9	2126
147196.0	120755.1	600.8	2996.4	11423.2		13695.9	1671.9	1900
56510.6	34972.6	540.5	9295.3	8569.3		14523.8	5414.0	2317
824249.3	783233.5	7109.8	-100401.8	-56981.6	93710.0	27867.7	77739.5	32860
806149.8	769727.6	6993.1	-102516.9	-60070.6	93698.4	23776.6	76854.1	32144
21699.8	14604.7	104.7	-828.0	-999.1	999.1	298.8	1193.2	1038
13520.9	13154.3	29.5	-2586.1	-4083.2	4083.2	-3210.6	843.1	689

12-19 分行业大中型工业企业主要经济效益指标

单位: % (2004 年)

行业	Sector	工业增加值率 Ratio of Value Added to Gross Industrial Output Value	资金利税率 Ratio of profits and Taxes to Capital	产值利税率 Ratio of profits and Taxes to Industrial Output Value
煤炭开采和洗选业	Coal Extracting and Dressing	54.6	6.4	14.5
石油和天然气开采业	Petroleum and Natural Gas Extraction	64.4	32.3	48.4
#天然原油和天然气开采	Crude Oil and Natural Gas Extraction	68.5	39.4	55.6
黑色金属矿采选业	Ferrous Metals Mining and Dressing	18.7	13.2	17.8
有色金属矿采选业	Nonferrous Metals Mining and Dressing	47.3	27.7	30.7
非金属矿采选业	Nonmetal Minerals Mining and Dressing	29.8	7.1	12.4
#采 盐	Salt Extraction			
其他采矿业	Other Ore Extraction			
农副食品加工业	Farm and Non-staple Processing	21.2	5.9	7.0
#谷物磨制	Grain Grinding	7.9	-2.7	-2.5
饲料加工	Fodder Processing	16.8	14.1	9.6
制 糖	Sugar Making	24.8	7.0	9.2
食品制造业	Food Manufacturing	23.9	6.7	11.6
#罐头制造	Beverage Production	23.8	5.9	11.2
饮料制造业	Beverage Production	42.0	10.7	24.3
#酒的制造	Wine Manufacturing	42.0	10.7	24.3
烟草制品业	Tobacco Products	60.5	51.8	56.2
纺织业	Textile Industry	19.6	-1.7	-2.6
#棉、化纤纺织及印染精加工	Cotton, Chemical Fiber, Dyeing, Printing and Dressing	18.4	-1.7	-2.3
毛纺织和染整精加工	Wool Textile, Dyeing and Printing	25.6	-1.2	-7.2
纺织服装、鞋、帽制造业	Textile Garment, Shoe and Hat			
皮革、毛皮、羽毛(绒)及其制品业	Leather, Fur, Feather (down) its Products	20.0	8.1	8.7
#皮革鞣制加工	Leather Tanning and Processing	20.0	8.1	8.7
皮革制品制造	Leather Products Manufacturing			
木材加工及木、竹、藤、棕、草制品业	Timber Processing, Wood, Bamboo, Cane, Grass Products			
家具制造业	Furniture Manufacturing	22.8	12.7	14.0
造纸及纸制品业	Papermaking and Paper Products	41.4	7.2	13.4
印刷业和记录媒介的复制	Printing and Copying of Medium for Record	50.1	4.7	11.3
文教体育用品制造业	Cultural, Educational and Sports Goods			
石油加工、炼焦及核燃料加工业	Oil Processing, Coking and Nuclear Fuel Processing	15.3	11.6	7.7
#炼 焦	Coking	37.0	8.0	14.8
化学原料及化学制品制造业	Raw Chemical Material and Chemical Products	31.5	14.3	16.1
#基础化学原料制造	Basic Chemical Material	29.7	18.0	19.0
肥料制造	Fertilizer Making	40.3	8.7	17.8
医药制造业	Medical and Pharmaceutical Products	41.9	13.3	41.4
化学纤维制造业	Chemical Fiber	27.8	17.4	11.7
橡胶制品业	Rubber Products	16.6	4.2	5.4
塑料制品业	Plastic Products	30.1	4.1	14.2
非金属矿物制品业	Nonmetal Mineral Products	31.3	6.6	15.4
#水泥制造	Cement Manufacturing	32.9	1.6	4.3
黑色金属冶炼及压延加工业	Smelting and Pressing of Ferrous Metals	26.6	35.5	21.4
有色金属冶炼及压延加工业	Smelting and Pressing of Nonferrous Metals	23.7	12.1	14.3
金属制品业	Metal Products	23.3	7.7	5.9
通用设备制造业	Ordinary Equipment Production	26.5	7.6	13.3
专用设备制造业	Special Purposes Equipment	12.6	-3.8	-13.4
交通运输设备制造业	Transport Equipment	8.7	-2.5	-2.8
电气机械及器材制造业	Electric Equipment and Machinery	17.2	7.0	9.9
通信设备、计算机及其他电子设备制造业	Telecom Equipment, Computer and Other Electronic Equipment	22.7	12.4	23.5
仪器仪表及文化、办公用机械制造业	Equipment, Meter and Cultural and Office Machinery			
工艺品及其他制造业	Art and Handicraft as well as Other Manufacturing Sector			
废弃资源和废旧材料回收加工业	Recycling and Processing of Deserted Resources and Waste Material			
电力、热力的生产和供应业	Electric and Thermal Production and Supply	38.7	1.2	3.6
#电力生产和电力供应	Electric Power Production and Supply	38.9	1.1	3.1
燃气生产和供应业	Gas Production and Supply	24.2	0.4	1.1
水的生产和供应业	Water Production and Supply	56.8	-4.7	-38.9

Main Indicators on Economic Benefit of Large-scale and Medium-scale Industrial Enterprises by Industry Sectors

(%)

总资产贡献率 Ratio of Total Assets to Industrial Output Value	资本保值增值率 Ratio of Capital Held and Rise	资产负债率 Assets Liability Ratio	流动资产周转次数(次/年) Number of Times of Annual Turnover Circulating Funds (times/year)	成本费用利润率 Ratio of Profits to Industrial Cost	全员劳动生产率(元/人·年) Overall Labor Productivity (yuan/person-year)	工业经济效益综合指数 Comprehensive Index of Industry Economic Results
5.3	103.1	48.0	1.0	5.1	36415.8	99.9
33.7	135.8	43.5	3.6	65.9	475538.7	678.8
37.5	115.7	41.6	5.7	105.0	1070206.0	1211.6
11.5	113.9	56.7	1.1	11.0	58750.9	150.5
29.5	93.2	69.3	1.4	25.9	64051.8	240.5
5.7	65.1	61.4	0.4	15.2	24844.5	115.0
6.5	138.5	71.6	1.4	4.5	48675.4	111.3
-1.8	100.0	73.7	3.2	-2.7	25795.8	67.9
12.3	121.9	52.7	2.2	84.2	109055.1	469.9
6.3	110.2	78.5	1.2	4.5	45283.8	101.6
8.8	146.4	68.5	1.0	11.3	112259.3	175.8
8.8	103.4	75.3	0.9	12.3	225790.1	238.5
9.0	97.5	56.7	0.6	14.4	126783.0	191.2
9.0	97.5	56.7	0.6	14.4	126783.0	191.2
53.7	138.4	58.4	1.3	16.9	1054033.3	859.9
-0.2	98.6	69.6	1.1	-6.6	21978.0	33.7
-0.2	102.7	71.6	1.3	-6.5	21111.4	35.9
-1.0	100.0	85.1	0.2	-9.3	12787.7	5.1
13.0	110.1	54.7	1.4	3.4	119369.2	162.0
13.0	110.1	54.7	1.4	3.4	119369.2	162.0
9.0	113.1	10.8	1.4	14.8	70329.6	169.4
6.8	83.3	54.6	0.8	7.0	62819.6	120.6
4.9	102.3	58.6	1.6	1.5	39067.1	94.4
11.5	104.8	37.6	4.9	0.5	325488.6	308.2
6.6	191.4	52.7	2.2	14.6	47189.6	169.4
11.2	110.8	48.3	2.2	9.9	97837.1	179.0
15.5	92.3	66.4	2.3	10.8	91850.0	183.7
9.5	262.5	22.7	1.3	14.5	72022.0	189.5
10.9	68.1	56.0	0.6	35.0	50758.0	223.5
16.1	197.7	60.8	2.4	12.0	120948.7	222.3
4.5	77.4	64.8	1.0	0.5	42204.9	79.9
6.1	119.3	53.9	1.2	3.8	75443.5	124.3
6.2	95.2	54.4	0.8	9.0	55855.8	125.7
3.3	80.9	62.7	0.8	-4.0	47812.9	63.7
31.4	120.4	44.1	3.6	17.3	194447.1	319.1
9.6	78.4	62.0	2.7	9.5	80467.8	165.2
7.1	160.2	46.1	1.8	3.2	54629.2	120.1
12.9	120.0	66.1	0.7	4.6	42369.1	113.5
-2.4	38.8	87.6	0.5	-14.0	16588.7	-19.9
-1.2	90.1	77.1	1.0	-5.0	29121.8	38.7
6.5	141.5	56.7	1.0	7.9	145831.6	184.5
13.4	100.0	72.9	1.4	18.2	69633.2	184.5
4.2	82.1	79.6	1.9	-6.2	105175.3	97.9
4.1	80.6	80.4	2.0	-6.6	105810.1	96.6
1.1	133.6	46.2	0.7	-4.0	71159.0	80.3
-4.6	117.2	46.3	1.0	-25.1	77104.5	-6.0

12-20 主要工业产品产量

Output of Major Industrial Products

产品名称	Item	2003	2004
原煤(吨)	Raw Coal (ton)	34828620	37493992
天然原油(吨)	Crude Oil (ton)	21413933	22530197
天然气(万立方米)	Natural Gas (10 000 cu.m)	502942	574805
铁矿石原矿量(吨)	Crudeiron Ore (ton)	2690758	3870807
铜精矿含铜量(吨)	Cuproaurite (ton)	7530	21802
硫铁矿(折含 S 35%)(吨)	Pyritel with Content of (S35%)(ton)	53137	142234
原盐(吨)	Salt (ton)	527087	873219
发电量(万千瓦小时)	ElectriCity (10 000 kwh)	2346221	2662976
#火 电	Thermalpower	1962827	2267387
水 电	Hydropower	361980	370824
供热量(万百万千焦)	Heat Supply (10 000 million kj)	9240	9984
大米(吨)	Rice (ton)	153316	128225
小麦粉(万吨)	Wheate Flour (10 000 ton)	292	274
精制食用植物油(吨)	Refined edible oil		320013
机制糖(吨)	Sugar (ton)	454256	372605
配混合饲料(吨)	Forage (ton)	1180284	1028023
糖果(吨)	Candy (ton)	3536	1993
乳制品(吨)	Dairy products (ton)	14846	26062
罐头(吨)	Canned Food (ton)	474825	664085
味精(吨)	Mono sodium glutamate (ton)	6693	7427
酱油(吨)	Soy (ton)	8853	12200
发酵酒精(千升)	Zymolytic Alcohol (kilo-liter)	40867	28658
饮料酒(千升)	Alcohol Beverage(kilo-liter)	317260	345770
#白 酒	Liquor	56449	60780
啤 酒	Beer	229497	249003
葡萄酒	Grape Wine	30290	34984
软饮料(吨)	Soft Drink (ton)	147405	306996
冷冻饮品(吨)	Ice Beverage (ton)	10952	14233
卷烟(万支)	Cigarettes (10 000 pieces)	625000	700000
纱(吨)	Yarn (ton)	292713	291386
布(万米)	Cloth (10 000 m)	15239	13989
#棉 布	Pure Cotton Cloth	15239	13989
印染布(万米)	Printing and dyeing Cloth (10 000 m)	460	311
绒线(毛线)(吨)	Knitting Wool (ton)	744	980
呢绒(万米)	Woolen Cloth Goods (10 000 m)	206	206
丝(吨)	Silk (ton)	110	39

12-20 续表 1 Continued

产品名称	Item	2003	2004
丝织品(万米)	Silk Produces (10 000 m)	193	177
针棉织品折用纱线量(吨)	Cotton Knitwear (ton)	1132	
服装(万件)	Garments (10 000 units)	1168	1036
轻革(平方米)	Light leather (sq.meter)	4931864	3612929
皮鞋(万双)	Leather Shoes (10 000)	44	30.16
革皮服装(件)	Leather Garment (unit)	37125	26977
人造板(立方米)	Artificial Board (cu.m)	136458	342770
＃胶合板	Plywood	44534	52909
纤维板	Fiberboard	48268	218852
刨花板	Chip Board	38211	26054
家具(件)	Furniture (unit)	2966417	2608055
＃木制家具	Wooden furniture	2422745	2260813
金属家具	Steal Furniture	440498	305501
纸浆(吨)	Paper pulp (ton)	236905	177790
机制纸及纸板(吨)	Machine-made Paper and Paperboard (ton)	233365	263066
＃机制纸	Machine-made Paper	132950	
机制纸板	Machine-made Paperboard	100415	
本册(万本)	Copy (10 000 copy)	1918	3770
原油加工量(吨)	Processed Crude oil (ton)	11339137	12201800
汽油(吨)	Gasoline (ton)	2208756	2358451
溶剂油(吨)	Megilp (ton)	192997	160929
煤油(吨)	Kerosene (ton)	195600	244526
柴油(吨)	Diesel Oil (ton)	4474525	5230965
润滑油(吨)	Lubricating oil (ton)	494488	601112
燃料油(吨)	Fuel Oil (ton)	274849	288843
石油沥青(吨)	Petroleum Bitumen (ton)	1009077	1105787
液化石油气(吨)	Liquefied petroleum gas (ton)	475658	505732
炼厂干气(吨)	Refinery Gas (ton)	332109	332872
焦炭(吨)	Coke (ton)	1286538	1790385
＃机械化焦炉生产的焦炭(吨)	Coke Turned out by Mechanized Coke Oven (ton)	630847	1133797
煤气(万立方米)	Coal gas (10 000 cu.m)	267494	334685
硫酸(折 100%)(吨)	Sulfuric Acid (ton)	85322	114046
盐酸(含量 31%以上)(吨)	Hydrochloric Acid (With Content of 31%) (ton)	87467	132417
氢氧化钠(烧碱)(折 100%)(吨)	Caustic Soda (ton)	114110	174445
碳酸钠(纯碱)(吨)	Soda Ash (ton)	95919	113178
硫化碱(吨)	Alkali sulfide (ton)	147682	163547

12-20 续表 2 Continued

产品名称	Item	2003	2004
碳化钙(电石)(折 300 升/千克)(吨)	Calcium Carbide (ton)	82057	115991
合成氨(吨)	Synthetic Ammonia (ton)	1082601	1015630
农用氮、磷、钾化学肥料总计(折纯)(吨)	Chemical Fertilizers (ton)	854530	869795
#氮肥(折含 N 100%)	Nitrogen Fertilizers	845828	808500
#尿 素	Carbamide	827841	776202
磷肥(折合 P_2O_5 100%)	Phosphate Fertilizers	1599	18186
乙烯(吨)	Ethylene(ton)	235921	253711
油漆(吨)	Oil Paint (ton)	13417	17925
塑料树脂及共聚物(吨)	Plastics (ton)	533534	624573
肥皂(吨)	Soap (ton)	87	629
合成洗涤剂(吨)	Synthetic Detergents (ton)	26915	34284
火柴(件)	Match (units)	209877	
化学原料药(吨)	Chemical Medicine (ton)	300	291
中成药(吨)	Traditional Chinese Medicine (ton)	4380	3712
轮胎外胎(条)	Outer Tyres (units)	696026	870913
胶鞋(万双)	Rubber Shoes (10 000 pairs)	16	46
塑料制品(吨)	Plastic Produces (ton)	314891	388270
#塑料薄膜	Plastic Film	99729	105131
#农用薄膜	Farm Plastic Sheet	78125	
塑料型材(含板片材)	Plastic Moulding Material	31914	10056
水泥(万吨)	Cement (10 000 ton)	1129	1213
水泥排水管(千米)	Cement Sewage Duct (1000 m)	836	760
水泥压力管(千米)	Cement Pressure Duct (1000 m)	1015	41
水泥电杆(吨)	Cement Electric Pole Piece (ton)	200512	111087
砖(折标准砖)(万块)	Brick (Standard Brick) (10 000 pieces)	877997	758256
瓦(万片)	Tile (10 000 pieces)	8322	1170
大理石板材(平方米)	Marble Slab (sq.meter)	117306	109663
花岗石板材(平方米)	Granite Sheet (sq.meter)	2449083	1513215
平板玻璃(重量箱)	Plate Glass (weight case)	675987	1226528
日用玻璃制品(吨)	Household Glass Products (ton)	63074	58716
日用陶瓷(万件)	Household Ceramics (10 000 pcs)	392	16
耐火材料制品(吨)	Fire Proof Material (ton)	52510	68670
生铁(吨)	Pig Iron (ton)	1448577	1938948

12-20 续表 3 Continued

产品名称	Item	2003	2004
粗钢(吨)	Steel (ton)	2041153	2491278
#普通低合金钢(吨)	Ordinary Low-Alloy Steel (ton)		1018576
合金钢(吨)	Low-Alloy Steel (ton)		44010
钢材(吨)	Steel Produces (ton)	2031049	2385191
#大型型钢	Large Fashioned Steel	2559	4432
中小型型钢	Medium and Small Fasioned Steel	75761	81064
钢　筋	Concrete Iron	991921	1070135
盘　条(线材)	Wire Rod	807151	941345
铁合金(吨)	Ferroalloy (ton)	27521	33989
铜(吨)	Copper (ton)	2894	3453
镍(吨)	Nickel (ton)	2050	
铝(吨)	Aluminium (ton)	50171	57046
铝材(吨)	Aluminium Material (ton)	18392	9359
铸铁管(吨)	Cost Iron Tube (ton)		
手工工具(万把)	Hand Tools (10 000)	13	1
日用不锈钢制品(吨)	Household Steinless Steel Products (ton)	83	72
工业锅炉(蒸发量吨)	Industrial Boiler (Evaporating Quantity)	555	2266
金属切削机床(台)	Metal-cutting Machine Tools (unit)	5	
输送机械(米)	Conveying Machinery (m)	2930	70527
泵(台)	Pump (unit)	4330	4385
风机(台)	Fan (unit)	2663	3665
轴承(万套)	Bearing (10 000)	121	98
小型拖拉机(台)	Small-Size Tractor (unit)		1407
收获机械(台)	Harvesting Machinery (unit)	3625	59
汽车(辆)	Motor Vehicles(unit)	1615	2155
改装汽车(辆)	Modified Truck (unit)	1280	1923
发电设备(千瓦)	Power Generating Equipment (kw)	28100	74290
交流电动机(千瓦)	Alternating Current Motor (kw)	31300	51800
变压器(千伏安)	Transformer (kev)	11738706	11357474
电力电缆(公里)	Electric Cable (km)	36660	21788
通讯电缆(公里)	Comrnunicating cable (km)	5666	
钢芯铝绞线(吨)	Aluminium Strand Wire with Steel Core (ton)	22213	
蓄电池(千伏安时)	Battery (KVAh)	204903	106821
干电池(折一号电池)(万只)	Primary Battery(10 000 units)	3646	3037
发光源(灯泡)(万只)	Bulb (10 000 units)	496	

12-21 各地、州、市主要工业产品产量

年 份 Year	地 区 Region	纱 (吨) Yarn (ton)	布 (万米) Cloth (10 000 m)	毛 线 (吨) Knitting Wool (ton)	呢 绒 (万米) Woolen Piece Goods (10 000 m)	丝 (吨) Silk (ton)
	1978	28008	15616	1239	189.37	144
	1980	31272	16931	1614	240.08	86
	1985	39130	21150	2396	680.00	96
	1990	101941	30017	2179	1230.00	190
	1991	135771	27851	2040	1228.00	316
	1992	142682	24006	1570	1205.00	319
	1993	125362	23250	2226	1228.90	379
	1994	197553	28171	2570	1352.00	442
	1995	244689	30460	2286	1262.00	421
	1996	208526	27186	2202	1361.00	283
	1997	247143	29862	2393	1227.00	352
	1998	220332	26719	1361	979.00	304
	1999	294378	27450	1349	798.00	267
	2000	334307	28060	1184	754.00	149
	2001	302654	25380	843	399.00	214
	2002	316095	20679	811	264.58	201
	2003	292713	15239	744	205.58	110
	2004	291386	13989	980	205.92	39
乌鲁木齐市	Urumqi City	40421	1612	454	18.47	
克拉玛依市	Karamay City					
石河子市	Shihezi City	39967	4272	167	101.00	
阿拉尔市	Alar City	5892				
图木舒克市	Tumxuk City					
五家渠市	Wujiaqu City	7512				
吐鲁番地区	Turpan Administrative Offices	8904				
哈密地区	Hami [Kumul] Administrative Offices	14374	44			
昌吉回族自治州	Changji Hui Autonomous Prefecture	46541	1531		86.45	
伊犁哈萨克自治州	Ili Kazak Autonomous Prefecture	48703	2534	359		
伊犁州直属县(市)	Counties (Cities) Direct Under Ili Prefecture	26309	1183			
塔城地区	Tacheng [Tarbagatai] Administrative Offices	22394	1351	332		
阿勒泰地区	Altay Administrative Offices			27		
博尔塔拉蒙古自治州	Bortala Mongol Autonomous Prefecture	11320	168			
巴音郭楞蒙古自治州	Bayangol Mongol Autonomous Prefecture	25076	1308			
阿克苏地区	Aksu Administrative Offices	17695	945			
克孜勒苏柯尔克孜自治州	Kizilsu Kirgiz Autonomous Prefecture					
喀什地区	Kashgar [Kaxgar] Administrative Offices	19816	1260			
和田地区	Hotan Administrative Offices	5165	316			39

注：卷烟计量单位从 2003 年开始改为亿支。

Output of Major Industrial Products by Prefecture, Autonomous Prefecture and City

机制纸及纸板(吨) Machine-made Paper and Paperboard (ton)	原盐(万吨) Salt (10 000 ton)	糖(万吨) Sugar (10 000 ton)	饮料酒(千升) Alcohol Beverage (kilo-liter)	卷烟(万箱) Cigarettes (10 000 cases)	原煤(万吨) Coal (10 000 ton)	原油(万吨) Crude Oil (10 000 ton)	天然气(万立方米) Natural gas (10 000 cu.m)	发电量(亿千瓦时) ElectriCity (100 million kwh)	#水电 Hydropower
19851	51.71	2.08		3.01	1079.01	353.05	25100	21.17	4.64
23838	38.18	4.43		3.11	1136.84	390.58	35298	23.58	5.25
41521	35.09	7.18		8.04	1600.22	499.00	54556	38.11	8.64
90857	159.00	16.84		12.34	2100.00	695.00	50161	69.79	14.25
101721	150.00	26.12		12.39	2111.00	762.00	55432	78.04	14.67
118113	111.48	32.17		12.09	2204.46	831.66	67472	86.80	17.55
135038	71.49	33.53		13.00	2392.29	1065.50	84330	95.78	20.24
145674	39.94	28.39		12.78	2633.29	1156.62	90556	106.17	21.60
180440	25.98	30.18		13.61	2720.74	1267.83	114821	120.43	22.82
169789	36.54	36.34		13.56	2986.00	1457.10	140609	136.03	24.49
161659	39.85	42.28		13.21	3021.37	1629.25	213006	150.58	26.97
168799	27.53	47.59		12.04	2926.91	1628.38	237826	157.76	28.23
180138	36.14	46.36		11.00	2778.16	1739.65	310600	169.30	30.06
176477	31.78	30.76		10.50	2798.90	1848.43	353930	182.98	30.53
193389	46.02	41.98		11.04	2819.61	1946.95	417429	197.62	34.10
226950	50.75	51.84		12.00	3098.67	2036.19	485237	212.24	34.67
233365	52.71	45.43	317260	62.50	3482.86	2141.39	502942	234.62	36.20
263066	87.32	37.26	345770	70.00	3749.40	2253.02	574805	266.30	37.08
42733	12.57		139882		894.08	358.17	49003	88.68	
20	0.01		1698		7.28	1115.35	255031	22.70	
33972			4350					13.62	2.43
								0.02	0.02
								0.01	0.01
2980					37.63				
	11.25		4474		151.08	225.00	132646	0.88	0.06
	24.51		1734		460.46			13.36	0.03
104700	0.05	2.21	18796		866.29			48.39	0.68
15162	29.79	22.78	129715	70.00	758.17			27.48	10.72
6484		12.43	68781	70.00	296.18			14.03	4.21
3965	29.60	8.78	59670		453.88			7.90	1.62
4713	0.19	1.57	1264		8.12			5.55	4.89
	4.50	1.69	753					3.61	2.07
60203	3.16	8.13	6506		116.18	554.38	138125	20.45	7.20
696	0.25	2.44	18938		388.47	0.12		11.72	3.62
	1.21				3.83			0.43	0.26
2600			17879		12.09			11.79	6.96
	0.03		1025		53.84			3.14	3.04

Note: The metering unit of tobacco has been changed into 100, 000, 000 from the year 2003.

12-21 续表

年 份 Year	地 区 Region	生 铁 (万吨) Pig Iron (10 000 tons)	粗钢 (万吨) Steel (10 000 tons)	大理石板 材 (平方米) Marble Plate (sq.m.)	钢 材 (万吨) Steel Produces (10 000 tons)
	1978	17.52	8.46		6.83
	1980	15.81	10.74		8.59
	1985	22.87	19.79		16.73
	1990	40.57	36.49	9589	28.48
	1991	41.31	40.57	6779	33.80
	1992	46.47	47.49	11407	40.30
	1993	56.54	53.63	20332	45.98
	1994	68.44	66.39	20112	57.71
	1995	69.53	70.59	34169	66.55
	1996	85.64	87.47	6420	86.70
	1997	93.82	97.21	53588	99.89
	1998	100.40	107.67	9197	116.19
	1999	101.30	105.60	7807	117.30
	2000	106.42	109.70	6294	131.26
	2001	111.73	131.83	22786	134.42
	2002	122.78	175.45	34185	173.07
	2003	144.86	204.12	117306	203.10
	2004	193.89	249.13	109663	238.52
乌鲁木齐市	Urumqi City	166.04	227.84	4000	226.40
克拉玛依市	Karamay City			500	
石河子市	Shihezi City				
阿拉尔市	Alar City				
图木舒克市	Tumxuk City				
五家渠市	Wujiaqu City				
吐鲁番地区	Turpan Administrative Offices	5.69		19480	
哈密地区	Hami [Kumul] Administrative Offices	0.79			
昌吉回族自治州	Changji Hui Autonomous Prefecture	1.24	7.22		4.11
伊犁哈萨克自治州	Ili Kazak Autonomous Prefecture	6.90	12.44	79207	5.40
伊犁州直属县(市)	Counties (Cities) Direct Under Ili Prefecture	6.51	6.84		
塔城地区	Tacheng [Tarbagatai] Administrative Offices		5.60		5.40
阿勒泰地区	Altay Administrative Offices	0.38		79207	
博尔塔拉蒙古自治州	Bortala Mongol Autonomous Prefecture	8.63			
巴音郭楞蒙古自治州	Bayangol Mongol Autonomous Prefecture	4.60	1.62	6476	2.60
阿克苏地区	Aksu Administrative Offices				
克孜勒苏柯尔克孜自治州	Kizilsu Kirgiz Autonomous Prefecture				
喀什地区	Kashgar [Kaxgar] Administrative Offices				
和田地区	Hotan Administrative Offices				0.01

Continued

水 泥 (万吨) Cement (10 000 tons)	硫 酸 (吨) Sulfuric Acid (ton)	烧 碱 (吨) Caustic Soda (ton)	合成氨 (吨)(折纯) Synthetic Ammonia (ton)	农用氮、磷、钾化肥(吨) Farm Nitrogen Phophate and Potassium (ton)	碳化钙 (电石)(吨) Calcium Crbide (ton)	塑料制品 (吨) Plastic Products (ton)	小型拖拉机 (台) Small Tractor (unit)
78.15	20262	4164	33155	20276	4895	3194	843
90.89	19153	3542	13762	9207	4486	2051	137
201.05	23921	5045	85728	58080	5989	17974	11117
285.00	47732	15063	397062	287640	15976	40958	17081
328.00	57732	16700	449832	331692	12636	50805	27462
375.20	60396	18737	466615	356014	14344	75044	22398
418.70	54506	19010	440469	334599	9995	62484	15516
448.26	71329	21004	450439	345700	12040	75601	22601
489.88	88491	24732	492754	383279	12344	100739	30352
562.87	76413	28008	488337	372056	15901	129059	26671
628.00	77187	35544	581449	428711	28350	143916	14780
728.94	64836	39614	688069	520681	28999	168372	19017
805.83	68169	42161	896632	685587	40216	139497	17048
895.67	71458	51831	947511	754668	51749	197756	13472
981.29	72511	68589	884340	729034	65763	262873	12672
1029.71	70407	93362	956732	766291	73680	230729	4019
1128.98	85322	114110	1082601	854530	82057	314891	
1212.99	114046	174445	1015630	869795	115991	388270	1407
267.64	298	114718	745443	598734	106514	83310	
						36431	
	22236	56192				61653	
						17919	
4.24						1083	
						4939	
26.74	49096			200		690	
28.80	2297			3624		6009	
161.44	14500			7723	9477	72824	1262
265.16	11950			2608		52325	145
102.64	11950			2555		20730	120
129.56						29557	25
32.97				53		2038	
25.79						13194	
113.30		3535	270187	250096		10488	
188.20	13669			6810		9084	
3.27						373	
92.73						16773	
35.69						1173	

12-22 国有及国有控股企业主要指标占全区规模以上工业比重

Percentage of State-ownership and State-owned Holding Enterprises to the Industry at a Scale in Terms of Major Quota

单位：万元 (2004 年) (10 000yuan)

指 标	Item	全区规模以上企业 Enterprises at Considerable Scale	国有及国有控股企业 State-Ownership and State-Holding Enterprises	国有及国有控股企业占全区比重 (%) Percentage of State Ownership and State-Holding Enterprises to the Enterprises in Xinjiang
从业人员(人)	Employment Staff (person)	449761	301025	66.9
工业总产值	Gross Industrial Output Value	15718444.4	12535046.5	79.7
工业增加值	Added Industrial Value	6689966.6	5850758.9	87.5
资产总计	Total Sum of Asset	24880833.1	19682108.1	79.1
流动资产年平均余额	Average Annual Balance of Circulating Asset	7236560.6	5003834.0	69.1
固定资产净值年平均余额	Average Balance of Net Fixed Asset	13939098.1	12071356.7	86.6
负债合计	Total Sum of Debt	13253592.9	10154988.6	76.6
所有者权益	Owner's Right and Interest	11614702.1	9514581.4	81.9
实收资本	Substantial Capital	7274478.1	5971047.0	82.1
产品销售收入	Sales Income	15834415.5	12779766.5	80.7
产品销售税金及附加	Product Sales Income and Tax and Additon	315383.3	292037.3	92.6
利润总额	Total Sum of Profit	2263156.6	2084933.2	92.1
利税总额	Total Sum of Profit and Tax	3494005.3	3182621.6	91.1
全员劳动生产率(元/人)	Productivity of Labor for the Staff (yuan/man)	148744.9	194361.2	
亏损单位数(个)	Number of Loss Enterprises (unit)	539	281	52.1
亏损企业亏损额	Number of Loss for Loss Enterprises	431474.2	365370.5	84.7

12-23 重点行业主要指标占全区规模以上工业比重

Percentage of Major Indicators in Key Industrial Sectors to Xinjiang's Industry at Considerable Scale

(2004 年)

指 标	Item	合 计 Total	占全区比重 (%) Percentage (%)
从业人员(人)	**Employed staff (person)**	**247868**	**55.1**
石油和天然气开采业	Oil and Natural Gas Extraction	80965	18.0
石油加工、炼焦及核燃料加工业	Oil Processing	20586	4.6
黑色金属冶炼及压延加工业	Ferrous Metal Smeltering and Rolling Process	20748	4.6
电力、热力的生产和供应业	Electric Power, Thermal Power Production and Supply	44464	9.9
纺织业	Textile Industry	60320	13.4
农副食品加工业	Agricultural and Side-line Food Production	20785	4.6
工业总产值(万元)	**Gross Industrial Output Value (10 000 yuan)**	**12071731.1**	**76.8**
石油和天然气开采业	Oil and Natural Gas Extraction	5110995.9	32.5
石油加工、炼焦及核燃料加工业	Oil Process, Coke and Nuclear Fuel Processing Industry	3545412.7	22.6
黑色金属冶炼及压延加工业	Ferrous Metal Smeltering and Rolling Process	1178679.2	7.5
电力、热力的生产和供应业	Electri Power and Thermal Production and Supply	987051.8	6.3
纺织业	Textile Industry	595723.2	3.8
农副食品加工业	Agricultural and Side-line Food Process	653868.3	4.2
工业增加值(万元)	**Added Industrial Output Value (10 000 yuan)**	**5496130.2**	**82.2**
石油和天然气开采业	Oil and Natural Gas Extraction	3810058.3	57.0
石油加工、炼焦及核燃料加工业	Oil Process, Coking and Nuclear Fuel Process	659181.9	9.9
黑色金属冶炼及压延加工业	Ferrous Metal Smeltering and Rolling Process	354804.2	5.3
电力、热力的生产和供应业	Electric Power, Thermal Production and Supply	435717.4	6.5
纺织业	Textile Industry	121805.0	1.8
农副食品加工业	Agricultural and Side-line Food Process	114563.4	1.7

12-23 续表 Continued

指　标	Item	合　计 Total	占全区比重(%) Percentage(%)
资产总计(万元)	**Total Sum of Asset (10 000 yuan)**	**17207755.4**	**69.2**
石油和天然气开采业	Oil and Natural Gas Extraction	8799967.2	35.4
石油加工、炼焦及核燃料加工业	Oil Process, Coking and Nuclear Fuel Processing	2466232.5	9.9
黑色金属冶炼及压延加工业	Ferrous Metal Smeltering and Rolling Industry	959071.8	3.9
电力、热力的生产和供应业	Electric Power and Thermal Production and Supply	3165219.3	12.7
纺织业	Textile Industry	1043290.5	4.2
农副食品加工业	Agricultural and Side-line Food Processing	773974.1	3.1
利润总额(万元)	**Total Sum of Profit (10 000 yuan)**	**2042085.2**	**90.2**
石油和天然气开采业	Oil and Natural Gas Extraction	1924736.9	85.0
石油加工、炼焦及核燃料加工业	Oil Processing, Coking and Nuclear Fuel Processing	49659.9	2.2
黑色金属冶炼及压延加工业	Ferrous Metal Smeltering and Rolling Process	158416.2	7.0
电力、热力的生产和供应业	Electric Power and Thermal Power Production and Supply	-63206.8	
纺织业	Textile Industry	-40142.3	
农副食品加工业	Agricultural and Side-line Food Processing	12621.3	0.6
利税总额(万元)	**Total Sum of Profit and Tax (10 000 yuan)**	**3030401.0**	**86.7**
石油和天然气开采业	Oil and Natural Gas Extraction	2463574.0	70.5
石油加工、炼焦及核燃料加工业	Oil Procesing, Coking and Nuclear Fuel Industry	294728.5	8.4
黑色金属冶炼及压延加工业	Ferrous Metal Smeltering and Rolling Process	231068.2	6.6
电力、热力的生产和供应业	Electric Power and Thermal Power Production and Supply	32131.6	0.9
纺织业	Textile Industry	-17087.7	
农副食品加工业	Agricultural and Side-line Food Processing	25986.4	0.7
主营业务收入(万元)	**Income of Major Business (10 000 Yuan)**	**12182296.7**	**76.9**
石油和天然气开采业	Oil and Natural Gas Extraction	5246456.9	33.1
石油加工、炼焦及核燃料加工业	Oil Processing, Coking and Nuclear Fuel Processing	3507205.6	22.1
黑色金属冶炼及压延加工业	Ferrous Metal Smeltering and Rolling Industry	1192885.9	7.5
电力、热力的生产和供应业	Electric Power and Thermal Production and Supply	1006971.0	6.4
纺织业	Textile Industry	557474.5	3.5
农副食品加工业	Agricultural and Side-line Food Processing Industry	671302.8	4.2

主要统计指标解释

工业 指从事自然资源的开采，对采掘品和农产品进行加工和再加工的物质生产部门。具体包括：(1)对自然资源的开采，如采矿、晒盐、森林采伐等(但不包括禽兽捕猎和水产捕捞)；(2)对农副产品的加工、再加工，如粮油加工、食品加工、轧花、缫丝、纺织、制革等；(3)对采掘品的加工、再加工，如炼铁、炼钢、化工生产、石油加工、机器制造、木材加工等，以及电力、自来水、煤气的生产和供应等；(4)对工业品的修理、翻新，如机器设备的修理、交通运输工具(包括小卧车)的修理等。

1984年以前农村的村及村以下办工业归属农业，1984年以后划归工业。

工业统计调查单位为独立核算法人工业企业。

独立核算法人工业企业指从事工业生产经营活动的单位。独立核算法人工业企业应同时具备以下条件：①依法成立，有自己的名称、组织机构和场所，能够承担民事责任；②独立拥有和使用资产，承担负债，有权与其他单位签订合同；③独立核算盈亏，并能够编制资产负债表。本年鉴中涉及的企业登记注册类型：

国有及国有控股企业 指国有企业加上国有控股企业。国有企业(即原全民所有制工业或国营工业)指企业全部资产归国家所有，并按《中华人民共和国企业法人登记管理条例》规定登记注册的非公司制的经济组织。包括国有企业、国有独资公司和国有联营企业。1957年以前的公私合营和私营工业，后均改造为国营工业，1992年改为国有工业，这部分工业的资料不单独分列时，均包括在国有企业内。国有控股企业是对混合所有制经济的企业进行的"国有控股"分类。它是指这些企业的全部资产中国有资产(股份)相对其他所有者中的任何一个所有者占资(股)最多的企业。该分组反映了国有经济控股情况。

集体企业 指企业资产归集体所有，并按《中华人民共和国企业法人登记管理条例》规定登记注册的经济组织。是社会主义公有制经济的组成部分。包括城乡所有使用集体投资举办的企业，以及部分个人通过集资自愿放弃所有权并依法经工商行政管理机关认定为集体所有制的企业。

股份合作企业 指以合作制为基础，由企业职工共同出资入股，吸收一定比例的社会资产投资组建，实行自主经营，自负盈亏，共同劳动，民主管理，按劳分配与按股分红相结合的一种集体经济组织。

联营企业 指两个及两个以上相同或不同所有制性质的企业法人或事业单位法人，按自愿、平等、互利的原则，共同投资组成的经济组织。联营企业包括：

国有联营企业指国有企业与国有企业间的联营；

集体联营企业指集体企业与集体企业间的联营；

国有与集体联营企业指国有企业与集体企业间的联营。

有限责任公司 指根据《中华人民共和国公司登记管理条例》规定登记注册，由两个以上，五十个以下的股东共同出资，每个股东以其所认缴的出资额对公司承担有限责任，公司以其全部资产对其债务承担责任的经济组织。有限责任公司包括国有独资公司以及其他有限责任公司。

股份有限公司 指根据《中华人民共和国企业法人登记管理条例》规定登记注册，其全部注册资本由等额股份构成并通过发行股票筹集资本，股东以其认购的股份对公司承担有限责任，公司以其全部资产对其债务承担责任的经济组织。

私营企业 指由自然人投资设立或由自然人控股，以雇佣劳动为基础的营利性经济组织。包括按照《公司法》、《合伙企业法》、《私营企业暂行条例》规定登记注册的私营有限责任公司、私营股份有限公司、私营合伙企业和私营独资企业。

港、澳、台商投资企业 指企业注册登记类型中的港、澳、台资合资、合作、独资经营企业和股份有限公司之和。

外商投资企业 指企业注册登记类型中的中外合资、合作经营企业、外资企业和外商投资股份有限公司之和。"三资"企业系指港、澳、台商投资企业和外资企业的简称。

轻工业 指主要提供生活消费品和制作手工工具的工业。按其所使用的原料不同，可分为两大类：(1)以农产品为原料的轻工业，是指直接或间接以农产品为基本原料的轻工业。主要包括食品制造、饮料制造、烟草加工、纺织、缝纫、皮革和毛皮制作、造纸以及印刷等工业；(2)以非农产品为原料的轻工业，是指以工业品为原料的轻工业。主要包括文教体育用品、化学药品制造、合成纤维制造、日用化学制品、日用玻璃制品、日用金属制品、手工工具制造、医疗器械制造、文化和办公用机械制造等工业。

重工业 指为国民经济各部门提供物质技术基础的主要生产资料的工业。按其生产性质和产品用途，可以分为下列三类：(1)采掘(伐)工业，是指对自然资源的开采，包括石油开采、煤炭开采、金属矿开采、非金属矿开采和木材采伐等工业；(2)原材料工业，指向国民经济各部门提供基本材料、动力和燃料的工业。包括金属冶炼及加工、炼焦及焦炭、化学、化工原料、水泥、人造板以及电力、石油和煤炭加工等工业；(3)加工工业，是指对工业原材料进行再加工制造的工业。包括装备国民经济各部门的机械设备制造工业、金属结构、水泥制品等工业，以及为农业提供的生产资料如化肥、农药等工业。根据上述划分原则，修理业中以重工业产品为修理作业对象的划为重工业，反之划为轻工业。

工业总产值

(1)定义：工业总产值是以货币形式表现的，工业企业在518一定时期内生产的工业最终产品或提供工业性劳务活动的总价值量。它反映一定时间内工业生产的总规模和总水平。

(2)计算原则：工业生产的原则，即凡是企业在报告期生产的经检验合格的产品，不管是否在报告期销售，均包括在内。

最终产品的原则，即凡是计入工业总产值的产品，必须是本企业生产的经检验合格的，不需要再进行任何加工的最终产品。如果企业有中间产品(半成品)对外销售，则对外销售的中间产品应视为企业的最终产品。

工厂法原则，即工业总产值是以工业企业作为基本计算(核算)单位，即按企业的最终产品计算工业总产值。按这种方法计算的工业总产值，不允许同一产品价值在企业内部重复计算，不能把企业内部各个车间(分厂)生产的成果相加，但允许企业间的重复计算。

(3)内容及计算方法：1995年全国工业普查对工业总产值(原规定)的内容及计算原则和方法做了某些修订，修订后的工业总产值(新规定)包括三项内容：即本期生产成品价值、对外加工费收入、在制品半成品期末期初差额价值三部分。本期生产成品价值：指企业本期生产，并在报告期内不再进行加工，经检验、包装入库的全部工业成品(半产品)价值合计，包括企业生产的自制设备及提供给本企业在建工程、其他非工业部门和福利部门等单位使用的成品价值。

本期生产成品价值为按自备原材料生产的产品的数量乘以本期不含增值税(销项税额)的产品实际销售平均单价计算；会计核算中按成本价格转帐的自制设备和自产自用的成品，按成本价格计算生产成品价值。生产成品价值中不包括用定货者来料加工的成品(半产品)价值。

对外加工费收入：指企业在报告期内完成的对外承接的工业品加工(包括用定货者来料加工产品)的加工费收入和对外工业修理作业所取得的加工费收入。对外加工费收入按不含增值税(销项税额)的价格计算，可根据会计“产品销售收入”科目的有关资料取得。

对于本企业对内非工业部门提供的加工修理、设备安装的劳务收入，如果企业会计核算基础较好，能取得这部分资料，而且这部分价值所占比重较大，应包括在对外加工费收入中。

自制半成品在制品期末期初差额价值：指企业报告期在制品期末减期初的差额价值，本指标一般可以从会计核算资料中取得。如果会计产品成本核算中不计算半成品、在制品的成本，则总产值中也不包括这部分价值，反之则包括。

(4)工业总产值统计范围变化和计算方法修订情况：

1984年以前工业总产值不包括村办工业，村办工业总产值划归农业。1984 年以后工业总产值包括村办工业。

1995年工业普查对工业总产值计算方法做了修订，即从1995年始按新修订(新规定)方法计算工业总产值。新规定与原规定的区别如下：

全价与加工费的计算原则不同：新规定为凡自备原材料，不论其生产繁简程度如何，一律按全价计算工业总产值；凡来料加工，允许按加工费计算工业总产值。原规定则视生产加工的繁简程度不同，规定哪些行业按全价，哪些行业按加工费计算工业总产值。

自制半成品、在产品期末期初差额价值的计算原则不同：新规定要求，凡会计产品成本核算时计算了成本的差额价值，总产值中就应包括，否则可不包括；原规定则按生产周期六个月的界限区分，凡生产周期六个月以上的企业，总产值计算中应包括这部分差额价值，否则可不包括。

计算价格不同：新规定按不含增值税(销项税额)的价格计算；原规定则按含增值税(销项税额)的价格计算。

工业增加值 指工业企业在报告期内以货币表现的工业生产活动的最终成果。

工业增加值有两种计算方法：一是生产法，即工业总产出减去工业中间投入加上应交增值税；二是收入法，即从收入的角度出发，根据生产要素在生产过程中应得到的收入份额计算，具体构成项目有固定资产折旧、劳动者报酬、生产税净额、营业盈余，这种方法也称要素分配法。本年鉴中的

工业增加值是以生产法计算的。

生产法工业增加值的计算方法为：

工业增加值= 工业总产出- 工业中间投入+ 应交增值税

(1)工业总产出：指工业企业在一定时期内工业生产活动的总成果。工业总产出包括：成品生产价值，对外加工费收入，自制半成品、在产品期末期初差额价值。1995年后用新规定计算的工业总产值代替。

(2)工业中间投入：指工业企业在工业生产活动中消耗的外购物质产品和对外支付的服务费用。服务费用包括支付给物质生产部门(工业、农业、批发零售贸易业、建筑业、运输邮电业)的服务费用和支付给非物质生产部门(如保险、金融、文化教育、科学研究、医疗卫生、行政管理等)的服务费用。

工业中间投入的确定须遵循以下原则：必须从外部购入的，并已计入工业总产出的产品和服务价值；必须是本期投入生产，并一次性消耗掉(包括本期摊销的低值易耗品等)的产品和服务价值。工业中间投入包括直接材料费用、制造费用中的工业中间投入、管理费用中的工业中间投入、销售费用中的工业中间投入和利息支出五部分。

实收资本 业实际收到投资者的可作为长期周转使用的经营资金。根据现行会计制度规定，实收资本按投资主体分为：国家资本、集体资本、法人资本、个人资本、港澳台资本和外商资本。

国家资本：指有权代表国家投资的政府部门或者机构以国有资产投入企业形成的资本。

集体资本：指有权代表国家投资的集体部门或者机构以国有资产投入企业形成的资本。

法人资本：指其他法人单位以其依法可以支配的资产投入企业形成的资本。

个人资本：指社会个人或者本企业内部职工以个人合法财产投放到企业形成的资本。

港澳台资本：指我国香港、澳门和台湾地区投资者以各种形式的资产进行投资形成的资本。

外商资本：指外国投资者对企业投资形成的资本。

资产合计 业拥有或控制的能以货币计量的经济资源，包括各种财产、债权和其他权利。资产按流动性分为流动资产、长期投资、固定资产、无形资产、递延资产和其他资产。该指标根据企业会计“资产负债表”中“资产总计”项目的期末数增列。

流动资产合计 指可以在一年或者超过一年的一个营业周期内变现或者耗用的资产，包括现金及各种存款、短期投资、应收及预付货款、存款等。流动资产平均余额指企业在报告期内全部流动资产的平均余额。

固定资产原价 指企业在建造、购置、安装、改建、扩建、技术改造某项固定资产时所支出的全部货币总额。它一般包括买价、包装费、运杂费和安装费等。

固定资产净值年平均余额 指固定资产净值在报告期内余额的平均数。计算公式为：

固定资产净值年平均余额=1至12月各月月初、月末固定资产净值之和/24

该指标根据“资产负债表”中“固定资产原价”、“累计折旧”指标的期初、期末数计算填列。

固定资产净值指固定资产原价减去历年已提折旧额后的净额。计算公式为：

固定资产净值= 固定资产原价- 累计折旧

流动负债合计 在一年或超过一年的一个营业周期内偿还的债务。流动负债包括短期负债、应付票据、应付帐款、预收帐款、应付工资、应付福利费、应交税金、应付利润、其他应付款、预提费用等。

流动负债具有偿还期限短，在债权人提出要求时即期偿付，或在一年内必须偿还的特点。该指标根据“资产负债表”中“流动负债”项的期末数填列。

长期负债合计 还期在一年或超过一年的一个营业周期以上的债务，它是除了投资人投入企业的资本以外，企业向债权人筹集、可供企业长期使用的资金，是企业必须以资产或劳务偿还的经济责任，包括长期借款、应付债款、长期应付款、其他长期负债等。与流动负债相比，长期负债具有为数较大、偿还期限较长的特点，且对投资者来说可带来更大的利益。指标根据“资产负债表”中“长期负债合计”项的期末数填列。

所有者权益 业投资人对企业净资产的所有权。企业净资产等于企业全部资产减去全部负债后的余额，包括企业投资人对企业的最初投入的实际到位的资产及资本公积金、盈余公积金和未分配利润。所有者权益合计数小于零，表示企业资不抵债。

产品销售收入 指企业在报告期内生产的成品、自制半成品和工业性劳务取得的收入。

产品销售成本 指企业在报告期内销售本企业生产的成品、自制半成品和工业性劳务等的实际成本。

产品销售税金及附加 指企业在报告期内销售产品、提供的劳务等主要经营业务应负担的城市维护建设税、消费税、资源税和教育费附加等。

产品销售利润 业销售产品、提供的劳务等主要经营业务收入扣除其成本、费用、税金的利润。

利润总额 指企业生产经营活动的最终成果，是企业在一定时期内实现的盈亏相抵后的利润总额(亏损以"-"号表示)，它等于营业利润加上补贴收入加上投资收益加上营业外净收入再加上以前年度损益调整。

本年应交增值 企业在报告期内应交纳的增值税额。它等于本年销项税额加上出口退税加上进项税额转出数减去本年进项税额。小规模纳税企业直接按全年计税销售额乘以征收率计算取得。

总资产贡献率 业全部资产的获利能力，是企业经营业绩和管理水平的集中体现，是评价和考核企业盈利能力的核心指标。计算公式为:

总资产贡献率(%)=(利润总额+税金总额+利息支出)/平均资产总额 × 100%

公式中：税金总额为产品销售税金及附加与应交增值税之和；平均资产总额为期初期末资产之和的算术平均值。

资产负债率 该指标既反映企业经营风险的大小，也反映企业利用债权人提供的资金从事经营活动的能力。计算公式为:

资产负债率(%)=(负债总额/资产总额) × 100%

资产与负债均为报告期期末数。

流动资产周转次数 指一定时期内流动资产完成的周转次数，反映投入工业企业流动资金的周转速度。计算公式为:

流动资金周转次数=产品销售收入/全部流动资产平均余额

公式中：全部流动资产平均余额为期初和期末的流动资产之和的算术平均值。

成本费用利润率 反映企业投入的生产成本及费用的经济效益，同时也反映企业降低成本所取得的经济效益。计算公式为:

成本费用利润率(%)=(利润总额/成本费用总额) × 100%

公式中：成本费用总额为产品销售成本、销售费用、管理费用、财务费用之和。

全员劳动生产率 标反映企业的生产效率和劳动投入的经济效益。计算公式为:

全员劳动生产率(元/人)=工业增加值/全部从业人员平均人数

产品销售率 该反映工业产品已实现销售的程度，是分析工业产销衔接情况、研究工业产品满足社会需求的指标。计算公式为:

产品销售率(%)=工业销售产值/工业总产值(现价) × 100%

Explanatory Notes on Main Statistical Indicators

Indus try refers to the material production sector which is engaged in extraction of natural resources and processing and reprocessing of minerals and agricultural product s, including (1) extraction of natural resources, such as mining, salt product ion, logging (but not including hunting and fishing); (2) processing and reprocessing of farm and sideline produces, such as rice husking, flour milling, wine making, oil pressing, cotton ginning, silk reeling, spinning and weaving, and leather making; (3) manufacture of industrial products, such as steel making, iron smelting, chemicals manufacturing, petroleum processing, machine building, timber processing; water and gas production and electriCity generation and supply; (4)repairing of industrial products such as the repairing of machinery and means of transport (including cars).

Prior to 1984, the rural industry run by villages and cooperative organizations under village was classified into agriculture. Since 1984, it has been group ed into industry.

Units of industrial statistics survey corporate industrial enterprises with independent accounting system.

Corporate industrial enterprises with independent accounting system refer to enterprises engaging in industrial production activities, which meet the following requirements : ① They are established legally, having their own names, organizations, location, able t o take civil liability ; ② They possess and use their assets independently, assume liabilities, and are entitled to sign contracts with other units; ③ They are financially independent and compile their own balance sheets.

Enterprises covered in the industrial statistics in the Year book in clued following categories by their registration:

State-owned Enterprises refer to industrial enterprises where the means of production or income are owned by the state. Joint state-private industries and private industries, which existed before 1957, have been transformed into state industries. Statistics on these enterprises has been included in the state owned industries since 1957 when separation of data was no longer necessary.

Collective-owned Enterprises refer to industrial enterprises where t he means of production are owned collectively, including urban and rural enterprises invested by collectives and some enterprises which were formerly owned privately but have been registered in industrial and commercial administration agency as collective units through raising fund from the public.

Share-holding Cooperative Enterprises refer to economic units set up on cooperative basis, wit h funding partly from members of the enterprise and partly from outside investment, where the operation and management is decided by the members who also participate in the production, and the distribution of income is based both on work (lab our input) and on shares (capital input).

Joint-operation enterprises refer to economic units that are established by joint investment by two or more corporate enterprises or institutions of the same or different types of owner ship on voluntary, equal and mutual-beneficial basis. They include:

a) state-owned joint-operation enterprises (joint operation between state-owned enterprises);

b) collective joint -operation enterprises (joint operation between collective enterprises; and

c) stat e-collective joint-operation enterprises (joint operation between state and collective enterprises).

Limited Liability Corporations refer to economic units registered in accordance with the Regulation of the People's Republic of China on the Management of Registration of Corporations, wit h capitals from 2 t o 49 investors, each investor bears limited liability to the corporation depending on his/her holding of shares, and the corporation bears liability to its debt to the maximum of its total as sets.

Share-holding Corporations Ltd. refer to economic units registered in accordance with the Regulation of the People's Republic of China on the Management of Registration of Corporate Enterprises, with total registered capitals divided into equal shares and raised through issuing stocks. Each investor bears limited liability to the corporation depending on the holding of shares, and the corporation bears liability to its debt to the maximum of its total assets.

Private Enterprises refer to economic unit s invested or controlled (by holding the majority of the shares) by natural persons who hire lab ours for profit-making activities. Included in this category are private limited liability corporations, private share-holding corporations Ltd., private partnership enterprises and private sole investment enterprises registered in accordance with the Corporation Law, Partnership Enterprise Law and Tentative Regulation on Private Enterprises.

Enterprises with Funds form Hong Kong, Macao and Taiwan refers to all industrial enterprises registered as the joint venture, cooperative, sole (exclusive) investment industrial enterprises and limited liability corporations with funds from Hong Kong, Macao and Taiwan.

Foreign Funded Enterprises refers to all industrial enterprises registered as the joint- venture, cooperative, sole (exclusive) investment industrial enterprises and limited liability corporations with foreign funds.

Light Industry refers to the industry that produces consumer goods and hand tools. It consists of two categories, depending on the materials used:

(1) Industries using farm products as raw materials. The se are branches of light industry which directly or indirectly use farm products as basic raw materials, including the manufacture of food and beverages, tobacco processing, textile, clothing, fur and leather manufacturing, paper making, printing, etc.

(2) Industries using non farm products as raw materials. These are branches of light industry which use manufactured goods as raw materials, including the manufacture of cultural, educational articles and sports goods, chemicals, synthetic fiber, chemical products for daily use, glass products for daily use, metal products for daily use, hand tools, medical apparatus and instruments, and the manufacture of cultural and clerical machinery.

Heavy Industry refers to the industry which produces capital goods, and provides various sect ors of the national economy with necessary material and technical basis. It consists of the following three branches according to the purpose of production or the use of products:

(1) Mining, quarrying and logging industry refers to the industry that extract s natural resources, including extract ion of petroleum, coal, metal and non-metal ores and logging.

(2) Raw materials industry refers t o the industry that provides various sectors of the national economy with raw materials, fuels and power. It includes smelting and processing of metals, coking and coke chemistry, chemical materials and building materials such as cement, plywood, and power, petroleum refining and coal dressing.

(3) Manufacturing industry refers to the industry that processes raw materials. It includes machine building industry which equips sectors of the national economy, industries of metal structure and cement products, industries producing means of agricultural production, such as chemical fertilizers and pesticides. According to the above principle of classification, the repairing trades which are engaged primarily in repairing products of heavy industry are classified into heavy industry while these engaged in repairing products of light industry are classified into light industry.

Gross Industrial Output Value

(1) Definition: Gross industrial output value is the total volume of final industrial products produced and industrial services provided during a given period. It reflects the total achievements and overall scale of industrial production during a given period.

(2) Principles for calculation:

Statistics on industrial production follow the principle that all products produced by the enterprises and accepted during the reference period are to be included no matter whether they are sold or not during the reference period.

Determination of final products follow the principle that all products that are included in the calculation of grow industrial output value are the final products of the enterprise which have been accepted through quality check and require no further processing. If an enterprise has intermediate (semi-finished) products to sell, the se intermediate products are considered as the final products of the enterprise.

Gross industrial out put value is calculated following the principle of factory approach, i.e. industrial enterprise is used as the basic accounting unit in calculating the gross industrial output value. By this approach, value of the same product is not to be double counted, and the output value of different workshops (branch factories) should not be added. However, this approach does not exclude the possibility of double counting between enterprises.

(3) Content and calculation method: The old definition of gross industrial output value was modified during the national industrial census in 1995. The revised (new) definition of gross industrial output value consists of 3 components: value of the finished products during the reference period, income from external processing, and value of change in semi-finished products at the end and at t he beginning of the reference period.

Value of the finished products during the reference period: refers to the value of all finished (semi-finished) industrial products that are produced during the reference period without the need for further processing, checked for acceptance, packed and put into the warehouse of the enterprise, including the value of own-produced equipment and the value of products provided to the projects under const ruction of the enterprise, and to other non-industrial or welfare units. Value of finished products during the reference period is calculated by the quantity of products produced using own materials multiplied by t he average unit prices at which products are sold (excluding value-added tax). Own-produced equipment and products produced for own use are value at cost prices as in the case of enterprise accounting. Value of finished products does not include t he value of finished products (semi-finished products) that are produced using the materials from the clients who make the orders.

Income from external processing: refers to income from contracted external processing of industrial products (including processing of industrial products using materials from the clients), and the income from industrial repairing work provided to other units. Income from external processing is calculated using information from the item "products sales income" in the enterprise accounting at the prices excluding value-added tax.

For income from services such as processing, repairing and installation of equipment provided to non-industrial units with in the enterprise, if the accounting work of the enterprise is good enough to separate it from other records, and t he share of such services is significant, it should also be included in the income from external processing.

Value of change in semi-finished products at the end and at the beginning of the reference period: refers to the value of change in semi-finished products at the end and at the beginning of the reference period, which generally can be obtained from accounting records of enterprises. If the enterprise accounting excludes the cost of semi-finished products, then it should not be included in the gross industrial out put value, and vice versa.

(4) Changes in the coverage and method of calculation of gross industrial output value

Prior t o 1984, the value of rural industry run by villages was classified into agriculture instead of industry. Since 1984, it has been included in the gross industrial output value.

Method of calculation for the gross industrial output value was modified in the industrial census in 1995. The difference in the new method as compared with the old one is outlined below:

Principle in using full value vs. processing fee: The new method stipulates that all products produced using own materials are to be calculated with full value in reporting t he gross industrial output value irrespective of sophistication of production, and for external processing, it allows calculation using processing fee. In the old method, however, the use of full value or processing fee was determined by the degree of sophistication of production in different branches of industries.

Principle in determining the value of change in semi-finished products: The new method requires that value of the change in semi-finished products should be included in the gross industrial output value if it is included in the accounting record of the enterprise, otherwise it should not be included. By the old method, it is determined by the type of enterprises in terms of production cycle. If t he production cycle is over 6 months, t he value of change in semi-finished products is included in the gross industrial output value, other wise it is excluded.

Difference in prices: The new method uses prices excluding value-added tax in the calculation of gross industrial output value, while the old method used prices including value-added tax.

Value-added of Industry refers to the final results of industrial production of industrial enterprises in money terms during the reference period.

Industrial value-added can be calculated by two approaches: the production approach, i.e. gross industrial output value minus intermediate input plus value-added tax, and the income approach, i.e. income for various factors used in the course of production, including depreciation of fixed assets, remuneration of labourers, net of product ion tax, and operating surplus. Value-added of industry in the Yearbook is calculated by production approach as following:

Value-added of industry = gross industrial output – industrial intermediate input + value-added tax

(1) Gross industrial output: refers to the total achievements of industrial production during a given period. Gross industrial output includes value of finished products, income from external processing, and value of change in semi-finished products at the end and at the beginning of the reference period. Since 1995, it was substituted by the gross industrial output value by new method.

(2) Industrial intermediate input: refers to purchased good sand paid services consumed during t he industrial production of enterprises. Fees paid for services include fees paid for the services provided by material production sectors (industry, agriculture, wholesale and retail trade, construction, transport, post and telecommunications) and by non-material product ion sectors (insurance, banking, culture, education, scientific research, health and medical care, public administration, etc.). The determination of industrial intermediate input follows the principle that the goods and services must be purchased from outside and included in the gross industrial output, and that the goods and services are inputted into product ion and consumed (include low-value consumables) during the reference period.

Industrial intermediate input includes 5 components, namely direct consumption of materials, industrial intermediate input in manufacturing cost, industrial intermediate input in management cost, industrial intermediate input in marketing cost and expenditure on interest.

Capitals Obtained refers to capital actually received by the enterprise from investors that could be used as operational capitals for a long period. According t o the current accounting system, capitals obtained can be classified by investors as state capital, collective cap ital, corporate capital, individual capital, capital from Hong Kong, Mac au and Taiwan and foreign capital.

State capital: refers to capital which is formed through state owned investment into the enterprise by government agencies or institutions that could represent the state in the investment.

Collective capital: refers to capital which is formed through state-owned investment into the enterprise by collective institutions or units that could represent the state in the investment.

Corporate capital: refers to capital which is formed through investment by other corporate units using assets which is at their disposal by law. Individual capital: refers to capital which is formed through investment by individuals outside the enterprise or employees of the enterprise using their personal legal properties.

Capital from Hong Kong, Mac au and Taiwan: refers to capital which is formed through investment by investors from Hong Kong, Mac au and Taiwan of China using t heir assets of various forms.

Foreign capital: refers to capital which is formed through investment by foreign investors.

Total Assets refer to all economic resources, in monetary terms, that is owned or controlled by enterprises, including properties, creditors equity and other economic rights of all forms. Classified by the degree of equitability, total assets include circulating assets, long-term investment, fixed assets, intangible assets and deferred assets, and other as sets. Data on this indicator can be obtained by the year-end figures of tot al assets in the Assets and Liability Table of accounting records of enterprises.

Total of Working Capitals refer to capitals which can be cashed in or spent or consumed in an operating cycle of one year or over one year, including cash, all kinds of deposits, short term investment, receivable and payable payment for goods or deposits.

Average Value of Working Capitals refers to the average value of all working capitals of t he enterprise during the reference period.

Original Value of Fixed As sets refers to the value of payment by t he enterprise in building, purchasing installing reconstructing, expending or transforming a particular item of fixed assets. In general, it includes value of purchase, cost for packaging, transportation, installation, etc.

Annual Average of Net Value of Fixed Assets refer to average of the net value of fixed as sets during t he reference period, calculated with the following formula:

Annual Average of Net Value of Fixed Assets = sum of net value of fixed assets at the beginning and at the end of each month from January to December / 24.

Information on this indicator can be obtained from the beginning and ending figures of the original value of fixed assets and cumulative depreciation from the Assets and Liability Table of enterprises.

Net value of fixed assets refers to the original value of fixed assets minus depreciation over the years, i.e.:

Net value of fixed assets = original value of fixed asset s -cumulative depreciation

Total Liquid Liabilities refer to enterprises' total debt payable within an operating cycle of one year or over one year, including short-term loans, notes and accounts payable, advance payments received, wages and welfare funds pay able, taxes and profit payable, other payables, fees received by advance payment, etc.

Liquid liabilities feature in the short term of payment , immediate payment at the request of creditors, or pay able with in one year. Data on this item can be obtained from the ending figures on liquid liabilities from the Assets and Liability Table of enterprises.

Total Long-term Liabilities refers to the debt payable within an operating cycle of one year or over one year. It is the cap ital that enterprises raised from creditors for the long-term use of enterprises in addition to capitals put into the enterprise by investors, and constitutes the economic liabilities that enterprises have to repay by assets or lab our services, including long-term loans, payable liabilities, long-term pay able, other long-term liabilities, etc. Compared with the liquid liabilities, the long-term liabilities feature in large volume, longer term for repayment, and larger benefits for investors. Data on this item can be obtained from the ending figures on long-term liabilities from the Assets and Liability Table of enterprises.

Creditors' Equity refers to investors ownership of net assets of the enterprise, which is equal to the total assets of the enterprise minus its total liabilities, including the primary input actually received at the enterprise from invest ors, capital accumulation fund, surplus accumulation fund and undistributed pr of it. When the total of creditors' equity is les s than zero, that indicates the liability of the enterprise is larger that its assets.

Sales Revenue of Industrial Products refers to the revenue from the sales of finished and semi-finished products and from rendering of industrial services by industrial enterprises during the reference period.

Cost of Industrial Products Sold refers to the actual cost of finished and semi-finished products sold and industrial services rendered by industrial enterprises during t he reference period.

Tax and Extra Charges on Sales of Products refer to the tax on City maintenance and construction, consumption tax, resources tax and extra charges for education, which should be borne by the enterprises in selling products and providing industrial services during the reference period.

Profit from Sal es of Products refers to the profit gained by the enterprises by deducting cost, charges and taxes from the business income of the enterprises obtained in selling products and providing industrial services.

Total Profits refer to the final achievements of production and operation of the enterprises, represented by the total profits after deducting losses (loss is expressed by the negative figure). It is the sum of profits from operation, income from subsidies, investment earnings, net income from activities other than operation, and adjustment of profits and losses of previous y ears.

Value-added Tax Payable refers t o t he amount of the value-added tax which should be paid by the enterprises during the reference period. It is the sum of tax on sales, export rebate, and transferred tax on purchases of the current year, minus the tax on purchases of the current year. Value-added tax payable of 524 small-size enterprises is determined by the taxable sales of the year multiplied by the tax rate.

Ratio of Profits, Taxes and Interests to Average Assets reflects the profit-making cap ability of all assets of the enterprise and is a key indicator manifesting the performance and management and evaluating the profit -making potential of the enterprise. It is calculated as follows:

Ratio of profits, taxes and interests to average as sets (%) =[(total profits + total taxes + interest payment) / average assets]× 100%

In the above formula, total taxes is t he sum of tax and extra charges on the s ales of products and value-added t ax payable; and average assets is the arithmetic mean of the sum of beginning assets and ending assets.

Ratio of Debts to Assets reflect both the operation risk and the capability of the enterprise in making use of the capital from the credit ors. It is calculated as follows:

Ratio of debts to assets (%) = (total debts / total assets)×100%

Both assets and debts are figures at the end of the reference period.

Turnover of Working Capital refers to the number of times of turnover of working cap ital in a given period of time, which reflects t he speed of t he turnover of working cap ital of industrial enterprises, and is calculated as follows:

Turnover of working capit al=(sales revenue of products)/(average balance of total working capital)

In the above formula, average balance of total working capital refers to the arithmetic mean of the sum of working capital at the beginning and at the end of the reference period.

Ratio of Profits to Total Industrial Costs refers to the ratio of profits realized in a given period to the total costs in the same period, which reflects the economic efficiency of input cost and is calculated as follows:

Ratio of profits to total industrial cost (%)=(total profits/total cost s)× 100%

Total costs in the above formula is the sum of cost of products sold, marketing cost, management cost and financial cost.

Overall Labour Productivity of Industrial Enterprises reflects efficiency of production and economic results of lab our input of enterprises. The formula us ed is:

Overall lab our productivity=(value added of industry) / (average number of staff and workers)

Ratio of Sales to Gross Output Value reflects the degree at which industrial products are sold. It help s to analyze the linkage between production and sales and the extent of t he needs of the society that has been met by t he sup ply of industrial products. It is calculated as follows:

Ratio of Sales to Gross Output Value=[Industrial sales /Gross industrial output value (at current prices)]× 100%

第十三篇
CHAPTER 13

建筑业

CONSTRUCTION

13-1 建筑企业概况

Main Indicators on Construction Enterprises

年份 Year	地区 Region	企业个数(个) Number of Enterprises (unit)				从业人员(万人) Number of Employees (10 000 persons)			
		合计 Total	国有 State-owned	集体 Collective	其他经济 Other Economy	合计 Total	国有 State-owned	集体 Collective	其他经济 Other Economy
1983		181	98	83		18.71	16.96	1.75	
1984		195	102	93		20.21	17.37	2.84	
1985		275	117	158		25.85	19.21	6.64	
1986		326	125	201		22.37	17.42	4.95	
1987		371	135	236		23.97	17.82	6.15	
1988		416	171	245		26.08	20.19	5.89	
1989		348	199	149		21.87	17.67	4.20	
1990		353	183	170		22.86	18.36	4.50	
1991		496	328	168		26.39	21.58	4.81	
1992		526	328	198		28.76	22.77	5.99	
1993		817	441	356	20	34.55	25.75	8.53	0.27
1994		920	496	401	23	31.25	23.29	7.71	0.25
1995		928	481	432	15	35.33	26.33	8.72	0.28
1996		886	478	386	22	24.97	18.53	6.09	0.35
1997		650	313	312	25	30.75	20.39	8.56	1.80
1998		682	269	348	65	22.14	14.83	6.42	0.89
1999		711	272	344	95	19.35	13.00	4.94	1.41
2000		690	226	293	171	26.16	17.69	4.25	4.22
2001		594	175	152	267	25.27	14.77	2.68	7.82
2002		730	146	109	475	23.57	8.64	1.89	13.04
2003		776	112	77	587	20.81	6.16	1.12	13.53
2004		932	105	51	776	33.22	7.21	0.84	25.17
乌鲁木齐市	Urumqi City	475	57	29	389	11.65	3.81	0.33	7.51
克拉玛依市	Karamay City	41	3	6	32	2.85	0.47	0.27	2.12
石河子市	Shihezi City	56	9		47	3.68	1.58		2.11
吐鲁番地区	Turpan Administrative Offices	10	1		9	0.43	0.05		0.38
哈密地区	Hami [Kumul] Administrative Offices	31	3	2	26	0.71	0.11	0.02	0.58
昌吉回族自治州	Changji Hui Autonomous Prefecture	59	2	4	53	2.59	0.07	0.08	2.44
伊犁哈萨克自治州	Ili Kazak Autonomous Prefecture	93	10	7	76	3.40	0.70	0.08	2.62
伊犁州直属县(市)	Counties (Cities) Direct Under Ili Prefecture	58	7	5	46	1.97	0.54	0.06	1.37
塔城地区	Tacheng [Tarbagatai] Administrative Offices	18	3	2	13	0.93	0.16	0.02	0.74
阿勒泰地区	Altay Administrative Offices	17			17	0.51			0.51
博尔塔拉蒙古自治州	Bortala Mongol Autonomous Prefecture	18	5	1	12	0.32	0.08	0.05	0.19
巴音郭楞蒙古自治州	Bayangol Mongol Autonomous Prefecture	46	3	1	42	3.34	0.10		3.24
阿克苏地区	Aksu Administrative Offices	40	6		34	1.51	0.15		1.36
克孜勒苏柯尔克孜自治州	Kizilsu Kirgiz Autonomous Prefecture	8	1	1	6	0.30	0.04		0.25
喀什地区	Kashgar [Kaxgar] Administrative Offices	33	3		30	1.78	0.03		1.75
和田地区	Hotan Administrative Offices	22	2		20	0.65	0.03		0.62

注：①2000 年至 2002 年建筑业所有指标数据均包括克拉玛依石油管理局工业部分，2003 年起将此部分扣除(以下同)。
②2004 年建筑业所有数据为经济普查数，企业个数及其他指标包括没有工作量或者停业企业，往年未包括(以下同)。

Note: a) All the quota indices in building sector from 2000 to 2002 include the industrial part of Karamay Oil Administration. From the year 2003, this part was omitted. (the same case with the following) . b) All the data in architectural sector are the statistics of economic census, enterprise numbers and other quota exclude work volume or closed enterprises except for previous years. (the same as below) .

13-2 按登记注册类型分的建筑业总产值

Total Output Value of Construction by Registration

单位：万元 (10 000 yuan)

年 份 Year	地 区 Region	合 计 Total	国有经济 State-owned	集体经济 Collective	其他经济 Other Economy
	1983	84017	74330	9687	
	1984	110900	87458	23442	
	1985	175165	138138	37027	
	1986	178237	143634	34594	
	1987	197551	155332	42219	
	1988	234702	186308	48394	
	1989	240076	198912	41164	
	1990	273893	220574	53319	
	1991	362544	291965	70579	
	1992	494945	389230	105715	
	1993	811163	618836	180727	11600
	1994	910718	694786	202908	13024
	1995	1070085	816396	238387	15302
	1996	1284669	977358	283776	23535
	1997	1141318	828482	288081	24755
	1998	1434787	1002235	378956	53596
	1999	1569486	1085080	365588	118818
	2000	2349506	1436653	362649	550204
	2001	2742800	1394099	252076	1096625
	2002	3136257	1270601	170319	1695337
	2003	3221502	739953	147256	2334293
	2004	3439968	910264	89189	2440515
乌鲁木齐市	Urumqi City	1353261	547697	27647	777917
克拉玛依市	Karamay City	404610	75965	39349	289296
石河子市	Shi Hezi City	234417	109705		124712
吐鲁番地区	Turpan Administrative Offices	61549	2531		59018
哈密地区	Hami [Kumul] Administrative Offices	45399	12952	2405	30042
昌吉回族自治州	Changji Hui Autonomous Prefecture	207117	5676	10020	191421
伊犁哈萨克自治州	Ili Kazak Autonomous Prefecture	282509	70826	6663	205020
伊犁州直属县(市)	Counties (Cities) Direct Under Ili Prefecture	185353	55195	5528	124630
塔城地区	Tacheng [Tarbagatai] Administrative Offices	65749	15631	1135	48983
阿勒泰地区	Altay Administrative Offices	31407			31407
博尔塔拉蒙古自治州	Bortala Mongol Autonomous Prefecture	30929	10952	2728	17249
巴音郭楞蒙古自治州	Bayangol Mongol Autonomous Prefecture	477943	45134	238	432571
阿克苏地区	Aksu Administrative Offices	147291	19641		127650
克孜勒苏柯尔克孜自治州	Kizilsu Kirgiz Autonomous Prefecture	14241	2062	139	12040
喀什地区	Kashgar [Kaxgar] Administrative Offices	123878	2620		121258
和田地区	Hotan Administrative Offices	56824	4503		52321

13-3 按构成分的建筑业总产值

Total Output Value of Construction by Composition

单位：万元 (10 000 yuan)

年份 Year	地区 Region	建筑业总产值 Total Output Value of Construction	建筑工程 Construction Works	安装工程 Works of Installation	其他 Others
	1983	84017	73391	7813	2813
	1984	110900	97814	11423	1663
	1985	175165	154496	18042	2627
	1986	178237	157204	18359	2674
	1987	197551	174245	20343	2963
	1988	234072	206508	24060	3504
	1989	240076	211747	24728	3601
	1990	273893	241574	28211	4108
	1991	362544	319764	37343	5438
	1992	494945	436542	50979	7424
	1993	811163	715473	83531	12159
	1994	910718	824232	74119	12367
	1995	1070085	942158	106744	21183
	1996	1284669	1124271	132079	28319
	1997	1141318	1009082	105891	26345
	1998	1434787	1270483	139104	25200
	1999	1569486	1398179	146154	25153
	2000	2349506	2073166	214425	61915
	2001	2742800	2403688	279909	59203
	2002	3136257	2637362	405115	93780
	2003	3221502	2708269	336535	176698
	2004	3439968	2836668	396509	206791
乌鲁木齐市	Urumqi City	1353261	1129233	150765	73263
克拉玛依市	Karamay City	404610	235325	132870	36415
石河子市	Shihezi City	234417	225756	6121	2540
吐鲁番地区	Turpan Administrative Offices	61549	22424	34200	4925
哈密地区	Hami [Kumul] Administrative Offices	45399	37136	2642	5621
昌吉回族自治州	Changji Hui Autonomous Prefecture	207117	189062	15326	2729
伊犁哈萨克自治州	Ili Kazak Autonomous Prefecture	282510	265775	11099	5636
伊犁州直属县(市)	Counties (Cities) Direct Under Ili Prefecture	185353	173446	8257	3650
塔城地区	Tacheng [Tarbagatai] Administrative Offices	65750	62011	2516	1223
阿勒泰地区	Altay Administrative Offices	31407	30318	326	763
博尔塔拉蒙古自治州	Bortala Mongol Autonomous Prefecture	30929	30030	438	461
巴音郭楞蒙古自治州	Bayangol Mongol Autonomous Prefecture	477943	404627	20672	52644
阿克苏地区	Aksu Administrative Offices	147290	128158	4697	14435
克孜勒苏柯尔克孜自治州	Kizilsu Kirgiz Autonomous Prefecture	14241	13153	150	938
喀什地区	Kashgar [Kaxgar] Administrative Offices	123878	103723	13945	6210
和田地区	Hotan Administrative Offices	56824	52266	3584	974

13-4 按行业和登记注册类型分的建筑业总产值

Main Economic Indicators on Construction Enterprises by Registered Sector

单位：万元　　(2004 年)　　(10 000 yuan)

项　目	Item	建筑业总产值 Total Value of Construction	#在外省完成的产值 Output Value Realized in Other Provinces	#装修装饰产值 Output Value of Decoration
总　计	**Total**	**3439968**	**195406**	**95339**
#一、二级企业	First, Second Enterprises	2504863	189749	50768
国有及国有控股	State-ownership and State-holding	1791266	177380	18288
按登记注册类型分组	**Construction Enterprises**			
内资企业	Domestic Funede	3438507	195406	95228
国有企业	State-owned Enterprises	796261	141754	9085
集体企业	Collective-owned Enterprises	89189		933
股份合作企业	Share Cooperative	1925		
联营企业	Joint Ownership Enterprises	4553		553
国有与集体联营企业	Private and Partnership Enterprise			
有限责任公司	Limited Liability Corporations	1926167	52868	53080
国有独资公司	Sole State -funded Company	114003	2550	1070
其他有限责任公司	Other Limited Liability Companies	1812165	50318	52010
股份有限公司	Share-holding Corporations Ltd	133742		403
私营企业	Private Enterprises	486669	784	31175
私营有限责任公司	Private Limited Liability Companies	479184	716	31036
私营股份有限公司	Private Stock Limited Company	3245	68	68
其他企业	Other Enterprises			
港、澳、台商投资企业	Enterprises With Investment from Hong Kong, Macao and Taiwan	1461		111
#合资经营企业	Joint-Venture	1461		111
按国民经济行业分组	**Grouped by National Economic Sectors**			
房屋和土木工程建筑业	Buildings and Givil Engineering Construction	3021389	173392	50790
房屋工程建筑	House and Works Construction	1984645	37881	46843
土木工程建筑	Civil Works Construction	1036744	135511	3947
铁路、道路、隧道和桥梁	Railway, Road, Tunnel and Bridge	599230	100592	979
水利和港口建筑	Water Conservancy and Seaport Construction	166329	1865	1751
工矿工程建筑	Mine Project	198579	33054	316
架线和管道工程建筑	Cabling and Piping Project	48298		822
其他土木工程建筑	Other Civil Works	24308		79
建筑安装业	Construction and Installation	312715	21740	7043
建筑装饰业	Construction and Installation	47027	68	37361
其他建筑业	Other Construction Sector	58837	206	145
按隶属关系分组	**Classification on Subordination**			
中　央	Central Government	891405	154184	7589
地　方	Local	2548563	41222	87750
按企业资质等级分组	**Classification on Enterprise Qualification**			
#施工总承包	Undertaking Porject	3131314	192917	50220
特　级	Special	87088	3501	51
一　级	First Class	1436440	182705	14925
二　级	Second Class	918793	4871	13051
三　级	Third Class	688993	1840	22193
专业承包	Specialized Undertaking	285780	2489	44101
特　级	Special			
一　级	First Class	53765	2173	4186
二　级	Second Class	74804		17588
三　级	Third Class	153461	316	21838

13-4 续表 Continued

单位：万元 (10 000 yuan)

项 目	Item	按构成分的建筑业总产值 Total Output Value of Construction Sectors		
		建筑工程 Construction Works	安装工程 Installation Works	其 他 Others
总 计	**Total**	**2836668**	**396509**	**206791**
#一、二级企业	First, Second Enterprises	2022370	332934	149558
国有及国有控股	State-ownership and State-holding	1554754	190986	45526
按登记注册类型分组	**Construction Enterprises**			
内资企业	Domestic Funede	2836557	395159	206791
国有企业	State-owned Enterprises	660167	107563	28531
集体企业	Collective-owned Enterprises	44210	31408	13571
股份合作企业	Share Cooperative	1925		
联营企业	Joint Ownership Enterprises	603	3950	
国有与集体联营企业	Private and Partnership Enterprise			
有限责任公司	Limited Liability Corporations	1625213	211318	89636
国有独资公司	Sole State -funded Company	95415	17322	1266
其他有限责任公司	Other Limited Liability Companies	1529798	193996	88371
股份有限公司	Share-holding Corporations Ltd	124722	343	8677
私营企业	Private Enterprises	379716	40578	66375
私营有限责任公司	Private Limited Liability Companies	374412	40331	64441
私营股份有限公司	Private Stock Limited Company	1151	160	1934
其他企业	Other Enterprises			
港、澳、台商投资企业	Enterprises With Investment from Hong Kong, Macao and Taiwan	111	1350	
#合资经营企业	Joint-Venture	111	1350	
按国民经济行业分组	**Grouped by National Economic Sectors**			
房屋和土木工程建筑业	Buildings and Givil Engineering Construction	2659089	212908	149392
房屋工程建筑	House and Works Construction	1833761	68936	81948
土木工程建筑	Civil Works Construction	825328	143972	67444
铁路、道路、隧道和桥梁	Railway, Road, Tunnel and Bridge	572711		26519
水利和港口建筑	Water Conservancy and Seaport Construction	143219	5922	17188
工矿工程建筑	Mine Project	72949	116116	9514
架线和管道工程建筑	Cabling and Piping Project	24325	21516	2457
其他土木工程建筑	Other Civil Works	12124	418	11766
建筑安装业	Construction and Installation	105594	177435	29686
建筑装饰业	Construction and Installation	36401	5606	5020
其他建筑业	Other Construction Sector	35584	560	22693
按隶属关系分组	**Classification on Subordination**			
中 央	Central Government	769650	95219	26536
地 方	Local	2067018	301290	180255
按企业资质等级分组	**Classification on Enterprise Qualification**			
#施工总承包	Undertaking Porject	2691353	288373	151588
特 级	Special	87065	8	15
一 级	First Class	1212983	173096	50361
二 级	Second Class	766803	90704	61286
三 级	Third Class	624502	24565	39926
专业承包	Specialized Undertaking	145315	108137	32328
特 级	Special			
一 级	First Class	17810	35853	102
二 级	Second Class	24774	33282	16748
三 级	Third Class	99841	38992	14628

13-5 建筑业增加值

Added Value of Construction

单位：万元 (10 000 yuan)

年份 Year	地区 Region	按经济类型分 Grouped by Ownership				按隶属关系分 By Administrative Relationship		
		合计 Total	国有企业 State-owned Enterprise	集体企业 Collective Enterprises	其他企业 Other Enterprises	中央企业 Central Enterprises	地方企业 Local Enterprises	#兵团 XGPCC
	1985	60152	52022	8130				
	1986	64924	53839	11085				
	1987	73062	59585	13477				
	1988	83489	68497	14992				
	1989	87786	74446	13340				
	1990	109923	91983	17940				
	1991	142690	121173	21517				
	1992	179949	148759	31190				
	1993	206686	164305	42381				
	1994	239598	178031	58775	2792	75305	164293	54827
	1995	283882	207212	72598	4072	92259	191623	59128
	1996	303370	218532	78973	5865	96996	206374	64581
	1997	380806	284938	87437	8431	133287	247519	105256
	1998	296444	182903	89375	24166	84239	212205	54148
	1999	323714	198463	87477	37774	92459	213255	5668
	2000	587341	386475	84268	116598	274836	312505	73025
	2001	637472	340470	49298	247703	260784	376688	81382
	2002	621430	223509	37383	360538	211988	409442	103855
	2003	672531	143473	29333	499725	161523	511008	117505
	2004	693070	158801	18938	515331	157382	535688	120633
乌鲁木齐市	Urumqi City	264186	97265	6756	160165	67896	196291	28029
克拉玛依市	Karamay City	89862	19424	8279	62159		89862	
石河子市	Shi Hezi City	51389	22142		29247	44536	6853	51389
吐鲁番地区	Turpan Administrative Offices	5409	858		4551	2956	2453	
哈密地区	Hami [Kumul] Administrative Offices	13284	1285	424	11575	1621	11663	456
昌吉回族自治州	Changji Hui Autonomous Prefecture	49000	715	1601	46684	4018	44982	4018
伊犁哈萨克自治州	Ili Kazak Autonomous Prefecture	51815	7639	985	43192	17293	34523	17878
伊犁州直属县(市)	Counties (Cities) Direct Under Ili Prefecture	33424	5607	652	27164	13517	19906	14103
塔城地区	Tacheng [Tarbagatai] Administrative Offices	12198	2031	333	9834	3775	8423	3775
阿勒泰地区	Altay Administrative Offices	6194			6194		6194	
博尔塔拉蒙古自治州	Bortala Mongol Autonomous Prefecture	6318	2608	757	2953	2066	4252	2499
巴音郭楞蒙古自治州	Bayangol Mongol Autonomous Prefecture	84662	2699	70	81893	13117	71545	7883
阿克苏地区	Aksu Administrative Offices	32879	2511		30368		32879	5232
克孜勒苏柯尔克孜自治州	Kizilsu Kirgiz Autonomous Prefecture	4148	621	67	3461		4148	
喀什地区	Kashgar [Kaxgar] Administrative Offices	30499	776		29723	2623	27876	1992
和田地区	Hotan Administrative Offices	9619	258		9360	1258	8361	1258

13-6 建筑企业技术装备情况

Number and Power of Machinery and Equipment Owned by Construction Enterprises

年份 Year	地区 Region	自有机械设备总台数(台) Total number of Self-owned Machinery (set)	自有机械设备总功率(万千瓦) Total Power of Self-owned Machinery (10 000 kw)	#施工机械功率 Construction Machinery Power	自有机械设备净值(万元) Net Value of Self-owned Machinery and Equipment (10 000 yuan)	技术装备率(元/人) Ratio of Technical Equipment (yuan/person)	动力装备率(千瓦/人) Ratio of Power Equipment (kw/person)
	1983	20282	57	21	28121	1160	3
	1984	25048	62	26	28978	1160	5
	1985	30307	105	35	29308	1332	6
	1986	25843	67	40	31983	1535	4
	1987	29369	69	41	32528	1710	4
	1988	27520	98	45	35433	1832	4
	1989	32180	97	45	42183	2387	4
	1990	34806	91	47	46098	2511	5
	1991	39425	100	54	52417	2429	5
	1992	38478	116	63	63719	2798	5
	1993	28800	102	53	42001	2403	6
	1994	46805	121	61	93371	3721	5
	1995	55455	138	86	106383	4211	5
	1996	60567	129	84	127572	4478	5
	1997	64252	149	96	139617	4747	5
	1998	72606	148	108	164157	7415	7
	1999	73735	155	111	184559	9543	8
	2000	77975	182	128	224485	8582	7
	2001	85981	177	133	238142	9425	7
	2002	96116	207	155	442787	18996	9
	2003	100913	207	143	395865	11866	6
	2004	98541	239		358397	11389	8
乌鲁木齐市	Urumqi City	24749	68		133991	12355	6
克拉玛依市	Karamay City	6584	32		49700	17622	11
石河子市	Shi Hezi City	4647	10		10636	2998	3
吐鲁番地区	Turpan Administrative Offices	2010	6		10702	28538	15
哈密地区	Hami [Kumul] Administrative Offices	3152	5		7818	14875	10
昌吉回族自治州	Changji Hui Autonomous Prefecture	11016	19		29247	11609	8
伊犁哈萨克自治州	Ili Kazak Autonomous Prefecture	16685	25		25486	7846	8
伊犁州直属县(市)	Counties (Cities) Direct Under Ili Prefecture	10236	10		13375	6932	5
塔城地区	Tacheng [Tarbagatai] Administrative Offices	3457	11		4923	5569	12
阿勒泰地区	Altay Administrative Offices	2992	4		7188	16531	10
博尔塔拉蒙古自治州	Bortala Mongol Autonomous Prefecture	2281	3		6221	20618	11
巴音郭楞蒙古自治州	Bayangol Mongol Autonomous Prefecture	10223	45		42430	12857	13
阿克苏地区	Aksu Administrative Offices	5515	14		23386	16641	10
克孜勒苏柯尔克孜自治州	Kizilsu Kirgiz Autonomous Prefecture	634	1		1642	5601	2
喀什地区	Kashgar [Kaxgar] Administrative Offices	7630	8		13129	7542	4
和田地区	Hotan Administrative Offices	3415	4		4011	7346	7

13-7 按登记注册类型分的建筑企业技术装备情况

Technical Equipment of Construction Enterprises by Registration

(2004 年)

项目	Item	自有机械设备年末总台数(台) Year-end Total of Self-owned Machinery and Equipment (set)	自有机械设备年末总功率(千瓦) End-year Total Power of Self-Owned Machinery and Equipment (kw)	自有机械设备年末净值(万元) End-year Net Value of Self-owned Machinery and Equipment (10 000 yuan)
总计	**Total**	**98541**	**2388382**	**358397**
#一、二级企业	First, Second Enterprises	53632	1585552	246158
国有及国有控股	State-ownership and State-holding	37953	1133557	182076
按登记注册类型分组	**Construction Enterprises**			
内资企业	Domestic Funede	98472	2385372	358258
国有企业	State-owned Enterprises	17779	503293	92776
集体企业	Collective-owned Enterprises	2925	52205	11875
股份合作企业	Share Cooperative			
联营企业	Joint Ownership Enterprises	163	3819	2071
国有与集体联营企业	Private and Partnership Enterprise			
有限责任公司	Limited Liability Corporations	53497	1404908	185823
国有独资公司	Sole State -funded Company	2391	107974	14660
其他有限责任公司	Other Limited Liability Companies	51106	1296934	171163
股份有限公司	Share-holding Corporations Ltd	3448	96281	6300
私营企业	Private Enterprises	20660	324866	59413
#私营有限责任公司	Private Limited Liability Companies	20069	321111	58477
私营股份有限公司	Private Stock Limited Company	60	3192	325
其他企业	Other Enterprises			
港、澳、台商投资企业	Enterprises With Investment from Hong Kong, Macao and Taiwan	69	3010	139
#合资经营企业	Joint-Venture	69	3010	139
按国民经济行业分组	**Grouped by National Economic Sectors**			
房屋和土木工程建筑业	Buildings and Givil Engineering Construction	85042	2057336	312767

13-7 续表 Continued

项 目	Item	自有机械设备年末总台数（台）Year-end Total of Self-owned Machinery and Equipment (set)	自有机械设备年末总功率（千瓦）End-year Total Power of Self-Owned Machinery and Equipment (kw)	自有机械设备年末净值（万元）End-year Net Value of Self-owned Machinery and Equipment (10 000 yuan)
房屋工程建筑	House and Works Construction	67522	1176466	157444
土木工程建筑	Civil Works Construction	17520	880870	155324
铁路、道路、隧道和桥梁	Railway, Road, Tunnel and Bridge	6989	509550	93729
水利和港口建筑	Water Conservancy and Seaport Construction	5807	135065	19208
工矿工程建筑	Mine Project	3238	188172	34769
架线和管道工程建筑	Cabling and Piping Project	819	31838	6071
其他土木工程建筑	Other Civil Works	667	16245	1547
建筑安装业	Construction and Installation	9995	252257	36557
建筑装饰业	Construction and Installation	2378	34683	3932
其他建筑业	Other Construction Sector	1126	44106	5141
按隶属关系分组	**Classification on Subordination**			
中 央	Central Government	17495	501282	74276
地 方	Local	81046	1887100	284121
按企业资质等级分组	**Classification on Enterprise Qualification**			
#施工总承包	Undertaking Porject	87766	2087036	314560
特 级	Special	1407	60840	5534
一 级	First Class	23271	645584	122502
二 级	Second Class	26334	815786	107410
三 级	Third Class	36754	564826	79115
专业承包	Specialized Undertaking	10775	301346	43837
特 级	Special			
一 级	First Class	1567	77137	5914
二 级	Second Class	2460	47045	10333
三 级	Third Class	6590	176129	27441

13-8 建筑企业工程施工情况

Condition of Building Works by Construction Enterprise

单位：万平方米　　　　(2004 年)　　　　(10 000 sq.m)

项 目	Item	房屋建筑施工面积 FloorSpace of Buildings Constructing	#本年新开工面积 Space of New-opened Works	实行投标承包面积 Space of Bidding and Contracting	#本 年 新开工 面 积 New-opened Work for This Year	房屋建筑竣工面积 FloorSpace of Buildings Completed
总 计	**Total**	**2812.30**	**1791.50**	**2426.79**	**1613.19**	**1483.35**
#一、二级企业	First, Second Enterprises	1775.95	1063.65	1544.40	982.19	858.64
国有及国有控股	State-ownership and State-holding	1330.49	767.63	1150.05	661.80	627.02
按登记注册类型分组	**Construction Enterprises**					
内资企业	Domestic Funede	2812.30	1791.50	2426.79	1613.19	1483.35
国有企业	State-owned Enterprises	387.84	234.06	315.42	195.66	162.53
集体企业	Collective-owned Enterprises	18.86	15.27	16.80	13.97	11.08
股份合作企业	Share Cooperative	3.02	2.86			1.81
联营企业	Joint Ownership Enterprises					
国有与集体联营企业	Private and Partnership Enterprise					
有限责任公司	Limited Liability Corporations	1967.35	1216.17	1690.85	1114.29	1064.94
国有独资公司	Sole State -funded Company	47.21	33.17	44.02	32.74	25.43
其他有限责任公司	Other Limited Liability Companies	1920.14	1183.00	1646.83	1081.55	1039.51
股份有限公司	Share-holding Corporations Ltd	100.97	56.81	93.31	55.81	40.42
私营企业	Private Enterprises	334.27	266.33	310.41	233.47	202.57
#私营有限责任公司	Private Limited Liability Companies	326.20	258.77	302.71	226.00	198.03
私营股份有限公司	Private Stock Limited Company	0.09	0.09	0.09		0.09
其他企业	Other Enterprises					
按国民经济行业分组	**Grouped by National Economic Sectors**					
房屋和土木工程建筑业	Buildings and Givil Engineering Construction	2674.51	1674.70	2316.64	1519.48	1396.40
房屋工程建筑	House and Works Construction	2570.17	1587.76	2235.18	1443.60	1345.44
土木工程建筑	Civil Works Construction	104.34	86.93	81.46	75.89	50.96
铁路、道路、隧道和桥梁	Railway, Road, Tunnel and Bridge	27.15	22.83	19.77	17.87	15.03
水利和港口建筑	Water Conservancy and Seaport Construction	50.11	38.89	42.02	38.82	25.03
工矿工程建筑	Mine Project	25.81	24.38	18.80	18.80	9.68
架线和管道工程建筑	Cabling and Piping Project	0.70	0.70	0.40	0.40	0.70
其他土木工程建筑	Other Civil Works	0.57	0.14	0.46		0.53
建筑安装业	Construction and Installation	92.97	74.80	71.14	54.70	51.78
其他建筑业	Other Construction Sector	44.82	42.01	39.01	39.01	35.17
按隶属关系分组	**Classification on Subordination**					
中 央	Central Government	550.90	360.23	433.79	307.32	305.33
地 方	Local	2261.40	1431.28	1993.00	1305.87	1178.02
按企业资质等级分组	**Classification on Enterprise Qualification**					
#施工总承包	Undertaking Porject	2757.04	1746.20	2388.03	1589.10	1455.58
特 级	Special	177.54	73.69	177.54	73.69	72.39
一 级	First Class	944.92	521.73	844.14	492.80	417.43
二 级	Second Class	808.92	524.15	682.53	480.45	434.96
三 级	Third Class	825.66	626.64	683.82	542.15	530.80
专业承包	Specialized Undertaking	55.26	45.30	38.75	24.09	27.77
特 级	Special					
一 级	First Class	0.36	0.36	0.36	0.36	0.36
二 级	Second Class	21.75	17.41	17.37	8.57	5.89
三 级	Third Class	29.34	26.46	17.49	14.17	17.71

13-9 建筑企业竣工房屋建筑面积

Floor Space of Completed Houses by Construction Enterprise

单位：万平方米 (10 000 sq.m)

时期(年份)	Period (Year)	合计 Total	厂房 Workshop	住宅 Flat	办公用房 House for Office
"五五"时期	**Fifth Five-Year Plan Period**	**527.31**	**58.53**	**274.62**	**39.81**
"六五"时期	**Sixth Five-Year Plan Period**	**1297.63**	**271.01**	**127.61**	**184.40**
"七五"时期	**Seventh Five-Year Plan Period**	**2120.30**	**324.20**	**925.20**	**193.90**
"八五"时期	**Eighth Five-Year Plan Period**	**2914.41**	**321.35**	**1448.92**	**285.54**
"九五"时期	**Ninth Five-Year Plan Period**	**4576.72**	**262.63**	**2891.37**	**405.71**
	1996	645.88	54.90	340.51	72.47
	1997	747.24	61.29	407.93	75.78
	1998	879.67	48.75	564.30	78.30
	1999	1042.51	42.07	727.14	69.57
	2000	1261.42	55.62	851.49	109.59
"十五"时期	**Tenth Five-Year Plan Period**				
	2001	1467.54	60.86	1012.33	110.98
	2002	1469.60	60.98	945.33	103.85
	2003	1450.81	70.48	740.17	159.71
	2004	1483.35	97.37	833.23	136.68

时期(年份)	Period (Year)	商业、居民服务业用房 House for Commerce and Residents' Service	文化教育业用房 House for Culture and Education	医疗用房 House for Medical Care	科研用房 House for Scientific research	其他 Other
"五五"时期	**Fifth Five-Year Plan Period**	**22.94**	**56.85**	**11.07**	**4.80**	**58.69**
"六五"时期	**Sixth Five-Year Plan Period**	**106.09**	**263.23**	**51.22**	**22.14**	**271.93**
"七五"时期	**Seventh Five-Year Plan Period**	**140.40**	**258.10**	**51.20**	**24.80**	**202.50**
"八五"时期	**Eighth Five-Year Plan Period**	**261.87**	**246.55**	**60.55**	**12.28**	**277.35**
"九五"时期	**Ninth Five-Year Plan Period**	**351.83**	**287.12**	**63.43**	**13.31**	**301.32**
	1996	59.87	39.44	14.07	1.06	63.56
	1997	61.77	57.36	8.76	4.51	69.84
	1998	62.95	52.69	14.06	1.71	56.89
	1999	80.43	57.77	9.93	3.00	52.60
	2000	86.81	79.86	16.61	3.03	58.42
"十五"时期	**Tenth Five-Year Plan Period**					
	2001	121.21	76.50	13.29	1.63	70.74
	2002	160.63	98.16	21.29	2.73	76.63
	2003	217.96	132.84	31.22	3.10	95.33
	2004	192.48	113.95	31.11	3.39	75.14

13-10 建筑企业总收入

Total Income of Construction Enterprises

单位：万元 (10 000 yuan)

年份 Year	地区 Region	企业总收入 Total Income of Enterprises	工程结算收入 Revenue of Project Settlement Accounts	#工程结算成本 Costs of Project Settlement Accounts	#工程结算利润 Profits of Project Settlement Accounts	其他业务收入 Other Revenue from Business	#其他业务利润 Other Profit from Business
	1993	642453	558473	493525	49542	83979	11020
	1994	813369	714469	627830	66444	98900	9332
	1995	898810	821713	713940	82858	77097	9445
	1996	983170	904800	799183	78801	78370	8765
	1997	1210813	1081666	950091	98216	129147	17368
	1998	1454758	1346748	1193276	112310	108010	19146
	1999	1595986	1500818	1320898	130925	95167	14882
	2000	2659696	2514011	2252154	197243	145686	30012
	2001	2961754	2807549	2521902	211441	154205	34532
	2002	3360613	3199880	2854350	254428	160733	30853
	2003	3221521	3090768	2716009	254015	130753	21692
	2004	3395793	3276421	2900842	253783	119372	21601
乌鲁木齐市	Urumqi City	1421570	1365594	1205694	108468	55976	9852
克拉玛依市	Karamay City	433339	415190	366814	36789	18149	1627
石河子市	Shihezi City	223396	214465	195080	13034	8931	2607
吐鲁番地区	Turpan Administrative Offices	35266	34997	35655	-1515	269	83
哈密地区	Hami [Kumul] Administrative Offices	39532	39296	34556	3333	236	51
昌吉回族自治州	Changji Hui Autonomous Prefecture	180772	177596	150164	19074	3176	499
伊犁哈萨克自治州	Ili Kazak Autonomous Prefecture	264929	249050	224476	15772	15879	3218
伊犁州直属县(市)	Counties (Cities) Direct Under Ili Prefecture	180905	171045	154560	10152	9860	2437
塔城地区	Tacheng [Tarbagatai] Administrative Offices	59351	54478	48704	4238	4873	734
阿勒泰地区	Altay Administrative Offices	24674	23528	21212	1382	1146	47
博尔塔拉蒙古自治州	Bortala Mongol Autonomous Prefecture	30107	29283	26651	1568	824	182
巴音郭楞蒙古自治州	Bayangol Mongol Autonomous Prefecture	431162	423363	371452	32720	7799	1229
阿克苏地区	Aksu Administrative Offices	146210	144320	126242	13124	1890	670
克孜勒苏柯尔克孜自治州	Kizilsu Kirgiz Autonomous Prefecture	15678	15618	14168	984	60	32
喀什地区	Kashgar [Kaxgar] Administrative Offices	121336	119103	105395	8224	2233	605
和田地区	Hotan Administrative Offices	52495	48545	44495	2208	3950	946

13-11 建筑企业利税总额

Total Pre-tax Profits of Constrution Enterprises

单位：万元 (10 000 yuan)

年 份 Year	地 区 Region	利税总额合计 Total Pre-tax Profits	利润总额 Total Profits	工程结算税金及附加 Taxes and Extra Charges on Project Settlement Accounts	管理费用中的税金 Taxes in Management Expenses	产值利税率 (%) Ratio of Pretax Profits to Output Value (%)	资金利税率 (%) Ratio of Pretax Profits to Assets (%)
	1994	28199	5535	20195	2469	3.81	4.11
	1995	30156	2974	24916	2266	3.44	3.46
	1996	20752	-8625	26816	2561	1.97	-0.93
	1997	31970	-4347	33360	2957	2.80	2.51
	1998	37596	-5875	41162	2309	2.62	2.41
	1999	64777	13359	48995	2423	4.13	3.72
	2000	19274	-48005	64614	2665	0.82	0.63
	2001	28688	-47485	74206	1967	1.05	0.84
	2002	84833	-11089	92484	3438	2.70	2.18
	2003	169594	67146	96888	5560	5.26	5.51
	2004	174255	65037	102990	6228	5.07	5.65
乌鲁木齐市	Urumqi City	62023	17080	43362	1580	4.58	4.16
克拉玛依市	Karamay City	29131	15791	11467	1872	7.20	7.14
石河子市	Shihezi City	9489	3179	6051	260	4.05	4.82
吐鲁番地区	Turpan Administrative Offices	-4501	-5278	753	24	-7.31	-13.35
哈密地区	Hami [Kumul] Administrative Offices	1791	477	1293	21	3.94	4.33
昌吉回族自治州	Changji Hui Autonomous Prefecture	13644	7200	6175	269	6.59	7.31
伊犁哈萨克自治州	Ili Kazak Autonomous Prefecture	12871	4757	7877	237	4.56	7.46
伊犁州直属县(市)	Counties (Cities) Direct Under Ili Prefecture	8956	3360	5459	136	4.83	8.87
塔城地区	Tacheng [Tarbagatai] Administrative Offices	3002	1405	1507	90	4.57	5.82
阿勒泰地区	Altay Administrative Offices	913	-8	911	11	2.91	4.54
博尔塔拉蒙古自治州	Bortala Mongol Autonomous Prefecture	1418	391	1009	18	4.59	6.05
巴音郭楞蒙古自治州	Bayangol Mongol Autonomous Prefecture	28690	14638	12950	1103	6.00	10.95
阿克苏地区	Aksu Administrative Offices	9636	4742	4765	130	6.54	7.84
克孜勒苏柯尔克孜自治州	Kizilsu Kirgiz Autonomous Prefecture	606	78	463	66	4.26	4.06
喀什地区	Kashgar [Kaxgar] Administrative Offices	6734	1527	5046	161	5.44	6.42
和田地区	Hotan Administrative Offices	2723	455	1781	488	4.79	9.78

13-12 建筑企业负债及所有者权益

Liability of Construction Enterprises and Owner's Right and Interest

单位：万元 (10 000 yuan)

年份 Year	地区 Region	负债合计 Total Liabilities	#流动负债 Liquid Liabilities	#长期负债 Long-term Liabilities	所有者权益 Owner's Right And Interest
	1993	505834	355021	150813	148728
	1994	540403	467895	72508	192618
	1995	699997	614110	84378	239208
	1996	815330	714429	98342	324051
	1997	1018007	901138	115032	350659
	1998	1175839	1044115	131724	385913
	1999	1325825	1205880	119945	415026
	2000	2068439	1941268	127171	1187982
	2001	2300621	2168441	132181	1439690
	2002	2717728	2585374	132354	1526859
	2003	2327382	2206412	120970	1047948
	2004	2631252	2517755	105621	1174864
乌鲁木齐市	Urumqi City	1366728	1315837	43711	462373
克拉玛依市	Karamay City	370800	348625	22175	134657
石河子市	Shihezi City	168299	163286	4684	53350
吐鲁番地区	Turpan Administrative Offices	34491	34135	356	12144
哈密地区	Hami [Kumul] Administrative Offices	28281	27776	190	25678
昌吉回族自治州	Changji Hui Autonomous Prefecture	144733	137599	7134	100122
伊犁哈萨克自治州	Ili Kazak Autonomous Prefecture	125081	122847	2234	77396
伊犁州直属县(市)	Counties (Cities) Direct Under Ili Prefecture	75254	74454	801	44150
塔城地区	Tacheng [Tarbagatai] Administrative Offices	40477	39222	1254	18013
阿勒泰地区	Altay Administrative Offices	9350	9171	179	15233
博尔塔拉蒙古自治州	Bortala Mongol Autonomous Prefecture	15244	12766	2478	12198
巴音郭楞蒙古自治州	Bayangol Mongol Autonomous Prefecture	184247	172742	11453	132944
阿克苏地区	Aksu Administrative Offices	79988	74990	4998	73604
克孜勒苏柯尔克孜自治州	Kizilsu Kirgiz Autonomous Prefecture	8665	8592	73	10144
喀什地区	Kashgar [Kaxgar] Administrative Offices	85877	81178	4698	61275
和田地区	Hotan Administrative Offices	18819	17381	1438	18979

13-13 建筑企业资产及资本金

Assets and Capital Principal of Construction Enterprise

单位：万元 (10 000 yuan)

年份 Year	地区 Region	资产合计 Total of Asset	#流动资产 Circulating Asset	固定资产原值 Original Value of Fixed Asset	固定资产净值 Net Value of Fixed Asset	专项工程 Special Works	无形及递延资产 Intangible Asset and deferred Asset	资本金合计 Total of Principal Value	#国家资本金 National Principal
1994		745843	511737	261305	193287	7425	4165	194259	109647
1995		939205	647608	323540	225084	14297	3132	221212	110987
1996		1139380	727336	457631	325229	17072	3837	264390	125332
1997		1368666	896643	536120	377251	18374	5154	309044	219732
1998		1561752	1067004	586000	402995	25251	9103	315532	214300
1999		1740851	1186433	643419	443518	30923	10762	346605	212237
2000		3256421	1855185	1762866	1106384	28496	35063	892851	208214
2001		3740312	2187385	1598991	1048023	32325	138976	1055531	227457
2002		4244587	2527414	1810695	1179599		184827	1327186	227601
2003		3375330	2292828	1000516	675947	17231	165349	835618	219826
2004		3810825	2632242	1094893	722019		163384	929293	225884
	乌鲁木齐市 Urumqi City	1832843	1314505	483293	300838		82902	399995	117136
	克拉玛依市 Karamay City	505457	365357	131513	83199		4844	93725	24599
	石河子市 Shihezi City	222224	171027	47923	31427		1174	46913	29646
	吐鲁番地区 Turpan Administrative Offices	46635	27405	28601	17459		894	25549	
	哈密地区 Hami [Kumul] Administrative Offices	54118	29540	24695	18037		1269	23326	4750
	昌吉回族自治州 Changji Hui Autonomous Prefecture	244855	154576	59742	43067		27334	69638	1982
	伊犁哈萨克自治州 Ili Kazak Autonomous Prefecture	202477	139180	74318	51836		2705	57908	13491
	伊犁州直属县(市) Counties (Cities) Direct Under Ili Prefecture	119405	80663	43478	30650		1947	33614	9778
	塔城地区 Tacheng [Tarbagatai] Administrative Offices	58489	45361	18399	11630		15	12747	3713
	阿勒泰地区 Altay Administrative Offices	24583	13156	12441	9556		743	11547	
	博尔塔拉蒙古自治州 Bortala Mongol Autonomous Prefecture	27442	16247	11886	8953		896	11080	1794
	巴音郭楞蒙古自治州 Bayangol Mongol Autonomous Prefecture	317423	207267	113366	82474		13680	76850	20218
	阿克苏地区 Aksu Administrative Offices	153592	97398	62501	42424		5483	59753	5478
	克孜勒苏柯尔克孜自治州 Kizilsu Kirgiz Autonomous Prefecture	18809	11297	5672	4282		1971	8949	676
	喀什地区 Kashgar [Kaxgar] Administrative Offices	147152	80678	36745	27486		16804	39474	5481
	和田地区 Hotan Administrative Offices	37798	17765	14638	10537		3428	16133	633

13-14 建筑企业劳动生产率
Labor Productivity of Construction Enterprises

单位：元/人 (yuan/person)

年份 Year	地区 Region	按建筑业总产值计算的劳动生产率 Overall Labor Productivity in Terms of Total Output Value	#国有经济 State-owned Units	#集体经济 Collective-owned Units	按建筑业增加值计算的劳动生产率 Overall Labor Productivity in Terms of Added-Value	#国有经济 State-owned Units	#集体经济 Collective-owned Units
	1993	25871	27064	23484	6607	7499	4724
	1994	29871	32616	23023	9499	10546	7186
	1995	34668	38483	26617	11238	12505	8673
	1996	32606	36557	25291	10648	12286	7719
	1997	38808	40629	33658	12948	13973	10215
	1998	47698	51465	40819	9855	10044	9627
	1999	55593	61196	44235	11466	11766	10584
	2000	74994	87999	48767	25208	32781	14138
	2001	84666	94344	62458	19678	23041	12215
	2002	86302	108857	66231	17100	19149	14537
	2003	94165	98095	86190	19659	19020	17169
	2004	107150	112145	107185	21588	22365	22759
乌鲁木齐市	Urumqi City	119299	135724	84858	23290	26135	20737
克拉玛依市	Karamay City	143459	121269	150300	31862	41638	31625
石河子市	Shihezi City	64733	69522		14191	14032	
吐鲁番地区	Turpan Administrative Offices	164131	61732		14423	20922	
哈密地区	Hami [Kumul] Administrative Offices	77222	122184	122704	22596	12123	21607
昌吉回族自治州	Changji Hui Autonomous Prefecture	82212	90097	123400	19450	11344	19716
伊犁哈萨克自治州	Ili Kazak Autonomous Prefecture	86972	72313	79611	15952	11013	11769
伊犁州直属县(市)	Counties (Cities) Direct Under Ili Prefecture	96063	64436	93536	17323	10465	11030
塔城地区	Tacheng [Tarbagatai] Administrative Offices	74377	99058	46154	13799	12872	13545
阿勒泰地区	Altay Administrative Offices	72234			14245		
博尔塔拉蒙古自治州	Bortala Mongol Autonomous Prefecture	102515	131315	50519	20942	31275	14009
巴音郭楞蒙古自治州	Bayangol Mongol Autonomous Prefecture	144761	140054	57951	25643	27461	16951
阿克苏地区	Aksu Administrative Offices	104811	130416		23396	16673	
克孜勒苏柯尔克孜自治州	Kizilsu Kirgiz Autonomous Prefecture	48588	51548	73316	14152	15518	35000
喀什地区	Kashgar [Kaxgar] Administrative Offices	71161	82132		17520	24320	
和田地区	Hotan Administrative Offices	104072	171217		17617	9825	

13-15 建筑企业亏损额及从业人数

Condition of Building Works by Construction Enterprise

(2004 年)

项　目	Item	企业数（个）Number of Enterprises (unit)	#亏损企业个数 Number of loss-making enterprises	亏损额（万元）Amount of Total loss (10 000 yuan)	计算劳动生产率的平均人数（人）Average number of staff for calculation of Labour Productivity (person)	期末从业人数（人）Employees at year-end (person)	#工程技术人员 Engineers and technicians
总　计	**Total**	**932**	**383**	**27922**	**321041**	**332201**	**40869**
#一、二级企业	First, Second Enterprises	301	115	19824	216070	222228	25153
国有及国有控股	State-ownership and State-holding	213	87	18380	150306	156465	19159
按登记注册类型分组	**Construction Enterprises**						
内资企业	Domestic Funede	928	380	27894	320862	332022	40838
国有企业	State-owned Enterprises	105	40	7458	71003	72132	8903
集体企业	Collective-owned Enterprises	51	22	1451	8321	8370	1030
股份合作企业	Share Cooperative	2			380	480	60
联营企业	Joint Ownership Enterprises	3	2	7	466	466	19
国有与集体联营企业	Private and Partnership Enterprise						
有限责任公司	Limited Liability Corporations	347	109	14495	176691	183814	21544
国有独资公司	Sole State -funded Company	14	8	2573	6468	7031	1048
其他有限责任公司	Other Limited Liability Companies	333	101	11922	170223	176783	20496
股份有限公司	Share-holding Corporations Ltd	10	2	47	14968	16271	1304
私营企业	Private Enterprises	410	205	4436	49033	50489	7978
#私营有限责任公司	Private Limited Liability Companies	396	200	4113	47963	49412	7728
私营股份有限公司	Private Stock Limited Company	7	2	255	394	401	99
其他企业	Other Enterprises						
港、澳、台商投资企业	Enterprises With Investment from Hong Kong, Macao and Taiwan	4	3	28	179	179	31
#合资经营企业	Joint-Venture	4	3	28	179	179	31
按国民经济行业分组	**Grouped by National Economic Sectors**						
房屋和土木工程建筑业	Buildings and Givil Engineering Construction	527	181	22969	277336	288504	34152

13-15 续表 Continued

项 目	Item	企业数（个） Number of Enterprises (unit)	#亏损企业个数 Number of loss-making enterprises	亏损额（万元） Amount of Total loss (10 000 yuan)	计算劳动生产率的平均人数（人） Average number of staff for calculation of Labour Productivity (person)	期末从业人数（人） Employees at year-end (person)	#工程技术人员 Engineers and technicians
房屋工程建筑	House and Works Construction	326	106	7029	209089	218423	23519
土木工程建筑	Civil Works Construction	201	75	15940	68247	70081	10633
铁路、道路、隧道和桥梁	Railway, Road, Tunnel and Bridge	76	29	6354	35471	36410	5372
水利和港口建筑	Water Conservancy and Seaport Construction	37	8	978	15176	15498	2467
工矿工程建筑	Mine Project	16	8	7238	10238	10529	1319
架线和管道工程建筑	Cabling and Piping Project	29	9	756	4110	4138	973
其他土木工程建筑	Other Civil Works	43	21	613	3252	3506	502
建筑安装业	Construction and Installation	170	82	2905	30228	32109	5092
建筑装饰业	Construction and Installation	169	93	1154	5721	6052	1087
其他建筑业	Other Construction Sector	66	27	894	7756	5536	538
按隶属关系分组	**Classification on Subordination**						
中 央	Central Government	80	25	9476	81864	83844	8994
地 方	Local	852	358	18446	239177	248357	31875
按企业资质等级分组	**Classification on Enterprise Qualification**						
#施工总承包	Undertaking Porject	442	135	21001	288399	300214	34960
特 级	Special	1			2714	2799	804
一 级	First Class	42	11	10663	112918	116729	12189
二 级	Second Class	110	29	6233	87618	91718	10631
三 级	Third Class	289	95	4106	85149	88968	11336
专业承包	Specialized Undertaking	406	208	6430	26279	27757	5636
特 级	Special						
一 级	First Class	12	6	156	3343	3343	611
二 级	Second Class	65	35	2339	6146	6524	1475
三 级	Third Class	326	164	3929	16424	17524	3504

主要统计指标解释

建筑业统计单位 指从事房屋、构筑物建造和设备安装活动的法人企业。建筑业法人企业应同时具备的条件是：①依法成立，有自己的名称、组织机构和场所，能够承担民事责任；②独立拥有和使用资产，承担负债，有权与其他单位签订合同；③独立核算盈亏，能够编制资产负债表。

建筑业总产值(即自行完成施工产值) 是以货币表现的建筑安装企业在一定时期内生产的建筑业产品的总和。建筑业总产值包括：

(1)建筑工程产值：指列入建筑工程预算内的各种工程价值。

(2)设备安装工程产值：指设备安装工程价值，不包括被安装设备本身价值。

(3)房屋、构筑物修理产值：指房屋、构筑物修理所完成的价值，但不包括被修理房屋、构筑物本身的价值和生产设备的修理价值。

(4)非标准设备制造产值：指加工制造没有定型的、非标准的生产设备的加工费和原材料价值，以及附属加工厂为本企业承建工程制作的非标准设备的价值。

建筑业增加值 指建筑业企业在报告期内以货币表现的建筑业生产经营活动的最终成果。目前建筑业增加值采用分配法(收入法)计算，即从收入的角度出发，根据生产要素在生产过程中应得的收入份额计算。具体计算公式为：

建筑业增加值＝本年提取的固定资产折旧+主营业务应付工资+主营业务应付福利费+管理费用中的劳动待业保险费、税金+工程结算税金及附加+营业利润

房屋建筑施工面积 指在报告期内施工的全部房屋建筑面积，包括本期新开工的房屋面积、上期施工跨入本期继续施工的房屋面积、上期停缓建在本期恢复施工的房屋面积、本期竣工的房屋面积及本期施工后又停缓建的房屋面积。

房屋建筑竣工面积 指在报告期内房屋建筑按照设计要求全部完工，达到了住人和使用条件，经验收鉴定合格，正式移交使用单位的房屋建筑面积。

自有机械设备年末总台数 指归本企业所有，属于本企业固定资产的生产性机械设备年末总台数。包括施工机械、生产设备、运输设备以及其他设备。

自有机械设备年末总功率 指本企业自有施工机械、生产设备、运输设备以及其他设备等列为在册固定资产的生产性机械设备年末总功率，按设定能力或查定能力计算。包括机械本身的动力和为该机械服务的单独动力设备，如电动机等。计算单位用千瓦，动力换算可按1马力＝0.735千瓦折合成千瓦数。电焊机、变压器、锅炉不计算动力。

工程结算收入 指企业承包工程实现的工程价款结算收入，以及向发包单位收取的除工程价款以外的按规定列作营业收入的各种款项，如临时设施费、劳动保险费、施工机械调迁费等以及向发包单位收取的各种索赔款。

工程结算利润 指已结算工程实现的利润，如亏损以“－”号表示。计算公式为：

工程结算利润＝工程结算收入－工程结算成本－工程结算税金及附加

企业总收入 指与企业生产经营直接有关的各项收入，包括工程结算收入和其他业务收入。计算公式为：

企业总收入＝工程结算收入＋其他业务收入

Explanatory Notes on Main Statistical Indicators

Statistical Unit in Construction refers to corporate enterprise engaged in the construction of buildings and structures and in the installation of equipment.A corporate construction enterprise should meet the following 3 requirements:①being set up in line with relevant legal basis,having its full name,organization and location,and capable of taking civil liabilities;②independently possessing and using its assets and assuming its liabilities,and entitled to sign contracts with other institutions;and ③ making independent accounts of its profits and losses,and capable of compiling its own balance sheet.

Gross Output Value of Construction (Output Value of Projects Under Construction) refers to total of construction products, expressed in money terms, completed by construction and installation enterprises during a given period of time. It includes:

(1) Output value of construction projects, that is the value of projects covered by the project budgets;

(2) Output value of installation projects, that is the value of the installation of equipment, (excluding the value of the equipment to be installed);

(3) Output value of repair of buildings and structures, that is the value created through the repairs of buildings or structures,but does not include the value of buildings or structures being repaired and the value of the repair of production equipment;

(4) Output value of manufactured non-standard equipment, that is the value of non-standard production equipment (including raw materials and manufacturing cost) made for the construction project, and the equipment manufactured by subsidiary workshops.

Value-added of Construction refers to the final result of the activities of production and management of construction in monetary terms in the reference period. At present, the value-added of construction is calculated with the income approach. In other words, it is the sum of income of various production factors in the production process. The formula is as follows:

Value-added of construction=depreciation of fixed assets in the year+wages payable+welfare expenses payable+insurance premium and tax for waiting for employment in the administrative expenses +taxes and surcharges on project settlement+profit gained from project settlement.

Floor Space of Buildings Under Construction refers to floor space of buildings under construction during the reference period, including newly started buildings,buildings started earlier and Continued during the reference period,and buildings suspended earlier but restarted during the reference period, buildings completed during the reference period, and buildings under construction and then suspended during the reference period.

Floor Space of Buildings Completed refers to the floor space of buildings that are completed in the reference period in accordance with the requirements of the design, up to the standard for putting them into use, and have been checked and accepted by concerned departments as qualified ones.

Total Number of Machinery and Equipment Owned by the End of Year refers to the number of machines and equipment owned by the enterprises, and listed as the fixed assets of the enterprises by the end of the year, including machinery and equipment for construction, production and transportation.

Total Power of Machinery and Equipment Owned by the End of Year refers to the total power of machinery and equipment owned by the enterprises,and listed as the fixed assets of the enterprises by the end of the year, including machinery and equipment for construction,production and transportation.The power of the machinery is calculated on basis of the designed or verified capaCity,covering the power of the machinery/equipment and the separate power equipment serving the machinery/equipment (such as electric motors), but excluding welders, transformers and boilers.The unit used for the calculation of power is kilowatt, with horsepower converted to kilowatt by 1 horsepower=0.735 kilowatt.

Income from Settlement of Projects refers to the income received by the construction enterprise from the contracted project through settlement procedures, and other charges to the contractoree as operational costs in addition to the value of the project, such as temporary facility fee,labour insurance premium,moving cost of construction equipment,as well as various types of claims to the contractee.

Profit from Settlement of Projects refers to profit realized through settled projects. It is calculated with the following formula:

Profit from Settlement of Projects=Income from Settlement of Projects−Settled Cost−Settled Taxes and Other Cost

Total Revenue of Enterprises refers to the sum of income from production and operation of enterprises, including income from settlement of projects and other operational income, namely:

Total Revenue of Enterprises=Income from Settlement of Projects+Other Operational Income

第十四篇

CHAPTER 14

运输和邮电

TRANSPORTATION POSTAL AND TELECOMMUNICATIONS SERVICES

14-1 交通运输业基本情况

Basic Conditions of Transportation

指　标	Item	1995	2000	2004
运输线路长度(公里)	**Length of Transportation Routes (km)**	**101665**	**190070**	**201591**
国家铁路营业里程	Railways in Operation	1578	2544	2999
电气化里程	Electrified Railways			
公　路	Highways	30298	80875	86824
民　航	Total Civil Aviation Routes	69789	152941	111768
客运量总计(万人)	**Total Passenger Traffic (10 000 persons)**	**17533**	**23191**	**29782**
铁　路	Railways	672	1147	1023
公　路	Highways	16739	21877	28473
民用航空	Civil Aviation	122	167	286
旅客周转量总计(亿人公里)	**Total Passenger-Kilometers (100 million passenger-km)**	**204.89**	**292.80**	**423.80**
铁　路	Railways	58.00	97.40	121.90
公　路	Highways	117.17	158.20	249
民用航空	Civil Aviation	29.68	37.20	52.90
货运量总计(万吨)	**Total Freight Traffic (10 000tons)**	**25406**	**33091**	**38886**
铁　路	Railways	2733	4199	5083
公　路	Highways	21754	27048	31700
民用航空	Civil Aviation	2	4	3
管　道	Petroleum and Gas Pipelines	917	1840	2100
货物周转量总计(亿吨公里)	**Total Freight Ton-kilometers (100 million tons km)**	**474.39**	**660.90**	**947.24**
铁　路	Railways	240.88	355.00	548.50
公　路	Highways	219.72	272.90	361.00
民用航空	Civil Aviation	0.57	0.98	0.74
管　道	Petroleum and Gas Pipelines	13.22	32.00	37.00
民用汽车拥有量(万辆)	**Number of Civil Motor Vehicles Owned (10 000 units)**	**24.7**	**37.0**	**50.1**
#载客汽车辆数	Number of Buses and Cars	9.4	18.0	26.9
载货汽车辆数	Number of Trucks	14.3	17.5	20.2
#普通载货汽车	Ordinary Trucks	12.5	16.5	14.7
#私人汽车拥有量	Number of Motor Vehicles Owned by Individuals	5.6	13.9	21.3

注：1.2004 年，运输线路长度减少的原因是南航新疆航空公司取消了一些经济效益差的航线的飞行。
2.2000 年、2004 年公路里程包括兵团数据，与 2000 年以前不可比。

Note: a) In 2004, the reduced length of transport line is due to that fact Xinjiang Airline has cancelled some airline with poor economic efficiency.
b)the highway mileage for the years 2000 and 2004 cover the data of XJPCC unlike that before 2000.

14-2　运输线路长度
Length of Transportation Routes

单位:公里　(km)

年份 Year	铁路营业里程 Length of Railways in Operation	#新疆境内 Inside Xinjiang	公路通车里程 Length of Highway	#高级次高级 High Grade & Seond High Grade	民航通航里程 Length of the Civil Aviation	#新疆境内 Inside Xinjiang	输油里程 Length of Oil Transportation
1978	1031	796	23818	5810	4783	4783	443
1980	1103	868	21148	6390	4412	4412	443
1985	1579	1344	22232	8369	4527	4527	473
1986	1579	1344	22227	8897	6843	5159	518
1987	1578	1343	25049	10270	22836	5159	518
1988	1578	1343	25406	11189	28417	5159	708
1989	1579	1343	25374	11921	30597	5159	740
1990	1578	1343	25425	12566	36465	5159	740
1991	1578	1343	25697	13270	40538	5159	849
1992	1578	1343	26024	13793	45212	5159	876
1993	2038	1803	27961	15798	48880	5159	876
1994	2038	1803	28611	16888	53715	6693	875
1995	2038	1803	30298	19013	69789	6693	875
1996	2038	1803	31609	20461	122089	9183	928
1997	2038	1803	32053	21495	123664	9717	1373
1998	2038	1803	32762	22485	150473	9717	1955
1999	3008	2780	33484	23214	141872	9719	2496
2000	3010	2775	80875	31059	152941	9719	2696
2001	3010	2774	80947	31635	161814	9719	2965
2002	3010	2775	82929	32541	132483	9898	3153
2003	3009	2775	83633	33891	141456	9898	3008
2004	2999	2763	86824	40679	111768	8664	3003

注：2000 年～2004 年公路通车里程中含兵团数据。
Note: From 2000 to 2004 highway mileage for traffic contains data of XJPCC.

14-3　运输线路质量
Quality of Transportation Routes

指标	Item	1995	2000	2004
铁路营业里程(公里)	Length of Railways in Operation (km)	2038	3010	2999
#复线里程	Double-Tracking Length		986	986
#自动闭塞里程	Automatic Blocking Length	273	685	988
公路线路里程(公里)	Length of Highways (km)	30298	34585	86824
#有路面里程	Paved Highways	27982	33035	40679
有路面里程比重(%)	Proportion (%)	92	96	47

注：2004 年有路面里程改为已铺装路面，与 2003 年前不可比。
Note: The road-surface mileage for 2004 has been changed into a paved road, incomparable to that before 2003.

14-4 客运量及周转量

Passenger Volume and Turn-over

年 份 Year	客运量(万人) Passenger Traffic (10 000 persons)				旅客周转量(亿人公里) Passenger-Kil ometers (100 million passenger-km)			
	总 计 Total	铁 路 Railways	公 路 Highways	民 航 Civil Aviation	总 计 Total	铁 路 Railways	公 路 Highways	民 航 Civil Aviation
1978	941	148	786	7	25.23	13.72	10.96	0.55
1980	1356	193	1152	10	30.49	18.83	10.83	0.83
1985	3728	320	3399	9	63.16	33.16	29.13	0.87
1986	4058	362	3674	22	73.87	36.40	34.00	3.74
1987	4439	377	4327	34	83.67	37.14	39.44	7.09
1988	5205	459	4698	48	99.17	42.86	46.35	9.96
1989	8740	453	8240	47	120.69	44.52	66.37	9.80
1990	9602	388	9161	53	103.80	37.96	55.11	10.73
1991	14582	383	14142	56	122.08	41.94	68.05	12.09
1992	14997	425	14490	82	138.24	44.48	75.38	18.38
1993	16352	513	15749	90	174.23	50.00	103.51	20.73
1994	17181	670	16405	106	195.58	58.08	112.50	25.00
1995	17533	672	16739	122	204.89	58.00	117.17	29.68
1996	18858	610	18110	138	218.79	57.80	128.58	32.20
1997	20237	748	19360	129	233.39	64.70	139.00	29.69
1998	21747	878	20735	134	256.90	76.90	149.60	30.40
1999	22763	1000	21618	145	270.74	81.90	157.05	31.79
2000	23191	1147	21877	167	292.80	97.40	158.20	37.20
2001	24344	932	23255	157	309.70	104.10	170.30	35.30
2002	26016	950	24883	183	330.80	106.00	185.60	39.20
2003	26972	879	25878	215	342.00	106.10	195.00	40.90
2004	29782	1023	28473	286	423.80	121.90	249.00	52.90

注：2004 年民航旅客吞吐量为 516.4 万人。
Note: Air passenger handling capacity is 5,164,000 persons in 2004.

14-5 货运量及货物周转量

Volume of Cargo Transportation and Freight Turnover

年 份 Year	货运量(万吨) Freight Volume (10 000 tons)				
	总 计 Total	铁 路 Railways	公 路 Highways	民 航 Civil Aviation	管 道 Petroleum and Gas Pipelines
1978	6064.52	923.33	4842.90	0.12	298.17
1980	8420.98	883.50	7208.60	0.16	328.72
1985	10681.21	1278.10	8847.00	0.11	556.00
1990	13919.51	1690.68	11550.96	0.87	677.00
1991	16986.88	1762.77	14536.59	0.85	686.67
1992	16042.30	1889.72	13390.07	1.24	761.24
1993	23083.00	2018.00	20253.00	1.00	781.00
1994	24298.00	2318.00	21097.00	2.00	881.00
1995	25406.00	2733.00	21754.00	2.00	917.00
1996	26676.00	2951.00	22505.00	2.00	1218.00
1997	28790.00	3190.00	24125.00	3.00	1472.00
1998	30484.00	3324.00	25573.00	3.00	1584.00
1999	32076.00	3777.20	26596.00	3.17	1700.00
2000	33090.70	4199.20	27048.00	3.50	1840.00
2001	33589.00	3904.00	27751.00	2.00	1932.00
2002	34966.90	4121.20	28861.00	2.70	1982.00
2003	37484.80	4601.60	30881.00	2.20	2000.00
2004	38885.70	5083.20	31700.00	2.50	2100.00

年 份 Year	货物周转量(亿吨公里) Turnover of Cargo (100 million ton-km)				
	总 计 Total	铁 路 Railways	公 路 Highways	民航(万吨公里) Civil Aviation (10 000 ton-km)	管 道 Petroleum and Gas Pipelines
1978	106.96	67.76	32.06	98.10	7.13
1980	121.14	67.27	45.89	137.80	7.97
1985	174.75	102.03	61.26	104.00	11.45
1990	262.29	141.16	108.09	2048.00	12.84
1991	305.16	163.34	129.07	2100.00	12.54
1992	308.99	173.48	121.92	3150.00	13.28
1993	391.53	184.30	194.10	3772.00	12.75
1994	429.24	207.64	208.10	5000.00	13.00
1995	474.39	240.88	219.72	5744.00	13.22
1996	507.15	260.96	229.55	6475.00	16.00
1997	541.40	269.70	247.00	7000.00	24.00
1998	553.60	264.20	262.80	7000.00	25.90
1999	602.94	303.60	270.46	8800.00	28.00
2000	660.88	355.00	272.90	9776.00	32.00
2001	714.43	403.90	275.90	6300.00	34.00
2002	759.62	425.30	298.00	8238.00	35.50
2003	837.04	475.00	325.00	6400.00	36.40
2004	947.24	548.50	361.00	7400.00	37.00

14-6 货物运输平均运距
Average Transport Distance of Cargo

单位：公里 (km)

年 份 Year	合 计 Total	铁 路 Railways	公 路 Highways	民 航 Civil Aviation	管 道 Petroleum and Gas Pipelines
1978	168	565	66	818	239
1980	139	566	64	861	242
1985	158	624	69	945	206
1990	188	835	94	2354	190
1991	180	927	89	2471	183
1992	193	918	91	2540	174
1993	169	913	95	3772	163
1994	177	896	99	2500	148
1995	187	881	101	2872	144
1996	190	884	102	3238	131
1997	188	845	102	2333	163
1998	182	795	102	2332	164
1999	188	804	102	2776	165
2000	200	845	101	2857	174
2001	211	1023	99	3150	176
2002	217	1032	103	3051	179
2003	224	865	105	2909	182
2004	244	904	114	2960	176

14-7 铁路运输主要财务指标
Main Financial Indicators of Railway Transportation

单位：万元 (10 000 yuan)

指 标	Item	1985	1990	1995	2000	2004
运输总收入	**Total Transportation Revenue**	**40410**	**86686**	**192555**	**509480**	**756947**
客运收入	Revenue from Passenger Traffic	8412	18763	33560	82121	138508
货运收入	Revenue from Freight Traffic	29564	62516	142168	318485	602454
运输清算收入	**Transportation Claring Revenue**	**28530**	**59765**		**467142**	**744833**
运输总支出	**Toatl Transportation Costs**	**22740**	**51875**	**193693**	**418497**	**739896**
工 资	Wages and Salaries	4538	11163	38429	98293	100749
材 料	Materials	2697	6702	23183	36210	93606
燃 料	Fuel	5441	9308	32996	74487	103892
电 力	Electricity	346	666	2433	4701	3477
折 旧	Depreciation	8756	17174	13137	60859	60780
营业外收支净额	**Non-operating Net Revenue or Expenditure**	**2241**	**6886**	**14503**	**23236**	**37695**
实现利润	**Profits**	**2326**	**6291**	**-12591**	**34130**	**-14631**
运输利润	Transportation Profits	1684	5501	-11649	33195	-15161

14-8　铁路运输技术经济主要指标

Main Technological and Economic Indicators of Railway Transportation

指　标	Item	2000	2004
货运机车日产量(万吨公里)	Average Daily Ton-kilometers of Freight Locomotives (10 000 ton-km)	107.1	98.1
#内燃机车	Diesel Locomotives	107.1	98.1
货运机车平均牵引总重(吨)	Average Total Tonnage of Freight Locomotives (ton)	2327	2354
#内燃机车	Diesel Locomotives	2327	2354
货运机车日车公里(公里)	Daily Distance per Freight Locomotive (km)	610	571
客运机车日车公里(公里)	Daily Distance per Passenger Locomotive (km)	627	736
内燃机车每万吨公里耗油(公斤)	Oil Consumption of Diesel Locomotives (kg/10 000 ton-km)	27.6	29.5
货物列车出发正点率(%)	Punctuality Rate of Freight Trains at Departure (%)	99.4	99.4
货物列车运行正点率(%)	Punctuality Rate of Freight Trains in Running (%)	97.2	99.4
旅客列车出发正点率(%)	Punctuality Rate of Passenger Trains at Departure (%)	99.7	97.0
旅客列车运行正点率(%)	Punctuality Rate of Passenger Trains in Running (%)	99.5	91.4
旅客列车技术速度(公里/小时)	Technical Speed of Passenger Trains (km/hr)	62.3	72.0
旅客列车旅行速度(公里/小时)	Travelling Speed of Passenger Trains (km/hr)	57.7	63.5
客运密度(万人公里/公里)	Density of Passenger Transport (10 000 passenger-km/km)	323.6	422.0
货物列车技术速度(公里/小时)	Technical Speed of Freight Trains (km/hr)	46.9	47.5
货物列车旅行速度(公里/小时)	Running Speed of Freight Trains (km/hr)	43.6	39.6
货运密度(万吨公里/公里)	Density of Freight Transport (10 000 ton-km/km)	1179.3	1795.3
货车周转时间(天)	Turning Around Time of Freight Cars (day)	4.65	5.10
一次货物作业时间(小时)	Handling Time of Freight (hour)	38.9	18.0
货车中转停留时间(小时)	Transfer Waiting Time per Car (hour)	3.6	4.0
货车静载重(准轨) (吨)	Static Load of Freight Cars (Standard Gauge)　(ton)	52.8	55.1

14-9　民用车辆拥有量

Number of Civil Motor Vehicles Owned

单位：辆　(unit)

指　标	Item	民用汽车拥有量 Number of Automible for Civil Purpose			
		2003		2004	
		汽车总计 Total Number Of Automible	#私 人 Private	汽车总计 Total Number Of Automobile	#私 人 Private
民用汽车	**Civil Automobile**	**467649**	**192043**	**500739**	**212949**
载客汽车	Passenger Vehicles	256449	139489	269482	146308
#大 型	Large	16949	1375	18864	2601
中 型	Medium	5836	1751	19182	7136
小 型	Small	216493	124219	210167	115709
微 型	Mini	17171	12144	21269	20862
#轿 车	Car	153375	102370	187238	94881
载货汽车	Buses and Cars	189921	51845	201470	64941
#重 型	Large	60174	11306	55486	13647
中 型	Medium	39815	8083	41361	12339
轻 型	Light	79263	28248	83851	26916
微 型	Mini	10669	4208	20772	12039
其它汽车	**Other Cars**	**21279**	**709**	**29787**	**1700**

14-10 邮电事业情况
Basic Conditions of Post and Telecommunications Services

指　　标	Item	1995	2000	2004
邮政局及电信营业网点(处)	**Number of Post & Telecommunications Offices (unit)**	**1565**	**2689**	**1344**
邮路长度(单程)(公里)	**Length of Postal Routes (km)**	**100425**	**134109**	**123996**
#农 村	Rural	55856	55852	95520
邮电业务总量(万元)	**Business Volume of Post and Telecommunications (10 000 yuan)**	**90226**	**473000**	**1531835**
函件(万件)	Number of Letters (10 000 pcs)	9007	7148	4757
包件(万件)	Number of Parcels (10 000 pcs)	201	163	321
特快专递(万件)	Pieces of Express Mail Services (10 000 pcs)	94	124	238
报刊期发数(万份)	Number of Newspapers and Magazines Circulation (10 000 copies)	478.1	534.5	633.3
长途电话(万次)	Number of Long-distance Calls (10 000 times)	11766	34712.	62526
本地电话年末用户(万户)	Local Telephone Subscribers at Year-end (10 000 subscribers)	44.6	191.0	516.7
城市电话年末数	Urban Telephone Subscribers at Year-end	42.0	136.3	387.0
乡村电话年末数	Number of Rural Telephones Subscribers at Year-end	2.6	54.7	108.2
#住宅电话年末数	Residential Telephone Subscribers	26.0	101.1	297.4
年末无线寻呼用户(万户)	Number of Subscribers of Pageing Service at Year-end (10 000 subscribers)	12.4	167.5	13.9
年末移动电话用户(万户)	Number of Mobile Telephones Subscribers at Year-end (10 000 Subscribers)	2.7	78.0	489.7
邮电通信电路及长途电信线路	**Telecommunications Facilities**			
长途电话电路数(路)	Long Distance Telephone Lines (line)	10019	79679	82494
#光缆电路	Optical Cable Lines	6399	71969	
数字电路	Digital Lines	9329		
长途光缆线路长度(公里)	Length of Long Distance Optical Cable Lines (km)	592.5	10828.0	27300.0
长途微波线路长度(公里)	Length of Long Distance Microwave Lines (km)	7029.6	4889.0	3000.0
邮电通信设备	**Telecommunications Facilities**			
长途自动交换机容量(路端)	Capacity of Long-distance Telephone Exchanges (circuit)	38490	102540	191000
本地电话局用交换机容量(万门)	Capacity of Local Office Telephone Exchanges (10 000 line)	85.8	241.7	447.0
中央国有	Central State-owned	83.6	241.7	447.0
地方国有	Local State-owned	2.2		
电话机(万部)	Number of Telephone (10 000 sets)	44.2	190.0	
中央国有	Central State-owned	43.1	190.0	
地方国有	Local State-owned	1.1		
全区邮电通信水平	**Level of Postal and Telecommunications Services**			
平均每百人每年发函件数(件)	Arerage Number of Letters Mailed Per 100 (pieces/100 persons)	554.0	387.0	242.3
平均每百人每年订报刊数(份)	Arerage Number of Newspaper Subscribed Per 100 (pieces/100 persons)	28.8	28.9	32.3
平均每百人拥有电话机数(部)(固定)	Number of Telephone Sets Owned per 100 Persons(sets)(stable)	4.0	15.0	26.3
平均每百人拥有电话机数(部)(移动)	Number of Telephone Sets Owned per 100 Persons (sets)(mobile)			24.9
每一局所平均服务人口数(万人/处)	Average Number of People Served by every Offices (10 000 person/unit)	1.0	0.7	0.68
农村邮电通信水平	**Rural Level**			
设有邮电局、所的乡(镇)比重(%)	Percentage of Townships with Post and Telecommunication Offices (%)	69	42	73
通电话的乡(镇)比重(%)	Percentage of Townships with Telephone Communication (%)	96	100	100
进入长话自动网的乡(镇)比重(%)	Percentage of Townships with Access to Auto-exchange Net of Long Distance Call (%)	31	100	100

注：1、2003 年后，电信部门取消营业网点统计；2、2000 年后，电信部门取消电话机部数统计；3、2000 年后，电信部门取消长途电话电路中光缆及数字电路统计；4.2004 年营业网点数及每一局所平均服务人口数均为邮政数。

Note: a) After 2003, the telecom munication authority has cancelled the statistics for business outlets. b) After 2000, the telecommunication authority has cancelled the statistics for telephone subscribers. c) After 2000, the telecommunication authority has cancelled the statistics for optical cable and digital circuit for long-distance telephones. d) Number of business outlets for the year 2004 and average population served by each bureau is postal statistics.

14-11 主要年份邮电业务情况

Postal and Telecommunications Services in main years

年 份 Year	邮电业务总量（万元） Business Volume of Post and Telecommunications (10 000 yuan)	邮政业务总量 Business Volume of Post	电信业务总量 Business Volume of Telecommunications	函 件（万件） Number of Letters (10 000 pcs)
1978	4742.7			4842.7
1980	5211.5			5890.8
1985	7970.5			7032.6
1990	17371.6	8203.2	8311.8	7380.5
1991	21445.0	9606.1	10867.2	7422.5
1992	28781.9	11800.0	15700.4	8070.7
1993	39969.4	13894.6	24357.0	9750.2
1994	56082.0	15103.0	39087.2	9947.2
1995	90225.5	17322.2	71219.8	9041.8
1996	132128.5	20545.6	111582.9	8373.0
1997	171552.0	42144.0	129408.0	6985.0
1998	250595.0	49296.0	201299.0	6582.1
1999	347000.0	56717.0	290283.0	6524.0
2000	473000.0	59370.0	413630.0	7148.0
2001	634338.0	62265.0	572073.0	5601.0
2002	947000.0	68032.0	878968.0	6814.0
2003	1144837.5	72006.5	1072831.0	5987.0
2004	1531835.0	74834.9	1457000.0	4756.7

年 份 Year	特快专递（件） Pieces of Express Mail Services (pcs)	报刊期发数（万份） Newspapers and Magazines Circulation (10 000 copies)	集邮业务（万枚） Philately (10 000 pieces)	长途电话（万次） Number of Long Distance Telephone Calls (10 000 times)
1978		223.8		258.8
1980		329.6		276.5
1985		578.9		425.1
1990	26	805.7	1034.5	762.5
1991	92336	456.7	1899.3	1075.8
1992	202192	476.1	22933.3	1734.2
1993	266808	465.0	2767.2	2833.2
1994	649351	466.8	3367.5	5280.6
1995	936418	478.1	3086.6	11705.9
1996	1022472	422.3	3634.2	19465.0
1997	960000	376.0	4497.0	24078.0
1998	960000	370.6	6412.0	29857.8
1999	1030000	595.6	7537.0	35739.4
2000	1240000	534.5	5766.0	34712.0
2001	1470000	358.0	5491.0	89844.0
2002	1630000	399.0	4620.0	45769.0
2003	1990000	587.3	3112.8	35554.2
2004	2381412	633.4	3141.3	62526.0

注：从 1997 年起，市内电话户数统计口径有了较大调整，故农村电话户数增幅较大。

14-11 续表 Continued

年 份 Year	无线寻呼用户(户) Number of Subscribers of Pageing Services (subscriber)	移动电话用户(户) Number of Mobile Telephone Subscribers (subscriber)	国际互联网络用户(户) Number of Subscribers of Internet Services (subscriber)	本地电话年末用户(户) Number of Subscribers of Local Telephone at Year-end (subscriber)
1978				29126
1980				31664
1985				47176
1990	1836			89397
1991	4624			107188
1992	18528	8		132779
1993	47435	4604		179328
1994	69845	13398		269024
1995	123970	26879		446226
1996	196343	42461		704725
1997	317276	75288		950080
1998	428447	156537		1193631
1999	610000	326000		1475383
2000	1675000	780000		1910256
2001	2010000	1809000	128000	2626000
2002	1389000	2970000	173000	3375000
2003	413580	4212013	607872	4310000
2004	138452	4897000	780499	5167000

年 份 Year	城市电话用户(户) Number of Urban Telephone Subscribers (subscriber)	#住宅电话 Residential Telephone Subscribers	乡村电话用户(户) Rural Telephone Subscribers (subscriber)	#住宅电话 Residential Telephone Subscribers	公用电话(户) Public Telephone (subscriber)
1978	18594		10532		
1980	21483		10181		
1985	37385		9791		
1990	78879	11500	10518		257
1991	96073	19028	11115	297	281
1992	119818	31593	12961	665	415
1993	161792	60006	17536	2596	734
1994	252554	122620	16470	3839	1874
1995	420361	260498	25865	11500	5612
1996	697925	495127	6800	2577	11819
1997	726539	540166	223541	185607	22808
1998	881020	653079	312611	266253	38795
1999	1067373	795426	408010	354898	46856
2000	1362838	1011204	547418	482275	70753
2001	1961000	1243341	665000	577707	84309
2002	2383000	1799000	795000	734000	166000
2003	2938893	1799600	934570	886139	281632
2004	3870000	1940000	1082000	1034000	432000

Note: From 1997 on, greater readjustment has been made on the Statistic Method about the number of telephone Subscribers and the number of rural Subscribers has gone up by a bigger margin.

主要统计指标解释

铁路营业里程 又称营业长度(包括正式营业和临时营业里程)，指办理客货运输业务的铁路正线总长度。凡是全线或部分建成双线及以上的线路，以第一线的实际长度计算复线、站线、段管线、岔线和特殊用途线以及不计算运费的联络线都不计算营业里程。该指标可以反映铁路运输业基础设施的发展水平，也是计算客货周转量、运输密度和机车车辆运用效率等指标的基础资料。

铁路电气化里程 指在全部铁路营业里程中已安装了供电线路及设备，可以供电力机车牵引列车运行的区段的总里程。

铁路自动、半自动闭塞里程 指装有列车自动或人工完成闭塞状态的铁路设备里程。为保证列车安全运行，在一个区间、同一时间内，一般只允许一列列车运行，这种保证列车在这个区间安全间隔运行的技术方法称为"闭塞"。自动或半自动闭塞里程占铁路营业里程的比重是反映铁路现代化的重要标志之一。

公路里程 指在一定时期内实际达到《公路工程 [WTBZ] 技术标准JTJ01-88》规定的等级公路，并经公路主管部门正式验收交付使用的公路里程数。包括大中城市的郊区公路以及通过小城镇街道部分的公路里程和桥梁、渡口的长度，不包括大中城市的街道、厂矿、林区生产用道和农业生产用道的里程。两条或多条公路共同经由同一路段，只计算一次，不得重复计算里程长度。该指标可以反映公路建设的发展规模，也是计算运输网密度等指标的基础资料。

民用航空航线里程 指民航运输定期班机飞行的航线长度的总和。航线长度按机场之间的距离计算，通常有两种计算方法：一是将每条航线长度相加称为重复计算航线里程;一是将两线或两条以上航线经过同一区段里程，只计算一次航线长度称为不重复计算航线里程。一般常用的是后者，该指标可以确切反映民航运输网的规模，是表明民航事业为国民经济服务和方便人民生活程度的主要指标。

输油(气)管道长度 也称输油(气)里程，指油品(或天然气)的实际输送距离，一般按输油(气)管道的单线长度计算。若包括复线和备用线长度则称为输油(气)管道延展长度，是指管道铺设的实际长度。我们通常使用的是不包括复线的"输油(气)管道里程"，该指标可以反映管道运输的发展规模和水平。

货(客)运量 指在一定时期内，各种运输工具实际运送的货物(旅客)数量。该指标是反映运输业为国民经济和人民生活服务的数量指标，也是制定和检查运输生产计划、研究运输发展规模和速度的重要指标。货运按吨计算，客运按人计算。货物不论运输距离长短、货物类别，均按实际重量统计。旅客不论行程远近或票价多少，均按一人一次客运量统计；半价票、小孩票也按一人统计。

货(客)运密度 指在一定时期内某种运输方式在营运线路的某一区段平均每公里线路通过的货物(旅客)运输周转量。计算公式为：

货(客)运密度=Σ货物(旅客)周转量/营业线路长度

该指标可以反映交通运输线路上的货物(旅客)运输量运输繁忙程度，是平衡运输线路运输能力和通过能力，规划线路建设及改造、配备技术设备，研究运输网布局的重要依据。

货物(旅客)周转量 指在一定时期内，由各种运输工具运送的货物(旅客)数量与其相应运输距离的乘积之总和。该指标可以反映运输业生产的总成果，也是编制和检查运输生产计划，计算运输效率、劳动生产率以及核算运输单位成本的主要基础资料。计算货物周转量通常按发出站与到达站之间的最短距离，也就是计费距离计算。计算公式为：

货物(旅客)周转量= 货物(旅客)运输量×运输距离

铁路货车平均静载重 指铁路货车在始发站静止状态下平均每车装载的货物重量，用以分析货车完成装车时车辆载重力的利用情况。计算公式为：

货车平均静载重=货物发送吨数/装车数

静载重的多少取决于运送货物的性质、种类、车辆的类型和装载技术的高低。根据货车的平均标记载重与静载重进行对比，可以反映货车载重能力的利用程度。计算公式为：

货车载重力利用率(%)=货车平均静载重/货车平均标记载重×100%

铁路货运机车日产量 指在一定时期内，平均每台货运机车在一昼夜内所完成的总重吨公里数，包括载运货物的重量和车辆本身的自重。该指标从时间和牵引能力两方面反映了机车运用效率。计算公式为：

货运机车平均日产量=货运总重吨公里数/货运机车台日数

民用汽车拥有量 指报告期末，在公安交通管理部门按照《机动车注册登记工作规范》，已注册登记领有民用车辆牌照的全部汽车数量。汽车拥有量统计的主要分类：根据汽车结构分为载客汽车、载货汽车及其他汽车；根据汽车所有者不同分为个人(私人)汽车、单位汽车；根据汽车的使用性质分为营运汽车、非营运汽车和特种汽车；根据汽车大小规格不同载客汽车分为大型、中型、小型和微型，载货汽车分为重型、中型、轻型和微型。

邮电业务总量 指以价值量形式表现的邮电通信企业为社会提供各类邮电通信服务的总数量。邮电业务量按专业分类包括函件、包件、汇票、报刊发行、邮政快件、特快专递、邮政储蓄、集邮、公众电报、用户电报、传真、长途电话、出租电路、无线寻呼、移动电话、分组交换数据通信、出租代维等。计算方法为各类产品乘以相应的平均单价(不变价)之和，再加上出租电路和设备、代用户维护电话交换机和线路等的服务收入。该指标综合反映了一定时期邮电业务发展的总成果，是研究邮电业务量构成和发展趋势的重要指标。计算公式为：

邮电业务总量= Σ(各类邮电业务量×不变单价)+ 出租代维及其他业务收入= 邮电业务总量+ 电信业务总量

无线寻呼用户 无线寻呼是指电话用户通过无线寻呼中心，在规定范围内向携带小型寻呼机的用户发出声音、数字或文字显示信息。在寻呼台办理登记手续携带小型寻呼机的用户，称为无线寻呼用户。

移动电话用户 指通过移动电话交换机进入移动电话网、占用移动电话号码的各类电话用户。包括签约用户和智能网预付费用户。一个移动电话号码统计为一户。

本地电话用户 指接入本地电信运营商固定电话网上的电话用户。包括：住宅用户、单位用户、公用电话用户等。按电话用户位置又分为市内电话用户和农村电话用户。1997年以前，"市内电话用户"是指接入县城及县以上城市的电话网上的电话用户；"农村电话用户"是指接入县邮电局农话台及县以下农村电话交换点，以县城为中心(除市话用户外)联通县、乡(镇)、行政村、村民小组的用户。从1997年起，电话用户数分组调整为以用户所在区域划分为"城市电话用户"和"乡村电话用户"，与过去的按市内电话和农村电话划分方法不同。而电话用户总数、电话机总部数统计范围不变。

城市电话用户 指直辖市、省辖市、地级市、县级市的市区、市郊区及县城(包括县人民政府所在地的县城关区或行政建制相当于县人民政府所在地的镇)范围内接入局用交换机的电话用户数，包括分布在农村地区的独立工矿区、林区、驻军等电话用户数。

乡村电话用户 指按行政区划属于城市范围以外的乡(镇)、村的电话用户数。

住宅电话用户 指安装在居民住宅或农民家里并按照住宅电话用户登记注册和收费的电话用户。包括私人付费、单位付费和按规定免费安装的住宅电话用户。

长途电话交换机容量 指用于接入长途电话网的电话交换机设备的额定容量，包括国际电话交换机容量。局用交换机容量指安装在电信运营企业内用于接续本地固定电话的电话交换机容量，包括现用和备用的人工或自动交换机的全部容量。不包括用户交换机容量。

移动电话交换机容量 指移动电话交换机根据一定话务模型和交换机处理能力计算出来的最大同时服务用户的数量。

Explanatory Notes on Main Statistical Indicators

Length of Railways in Operation refers to the total length of the trunk line under passenger and freight transportation (including both full operation and temporary operation). The calculation is based on the actual length of the first line even if this line has a full or partial double track or more tracks, excluding double tracks, station sidings, tracks under the charge of stations, branch lines, special-purpose lines and the non-payable connecting lines. The length of railways in operation is an important indicator to show the development of the infrastructure for the railway transport, and also the essential data to calculate volume of passenger freight transport, traffic density and utilization efficiency of the locomotives and carriages.

Length of Electrified Railways refers to the length of the section of railways in operation in which the power supply lines and other equipment are installed for the running of electrified locomotives. The proportion of the length of electrified railways to the total length of railways in operation is an important indicator to show the modernization of railways.

Automatic-blocking and Semi-automatic-blocking Length of Railways refer to length of railways installed with equipment to perform automatic or manual blocking of trains. Blocking is a spacing technique by which a section of the railway only allows one train to pass at a time in the aim of ensuring the traffic safety. the proportion of automatic/semi-automatic blocking length to the total length of railways in operation is an important indicator to show the modernization of railways.

Length of Highways refers to the length of highways which are built in conformity with the grades specified by the highway engineering standard formulated by the Ministry of Communications, and have been formally checked and accepted by the departments of highways and put into use. The length of highways includes that of the suburb highways at large and medium sized cities, highways passing through streets at small cities and towns, and also the length of bridges and ferries. It does not include the length of streets in big and medium-sized cities and highways built for the production purpose at factories, mines, forest areas and agricultural areas. If two or more highways go the same section of the way, the length of the section is only calculated for once and no duplication is allowed. The length of highways is an important indicator to show the development of the highway construction and to provide essential information to calculate the transport network density.

Length of Navigable Inland Waterways it is an indicator reflecting the size and development of inland water network, it refers to the length of the natural rivers, lakes, reservoirs, canals, and ditches open to navigation during a given period, which enables the transport by ships and rafts. It includes the channels open to navigation for over an accumulative 3 months in a year, yet this does not include the river courses, which are only used to float odd logs and bamboo rafts. This indicator can reflect the scale, level and development situation of the inland waterway network.

Length of Civil Aviation Routes refers to the length of all routes for regular civil aviation flights. There are usually two ways to calculate the distance between airports connected by the route length: One is to put the length of all air routes together, called duplicated calculation of the length of the routes; the other is not to allow the duplication in calculation when two or more routes passing the same section of aviation routes. The latter is usually used, as it can precisely show the size of the civil aviation network and indicate the extent of civil aviation serving the national economy and the people.

Length of Oil (Gas) Pipelines used as an indicator to show the development, scale and level of the pipeline transportation, it refers to the actual transport distance of oil (or gas) products, and is in general calculated in the length of single pipeline. If the length of the double pipelines and alternate pipeline are included, it is called the extension length of the oil (gas) pipelines, which indicates the actual length of the pipelines built, excluding double pipelines.

Freight (Passenger) Traffic refers to the volume of freight (passenger) transported with various means. Freight transport is calculated in tons and passenger traffic is calculated in the number of persons. Despite the type of freight and traveling distance, the freight transport is calculated in t he actual weight of the goods: and despite the traveling distance and ticket price, the passenger traffic is calculated by the principle that one person can be counted only once in one travel. The passengers who travel with a half price ticket or a child ticket is also calculate das one person. The freight (passenger) traffic provides a quantitative measure to show how the transport industry serves the national economy and people, and is also an important indicator for planning the transport industry and for studying the development scale and speed of the transport industry.

Freight (Passenger) Traffic Density refers to the freight (passenger) traffic volume carried by a particular means of transportation during a given period through one kilometer of a specific section of transportation route. The formula is as follows:

Freight (Passenger) Traffic Density =[Freight Ton-kilometers (Passenger-kilometers)] / (Length of Rout e in Operation)

Measuring unit: ton-kilometer / kilometer (or person-kilometer/ kilometer)

Freight (passenger) traffic density reflects the degree of business of freight (passenger) traffic on transportation routes, and therefore provides important information for balancing transport cap ability, planning const ruction and up grading of transport routes and studying t he distribution of transport network.

Freight Ton-kilometers (Passenger-kilometers) refer to the sum of the products of the volume of transported cargo (passengers) multiplying by the transport distance. It is an important indicator to reflect the achievement of transportation industry. Normally, the shortest distance between the departure station and the destination station (i.e., the payable distance) is the basis to calculate the freight ton-kilometers. This is an import ant indicator to show the total results of the transport industry, to prepare and examine the transport plan and to measure the efficiency, the lab our productivity and t he unit cost of transport.

The formula is as follows:

Freight Ton-kilometers (Passenger-kilometers) = $\sum$ {Freight(Passenger) Traffic $\times$ Distance of Transportation}

Measuring unit: ton-kilometer (person-kilometer)

Static Load of Freight Cars refers to the average cargo weight as loaded by each freight car under the static condition at the departure station. It is used to show the utilization extent of the loading capacity of the freight cars. The formula is:

Static Load (ton) of Freight Car= (Tonnage of Goods Dispatched)/ (Number of Freight Cars Loaded)

The static load of freight cars is determined by the nature and type of goods loaded, the type of vehicles, and the technique of loading. The difference between the average marked load and the static load of freight cars reflects the utilization of loading capacity of freight cars. For its calculation the following formula is app lied:

Utilization Rate of Capacity of Freight Cars(%)=[(Average Static Load)× 100%] / (Average Marked Load)

Average Daily Haul of Freight Locomotives refers to the average total ton-kilometers accomplished by each freight transport locomotive over day and night during a given period of time. It includes both the weight of the goods carried and the deadweight of the train itself. It is a comprehensive indicator reflecting the locomotive efficiency in terms of both time and the pulling force.

Average Daily Haul of Freight Transport Locomotive (ton kilometer)=[(Total Ton/(Kilometers of Freight)) / (Daily Number of Freight Transport Locomotive)

Volume of Freight Handled in Major Coastal Ports refers to the volume of cargo passing in and out the harbor area of the major coastal port s and having been loaded and unloaded. The volume includes that of the postal matters, registered luggage and fuels, materials and fresh water as supplies of the ships. The volume of freight handled may be classified by direction of flow as freight for import and freight for export, or by nature of cargo as freight for domestic trade and freight for foreign trade. As an important indicator, the volume of freight handled by type of cargo and by main flow direction reflects the production capacity of ports.

Possession of Civil Motor Vehicles refer to the total numbers of vehicles that are registered and received vehicles' license tags according to the Work Standard for Motor Vehicles Registration formulated by transport management office under department of public security at the end of reference period. They are divided into following categories according to the structure of motor vehicles: passenger vehicles, trucks and others; and private vehicles and vehicles for units use according to ownerships; working vehicles, non-working vehicles and special motor vehicles according to kind of usage; large passenger vehicles, medium passenger vehicles and small passenger vehicles, heavy trucks, light-heavy trucks and light trucks according to sizes of vehicles.

Business Volume of Post and Telecommunications refers to the total amount of post and telecommunication services, expressed in value terms, provided by the post and telecommunications departments for the society. Post and telecommunication services can be classified as letters, parcels, remittance, issue of newspapers and magazines, fast mail service, express mail service, savings deposits, stamps for collection, public and individual telegraph service, facsimiles, long-distance telephone service, leasing of telephone lines, urban paging service, mobile telephone service, data transfer and transmission, etc. The accounting approach is to multiply the service products of all types with their average unit price (constant price) to get sum of business value, plus income from other services such as leasing of telephone lines and equipment, maintenance of telephone switchboards and lines on behalf of customers . This indicator reflects the overall results of post and telecommunications service during a given period, and is important to study the composition of business service and the development of post and telecommunications service.

The formula is as follows:

Business Volume of Post and Telecommunications= Σ(Transaction of Post and Telecommunication Service × Constant Price) + Income from Leasing, Maintenance and other Services

Subscribers of Wireless Paging Services Wireless paging service refers the service by which telephone users send audio, digital or character signals to persons carrying small-size pagers within the designated areas through wireless paging centers. The page carriers who have registered in paging centers are count ed as paging subscribers.

Mobil e Telephone Subscribers refer to the persons who own mobile telephone numbers and are connected with the mobile telephone communication network through the mobile telephones witch boards, including contracted subscribers and prepaid subscribers for intelligent network. One mobile telephone is taken as a subscriber.

Local Telephone Subscribers refer to subscribers that are connected to the local telecommunication service provider through fix line network, including household subscribers, institutional subscribers and public telephones. They are also classified as city subscribers and rural subscribers according to locations. Before 1997, city subscribers referred to those connected to city telephone networks in county towns and cities, while village subscribers referred to those connected to village telephone stations at and below counties. Since 1997, the classification of telephone subscribers was modified on the basis of physical location of the subscribers as urban telephone subscribers and rural telephone subscribers , which is different from the previous classification of categorizing local telephones and rural telephones , while the definition of total subscribers and total number of telephones remain unchanged.

Urban Telephone Subscribers refer to number of telephone subscribers, located at municipalities, cities under the jurisdiction of province, cities at prefecture level, downtown and suburb of city at county level town and county towns (including country towns where county government located, and towns of count y level according to the administrative organizational system),that are connected to the public line telephone network, including rural mineral area, forest area, military area.

Rural Telephone Subscribers refer to telephone subscribers, located at counties (towns) and villages out side the range of cities according to administrative jurisdiction.

Household Telephone Subscribers refer to telephone sets in stalled in the dwelling units of urban or rural residents, and registered as residence subscribers for payment, including 3 types of payment for the service: private payment, public payment and free service. Capacity of Long Distance Telephone Exchanges: refers to the rated cap a city of telephone exchanges to connect long distance telephone network, including capacity of international telephone exchanges.

Capacity of Office Telephone Exchanges refers to the capacity (measured in gate) of telephone exchanges installed in the offices of telecommunication service providers for communication between fixed telephones. It includes the capacity of both manual and automatic exchanges in use and for stand-by purpose, excluding the capacity of subscribers' exchanges.

Capacity of Mobile Telephone Exchanges refers to the capacity of the maximum services provided to subscribers at onetime basing on a certain model and transacting capacity of the mobile telephone exchanges.

第十五篇

CHAPTER 15

批发零售贸易和餐饮业

WHOLESALE AND RETAIL TRADE AND CATERING TRADE

15-1 限额以上批发和零售业、住宿和餐饮业基本情况

Basic Conditions of Wholesale, Retail, Accommodation and Catering Trade

指标	Item	1999	2000	2001	2002	2003	2004
法人机构(个)	**Number of Corporate (unit)**	**471**	**394**	**502**	**502**	**518**	**1236**
批发零售贸易业	Wholesale and Retail Trade	443	370	479	477	483	936
住宿餐饮业	Accommodation and Caetring Trade						300
#餐饮业	Catering Trade	28	24	23	25	35	65
产业活动单位(个)	**Number of Economic Active Unit (unit)**	**499**	**431**	**571**	**595**	**610**	**1323**
批发零售业	Wholesale and Retail Trades	456	382	511	524	530	1014
住宿餐饮业	Accommodation and Caetring Trade						309
#餐饮业	Catering Trade	43	49	60	71	80	74
批发零售业	**Wholesale and Retail Trades**						
商品销售总额（亿元）	Total sales (100 million yuan)	463.2	478.3	506.2	624.8	776.4	1078.7
社会消费品零售总额(亿元)	**Total Retail Sales of Consumer Goods (100 million yuan)**	**347.4**	**374.5**	**406.3**	**442.9**	**421.2**	**563.7**
按销售单位所在地分	**By Location of Establishments**						
市	City	214	233.7	256.6	284.8	311.3	382.8
县	County	61.5	65.2	69.7	74.3	49.2	87.2
县以下	Below County Level	71.9	75.6	80.0	83.8	60.7	93.7
按行业分	**By Sector**						
批发零售贸易业	Wholesale and Retail Trade	222.6	242.3	266.4	296.2	341.9	448.3
餐饮业	Catering Trade	32.7	38.2	44.5	53.0	60.6	78.8
其他行业	Others	92.1	94.0	95.4	93.7	18.7	36.6

注：2004 年为经济普查数据(以下同)；1999—2003 年法人机构、产业活动单位不包括住宿业。
Note: Economic Census data for the year 2004 (the same as below); The corporate agency and industrial units from 1999 to 2003 exclude accommodation.

15-2　社会消费品零售总额
Total Retail Sale of Consumer Goods

单位：亿元　　(100 million yuan)

年　份 Year	社会消费品零售总额 Total Retail Sales of Consumer Goods	按销售单位所在地分 Location of Retailers		
		市 City	县 County	县以下 Under County Level
1978	21.89	7.44	4.80	9.65
1980	29.36	11.06	6.05	12.25
1985	57.38	24.55	10.70	22.13
1990	104.30	57.17	24.27	22.86
1991	121.52	68.79	27.29	25.44
1992	138.25	78.10	31.07	29.08
1993	168.37	96.14	37.94	34.29
1994	197.11	114.04	42.18	40.89
1995	253.65	145.74	50.03	57.88
1996	295.36	171.51	55.38	68.47
1997	310.42	186.37	57.54	66.51
1998	327.52	197.89	59.89	69.74
1999	347.40	213.96	61.51	71.93
2000	374.50	233.66	65.15	75.69
2001	406.35	256.58	69.73	80.04
2002	442.88	284.74	74.32	83.82
2003	421.16	311.33	49.20	60.63
2004	563.65	382.67	87.23	93.75

年　份 Year	按行业分 Sector		
	批发零售贸易业 Wholesale and Retail Trade	餐饮业 Catering Service	其他行业 Others
1978	17.34	0.57	3.98
1980	22.95	0.94	5.47
1985	40.83	2.51	14.04
1990	72.68	6.06	25.56
1991	87.21	6.48	27.83
1992	105.62	7.44	25.19
1993	127.96	8.70	31.71
1994	146.22	10.85	40.04
1995	169.16	17.27	67.22
1996	191.14	19.44	84.78
1997	198.73	22.22	89.47
1998	206.92	27.84	92.76
1999	222.57	32.76	92.07
2000	242.29	38.21	94.00
2001	266.38	44.57	95.40
2002	296.13	53.04	93.71
2003	341.90	60.64	18.62
2004	448.29	78.82	36.54

15-3 分类型、分地区限额以上批发零售贸易业、餐饮业基本情况

Basic Conditions of Enterprises above Designated Size in Wholesale and Retail Trades and Catering Trade

(2004 年)

指　标	Item	法人企业数(个) Number of Corporate Enterprises (unit)	产业活动单位数(个) Number of Economic Active (unit)	从业人员数(人) Persons Engaged (person)
总　计	**Total**	**1236**	**1323**	**108338**
批发业	**Wholesale Trade**	**616**	**660**	**44675**
内资企业	Domestic-Funded Enterprises	614	658	44577
国有企业	State-owned Enterprises	111	141	10547
集体企业	Collective-owned Enterprises	41	41	6626
股份合作企业	Share Cooperative	2	2	81
联营企业	Joint Ownership Enterprises	2	2	113
有限责任公司	Limited Liability Corporations	200	210	18914
股份有限公司	Share-holding Corporations Ltd	18	19	2694
私营企业	Private Enterprises	239	242	5587
其他行业	Others	1	1	15
港、澳、台投资企业	Enterprises With Investment from Hong Kong, Macao and Taiwan	1	1	48
外商投资企业	Foreign Funded Enterprises	1	1	50
零售业	**Retail Trade**	**320**	**354**	**30933**
内资企业	Domestic-Funded Enterprises	317	350	30022
国有企业	State-owned Enterprises	56	75	6232
集体企业	Collective-owned Enterprises	7	9	255
有限责任公司	Limited Liability Corporations	97	105	7194
股份有限公司	Share-holding Corporations Ltd	12	13	5053
私营企业	Private Enterprises	145	148	11288
港、澳、台商投资企业	Enterprises With Investment from Hong Kong, Macao and Taiwan	1	2	36
外商投资企业	Foreign Funded Enterprises	2	2	875
住宿业	**Accommodation**	**235**	**235**	**26252**
内资企业	Domestic-Funded Enterprises	226	226	23162
国有企业	State-owned Enterprises	117	117	13424
集体企业	Collective-owned Enterprises	9	9	1171
股份合作企业	Cooperative Enterprises	3	3	269
联营企业	Joint Ownership Enterprises	1	1	140
有限责任公司	Limited Liability Corporations	41	41	3803
股份有限公司	Share-holding Corporations Ltd	5	5	496

15-3 续表 Continued

指 标	Item	法 人 企业数（个） Number of Corporate Enterprises (unit)	产业活动单位数（个） Number of Economic Active (unit)	从 业 人员数（人） Persons Engaged (person)
私营企业	Private Enterprises	49	49	3788
其他行业	Others	1	1	71
港、澳、台商投资企业	Enterprises With Investment from Hong Kong, Macao and Taiwan	6	6	1788
外商投资企业	Foreign Funded Enterprises	3	3	1302
餐饮业	**Catering Trade**	**65**	**74**	**6478**
内资企业	Domestic-Funded Enterprises	64	73	6422
国有企业	State-owned Enterprises	2	3	235
集体企业	Collective-owned Enterprises	1	1	30
有限责任公司	Limited Liability Corporations	8	12	1274
股份有限公司	Share-holding Corporations Ltd		1	324
私营企业	Private Enterprises	52	55	4479
其他行业	Others	1	1	80
外商投资企业	Foreign Funded Enterprises	1	1	56
按地区分	**By Region**			
乌鲁木齐市	Urumqi City	514	529	42832
克拉玛依市	Karamay City	38	46	3948
石河子市	Shihezi City	2	2	377
吐鲁番地区	Turpan Administrative Offices	27	28	2158
哈密地区	Hami [Kumul] Administrative Offices	42	45	2931
昌吉回族自治州	Changji Hui Autonomous Prefecture	81	87	6162
伊犁哈萨克自治州	Ili Kazak Autonomous Prefecture	140	141	9697
伊犁州直属县(市)	Counties (Cities) Direct Under Ili Prefecture	86	86	6092
塔城地区	Tacheng [Tarbagatai] Administrative Offices	29	29	1842
阿勒泰地区	Altay Administrative Offices	25	26	1763
博尔塔拉蒙古自治州	Bortala Mongol Autonomous Prefecture	20	20	1382
巴音郭楞蒙古自治州	Bayangol Mongol Autonomous Prefecture	73	78	6968
阿克苏地区	Aksu Administrative Offices	81	85	8475
克孜勒苏柯尔克孜自治州	Kizilsu Kirgiz Autonomous Prefecture	5	5	287
喀什地区	Kashgar [Kaxgar] Administrative Offices	37	38	8688
和田地区	Hotan Administrative Offices	9	10	842
生产建设兵团	Xinjiang Production and Construction Corps	167	209	13591

15-4 分行业、分地区限额以上批发零售贸易业商品销售额

Total Purchases, Sales and Inventory of Enterprise above Designated Size inWholesale and Retail Trade by Sector

单位：万元 (2004 年) (10 000 yuan)

指　标	Item	销售总额 Total Sales	批 发 Wholesale Trade	零 售 Retail Trade
总　计	**Total**	**10787153**	**8890099**	**1897054**
批发业	**Wholesale Trade**	**9044857**	**8735726**	**309131**
农畜产品批发业	Wholesale of Farming and Stock-raising Products	1995540	1990550	4990
食品、饮料及烟草制品批发业	Wholesale of Food,Beverages and Tobaccos	667008	663441	3567
#米、面制品及食用油批发业	Wholesale of Rice, Flour Products and Cooking Oil	48485	48337	148
烟草制品批发业	Wholesale of tobaccos	525266	524103	1163
纺织、服装及日用品批发业	Wholesale of Textitle, Garment and Daily Necessities	277241	275239	2002
#服装批发业	Garment Wholesale	153401	153401	
文化、体育用品及器材批发业	Culture, Sports Goods and Apparatus Wholesale	101923	99870	2053
医药及医疗器械批发业	Wholesale of Medicines and Medical Appliances	182201	182201	
矿产品、建材及化工产品批发业	Wholesale of Mineral Product, Construction Material and Chemical Products	3993102	3746523	246579
#石油及制品批发业	Wholesale of Petroleum and Related Products	1195848	975976	219872
金属及金属矿批发业	Wholesale of Metal and Metal Ore Products	1266308	1264250	2058
建材批发业	Wholesale of Building Materials	156603	141210	15393
化肥批发业	Wholesale of Minerial Prosucts	766420	762521	3899
机械设备、五金交电及电子产品批发	Wholesale of Machinery Equipment, Hardware and Electronic Products	1263457	1213910	49547
#汽车、摩托车及零配件批发业	Wholesale of Motor Vehicles, Motorcycles and Parts	312031	278076	33955
家用电器批发业	Wholesale of Household Appliance	77989	77269	720
计算机、软件及辅助设备批发业	Wholesale of Computer, Software and Accessory Equipment	70789	57147	13642
贸易经纪与代理	Trade Broker and Agent	126457	126457	
其他批发业	Other Wholesales not	437928	437535	393
零售业	**Retail Trade**	**1742296**	**154373**	**1587923**
综合零售业	Comprehensive Retail Sector	301950	9137	292813
百货零售业	Merchandile Retail	173596	2792	170804
超级市场零售业	Retail of Super Market	128354	6345	122009
食品、饮料及烟草制品专门零售业	Retail of Food, Beverage and Tobacco Products	22012	3141	18871
纺织、服装及日用品专门零售业	Retail of Textile, Garment and Daily Necessities	69689	351	69338
#服装零售业	Garment Retail	39424	351	39073

15-4 续表 Continued

单位：万元　　(10 000 yuan)

指　　标	Item	销售总额 Total Sales	批 发 Wholesale Trade	零 售 Retail Trade
文化、体育用品及器材专门零售业	Special Retail of Cultural, Sports and Apparatus	71916	3757	68159
#体育用品零售业	Sports Goods Retail	2540		2540
图书零售业	Books Retail	57789	3288	54501
医药及医疗器材专门零售业	Retail of Medicine and Medical-care Apparatus	147966	32822	115144
#药品零售业	Medcine Retail	145459	32822	112637
汽车、摩托车、燃料及零配件专门零售业	Car, Motor, Fuel and Parts as Well as Components	885769	78399	807370
#汽车零售业	Car Retail	451822	13169	438653
机动车燃料零售业	Auto Fuel Retail	394192	63466	330726
家用电器及电子产品专门零售业	Retail of Motor Vehicles,Motorcycles and Parts	193665	23786	169879
#家用电器零售业	Retail of Household Appliance	74708	20586	54122
计算机、软件及辅助设备零售业	Retail of Cumputers,Software and Office Appliances	45734	1462	44272
通讯设备零售业	Retail of Telecommunication Equipment	72416	1738	70678
五金、家俱及室内装修材料专门零售业	Retail of Hardware, Furniture and Indoor Decorating Material	16599		16599
无店铺及其他零售业	Non-shop and Other Retail	32730	2980	29750
按地区分	**By Region**			
乌鲁木齐市	Urumqi City	4188389	3122432	1065957
克拉玛依市	Karamay City	525742	478442	47300
石河子	Shihezi City	7769	2449	5320
吐鲁番地区	Turpan Administrative Offices	79323	45011	34312
哈密地区	Hami [Kumul] Administrative Offices	167321	98623	68698
昌吉回族自治州	Changji Hui Autonomous Prefecture	371015	279412	91603
伊犁哈萨克自治州	Ili Kazak Autonomous Prefecture	1017199	939927	77272
伊犁州直属县(市)	Counties (Cities) Direct Under Ili Prefecture	451117	405415	45702
塔城地区	Tacheng [Tarbagatai] Administrative Offices	349715	331268	18447
阿勒泰地区	Altay Administrative Offices	216367	203245	13122
博尔塔拉蒙古自治州	Bortala Mongol Autonomous Prefecture	528635	509159	19476
巴音郭楞蒙古自治州	Bayangol Mongol Autonomous Prefecture	460667	353843	106824
阿克苏地区	Aksu Administrative Offices	479744	358779	120965
克孜勒苏柯尔克孜自治州	Kizilsu Kirgiz Autonomous Prefecture	11049	10193	856
喀什地区	Kashgar [Kaxgar] Administrative Offices	263643	199571	64072
和田地区	Hotan Administrative Offices	67951	30852	37099
生产建设兵团	Xinjiang Production and Construction Group	2618706	2461406	157300

15-5 餐饮企业销售情况

Sales of Catering Service

单位：万元 (2004 年) (10 000 yuan)

项 目	Item	法人企业数(个) Number of Corporate Enterprise (unit)	产业活动单位数(个) Number of Economic Active (unit)	营业总收入 Business Revenue	#商品零售额 Retail Sales of Commodities
总 计	**Total**	**311**	**391**	**70512**	**69232**
限额以上企业(单位)	**above Designated Size**	**65**	**74**	**51984**	**51433**
正 餐	Dinner	62	71	50230	49679
快 餐	Snack	3	3	1754	1754
限额以下企业(单位)	**Below Designated Size**	**246**	**317**	**18528**	**17799**
按地区分	**By Region**				
乌鲁木齐市	Urumqi City	133	152	47450	46864
克拉玛依市	Karamay City	6	20	2818	2819
吐鲁番地区	Turpan Administrative Offices	5	8	517	517
哈密地区	Hami [Kumul] Administrative Offices	7	10	935	933
昌吉回族自治州	Changji Hui Autonomous Prefecture	35	40	3519	3373
伊犁哈萨克自治州	Ili Kazak Autonomous Prefecture	25	33	1902	1882
伊犁州直属县(市)	Counties (Cities) Direct Under Ili Prefecture	15	15	911	899
塔城地区	Tacheng [Tarbagatai] Administrative Offices	9	14	923	915
阿勒泰地区	Altay Administrative Offices	1	4	68	68
博尔塔拉蒙古自治州	Bortala Mongol Autonomous Prefecture	2	2	185	185
巴音郭楞蒙古自治州	Bayangol Mongol Autonomous Prefecture	26	31	3967	3878
阿克苏地区	Aksu Administrative Offices	5	7	675	400
喀什地区	Kashgar [Kaxgar] Administrative Offices	23	25	2280	2260
和田地区	Hotan Administrative Offices	4	4	285	285
生产建设兵团	Xinjiang Production and Construction Corps	40	59	5979	5836

15-6 限额以上住宿企业经营情况

Operation of Hospitality Enterprises

(2004 年)

项　　目	Item	营业额 (万元) Business Volume (10 000 yuan)	客房收入 Income of Guest Rooms	餐费收入 Catering Income
总　计	**Total**	**182357**	**81350**	**75815**
按星级分	**Classified by Stars**			
一 星	One-Star	4530	1818	2147
二 星	Two-Star	21918	13022	7139
三 星	Three-Star	72413	37580	28833
四 星	Four-Star	39409	16607	14647
五 星	Five-Star	44087	12323	23047
按地区分	**By Region**			
乌鲁木齐市	Urumqi City	107829	42849	46183
克拉玛依市	Karamay City	2644	974	1233
吐鲁番地区	Turpan Administrative Offices	4264	2270	1730
哈密地区	Hami [Kumul] Administrative Offices	3524	1548	1748
昌吉回族自治州	Changji Hui Autonomous Prefecture	3408	1480	1394
伊犁哈萨克自治州	Ili Kazak Autonomous Prefecture	17635	8771	6904
伊犁州直属县(市)	Counties (Cities) Direct Under Ili Prefecture	13035	6527	4982
塔城地区	Tacheng [Tarbagatai] Administrative Offices	1489	613	769
阿勒泰地区	Altay Administrative Offices	3111	1631	1153
博尔塔拉蒙古自治州	Bortala Mongol Autonomous Prefecture	2359	953	1065
巴音郭楞蒙古自治州	Bayangol Mongol Autonomous Prefecture	10892	5466	4392
阿克苏地区	Aksu Administrative Offices	5174	3831	1075
克孜勒苏柯尔克孜自治州	Kizilsu Kirgiz Autonomous Prefecture	357	143	207
喀什地区	Kashgar [Kaxgar] Administrative Offices	4543	2599	1807
和田地区	Hotan Administrative Offices	286	229	
生产建设兵团	Xinjiang Production and Construction Group	19442	10237	8077

注：限额以上住宿企业指星级以上宾馆。

Note: The hospitality enterprises refer to starred enterprises.

15-6 续表 Continued

项　　目	Item			客房数（间）Number of rooms	床位数（张）Number of beds
		商品销售收入 Sales volum of commodity	其他收入 Others		
总　计	**Total**	**5156**	**20036**	**29014**	**56006**
按星级分	**Classified by Star**				
一 星	One-Star	56	508	785	1671
二 星	Two-Star	509	1249	10408	21122
三 星	Three-Star	1469	4531	12468	24439
四 星	Four-Star	1113	7041	3467	5880
五 星	Five-Star	2009	6707	1886	2894
按地区分	**By Region**				
乌鲁木齐市	Urumqi City	3035	15762	9786	17632
克拉玛依市	Karamay City	221	216	360	691
吐鲁番地区	Turpan Administrative Offices	20	244	4268	8701
哈密地区	Hami [Kumul] Administrative Offices	49	179	841	1699
昌吉回族自治州	Changji Hui Autonomous Prefecture	256	278	849	1766
伊犁哈萨克自治州	Ili Kazak Autonomous Prefecture	577	1383	4669	9279
伊犁州直属县(市)	Counties (Cities) Direct Under Ili Prefecture	349	1177	2905	5653
塔城地区	Tacheng [Tarbagatai] Administrative Offices	54	53	439	995
阿勒泰地区	Altay Administrative Offices	174	153	1325	2631
博尔塔拉蒙古自治州	Bortala Mongol Autonomous Prefecture	145	196	532	1170
巴音郭楞蒙古自治州	Bayangol Mongol Autonomous Prefecture	379	655	1636	3158
阿克苏地区	Aksu Administrative Offices	130	138	1417	2725
克孜勒苏柯尔克孜自治州	Kizilsu Kirgiz Autonomous Prefecture	1	6	118	220
喀什地区	Kashgar [Kaxgar] Administrative Offices		137	1398	2623
和田地区	Hotan Administrative Offices		57	66	132
生产建设兵团	Xinjiang Production and Construction Group	343	785	3074	6210

15-7 各地、州、市、县(市)社会消费品零售总额

Total Retail Sales of Consumer Goods by Prefecture, Autonomous Prefecture, City and County

单位：万元 (2004 年) (10 000 yuan)

地 区	Region	社会消费品零售总额 Total Retail Sales of Consumer Goods	市 City	县 County	县以下 Under-County Level
总 计	**Total**	**5636520**	**3826693**	**872337**	**937490**
乌鲁木齐市	**Urumqi City**	**1909693**	**1864947**		**44746**
乌鲁木齐县	Urumqi County	20574	6610		13964
克拉玛依市	**Karamay City**	**169603**	**114793**	**53370**	**1440**
吐鲁番地区	**TurpanAdministrative Offices**	**132848**	**51802**	**39974**	**41072**
吐鲁番市	Turpan City	64753	51802		12951
鄯善县	Shanshan County	49483		27317	22166
托克逊县	Toksun County	18612		12657	5955
哈密地区	**Hami Administrative Offices**	**169550**	**152236**	**7240**	**10074**
哈密市	Hami City	156649	152236		4413
巴里坤哈萨克自治县	Barkol KazakAutonomous County	8904		4958	3946
伊吾县	Yiwu County	3997		2282	1715
昌吉回族自治州	**Changji Hui Autonomous Prefecture**	**493332**	**233295**	**113944**	**146093**
昌吉市	Changji City	228423	163541		64882
阜康市	Fukang City	42664	30156		12508
米泉市	Miquan City	56168	39598		16570
呼图壁县	Hutubi County	43541		30966	12575
玛纳斯县	Manas County	43082		28986	14096
奇台县	Qitai County	45042		30939	14103
吉木萨尔县	Jimsar County	21166		13946	7220
木垒哈萨克自治县	Mori Kazak Autonomous County	13246		9107	4139
伊犁哈萨克自治州	**Ili Kazak Autonomous Prefecture**	**716844**	**283696**	**250792**	**182356**
伊犁州直属县(市)	**Counties (Cities) Direct Under Ili Prefecture**	**411834**	**190330**	**123740**	**97764**
伊宁市	Yining City	132714	127592		5122
奎屯市	Kuytun City	62738	62738		
伊宁县	Yining County	37386		20936	16450
察布查尔锡伯自治县	Qapqal Xibe Autonomous County	6652		4435	2217
霍城县	Huocheng County	44756		26854	17902
巩留县	Gongliu County	15715		12283	3432
新源县	Xinyuan County	54805		24114	30691
昭苏县	Zhaosu County	14566		7884	6682
特克斯县	Tekes County	23593		17023	6570
尼勒克县	Nilka County	18909		10211	8698
塔城地区	**Tacheng [Tarbagatai] Administrative Offices**	**168433**	**52490**	**58146**	**57797**
塔城市	Tacheng [Qoqek] City	40540	26156		14384
乌苏市	Usu City	37823	26334		11489
额敏县	Emin [Dorbiljin] County	28287		16972	11315
沙湾县	Shawan County	37223		24534	12689
托里县	Toli County	10969		8112	2857
裕民县	Yumin [Qagantokay] County	6292		4076	2216
和布克赛尔蒙古自治县	Hoboksar Mongol Autonomous County	7299		4452	2847
阿勒泰地区	**Altay Administrative Offices**	**136577**	**40876**	**68906**	**26795**
阿勒泰市	Altay City	55995	40876		15119
布尔津县	Burqin County	33148		30496	2652
富蕴县	Fuyun [Koktokay] County	12346		10124	2222
福海县	Fuhai [Burultokay] County	12529		9773	2756
哈巴河县	Habahe [Kaba] County	12508		11258	1250
青河县	Qinghe [Qinggil] County	7417		5859	1558
吉木乃县	Jeminay County	2634		1396	1238

15-7 续表 Continued

单位：万元 (10 000 yuan)

地 区	Region	社会消费品零售总额 Total Retail Sales of Consumer Goods	市 City	县 County	县以下 Under-County Level
博尔塔拉蒙古自治州	**Bortala Mongol Autonomous Prefecture**	**88477**	**55058**	**8445**	**24974**
博乐市	Bole [Bortala] City	68823	55058		13765
精河县	Jinghe [Jing] County	12638		6935	5703
温泉县	Wenquan [Araxang] County	7016		1510	5506
巴音郭楞蒙古自治州	**Bayangol Mongol Autonomous Prefecture**	**390348**	**236417**	**99341**	**54590**
库尔勒市	Korla City	271621	236417		35204
轮台县	Luntai [Bugur] County	26368		21844	4524
尉犁县	Yuli [Lopnur] County	15868		13146	2722
若羌县	Ruoqiang [Qarkilik] County	9265		8770	495
且末县	Qiemo [Qarqan] County	15874		15458	416
焉耆回族自治县	Yanji Hui Autonomous County	16822		14735	2087
和静县	Hejing County	14641		10257	4384
和硕县	Hoxud County	15875		12029	3846
博湖县	Bohu [Bagrax] County	4014		3102	912
阿克苏地区	**Aksu Administrative Offices**	**327749**	**154297**	**152604**	**20848**
阿克苏市	Aksu City	160382	154297		6085
温宿县	Wensu [Onsu] County	14451		13966	485
库车县	Kuqa County	48700		38618	10082
沙雅县	Xayar County	27545		26548	997
新和县	Xinhe [Toksu] County	18364		17400	964
拜城县	Baicheng [Bay] County	26875		25877	998
乌什县	Wushi [Uxturpan] County	7969		7727	242
阿瓦提县	Awat County	20540		19590	950
柯坪县	Kalpin County	2923		2878	45
克孜勒苏柯尔克孜自治州	**Kizilsu Kirgiz Autonomous Prefecture**	**37920**	**20565**	**11265**	**6090**
阿图什市	Artux City	24193	20565		3628
阿克陶县	Akto County	6487		5300	1187
阿合奇县	Akqi County	3460		2941	519
乌恰县	Wuqia [Ulugqat] County	3780		3024	756
喀什地区	**Kashgar [Kaxgar] Administrative Offices**	**265480**	**123416**	**89250**	**52814**
喀什市	Kashgar [Kaxgar] City	123416	123416		
疏附县	Shufu County	3823		1799	2024
疏勒县	Shule County	15865		7217	8648
英吉沙县	Yengisar County	8946		5576	3370
泽普县	Zepu [Poskam] County	11219		7468	3751
莎车县	Shache [Yarkant] County	27393		16550	10843
叶城县	Yecheng [Kagilik] County	21614		17473	4141
麦盖提县	Makit County	13137		8061	5076
岳普湖县	Yopurga County	7734		4891	2843
伽师县	Jiashi [Payzawat] County	8773		5115	3658
巴楚县	Bachu [Maralbexi] County	20489		12029	8460
塔什库尔干塔吉克自治县	Taxkorgan Tajik Autonomous County	3071		3071	
和田地区	**Hotan Administrative Offices**	**120851**	**72185**	**24104**	**24562**
和田市	Hotan City	72185	72185		
和田县	Hotan County	6202		733	5469
墨玉县	Moyu [Karakax] County	11608		6560	5048
皮山县	Pishan [Guma] County	5225		2122	3103
洛浦县	Lop County	9220		3969	5251
策勒县	Qira County	6974		4830	2144
于田县	Yutian [Keriya] County	7265		4422	2843
民丰县	Minfeng [Niya] County	2172		1468	704
生产建设兵团	**Xinjiang Production & Construction Group**	**813825**	**463986**	**22008**	**327831**

15-8 各地、州、市、县(市)社会消费品零售总额(按行业分)

Total Retail Sale of Consumer Goods by Sector and by Prefecture, Autonomous Prefecture, City and County

单位：万元　　(2004 年)　　(10 000 yuan)

地区	Region	社会消费品零售总额 Total Retail Sales of Consumer Goods	批发零售贸易业 Wholesale And Retail Sale Trade	餐饮业 Catering Trade	其他行业 Others
总　计	**Total**	**5636520**	**4482946**	**788185**	**365389**
乌鲁木齐市	**Urumqi City**	**1909693**	**1575836**	**259987**	**73870**
乌鲁木齐县	Urumqi County	20574	18722	1852	
克拉玛依市	**Karamay City**	**169603**	**141983**	**26169**	**1451**
吐鲁番地区	**TurpanAdministrative Offices**	**132848**	**107607**	**24620**	**621**
吐鲁番市	Turpan City	64753	51434	12823	496
鄯善县	Shanshan County	49483	41319	8062	102
托克逊县	Toksun County	18612	14854	3735	23
哈密地区	**Hami Administrative Offices**	**169550**	**130608**	**14952**	**23990**
哈密市	Hami City	156649	120069	13429	23151
巴里坤哈萨克自治县	Barkol KazakAutonomous County	8904	7590	973	341
伊吾县	Yiwu County	3997	2949	550	498
昌吉回族自治州	**Changji Hui Autonomous Prefecture**	**493332**	**399070**	**68514**	**25748**
昌吉市	Changji City	228423	194994	23651	9778
阜康市	Fukang City	42664	31956	9262	1446
米泉市	Miquan City	56168	41266	11522	3380
呼图壁县	Hutubi County	43541	34853	5779	2909
玛纳斯县	Manas County	43082	33345	5983	3754
奇台县	Qitai County	45042	36847	6235	1960
吉木萨尔县	Jimsar County	21166	16394	3751	1021
木垒哈萨克自治县	Mori Kazak Autonomous County	13246	9415	2331	1500
伊犁哈萨克自治州	**Ili Kazak Autonomous Prefecture**	**716844**	**565732**	**106551**	**44561**
伊犁州直属县(市)	**Counties (Cities) Direct Under Ili Prefecture**	**411834**	**332311**	**56184**	**23339**
伊宁市	Yining City	132714	104784	20826	7104
奎屯市	Kuytun City	62738	52878	7345	2515
伊宁县	Yining County	37386	30412	3028	3946
察布查尔锡伯自治县	Qapqal Xibe Autonomous County	6652	4612	1985	55
霍城县	Huocheng County	44756	36309	6881	1566
巩留县	Gongliu County	15715	11705	2076	1934
新源县	Xinyuan County	54805	45959	8147	699
昭苏县	Zhaosu County	14566	9461	2309	2796
特克斯县	Tekes County	23593	20156	2408	1029
尼勒克县	Nilka County	18909	16035	1179	1695
塔城地区	**Tacheng [Tarbagatai] Administrative Offices**	**168433**	**129178**	**25498**	**13757**
塔城市	Tacheng [Qoqek] City	40540	29804	5280	5456
乌苏市	Usu City	37823	27896	5662	4265
额敏县	Emin [Dorbiljin] County	28287	24858	2210	1219
沙湾县	Shawan County	37223	27468	8495	1260
托里县	Toli County	10969	8684	1384	901
裕民县	Yumin [Qagantokay] County	6292	5223	857	212
和布克赛尔蒙古自治县	Hoboksar Mongol Autonomous County	7299	5245	1610	444
阿勒泰地区	**Altay Administrative Offices**	**136577**	**104243**	**24869**	**7465**
阿勒泰市	Altay City	55995	47428	7589	978
布尔津县	Burqin County	33148	21433	10204	1511
富蕴县	Fuyun [Koktokay] County	12346	9441	2037	868
福海县	Fuhai [Burultokay] County	12529	7241	1462	3826
哈巴河县	Habahe [Kaba] County	12508	10187	2187	134
青河县	Qinghe [Qinggil] County	7417	6496	872	49
吉木乃县	Jeminay County	2634	2017	518	99

15-8 续表 Continued

单位：万元 (10 000 yuan)

地　　区	Region	社会消费品零售总额 Total Retail Sales of Consumer Goods	批发零售贸易业 Wholesale And Retail Sale Trade	餐饮业 Catering Trade	其他行业 Others
博尔塔拉蒙古自治州	**Bortala Mongol Autonomous Prefecture**	**88477**	**76976**	**10546**	**955**
博乐市	Bole [Bortala] City	68823	61754	7069	
精河县	Jinghe [Jing] County	12638	10221	2417	
温泉县	Wenquan [Araxang] County	7016	5001	1060	955
巴音郭楞蒙古自治州	**Bayangol Mongol Autonomous Prefecture**	**390348**	**335850**	**47641**	**6857**
库尔勒市	Korla City	271621	237620	29533	4468
轮台县	Luntai [Bugur] County	26368	21150	4670	548
尉犁县	Yuli [Lopnur] County	15868	13489	2284	95
若羌县	Ruoqiang [Qarkilik] County	9265	8059	819	387
且末县	Qiemo [Qarqan] County	15874	14722	1026	126
焉耆回族自治县	Yanji Hui Autonomous County	16822	14195	2488	139
和静县	Hejing County	14641	11210	3116	315
和硕县	Hoxud County	15875	12454	2671	750
博湖县	Bohu [Bagrax] County	4014	2951	1034	29
阿克苏地区	**Aksu Administrative Offices**	**327749**	**207792**	**47393**	**72564**
阿克苏市	Aksu City	160382	119504	18906	21972
温宿县	Wensu [Onsu] County	14451	7948	2073	4430
库车县	Kuqa County	48700	26282	9874	12544
沙雅县	Xayar County	27545	14030	7432	6083
新和县	Xinhe [Toksu] County	18364	9281	2106	6977
拜城县	Baicheng [Bay] County	26875	13546	2953	10376
乌什县	Wushi [Uxturpan] County	7969	5310	1227	1432
阿瓦提县	Awat County	20540	11131	2456	6953
柯坪县	Kalpin County	2923	760	366	1797
克孜勒苏柯尔克孜自治州	**Kizilsu Kirgiz Autonomous Prefecture**	**37920**	**33093**	**4048**	**779**
阿图什市	Artux City	24193	21539	2371	283
阿克陶县	Akto County	6487	5252	862	373
阿合奇县	Akqi County	3460	2970	456	34
乌恰县	Wuqia [Ulugqat] County	3780	3332	359	89
喀什地区	**Kashgar [Kaxgar] Administrative Offices**	**265480**	**193620**	**29806**	**42054**
喀什市	Kashgar [Kaxgar] City	123416	100237	4505	18674
疏附县	Shufu County	3823	2336	443	1044
疏勒县	Shule County	15865	8264	4501	3100
英吉沙县	Yengisar County	8946	4640	1781	2525
泽普县	Zepu [Poskam] County	11219	6149	1593	3477
莎车县	Shache [Yarkant] County	27393	19297	4154	3942
叶城县	Yecheng [Kagilik] County	21614	16381	4442	791
麦盖提县	Makit County	13137	8560	2307	2270
岳普湖县	Yopurga County	7734	5985	1709	40
伽师县	Jiashi [Payzawat] County	8773	3106	2043	3624
巴楚县	Bachu [Maralbexi] County	20489	15594	2328	2567
塔什库尔干塔吉克自治县	Taxkorgan Tajik Autonomous County	3071	3071		
和田地区	**Hotan Administrative Offices**	**120851**	**98220**	**13426**	**9205**
和田市	Hotan City	72185	66570	4682	933
和田县	Hotan County	6202	4421	1181	600
墨玉县	Moyu [Karakax] County	11608	8014	1372	2222
皮山县	Pishan [Guma] County	5225	3472	1021	732
洛浦县	Lop County	9220	6237	1434	1549
策勒县	Qira County	6974	4496	1540	938
于田县	Yutian [Keriya] County	7265	3639	1605	2021
民丰县	Minfeng [Niya] County	2172	1372	591	209
生产建设兵团	**Xinjiang Production & Construction Group**	**813825**	**616559**	**110254**	**87012**

15-9 限额以上批发贸易业机构数、从业人员数

(2004 年)

指标	Item	合计 Total 法人单位(个) Number of Corporate Enterprise (unit)	产业活动单位(个) Number of Economic Active (unit)	人员(人) Persons Engaged (person)
总计	**Total**	**616**	**660**	**44675**
#国有及国有控股	State Owned and Holding Company	221	264	21831
按登记注册类型分	**By Type of Registration**			
内资企业	Domestic-funded Enterprise	614	658	44577
国有企业	State – owned	111	141	10547
集体企业	Collective Owned	41	41	6626
股份合作企业	Share Cooperative	2	2	81
联营企业	Joint Ownership Enterprises	2	2	113
有限责任公司	Limited Liability Company	200	210	18914
股份有限公司	Share Holding Limited Company	18	19	2694
私营企业	Private Enterprise	239	242	5587
其他行业	Others	1	1	15
港、澳、台商投资企业	Enterprises With Investment from Hong Kong, Macao and Taiwan	1	1	48
外商投资企业	Foreign Funded Enterprises	1	1	50
按国民经济行业分	**By Sector**			
农畜产品批发业	Wholesale of Farming and Stock-raising Products	154	158	19890
食品、饮料及烟草制品批发业	Wholesale of Food, beverages and tobaccos	53	56	4408
#米、面制品及食用油批发业	Wholesale of Rice, Flour Products and Cooking Oil	13	13	715
烟草制品批发业	Wholesale of tobaccos	18	19	2545
纺织、服装及日用品批发业	Wholesale of Textile, Garment and Daily Necessities	15	15	429
#服装批发业	Garment Wholesale	2	2	29
文化、体育用品及器材批发业	Wholesale of Culture, Sports Goods and Apparatus	6	6	559
医药及医疗器械批发业	Wholesale of Medicines and Medical Appliances	14	14	1112
矿产品、建材及化工产品批发业	Ore Products, Building Material and Chemical Products	225	258	12242
#石油及制品批发业	Wholesale of Petroleum and Related Products	49	54	5386
金属及金属矿批发业	Metal and Metal Ore Wholesale	81	81	1509
建材批发业	Wholesale of Building Materials	16	18	353
化肥批发业	Wholesale of Minerial Prosucts	48	69	3259
机械设备、五金交电及电子产品批发业	Machinery Equipment, Hardware and Electronic Products	122	125	5200
#汽车、摩托车及零配件批发业	Wholesale of Motor Vehicles, Motorcycles and Parts	54	55	1606
家用电器批发业	Household Appliance	6	6	805
计算机、软件及辅助设备批发业	Computer, Software and Accessory Equipment	10	10	465
贸易经纪与代理	Trade Broker and Agent	5	5	174
其他批发业	Other Wholesales	22	23	661
按地区分	**By Region**			
乌鲁木齐市	Urumqi City	265	272	10558
克拉玛依市	Karamay City	18	18	1455
吐鲁番地区	TurpanAdministrative Offices	4	4	412
哈密地区	Hami [Kumul] Administrative Offices	11	14	1459
昌吉回族自治州	Changji Hui Autonomous Prefecture	42	44	2918
伊犁哈萨克自治州	Ili Kazak Autonomous Prefecture	59	59	4141
伊犁州直属县(市)	Counties (Cities) Direct Under Ili Prefecture	38	38	2513
塔城地区	Tacheng [Tarbagatai] Administrative Offices	14	14	1067
阿勒泰地区	Altay Administrative Offices	7	7	561
博尔塔拉蒙古自治州	Bortala Mongol Autonomous Prefecture	12	12	768
巴音郭楞蒙古自治州	Bayangol Mongol Autonomous Prefecture	30	32	3004
阿克苏地区	Aksu Administrative Offices	35	38	5132
克孜勒苏柯尔克孜自治州	Kizilsu Kirgiz Autonomous Prefecture	2	2	136
喀什地区	Kashgar [Kaxgar] Administrative Offices	18	18	6305
和田地区	Hotan Administrative Offices	4	4	376
生产建设兵团	Xinjiang Production and Construction Group	116	143	8011

Enterprises and Employees of Wholesale above Designated Size

市 City			县 County			县以下 Under County Level		
法人单位(个) Number of Corporate (unit)	产业活动单位(个) Number of Economic Entity (unit)	人员(人) Persons Engaged (person)	法人单位(个) Number of Corporate (unit)	产业活动单位(个) Number of Economic Entity (unit)	人员(人) Persons Engaged (person)	法人单位(个) Number of Corporate (unit)	产业活动单位(个) Number of Economic Entity (unit)	人员(人) Persons Engaged (person)
504	**536**	**28051**	**82**	**91**	**14067**	**30**	**33**	**2557**
189	220	17475	29	38	3987	3	6	369
503	535	28001	81	90	14019	30	33	2557
94	116	8854	15	23	1553	2	2	140
18	18	1204	18	18	4919	5	5	503
2	2	81						
1	1	13	1	1	100			
151	158	10840	36	36	6605	13	16	1469
17	18	2211	1	1	483			
220	222	4798	9	10	344	10	10	445
			1	1	15			
			1	1	48			
1	1	50						
86	87	5535	56	57	12709	12	14	1646
49	51	4100	4	4	178		1	130
9	9	537	4	4	178			
18	19	2545						
14	14	421	1	1	8			
2	2	29						
6	6	559						
14	14	1112						
198	223	10619	19	27	1137	8	8	486
47	51	5224	1	2	20	1	1	142
81	81	1509						
13	15	319	3	3	34			
30	45	2027	14	20	1036	4	4	196
112	115	4901	2	2	35	8	8	264
49	50	1499				5	5	107
5	5	793	1	1	12			
10	10	465						
5	5	174						
20	21	630				2	2	31
255	262	10144				10	10	414
18	18	1455						
1	1	69	1	1	106	2	2	237
10	13	1413	1	1	46			
25	26	828	8	8	794	9	10	1296
38	38	2960	20	20	1151	1	1	30
23	23	1780	14	14	703	1	1	30
9	9	658	5	5	409			
6	6	522	1	1	39			
11	11	465	1	1	303			
22	24	2318	5	5	420	3	3	266
14	14	752	19	20	4225	2	4	155
1	1	27	1	1	109			
2	2	189	16	16	6116			
1	1	71	3	3	305			
106	125	7360	7	15	492	3	3	159

15-10 限额以上零售贸易业机构数、从业人员数

(2004 年)

指 标	Item	合 计 Total 法人单位(个) Number of Corporate (unit)	产业活动单位(个) Number of Economic Entity (unit)	人 员(人) Persons Engaged (person)
总 计	**Total**	**320**	**354**	**30933**
#国有及国有控股	State Owned and Holding Company	82	116	13458
按登记注册类型分	**By Type of Registration**			
内资企业	Domestic-funded Enterprise	317	350	30022
国有企业	State – owned	56	75	6232
集体企业	Collective Owned	7	9	255
有限责任公司	Limited Liability Company	97	105	7194
股份有限公司	Share Holding Limited Company	12	13	5053
私营企业	Private Enterprise	145	148	11288
港、澳、台商投资企业	Enterprises With Investment from HongKong, Macao and Taiwan	1	2	36
外商投资企业	Foreign Funded Enterprises	2	2	875
按国民经济行业分	**By National Economy Sector**			
综合零售业	Compreehnsive Retail	59	65	11940
百货零售业	Merchandile Retail	28	34	6246
超级市场零售业	Super-market Retail	31	31	5694
食品、饮料及烟草制品专门零售业	Food, Drinks and Tobacco Products	10	11	823
纺织、服装及日用品专门零售业	Textile, Garment and Daily Necessities	13	14	1206
#服装零售业	Garment Retail	10	10	1136
文化、体育用品及器材专门零售业	Culture, Sports Goods and Appratus	26	27	1708
#体育用品零售业	Retail of Sports Goods	2	2	115
图书零售业	Books Retail	18	18	1395
医药及医疗器材专门零售业	Drugs and Medical-care Appratus	25	25	2264
#药品零售业	Rotail of medcine	23	23	2216
汽车、摩托车、燃料及零配件专门零售业	Car, Motor, Fuel, Parts and Components	108	124	7769
#汽车零售业	Auto Retail	65	67	2298
机动车燃料零售业	Auto Fuel Retail	31	43	5206
家用电器及电子产品专门零售业	Retail of Motor Vehicles, Motorcycles and Parts	56	56	3861
#家用电器零售业	Household Electric Appliance	18	18	825
计算机、软件及辅助设备零售业	Retail of Cumputers, Software and Office Appliances	25	25	450
通讯设备零售业	Retail of Telecommunication Equipment	12	12	2566
五金、家俱及室内装修材料专门零售业	Hardware, Furniture and Indoor Decorating Material	9	11	406
无店铺及其他零售业	Non-shop and Other Retail	14	21	956
按地区分	**By Region**			
乌鲁木齐市	Urumqi City	136	141	15697
克拉玛依市	Karamay City	14	18	1669
石河子市	Shihezi City	2	2	377
吐鲁番地区	Turpan Administrative Offices	11	12	813
哈密地区	Hami [Kumul] Administrative Offices	21	21	768
昌吉回族自治州	Changji Hui Autonomous Prefecture	23	27	2179
伊犁哈萨克自治州	Ili Kazak Autonomous Prefecture	27	28	2101
伊犁州直属县(市)	Counties (Cities) Direct Under Ili Prefecture	19	19	1232
塔城地区	Tacheng [Tarbagatai] Administrative Offices	6	6	282
阿勒泰地区	Altay Administrative Offices	2	3	587
博尔塔拉蒙古自治州	Bortala Mongol Autonomous Prefecture	1	1	177
巴音郭楞蒙古自治州	Bayangol Mongol Autonomous Prefecture	18	21	1396
阿克苏地区	Aksu Administrative Offices	29	30	2348
克孜勒苏柯尔克孜自治州	Kizilsu Kirgiz Autonomous Prefecture	1	1	36
喀什地区	Kashgar [Kaxgar] Administrative Offices	7	7	1308
和田地区	Hotan Administrative Offices	4	5	389
生产建设兵团	Xinjiang Production and Construction Group	26	40	1675

Enterprises and Employees of Retail above Designated Size

市 City			县 County			县以下 Under County Level		
法人单位（个） Number of Corporate (unit)	产业活动单位（个） Number of Economic Entity (unit)	人 员（人） Persons Engaged (person)	法人单位（个） Number of Economic Entity (unit)	产业活动单位（个） Number of Economic Active (unit)	人 员（人） Persons Engaged (person)	法人单位（个） Number of Economic Entity (unit)	产业活动单位（个） Number of Economic Active (unit)	人 员（人） Persons Engaged (person)
295	**322**	**29401**	**21**	**27**	**1389**	**4**	**5**	**143**
68	95	12525	13	19	897	1	2	36
292	318	28490	21	27	1389	4	5	143
45	59	5541	10	15	675	1	1	16
7	8	254		1	1			
88	95	6428	7	7	644	2	3	122
12	13	5053						
140	143	11214	4	4	69	1	1	5
1	2	36						
2	2	875						
57	62	11576	2	3	364			
26	31	5882	2	3	364			
31	31	5694						
5	6	380	5	5	443			
13	14	1206						
10	10	1136						
23	23	1648	3	4	60			
2	2	115						
15	15	1336	3	3	59			
22	22	2154	3	3	110			
20	20	2106	3	3	110			
101	114	7436	4	7	215	3	3	118
63	65	2149	1	1	67	1	1	82
27	37	5062	2	4	108	2	2	36
55	55	3838	1	1	23			
17	17	802	1	1	23			
25	25	450						
12	12	2566						
8	10	401				1	1	5
11	16	762	3	4	174		1	20
135	140	15681				1	1	16
14	18	1669						
2	2	377						
7	7	654	2	3	72	2	2	87
20	20	752	1	1	16			
16	20	1703	6	6	456	1	1	20
25	26	1999	2	2	102			
18	18	1142	1	1	90			
5	5	270	1	1	12			
2	3	587						
1	1	177						
17	20	1342	1	1	54			
24	24	2034	5	5	294		1	20
			1	1	36			
5	5	1124	2	2	184			
3	3	370	1	2	19			
26	36	1519		4	156			

15-11 限额以上餐饮业机构数、从业人员数

(2004 年)

指标	Item	合计 Total 法人单位(个) Number of Corporate (unit)	产业活动单位(个) Number of Economic Entity (unit)	人员(人) Persons Engaged (person)
总计	**Total**	**65**	**74**	**6478**
#国有及国有控股	State Owned and Holding Company	5	14	1449
按登记注册类型分	**By Type of Registration**			
内资企业	Domestic-funded Enterprise	64	73	6422
国有企业	State – owned	2	3	235
集体企业	Collective Owned	1	1	30
有限责任公司	Limited Liability Company	8	12	1274
股份有限公司	Share Holding Limited Company		1	324
私营企业	Private Enterprise	52	55	4479
其他行业	Others	1	1	80
外商投资企业	Enterprises With Foreign Investment	1	1	56
按国民经济行业分	**By Sector**			
正餐	Dinner	62	71	6160
快餐	Snack	3	3	318
按地区分	**By Region**			
乌鲁木齐市	Urumqi City	48	51	4034
克拉玛依市	Karamay City	1	5	331
哈密地区	Hami [Kumul] Administrative Offices	1	1	93
昌吉回族自治州	Changji Hui Autonomous Prefecture	4	4	364
伊犁哈萨克自治州	Ili Kazak Autonomous Prefecture	2	2	158
伊犁州直属县(市)	Counties (Cities) Direct Under Ili Prefecture	1	1	45
塔城地区	Tacheng [Tarbagatai] Administrative Offices	1	1	113
巴音郭楞蒙古自治州	Bayangol Mongol Autonomous Prefecture	6	6	524
阿克苏地区	Aksu Administrative Offices	1	1	179
喀什地区	Kashgar [Kaxgar] Administrative Offices		1	113
生产建设兵团	Xinjiang Production and Construction Group	2	3	682

Enterprises and Employees of Catering Trade above Designated Size

市 City			县 County		
法人单位（个）Number of Corporate (unit)	产业活动单位（个）Number of Economic Entity (unit)	人 员（人）Persons Engaged (person)	法人单位（个）Number of Corporate Unit	产业活动单位（个）Number of Economic Entity (unit)	人 员（人）Persons Engaged (person)
63	**72**	**6320**	**2**	**2**	**158**
4	13	1404	1	1	45
62	71	6264	2	2	158
1	2	190	1	1	45
1	1	30			
8	12	1274			
	1	324			
51	54	4366	1	1	113
1	1	80			
1	1	56			
60	69	6002	2	2	158
3	3	318			
48	51	4034			
1	5	331			
1	1	93			
4	4	364			
			2	2	158
			1	1	45
			1	1	113
6	6	524			
1	1	179			
	1	113			
2	3	682			

15-12　限额以上住宿业机构、人员数

(2004 年)

指　标	Item	合　计 Total		
		法人单位(个) Number of Corporate (unit)	产业活动单位(个) Number of Economic Entity (unit)	人员(人) Persons Engaged (person)
总　计	**Total**	**235**	**235**	**26252**
#国有及国有控股	State Owned and Holding Company	124	124	15618
按登记注册类型分	**By Type of Registration**			
内资企业	Domestic-funded Enterprise	226	226	23162
国有企业	State – owned	117	117	13424
集体企业	Collective Owned	9	9	1171
股份合作企业	Share Cooperative	3	3	269
联营企业	Joint Ownership Enterprises	1	1	140
有限责任公司	Limited Liability Company	41	41	3803
股份有限公司	Share Holding Limited Company	5	5	496
私营企业	Private Enterprise	49	49	3788
其他行业	Others	1	1	71
港、澳、台投资企业	Enterprises With Investment from Hong Kong, Macao and Taiwan	6	6	1788
外商投资企业	Enterprises With Foreign Investment	3	3	1302
按地区分	**By Region**			
乌鲁木齐市	Urumqi City	65	65	12543
克拉玛依市	Karamay City	5	5	493
吐鲁番地区	Turpan Administrative Offices	12	12	933
哈密地区	Hami [Kumul] Administrative Offices	9	9	611
昌吉回族自治州	Changji Hui Autonomous Prefecture	12	12	701
伊犁哈萨克自治州	Ili Kazak Autonomous Prefecture	52	52	3297
伊犁州直属县(市)	Counties (Cities) Direct Under Ili Prefecture	28	28	2302
塔城地区	Tacheng [Tarbagatai] Administrative Offices	8	8	380
阿勒泰地区	Altay Administrative Offices	16	16	615
博尔塔拉蒙古自治州	Bortala Mongol Autonomous Prefecture	7	7	437
巴音郭楞蒙古自治州	Bayangol Mongol Autonomous Prefecture	19	19	2044
阿克苏地区	Aksu Administrative Offices	16	16	816
克孜勒苏柯尔克孜自治州	Kizilsu Kirgiz Autonomous Prefecture	2	2	115
喀什地区	Kashgar [Kaxgar] Administrative Offices	12	12	962
和田地区	Hotan Administrative Offices	1	1	77
生产建设兵团	Xinjiang Production and Construction Group	23	23	3223

Enterprises and Employees of Catering Trade above Designated Size

市 City			县 County			县以下 Under County Level		
法人单位（个）Number of Corporate (unit)	产业活动单位（个）Number of Economic Entity (unit)	人员（人）Persons Engaged (person)	法人单位（个）Number of Corporate Unit	产业活动单位（个）Number of Economic Entity (unit)	人员（人）Persons Engaged (person)	法人单位（个）Number of Corporate Unit	产业活动单位（个）Number of Economic Entity (unit)	人员（人）Persons Engaged (person)
177	**177**	**23536**	**52**	**52**	**2465**	**6**	**6**	**251**
101	101	14485	20	20	1007	3	3	126
168	168	20446	52	52	2465	6	6	251
90	90	12054	25	25	1264	2	2	106
9	9	1171						
3	3	269						
1	1	140						
31	31	3475	8	8	292	2	2	36
3	3	383	1	1	31	1	1	82
30	30	2883	18	18	878	1	1	27
1	1	71						
6	6	1788						
3	3	1302						
65	65	12543						
5	5	493						
6	6	519	4	4	316	2	2	98
7	7	496	2	2	115			
9	9	535	3	3	166			
30	30	2617	21	21	656	1	1	24
22	22	2091	6	6	211			
5	5	295	3	3	85			
3	3	231	12	12	360	1	1	24
5	5	365	2	2	72			
10	10	1469	7	7	528	2	2	47
7	7	343	9	9	473			
2	2	115						
8	8	785	3	3	95	1	1	82
1	1	77						
22	22	3179	1	1	44			

15-13　限额以上批发贸易企业资产及负债情况

Assets and Liability of Enterprises above Designated Size in Wholesale and Retail Trade

单位：万元　　(2004 年)　　(10 000 yuan)

指　标	Item	资产合计 Total Asset	#流动资产 Circulating Funds	#固定资产 Fixed Asset	负债合计 Total Liabilities
总　计	**Total**	**6414478.3**	**4904158.7**	**614565.7**	**5140104.2**
按登记注册类型分	**By Type of Registration**				
内资企业	Domestic-funded Enterprise	6389290.3	4883147.1	611593.8	5118378.9
国有企业	State – owned	1504936.6	1228176.5	169963.9	1367166.9
集体企业	Collective Owned	602826.1	493670.6	71965.7	624245.5
股份合作企业	Share Holding Cooperative Operation	3848.0	2526.6	889.0	2841.6
联营企业	Joint Ownership Enterprises	7207.5	6841.1	344.4	9503.4
有限责任公司	Limited Liability Company	2556171.7	1978172.2	206674.7	1926962.3
股份有限公司	Share Holding Limited Company	914138.5	565279.2	73489.4	621412.5
私营企业	Private Enterprise	799679.8	608004.3	88261.3	565917.0
其他行业	Others	482.1	476.6	5.4	329.7
港、澳、台投资企业	Enterprises With Investment from Hong Kong, Macao and Taiwan	20066.8	17469.6	2381.9	19061.7
外商投资企业	Enterprises With Foreign Investment	5121.2	3542.0	590.0	2663.6
按国民经济行业分	**By Sector**				
农畜产品批发业	Farming and Stock-raising Products	2742081.9	2285557.2	240705.5	2630193.5
食品、饮料及烟草制品批发业	Wholesale of Food Beverages and Tobaccos	286082.9	178633.6	53838.0	192858.5
#米、面制品及食用油批发业	Rice, Flour Products and Cooking Oil	82309.2	53507.3	8656.2	70618.2
烟草制品批发业	Wholesale of Tobaccos	110398.8	66464.0	30633.0	44213.5
纺织、服装及日用品批发业	Textile, Garment and Daily Necessities	168798.2	152404.0	7348.1	150467.7
#服装批发业	Garment Whoelsale	9329.7	8465.2	531.5	4406.6
文化、体育用品及器材批发业	Culture, Sport Goods and Apparatus	61864.2	35560.8	14964.1	40436.8
医药及医疗器械批发业	Wholesale of Medicines and Medical Appliances	87123.6	69199.5	9241.6	67759.4
矿产品、建材及化工产品批发业	Ore Products, Building Material and Chemical products	2170813.7	1524168.7	232025.2	1470287.2
#石油及制品批发业	Wholesale of Petroleum and Related Products	397034.2	212243.9	89527.5	234066.3
金属及金属矿批发业	Wholesale of Metal and Metal Ore	846284.0	545996.8	70558.9	501297.4
建材批发业	Wholesale of Building Materials	149478.3	132099.1	6501.4	97625.7
化肥批发业	Wholesale of Minerial Prosucts	529681.7	447252.9	32379.7	442042.5
机械设备、五金交电及电子产品批发业	Machinery Equipment, Hardware and Electronic Products	712320.3	532017.0	41575.8	456615.4
#汽车、摩托车及零配件批发业	Wholesale of Motor Vehicles, Motorcycles and Parts	170724.3	126324.5	19020.4	108051.7
家用电器批发业	Household Appliance Wholesale	28056.2	26089.1	1782.9	24471.3
计算机、软件及辅助设备批发业	Wholesale of Computer, Software and Accessory Equipment	15218.2	14243.0	585.8	11999.8
贸易经纪与代理	Trade Broker and Agent	83064.6	35003.8	10938.3	64624.0
其他批发业	Other Wholesales not	102328.9	91614.1	3929.1	66861.7
按地区分	**By Region**				
乌鲁木齐市	Urumqi City	1731506.7	1286896.9	175940.0	1218610.0
克拉玛依市	Karamay City	100743.5	55313.6	19595.9	76364.4
吐鲁番地区	Turpan Administrative Offices	50087.4	45673.2	2440.5	41775.7
哈密地区	Hami [Kumul] Administrative Offices	29683.1	15622.1	9113.2	24819.4
昌吉回族自治州	Changji Hui Autonomous Prefecture	330516.6	260783.6	34203.4	276346.8
伊犁哈萨克自治州	Ili Kazak Autonomous Prefecture	485921.2	382283.8	54676.2	519111.6
伊犁州直属县(市)	Counties (Cities) Direct Under Ili Prefecture	225128.2	157641.1	36775.3	276525.9
塔城地区	Tacheng [Tarbagatai] Administrative Offices	227090.6	203770.0	10767.3	213173.6
阿勒泰地区	Altay Administrative Offices	33702.4	20872.7	7133.6	29412.1
博尔塔拉蒙古自治州	Bortala Mongol Autonomous Prefecture	179651.3	160332.3	7061.6	128391.7
巴音郭楞蒙古自治州	Bayangol Mongol Autonomous Prefecture	314512.6	233154.4	61851.4	258535.7
阿克苏地区	Aksu Administrative Offices	463790.6	348934.7	60565.4	379674.8
克孜勒苏柯尔克孜自治州	Kizilsu Kirgiz Autonomous Prefecture	9089.6	8284.8	781.4	9853.4
喀什地区	Kashgar [Kaxgar] Administrative Offices	279216.1	222826.7	38566.5	328120.1
和田地区	Hotan Administrative Offices	24513.8	11578.2	7668.2	18744.0
生产建设兵团	Xinjiang Production and Construction Group	2415245.8	1872474.4	142102.0	1859756.6

15-14 限额以上零售贸易企业资产及负债情况

Assets and Liability of Enterprises above Designated Size in Retail Trade

单位：万元 (2004 年) (10 000 yuan)

指 标	Item	资产合计 Total Asset	#流动资产 Circulating Funds	#固定资产 Fixed Asset	负债合计 Total Liabilities
总 计	**Total**	**1144071.3**	**541774.0**	**375708.9**	**844581.0**
按登记注册类型分	**By Type of Registration**				
内资企业	Domestic-funded Enterprise	1128355.3	533254.1	372261.5	833167.5
国有企业	State – owned	200619.4	81339.7	88805.7	214767.7
集体企业	Collective Owned	7295.8	5243.8	328.6	5667.8
有限责任公司	Limited Liability Company	308827.6	195037.7	67672.1	211912.8
股份有限公司	Share Holding Limited Company	266509.9	59072.3	114462.6	172985.5
私营企业	Private Enterprise	345102.6	192560.6	100992.5	227833.7
港、澳、台商投资企业	Enterprises With Investment from HongKong, Macao and Taiwan	488.0	80.2	6.9	491.4
外商投资企业	Foreign Funded Enterprises	15228.0	8439.7	3440.5	10922.1
按国民经济行业分	**By Sector**				
综合零售业	Comprehensive Retail	353449.7	110511.4	139577.6	256433.5
百货商店	Department Store	278386.5	72489.8	117683.1	201973.9
超级市场	Super-Market	75063.2	38021.6	21894.5	54459.6
食品、饮料及烟草制品专门零售业	Food, Drinks and Tobacco Products	43672.9	35646.5	6412.8	77867.6
纺织、服装及日用品专门零售业	Textile, Garment and Daily Necessities	54182.5	27729.9	15168.1	42291.3
文化、体育用品及器材专门零售业	Culture, Sports Goods and Appartus	56945.3	27625.0	24154.7	37562.2
#图书零售业	Books Retail	48416.1	20072.0	23525.0	29559.2
医药及医疗器材专门零售业	Medcine and Medical-care Apparatus	94818.1	70427.0	16125.5	68211.9
#药品零售业	Retail of Medcine	93074.2	68805.4	16007.2	66571.1
汽车、摩托车、燃料及零配件专门零售业	Car, Motor, Fuel and Parts and Components	361840.3	172311.3	112360.1	258674.1
#汽车零售业	Car Retail	190201.1	129357.2	34258.0	121886.3
家用电器及电子产品专门零售业	Retail of Motor Vehicles, Motorcycles and Parts	125585.0	75080.2	35760.1	72855.0
#家用电器零售业	Household Appliance Retail	53855.2	32127.0	14806.1	32323.4
计算机、软件及辅助设备零售业	Retail of Cumputers,Software and Office Appliances	12383.3	11354.4	556.9	7357.1
通讯设备零售业	Telecommunication Equipment Retail	59027.6	31352.4	20384.7	32925.9
五金、家俱及室内装修材料专门零售业	Hardware, Furniture and Indoor Decorating Material	29465.5	14260.5	11053.1	15589.8
无店铺及其他零售业	Non-shop and Other Retail	24112.0	8182.2	15096.9	15095.6
按地区分	**By Region**				
乌鲁木齐市	Urumqi City	754617.5	374539.0	232576.8	509119.5
克拉玛依市	Karamay City	16005.7	9213.4	4507.7	10993.5
石河子市	Shihezi City	9009.4	2666.4	4844.2	11952.5
吐鲁番地区	Turpan Administrative Offices	21934.7	4691.6	7727.2	13461.8
哈密地区	Hami [Kumul] Administrative Offices	15237.2	10808.3	3853.0	12607.6
昌吉回族自治州	Changji Hui Autonomous Prefecture	71196.8	29055.8	23924.4	49661.4
伊犁哈萨克自治州	Ili Kazak Autonomous Prefecture	39863.7	23792.4	12603.7	50935.4
伊犁州直属县(市)	Counties (Cities) Direct Under Ili Prefecture	27048.2	19163.9	6403.2	42826.2
塔城地区	Tacheng [Tarbagatai] Administrative Offices	11969.3	4144.6	5840.5	7906.0
阿勒泰地区	Altay Administrative Offices	846.2	483.9	360.0	203.2
博尔塔拉蒙古自治州	Bortala Mongol Autonomous Prefecture	4032.5	1752.4	2280.1	1562.7
巴音郭楞蒙古自治州	Bayangol Mongol Autonomous Prefecture	43869.5	16891.3	21768.6	28229.6
阿克苏地区	Aksu Administrative Offices	76036.0	30171.9	27140.6	79838.1
克孜勒苏柯尔克孜自治州	Kizilsu Kirgiz Autonomous Prefecture	1160.6	1078.8	81.8	6135.9
喀什地区	Kashgar [Kaxgar] Administrative Offices	47045.8	15039.0	16024.8	33361.3
和田地区	Hotan Administrative Offices	12268.2	4936.8	5312.0	9990.1
生产建设兵团	Xinjiang Production and Construction Group	31793.7	17136.9	13064.0	23731.6

15-15　限额以上餐饮企业资产及负债情况

Assets and Liability of Enterprises above Designated Size in Catering Services

单位：万元　　(2004 年)　　(10 000 yuan)

指　　标	Item	资产合计 Total Asset	#流动资产 Circulating Funds	#固定资产 Fixed Asset	负债合计 Total Liabilities
总　计	**Total**	**44270.7**	**9878.9**	**18737.1**	**26356.7**
按登记注册类型分	**By types of registration**				
内资企业	Domestic-funded Enterprise	42611.8	9728.9	18694.1	24720.5
国有企业	State – owned	3802.9	511.2	3125.6	1183.8
集体企业	Collective Owned	92.5			7.3
有限责任公司	Limited Liability Company	7020.7	1333.6	5272.1	5868.8
私营企业	Private Enterprise	31512.7	7759.4	10254.5	17564.9
其他行业	Others	183.0	124.7	41.9	95.7
外商投资企业	Foreign Funded Enterprises	1658.9	150.0	43.0	1636.2
按国民经济行业分	**By sector**				
正　餐	Dinner	43048.3	9125.2	18543.3	25718.4
快　餐	Snack	1222.4	753.7	193.8	638.3
按地区分	**By Region**				
乌鲁木齐市	Urumqi City	30135.8	7240.7	8626.8	16955.4
克拉玛依市	Karamay City	80.0	70.0	10.0	
哈密地区	Hami [Kumul] Administrative Offices	93.2	37.4	55.8	
昌吉回族自治州	Changji Hui Autonomous Prefecture	3975.8	602.8	2494.0	2317.2
伊犁哈萨克自治州	Ili Kazak Autonomous Prefecture	2425.5	193.3	2043.1	536.4
伊犁州直属县(市)	Counties (Cities) Direct Under Ili Prefecture	519.6	101.8	415.5	44.3
塔城地区	Tacheng [Tarbagatai] Administrative Offices	1905.9	91.5	1627.6	492.1
巴音郭楞蒙古自治州	Bayangol Mongol Autonomous Prefecture	2750.8	1443.5	1273.0	1929.4
阿克苏地区	Aksu Administrative Offices	4314.3	132.8	4172.3	4314.3
生产建设兵团	Xinjiang Production and Construction Group	495.3	158.4	62.1	304.0

15-16 限额以上住宿企业资产及负债情况

Assets and Liability of Enterprises above Designated Size in Catering Services

单位：万元　　(2004 年)　　(10 000 yuan)

指　　标	Item	资产合计 Total Asset	#流动资产 Circulating Funds	#固定资产 Fixed Asset	负债合计 Total Liabilities
总　计	**Total**	**658700.2**	**102415.2**	**472713.7**	**361441.2**
按登记注册类型分	**By types of registration**				
内资企业	Domestic-funded Enterprise	559034.9	83146.7	396714.2	295609.2
国有企业	State – owned	342231.9	47133.8	240465.9	164512.1
集体企业	Collective Owned	17274.3	2599.3	14317.6	21827.7
股份合作企业	Share Holding Cooperative Operation	4033.3	333.8	1614.0	2760.9
联营企业	Joint Ownership Enterprises	3151.6	1226.3	1884.8	1358.8
有限责任公司	Limited Liability Company	94297.6	12797.9	73155.7	40328.9
股份有限公司	Share Holding Limited Company	17922.8	2509.1	10067.9	13339.8
私营企业	Private Enterprise	78992.9	16416.0	54208.3	51364.2
其他行业	Others	1130.5	130.5	1000.0	116.8
港、澳、台投资企业	Enterprises With Investment from Hong Kong, Macao and Taiwan	79670.5	14503.1	61129.5	60962.2
外商投资企业	Enterprises With Foreign Investment	19994.8	4765.4	14870.0	4869.8
按星级等级分	Classified by Stars				
一 星	One-Star	21234.1	2074.3	18713.4	15281.0
二 星	Two-Star	114199.0	16521.9	61170.0	68057.2
三 星	Three-Star	237786.9	42779.1	166990.2	118744.0
四 星	Four-Star	140251.7	20559.0	109095.0	77922.1
五 星	Five-Star	145228.5	20480.9	116745.1	81436.9
按地区分	**By Region**				
乌鲁木齐市	Urumqi City	370127.0	57556.3	267220.8	200896.0
克拉玛依市	Karamay City	5615.3	1105.4	3162.0	2069.0
吐鲁番地区	Turpan Administrative Offices	14298.1	3455.7	10196.4	9879.9
哈密地区	Hami [Kumul] Administrative Offices	14248.4	2541.5	10528.9	5982.3
昌吉回族自治州	Changji Hui Autonomous Prefecture	11054.8	1767.9	8453.8	9228.5
伊犁哈萨克自治州	Ili Kazak Autonomous Prefecture	76052.8	8912.6	55869.1	41998.0
伊犁州直属县(市)	Counties (Cities) Direct Under Ili Prefecture	56096.0	5180.3	43162.3	31065.1
塔城地区	Tacheng [Tarbagatai] Administrative Offices	7236.0	1724.8	3397.5	5334.0
阿勒泰地区	Altay Administrative Offices	12720.8	2007.5	9309.3	5598.9
博尔塔拉蒙古自治州	Bortala Mongol Autonomous Prefecture	6939.3	1426.3	4663.7	2870.7
巴音郭楞蒙古自治州	Bayangol Mongol Autonomous Prefecture	36197.1	5927.9	23707.7	28655.6
阿克苏地区	Aksu Administrative Offices	14432.0	1908.0	9956.8	7067.1
克孜勒苏柯尔克孜自治州	Kizilsu Kirgiz Autonomous Prefecture	685.0	245.1	172.7	292.8
喀什地区	Kashgar [Kaxgar] Administrative Offices	17361.9	3644.2	9659.2	13407.7
和田地区	Hotan Administrative Offices	2182.0	386.4	1529.0	967.4
生产建设兵团	Xinjiang Production and Construction Group	89506.5	13537.9	67593.6	38126.2

15-17　限额以上批发贸易企业主要财务指标

Main Financial Indicators of Enterprises above Designated Size in Wholesale

单位：万元　　(2004 年)　　(10 000 yuan)

指　　标	Item	商品销售收入 Sales Revenue	商品销售成本 Cost of Sales	商品销售税金及附加 Sales Tax and Extra Changes	商品销售利润 Total Profits
总　　计	**Total**	**7815556.7**	**7010946.0**	**8571.7**	**405472.1**
按登记注册类型分	**By types of registration**				
内资企业	Domestic-funded Enterprise	7804619.0	7000674.9	8569.0	404808.2
国有企业	State－owned	2047535.8	1761826.1	1643.2	77978.6
集体企业	Collective Owned	372336.3	325773.4	583.5	16211.6
股份合作企业	Share Holding Cooperative Operation	13638.3	12916.2	3.5	292.8
联营企业	Joint Ownership Enterprises	4646.2	4045.7	4.5	288.2
有限责任公司	Limited Liability Company	2703212.8	2416042.8	4253.2	199817.8
股份有限公司	Share Holding Limited Company	827288.2	722125.1	975.4	44185.9
私营企业	Private Enterprise	1832714.4	1754891.8	1105.7	65934.2
其他行业	Others	3247.0	3053.8		99.1
港、澳、台投资企业	Enterprises With Investment from Hong Kong, Macao and Taiwan	6432.0	6104.0		328.0
外商投资企业	Enterprises With Foreign Investment	4505.7	4167.1	2.7	335.9
按国民经济行业分	**By Sector**				
农畜产品批发业	Farming and Stock-raising Products	1920189.6	1693864.6	1025.2	84104.6
食品、饮料及烟草制品批发业	Wholesale of Food, Beverages and Tobaccos	470890.5	413057.1	1076.9	50703.8
#米、面制品及食用油批发业	Rice, Flour Products and Cooking Oil	47380.3	43822.5	7.9	1299.7
烟草制品批发业	Wholesale of tobaccos	345917.2	299984.8	724.9	43799.3
纺织、服装及日用品批发业	Textile, Garment and Daily Necessities	270537.7	211817.3	25.3	4063.5
#服装批发业	Garment Wholesale	153400.5	152838.9	3.3	-30.3
文化、体育用品及器材批发业	Culture, Sports Goods and Apparatus	73310.4	65650.0	107.5	7552.9
医药及医疗器械批发业	Wholesale of Medicines and Medical Appliances	156620.7	147314.7	133.6	8058.2
矿产品、建材及化工产品批发业	Ore Products, Building Material and Chemical Products	3309265.2	2953966.2	4365.8	178456.9
#石油及制品批发业	Wholesale of Petroleum and Related Products	1025535.8	947079.0	1206.2	55652.5
金属及金属矿批发业	Metal and Metal Ore Wholesale	1134012.6	1051917.8	953.8	67385.7
建材批发业	Wholesale of Building Materials	116763.9	111646.6	111.6	4352.7
化肥批发业	Wholesale of Minerial Prosucts	647510.8	563951.3	1694.1	31119.8
机械设备、五金交电及电子产品批发业	Machinery Equipment, Hardware and Electronic Products	1101859.3	1049721.6	1340.3	39861.7
#汽车、摩托车及零配件批发业	Wholesale of Motor Vehicles, Motorcycles and Parts	276507.7	261725.0	781.7	12350.7
家用电器批发业	Wholesale of Household Appliance	68204.4	61827.9	37.3	5980.4
计算机、软件及辅助设备批发业	Computer, Software and Supporting Equipment	57776.1	55561.0	24.1	2191.0
贸易经纪与代理	Trade Broker and Agent	127066.8	123096.3	170.6	3758.9
其他批发业	Other Wholesales not	385816.5	352458.2	326.5	28911.6
按地区分	**By Region**				
乌鲁木齐市	Urumqi City	2479442.8	2344277.6	2456.1	131354.8
克拉玛依市	Karamay City	478323.8	439678.0	647.6	31451.2
吐鲁番地区	Turpan Administrative Offices	37966.6	35334.1	58.4	1019.4
哈密地区	Hami [Kumul] Administrative Offices	107906.5	101147.6	152.2	4462.3
昌吉回族自治州	Changji Hui Autonomous Prefecture	262133.6	227717.0	171.1	12637.5
伊犁哈萨克自治州	Ili Kazak Autonomous Prefecture	928028.2	868414.5	800.0	35430.9
伊犁州直属县(市)	Counties (Cities) Direct Under Ili Prefecture	396554.7	376466.8	541.0	6836.6
塔城地区	Tacheng [Tarbagatai] Administrative Offices	320250.8	286643.4	183.5	26895.0
阿勒泰地区	Altay Administrative Offices	211222.7	205304.3	75.5	1699.3
博尔塔拉蒙古自治州	Bortala Mongol Autonomous Prefecture	434155.9	380926.3	516.7	40483.7
巴音郭楞蒙古自治州	Bayangol Mongol Autonomous Prefecture	347178.0	318784.3	463.9	11836.6
阿克苏地区	Aksu Administrative Offices	329638.5	284964.2	1736.3	19471.4
克孜勒苏柯尔克孜自治州	Kizilsu Kirgiz Autonomous Prefecture	8168.1	7424.5	7.5	224.0
喀什地区	Kashgar [Kaxgar] Administrative Offices	187301.6	140508.8	219.3	20599.4
和田地区	Hotan Administrative Offices	26076.1	21883.7	43.7	3846.4
生产建设兵团	Xinjiang Production and Construction Group	2189237.0	1839885.4	1298.9	92654.5

15-18 限额以上零售贸易企业主要财务指标

Main Financial Indicators of Enterprises above Designated Size in Wholesale and Retail Trade

单位：万元 (2004 年) (10 000 yuan)

指 标 Item	商品销售收入 Sales Revenue	商品销售成本 Cost of Sales	商品销售税金及附加 Sales Tax and Extra Changes	商品销售利润 Total Profits
总 计 **Total**	**1524839.0**	**1361783.0**	**3739.9**	**128951.9**
按登记注册类型分 **By types of registration**				
内资企业 Domestic-funded Enterprise	1480304.8	1325912.7	3739.4	120288.5
国有企业 State – owned	219890.4	185099.3	491.4	20078.7
集体企业 Collective Owned	8751.6	7481.7	15.1	584.0
有限责任公司 Limited Liability Company	445107.6	406524.3	1079.5	29302.1
股份有限公司 Share Holding Limited Company	301305.1	263840.6	980.8	33514.5
私营企业 Private Enterprise	505250.1	462966.8	1172.6	36809.2
港、澳、台商投资企业 Enterprises With Investment from HongKong, Macao and Taiwan	3298.0	2466.7	0.5	830.8
外商投资企业 Foreign Funded Enterprises	41236.2	33403.6		7832.6
按国民经济行业分 **By Sector**				
综合零售业 Comprehensive Retail	256438.1	215206.6	1212.6	35789.7
百货零售业 Department Store	141827.5	114544.8	952.3	25760.2
超级市场零售业 Super-Market	114610.6	100661.8	260.3	10029.5
食品、饮料及烟草制品专门零售业 Food, Drinks and Tobacco	20366.4	17392.7	14.7	-3690.1
纺织、服装及日用品专门零售业 Textile, Garment and Daily Necessities	59856.3	48741.3	130.5	10763.1
文化、体育用品及器材专门零售业 Culture, Sport Goods and Appratus	59497.7	43427.2	265.7	11326.7
#图书零售业 Books Retail	50604.8	36178.8	174.7	9773.2
医药及医疗器材专门零售业 Medicine and Medical-care Appratus	127922.7	114531.3	174.8	11992.6
#药品零售业 Rotail of medcine	125760.7	112673.3	160.8	11702.6
汽车、摩托车、燃料及零配件专门零售业 Auto, Motor, Fuel and Parts and Components	801100.6	742176.5	1185.5	46751.8
#汽车零售业 Auto Retail	393789.4	373713.3	254.1	16987.3
家用电器及电子产品专门零售业 Retail of Motor Vehicles,Motorcycles and Parts	175506.7	162392.1	493.5	10725.9

15-18 续表 Continued

单位：万元 (10 000 yuan)

指 标 Item	商品销售收入 Sales Revenue	商品销售成本 Cost of Sales	商品销售税金及附加 Sales Tax and Extra Changes	商品销售利润 Total Profits
#家用电器零售业 Household Appliance	65496.1	63319.5	35.6	1589.9
计算机、软件及辅助设备零售业 Retail of Cumputers,Software and Office Appliances	40349.1	38590.2	75.4	1164.4
通讯设备零售业 Telecommunication Equipment	68970.9	59856.3	378.7	7910.9
五金、家俱及室内装修材料专门零售业 Hardware, Furniture and Indoor Decoration Material	13202.9	9028.8	6.1	4057.5
无店铺及其他零售业 Non-shop and Other Retail	10947.6	8886.5	256.5	1234.7
按地区分 **By Region**				
乌鲁木齐市 Urumqi City	919472.5	824680.5	2108.3	92133.3
克拉玛依市 Karamay City	23290.7	16623.7	101.3	963.7
石河子市 Shihezi City	39389.2	36182.9	57.2	2847.6
吐鲁番地区 Turpan Administrative Offices	35411.6	31474.9	61.9	783.5
哈密地区 Hami [Kumul] Administrative Offices	23501.1	21317.0	61.7	749.6
昌吉回族自治州 Changji Hui Autonomous Prefecture	82275.8	73572.6	144.3	7660.8
伊犁哈萨克自治州 Ili Kazak Autonomous Prefecture	61178.4	53783.9	94.3	-3329.6
伊犁州直属县(市) Counties (Cities) Direct Under Ili Prefecture	34725.2	30900.9	56.0	-4214.1
塔城地区 Tacheng [Tarbagatai] Administrative Offices	25162.8	21805.7	36.3	801.0
阿勒泰地区 Altay Administrative Offices	1290.4	1077.3	2.0	83.5
博尔塔拉蒙古自治州 Bortala Mongol Autonomous Prefecture	17947.5	16246.8	23.1	1677.6
巴音郭楞蒙古自治州 Bayangol Mongol Autonomous Prefecture	42168.9	38152.6	114.5	2348.5
阿克苏地区 Aksu Administrative Offices	135108.8	122692.0	774.9	10039.4
克孜勒苏柯尔克孜自治州 Kizilsu Kirgiz Autonomous Prefecture	1702.5	2042.0		-734.3
喀什地区 Kashgar [Kaxgar] Administrative Offices	75744.0	64889.3	96.3	10150.6
和田地区 Hotan Administrative Offices	32508.9	28573.1	50.8	885.3
生产建设兵团 Xinjiang Production and Construction Group	35139.1	31551.7	51.3	2775.9

15-19 限额以上餐饮企业主要财务指标

Main Financial Indicators of Enterprises above Designated Size in Catering Services

单位：万元　　(2004 年)　　(10 000 yuan)

指　　标	Item	营业收入 Sales Revenue	营业成本 Cost of Sales	营业税金及附加 Sales Tax and Extra Changes	经营利润 Total Profits
总　　计	**Total**	**48433.9**	**28737.2**	**3031.9**	**15103.3**
按登记注册类型分	**By types of registration**				
内资企业	Domestic-funded Enterprise	47633.9	28427.2	2991.9	14653.3
国有企业	State – owned	1388.5	561.5	65.0	762.0
集体企业	Collective Owned	247.6	127.1	13.6	106.9
有限责任公司	Limited Liability Company	5213.8	2190.5	325.5	1540.6
私营企业	Private Enterprise	40043.0	25005.0	2547.1	12086.6
其他行业	Others	741.0	543.1	40.7	157.2
外商投资企业	Foreign Funded Enterprises	800.0	310.0	40.0	450.0
按国民经济行业分	**By sector**				
正　餐	Dinner	46679.9	27819.8	2920.3	14378.3
快　餐	Snack	1754.0	917.4	111.6	725.0
按地区分	**By Region**				
乌鲁木齐市	Urumqi City	39715.9	24053.2	2505.5	13157.2
克拉玛依市	Karamay City	480.0	453.6	26.4	
哈密地区	Hami [Kumul] Administrative Offices	425.5	200.0	2.4	223.1
昌吉回族自治州	Changji Hui Autonomous Prefecture	1692.0	1140.5	98.7	452.8
伊犁哈萨克自治州	Ili Kazak Autonomous Prefecture	585.5	392.4	20.8	172.3
伊犁州直属县(市)	Counties (Cities) Direct Under Ili Prefecture	267.1	113.9	3.4	149.8
塔城地区	Tacheng [Tarbagatai] Administrative Offices	318.4	278.5	17.4	22.5
巴音郭楞蒙古自治州	Bayangol Mongol Autonomous Prefecture	2719.7	1400.0	219.0	405.5
阿克苏地区	Aksu Administrative Offices	1235.9	311.3	53.5	4.8
生产建设兵团	Xinjiang Production and Construction Group	1579.4	786.2	105.6	687.6

15-20 限额以上住宿企业主要财务指标

Main Financial Indicators of Enterprises above Designated Size in Catering Services

单位：万元 (2004 年) (10 000 yuan)

指 标	Item	主营业务收入 Income of Major Business	主营业务成本 Cost of Major Business	主营业务税金及附加 Major Business, Tax and Addition	主营业务利润 Major Business Profit
总 计	**Total**	**180619.1**	**58470.6**	**11288.3**	**95320.9**
按登记注册类型分	**By types of registration**				
内资企业	Domestic-funded Enterprise	154310.3	52825.2	9769.2	76527.5
国有企业	State – owned	96309.6	34126.5	6077.7	48064.2
集体企业	Collective Owned	7000.5	1499.2	456.1	4602.0
股份合作企业	Share Holding Cooperative Operation	1521.4	739.2	127.0	-164.9
联营企业	Joint Ownership Enterprises	860.7	155.9	49.0	194.5
有限责任公司	Limited Liability Company	23629.7	6849.1	1629.1	12856.1
股份有限公司	Share Holding Limited Company	3938.8	2313.4	265.8	759.3
私营企业	Private Enterprise	21030.6	7130.8	1164.5	10208.5
其他行业	Others	19.0	11.1		7.8
港、澳、台投资企业	Enterprises With Investment from Hong Kong, Macao and Taiwan	17116.3	3868.6	902.3	11994.5
外商投资企业	Foreign Funded Enterprises	9192.5	1776.8	616.8	6798.9
按星级等级分	**Classified by Stars**				
一 星	One-Star	4473.1	1473.9	244.8	2596.0
二 星	Two-Star	21091.8	8144.6	1194.4	7029.9
三 星	Three-Star	73088.0	25141.0	4122.2	35959.1
四 星	Four-Star	35250.2	12629.1	2689.1	17165.0
五 星	Five-Star	46716.0	11082.0	3037.8	32570.9
按地区分	**By Region**				
乌鲁木齐市	Urumqi City	107447.1	27602.1	7157.5	72687.5
克拉玛依市	Karamay City	2644.1	1420.9	170.4	1052.8
吐鲁番地区	Turpan Administrative Offices	4193.6	1282.4	274.0	808.9
哈密地区	Hami [Kumul] Administrative Offices	3419.5	1241.2	169.2	1241.1
昌吉回族自治州	Changji Hui Autonomous Prefecture	3263.3	1244.4	171.6	1210.5
伊犁哈萨克自治州	Ili Kazak Autonomous Prefecture	17319.8	6624.4	977.4	3781.7
伊犁州直属县(市)	Counties (Cities) Direct Under Ili Prefecture	12766.5	4681.3	696.7	3459.5
塔城地区	Tacheng [Tarbagatai] Administrative Offices	1547.5	862.6	121.6	-574.1
阿勒泰地区	Altay Administrative Offices	3005.8	1080.5	159.1	896.3
博尔塔拉蒙古自治州	Bortala Mongol Autonomous Prefecture	2352.5	1498.9	136.2	358.5
巴音郭楞蒙古自治州	Bayangol Mongol Autonomous Prefecture	10211.3	6091.3	602.3	1061.7
阿克苏地区	Aksu Administrative Offices	5285.6	2109.9	259.3	2224.8
克孜勒苏柯尔克孜自治州	Kizilsu Kirgiz Autonomous Prefecture	355.9	233.5	10.0	61.4
喀什地区	Kashgar [Kaxgar] Administrative Offices	4478.1	2091.3	267.6	1185.6
和田地区	Hotan Administrative Offices	285.5	188.6	22.5	74.4
生产建设兵团	Xinjiang Production and Construction Group	19362.8	6841.7	1070.3	9572.0

15-21 限额以上批发零售贸易业商品销售类值

Total Sales of Enterprises above Designated Size in Wholesale and Retail Trades by Category of Commodities

单位：万元 (10 000 yuan)

项目	Item	销售合计 Total Sales		批发 Wholesale Trade		零售 Retail Trade	
		2003	2004	2003	2004	2003	2004
总计	**Total**	**7021618**	**10787153**	**5823375**	**8890098**	**1198243**	**1897055**
食品、饮料、烟酒类	Food, Beverage, Tobacco and Liquor	517577	956724	438494	804414	79083	152310
服装、鞋帽类、针、纺织品类	Garments, Shoes and Hats, Knitted Goods and Textiles	314937	349106	225179	223563	89758	125543
化妆品类	Cosmetics	14941	43451	1749	13209	13192	30242
金银珠宝类	Gold, Silver and Jewelry	10294	16162		469	10294	15693
日用品类	Articles for Daily Use	27691	73286	4749	33999	22942	39287
五金、电料类	Hardwares, Electrc Appliances	25781	33765	21633	30187	4149	3578
体育、娱乐用品类	Sports and Recreational Articles	2016	8638	3	6029	2014	2609
书报杂志类	Books and Newspapers	102831	154235	70315	100894	32517	53341
电子出版物及音像制品类	E-journal and Video Products	370	3128	2	448	368	2680
家用电器及音像器材类	Household Appliances and Video Appliances	132431	218284	71537	134701	60894	83583
中西药品类	Traditional Chinese and Western Medicines	246216	339001	142668	220154	103548	118847
文化办公用品类	Culture and Office Use	74836	114655	46668	55767	28169	58888
家俱类	Furnitures	1570	10158	393	999	1177	9159
通讯器材类	Telecommunication Apparatus	38942	172463	3538	98870	35405	73593
煤炭及制品类	Coal and its Products	6401	77540	4294	68814	2107	8726
木材及制品类	Wood and Wooden Products	55	43	55	43		
石油及制品类	Petroleum and Petroleum Products	1062911	1367629	647967	808298	414944	559331
化工材料及制品类	Chemical Materials and Products	559393	1401423	559357	1400873	37	550
金属材料类	Metal Matterials	656573	1790276	654129	1767878	2444	22398
建筑装潢材料类	Building and Decorative Materials	82650	88759	82602	86202	48	2557
机电产品及设备类	Mechanical and Electrical Products and Accessories	255951	263566	237284	256948	18667	6618
汽车类	Auto Category	540389	773153	289736	269783	250653	503370
种子饲料类	Seeds and Forage	16140	48126	16140	48126		
棉麻类	Cotton, Flax, Local and Livestock	1701819	1923183	1701819	1923183		
其他类	Others	628901	560399	603067	536247	25833	24152

15-22 个体工商业基本情况

Basic Conditions of Urban and Rural Self-Employment Business

(2004 年)

项　　目	Item	户 数 (户) Number of Individual (door)	从业人员 (人) Persons Engaged (person)	营业收入 (万元) Business Income (10 000 yuan)
总　计	**Total**	**556847**	**981175**	**6269055**
工　业	Industry	30252	98039	495609
建筑业	Construction	1136	13652	75820
交通运输业	Transportation	118743	161724	961126
批发业	Wholesale Trade	13919	27072	1171427
零售业	Retail Trade	240952	360255	2474727
住宿业	Accommodation	3294	8007	34682
餐饮业	Catering Trade	52975	153008	573134
房地产业	Real Estate management	5432	5779	16850
租赁和商务服务业	Leasing and Business Service	5425	7863	27039
教　育	Education	579	2560	6017
卫生和福利业	Health and Welfare Undertaking	6624	12435	46924
居民服务业	Resident Service	42280	69916	185977
文化体育和娱乐业	Culture, Sports and Enterteinment	6243	12189	45555
其他服务业	Other Service	28993	48676	154168

主要统计指标解释

社会消费品零售总额 指国民经济各行业直接售给城乡居民和社会集团的消费品总额。它是反映各行业通过多种商品流通渠道向居民和社会集团供应的生活消费品总量，是研究国内零售市场变动情况、反映经济景气变化程度的重要指标。

社会消费品零售总额包括：(1)售给城乡居民作为生活用的商品和修建房屋用的建筑材料；(2)售给社会集团的各种办公用品和公用消费品；(3)售给机关、团体、学校、部队、企业、事业单位的职工食堂和旅店(招待所)附设专门供本店旅客食用，不对外营业的食堂的各种食品、燃料；企业、单位和国营农场直接售给本单位职工和职工食堂的自己生产的产品；(4)售给部队干部、战士生活用的粮食、副食品、衣着品、日用品、燃料；(5)售给来华的外国人、华侨、港澳台同胞的消费品；(6)居民自费购买的中、西药品、中药材及医疗用品;(7)报社、出版社直接售给居民和社会集团的报纸、图书、杂志，集邮公司出售的新、旧纪念邮票、特种邮票、首日封、集邮册、集邮工具等；(8)旧货寄售商店自购、自销部分的商品;(9)煤气公司、液化石油气站售给居民和社会集团的煤气灶具和罐装液化石油气；(10)农民售给非农业居民和社会集团的商品。不包括售给国民经济各部门企业、事业单位(包括国有经济的农场)生产经营用的各种原材料、燃料、设备、工具等和售给批发零售贸易业、餐饮业作为转卖用的商品，旧货寄售商店受托寄售卖出的商品，服务业的营业收入，邮局出售邮票的收入，自来水、电力、煤气生产(供应)单位的产品供应收入，也不包括农民之间的商品销售。

批发零售贸易业商品购、销、存总额 指各种登记注册类型的批发、零售贸易业企业(单位)以本企业(单位)为总体的，从国内、国外市场购进的商品总量、销售和出口的商品总量、库存商品总量等情况。该指标对促进工农业生产发展、活跃市场、平抑物价、保障供给、满足需求具有举足轻重的作用。该指标可以反映商品流转过程中商品的购进、销售、库存之间的比例关系和存在的问题。

商品购进总额 指从本企业(单位)以外的单位和个人购进(包括从境外直接进口)作为转卖或加工后转卖的商品总额。它反映批发零售贸易业从国内、国外市场上购进商品的总量。商品购进总额包括：(1)从工农业生产者购进的商品；(2)从出版社、报社的出版发行部门购进的图书、杂志和报纸;(3)从各种登记注册类型的批发零售贸易企业(单位)购进的商品；(4)从其他单位购进的商品，如从机关、团体、企业等单位购进的剩余物资，从餐饮业、服务业购进的商品，从海关、市场管理部门购进的缉私和没收的商品，从居民手中收购的废旧商品等；(5)从国(境)外直接进口的商品。不包括企业(单位)为自身经营用和未通过买卖行为而收入的商品以及销售退回、商品升溢等。

商品销售总额 指对本企业(单位)以外的单位和个人出售(包括对境外直接出口)的商品总额。它反映批发零售贸易业在国内市场上销售商品以及出口商品的总量。商品销售总额包括：(1)售给城乡居民和社会集团消费用的商品；(2)售给工业、农业、建筑业、运输邮电业、批发零售贸易业、餐饮业、服务业等作为生产、经营使用的商品；(3)售给批发零售贸易业作为转卖或加工后转卖的商品；(4)对国(境)外直接出口的商品。不包括出售本企业(单位)自用的废旧包装用品；未通过买卖行为付出的商品；经本单位介绍，由买卖双方直接结算，本单位只收取手续费的业务；购货退出的商品以及商品损耗和损失等。

批发零售贸易业库存 指报告期末各种登记注册类型的批发零售贸易企业(单位)已取得所有权的商品。它反映批发零售贸易企业(单位)的商品库存情况和对市场商品供应的保证程度。期末库存包括：(1)存放在批发零售贸易业经营单位(如门市部、批发站、经营处)仓库、货场、货柜和货架中的商品；(2)挑选、整理、包装中的商品；(3)已记入购进而尚未运到本单位的商品，即发货单或银行承兑凭证已到而货未到的部分；(4)寄放他处的商品，如因购货方拒绝承付而暂时存放在购货方的商品和已办完加工成品收回手续而未提回的商品；(5)委托其他单位代销(未作销售或调出)尚未售出的商品；(6)代其他单位购进尚未交付的商品。不包括所有权不属于本单位的商品、拨付除批发零售贸易业以外的其他行业所属独立核算加工厂等加工生产尚未收回成品的商品、代国家物资储备部门保管的商品等。

库存总额采用的计算价格是：农副产品采购单位按购进价计算；批发单位按进货价计算；零售单位按核算价格计算，即按什么价格核算就按什么价格计算。

餐饮业营业收入 指餐饮企业、活动单位或个体户的全部营业额，包括商品零售额和其他服务性收入。其主要反映餐饮企业、活动单位或个体户的经营情况及发展变化趋势。

餐饮业商品零售额 指餐饮企业、活动单位或个体户直接对居民和社会集团零售的各种商品。包括：(1)经烹饪、调制加工后出售的各种食品，如主食、炒菜、凉拌菜等；(2)不经加工直接转卖的各种外购商品，如卷烟、酒、饮料、熟食、水果等；(3)附设非独立核算的专门销售商品的小卖部出售的各种食品及其他商品。

消费品市场成交额 指在全国消费品交易市场成交的全部商品金额。消费品市场包括农副产品市场和工业消费品市场。

Explanatory Notes on Main Statistical Indicators

Total Retail Sales of Consumer Goodsrefer to the sum of retail sales of consumer goods sold by all sectors of the national economy to urban and rural residents and social groups. This indicator is used to show t he supply of consumer goods through various channels to households and institutions, and is very important for t he study on changes at the domestic retail market, and on economic cycles.

The retail sales of consumer goods include: (1) commodities old to urban and rural residents for t heir daily use and building materials sold to them for t he const ruction or repair of houses; (2) office appliances and supp lies sold t o institutions; (3) food and fuels sold to canteens of institutions, enterprises, schools, military units and to canteens of hotels and hostels that only serve t heir guests, and commodities produced by enterprises, institutions or state farms and sold directly to their employees or their canteens; (4) grain and non-staple food, clothing, daily articles and fuels sold to military personnel; (5) consumer goods sold to foreigners, overseas Chinese, and Chinese compatriots from Taiwan, Hong Kong and Macao during their stay in the mainland of China; (6) Chinese and western medicines, herbs and medical facilities purchased by residents; (7) newspapers, books and magazines directly sold to residents and social groups by publishers , new and old commemorative stamps, specials tamps , first-day covers, stamp albums and other stamp-collection articles sold by stamp companies; (8) consumer goods purchased and then sold by second-hand shops; (9) stoves and other heating facilities and liquefied gas sold by gas companies to households and institutions; and (10) commodities sold by farmers to non-agricultural residents and social groups. Excluded under this heading are: raw materials, fuels, equipment, tools sold to enterprises, institutions and state farms for production purpose; commodities old to trade establishments for re-selling; commissioned sales at second-hand shops; operational income of urban public utilities; stamps sold at post offices; income of water, power, gas production and supply establishments from the supply of their products; and s ales of commodities among farmers.

Purchase, Sales and Stock of Commodities by Wholesale and Retail Tradesrefer to the total volume of commodities purchased, total volume of s ales and exports, and the stock of commodities by wholesale and ret ail enterprises (establishments) of different status of registration from domestic and overseas markets. This indictor plays an important role in promoting industrial and agricultural production, thriving market, stabilizing prices, ensuring market supply and meeting the needs of consumers. It also reflects the relationship among purchase, sales and stock of commodities in the circulation of goods and reveals the existing problems.

Total Purchases of Commoditiesrefer to the total value of purchases of commodities by t he enterprises (establishments) from other establishments or individuals (including direct import from abroad) for the purpose of re-selling, either with or without further processing of the commodities purchased. This indicator is us ed to show the total value of purchases of commodities by wholes ale and retail establishments from domes tic and overseas markets. The total purchases include: (1) agricultural and industrial products purchased from producers; (2) books, magazines and news papers purchased from distribution departments of the publishers; (3) commodities purchased from wholesale and retail establishments of different status of registration; (4) commodities purchased from other units, such as surplus materials purchased from government agencies, enterprises or institutions, commodities purchased from catering and service establishments, confiscated goods purchased from customs authorities or market management agencies, second-hand goods and wastes purchased from resident s; and (5) commodities directly imp ort ed from abroad. Excluded are commodities purchased by enterprises (establishments) for use in their own business operation, commodities obtained without buying or selling procedures, rejected commodities, etc.

Total Sales of Commoditiesrefer to value of commodities old by the establishments to other establishments and individuals (including direct export). This indicator is used to show the total value of sales of commodities at domestic market sand export. The total sales include: (1) commodities sold t o urban and rural residents and social groups for their consumption; (2) commodities sold to establishments in industry, agriculture, construction, transportation, post and telecommunications, wholesale and retail trades, catering trade and public utility for their production and operation; (3) commodities sold to wholesale and retail establishments for re selling, with or without further processing; and (4) commodities for direct export to other countries. Excluded are selling of waste packaging materials used by the establishments (units) themselves, commodities transferred without buying or selling procedures, commission income from brokerage in trans actions whose settlement is directly handled by buyers and sellers, rejected commodities in the purchase, loss in commodities, etc.

Commodity Stock of Wholesale and Retail Enterprisesrefers to total commodities possessed by wholesale and retail enterprises (units) of various types of registration status at the end of the reference period, which reflects the commodity stock level of various wholesale and ret ail enterprises and the potential for market supply. It includes: (1) commodities located in storage, garages, counters, and shelves of operating units (such as sale stores, wholesale centers, and operating offices) of wholesale and ret ail enterprises; (2) commodities in the process of selecting, sorting, and packing; (3) commodities not arrived but recorded as purchase in t he account, i.e. commodities not arrived but payment receipts for the commodities from the sellers or the banks arrived; (4) commodities deposited in other p laces rather than places mentioned above, for instance: commodities in the hold of purchasers temporarily due t o the refusal of payment and commodities not taken back after going through the formalities;(5) commodities entrusted to other units to sell but not sold yet; (6) commodities purchased for other units but not delivered yet. Commodities not included as stock are those not owned by the enterprises (unit s), those allocated to financially in dependent factories rather than wholesale and retail enterprises for processing but not taken back yet, and finally those put in stock by wholesale and retail enterprises on behalf of t he state material reserves units.

For t he calculation of the value of commodities stock, the value is calculated at purchasing prices in agricultural goods purchasing units and wholesale units, and at the accounting prices in retail units.

Business Income of Catering Industryrefer to the total turnover of catering businesses, establishments or individuals, including retail sales and other services income. It reflects the operational and managerial conditions and development trend of catering businesses, establishment s and individuals in t his sector.

Retail Sales of Commodities in Catering Indus tryrefer to retail sales to residents and social groups by catering enterprises, establishments and individual, including: (1) various food sold after cooking and processing, such as: staple food, cooked dishes, cold and dressed dishes and so on. (2) re-selling commodities without further processing, such as: cigarettes, liquor, beverage, cooked food, fruit s and son on. (3) various food and other commodities sold in and ascent buffets with dependant accounting system.

Volume of Transaction of Consumption Goods on Market refers to the value of trans action of all goods at national consumption goods market, including both markets for farm and sideline products and for industrial consumption goods.

第十六篇

CHAPTER 16

能源生产和消费

PRODUCTION AND CONSUMPTION OF ENERGY

16-1 能源生产总量及构成

Total Production of Energy and Its Composition

年 份 Year	能源生产总量（万吨标准煤） Total Energy Production (10 000 tons of SCE)	占能源生产总量的比重(%) Percentage of Total Energy Production (%)			
		原 煤 Raw Coal	原 油 Crude Oil	天然气 Natural Gas	水风电 Hydro and Wind Power
1978	1410.75	60.0	35.8	2.4	1.8
1980	1527.72	58.4	36.5	3.1	2.0
1985	2092.47	60.0	34.1	3.5	2.4
1990	2801.57	58.8	35.8	2.4	3.0
1991	2930.31	56.6	38.2	2.5	2.7
1992	3180.94	54.4	40.0	2.8	2.8
1993	3622.78	51.8	42.0	3.1	3.1
1994	3957.24	52.2	41.8	3.0	3.0
1995	4266.06	50.1	43.5	3.6	2.8
1996	4755.50	49.3	44.1	3.9	2.7
1997	5130.60	46.2	45.4	5.5	2.9
1998	5095.18	45.1	45.7	6.2	3.0
1999	5246.28	41.8	47.4	7.9	2.9
2000	5419.77	40.6	48.7	7.9	2.8
2001	5720.04	38.7	48.6	9.7	3.0
2002	6156.05	39.5	47.3	10.5	2.7
2003	6657.43	41.1	46.0	10.2	2.7
2004	7112.95	41.4	45.3	10.7	2.6

注：电力折算标准煤的系数根据当年平均发电煤耗计算，并将历史资料做了调整，下表同。

Note: The coefficient for conversion of electric power into SCE (standard coal equivalent) is calculated on the basic of the data on the average coal consumption in generating electric power in the same year. The same is as in the following tables.

16-2 能源消费总量及构成

Total Consumption of Energy and Its Composition

年 份 Year	能源消费总量（万吨标准煤） Total Energy consumption (10 000 tons of SCE)	占能源消费总量的比重(%) Consumption of Total Energy Consumption(%)			
		煤 炭 Coal	石 油 Crude Oil	天然气 Natural Gas	水风电 Hydro and Wind Power
1978	979.27	72.5	21.5	3.4	2.6
1980	1026.45	71.3	21.1	4.6	3.0
1985	1410.84	72.0	19.3	5.1	3.6
1990	1924.38	69.6	22.5	3.5	4.4
1991	2071.40	67.9	24.6	3.6	3.9
1992	2260.76	66.6	25.5	4.0	3.9
1993	2496.98	63.9	27.2	4.5	4.4
1994	2605.67	64.6	26.3	4.6	4.5
1995	2733.04	66.2	23.8	5.6	4.4
1996	3045.16	65.1	24.8	6.0	4.1
1997	3208.24	63.3	24.3	7.8	4.6
1998	3279.75	62.2	24.9	8.2	4.7
1999	3215.02	62.9	23.1	9.2	4.8
2000	3316.03	63.6	23.3	8.6	4.5
2001	3496.44	60.4	21.6	13.2	4.8
2002	3622.40	62.2	20.5	12.7	4.6
2003	4064.43	60.3	21.7	13.1	4.9
2004	4784.83	61.0	20.1	15.0	3.9

16-3　综合能源平衡表

Overall Energy Balance

单位:万吨标准煤　　(10 000 tons of SCE)

项　　目	Item	1985	1990	1995	2000	2004
可供消费的能源总量	**Total Energy Available for Consumption**	**1470.48**	**2045.32**	**2883.61**	**3430.05**	**4902.39**
一次能源生产量	Primary Energy Output	2092.47	2801.57	4266.06	5419.77	7112.95
进口量	Imports				107.39	56.24
外省调入量	Inflow from other Provinces (Autonomons Regions and Municipalities)	2.54	2.26	8.29	25.59	23.12
出口量(-)	Exports (-)	0.07	4.84	1.04	31.90	26.89
本区调出量(-)	Outflow (-)	583.47	694.89	1414.05	2144.79	2339.96
年初年末库存差额	Stock Changes in the Year	-40.99	-58.78	24.35	53.99	9.87
能源消费总量	**Total Energy Consumption**	**1410.89**	**1924.45**	**2733.01**	**3316.03**	**4784.83**
在总量中：	Consumption by Usage					
农、林、牧、渔、水利业	Farming, Forestry, Animal Husbandry, Fishery and Water Conservancy	127.30	134.91	189.13	274.97	273.69
工　业	Industry	679.58	1095.22	1571.88	1860.26	2747.05
建筑业	Construction	41.16	41.16	63.01	81.73	69.63
交通运输和邮电通讯业	Transportation, Post and Telecommunications Services	89.24	99.72	152.77	189.76	256.29
商业、饮食、物资供销和仓储业	Commerce, Catering Services, Materials Supply, Marketing and Storage	12.98	26.28	51.37	93.83	285.14
其　他	Others	104.98	99.12	205.04	164.57	165.29
生活消费	Residential Consumption	355.65	428.04	499.84	650.91	901.88
在总量中：	Consumption by Usage					
终端消费	Final Consumption	1337.20	1825.44	2587.35	3148.77	4526.52
#工　业	Industry	605.94	996.27	1426.22	1692.96	2574.59
加工转换损失量	Losses in Processing and Transformation	26.76	27.90	62.06	91.25	106.94
#炼　焦	Coking	13.86	13.00	27.56	72.05	40.76
炼　油	Petroleum Refining	7.41	13.16	33.49	75.99	66.18
损失量	Other Losses	46.68	71.05	83.60	76.05	85.86
平衡差额	**Balance**	**59.59**	**120.87**	**150.60**	**114.02**	**117.56**

注：①村办工业包括在工业中(下同)。
②电力、热力按等价热值折算，因此加工转换损失量中不包括发电、供热损失量。
③进口量包括新疆飞机在国外加油量，出口量包括外国飞机在新疆的加油量。

Note: a) Data on industry includes the data of village-run industry. (The same is as in the following tables).
b) Electric power and heat are converted on the basic of equal caloric value. Therefore, losses in processing and transformation exclude losses in power generation and heating.
c) Data on imports include the petroleum consumed by the Xinjiang airplanes in refueling abroad. Data on exports include the petroleum consumed by the foreign airplanes in refueling in Xinjiang.

16-4 石油平衡表

Petroleum Balance

单位:万吨 (10 000 tons)

项目	Item	1985	1990	1995	2000	2004
可供量	**Total Energy Available for Consumption**	**210.92**	**333.19**	**496.35**	**616.14**	**788.40**
生产量	Output	499.38	701.26	1299.83	1848.43	2253.02
进口量	Imports				75.16	38.85
外省调入量	Inflow from other Provinces (Autonomons Regions and Municipalities)	0.74	1.44	3.31	10.85	
出口量(-)	Exports (-)		3.29	0.63	11.17	0.75
本区调出量(-)	Outflow (-)	283.50	353.59	849.63	1285.38	1454.67
年初年末库存差额	Stock Changes in the Year	-5.70	-12.63	43.47	-21.75	46.89
消费量	**Total Energy Consumption**	**182.00**	**300.16**	**451.26**	**527.71**	**667.50**
在消费量中:	Consumption by Sector					
农、林、牧、渔、水利业	Farming, Forestry, Animal Husbandry, Fishery And Water Conservancy	22.85	42.46	44.56	63.65	48.11
工　业	Industry	91.43	171.96	269.79	273.95	232.45
建筑业	Construction	10.65	16.87	16.67	32.10	28.50
交通运输和邮电通讯业	Transportation, Post and Telecommunications Services	36.58	48.30	76.55	86.89	150.44
商业、饮食、物资供销和仓储业	Commerce, Catering Services, Materials Supply, Marketing and Storage	3.68	3.66	8.80	18.78	145.20
其　他	Others	11.42	8.48	20.25	32.70	32.30
生活消费	Residential Consumption	5.39	8.43	14.64	19.64	30.50
在消费量中:	Consumption by Sector					
终端消费	Final Consumption	161.23	257.06	411.94	457.99	620.00
#工　业	Industry	65.66	128.86	230.47	204.23	184.95
中间消费(用于加工转换)	Intermediate Consumption	8.01	15.69	10.01	17.34	47.50
发　电	Power Generation	8.01	15.69	10.01	2.10	4.03
供　热	Heating				1.24	0.04
此外：当年炼油投入量	Petroleum Refining Input	277.13	464.29	692.40	1001.32	1231.09
平衡差额	**Balance**	**28.92**	**33.03**	**45.09**	**88.43**	**120.90**

注：①生产量为原油产量。
　　②进口量包括新疆飞机在国外加油量，出口量包括外国飞机在新疆的加油量。

Note: a) Data on output refer to the output of crude oil.
　　b) Data on imports include the petroleum consumed by the Xinjiang Airplanes in refueling abroad. Data on exports include the petroleum consumed by the foreign airplanes in refueling in Xinjiang.

16-5 煤炭平衡表

Coal Balance Sheet

单位:万吨 (10 000 tons)

项 目	Item	1985	1990	1995	2000	2004
可供量	**Total Energy Available for Consumption**	**1321.41**	**1816.32**	**2444.21**	**2702.81**	**3602.16**
生产量	Output	1600.22	2100.20	2720.74	2798.90	3749.40
外省调入量	Inflow from other Provinces (Autonomons Regions and Municipalities)			1.40	10.70	22.90
出口量(-)	Exports (-)		0.01	0.14	0.22	
本区调出量(-)	Outflow (-)	237.10	232.76	221.00	203.12	244.18
年初年末库存差额	Stock Changes in the Year	-41.71	-51.11	-56.79	96.55	73.10
消费量	**Total Energy Consumption**	**1293.12**	**1716.11**	**2327.52**	**2702.40**	**3631.79**
在消费量中:	Consumption by Sector					
农、林、牧、渔、水利业	Farming, Forestry, Animal Husbandry, Fishery and Water Conservancy	80.06	23.96	80.44	100.00	116.00
工 业	Industry	639.42	1080.07	1452.19	1801.40	2731.79
建筑业	Construction	19.69	11.67	26.02	26.00	27.00
交通运输和邮电通讯业	Transportation, Post and Telecommunications Services	42.19	25.42	32.56	55.00	21.00
商业、饮食、物资供销和仓储业	Commerce, Catering Services, Materials Supply, Marketing and Storage	6.53	20.50	33.00	40.00	41.00
其 他	Others	83.51	79.48	176.31	90.00	90.00
生活消费	Residential Consumption	421.72	479.37	527.00	590.00	605.00
在消费量中:	Consumption by Sector					
终端消费	Final Consumption	1009.45	1163.46	1427.87	1502.63	1637.43
#工 业	Industry	355.75	523.06	552.54	601.63	737.43
中间消费(用于加工转换)	Intermediate Consumption	264.55	525.51	842.96	1199.77	1994.36
发 电	Power Generation	185.60	372.01	575.88	849.20	1251.37
供 热	Heating	6.99	32.32	102.93	204.46	504.41
炼 焦	Coking	71.96	111.39	158.93	137.77	229.03
平衡差额	**Balance**	**28.29**	**100.21**	**116.69**	**0.41**	**-29.63**

注：生产量为原煤产量。
Note: Data on output refer to the output of raw coal.

16-6 电力平衡表
Electricity Balance Sheet

单位:亿千瓦小时 (100 million kwh)

项目	Item	1985	1990	1995	2000	2004
可供量	**Total Energy Available for Consumption**	**38.11**	**69.79**	**120.43**	**182.98**	**265.90**
生产量	Output	38.11	69.79	120.43	182.98	265.90
水　电	Hydropower	8.64	14.25	22.82	30.54	37.08
风　电	Wind Power		0.08	0.34	1.73	2.48
火　电	Thermal Power	29.47	55.46	97.27	150.71	226.34
消费量	**Total Energy Consumption**	**38.11**	**69.79**	**120.37**	**182.98**	**265.90**
在消费量中:	Consumption by Sector					
农、林、牧、渔、水利业	Farming, Forestry, Animal Husbandry, Fishery and Water Conservancy	5.25	9.16	11.50	22.30	23.76
工　业	Industry	25.68	48.86	83.53	118.85	191.07
建筑业	Construction	1.64	1.18	3.20	3.50	1.41
交通运输和邮电通讯业	Transportation, Post and Telecommunications Services	0.40	1.48	2.73	4.00	3.90
商业、饮食、物资供销和仓储业	Commerce, Catering Services, Materials Supply, Marketing and Storage	0.16	0.81	2.30	6.90	11.76
其　他	Others	2.60	4.08	7.00	9.83	9.74
生活消费	Residential Consumption	2.38	4.22	10.11	17.60	24.26
在消费量中:	Consumption by Sector					
终端消费	Final Consumption	35.58	65.74	112.87	170.86	247.69
#工　业	Industry	23.15	44.81	76.03	106.73	172.86
输配电损失量	Losses in Transmission	2.53	4.05	7.50	12.12	18.21

16-7 分行业能源消费总量和主要能源消费量

(2004 年)

行 业	Sector	能源消费总量(万吨标准煤) Total Energy Consumption (10 000 tons of SCE)	煤炭消费量(万吨) Coal Consumption (10 000 tons)	焦炭消费量(万吨) Coke Consumption (10 000 tons)
消费总量	**Total Consumption**	**4784.83**	**3753.72**	**126.88**
农、林、牧、渔业	**Farming, Forestry, Animal Husbandry, and Fishery**	**273.69**	**116.00**	
工 业	**Industry**	**2832.91**	**2853.72**	**126.88**
采矿业	**Mining and Quarrying**	**981.48**	**269.69**	**1.97**
煤炭开采和洗选业	Coal Extracting and Dressing	165.34	215.91	0.01
石油和天然气开采业	Petroleum and Natural Gas Extraction	785.81	68.43	
黑色金属矿采选业	Ferrous Metals Mining and Dressing	10.55	6.10	
有色金属矿采选业	Nonferrous Metals Mining and Dressing	15.85	2.53	1.96
非金属矿采选业	Nonmetal Minerals Mining and Dressing	3.91	1.03	
其他采矿业	Others	0.02	0.01	
制造业	**Manufacturing**	**1552.74**	**1219.31**	**124.91**
农副食品加工业	Farm and Non-staple Food Processing	75.13	68.91	2.21
食品制造业	Food Production	49.98	46.88	
饮料制造业	Beverage Production	13.37	10.69	
烟草制品业	Tobacco Processing	1.12	1.00	
纺织业	Textile Industry	79.71	35.81	
纺织服装、鞋、帽制造业	Textile Garment, Shoe and Hat	0.57	0.36	
皮革、毛皮、羽绒及其制品业	Leather, Furs, Down and Related Products	0.96	1.20	
木材加工及木、竹、藤、棕、草制品业	Timber Production, Wood, Bamboo, Cane and Grass	9.39	7.26	
家具制造业	Furniture Manufacturing	2.01	0.75	
造纸及纸制品业	Papermaking and Paper Products	33.00	30.62	
印刷业和记录媒介的复制	Printing and Copying of Medium for Record	2.57	1.01	
石油加工、炼焦及核燃料加工业	Oil Processing, Coking and Nuclear Fuel Processing	457.95	318.51	

Consumption of Total Energy and Its Main Varieties by Sector

原油消费量 (万吨) Crude Oil Consumption (10 000 tons)	汽油消费量 (万吨) Gasoline Consumption (10 000 tons)	煤油消费量 (万吨) Kerosene Consumption (10 000 tons)	柴油消费量 (万吨) Diesel Oil Consumption (10 000 tons)	燃料油消费量 (万吨) Fuel Oil Consumption (10 000 tons)	天然气消费量 (亿立方米) Natural Gas Consumption (100 millioncu.m)	电力消费量 (亿千瓦小时) Electricity Consumption (100 millionkwh)
1314.13	**110.91**	**18.20**	**196.15**	**20.11**	**54.04**	**265.90**
	7.50		**39.06**			**23.76**
1314.13	**5.20**	**0.04**	**27.11**	**20.02**	**52.77**	**191.07**
124.96	**2.38**	**0.02**	**20.33**	**1.95**	**41.93**	**29.13**
78.85	0.36	0.01	1.39			3.32
46.11	1.86		17.45	1.95	41.93	21.89
	0.03		0.46			1.07
	0.07		0.36			2.42
	0.06		0.67			0.43
		0.01				
1189.11	**2.36**	**0.02**	**5.47**	**18.07**	**10.54**	**104.88**
	0.14		0.18	0.01		4.51
	0.19		0.38		0.07	2.28
	0.08		0.04			0.73
						0.07
	0.08		0.06			12.35
	0.01					0.04
	0.01		0.01			0.08
	0.01		0.04			0.76
	0.03		0.02			0.27
0.09	0.04		0.05			2.22
	0.09	0.01	0.01			0.22
1189.02	0.21		0.57	17.44	8.72	15.80

16-7 续表

行　　业	Sector	能源消费总量(万吨标准煤) Total Energy Consumption (10 000 tons of SCE)	煤炭消费量(万吨) Coal Consumption (10 000 tons)	焦炭消费量(万吨) Coke Consumption (10 000 tons)
化学原料及化学制品制造业	Raw Chemical Materials and Chemical Products	171.41	106.66	11.91
医药制造业	Medical and Pharmaceutical Products	3.74	3.22	
化学纤维制造业	Chemical Fiber	8.24	3.29	
橡胶制品业	Rubber Products	4.98	4.07	
塑料制品业	Plastic Products	30.00	8.21	0.01
非金属矿物制品业	Nonmetal Mineral Products	285.58	314.67	1.56
黑色金属冶炼及压延加工业	Smelting and Pressing of Ferrous Metals	221.98	166.97	106.22
有色金属冶炼及压延加工业	Smelting and Pressing of Nonferrous Metals	36.70	33.05	0.91
金属制品业	Metal Products	5.62	1.58	1.13
通用设备制造业	Ordinary Equipment Production	13.15	2.17	0.74
专用设备制造业	Special Purposes Equipment	5.22	6.67	0.13
交通运输设备制造业	Transport Equipment	3.86	2.45	0.05
电气机械及器材制造业	Electric Equipment and Machinery	4.63	2.23	0.04
通信设备、计算机及其他电子设备制造业	Telecom. Equipment, Computer and Other Electronic Equipment	31.15	40.88	
仪器仪表及文化办公用机械制造业	Equipment, Meter, Culture and Office Machinery	0.20		
工艺品及其他制造业	Arts and Handicraft, Other Manufacturing Sector	0.10	0.05	
废弃资源和废旧材料回收加工业	Recycling and Processing of Deserted Resources and Waste Material	0.42	0.14	
电力、燃气及水的生产和供应业	**Electric Power, Gas and Water Production and Supply**	**298.69**	**1340.40**	
电力、热力的生产和供应业	Production and Supply of Power, Steam and Hot Water	288.38	1339.34	
燃气生产和供应业	Gas Production and Supply	3.49		
水的生产和供应业	Water Production and Supply	6.82	1.06	
建筑业	**Construction**	**69.63**	**27.00**	
交通运输、仓储及邮电通信业	**Transportation, Storage, Postal & Telecommunications Services**	**256.29**	**21.00**	
批发和零售贸易业、餐饮业	**Wholesale, Retail Trade and Catering Services**	**285.14**	**41.00**	
其他行业	**Others**	**165.29**	**90.00**	
生活消费	**Residential Consumption**	**901.88**	**605.00**	

Continued

原油消费量 (万吨) Crude Oil Consumption (10 000 tons)	汽油消费量 (万吨) Gasoline Consumption (10 000 tons)	煤油消费量 (万吨) Kerosene Consumption (10 000 tons)	柴油消费量 (万吨) Diesel Oil Consumption (10 000 tons)	燃料油消费量 (万吨) Fuel Oil Consumption (10 000 tons)	天然气消费量 (亿立方米) Natural Gas Consumption (100 millioncu.m)	电力消费量 (亿千瓦小时) Electricity Consumption (100 millionkwh)
	0.44		1.20	0.01	1.68	13.28
	0.02		0.02		0.01	0.13
						1.20
	0.03		0.01			0.35
	0.11		0.04		0.03	4.40
	0.28		1.88	0.01	0.02	14.31
	0.12		0.14	0.50		15.74
	0.04		0.39		0.01	5.75
	0.09		0.06	0.01		0.56
	0.13	0.01	0.18			2.04
	0.06		0.03			0.73
	0.07		0.05			0.20
	0.05		0.03	0.09		0.44
	0.02		0.07			6.36
	0.01					0.02
						0.01
			0.01			0.03
0.06	**0.46**		**1.31**		**0.30**	**57.06**
0.06	0.40		1.25		0.06	55.78
	0.01		0.03		0.24	0.05
	0.05		0.03			1.23
	13.50		**15.00**			**1.41**
	40.21	**18.16**	**90.98**	**0.09**	**0.07**	**3.90**
	14.00		**11.00**		**0.20**	**11.76**
	20.00		**10.00**			**9.74**
	10.50		**3.00**		**1.00**	**24.26**

16-8　能源生产弹性系数

Elasticity Coefficient of Energy Production

年　份 Year	能源生产比上年增长(%) Growth Rate of Energy Production As Against Preceding Year(%)	电力生产比上年增长(%) Growth Rate of Electricity Production over Preceding Year(%)	新疆生产总值比上年增长(%) Growth Rate of Gross Domestic Product (GDP) over Preceding Year(%)	能源生产弹性系数 Elasticity Cofficient of Energy Production	电力生产弹性系数 Elasticity Ratio of Electricity Production
1980	7.8	3.6	7.2	1.08	0.50
1985	11.6	11.5	16.9	0.69	0.68
1990	5.8	10.8	11.7	0.50	0.92
1991	4.6	11.8	14.4	0.32	0.82
1992	8.6	11.2	13.1	0.66	0.85
1993	13.9	10.3	10.3	1.35	1.00
1994	9.2	10.8	10.9	0.84	0.99
1995	7.8	13.4	9.0	0.87	1.49
1996	11.5	12.9	6.4	1.80	2.02
1997	7.9	10.7	11.0	0.72	0.97
1998	-0.7	4.8	7.3		0.66
1999	3.0	7.3	7.1	0.42	1.03
2000	3.3	8.1	8.2	0.40	0.99
2001	5.5	8.0	8.1	0.68	0.99
2002	7.6	7.4	8.1	0.94	0.91
2003	8.1	10.5	10.8	0.75	0.97
2004	6.8	13.3	11.1	0.61	1.20

注：新疆生产总值按可比价格计算，下表同。

Note: The Gross Production Value is calculated at comparable prices and the same with that in the following tables.

16-9　能源消费弹性系数

Elasticity Coefficient of Energy Consumption

年　份 Year	能源消费比上年增长(%) Growth Rate of Energy Consumption Over Preceding Year(%)	电力消费比上年增长(%) Growth Rate of Electricity Consumption over Preceding Year(%)	新疆生产总值比上年增长(%) Growth Rate of Gross Domestic Product (GDP) over Preceding Year(%)	能源消费弹性系数 Elasticity Coefficient of Energy Consumption	电力消费弹性系数 Elasticity Coefficient of Electricity Consumption
1980	4.5	3.6	7.2	0.63	0.50
1985	13.6	11.5	16.9	0.80	0.68
1990	9.3	10.8	11.7	0.79	0.92
1991	7.6	11.8	14.4	0.53	0.82
1992	9.1	11.2	13.1	0.69	0.85
1993	10.4	10.3	10.3	1.01	1.00
1994	4.4	10.8	10.9	0.40	0.99
1995	4.9	13.4	9.0	0.54	1.49
1996	11.4	12.9	6.4	1.78	2.02
1997	5.4	10.7	11.0	0.49	0.97
1998	2.2	4.8	7.3	0.30	0.66
1999	-2.0	7.3	7.1		1.03
2000	3.1	8.1	8.2	0.38	0.99
2001	5.4	8.0	8.1	0.67	0.99
2002	3.6	7.4	8.1	0.44	0.91
2003	12.2	10.5	10.8	1.13	0.97
2004	17.7	13.3	11.1	1.59	1.20

16-10 平均每万元工业总产值能源消费量

The Energy Consumption of the Total Output Value Per Ten Thousand Yuan

(2004 年)

行业	Sector	能源消费总量(吨标准煤) Total Energy Consumption (ton of SCE)	煤炭(吨) Coal (ton)	电力(千瓦时) Electricity (kwh)
工业	**Industry**	**1.71**	**1.72**	**1153.79**
采矿业	**Mining and Quarrying**	**1.67**	**0.46**	**495.42**
煤炭开采和洗选业	Coal Extracting and Dressing	5.41	6.27	1086.03
石油和天然气开采业	Petroleum and Natural Gas Extraction	1.47	0.13	410.42
黑色金属矿采选业	Ferrous Metals Mining and Dressing	0.93	0.54	944.40
有色金属矿采选业	Nonferrous Metals Mining and Dressing	1.85	0.30	2827.10
非金属矿采选业	Nonmetal Minerals Mining and Dressing	0.94	0.25	1036.14
其他采矿业	Others	1.00	0.50	
制造业	**Manufacturing**	**1.62**	**1.27**	**1093.13**
农副食品加工业	Farm and Non-staple Food Processing	1.06	0.97	638.00
食品制造业	Food Production	1.25	1.17	568.30
饮料制造业	Beverage Production	0.65	0.52	352.49
烟草制品业	Tobacco Processing	0.16	0.14	98.04
纺织业	Textile Industry	1.30	0.59	2018.63
纺织服装、鞋、帽制造业	Textile Garment, Shoe and Hat	0.47	0.30	330.58
皮革、毛皮、羽绒及其制品业	Leather, Furs, Down and Related Products	0.22	0.27	179.78
木材加工及木、竹、藤、棕、草制品业	Timber Production, Wood, Bamboo, Cane and Grass	1.76	1.36	1425.89
家具制造业	Furniture Manufacturing	0.26	0.10	342.64
造纸及纸制品业	Papermaking and Paper Products	2.88	2.68	1940.56
印刷业和记录媒介的复制	Printing and Copying of Medium for Record	0.47	0.18	401.46
石油加工、炼焦及核燃料加工业	Petroleum Refining and Coking	1.29	0.90	444.58
化学原料及化学制品制造业	Raw Chemical Material and Chemical Products	3.02	1.88	2340.09
医药制造业	Medical and Pharmaceutical Products	0.98	0.84	340.31
化学纤维制造业	Chemical Fiber	1.92	0.77	2790.70
橡胶制品业	Rubber Products	0.91	0.75	642.20
塑料制品业	Plastic Products	0.98	0.27	1433.22
非金属矿物制品业	Nonmetal Mineral Products	5.08	5.60	2545.81
黑色金属冶炼及压延加工业	Smelting and Pressing of Ferrous Metals	1.87	1.41	1324.92
有色金属冶炼及压延加工业	Smelting and Pressing of Nonferrous Metals	2.13	1.92	3344.97
金属制品业	Metal Products	0.35	0.10	348.69
通用设备制造业	Ordinary Equipment Production	1.28	0.21	1986.37
专用设备制造业	Special Purposes Equipment	0.83	1.06	1155.06
交通运输设备制造业	Transport Equipment	0.39	0.25	204.50
电气机械及器材制造业	Electric Equipment and Machinery	0.18	0.09	174.95
通信设备、计算机及其他电子设备制造业	Telecom. Equipment, Computer and Other Electronic Equipment	4.99	6.55	10192.31
仪器仪表及文化办公用机械制造业	Equipment, Meter, Culture and Office Machinery	0.27		273.97
工艺品及其他制造业	Arts and Handicraft, Other Manufacturing Sector	0.71	0.36	714.29
废弃资源和废旧材料回收加工业	Recycling and Processing of Deserted Resources and Waste Material	0.86	0.29	612.24
电力、燃气及水的生产和供应业	**Electric Power, Gas and Water Production and Supply**	**2.75**	**12.34**	**5255.11**
电力、热力的生产和供应业	Electric and Thermal Power Production and Supply	2.85	13.24	5513.49
燃气生产和供应业	Gas Production and Supply	0.92		132.28
水的生产和供应业	Water Production and Supply	1.88	0.29	3388.43

16-10 续表 Continued

行 业	Sector	焦 炭(吨) Coke (ton)	原 油(吨) Crude Oil (ton)	燃料油(重油)(吨) Fuel Oil (ton)
工 业	**Industry**	**0.08**	**0.79**	**0.01**
采 矿 业	**Mining and Quarrying**		**0.21**	
煤炭开采和洗选业	Coal Extracting and Dressing		2.58	
石油和天然气开采业	Petroleum and Natural Gas Extraction		0.09	
黑色金属矿采选业	Ferrous Metals Mining and Dressing			
有色金属矿采选业	Nonferrous Metals Mining and Dressing	0.23		
非金属矿采选业	Nonmetal Minerals Mining and Dressing			
其他采矿业				
制 造 业	**Manufacturing**	**0.13**	**1.24**	**0.02**
农副食品加工业	Farm and Non-staple Food Processing	0.03		
食品制造业	Food Production			
饮料制造业	Beverage Production			
烟草制品业	Tobacco Processing			
纺织业	Textile Industry			
纺织服装、鞋、帽制造业	Textile Garment, Shoe and Hat			
皮革、毛皮、羽绒及其制品业	Leather, Furs, Down and Related Products			
木材加工及木、竹、藤、棕、草制品业	Timber Production, Wood, Bamboo, Cane and Grass			
家具制造业	Furniture Manufacturing			
造纸及纸制品业	Papermaking and Paper Products		0.01	
印刷业和记录媒介的复制	Printing and Copying of Medium for Record			
石油加工、炼焦及核燃料加工业	Petroleum Refining and Coking		3.35	0.05
化学原料及化学制品制造业	Raw Chemical Material and Chemical Products	0.21		
医药制造业	Medical and Pharmaceutical Products			
化学纤维制造业	Chemical Fiber			
橡胶制品业	Rubber Products			
塑料制品业	Plastic Products			
非金属矿物制品业	Nonmetal Mineral Products	0.03		
黑色金属冶炼及压延加工业	Smelting and Pressing of Ferrous Metals	0.89		
有色金属冶炼及压延加工业	Smelting and Pressing of Nonferrous Metals	0.05		
金属制品业	Metal Products	0.07		
通用设备制造业	Ordinary Equipment Production	0.07		
专用设备制造业	Special Purposes Equipment	0.02		
交通运输设备制造业	Transport Equipment	0.01		
电气机械及器材制造业	Electric Equipment and Machinery			
通信设备、计算机及其他电子设备制造业	Telecom. Equipment, Computer and Other Electronic Equipment			
仪器仪表及文化办公用机械制造业	Equipment, Meter, Culture and Office Machinery			
工艺品及其他制造业	Arts and Handicraft, Other Manufacturing Sector			
废弃资源和废旧材料回收加工业	Recycling and Processing of Deserted Resources and Waste Material			
电力、燃气及水的生产和供应业	**Electric Power, Gas and Water Production and Supply**			
电力、热力的生产和供应业	Electric and Thermal Power Production and Supply			
燃气生产和供应业	Gas Production and Supply			
水的生产和供应业	Water Production and Supply			

16-11 能源加工转换效率

Efficiency of Energy Procession and Conversion

单位：% (%)

年 份 Year	总效率 Total Efficiency	发 电 Electricity Generation	供 热 Heating	炼 焦 Coking	炼 油 Petroleum Refining
1980	73.9	21.2		72.0	96.9
1985	74.9	21.1		75.5	98.1
1990	73.9	20.9	69.4	85.5	98.0
1991	73.9	22.4	60.7	81.3	98.1
1992	73.5	24.4	60.5	83.6	95.4
1993	73.3	22.7	49.9	90.0	94.2
1994	74.0	24.8	49.9	80.8	95.9
1995	72.7	23.6	71.2	78.6	96.6
1996	71.0	24.3	57.0	79.5	94.5
1997	70.6	22.9	54.7	90.0	95.5
1998	71.9	23.6	58.8	94.8	95.9
1999	72.3	25.4	69.8	92.2	94.0
2000	73.6	26.6	75.0	89.4	94.7
2001	73.7	26.1	74.6	78.2	97.4
2002	73.6	26.8	73.5	83.4	96.8
2003	73.8	26.0	78.0	92.0	97.9
2004	70.2	25.9	70.3	78.8	96.2

16-12 平均每天各种能源消费量

Average Daily Energy Consumption by Variety

能源品种	Variey of Energy	1980	1985	1990	1995	2000	2004
总计(万吨标准煤)	**Total (10 000 tons of SCE)**	**2.84**	**3.87**	**5.41**	**7.60**	**9.09**	**13.11**
煤炭(万吨)	Coal (10 000 tons)	2.57	3.54	5.04	6.67	7.48	9.95
焦炭(万吨)	Coke (10 000 tons)	0.09	0.12	0.16	0.20	0.20	0.43
原油(万吨)	Crude Oil (10 000 tons)	0.57	0.82	1.33	1.99	2.94	3.60
燃料油(万吨)	Fuel Oil (10 000 tons)	0.05	0.07	0.25	0.32	0.16	0.06
汽油(万吨)	Gasoline (10 000 tons)	0.12	0.15	0.20	0.28	0.28	0.30
煤油(万吨)	Kerosene (10 000 tons)	0.01	0.01	0.01	0.04	0.06	0.05
柴油(万吨)	Diesel Oil (10 000 tons)	0.13	0.16	0.24	0.33	0.43	0.54
天然气(万立方米)	Natural Gas (10 000 cu.m)	96.71	149.59	137.53	314.52	642.19	1480.55
电力(亿千瓦时)	Electricity (100 million kwh)	0.06	0.10	0.19	0.33	0.50	0.73

16-13　分品种生活能源年消费总量

Average Annual Energy Consumption for Non-Production Purposes by Variety

年　份 Year	合计（万吨标准煤） Total (10 000 tons of SCE)	煤炭（万吨） Coal (10 000 tons)	煤油（万吨） Kerosene (10 000 tons)	液化石油气（万吨） Liquefied Petroleum Gas (10 000 tons)	天然气（亿立方米） Natural Gas (100million cu.m)	热力（万百万千焦） Heat (10 billion kilo-joule)	电力（亿千瓦小时） Electricity (100 million kwh)
1980	330.44	404.10					1.70
1985	355.65	421.72	0.71	3.00			2.38
1990	428.04	479.37	0.58	5.35		160.02	4.22
1991	438.67	486.09	0.50	6.85		147.11	5.60
1992	457.27	498.20	0.60	6.66		161.64	7.18
1993	480.07	510.00	0.50	8.78		185.17	7.81
1994	491.37	520.00	0.60	8.90		171.53	8.33
1995	499.84	527.00	0.50	8.94		177.29	10.11
1996	522.59	537.33	0.56	9.59		180.55	12.35
1997	594.82	549.00	0.50	8.66		1000.00	14.06
1998	617.55	570.00	0.65	9.82	0.05	1000.00	15.98
1999	609.22	580.00	0.75	10.10	0.11	864.00	16.83
2000	650.91	590.00	0.75	10.89	0.13	1611.81	17.60
2001	703.97	600.00	0.67	12.31	0.46	2209.66	19.50
2002	752.10	610.00	0.10	14.22	0.32	3112.58	19.20
2003	782.21	625.04		16.62	0.60	3191.14	20.37
2004	901.88	605.00		17.00	1.00	3363.45	24.26

16-14　每人年平均生活用能源

Annual Average Per-Capital Energy Consumption for Non-Production Purpose

年　份 Year	平均每人生活消费能源（公斤标准煤/人） Annual Average Non-productive Consumption Per-Capital (kg of SCE/person)	煤炭（公斤） Coal (kg)	电力（千瓦小时） Electricity (kwh)	煤油（公斤） Kerosene (kg)	液化石油气（公斤） Liquefied Petroleum Gas (kg)	天然气（立方米） Natural Gas (cu.m)
1980	258	315	13.25			
1985	261	310	17.49	0.52	2.20	
1990	268	313	27.60	0.38	3.50	
1991	285	313	36.00	0.32	4.41	
1992	255	315	45.40	0.38	4.21	
1993	275	318	48.70	0.31	5.47	
1994	276	318	51.00	0.40	5.45	
1995	301	317	65.60	0.30	5.33	
1996	299	318	73.10	0.33	5.67	
1997	330	331	81.80	0.29	5.04	
1998	353	326	91.45	0.37	5.61	0.03
1999	343	327	94.82	0.42	5.69	0.62
2000	353	320	95.33	0.41	5.90	0.70
2001	375	320	103.93	0.36	6.56	2.45
2002	395	320	100.78	0.05	7.46	1.68
2003	404	323	105.33		8.59	3.10
2004	459	308	123.58		8.66	5.09

16-15 各地、州、市规模以上工业能源消费量

Energy Consumption of Industry Above Designated Size by Prefecture, Autonomous Prefecture and City

(2004 年)

能源品种	Variey of Energy	合计 Total	乌鲁木齐市 Urumqi City	克拉玛依市 Karamay City	石河子市 Shi Hezi City	阿拉尔市 Alar City
原煤(吨)	Coal (ton)	25290062	9579490	1687794	1309525	4485
洗精煤(吨)	Washed Coal(ton)	1095631	1067338			
其他洗煤(吨)	Other Washed Coal (ton)	105064	105000			
焦炭(吨)	Coke (ton)	1230116	878959		4	
焦炉煤气(万立方米)	Coke Oven Gas (10 000 cu.m)	19408	19408			
高炉煤气(万立方米)	High Oven Gas (10 000 cu.m)	11893	11893			
天然气(万立方米)	Natural Gas (10 000 cu.m)	456120	103261	217578		
原油(吨)	Coal (ton)	13138335	4261417	7610711		
汽油(吨)	Gasoline (ton)	42266	11713	11823	1197	3
煤油(吨)	Kerosene (ton)	172	113	2	4	
柴油(吨)	Diesel Oil (ton)	203779	28798	104712	2799	
燃料油(吨)	Fuel Oil (ton)	249019	212844	31282		
液化石油气(吨)	Liquefied Petroleum Gas (ton)	98408	49964	341		
炼厂干气(吨)	Refinary Dry Gas (ton)	362984	193112	147654		
其他石油制品(吨)	Other Oil Product (ton)	749407	156792			
热力(百万千焦)	Heat (million KJ)	65160348	3187838	41941100	4007876	
电力(万千瓦时)	Electricity (10 000 kwh)	1604095	555470	218421	66882	387
其他燃料(吨标准煤)	Other (tons of SCE)	35153				
能源合计(吨标准煤)	Energy Total (tons of SCE)	56957722	19940020	17851226	1348114	4772

能源品种	Variey of Energy	图木舒克市 Tumxuk City	五家渠市 Wujiaqu City	吐鲁番地区 Turpan Administrative Offices	哈密地区 Hami [kumul] Administrative Offices	昌吉州 Changji Hui Autonomous Prefecture
原煤(吨)	Coal (ton)	10689	25418	352679	1422530	4337202
洗精煤(吨)	Washed Coal (ton)			3061		55
其他洗煤(吨)	Other Washed Coal (ton)					64
焦炭(吨)	Coke (ton)			37173	40480	7521
焦炉煤气(万立方米)	Coke Oven Gas (10 000 cu.m)					
高炉煤气(万立方米)	High Oven Gas (10 000 cu.m)					
天然气(万立方米)	Natural Gas (10 000 cu.m)			30430		1217
原油(吨)	Coal (ton)			182381		16657
汽油(吨)	Gasoline (ton)	39	121	636	1620	4319
煤油(吨)	Kerosene (ton)		1		13	3
柴油(吨)	Diesel Oil (ton)	27	30	7052	12798	8016
燃料油(吨)	Fuel Oil (ton)			6		966
液化石油气(吨)	Liquefied Petroleum Gas (ton)				27	46317
炼厂干气(吨)	Refinary Dry Gas (ton)					
其他石油制品(吨)	Other Oil Product (ton)		9			1844
热力(百万千焦)	Heat (million KJ)		4405	90733	3	287997
电力(万千瓦时)	Electricity (10 000 kwh)	9381	3192	45392	72510	284835
其他燃料(吨标准煤)	Other (tons of SCE)			34624		
能源合计(吨标准煤)	Energy Total (tons of SCE)	45631	31433	1185449	1400928	4385952

注：1.本表为全部国有及年产品销售收入 500 万元以上的非国有工业企业；2.各地区数含兵团工业在内。

Note: a) This table is for all the state-owned and non-state owned enterprises with sales revenue of over 5 million yuan; b) Figures in different prefectures include XPCG enterprises.

16-15 续表 Continued

名 称	Variey of Energy	伊犁州直属县(市) Counties (Cities) Direct Under Ili Prefecture	塔城地区 Tacheng [Tarbagatai] Administrative Office	阿勒泰地区 Altay Administrative Offices	博尔塔拉州 Bortala Mongol Autonomous Prefecture
原煤(吨)	Coal (ton)	1633754	1131303	240707	289379
洗精煤(吨)	Washed Coal (ton)				
其他洗煤(吨)	Other Washed Coal (ton)				
焦炭(吨)	Coke (ton)	100144	4575	20633	62719
焦炉煤气(万立方米)	Coke Oven Gas (10 000 cu.m)				
高炉煤气(万立方米)	High Oven Gas (10 000 cu.m)				
天然气(万立方米)	Natural Gas (10 000 cu.m)	26			
原油(吨)	Coal (ton)				
汽油(吨)	Gasoline (ton)	1204	958	609	223
煤油(吨)	Kerosene (ton)	13			
柴油(吨)	Diesel Oil (ton)	2504	2085	910	634
燃料油(吨)	Fuel Oil (ton)	769			
液化石油气(吨)	Liquefied Petroleum Gas (ton)				
炼厂干气(吨)	Refinary Dry Gas (ton)				
其他石油制品(吨)	Other Oil Product (ton)	298			
热力(百万千焦)	Heat (million KJ)	4047	1421526		161523
电力(万千瓦时)	Electricity (10 000 kwh)	61665	41608	23330	11878
其他燃料(吨标准煤)	Other (tons of SCE)				
能源合计(吨标准煤)	Energy Total (tons of SCE)	1509547	1033551	287472	322376

名 称	Variey of Energy	巴音郭楞州 Bayangol Mongol Autonomous Prefecture	阿克苏地区 Aksu Administrative Offices	克孜勒苏州 Kizilsu Kirgiz Autonomous Prefecture	喀什地区 Kashgar [kaxgar] Administrative Offices	和田地区 Hotan Administrative Offices
原煤(吨)	Coal (ton)	1431009	1089149	67109	515577	162263
洗精煤(吨)	Washed Coal (ton)	25177				
其他洗煤(吨)	Other Washed Coal (ton)					
焦炭(吨)	Coke (ton)	69372	8472	1	64	
焦炉煤气(万立方米)	Coke Oven Gas (10 000 cu.m)					
高炉煤气(万立方米)	High Oven Gas (10 000 cu.m)					
天然气(万立方米)	Natural Gas (10 000 cu.m)	92203	11405			
原油(吨)	Coal (ton)	872122	195047			
汽油(吨)	Gasoline (ton)	5704	1045	118	392	543
煤油(吨)	Kerosene (ton)	11	13			
柴油(吨)	Diesel Oil (ton)	23689	6660	535	628	1903
燃料油(吨)	Fuel Oil (ton)	2	3150		1	
液化石油气(吨)	Liquefied Petroleum Gas (ton)	756	1000		4	
炼厂干气(吨)	Refinary Dry Gas (ton)	19568	2650			
其他石油制品(吨)	Other Oil Product (ton)		590438		28	
热力(百万千焦)	Heat (million KJ)	13685796	367504			
电力(万千瓦时)	Electricity (10 000 kwh)	112602	65040	3757	21147	6597
其他燃料(吨标准煤)	Other (tons of SCE)				529	
能源合计(吨标准煤)	Energy Total (tons of SCE)	4597293	2351549	64069	453287	145055

主要统计指标解释

能源生产总量 指一定时期内一次能源生产量的总和，是观察能源生产水平、规模、构成和发展速度的总量指标。一次能源生产量包括原煤、原油、天然气、水电、核能及其他动力能(如风能、地热能等)发电量，不包括低热值燃料生产量、生物质能、太阳能等的利用和由一次能源加工转换而成的二次能源产量。

能源消费总量 指一定时期内物质生产部门、非物质生产部门和生活消费的各种能源的总和，是观察能源消费水平、构成和增长速度的总量指标。能源消费总量包括原煤和原油及其制品、天然气、电力，不包括低热值燃料、生物质能和太阳能等的利用。能源消费总量分为终端能源消费量、能源加工转换损失量和损失量三部分。

(1)终端能源消费量：指一定时期内生产和生活消费的各种能源在扣除了用于加工转换二次能源消费量和损失量以后的数量。

(2)能源加工转换损失量：指一定时期内投入加工转换的各种能源数量之和与产出各种能源产品之和的差额，是观察能源在加工转换过程中损失量变化的指标。

(3)能源损失量：指一定时期内能源在输送、分配、储存过程中发生的损失和由客观原因造成的各种损失量，不包括各种气体能源放空、放散量。

能源生产弹性系数 是研究能源生产增长速度与国民经济增长速度之间关系的指标。计算公式为：

能源生产弹性系数＝能源生产总量年平均增长速度／国民经济年平均增长速度

国民经济年平均增长速度，可根据不同的目的或需要，用国民生产总值、国内生产总值等指标来计算，本年鉴是采用国内生产总值指标计算的。

电力生产弹性系数 是研究电力生产增长速度与国民经济增长速度之间关系的指标。一般来说，电力的发展应当快于国民经济的发展，也就是说电力应超前发展。计算公式为：

电力生产弹性系数＝电力生产量年平均增长速度／国民经济年平均增长速度

能源消费弹性系数 是反映能源消费增长速度与国民经济增长速度之间比例关系的指标。计算公式为：

能源消费弹性系数＝能源消费量年平均增长速度／国民经济年平均增长速度

电力消费弹性系数 反映电力消费增长速度与国民经济增长速度之间比例关系的指标。计算公式为：

电力消费弹性系数＝电力消费量年平均增长速度／国民经济年平均增长速度

能源加工转换效率 指一定时期内能源经过加工、转换后，产出的各种能源产品的数量与同期内投入加工转换的各种能源数量的比率。它是观察能源加工转换装置和生产工艺先进与落后、管理水平高低等的重要指标。计算公式为：

能源加工转换效率＝能源加工、转换产出量／能源加工、转换投入量×100%

Explanatory Notes on Main Statistical Indicators

Total Energy Production refers to the total production of primary energy by all energy producing enterprises in the region in a given period of time. It is a comprehensive indicator to show the capacity, scale, composition and development of energy production of the region. The production of primary energy includes that of coal, crude oil, natural gas, hydropower and electricity generated by nuclear energy and other means such as wind power and geothermal power. However, it excludes the production of fuels of low calorific value, bio-energy, solar energy and the secondary energy converted from the primary energy.

Total Domestic Energy Consumption refers to the total consumption of energy of various kinds by material production sectors, non material production sectors and households in the region in a given period of time. It is a comprehensive indicator to show the scale, composition and development of energy consumption. The total energy consumption includes that of coal, crude oil and their products, natural gas and electricity. However it excludes the consumption of fuel of low calorific value, bio-energy and solar energy. Total domestic energy consumption can be divided into three parts:

(1) Final Energy Consumption: It refers to the total energy consumption by material production sectors, non material production sectors and households in the region (region) in a given period of time, but excludes the consumption in conversion of the primary energy into the secondary energy and the loss in the process of energy conversion.

(2) Loss During the Process of Energy Conversion: It refers to the total input of various kinds of energy for conversion, minus the total output of various kinds of energy in the region in a given period of time. It is an indicator to show the loss that occurs during the process of energy conversion.

(3) Loss: It refers to the total of the loss of energy during the course of energy transport, distribution and storage and the loss caused by any objective reason in a given period of time. The loss of various kinds of gas due to gas discharges and stocktaking is excluded.

Elasticity Ratio of Energy Production is an indicator to show the relationship between the growth rate of energy production and the growth rate of the national economy. The formula is:

Elasticity Ratio of Energy Production=Average Annual Growth Rate of Energy Production ÷Average Annual Growth Rate of National Economy

The average annual growth rate of the national economy can be shown by the gross national product, gross domestic product and other indicators, depending upon the purposes or needs. The gross domestic product is used in calculation of the ratio in this chapter.

Elasticity Ratio of Electricity Production is an indicator to show the relationship between the growth rate of electricity production and the growth rate of the national economy. Generally speaking, the growth rate of electricity production should be higher than that of the national economy.

Its formula is:

Elasticity Ratio of Electricity Production=Average Annual Growth Rate of Electricity Production ÷Average Annual Growth Rate of National Economy

Elasticity Ratio of Energy Consumption is an indicator to show the relationship between the growth rate of energy consumption and the growth rate of the national economy. The formula is:

Elasticity Ratio of Energy Consumption=Average Annual Growth Rate of Energy Consumption ÷Average Annual Growth Rate of National Economy

Elasticity Ratio of Electricity Consumption is an indicator to show the relationship between the growth rate of electricity consumption and the growth rate of the national economy. The formula is:

Elasticity Ratio of Electricity Consumption=Average Annual Growth Rate of Electricity ÷Average Annual Growth Rate of National Economy

Efficiency of Energy Processing and Conversion refers to the ratio of the total output of energy products of various kinds after processing and conversion and the total input of energy of various kinds for processing and conversion in the same reference period. It is an important indicator to show the current conditions of energy processing and conversion equipment, production technique and management. The formula is:

Efficiency of Energy Processing & Conversion=Output of Energy After Processing & Conversion÷Input of Energy for Processing & Conversion×100%

第十七篇

CHAPTER 17

对外经济贸易和旅游

FOREIGN TRADE AND ECONOMIC COOPERATION AND TOURISM

17-1 进出口贸易总额

Total Sum of Imports and Exports

单位：万美元 (USD 10 000)

年 份 Year	地 区 Region	进出口总额 Total Imports and Exports	出口总额 Total Exports	#一般贸易 General Trade	#边境贸易 Border Trade Volume	进口总额 Total Imports	#一般贸易 General Trade	#边境贸易 Border Trade Volume
	1985	29197	18020			11177		
	1990	41025	33530		3506	7495		3416
	1991	45933	36317		5025	9616		4931
	1992	75039	45386		16474	29653		15555
	1993	92210	49509		28906	42701		28806
	1994	104053	57612	29106	23932	46441	16036	27335
	1995	142798	76880	44550	27562	65918	17640	41888
	1996	140367	54975	30281	18647	85392	25982	54484
	1997	144667	66547	36061	22962	78120	24061	52031
	1998	153214	80789	32268	37599	72425	20972	49354
	1999	176534	102473	37120	57329	73791	25723	44976
	2000	226399	120408	55060	58020	105991	28020	73950
	2001	177148	66849	29523	18418	110299	24895	79661
	2002	269186	130849	54404	47218	138337	26028	107152
	2003	477198	254221	71115	160411	222977	72510	143504
	2004	563563	304658	50194	223782	258905	101540	147058
乌鲁木齐市	Urumqi City	165261	91704			73557		
克拉玛依市	Karamay City	6508	2538			3970		
石河子市	Shihezi City	14898	8863			6035		
吐鲁番地区	Turpan Administrative Offices	539	234			305		
哈密地区	Hami [Kumul] Administrative Offices	2882	1678			1204		
昌吉回族自治洲	Changji Hui Autonomous Prefecture	31057	23947			7110		
伊犁哈萨克自治州	Ili Kazak Autonomous Prefecture	156582	124076			32506		
伊犁州直属县(市)	Counties (Cities) Direct Under Ili Prefecture	96443	80952			15491		
塔城地区	Tacheng [Tarbagatai] Administrative Offices	46942	32727			14215		
阿勒泰地区	Altay Administrative Offices	13197	10397			2800		
博尔塔拉蒙古自治州	Bortala Mongol Autonomous Prefecture	169050	42162			126888		
巴音郭楞蒙古自治州	Bayangol Mongol Autonomous Prefecture	4105	2448			1657		
阿克苏地区	Aksu Administrative Offices	491	191			300		
克孜勒苏柯尔克孜自治州	Kizilsu Kirgiz Autonomous Prefecture	5653	1856			3797		
喀什地区	Kashgar [Kaxgar] Administrative Offices	6537	4961			1576		
和田地区	Hotan Administrative Offices							

注：①1998 年以前的资料由外经贸厅提供，1998 年以后资料由乌鲁木齐海关提供(17-2、17-3、17-4、17-5、17-6 表相同)。
②补充了 1990—1993 年的边境贸易进口、出口数。由于 1990—1993 年新疆进出口只按大贸和边贸分类，故没有一般贸易数。

Note: a) The data prior to 1998 is offered by the bureau of foreign economic and trade and data after 1998 is offered by Urumqi Customs House (The same case with that in the 17-2, 17-3, 17-4, 17-5, 17-6 tables). b) The figures of frontier-trade import and export from 1990 to 1993 have been supplanted. As XJ import and export trades were classified by international trade and frontier trade during that period, no general trade figures are available.

17-2 主要进出口商品数量和金额
Main Imports and Exports in Volume and Value

单位：万美元 (USD 10 000)

项　　目	Item	2004 年 数　量 Volume	2004 年 金　额 Value	2004 年比 2003 年增减% Increase Rate in 2004 Over 2003 Decrease(%) 数　量 Volume	金　额 Value
主要出口商品	**Main Export Commodities**				
棉花(原棉)(吨)	Cotton，Raw Cotton (ton)	5669	1030	-89.4	-82.4
棉纱(吨)	Cotton Yarn (ton)	7794	2370	-51.4	-43.0
棉坯布(千米)	Cotton Clothing (thousand m)	3804	255	38.3	60.4
肠衣(吨)	Casings (ton)	571	1921	3.6	15.5
食糖(吨)	Sugar (ton)	2821	86	-74.1	-73.5
番茄酱(吨)	Tomato jam (ton)	345991	17437	0.6	-0.1
电视机(万台)	TV sets (10 000 set)	107	4407	3.9	36.9
地毯(百平方米)	Carpets (100 sp.m)	128	40	-84.3	-16.7
药材(吨)	Medical Materials (ton)	3345	533	215.0	170.4
鞋　类	Leather Shoes		37100		-17.7
主要进口商品	**Main Import Commodities**				
羊毛及条(吨)	Wool and Wool Tops (ton)	2243	270	-54.8	-54.4
钢材(万吨)	Rolled Steel (10 000tons)	53	24232	-48.0	-31.0
纸及纸板(未切成型的)(万吨)	Paper and Paperboard in Rolls (10 000tons)	871	75	-91.3	-86.9
原木(万立方米)	Logs (10 000cu.m)	11	846	-2.7	6.9
医疗仪器及器械	Medical Equipment and Apparatus		2136		-1.7
农药(吨)	Pestilizers (ton)	77	47	5.5	-15.8
肥料(万吨)	Fertilizers (10 000tons)	31	4889	106.7	149.2
原油(万吨)	Crude Oil (10 000 tons)	39	8567	34.5	82.6
成品油(万吨)	Oil Product (10 000 tons)	16	3538	1.9	70.2
牛皮革及马皮革(吨)	Cattle and Horse Leather (ton)	27545	3352	134.5	138.7

17-3 出口商品分类金额

Value of Exports by Category of Commodities

单位：万美元 (USD 10 000)

年 份 Year	总 额 Total	初级产品 Primary Goods	食品及活动物 Food and Live Animals Used Chiefly for Food	饮料及烟草 Beverges and Tobacco	非食用原料 Non-Edible Raw Mateials	矿物燃料润滑油及有关原料 Mineral Fuels, Lubricants and Related Materials	动、植物油脂及蜡 Animal and Vegetable Oils, Fats and Wax	其 他 Others
1981	4730	2738	561		2128	33	8	8
1985	18020	13117	1126		11825	26	140	
1990	33530	20000	2669		16965	294	72	
1991	36317	22631	4739	1	15781	310		1800
1992	45386	27195	14276	306	12415	182	16	
1993	49509	32032	20450	1111	9416	170	724	161
1994	57612	32744	12893	4485	13644	1374	233	115
1995	76880	38678	13173	4359	10877	2540	397	132
1996	54975	16395	8832	1028	4014	2450	71	
1997	66547	18590	9623	3447	2167	3179	174	
1998	80789	17693	10078	1290	3546	2603	176	
1999	102743	23043	7043	787	14031	1182		
2000	120408	36002	7128	975	25554	2344	1	
2001	66849	22152	12673	638	5997	2638	206	
2002	130849	40228	20068	385	17338	2334	103	
2003	254221	35739	22924	416	9036	3270	93	
2004	304658	37709	23735	451	4176	9340	7	

年 份 Year	工业制成品 Manufactured Goods	化学品及有关产品 Chemicals and Related Products	轻纺产品、橡胶制品矿冶产品及其制品 Light and Textile Industrial Products, Rubber products Minerals Metal-lurgical products	机械及运输设备 Machinery and Transport Equipment	杂项制品 Miscellaneous Products	未分类商品 Non-Classified Products	其 他 Others
1981	1992	485	343	3	1158	9	
1985	4903	1077	140	1	3674	11	
1990	13530	1322	670	650	10888		
1991	13686	1368	316	636	9580	1786	
1992	18191	1722	766	1222	14481		
1993	17477	1249	487	1996	13677	68	
1994	24868	1517	1455	3294	18487	115	
1995	38202	2998	1864	4473	28734	133	
1996	38580	4450	1937	3412	28202	579	
1997	47957	5653	1790	3572	36717	225	
1998	63096	3899	2934	3665	52476	122	
1999	79700	3824	20892	3051	51900	33	
2000	84406	3910	25540	6595	48308	53	
2001	44697	4988	14099	9928	15682		
2002	90621	4835	19112	10760	55827	87	
2003	218482	9467	34280	16374	158355	6	
2004	266949	11388	40833	17285	197443		

17-4　进口商品分类金额

Value of Imports by Category of Commodities

单位：万美元　　　　(USD 10 000)

年　份 Year	总　额 Total Amount	初级产品 Pirmary Goods	食品及活动物 Food and Live Animals Used Chiefly For Food	饮料及烟　草 Beverages and Tobacco	非食用原　料 Non-Edible Raw Mateials	矿物燃料润滑油及有关原料 Minerl Fuels，Lubricants And Related Materials	动、植物油脂及蜡 Animal and Vegetable Oils，Fats And Wax	其　他 Others
1981	1526	144	12	132				
1985	11177	158	5		12			141
1990	7495	179	170		5			4
1991	9616	845	49		796			
1992	29653	2315	159		1481	675		
1993	42701	4742	687	368	1829	688		1170
1994	46441	14164	97	49	10722	2637	248	411
1995	65918	27515	143		19722	7608		42
1996	85392	16782	207	19	16255	34		267
1997	78120	17947	410		17531	6		
1998	72425	11805	143	25	11551	86		
1999	73791	28643	955	115	27295	275	3	
2000	105991	46502	1053	83	45018	296	52	
2001	110299	38294	2730	113	34765	680	6	
2002	138337	28782	1736	15	24197	2808	26	
2003	222977	41729	2550	5	33615	5557	2	
2004	258905	70535	531		59319	10600	85	

年　份 Year	工业制成品 Manufactured Goods	化学品及有关产品 Chemicals and Related Products	轻纺产品、橡胶制品矿冶产品及其制品 Light and Textile Industrial ProductsRubber Products Minerals Metal-lurgical products	机械及运输设备 Machinery and Transport Equipment	杂　项制　品 Miscellaneous Products	未分类商品 Non-Classified Products	其　他 Others
1981	1382	63	340	653	326		
1985	11019	1915	3021	5562	255	266	
1990	7316	3887	1951	1149	329		
1991	8771	5478	1534	1491	268		
1992	27338	17324	3547	3976	2491		
1993	37959	6546	17386	12284	1734	9	
1994	32277	4850	9576	10708	3378	3765	
1995	38403	9193	12486	13723	2072	929	
1996	68610	16463	30031	17301	4293	255	267
1997	60173	10549	33157	12069	3916	482	
1998	60620	13906	32704	9657	4195	158	
1999	45148	7644	23518	12640	1346		
2000	59489	5991	35016	16541	1941		
2001	72005	7033	46124	16159	2689		
2002	109555	7127	86402	14158	1868		
2003	181248	10987	133756	33579	2926		
2004	188370	20195	136340	27914	3921		

17-5 新疆同各国(地区)海关进出口总额

Total Sum of Xinjiang's Imports and Exports with Related Countries and Territories (Customs Statistics)

单位：万美元 (USD 10 000)

国 别 (地 区)	Country (Territory)	2003			2004		
		进出口总额 Total Imports and Exports	出口总额 Total Exports	进口总额 Total Imports	进出口总额 Total Imports and Exports	出口总额 Total Exports	进口总额 Total Imports
总 计	**Total**	**477198**	**254221**	**222977**	**563563**	**304658**	**258905**
亚 洲	**Asia**	**72427**	**51110**	**21317**	**58316**	**39965**	**18351**
阿富汗	Afghanistan	127	127		286	286	
巴 林	Bahrain	32	32		25	25	
孟加拉国	Bangladesh	144	144		85	85	
不 丹	Bhutan	116	116				
文 莱	Brunei	4	4		1	1	
缅 甸	Myanmar	37	37		59	59	
柬埔寨	Cambodia	53	53		29	5	24
塞浦路斯	Cyprus	15	15		1	1	
朝鲜民主主义共和国	D.P.R Korea	22	22				
中国香港	Hong Kong, China	7314	7194	120	4663	4596	67
印 度	India	2260	769	1491	1087	325	762
印度尼西亚	Indonesia	2210	2091	119	1077	938	139
伊 朗	Iran	230	174	56	654	551	103
以色列	Israel	736	203	533	438	207	231
日 本	Japan	15118	4176	10942	8999	5664	3335
约 旦	Jordan	29	29		44	44	
科威特	Kuwait	163	99	64	281	61	220
黎巴嫩	Lebanon	35	35		56	56	
中国澳门	Macao, China	18	18				
马来西亚	Malaysia	587	298	289	1556	627	929
蒙 古	Mongolia	878	483	395	1644	964	680
尼泊尔	Nepal	50	50		70	70	
阿 曼	Aman	113	113		218	218	
巴基斯坦	Pakistan	25539	25067	472	16315	16159	156
菲律宾	The Philppines	2875	671	2204	4119	1300	2819
卡塔尔	Qatar	3	3		8	8	
沙特阿拉伯	Saudi Arbia	1150	834	316	1409	844	565
新加坡	Singapore	1832	1346	486	858	217	641
韩 国	Republic of Korea	4619	3029	1590	4676	2160	2516
斯里兰卡	Sri Lanka	57	57		43	43	
叙利亚	Syria	17	17		40	40	
泰 国	Thailand	2005	1487	518	863	494	369
土耳其	Turkey	175	104	71	309	142	167
阿拉伯联合酋长国	Unitd Arab Emirates	613	612	1	1719	1646	73
也门共和国	Arab Republic of Yemen	249	249		479	479	
越 南	Viet Nam	785	785		1201	1199	2
中华人民共和国	China	33		33	128		128
中国台湾	Taiwan, China	2184	567	1617	4876	451	4425
非 洲	**Africa**	**1476**	**1432**	**44**	**7160**	**5259**	**1901**
阿尔及利亚	Algeria				293	293	
安哥拉	Angola	1	1				
贝 宁	Benin	11	11		2	2	
博茨瓦纳	Botswana				1	1	
喀麦隆	Cameroon				1	1	
吉布提	Djibouti				2	2	
埃 及	Egypt	101	58	43	329	320	9
埃塞俄比亚	Ethiopia	1	1		56	56	
加 纳	Gambia	163	163		420	420	
冈比亚	Gambia				1	1	
几内亚	Guinea	3	3		2	2	

17-5 续表 1 Continued

单位：万美元 (USD 10 000)

国别（地区）	Country (Territory)	2003			2004		
		进出口总额 Total Imports and Exports	出口总额 Total Exports	进口总额 Total Imports	进出口总额 Total Imports and Exports	出口总额 Total Exports	进口总额 Total Imports
可特迪瓦共和国	Cote d'ivoir				4	4	
肯尼亚	Kenya	12	12		31	31	
利比亚	Libya	9	9		65	65	
马达加斯加	Madagascar				1	1	
马　里	Mali				2	2	
毛里求斯	Mauritius	14	14		31	31	
摩洛哥	Morocco	78	77	1	35	35	
莫桑比亚	Mozambique	231	231		15	15	
纳米比亚	Mozanmbique				61	61	
尼日利亚	Nigeria	1	1		61	61	
留尼汪	Reunion	1	1				
塞内加尔	Senegal				186	186	
塞拉利昂	Sierra Leone				1	1	
南　非	South Africa	255	255		824	678	146
苏　丹	Sudan	556	556		2884	2884	
坦桑尼亚	Tanzania	6	6		31	31	
多　哥	Togo	7	7		64	64	
突尼斯	Tunisia	22	22		8	8	
民主刚果	Congo DR	1	1				
赞比亚	Zambia	1	1		1747	1	1746
津巴布韦	Zimbabwe	2	2		2	2	
欧 洲	**Europe**	**366696**	**186508**	**180188**	**451088**	**245267**	**205821**
比利时	Belgium	455	280	175	340	72	268
丹　麦	Denmark	722	37	685	251	22	229
英　国	United Kingdom	2570	1723	847	2401	1507	894
德　国	Federal Republic of Germany	8126	2356	5770	8826	1978	6848
法　国	France	3308	1459	1849	1829	515	1314
爱尔兰	Ireland	43	17	26	76	55	21
意大利	Italy	14326	7540	6786	10409	4393	6016
荷　兰	Netherlands	1212	975	237	1365	1022	343
希　腊	Greece	124	124		83	83	
葡萄牙	Portugal	129	123	6	87	28	59
西班牙	Spain	740	710	30	559	404	155
奥地利	Austria	257	38	219	472	105	367
保加利亚	Bulgaria				10	10	
芬　兰	Finland	266	125	141	431	218	213
匈牙利	Hungary	192	181	11	168	168	
马尔他	Malta	38	38		31	31	
挪　威	Norway	239	157	82	293	178	115
波　兰	Poland	804	363	441	767	694	73
罗马尼亚	Romania	572	422	150	325	293	32
瑞　典	Sweden	1179	308	871	1156	327	829
瑞　士	Switzerland	1188	593	595	1995	711	1284
爱沙尼亚	Estonia				16	6	10
拉脱维亚	Latvia	77	77		70	68	2
立陶宛	Lithuania	138	138		76	76	
格鲁吉亚	Georgia	560	560		19	19	
亚美尼亚	Argentina				4	4	
阿塞拜疆	Azerbajan	15222	15222		9050	9046	4
白俄罗斯	Belorussia				158	21	137
哈萨克斯坦	Kazakhstan	254613	127293	127320	328607	178166	150441
吉尔吉斯	Kirgizistan	23094	16266	6828	46206	35771	10435

17-5 续表 2 Continued

单位：万美元 (USD 10 000)

国别(地区)	Country (Territory)	2003			2004		
		进出口总额 Total Imports and Exports	出口总额 Total Exports	进口总额 Total Imports	进出口总额 Total Imports and Exports	出口总额 Total Exports	进口总额 Total Imports
俄罗斯	Russia	27453	5460	21993	22314	4789	17525
塔吉克斯坦	Tajikistan	873	329	544	3088	2264	824
土库曼斯坦	Turkmenistan	2472	2397	75	359	236	123
乌克兰	Ukraine	1215	88	1127	313	148	165
乌兹别克斯坦	Uzbekistan	3773	799	2974	8576	1648	6928
南斯拉夫联盟	Yugoslavia	26		26	153	18	135
斯洛文尼亚	Slovenia	40	40		21	21	
克罗地亚	Croatia	10	10		51	21	30
捷 克	Czecho	314	249	65	125	123	2
斯洛伐克	Slovakia	326	11	315	8	8	
拉丁美洲	**Latin America**	**12491**	**2666**	**9825**	**20080**	**1617**	**18463**
阿根廷	Argentina	212	163	49	94	21	73
玻利维亚	Bolivia	4	4				
伯里兹	Belize				1	1	
巴 西	Brazil	852	286	566	1553	255	1298
智 利	Chile	9263	143	9120	15459	61	15398
哥伦比亚	Colombia	40	40		504	504	
哥斯达黎加	Costarica	49	49		19	19	
多米尼克	Commonwealth of Dominica				4	4	
古 巴	Cuba	310	310		49	49	
多米加共和国	Dominican Republic	12	12				
多米尼加	Dominica				16	16	
希腊索岛	Curacao	4	4				
厄瓜多尔	Ecuador	23	23		63	63	
瓜德罗普	Guadeloupe	2	2				
洪都拉斯	Honduras	58	58		29	29	
危地马拉	Guatemala	29	29		22	22	
圭亚那	Guyana				2	2	
海 地	Hayti				21	21	
牙买加	Jamaica	29	29		35	35	
墨西哥	Mexico	209	206	3	225	211	14
巴拿马	Panama	778	778		139	139	
巴拉圭	Paraguay				361	17	344
秘 鲁	Peru	528	441	87	1332	45	1287
波多黎各	Puerto Rico	57	57		61	61	
圣卢西亚	Saint Lucia				2	2	
萨尔瓦多	El. Salvador	4	4		4	4	
特立尼达和多巴哥	Trinidada and Tobago				5	5	
乌拉圭	Uruguay	5	5		5	5	
委内瑞拉	Venezuela	23	23		75	26	49
北美洲	**North America**	**20443**	**11189**	**9254**	**24987**	**11742**	**13245**
加拿大	Canada	953	503	450	2175	1355	820
美 国	United States	19489	10685	8804	22812	10387	12425
格陵兰	Greenland	1	1				
大洋洲	**Oceania**	**3665**	**1316**	**2349**	**1932**	**808**	**1124**
澳大利亚	Australia	2717	1037	1680	1047	534	513
斐 济	Fiji	8	8		11	11	
新喀里多尼亚	Newcaledonia	2	2				
新西兰	New Zealand	901	232	669	857	246	611
巴布亚新几内亚	Papua New Guinea	21	21		17	17	
汤 加	Tonda	14	14				
法属波利尼亚	Bolivia surbodinate to France	2	2				

17-6 按贸易方式和登记注册类型分的海关进出口额

Total Imports and Exports by Trade Mode and Registration (Customs Statiatics)

单位：万美元 (USD10 000)

项　目	Item	2003			2004		
		进出口总额 Total Imports and Exports	出口总额 Total Exports	进口总额 Total Imports	进出口总额 Total Imports and Exports	出口总额 Total Exports	进口总额 Total Imports
总　计	**Total**	**477198**	**254221**	**222977**	**563563**	**304658**	**258905**
按贸易方式分	**By Trade Mode**						
一般贸易	General Trade	143625	71115	72510	151734	50194	101540
加工贸易	Processing Trade	23294	20188	3106	31839	26643	5196
边境小额贸易	Petty-volume Border Trade	303915	160411	143504	370840	223782	147058
其它贸易	Other Trade	6364	2507	3857	9150	4039	5111
按登记注册类型分	**By Registration**						
国有经济	State-owned Units	265058	155317	109741	243242	109760	133482
集体经济	Collective-owned Units	103114	40863	62251	80348	50843	29505
私营经济	Private-owned Units	94161	48656	45505	222156	133008	89148
三资企业	Three Kinds of Ventures	14779	9382	5397	17758	11046	6712
其它经济	Other Types of Ownership	86	3	83	59	1	58

17-7 人民币对主要外币年平均汇价(中间价)

Average Exchange Rate of RMB Yuan Against Main Convertible Currences (Medium Rate)

单位：人民币元 (RMB yuan)

年 份 Year	100 美元 100 US Dollars	100 日元 100 Japanese Yen	100 港元 100 Hong Kong Dollars	100 欧元 100 Euros
1985	293.66	1.2457	37.57	
1990	478.32	3.3233	61.39	
1991	532.33	3.9602	68.45	
1992	551.46	4.3608	71.24	
1993	576.20	5.2020	74.41	
1994	861.87	8.4370	111.53	
1995	835.10	8.9225	107.96	
1996	831.42	7.6352	107.51	
1997	828.98	6.8600	107.09	
1998	827.91	6.3488	106.88	
1999	827.83	7.2932	106.66	
2000	827.84	7.6864	106.18	
2001	827.70	6.8075	106.08	
2002	827.70	6.6237	106.07	800.58
2003	827.70	7.1466	106.24	936.13
2004	827.68	7.6552	106.23	1029.00

17-8 对外承包工程和劳务合作
Contracted Projects in Foreign Countries or Territories

项目	Item	2003	2004
承包工程	**Contracted Projects**		
新签合同数(个)	Newly Signed Number of Contract (Units)	18	10
新签合同金额(万美元)	Newly Signed Contracted Value (USD 10 000)	18910	10195
实际营业额	Actual Business Volume		

17-9 利用外资(按方式分)
Utilization of Foreign Capital by Mode

单位：个、万美元 (unit, USD 10 000)

指标	Item	2003			2004		
		项目 Number of Projects	合同金额 Contract Value	实际使用金额 Used Value	项目 Number of Projects	合同金额 Contract Value	实际使用金额 Used Value
总计	**Total**	**65**	**16147**	**4005**	**74**	**25786**	**4586**
外商直接投资	**Foreign Direct Investments**	**65**	**16147**	**4005**	**74**	**25786**	**4586**
外资企业	Foreign Investment Enterprises	31	6643	1603	27	8202	1588
合资经营企业	Joint Ventures Enterprises	9	5025	345	31	9764	2712
合作经营企业	Cooperative Operation Enterprises	25	4395	1973	16	7820	25
股份制企业	Foreign Investment Share Enterprises		84	84			261

17-10 外国和港澳台地区在华直接投资情况

Basic Conditions of Direct Investment in China by Foreign Countries and Compatriots From Hongkong，Macao and Taiwan

单位：个、万美元　　　　(2004 年)　　　　(Unit, USD 10 000)

项 目	Item	签订协议情况 Signed Agreements		客商实际投资额	年末实有企业个数
		合同数 Number of Contracts	客商投资额 Actually Used Amount of Region Investment	Used Amount of Foreign Investment	Year-end number of Enterprises
总 计	**Total**	**74**	**25786**	**4586**	**331**
按投资方式分	**Grouped by Investment Mode**				
外资企业	Foreign Investment Enterprises	27	8202	1588	80
合资经营企业	Joint Ventures Enterprises	31	9764	2712	213
合作经营企业	Cooperative Operation Enterprises	16	7820	25	32
外商投资股份制企业	Foreign Investment Share Enterprises			261	6
按国民经济行业分	**Grouped by Economic Sector**				
农、林、牧、渔业	Farming, Forestry, Animal Husbandry and Fishery	10	6153	366	31
采掘业	Mining and Quarrying	11	2512	37	11
制造业	Manufacturing	28	9417	2412	179
电力、煤气及水的生产和供应业	Production and Supply of ElectiCity, Gas and Water	1	500	204	2
建筑业	Construction			64	9
交通运输、仓储及邮电通讯业	Transport, Storage, Post and Telecommunications			639	6
信息传输、计算机服务和软件业	Information Transmission, Computer Service and Software	1	27		4
批发和零售业	Wholesale and Retail Trade and Catering Services	2	657	655	1
住宿和餐饮业	Accommodation and Catering Service	7	352	2	19
金融业	Finance				
房地产业	Real Estate	5	4532	206	21
租赁和商务服务业	Social Services	5	199	1	11
科学研究、技术服务和地质勘察业	Scientific Research, Technical Service and Geological Survey	3	1335		9
水利、环境和公共设施管理业	Water Conservancy, Environment and Public Facility Management				
居民服务和其他服务业	Community Service and Other Service	1	459		15
教 育	Education		-32		
卫生、社会保障和社会福利业	Health Care, Sports and Social Welfare				1
文化、体育和娱乐业	Education, Culture and Arts		-325		6
公共管理和社会组织	Public Management and Social Organization				
其他行业	Others Sectors				6
按国别、地区分	**By Country or Territory**				
中国香港	Hong Kong，China	25	13604	1320	127
中国澳门	Macao，China				4
中国台湾	Taiwan，China	2	-268		22
日 本	Japan	1	26		9
美 国	United States	6	2280	73	32
加拿大	Canada	3	1444		9
德 国	Federal Republic of Germany	1	44		9
土耳其	Turkey	2	155		6
英 国	United Kingdon	3	57	121	6
泰 国	Thailand				5
新加坡	Singapore	4	1497	1023	7
澳大利亚	Australia	8	2429	160	17
独联体	Commonwealth of Independent States	5	306	206	16
马来西亚	Malaysia				5
韩 国	Republic of Korea	3	1903		9

17-11 各地、州、市利用外商直接投资情况

Foreign Direct Investment Used by Prefecture, Autonomous Prefecture and City

单位：个、万美元 (unit, USD 10 000)

地　区	Region	2003			2004		
		签　订合同数 Number of Contracts	合同金额 Contract Value	实际利用投资 Amount of Foreingn Capital Actually Used	签　订合同数 Number of Contracts	合同金额 Contract Value	实际利用投资 Amount of Foreingn Capital Actually Used
总　计	**Total**	**65**	**16147**	**4005**	**74**	**25786**	**4586**
乌鲁木齐市	Urumqi City	37	5662	759	33	15324	2130
克拉玛依市	Karamay City	1	85	60	2	757	
石河子市	Shi Hezi City	3	684	125	3	967	400
吐鲁番地区	Turpan Administrative Offices	1	18	114	3	473	
哈密地区	Hami [Kumul] Administrative Offices	3	80	8	4	1101	108
昌吉回族自治洲	Changji Hui Autonomous Prefecture	5	1481	829	4	1925	398
伊犁哈萨克自治州	Ili Kazak Autonomous Prefecture	2	1530	15	10	2084	538
伊犁州直属县(市)	Counties (Cities) Direct Under Ili Prefecture	1	242	15	7	1981	538
塔城地区	Tacheng [Tarbagatai] Administrative Offices	1	1288		1	11	
阿勒泰地区	Altay Administrative Offices				2	92	
博尔塔拉蒙古自治州	Bortala Mongol Autonomous Prefecture	2	30	2	4	136	
巴音郭楞蒙古自治州	BayangolMongol Autonomous Prefecture	5	4371	655	4	675	241
阿克苏地区	Aksu Administrative Offices	3	1240	1358	4	1570	640
克孜勒苏柯尔克孜自治州	Kizilsu Kirgiz Autonomous Prefecture	1	2				2
喀什地区	Kashgar [Kaxgar] Administrative Offices	1	664	80	2	740	129
和田地区	Hotan Administrative Offices	1	300		1	34	

17-12 新疆在外国和港澳台地区直接投资

Direct Investment in Foreign Countries and Hong Kong，Macao and Talwan Made by Xinjiang's Partner

单位：个、万美元 (unit, USD 10 000)

项　目	Item	2003			2004		
		签订协议情况 Signed Agreements		我方实际投资 Actually National Investment	签订协议情况 Signed Agreements		我方实际投资 Actually National Investment
		合同数 Number of Contracts	我方投资额 National Investment		合同数 Number of Contracts	我方投资额 National Investment	
总　计	**Total**	**17**	**1742**		**25**	**2330**	
独资经营	Foreign Investment Enterprises	10	1236		16	1189	
合资经营	Joint Ventures Enterprises	5	357		9	1141	
合作经营	Cooperative Operation Enterprises	2	149				

17-13 经济技术开发(合作)区主要情况

Main Conditions of Economic and Technological Development and Cooperation Zones

项 目 Item	2004	项 目 Item	2004
工业总产值(现价、万元) Gross Industrial Output Value (10 000 yuan)	**1438072**	新签合同数(个) Number of New signed Contracts (unit)	158
#外商投资企业 Foreign Funded Enterprises	291353	注册资本(万元) Registered Capital (10 000 yuan)	488193
工业企业销售收入(万元) Industral Enterprises (10 000 yuan)	**1101849**	#吸引外省资金(万元) Absorb Fund from Other Provinces (10 000 yuan)	133072
#外商投资企业 Foreign Funded Enterprises	266709	**年末全部投产企业数(个) Total Numberof Operated Enterprises Year-end (unit)**	**1934**
税收总额 (万元) Total Tax Rerenue (10 000 yuan)	**139513**	#外商投资企业(个) Foreign Funded Enterprises (unit)	79
#外商投资企业 Foreign Funded Enterprises	2284	内联企业(个) Internal United Enterprise (unit)	1787
工业企业 Industrial Enteprises	13443	**从业人员平均人数(人) Average Numbers of Employees (person)**	**97233**
财政收入(万元) Government Revenue (10 000 yuan)	**110939**	#外商投资企业(人) Foreign Funded Enterprises (person)	1137
出口总额(万美元) Total Exports (USD 10 000)	**98106**	**基本建设完成投资额(万元) Investment in Capital Construction Completed (10 000 yuan)**	**470076**
#外商投资企业 Foreign Funded Enterprises	14755	#基础设施 Infrastructure	55337
进口总额(万美元) Imports (USD 10 000)	**38332**	#水 Watar	2142
#外商投资企业 Foreign Funded Enterprises	5466	电 Electricity	14335
外商投资企业利润总额(正负相抵、万元) Total Profit of Foreign Investment Enterprises (10 000 yuan)	**24602**	路 Road	17954
#盈利额 Profit Volume	24556	通 信 Correspondence	96
外引内联 Introduce i nvestment from abroad and establish lateral Cooperation		其 他 Other	20810
#外商投资企业 Foreign Funded Enterprises		**在固定资产投资完成额中 The completetd sum of investment in Fixed Assets**	
新签合同数(个) New Signed Number of Countracts (unit)	10	房屋建设投资额 (万元) Investment in Building Construction (10 000 yuan)	191753
新签投资总额(万美元) New Signed Contracted Value (USD 10 000)	6877	房屋竣工面积(万平方米) Space of Buildings Completed (10 000 sp.m)	74.41
#外资金额(万美元) Foreign Capital (USD 10 000)	3807	**出让土地面积(万平方米) Sold Land Areas (10 000 sp.m)**	**228**
实际利用外资(万美元) Amount of Foreign Capital Actually Utilized (USD 10 000)	873	**吸取土地出让金(万元) Absorbing Money For Land Sold (10 000 yuan)**	**18913**
#内联企业 Internal United Enterprise			

17-14 边境地区边民互市情况
Mutual Exchange Goods in Border Areas

项　　目	Item	2003	2004	2004 年比 2003 年增减(%) Increase Rate in 2004 Over 2003 Decrease(%)
交易总额(万元)	**Total Transaction (10 000 yuan)**	**122438**	**69049**	**-43.6**
出　口	Exports	122414	66279	-45.9
进　口	Imports	24	2770	114.4 倍
参市的外国人（人次）	**Number of Persons Joined (person)**	**42887**	**79753**	**86.0**
税收总额(万元)	**Total Revenue (10 000 yuan)**	**12**	**25**	**1.1 倍**

17-15 旅游事业发展情况
Development of Tourism

项　　目	Item	1995	2000	2004
旅游社总数（个）	**Total Number of Travel Agencies (unit)**	**79**	**130**	**322**
国际旅行社	International Travel Agencies	9	38	39
国内旅行社	Domestic Travel Agencies	18	92	283
旅行社职工人数（人）	**Number of Staff and Workers of Travel Agencies (person)**	**1007**	**1219**	**1280**
国际旅行社	International Travel Agencies	446	1219	1280
国内旅行社	Domestic Travel Agencies	307		
涉外饭店总数（个）	**Total Number of Tourist Hotel (unit)**	**79**	**208**	**298**
入境旅游人数（人）	**Total Number of International Tourists Inbound (person)**	**203579**	**256082**	**316900**
外 国 人	Foreigners	185514	208374	270959
华　　侨	Overseas Chinese	3522		
港、澳同胞	Compatriots, from Hong Kong and Macao	5727		
香　　港	Compatriots from Hong Kong		12710	21787
澳门同胞	Compatriots from Macao		1387	327
台湾同胞	Compatriots from Taiwan	8816	33611	23827
国内旅游人数（万人）	**Total Number of Domestic Tourist (10 000 persons)**	**514.14**	**757.81**	**1241.58**
疆内居民出境游（人）	**Total Number of Domestic Resident Outbound (person)**	**591**	**4535**	**16511**
旅游收入	**Income of Tourism**			
国际旅游收入(万美元)	Earnings from International Tourism (USD 10 000)	5268	9494	9108.29
国内旅游收入(亿元)	Earnings from Domestic Tourism (100 million yuan)	7.10	62.67	108.96

17-16 国际旅游事业发展情况

Development of International Tourism

项　　目	Item	1995	2000	2004
旅游人数合计（人）	**Number of Tourists (person)**	**203579**	**256082**	**316900**
按国别分	**By Country**			
外国人	Foreigners	185514	208374	270959
#日　本	Japan	43983	51974	44130
新加坡	Singapore	2048	5137	3288
美　国	United States	5595	10231	13478
英　国	United Kingdom	2422	3702	4148
法　国	France	3062	5218	7347
德　国	Federal Republic of Germany	4892	6310	5932
独联体	Commonwealth of Independent States	93578	76966	131355
华　侨	Overseas Chinese	3522		
港澳同胞和台湾同胞	Compatriots from Hong Kong，Macao and Taiwan	14543	47708	45941
按地区分	**By Regions**			
乌鲁木齐市	Urumqi City	63275	144830	130649
克拉玛依市	Karamay City		505	650
石河子市	Shihezi City		532	232
吐鲁番地区	Turpan Administrative Offices	27230	43641	22844
哈密地区	Hami [Kumul] Administrative Offices	1220	624	2970
昌吉回族自治州	Changji Hui Autonomous Prefecture	224	213	316
伊犁哈萨克自治州	Ili Kazak Autonomous Prefecture	68948	18204	93552
伊犁州直属县(市)	Counties (Cities) Direct Under Ili Prefecture	67651	15356	63947
塔城地区	Tacheng [Tarbagatai] AdministrativeOffices	1297	298	878
阿勒泰地区	Altay Administrative Offices		2550	28727
博尔塔拉蒙古自治州	Bortala Mongol Autonomous Prefecture	354	672	338
巴音郭楞蒙古自治州	BayangolMongol Autonomous Prefecture	1738	7313	3834
阿克苏地区	Aksu Administrative Offices	5737	6028	4179
克孜勒苏柯尔克孜自治州	Kizilsu Kirgiz Autonomous Prefecture	2485	2100	503
喀什地区	Kashgar [Kaxgar] Administrative Offices	31102	27510	44118
和田地区	Hotan Administrative Offices	1266	3910	12715

注：1998 年以后的旅游外汇收入根据抽样调查取得。
Note: The Foreign Exchange Earnings from Tourism after 1998 are obtained from Sampled Survey.

17-17 各地、州、市国际旅行社及旅游宾馆(酒店)基本情况

Accommodation of International Travel Agencies and Tourist Hotels by Prefecture, Autonomous Prefecture and City

(2004 年)

地　　区	Region	国际旅行社 (个) Number of International Travel Agencies (unit)	旅游宾馆从业人员 (人) Persons Engaged from Tourist Hotels (person)	客 房 (间) Number of Room	床 位 (张) Number of Bed
总　计	**Total**	**39**	**27307**	**30117**	**59358**
乌鲁木齐市	Urumqi City	24	13325	12444	23557
克拉玛依市	Karamay City		1493	1064	2120
石河子市	Shihezi City		763	765	1624
吐鲁番地区	Turpan Administrative Offices	1	933	1175	2542
哈密地区	Hami [Kumul] Administrative Offices		1199	1159	2175
昌吉回族自治州	Changji Hui Autonomous Prefecture	1	934	1500	2824
伊犁哈萨克自治州	Ili Kazak Autonomous Prefecture	6	4144	5383	10915
伊犁州直属县(市)	Counties (Cities) Direct Under Ili Prefecture	3	2719	2974	6063
塔城地区	Tacheng [Tarbagatai] Administrative Offices	2	610	791	1572
阿勒泰地区	Altay Administrative Offices	1	815	1618	3280
博尔塔拉蒙古自治州	Bortala Mongol Autonomous Prefecture	1	518	839	1842
巴音郭楞蒙古自治州	Bayangol Mongol Autonomous Prefecture	1	1663	1957	4002
阿克苏地区	Aksu Administrative Offices	1	804	1487	3112
克孜勒苏柯尔克孜自治州	Kizilsu Kirgiz Autonomous Prefecture		54	96	201
喀什地区	Kashgar [Kaxgar] Administrative Offices	3	1122	1677	3304
和田地区	Hotan Administrative Offices	1	355	571	1140

17-18 各地、州、市旅游收入情况

Income of Tourism by Prefecture, Autonomous Prefecture and City

(2004 年)

地　　区	Region	国际旅游收入 (万美元) Earnings from International Tourism (USD 10 000)	国内旅游收入 (万元) Earnings from Domestic Tourism (10 000 yuan)
总　计	**Total**	**9108.29**	**1089595**
乌鲁木齐市	Urumqi City	4846.17	499681
克拉玛依市	Karamay City	16.65	32299
石河子市	Shihezi City	3.47	44256
吐鲁番地区	Turpan Administrative Offices	1114.67	44736
哈密地区	Hami [Kumul] Administrative Offices	59.07	40268
昌吉回族自治州	Changji Hui Autonomous Prefecture	8.20	41817
伊犁哈萨克自治州	Ili Kazak Autonomous Prefecture	506.61	163106
伊犁州直属县(市)	Counties (Cities) Direct Under Ili Prefecture	346.16	65299
塔城地区	Tacheng [Tarbagatai] Administrative Offices	47.32	28506
阿勒泰地区	Altay Administrative Offices	113.13	69301
博尔塔拉蒙古自治州	Bortala Mongol Autonomous Prefecture	8.25	17574
巴音郭楞蒙古自治州	BayangolMongol Autonomous Prefecture	125.55	46532
阿克苏地区	Aksu Administrative Offices	283.76	39128
克孜勒苏柯尔克孜自治州	Kizilsu Kirgiz Autonomous Prefecture	7.60	8611
喀什地区	Kashgar [Kaxgar] Administrative Offices	1927.81	84140
和田地区	Hotan Administrative Offices	200.48	27417

17-19 国际旅游外汇收入及构成

Foreign Exchange Earnings and Its Composition

单位：万美元 (USD 10 000)

指 标	Item	2003		2004	
		金 额 Value	比 重(%) Percentage (%)	金 额 Value	比 重(%) Percentage (%)
总 计	**Total**	**4857.63**	**100**	**9108.32**	**100**
长途交通费	Long Distance Transportation	1350.84	27.8	3100.48	34.0
民 航	Air	867.21	17.8	1683.12	18.4
铁 路	Railway	124.66	2.6	708.68	7.8
汽 车	Highway	358.97	7.4	708.68	7.8
游 览	Visiting	96.24	2.0	265.76	2.9
住 宿	Accommodation	393.86	8.1	708.68	7.8
餐 饮	Cater	455.30	9.4	797.27	8.8
商品销售	Commodity Sales	1850.30	38.1	3189.06	35.0
娱 乐	Entertainment	159.04	3.3	354.34	3.9
邮电通信	Postal and Communication	137.52	2.8	265.76	2.9
市内交通	Local Transportation	57.85	1.2	177.17	2.0
其他服务	Other Service	356.68	7.3		
一日游		133.56	2.8	249.8	2.7

注：2003 年的商品销售中剔除了一日游。
Note: One-day Tour in tourist programs for the year 2003

17-20 接待外国旅游人数(按国别分)

Number of Foreign Tourists Received by Country

单位：人 (person)

国 别	Country	2003	2004	国 别	Country	2003	2004
总 计	**Total**	**149916**	**270959**	意大利	Italy	1236	2683
亚 洲	**Asia**	**34780**	**74731**	荷 兰	Netherlands	708	
印 度	India	123	220	西班牙	Spain	181	1226
印度尼西亚	Indonesia	280	1189	瑞 典	Sweden	179	457
日本	Japan	16309	44130	瑞 士	Switzerland	556	1668
马来西亚	Malaysia	1715	2419	独联体	Commonwealth of Independent States	91732	131355
蒙 古	Mongolia	436	138	其 他	Other	1989	9420
菲律宾	The Philippines	276	130	**北美洲**	**North America**	**6794**	**16968**
新加坡	Singapore	1073	3288	加拿大	Canada	1113	2894
韩 国	Republic of Korea	3392	6680	美 国	United States	5225	13478
泰 国	Thailand	490	730	其 他	Other	456	596
其 他	Other	10686	15807	**大洋洲**	**Oceania**	**2864**	**4430**
非 洲	**Africa**	**107**	**312**	澳大利亚	Australia	2134	3712
欧 洲	**Europe**	**103456**	**164236**	新西兰	New Zealand	238	451
英 国	United Kingdom	2150	4148	其 他	Other	492	267
德 国	Federal Republic of Germany	2757	5932	**其他小计**	**Other sub-total**	**1915**	**10282**
法 国	France	1968	7347				

主要统计指标解释

进出口总额、海关进出口总额 指实际进出我国国境的货物总金额。包括对外贸易实际进出口货物，来料加工装配进出口货物，国家间、联合国及国际组织无偿援助物资和赠送品，华侨、港澳台同胞和外籍华人捐赠品，租赁期满归承租人所有的租赁货物，进料加工进出口货物，边境地方贸易及边境地区小额贸易进出口货物(边民互市贸易除外)，中外合资企业、中外合作经营企业、外商独资经营企业进出口货物和公用物品，到、离岸价格在规定限额以上的进出口货样和广告品(无商业价值、无使用价值和免费提供出口的除外)，从保税仓库提取在中国境内销售的进口货物，以及其他进出口货物。进出口总额用以观察一个国家在对外贸易方面的总规模。我国规定出口货物按离岸价格统计，进口货物按到岸价格统计。

商品经营单位所在地进、出口额 指所在地海关注册登记的有进出口经营权的企业实际进、出口额。

商品目的地进口额和商品货源地出口额、目的地进口额 指进口货物的消费、使用或最终抵运地的实际进口额，货源地出口额是指出口货物的产地或原始发货地的实际出口额。

利用外资 指我国各级政府、部门、企业和其他经济组织通过对外借款、吸收外商直接投资以及用其他方式筹措的境外现汇、设备、技术等。

对外借款 是我国利用外资的重要部分。指通过对外正式签订借款协议，从境外筹措的资金，包括外国政府贷款、国际金融组织贷款、外国银行商业贷款、出口信贷以及对外发行债券等。1996年及以前还包括对外发行股票。

外商直接投资 指外国企业和经济组织或个人(包括华侨、港澳台胞以及我国在境外注册的企业)按我国有关政策、法规，用现汇、实物、技术等在我国境内开办外商独资企业、与我国境内的企业或经济组织共同举办中外合资经营企业、合作经营企业或合作开发资源的投资(包括外商投资收益的再投资)，以及经政府有关部门批准的项目投资总额内企业从境外借入的资金。

外商其他投资 指除对外借款和外商直接投资以外的各种利用外资的形式。包括企业在境内外股票市场公开发行的以外币计价的股票(目前主要是在香港证券市场发行的H股和在境内证券市场发行的B股)发行价总额，国际租赁进口设备的应付款，补偿贸易中外商提供的进口设备、技术、物料的价款，加工装配贸易中外商提供的进口设备、物料的价款。

对外承包工程 指各对外承包公司以招标议标承包方式承揽的下列业务：(1)承包国外工程建设项目，(2)承包我国对外经援项目，(3)承包我国驻外机构的工程建设项目，(4)承包我国境内利用外资进行建设的工程项目，(5)与外国承包公司合营或联合承包工程项目时我国公司分包部分，(6)对外承包兼营的房屋开发业务。对外承包工程的营业额是以货币表现的本期内完成的对外承包工程的工作量，包括以前年度签订的合同和本年度新签订的合同在报告期内完成的工作量。

对外劳务合作 指以收取工资的形式向业主或承包商提供技术和劳动服务的活动。我国对外承包公司在境外开办的合营企业，中国公司同时又提供劳务的，其劳务部分也纳入劳务合作统计。劳务合作营业额按报告期内向雇主提交的结算数(包括工资、加班费和奖金等)统计。

对外设计咨询 指以服务成果向业主收费的技术服务项目。包括承担地形地貌测绘，地质资源勘探与普查，建设区域规划，提供设计文件、图纸、生产工艺技术资料和工程技术经济咨询，工程项目的可行性考察、研究和评估，进行技术指导和培训人员等；也包括承担国(境)内利用外资进行建设的工程项目的上述规定的设计咨询项目的收取外币部分。

旅游者人数 包括入境国际旅游者人数、出境居民人数和国内旅游者人数。

(1)入境国际旅游者人数：指来中国参观、访问、旅行、探亲、访友、休养、考察、参加会议和从事经济、科技、文化、教育、宗教等活动的外国人、华侨、港澳同胞和台湾同胞的人数。不包括外国在我国的常驻机构，如使领馆、通讯社、企业办事处的工作人员；来我国常住的外国专家、留学生以及在岸逗留不过夜人员。

(2)出境居民人数：指大陆居民因公务活动或私人事务短期出境的人数。公务活动出境居民人数包括在国际交通工具上的中国服务员工，因私出境居民人数不包括在国际交通工具上的中国服务员工。

(3)国内旅游者人数：指我国大陆居民和在我国常住1年以上的外国人、华侨、港澳台同胞离开常住地在境内其他地方的旅游设施内至少停留一夜，最长不超过6个月的人数。

国际旅游(外汇)收入 指入境旅游的外国人、华侨、港澳同胞和台湾同胞在中国大陆旅游过程中发生的一切旅游支出，对于国家来说就是国际旅游(外汇)收入。

国际旅行社 指经营对外招徕并接待外国人、华侨、港澳同胞和台湾同胞来中国、归国或回内地旅游业务的旅行社。

国内旅行社 指负责经营招徕、组团、接待国内旅客的旅游业务，以及不对外招徕，负责经营接待国际旅行社或其它涉外部门组织的外国人、华侨、港澳同胞和台湾同胞来中国、归国或回内地的旅游业务的旅行社。

涉外饭店 指经有关部门批准，允许接待外国人、华侨、港澳同胞和台湾同胞的饭店。

Explanatory Notes on Main Statistical Indicators

Total Imports and Exports at Customs refer to the value of commodities imported into and exported from the boundary of China. They include the actual imports and exports through foreign trade, imported and exported goods under the processing and assembling trades and materials, supplies and gifts as aid given gratis between governments and by the United Nations and other international organizations, and contributions donated by overseas Chinese, compatriots in Hong Kong and Macao and Chinese with foreign citizenship, leasing commodities owned by tenant at the expiration of leasing period, the imported and exported commodities processed with imported materials, commodities trading in border areas(excluding mutual exchange goods), the imported and exported commodities and articles for public use of the Sino-foreign joint ventures, cooperative enterprises and ventures exclusively with foreign own investment .Also included are import or export of samples and advertising goods for whose CIF or FOB value are beyond the permitted ceiling (excluding goods of no trading or use value and free commodities for export),imported goods sold in China from bonded warehouses and other imported or exported goods.The indicator of the total imports and exports at customs can be used to observe the total size of external trade in a country.In accordance with the stipulation of the Chinese government,imports are calculated at CIF, while exports are calculated at FOB

Import Export Value by Location of China Foreign Trade Managing Units refers to actual value of imports and exports carried out by corporations which have been registered by the local customhouse and are vested with right to run import export business.

Import Value of Commodities by the Places of their Destination and Export Value of Commodities by the Places of their Origin in China: The former indicator refers to the value of import commodities of the places of their consumption, utilization or the places of their final destination. The latter indicator refers to the value of export commodities of the places of their origin or the places of the commodities dispatched.

Utilization of Foreign Capital refers to remittance, equipment and technology financed from abroad, by loans, foreign direct investment and other forms undertaken by the Chinese governments at all levels, by various departments, enterprises and other economic units.

Foreign Borrowings an important part of China扭 utilization of foreign capital,it refer to funds borrowed from abroad through formal signing of borrowing agreements with foreign institutions, including loans of foreign governments, loans of international financial institutions,commercial loans of foreign banks, export credit, and funds raised by Chinese bonds (and shares before 1996) issued abroad.

Direct Investment by Foreign Entrepreneurs refers to the investments inside China by foreign enterprises and economic organizations or individuals(including overseas Chinese,compatriots from Hong Kong and Macao,and Chinese enterprises registered abroad), following the relevant policies and laws of China, for the establishment of ventures exclusively with foreign own investment, Sino-foreign joint ventures and cooperative enterprises or for co-operative exploration of resources with enterprises or economic organizations in China. It includes the re investment of the foreign entrepreneurs with the profits gained from the investment and the funds that enterprises borrow from abroad in the total investment of projects which are approved by the relevant department of the government.

Other Investment by Foreign Entrepreneurs refers to all forms of utilization of foreign capitals other than foreign borrowings and foreign direct investment. It includes the total value of stock shares in foreign currencies issued by enterprises at domestic or foreign stock exchanges (now mainly consisting of H shares issued at Hong Kong Security Market and B shares issued at domestic security markets), rent payable for the imported equipment through international leasing arrangement, cost of imported equipment, technology and materials provided by foreign counterparts in compensation trade and processing and assembly trade.

Contracted Projects with Foreign Countries refer to projects undertaken by Chinese contractors (project contracting companies)through bidding process.They include: (1)overseas civil engineering construction projects financed by foreign investors; (2)overseas projects financed by the Chinese government through its foreign aid programs; (3)construction projects of Chinese diplomatic missions,trade offices and other institutions stationed abroad; (4)construction projects in China financed by foreign investment; (5)sub-contracted projects to be taken by Chinese contractors through a joint umbrella project with foreign contractor(s); (6)housing development projects.The business income from international contracted projects is the work volume of contracted projects completed during the reference period, expressed in monetary terms, including completed work on projects signed in previous years.

Service Cooperation with Foreign Countries refers to the activities of providing technology and labour services to employers or contractors in the forms of receiving salaries and wages. Labour services providing by contractual joint ventures of Chihe statistics of service co operation with foreign countries.The business income of labour service co operation is the income in the form of wages and salaries, overtime pay, bonuses and other remuneration received from the employers during the reference period.

Overseas Design and Consultation Service refers to projects with charges for technical services from overseas operators. It includes geographic and topographic mapping, geological resource prospecting and survey, planning of construction areas, provision of design documents, blueprints, materials on production process and techniques, as well as engineering, technical and economic consultation, and feasibility study, research and evaluation of projects. Also included under this category are the above-mentioned services of foreign-financed projects in China that are paid in foreign currencies.

Number of Tourists include international tourists entering into China, Chinese residents going abroad and domestic tourists.

(1) International tourists refer to foreigners, overseas Chinese, Chinese compatriots from Hong Kong, Macao and Taiwan coming to China for sightseeing, visits, tours, family reunions, vacations, study tours, conferences and other activities of a business, scientific and technological, cultural, educational and religious nature. It does not include representatives and employees of resident institutions of foreign countries in China such as embassies, consulates, news agencies and offices of foreign companies and organizations, nor does it include long-term foreign experts or students residing in China, or persons in transition without spending a night in China.

(2) Chinese residents going abroad refer to Chinese residents going abroad for short terms for either public business or private purposes. Chinese employees working on international transport carriers are included in those going abroad for public business purpose, not in those for private purpose.

(3) Domestic tourists refer to residents of the mainland of China who stay for one night at least but no more than 6 months at tourist facilities in other places than their permanent residence within the territory of the mainland China, including foreigners, overseas Chinese and Chinese compatriots from Hong Kong, Macao and Taiwan who have resided in China for over one year.

Foreign Exchange Earnings from International Tourism refer to the total expenditures of foreigners, overseas Chinese, Chinese compatriots from Hong Kong, Macao and Taiwan during their stay in the mainland of China, which are earnings of foreign exchange from international tourism from the point of view from China.

International Travel Agencies refer to travel agencies engaged in the promotion, solicitation, organization and reception of tours to the mainland of China by foreigners, overseas Chinese, Chinese compatriots from Hong Kong, Macao and Taiwan.

Domestic Travel Agencies refer to travel agencies engaged in the promotion, solicitation, organization and reception of domestic tourists, and in the reception of foreigners, overseas Chinese, Chinese compatriots from Hong Kong, Macao and Taiwan organized by international travel agencies or other departments concerned, without their own promotion and solicitation programmes.

Tourist Hotels refer to hotels that are able, with the approval of departments concerned, to accommodate foreigners, overseas Chinese, Chinese compatriots from Hong Kong, Macao and Taiwan Province.

第十八篇

CHAPTER 18

教育、科技和文化

EDUCATION SCIENCE AND CULTURE

18-1 各级各类学校数
Number of Schools by Level and Type

单位：所 (unit)

年 份 Year	普通高等学校 Regular Institutions of Higher Education	中等学校 Secondary Schools	中等专业学校 Specialized Secondary Schools	普通中学 Regular Secondary Schools	#高中 Senior Secondary Schools	职业中学 Vocational Secondary Schools	技工学校 Technical Schools	小学 Primary Schools	盲聋哑学校 Special Schools
1978	10	2078	78	1997	673		10	9891	1
1985	14	2360	97	2147	794	65	51	8104	3
1990	21	2274	112	1958	766	134	70	7247	6
1991	21	2229	112	1915	752	140	62	7132	6
1992	21	2239	112	1903	715	160	64	7122	6
1993	21	2206	113	1851	650	170	72	7088	6
1994	21	2168	114	1830	586	157	67	7117	6
1995	21	2121	115	1792	554	145	69	7086	6
1996	18	2092	115	1776	536	137	64	7047	7
1997	18	2090	115	1770	531	131	74	6962	8
1998	17	2066	115	1763	517	121	67	6837	7
1999	17	2022	113	1725	488	116	68	6796	7
2000	20	2000	112	1711	484	112	65	6718	7
2001	21	2179	99	1929	472	89	62	6221	7
2002	24	2173	87	1945	507	83	58	6043	7
2003	26	2154	78	1932	500	86	58	5832	8
2004	28	2186	78	1965	498	84	59	5451	8

18-2 各级各类学校教师数
Number of Teachers by Level and Type of School

单位：人 (person)

年 份 Year	普通高等学校 Regular Institutions of Higher Education	中等学校 Secondary Schools	中等专业学校 Specialized Secondary Schools	普通中学 Regular Secondary Schools	#高中 Senior Secondary Schools	职业中学 Vocational Secondary Schools	技工学校 Technical Schools	小学 Primary Schools	盲聋哑学校 Special Schools
1978	2458	44417	2543	41661	8064		213	82616	28
1980	3149	50056	3459	45232	9292	77	1288	89027	54
1985	5473	69185	4554	60942	15059	1567	2122	98294	67
1990	7002	78596	6158	65814	19318	3117	3507	95060	139
1991	7269	78339	6134	64923	19488	3580	3702	95565	145
1992	7280	78403	6210	64465	19000	3769	3959	96729	154
1993	7158	77200	6271	63448	17142	3853	3628	99297	129
1994	7554	75546	6383	62087	15011	3531	3545	101863	145
1995	7687	76584	6540	62934	14434	3494	3616	106001	162
1996	7835	79424	6791	65228	14781	3685	3720	112149	114
1997	7837	82459	7089	68115	15111	3568	3687	119184	156
1998	7587	83952	7194	69845	15734	3641	3272	123308	163
1999	7516	86667	7229	72195	15673	3598	3645	126401	171
2000	7924	89211	6786	75895	16069	3104	3426	131259	183
2001	9123	92264	6842	79419	17025	2546	3457	132137	187
2002	10369	96469	6031	84714	19031	2399	3325	132435	200
2003	11237	100573	5157	89332	20976	2440	3644	132284	237
2004	12239	106839	5494	94381	22809	3079	3885	134915	257

18-3 各级各类学校在校学生数

Number of Student Enrollment by Level and Type of School

单位：人 (person)

年份 Year	普通高等学校 Regular Institutions of Higher Education	中等学校 Secondary Schools	中等专业学校 Specialized Secondary Schools	普通中学 Regular Secondary Schools	#高中 Senior Secondary Schools	职业中学 Vocational Secondary Schools	技工学校 Technical Schools	小学 Primary Schools	盲聋哑学校 Special Schools
1980	14308	886740	42362	823161	147446	1416	19801	2055513	371
1985	26500	1054293	33251	955356	223405	41825	23861	1966306	706
1990	31271	1015214	45985	863118	251067	65862	40249	1857246	610
1991	31374	963948	47129	806702	246950	68460	41657	1955216	652
1992	33857	941656	52102	783130	212942	65330	41094	1980686	624
1993	39422	884083	63314	718607	166203	58509	43653	2039409	549
1994	43687	892041	73922	723596	137870	50894	43629	2105911	590
1995	44918	912597	68586	749788	141330	54122	40101	2301274	643
1996	44928	967253	72782	803856	149937	51952	38663	2301764	407
1997	46342	1045980	77837	876720	168483	54038	37385	2419700	629
1998	47464	1121675	82262	958420	183230	51458	29535	2502691	613
1999	54959	1233288	93445	1062380	189037	49871	27592	2507406	681
2000	72867	1311845	105255	1132912	198639	51270	22408	2477413	674
2001	109815	1390360	97321	1228566	225411	47673	16800	2435667	922
2002	134831	1493580	83902	1338836	272381	50787	20055	2359788	3876
2003	151256	1584700	71499	1448531	315178	45330	19340	2289066	1863
2004	168247	1676971	71324	1517948	359147	61502	26197	2218109	2549

注：1.高等学校含研究生数。2.盲聋哑学校 2002 年新增随班就读。(以下同)

Note: a) Regular Institutions of Higher Education include number of Postgraduates.

b) In Special Schools for the blind,deaf, mute, new comers may follow the classes accordingly from the year 2002 (The same as follows).

18-4 各级各类学校招生数

New Student Enrollment by Level and Type of School

单位：人 (person)

年份 Year	普通高等学校 Regular Institutions of Higher Education	中等学校 Secondary Schools	中等专业学校 Specialized Secondary Schools	普通中学 Regular Secondary Schools	#高中 Senior Secondary Schools	职业中学 Vocational Secondary Schools	技工学校 Technical Schools	小学 Primary Schools	盲聋哑学校 Special Schools
1980	3767	336402	14688	310931	73959	792	10531	433089	90
1985	9298	386074	13919	341123	93692	20429	10603	374643	91
1990	8034	356615	15586	297641	84567	27968	15420	335552	103
1991	8179	302489	16902	239511	77525	29354	16722	344432	15
1992	10985	334705	20611	269859	61673	27041	17194	359302	119
1993	13359	331884	26572	263683	56180	24778	16851	385535	102
1994	12099	326160	29248	259237	44552	21350	16325	400700	102
1995	12307	356814	25260	286318	58203	25643	19593	419717	165
1996	12421	366772	26311	299348	59400	23003	18110	428651	67
1997	12673	392571	27302	326494	64377	21741	17034	443238	120
1998	12880	426400	27497	365234	71302	19862	13807	429247	130
1999	19821	463579	36014	399516	69801	18828	9221	391298	175
2000	30689	486763	38866	418790	76744	20027	9080	364193	177
2001	42253	510469	26763	459878	93519	16621	7207	352975	135
2002	42808	551353	22241	501924	113366	16746	10442	346386	874
2003	44733	583033	24016	532987	126163	15378	10652	347619	369
2004	53204	606666	27990	536405	138315	27585	14686	347364	390

18-5 各级各类学校毕业生数

Number of Graduates by Level and Type of School

单位：人 (person)

年 份 Year	普通高等学校 Regular Institutions of Higher Education	中等学校 Secondary Schools	中等专业学校 Specialized Secondary Schools	普通中学 Regular Secondary Schools	#高 中 Senior Secondary Schools	职业中学 Vocational Secondary Schools	技工学校 Technical Schools	小 学 Primary Schools	盲聋哑学校 Special Schools
1957	525	7762	1378	6353	593	31		53122	
1962	697	35228	6554	28455	4605	219		117864	
1965	1282	26123	1196	24607	3848	320		77080	
1970	1661	45201	437	44764	898			173553	
1975	723	128368	5497	122871	33519			194283	50
1978	1509	205862	8801	195542	53970		1519	388359	195
1980	814	264626	11946	246382	60370	341	5957	292515	37
1981	779	280171	17039	257478	67114	367	5287	397524	37
1982	4108	269927	17201	244853	69504	385	7488	310025	32
1983	4823	283120	11584	260906	77546	1144	9486	317227	27
1984	3426	275788	8130	257833	72191	2764	7061	295993	48
1985	3511	290077	8097	267302	68096	7424	7254	289045	73
1986	4797	296360	11551	268402	58585	8543	7864	307047	52
1987	8001	321981	10623	289556	73947	12280	9522	317820	101
1988	7792	346072	12026	311224	85718	12758	10064	288594	68
1989	6900	347719	12441	308467	86489	14650	12161	249888	57
1990	8603	343313	14260	297235	81062	17938	13880	259301	98
1991	7919	324031	15571	274913	79664	17505	16042	183350	159
1992	8402	310076	14950	260953	84518	18999	15174	268074	157
1993	7741	312284	16760	261502	78675	18558	15464	259468	104
1994	7734	250909	16206	198839	57090	18100	17764	262215	55
1995	10505	271992	18981	215756	44589	16490	20765	271227	57
1996	12272	271267	21701	215295	43478	15424	18847	279866	39
1997	10908	284580	21936	228287	37966	17181	17176	294420	71
1998	11401	313807	23090	259910	49702	18038	12769	321044	100
1999	11886	341434	25118	282486	52403	18826	15004	357801	84
2000	10985	363503	25879	308225	54985	17341	12058	371758	70
2001	16121	380946	26403	329801	59251	13881	10861	395010	104
2002	16380	410299	31598	356203	61932	15087	7411	411626	848
2003	25785	434523	31304	379269	70824	15685	8265	421443	264
2004	31013	468849	24758	420583	84418	15475	8033	417588	382

18-6 研究生数

Number of Postgraduates

单位：人 (person)

年 份 Year	招生数 New Student Enrollment	在校学生数 Student Enrollment	攻读博士学位 Working for Doctorate	攻读硕士学位 Working for Master's Degree	毕业生数 Graduates	攻读博士学位 Working for Doctorate	攻读硕士学位 Working for Master's Degree
1978	16	16		16			
1980	15	66		66			
1985	120	179		174	21		21
1990	73	256	3	253	112		112
1991	76	229	4	225	108		108
1992	93	257	5	252	63		63
1993	127	315	6	309	68	1	67
1994	166	421	9	412	89	1	88
1995	180	509	14	295	91		91
1996	217	535	16	519	142	3	139
1997	234	647	18	629	158	3	155
1998	276	747	19	728	173	7	166
1999	386	901	29	872	229	5	224
2000	544	1196	48	1148	235	5	230
2001	827	1749	80	1669	277	8	269
2002	1104	2495	112	2383	355	11	344
2003	1664	3629	186	3443	521	18	503
2004	2336	5120	283	4837	832	30	802

18-7 高等学校基本情况

Basic Statistics on Institutions of Higher Education by Type

单位：人 (2004 年) (person)

项 目	Item	学校数(所) Schools (unit)	毕业生数 Graduates	招生数 New Student Enrollment	在校学生数 Student Enrollment	教职工数 Staff and Teachers	#专任教师 Full-time Teachers
总 计	**Total**	**28**	**30181**	**50868**	**163127**	**23265**	**12239**
综合大学	Multiversity	6	8580	15108	52001	8581	4525
理工院校	Science Engineering	8	2632	8835	18571	2622	1536
农业院校	Agriculture	3	3707	5680	19579	2699	1514
医药院校	Medicine	2	1544	2216	9353	1810	656
师范院校	Normal Institutions	5	7939	11570	39818	4760	2676
财经学院	Economics and Finance	1	1714	2560	11162	1475	710
政法院校	Politics & Law	2	346	1245	3169	723	313
艺术院校	Art	1	313	690	2197	595	309
成人高校普通班	Ordinary Class for Adult Higher Education		3406	2964	7277		
总计中：高职学院	In total: Vocational Training	12	2906	11192	22909	4238	2448

18-8 中等专业学校基本情况

Basic Statistics on Specialized Secondary Schools by Type

单位：人 (2004 年) (person)

项 目	Item	毕业生数 Graduates	招生数 New Student Enrollment	在校学生数 Student Enrollment	#专业课教师 Teachers of Various Subjects
总 计	**Total**	**24758**	**27990**	**71324**	**3232**
农业类	Agriculture	2459	1612	4199	337
资源与环境类	Resource and Environment	477	396	584	12
能源类	Energy Source	220	1147	2451	35
土木水利工程类	Civil-Works and Water Conservance	1542	2404	4803	170
加工制造类	Processing and Manufacturing	1196	4206	7494	129
交通运输类	Traffic and Communication	588	1143	3046	67
信息技术类	Information Technology	1401	2075	4757	106
医药卫生类	Medcine and Health	2818	6514	14889	415
商贸与旅游类	Commerce, Trade and Tourism	1030	2099	4831	35
财经类	Economics and Finance	810	771	1467	256
文化艺术与体育类	Physical Culture	3127	2074	7580	354
社会公共事业类	Scoial and Public Undertaking	1635	975	3019	149
师范类	Normal Shools	5349	1242	8116	1028
其 他	Others	2106	1332	4088	139

18-9 普通中学和其他学校基本情况

Basic Statistics on Regular Secondary Schools and Other Schools by Type

单位：人 (2004 年) (person)

项 目	Item	学校数(所) Schools (unit)	毕业生数 Graduates	招生数 New Student Enrollment	在校学生数 Student Enrollment	教职工数 Staff and Teachers	#专任教师 Full-time Teachers
普通中学	**Regular Secondary Schools**	**1965**	**420583**	**536405**	**1517948**	**113047**	**94381**
高 中	Senior Secondary Schools	498	84418	138315	359147		22809
初 中	Junior Secondary Schools	1467	336165	398090	1158801		71572
职业中学	**Vocational Secondary Schools**	**84**	**15475**	**27585**	**61502**	**4732**	**3079**
技工学校	**Technical Shools**	**59**	**8033**	**14686**	**26197**	**5835**	**3885**
小 学	**Primary Schools**	**5451**	**417588**	**347364**	**2218109**	**150308**	**134915**
盲聋哑学校	**Special Schools**	**8**	**382**	**390**	**2549**	**356**	**257**

18-10 各类成人教育情况

Basic Statistics on Adult Education by Type

单位: 人 (2004 年) (person)

项 目	Item	学校数(所) Schools (unit)	毕业生数 Graduates	在校学生数 Student Enrollment	教职工数 Staff and Teachers	#专任教师 Full-time Teachers
成人高等教育	**Adult Education Schools**	**11**	**46465**	**84583**	**5578**	**3064**
广播电视大学	Radio and TV Universities	2	4761	2190	3065	1512
职工大学	Schools of Higher Education for Staff Workers	3	3006	4646	561	383
教育学院	Pedagogical Colleges	6	8331	11985	1952	1169
普通高校办的成人班	Adult Classes run by Ordinary Colleges and Universities		30367	65762		
成人中等教育	**Secondary Schools for Adults**	**26**	**2663**	**7146**	**1859**	**1137**
成人中学	**Secondary Schools for Adults**	**29**	**2454**	**5384**	**87**	**47**
成人技术培训学校	**Technical adult college**	**1291**	**792061**	**892080**	**2486**	**600**
成人初等学校	**Primary Schools for Adults**	**357**	**83888**	**141927**	**2526**	**440**
扫盲班	Literacy Courses		47873	95857	2072	397

18-11 教育发展水平

Development Level of Education

年 份 Year	各类学校在校生占全区人口比重(%) Students as Percentage of Total Population (%)	平均每万人口中(人) Number of Students per 10 000 Population (person)			大中小学生各占学生总数的比重(%) Students of Different Level as Percentage of Total Students(%)		
		大学生 University and College Students	中学生 Secondary School tudents	小学生 Primary School Students	大学生 University and College Students	中学生 Secondary School Students	小学生 Primary School Students
1978	23.34	8.30	654.00	1645.38		28.02	70.50
1980	23.04	11.15	641.47	1601.82		27.80	69.52
1985	22.39	19.47	701.88	1444.60		31.35	64.52
1990	18.99	20.45	564.44	1208.01	1.08	29.72	63.94
1991	18.98	20.18	518.92	1257.72	1.06	27.33	66.25
1992	18.71	21.42	495.45	1253.10	1.15	26.49	66.99
1993	18.46	24.56	447.66	1270.45	1.33	24.25	68.82
1994	18.63	26.76	443.19	1289.83	1.44	23.79	69.22
1995	19.61	26.84	453.23	1330.61	1.38	23.00	70.60
1996	19.62	26.60	475.85	1362.56	1.36	24.26	69.46
1997	20.44	26.97	510.29	1408.37	1.32	24.96	68.89
1998	21.02	27.16	548.49	1432.28	1.29	26.10	68.15
1999	21.39	30.96	598.52	1412.62	1.45	27.98	66.05
2000	22.84	41.05	638.26	1395.72	1.82	27.93	61.09
2001	20.98	58.53	654.84	1298.22	2.79	31.21	61.87
2002	23.14	70.04	702.72	1238.61	3.21	31.87	56.18
2003	22.53	76.33	749.00	1183.62	3.39	33.25	52.54
2004	21.91	83.09	773.23	1129.89	4.18	38.92	56.90

18-12 各级学校教师负担学生数

Student-Teacher Ratio by Level of School

单位：人 (person)

年 份 Year	高等学校 University and College		普通中学 Secondary Schools		小 学 Primary Schools	
	教师数 Number of Teachers	平均每个教师负担学生数 Student-Teacher Ratio	教师数 Number of Teachers	平均每个教师负担学生数 Student-Teacher Ratio	教师数 Number of Teachers	平均每个教师负担学生数 Student-Teacher Ratio
1978	2458	4.16	41661	19.36	82616	24.56
1980	3149	4.54	45232	18.20	89027	23.09
1985	5473	4.84	60942	15.68	98294	20.00
1990	7002	4.47	65814	13.12	95060	19.54
1991	7269	4.32	64923	12.43	95565	20.46
1992	7280	4.65	64465	12.15	96729	20.48
1993	7158	5.51	63448	11.33	99297	20.54
1994	7554	5.78	62087	11.66	101863	20.67
1995	7687	5.78	62934	11.91	106001	20.77
1996	7835	5.73	65228	12.32	112149	20.52
1997	7837	5.91	68115	12.87	119184	20.30
1998	7887	6.26	69845	13.72	123308	20.30
1999	7516	7.31	72195	14.72	126401	19.84
2000	7924	9.34	75895	14.92	131259	18.87
2001	9123	12.04	79419	15.47	132137	18.43
2002	10369	13.00	84714	15.80	132435	17.82
2003	11237	13.46	89332	16.22	132284	17.30
2004	12239	13.74	94381	16.08	134915	16.44

18-13 各级学校女学生和女教师数

Number of Female Students and Teachers by Level of School

单位：人 (person)

项 目	Item	1995	2000	2004
女学生	**Number of Female Students**	**1553655**	**1889552**	**1993031**
高等学校	Institutions of Higher Education	21268	38419	85100
中等专业学校	Specialized Secondary Schools	35927	49892	39581
普通中学	Regular Secondary Schools	379171	568060	765518
职业中学	Vocational Secondary Schools	28495	23670	27531
技工学校	Technical Shools	12191	8740	8444
小学	Primary Schools	1076333	1200513	1065871
盲聋哑学校	Special Schools for the Blind, Mute and Deaf	270	258	986
女学生占学生总数的比重(%)	**Percentage of Female Students to Total Students (%)**	**49.2**	**48.9**	**49.0**
女教师	**Number of Female Teachers**	**106877**	**134563**	**153376**
高等学校	Institutions of Higher Education	2857	3192	5728
中等专业学校	Specialized Secondary Schools	3079	3408	2881
普通中学	Regular Secondary Schools	30508	40030	51792
职业中学	Vocational Secondary Schools	1613	1601	1562
技工学校	Technical Schools	1085	1264	1568
小学	Primary Schools	67617	84944	89645
盲聋哑学校	Special Schools for the Blind, Mute and Deaf	118	124	200
女教师占教师总数的比重(%)	**Percentage of Female Teachers to Total Teachers (%)**	**56.5**	**58.9**	**61.3**

18-14 初中毕业生和小学生升学率及小学学龄儿童入学率

Percentage of Graduates of Junior Secondary Schools and Primary Schools Entering Higher Level Schools, Percentage of School-age Children Enrolled

年份 Year	初中毕业生升高中情况 Student of Graduates of Junior Secondary Schools Entering Senior Secondary Schools			小学毕业生升学情况 Student of Graduates of Primary Schools Entering Junior Secondary Schools			小学学龄儿童入学情况 Student of School-Age Children Enrolled		
	初中毕业生数(人) Graduates of Junior Secondary Schools (person)	高中招生数(人) Students Entering Senior Secondary Schools (person)	升学率(%) Percentage of Graduates of Primary Schools Entering Junior Secondary Schools (%)	小学毕业生数(人) Graduates of Primary Schools (person)	初中招生数(人) Students Entering Junior Secondary Schools (person)	升学率(%) Percentage of Graduates of Primary Schools Entering Junior Secondary Schools (%)	学龄儿童数(人) School-Age Children (person)	已入学学龄儿童数(人) School-Age Children Enrolled in Schools (person)	入学率(%) Enrollment Rate (%)
1978	141572	68261	48.22	788359	255687	88.67	1541148	1480400	96.00
1980	186012	73989	39.76	292515	236432	80.83	1637610	1548653	94.57
1985	199206	93692	47.03	289045	247431	85.60	1645055	1569328	95.40
1990	216173	84567	39.12	259301	213074	82.17	1502163	1465325	97.50
1991	195249	77525	39.71	183350	161986	88.35	1799056	1723725	95.80
1992	176435	61673	34.96	268074	208186	77.66	1819546	1747470	96.00
1993	182827	56810	30.73	259468	207503	79.97	1868759	1804304	96.60
1994	141749	44552	31.43	262215	214685	81.87	1943216	1886075	97.06
1995	171167	58203	34.00	271227	228115	84.10	2036541	1976120	97.03
1996	171817	59400	34.57	279866	239948	85.74	2136336	2081199	97.42
1997	190321	64377	33.82	294420	266943	90.66	2259742	2182537	96.58
1998	210208	71302	33.92	321044	300066	93.47	2326765	2272701	97.68
1999	230083	69801	30.33	357801	337290	94.27	2345897	2277524	97.09
2000	253240	76744	30.30	371758	342046	92.01	2313890	2245190	97.03
2001	270550	93519	34.56	395010	366359	92.75	2257795	2212477	97.41
2002	294271	113366	38.52	411626	388558	94.39	2184260	2136643	97.82
2003	308445	126163	40.90	421443	406824	96.53	2122900	2087775	98.34
2004	336165	138315	41.14	417588	398090	95.33	2063210	2038258	97.79

18-15 各级各类学校少数民族在校学生数

Number of Student Enrollment of Minority Nationalities by Level and Type of School

单位: 人 (person)

年份 Year	高等学校 Institutions of Higher Education	中等学校 Secondary Schools	中等专业学校 Specialized Secondary Schools	职业中学 Vocational Secondary Schools	技工学校 Technical Schools	普通中学 Regular Secondary Schools	#高中 Senior Secondary Schools	#初中 Junior Secondary Schools	小学(万人) Primary Schools (10 000 persons)
1978	4890	310987	10807			300180	38837	261343	106.58
1980	6455	311213	22263	592	4514	283844	50340	233504	101.73
1985	13996	346833	17888	4915	7649	316381	71199	245182	116.43
1990	17542	439140	23897	13577	13685	387981	94579	293402	126.78
1991	17694	406750	24433	14465	14163	353689	99363	254326	138.80
1992	18704	416976	27039	15524	13972	360441	93868	266573	143.05
1993	21045	409016	31696	18094	14842	344384	74171	270213	147.54
1994	23166	437432	32671	16299	17452	371123	53103	318020	151.76
1995	24125	477379	33264	20013	16040	408062	52570	355492	157.84
1996	24171	538467	36928	22997	15464	463078	60430	402648	163.04
1997	21611	617750	38875	25797	14952	538126	77628	460498	170.43
1998	20941	695845	41617	26133	16275	611820	87326	524494	174.39
1999	23224	784981	49700	28551	15105	691625	89411	602214	174.30
2000	31989	834390	62572	34992	12260	724566	91843	632723	171.44
2001	47689	867582	58971	37013	9191	762407	103658	658749	165.84
2002	61610	913720	51204	40938	10971	810607	121523	689084	158.25
2003	65394	954789	42146	33997	10579	868067	137714	730353	151.53
2004	70340	985148	31566	49693	13407	890482	148398	742084	143.62

18-16 各地、州、市各级各类学校数

Number of Schools by Level, Type and by Prefecture, Autonomous Prefecture and City

单位：所 (2004 年) (unit)

地区	Region	普通高等学校 Regular Institutions of Higher Education	中等专业学校 Specialized Secondary Schools	#中等师范学校 Normal Secondary Schools
总计	**Total**	**28**	**78**	**19**
乌鲁木齐市	Urumqi City	14	22	3
克拉玛依市	Karamay City	1	2	1
石河子市	Shihezi City	1	2	1
吐鲁番地区	Turpan Administrative Offices		3	1
哈密地区	Hami [Kumul] Administrative Offices		4	1
昌吉回族自治州	Changji Hui Autonomous Prefecture	3	2	1
伊犁哈萨克自治州	Ili Kazak Autonomous Prefecture	2	12	3
伊犁州直属县(市)	Counties (Cities) Direct Under Ili Prefecture	2	5	1
塔城地区	Tacheng [Tarbagatai] Administrative Offices		4	1
阿勒泰地区	Altay Administrative Offices		3	1
博尔塔拉蒙古自治州	Bortala Mongol Autonomous Prefecture		2	1
巴音郭楞蒙古自治州	Bayangol Mongol Autonomous Prefecture	1	3	1
阿克苏地区	Aksu Administrative Offices	2	2	1
克孜勒苏柯尔克孜自治州	Kizilsu Kirgiz Autonomous Prefecture		3	1
喀什地区	Kashgar [Kaxgar] Administrative Offices	1	8	2
和田地区	Hotan Administrative Offices	2	5	1
生产建设兵团	Production and Construction Group	1	8	1
塔西南油田	Tarim Oil Field Southwest			

地区	Region	普通中学 Regular Secondary Schools	#高中 Senior Secondary Schools	职业中学 Vocational Secondary Schools	小学 Primary Schools	盲聋哑学校 Special Schools
总计	**Total**	**1965**	**498**	**84**	**5451**	**8**
乌鲁木齐市	Urumqi City	123	61	6	168	2
克拉玛依市	Karamay City	24	17		30	1
石河子市	Shihezi City	11	7		12	
吐鲁番地区	Turpan Administrative Offices	95	23	4	118	
哈密地区	Hami [Kumul] Administrative Offices	72	19	3	55	
昌吉回族自治州	Changji Hui Autonomous Prefecture	125	36	9	255	1
伊犁哈萨克自治州	Ili Kazak Autonomous Prefecture	460	108	21	951	1
伊犁州直属县(市)	Counties (Cities) Direct Under Ili Prefecture	254	67	12	545	
塔城地区	Tacheng [Tarbagatai] Administrative Offices	110	25	6	273	1
阿勒泰地区	Altay Administrative Offices	96	16	3	133	
博尔塔拉蒙古自治州	Bortala Mongol Autonomous Prefecture	39	11	2	98	
巴音郭楞蒙古自治州	Bayangol Mongol Autonomous Prefecture	127	23		264	1
阿克苏地区	Aksu Administrative Offices	156	42	4	874	1
克孜勒苏柯尔克孜自治州	Kizilsu Kirgiz Autonomous Prefecture	64	13	1	217	
喀什地区	Kashgar [Kaxgar] Administrative Offices	236	40	16	1212	1
和田地区	Hotan Administrative Offices	150	15	9	856	
生产建设兵团	Production and Construction Group	281	81	9	338	
塔西南油田	Tarim Oil Field Southwest	2	2		3	

18-17 各地、州、市各级各类学校教职工数

Number of Teachers and Staff by Level and Type of School and by Prefecture, Autonomous Prefecture and City

单位：人 (2004 年) (person)

地　区	Region	普通高等学校 Regular Institutions of Higher Education	中等专业学校 Specialized Secondary Schools	#中等师范学校 Normal Secondary Schools
总　计	**Total**	**23265**	**9116**	**2927**
乌鲁木齐市	Urumqi City	13949	2909	409
克拉玛依市	Karamay City	458	279	199
石河子市	Shihezi City	2540	97	97
吐鲁番地区	Turpan Administrative Offices		242	178
哈密地区	Hami [Kumul] Administrative Offices		562	141
昌吉回族自治州	Changji Hui Autonomous Prefecture	1309	137	
伊犁哈萨克自治州	Ili Kazak Autonomous Prefecture	1828	1639	559
伊犁州直属县(市)	Counties (Cities) Direct Under Ili Prefecture	1828	759	245
塔城地区	Tacheng [Tarbagatai] Administrative Offices		454	145
阿勒泰地区	Altay Administrative Offices		426	169
博尔塔拉蒙古自治州	Bortala Mongol Autonomous Prefecture		186	148
巴音郭楞蒙古自治州	Bayangol Mongol Autonomous Prefecture	282	692	151
阿克苏地区	Aksu Administrative Offices	1342	302	222
克孜勒苏柯尔克孜自治州	Kizilsu Kirgiz Autonomous Prefecture		301	146
喀什地区	Kashgar [Kaxgar] Administrative Offices	896	1083	359
和田地区	Hotan Administrative Offices	515	277	184
生产建设兵团	Production and Construction Group	146	410	134
塔西南油田	Tarim Oil Field Southwest			

地　区	Region	普通中学 Regular Secondary Schools	小学 Primary Schools	盲聋哑学校 Special Schools
总　计	**Total**	**113047**	**150308**	**356**
乌鲁木齐市	Urumqi City	9899	9311	171
克拉玛依市	Karamay City	2297	1925	15
石河子市	Shihezi City	1029	778	
吐鲁番地区	Turpan Administrative Offices	4419	4654	
哈密地区	Hami [Kumul] Administrative Offices	3338	4172	8
昌吉回族自治州	Changji Hui Autonomous Prefecture	9022	9506	38
伊犁哈萨克自治州	Ili Kazak Autonomous Prefecture	23207	33150	4
伊犁州直属县(市)	Counties (Cities) Direct Under Ili Prefecture	12897	17756	
塔城地区	Tacheng [Tarbagatai] Administrative Offices	6166	9123	4
阿勒泰地区	Altay Administrative Offices	4144	6271	
博尔塔拉蒙古自治州	Bortala Mongol Autonomous Prefecture	2704	3463	
巴音郭楞蒙古自治州	Bayangol Mongol Autonomous Prefecture	6717	9543	42
阿克苏地区	Aksu Administrative Offices	8936	15626	26
克孜勒苏柯尔克孜自治州	Kizilsu Kirgiz Autonomous Prefecture	3198	5175	
喀什地区	Kashgar [Kaxgar] Administrative Offices	14112	23229	52
和田地区	Hotan Administrative Offices	7110	12115	
生产建设兵团	Production and Construction Group	16897	17514	
塔西南油田	Tarim Oil Field Southwest	162	147	

18-18 各地、州、市各级各类学校教师数

Number of Teachers by Level and Type of School and by Prefecture, Autonomous Prefecture and City

单位：人 (2004 年) (person)

地区	Region	普通高等学校 Regular Institutions of Higher Education	中等专业学校 Specialized Secondary Schools	#中等师范学校 Normal Secondary Schools
总 计	**Total**	**12239**	**5494**	**1937**
乌鲁木齐市	Urumqi City	7070	1670	258
克拉玛依市	Karamay City	209	144	113
石河子市	Shihezi City	1439	49	49
吐鲁番地区	Turpan Administrative Offices		183	130
哈密地区	Hami [Kumul] Administrative Offices		303	72
昌吉回族自治州	Changji Hui Autonomous Prefecture	763	78	
伊犁哈萨克自治州	Ili Kazak Autonomous Prefecture	908	977	392
伊犁州直属县(市)	Counties (Cities) Direct Under Ili Prefecture	908	427	172
塔城地区	Tacheng [Tarbagatai] Administrative Offices		278	107
阿勒泰地区	Altay Administrative Offices		272	113
博尔塔拉蒙古自治州	Bortala Mongol Autonomous Prefecture		106	88
巴音郭楞蒙古自治州	Bayangol Mongol Autonomous Prefecture	166	454	107
阿克苏地区	Aksu Administrative Offices	711	204	138
克孜勒苏柯尔克孜自治州	Kizilsu Kirgiz Autonomous Prefecture		216	105
喀什地区	Kashgar [Kaxgar] Administrative Offices	543	736	264
和田地区	Hotan Administrative Offices	342	200	134
生产建设兵团	Production and Construction Group	88	174	87
塔西南油田	Tarim Oil Field Southwest			

地区	Region	普通中学 Regular Secondary Schools	#高中 Senior Secondary Schools	小学 Primary Schools	盲聋哑学校 Special Schools
总 计	**Total**	**94381**	**22809**	**134915**	**257**
乌鲁木齐市	Urumqi City	7386	2809	8428	116
克拉玛依市	Karamay City	1725	687	1692	13
石河子市	Shihezi City	761	345	670	
吐鲁番地区	Turpan Administrative Offices	4023	975	4422	
哈密地区	Hami [Kumul] Administrative Offices	2863	1036	3707	6
昌吉回族自治州	Changji Hui Autonomous Prefecture	7359	2161	8988	30
伊犁哈萨克自治州	Ili Kazak Autonomous Prefecture	19912	5099	29474	4
伊犁州直属县(市)	Counties (Cities) Direct Under Ili Prefecture	11209	2897	15981	
塔城地区	Tacheng [Tarbagatai] Administrative Offices	5281	1487	8018	4
阿勒泰地区	Altay Administrative Offices	3422	715	5475	
博尔塔拉蒙古自治州	Bortala Mongol Autonomous Prefecture	2292	628	3047	
巴音郭楞蒙古自治州	Bayangol Mongol Autonomous Prefecture	5829	1443	8878	32
阿克苏地区	Aksu Administrative Offices	7810	1220	14567	17
克孜勒苏柯尔克孜自治州	Kizilsu Kirgiz Autonomous Prefecture	2868	560	4481	
喀什地区	Kashgar [Kaxgar] Administrative Offices	12482	1628	20702	39
和田地区	Hotan Administrative Offices	6028	607	10752	
生产建设兵团	Production and Construction Group	12904	3541	14977	
塔西南油田	Tarim Oil Field Southwest	139	70	130	

18-19 各地、州、市各级各类学校在校学生数

Number of Student Enrollment by Level and Type of School and by Prefecture, Autonomous Prefecture and City

单位：人 (2004 年) (person)

地区	Region	普通高等学校 Regular Institutions of Higher Education	中等专业学校 Specialized Secondary Schools	#中等师范学校 Normal Secondary Schools
总 计	**Total**	**168247**	**71324**	**8686**
乌鲁木齐市	Urumqi City	103378	29991	1752
克拉玛依市	Karamay City	4399	858	
石河子市	Shihezi City	19875	945	503
吐鲁番地区	Turpan Administrative Offices		945	346
哈密地区	Hami [Kumul] Administrative Offices		764	293
昌吉回族自治州	Changji Hui Autonomous Prefecture	9973	8124	
伊犁哈萨克自治州	Ili Kazak Autonomous Prefecture	8507	5971	845
伊犁州直属县(市)	Counties (Cities) Direct Under Ili Prefecture	8507	4349	603
塔城地区	Tacheng [Tarbagatai] Administrative Offices		825	198
阿勒泰地区	Altay Administrative Offices		797	44
博尔塔拉蒙古自治州	Bortala Mongol Autonomous Prefecture		489	329
巴音郭楞蒙古自治州	Bayangol Mongol Autonomous Prefecture	432	7200	1077
阿克苏地区	Aksu Administrative Offices	7314	3770	1665
克孜勒苏柯尔克孜自治州	Kizilsu Kirgiz Autonomous Prefecture		791	653
喀什地区	Kashgar [Kaxgar] Administrative Offices	9294	5249	364
和田地区	Hotan Administrative Offices	3952	763	512
生产建设兵团	Production and Construction Group	1123	5464	347
塔西南油田	Tarim Oil Field Southwest			

地区	Region	普通中学 Regular Secondary Schools	#高中 Senior Secondary Schools	职业中学 Vocational Secondary Schools	小学 Primary Schools	盲聋哑学校 Special Schools
总 计	**Total**	**1517948**	**359147**	**61502**	**2218109**	**2549**
乌鲁木齐市	Urumqi City	116429	46435	1334	148338	616
克拉玛依市	Karamay City	19825	7896		24043	49
石河子市	Shihezi City	12529	6219		12565	
吐鲁番地区	Turpan Administrative Offices	44297	11876	694	54858	
哈密地区	Hami [Kumul] Administrative Offices	34321	12886	345	36425	58
昌吉回族自治州	Changji Hui Autonomous Prefecture	98374	33009	3895	109601	221
伊犁哈萨克自治州	Ili Kazak Autonomous Prefecture	272605	80824	2332	388203	45
伊犁州直属县(市)	Counties (Cities) Direct Under Ili Prefecture	158442	47394	1257	249466	
塔城地区	Tacheng [Tarbagatai] Administrative Offices	68781	22160	499	87810	45
阿勒泰地区	Altay Administrative Offices	45382	11270	576	50927	
博尔塔拉蒙古自治州	Bortala Mongol Autonomous Prefecture	27664	9589	2015	33195	
巴音郭楞蒙古自治州	Bayangol Mongol Autonomous Prefecture	77452	23439		92684	172
阿克苏地区	Aksu Administrative Offices	176606	23274	2364	247547	297
克孜勒苏柯尔克孜自治州	Kizilsu Kirgiz Autonomous Prefecture	46876	9236		56761	
喀什地区	Kashgar [Kaxgar] Administrative Offices	271727	29166	42126	496381	1091
和田地区	Hotan Administrative Offices	114722	9378	4104	232998	
生产建设兵团	Production and Construction Group	202967	55210	2293	282872	
塔西南油田	Tarim Oil Field Southwest	1554	710		1638	

18-20 各地、州、市各级各类学校招生数

Number of New Student Enrollment by Level and Type of School and by Prefecture, Autonomous Prefecture and City

单位：人 (2004 年) (person)

地　区	Region	普通高等学校 Regular Institutions of Higher Education	中等专业学校 Specialized Secondary Schools	#中等师范学校 Normal Secondary Schools
总　计	**Total**	**53204**	**27990**	**1042**
乌鲁木齐市	Urumqi City	31416	12017	419
克拉玛依市	Karamay City	2409	746	
石河子市	Shihezi City	5300		93
吐鲁番地区	Turpan Administrative Offices		270	75
哈密地区	Hami [Kumul] Administrative Offices		327	
昌吉回族自治州	Changji Hui Autonomous Prefecture	4640	3486	
伊犁哈萨克自治州	Ili Kazak Autonomous Prefecture	2208	1925	
伊犁州直属县(市)	Counties (Cities) Direct Under Ili Prefecture	2208	1375	
塔城地区	Tacheng [Tarbagatai] Administrative Offices		275	
阿勒泰地区	Altay Administrative Offices		275	
博尔塔拉蒙古自治州	Bortala Mongol Autonomous Prefecture		265	105
巴音郭楞蒙古自治州	Bayangol Mongol Autonomous Prefecture	216	3259	107
阿克苏地区	Aksu Administrative Offices	2493	858	
克孜勒苏柯尔克孜自治州	Kizilsu Kirgiz Autonomous Prefecture		148	98
喀什地区	Kashgar [Kaxgar] Administrative Offices	2721	2031	
和田地区	Hotan Administrative Offices	1264	283	70
生产建设兵团	Production and Construction Group	537	2375	75
塔西南油田	Tarim Oil Field Southwest			

地　区	Region	普通中学 Regular Secondary Schools	#高中 Senior Secondary Schools	职业中学 Vocational Secondary Schools	小学 Primary Schools	盲聋哑学校 Special Schools
总　计	**Total**	**536405**	**138315**	**27585**	**347364**	**390**
乌鲁木齐市	Urumqi City	41391	18143	437	26036	45
克拉玛依市	Karamay City	6989	2905		4308	6
石河子市	Shihezi City	4425	2317		2039	
吐鲁番地区	Turpan Administrative Offices	14716	4485	305	8976	
哈密地区	Hami [Kumul] Administrative Offices	11649	4752	97	5804	
昌吉回族自治州	Changji Hui Autonomous Prefecture	34100	12621	1776	18680	25
伊犁哈萨克自治州	Ili Kazak Autonomous Prefecture	95720	31238	1309	64668	9
伊犁州直属县(市)	Counties (Cities) Direct Under Ili Prefecture	57083	18550	664	42955	
塔城地区	Tacheng [Tarbagatai] Administrative Offices	23719	8491	368	14039	9
阿勒泰地区	Altay Administrative Offices	14918	4197	277	7674	
博尔塔拉蒙古自治州	Bortala Mongol Autonomous Prefecture	9725	3741	695	5385	
巴音郭楞蒙古自治州	Bayangol Mongol Autonomous Prefecture	27226	8997		14865	30
阿克苏地区	Aksu Administrative Offices	62677	9252	1171	36844	105
克孜勒苏柯尔克孜自治州	Kizilsu Kirgiz Autonomous Prefecture	16143	3503		8664	
喀什地区	Kashgar [Kaxgar] Administrative Offices	94745	11835	19883	71301	170
和田地区	Hotan Administrative Offices	43845	3377	1053	36829	
生产建设兵团	Production and Construction Group	72517	20893	859	42648	
塔西南油田	Tarim Oil Field Southwest	537	256		317	

18-21 各地、州、市各级各类学校毕业生数

Number of Graduates by Level and Type of School and by Prefecture, Autonomous Prefecture and City

单位：人 (2004 年) (person)

地 区	Region	普通高等学校 Regular Institutions of Higher Education	中等专业学校 Specialized Secondary Schools	#中等师范学校 Normal Secondary Schools
总 计	**Total**	**31013**	**24758**	**7097**
乌鲁木齐市	Urumqi City	20523	9236	698
克拉玛依市	Karamay City	460	62	
石河子市	Shihezi City	1902		382
吐鲁番地区	Turpan Administrative Offices		433	296
哈密地区	Hami [Kumul] Administrative Offices		665	297
昌吉回族自治州	Changji Hui Autonomous Prefecture	1653	1731	
伊犁哈萨克自治州	Ili Kazak Autonomous Prefecture	1155	3005	1104
伊犁州直属县(市)	Counties (Cities) Direct Under Ili Prefecture	1155	2115	833
塔城地区	Tacheng [Tarbagatai] Administrative Offices		252	117
阿勒泰地区	Altay Administrative Offices		638	154
博尔塔拉蒙古自治州	Bortala Mongol Autonomous Prefecture		100	100
巴音郭楞蒙古自治州	Bayangol Mongol Autonomous Prefecture		1583	820
阿克苏地区	Aksu Administrative Offices	931	1236	496
克孜勒苏柯尔克孜自治州	Kizilsu Kirgiz Autonomous Prefecture		619	339
喀什地区	Kashgar [Kaxgar] Administrative Offices	1450	3427	1577
和田地区	Hotan Administrative Offices	2189	1176	744
生产建设兵团	Production and Construction Group	750	1485	244
塔西南油田	Tarim Oil Field Southwest			

地 区	Region	普通中学 Regular Secondary Schools	#高中 Senior Secondary Schools	职业中学 Vocational Secondary Schools	小学 Primary Schools	盲聋哑学校 Special Schools
总 计	**Total**	**420583**	**84418**	**15475**	**417588**	**382**
乌鲁木齐市	Urumqi City	31877	10820	274	23134	147
克拉玛依市	Karamay City	5585	1816		3526	7
石河子市	Shihezi City	3265	1488		2011	
吐鲁番地区	Turpan Administrative Offices	15004	3210	218	10611	
哈密地区	Hami [Kumul] Administrative Offices	10265	3162	56	6643	
昌吉回族自治州	Changji Hui Autonomous Prefecture	27929	8105	678	20627	29
伊犁哈萨克自治州	Ili Kazak Autonomous Prefecture	79831	20235	683	68545	5
伊犁州直属县(市)	Counties (Cities) Direct Under Ili Prefecture	45205	11467	347	41969	
塔城地区	Tacheng [Tarbagatai] Administrative Offices	20594	5927	205	15643	5
阿勒泰地区	Altay Administrative Offices	14032	2841	131	10933	
博尔塔拉蒙古自治州	Bortala Mongol Autonomous Prefecture	7563	2129	380	6019	
巴音郭楞蒙古自治州	Bayangol Mongol Autonomous Prefecture	20036	4016		17729	2
阿克苏地区	Aksu Administrative Offices	46758	5413	597	51842	68
克孜勒苏柯尔克孜自治州	Kizilsu Kirgiz Autonomous Prefecture	12440	2244		13358	
喀什地区	Kashgar [Kaxgar] Administrative Offices	74276	7150	10286	102667	124
和田地区	Hotan Administrative Offices	33328	2606	1800	40163	
生产建设兵团	Production and Construction Group	51940	11820	503	50432	
塔西南油田	Tarim Oil Field Southwest	486	204		281	

18-22 各类学校教育经费情况
Educational Funds in Various Schools

单位：万元　　(2004 年)　　(10 000 yuan)

指　标	Item	合　计 Total	国家财政性教育经费 Government Appropriation for Education	#预算内教育经费 Budgetary Education Expense	社会团体和公民个人办学经费 Funds of Social Organizations and Citizens for Running Schools	社会捐资和集资办学经费 Donations and Fund-Raising for Running Schools	学费和杂费 Tuition and Miscellaneous Fee	其它教育经费 Other Educational Funds
总　计	**Total**	**1140571**	**880081**	**793660**	**23396**	**3109**	**133534**	**100451**
中 央	Central Government	20748	19588	8658			100	1060
地 方	Local Government	1119823	860493	785002	23396	3109	133434	99391
按学校类别分组	**Grouped by Type of Schools**							
高等学校	**Institutions of Higher Education**	**191556**	**82747**	**75368**	**1118**	**1185**	**72455**	**34051**
普通高等学校	Regular Institutions of Higher Education	168428	73790	66464	1118	734	61831	30955
成人高等学校	Institutions of Higher Education for Adults	23128	8957	8904		451	10624	3096
中等专业学校	**Specialized Secondary Schools**	**56890**	**32066**	**31615**		**29**	**18949**	**5846**
中等技术学校	Technical Schools	37606	20887	20695		1	12725	3993
中等师范学校	Normal Secondary Schools	14446	8141	7963		28	4874	1403
成人中专学校	Specialized Secondary Schools for Adults	4838	3038	2957			1350	450
技工学校	**Technical Schools**	**15015**	**8688**	**8859**			**3417**	**2910**
中 学	**Secondary Schools**	**360669**	**289179**	**258132**	**14892**	**862**	**30514**	**25222**
普通中学	Regular Secondary Schools	360441	289018	258001	14858	862	30488	25215
高级中学	Senior Secondary Schools	35994	22328	20062	1709	17	8154	3786
完全中学	Whole Secondary Schools	153348	112393	97393	11051	464	18305	11135
初级中学	Junior Secondary Schools	171099	154297	140546	2098	381	4029	10294
#农 村	Rural Areas	108872	104300	98801		180	1376	3016
成人中学	Secondary Schools for Adults	228	161	131	34		26	7
职业中学	**Vocational Schools**	**7246**	**5161**	**4950**		**11**	**1202**	**872**
小 学	**Primary Schools**	**409036**	**384016**	**359193**	**7386**	**736**	**6981**	**9917**
普通小学	Regular Primary Schools	409036	384016	359193	7386	736	6981	9917
#农 村	Rural Areas	263265	257626	251046		479	2030	3130
成人小学	Primary Schools for Adults							
特殊教育学校	**Special Education Schools**	**1812**	**1450**	**1280**		**47**	**17**	**298**
幼儿园	**Kindergartens**	**23680**	**18537**	**18257**		**21**		**5122**
其 它	**Others**	**74667**	**58237**	**36005**		**218**		**16212**

18-23　科技活动基本情况

Basic Statistics on Scientific and Technological Activities

指　　标	Item	2003	2004
科技活动人员(人)	**Number of Persons Engaged in Scientific and Technological Activities (person)**	**25246**	**25071**
#科学家与工程师	Scientists and Engineers	16871	16575
研究与试验发展全时人员(人年)	**Number of Persons Engaged in Research and Development (person year)**	**5335**	**5788**
#科学家与工程师	Scientists and Engineers	4628	5030
科技经费筹集额(万元)	**Funding for Scientific and Technological Activities (10 000 yuan)**	**189930**	**268453**
#政府资金	Government Funds	49072	52267
企业资金	Funds Self-raised by Enterprises	117487	190607
银行贷款	Bank Loans	8852	8400
科技经费内部支出(万元)	**Expenditures for Scientific and Technological Activities (10 000 yuan)**	**173994**	**254746**
#劳务费	Service Fees	54114	64859
固定资产购建费	Purchases of Fixed Assets	49219	66306
#研究与试验发展经费支出	Research and Development Expenses	37957	60135
基础研究	Fundamental Research	3223	3521
应用研究	Applied Research	8782	17169
试验发展	Experimental Development	25952	39445
研究与试验发展经费支出占新疆生产总值比重(%)	**Proportion of Research and Development Expenses to GDP (%)**	**0.20**	**0.28**

18-24　县级以上政府部门属研究与开发机构及科技信息与文献机构数、人员数

State-Owned Research and Development Institutions and Information and Literature Institutions at and Above County Level and Persons Engaged

(2004 年)

指　　标	Item	合　计 Total	自然科学技术领域 Field of Natural Sciences and Technology	社会、人文科学技术领域 Field of Social Sciences and Humanities	科技信息和文献机构 Scientific-technical Information and Document Institutions
机构数(个)	**Institutions (unit)**	**108**	**92**	**8**	**8**
科技活动人员(人)	**S&T Personnel (person)**	**5011**	**4472**	**300**	**239**
#科学家工程师	Scientists and Engineers	3560	3120	255	185
研究与试验发展全时人员(人年)	**Number of Persons Engaged in Research and Development (person year)**	**2056**	**1852**	**155**	**49**
#科学家工程师	Scientists and Engineers	1727	1561	134	32
科技经费筹集额(万元)	**Sources of Funds for S&T(10 000 yuan)**	**46877**	**41910**	**3025**	**1942**
#政府拨款	Government Funds	35699	31105	2844	1750
银行贷款	Bank Loans	180	180		
科技经费内部支出额(万元)	**Intramural Expenditure for S&T (10 000 yuan)**	**44537**	**39923**	**2721**	**1893**
#劳务费	Labor Expenses	15434	13376	1337	721
固定资产购建费	Expenses on Fixed Assets	7726	7508	99	119
#研究与发展经费支出	R&D Expenditure	19687	18150	940	597
基础研究	Fundamental Research	2540	1622	918	
应用研究	Applied Research	11628	11009	22	597
试验发展	Experimental Development	5519	5519		

18-25 重大科学技术研究成果及奖励数

Number of Major Achievements in Scientific and Technological Research and Awarded Prizes

单位：项 (item)

年 份 Year	重大科技成果 Number of Major Achievements in Science ang Technology		奖励情况 Awarded Prizes					
	国家级 National	自治区级 Autonomous Regional	国家级 National	自治区级 Autonomous Regional	一等奖 Frist Class Awards	二等奖 Second Class Awards	三等奖 Third Class Awards	四等奖 Fourth Class Awards
1978 年以前		1551	88	610				
1979		270		117	13	35	69	
1980-1985		1173	16	356	5	31	102	218
1986	10	266	6	103	2	16	31	54
1987		271	7	31		2	9	20
1988		288	7	277	3	48	88	138
1989		378	12	168	2	27	59	80
1990		444	3	129		18	56	55
1991		255	9	137	2	21	48	66
1992		172	9	140	3	24	57	56
1993		330	6	124	4	25	45	50
1994		296		177	1	31	67	78
1995		218	3	137	4	26	53	54
1996		276	15	135	2	27	46	60
1997		230	9	131	5	25	47	54
1998		219	4	105	2	27	38	38
1999		215	5	108	9	32	49	18
2000		250	2	90	5	18	67	
2001		285	6	92	4	23	65	
2002		207	5	99	5	30	64	
2003		232	3	111	8	34	69	

18-26 专利申请和批准数

Number of Patent Applications Examined and Approved

单位：件 (case)

年 份 Year	申请数 Number of Patent Applications Examined				批准数 Number of Patent Applications Granted				代理机构（个） Agency (unit)
	合计 Total	发明 Inventions	实用新型 Utility Models	外观设计 Designs	合计 Total	发明 Inventions	实用新型 Utility Models	外观设计 Designs	
1985	36								
1990	250	38	203	9	139	3	135	1	5
1991	402	64	302	36	135	2	124	9	5
1992	502	91	374	37	196	6	180	10	5
1993	642	144	467	31	454	22	398	34	5
1994	608	104	479	25	358	9	326	23	6
1995	609	92	467	50	312	11	285	16	6
1996	713	113	531	69	362	9	316	37	7
1997	799	139	544	116	328	12	246	70	7
1998	978	166	600	212	462	14	337	111	7
1999	881	139	552	190	859	32	630	197	7
2000	1088	179	699	210	717	66	475	176	7
2001	1088	189	683	216	755	90	522	143	5
2002	1239	216	779	244	627	61	407	159	4
2003	1472	253	940	279	751	75	520	156	5
2004	1492	272	870	350	792	75	530	187	5

18-27 高等学校科技活动情况

Basic Statistics on Higher Education for Scientific and Technological Activities

指　　标	Item	2003	2004
科技活动人员(人)	**S&T Personnel (person)**	**3586**	**3136**
#科学家工程师	Scientists and Engineers	3582	2623
研究与发展机构(个)	**R&D Institutions (unit)**	**21**	**17**
研究与发展人员全时当量(人・年)	**Full-time Equivalent of R&D Personnel (person.year)**	**1644**	**1555**
#科学家工程师	Scientists and Engineers	1644	1479
#基础研究	Fundamental Research	519	530
应用研究	Applied Research	860	811
试验发展	Experimental Development	265	214
科技经费筹集额(万元)	**Sources of Funds for S&T(10 000 yuan)**	**5018**	**6033**
#政府拨款	Government Funds	4366	4947
银行贷款	Bank Loans		
科技经费内部支出额(万元)	**Intramural Expenditure for S&T (10 000 yuan)**	**3823**	**5982**
#劳务费	Labor Expenses	1600	1787
固定资产购建费	Expenses on Fixed Assets	675	1459
#研究与发展经费支出	R&D Expenditure (10 000 yuan)	2032	3250
基础研究	Fundamental Research	684	1045
应用研究	Applied Research	1226	1764
试验发展	Experimental Development	122	441

18-28 企事业单位专业技术人员数

Number of Scientific and Technical Personnel in Enterprises And Institutions

单位：人 (person)

年 份 Year	总 计 Total	工程技术人员 Engineering	农业技术人员 Agriculture	卫生技术人员 Health Care	科学研究人员 Scientific Researcn	教学人员 Teaching
1978.6月末	85063	22198	13141	31741	3042	14941
1985	158709	51636	20730	57559	3416	25368
1990	241524	92383	25089	71906	4326	47820
1991	394931	91438	24106	72435	5016	201936
1992	404540	95814	25432	74149	5094	204051
1993	411073	100105	24668	75377	5090	205833
1994	424318	104209	26709	78466	5051	209883
1995	437209	109463	28096	79014	4825	215811
1996	325286	58108	22306	55332	2691	186849
1997	345273	60324	24434	58787	2933	198795
1998	355878	59009	27727	6008	2701	206433
1999	367125	75276	25856	57054	2515	206424
2000	368262	58576	27764	62338	2409	217175
2001	385129	59913	30043	65585	2492	227096
2002	387726	58011	31867	65364	2337	230147
2003	385705	57506	30808	65622	2236	229533
2004	398318	55421	32831	68604	2928	238534

注：① 1991年起专业技术人员包括企事业单位(不含行政机关)人员数,教学人员包括社会和自然科技领域及小学教师人数。
② 1996年后数据不包括中央单位的专业技术从员数，故人员减少较多。

Note: a) The Specialezed and technical personnel include those who work in enterprises and institutions (excluding administrative organs), teaching Staff, those work in social and nature scientific fields as well as elementary school teachers from 1991 on.
b) After 1996, the data exclude the figure of professionals with national establishments stationed to Xinjiang and thus the number of staff is reduced a lot.

18-29 企事业单位专业技术人员比重

Proportion of Scientific and Technical Personnel in Enterprises and Institutions

单位：% (%)

年 份 Year	总 计 Total	工程技术 Engineering	农业技术 Agriculture	卫生技术 Health Care	科学研究 Scientific Research	教 学 Teaching
1978.6月末	100	26.10	15.45	37.31	3.58	17.56
1985	100	32.54	13.06	36.27	2.15	15.98
1990	100	38.25	10.39	29.77	1.79	19.80
1991	100	23.16	6.10	18.34	1.27	51.13
1992	100	23.68	6.29	18.33	1.26	50.44
1993	100	24.35	6.00	18.34	1.24	50.07
1994	100	24.56	6.30	18.49	1.19	49.46
1995	100	25.04	6.43	18.07	1.10	49.36
1996	100	17.86	6.86	17.01	0.83	57.44
1997	100	17.47	7.08	17.03	0.85	57.57
1998	100	16.58	7.79	16.86	0.76	58.00
1999	100	20.50	7.04	15.54	0.69	56.23
2000	100	15.91	7.54	16.93	0.65	58.97
2001	100	15.55	7.80	17.03	0.65	58.97
2002	100	14.96	8.22	16.86	0.60	59.36
2003	100	14.91	7.99	17.01	0.58	59.51
2004	100	13.91	8.24	17.22	0.74	59.89

18-30 工业企业科技活动情况

(2004 年)

项 目	Item	企业数(个) Nnmber of Industrial Enterprises (unit)	科技机构数(个) Number of Scientific Technological Agencies (unit)	从事科技活动人员数(人) Number of Persons Engaged in Scientific and Technological Activities (person)
总 计	**Total**	**1430**	**78**	**9986**
按企业规模分	**Grouped by Size of Enterprises**			
大中型企业	Large and Medium-size Enterprises	203	60	9069
小型企业	Small Enterprises	1227	18	917
按登记注册类型分	**Grouped by Ownership**			
国有企业	State-owned	384	22	2332
集体企业	Collective-owned	46	1	40
股份制企业	Share-holding Corporations Ltd	9		
联营企业	Joint-run Enterprises	8		
有限责任公司	Liability Ltd. Co	571	28	1936
股份有限责任公司	Share-holding Corporations	41	21	5059
私营企业	Private-run Enterprises	308	4	242
港澳台商投资	Investment from Hong Kong, Taiwan and Maccao	17		18
外商投资企业	Foreign Funded Enterprises	46	2	359
按企业所在地区划分	**Grouped by Region of Enterprises**			
乌鲁木齐市	Urumqi City	332	25	2217
克拉玛依市	Karamay City	74	17	4522
石河子市	Shihezi City	73	6	570
吐鲁番地区	Turpan Administrative Offices	55	1	524
哈密地区	Hami [Kumul] Administrative Offices	70	3	176
昌吉回族自治州	Changji Hui Autonomous Prefecture	240	9	522
伊犁哈萨克自治州	Ili Administrative Offices	247	9	404
伊犁州直属县(市)	Counties (Cities) Direct Under Ili Prefecture	126	3	223
塔城地区	Tacheng [Tarbagatai] Administrative Offices	77	4	145
阿勒泰地区	Altay Administrative Offices	44	2	36
博尔塔拉蒙古自治州	Bortala Mongol Autonomous Prefecture	29		
巴音郭楞蒙古自治州	Bayangol Mongol Autonomous Prefecture	118	5	635
阿克苏地区	Aksu Administrative Offices	87	3	416
克孜勒苏柯尔克孜自治州	Kizilsu Kirgiz Autonomous Prefecture	17		
喀什地区	Kashi Administrative Offices	59		
和田地区	Hotan Administrative Offices	29		
按工业行业大类分	**Grouped by Sector**			
煤炭开采和洗选业	Coal Extracting and Dressing	69	3	441
石油和天然气开采业	Petroleum and Natural Gas Extraction	14	13	4902

Statistics on Technical Activities of Large and Medium-Sized Industrial Enterprises

科学家工程师 Scientists and Engineers	研究与试验发展人员 Number of Persons in Research and Experiment	机构中从事科技活动人员数 Number of Persons Engaged in Scientific and Technological Activities	经费筹集额(万元) Funding for Scientific and Technological Activities (10 000 yuan)	#企业资金 Enterprise Funds	支出总额(万元) Funding for Scientific and Technological Expenses (10 000 yuan)	#研究与试验发展经费 Research and Development Expenses	科技项目数(项) Number of Science and Technology (item)	#研究与试验发展项目数 Number of Research and Development
7093	**3115**	**5444**	**183324.9**	**173111.6**	**173196.6**	**36007.8**	**1029**	**418**
6509	3075	5170	174569.5	167241.8	165229.7	35529.6	951	412
584	40	274	8755.4	5869.8	7966.9	478.2	78	6
1923	929	1256	12353.2	11053.0	11464.9	4358.1	215	90
6		13	456.9	456.9	456.9		3	
1224	107	763	17739.6	14235.9	15415.5	731.5	213	19
3651	2065	2921	147762.9	142633.6	141170.0	30607.9	543	308
108	14	142	2911.7	2740.6	2639.7	310.3	48	1
18			120.0	120.0	120.0		1	
163		349	1980.6	1871.6	1929.6		6	
1517	108	1240	24285.6	21980.5	18783.6	557.2	288	32
3396	2862	2267	69250.7	68460.3	68838.3	23680.6	487	377
380		430	8713.5	7272.0	8503.5		49	
451		339	5227.1	4230.1	2317.0		55	
79		52	306.0	306.0	261.8		9	
365	91	275	21219.4	18455.6	20288.1	5513.0	34	3
248		237	5532.4	3763.2	5500.6		31	
111		95	2809.0	1958.0	2783.5		17	
132		135	1452.6	1452.6	1451.3		12	
5		7	1270.8	352.6	1265.8		2	
436	54	513	47287.1	47167.1	47275.6	6257.0	58	6
221		91	1503.1	1476.8	1428.1		18	
278	34	133	2158.5	2086.5	1919.1	147.6	50	5
3822	2488	2893	91228.2	90243.2	86780.4	25147.5	497	328

18-30 续表

项　　目	Item	企业数（个）Nnmber of Industrial Enterprises (unit)	科技机构数（个）Number of Scientific Technological Agencies (unit)	从事科技活动人员数（人）Number of Persons Engaged in Scientific and Technological Activities (person)
黑色金属矿采选业	Ferrous Metals Mining and Dressing	21		
有色金属矿采选业	Nonferrous Metals Mining and Dressing	18	4	82
非金属矿采选业	Nonmetal Minerals Mining and Dressing	16	1	8
农副食品加工业	Farm and Non-staple Processing	170	2	103
食品制造业	Food Manufacturing	84	3	143
饮料制造业	Beverage Production	36	4	421
烟草制品业	Tobacco Products	2	1	24
纺织业	Textile Industry	73	4	269
纺织服装、鞋、帽制造业	Textile Garment, Shoe and Hat	9		
皮革、毛皮、羽毛(绒)及其制品业	Leather, Fur, Feather (down) its Products	6		
木材加工及木、竹、藤、棕、草制品业	Timber Processing, Wood, Bamboo, Cane, Grass Products	13		
家具制造业	Furniture Manufacturing	9	1	33
造纸及纸制品业	Papermaking and Paper Products	36		17
印刷业和记录媒介的复制	Printing and Copying of Medium for Record	49		38
石油加工、炼焦及核燃料加工业	Oil Processing, Coking and Nuclear Fuel Processing	43	4	585
化学原料及化学制品制造业	Raw Chemical Material and Chemical Products	98	6	692
医药制造业	Medical and Pharmaceutical Products	15	3	72
化学纤维制造业	Chemical Fiber	4	1	11
橡胶制品业	Rubber Products	4	1	36
塑料制品业	Plastic Products	68	3	350
非金属矿物制品业	Nonmetal Mineral Products	120	4	404
黑色金属冶炼及压延加工业	Smelting and Pressing of Ferrous Metals	37	1	104
有色金属冶炼及压延加工业	Smelting and Pressing of Nonferrous Metals	18		
金属制品业	Metal Products	52	1	65
通用设备制造业	Ordinary Equipment Production	40		16
专用设备制造业	Special Purposes Equipment	27	4	114
交通运输设备制造业	Transport Equipment	20	3	238
电气机械及器材制造业	Electric Equipment and Machinery	38	7	357
通信设备、计算机及其他电子设备制造业	Telecom Equipment, Computer and Other Electronic Equipment	1	1	48
仪器仪表及文化、办公用机械制造业	Equipment, Meter and Cultural and Office Machinery	3		10
废弃资源和废旧材料回收加工业	Recycling and Processing of Deserted Resources and Waste Material	2		
电力、热力的生产和供应业	Electric and Thermal Production and Supply	131	3	383
燃气生产和供应业	Gas Production and Supply	9		
水的生产和供应业	Water Production and Supply	75		20

Continued

科学家工程师 Scientists and Engineers	研究与试验发展人员 Number of Persons in Research and Experiment	机构中从事科技活动人员数 Number of Persons Engaged in Scientific and Technological Activities	经费筹集额(万元) Funding for Scientific and Technological Activities (10 000 yuan)	#企业资金 Enterprise Funds	支出总额(万元) Funding for Scientific and Technological Expenses (10 000 yuan)	#研究与试验发展经费 Research and Development Expenses	科技项目数(项) Number of Science and Technology (item)	#研究与试验发展项目数 Number of Research and Development
35		53	1370.8	452.6	1373.8		8	
6		6	14.7	14.7	14.7		1	
57		36	864.0	475.0	861.0		5	
78		71	333.3	193.3	276.7		11	
191		398	2802.6	2763.9	2802.6		9	
8		16	369.5	369.5	369.5		2	
135		148	1458.4	1446.9	1458.4		14	
7		33	1014.5	1014.5	1014.5		3	
17			480.5	480.5	480.5		6	
3			700.0	200.0	700.0		1	
296	181	360	33389.4	32722.0	29726.2	3569.6	106	49
573	232	147	8074.0	6553.3	8106.7	962.8	43	15
54		50	785.0	442.0	556.0		7	
11	8	11	110.0	110.0	107.0	107.0	2	2
5		36	820.6	820.6	820.6		10	
330	20	254	7471.6	6796.6	6782.4	21.5	49	4
194		122	1265.4	1265.4	1185.4		17	
98	28	50	363.6	295.1	294.1	103.0	31	9
58	27	4	647.4	617.4	596.1	420.0	15	2
6			56.0		56.0		1	
92	6	105	529.8	213.0	509.1	15.8	21	1
163		153	3397.7	3367.7	3299.2		65	
284	91	173	17951.3	15732.8	17528.5	5513.0	27	3
48		28	2585.0	2185.0	2585.0		5	
9			313.0	280.0	223.0		1	
226		164	2695.9	1895.9	2695.9		20	
9			74.2	74.2	74.2		2	

18-31 各类技术合同签定及执行情况

Statistics on Signing and Implementing Technical Contracts by Type

项 目	Item	合同数(项) Number of Contracts (item)		合同金额(万元) Revenue from fulfilment of Contracts (10 000 yuan)		#技术交易额 Transaction Value in Technical Market	
		2003	2004	2003	2004	2003	2004
总 计	**Total**	**1516**	**1619**	**120394.88**	**133370.61**	**107897.74**	**92047.06**
技术开发合同	Technology Development	401	336	51215.25	30003.52	50918.82	28503.55
技术转让合同	Technology Transfer	161	121	29973.72	53864.58	19900.04	22479.47
技术咨询合同	Technology Consultation	466	573	7052.31	13456.82	6844.21	12657.75
技术服务合同	Technology Service	488	589	32153.60	36045.69	30234.67	28406.29

18-32 各级技术计划项目进入技术市场情况

Statistics on Projects for Technical Plan Entering Technical Market by Level

单位：项、万元 (2004 年) (item,10 000 yuan)

项 目	Item	合 计 Total		国家部门计划 National Plans		省、自治区计划 单列市计划 Provinces, Municipality Plans		地、市、县计划 Area City and County Plans	
		项 数 Number of Items	金 额 Values	项 数 Number of Items	金 额 Values	项 数 Number of Items	金 额 Values	项 数 Number of Items	金 额 Values
总 计	**Total**	**393**	**85426.61**	**109**	**19454.35**	**81**	**3436.94**	**203**	**62535.32**
科研机构	Scientific Research Institutions	143	10757.16	16	7344.50	54	581.81	73	2830.85
大中专院校	Institutions of Higher Education and Secondary Schools	2	45.00			2	45.00		
工业企业	Industrial Enterprises	200	62596.00	77	11114.60	15	2355.13	108	49126.27
技术贸易机构	Technology Trade Agencies	15	7426.96	9	473.96	2	196.00	4	6757.00
个体经营	Individual Operation	1	40.00	1	40.00				
其 他	Other	32	4561.49	6	481.29	8	259.00	18	3821.20

18-33 技术经济合同成交情况
Statistics on Transaction in Technical and Economic Contract

单位：项、万元 (2004 年) (item, 10 000 yuan)

卖方类别 Classification of Buyers ＼ 买方类别 Classification of Sellers		合计 Total		#工业企业 Industrial Enterprises						#科研机构 Scientific research Institutions	
				国有企业 State owned		集体企业 Collective owned		其他 Others			
		项数 Number of Items	金额 Values	项数 Number of Items	金额 Values	项数 Number of Items	金额 Values	项数 Number of Items	金额 Values	项数 Number of Items	金额 Values
总计	**Total**	**1619**	**133370.61**	**579**	**37631.60**	**29**	**441.00**	**524**	**12964.94**	**42**	**1378.03**
科研机构	Scientific Research Institutions	481	20857.98	93	3257.54	3	10.20	171	2841.87	14	752.87
大中专院校	Institutions of Higher Education And Secondary Schools	12	363.50	3	118.00			8	243.50	1	2.00
工业企业	Industrial Enterprises	365	72663.22	202	20585.65	10	168.56	78	4551.93	9	49.20
技术贸易机构	Technology Trade Agencies	595	26695.86	163	4694.87	9	26.03	255	4874.04	11	78.96
个人及个人合计	Individual or Total	4	93.50	2	53.00	1	0.50			1	40.00
其他	Other	162	12696.55	116	8922.54	6	235.71	12	453.60	6	455.00

18-34 技术流向地域情况
Statistics on Location of Technical Contract

单位：项、万元 (2004 年) (item, 10 000 yuan)

地区 Region		合同类别合计 Contracts of Classification Total		技术开发 Technology Development		技术转让 Technology Transfer		技术咨询 Technology Consultation		技术服务 Technology Service	
		项数 Number of Items	金额 Values	项数 Number of Items	金额 Values	项数 Number of Items	金额 Values	项数 Number of Items	金额 Values	项数 Number of Items	金额 Values
总计	**Total**	**1619**	**133370.61**	**336**	**30003.52**	**121**	**53864.58**	**573**	**13456.82**	**589**	**36045.69**
北京市	Beijing	8	528.80	1	25.00	2	440.00	2	24.00	3	39.80
天津市	Tianjing										
山西省	Shanxi										
辽宁省	Liaoning	1	0.35							1	0.35
上海市	Shanghai	1	5.00	1	5.00						
江苏省	Jiangsu	2	55.00	1	50.00					1	5.00
浙江省	Zhejiang	1	10.50							1	10.50
福建省	Fujian	2	348.20					2	348.20		
山东省	Shandong	4	87.49	1	20.00	1	40.00	1	22.49	1	5.00
河南省	Henan	1	3.95							1	3.95
湖北省	Hubei	1	3.00					1	3.00		
广东省	Guangdong	1	2.86	1	2.86						
云南省	Yunnan	1	2.10	1	2.10						
陕西省	Shanxi	1	0.80							1	0.80
甘肃省	Gansu										
青海省	Qinghai										
宁夏	Ningxia	2	49.00					1	1.00	1	48.00
新疆	Xinjiang	1589	132254.36	330	29898.56	114	53365.38	566	13058.13	579	35932.29
其他	Other	4	19.20			4	19.20				

18-35 图书、杂志、报纸出版数量
Number of Books, Magazines and Newspapers Published

项　目	Item	1995	2000	2004
图 书	**Books Published**			
种数(种)	Number of Publications (kind)	1881	3418	3750
新出版(种)	New Publications (kind)	870	1901	2426
总印数(万册)	Total Printed Copies (10 000 copies)	5653	7287	8250
总印张(万印张)	Total Printed Sheets (10 000 sheets)	25800	39108	63458
杂 志	**Magazines Published**			
种数(种)	Number of Publications (kind)	154	174	185
平均每期印数(万册)	Average Per Issue Printed Copies(10 000copies)	94	110	128
总印数(万册)	Total Printed Copies (10 000 copies)	972	1125	1450
总印张(万印张)	Total Printed Sheets (10 000 sheets)	3500	3914	5771
报 纸	**Newspapers Published**			
种数(种)	Number of Newspapers Published (kind)	87	94	88
平均每期印数(万份)	Average Per Issue Printed Number (10 000 copies)	116	163	154
总印数(万份)	Total Printed Copies (10 000 copies)	18700	29486	33910
总印张(万印张)	Total Printed Sheets (10 000 sheets)	18900	53028	81340

18-36 文化产业基本情况
Basic Statistics on Culture

项　目	Item	1995	2000	2004
文化产业机构数(个)	**Number of Culture Institutions (unit)**	**1174**	**7848**	**10889**
文化部门	Culture Departments	366	1055	2747
其他部门	Other Departments	808	6793	8142
文化产业人员数(人)	**Number of Person in Culture (person)**	**8348**	**26621**	**32141**
文化部门	Culture Departments	7372	9801	11799
其他部门	Other Departments	976	16820	20342
各类文化艺术事业单位数(个)	**Number of Institutions on Various Culture and Art (unit)**			
文化馆、艺术馆	Cultural Centers, Art Centers	107	108	108
公共图书馆	Public Libraries	66	80	92
博物馆	Museums	12	23	25
艺术表演场所	Art Performance Places	26	23	30
艺术表演团体	Art Performance Troupes	87	88	109
戏剧、电影观众(万人次)	**Spectators of Theater and Movie (10 000 person-times)**			
戏 剧	Theater	20	14	71
电 影	Movie	319	35	806
按总人口平均每人观看(次)	**Average Per-Capital Watch by Total Population (times)**			
戏 剧	Theater	0.01	0.01	0.04
电 影	Movie	0.20	0.02	0.41

18-37 文化艺术、文物事业机构和人员情况

Number of Institutions and Personnel in Culture, Art and Cultural Relics

(2004 年)

项 目	Item	机构数(个) Number of Institutions (unit)	从业人员数(人) Number of Persons Engaged (person)
艺术事业	**Art Institutions**	**139**	**4347**
艺术表演团体	Art Performance Troupes	109	4030
话剧、儿童剧、滑稽剧团	Drama, Children Plays and Comedy Troupes	3	294
歌剧、舞剧、歌舞剧团	Opera, Ballet and Dance Troupes	8	437
歌舞团、轻音乐团	Song and Dance Troupe, Light Music Troupe	41	1669
文工团、文宣队、乌兰牧骑	Cultural and Performance Troupes and Ulanmuchi (equestrain art troupes)	41	1064
戏曲剧团	Local Opera Troupes	12	433
#京 剧	Local Beijing Opera Troupes	2	98
曲艺、杂技、木偶、皮影团	Recitation and Ballad Troupes, Acrobatics and Circus Troupes, Puppet Show Troupes and Shadow Play Troupes	3	118
综合性	General	1	15
艺术表演场所	Art Centers	30	317
剧场、影剧院	Theaters and Music Halls	29	280
综合性	General	1	37
图书馆事业	**Libraries**	**92**	**909**
群众文化事业	**Mass Culture**	**1240**	**3045**
群众艺术馆	Mass Art Centers	16	363
文化馆	Cultural Centers	92	988
文化站	Cultural Stations	1132	1694
#乡镇文化站	Township Cultural Stations	994	1448
艺术教育事业	**Culture and Education**	**3**	**184**
艺术科研机构	**Art Research Institutions**	**2**	**52**
文化市场经营单位	**Entertainment Operators**	**8371**	**20341**
文化娱乐业	Entertainment Operators	3014	11161
文化市场其他经营单位	Cultural Market Operators	5357	9180
其他文化事业	**Other Cultural Units**	**12**	**37**
艺术创作机构	Art Creation Institutions	7	37
艺术展览机构	Art Exhibition Institutions		
其 他	Others	5	
文物事业合计	**Cultural Relics**	**107**	**930**
文物机构	Historical Relics Agency	81	612
文物保护管理机构	Agency of Historical Relics Preservation	78	467
文物科研机构	Scientific and Research Historical Relics Agency	2	130
其他文物机构	Other Historical Relics Agency	1	15
博物馆	Museums	25	277
艺术类	Art	1	25
综合类	General	3	20
历史类	History Museum	20	222
其他类	Other Museum	1	10
文物商店	Cultural Relics Agencies	1	41

18-38 电影、电视、广播事业基本情况

Basic Statistics on Feature Film, Television and Broadcasting

项　目	Item	2003	2004
电影制片厂(个)	**Number of Film Studios (unit)**	**1**	**1**
广播电台(座)	**Number of Broadcasting Stations (unit)**	**6**	**6**
发射台及转播台(座)	Broadcast Transmission Stations and Relaying Stations (unit)	40	41
发射机功率(千瓦)	Power of Transmitters (kw.)	2332	2582
节目(套)	Program (set)	111	93
制作广播节目(小时)	Production of Broadcasting (hour)	159380	162609
#新闻资讯类节目	News Programs	23558	28031
专题服务类节目	Feature Programs	34536	45893
综艺类节目	Variety Show	57721	51342
广播剧类节目	Radio Play	9350	3814
广告类节目	Advertisement Programs	15833	19959
其他类节目	Other Programs	18382	13570
乡广播站(个)	Number of Township Broadcast Stations in Country (unit)	774	769
广播喇叭数(万只)	Number of Loudspeaker (10 000units)	23.44	13.43
广播人口覆盖率((%)	Listener Rate (%)	92.8	92.87
电视台(座)	**Number of Television Stations (unit)**	**16**	**10**
广播电视台(座)	**Radio and TV Stations (unit)**	**24**	**30**
#县级广播电视台(座)	Radio and TV Station at County-Level (unit)	24	24
发射台及转播台(座)	Television Transmission Stations and Relaying Stations (unit)	878	878
发射机功率(千瓦)	Power of Transmitters (kw.)	356.214	364.659
节目(套)	Program (set)	166	135
制作电视节目(小时)	Production of TV Programs (hour)	79736	50387
#新闻资讯类节目	News Programs	15975	10690
专题服务类节目	Feature Programs	8429	11786
综艺类节目	Variety Show	5950	10084
影视剧类节目	Film and TV Play Programs	31870	8931
广告类节目	Advertisement Programs	13254	6527
其他类节目	Other Programs	4258	2369
电视人口覆盖率(%)	Viewer Rate (%)	92.51	92.53

主要统计指标解释

普通高等学校 指按照国家规定的设置标准和审批程序批准举办的，通过全国普通高等学校统一招生考试，招收高中毕业生为主要培养对象，实施高等教育的全日制大学、独立设置的学院和高等专科学校、高等职业学校和其他机构。

大学、独立设置的学院主要实施本科层次以上教育，高等专科学校、高等职业学校实施专科层次教育，其他机构是承担国家普通招生计划任务不计校数的机构。包括普通高等学校分校和批准筹建的普通高等学校等。

成人高等学校 指按照国家规定的设置标准和审批程序批准举办的，通过全国成人高等学校统一招生考试，招收具有高中毕业或同等学历的在职从业人员为主要培养对象，利用函授、业余、脱产等多种形式对其实施高等学历教育的学校。包括职工高等学校、农民高等学校、管理干部学院、教育学院、独立函授学院、广播电视大学、其他机构等。其他机构是承担国家成人招生计划任务不计校数的机构。

小学学龄儿童入学率 指调查范围内已入小学学习的学龄儿童占校内外学龄儿童总数(包括弱智儿童，不包括盲聋哑儿童)的比重。计算公式为：

小学学龄儿童入学率=已入小学学习的学龄儿童数/按内外学龄儿童总数 × 100%

科技活动 指在自然科学、农业科学、医药科学、工程与技术科学、人文与社会科学领域(简称科学技术领域)中，与科技知识的产生、发展、传播和应用密切相关的有组织的活动。可分为研究与试验发展(R&D)、研究与试验发展成果应用及相关的科技服务三类活动。该定义是联合国教科文组织考虑成员国特别是发展中国家开展科技统计工作的需要，而对科技活动所作的统计界定。

科技活动人员 指直接从事科技活动、以及专门从事科技活动管理和为科技活动提供直接服务，累计的实际工作时间占全年制度工作时间10%及以上的人员。(1)直接从事科技活动的人员包括：在独立核算的科学研究与技术开发机构、高等学校、各类企业及其他事业单位内设的研究室、实验室、技术开发中心及中试车间(基地)等机构中从事科技活动的研究人员、工程技术人员、技术工人及其它人员；虽不在上述机构工作，但编入科技活动项目(课题)组的人员；科技信息与文献机构中的专业技术人员；从事论文设计的研究生等。(2)专门从事科技活动管理和为科技活动提供直接服务的人员，包括：独立核算的科学研究与技术开发机构、科技信息与文

献机构、高等学校、各类企业及其他事业单位主管科技工作的负责人，专门从事科技活动的计划、行政、人事、财务、物资供应、设备维护、图书资料管理等工作的各类人员，但不包括保卫、医疗保健人员、司机、食堂人员、茶炉工、水暖工、清洁工等为科技活动提供间接服务的人员。该指标用来反映投入科技活动人力的规模。

科学家与工程师 指科技活动人员中具有高、中级技术职称(职务)的人员和不具有高、中级技术职称(职务)的大学本科及以上学历人员。该指标用来反映投入科技活动人力的素质。

研究与试验发展(R&D) 指在科学技术领域，为增加知识总量、以及运用这些知识去创造新的应用进行的系统的创造性的活动，包括基础研究、应用研究、试验发展三类活动。国际上通常采用R&D 活动的规模和强度指标反映一国的科技实力和核心竞争力。

基础研究 指为了获得关于现象和可观察事实的基本原理的新知识(揭示客观事物的本质、运动规律，获得新发现、新学说)而进行的实验性或理论性研究，它不以任何专门或特定的应用或使用为目的。其成果以科学论文和科学著作为主要形式。用来反映知识的原始创新能力。

应用研究 指为获得新知识而进行的创造性研究，主要针对某一特定的目的或目标。应用研究是为了确定基础研究成果可能的用途，或是为达到预定的目标探索应采取的新方法(原理性)或新途径。其成果形式以科学论文、专著、原理性模型或发明专利为主。用来反映对基础研究成果应用途径的探索。

试验发展 指利用从基础研究、应用研究和实际经验所获得的现有知识，为产生新的产品、材料和装置，建立新的工艺、系统和服务，以及对已产生和建立的上述各项作实质性的改进而进行的系统性工作。其成果形式主要是专利、专有技术、具有新产品基本特征的产品原型或具有新装置基本特征的原始样机等。在社会科学领域，试验发展是指把通过基础研究、应用研究获得的知识转变成可以实施的计划(包括为进行检验和评估实施示范项目)的过程。人文科学领域没有对应的试验发展活动。主要反映将科研成果转化为技术和产品的能力，是科技推动经济社会发展的物化成果。

研究与试验发展人员 指参与研究与试验发展项目研究、管理和辅助工作的人员， 包括项目(课题)组人员， 企业科技行政管理人员和直接为项目(课题)活动提供服务的辅助人员。反映投入从事拥有自主知识产权的研究开发活动的人力规模。

研究与试验发展人员全时当量 指全时人员数加非全时人员按工作量折算为全时人员数的总和。例如：有两个全时人员和三个非全时人员(工作时间分别为2０%、3０% 和70%)，则全时当量为2+0.2+0.3+0.7=3.2 人年。为国际上比较科技人力投入而制定的可比指标。

专业技术人员 指从事专业技术工作和专业技术管理工作的人员，即企事业单位中已经聘任专业技术职务从事专业技术工作和专业技术管理工作的人员，以及未聘任专业技术职务，现在专业技术岗位上工作的人员。包括工程技术人员，农业技术人员，科学研究人员，卫生技术人员，教学人× 100%员，经济人员，会计人员，统计人员，翻译人员，图书资料、档案、文博人员，新闻出版人员，律师、公证人员，广播电视播音人员，工艺美术人员，体育人员，艺术人员及企业政治思想工作人员，共十七个专业技术职务类别。用来反映科技人力资源情况。

科技活动经费筹集 指从各种渠道筹集到的计划用于科技活动的经费，包括政府资金、企业资金、事业单位资金、金融机构贷款、国外资金和其他资金等。反映各社会经济主体对促进科技进步所做的努力。

政府资金 指从各级政府部门获得的计划用于科技活动的经费，包括科学事业费、科技三项费、科研基建费、科学基金、教育等部门事

业费中计划用于科技活动的经费以及政府部门预算外资金中计划用于科技活动的经费等。

企业资金 指从自有资金中提取或接受其他企业委托的、科研院所和高校等事业单位接受企业委托获得的，计划用于科研和技术开发的经费。不包括来自政府、金融机构及国外的计划用于科技活动的资金。

金融机构贷款 指从各类金融机构获得的用于科技活动的贷款。科技活动经费内部支出指报告年内用于科技活动的实际支出，包括劳务费、科研业务费、科研管理费，非基建投资购建的固定资产、科研基建支出以及其他用于科技活动的支出。不包括生产性活动支出、归还贷款支出及转拨外单位支出。反映科技投入实际完成情况。

劳务费 指以货币或实物形式直接或间接支付给从事科技活动人员的劳动报酬及各种费用。包括各种形式的工

资、津贴、奖金、福利、离退休人员费用、人民助学金等。反映改善科技人员待遇情况。

固定资产购建费 指报告年内使用非基建投资购建的固定资产和用于科研基建投资的实际支出额，即固定资产实际支出和科研基建投资实际完成额之和。固定资产是指长期使用而不改变原有实物形态的主要物资设备、图书资料、实验材料和标本以及其他设备和家具、房屋、建筑物。反映用于改善科研条件和科研手段方面的投入情况。

新产品 指采用新技术原理、新设计构思研制、生产的全新产品，或在结构、材质、工艺等某一方面比原有产品有明显改进，从而显著提高了产品性能或扩大了使用功能的产品。既包括政府有关部门认定并在有效期内的新产品，也包括企业自行研制开发、未经政府有关部门认定，从投产之日起一年之内的新产品。用来反映科技产出及对经济增长的直接贡献。

专利 是专利权的简称，是对发明人的发明创造经审查合格后，由专利局依据专利法授予发明人和设计人对该项发明创造享有的专有权。包括发明、实用新型和外观设计。反映拥有自主知识产权的科技和设计成果情况。

发明 指对产品、方法或者其改进所提出的新的技术方案。是国际通行的反映拥有自主知识产权技术的核心指标。

实用新型 指对产品的形状、构造或者其结合所提出的适于实用的新的技术方案。反映具有一定技术含量的技术成果情况。

外观设计 指对产品的形状、图案、色彩或者其结合所作出的富有美感并适于工业上应用的新设计。反映拥有自主知识产权的外观设计成果情况。

文化事业机构 指从事专业文化工作和为专业文化工作服务的独立建制的单位。不包括这些单位另外举办独立核算的其他机构和各部门的业余文化组织。该指标主要反映文化事业机构发展规模水平。

艺术表演团体 指从事戏曲、音乐、舞蹈、杂技等专业艺术表演，有独立帐户的单位，不包括半工半艺、半农半艺和民间职业剧团。该指标主要反映全国专业艺术表演团体发展规模水平。

艺术表演观众人数(人次) 指售票、包场演出或民族地区免费演出的艺术表演观众人次数，不包括彩排审查和内部观摩演出的观看人次数。该指标主要反映全国观看专业艺术表演团体演出的效益规模。

Explanatory Notes on Main Statistical Indicators

Regular Institutions of Higher Learning refer to educational establishments set up according to the government evaluation and approval procedures, enrolling graduates from senior secondary schools and providing higher education courses and training for senior professionals. They include full-time universities, colleges, high professional schools, high professional vocational schools and others.

Universities and colleges are mainly providing undergraduate courses; those high profess ional schools and high professional vocational schools are mainly providing professional trainings; and others refer to educational establishments, which hare responsible for enrolling students but not covered in the total number of schools, including: branch schools of universities and colleges, and universities and colleges that have been proved and prepared to construct.

Institutions of Higher Learning for Adults refer to educational establishments, set up in line with relevant rules approved by the government, enrolling staff and workers wit h senior secondary school or equivalent education, and providing higher education courses in many forms of correspondence, spare time, or full time for adults. Professionals thus trained receive a qualification equivalent to graduates studying regular courses at regular universities, colleges and professional colleges. Institutions of higher learning for adults include schools of high education for staff and workers, schools of high education for peasants, colleges for management cadres, pedagogical colleges, independent correspondence colleges, Radio and TV universities and other educational establishments. Other educational establishments are responsible for enrolling adult students but not covered in the number of schools.

Enrollment Rate of Primary School Age Children refers to the proportion of school age children enrolled at schools to the total number of school age children both in and outside schools (including retarded children, but excluding blind, deaf and mute children). The formula is:

Enrollment Rate of Primary School-age Children = (Total Primary School-age Children at Schools)/(Total Primary School-age Children Both at and Outside Schools) × 100%

Scientific and Technological Activities (S&T Activities) refer to organized activities which are closely related with the creation, development, dissemination and application of the scientific and technical knowledge in t he fields of natural sciences, agricultural science, medical science, engineering and technological science, humanities and social sciences (referred to as scientific and technological fields). S&T activities can be classified in to 3 categories: research and development (R&D) activities, application of R&D results, and related S&T services. This statistical definition is made by UNICHIEF for scientific and technological activities to meet the need of carrying out statistical work in this field for its member countries in particular those developing countries.

Personnel Engaged in S&T Activities refer to personnel directly engaged in S&T activities, in the management of S&T activities, and in providing direct service to S&T activities, who sp end over 10% of the total working hours in a year in S&T activities. (1) Personnel directly engaged in S&T activities include researchers, engineers, technicians and other related personnel engaged in S&T activities in independent-accounting R&D institutions, institutions of higher learning, and in research institutes, laboratories, technology development centers and central experiment workshops under enterprises and institutions. Also included are people working in S&T research project teams, professional and technical personnel working in S&T information archiving institutes, and graduate students working on the design of their thesis. (2) Personnel engaged in the management of S&T activities and in providing direct service to S&T activities include senior management people responsible for S&T activities in independent -accounting R&D institutions, S&T information archiving institutes, institutions of higher learning, and in enterprises and institutions where S&T activities are undertaken. Also included are people responsible for the planning, administration, personnel management, financial management, logistics supply, equipment maintenance, information and library management that are related with S&T activities. People providing indirect services are excluded, such as security, medical service, drivers, plumbers, cleaners and those providing catering and related service. This indicator reflects the size of personnel engaged in S&T activities.

Scientists and Engineers refer to persons engaged in S&T activities who have obtained titles of senior and middle level professional positions, and those without such position but have completed university or higher education. This indicator reflects the quality of personnel engaged in S&T activities.

Research and Development (R&D) refers to systematic and creative activities in the field of science and technology aiming at increasing the knowledge and using the knowledge for new application. R&D includes 3 categories of activities: basic research, applied research and experiments and development. The scale and intensity of R&D are widely us ed internationally to reflect the strength of S&T and the core competitiveness of a country in the world.

Basic Re search refers to empirical or theoretical research aiming at obtaining new knowledge on the fundament al principles of phenomena of observable facts to reveal the nature and law of movement of object s and to acquire new discoveries or new theories. Basic research takes no specific or designated application as the aim of the research. Results of basic research are mainly released or disseminated in the form of scientific papers or monographs. This indicator reflects the original innovation capaCity of knowledge.

Applied research refers to creative research aiming at obtaining new knowledge on a specific objective or target. Purpose of the applied research is to identify the possible use of results from basic research, or to explore new (fundamental) methods or new approaches. Results of applied research are expressed in the form of scientific papers , monographs, fundamental models or invention patents. This indicator reflects the exploration of ways to apply the results of basic research.

Experiments and Development refer to systematic activities aiming at using the knowledge from basic and applied researches or from practical experience to develop new products, materials and equipment, to establish new production process, systems and services, or to make substantial improvement on the existing products, process or services. Results of experiment and development activities are embodied in patents, exclusive technology, and monotype of new products or equipment. In social sciences, experiment and development activities refer to the process of converting the knowledge from basic or applied researches in to feasible programs (including conduct of demonstration projects for assessment and evaluation). There are no experiment and development activities in the science of humanities. This indicator reflects the capability of transferring the results of S&T into technique and products, which is the materialized measurement of S&T pushing forward the economic and social development.

R&D Personnel refer to persons engaged in research, management and supporting activities of R&D, including persons in the project teams, persons engaged in the management of S&T activities of enterprises and sup porting staff providing direct service to the research projects. This indicator reflects the size of personnel engaged in R&D activities with independent intellectual property.

Full-time Equivalent of R&D Personnel refers to the sum of the full-time persons and the full-time equivalent of part time persons converted by workload. For instance, if there are 2full-time persons and 3 part time workers (20%, 30% and 70%of working hours respectively on R&D activities), the full-time equivalent is 2+0.2+0.3+0.7=3.2 person-years. This is an internationally comp arable indicator of input of personnel in S&T activities.

Professional and Technical Personnel refer to persons engaged in professional and technical work or in the management of professional and technical activities, i.e., people with professional or technical posit ions who are engaged in professional and technical work or in the management of professional and technical activities, and people without professional or technical positions but are working on professional or technical posts. They include professionals and technicians working in 17 categories of technical occupations including engineering, agriculture, scientific researches, medical service, teaching, economic research and application, accounting, statistics, translation, libraries, archives, cultural and museum service, journalism and publication, lawyers, notarization service, radio and television broadcasting, handicraft and fine arts, sports, performing art, and political workers in enterprises. This indicator reflects the condition of human resources in S&T.

Funding for S&T Activities refers to funds obtained from various sources for S&T activities, including government funds, self-raised funds by enterprises, self-raised funds by institutions, loans from financial institutions, foreign funds and other funds . This indicator reflects the efforts made by various social economic entities in promoting the development of S&T.

Government Funds refer to funds obtained from government agencies at all levels to be used for S&T activities, including fund for scientific undertakings, 3 kinds of fund for S&T activities, fund for capital const ruction for scientific researches, science fund, funds from education expenditures by education departments for S&T activities, and extra-budget fund from government agencies for S&T activities.

Self-raised Funds by Enterprises refers to self-raised funds by enterprises from their own expenditure or from other enterprises and funds received by universities or research institutions from enterprises for scientific research or technical development projects. Excluded in this category are funds from government agencies, financial institutions or from foreign institutions.

Loans from Financial Institutions refer to loans from various financial institutions for S&T activities.

Internal Expenditures on S&T activities refer to the actual expenditures on S&T activities during the reference year, including service fees, expenditure on research activities, expenditure on research management, purchase or const ruction of fixed assets not included in the investment for capital const ruction, expenditure on capital construction for scientific researches, and other expenditures on S&T activities. Not included are expenditure on production activities, repayment of loans and transfer expenditure. This indicator reflects the real accomplishment of input in S&T.

Service Fees refer to direct or indirect payment, in cash or in kind, made to personnel engaged in S&T activities as remuneration and other fees. They include, in various forms, salaries, subsidies, bonus, benefits, retirement pension, stipend, etc. This indicator reflects the improvement of treatment toward S&T personnel.

Purchase or Construction of Fixed Assets refers to the fixed assets purchased or constructed using funds other than the investment in capital construction, and the actual expenditure on capital construction for scientific researches. In other words, it is the sum of the actual expenditure on fixed as sets and the accomplished investment in capital construction for scientific researches. Fixed as sets refer to main materials and equipment, literatures and documents in libraries, materials for experiments, specimen, instruments, furniture, buildings and constructions that can be used for a long time without changing t he form and shape of those articles or constructions. This indictor reflects the input in improving t he condition of S&T and the means of scientific research.

New Products refer to new products produced with new technology and new design, or products that represent noticeable improvement in terms of structure, material, or production process so as to imp rove significantly the character or function of the older versions. They include new products certified by relevant government agencies within the period of certification, as well as new products designed and produced by enterprises within a year without certification by government agencies. This indictor reflects the direct contribution of S&T output to economic growth.

Patent is an abbreviation for the patent right and refers to the exclusive right of ownership by the inventors or designers for the creation or inventions, given from the patent offices after due process of assessment and approval in accordance wit h the Patent Law. Patents are grant ed for inventions, utility model sand designs. This indicator reflects the achievements of S&T and design with in dependent intellectual property.

Inventions refer to the new technical proposals to the products or methods or their modifications. This is universal core Indicator reflecting the technologies with independent intellectual property.

Utility Models refer to t he practical and new technical proposals on the shape and structure of the product or the combination of both. This indicator reflects the condition of technological results with certain technical content.

Designs refer to the aesthetics and industrially applicable new designs for the shape, pattern and color of the product, or their combinations. This indicator reflects the appearance design achievements with independent intellectual property.

Cultural Institutions refer to units, which have their own organizational system and independent accounting system and specialize in or serve cultural development. They exclude other establishments run by these cultural institutions and amateur cultural groups established by various departments. This indicator reflects the development of cultural units.

Art Troupe refers to t he troupe which is engaged in drama, opera, music, dance, acrobatics or other art performance, opens independent accounts with banks and has self-supporting accounting system; excluding the troupes which are engaged partly in industrial or agricultural activities, partly in art performance and the professional troupes organized by the people. This indicator reflects the development of national professional art troupes.

Number of Spectators at Art Performance refers to the number of attendants at commercial shows, completely booked shows or free shows given in minority national areas, and does not include the number of spectators at rehearsals for examination and internal shows for study. This indicator reflects beneficial results of.

第十九篇

CHAPTER 19

体育、卫生及其他

SPORTS PUBLIC HEALTH
AND OTHERS

19-1 体育局系统从业人员数

Number of Staff and Workers in Sports Bureau

单位：人 (2004 年) (person)

项 目	Item	合 计 Total	公务员 Government Officials	教练员 Coaches	运动员 Athletes	科研人员 Scientific Research Personnel
总 计	**Total**	**2603**	**549**	**604**	**387**	**22**
体育行政机关	Sports Executive Organs	637	549			
优秀运动队	Excellent Sports Teams	650		63	378	1
体育运动学校	Physical Education and Sports Schools	476		150		5
业余体校	Sparetime Sports Schools	536		383	8	
体育场馆	Gymnasium	143				
其他事业单位	Other Institutions	161		8	1	16

项 目	Item	医务人员 Medical Personnel	文化教师 Culture Teachers	管理人员 Administrative Personnel	其他人员 Others
总 计	**Total**	**31**	**164**	**372**	**474**
体育行政机关	Departments in Sports			44	44
优秀运动队	Excellent Sports Teams	22		103	83
体育运动学校	Physical Education and Sports Schools	9	159	67	86
业余体校	Sparetime Sports Schools		5	60	80
体育场馆	Gymnasium			53	90
其他事业单位	Other Institutions			45	91

19-2 按项目分等级裁判员发展人数

Number of Referees in Levels by Type of Sports

单位：人　　(2004 年)　　(person)

项　目	Item	合　计 Total	国家级裁判员 National Level Referee			一级裁判员 First Level Referee			二级裁判员 Second Level Referee		
			小 计 Sub-total	男 Male	女 Female	小 计 Sub-total	男 Male	女 Female	小 计 Sub-total	男 Male	女 Female
总　计	**Sum Total**	**814**	**17**	**14**	**3**	**254**	**188**	**66**	**543**	**412**	**131**
田　径	Track and Field	235	1	1		35	20	15	199	132	67
网　球	Tennis	9				9	7	2			
射　箭	Archery	16				11	6	5	5	4	1
射　击	Shooting	22	1	1		16	6	10	5	4	1
足　球	Football	78				23	23		55	54	1
篮　球	Basketball	84	1	1		28	27	1	55	48	7
排　球	Volleyball	31				11	7	4	20	17	3
乒乓球	Table Tennis	31	1	1		3	3		27	24	3
门　球	Croquet	26							26	19	7
柔　道	Judo	40	7	4	3	15	12	3	18	12	6
国际式摔跤	International Wrestling	55	2	2		12	11	1	41	37	4
武　术	Martial Art	72				27	21	6	45	25	20
其　他	Others	115	4	4		64	45	19	47	36	11

19-3 按项目分等级运动员发展人数

Number of Athletes at Levels by Type of Sports

单位：人　　(2004 年)　　(person)

项　目	Item	合　计 Total	国家级运动健将 National Level			一级运动员 First Grade			二级运动员 Second Grade		
			小 计 Sub-total	男 Male	女 Female	小 计 Sub-total	男 Male	女 Female	小 计 Sub-total	男 Male	女 Female
总　计	**Sum Total**	**215**	**10**	**8**	**2**	**20**	**6**	**14**	**185**	**123**	**62**
田　径	Track and Field	72	1		1	5	3	2	66	42	24
拳　击	Boxing	5	1	1					4	4	
游　泳	Swimming	17				1	1		16	8	8
柔　道	Judo	5							5	3	2
足　球	Football	2							2	2	
篮　球	Basketball	35	5	5					30	29	1
乒乓球	Table Tennis	24							24	13	11
手　球	Handball	10				10		10			
射　击	Shooting	23	1		1	4	2	2	18	10	8
射　箭	Archery	6	1	1					5	3	2
沙滩排球	Beach Volleyball	2							2		2
速度滑冰	Speed Skating	11	1	1					10	6	4
跆拳道	Taikuangdao	3							3	3	

19-4 各地、州、市体育局系统机构数

Number of Institutions in Sports Committees by Region

单位：个 (2004 年) (unit)

地 区	Region	合 计 Total	行政机关 Departments in Sports	优秀运动队 Excellent Sports Teams	体育运动学校 Physical Education and Sports Schools
总 计	**Total**	**214**	**107**	**7**	**7**
自治区直属	Under Autonomous Region	14	1	5	1
地区小计	Sub-total	200	106	2	6
乌鲁木齐市	Urumqi City	18	9		1
克拉玛依市	Karamay City	2	1		
吐鲁番地区	Turpan Administrative Offices	8	4		
哈密地区	Hami [Kumul] Administrative Offices	10	4		
昌吉回族自治州	Changji Hui Autonomous Prefecture	12	9		1
伊犁哈萨克自治州	Ili Kazak Autonomous Prefecture	51	27	2	2
伊犁州直属县(市)	Counties (Cities) Direct Under Ili Prefecture	23	11	1	2
塔城地区	Tacheng [Tarbagatai] Administrative Offices	10	8		
阿勒泰地区	Altay Administrative Offices	18	8	1	
博尔塔拉蒙古自治州	Bortala Mongol Autonomous Prefecture	7	4		
巴音郭楞蒙古自治州	Bayangol Mongol Autonomous Prefecture	16	10		
阿克苏地区	Aksu Administrative Offices	17	10		1
克孜勒苏柯尔克孜自治州	Kizilsu Kirgiz Autonomous Prefecture	12	5		
喀什地区	Kashgar [Kaxgar] Administrative Offices	27	13		1
和田地区	Hotan Administrative Offices	18	9		
自治区直辖行政单位	Administrative Units under Autonomous Region	2	1		

地 区	Region	业余体校 Sparetime Sports Schools	体育场馆 Gymnasium	其他事业单位 Other Institutions
总 计	**Total**	**68**	**12**	**13**
自治区直属	Under Autonomous Region		1	6
地区小计	Sub-total	68	11	7
乌鲁木齐市	Urumqi City	5	1	2
克拉玛依市	Karamay City	1		
吐鲁番地区	Turpan Administrative Offices	4		
哈密地区	Hami [Kumul] Administrative Offices	3	1	2
昌吉回族自治州	Changji Hui Autonomous Prefecture	1	1	
伊犁哈萨克自治州	Ili Kazak Autonomous Prefecture	16	4	
伊犁州直属县(市)	Counties (Cities) Direct Under Ili Prefecture	6	3	
塔城地区	Tacheng [Tarbagatai] Administrative Offices	2		
阿勒泰地区	Altay Administrative Offices	8	1	
博尔塔拉蒙古自治州	Bortala Mongol Autonomous Prefecture	3		
巴音郭楞蒙古自治州	Bayangol Mongol Autonomous Prefecture	5	1	
阿克苏地区	Aksu Administrative Offices	5	1	
克孜勒苏柯尔克孜自治州	Kizilsu Kirgiz Autonomous Prefecture	4	1	2
喀什地区	Kashgar [Kaxgar] Administrative Offices	11	1	1
和田地区	Hotan Administrative Offices	9		
自治区直辖行政单位	Administrative Units under Autonomous Region	1		

19-5 各地、州、市体育局系统机构从业人员数

Number of Staff & Workers in Sports Bureau by Region

单位：人 (2004 年) (person)

地 区	Region	合 计 Total	行政机关 Departments in Sports	#公务员 Government Officials	优秀运动队 Excellent Sports Teams
总 计	**Total**	**2603**	**637**	**549**	**650**
自治区直属	Under Autonomous Region	900	49	44	595
地区小计	Sub-total	1703	588	505	55
乌鲁木齐市	Urumqi City	265	44	35	
克拉玛依市	Karamay City	26	12	12	
吐鲁番地区	Turpan Administrative Offices	69	36	24	
哈密地区	Hami [Kumul] Administrative Offices	86	25	24	
昌吉回族自治州	Changji Hui Autonomous Prefecture	84	52	46	
伊犁哈萨克自治州	Ili Kazak Autonomous Prefecture	456	134	114	55
伊犁州直属县(市)	Counties (Cities) Direct Under Ili Prefecture	259	54	40	25
塔城地区	Tacheng [Tarbagatai] Administrative Offices	58	26	20	
阿勒泰地区	Altay Administrative Offices	139	54	54	30
博尔塔拉蒙古自治州	Bortala Mongol Autonomous Prefecture	50	27	27	
巴音郭楞蒙古自治州	Bayangol Mongol Autonomous Prefecture	96	39	35	
阿克苏地区	Aksu Administrative Offices	172	66	53	
克孜勒苏柯尔克孜自治州	Kizilsu Kirgiz Autonomous Prefecture	70	25	25	
喀什地区	Kashgar [Kaxgar] Administrative Offices	256	98	80	
和田地区	Hotan Administrative Offices	43	27	27	
自治区直辖行政单位	Administrative Units under Autonomous Region	30	3	3	

地 区	Region	体育运动学 校 Physical Education and Sports Schools	业余体校 Sparetime Sports Schools	体育场馆 Gymnasium	其他事业单 位 Other Institutions
总 计	**Total**	**476**	**536**	**143**	**161**
自治区直属	Under Autonomous Region	131		20	105
地区小计	Sub-total	345	536	123	56
乌鲁木齐市	Urumqi City	98	82	10	31
克拉玛依市	Karamay City		14		
吐鲁番地区	Turpan Administrative Offices		33		
哈密地区	Hami [Kumul] Administrative Offices		33	14	14
昌吉回族自治州	Changji Hui Autonomous Prefecture	21	8	3	
伊犁哈萨克自治州	Ili Kazak Autonomous Prefecture	83	125	59	
伊犁州直属县(市)	Counties (Cities) Direct Under Ili Prefecture	83	53	44	
塔城地区	Tacheng [Tarbagatai] Administrative Offices		32		
阿勒泰地区	Altay Administrative Offices		40	15	
博尔塔拉蒙古自治州	Bortala Mongol Autonomous Prefecture		23		
巴音郭楞蒙古自治州	Bayangol Mongol Autonomous Prefecture		46	11	
阿克苏地区	Aksu Administrative Offices	67	35	4	
克孜勒苏柯尔克孜自治州	Kizilsu Kirgiz Autonomous Prefecture		27	10	8
喀什地区	Kashgar [Kaxgar] Administrative Offices	76	67	12	3
和田地区	Hotan Administrative Offices		16		
自治区直辖行政单位	Administrative Units under Autonomous Region		27		

19-6 主要年份卫生机构数

Number of Health Institutions in Main Years

单位：个 (unit)

年 份 Year	合 计 Total	医院、卫生院 Hospitals	#县及县以上医院 At and Above County Level	疗养院 Sanato-riums	门诊部 Clinics	专科防治所、站 Specialized Prevention & Treatment Centers or Stations	卫生防疫站 Sanitation and Antiepide-mic Agencies	妇幼保健所、站 Maternity and Child Care Centers	社区卫生服务中心 Community Sanitation Service Center	医学科学研究机构 Research Institutes of Medical Science	其他卫生机构 Other Institutions	诊所、医务保健室、医务室 Clinics Health Care Room Infirmary	#私营、个体机构 Institutions of Privately Owned & Individual
1978	2581	806		2	1609	1	104	12		1	46		
1980	2818	884		4	1756	4	102	12		1	55		
1985	3320	947		5	2125	2	139	27		2	73		
1990	3945	1049		6	2536	13	191	59		3	88		
1995	3932	1292		8	2247	16	216	69		6	78		
1996	7259	1320		8	5541	16	215	75		6	78		3293
1997	6614	1345		8	4859	16	217	75		7	87		2701
1998	6615	1351		8	4850	16	218	75		7	90		2703
1999	6608	1357	530	8	162	16	213	72		7	90	4683	2704
2000	7314	1352	522	8	154	16	210	74		7	89	5404	3653
2001	7309	1357	523	8	149	17	207	75		6	86	5404	3657
2002	10297	1459	622	10	352	17	226	96	24	3	135	7975	4398
2003	9434	1471	632	7	316	17	207	88	22	3	136	7167	4475
2004	9087	1525	682	6	286	12	193	85	46	3	138	6793	4775

注：1. 从 1996 年起含私营、个体机构。2.2002 年起卫生部新制度规定持有"医疗执业许可证"所有卫生机构算为一个机构,兵团连队卫生室统计到卫生所中,所以卫生机构总数增加.

Note: 1.Since 1996 Institutions of Privately Owned and Individuals has been Contained.

2.From 2002, in line with new regulations of Ministry of Public Health,all the health institutions that have Medical Service Permit Shall be counted as one and health care rooms Shall be counted in health clinics,therefore the total number of health institutions increased.

19-7 主要年份卫生人员数

Number of Persons Engaged in Health Institutions in Main Years

单位：人 (person)

年 份 Year	合 计 Total	#卫生技术人员 Medical Technical Personnel	#医 生 Doctors	执业医师 Doctors with License	执业助理医师 Assistant Doctors with License	#注册护士 Registered Nurses	平均每万人口医生数 Number of Doctors per 10 000 Population	在合计中私人个体开业人员 Persons of Privately Owned & Individual
1978	66252	51050	16898	7368	9530	10765	14	
1980	74627	57949	20614	10092	10522	12077	16	
1985	88460	68961	25721	13330	12391	17136	19	188
1990	102053	79853	33683	24967	8716	23386	22	2034
1995	116856	92028	39636	30038	9598	26350	24	4252
1996	119653	94542	41687	31277	10410	27630	25	4457
1997	122695	97568	42981	31921	11060	29359	25	3602
1998	122642	97591	43236	32054	11182	29990	25	3644
1999	122178	97514	43988	32978	11010	30116	25	3681
2000	122064	98093	45402	34892	10510	30850	25	5835
2001	121374	97476	45366	35723	9643	30982	24	5972
2002	110227	89789	37617	28076	9541	28116	20	7928
2003	116572	95759	40430	31008	9422	30279	21	9731
2004	120502	99788	43053	33792	9261	30908	22	12258

注：2002 年以前执业医师为中医师、西医师，中西医结合医师，执业助理医师为中医士、西医士，中西医结合医士、注册护士为护师、护士。(以下同)

Note: Prior to 2002,doctors with license were doctors trained in Western medicine,assistant doctors are practioners with Secondary Western medical education,and registered nurses are master nurses and nurses (The following is the same as below) .

19-8 卫生机构、床位、人员数

(2004 年)

项 目	Item	机构数（个）Type of Institutions (unit)	床位数（张）Beds (unit)	卫生人员合计（人）Total Number of Medical Personnel (person)	卫生技术人员 Medical Technical Personnel
总 计	**Total**	**9087**	**78054**	**120502**	**99788**
按市县分	**By City and County Areas**				
市	City	1041	49222	67359	54242
县	County	1253	28832	39936	32339
按经济类型分	**By Economic Sectors**				
国 有	State-owned	3647	68708	99139	81059
集 体	Couective-owned	522	4539	7112	5754
联 营	Joint Operation	43	79	249	226
私 营	Private-owned	4775	3619	12258	11516
其 他	Others	100	1109	1744	1233
按设置主办单位分	**By sponsors**				
政府办	Government sponsored	1623	61810	87965	71019
#卫生部门	Health Departments	1487	55368	79466	64007
企业办	EnterPrises sponsored	1308	9108	13437	11499
其 他	Others	6156	7136	19100	17270
按机构分	**By Organizations**				
医院合计	Total Number of Hospitals	682	61192	75651	60869
市	City	416	43949	53913	43253
县	County	266	17243	21738	17616
综合医院	Comprehensive Hospitals	542	50788	64331	52272
中医医院	Hospitals of Traditional Chinese Medicine	38	3204	3988	3323
中西医综合医院	TCM and Western Medicine Hospital	2	20	18	13
民族医院	Hospitals for Nationalities	42	2104	2767	2061
专科医院	Specialist Hospitals	58	5076	4547	3200
口腔医院	Nonnasality Hospitals	2	50	167	129
眼科医院	Ophthalmology Hospitals	3	145	160	119
耳鼻喉科医院	Otolaryngology Hospitals	1	20	17	11
肿瘤医院	Tumour Hospital	1	920	468	369
心血管病医院	Cardiovascular Hospitals	2	309	529	335
胸科医院	Chest Hospital	1	246	325	248
血液病医院	Hospital for Blood Diseases	1	20	40	28
妇产(科)医院	Hospitals for Gynaecology and Obsterics	5	117	156	130
儿童医院	Hospital for Children	1	40	20	16
精神病医院	Mental Hospitals	10	1919	1067	701
传染病医院	Infectous Diseases Hospitals	2	85	157	115
皮肤病医院	Dermatology Hospital	1	50	48	32
结核病医院	Tubercuiosis Hospitals	1	120	125	100
骨科医院	Hospital of Orthopedics	4	145	236	168
康复医院	Recovery Hospitals	6	260	216	153
其他专科医院	Other Specialist Hospitals	17	630	816	546
疗养院	Sanatoriums	6	786	357	183
社区卫生服务中心	Community Sanitation Service Center	46	155	510	438
卫生院合计	Total Number of Public Health Center	843	12830	17664	14639
街道卫生院	Public Health Center in Neighbourhood	7	13	177	158
乡、镇卫生院	Public Health Center in Township and Towns	836	12817	17487	14481
中心卫生院	Public Health Center in Rural Area	94	2156	2494	2096
乡卫生院	Public Health Center in Township and Towns	742	10661	14993	12385
门诊部	Out-patients Department	286	718	2034	1732
急救中心(站)	First-Aid-Stations(Center)	2	50	80	58
采供血机构	Blood Collection & Supply Organs	15		382	261
妇幼保健院(所、站)	Hospitals for Maternity and Child Care	85	1124	2780	2286
专科疾病防治院(所、站)	Specialized Stations	12	817	277	146
疾病预防控制中心(防疫站)	Diseases Preventing & Controlling Center (Epidemic Prevention Station)	193	24	6436	5152
卫生监督所	Sanitation Superintendence Office	16		358	291
卫生监督检验(监测、检测)所(站)	Sanitation Superintendence & Examining(monitoring,testing)office(station)	2	2	17	12
医学科学研究机构	Research Institutes of Medical Sciences	3		84	28
健康教育所(站、中心)	Health Education Center (station,center)	2		9	5
其它卫生事业机构	Other Health Institutions	101	356	656	481

Number of Health Institutions, Beds and Persons Engaged by Type of Institutons

执业医师 Doctors with license	执业助理医师 Assistant Doctors with license	注册护士 Registered Nurses	药剂人员 Druggist of Medicine	检验人员 Laboratory Technicians	其他 Others	其他技术人员 Other Technicians	管理人员 Managerial Personnel	工勤人员 Logistics Workers
33792	**9261**	**30908**	**6015**	**5139**	**14673**	**4340**	**6441**	**9933**
19596	3315	18309	3589	3329	6104	2655	4399	6063
8395	4234	9528	2035	1664	6483	1685	2042	3870
26887	7100	26241	5054	4596	11181	3823	5597	8660
1670	734	1618	329	225	1178	255	305	798
77	40	69	15	7	18	5	12	6
4780	1298	2615	538	240	2045	170	318	254
378	89	365	79	71	251	87	209	215
22822	6415	22786	4452	4141	10403	3593	4885	8468
20710	5694	20171	4036	3799	9597	3377	4298	7784
4233	873	3994	681	486	1232	382	817	739
6737	1973	4128	882	512	3038	365	739	726
20411	3987	22501	4494	2834	6642	2922	4613	7247
15529	2249	16193	3148	2025	4109	2041	3504	5115
4882	1738	6308	1346	809	2533	881	1109	2132
17402	3433	19983	3604	2435	5415	2292	3893	5874
1287	219	967	371	147	332	158	197	310
3	2	4	1	1	2		1	4
688	188	467	308	92	318	185	131	390
1031	145	1080	210	159	575	287	391	669
72	7	37	3	2	8	2	14	22
49	7	47	7	4	5	17	14	10
1	3	3	1	1	2	1	2	3
184	3	112	18	16	36	39	14	46
78	4	102	11	12	128	17	85	92
110		94	14	10	20	19	9	49
6	1	13	2	2	4	5	3	4
47	12	35	9	8	19	9	12	5
2		5	1	2	6	1	2	1
164	22	304	45	21	145	66	78	222
20	1	16	7	6	65	8	17	17
9	2	14	3	3	1	8	7	1
17	21	47	6	6	3	5	6	14
43	13	63	20	10	19	24	27	17
54	11	40	12	6	30	12	24	27
175	38	148	51	50	84	54	77	139
61	8	77	13	11	13	11	66	97
158	17	160	31	7	65	20	7	45
3064	2328	3738	778	607	4124	768	783	1474
42	15	38	12	10	41	2	11	6
3022	2313	3700	766	597	4083	766	772	1468
438	329	610	110	103	506	125	100	173
2584	1984	3090	656	494	3577	641	672	1295
744	117	465	134	102	170	62	166	74
31		22	1		4	5	3	14
38	11	54	9	119	30	38	33	50
813	362	437	99	187	388	131	155	208
47	37	17	3	9	33	21	63	47
2364	604	233	49	1049	853	237	469	578
146	36	8	1	14	86	13	23	31
1			1	10		4		1
					28	40	7	9
					5	3	1	
113	42	125	11	44	146	65	52	58

19-9　卫生机构床位数

Number of Sick-Beds in Health Institutions

单位：张　(unit)

年 份 Year	合 计 Total	医院卫生院 Hospitals	# 县及县以上医院 At and above County Level	疗养院 Sanatoriums	其他卫生机构 Other Health Institutions	每万人口医院、卫生院床位数 Number of Hospital Beds per 10 000 Population
1978	57647	39179		108	18360	31.8
1980	61075	47236		682	13157	36.8
1985	60930	55298		870	4762	40.6
1990	67414	60707	47924	1010	5697	40.5
1991	68504	62363	49211	918	5223	40.8
1992	70382	63935	50792	1118	5329	40.4
1993	72397	66289	52649	1291	4817	41.3
1994	72474	66727	53516	1333	4414	40.9
1995	72955	66696	53336	1233	5026	40.1
1996	71971	67355	54021	1283	3333	39.9
1997	71558	67096	53394	1183	3279	39.1
1998	71095	66495	52868	1305	3295	38.1
1999	71436	66627	52958	1421	3388	37.5
2000	70542	65916	52438	1301	3325	35.7
2001	70898	66008	52274	1216	3674	35.1
2002	67535	64878	52458	495	2162	34.1
2003	72845	69795	57177	702	2348	36.1
2004	78054	74022	61192	786	3246	37.7

19-10　医疗机构病床使用情况

Utilization of Beds in Medical Care Institutions

(2004 年)

项　目	Item	实际开放总床日数(日) Beds Open to Patients (day)	平均开放病床(张) Average Beds Open to Patients (unit)	病床周转次数(次) Turnover of Beds (times)	病床工作日(日) Number of Days per Bed in Use in a Year (day)	病床使用率(%) Utilization Rate of Beds (%)	出院者平均住院日(日) Average Hospitalization Period (day)
总　计	**Total**	**24653366**	**67543**	**23.74**	**253.82**	**69.54**	**9.66**
医　院	Total Number of Hospitals	20132337	55157	23.86	268.82	73.65	10.58
疗养院	Sanatoriums	230850	632	8.92	223.67	61.28	6.07
社区卫生服务中心	Community Sanitation Service Center	7550	21	13.29	132.95	36.42	10.00
卫生院	Total Number of Public Health Center	3590141	9836	22.95	169.77	46.51	5.95
门诊部	Out-patients Department	95364	261	108.4	181.04	49.60	1.07
妇幼保健院(所、站)	Hospitals for Maternity and Child Care	298559	818	31.37	211.69	58.00	5.45
专科疾病防治院(所、站)	Specialized Stations	298565	818	2.79	344.87	94.49	9.97

19-11 医疗机构、诊疗人次及入院出院人数

Number of Health Institutions, Patients Treated, Hospital Admissions and Patients Discharged

(2004 年)

项 目	Item	机构数(个) Institutions (unit)	诊疗人次(万人次) Total Number of Patients Treated (10 000 patient-times)	#门、急诊人次 Out-patients and Emergency Patients	#急诊人次 Emergency Patients
总 计	**Total**	**1868**	**3992.97**	**3605.22**	**131.57**
医 院	Total Number of Hospitals	664	2731.87	2418.26	125.19
疗养院	Sanatoriums	6	6.03	5.57	
社区卫生服务中心	Community Sanitation Service Center	18	85.62	85.59	
卫生院	Total Number of Public Health Center	843	884.26	837.84	4.82
门诊部	Out-patients Department	243	143.81	141.32	0.80
妇幼保健院(所、站)	Hospitals for Maternity and Child Care	85	126.39	101.73	0.71
专科疾病防治院(所、站)	Specialized Stations	9	14.99	14.91	0.05

项 目	Item	门、急诊诊次占总诊次的比重(%) Percentage of Clinic Case and Emergence Case Among the Total Cases (%)	入院人数(万人) Hospital Admissions (10 000 patients)	出院人数(万人) Patients Discharged (10 000 patients)	治愈率(%) Cure rate (%)
总 计	**Total**	**90.29**	**162.00**	**160.37**	**64.50**
医 院	Total Number of Hospitals	88.52	131.69	131.58	61.91
疗养院	Sanatoriums	92.37	0.57	0.56	93.03
社区卫生服务中心	Community Sanitation Service Center	99.96	0.03	0.03	75.64
卫生院	Total Number of Public Health Center	94.75	24.00	22.57	73.32
门诊部	Out-patients Department	98.27	2.84	2.83	92.55
妇幼保健院(所、站)	Hospitals for Maternity and Child Care	80.49	2.58	2.57	87.89
专科疾病防治院(所、站)	Specialized Stations	99.47	0.29	0.23	0.48

19-12 各地、州、市卫生机构、床位和人员数

Number of Health Institutions，Beds and Personnel by Prefecture, Autonomous Prefecture and City

(2004 年)

地区	Region	机构数(个) Type of Institutions (unit)	床位数(张) Beds (unit)	卫生人员合计(人) Total Number of Medical Personnel (person)	卫生技术人员 Medical Technical Personnel
总计	**Total**	**9087**	**78054**	**120502**	**99788**
乌鲁木齐市	Urumqi City	1449	17710	25570	20947
克拉玛依市	Karamay City	96	1868	2923	2290
石河子市	Shihezi City	866	3909	6122	5131
吐鲁番地区	Turpan Administrative Offices	221	1982	3636	3032
哈密地区	Hami [Kumul] Administrative Offices	295	2629	4803	4054
昌吉回族自治州	Changji Hui Autonomous Prefecture	1165	6783	10741	9047
伊犁哈萨克自治州	Ili Kazak Autonomous Prefecture	2536	14226	25485	21519
伊犁州直属县(市)	Counties (Cities) Direct Under Ili Prefecture	1770	8734	15374	12941
塔城地区	Tacheng [Tarbagatai] Administrative Offices	557	3207	5920	4989
阿勒泰地区	Altay Administrative Offices	209	2285	4191	3589
博尔塔拉蒙古自治州	Bortala Mongol Autonomous Prefecture	287	1932	3427	2878
巴音郭楞蒙古自治州	Bayangol Mongol Autonomous Prefecture	379	5186	7816	6526
阿克苏地区	Aksu Administrative Offices	347	6854	9572	7950
克孜勒苏柯尔克孜自治州	Kizilsu Kirgiz Autonomous Prefecture	76	1443	2639	2154
喀什地区	Kashgar [Kaxgar] Administrative Offices	1089	8811	11721	9698
和田地区	Hotan Administrative Offices	281	4721	6047	4562

地区	Region	其他技术人员 Other Technicians	管理人员 Managerial Personnel	工勤人员 Logistics Workers	平均每万人口医院床位数(张) Number of Hospital Beds per 10000 Population(unit)
总计	**Total**	**4340**	**6441**	**9933**	**39.76**
乌鲁木齐市	Urumqi City	995	1470	2158	95.24
克拉玛依市	Karamay City	158	186	289	73.58
石河子市	Shihezi City	186	359	446	60.81
吐鲁番地区	Turpan Administrative Offices	150	176	278	34.19
哈密地区	Hami [Kumul] Administrative Offices	177	249	323	49.98
昌吉回族自治州	Changji Hui Autonomous Prefecture	149	769	776	43.36
伊犁哈萨克自治州	Ili Kazak Autonomous Prefecture	878	1222	1866	34.31
伊犁州直属县(市)	Counties (Cities) Direct Under Ili Prefecture	498	764	1171	34.16
塔城地区	Tacheng [Tarbagatai] Administrative Offices	269	190	472	33.19
阿勒泰地区	Altay Administrative Offices	111	268	223	36.68
博尔塔拉蒙古自治州	Bortala Mongol Autonomous Prefecture	77	215	257	42.75
巴音郭楞蒙古自治州	Bayangol Mongol Autonomous Prefecture	313	391	586	45.16
阿克苏地区	Aksu Administrative Offices	492	392	738	30.77
克孜勒苏柯尔克孜自治州	Kizilsu Kirgiz Autonomous Prefecture	148	131	206	30.83
喀什地区	Kashgar [Kaxgar] Administrative Offices	330	684	1009	24.37
和田地区	Hotan Administrative Offices	287	197	1001	26.64

19-13 各地、州、市卫生技术人员数

Number of Medical Technical Personnel by Prefecture, Autonomous Prefecture and City

单位:人 (2004 年) (person)

地 区	Region	卫生技术人员合计 Number of Medical Technical Personnel	执业医师 Doctors with License	执业助理医师 Assistant Doctors with License	注册护士 Registered Nurses
总 计	**Total**	**99788**	**33792**	**9261**	**30908**
乌鲁木齐市	Urumqi City	20947	8586	927	6933
克拉玛依市	Karamay City	2290	981	66	929
石河子市	Shihezi City	5131	1657	707	1659
吐鲁番地区	Turpan Administrative Offices	3032	994	272	1024
哈密地区	Hami [Kumul] Administrative Offices	4054	1383	385	1258
昌吉回族自治州	Changji Hui Autonomous Prefecture	9047	2888	918	2752
伊犁哈萨克自治州	Ili Kazak Autonomous Prefecture	21519	7409	2339	6139
伊犁州直属县(市)	Counties (Cities) Direct Under Ili Prefecture	12941	4541	1258	3640
塔城地区	Tacheng [Tarbagatai] Administrative Offices	4989	1614	544	1556
阿勒泰地区	Altay Administrative Offices	3589	1254	537	943
博尔塔拉蒙古自治州	Bortala Mongol Autonomous Prefecture	2878	939	354	807
巴音郭楞蒙古自治州	Bayangol Mongol Autonomous Prefecture	6526	2146	562	1980
阿克苏地区	Aksu Administrative Offices	7950	2111	795	2606
克孜勒苏柯尔克孜自治州	Kizilsu Kirgiz Autonomous Prefecture	2154	573	317	676
喀什地区	Kashgar [Kaxgar] Administrative Offices	9698	2788	1199	3050
和田地区	Hotan Administrative Offices	4562	1337	420	1095

地 区	Region	药剂人员 Druggist of Medicine	检验人员 Laboratory Technicians	其 他 Others	平均每万人口医生数 Number of Doctors per 10 000 Population
总 计	**Total**	**6015**	**5139**	**14673**	**21.93**
乌鲁木齐市	Urumqi City	1304	1195	2002	51.16
克拉玛依市	Karamay City	136	96	82	41.24
石河子市	Shihezi City	271	212	625	36.77
吐鲁番地区	Turpan Administrative Offices	202	161	379	21.84
哈密地区	Hami [Kumul] Administrative Offices	258	215	555	33.61
昌吉回族自治州	Changji Hui Autonomous Prefecture	721	405	1363	24.33
伊犁哈萨克自治州	Ili Kazak Autonomous Prefecture	1160	1111	3361	23.51
伊犁州直属县(市)	Counties (Cities) Direct Under Ili Prefecture	742	660	2100	22.68
塔城地区	Tacheng [Tarbagatai] Administrative Offices	258	256	761	22.33
阿勒泰地区	Altay Administrative Offices	160	195	500	28.75
博尔塔拉蒙古自治州	Bortala Mongol Autonomous Prefecture	186	149	443	28.61
巴音郭楞蒙古自治州	Bayangol Mongol Autonomous Prefecture	400	382	1056	23.58
阿克苏地区	Aksu Administrative Offices	457	425	1556	13.05
克孜勒苏柯尔克孜自治州	Kizilsu Kirgiz Autonomous Prefecture	128	107	353	19.01
喀什地区	Kashgar [Kaxgar] Administrative Offices	512	463	1686	11.03
和田地区	Hotan Administrative Offices	280	218	1212	9.91

19-14 分市县医院床位和专业卫生技术人员数

Hospital Beds and Medical Technical Personnel by City and County Areas

年 份 Year	医院、卫生院床位(张) Number of Hospital Beds (unit)		专业卫生技术人员(人) Number of Medical Technical Personnel (person)		#执业医师、执业助理医师 Doctors & Assistant Doctors with License		#注册护士 Registered Nurses	
	市 City	县 County	市 City	县 County	市 City	县 County	市 City	县 County
2000	38398	27518	44115	31138	18408	13225	16805	9918
2001	38323	27685	44113	31055	18811	13271	16714	10105
2002	38700	26178	41850	27932	16689	10578	15965	8840
2003	42880	26915	44678	28228	17883	10916	17015	9087
2004	46300	27722	46956	28552	19207	10583	17185	9054

19-15 全区法定报告传染病发病及死亡情况

Confirmed Incidence and Death from Infectious Diseases in Xinjiang

(2004 年)

项 目	Item	发病率(1/10 万) Incidence (1/100 000)	死亡率(1/10 万) Death Rate (1/100 000)	病死率(%) Mortality Rate (%)
总 计	**Total**	**435.31**	**0.468**	**0.107**
霍 乱	Cholera	0.02		
肝 炎	Viral Hepatitis	137.53	0.054	0.039
痢 疾	Dysentery	80.74	0.038	0.047
伤 寒	Typhoid	4.82		
艾滋病	AIDS	0.10	0.027	27.778
淋 病	Gonorrhea	16.78		
梅 毒	Syphilis	6.58		
麻 疹	Measles	34.95	0.016	0.046
百日咳	Pertussis	3.44	0.016	0.469
流 脑	Epidemic Encephalitis	0.31	0.016	5.263
猩红热	Scarlet Fever	3.36		
布氏杆菌病	Brucellosis	1.69		
炭 疽	Anthrax	0.79	0.005	0.680
斑疹伤寒	Typhus Fever	0.01		
黑热病	Kala-Azar	0.95		
新生儿破伤风	Newborn Baby Tetanus	59.00	9.000	15.333
肺结核	Pulmonary Tuberculosis	142.02	0.172	0.121

19-16 城市前十位疾病死亡原因及构成

Death Causes and Percentage of Top10 Diseases in Urban Areas

(2004 年)

疾病死亡原因	Cause of Death	占死亡总人数的比重 (%) Persentage of Total Deaths (%)
十种死因合计	**Total**	**90.75**
恶性肿瘤	Malignant Tumour	22.74
脑血管病	Cerebrovasular Disease	15.13
心脏病	Heart Trouble	24.92
呼吸系统疾病	Respiratory Disease	11.00
损伤和中毒	Trauma and Toxicosis	7.20
消化系统疾病	Digestive Disease	3.57
内分泌、营养、代谢及免疫疾病	Internal System, Nutrition, Metabolite and Immunity Disease	3.27
泌尿、生殖系病	Urinary Disease	1.59
精神病	Mental Disease	0.17
神经病	Neuropathy	1.16

注：统计范围包括乌鲁木齐市及辖区资料。
Note: Statistics in Data Covers Urumqi and its Districts.

19-17 离休、退休、退职人员年底人数

Number of Retired and Resigned Persons at the Year-end

单位:人 (person)

年份 Year	总计 Total				#企业 Enterprises			
	合计 Total	离休人员 Retired Veterans	退休人员 Retired Persons	退职人员 Resigned Persons	合计 Total	离休人员 Retired Veterans	退休人员 Retired Persons	退职人员 Resigned Persons
1990	535736	63742	443669	28326	399764	47008	331514	21242
1991	552629	64949	460408	27272	416336	48468	346266	21602
1992	610517	69026	516681	24810	481485	51461	410048	19976
1993	722494	83184	610758	28552	570801	62065	485760	22976
1994	717170	80016	606926	30228	558839	64311	469441	25087
1995	773688	76834	668482	28372	611054	61399	526236	23419
1996	799205	75591	695551	28063	624877	61167	540360	23350
1997	842722	78472	733099	31151	655491	64036	566101	25354
1998	894588	74509	787930	32149	715276	61147	626570	27559
1999	951600	72799	847560	31241	749909	59158	663200	27551
2000	1003360	63260	905390	34710	783148	49083	703058	31007
2001	995882	54990	907178	33714	754933	41937	683293	29703
2002	1002836	52272	920401	30163	739035	39606	673844	25585
2003	1027896	50995	946583	30318	803436	39813	737054	26569
2004	1062388	47238	980378	34772	778236	35626	713634	28976

19-18 离休、退休、退职费

Pensions for Retired and Resigned Persons

年份 Year	合计(万元) Total (10 000 yuan)	国有单位 Funds of State-Owned Units	城镇集体单位 Funds of Urban Collective Owned Units	其他单位 Funds of Other Ownership Units	平均每人(元) Per Capita Funds (yuan)	#国有单位 State-Owned Units
绝对数 Absolute Figure						
1990	94304.10	90341.20	3907.60	55.30	1871	1837
1991	105953.77	101213.47	4671.30	69.00	1947	1950
1992	124466.87	118915.12	5371.20	180.55	2140	2142
1993	149088.70	141980.40	6685.40	422.90	2237	2226
1994	256946.60	248619.70	7718.80	608.10	3635	3674
1995	331522.30	321199.10	9881.60	441.60	4615	4667
1996	377781.50	363217.40	13631.40	932.70	5014	5059
1997	456596.30	443124.30	12970.30	501.70	5802	5904
1998	585609.07	568726.49	13461.79	3420.79	6860	6949
1999	681552.63	661271.30	14970.82	5310.51	7383	7478
2000	759880.38	740781.85	14005.06	5093.47	7774	7878
2001	837082.46	816688.54	13988.71	6405.21	8374	8464
2002	952163.00	928136.70	15187.20	8839.10	9495	9582
2003	1005080.79	958105.52	17464.48	29510.79	9778	9891
2004	1098304.25	1049374.82	18868.11	30061.32	10338	10531
比上年增长(%) Increase over Preceding Year (%)						
1990	22.8	23.7	8.1	-44.8	1.0	4.2
1991	12.4	12.0	19.5	24.8	4.1	6.2
1992	17.5	17.5	15.0	161.7	9.9	9.9
1993	19.8	19.4	24.5	134.2	4.5	3.9
1994	72.3	75.1	15.5	43.8	62.5	65.0
1995	29.0	29.2	28.0	-27.4	26.9	27.0
1996	14.0	13.1	37.9	111.2	8.6	8.4
1997	20.9	22.0	-4.8	-46.2	15.7	16.7
1998	28.3	28.3	3.8	581.8	18.2	17.7
1999	16.4	16.3	11.2	55.2	7.6	7.6
2000	11.5	12.0	-6.5	-4.1	5.3	5.3
2001	10.2	10.2	-0.1	25.8	7.7	7.4
2002	13.7	13.6	8.6	38.0	13.4	13.2
2003	5.6	3.2	15.0	233.9	3.0	3.2
2004	9.0	9.5	8.0	1.9	5.7	6.5

注:本表数字不包括离休、退休、退职职工的医疗卫生费。

Note: Figures in this table exclude medical expenditures of retired and resigned workers and staff.

19-19 离休、退休、退职人员保险福利费用构成情况
Figures of Total Social Insurance and Welfare Fund of Retirees

年份 Year	合计 Total	离休金 Pensions for Termination	退休金 Retirement Pensions	退职生活费 Resignation Allowances For Living Expenses	医疗卫生费 Medical Care Expenses	其他 Others
绝对数(万元) **Absolute Figure (10 000 yuan)**						
1990	118559.52	16565.78	76101.69	1636.63	9665.17	14590.25
1991	136817.09	17110.17	87179.33	1664.27	11491.77	19371.55
1992	168999.66	19281.65	102760.16	2425.06	14512.37	30020.42
1993	202405.50	26812.90	119391.00	2884.80	16490.20	36826.60
1994	310255.90	34366.60	218522.30	4057.70	30574.80	22734.50
1995	394514.40	40535.10	286032.30	4954.90	39422.80	23569.30
1996	450345.20	42148.40	330166.40	5466.70	46042.50	26521.20
1997	545914.20	55033.40	394642.20	6920.70	49565.70	39752.20
1998	680073.99	65655.00	509711.30	10242.77	69430.99	25033.93
1999	789707.40	71871.48	597635.77	12177.28	81602.16	26420.71
2000	867924.73	77968.35	667698.42	14213.61	79834.44	28209.91
2001	950372.68	87573.97	736006.76	13501.73	77711.40	35578.82
2002	1055177.40	90009.70	847885.80	14267.50	64261.50	38752.90
2003	1129406.74	93407.96	895008.59	16664.24	83722.25	40603.70
2004	1202101.71	102192.78	977477.70	18633.77	50595.71	53201.75
比上年增长(%) **Increase over Preceding Year (%)**						
1990						
1991	15.4	3.3	14.6	1.7	18.9	32.8
1992	23.5	12.7	17.9	45.7	26.3	55.0
1993	19.8	39.1	16.2	19.0	13.6	22.7
1994	53.3	28.2	83.0	40.7	85.4	-38.3
1995	27.2	17.9	30.9	22.1	28.9	3.7
1996	14.2	4.0	15.4	10.3	16.8	12.5
1997	21.2	30.6	19.5	26.6	7.7	49.9
1998	24.6	19.3	29.2	48.0	40.1	-37.0
1999	16.1	9.5	17.2	18.9	17.5	5.5
2000	9.9	8.5	11.7	16.7	-2.2	6.8
2001	9.5	12.3	10.2	-5.0	-2.7	26.1
2002	11.0	2.8	15.2	5.7	-17.3	8.9
2003	7.0	3.8	5.6	16.8	30.3	4.8
2004	6.4	9.4	9.2	11.8	-39.6	31.0
构成(以合计为 100) **Composition (Total=100)**						
1990	100	14.0	64.2	1.4	8.2	12.3
1991	100	12.5	63.7	1.2	8.4	14.2
1992	100	11.4	60.8	1.4	8.6	17.8
1993	100	13.2	59.0	1.4	8.1	18.2
1994	100	11.1	70.4	1.3	9.9	7.3
1995	100	10.3	72.5	1.3	10.0	6.0
1996	100	9.4	73.3	1.2	10.2	5.9
1997	100	10.1	72.3	1.3	9.1	7.3
1998	100	9.7	74.9	1.5	10.2	3.7
1999	100	9.1	75.7	1.5	10.3	3.3
2000	100	9.0	76.9	1.6	9.2	3.3
2001	100	9.2	77.4	1.4	8.2	3.7
2002	100	8.5	80.3	1.4	6.1	3.7
2003	100	8.3	79.2	1.5	7.4	3.6
2004	100	8.5	81.3	1.6	4.2	4.4

注：本表不包括民政部门支付的离休、退休、退职费。

Note: The Table excludes retired and resigned staff and workers paid by the civil administration organs.

19-20　社会福利事业单位基本情况

Basic Statistics on Social Welfare Institutions

(2004 年)

指　标	Item	院　数 (个) Number of Homes (unit)	工作人员数 (人) Number of Persons Engaged (person)	床位数 (张) Number of Beds (unit)	年末收养人数 (人) Number of Persons Housed (person)	#收养女性 Female
总　计	**Total**	**496**	**2468**	**13438**	**10356**	**3815**
社会福利院	Social Welfare Homes	23	375	1474	1196	448
儿童福利院	Children Welfare Institute	35	453	2971	2916	1119
光荣院	Homes for Disabled Veterans	6	37	168	109	21
精神病福利院	Psychopath Welfare Homes	7	438	1115	1079	532
社会办敬老院	Welfare Homes by Social Elderly	424	1143	7640	5044	1695
荣誉军人康复医院	Recuperative Hospital for Soldiers with Honour	1	22	70	12	

19-21　社会福利事业、企业单位数和工作人员数

Number of Social Welfare Institutions and Enterprises and Persons Engaged

(2004 年)

项　目	Item	机构数 (个) Number of Institutions or Enterprises (unit)	工作人员数 (人) Number of Persons Engaged (person)
收养性福利事业单位	Adopting Social Welfare Institutions	496	2468
国家办	Run by State	92	1495
集　体	Run by collective	393	872
民　办	Run by non-government sector	11	101
社会福利企业	Social Welfare Enterprises	161	5133
国　有	Run by State	23	623
集　体	Run by collective	88	2623
民　办	Run by non-government sector	50	1887
优抚安置事业单位	Administration Agencies for Martyrs	36	374
收容遣送单位	Collecting and Repatriation Units	23	245
殡葬服务事业单位	Funeral and Interment Institutions	71	534
福利彩票发行单位	Welfare Lottery-Ticked Issuance Unit	33	164
社区服务单位	Community Service Institutions	146	1108

19-22 社会救济情况
Basic Statistics on Social Relief Funds

指　　标	Item	2003	2004
城镇居民最低生活保障人数(人)	**Number of Persons Receiving Lowest Cost-of-living in Urban Area (person)**	**577991**	**588423**
#在职人员	# Full Employed Staff and Workers	15184	13074
下岗人员	Laid-offs	49216	32761
退休人员	Retired Persons	11757	10628
失业人员	Unemployment	111396	119856
“三无”人员	"Non-Three" Persons	34858	37361
其他人员	Others	355580	374743
城镇居民最低生活保障家庭数(户)	**Number of Family Receiving Lowest Cost-of-living in Urban Area (household)**	**220511**	**222333**

注：“三无”人员是指无依无靠、无生活来源、无劳动能力的人员。
Note:Non-three” persons refer to those with neither fiancial supopot, source of life nor work capability.

19-23 工会组织情况
Basic Statistics on Trade Unions

年　份 Year	工会基层组织个数(个) Number of Grassroots Unions (unit)	全区已建工会组织的基本单位职工与会员人数(万人) Membership and Number of Staff and Workers in Grassroots Unions (10 000persons)				专职工会干　部(万人) Number of Full-time Personnel of Unions (10 000 persons)
		职工人数 Number of Staff and Workers	#女职工 Female	会员人数 Number of Membership	#女职工 Female	
1980	3255	84.20	30.25	67.13	20.42	0.48
1985	6165	189.48	73.84	151.93	59.03	0.50
1990	10685	231.48	90.64	196.58	76.97	0.79
1995	14457	271.43	114.13	254.49	104.97	1.19
1996	11282	246.38	105.14	227.67	97.48	1.02
1997	11085	241.21	96.11	215.96	90.94	0.94
1998	10624	220.46	93.84	204.89	88.14	0.81
1999	10433	211.88	89.49	195.11	82.64	0.81
2000	13016	211.73	90.80	200.80	84.93	0.59
2001	18219	234.84	100.71	215.31	91.07	0.73
2002	20806	236.58	99.65	220.85	93.11	0.49
2003	11263	230.24	93.43	220.55	87.05	0.45
2004	11979	224.52	94.49	219.35	90.62	0.48

19-24 残疾人事业基本情况

Basic Conditions of People with Disabilities

项 目	Item	2003	2004
康 复	**Rehabilitation**		
白内障复明	Re-light of Cataract		
白内障复明手术(万例)	Operation (10 000 cases)	0.83	0.82
人工晶体植入率(%)	Embedded Rate of Artificial Crystal (%)	92.60	91.70
低视力配用助视器(人)	Low-eyesight Matched with Eyesight-aid Apparatus (person)	214	441
聋儿康复	Rehabilitation of Deaf Children		
年收训聋儿(人)	Annual Adoptive Deaf Children (person)	95	91
聋儿入普幼普小率(%)	Enrollment Rate to General Infant School or Elementary School (%)	17	33
培训家长(人)	Patriarch Trained (person)	145	120
精神病防治康复	Prevention, Cure and Rehabilitation of Psychosis		
开展精神病防治康复工作市县数(个)	Number of Counties Carried on the Works of Prevention, Cure and Rehabilitation (unit)	5	5
综合防治康复精神病人数(万人)	Number of Psychosis Sicks Synthetically Prevented, Cured and Rehabilitated (10 000 persons)	1.50	1.60
监护率(%)	Warding Rate (%)	94.00	82.16
显好率(%)	Rate of Getting Better (%)	62.11	68.96
社会参与率(%)	Social Participation Rate (%)	51.07	58.16
肇事率(%)	Rate of Causing Trouble (%)	0.09	0.14
救济贫困患者数(人)	Number of Poor Sufferer Relieved (person)	1636	1033
用品用具供应件数(万件)	Number of Appliances Supplied (10 000 units)	1.14	0.92
康复训练与服务(人)	Rehabilitation Training and Service (person)		
肢体残疾康复训练数	Rehabilitation Training of Body Disabilities	708	1040
智力残疾儿童康复训练数	Rehabilitation Training of Mental Disabilities Children	299	358
教 育	**Education**		
未入学适龄残疾儿童(万人)	Number of Uneducated Children (10 000 persons)	1.24	1.11
职业教育与培训机构数(个)	Vocational Education and Training Number of Institutions (unit)		
独立建制	Self Help	38	15
依托社会	Supported by Society	85	15
教育与培训人数(万人)	Number of Educated and Trained (10 000 persons)	0.35	0.65
就 业	**Employment**		
城镇残疾人就业状况(万人)	Employment of Urban Handicappeds (10 000 persons)		
当年安排就业	Persons Employed in the Year	0.31	0.37
按比例就业	Employment by Proportion	0.09	0.09
集中就业	Centralized Employment	0.07	0.10
个体就业	Individual Employment	0.13	0.16
未安排就业	Un-arranged Handicappeds	1.65	1.39
农村残疾人就业状况(万人)	Employment of Rural Handicapped (10 000 persons)		
就 业	Employed	8.24	21.01
未就业	Unemployed	1.30	1.97
残疾人就业服务机构(个)	Number of Institutions Engaging in Handicappeds Employment (unit)		
省	Provinces	1	1
地	Prefectures	12	12
市(含县级市)	Cities (Cities at County Level)	19	19
县	County	64	68
市辖区	Districts under the Jurisdiction of Cities	11	11
实施分散按比例就业的地区数(个)	Number of Regions Implemented the Policy of the Disperse Employment by Proportion (unit)		
省	Provinces	1	1
地	Prefectures	12	12
市(含县级市)	Cities (Cities at County Level)	19	19
县	County	67	67
市辖区	Districts under the Jurisdiction of Cities	11	11
扶 贫	**Poverty Alleviation**		
扶贫开发解决温饱(万人)	Number of Handicappeds Have Lived with Warmth Fill-bellies (10 000 persons)	0.82	1.57
尚未解决温饱贫困残疾人(万人)	Number of Handicappeds Have Lived without Warmth Fill-bellies yet (10 000 persons)	4.93	4.43
可扶持贫困残疾人(万人)	Number of Handicappeds Can Be Supported (10 000 persons)	5.02	5.16
残联组织建设	**Organization of Association for the Handicapped**		
残疾人工作者数(万人)	Number of Workers for the Handicappeds (10 000 persons)	0.21	0.21

19-25 历届全区人民代表大会代表人数

Number of Deputies to all the Previous People's Congresses of Xinjiang

项　目 Item	第一届 (1954) First Congress	第二届 (1959) Second Congress	第三届 (1964) Third Congress	第四届 (1975) Fourth Congress	第五届 (1978) Fifth Congress	第六届 (1983) Sixth Congress	第七届 (1988) Seventh Congress	第八届 (1993) Eighth Congress	第九届 (1998) Ninth Congress	第十届 (2003) Tenth Congress
代表总数(人) Total Number of All Deputies (person)	**376**	**386**	**453**	**809**	**672**	**550**	**550**	**542**	**550**	**550**
#中国共产党党员 Deputies from the Communist Party of China	178		240			374	357	381	396	396
占总数比重(%) Percentage to Total (%)	47.3		53.0			68.0	64.9	70.3	72.0	72.0
#少数民族 Deputies from National Minorities	331		383	510	430	357	363	355	363	363
占总数比重(%) Percentage to Total(%)	88.0		84.5	63.8	64.0	64.9	66.0	65.5	66.0	66.0
#妇 女 Female Deputies	52	61	89	200	146	17	126	123	135	135
占总数比重(%) As Percentage to Total(%)	13.8	15.8	19.6	24.7	21.7	21.3	22.9	22.7	24.5	24.5

19-26 历届全区政治协商会议委员人数

Number of Deputies to all the Previous People's Political Consultative Conferences of Xinjiang

项　目 Item	第一届 (1954) First Congress	第二届 (1959) Second Congress	第三届 (1964) Third Congress	第四届 (1978) Fourth Congress	第五届 (1983) Fifth Congress	第六届 (1988) Sixth Congress	第七届 (1993) Seventh Congress	第八届 (1998) Eighth Congress	第九届 (2003) Ninth Congress
委员总数(人) Total Number of All Deputies (person)	**141**	**275**	**303**	**407**	**441**	**429**	**416**	**444**	**470**
#中国共产党党员 Deputies from the Communist Party of China	28	57	65	149	158	157	161	183	196
占总数比重(%) Percentage to Total(%)	19.9	20.7	21.5	36.6	35.8	36.6	38.7	41.2	41.7
#少数民族 Deputies from National Minorities(%)	121	196	205	221	253	245	204	246	246
占总数比重(%) Percentage to Total	85.8	71.3	67.7	54.3	57.4	57.0	49.0	55.4	52.3
#妇 女 Female Deputies	10	28	28	40	49	63	66	82	95
占总数比重(%) Percentage to Total(%)	7.1	10.2	9.2	9.8	11.1	14.7	15.9	18.5	20.2

19-27　律师、公证、调解工作基本情况

Basic Statistics on Lawyers, Notarization and Mediation

项　　目	Item	1985	1990	1995	2000	2004
律师工作	**Lawyers**					
律师事务所(个)	Number of Law Offices (unit)	113	130	169	227	241
律师(人)	Number of Lawyers (person)	694	780	1705	2414	2529
专职律师(人)	Full-time Lawyers (person)	280	435	1209	1508	1937
兼职和特邀律师(人)	Part-time Lawyers (person)	414	345	336	418	103
聘请担任常年法律顾问的单位(处)	Number of Units with Permanent Legal Advisors (unit)	1263	1748	2560	2613	2733
民事诉讼代理(件)	Agent of Civil Cases (case)	1937	6306	6380	16165	22114
刑事辩护及代理(件)	Defender and Agent of Criminal Cases (case)	2310	6237	5850	5826	5533
非诉讼法律事务(件)	Agent of Non-Litigious Legal Affairs (case)	979	614	5357	4810	9457
解答法律咨询(万件)	Agent of Legal Advisory Services (10 000 cases)	1.83	4.62	4.21	7.45	9.01
代写法律事务文书(万件)	Agent of Legal Documents Written on Behalf of Clients (10 000 cases)	0.43	0.69	1.06	1.94	3.18
公证工作	**Notarization**					
公证处(个)	Number of Notary Offices (unit)	90	113	126	131	126
公证员	Notaries	101	173	266	332	417
公证员助理(人)	Assistant Notaries (person)	22	76	49	43	59
办理公证文书(万件)	Number of Notarized Document (10 000 cases)	5.18	6.79	10.11	18.85	21.06
人民调解工作	**Number of People's Mediation**					
专职司法助理员(人)	Number of Full-time Judicial Assistants (person)	1061	939	1515	1750	1566
人民调解委员会(个)	Number of People's Mediation Committees (unit)	16070	17422	19045	22294	16441
调解人员(万人)	Number of Mediators (10 000 persons)	7.88	7.11	12.04	10.04	8.17
调解民间纠纷(万件)	Number of Civil Disputes Mediated (10 000 cases)	8.43	11.86	9.18	8.09	7.93

19-28 调解民间纠纷分类

Number of Civil Disputes Mediated by Type

(2004 年)

项 目	Item	调解纠纷(件) Civil Disputes (case)	各类纠纷所占比重(%) Percentage (%)
总 计	**Total**	**79332**	**100**
婚姻家庭	Marriage and Family	23229	29.28
合 同	Contract	4713	5.94
劳 动	Labor	4841	6.10
村务管理	Village-affair Management	2103	2.65
土 地	Land	6515	8.21
征地拆迁	Requisitioned Land Demolition	1437	1.81
房屋宅基地	Housing and Housing Sites	3757	4.74
计划生育	Family Planning	929	1.17
邻 里	Neighbour	14803	18.66
损害赔偿	Compensation for Damages	5686	7.17
施工扰民	Construction Noise	671	0.85
其 他	Others	10648	13.42

19-29 火灾事故发生情况

Basic Statistics on Fire Accidents

(2004 年)

指 标	Item	合 计 Total	按事故发生程度分 By Serious Dgree of Fires		
			特 大 Extraordinarily Serious	重 大 Serious	一 般 Ordinary
发生起数(起)	Fires (case)	4338	1	5	4332
死亡(人)	Death (person)	28		3	25
受伤(人)	Injuries (person)	95		8	87
损失折款(万元)	Losses Converted into Cash (10 000 yuan)	2432.1	489.9	336.8	1605.4
平均每起事故损失(元)	Average Loss per Fire (yuan)	5607	4899000	673600	3706

19-30 交通事故发生情况

Basic Statistics on Traffic Accidents

(2004 年)

指 标	Item	合 计 Total	按事故发生程度 By Serious Dgree for Traffic Accidents			按事故发生地区分 By Area for Traffic Accidents	
			特 大 Extraordinarily Serious	重 大 Serious	一 般 Ordinary	城 市 Cities	郊区、县(农村) Counties (Rural Areas)
发生起数(起)	Traffic Accidents (case)	8374	2441	5066	867	2679	5695
死亡(人)	Death (person)	2892	2892			649	2243
受伤(人)	Injuries (person)	8918	1556	7362		2483	6435
损失折款(万元)	Losses Converted into Cash (10 000 yuan)	2974.17	1306.86	1216.94	450.37	559.85	2414.32
平均每起事故损失(元)	Average Loss per Fire (yuan)	3552	5354	2402	5195	2089	4239

19-31 公安机关受理查处治安案件情况

Offense Cases Against Public Order Handled by Public Security Organs

单位：起 (case)

案件类别	Category of Cases	2003 受理 Number of Cases Accepted to be Treated	2003 查处 Number of Cases Investigated and Treated	2004 受理 Number of Cases Accepted to be Treated	2004 查处 Number of Cases Investigated and Treated
总计	**Total**	**120337**	**83213**	**146923**	**104486**
扰乱工作、公共秩序	Disturbing Work or Public Order	2845	2564	1717	1505
结伙斗殴、寻衅滋事	Gang Fighting or Picking Quarrels and Making Troubles	2950	2332	3522	2972
侮辱妇女及其他流氓活动	Acting Indecently Towards Women	471	410	505	444
阻碍国家工作人员执行公务	Obstructing the Government Workers to Perform their Duty	826	765	817	775
违反枪支管理规定	Violating Regulations on Management of Firearms	57	99	42	40
违反爆炸物品管理规定	Violating Regulations on Management of Explosives	147	142	103	99
殴打他人	Beating Other Body	35352	21684	44204	29155
偷窃财物	Robbing Other People of their Valuables	26744	7931	33767	10433
骗取、抢夺、敲诈勒索财物	Defrauding, Snatching or Extorting and Racketeering Valuables	2347	707	3285	1085
哄抢公私财物	Making Stirs and then Robbing Public or Private Valuables	79	45	67	45
故意损坏公私财物	Intentionally Damaging Public or Private Valuables	2278	1532	3370	2264
伪造倒卖票券、证件	Forging and Fraudulently Selling Bills or Certificates	35	23	30	30
利用迷信扰乱秩序或骗财	Disturbing Public Order or Defrauding People of their Valuables by Making Use of their Superstition	45	34	89	81
卖淫、嫖娼	Prostitution or Going Whoring	2272	2256	2151	2128
赌博	Gambling	3638	3460	3101	3043
违反户口、居民身份证管理	Violating Regulations on Management of Residence or Identity Cards	13160	13140	11274	11255
其他	Others	27091	26089	38879	39132

19-32 刑事案件中青少年犯罪情况

Juvenile Delinquency Among Criminal Cases

年份 Year	刑事罪犯总数（人） Offenders (person)	#青少年罪犯 Young Offenders	#不满 18 岁 Less than 18	#18 岁至 25 岁 Between 18 to 25	青少年罪犯占刑事罪犯（%） Persentage of Proportion to Total (%)
2001	29704	15214	4431	10783	51.22
2002	31529	16590	5655	10935	52.61
2003	35242	18749	6541	12209	53.20
2004	39665	21040	7923	13117	53.04

主要统计指标解释

等级运动员人数 指经考核正式批准授予等级运动员称号的人数。运动员等级分为国际级运动健将、运动健将、一级运动员、二级运动员、三级运动员、少年级运动员。该指标主要反映运动员队伍的技术质量水平。

等级裁判员人数 指经考核正式批准授予等级裁判员称号的人数。裁判员等级分为国际裁判、国家级裁判、一级裁判、二级裁判、三级裁判。该指标主要反映裁判员队伍的技术质量水平。

体育场 指有400米跑道(中心含足球场)，有固定道牙，跑道6条以上，并有固定看台的室外田径场地。体育场按看台容纳观众人数分为：甲级25000人以上，乙级15000-25000人，丙级5000-15000人，丁级5000人以下。该指标主要反映大中型体育场数量水平。

体育馆 指有固定看台，可供篮球、排球、羽毛球、乒乓球、体操等项目训练比赛活动用的室内运动场地。体育馆按看台容纳观众人数分为：甲级6000人以上，乙级4000-6000人，丙级2000-4000人，丁级2000人以下。该指标主要反映大中型体育馆数量水平。

卫生机构 包括医疗机构、疾病预防控制中心(防疫站)、采供血机构、卫生监督及监测(检验)机构、医学科研和在职培训机构、健康教育所等。医疗机构包括医院、社区卫生服务中心(站)、疗养院、卫生院、门诊部、诊所(卫生所、医务室)、妇幼保健院(所、站)、专科疾病防治院(所、站)、急救中心(站)和临床检验中心。医疗机构分为非赢利性医疗机构和赢利性医疗机构。

医院 包括综合医院、中医医院、中西医结合医院、民族医院、各类专科医院和护理院。

卫生技术人员 指卫生机构中医生、护理人员、药剂人员、检验人员等卫生技术人员。

医生 指在医疗、预防保健机构工作且取得《执业医师证书》的执业医师和执业助理医师。

卫生服务总费用 反映全国当年用于医疗卫生保健服务所消耗的资金总额，用筹资来源法测算。政府预算卫生支出指各级政府用于卫生事业的财政预算拨款。社会卫生支出指政府预算外的卫生资金投入，主要表现为社会医疗保险。其中包括如企事业单位和乡村集体经济单位举办医疗卫生机构设施建设费，企业职工医疗卫生费，行政事业单位负担的职工公费医疗超支部分等。居民个人卫生支出指城乡居民用自己可支配的经济收入支付的各项医疗卫生费用和医疗保险费用。

社会福利事业单位 指集中收养社会孤老、残、幼的机构，包括由民政部门管理的社会福利院、儿童福利院、精神病人福利院和城镇集体举办的福利院及农村集体举办的敬老院以及优抚医院和具有收养能力的社区服务中心等。该指标主要反映我国在社会福利性单位投入的水平。

社会福利事业单位收养人数 包括民政部门管理和城镇、农村集体举办的社会福利事业单位中收养的老人、少年儿童、缺乏生活自理能力的残疾人员和精神病人。该指标主要反映收养性社会福利单位的收养能力。

社会福利企业单位 指以安置城镇有一定劳动能力的盲、聋、哑和肢体残疾人员就业为目的，享受国家减免税待遇的国有或集体企业。包括福利工厂、福利商业和服务业、假肢厂和安置农场等单位。该指标主要反映我国对残疾人照顾的特殊政策。

农村五保户 指农村中既无劳动能力，又无经济来源的老、弱、孤、残的农民，其生活由集体供养，实行保吃、保穿、保住、保医、保葬(孤儿保教)，简称“五保”，享受五保待遇的家庭叫五保户。该指标主要反映农村弱势群体的人员数量。

聋儿入普幼普小率 指本年度内进入普通幼儿园、普通小学的聋儿数与在训聋儿数(不含当年新收训聋儿数)之比。该指标主要反映经过康复训练的聋儿进入普通幼儿园和普通小学的情况。

综合防治康复精神病人数 指在开展精神病防治康复工作地区，采取不同形式，接受综合性防治康复措施、开放式管理的精神病人数。该指标主要反映精神病患者接受治疗康复情况。

监护率 指通过监护小组、家庭病床、工疗站、社会就业以及精神卫生机构，接受社会化、综合性、开放式治疗与康复的精神病人占经调查摸底、登记在册的精神病人数的百分比。该指标主要反映对精神病患者落实治疗康复措施的情况。

社会参与率 指生活能自理，并参加生产劳动和社会生活的精神病人数占监护精神病人数的百分比。该指标主要反映精神病人康复状况和参与社会的情况。

未入学适龄残疾儿童少年 指根据义务教育法规定应接受义务教育，但因各种原因未能入学的适龄视力残疾、听力与言语残疾、智力残疾、肢体残疾、精神残疾、多重残疾儿童少年。适龄残疾儿童少年的年龄段参照各省级人民政府依照义务教育法规定的入学年龄。该指标主要反映因各种原因未能入学的适龄残疾儿童的年度变化，为制定残疾儿童义务教育发展规划及其应采取的方针、政策和措施提供依据，同时为各地开展资助残疾儿童就学工作提供依据。

律师 指依法取得律师执业证书，担任法律顾问，民事(刑事、行政)案件代理人、刑事案件辩护人、办理非诉讼业务，解答法律询问，代写法律事务文书等，为社会提供法律服务的人员。

公证人员 指在公证处工作的人员总称，包括公证处主任、副主任、公证员、公证员助理(助理公证员)和其他从事辅助性工作的人员。

公证文书 指公证处根据当事人申请，依照事实和法律，按照法定程序制作的，具有法律效力的司法证明文书。根据公证书用途和使用地，公证书分为国内公证书、国内经济公证书、涉外民事公证书、涉外经济公证书四类。

调解员 指在人民调解委员会担负调解民间纠纷工作的人员，包括调解委员会的委员和调解小组的调解员。该指标主要反映从事人民调解工作的人员数量。

调解民间纠纷 指调解委员会按照法律规定，根据自愿原则，用说服教育的方法调解民间发生的有关民事权利和义务争执的件数，包括调解成功数和调解未成功数。该指标主要反映人民调解委员会的工作量。

立案 指人民检察院对受理的报案、控告、举报或自首及自行发现的犯罪线索、犯罪嫌疑人进行初步调查后，认为存在职务犯罪事实和应追究刑事责任，并决定作为刑事案件进行侦查的诉讼活动，是追究犯罪的开始。该指标主要反映人民检察院依法将职务犯罪线索作为刑事案件进行侦查的诉讼活动。

大案 指贪污、贿赂案数额在5万元以上，挪用公款案数额在10万元以上，集体私分、巨额财产来源不明、隐瞒境外存款案数额在50万元以上以及按照《人民检察院直接受理的渎职、侵权重、特大案件标准(试行)》认定的案件。该指标主要反映人民检察院立案查办的职务犯罪案件中经济损失大、社会危害严重的案件。

要案 指县、处级以上干部的犯罪案件。该指标主要反映国家工作人员中县、处级以上干部因职务犯罪被人民检察院依法立案侦查的情况。

决定逮捕 指人民检察院对直接受理、自行侦查的案件，认为需要逮捕犯罪嫌疑人时，依据法律做出的逮捕决定。该指标主要反映人民检察院对直接受理的案件行使决定逮捕权的情况。

批准逮捕 指人民检察院对公安机关、国家安全机关、监狱管理机关提出逮捕的犯罪嫌疑人进行审查，根据事实，依法做出逮捕决定。该指标主要反映人民检察院对提请逮捕机关提请逮捕犯罪嫌疑人进行审查后依法做出批准逮捕决定的情况。

决定起诉 指人民检察院对公安机关、国家安全机关、监狱管理机关和检察机关内设机构反贪污贿赂部门等移送起诉的案件进行审查，根据事实，做出提起公诉的案件。该指标主要反映人民检察院对各种刑事案件向人民法院提起公诉的情况。

受理劳动争议案件数 指劳动争议仲裁委员会根据国家有关规定，对劳动争议当事人的申请予以审查，符合受理条件而正式立案、准备处理的劳动争议案件数。

基本养老保险

1.参加保险人数：指报告期末按照国家法律、法规和有关政策规定参加基本养老保险的职工人数。包括不能正常缴费、已中断缴费但未终止保险关系的职工人数。

2.社会统筹基金收入：指根据国家规定，由纳入基本养老保险范围的单位，按照国家规定的缴费基数和缴费比例缴纳的社会统筹基金，以及通过其他方式取得的形成基金来源的收入，包括：单位缴纳的社会统筹基金收入、财政补贴收入、利息收入、其他收入。

3.社会统筹基金支出：指按照国家政策规定的开支范围和开支标准从社会统筹基金中支付给参加基本养老保险的离休、退休、退职人员个人的养老金、丧葬抚恤补助，以及由于保险关系转移、上下级之间调剂资金等原因而发生的支出。包括：基础性养老金、过渡性养老金、离休金、退休金、退职金、补贴、丧葬抚恤补助、其他支出。

4.社会统筹基金结余：指截止报告期末基本养老保险的社会统筹基金结余金额。包括银行存款、财政专户、债券投资和其他。

离休、退休、退职人员　指正式办理了离休、退休、退职手续，并享受相应的离休、退休、退职待遇的人员。

基本医疗保险

1.参加保险人数：指报告期末按国家有关规定参加基本医疗保险的人数。包括参加保险的职工人数和退休人员人数。

2.社会统筹基金收入：指根据国家有关规定，由纳入基本医疗保险范围的缴费单位，按国家规定的缴费基数和缴费比例缴纳的社会统筹基金，以及通过其他方式取得的形成基金来源的款项，包括：单位缴纳的社会统筹基金收入、财政补贴收入、利息收入、其他收入。

3.社会统筹基金支出：指按照国家政策规定的开支范围和开支标准从社会统筹基金中支付给参加基本医疗保险的职工和退休人员的医疗保险待遇支出及其他支出。包括：住院医疗费用支出、门急诊医疗费用支出、其他支出。

4.社会统筹基金结余：指截止报告期末基本医疗保险的社会统筹基金结余金额。包括银行存款、财政专户、债券投资和其他。

失业保险

1.参加保险人数：指报告期末按照国家法律、法规和有关政策规定参加了失业保险的城镇企业事业单位的职工及地方政府规定参加失业保险的其他人员的人数。

2.失业保险金：指为保障失业人员的基本生活而按规定支付的失业保险金金额。保险福利费用总额指各单位在工资以外支付给职工和离休、退休、退职人员个人和用于集体的保险福利费用，不包括用于职工的劳动保护费用，由保险福利费用开支的医务人员工资，集体福利机构工作人员和病伤休息期满 6 个月以上人员的工资。

离休、退休、退职人员保险福利费用包括:

1.离休金：指发给离休干部的工资和按 1982 年国务院《关于老干部离职休养制度的几项规定的通知》发给符合规定的离休干部相当于一至两个月标准工资的生活补贴及 1988 年增发的生活补贴。

2.退休金：指按照国家有关规定发给退休职工的退休费和 1988 年增发的生活补贴。

3.退职生活费：指按照 1978 年国务院《关于工人退休、退职的暂行办法》发给退职人员的生活费用和 1988 年增发的生活补贴。

以上离退休、退职人员的离退休金、退职生活费还应包括发给离退休、退职人员的生活补贴和物价补贴。

4.医疗卫生费：指离休、退休、退职人员的医疗费、住院费以及住院伙食补助等费用。

5.其他：指上述费用以外的其他保险福利费用，如丧葬抚恤救济费、交通费补贴、冬季取暖补贴等。

工业废水排放量　指经过企业厂区所有排放口排到企业外部的工业废水量。包括生产废水、外排的直接冷却水、超标排放的矿井地下水和与工业废水混排的厂区生活污水，不包括外排的间接冷却水(清污不分流的间接冷却水应计算在内)。

工业废水排放达标量　指报告期内废水中各项污染物指标都达到国家或地方排放标准的外排工业废水量，包括未经处理外排达标的，经废水处理设施处理后达标排放的，以及经污水处理厂处理后达标排放的。

工业废水排放达标率　指工业废水排放达标量占工业废水排放量的百分率，计算公式为:

工业废水排放达标率=工业废水排放达标量/工业废水排放量 × 100%

城镇生活污水排放量　指城镇居民每年排放的生活污水。用人均系数法测算。测算公式为:

城镇生活污水排放量=城镇生活污水排放系数+市镇非农业人口 × 365

城镇生活污水中化学需氧量(COD)产生量　指城镇居民每年排放的生活污水中的 COD 的产生量。用人均系数法测算。测算公式为:

城镇生活污水中 COD 产生量=城镇生活污水排放系数+市镇非农业人口 × 365

工业废气排放量　指报告期内企业厂区内燃料燃烧和生产工艺过程中产生的各种排入大气的含有污染物的气体的总量，以标准状态(273K，101325Pa)计算。测算公式为:

废气排放量=燃料燃烧过程中的废气排放量+生产工艺过程中的废气排放量

工业二氧化硫排放量　指报告期内企业在燃料燃烧和生产工艺过程中排入大气的二氧化硫总量。测算公式为:

工业二氧化硫排放量=燃料燃烧过程中二氧化硫排放量+生产工艺过程中二氧化硫排放量

生活及其他二氧化硫排放量　以生活及其他煤炭消费量为基础进行测算。

生活及其他工业烟尘排放量　指企业厂区内燃料燃烧过程中产生的烟气中夹带的颗粒物排放量。

生活及其他烟尘排放量　指除工业生产活动以外的所有社会、经济活动及公共设施的经营活动中燃烧所排放的烟尘纯重量。以生活及其他煤炭消费量为基础进行测算。

工业粉尘排放量　指企业在生产工艺过程中排放的能在空气中悬浮一定时间的固体颗粒物排放量。如钢铁企业的耐火材料粉尘、焦化企业的筛焦系统粉尘、烧结机的粉尘、石灰窑的粉尘、建材企业的水泥粉尘等。不包括电厂排入大气的烟尘。

工业固体废物产生量　指报告期内企业在生产过程中产生的固体状、半固体状和高浓度液体状废弃物的总量，包括危险废物、冶炼废渣、粉煤灰、炉渣、煤矸石、尾矿、放射性废物和其他废物等；不包括矿山开采的剥离废石和掘进废石(煤矸石和呈酸性或碱性的废石除外)。酸性或碱性废石指采掘的废石其流经水、雨淋水的 pH 值小于 4 或 pH 值大于 10.5 者。

危险废物　指列入国家危险废物名录或根据国家规定的危险废物鉴别标准和鉴别方法认定的，具有爆炸性、易燃性、易氧化性、毒性、腐蚀性、易传染疾病等危险特性之一的废物。

工业固体废物综合利用量　指报告期内企业通过回收、加工、循环、交换等方式，从固体废物中提取或者使其转化为可以利用的资源、能源和其他原材料的固体废物量(包括当年利用往年的工业固体废物贮存量)，如用作农业肥料、生产建筑材料、筑路等。综合利用量由原产生固体废物的单位统计。

工业固体废物综合利用率　指工业固体废物综合利用量占工业固体废物产生量(包括综合利用往年贮存量)的百分率。计算公式为:

工业固体废物综合利用率=工业固体废物综合利用量/(工业固体废物产生量+综合利用往年贮存量) × 100%

工业固体废物贮存量　指报告期内企业以综合利用或处置为目的，将固体废物暂时贮存或堆存在专设的贮存设施或专设的集中堆存场所内的数量。专设的固体废物贮存场所或贮存设施必须有防扩散、防流失、防渗漏、防止污染大气、水体的措施。

工业固体废物处置量　指报告期内企业将固体废物焚烧或者最终置于符合环境保护规定要求的场所，并不再回取的工业固体废物量(包括当年处置往年的工业固体废物贮存量)。处置方式有填埋(其中危险废物应安全填埋)、焚烧、专业贮存场(库)封场处理、深层灌注、回填矿井及海洋处置(经海洋管理部门同意投海处置)等。

工业固体废物排放量　指报告期内企业将所产生的固体废物排到固体废物污染防治设施、场所以外的数量，不包括矿山开采的剥离废石和掘进废石(煤矸石和呈酸性或碱性的废石除外)。

"三废"综合利用产品产值　指报告期内利用"三废"作为主要原料生产的产品价值(现行价)；已经销售或准备销售的应计算产品价值，留作生产自用的不应计算产品价值。

环境污染与破坏事故　指由于违反环境保护法规的经济、社会活动与行为，以及意外因素的影响或不可抗拒的自然灾害等原因，致使环境受到污染，国家重点保护的野生动植物、自然保护区受到破坏，人体健康受到危害，社会经济和人民财产受到损失，造成不良社会影响的突发性事件。

自然保护区　指对有代表性的自然生态系统、珍稀濒危野生动植物物种的天然分布区、水源涵养区、有特殊意义的自然历史遗迹等保护对象所在的陆地、陆地水体或海域，依法划出一定面积进行特殊保护和管理的区域。以县及县以上各级人民政府正式批准建立的自然保护区为准(包括"六五"以前由部门或"革委会"批准且现仍存在的自然保护区)。风景名胜区、文物保护区不计在内。自然保护区分国家级、省级、地市级和县级。按主管部门分属：环保、林业、农业、地矿、海洋、水利和其他部门。

Explanatory Notes on Main Statistical Indicators

Number of Athletes in Grades refers to the number of athletes who have been given tit les through examination. The titles of athletes include international masters of sports, masters of sports, first-grade, second- grade and third-grade sportsmen and young athletes. This indicator reflects skill of the athletes.

Number of Referees in Grades refers to the number of referees who have been given tit les after examination. They are classified as international referees, national referees and referees of the first, second and third grades. This indicator reflects the skill of referees.

Stadiums refer to stadiums for track and field events with six lane 400-meter tracks around soccer fields, permanent track marks and permanent bleachers. Stadiums are classified according to seating capaCity. They include: Class A stadiums have the capaCity of seating 25000 people each. Class B stadiums have the capaCity of seating 15000 to 25000 people each. Class C stadiums have the capaCity of s eating 5000 to 15000 people each, and Class D stadiums have the capaCity of seating fewer than 5000 people. This indicator reflects numbers of large and medium-sized stadiums.

Gymnasiums refer to indoor sports grounds with permanent seats in which basketball, volleyball. Badminton, table tennis and gymnastics competitions can be held. Gymnasiums are classified according to seating capaCity. They include: Class Agymnasiums with seating over 6000 people. Class B gymnasiums with seating 4000 to 6000 people. Class Cgymnasiums with seating 2000 to 4000 people, and Class D gymnasiums with eating fewer than 2000 people. This indicator reflects the total number of large and medium-sized gymnasiums Health Care Institutions include: medical institutions, disease prevent ion and control centers (epidemic prevention stations), blood gathering and supplying institutions, health supervision and inspection (checkup) institutions, medicinal scientific research and on-job training institutions, health education and son on.

Medical Organizations include: hospitals, health service centers (stations) of communities, nursing homes, health centers, clinics, clinics (health stations and infirmaries), maternity and child care agencies (centers and stations), special disease prevention and curing agencies (centers and stations), first aid centers (stations) and clinical inspection centers. Medical organizations are grouped by two types: profit- making and non- profit- making medical organizations.

Hospitals include: polyclinics, traditional Chinese medical hospitals, hospitals integrated with traditional Chinese therapeutics and western therapeutics, ethical hospitals, various specialties hospitals and nursing hospitals.

Medical Technical Personnel refers to doctors, assistant nurses, pharmacists, and laboratory technicians working in medical institutions.

Doctors refer to certified physicians and certified assistant physicians with certifications working in medical and health care and prevention agencies.

Total Cost of Health Services reflects the total expenditures on medical and health care services for the whole country, calculated on basis of sources of funding. Health expenditure from government budget refers to budgetary allocation for health undertakings by governments at all levels. Social health expenditure refers to non-government budgetary cap ital input, mainly the health insurance. It includes expenditure on health institutions run by enterprises and rural collective entities, expenditure on medical and health care of employees of enterprises, and excessive health expenditure of government employees that could be covered by the government health care system. Health expenditure on individuals refers to expenditure on health service and health insurance paid by residents from their disposable income.

Social Welfare Institutions refer to institutions taking care of old pople without children, handicapped people and orphans. They include social welfare institutions run by civil affairs departments, children welfare institutions, social welfare institutions for mental patients, collective-owned old peoples homes in rural areas, convalescent homes and community service centers with the capaCity of receiving those people. This indicator reflects the input in social welfare institutions.

Number of People Taken in by Social Welfare Institutions refers to the number of old people, children, totally dependent handicapped people and mental patients taken in by social welfare institutions run by civil affairs departments and those run by collective units in urban and rural areas. This indicator reflects the cap a City of social welfare institutions.

Social Welfare Enterprises are collective owned enterprises which employ the blind, deaf-mute, and other handicapped people who are able to work in cities and towns and enjoy exemption from state taxes, including welfare plants, welfare commercial services, artificial limb plants and farms, etc. This indicator reflects the preferential policies toward disabled persons.

Rural Households with Livelihood Guaranteed in Five Aspects refer to the households in which t here are old people without child, orphans and handicapped people who are unable to work and without financial resources in rural areas. They are taken care of by t he collective units and their food, clothing, housing, medical care, funeral expenses (or schooling for orphans) are guaranteed to be provided for. This indicator reflects the total number of disadvantageous groups of rural population.

Proportion of Deaf Children Enrolled in Ordinary Preschool and Primary Education refers to the proportion of deaf children who are enrolled in ordinary kindergartens or primary schools during the year in the total number of deaf children under rehabilitation programs (not including new comers into the rehabilitation programs during the year). This indicator mainly reflects number of rehabilitated deaf children entering ordinary kindergartens or primary schools.

Number of Mental Patients under Integrated Prevention and Rehabilitation Program refers to mental disease patients receiving integrated prevention and rehabilitation treatment of various forms under open environment in areas with mental disease rehabilitation programs. This indicator reflects the condition of metal patients receiving rehabilitation treatment.

Supervision Rate refers to the percentage of patients among the total number of registered mental disease patients, who participate in social integrated and open treatment and rehabilitation programs through various forms such as supervision groups, family treatment, employment or guidance from psychiatric institutions. This indicator reflects the implementation of various measures aimed at rehabilitating those metal patients.

Social Participation Rate refers to proportion of mental disease patients who are able to manage their daily life and participate in economic activities to the total number of mental disease patients under supervision. This indicator reflects the condition of recovery of those metal patient sand their participation in social activities.

School-age Disabled Children not in Schools refer to children with disability in sight, listening, speaking, mentality, limbs or multi-disability who are obliged to compulsory education by law but have not been enrolled in schools due to various reasons. The definition of school age for disabled children is decided by the definition of school age as specified by provincial governments in line wit h the local laws on compulsory education. This indicator reflects the annual change of school-age disable children not entering schools by various reasons. It will provide foundation for the formulation of development plans of compulsory education for those disable children, and for related principles, policies and measures as well. It is also t he base for the job of funding t hose disabled children back to schools across the countries.

Lawyers are certified legal workers according to law, and who are employed by legal counseling firms to act as legal advisers, agents in criminal or civil lawsuits, or defenders in criminal lawsuits, or to handle non-litigious legal affairs, to advise on matters of law or t o write legal papers for others, and provide service to the public.

Notary Personnel refers to people working for notary offices including: directors, deputy direct or, notaries, assistant notaries, and other people providing assistance.

Notary Documents refer to the judicatory notary documents drawn up by the request of the party and are in accordance with facts and laws and following certain legal proceedings. According to usage and locality, the notary documents are divided into following 4 types: domestic notary documents, domestic economic notary documents, foreign-related civil notary documents and foreign-related economic notary documents.

Mediators refer to workers on peoples mediation committees responsible for mediating in civil disputes and cases of slight infraction of the law. They include members of the mediation committees and mediators of mediation groups. This indicator reflects the number of people engaged in meditation.

Mediation of Civil Disputes refers to number of cases made by mediation committees in mediating in civil disputes concerning civil rights and duties through persuasion and education in accordance wit h t he provisions of law on a voluntary basis, so as t o solve disputes by helping the parties involved come to an agreement and understanding, including those unsuccessful ones. This indicator reflects the workload of the mediation committees.

Acceptance of Case refers t o t he decision made by the people's procurator ate office on reported cases, prosecution, impeachment, surrender, self-found criminal clues or suspects after initial investigation to confirm t he act of crime and to start legal proceedings of the case as criminal case.

Large Case refers to the case involves a corruption or bribery of over 50,000 yuan, or a misappropriation of over 100,000 yuan. Cases of collectively illegal possess ion of public funds, unstated sources of large properties, or disguised overseas savings deposits involving 500,000 yuan, or a case that has been defined by the "Standard on Serious and Large Cases of Misconduct and Tortious that Directly Accepted by People's Procurators Office (try out)". This indicator mainly reflects number of accepted cases of job-related criminals that caused serious economic losses or extremely harmful to the society.

Key Case refers to a case committed by government officials with a ranking of division director or county administrator. This indicator mainly reflects the recorded and spied on cases by the people's procurators offices toward government official with a ranking of division director or county administrator.

Decision on Arrest refers to decision made by people's procurators office, in accordance with laws, to arrest the suspect (s) in the cases that are accepted and to be investigated by procurators office. This indicator mainly reflects the implementation of the decision on arrest by people's procurators office.

Approval for Arrest refers to the decision made by people's procurators office, in accordance with laws and relevant facts, to approve t he arrest of the suspect(s) that is propos ed by the public security departments, state security departments or authority of prisons. This indicator reflects approved arrests made by people's procurators office that are proposed by related departments.

Decision on Prosecution refers to the decision made by people's procurators office, in accordance with laws and relevant facts, to institute proceedings to the people's court against the suspect (s) of criminal cases handed over by the public security departments, state security departments or authority of prisons, or by t he anti-corruption department s within the procurators office. This indicator reflects t he condition of the prosecutions made by people's procurators office toward the people's court.

Number of Labor Dispute Cases Accepted refers to the number of cases of labor dispute submitted that, after being reviewed by the labor dispute arbitration committees in line with the relevant stat e regulations, are accepted and registered or treatment.

Basic Endowment Insurance

1. Number of people participating in the insurance program: by the end of reference period, number of staff and workers participating in the insurance program in line with national laws, regulations and related policies, including those who can not make regular payment or interrupt payment but not terminate the insurance program.

2. Revenue of social comprehensive funds: according to national provision, payments made by units covered in basic endowment insurance program, and income from other resources, including: income of social comprehensive funds paid by unites, financial subsidies, interest income and others.

3. Expenditure of social comprehensive funds: refer to payment made to those retired and resigned people covered in endowment insurance program in terms of pens ion or compensation within the expenditure scope and standards according to related national policies, and the expenditure occurred due to shift of the insurance relationship or adjustment funds among agencies, including: basic pension, transitional pension, pension for

resigned people, pension for retired people, pension for people quitting jobs, subsidies, funeral subsidies and other expenditure.

4. Balance of social comprehensive funds: refer to the balance of basic endowment insurance of social comprehensive funds at the end of the reference period, including: bank savings, special fiscal account, investment in bonds and others.

Retired or Resigned Personnel refers to people who have formally gone through the formalities for their retirement or quitting work and enjoy the corresponding treatments.

Basic Medical Care Insurance:

1. Number of people participated in the insurance program: refer to number of people participated in the basic medical care insurance program according to related regulation by the end of reference period, including: number of staff and workers and retired persons participated in this insurance program.

2. Revenue of social comprehensive funds: according to national provision, payments made by units covered in basic medical care insurance program, and income from other resources, including: income of social comprehensive funds paid by unites, financial subsidies, interest income and others.

3. Expenditure of social comprehensive funds: refer to payment made to those retired and resigned people covered in basic medical care insurance within the expenditure scope and standards according to related national policies, including: expenditure on fee-for-service in hospital, expenditure on fee-for-service in clinic and other expenditure.

4. Balance of social comprehensive funds: refer to the balance of medical care insurance of social comprehensive funds at the end of the reference period, including: bank savings, special fiscal account, investment in bonds and others.

Unemployment Insurance

1. Number of people participated in unemployment insurance program: number of staff and workers in urban enterprises or institutions and other people according to local government regulations participated in unemployment insurance program in line with national law, regulations and related policies by the end of the reference period.

2. Sum of Unemployment Insurance: refer to total amount of insurance paid to un-employees to guarantee their basic lives according to related regulations.

Insurance and Welfare Funds refers to labor insurance and welfare fund paid by enterprises, organizations and institutions to their staff and workers as well as retired and resigned persons in addition to their wages and salaries excluding labor protection fees, wages paid to medical workers from insurance and welfare fund and wages paid to staff members working in collective welfare agencies and to people with over 6 months of sick-leave.

Insurance and Welfare Funds for Retired and Resigned Staff and Workers

1. Pensions for retired veteran cadres: They refer to pensions, other subsidies, and additional allowances paid to retired in line with relevant government documents.

2. Pensions for Retirement: They refer to living allowance; other subsidies and additional allowances paid to retired staff and workers in line with the relevant government documents.

3. Resignation Allowances for Living Expenses: They refer to living allowance, and additional allowances subsidies paid to resigned staff and workers in line with relevant government instructions.

It also includes living subsidies and prices subsidies paid to retired and resigned staff and workers.

4. Medical Care Allowance: refer to fee-for-service, cost of medical care and per diem subsidies during hospitalizations of retired and resigned staff and workers.

5. Others: They refer to other expenses, including other types of insurance and welfare fund, fees for funerals, traveling subsidies and heating subsidies during the winter time.

Volume of Industrial Waste Water Discharged refers to the volume of industrial waste water discharged, through all outlets, to the outside of industrial enterprises, including waste water produced, direct-cooling water, underground water from mines that does not meet t he standard of discharge, and the domes tic sewage mixed up with industrial waste water when discharged, but excluding discharged indirect -cooling water.

Volume of Waste Water up to the Standard for Discharge refers to the volume of discharged industrial wastewater that, with or without treatment, has come up to the national or local standards for discharge.

Ratio of Standard Waste Water Discharged to the Total Discharge: refer to the share of the volume of wastewater up to the standard for discharge of the total volume. The formula is as follows:

Ratio of Standard Waste Water Discharged to the Total Discharge= Volume of Waste Water up to the Standard for Discharge/Volume of Industrial Waste Water Discharged × 100%

Volume of Waste Water Discharged from Urban Daily Life: refer to the wastewater discharged by urban residents each year. Estimated according to per capita coefficient method. The formula is:

Volume of waste water discharged from urban daily life=coefficient of waste water discharged from urban daily life x urban population × 365

Volume of COD from Urban Waste Water: refer to the COD from wastewater discharged by urban residents each year. Estimated according to per capita coefficient method. The formula is:

COD from waste water discharged from urban daily life=coefficient of the COD × urban population × 365

Volume of Waste Industrial Gas Emission refers to waste gas emitted from burning of fuels and from production process in t he area of the factory, and is measured by 10000 standard cubic meters during the reference period under normal condition (273k, 101325Pa). The formula is:

Volume of waste industrial gas emission= waste gas emitted from burning + waste gas emitted from production process

Volume of Industrial Sulphur Dioxide Discharged refers to the volume of sulphur dioxide discharged to the air in the process of fuel burning or in the production process during the reference period. The formula is:

Volume of industrial sulphur dioxide discharged=sulphur dioxide discharged from burning + sulphur dioxide discharged from production process

Volume of Sulphur Dioxide Discharged from Daily

Life: refers to sulphur dioxide discharged from daily life and other coal consumption.

Volume of Industrial Soot Discharged refers to the volume of solid soot in the smoke discharged in the process of fuel burning in the area of the factory.

Volume of Soot Discharged from Daily Life and Others: refer to the net volume of soot discharged from burning of social and economic activities and public facilities other than industrial production activities.

Industrial Dust Discharged refers to the total weight of solid dust discharged by industrial enterprises in the production process during the reference period, such as dust of refractory materials from iron plants, dust from coke-screening system or from sintering machines of coking plants, dust from lime kilns, cement dust from building material enterprises, etc., but excluding smoke and dust discharged by power plants.

Volume of Industrial Sol id Wastes Produced refers to the total volume of solid, semi-solid or high concentration liquid residue produced by industrial enterprises in their production process during the reference period, including dangerous wastes, residues from melting, slag, powdered coal ash, gangue, chemical residues, tailings, radioactive residues and other residues, but excluding stripped or dug stones in mining (except gangue and acid or alkali s tones which are stones washed or soaked by water with a pH value smaller than 4 or larger than 10.5)

Dangerous Wastes refers to the wastes which are listed by the government as the dangerous wastes or the wastes which are explosive, inflammable, oxidizable, poisonous, corrosive or liable to cause infectious diseases or have other dangerous characteristics specified in accordance with the standards or methods stipulated by the government for identifying the dangerous wastes.

Volume of Industrial Solid Wastes Utilized in a Comprehensive Way refers to the volume of solid wastes from which useful materials can be extracted or which can be changed to be utilizable resources, energy or other materials, including the volume of industrial solid wastes stored up in the previous years and utilized in the current year, such as the solid wastes utilized as fertilizers, building materials, for making roads or for other purpose. Statistical data on utilization of industrial solid wastes are collected by solid wastes producing units.

Rate of Industrial Solid Wastes Utilized in a Comprehensive Way: refer to the proportion of the industrial solid wastes utilized in a comprehensive way to the total industrial solid wastes (including stored solid wastes utilized in a comprehensive way in the past years). The formula is:

Rate of Industrial Solid Wastes Utilized in a Comprehensive Way= Industrial Solid Wastes Utilized in a Comprehensive Way/(Volume of Industrial Solid Wastes Produced + stored solid wastes utilized in a comprehensive way in the previous years) × 100

Volume of Industrial Stored up Solid Wastes refers to the volume of industrial solid wastes temporarily stored up or piled with special facilities or piled in the special sites for the purpose of utilization or treatment in future during the reference period. The special facilities or special sites for storing up solid wastes should have t he measures against spreading or being washed away to other places, permeating the soil or causing air pollution or water contamination.

Volume of Industrial Solid Wastes Treated refers to solid wastes disposed of in a non-recoverable place that meet the requirement of environmental protection during the reference period, such as burying (t he dangerous wastes should be buried safely), burning, piling in designated sites, pouring water into the deep strata, filling of old mines, and oceanic treatment (being approved by oceanic management agencies) etc. (including treatment of solid wastes piled up in the previous y ears).

Volume of Industrial Solid Wastes Discharged refers to the volume of industrial solid wastes produced and discharged at the places outside the special facilities or special sites for preventing against pollution, excluding stripped or dugs tones in mining during the reference period (except gangue and acid or alkali waste stones).

Output Value of Products Made from Utilization of Waste Gas, Waste Water and Industrial Solid Wastes refers to the value of products (calculated at current prices) made by industrial enterprises using recovered waste water, waste gas or solid wastes as main raw materials during the reference period. Only the value of t he products, which have been sold or are ready to be sold should be included. The value of t he products, which will be used in the production of the enterprises, should not be included.

Accidents of Environment Pollution and Destruction refer to sudden accidents, due to economic and social behavior or activities in contrast wit h environment protection legislation, unexpected factors or irresistible natural disasters, that cause the pollution of environment, the destruct ion of natural protection zones, wild plants and animals, the danger to the health of people, and the loss in the property of the society and people.

Natural Reserves refer to all the land, water areas on land and sea areas are under special protection or management due to the possess ion of representative natural ecological system, natural distribution of rare and dying out animal zones, water-resource conservation areas, and natural historical relics. Also included are natural reserves formally approved by people's governments at various levels at and above county level (including those approved before the Sixth-five-year Program and still active natural reserves). Scenic spots and historical sites and zones for preservation of cultural relics are not included. Natural reserves are classified as national level, provincial level, prefecture level and county level ones. They are under the jurisdiction of different departments, such as: environment protection, forestry, agriculture, geological and mining, oceanic and water conservancy and so on.

第二十篇

CHAPTER 20

企业集团及企业景气指数

ENTERPRISES GROUP AND ENTERPRISES CLIMATE INDEX

20-1 企业集团主要经济指标
Main Economic Indicators of Enterprise Group

指　　标	Item	2003	2004
农林牧渔业总产值(万元)	Gross Output Value of Farming, Forestry, Animal Husbandry and Fishery (10 000 yuan)	39723	55491
采掘业总产值(万元)	Gross Output Value of Mining and Quarrying (10 000 yuan)	162832	264005
制造业总产值(万元)	Gross Output Value of Manufacturing (10 000 yuan)	2619289	2576184
电力、煤气及水的生产和供应业总产值(万元)	Gross Output Value of Production and Supply of Electric Power, Gas and Water (10 000 yuan)	31623	49825
建筑业总产值(万元)	Gross Output Value of Construction (10 000 yuan)	779762	791928
交通运输业货运量(万吨)	Freight Traffic (10 000 ton)	1822	3343
交通运输业客运量(万人)	Passenger Traffic (10 000 person)	182	2100
批发零售贸易业（万元）	Total Sales of Commodity (10 000 yuan)	1416170	2091219
外贸企业进出口总额(万美元)	Total Exports and Imports (USD 10 000)	13343	6150
#出　口	Exports	6235	4759
从业人员（人）	Employment (person)	183659	203296
在岗职工	Fully-employed Staff and Workers	167725	189575
其他从业人员	Other Employed Persons	15934	13721
从业人员劳动报酬(万元)	Remuneration Payment of Employment (10 000 yuan)	264225	323686
在岗职工	Fully-Employed Staff and Workers	259178	311558
其他从业人员	Other Employed Persons	14590	12128

注：1.2003 年企业集团统计范围包括：由国务院批准的国家试点企业集团和国务院主管部门、自治区人民政府及有关部门、各地州市人民政府及有关部门批准以及年末资产总计、年营业收入均达到 5 亿元以上的各类企业集团。

2. 本表 2003 年数据汇总范围有调整。

Note：a) The statistical coverage of enterprises group in 2003 include the state pilot enterprises groups ratified by the State Council and the enterprises of various types ratified by the government department and the department concerned of autonomous region, prefecture, autonomous prefecture and city with both total assets (year - end) and annual operation income of over 5 hundred million yuan.

b) The data covered in this table for the year 2003 has been subject to change.

20-2　企业集团主要财务指标

Main Indicators in Finance of Enterprises Group

单位：万元　　(2004 年)　　(10 000 yuan)

指　标	Item	单位数(个) Number of Enterprises (unit)	年末资产总计 Total Assets	固定资产原价 Original Value of Fixed Assets	累计折旧 Accumu-Lative Depre-ciation	累计对外投资 Accumulative External Investment
总　计	**Total**	**76**	**10486915**	**4370230**	**1280166**	**327386**
按集团审批部门分	**Grouped by Examining and Approving Department**					
自治区人民政府	Government of Autonomous Region	10	2758589	1406343	458114	75861
自治区政府主管部门	Responsible Government Department of Autonomous Region	30	4368055	1609148	505732	111161
其　他	Others	36	3360271	1354739	316320	140364
按集团主营行业分	**Grouped by Sector of Major Business**					
农、林、牧、渔业	Farming, Forestry, Animal Husbandry and Fishery	4	259741	234006	44922	2919
采掘业	Mining and Quarrying	3	408120	286403	110726	3023
制造业	Manufacturing	23	4242983	2216458	660744	226857
建筑业	Construction	7	981776	246657	73120	26077
运输邮电业	Transportation and Post	7	335729	112811	33652	2312
信息传输、计算机服务和软件业	Message Transmission, Computer and Software Service	1	138841	30164	7489	500
批发和零售贸易业	Wholesale and Retail Trade	13	1842922	449212	138899	50284
住宿和餐饮业	Hotel and Catering	2	129631	61924	11330	2426
房地产业	Real Estate	15	2048228	663946	181925	12988
其　他	Others	1	98944	68649	17359	
按母公司控股情况分	**Grouped by Share-holding Situation of Parent Company**					
国有绝对控股	State-owned Absolutely Holding Shares	25	4181464	2133393	712623	84919
国有相对控股	State-owned Relatively Holding Shares	3	288215	187200	55580	19511
集体绝对控股	Collective-owned Absolutely Holding Shares	9	1270261	218642	71665	26126
集体相对控股	Collective-owned Relatively Holding Shares	1	603414	190830	34470	27439
其　他	Others	38	4143561	1640165	405828	169391
按母公司登记注册类型分	**Grouped by Registration Status and Region of Parent Company**					
国有企业	State-owned	4	139241	69078	21184	1091
国有独资公司	State-owned Exclusive Investment Company	16	2476886	1134817	371628	41920
其他有限责任公司	Other Limited Liability Corporations	48	6183527	2448111	707837	156756
股份有限公司	Share-holding Corporation Ltd.	5	926787	366148	81455	62021
其　他	Others	3	760474	352076	98062	65598
按企业规模分	**Grouped by Size of Enterprises**					
大　型	Large Sized	26	6644111	3150622	967870	173028
中　型	Medium Sized	33	3201238	992429	265504	119457
小　型	Small Sized	15	510153	164442	35930	32512
其　他	Others	2	131413	62737	10862	2389

注：企业集团的财务指标来源于企业集团母公司按财政部门制定的“企业集团合并会计报表”的有关数据，合并会计报表中没有的指标按母公司与各子公司相加汇总的数据。

Note：The data sources of enterprises group financial indicators are obtained by parent company in accordance with Merge Financial Report Forms compiled by the Ministry of Finace, with the indicators excluded from Merge Financial Report Forms according to data collected from parent company and all subsidiary company.

20-2 续表 1 Continued

单位：万元 (10 000 yuan)

指　标	Item	流动资产年平均余额 Average Balance of Circulating Funds	年末负债合计 Total Liabilites at year-end	年末少数股东权益 Year-end Share-holder's Rights in Small Number	年末股东(所有者)权益 Ownership Interest
总　计	**Total**	**4930411**	**6981410**	**596378**	**2909127**
按集团审批部门分	**Grouped by Examining and Approving Department**				
自治区人民政府	Government of Autonomous Region	1216070	1858754	172105	727730
自治区政府主管部门	Responsible Government Department of Autonomous Region	2076678	2912344	227693	1228018
其　他	Others	1637663	2210312	196580	953379
按集团主营行业分	**Grouped by Sector of Major Business**				
农、林、牧、渔业	Farming, Forestry, Animal Husbandry and Fishery	32414	49030	632	210079
采掘业	Mining and Quarrying	129690	178802	204	229114
制造业	Manufacturing	1755920	2828619	329866	1084498
建筑业	Construction	627886	696331	50676	234769
运输邮电业	Transportation and Post	210826	278970	4147	52612
信息传输、计算机服务和软件业	Message Transmission, Computer and Software Service	76471	115230		23611
批发和零售贸易业	Wholesale and Retail Trade	1048256	1521694	35090	286138
住宿和餐饮业	Hotel and Catering	39688	71019	14209	44403
房地产业	Real Estate	1007039	1181532	155126	711570
其　他	Others	2221	60183	6428	32333
按母公司控股情况分	**Grouped by Share-holding Situlation of Parent Company**				
国有绝对控股	State-owned Absolutely Holding Shares	1855775	2841349	222848	1117267
国有相对控股	State-owned Relatively Holding Shares	127188	175581	13016	99618
集体绝对控股	Collective-owned Absolutely Holding Shares	776822	1120908	14259	135094
集体相对控股	Collective-owned Relatively Holding Shares	333651	418102	46685	138627
其　他	Others	1836975	2425470	299570	1418521
按母公司登记注册类型分	**Grouped by Registration Status and Region of Parent Company**				
国有企业	State-owned	43798	111342	2462	25437
国有独资公司	State-owned Exclusive Investment Company	1256918	1720875	67518	688493
其他有限责任公司	Other Limited Liability Corporations	2778359	3927075	411955	1844497
股份有限公司	Share-holding Corporation Ltd.	479042	596493	68739	261555
其　他	Others	372294	625625	45704	89145
按企业规模分	**Grouped by Size of Enterprises**				
大　型	Large Sized	3034315	4240049	424301	1979761
中　型	Medium Sized	1639393	2397654	136385	667199
小　型	Small Sized	222941	266164	22395	221594
其　他	Others	33762	77543	13297	40573

20-2 续表 2 Continued

单位：万元 (10 000 yuan)

指　标	Item	主营业务收入 Majior Business Income	主营业务成本 Cost of Major Business	#主营业务税金及附加 Tax and Addition for Major Business	新产品销售收入 Sales income of new products	出口销售总额 Total Exports
总　计	**Total**	**5583316**	**4582219**	**73284**	**231282**	**265849**
按集团审批部门分	**Grouped by Examining and Approving Department**					
自治区人民政府	Government of Autonomous Region	1555683	1202425	23672	52320	9430
自治区政府主管部门	Responsible Government Department of Autonomous Region	2530327	2159145	25843	7552	162733
其　他	Others	1497306	1220649	23769	171410	93686
按集团主营行业分	**Grouped by Sector of Major Business**					
农、林、牧、渔业	Farming, Forestry, Animal Husbandry and Fishery	29292	20987	160	3240	646
采掘业	Mining and Quarrying	126809	89691	1303		
制造业	Manufacturing	2133908	1621258	18558	220573	235343
建筑业	Construction	613356	530862	19587		
运输邮电业	Transportation and Post	100617	89140	1752		
信息传输、计算机服务和软件业	Message Transmission, Computer and Software Service	75336	61858	1639		
批发和零售贸易业	Wholesale and Retail Trade	1214837	1094391	4200		29206
住宿和餐饮业	Hotel and Catering	33848	18116	1373		169
房地产业	Real Estate	1240168	1045716	24437	7469	485
其　他	Others	15145	10200	275		
按母公司控股情况分	**Grouped by Share- holding Situalion of Parent Company**					
国有绝对控股	State-owned Absolutely Holding Shares	2020483	1551618	31276	52320	15365
国有相对控股	State-owned Relatively Holding Shares	159017	133319	1149		10319
集体绝对控股	Collective-owned Absolutely Holding Shares	915235	839415	5277		18419
集体相对控股	Collective-owned Relatively Holding Shares	367408	295590	1149	165334	19695
其　他	Others	2121173	1762277	34433	13628	202051
按母公司登记注册类型分	**Grouped by Registration Status and Region of Parent Company**					
国有企业	State-owned	32460	27552	1024		
国有独资公司	State-owned Exclusive Investment Company	1123249	928995	18263		7396
其他有限责任公司	Other Limited Liability Corporations	3688290	3037540	49631	65948	165413
股份有限公司	Share-holding Corporation Ltd.	527182	421740	3364	165334	30014
其　他	Others	212135	166392	1002		63026
按企业规模分	**Grouped by Size of Enterprises**					
大　型	Large Sized	3477718	2792519	51967	65865	88366
中　型	Medium Sized	1857151	1598505	16666	165417	177314
小　型	Small Sized	212281	171840	3302		
其　他	Others	36166	19355	1349		169

20-2 续表 3 Continued

单位：万元　　(10 000 yuan)

指标	Item	投资收益 Investment Income	利润总额 Total Profits	应交所得税 Due income tax	应交增值税 Due value-adding tax	固定资产投资完成额 Sum of Completed Investment in Fixed Asset
总　计	**Total**	**-36071**	**156317**	**56323**	**141395**	**521382**
按集团审批部门分	**Grouped by Examining and Approving Department**					
自治区人民政府	Government of Autonomous Region	-20892	74069	21807	92170	178324
自治区政府主管部门	Responsible Government Department of Autonomous Region	8457	93000	20347	29261	209508
其　他	Others	-23636	-10752	14169	19964	133550
按集团主营行业分	**Grouped by Sector of Major Business**					
农、林、牧、渔业	Farming, Forestry, Animal Husbandry and Fishery	755	1165	2	36	3340
采掘业	Mining and Quarrying	-3462	3156	4160	10798	26189
制造业	Manufacturing	-50586	50105	27976	114837	280530
建筑业	Construction	3724	24184	5253	1185	19908
运输邮电业	Transportation and Post	76	-522	347	-547	7026
信息传输、计算机服务和软件业	Message Transmission, Computer and Software Service	3	-7240	52	523	
批发和零售贸易业	Wholesale and Retail Trade	8086	20038	4565	6861	37253
住宿和餐饮业	Hotel and Catering	1155	2954	221	774	
房地产业	Real Estate	2719	61786	13576	6387	140207
其　他	Others	1459	691	171	541	6929
按母公司控股情况分	**Grouped by Share-holding Situation of Parent Company**					
国有绝对控股	State-owned Absolutely Holding Shares	-20270	90281	28556	118938	222130
国有相对控股	State-owned Relatively Holding Shares	908	2997	1248	6250	15032
集体绝对控股	Collective-owned Absolutely Holding Shares	6792	15034	1202	10	5927
集体相对控股	Collective-owned Relatively Holding Shares	2588	18665	4959	5710	4767
其　他	Others	-26089	29340	20358	10487	273526
按母公司登记注册类型分	**Grouped by Registration Status and Region of Parent Company**					
国有企业	State-owned	-38	-2102	86	80	4454
国有独资公司	State-owned Exclusive Investment Company	-3749	43081	9961	37743	75973
其他有限责任公司	Other Limited Liability Corporations	-2851	155786	38698	95282	350199
股份有限公司	Share-holding Corporation Ltd.	6833	22935	6571	9861	13760
其　他	Others	-36266	-63383	1007	-1571	76996
按企业规模分	**Grouped by Size of Enterprises**					
大　型	Large Sized	-50896	102325	44298	123062	441952
中　型	Medium Sized	9551	39342	9815	16386	73389
小　型	Small Sized	4119	11220	2003	1174	6041
其　他	Others	1155	3430	207	773	

20-3 企业家信心指数

Entrepreneur Confidence Index

单位：%　　(2004 年)　　(%)

经济类型及行业	Ownership and Sector	一季度 First Quarter		二季度 Second Quarter	
		本期实际 Index	比上年同期增减 as±of Last Same Period Index	本期实际 Index	比上年同期增减 as±of Last Same Period Index
企业家信心指数	**Entrepreneur Confidence Index**	**125.6**	**4.2**	**124.5**	**12.8**
按企业登记注册类型分	**Grouped by Status of Registration**				
国有企业	State-owned Enterprises	118.9	6.5	127.6	25.7
集体企业	Collective-owned Enterprises	106.9	-3.9	93.1	12.0
股份合作企业	Share Holding	133.3	16.6	133.3	13.3
有限责任公司	Limited-Liability Corporations	121.0	4.7	114.0	9.3
股份有限公司	Share Holding Corporations Ltd.	165.1	8.5	152.2	2.7
私营企业	Private Enterprises	133.5	-1.9	123.3	9.3
外商及港澳台投资企业	Foreign, Hogkong, Macao and Taiwan Funded	125.0	10.7	125.0	39.3
按行业分	**Grouped by Sector**				
工　业	Industry	130.1	2.8	132.2	8.4
建筑业	Construction	108.1	0.4	111.9	7.6
交通运输、仓储和邮政业	Transportation,Storage,Posts and Telecommunications	127.8	6.8	124.1	31.5
批发和零售业	Wholesale,Retail and Catering	129.1	8.8	113.2	5.3
房地产业	Real Estate	133.1	38.8	112.6	5.5
社会服务业	Social Services	144.5	2.8	116.2	30.1
信息传输、计算机服务和软件业	Information Transmission, Computer Servcie and Software Industries	146.2	8.4	150.6	-5.8
住宿和餐饮业	Hotel and Eateries	109.1	4.4	118.2	76.3
按企业规模分	**Grouped by Size of Enterprises**				
大　型	Large Enterprises	154.4	2.6	156.1	15.8
中　型	Medium	124.7	12.0	116.0	10.2
小　型	Small	117.7	4.7	114.6	17.8
按特殊群体分	**Grouped by Special Group**				
乡镇企业	Town and Township Enterprises	108.0	-14.4	125.4	-3.2
上市公司	Listed Companies	168.2	8.6	161.9	9.8
国有控股企业	State-Owned Holding Enterprise	128.3	10.2	130.0	18.6

20-3 续表 Continued

单位：%　　　　(%)

经济类型及行业	Ownership and Sector	三季度 Third Quarter		四季度 Fourth Quarter	
		本期实际 Index	比上年同期增减 as±of Last Same Period Index	本期实际 Index	比上年同期增减 as±of Last Same Period Index
企业家信心指数	**Entrepreneur Confidence Index**	**125.2**	**0.1**	**123.4**	**-1.2**
按企业登记注册类型分	**Grouped by Status of Registration**				
国有企业	State-owned Enterprises	129.7	7.8	121.0	2.1
集体企业	Collective-owned Enterprises	110.3	10.3	96.6	-3.4
股份合作企业	Share Holding	133.3	-6.7	133.3	13.3
有限责任公司	Limited-Liability Corporations	112.9	-5.6	116.5	-5.2
股份有限公司	Share Holding Corporations Ltd.	153.2	-8.8	144.6	-12.0
私营企业	Private Enterprises	131.9	10.3	126.4	-0.1
外商及港澳台投资企业	Foreign,Hogkong,Macao and Taiwan Funded	137.5	23.2	125.0	20.2
按行业分	**Grouped by Sector**				
工　业	Industry	129.4	5.0	131.2	3.6
建筑业	Construction	104.3	-15.8	106.8	-4.9
交通运输、仓储和邮政业	Transportation,Storage, Posts and Telecommunications	135.3	6.6	130.8	-0.6
批发和零售业	Wholesale,Retail and Catering	117.7	-5.2	109.2	-19.8
房地产业	Real Estate	122.8	15.7	122.8	13.1
社会服务业	Social Services	136.8	2.5	121.5	-21.2
信息传输、计算机服务和软件业	Information Transmission,Computer Servcie and Software Industries	158.5	-7.5	166.6	19.2
住宿和餐饮业	Hotel and Eateries	136.4	13.1	97.6	4.6
按企业规模分	**Grouped by Size of Enterprises**				
大　型	Large Enterprises	154.0	0.2	144.9	-7.4
中　型	Medium	124.9	4.0	120.7	-1.0
小　型	Small	116.1	0.7	115.2	0.7
按特殊群体分	**Grouped by Special Group**				
乡镇企业	Town and Township Enterprises	121.0	-7.6	125.4	-0.2
上市公司	Listed Companies	158.8	-2.9	153.6	-1.6
国有控股企业	State-Owned Holding Enterprise	133.7	6.7	127.5	1.4

20-4　企业景气指数

Enterprises Business Climate Index

单位：%　　　　(2004 年)　　　　(%)

经济类型及行业	Ownership and Sector	一季度 First Quarter		二季度 Second Quarter	
		本期实际 Index	比上年同期增减 as±of Last Same Period Index	本期实际 Index	比上年同期增减 as±of Last Same Period Index
企业景气指数	**Enterprises Business Climate Index**	**115.7**	**2.4**	**121.1**	**14.8**
按企业登记注册类型分	**Grouped by Status of Registration**				
国有企业	State-owned Enterprises	113.1	7.2	124.8	35.5
集体企业	Collective-owned Enterprises	96.6	-3.8	82.8	-20.3
股份合作企业	Share Holding	133.3	16.6	166.7	46.7
有限责任公司	Limited-Liability Corporations	119.6	5.8	112.6	1.2
股份有限公司	Share Holding Corporations Ltd.	144.4	-15.3	156.0	12.2
私营企业	Private Enterprises	121.3	-8.6	119.4	25.1
外商及港澳台投资企业	Foreign, Hogkong, Macao and Taiwan Funded	108.3	17.8	120.8	54.1
按行业分	**Grouped by Sector**				
工　业	Industry	117.5	0.7	123.3	3.5
建筑业	Construction	95.1	5.0	112.5	12.0
交通运输、仓储和邮政业	Transportation,Storage, Posts and Telecommunications	125.0	4.8	119.6	51.7
批发和零售业	Wholesale Retail and Catering	128.5	7.8	112.5	2.5
房地产业	Real Estate	130.6	2.4	148.6	22.4
社会服务业	Social Services	137.0	11.3	125.3	46.1
信息传输、计算机服务和软件业	Information Transmission, Computer Servcie and Software Industries	150.9	2.7	151.9	-2.0
住宿和餐饮业	Hotel and Eateries	86.4	-9.0	120.5	94.9
按企业规模分	**Grouped by Size of Enterprises**				
大　型	Large Enterprises	147.4	-2.0	149.8	22.0
中　型	Medium	119.9	12.6	118.8	12.2
小　型	Small	106.2	-1.1	113.4	21.1
按特殊群体分	**Grouped by Special Group**				
乡镇企业	Town and Township Enterprises	108.0	-4.8	125.4	3.1
上市公司	Listed Companies	150.9	-9.4	163.9	11.2
国有控股企业	State-Owned Holding Enterprise	118.3	4.1	127.7	22.4
按观察指标分	**Grouped by Indicator Observed**				
生　产	Production (Operation)	98.6	0.4	134.7	19.4
盈利(亏损)变化	Changes of Profit(Loss)	93.5	2.0	119.0	29.6
流动资金	Funds	72.0	3.9	67.7	2.9
货款拖欠	Paymeny for Goods in Arrears	111.1	-1.1	99.2	6.2
劳动力需求	Demond on Labors	86.4	2.3	110.7	10.1
固定资产投资	Investment	94.7	-1.2	113.5	-6.4

20-4 续表 Continued

单位：% (%)

经济类型及行业	Ownership and Sector	三季度 Third Quarter		四季度 Fourth Quarter	
		本期实际 Index	比上年同期增减 as±of Last Same Period Index	本期实际 Index	比上年同期增减 as±of Last Same Period Index
企业景气指数	**Enterprises Business Climate Index**	**126.9**	**1.3**	**120.0**	**-2.5**
按企业登记注册类型分	**Grouped by Status of Registration**				
国有企业	State-owned Enterprises	130.2	10.9	119.2	1.3
集体企业	Collective-owned Enterprises	89.7	-18.4	93.1	-17.7
股份合作企业	Share Holding	183.3	43.3	200.0	60.0
有限责任公司	Limited-Liability Corporations	122.8	-2.8	115.1	-8.1
股份有限公司	Share Holding Corporations Ltd.	149.8	-15.6	143.9	-13.2
私营企业	Private Enterprises	131.9	6.1	125.0	-3.2
外商及港澳台投资企业	Foreign,Hogkong ,Macao and Taiwan Funded	116.7	2.4	95.8	10.1
按行业分	**Grouped by Sector**				
工　业	Industry	127.5	4.2	122.7	-4.8
建筑业	Construction	109.4	-8.9	110.2	5.2
交通运输、仓储和邮政业	Transportation, Storage, Posts and Telecommunications	136.4	6.6	125.0	-1.6
批发和零售业	Wholesale, Retail and Catering	116.3	-7.3	116.6	-5.9
房地产业	Real Estate	140.9	10.1	125.5	-10.4
社会服务业	Social Services	152.2	5.4	133.0	-8.7
信息传输、计算机服务和软件业	Information Transmission,Computer Servcie and Software Industries	159.2	-6.5	163.0	9.4
住宿和餐饮业	Hotel and Eateries	154.6	22.0	83.3	-2.8
按企业规模分	**Grouped by Size of Enterprises**				
大　型	Large Enterprises	149.2	-3.4	145.1	-9.9
中　型	Medium	126.5	-1.4	122.3	0.6
小　型	Small	121.8	8.6	107.9	-1.1
按特殊群体分	**Grouped by Special Group**				
乡镇企业	Town and Township Enterprises	112.3	-21.0	116.7	-7.1
上市公司	Listed Companies	151.8	-12.8	155.8	-10.3
国有控股企业	State-Owned Holding Enterprise	133.6	5.5	127.6	4.0
按观察指标分	**Grouped by Indicator Observed**				
生　产	Production(Operation)	132.8	0.9	100.8	-1.8
盈利（亏损）变化	Changes of Profit (Loss)	120.7	2.2	109.0	8.5
流动资金	Funds	69.7	3.5	66.3	-0.3
货款拖欠	Paymeny for Goods in Arrears	97.0	2.4	100.6	-1.0
劳动力需求	Demond on Labors	112.0	2.2	77.5	-4.5
固定资产投资	Investment	116.7	-1.3	101.8	2.3

主要统计指标解释

企业集团：是以母子公司为主体，通过投资及生产经营协作等多种方式，与众多的企事业单位共同组成的经济联合体。

母 公 司：是企业集团中起主导作用的核心企业，通过投资和生产经营协作等多种联结纽带，决定和影响着集团内其他成员企业，是居于控制地位的控股公司。

所属成员企业(单位)：指企业集团所属的成员企事业单位，包括企业集团的母公司、全资子公司(单位)、绝对控股子公司(单位)、相对控股子公司(单位),不包括参股企业、协作企业(单位)。但如果企业集团的子公司(单位)是一个纯粹管理型的公司,那么该子公司的二级控股子公司(单位)可作为企业集团所属成员单位进行统计。上述企业集团的各类子公司(单位)中应包括在中国境内和境外的子公司(单位)。

登记注册类型：是指在工商行政管理机关登记注册的具有法人资格的各类企业。包括国有企业、国有独资公司、其他有限责任公司、股份有限公司、中外合资企业、港澳台合资企业、其它。

国有企业：是指企业全部资产归国家所有,并按《中华人民共和国企业法人登记管理条例》规定登记注册的非公司制的经济组织。不包括有限责任公司中的国有独资公司。

国有独资公司：是指国家授权的投资机构或者国家授权的部门单独投资设立的有限责任公司。

其他有限责任公司：是指根据《中华人民共和国公司登记管理条例》规定登记注册,由两个以上,五十个以下的股东共同出资,每个股东以其所认缴的出资额对公司承担有限责任,公司以其全部资产对其债务承担责任的经济组织。其他有限责任公司不包括国有独资公司。

股份有限公司：是指根据《中华人民共和国公司登记管理条例》规定登记注册,其全部注册资本由等额股份构成并通过发行股票筹集资本,股东以其认购的股份对公司承担有限责任,公司以其全部资产对其债务承担责任的经济组织。

中外合资企业：是指外国企业或外国人与中国内地企业依照《中华人民共和国中外合资经营企业法》及有关法律的规定，按合同规定的比例投资设立，分享利润和分担风险的企业。

港澳台合资企业：是指港澳台地区投资者与内地企业依照《中华人民共和国中外合资经营企业法》及有关法律的规定，按规定的比例投资设立，分享利润和分担风险的企业。

少数股东权益：指子公司所有者权益中由母公司以外的其他投资者拥有的份额,在合并资产负债表中应单独列示。

股东(所有者)权益合计：指企业集团投资人对企业净资产的所有权,企业集团净资产等于企业集团全部资产减去负债合计和少数股东权益后的余额,其中包括企业投资人对企业的最初投入以及资本公积金、盈余公积金和未分配利润。

股本(实收资本)：指股份制企业集团以发行股票的方式筹集的资本。非股份制企业集团指实际收到的投资人投入的资本。

主营业务收入：指企业集团从事某种主要生产、经营活动所取得的营业收入。本项指标在各行业会计制度中的名称叫法不同,但一律按各行业会计制度或报表定义的口径进行填报。农业企业是指“主营业务收入”；工业企业是指“产品销售收入”；交通运输企业指“主营业务收入”；建筑企业指“工程结算收入”；批发零售贸易企业指“商品销售收入”；房地产企业指“房地产经营收入”；其他企业指“经营(营业)收入”。

从业人员：指在企业集团(包括母公司和子公司)工作并领取工资或其他形式的劳动报酬的全部人员数,包括在岗职工、再就业的离退休人员以及在企业集团中工作的外方人员和港澳台方人员、兼职人员、借用的外单位人员和第二职业者。不包括离开本企业集团仍保留劳动关系的职工。

企业景气调查：是通过对部分企业家定期进行问卷调查，并根据企业家对企业经营状况及宏观经济形势的判断和预期来编制景气指数，从而对现实经济运行状况及其发展趋势进行分析和预测的一种统计调查方法。

景气指数：又称为景气度，它是对企业景气调查中的定性指标通过定量方法加工汇总，综合反映某一特定调查群体或某一社会经济现象所处的状态或发展趋势的一种指标。通过其上升和下降的动态变化，反映经济发展状态及其变化过程。景气指数取值于 0--200 之间，100 为景气指数的临界值；当景气指数大于 100 时，表明经济状况趋于上升或改善，处于景气状态；当景气指数小于 100 时，表明经济状况趋于下降或恶化，处于不景气状态。

企业家信心指数：也称宏观经济景气指数，是根据企业家对企业外部市场经济环境与宏观政策的认识、看法、判断与预期而编制的指数，用以综合反映企业家对宏观经济环境的感受与信心。

企业景气指数：也称企业综合生产经营景气指数，是根据企业家对本企业综合生产经营情况的判断与预期而编制的指数，用以反映企业的综合生产经营状况。

Explanatory Notes on Main Statistical Indicators

Enterprises Group an economic association consists of numerous enterprises and institution, with parent company and subsidiary company as its main body, they join together by means of various methods, investment and business cooperation, etc.

Parent Company the nuclear enterprise, which plays a leading role in enterprises group. It occupies the holding company position, determines and affects other members of group by various ties of join, investment and business cooperation, etc.

Subordinate Enterprises (Units) refer to enterprises and institutions under enterprises group, include parent company of enterprises group, subsidiary companies(units) with exclusive investment, absolutely holding shares companies(units), relatively holding shares companies(units), exclude own shares enterprises, cooperate enterprises(units), If the subsidiary company(unit) is a pure management company, the companies(units) under the subsidiary company can be statistics as subordinate enterprises(units). The above-mention subsidiary company (units) include all companies those within and out of the boundaries of China.

Registration Status of Enterprises refer to different enterprises, which have registered in industrial and commercial administration agencies. Include state-owned enterprises, Sole State-Funded enterprises, other limited liability corporation, share-holding corporation Ltd. Joint-venture enterprises with foreign investment, Joint-venture enterprises with funds from Hong Kong, Macao and Taiwan, and Others.

State-owned Enterprises refer to non-corporation economic units where the entire assets are owned by the state and which have registered in accordance with the Regulation of the People's Republic of China on the Management of Registration of Corporation Enterprises. Excluded from this category are sole state-funded corporation in the limited liability corporations.

Exclusive State-Funded Company refer to limited liability corporations established with exclusive investment from investment institutions or departments authorized by the state.

Other Limited Liability Corporations refer to economic units established with investment from 2-50 investors and registered in accordance with the Regulation of the People's Republic of China on the Management of Registration of Corporations, each investor bearing limited liability to the corporation depending on its share of investment, and the corporation bearing liability to its debt to the maximum of its total assets. Excluded from this category are exclusive state-funded corporations.

Share-holding Corporations Ltd. Refer to economic units registered in accordance with the Regulation of the People's Republic of China on the Management of Registration of Corporations, with total registered capitals divided into equal shares and raised through issuing stocks. Each investor bears limited liability to the corporation depending on the holding shares, and the corporation bears liability to its debt to the maximum of its total assets.

Joint-venture Enterprises with Foreign Investment refer to enterprises jointly established by foreign enterprises or foreigners with enterprises in the mainland of China in accordance with the Low of the People's Republic of China on Sino-foreign Joint Venture Enterprises and other relevant lows, where the share of investment, profits and risks is stipulated in the contract.

Joint-venture Enterprises with Funds from Hong Kong, Macao and Taiwan refer to enterprises jointly established by investor from Hong Kong, Macao and Taiwan with enterprises in the mainland of China in accordance with the Low of the People's Republic of China on Sino-foreign Joint Venture Enterprises and other relevant lows, where the share of investment, profits and risks is stipulated in the contract.

Minority Share-holder's Equity refer to the owner shares of subsidiary company which not owned to parent company but to other investors, it must be arranged independently on merge balance sheet.

Total of Share-holder's (or Owner's) equity refer to enterprises group investor's title to net funds, the balance of total liabilities and minority share-holding equity from entire funds is net funds, it includes initial investment, accumulation fund, surplus of accumulation and undistributed profits.

Capital Stock (Capital Obtained) refer to capital raised through issuing stocks by the joint-stock enterprises group. It refers to capital actually received from investors in non-joint-stock enterprises group.

Major Business Revenue refer to the revenue earned from certain major action of production and management by enterprises group. This indicator has different account name in various sectors, but it must be filled and submitted in accordance with account system of various sector, or the concepts, definitions and coverage of report schedule. It refers to major business revenue in agriculture enterprises; It refers to production sales revenue in industry enterprises; It refers to major business revenue in transport enterprises; It refers to revenue of project settle accounts in construction; It refers to commodity sales revenue in wholesale and retail trade enterprises; It refers to real estate operation revenue in real estate trade enterprises, In other enterprises It refers to business revenue.

Employed Persons refer to all persons who work in ,and receive wages or other remuneration payment from enterprises group(include parent company and subsidiary company), they include fully employed staff and workers, re-employed retirees, foreigners and Chinese compatriots from Hong Kong, Macao and Taiwan part-time employees, employees of other units working temporarily at current posts, and employees holding the second job, but exclude staff and workers who have left their work units while keeping their labour contract (employment relation) unchanged.

Enterprises Climate Survey It is a statistics survey, which compile the climate index by regular paper survey to a section of entrepreneurs, based on entrepreneur's judgement and forecast to the production situation of their own enterprises and the macro-economy situation, and thus we can analyse and predict the current situation and future trend of the economic performance.

Business climate index It is the quantitative disposition and compilation of the qualitative economic indicators of the business climate survey, which can improve a comprehensive description of the real situation or the future trend of a special survey group or a social and economic phenomenon. The business climate index is ranging from 0 to 200. 100 is the critical value, when the climate index is larger than 100, it shows that the economic performance is picking up or improving. When it is lower than 100, it shows that the economic performance is declining or worsening.

Entrepreneur confidence index also called as the macro-economy climate index. It is a index based on entrepreneur's recognition, opinion, judgement and forecast to the market circumstances and macro-policies, It is a comprehensive description of the entrepreneur's impression and confidents of the macro-economy circumstances .

Business climate index also called as the comprehensive production and management climate index of enterprises. It is compiled basing on entrepreneur's judgement on production situation of their own expectation for the future performance. It is the description of the comprehensive production and management situation of the enterprises.

第二十一篇

CHAPTER 21

各地州市主要经济指标排序

RANKING OF MAIN ECONOMIC INDICATORS BY REGION OF XINJIANG

21-1 各地、州、市地区生产总值

Gross Domestic Product by Prefecture, Autonomous Prefecture and City

单位：万元 （2004 年） (10 000 yuan)

地　区	Region	地区生产总值 Gross Domestic Product	位次 Rank	人均地区生产总值（元） Per-Capital GDP (Yuan)	位次 Rank
乌鲁木齐市	Urumqi city	4842599	1	22820	2
克拉玛依市	Karamay city	2962019	2	66674	1
石河子市	Shihezi city	446120	12	15016	5
吐鲁番地区	Turpan Administrative Offices	972095	9	16887	4
哈密地区	Hami [Kumul] Administrative Offices	523636	11	9965	8
昌吉回族自治州	Changji Hui Autonomous Prefecture	2119163	4	12910	6
伊犁哈萨克自治州	Ili Kazak Autonomous Prefecture	3190201		7544	
伊犁州直属县(市)	Counties (Cities) Direct Under Ili Prefecture	1368108	6	5754	12
塔城地区	Tacheng [Tarbagatai] Administrative Offices	1296213	7	9992	7
阿勒泰地区	Altay Administrative Offices	525880	10	9492	9
博尔塔拉州	Bortala Mongol Autonomous Prefecture	386626	14	8554	10
巴音郭楞蒙古自治州	Bayangol Mongol Autonomous Prefecture	2294733	3	19620	3
阿克苏地区	Aksu Administrative Offices	1535741	5	6771	11
克孜勒苏柯尔克孜自治州	Kizilsu Kirgiz Autonomous Prefecture	143312	15	3054	14
喀什地区	Kashgar [Kaxgar] Administrative Offices	1195550	8	3497	13
和田地区	Hotan Administrative Offices	429831	13	2445	15

地　区	Region	第一产业增加值 Primary Industry	位次 Rank	第二产业增加值 Secondary Industry	位次 Rank	第三产业增加值 Tertiary Industry	位次 Rank
乌鲁木齐市	Urumqi city	70874	12	1868707	2	2903018	1
克拉玛依市	Karamay city	8374	15	2591811	1	361834	8
石河子市	Shihezi city	42235	14	188681	11	215204	11
吐鲁番地区	Turpan Administrative Offices	109903	10	643555	5	218637	10
哈密地区	Hami [Kumul] Administrative Offices	93097	11	190362	10	240177	9
昌吉回族自治州	Changji Hui Autonomous Prefecture	643207	1	880995	4	594961	2
伊犁哈萨克自治州	Ili Kazak Autonomous Prefecture	1052106		1009560		1128535	
伊犁州直属县(市)	Counties (Cities) Direct Under Ili Prefecture	406024	5	486416	6	475668	5
塔城地区	Tacheng [Tarbagatai] Administrative Offices	479174	4	340624	8	476415	4
阿勒泰地区	Altay Administrative Offices	166908	8	182520	12	176452	12
博尔塔拉州	Bortala Mongol Autonomous Prefecture	157060	9	79195	13	150371	14
巴音郭楞蒙古自治州	Bayangol Mongol Autonomous Prefecture	403318	6	1450017	3	441398	7
阿克苏地区	Aksu Administrative Offices	580375	2	373415	7	581951	3
克孜勒苏柯尔克孜自治州	Kizilsu Kirgiz Autonomous Prefecture	43185	13	28926	15	71201	15
喀什地区	Kashgar [Kaxgar] Administrative Offices	528772	3	220993	9	445785	6
和田地区	Hotan Administrative Offices	197609	7	75710	14	156512	13

21-2 各地、州、市人口状况

Population Status by Prefecture, Autonomous Prefecture and City

(2004 年)

地区	Region	总人口(万人) Total (10 000 person)	位次 Rank	城镇人口(万人) Urban Population (10 000 person)	位次 Rank
乌鲁木齐市	Urumqi City	185.96	4	182.26	1
克拉玛依市	Karamay City	25.39	15	25.39	15
石河子市	Shihezi City	64.29	9	64.29	8
吐鲁番地区	Turpan Administrative Offices	57.97	11	41.44	11
哈密地区	Hami [Kumul] Administrative Offices	52.60	12	45.93	10
昌吉回族自治州	Changji Hui Autonomous Prefecture	156.44	6	123.93	4
伊犁哈萨克自治州	Ili Kazak Autonomous Prefecture	414.58		228.32	
伊犁州直属县(市)	Counties (Cities) Direct Under Ili Prefecture	255.65	2	126.66	3
塔城地区	Tacheng [Tarbagatai] Administrative Offices	96.63	8	67.43	7
阿勒泰地区	Altay Administrative Offices	62.30	10	34.22	12
博尔塔拉州	Bortala Mongol Autonomous Prefecture	45.20	14	31.50	13
巴音郭楞蒙古自治州	Bayangol Mongol Autonomous Prefecture	114.85	7	71.31	6
阿克苏地区	Aksu Administrative Offices	222.77	3	139.99	2
克孜勒苏柯尔克孜自治州	Kizilsu Kirgiz Autonomous Prefecture	46.81	13	26.54	14
喀什地区	Kashgar [Kaxgar] Administrative Offices	361.54	1	112.69	5
和田地区	Hotan Administrative Offices	177.21	5	48.31	9

地区	Region	乡村人口(万人) Rural Population (10 000 person)	位次 Rank	人口自然增长率(‰) Illiterate and Semi-Iliterate Population (‰)	位次 Rank
乌鲁木齐市	Urumqi City	3.70	13	2.59	14
克拉玛依市	Karamay City			4.05	13
石河子市	Shihezi City			2.23	15
吐鲁番地区	Turpan Administrative Offices	16.52	10	10.41	4
哈密地区	Hami [Kumul] Administrative Offices	6.67	12	5.81	12
昌吉回族自治州	Changji Hui Autonomous Prefecture	32.51	6	6.96	11
伊犁哈萨克自治州	Ili Kazak Autonomous Prefecture	186.26		10.99	
伊犁州直属县(市)	Counties (Cities) Direct Under Ili Prefecture	128.99	2	12.29	2
塔城地区	Tacheng [Tarbagatai] Administrative Offices	29.19	7	8.11	8
阿勒泰地区	Altay Administrative Offices	28.08	8	10.11	6
博尔塔拉州	Bortala Mongol Autonomous Prefecture	13.70	11	9.68	7
巴音郭楞蒙古自治州	Bayangol Mongol Autonomous Prefecture	43.53	5	7.33	10
阿克苏地区	Aksu Administrative Offices	82.77	4	10.23	5
克孜勒苏柯尔克孜自治州	Kizilsu Kirgiz Autonomous Prefecture	20.27	9	7.37	9
喀什地区	Kashgar [Kaxgar] Administrative Offices	248.85	1	10.72	3
和田地区	Hotan Administrative Offices	128.89	3	12.37	1

注：全区城镇、乡村人口按“五普”口径计算，其余的按公安年报口径计算。

Note: The urban and rural population in Xinjiang are calculated on the 5th National population census, Others are calculated on the annals of public security.

21-3 各地、州、市固定资产投资

Investmment in Fixed Assets by Prefecture, Autonomous Prefecture and City

单位：万元　　(2004 年)　　(10 000 yuan)

地　区	Region	固定资产投资 Total Investment in Fixed Assets	位次 Rank	基本建设投资 Capital Construction	位次 Rank
乌鲁木齐市	Urumqi City	2066810	1	1015845	3
克拉玛依市	Karamay City	1250936	3	1148828	2
石河子市	Shihezi City	262875	11	186707	11
吐鲁番地区	Turpan Administrative Offices	426121	8	359380	8
哈密地区	Hami [Kumul] Administrative Offices	188604	13	129950	13
昌吉回族自治州	Changji Hui Autonomous Prefecture	829589	4	481333	5
伊犁哈萨克自治州	Ili Kazak Autonomous Prefecture	1318709		986534	
伊犁州直属县(市)	Counties (Cities) Direct Under Ili Prefecture	639878	6	448649	6
塔城地区	Tacheng [Tarbagatai] Administrative Offices	410719	9	298815	9
阿勒泰地区	Altay Administrative Offices	268112	10	239070	10
博尔塔拉州	Bortala Mongol Autonomous Prefecture	158681	14	105008	14
巴音郭楞蒙古自治州	Bayangol Mongol Autonomous Prefecture	1586819	2	1288439	1
阿克苏地区	Aksu Administrative Offices	688063	5	437100	7
克孜勒苏柯尔克孜自治州	Kizilsu Kirgiz Autonomous Prefecture	76658	15	58283	15
喀什地区	Kashgar [Kaxgar] Administrative Offices	614033	7	482521	4
和田地区	Hotan Administrative Offices	204771	12	184308	12

地　区	Region	更新改造投资 Innovation	位次 Rank	房地产开发投资 Real Estate Development	位次 Rank
乌鲁木齐市	Urumqi City	498755	1	453420	1
克拉玛依市	Karamay City	12027	13	88877	6
石河子市	Shi Hezi City	43053	8	30599	7
吐鲁番地区	Turpan Administrative Offices	55569	7	4876	15
哈密地区	Hami [Kumul] Administrative Offices	33030	10	20783	9
昌吉回族自治州	Changji Hui Autonomous Prefecture	181350	2	102802	3
伊犁哈萨克自治州	Ili Kazak Autonomous Prefecture	166213		123144	
伊犁州直属县(市)	Counties (Cities) Direct Under Ili Prefecture	67666	6	99503	4
塔城地区	Tacheng [Tarbagatai] Administrative Offices	81850	5	16675	11
阿勒泰地区	Altay Administrative Offices	16697	11	6966	14
博尔塔拉州	Bortala Mongol Autonomous Prefecture	13535	12	20511	10
巴音郭楞蒙古自治州	Bayangol Mongol Autonomous Prefecture	125186	4	138713	2
阿克苏地区	Aksu Administrative Offices	128152	3	93835	5
克孜勒苏柯尔克孜自治州	Kizilsu Kirgiz Autonomous Prefecture			12421	12
喀什地区	Kashgar [Kaxgar] Administrative Offices	34833	9	28282	8
和田地区	Hotan Administrative Offices	6528	14	7314	13

21-4　各地、州、市农林牧渔业总产值

Gross Output Value of Farming, Forestry, Animal Husbandry and Fishery by Prefecture, Autonomous Prefecture and City

单位：万元　(2004 年)　(10 000 yuan)

地　区	Region	农林牧渔业总产值 Total	位次 Rank	农业产值 Farming	位次 Rank	林业产值 Forestry	位次 Rank
乌鲁木齐市	Urumqi City	87789	13	36461	13	.845	14
克拉玛依市	Karamay City	22776	14	9543	14	2788	10
吐鲁番地区	Turpan Administrative Offices	182982	10	136555	8	1748	12
哈密地区	Hami [Kumul] Administrative Offices	105009	11	62348	11	2613	11
昌吉回族自治州	Changji Hui Autonomous Prefecture	843990	2	431158	3	17001	4
伊犁哈萨克自治州	Ili Kazak Autonomous Prefecture	1388266		744099		31393	
伊犁州直属县(市)	Counties (Cities) Direct Under Ili Prefecture	603376	4	298992	6	14847	5
塔城地区	Tacheng [Tarbagatai] Administrative Offices	548323	5	355240	5	7999	8
阿勒泰地区	Altay Administrative Offices	236567	8	89866	10	8547	7
博尔塔拉州	Bortala Mongol Autonomous Prefecture	185272	9	120818	9	3179	9
巴音郭楞蒙古自治州	Bayangol Mongol Autonomous Prefecture	539000	6	362830	4	8899	6
阿克苏地区	Aksu Administrative Offices	778039	3	567025	2	33377	2
克孜勒苏柯尔克孜自治州	Kizilsu Kirgiz Autonomous Prefecture	96190	12	51067	12	1456	13
喀什地区	Kashgar [Kaxgar] Administrative Offices	952840	1	624649	1	52844	1
和田地区	Hotan Administrative Offices	408090	7	294515	7	21606	3

地　区	Region	牧业产值 Animal Husbandry	位次 Rank	渔业产值 Fishery	位次 Rank
乌鲁木齐市	Urumqi City	45193	10	1873	8
克拉玛依市	Karamay City	4841	14	371	12
吐鲁番地区	Turpan Administrative Offices	40738	11	215	13
哈密地区	Hami [Kumul] Administrative Offices	37297	12	752	10
昌吉回族自治州	Changji Hui Autonomous Prefecture	372106	1	9556	1
伊犁哈萨克自治州	Ili Kazak Autonomous Prefecture	570645		11218	
伊犁州直属县(市)	Counties (Cities) Direct Under Ili Prefecture	268447	2	5622	2
塔城地区	Tacheng [Tarbagatai] Administrative Offices	175048	4	2301	7
阿勒泰地区	Altay Administrative Offices	127151	6	3295	6
博尔塔拉州	Bortala Mongol Autonomous Prefecture	57408	9	510	11
巴音郭楞蒙古自治州	Bayangol Mongol Autonomous Prefecture	140886	5	4220	4
阿克苏地区	Aksu Administrative Offices	126436	7	5119	3
克孜勒苏柯尔克孜自治州	Kizilsu Kirgiz Autonomous Prefecture	33771	13	146	14
喀什地区	Kashgar [Kaxgar] Administrative Offices	250233	3	3359	5
和田地区	Hotan Administrative Offices	84272	8	884	9

注：本表按当年价格计算；全区合计不等于各地、州汇总数。

Notes：The number in this form is computed by current price. Gross output value of autonomous region is not equal to the sum of output value of every prefecture.

21-5 各地、州、市主要农产品产量

Yield of Major Farm Crops by Prefecture, Autonomous Prefecture and City

单位：吨 (2004 年) (ton)

地区	Region	粮食 Grain	位次 Rank	棉花 Cotton	位次 Rank	油料 Oil Bearing Crops	位次 Rank	甜菜 Beetroots	位次 Rank
乌鲁木齐市	Urumqi City	40228	13	105	13	2345	10	998	8
克拉玛依市	Karamay City	2735	14	5841	12	324	14		
吐鲁番地区	Turpan Administrative Offices	77905	11	18519	8	582	13		
哈密地区	Hami [Kumul] Administrative Offices	64950	12	14356	9	1883	11		
昌吉回族自治州	Changji Hui Autonomous Prefecture	711675	5	118099	4	39129	3	207847	4
伊犁哈萨克自治州	Ili Kazak Autonomous Prefecture	1923627		119955		212902		1507933	
伊犁州直属县(市)	Counties (Cities) Direct Under Ili Prefecture	1117903	3	6773	11	113763	1	1073907	1
塔城地区	Tacheng [Tarbagatai] Administrative Offices	580442	6	113182	5	68298	2	343056	2
阿勒泰地区	Altay Administrative Offices	225282	8			30841	4	90970	7
博尔塔拉州	Bortala Mongol Autonomous Prefecture	201550	9	58764	6	14867	6	96994	6
巴音郭楞蒙古自治州	Bayangol Mongol Autonomous Prefecture	266217	7	144543	3	6376	8	258993	3
阿克苏地区	Aksu Administrative Offices	1152211	2	281692	1	17634	5	185265	5
克孜勒苏柯尔克孜自治州	Kizilsu Kirgiz Autonomous Prefecture	165418	10	8244	10	979	12		
喀什地区	Kashgar [Kaxgar] Administrative Offices	1658000	1	263334	2	11214	7		
和田地区	Hotan Administrative Offices	882002	4	38339	7	3223	9		

21-6 各地、州、市工业总产值和工业增加值

Gross Industrial Ouput Value and Added-Value of Industry by Prefecture, Autonomous Prefecture and City

单位：万元 (2004 年) (10 000 yuan)

地区	Region	工业总产值(当年价格) Gross Industrial Output Value At Current Prices	位次 Rank	工业增加值 Value Added of Industry	位次 Rank
乌鲁木齐市	Urumqi City	4355365.2	2	1323619.8	2
克拉玛依市	Karamay City	5330473.7	1	2651371.8	1
石河子市	Shihezi City	388727.0	8	115823.0	9
吐鲁番地区	Turpan Administrative Offices	745980.2	5	534595.7	4
哈密地区	Hami [Kumul] Administrative Offices	305940.4	9	128039.1	8
昌吉回族自治州	Changji Hui Autonomous Prefecture	1224291.1	4	347961.0	5
伊犁哈萨克自治州	Ili Kazak Autonomous Prefecture	896854.3		325190.7	
伊犁州直属县(市)	Counties (Cities) Direct Under Ili Prefecture	560395.5	6	216316.7	6
塔城地区	Tacheng [Tarbagatai] Administrative Offices	221186.2	10	68515.5	10
阿勒泰地区	Altay Administrative Offices	115272.6	12	40358.5	12
博尔塔拉蒙古自治州	Bortala Mongol Autonomous Prefecture	101830.5	13	17686.6	13
巴音郭楞蒙古自治州	Bayangol Mongol Autonomous Prefecture	1678695.3	3	1031353.9	3
阿克苏地区	Aksu Administrative Offices	442996.2	7	143414.7	7
克孜勒苏柯尔克孜自治州	Kizilsu Kirgiz Autonomous Prefecture	17641.1	15	3961.3	15
喀什地区	Kashgar [Kaxgar] Administrative Offices	146652.6	11	43082.9	11
和田地区	Hotan Administrative Offices	43932.0	14	17039.6	14

21-7 各地、州、市全部国有及规模以上非国有工业经济效益指标
Main Indicators on Economic Benefit of Industrial Enterprises With Independent Accounting System by Prefecture, Autonomous Prefecture and City

单位：% (2004 年) (%)

地 区	Region	工业增加值率 Ratio of Value Added to Gross Industrial Output Value	位次 Rank	资金利税率 Ratio of profits And Taxes to Capital	位次 Rank
乌鲁木齐市	Urumqi City	26.2	12	10.1	4
克拉玛依市	Karamay City	41.9	3	25.8	2
石河子市	Shihezi City	27.1	9	3.7	11
吐鲁番地区	Turpan Administrative Offices	61.7	1	41.2	1
哈密地区	Hami [Kumul] Administrative Offices	36.9	4	5.8	9
昌吉回族自治州	Changji Hui Autonomous Prefecture	25.2	13	5.6	10
伊犁哈萨克自治州	Ili Kazak Autonomous Prefecture	31.6		6.8	
伊犁州直属县(市)	Counties (Cities) Direct Under Ili Prefecture	33.7	6	9.0	5
塔城地区	Tacheng [Tarbagatai] Administrative Offices	26.9	10	2.2	12
阿勒泰地区	Altay Administrative Offices	30.8	7	6.5	8
博尔塔拉蒙古自治州	Bortala Mongol Autonomous Prefecture	15.6	15	0.3	13
巴音郭楞蒙古自治州	Bayangol Mongol Autonomous Prefecture	55.2	2	25.3	3
阿克苏地区	Aksu Administrative Offices	28.6	8	8.9	6
克孜勒苏柯尔克孜自治州	Kizilsu Kirgiz Autonomous Prefecture	20.0	14	-1.8	15
喀什地区	Kashgar [Kaxgar] Administrative Offices	26.5	11	6.6	7
和田地区	Hotan Administrative Offices	34.5	5	-1.2	14

地 区	Region	总资产贡献率 Ratio of Total Assets To Industrial OutputValue	位次 Rank	资本保值增值率 Ratio of Capital Holding And Rise	位次 Rank
乌鲁木齐市	Urumqi City	10.3	4	115.6	9
克拉玛依市	Karamay City	27.6	2	128.4	4
石河子市	Shihezi City	4.6	11	93.5	12
吐鲁番地区	Turpan Administrative Offices	39.7	1	116.4	8
哈密地区	Hami [Kumul] Administrative Offices	7.4	8	117.7	7
昌吉回族自治州	Changji Hui Autonomous Prefecture	6.1	10	100.2	11
伊犁哈萨克自治州	Ili Kazak Autonomous Prefecture	7.9		118.6	
伊犁州直属县(市)	Counties (Cities) Direct Under Ili Prefecture	10.1	5	111.1	10
塔城地区	Tacheng [Tarbagatai] Administrative Offices	3.6	12	135.2	2
阿勒泰地区	Altay Administrative Offices	7.8	7	134.4	3
博尔塔拉蒙古自治州	Bortala Mongol Autonomous Prefecture	1.7	13	118.2	6
巴音郭楞蒙古自治州	Bayangol Mongol Autonomous Prefecture	23.7	3	126.3	5
阿克苏地区	Aksu Administrative Offices	9.8	6	147.8	1
克孜勒苏柯尔克孜自治州	Kizilsu Kirgiz Autonomous Prefecture	-0.8	15	80.2	14
喀什地区	Kashgar [Kaxgar] Administrative Offices	7.3	9	49.9	15
和田地区	Hotan Administrative Offices	0.9	14	85.3	13

21-7 续表 Continued

单位：% (%)

地区	Region	资产负债率 Assets Liability Ratio	位次 Rank	成本费用利润率 Ratio of Profits to Industrial Cost	位次 Rank
乌鲁木齐市	Urumqi City	53.4	12	7.4	6
克拉玛依市	Karamay City	39.6	15	26.5	3
石河子市	Shihezi City	66.1	7	2.4	11
吐鲁番地区	Turpan Administrative Offices	49.2	14	65.8	1
哈密地区	Hami [Kumul] Administrative Offices	64.6	9	3.3	8
昌吉回族自治州	Changji Hui Autonomous Prefecture	65.9	8	3.1	9
伊犁哈萨克自治州	Ili Kazak Autonomous Prefecture	65.6		1.0	
伊犁州直属县(市)	Counties (Cities) Direct Under Ili Prefecture	61.8	10	2.4	10
塔城地区	Tacheng [Tarbagatai] Administrative Offices	70.5	6	-3.3	12
阿勒泰地区	Altay Administrative Offices	71.4	5	4.2	7
博尔塔拉蒙古自治州	Bortala Mongol Autonomous Prefecture	75.3	3	-3.4	13
巴音郭楞蒙古自治州	Bayangol Mongol Autonomous Prefecture	51.5	13	47.5	2
阿克苏地区	Aksu Administrative Offices	58.8	11	9.6	5
克孜勒苏柯尔克孜自治州	Kizilsu Kirgiz Autonomous Prefecture	87.8	2	-8.3	14
喀什地区	Kashgar [Kaxgar] Administrative Offices	88.6	1	9.9	4
和田地区	Hotan Administrative Offices	75.0	4	-12.6	15

地区	Region	全员劳动生产率(元/人年) Overall Labor Productivity (yuan/person -year)	位次 Rank	工业经济效益综合指数 Compre hensive Index of Industry Economic Results	位次 Rank
乌鲁木齐市	Urumqi City	122671.0	4	183.6	4
克拉玛依市	Karamay City	313367.6	2	418.5	3
石河子市	Shihezi City	52179.6	10	95.9	11
吐鲁番地区	Turpan Administrative Offices	389419.9	1	639.2	1
哈密地区	Hami [Kumul] Administrative Offices	52686.7	9	109.5	9
昌吉回族自治州	Changji Hui Autonomous Prefecture	76518.7	5	121.0	7
伊犁哈萨克自治州	Ili Kazak Autonomous Prefecture	55932.4		105.6	
伊犁州直属县(市)	Counties (Cities) Direct Under Ili Prefecture	68930.2	6	122.8	6
塔城地区	Tacheng [Tarbagatai] Administrative Offices	34892.8	12	68.6	12
阿勒泰地区	Altay Administrative Offices	56667.4	8	119.3	8
博尔塔拉蒙古自治州	Bortala Mongol Autonomous Prefecture	23664.2	14	54.8	13
巴音郭楞蒙古自治州	Bayangol Mongol Autonomous Prefecture	255355.2	3	441.6	2
阿克苏地区	Aksu Administrative Offices	66108.0	7	155.7	5
克孜勒苏柯尔克孜自治州	Kizilsu Kirgiz Autonomous Prefecture	19796.6	15	17.8	14
喀什地区	Kashgar [Kaxgar] Administrative Offices	35827.8	11	106.1	10
和田地区	Hotan Administrative Offices	28974.0	13	9.2	15

21-8　各地、州、市主要工业产品产量

Output of Major Industrial Products by Prefecture, Autonomous Prefecture and City

(2004 年)

地　区	Region	纱 (吨) Yarn (ton)	位次 Rank	布 (万米) Cloth (10 000 m)	位次 Rank	呢绒 (万米) Woolen Piece Goods (10 000 m)	位次 Rank
乌鲁木齐市	Urumqi City	40421	2	1612	2	18.47	3
克拉玛依市	Karamay City						
石河子市	Shihezi City	39967	3	4272	1	101.00	1
吐鲁番地区	Turpan Administrative Offices	8904	11				
哈密地区	Hami [Kumul] Administrative Offices	14374	9	44	11		
昌吉回族自治州	Changji Hui Autonomous Prefecture	46541	1	1531	3	86.45	2
伊犁哈萨克自治州	Ili Kazak Autonomous Prefecture	48703		2534			
伊犁州直属县(市)	Counties (Cities) Direct Under Ili Prefecture	26309	4	1183	7		
塔城地区	Tacheng [Tarbagatai] Administrative Offices	22394	6	1351	4		
阿勒泰地区	Altay Administrative Offices						
博尔塔拉蒙古自治州	Bortala Mongol Autonomous Prefecture	11320	10	168	10		
巴音郭楞蒙古自治州	Bayangol Mongol Autonomous Prefecture	25076	5	1308	5		
阿克苏地区	Aksu Administrative Offices	17695	8	945	8		
克孜勒苏柯尔克孜自治州	Kizilsu Kirgiz Autonomous Prefecture						
喀什地区	Kashgar [Kaxgar] Administrative Offices	19816	7	1260	6		
和田地区	Hotan Administrative Offices	5165	12	316	9		

地　区	Region	糖 (万吨) Sugar (10 000 ton)	位次 Rank	饮料酒 (千升) Alcohol Beverage (kilo-liter)	位次 Rank	塑料制品 (吨) Plastic Products (ton)	位次 Rank
乌鲁木齐市	Urumqi City			139882	1	83310	1
克拉玛依市	Karamay City			1698	11	36431	4
石河子市	Shihezi City			4350	9	61653	3
吐鲁番地区	Turpan Administrative Offices			4474	8	690	14
哈密地区	Hami [Kumul] Administrative Offices			1734	10	6009	11
昌吉回族自治州	Changji Hui Autonomous Prefecture	2.21	5	18796	5	72824	2
伊犁哈萨克自治州	Ili Kazak Autonomous Prefecture	22.78		129715		52325	
伊犁州直属县(市)	Counties (Cities) Direct Under Ili Prefecture	12.43	1	68781	2	20730	6
塔城地区	Tacheng [Tarbagatai] Administrative Offices	8.78	2	59670	3	29557	5
阿勒泰地区	Altay Administrative Offices	1.57	7	1264	12	2038	12
博尔塔拉蒙古自治州	Bortala Mongol Autonomous Prefecture	1.69	6	753	14	13194	8
巴音郭楞蒙古自治州	Bayangol Mongol Autonomous Prefecture	8.13	3	6506	7	10488	9
阿克苏地区	Aksu Administrative Offices	2.44	4	18958	4	9084	10
克孜勒苏柯尔克孜自治州	Kizilsu Kirgiz Autonomous Prefecture					373	15
喀什地区	Kashgar [Kaxgar] Administrative Offices			17879	6	16773	7
和田地区	Hotan Administrative Offices			1025	13	1173	13

21-8 续表 Continued

地　区	Region	机制纸及纸板（吨）Machine-made Paper and Paper board (ton)	位次 Rank	原煤（万吨）Coal (10 000 ton)	位次 Rank	原油（万吨）Crude Oil (10 000 ton)	位次 Rank
乌鲁木齐市	Urumqi City	42733	3	894.08	1	358.17	3
克拉玛依市	Karamay City	20	10	7.28	12	1115.35	1
石河子市	Shihezi City	33972	4				
吐鲁番地区	Turpan Administrative Offices			151.08	7	225.00	4
哈密地区	Hami [Kumul] Administrative Offices			460.46	3		
昌吉回族自治州	Changji Hui Autonomous Prefecture	104700	1	866.29	2		
伊犁哈萨克自治州	Ili Kazak Autonomous Prefecture	15162		758.17			
伊犁州直属县(市)	Counties (Cities) Direct Under Ili Prefecture	6484	5	296.18	6		
塔城地区	Tacheng [Tarbagatai] Administrative Offices	3965	7	453.88	4		
阿勒泰地区	Altay Administrative Offices	4713	6	8.12	11		
博尔塔拉蒙古自治州	Bortala Mongol Autonomous Prefecture						
巴音郭楞蒙古自治州	Bayangol Mongol Autonomous Prefecture	60203	2	116.18	8	554.38	2
阿克苏地区	Aksu Administrative Offices	696	9	388.47	5	0.12	5
克孜勒苏柯尔克孜自治州	Kizilsu Kirgiz Autonomous Prefecture			3.83	13		
喀什地区	Kashgar [Kaxgar] Administrative Offices	2600	8	12.09	10		
和田地区	Hotan Administrative Offices			53.84	9		

地　区	Region	水泥（万吨）Cement (10 000 ton)	位次 Rank	发电量（亿千瓦小时）ElectriCity (100 million kwh)	位次 Rank	农用化肥（吨）Chemical Fertilizers (ton)	位次 Rank
乌鲁木齐市	Urumqi City	267.64	1	88.68	1	598734	1
克拉玛依市	Karamay City			22.70	3		
石河子市	Shihezi City			13.62	6		
吐鲁番地区	Turpan Administrative Offices	26.74	11	0.88	14	200	7
哈密地区	Hami [Kumul] Administrative Offices	28.80	10	13.36	7	3624	5
昌吉回族自治州	Changji Hui Autonomous Prefecture	161.44	3	48.39	2	7723	3
伊犁哈萨克自治州	Ili Kazak Autonomous Prefecture	265.16		27.48		2608	
伊犁州直属县(市)	Counties (Cities) Direct Under Ili Prefecture	102.64	6	14.03	5	2555	6
塔城地区	Tacheng [Tarbagatai] Administrative Offices	129.56	4	7.90	10		
阿勒泰地区	Altay Administrative Offices	32.97	9	5.55	11	53	8
博尔塔拉蒙古自治州	Bortala Mongol Autonomous Prefecture	25.79	12	3.61	12		
巴音郭楞蒙古自治州	Bayangol Mongol Autonomous Prefecture	113.30	5	20.45	4	250096	2
阿克苏地区	Aksu Administrative Offices	188.20	2	11.72	9	6810	4
克孜勒苏柯尔克孜自治州	Kizilsu Kirgiz Autonomous Prefecture	3.27	13	0.43	15		
喀什地区	Kashgar [Kaxgar] Administrative Offices	92.73	7	11.79	8		
和田地区	Hotan Administrative Offices	35.69	8	3.14	13		

21-9　各地、州、市社会消费品零售总额

Total Retail Sales of Consumer Goods by Prefecture, Autonomous Prefecture and City

单位：万元　(2004 年)　(10 000 yuan)

地　区	Region	社会消费品零售总额 Total Retail Sales of Consumer Goods	位次 Rank	市 City	位次 Rank
乌鲁木齐市	Urumqi City	1909693	1	1864947	1
克拉玛依市	Karamay City	169603	7	114793	8
吐鲁番地区	Turpan Administrative Offices	132848	11	51802	12
哈密地区	Hami [Kumul] Administrative Offices	169550	8	152236	6
昌吉回族自治州	Changji Hui Autonomous Prefecture	493332	2	233295	3
伊犁哈萨克自治州	Ili Kazak Autonomous Prefecture	716844		281390	
伊犁州直属县(市)	Counties (Cities) Direct Under Ili Prefecture	411834	3	190330	4
塔城地区	Tacheng [Tarbagatai] Administrative Offices	168433	9	52490	11
阿勒泰地区	Altay Administrative Offices	136577	10	40876	13
博尔塔拉蒙古自治州	Bortala Mongol Autonomous Prefecture	88477	13	55058	10
巴音郭楞蒙古自治州	Bayangol Mongol Autonomous Prefecture	390348	4	236417	2
阿克苏地区	Aksu Administrative Offices	327749	5	154297	5
克孜勒苏柯尔克孜自治州	Kizilsu Kirgiz Autonomous Prefecture	37920	14	20565	14
喀什地区	Kashgar [Kaxgar] Administrative Offices	265480	6	123416	7
和田地区	Hotan Administrative Offices	120851	12	72185	9

地　区	Region	县 County	位次 Rank	县以下 Under County Level	位次 Rank
乌鲁木齐市	Urumqi City			44746	6
克拉玛依市	Karamay City	53370	8	1440	14
吐鲁番地区	Turpan Administrative Offices	39974	9	41072	7
哈密地区	Hami [Kumul] Administrative Offices	7240	13	10074	12
昌吉回族自治州	Changji Hui Autonomous Prefecture	113944	3	146093	1
伊犁哈萨克自治州	Ili Kazak Autonomous Prefecture	284375		190031	
伊犁州直属县(市)	Counties (Cities) Direct Under Ili Prefecture	123740	2	97764	2
塔城地区	Tacheng [Tarbagatai] Administrative Offices	58146	7	57797	3
阿勒泰地区	Altay Administrative Offices	68906	6	26795	9
博尔塔拉蒙古自治州	Bortala Mongol Autonomous Prefecture	8445	12	24974	8
巴音郭楞蒙古自治州	Bayangol Mongol Autonomous Prefecture	99341	4	54590	4
阿克苏地区	Aksu Administrative Offices	152604	1	20848	11
克孜勒苏柯尔克孜自治州	Kizilsu Kirgiz Autonomous Prefecture	11265	11	6090	13
喀什地区	Kashgar [Kaxgar] Administrative Offices	89250	5	52814	5
和田地区	Hotan Administrative Offices	24104	10	24562	10

21-10 各地、州、市海关进出口总额

Total Imports and Exports by Prefecture, Autonomous Prefecture and City

单位：万美元 (2004 年) (USD 10 000)

地　　区	Region	进出口总额 Total Imports and Exports	位 次 Rank	出口总额 Total Exports	位 次 Rank	进口总额 Total Lmports	位 次 Rank
乌鲁木齐市	Urumqi City	165261	2	91704	1	73557	2
克拉玛依市	Karamay City	6508	9	2538	9	3970	7
石河子市	Shihezi City	14898	6	8863	7	6035	6
吐鲁番地区	Turpan Administrative Offices	539	13	234	13	305	13
哈密地区	Hami [Kumul] Administrative Offices	2882	12	1678	12	1204	12
昌吉回族自治洲	Changji Hui Autonomous Prefecture	31057	5	23947	5	7110	5
伊犁哈萨克自治州	Ili Administrative Offices	156582		124076		32506	
伊犁州直属县(市)	Counties (Cities) Direct Under Ili Prefecture	96443	3	80952	2	15491	3
塔城地区	Tacheng [Tarbagatai] Administrative Offices	46942	4	32727	4	14215	4
阿勒泰地区	Altay Administrative Offices	13197	7	10397	6	2800	9
博尔塔拉蒙古自治州	Bortala Mongol Autonomous Prefecture	169050	1	42162	3	126888	1
巴音郭楞蒙古自治州	Bayangol Mongol Autonomous Prefecture	4105	11	2448	10	1657	10
阿克苏地区	Aksu Administrative Offices	491	14	191	14	300	14
克孜勒苏柯尔克孜自治州	Kizilsu Kirgiz Autonomous Prefecture	5653	10	1856	11	3797	8
喀什地区	Kashgar [Kaxgar] Administrative Offices	6537	8	4961	8	1576	11
和田地区	Hotan Administrative Offices						

21-11 各地、州、市在岗职工工资总额和平均工资

Total Wages of Employed Staff and Workers and Avarage Wage by Prefecture, Autonomous Prefecture and City

(2004 年)

地　　区	Region	在岗职工工资总额(万元) Total Wages of Statt and Workers (10 000 yuan)	位 次 Rank	在岗职工平均工资(元) Average On-the-Job Wage (yuan)	位 次 Rank
乌鲁木齐市	Urumqi City	953235.7	1	19052	2
克拉玛依市	Karamay City	247807.8	7	19893	1
石河子市	Shihezi City	111937.9	12	13234	10
吐鲁番地区	Turpan Administrative Offices	124707.1	10	17849	3
哈密地区	Hami [Kumul] Administrative Offices	108071.6	13	14220	6
昌吉回族自治州	Changji Hui Autonomous Prefecture	265686.0	5	11880	11
伊犁哈萨克自治州	Ili Kazak Autonomous Prefecture	642110.1		11138	
伊犁州直属县(市)	Counties (Cities) Direct Under Ili Prefecture	280520.9	4	11354	14
塔城地区	Tacheng [Tarbagatai] Administrative Offices	234769.4	8	10550	15
阿勒泰地区	Altay Administrative Offices	126819.8	9	11863	12
博尔塔拉蒙古自治州	Bortala Mongol Autonomous Prefecture	105215.7	14	11799	13
巴音郭楞蒙古自治州	Bayangol Mongol Autonomous Prefecture	281682.3	3	13938	8
阿克苏地区	Aksu Administrative Offices	288334.6	2	13940	7
克孜勒苏柯尔克孜自治州	Kizilsu Kirgiz Autonomous Prefecture	53492.7	15	16012	4
喀什地区	Kashgar [Kaxgar] Administrative Offices	260453.0	6	13565	9
和田地区	Hotan Administrative Offices	120577.3	11	14843	5

21-12 各地、州、市地方财政一般预算收支

Government Revenue and Expenditures by Prefecture, Autonomous Prefecture and City

单位：万元 (2004 年) (10 000 yuan)

地　区	Region	地方财政一般预算收入 Local Financial Revenue	位 次 Rank	地方财政一般预算支出 Local Financial Expenditure	位 次 Rank
乌鲁木齐市	Urumqi City	463395	1	393022	1
克拉玛依市	Karamay City	202145	2	206937	5
石河子市	Shihezi City	32345	10	48100	15
吐鲁番地区	Turpan Administrative Offices	50296	9	81277	12
哈密地区	Hami [Kumul] Administrative Offices	29749	11	75752	13
昌吉回族自治州	Changji Hui Autonomous Prefecture	100499	4	193226	7
伊犁哈萨克自治州	Ili Kazak Autonomous Prefecture	154917		548273	
伊犁州直属县(市)	Counties (Cities) Direct Under Ili Prefecture	75248	6	267542	3
塔城地区	Tacheng [Tarbagatai] Administrative Offices	57557	7	159280	9
阿勒泰地区	Altay Administrative Offices	22112	13	121451	10
博尔塔拉蒙古自治州	Bortala Mongol Autonomous Prefecture	23643	12	72631	14
巴音郭楞蒙古自治州	Bayangol Mongol Autonomous Prefecture	106904	3	202238	6
阿克苏地区	Aksu Administrative Offices	98295	5	259597	4
克孜勒苏柯尔克孜自治州	Kizilsu Kirgiz Autonomous Prefecture	6750	15	87532	11
喀什地区	Kashgar [Kaxgar] Administrative Offices	57064	8	293124	2
和田地区	Hotan Administrative Offices	19956	14	178839	8

注:各地、州、市合计不等于总计。

Note: The total amount of different administrative office, autonomous prefectures and cities is not equal to the total.

21-13 分城镇居民消费价格指数和商品零售价格指数

General Retail Price and Consumer Price Index by City/County

(上年=100) (2004 年)(抽样调查) (Sampled Survey) (Preceding year=100)

地　区	Region	商品零售价格指数 General Retail Price Index	位 次 Rank	居民消费价格指数 General Consumer Price Index	位 次 Rank
乌鲁木齐市	Urumqi City	101.1	15	100.9	14
喀什市	Kashgar [Kaxgar] City	100.9	16	101.6	13
伊宁市	Yining [Gulja] City	103.3	5	104.0	4
和田市	Hotan City	102.9	8	103.0	9
克拉玛依市	Karamay City	101.7	13	103.7	6
哈密市	Hami [Kumul] City	101.3	14	102.2	12
昌吉市	Changji City	103.0	7	103.3	7
库尔勒市	Korla City	104.3	3	103.9	5
阿克苏市	Aksu City	101.8	12	102.2	12
焉耆回族自治县	Yanji Hui Autonomous County	103.2	6	103.2	8
塔城市	Tacheng [Qoqek] City	100.4	17	100.7	15
阿勒泰市	Altay City	103.7	4	103.2	8
乌苏市	Usu City	104.3	3	104.7	3
博乐市	Bole [Bortala] City	102.2	11	102.8	10
吐鲁番市	Turpan City	103.0	7	104.7	3
库车县	Kuqa County	105.1	2	107.0	1
阿图什市	Artux City	102.6	10	103.3	7
莎车县	Shache [Yarkant] County	105.4	1	106.4	2
奎屯市	Kuytun City	102.2	11	102.7	11
石河子市	Shihezi City	102.7	9	102.8	10

21-14 各地、州、市各类学校在校学生数

Number of Student Enrollment by Type of School and by Prefecture, Autonomous Prefecture and City

单位：人 (2004 年) (person)

地 区	Region	普通高等学校 Regular Institutions of Higher Education	位次 Rank	中等专业学校 Specialized Secondary Schools	位次 Rank
乌鲁木齐市	Urumqi City	103378	1	29991	1
克拉玛依市	Karamay City	4399	7	858	9
石河子市	Shihezi City	19875	2	945	7
吐鲁番地区	Turpan Administrative Offices			945	8
哈密地区	Hami [Kumul] Administrative Offices			764	13
昌吉回族自治州	Changji Hui Autonomous Prefecture	9973	3	8124	2
伊犁哈萨克自治州	Ili Kazak Autonomous Prefecture	8507		5971	
伊犁州直属县(市)	Counties (Cities) Direct Under Ili Prefecture	8507	5	4349	5
塔城地区	Tacheng [Tarbagatai] Administrative Offices			825	10
阿勒泰地区	Altay Administrative Offices			797	11
博尔塔拉蒙古自治州	Bortala Mongol Autonomous Prefecture			489	15
巴音郭楞蒙古自治州	Bayangol Mongol Autonomous Prefecture	432	9	7200	3
阿克苏地区	Aksu Administrative Offices	7314	6	3770	6
克孜勒苏柯尔克孜自治州	Kizilsu Kirgiz Autonomous Prefecture			791	12
喀什地区	Kashgar [Kaxgar] Administrative Offices	9294	4	5249	4
和田地区	Hotan Administrative Offices	3952	8	763	14

地 区	Region	普通中学 Regular Secondary Schools	位次 Rank	小 学 Primary Schools	位次 Rank
乌鲁木齐市	Urumqi City	116429	4	148338	5
克拉玛依市	Karamay City	19825	14	24043	14
石河子市	Shihezi City	12529	15	12565	15
吐鲁番地区	Turpan Administrative Offices	44297	11	54858	10
哈密地区	Hami [Kumul] Administrative Offices	34321	12	36425	12
昌吉回族自治州	Changji Hui Autonomous Prefecture	98374	6	109601	6
伊犁哈萨克自治州	Ili Kazak Autonomous Prefecture	272605		388203	
伊犁州直属县(市)	Counties (Cities) Direct Under Ili Prefecture	158442	3	249466	2
塔城地区	Tacheng [Tarbagatai] Administrative Offices	68781	8	87810	8
阿勒泰地区	Altay Administrative Offices	45382	10	50927	11
博尔塔拉蒙古自治州	Bortala Mongol Autonomous Prefecture	27664	13	33195	13
巴音郭楞蒙古自治州	Bayangol Mongol Autonomous Prefecture	77452	7	92684	7
阿克苏地区	Aksu Administrative Offices	176606	2	247547	3
克孜勒苏柯尔克孜自治州	Kizilsu Kirgiz Autonomous Prefecture	46876	9	56761	9
喀什地区	Kashgar [Kaxgar] Administrative Offices	271727	1	496381	1
和田地区	Hotan Administrative Offices	114722	5	232998	4

21-15 各地、州、市每万人口医院床位数和医生数

Number of Doctors and Hospital Beds Per 10 000 Population by Prefecture, Autonomous Prefecture and City

(2004 年)

地 区	Region	每万人口医院床位数(张) Number of Hospital Beds per 10 000 Population (unit)	位 次 Rank	平均每万人口医生数(人) Number of doctors Per 10 000 Population (person)	位 次 Rank
乌鲁木齐市	Urumqi City	95.24	1	51.16	1
克拉玛依市	Karamay City	73.58	2	41.24	2
石河子市	Shihezi City	60.81	3	36.77	3
吐鲁番地区	Turpan Administrative Offices	34.19	9	21.84	11
哈密地区	Hami [Kumul] Administrative Offices	49.98	4	33.61	4
昌吉回族自治州	Changji Hui Autonomous Prefecture	43.36	6	24.33	7
伊犁哈萨克自治州	Ili Kazak Autonomous Prefecture	34.31		23.51	
伊犁州直属县(市)	Counties (Cities) Direct Under Ili Prefecture	34.16	10	22.68	9
塔城地区	Tacheng [Tarbagatai] Administrative Offices	33.19	11	22.33	10
阿勒泰地区	Altay Administrative Offices	36.68	8	28.75	5
博尔塔拉蒙古自治州	Bortala Mongol Autonomous Prefecture	42.75	7	28.61	6
巴音郭楞蒙古自治州	Bayangol Mongol Autonomous Prefecture	45.16	5	23.58	8
阿克苏地区	Aksu Administrative Offices	30.77	13	13.05	13
克孜勒苏柯尔克孜自治州	Kizilsu Kirgiz Autonomous Prefecture	30.83	12	19.01	12
喀什地区	Kashgar [Kaxgar] Administrative Offices	24.37	15	11.03	14
和田地区	Hotan Administrative Offices	26.64	14	9.91	15

21-16 各地、州、市卫生技术人员和医生数

Medical Technical Personnel and Doctors by Prefecture, Autonomous Prefecture and City

单位：人 (2004 年) (person)

地 区	Region	卫生技术人员 Medical Technical Personnel	位 次 Rank	#医 生 Doctors	位 次 Rank
乌鲁木齐市	Urumqi City	20947	1	9513	1
克拉玛依市	Karamay City	2290	14	1047	14
石河子市	Shihezi City	5131	7	2364	7
吐鲁番地区	Turpan Administrative Offices	3032	12	1266	13
哈密地区	Hami [Kumul] Administrative Offices	4054	10	1768	10
昌吉回族自治州	Changji Hui Autonomous Prefecture	9047	4	3806	4
伊犁哈萨克自治州	Ili Kazak Autonomous Prefecture	21519		9748	
伊犁州直属县(市)	Counties (Cities) Direct Under Ili Prefecture	12941	2	5799	2
塔城地区	Tacheng [Tarbagatai] Administrative Offices	4989	8	2158	8
阿勒泰地区	Altay Administrative Offices	3589	11	1791	9
博尔塔拉蒙古自治州	Bortala Mongol Autonomous Prefecture	2878	13	1293	12
巴音郭楞蒙古自治州	Bayangol Mongol Autonomous Prefecture	6526	6	2708	6
阿克苏地区	Aksu Administrative Offices	7950	5	2906	5
克孜勒苏柯尔克孜自治州	Kizilsu Kirgiz Autonomous Prefecture	2154	15	890	15
喀什地区	Kashgar [Kaxgar] Administrative Offices	9698	3	3987	3
和田地区	Hotan Administrative Offices	4562	9	1757	11

附 录

APPENDIX

各省市区主要经济指标排序

RANKING OF MAIN ECONOMIC INDICATORS BY REGION

各省市区主要经济指标排序
Ranking of Main Economic Indicators by Region

(2004 年)

地　区	Region	地区生产总值(亿元) Prefecture Gross Production (100 million yuan)	位　次 Rank	地区生产总值比上年增长(%) Higher Prefecture Gross Production than that by (%) in the previous year	位　次 Rank
全　国	**China**	**136515.0**		**9.5**	
北　京	Beijing	4283.3	15	13.2	10
天　津	Tianjin	2931.9	21	15.7	2
河　北	Hebei	8768.8	6	12.5	15
山　西	Shanxi	3042.4	18	14.1	7
内蒙古	Inner Mongolia	2712.1	23	19.4	1
辽　宁	Liaoning	6872.7	8	12.8	13
吉　林	Jilin	2958.2	20	12.2	20
黑龙江	Heilongjiang	5303.0	13	11.7	24
上　海	Shanghai	7450.3	7	13.6	9
江　苏	Jiangsu	15403.2	3	14.9	4
浙　江	Zhejiang	11243.0	4	14.3	5
安　徽	Anhui	4812.7	14	12.5	16
福　建	Fujian	6053.1	11	12.1	21
江　西	Jiangxi	3495.9	16	13.2	11
山　东	Shandong	15490.7	2	15.3	3
河　南	Henan	8815.1	5	13.7	8
湖　北	Hubei	6309.9	10	11.3	27
湖　南	Hunan	5612.3	12	12.0	22
广　东	Guangdong	16039.5	1	14.2	6
广　西	Guangxi	3320.1	17	11.8	23
海　南	Hainan	769.4	28	10.4	31
重　庆	Chongqing	2665.4	24	12.2	19
四　川	Sichuan	6556.0	9	12.7	14
贵　州	Guizhou	1591.9	26	11.4	26
云　南	Yunnan	2959.5	19	11.5	25
西　藏	Tibet	211.5	31	12.2	18
陕　西	Shaanxi	2883.5	22	12.9	12
甘　肃	Gansu	1558.9	27	10.9	30
青　海	Qinghai	465.7	29	12.3	17
宁　夏	Ningxia	460.4	30	11.0	29
新　疆	Xinjiang	2200.2	25	11.1	28

续表 1

地　区	Region	第一产业增加值(亿元) Primary Industry Product (100 million yuan)	位　次 Rank	第二产业增加值(亿元) Secondary Industry Product (100 million yuan)	位　次 Rank	第三产业增加值(亿元) Tertiary Industry Product (100 million yuan)	位　次 Rank
全　国	**China**	**20744.0**		**72387.0**		**43384.0**	
北　京	Beijing	102.9	26	1610.4	16	2570.0	9
天　津	Tianjin	102.3	27	1560.2	18	1269.4	16
河　北	Hebei	1370.4	4	4635.2	5	2763.2	7
山　西	Shanxi	253.4	25	1810.1	15	979.0	23
内蒙古	Inner Mongolia	506.1	18	1332.5	21	873.5	24
辽　宁	Liaoning	769.9	13	3278.9	8	2823.9	6
吉　林	Jilin	561.0	17	1379.3	20	1017.9	22
黑龙江	Heilongjiang	587.8	16	3155.3	9	1559.9	15
上　海	Shanghai	96.7	28	3788.2	7	3565.3	5
江　苏	Jiangsu	1315.4	5	8716.1	3	5371.7	2
浙　江	Zhejiang	816.0	10	6045.0	4	4382.0	4
安　徽	Anhui	932.4	9	2169.8	14	1710.4	14
福　建	Fujian	777.9	12	2950.3	11	2324.9	11
江　西	Jiangxi	711.7	14	1595.7	17	1188.5	18
山　东	Shandong	1778.3	1	8724.5	2	4987.9	3
河　南	Henan	1647.5	2	4515.4	6	2652.3	8
湖　北	Hubei	1020.1	8	2994.7	10	2295.2	12
湖　南	Hunan	1155.9	7	2214.4	13	2242.0	13
广　东	Guangdong	1245.4	6	8890.3	1	5903.8	1
广　西	Guangxi	811.4	11	1288.3	23	1220.5	17
海　南	Hainan	283.8	23	180.4	30	305.1	28
重　庆	Chongqing	431.3	20	1181.2	24	1052.8	20
四　川	Sichuan	1394.3	3	2690.0	12	2471.8	10
贵　州	Guizhou	334.1	22	714.7	27	543.1	26
云　南	Yunnan	604.3	15	1314.2	22	1041.0	21
西　藏	Tibet						
陕　西	Shaanxi	395.0	21	1416.8	19	1071.7	19
甘　肃	Gansu	281.4	24	758.2	26	519.4	27
青　海	Qinghai	57.8	30	227.1	29	180.9	29
宁　夏	Ningxia	65.1	29	239.4	28	155.8	30
新　疆	Xinjiang	444.7	19	1010.1	25	745.4	25

Continued

第一产业占GDP比重(%) Composition of Primary Industry Product to GDP	位次 Rank	第二产业占GDP比重(%) Composition of Secondary Industry Product to GDP	位次 Rank	#工业占GDP比重(%) Composition of Industry Product to GDP	位次 Rank	#建筑业占GDP比重(%) Composition of Constuction Product to GDP	位次 Rank	第三产业占GDP比重(%) Composition of Tertiary Industrial Product to GDP	位次 Rank
15.2		**53.0**		**46.0**		**7.0**		**31.8**	
2.4	29	37.6	29	30.1	29	7.5	17	60.0	1
3.5	28	53.2	7	49.0	6	4.2	29	43.3	3
15.6	16	52.9	8	46.6	9	6.3	25	31.5	28
8.3	25	59.5	2	51.6	2	7.9	14	32.2	27
18.7	12	49.1	13	37.4	16	11.7	5	32.2	25
11.2	22	47.7	17	41.2	12	6.5	22	41.1	4
19.0	10	46.6	19	38.6	15	8.0	12	34.4	19
11.1	23	59.5	1	53.1	1	6.4	23	29.4	30
1.3	30	50.8	11	46.9	8	3.9	30	47.9	2
8.5	24	56.6	3	50.1	4	6.5	21	34.9	18
7.3	27	53.8	6	47.9	7	5.9	27	39.0	8
19.4	9	45.1	22	36.1	20	9.0	9	35.5	16
12.9	19	48.7	15	41.8	11	6.9	20	38.4	10
20.4	7	45.6	21	31.7	27	13.9	2	34.0	21
11.5	21	56.3	4	50.3	3	6.0	26	32.2	26
18.7	11	51.2	10	43.8	10	7.4	18	30.1	29
16.2	15	47.5	18	41.1	13	6.4	24	36.4	15
20.6	5	39.5	27	31.8	26	7.7	16	39.9	5
7.8	26	55.4	5	49.9	5	5.5	28	36.8	13
24.4	2	38.8	28	31.5	28	7.3	19	36.8	14
36.9	1	23.4	30	15.5	30	7.9	15	39.7	6
16.2	14	44.3	25	34.8	22	9.5	8	39.5	7
21.3	3	41.0	26	33.0	25	8.0	13	37.7	11
21.0	4	44.9	23	36.1	19	8.8	11	34.1	20
20.4	6	44.4	24	35.6	21	8.8	10	35.2	17
13.7	18	49.1	12	36.9	17	12.2	3	37.2	12
18.1	13	48.6	16	36.9	18	11.7	6	33.3	24
12.4	20	48.8	14	34.1	23	14.7	1	38.8	9
14.2	17	52.0	9	40.5	14	11.5	7	33.8	23
20.2	8	45.9	20	33.9	24	12.0	4	33.9	22

续表 2

地　区	Region	总人口(万人) Total Population (10 000 persons)	位　次 Rank	地方财政收　入(亿元) Local Government Revenue (100 million yuan)	位　次 Rank	地方财政支　出(亿元) Local Government Expenditures (100 million yuan)	位　次 Rank
全　国	**China**	**129988**		**11693.4**		**20592.8**	
北　京	Beijing	1493	26	744.5	6	898.3	7
天　津	Tianjin	1024	27	246.2	18	375.0	26
河　北	Hebei	6809	6	407.8	9	785.6	10
山　西	Shanxi	3335	19	256.4	17	519.1	17
内蒙古	Inner Mongolia	2384	23	196.8	23	564.1	16
辽　宁	Liaoning	4217	14	529.6	7	931.4	6
吉　林	Jilin	2709	21	166.3	24	507.8	20
黑龙江	Heilongjiang	3817	16	289.4	14	697.6	12
上　海	Shanghai	1742	25	1106.2	2	1382.5	2
江　苏	Jiangsu	7433	5	980.5	3	1312.0	3
浙　江	Zhejiang	4720	11	806.0	5	1062.9	5
安　徽	Anhui	6461	8	274.6	15	601.5	15
福　建	Fujian	3511	18	333.5	11	516.7	18
江　西	Jiangxi	4284	13	205.8	21	454.1	22
山　东	Shandong	9180	2	828.3	4	1189.4	4
河　南	Henan	9717	1	428.8	8	880.0	9
湖　北	Hubei	6016	9	310.5	13	646.3	14
湖　南	Hunan	6698	7	320.6	12	719.5	11
广　东	Guangdong	8304	4	1418.5	1	1853.0	1
广　西	Guangxi	4889	10	237.8	19	507.5	21
海　南	Hainan	818	28	57.0	28	127.2	30
重　庆	Chongqing	3122	20	200.6	22	395.7	25
四　川	Sichuan	8725	3	385.8	10	895.3	8
贵　州	Guizhou	3904	15	149.3	26	418.4	24
云　南	Yunnan	4415	12	263.4	16	663.6	13
西　藏	Tibet	274	31	10.0	31	133.8	29
陕　西	Shaanxi	3705	17	215.0	20	516.3	19
甘　肃	Gansu	2619	22	104.2	27	356.9	27
青　海	Qinghai	539	30	27.0	30	137.3	28
宁　夏	Ningxia	588	29	37.5	29	123.0	31
新　疆	Xinjiang	1963	24	155.7	25	421.0	23

Continued

居民消费价格指数 Consumer Price Index	位次 Rank	全部职工平均货币工资(元) Average Wage of total Staff (yuan)	位次 Rank	#国有单位职工平均货币工资(元) Average Wage of Staff in State-owned Units (yuan)	位次 Rank	城镇居民年人均可支配收入(元) Per-Capitall Annual Disposable Income of Urban households (yuan)	位次 Rank	城镇居民年人均消费性支出(元) Per-Capitall Annual living Expenditures for Consumption (yuan)	位次 Rank
103.9		**16024**		**16729**		**9422**		**7182**	
101.0	31	29674	3	34009	1	15638	2	12200	2
102.3	29	21754	6	23086	6	11467	5	8802	5
104.3	9	12925	25	13576	22	7951	17	5819	22
104.1	10	12943	23	13353	24	7903	18	5654	27
102.9	25	13324	21	14209	20	8123	14	6219	18
103.5	21	14921	11	15715	14	8008	16	6543	13
104.1	11	12431	28	12540	31	7841	19	6069	19
103.8	16	12557	27	12675	29	7471	27	5568	28
102.2	30	30085	2	31507	3	16683	1	12631	1
104.1	12	18202	7	20876	7	10482	7	7332	9
103.9	15	23506	4	33426	2	14546	3	10636	4
104.5	6	12928	24	13522	23	7511	24	5711	26
104.0	13	15603	10	18529	9	11175	6	8161	7
103.5	20	11860	31	12291	32	7560	23	5338	30
103.6	19	14332	16	16031	11	9438	8	6674	12
105.4	2	12114	30	12701	28	7705	22	5294	31
104.9	4	11855	32	13096	26	8023	15	6399	15
105.1	3	13928	18	14469	18	8617	13	6885	10
103.0	24	22116	5	25979	5	13628	4	10695	3
104.4	8	13579	20	14141	21	8690	12	6446	14
104.4	7	12652	26	12664	30	7736	20	5802	23
103.7	18	14357	15	15847	12	9221	9	7973	8
104.9	5	14063	17	15818	13	7710	21	6371	16
104.0	14	12431	28	12870	27	7322	29	5494	29
106.0	1	14581	13	15320	15	8871	11	6837	11
102.7	27	30873	1	30165	4	9167	10	8446	6
103.1	23	13024	22	13333	25	7492	26	6233	17
102.3	28	13623	19	14358	19	7377	28	5937	20
103.2	22	17229	8	18686	8	7320	30	5759	25
103.7	17	14620	12	15212	16	7218	31	5821	21
102.7	26	14484	14	14477	17	7503	25	5774	24

续表 3

地　区	Region	农民人均纯收入(元) Per-Capita Annual Net Income of Rural Households (yuan)	位　次 Rank	农民人均现金收入(元) Per-Capita Cash Income of Rural Households (yuan)	位　次 Rank	农民人均生活消费支出(元) Per-Capita Living Expenditure of Rural Households (yuan)	位　次 Rank
全　国	**China**	**2936**		**3234**		**2185**	
北　京	Beijing	6170	2	6973	3	4617	3
天　津	Tianjin	5020	4	6008	4	2642	7
河　北	Hebei	3171	10	3435	11	1835	20
山　西	Shanxi	2590	18	2524	24	1637	26
内蒙古	Inner Mongolia	2606	17	3293	12	2083	12
辽　宁	Liaoning	3307	9	4062	9	2073	13
吉　林	Jilin	3000	12	3224	13	1971	15
黑龙江	Heilongjiang	3005	11	3663	10	1837	19
上　海	Shanghai	7066	1	7262	1	6329	1
江　苏	Jiangsu	4754	5	5187	5	2993	6
浙　江	Zhejiang	5944	3	7070	2	4659	2
安　徽	Anhui	2499	22	2588	22	1814	21
福　建	Fujian	4089	7	4433	7	3016	5
江　西	Jiangxi	2787	16	2886	19	2096	10
山　东	Shandong	3507	8	4322	8	2389	9
河　南	Henan	2553	19	2563	23	1664	25
湖　北	Hubei	2890	13	2971	17	2089	11
湖　南	Hunan	2838	14	3135	14	2472	8
广　东	Guangdong	4366	6	4794	6	3241	4
广　西	Guangxi	2305	24	2603	21	1929	16
海　南	Hainan	2818	15	3117	15	1745	22
重　庆	Chongqing	2510	21	2268	25	1854	18
四　川	Sichuan	2519	20	2668	20	2016	14
贵　州	Guizhou	1722	31	1623	30	1296	31
云　南	Yunnan	1864	28	1860	29	1571	28
西　藏	Tibet	1861	29	1564	31	1471	29
陕　西	Shaanxi	1867	27	2077	26	1618	27
甘　肃	Gansu	1852	30	1864	28	1464	30
青　海	Qinghai	1958	26	1957	27	1676	24
宁　夏	Ningxia	2320	23	2979	16	1927	17
新　疆	Xinjiang	2245	25	2945	18	1690	23

注：现金收支为不含储蓄借贷后的现金收支。

Note: The cash income and expenditure refer to the one abscent of deposit loan.

Continued

农林牧渔业总产值(亿元) Gross Output Value of Farming, Forestry, Animal Husbandry and Fishery (100 million yuan)	位 次 Rank	农林牧渔业总产值比上年增长(%) Output Value Increase Rate in 2004 over 2003 of Farming,Forestry, Animal Husbandry and Fishery	位 次 Rank	粮食产量(万吨) Grain (10 000 ton)	位 次 Rank	棉花产量(万吨) Cotton (10 000 ton)	位 次 Rank	油料产量(万吨) Oilbearing Crops (10 000 ton)	位 次 Rank
36239.0		**7.5**		**46947.0**		**632.4**		**3065.9**	
262.0	26	0.4	30	70.2	31	0.8	16	2.9	30
241.0	28	4.3	28	122.8	27	12.0	9	1.6	31
2375.9	4	6.8	15	2480.1	9	66.5	4	154.3	7
481.8	23	6.8	16	1062.0	19	12.0	10	28.2	24
851.3	18	15.0	2	1505.3	14	0.7	17	103.7	9
1510.5	10	7.9	10	1720.0	11	0.5	18	45.9	18
940.7	17	5.4	22	2510.0	8			38.1	21
1136.6	14	19.3	1	3001.0	4			46.0	17
248.9	27	-7.2	31	106.3	28	0.2	19	7.4	28
2417.6	3	8.9	7	2829.1	5	50.3	5	238.4	5
1332.3	11	4.4	27	834.9	21	2.3	15	48.8	14
1644.4	9	8.9	6	2743.0	6	41.2	6	299.7	4
1317.3	12	5.0	25	736.5	24			27.8	25
1055.0	15	8.0	9	1663.0	12	8.5	12	74.5	12
3453.9	1	6.0	20	3516.7	2	109.8	2	369.7	2
2963.9	2	12.9	3	4260.0	1	66.7	3	408.8	1
1695.4	8	5.5	21	2100.1	10	39.5	7	314.4	3
1913.3	7	7.5	11	2640.0	7	20.3	8	139.6	8
2154.8	6	4.5	26	1390.0	16			77.5	11
1294.5	13	6.2	19	1398.5	15	0.1	20	58.3	13
438.7	25	9.2	4	190.1	26			9.1	27
612.8	21	5.2	23	1144.5	18			41.8	20
2252.3	5	7.1	12	3146.7	3	3.3	14	226.3	6
524.6	22	2.6	29	1149.6	17	0.1	21	82.7	10
965.2	16	6.8	17	1509.5	13			33.4	22
62.7	31	7.0	13	96.0	29			5.4	29
651.2	20	9.1	5	1040.0	20	8.2	13	46.1	16
477.4	24	7.0	14	805.8	23	11.0	11	48.5	15
86.7	30	5.1	24	88.5	30			28.9	23
125.5	29	8.3	8	290.5	25			13.8	26
750.7	19	6.4	18	828.53	22	175.3	1	44.5	19

续表 4

地　区	Region	工业增加值(亿元) Industrial Added Value (100 million yuan)	位　次 Rank	原 煤(万吨) Raw Coal (10 000 tons)	位　次 Rank	原 油(万吨) Crude Oil (10 000 tons)	位　次 Rank
全　国	**China**	54805.1		195600.0		17500.0	
北　京	Beijing	1259.5	14	908.4	22		
天　津	Tianjin	1395.6	13			1443.0	6
河　北	Hebei	2459.2	6	7156.2	9	535.6	8
山　西	Shanxi	1242.8	15	37231.6	1		
内蒙古	Inner Mongolia	776.8	21	17171.4	2		
辽　宁	Liaoning	2255.7	8	6232.5	10	1296.4	7
吉　林	Jilin	994.3	18	2396.5	16	478.9	10
黑龙江	Heilongjiang	1619.6	11	7162.6	8	4672.2	1
上　海	Shanghai	3427.0	5			31.9	15
江　苏	Jiangsu	6447.5	3	2747.0	15	168.9	12
浙　江	Zhejiang	4173.4	4	56.3	27		
安　徽	Anhui	1082.2	17	7868.1	7		
福　建	Fujian	1845.8	9	1076.1	21		
江　西	Jiangxi	617.8	23	1232.6	20		
山　东	Shandong	6498.3	2	14646.2	3	2674.3	2
河　南	Henan	2332.7	7	14445.5	4	523.4	9
湖　北	Hubei	1664.7	10	395.6	25	78.2	13
湖　南	Hunan	1198.1	16	3036.2	14		
广　东	Guangdong	7086.4	1	219.4	26	1467.5	5
广　西	Guangxi	595.6	24	521.3	23	3.6	18
海　南	Hainan	102.7	30			8.0	17
重　庆	Chongqing	579.7	25	1764.2	18		
四　川	Sichuan	1546.5	12	4429.9	11	14.3	16
贵　州	Guizhou	438.4	27	9756.6	5		
云　南	Yunnan	881.2	19	1718.6	19		
西　藏	Tibet	14.4	31	1.6	28		
陕　西	Shaanxi	870.7	20	8426.0	6	1528.0	4
甘　肃	Gansu	505.1	26	3083.8	13	76.3	14
青　海	Qinghai	132.4	29	418.8	24	222.0	11
宁　夏	Ningxia	147.0	28	2354.6	17		
新　疆	Xinjiang	669.0	22	3749.4	12	2253.02	3

注：工业增加值为规模以上工业企业。

Note: Industrial Added Value for Industrial Enterprise at Certain Scale.

Continued

社会消费品零售总额(亿元) Total Retail Sales of Consumer Goods (100 million yuan)	位次 Rank	社会消费品零售总额比上年增长(%) Increase Rate in 2004 over 2003of Total Retail Sales of Consumer Goods	位次 Rank	进出口总额(亿美元) Total Imports and Exports (USD 100 million)	位次 Rank	#出口总额(亿美元) Total Exports (USD 100 million)	位次 Rank	外商直接投资(万美元) Foreign Direct Investments (USD 10 000)	位次 Rank
53950.1		**13.3**		**11547.9**		**5933.7**		**6062998**	
2191.8	11	14.4	11	946.6	4	205.8	8	255974	7
1052.7	18	14.1	13	420.4	8	208.6	7	172091	11
2522.9	8	15.8	4	135.3	10	93.4	10	69954	13
884.8	24	21.3	2	53.8	19	40.4	12	9022	25
892.0	22	22.7	1	37.2	23	13.6	25	34297	17
2642.8	7	13.4	20	344.4	9	189.2	9	540677	6
1252.6	16	12.8	27	67.9	13	17.2	24	19237	21
1555.4	14	13.0	24	67.9	14	36.8	15	33917	18
2454.6	9	10.5	30	1600.2	3	735.1	3	631087	4
4159.7	3	16.6	3	1708.6	2	875.0	2	894830	2
3645.4	4	15.5	6	852.3	5	581.6	4	573256	5
1503.1	15	12.9	25	72.1	11	39.4	14	42850	14
1995.8	13	14.7	9	475.5	7	294.0	6	192384	9
1059.9	17	14.8	8	35.3	25	20.0	23	204487	8
4483.5	2	13.9	17	606.7	6	358.5	5	866423	3
2808.2	5	15.7	5	66.2	16	41.8	11	42211	15
2667.5	6	13.1	22	67.7	15	33.8	16	174441	10
2069.8	12	14.0	16	54.3	18	31.0	17	141803	12
6370.4	1	13.6	18	3571.3	1	1915.6	1	1001158	1
973.4	19	13.5	19	42.8	20	23.9	20	29579	19
220.2	28	14.9	7	34.0	26	10.9	26	11926	24
955.0	21	14.3	12	38.6	21	20.9	22	25196	20
2384.0	10	14.0	15	68.7	12	39.8	13	36503	16
517.6	27	12.8	28	15.1	28	8.7	28	6271	27
884.9	23	13.1	23	37.5	22	22.4	21	14153	22
63.7	31	9.3	31	2.0	31	1.3	31		
966.5	20	13.3	21	36.4	24	24.0	19	14132	23
535.8	26	12.9	26	17.7	27	10.0	27	3539	29
115.6	30	12.6	29	5.8	30	4.6	30		
137.8	29	14.1	14	9.1	29	6.5	29	6704	26
563.7	25	14.5	10	56.4	17	30.5	18	4586	28

续表 5 Continued

地 区	Region	国际旅游人数(万人次) Total Number of Inbound International Tourists (10 000 persons)	位 次 Rank	旅游外汇收入(亿美元) Earnings from International Tourism (USD 100 million)	位 次 Rank
全 国	**China**	**10904.0**		**257.0**	
北 京	Beijing	315.5	3	31.7	2
天 津	Tianjin	61.6	15	4.1	10
河 北	Hebei	58.1	17	1.9	19
山 西	Shanxi	29.6	25	0.8	25
内蒙古	Inner Mongolia	80.0	13	2.5	16
辽 宁	Liaoning	108.1	10	6.1	7
吉 林	Jilin	32.4	22	1.0	22
黑龙江	Heilongjiang	73.3	14	3.0	13
上 海	Shanghai	385.5	2	30.4	3
江 苏	Jiangsu	306.6	4	17.6	4
浙 江	Zhejiang	276.7	5	13.0	5
安 徽	Anhui	50.1	19	1.4	21
福 建	Fujian	172.9	6	10.7	6
江 西	Jiangxi	28.8	26	0.8	27
山 东	Shandong	119.3	7	5.7	8
河 南	Henan	45.0	20	1.6	20
湖 北	Hubei	61.2	16	1.9	18
湖 南	Hunan	55.3	18	3.1	12
广 东	Guangdong	1563.7	1	53.8	1
广 西	Guangxi	117.6	8	2.9	15
海 南	Hainan	30.9	24	0.8	24
重 庆	Chongqing	43.4	21	2.0	17
四 川	Sichuan	96.6	11	2.9	14
贵 州	Guizhou	23.1	28	0.8	26
云 南	Yunnan	110.1	9	4.2	9
西 藏	Tibet	9.6	29	0.4	29
陕 西	Shaanxi	80.0	12	3.6	11
甘 肃	Gansu	23.7	27	0.4	28
青 海	Qinghai	2.9	30	0.1	30
宁 夏	Ningxia	0.7	31	0.0	31
新 疆	Xinjiang	31.7	23	0.9	23

中国统计出版社最新资料书简目

New Published Statistical Yearbook by China Sta tistics Press

自治区劳动和社会保障厅

自治区政协副主席、自治区劳动和社会保障厅党组书记　黄昌元

自治区劳动和社会保障厅厅长　艾拉提·艾山

2004年，自治区劳动和社会保障厅以“三个代表”重要思想为指导，坚持立党为公，执政为民，认真落实科学发展观和正确的政绩观，使全区劳动和社会保障事业取得了长足的发展：就业再就业工作成效显著，全区实现就业再就业36.89万人，完成全年目标任务的119%；继续巩固两个确保，全年进中心国有企业下岗职工0.91万人，出中心3.17万人，截止年底仍在中心1.88万人，支付国有企业下岗职工基本生活保障费并代缴社会保险费1.81亿元，为企业离退休人员发放养老金38.75亿元；社会保险扩面征缴力度进一步加大，各项社会保险参保人数达628.47万人；职业技能培训取得新成效，全年培训各类人员103.96万人，完成全年目标任务的121%；劳动关系进一步规范，全区国有及国有控股企业劳动合同签订率达到95%以上，非国有企业劳动合同签订率达到70%以上，受理劳动争议案件结案率达96.9%；劳动保障监察执法力度不断加大，对1.87万户用人单位用工情况进行了审查，追缴拖欠农民工工资12.38亿元；基础工作取得新成果，自治区金保工程已建成，实现了与劳动保障部联网，开通了与劳动保障部的IP电话和视频会议系统；劳动保障部门能力建设不断加强，通过开展业务培训和思想政治教育等，建成了一流队伍，一流班子，创出了一流业绩。

自治区领导参加自治区劳动和社会保障工作会议

艾拉提·艾山厅长在检查自治区再就业基地

艾拉提·艾山厅长在和田地区调研

蓬勃向上的新疆审计事业

朱登云厅长在作财政审计工作报告

朱登云厅长代表政府作审计工作报告

2004 年，在自治区党委、人民政府和国家审计署的正确领导下，自治区审计厅以十六大和十六届四中全会精神为指导，坚持“全面审计、突出重点”工作方针，努力强化创新意识，突出对重点领域、重点部门、重点资金的审计监督，努力加大对重大违纪违规问题的查处力度，进一步提高审计工作质量和水平，审计监督工作取得了新的进展。一是围绕促进财政改革，加强财政监督和部门单位财务管理，组织开展了对自治区本级和各地财政预决算审计。二是围绕与人民群众切身利益紧密相关的事项，积极开展了社保资金、扶贫资金使用和相关政策执行情况的审计。三是围绕西部大开发战略实施，积极开展重点建设项目和外资项目审计。四是围绕加强干部管理监督、强化监督制约机制，继续推进经济责任审计。2004 年，全区各级审计机关共审计 2351 个单位，查出违规资金 52 亿元，收缴财政 1.4 亿元，向司法纪检部门移交 78 件、涉案人员 89 人，提交审计报告及信息 1341 篇。维护了正常的财政经济秩序，促进了依法行政和党风廉政建设，为自治区党委政府宏观决策管理发挥了积极作用。

自治区审计厅举办传达学习十六届四中全会精神培训班

一年来，我区审计工作呈现出一派蓬勃向上的景象，在四个方面取得了

审计厅领导干部反腐倡廉学习班动员会

自治区大专院校财务与审计专题研讨班

朱登云厅长在库车县调研

显著成绩：第一，全面推进依法审计。针对不同人员开展法制培训，对全疆审计干部进行定期轮训，依法行政水平有了较大提高；从内控制度入手，加强管理，做到依法行政、依法审计；认真落实审计项目三级复核制度，加强审计质量和执法检查工作。第二，审计为宏观调控和大局服务的意识明显增强。对审计中发现的影响自治区改革和经济健康发展的突出问题，及时向自治区人民政府报送专题报告，并深入分析产生问题的原因，从机制、制度和管理上提出建议，分别被王乐泉书记、司马义·铁力瓦尔地主席等自治区党政领导批示，要求有关部门制定措施、积极整改，为领导宏观决策管理发挥了积极作用。第三，加大了审计结果公开力度。在新闻媒体上公布了《关于抗震救灾重建资金审计情况公告》，并且首次在《新疆日报》、《新疆经济报》和自治区人民政府网站上全面披露了《2003 年度自治区本级预算执行和其他财政收支情况审计工作报告》，在社会上引起广泛关注。第四，在人力资源整合上进行了创新。树立了全区审计机关"一盘棋"的思想，打破全区审计机关和厅机关各处室界限，统一编组，合理使用人力，并建立厅领导现场巡视协调制度，有力地推动了审计工作的顺利开展。

审计厅举办审计干部书画摄影作品展

新疆维吾尔自治区国土资源厅

自治区国土资源厅党组书记、副厅长王伟博

自治区国土资源厅党组副书记、厅长哈尼巴提·沙布开

2004年，在自治区党委、自治区人民政府和国土资源部的正确领导下，自治区国土资源工作紧紧围绕为自治区经济建设和社会发展提供资源保障和服务这个中心，认真贯彻落实党的十六届三中、四中全会和自治区党委六届七次、八次全委（扩大）会议精神，为保持自治区经济持续快速发展做出了积极的贡献。

截止2004年底，全区基本农田保护面积为3948.9万亩（不含兵团），以1996年自治区耕地面积4602.6万亩为基数，保护率达到了85.8%。全年安排土地开发整理项目经费预算5390万元，完成了12个国家投资的土地开发整理项目，建设总规模为4189公顷，新增耕地面积2080.3公顷。

地质勘查工作得到进一步加强，年度地质勘查资金投入预计达到68.2亿元（其中：非油气矿产地质勘查资金投入预计达到3.2亿元；石油天然气勘查资金投入预计达到65亿元左右）。发现一批新的重要矿产地。

窗口办公

在国土资源市场建设方面，2004年1至8月，全区共出让土地4180宗，面积24381亩，合同收入12.4624亿元。其中招标拍卖挂牌出让434宗，面积3358亩，合同收入6.95亿元。截止2004年9月，全区有偿出让采矿权194个，采矿权价款2.55亿元，收取采矿权价款2941万元。出让探矿权9个，收取价款2067万元。

国土资源规划管理、国土资源宏观调控、国土资源市场秩序治理整顿、国土资源测绘、地质环境保护和地质灾害治理工作，以及依法行政、党风廉政建设、精神文明建设和系统行风建设均得到全面加强，2004年12月3日，在自治区党政机关作风评议大会上，自治区国土资源厅被评为自治区列入行业作风评议八个部门的第一名。

社会宣传

新疆维吾尔自治区卫生厅

团结进取的党组一班人

2004 年，全区卫生系统在自治区党委、人民政府的领导下，团结一致，扎实工作，在疾病预防控制体系、医疗救治体系、传染病院（区）建设、新型农牧区合作医疗试点、城市医疗卫生体制改革、农村卫生、传染病防治、纠正行业不正之风、解决群众看病贵等方面做了大量富有成效的工作：

认真抓好公共卫生体系建设。2002–2004 年国家和自治区相继投资 5.7 亿元，组织实施了血站、传染病医院（病区）、紧急救援中心、农村巡回医疗车、乡镇卫生院建设项目 200 多个。

稳步推进新型合作医疗试点工作。2003 年确定于田、麦盖提、乌鲁木齐、玛纳斯、富蕴等五个县为新型农牧区合作医疗试点县。2004 年自治区党委、人民政府又新增了阿克陶、阿瓦提、焉耆、鄯善、哈密市、伊宁县、博乐市、沙湾 8 个试点县。2005 年自治区将再新增 40 个试点县。

2004 年自治区新型农牧区合作医疗会议在南疆喀什召开。图为卫生厅党组书记柯丽（右一）、卫生厅厅长买买明·牙生（左二）和与会代表进行现场观摩

切实抓好重点传染病的防治工作。对符合条件的 14751 名结核病患者进行了免费治疗。自治区人民政府还调整成立了“自治区艾滋病防治工作委员会”。

积极推进城镇医疗卫生体制改革。截止 2004 年 10 月底，全区有 94% 的县以上公立医院开展了药品集中招标采购工作，累计采购金额达到 10.8 亿元，占医院购药总金额的 67.4%，药价下降 20%，约 2 亿元；全区有 103 所县以上公立医疗机构开展了一次性医用耗材招标采购试点工作，采购金额 1.06 亿元，降低采购成本 1786 万元；二级医院和一级医院在现行价格的基础上分别降低了 15% 和 30%，部分大型医疗设备检查收费标准下降 6% 至 53%；全区 12 个大中城市建立社区卫生服务机构 304 个。

加强了卫生立法与法制监督工作。2004 年，自治区人民政府颁布了《新疆维吾尔自治区预防控制艾滋病性病办法》，完成了《自治区爱国卫生条例》的调研和立项工作，起草了《自治区突发公共卫生事件应急管理办法》，清理取消卫生行政许可项目 19 个，改变管理方式项目 4 个。

以行风评议为契机，进一步加大了卫生行风建设力度。2004 年，卫生纠风工作采取区、地、县三级联动的方式，在卫生厅的统一部署下，先后组织召开了“医疗机构向社会公开服务承诺发布会”。其中自治区 11 所大型医院向社会做出了十项服务承诺，122 名专家联名发出拒收红包、回扣、开单提成和诚信服务倡议书。

自治区卫生厅关爱百姓健康大型义诊咨询活动现场

2004 年国家安排国债资金 1900 万元为我区 85 个县市装备了 85 辆农村巡回医疗车，进一步改善农牧区的医疗服务水平，解决农牧民看病难问题

新疆维吾尔自治区司法厅

司法厅党组书记　杜建锡

司法厅厅长　哈斯木·马木提

新疆维吾尔自治区司法厅是自治区人民政府主管全区司法行政工作的职能部门，担负着管理、监督、指导全区监狱、劳教、律师、公证、基层法律服务、普法依法治理、人民调解、面向社会司法鉴定、司法考试、法学教育及法学研究等项工作任务。司法厅下设监狱工作管理局、劳动教养工作管理局(均为二级局)。全区所辖地、州、市司法局 15 个，县(市、区)司法局 95 个。全区现有 237 个律师事务所，2012 名执业律师；126 个公证处，417 名执业公证员；713 个基层法律服务所，2221 名执业法律服务工作者；面向社会服务司法鉴定机构 16 个，人员 286 名。

近年来，司法厅党委进一步解放思想、转变观念、深化改革、锐意进取，坚持以邓小平理论、“三个代表”重要思想和科学发展观为指导，深入学习贯彻党的十六届三中、四中全会精神，紧紧围绕自治区的中心工作，充分发挥法律保障和法律服务的职能作用，在加强自治区法制建设，保障国家法律的实施和公民的合法权益，打击犯罪活动，化解人民内部矛盾，维护社会秩序，促进经济发展等方面做出了积极贡献。

杜建锡书记在自治区劳教局检查指导工作并听取工作汇报

坚持把监狱、劳教工作放到突出位置来抓，全力维护了监所稳定；坚持“普”、“治”并举，依法治理工作稳步推进。深入开展了“民主法治示范村”创建活动和“法律进社区”活动。目前，全区各地、州、市、县(市、区)和 90%的行政村开展了依法治理工作；坚持以拓展和规范为主题，促进了法律服务工作的健康发展；基层基础工作进一步加强。全区已建成司法所 973 个，占总建制数的 96.6%；司法行政法制工作明显加强。积极开展了涉及司法行政工作的行政许可依据、项目、主体的清理工作，经自治区人民政府审核、确认了 9 件。此外，司法鉴定工作进一步规范。历次国家司法考试工作圆满完成，实现了司法部提出的“最权威、最规范、最严密、最廉洁”的要求。

2004 年 10 月，哈斯木·马木提厅长在巴音郭楞蒙古自治州和硕县司法局检查司法行政工作

新疆维吾尔自治区民政厅

自治区民政厅党组书记　莫　涓

自治区民政厅厅长　吾买尔江·米孜艾合买提

2004年自治区民政厅坚持以邓小平理论和“三个代表”重要思想为指导，深入贯彻党的十六大和十六届三中、四中全会精神，按照自治区党委、人民政府的统一部署，认真贯彻全国民政工作会议和自治区民政工作会议精神，落实“以人为本，为民解困”的工作宗旨，狠抓各项工作的落实，较好地完成了各项工作。

救灾救济工作成效显著，全年共投入救灾资金9100万元(包括中央、自治区及各地财政投入资金)。全区将有198万人(次)灾民和群众得到不同形式的救济。城市居民最低生活保障工作稳步推进。自治区民政厅根据各地州、市结合本地实际制定出台了《低保工作实施细则》，使低保工作有法可依，有章可循，并配合有关部门积极开展农村医疗救助试点工作，预计全年发放低保金5.1亿元，基本实现了应保尽保。

基层工作和城市社区建设工作得到加强，大力开展村民自治示范活动，其中8个村被国家民政部、司法部命名为“全国民主法治示范村”；社区服务业加快发展，研究和制定促进社区服务发展的新政策和新措施，更多地吸收下岗失业人员再就业、双拥优扶安置工作取得进展，及时下拨抚恤经费和定期定量补助金，确保重点优抚对象的生活。住房得到保障，改善部分光荣院和烈士陵园的条件；认真做好伤残证、新证，提高等级，换证、补证等工作，全力做好退役士兵安置工作。

社会福利和社会慈善事业工作扎实有效，启动并全面实施“残疾孤儿手术康复明天计划”，2004年内为70名残疾孤儿进行了手术矫治。

自治区民政厅在新的一年里，将以“开拓进取，扎实工作”为全面建设小康社会，为自治区的稳定发展作出应有的贡献。

自治区每年八一、春节都要组织慰问团走访慰问驻疆部队官兵，进一步密切了军政、军民关系。图为自治区慰问团在驻疆空军部队召开“八一”慰问座谈会。

自治区各级党政军领导十分重视双拥工作，把双拥工作作为维护社会稳定的首要任务，取得显著成绩。目前，我区有全国双拥模范城(县)12个。图为自治区双拥办领导检查指导阿克苏市的双拥工作。

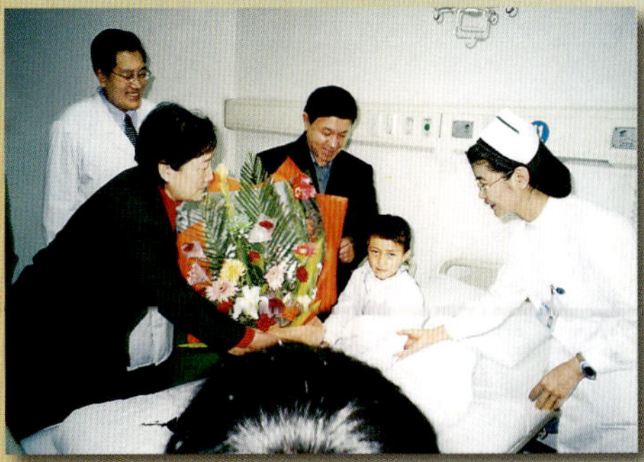

2004年12月31日，自治区民政厅副厅长热合木吐拉·尼牙孜探望“明天计划”为维吾尔族孤儿实施心脏手术。

新疆维吾尔自治区

交通厅党组成员、公路管理局党组书记郗志刚在阿勒泰抗风雪保交通一线检查工作

公路管理局局长甫拉提·伊敏诺夫看望生产一线驾驶人员

自治区公路管理局直接管养自治区列入国家统计范围的公路 15299 千米。其中:国道 7 条 7596 千米,省道 50 条 5313 千米,专用公路 57 条 2390 千米。

自治区公路管理局下设 12 个公路总段、6 个直属企业、1 个干部学校、3 个直属公路段。全区 12 个公路总段下设 69 个公路段,3 个收费所、221 个公路养护站(道班)。各类专业技术人员 1907 人。公路管理局下设 15 个基层党委,5 个党总支、144 个党支部,3566 名党员。

近年来,公路管理局各族干部职工认真贯彻党的十六大、十六届三中全会精神,努力践行“三个代表”重要思想,按照“建养并重,协调发展,强化管理,深化改革,调整结构,依靠科技,提高质量,依法治路,保障畅通”的工作方针,坚持一手抓建设,加快公路发展步伐,一手抓养护提高服务质量,克服重重困难和不利因素,圆满完成了各项工作任务。2004 年完成公路路况好路率 80.3%,同比提高了 3 个百分点。完成公路建设投资 50 亿元,公路基本建设项目总里程 4423 千米,农村公路建设项目总里程 9199 千米。目前公路管理局系统共有自治区级文明单位 99 个,地州级文明单位 49 个,县级文明单位 37 个。2001 年国家人事部、交通部授予公路管理局全国交通系统文明行业称号,2003 年 1 月被自治区人民政府命名为自治区级文明行业,2005 年 3 月被国家人事部、交通部授予全国交通系统先进集体。

抗洪抢险

疏通道路

公路管理局

自治区公路管理局领导班子成员参加 2005 年公路工作会议

公路路政执法队伍

文艺汇演

正确分析和把握形势
以科学发展观引领全行业全面协调可持续发展
——新疆维吾尔自治区通信管理局

2004年是全面落实十六大和十六届三中全会精神，继续向着“全面建设小康社会”奋斗目标迈进的一年，新疆维吾尔自治区通信管理局在信息产业部、自治区党委、人民政府的正确领导下，按照全国信息产业会议部署，以推进电信业与经济和社会的协调发展作为监管工作的出发点和立足点，以贯彻实施《行政许可法》为契机，进一步转变政府职能，提高依法行政水平；在实践工作中不断探索，认真落实信息产业部《关于加强依法治理电信市场的若干规定》等文件，将文件精神融汇到日常监管工作和依法行政过程中，有效解决了在互联互通、电信资费、电信服务质量、通信建设市场等方面存在的问题；维护空中电波秩序，保障民航飞行安全，无线电管理工作取得新的成绩；按照信息产业部和国务院纠风办的统一部署，以求真务实的作风全面完成电信行业民主评议行风活动，促进了全社会对电信行业的认识和了解，推进了电信行业信用体系的建立，为行业发展营造良好的政策环境和公平有序的市场竞争环境，为促进新疆电信业持续快速协调健康发展做出了积极贡献。

自2004年7月1日起，新疆通信管理局联合自治区人民政府纠风办在全区电信行业开展了为期半年的民主评议行风活动

2004年9月15日，由新疆通信管理局牵头，电信公司、移动公司、联通公司和铁道设计院组成通信行业精一伊一霍铁路修建实地考察团，确保铁路修建过程中通信顺畅

在全行业干部职工的共同努力下，我区电信业保持了快速、健康发展势头。截止2004年底，全行业完成业务收入76.56亿元，固定资产投资33.1亿元。全区固定电话用户新增85.7万户，总数达到516.7万户。移动电话新增68.5万户，总数达到489.7万户。互联网拨号用户达到54.9万户。全区固定电话普及率达到26.3部/百人，移动电话普及率达到24.9部/百人。以上两项均居西部十二省区前列。

为配合3·15国际消费者权益日活动，新疆通信管理局在乌鲁木齐市人民广场开展咨询服务活动

在改革中前进的新疆粮食

自治区副主席张舟在塔城市恰夏粮站调研

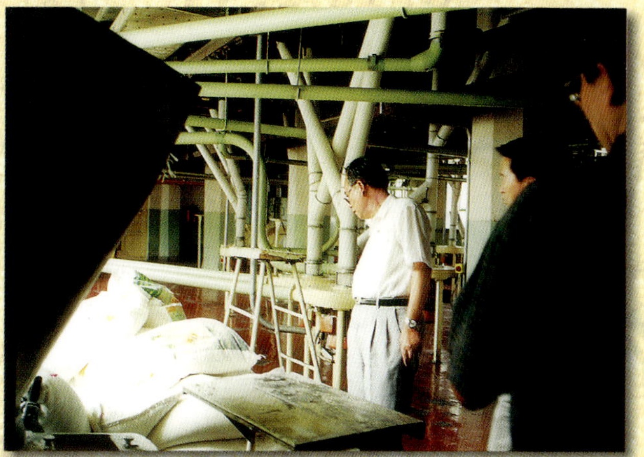

中国粮食行业协会会长白美清视察“金西域”有限责任公司面粉车间

新疆粮食是自治区国民经济的重要组成部分。1998年以来，全区粮食工作坚持以购销市场化改革为方向，开拓进取，与时俱进，初步形成了具有新疆特色的新的粮食市场化流通体系。粮食宏观调控能力不断增强，粮食库存充裕，建立了粮食风险基金，初步形成了较为完备的三级粮食储备体系和遍布各地、州(市)、县批发市场体系，粮食产销衔接日益紧密，粮食安全应急和预警机制已初步建立并正在逐步完善；国有粮食购销企业市场竞争力不断增强，目前，全区独立核算的国有粮食购销企业150户，职工1.5万余人，总资产91.5亿元(其中固定资产11.7亿元)，完好仓容30亿公斤，地坪(晒场)139万M^2,粮仓机械设备3260余台(套)；粮食产业化发展取得阶段性成果，全区面粉年加工能力达17亿公斤，油料年加工能力为9.8亿公斤。一批具备一定规模的粮食龙头企业在制粉、油脂加工、饲料加工和大米加工领域发挥着重要作用，出现了“金西域”、“天山”、“米全”、“金狮”、“泰昆”等新疆名牌产品。展望未来，新疆粮食将全面启动科技兴粮战略，以发展符合国际现代食品健康标准，具有市场前景的绿色食品为重点，以粮食产业化为改革和发展方向，以将资源优势转化经济效益为目标，进一步加大粮食企业改革力度，扶优、扶强、扶名牌、扶龙头企业，迎接挑战，再创新疆粮食经济的辉煌。我们也热耽希望国内外广大朋友和我们一起投身于这场世纪改革发展和西部大开发的洪流中，在新疆——这旧日丝绸之路的富饶之地，谱写出新千年更加灿烂的篇章！

粮食企业为部队生产加工高品质的面粉

乌鲁木齐市举办“放心粮油”展示会

丰富多彩的职工文化生活

新疆维吾尔自治区旅游局

2004 年 7 月 23 日，时任国家旅游局何光玮局长在自治区副主席张舟、自治区旅游局局长乃依木·亚森陪同下在喀纳斯检查指导工作

2004 年，自治区旅游局认真贯彻落实自治区党委六届八次全委扩大会议、自治区十届人大二次会议《政府工作报告》以及全国旅游工作会议精神。全力以赴作好旅游市场的恢复与振兴工作，全年完成了接待入境旅游者 29.8 万人次，创汇 9100 万美元；完成接待国内游客 1242 万人次，国内旅游收入 109 亿元人民币，旅游总收入达到 117.6 亿元人民币，比 2003 年增长 26.8%，较好地完成了各项任务。

1.旅游市场总体恢复明显。以日、韩、港澳台等传统客源市场和俄、哈、吉等周边国家为重点，同时加大对欧美市场的宣传力度，先后派员赴澳洲、韩国、美国、独联体、欧洲、港澳台、东南亚宣传促销，效果明显，特别是独联体一日游异常火爆，比 2002 年同期增长 2 倍多，国内旅游市场持续兴旺。2004 年春节、“五一”、“十一”三个黄金周持续兴旺，实现了“健康、安全、秩序、质量”四统一的目标。特别是“十一”黄金周旅游接待人数达到 97.55 万人次，比去年同期增长 48.99%；旅游收入 5.56 亿元人民币，比去年同期增长 44.79%。

2.旅游产业地位得到进一步提高，旅游产业规模不断扩大，地位日益提升。2004 年新增国内旅行社 55 家，全区旅行社达到 316 家，其中国际旅行社 42 家；华凌大饭店荣膺五星级宾馆饭店，新增四星级宾馆饭店 4 家，全区旅游星级宾馆饭店达 277 家；优秀旅游城市已达 6 家；新增旅游直接从业人员 10000 余人，新增导游 1500 余人，各类语种的导游达 6000 多人。新增 A 级景区 20 个，使我区的国家 A 级景区点达到 63 个。

3.成功接待了全国旅游工作座谈会。2004 年 7 月 20 日至 26 日，全国旅游工作座谈会在我区召开。全国 30 个省、市、自治区、10 个计划单列市、5 个副省级城市以及部分重点旅游城市的旅游局局长、中央以及新疆各大新闻媒体记者，共 120 余人参加了会议。

4.认真贯彻《行政许可法》，不断提高旅游行政管理部门依法行政的水平。

5.加快旅游厕所工程建设工作。

6.旅游行业管理力度进一步加大。2004 年以来，我局出台了“新疆旅游投诉暂行规定”、“自治区各旅游投诉电话管理办法”、“自治区旅游质量监督管理系统行政执法人员用语规范”，通过法规制度建设，加大了对旅游市场的监督管理力度，提高了行业管理水平，推动了新疆旅游业的发展。

7.旅游培训工作取得可喜成绩。2004 年，新疆旅游培训中心共举办了各类培训班 50 期，培训人员近 9000 人次。

国家旅游局孙钢副局长在自治区旅游局党组书记池重庆陪同下，考察我区旅游发展情况

自治区旅游局党组书记池重庆一行检查天池旅游市场

自治区旅游局局长乃依木·亚森在景区调研

2004 年自治区旅游工作会议会场

新疆邮政首届艺术节

奋进中的新疆邮政

新疆邮政自1999年邮电分营以来，经过五年的上下求索，进入了一个新的发展时期。全区1万3千名邮政职工坚定信心，同舟共济，锐意进取，走出了一条具有新疆特色邮政的可持续发展之路，为企业健康发展奠定了基础。全区邮政业务收入从1999年的5.34亿元提高到2004年的7.5亿元，累计完成32.45亿元。2003年初，被自治区文明委命名为自治区级"文明行业"。

以科技为先导，用信息化改造和提升传统邮政。先后投资建成了邮政综合计算机网，邮政储蓄计算机网，实现了全国邮政储蓄绿卡统一版本系统成功运行；构建了11185客户综合服务平台，初步建成了以邮政综合网和邮政储蓄网为主要网络，以电子化支局为基础，以11185综合服务平台为支撑的邮政信息化运行系统；全区所有邮政储蓄网点和主要邮政营业窗口实现了电子化，网络技术层迈上了新台阶。

以市场为导向，积极开拓邮政业务，服务地方经济。大力发展一体化物流，物流专业体系初具雏形，邮政物流品牌优势日益凸显；以服务三农为重点的农资分销业务在全区全面启动；充分体现速递业务"特、快、专"的业务特性，使身份证快证特快专递、普通护照特快专递寄送、中速快件业务、邮政特惠箱等业务稳步发展，推出了天山北坡经济带六城市之间的"限时递业务"；开发了两小时电子汇款、即时电子汇款、西联汇款等业务，增加了电子汇兑业务品种，增强了邮政汇兑的实力；成功设计发行了二组《走进新疆》系列邮资明信片(雪莲邮资图)，实现了《中邮专送广告》新疆版全疆联网，尝试开发了保险明信片，反映城市经济发展特色的明信片、系列化和个性化的精品专题明信片，大力发展了旅游门票明信片业务的发展，形成了门类较为齐全，各具特色的函件业务群体。

以服务为宗旨，长年履行普遍服务义务。实施"邮政服务形象工程"，实行规范服务，推进企业文化建设，文明建设硕果累累。全区邮政系统顺利通过自治区级"文明行业"复验，25个集体被授予全区邮政"规范化服务示范窗口"先进集体。

乌鲁木齐市邮政局威风锣鼓队

信函自动分拣机

邮政窗口服务

邮政普及服务

新疆维吾尔自治区妇女联合会

自治区妇联主席热孜万·艾拜陪同中共中央政治局委员、自治区党委书记王乐泉接见妇女“九大”代表

自治区党委、人大、政府、政协领导视察自治区妇女就业、创业成果展示会

自治区妇联始建于1951年8月，前身为“新疆省民主妇女联合会”和“新疆维吾尔自治区民主妇女联合会”。机关位于乌鲁木齐市民主路42号世纪大厦，内设办公室、组织部、宣传部、权益部、城乡部、儿童部、机关党委、纪检办、老干处、妇儿工委办公室和机关服务中心等11个部门；下属妇女干部学校、儿童发展中心、《新疆妇女》(维文)杂志社、《伴侣》(汉文)编辑部4个事业单位和1个企业单位——新疆妇女旅行社。机关有维、汉、哈、回、蒙、锡伯6个民族60余名在职干部职工。现全区15个地州市、93个县市、993个乡镇(街)均有妇联组织。有城乡基层村属妇代会9165个；乡镇企业妇代会200多个；个体劳协、私企协和专业市场妇委会以及其他新经济领域妇委会300多个；党政群机关、教科文卫等事业单位妇委会1663个，团体会员组织2061个，自治区级妇女联谊组织和学术团体10多个，形成了妇女组织网络化，妇女工作社会化的格局。

占全区人口半数的各族妇女是推动新疆经济和社会发展的重要力量。50多年来，作为党和政府联系妇女群众的桥梁和纽带，自治区妇联始终坚持马克思主义妇女观和民族观，把全心全意为各族妇女群众服务作为工作的出发点和落脚点，一手抓维权，一手抓发展，高举邓小平理论伟大旗帜，领导、动员、组织新疆各族妇女全面贯彻党的基本路线、方针、政策，努力实践“三个代表”重要思想，紧紧围绕自治区改革、发展、稳定的大局，推动了新疆妇女运动和妇女工作的发展。

自治区妇联九届领导班子成员陪同自治区党委副书记、纪检委书记胡家燕视察妇女维权部。胡家燕书记(左三)、妇联党组书记田文(左二)、主席热孜万·艾拜(左四)、副主席沙特甫汗·沙克泰(右四)、副主席涂凤英(右二)、副主席古丽夏提·阿不都哈德尔(右三)

自治区妇联党组书记田文陪同香港妇女发展联合会访问团参观新疆女子职业学校民族糕点班

新疆维吾尔自治区残疾人联合会

自治区残联成立于1989年，下属残疾人职业中专学校、自治区残疾人劳动就业服务中心（盲人按摩指导中心）、残疾人康复服务指导中心（聋儿康复中心）、残疾人用品用具供应服务站等4个正县级事业单位，职工总人数105人。

自治区残联2004年工作情况：

1.康复任务超额完成。至2004年底，组织实施了白内障复明、儿麻后遗症矫治、聋儿听力语言训练、低视力康复、精神病防治康复、肢体残疾人康复训练、智残儿童康复训练等康复工程，使12万余名残疾人得到不同程度的康复，各项康复任务均完成或超额完成国家下达的指标。

自治区副主席贾帕尔·艾比不拉为残疾人事业目标管理先进单位颁奖

2.就业工作全面展开。按比例安排残疾人就业工作全面推行，所有地、县均建立残疾人就业服务机构，按比例就业城市实施面达100%，县、市实施面96%。

自治区残联党组书记、理事长刘林亭慰问残疾人

残疾人法律援助活动普遍开展，图为自治区残联领导和新疆百丰律师事务所签订协议

3.扶贫解困成效显著。残疾人扶贫工作纳入了各级政府扶贫开发总体规划，有劳动能力的贫困残疾人被列入扶贫对象。

4.残疾人教育有发展。义务教育入学率提高，普通中小学普遍接收肢体残疾和轻度弱智、弱视残疾学生入学。

5.文化体育生活活跃。举办了自治区残疾人文艺汇演，15个地、州、市的200余名残疾人参加了舞蹈、声乐、器乐汇报演出，发现和培养了一批优秀残疾人艺术人才。

6.组织建设得到加强和完善。

《自治区残疾事业"十五"计划纲要》确定了今后五年我区残疾人工作的奋斗目标及主要业务领域的工作措施。"十五"期间，我区残疾人事业的总体思路是：

1.夯实基础，提高为残疾人服务的能力，加强残疾人事业法制建设，依法维护残疾人的合法权益，依法发展残疾人事业。

2.突出重点，全面推进，今后几年，我们将继续重点做好残疾人生存状况的康复、教育、就业、扶贫、社会保障工作。

3.进一步解放思想，转变观念，调整思路，开拓创新，抓住西部大开发的机遇，特别是中央11号文件对新疆稳定与发展全方位支持的好时机，加快残疾人事业的发展。

4.加强自身建设，不断适应新形势、新任务对残疾人工作的要求。按照"进一步加强残疾人工作与残联建设"的原则，切实加强基层工作，规范县、乡残联一体化工作机构，充实人员，完善制度。

总之，我们有决心和信心，在中残联的大力关爱和有力指导下，在自治区党委、政府的领导下，解放思想，与时俱进，以扎实的工作，顽强的作风，齐心协力做好各项残疾人工作，努力推动残疾人事业与全面建设小康社会协调发展，不断开创我区残疾人事业新局面。

新疆维吾尔自治区供销合作社联合社

2004 年 9 月，自治区供销社主办了首届“中国西部农村合作经济发展论坛”，自治区有关领导到会祝贺

党委书记、理事会主任马德同志在供销社直属单位民族团结教育月活动表彰大会上讲话

自治区党政领导参加自治区供销社 2004 年度棉花形势分析会

2004 年 11 月 10 日，自治区领导参加新疆果业集团有限公司成立揭牌仪式

新疆维吾尔自治区供销合作社联合社在自治区党委、政府的正确领导下，以党的十六大精神和“三个代表”重要思想为指导，坚持发展第一要务，坚定不移地推进“四项改造”，紧紧围绕自治区“三农”中心工作，通过实施“613”和“217”为农服务系统工程，大力参与农业产业化经营和农村流通现代化建设，积极探索新形势下合作经济发展的新路子，各项工作呈现良好发展势头。

经济运行呈现良好态势，为自治区“三农”发展做出了新贡献，2004 年 1–11 月，全区供销社系统购进实现 204.8 亿元，同比增长 35.8%，其中农副产品购进实现 137.9 亿元，同比增长 54.6%，实现销售收入 145.2 亿元，同比增长 14.8%，1–11 月全系统上缴国家税费 1.7 亿元。

参与农业产业化经营工作力度进一步加大，目前全系统已培育发展龙头企业 196 家，其中，全国供销系统龙头企业 15 家，自治区级重点龙头企业 4 家，自治区供销社龙头企业 27 家。

为完善农村经营体制开辟了新途径。目前供销社系统兴办各类专业合作社 175 个，入社农民 6500 多户，专业合作社助农增收 1.8 亿元。

网络建设实现了跨越式发展，农村流通现代化迈出新步伐。全系统已发展连锁企业 14 个，连锁网点 2549 个。以新疆农资集团为龙头的“农佳乐”农资连锁经营服务网络遍布区内各 15 个地州（市）、80 个县市和内地 10 个省市。

自治区供销社本级企业已全部完成产权制度改革，各地州（市）供销社 70%以上的社有企业已行了改制。通过资产重组，股权置换，产业整合，重组成立了农资、棉花、果业三大集团公司。

基层社改革取得新进展，为农服务意识增强。全区基层社改革面达到 35%。

2005 年，自治区供销社系统将进一步做好“三农”工作，继续实施“271”为农服务系统工程，实现“两个突破”（在促进农村合作经济组织，旅游业发展上有新突破），上“四个台阶”（在实现农业产业化、网络建设、深化企业改革、出口创汇四个方面上一个新台阶），在引领农村合作经济组织发展，带动农民增收致富奔小康进程中发挥更大作用。

2004 年 8 月，供销社系统首届行业技能大赛在喀什举行

新疆维吾尔自治区文学艺术界联合会

自治区领导为新疆文联成立50周年摄影、美术、书法展览开幕式剪彩

新疆维吾尔自治区文学艺术界联合会（简称新疆文联），是由自治区党委领导，自治区党委宣传部代管的人民团体。

新疆文联所属的团体会员有：新疆作家协会、新疆音乐家协会、新疆舞蹈家协会、新疆美术家协会、新疆戏剧家协会、新疆民间文艺家协会、新疆书法家协会、新疆摄影家协会、新疆电影家协会、新疆电视艺术家协会、新疆杂技家协会，以及各地、州、市文学艺术界联合会和全区性产业文联。

新疆文联设有办公室、组织人事部、纪检（监察室）、联络部、老干部处、机关党委、机关服务中心、工会、文艺理论研究室。新疆文联还设有《明星时代》、《西部》、《塔里木》（维吾尔文）、《曙光》（哈萨克文）、《启明星》（蒙古文）、《新疆柯尔克孜文学》（柯尔克孜文）、《新疆艺术》（维吾尔文）、《文学译丛》（维吾尔文）等五种文版的八个编辑部和杂志社。新疆民间艺术家协会主管编辑的杂志有《民族文汇》和两个民间文学期刊《美拉斯》（维吾尔文）、《木拉》（哈萨克文）。

新疆文联的宗旨是：以马列主义、毛泽东思想、邓小平理论和“三个代表”重要思想为指导，坚持文艺为人民服务、为社会主义服务的方向和“百花齐放、百家争鸣”的方针，致力于繁荣自治区多民族社会主义文学艺术事业，为建设社会主义先进文化和实现现代化而努力奋斗。

文艺工作者在表演“顶碗舞”

中国人民武装警察部队

中国人民武装警察部队新疆维吾尔自治区总队（简称：武警新疆总队，副军级），是驻守在祖国西北边陲的一支具有光辉历史、光荣传统的部队。主要担负看押（守）、守卫（护）、警卫等勤务及处置各类突发事件。

总队自1982年重新组建以来，总队党委带领广大官兵不负重托，不辱使命，忠实履行职责，在保卫和支援地方经济建设、在积极开展“三个文明”建设、在打击“三股势力”的殊死战斗中，充分发挥了“拳头”和“尖刀”作用。特别是近年来，在党中央、国务院、中央军委的亲切关怀下、在武警总部和自治区党委、政府的正确领导下，总队党委始终以邓小平理论和“三个代表”重要思想为指导，牢记“两个务必”，坚持用科学的发展观、政绩观来指导部队全面建设，部队各项事业蒸蒸日上，开创了部队建设的新局面。

坚持把思想政治建设摆在部队各项建设的首位，坚持党对武警部队的绝对领导，始终保持蓬勃朝气、昂扬锐气和浩然正气，部队建设始终保持了正确的发展方向。图为总队长潘昌杰与政治委员徐田有在党委中心组理论学习时交流心得

积极参加和支援西部大开发，新疆总队作为武警部队唯一代表出席“全军军队参加和支援西部大开发工作会议”。图为总队长潘昌杰在会议上介绍经验

走出国门，加强与世界其他国家军警部队的友好往来，相互借鉴，相互学习，共同提高。图为2004年9月14日到25日，总队政治委员徐田有少将出访土尔其时接受该国宪兵司令费维兹上将赠送的军牌

树立典型，表彰先进，极大地调动了广大官兵“扎根边疆、艰苦奋斗、戍边卫民、爱国奉献”的热情。喀什地区支队塔什库尔干塔吉克自治县中队被武警部队和自治区党委、政府分别授予“艰苦奋斗模范中队”和“高原创业为民模范中队”荣誉称号

以史为鉴，学史明理。总队以警史馆为窗口，坚持不懈地在官兵中开展革命传统教育并取得了良好的社会效益。一年多来，先后接待军内外参观者达5000多人次，充分发挥了爱国主义教育示范基地的作用

努力加强“三个文明”建设，与驻地共青团组织广泛开展“思想工作联抓、公益事业联做、人才培养联手、文体活动联谊”活动

新疆总队

“2004 年度国家反劫机演习”于 10 月 20 日在乌鲁木齐国际机场拉开帷幕。总队特战分队进行了反劫持人质、现场封控等课目的演示并获圆满成功

整装待发的特战队员

2004 年 11 月，武警新疆总队反恐特战大队入住新落成的反恐怖训练基地。至此，我区在反恐怖斗争领域里又迈出了重要的一步，反恐特战大队的诞生，标志着新疆总队建设进入了一个新的历史阶段

英勇善战的武警航空兵

紧 急 出 动

快速出击

风雨兼程五十载　开拓奋进谱华章

自治区高级人民法院

中共中央政治局委员、自治区党委书记王乐泉等自治区领导亲切看望“人民满意的好法官”

伴随着自治区50年前进的步伐，自治区人民法院也走过了半个世纪的光辉历程。目前全区共有法院151个，其中高级法院一个，高级法院分院两个（地方、兵团各1个），中级法院24个，基层法院124个。现有干警8077名，2004年审结各类案件达26万多件，逐步形成了组织机构健全、司法保障有力的良好局面。

50年来，各级法院在自治区党委的领导和人大的监督下，忠实履行宪法和法律赋予的职责，围绕“公正与效率”工作主题，落实司法为民要求，积极推进法院改革和创新，努力提高审判质量，充分发挥各项审判职能，全力维护社会稳定，促进自治区经济发展和社会文明进步，保障新疆经济发展和人民幸福，各项工作取得了令人瞩目的成绩，仅1995年至2004年的十年间，全区法院就审结刑事案件175309件、民商事案件1449358件，为自治区的改革、发展和稳定做出了积极贡献。

近年来，全区各级人民法院深入开展“优秀法院、优秀法官”创建活动，精神文明建设取得显著成效。1997年以来，全区法院系统共有47个集体获得国家级荣誉称号，有121个集体获得自治区级荣誉称号；有51名同志获得国家级荣誉称号，182名同志获得自治区级荣誉称号。到2004年年底，全区所有法院都已进入文明单位行列，其中自治区级文明单位79个。

自治区高级人民法院新闻发布会——聚焦人民陪审员

全区“人民满意的好法院、人民满意的好法官”表彰大会

自治区法院系统“人民满意的好法院、人民满意的好法官”颁奖、授牌仪式

自治区高级人民法院审判长颁证大会

新疆维吾尔自治区红十字会

2004年是中国红十字会建会100周年，也是新疆维吾尔自治区红十字会发展史上具有重要意义的一年。自治区党委批准成立中共新疆维吾尔自治区红十字会党组，任命王建共为党组书记。并胜利召开了新疆维吾尔自治区红十字会第三次会员代表大会。中共中央政治局委员、自治区党委书记王乐泉看望与会代表并发表重要讲话。大会选举产生了新一届理事会，聘请自治区党委副书记、自治区主席司马义·铁力瓦尔地为名誉会长，选举自治区副主席库热西·买合苏提为会长。全年向灾区下拨救灾款26万元，救灾物资价值74万元。巴楚—伽师地震灾区重建项目和加拿大二期小项目工作基本完成。与香港红十字会合作的“普及农牧区群众防灾防病知识、建立红十字会基层备灾机制项目”正式启动。召开了“纪念中国红十字会成立100周年暨‘双先’表彰大会”。与自治区党委宣传部联合下发了加强红十字会宣传工作的通知。为造血干细胞资料库建设募集专项资金113.47万元。全年在13期各类培训班上传播红十字运动基本知识，2000余人接受了培训。与自治区13个部门联合下发了《关于广泛深入开展救护工作的意见》的通知。举办了4期彩票公益金卫生救护师资培训班，培训141人。昌吉市被总会评为全国首批社区红十字服务示范市。春节、古尔邦节前，自筹资金65万元开展了“红十字博爱送万家”活动，对全疆3750户特困家庭进行了慰问。中国造血干细胞捐献者资料库新疆分库正式挂牌启动。全年有528人份检测数据入库。艾滋病预防工作方面，举办各类培训班100期，培训1798人。制作并在新疆卫视播出专题片“红十字会在行动”。

中共中央政治局委员、自治区党委书记王乐泉看望出席自治区红十字会第三次会员代表大会代表并发表重要讲话

2004年10月12日，自治区红十字会召开第三次会员代表大会

2005年1月29日，自治区红十字会向五家渠八一水库决堤受灾群众捐赠物资

香港红十字会为“普及农牧区群众防灾防病知识、建立红十字会基层备灾机制项目”捐赠6辆工作车

中共新疆维吾尔自治区委员会党校
新疆行政学院

自治区领导在自治区党校(学院)主体班次开学典礼上

校、院领导带队在昌吉州“四县市”参观考察

自治区党校(学院)学员在听辅导报告

中共新疆维吾尔自治区委员会党校创建于1950年3月。新疆行政学院于2000年9月在自治区党校挂牌成立,实行“两块牌子,一套班子”的体制。

自治区党校(行政学院)位于乌鲁木齐市中心区域,校(院)座落于西后街22号。校(院)实行校(院)务委员会领导体制,自治区党委副书记、自治区纪检委书记胡家燕同志兼任校长。设有哲学、政治学、经济学、党史党建、马克思主义民族宗教理论、法学、语文、行政学、新疆经济与社会发展研究中心等9个教学科研部门。

校(院)现有教职工478人,办学规模1000人。校(院)总面积74492平方米。各种教学设施齐全,图书馆6003平方米,现有藏书22万余册。教学活动中心8341平方米,融远程教学、多媒体教学、礼堂、文化健身娱乐设施为一体。新建的培训楼建筑面积9668平方米,共有160个标准间。全校现有教室30个,会议室9个,可同时接纳1200余人学习、研讨。校园内绿化、美化面积占总面积的40%以上,为学员提供了一个清新优雅的学习、休闲环境。

自治区党校、行政学院现有专职教师114人,其中,教授11人,副教授55人,具有博士、硕士学位研究生18人。2004年,校(院)共立项各级各类课题10项,7项科研成果获得全国党校系统、全国行政学院系统优秀科研成果一、二、三等奖,3项成果获得自治区第六届哲学社会科学评奖一、二、三等奖。全年共完成科研成果203项,出版专著3部,在各级刊物上发表论文166篇。2004年,共培训厅局级等主体班学员800余人,研究生315人,在校本专科函授学员12000余人。

当前,自治区党校、行政学院根据中央关于加强党的执政能力建设的部署,结合共产党员先进性教育,按照自治区党委的要求,正在拟定今后一个时期校(院)发展的战略和规划,深化教学科研改革,加强学科建设,积极推进人事制度改革,努力创造一流的工作水平和工作业绩。

校园一角

新疆储备物资管理局

新疆储备物资管理局是中央驻疆单位，隶属于国家发展与改革委员会国家物资储备局，主要负责国家战略储备物资的管理工作。国家物资储备的功能是：“服务国防建设，应对突发事件，参与宏观调控，维护国家安全”。新疆储备局自1974年建局以来，历届领导班子在国家物资储备局党组和自治区党委、人民政府的领导下，紧紧围绕物资储备工作的基本任务，励精图治，不辱使命，团结奋斗，扎实工作，圆满完成了以储备物资管理为中心的各项任务，国储物资管理达到了“保质、保量、保安全、保急需”的总要求。在抓好物资管理的同时，储备局把支援地方经济建设视为己任，积极发挥行业优势，采取收储、借贷储备物资等形式，在一定范围内调节市场，竭诚为地方经济建设服务，做出了一定的贡献。此外，积极开展以“四代一租”（代储、代管、代装卸、代发送，库房租赁）为主的经营服务性工作，利用铁路专用线、仓库等仓储设施及门吊、汽吊、叉车等装卸设备，积极发展物流业，并形成了一定规模，促进了新疆储备事业的发展。在新的历史时期，新疆储备局党组一班人积极贯彻十六大和十六届三中、四中全会精神，认真实践“三个代表”的重要思想，坚持“以储为主、多种经营”的储备工作方针，解放思想、不断进取、勇于实践、求真务实，积极研究和探索新疆储备事业发展的新问题，以饱满的热情向更高更新的目标而努力奋斗！

党组成员、纪检组长朱新利（左一），党组成员、副局长袁顺林（左二），党组书记、局长罗歆京（左三），助理巡视员艾克木·色依提（左四）

党组书记、局长罗歆京同志看望武警部队官兵并协商仓库安全保卫工作

党组书记、局长罗歆京同志出席国家物资储备会议时与国家物资储备局局长肖贵林同志签订责任书后亲切握手

新疆维吾尔自治区建筑材料行业管理办公室

团结奋进的领导班子:吕志坚主任(右二)、柳奇副主任(右三)、孙存稳副主任(右一)、艾斯哈尔·茹孜副主任(右四)

新疆维吾尔自治区建筑材料行业管理办公室为自治区经济贸易委员会管理的主管建材行业的行政机构。主要职责是:(一)研究拟定自治区建材工业发展战略和行业规划,提出发展自治区建材行业的方针、政策;推进行业结构调整,引导行业合理布局。(二)研究提出自治区建材工业的行业法规,组织制定行业管理规章、技术标准;汇集、分析和发布行业经济技术信息,提供信息咨询服务。(三)协调行业内部关系,维护公平竞争秩序;掌握、分析自治区建材生产动态,向有关部门提出政策建议;促进建材资源综合利用,推进新型建材及制品的开发和推广应用;组织有关的自治区建材行业经济技术合作与交流。(四)指导直属国有建材企事业改革和结构调整,指导自治区国有建材企业扭亏解困、减员增效和实施再就业工程。(五)负责自治区发展散装水泥、新型墙材和建筑节能工作;协助有关部门作好自治区非金属矿资源勘察、开采的监督管理工作。

2004年,自治区建材行办认真贯彻落实自治区党委、人民政府的总体部署和经贸委的工作安排,以市场为导向,以发展为主题,以结构调整为主线,以科技创新、体制创新为动力,加快新型工业化发展步伐,实现了年初制定的各项工作目标。全年实现工业增加值29亿元,同比增长13.5%;实现产品销售率98%;水泥产量1250万吨,增长11%。截止年末,全区有乡及乡以上建材企业1042家,全行业从业人数10万余人。建材行业作为自治区五大支柱产业之一,为我区经济的发展做出了贡献。

水泥企业生产区

石膏板车间

鄯善红荒料

加大高新技术应用力度
努力提升新疆机电工业

——新疆维吾尔自治区机械电子行业管理办公室

自治区机电行办主任张启曾在“新疆制造业信息化示范工程项目签约大会”上作专题演讲

自治区机电行办领导班子及各处室负责人在认真学习十六届三中全会精神

新疆机械电子行业管理办公室作为自治区机电工业的行业主管部门，根据自治区走新型工业化发展道路的总体战略部署要求，积极推进机电工业加快电子信息技术和高新技术应用步伐，努力培育创新能力，加大招商引资力度使机电工业近年来保持了平稳的发展速度。机电工业也被自治区列为制造业信息化示范行业。到2003年底，全区机电工业规模以上企业141家，实现工业增加值12亿元，完成销售收入42亿元，实现利税总额突破4亿元。全行业涌现出了一批积极应用高新技术、电子信息技术改造传统产业，并取得较好成效的骨干企业。特变电工股份有限公司的变压器年产量已达到6000万KVA，居中国首位，全球第三位，并研制出了智能化控制变压器、超高压720KV电线电缆、变压器远程监控自动系统等在行业居于领先水平的产品。新疆金风科技股份有限公司消化吸收德国等世界发达国家先进风力发电装备制造技术开发生产的600KW国产化风力发电机组已批量化生产，750KW国产化试验机组已研发成功并正式挂网运行，已成为国内最大的风力发电装备研制和制造基地。新疆众和股份有限公司生产的低压电子铝箔在全国市场占有率达到75%，也已成为国内电子新材料的重要生产基地。新疆第三机床厂开发的节能型抽油机具有多项专利技术，并走向了全国的油田市场。东风新疆汽车有限公司的重型车、沙漠越野车已成为了行业内的名牌产品。

行办机关近年来，通过加强理论学习、业务培训和贯彻落实行政许可法，依法行政的能力、为行业服务的水平不断提高，通过开展精神文明创建活动，保持了机关干部“高效、勤政、廉洁”的公务员形象。行办机关于2004年被评为自治区文明单位。

自治区机电行办主任张启曾、副主任王基友和自治区计委信息中心主任姜同海、自治区经贸委信息中心主任贺晓江参加“新疆机电制造业信息化建设发展论坛”

自治区机电行办主要领导与韩国SK集团下属SKTT株式会社主要负责人就引进韩国新型高端手机合作项目进行洽谈

自治区机电行办领导带队到新疆广汇集团工业园区调研

由自治区经贸委主持的“新疆机电工业‘十一五’发展规划论证会”在机电行办召开

中国民航新疆管理局
新疆空中交通管理局

2004年，是民航新疆管理局空中交通管理局（简称：空管局，下同）的开局之年。一年来，面对航班流量剧增和管理体系发生变革的局面，全局干部职工紧紧抓住机遇，开拓创新，团结奋斗，确保了空管安全，为新疆空管的健康发展奠定了坚实基础。

空管局始终坚持"安全第一，预防为主"的方针不动摇，积极开展安全法规制度建设，积极推进规范化、科学化安全管理；完善监督检查机制，积极开展了安全检查工作；加强协调与沟通，积极维护安全运行的系统性。严格落实各项规章制度，确保安全责任落到实处；积极建立系统预警机制，掌握规律性，努力做到防患于未然；较好地坚持了设备巡视维护制度，建立了设备应急备份机制；加强军民航协调，积极改善空域环境；积极开展了"民航空管安全管理年"等多项安全生产活动。通过夯实安全管理基础，强化安全运行，保持了全年空管安全形势的平稳。

民航总局空管局苏兰根局长在视察新疆空管局

新疆空管局召开半年工作会议

党委书记　彭　刚

局长　曹　琼

空管局先后完成了阿勒泰、塔城、阿克苏导航台工程建设、阿克苏空管站电源改造工程、乌鲁木齐国际机场气象自动观测系统设备招投标等一批通信、导航、监视、气象、航行情报基础设施设备的建设，改善了新疆空管硬件条件。

空管局根据行业要求，加大了技术骨干和各类专家人才的培训力度，满足生产发展的需要。加强了对管理人员的培训，积极培养一支具备先进管理理念和科学管理知识的管理队伍。通过培训教育，为空管安全工作提供了人力资源保证。

空管局认真学习贯彻十六大、十六届四中全会精神及“三个代表”重要思想。加强各级领导班子建设。强化了干部队伍的教育培训，加强了全局干部队伍建设。积极开展思想政治工作和宣传工作。建立健全各级工会组织和共青团组织，开展了各类工会和共青团主题活动。加强了党风廉政建设和反腐败工作，全局未发生违法违纪案件。通过加强党建、思想政治工作和精神文明建设，为保证飞行安全提供了强有力的组织保证和思想保证。

航空气象预报员在讲解天气

航行情报人员讲解航行情报资料

管制员在精心指挥

通信导航人员在维修设备

新疆维吾尔自治区监狱管理局

新疆维吾尔自治区监狱系统在自治区党委、人民政府和司法部、自治区司法厅的正确领导下，高举邓小平理论伟大旗帜，忠实践行“三个代表”重要思想，认真贯彻《监狱法》，始终坚持“惩罚与改造相结合，以改造人为宗旨”的监狱工作方针，以提高罪犯改造质量为中心，以监所安全稳定为首任，以民警队伍建设为保障，积极推进监狱工作的“法制化、科学化、社会化”建设。罪犯改造质量明显提高，监管改造场所持续安全稳定。各级领导班子更加坚强有力，建设了一支政治坚定、纪律严明、作风优良、业务过硬的特别能吃苦、能战斗、能奉献的监狱人民警察队伍。为自治区的社会稳定和经济发展做出了突出贡献。

跃马扬鞭锐意进取，扎实工作再创佳绩。自治区监狱管理局将继续加强队伍建设，将教育人、改造人为贯穿监狱工作的主线，认真贯彻监狱工作方针，切实把提高教育改造质量作为监狱工作的中心任务抓紧抓好。与时俱进，夯实基础，奋勇拼搏，再创新业绩，走向新辉煌。

司法厅副厅长、监狱管理局局长张爱国（右二），监狱管理局党委书记王爱国（右一）在第四监狱检查工作

警徽熠熠显风采

警官之歌

擒敌拳比赛

新疆维吾尔自治区道路运输管理局

局领导进行物流调研

50年来，在党和政府的关心支持下，新疆公路交通运输事业取得了辉煌的成绩，特别是改革开放20年来，道路运输行业发展一日千里。到2004年底，全区营运客车已达39902辆，货车已达172591辆，完成的客、货运输量在综合运输体系中分别占95.6%、81.5%；以省会通向地市的干线公路为骨架，以省辖市通向县(市)二、三级公路为基础的干支连接线，纵横交织，形成了以专业车站为主体、社会公用车站为补充的全区汽车站(场)格局，构筑了与铁路、水运、空运相衔接的立体运输网络。随着道路运输结构的不断调整和道路运输生产力的不断解放，道路运输业已成为多层次、多渠道、多种经济成份、多种经营方式并存的新型产业，出现在经济建设的主战场。客货运输不断壮大，国际汽车运输持续发展，汽车维修技术不断提高，机动车驾驶员培训工作广泛拓展，道路旅游运输蓬勃兴起，道路运输业户遍布全疆，展示了行业的整体实力，全行业呈现出一派欣欣向荣的景象。在发展中，全行业积极开展创建文明道路运输行业工作，积极推动三个文明建设协调发展。2004年7月1日，《中华人民共和国道路运输条例》颁布，为全区道路运输业发展提供了可靠的法律保障，行业管理全面步入法制轨道。随着运力的快速发展、竞争机制的逐步形成和“依法治运、依法兴运”方针的全面落实，道路运输市场日益显示出前所未有的活力，众所关注的“行路难、运货难”问题已基本解决，取而代之的是一种全新的景象；客货运输有序，站点星罗棋布，客运班线四通八达，车辆往返如梭，人便于行，货畅其流。公路运输在经济建设和人民生活中正发挥着越来越重要的作用。

职工文艺演出，展示运管风采

涉外道路运输蓬勃发展

运管局职工召开《中华人民共和国道路运输管理条例》宣传贯彻大会

新疆维吾尔自治区招生委员会办公室

2004 年自治区招生委员会第三次会议暨新闻发布会

2004 年自治区招生系统行风评议员会议

自治区招生办公室文明市民专题讲座

2004 年普通高校招生网上录取招生培训会

自治区招生办公室成立于 1980 年，主要承担普通、成人高校和硕士研究生全国统一考试任务。其中，普通、成人高考使用汉语、维吾尔语、哈萨克语、柯尔克孜语和蒙语共五种语言文字。二十多年来，在教育部和自治区党委、政府的领导下，新疆的招生考试事业取得了长足的进步：1999 年汉语言及少数民族语言文字高考（以下简称民、汉）同步完成“3+X”科目设置改革；2002 年民、汉同步完成局域网录取；2003 年民汉同步完成远程异地录取。目前，自治区招生办公室正积极筹建保密基地，网上阅卷的前期准备工作也在进行之中。相信在未来几年，新疆的招生考试工作会继续向前推进，心系考生，依法执招执考，维护公平、公正的录取原则，将会进一步体现于招生考试工作之中。

接待站查分

新疆维吾尔自治区盐务局

领导班子深入盐田检查原盐质量

新疆维吾尔自治区盐务局(盐业公司)是自治区人政府授权的盐业主管职能部门,担负着贯彻执行国家盐业工作方针政策、法规、自治区盐行业管理和盐政监督以及盐业生产、经营等职能,目前全区已有制盐企业17家,职工3500多人,原盐生产能力250万吨,其中食盐定点生产企业12家,加碘食盐20万吨,主要产品有真空精制盐、粉碎洗涤盐、日晒精盐、肠衣盐、味精盐和多品种食盐。

在国家盐业总局和自治区人民政府的支持下,已建立起了覆盖全疆的盐政管理体系,全区现有各级盐政管理机构80多个,盐政执法人员400多人,从成立至今,共查获各类盐业案件上万起,严厉打击了各类涉盐违法活动。全疆9个地州成立了盐业专营公司,85%以上的县市成立了盐业管理和经营机构,食盐专营工作中实施了"六统一",食盐生产销售、运输实行了"三证"管理。

作为碘缺乏病重灾区的新疆,在没有任何财政补贴的情况下,靠自己的努力,通过各种方式宣传食用加碘盐的重要性,积极组织各级盐业管理机构,大力宣传报道碘盐的重要作用,使各族群众食用碘盐的意识得到了加强,至2002年底,全区7-14岁儿童甲状腺肿大率由六十年代的87.5%下降到20.8%。群体尿碘水平也由24.3微克/升增高到202微克/升,消除碘缺乏危害工作取得了很大成就。

在进入新世纪之时,新疆维吾尔自治区盐务局(盐业公司)及所属企业紧紧抓住西部大开发的机遇,依托新疆丰富的盐资源优势,以盐为主,多种经营,使盐业生产、盐化工和盐田生物等方面都得到了很大的发展。新疆盐业公司也渴望与国内外的有识之士携手合作,共同开发新疆丰富的盐资源,实现自治区人民政府提出的优势资源转换战略,建设美好的新疆。

程宝和局长、热依木局长巡视第十届防治碘缺乏病宣传日活动现场

中国邮政
CHINA POST

乌鲁木齐邮区中心局

乌鲁木齐邮区中心局成立5年多来,在自治区邮政局的直接领导下,克服了基础设施薄弱、运行成本高、普遍服务压力大等困难,采取积极有效措施,不仅很好地履行了普遍服务的义务,而且促进了服务水平的不断提高。通过整合网络资源,先后进行了四次邮件大提速,加快了各类邮件的传递速度;通过流程再造,减少中间环节,使邮件内部处理更加快捷;通过信息化建设,建成了邮运网络专用计算机信息网,使邮政服务更加适应现代化社会的要求;通过不断强化管理创新,规范工作程序,巩固了发展成果,夯实了发展基础,增强了企业发展后劲。

雄关漫道真如铁,而今迈步从头越。国家邮政局明确了"以深化改革促进发展,以加快发展促进改革"的总体思路,强调通过深化改革和加快发展更好地履行普遍服务义务。当前,乌鲁木齐邮区中心局正按照国家邮政局的统一部署以旺盛的干劲和扎实的工作,稳步推进各项改革和发展,并取得了可喜成果。

我们完全相信,依靠全局职工同心同德和奋力拼搏,乌鲁木齐邮区中心局的明天会更加美好,在全面建设小康社会,促进新疆经济发展的进程中,必将做出新的更大的贡献。

国家邮政局谭小为副局长(右二)在新疆邮政局阿不来提局长(右三)陪同下,视察乌鲁木齐邮区中心局邮件处理中心

乌鲁木齐邮区中心局局长、党委书记肖建新慰问生产一线职工

交叉带式包件分拣机

依达良新型喷灌人工草料基地建设

新疆克孜勒苏柯尔克孜自治州

克孜勒苏柯尔克孜自治州（简称克州），是祖国最西部神秘的圣土。

这里，群山耸峙，雪峰林立，是被称作群山聚首的“万山之州”。

这里，天山的逶迤隽秀，帕米尔的巍峨雄奇；喀拉库勒湖畔迎高原日出，斯姆哈纳河岸送长河落日；玉其塔什草原纵马，奥依塔克冰川探险……这一切，已成为人们旅游、观光的胜地。

这里，以直通中亚、西亚的吐尔尕特、伊尔克什坦口岸而闻名遐迩，是向西开放的“桥头堡”。

克州党委书记、人大主任　闫汾新

克州党委副书记、州长　买买提艾山·托乎达力

2004年，克州认真贯彻落实“三个代表”重要思想、党的十六大和十六届三中、四中全会精神，全面落实科学发展观，与时俱进、开拓创新、艰苦奋斗、扎实工作，全面完成了年初确定的各项任务。克州生产总值14.28亿元，同比增长11%。地方财政收入7966万元，增长26.24%；年末总人口468079人，人口自然增长率为7.55‰；居民消费价格指数103.3%。

农村经济在结构调整中稳步发展。粮食44.67万亩，总产16.54万吨；棉花9.21万亩，总产8244吨。实有果树面积19.46万亩，总产量5万吨。年末牲畜存栏158.66万头（只），出栏91.11万头（只），商品率52.22%。

新建多功能的克州体育中心

位于乌恰县境内的喀克天然气主管网

工业生产稳步增长，行业结构得到进一步调整。国有工业企业改制不断深化，企业呈现良好发展势头。工业企业完成产值26300万元.，比上年增长10%；规模以上企业完成产值18200万元，同比增长86.1%。

固定资产投资较快增长，结构进一步改善。累计完成投资7.44亿元，比上年增长63%，加大了水利、交通、通讯和卫生、体育、教育、文化等基础设施和生态环境建设力度。

招商引资工作全方位、多渠道展开。引进各类项目57个，合同引资13.88亿元，当年执行合同3.23亿元，增长7.7%。外贸出口大幅度增长，全年进出口货物量达56.91万吨，增长88.7%，进出口货值39021万美元，增长108.6%。

旅游业加快发展，举办了自治州50年大庆和国际热气球比赛、国际大学生登山运动等系列活动。全年接待国内外游客12.17万人次，增长18.8%；旅游收入2433万元，增长26.7%。

自治州教育、科技、文化、卫生、体育、广播电视、计划生育等各项社会事业持续稳定协调发展。

农牧民收入有所增长，人民生活水平逐步改善。农牧民人均纯收入1406元，比上年增加86元；农村4055户、19283人越过低收入贫困标准；城镇居民可支配收入5200元；城镇贫困人口21669人享受了最低生活保障；实现就业6367人。医疗、养老、失业、工伤、生育等社会事业均衡发展。

神奇美丽的克州，正在撩开神秘的面纱，将美丽绝伦的容颜展现在世人面前，全国惟一的以柯尔克孜族为主体民族的自治州，正以海纳百川的胸怀迎接开放。克州明天更加美好，民族更加团结，经济更加繁荣，人民更加幸福。

抗震安居工程

常务副指挥李丕龙

中国石化
西部新区勘探指挥部

领导班子成员，从左至右依次是：总工程师赵殿栋，副指挥孙兆玉，常务副指挥李丕龙，中石化党组成员、股份公司高级副总裁、指挥部党工委书记、指挥牟书令，常务副书记苏文生，副指挥兼总地质师侯洪斌，总会计师胡国强

中国石化西部新区勘探指挥部成立于2001年12月21日。作为中国石油化工股份有限公司的派出机构，全面肩负着西部新区油气勘探的历史重任。该机构成立的主要目的是：响应党中央、国务院号召，积极投身西部大开发；全面贯彻国家"稳定东部、发展西部"油气资源战略方针，大力发展国家油气事业。

目前，中石化在准噶尔、塔里木、柴达木、吐哈及河西走廊诸盆地共取得探矿权区块69个，勘探面积29.8万km^2。参战职工逾万名，形成了万人会战找油找气、找大场面的宏大声势。西指成立三年来，坚持"集团化决策、项目化管理、市场化运行、社会化服务"的现代化运作模式，形成了一套有效的管理流程。面对新区勘探对象复杂，坚定不移地走"科学勘探之路"，开展联合科研会战，加强成果融合，实现了区块与区带、区带与盆地研究的整体性、系统性。大力加强企业文化建设，深入开展"三创三争"主题教育活动，逐步培育形成了"团结融合、艰苦创业、开拓创新、科学高效"中石化西部新区精神。

面对新形势、新任务，新一届领导班子审时度势，确立了实施新区勘探"三步走"的战略：即第一步到2006年实现"大突破"，力争拿到亿吨级储量规模的高产大油气田；第二步到2010年实现"大发展"，力争探明储量4-5亿吨，建成油气产能400-500万吨；第三步到2020年实现"大接替"，力争探明储量15亿吨以上，全面实现中石化资源战略接替的宏大目标。

管线"放喷"现象

新疆巴音郭楞蒙古自治州实施优势资源转换战略

巴音郭楞蒙古自治州简称巴州，是全国三十多个少数民族自治州之一，“巴音郭楞”系蒙语，意为“富饶的流域”。位于新疆东南部，总面积48.27万平方公里，占新疆的四分之一，全国的二十分之一，素有“华夏第一州”之称。其中沙漠、戈壁和山地占80%。2004年末全州总人口114.8万人，由蒙、汉、维、回等37个民族组成，其中：少数民族47.6万人，占总人口42.2%。1954年6月23日，经国务院批准，巴音郭楞蒙古自治州成立，现辖库尔勒市、焉耆、和静、和硕、博湖、尉犁、轮台、若羌、且末八县，首府设在库尔勒市。境内驻有部队和新疆生产建设兵团农二师及其17个团场、中国石油塔里木油田分公司、中国石化塔里木河南勘探公司、乌鲁木齐铁路局南疆铁路临管处、塔里木河流域管理局等中央、自治区单位。

巴州地理位置优越，石油石化、水土光热、矿产及旅游等资源优势突出，开发潜力较大，是自治区确定的重点发展的地区之一。经过50多年的建设和发展，城乡面貌发生了翻天覆地的变化，特别是西部大开发战略的实施，为巴州加快发展提供了大好机遇，全州国民经济保持快速发展，综合经济实力明显增强，人民生活水平大幅度提高。2004年，全州完成生产总值227亿元，同比增长13%，增速达到1998年以来的最高水平。其中第一产业40亿元，增长11.5%；第二产业144亿元，增长13.7%；第三产业43亿元，增长11%。全社会固定资产投资完成153亿元，增长33.1%；完成全口径财政收入28.39亿元，增长39.4%，其中地方财政收入达到11亿元，增长14.8%；城镇居民可支配收入8000元，比上年增长6.7%；农牧民人均纯收入达到3866元，比上年增长348元；社会消费品零售总额44亿元，比上年增长13.9%；外贸进出口总额3792万美元，比上年增长12.6%；全年实现再就业人数为2.16万人，完成就业目标计划的113.6%；城镇登记失业率控制在3.9%目标以内。在经济快速发展的时间，科技、教育、文化、卫生、体育、广播电视等社会各项事业全面进步。

2005年及“十一五”时期，是巴州经济社会快速发展的重要时期。在圆满完成“十五”规划目标的基础上，巴州各级党政及各族干部群众将认真贯彻落实中央、自治区、自治州各项方针政策和工作部署，按照科学发展观和构建和谐社会的要求，紧扣全面建设小康社会的总体目标，认真制订符合巴州实际的“十一五”规划基本思路。紧紧抓住发展这个第一要务，坚持以人为本，全面推进以市场为导向的优势资源转换战略，可持续发展战略和科教兴州战略及“123456”经济发展思路，以发展经济、致富百姓为己任，统筹县市、城乡、人与自然、经济与社会、近期与远期和“三个文明”协调发展，坚定不移地走好工业强州、农业稳州、商贸活州、生态立州、科教兴州、依法治州和融合发展的路子，努力建设富裕、文明、稳定、祥和的名副其实的“华夏第一州”。

重点抓好以下工作：一是实施优势资源转换战略，以四大产业开发为重点，加快推进工业化进程。重点抓好中石油大化肥、美克化工、轮台30万吨合成氨52万吨尿素、国投罗布泊钾肥、金特和钢、察汗乌苏水电站、

加快建设全面小康社会步伐

库尔勒热电厂、塔什店火电四期及冠农果茸、苇业股份、香梨股份、乡都酒业、红帆生物等项目建设，提升壮大工业经济总体实力。二是加快发展特色农业，努力提高综合效益。加大结构调整力度，稳定粮食种植面积，扩大棉花、工业番茄、色素辣椒、甜菜、芳香植物等特色经济作物面积；以六大畜产品基地建设为重点，突出发展特色畜牧业；加快100万亩香梨、20万亩葡萄、20万亩轮南杏、20万亩红枣等特色林果基地建设，2005年新增林果面积12万亩，使特色林果业逐步成为农民增收致富的支柱产业。三是加快发展现代服务业，加大招商引资力度，不断引大引强。重点做好博斯腾湖长堤景点、塔河森林公园、巴音布鲁克区等旅游资源开发。力争全年接待游客215万人次，增长13%；实现旅游总收入6.63亿元，增长25%。引进区外到位资金13亿元，增长30%。四是努力培植财源，加快实施“财政收入上台阶工程”。通过争取上级资金投入和落实地方资金，加快重点园区基础设施建设，扶持库尔勒、轮台、和静、焉耆等重点县市财源项目建设，努力实现财政收入迈上新台阶，做大财政经济“蛋糕”。五是加大固定资产投资，促进经济持续发展。加快和库高速公路、库尔勒机场、博斯腾湖综合治理等42个重点项目建设。确保收尾项目竣工发挥效益，续建项目加快工程进度，新开工项目尽快开工建设，积极做好预备项目前期工作。六是加快科技、教育、文化、卫生、体育等社会各项事业发展，着力打造和谐巴州。七是加强生态环境保护建设，统筹人与自然协调发展。

新疆生产建设兵团农五师

新疆生产建设兵团农五师位于博尔塔拉蒙古自治州境内,1953 年 5 月建师,全师下辖 11 个农牧团场(81 团–91 团),25 个师直工交建商企业,全师总面积 597.5 万亩,其中草场面积 228 万亩,耕地面积 75.6 万亩,总人口 10.8 万人。

自 1999 年以来,五师利用国家实施国有大中型企业三年脱困的政策,对全师 18 个工交建商中的 17 个企业进行了破产重组或以资抵债,处理不良资产 4.6 亿元,其中 15 个企业建立了现代企业制度。资产负债率下降到 76%,职工年收入从 6320 元上升到 13000 元以上,翻了一番,利润从 2000 年扭亏为盈后,每年以 1000 万元的速度递增。2000 年,五师一举甩掉了连续 8 年的亏损帽子。

五师农业确立了粮、棉、果、牧、特五大支柱产业。全师棉花总面积 40 余万亩,是全国优质棉生产基地。2000 年注册的“北疆”牌棉花连续两年荣获全国金奖。“北疆”牌红提葡萄产业从无到有,现已发展到 5 万亩,成为全国最大的红提葡萄生产基地,并被国家林业部命名为“中国红提葡萄之乡”,果品畅销国内外市场。金博种业已经跨入全国种子行业 50 强,名列第 27 位,成为新疆的知名品牌,产品畅销天山南北及内地。五师利用天然草场及农区幅员辽阔、水草丰茂的优势,已建立 20 万只超细羊毛基地。工业形成建材、电力、食品、纺织、节水设备等产业,2004 年 1 月 7 日,五师在新疆赛里木现代农业股份有限公司成功上市,融资 3.3 亿元,成为博州地区最大的龙头企业。五师在的发展经济的同时更注重精神文明建设,师部和团场小城镇建设已初见规模,确立了养老、医疗、失业、工伤、生育“五保合一”的社会保障体系,广播、电视覆盖率达到 98%。

2004 年,五师党委在前四年被评为兵团经济建设先进师、连续三年荣获全兵团综合考核第一的基础上,经济建设再度跨上新的台阶:一是生产总值突破 11 亿元,达到 11.29 亿元,同比增长 11.1%;人均生产总值首次突破万元,达到 1.04 万元。二是职工人均工资性收入 1.26 万元,农牧职工亏损倒挂户和 3000 元以下的低收入户首次控制在职工总数的 2%以内。三是盈利突破 5000 万元,达到 5069 万元,完成兵团计划指标的 1.69 倍。四是棉花总面积 44.66 万亩,总产首次突破 120 万担,达到 126 万担,实现了多年以来的奋斗目标。五是招商引资取得了重大突破,全年完成 25 个招商引资项目,引资 5.07 亿元,同比翻了两番。六是对外贸易进一步扩大,在 2003 年进出口总额突破 1 亿美元的基础上,2004 年达到 1.59 亿美元,增幅超过 56.6%,发展势头继续看好。

连续两年荣获全国金奖的“北疆”牌棉花

“北疆”牌红提成为全国最大的红提葡萄生产基地

“羚羊唛”高级烹调油

中共中央政治局委员、自治区党委书记王乐泉为怪石峪题字

五大产业中的畜牧业

新疆生产建设兵团农十四师

和田，古老、神奇而美丽的地方。

兵团农十四师，一片充满生机、蕴含商机的热土。

毛泽东主席“一唱雄鸡天下白，万方乐奏有于阗”的“于阗”即和田古称。这里光热资源充足，土地肥沃，物产丰富，民风淳朴。和田玉器、玉雕名甲天下，举世无双。

兵团农十四师是党政军企合一的特殊组织，师机关驻和田市。全师现辖四个农牧团场、11个独立核算工交建商企业，土地面积150.1千公顷，其中耕地3.95千公顷，牧草地84.13千公顷，园地5.96千公顷。是农工商贸一体的大型农垦集团。

为适应加快西部大开发战略，兵团农十四师计划在2020年以前建成皮墨、于田、民丰三大垦区，开发良田100万亩，建成全疆一流的特色林果基地、特色畜牧饲草基和果品畜产品加工四大基地。2002年皮墨生态农业示范区（224团）全面开始建设，计划总投资14亿元，截止2004年底已完成投资6.47亿元。农十四师坚持“投资主体多元化，招商引资多样化，项目运作市场化，行政管理规范化，建设资金社会化”的原则，积极创造“让别人发财，求自己发展”的宽松投资环境，吸引外部资金到农十四师投资。

西部大开发，兵团农十四师商机无限！

师党委领导班子共商农十四师改革、发展大计

1949年12月5–22日，中国人民解放军第一兵团二军五师十五团1800多名指战员徒步横穿塔克拉玛干沙漠，行程1550里，进军和田。图为农十四师四十七团的中国人民解放军进军和田纪念碑。

2003年9月6日，意大利政府与兵团农十四师达成贷款协议。图为师政委杨福林和意大利政府代表卜卡奇在喀什贷款初评会上签字。

兵团农十四师党政办公大楼（行政中心）

绿意相伴，百花相映，合作区道路绿化点缀园区建设

快速发展的伊宁边境经济合作区

哈萨克斯坦总统纳扎尔巴耶夫莅临伊宁边境经济合作区考察

教育的明珠，人才的摇篮——合作区英才私立学校

名校换新貌，软硬件环境日益完善的伊宁市三中

合作区园区建设成绩显著，人居环境焕然一新

国家级伊宁边境经济合作区于1992年经国务院批准设立，规划面积6.5平方公里，控制面积22平方公里。经过13年的开发建设，建成区5.1平方公里，地面建筑面积近90万平方米，基础设施建设及固定投资13.4亿元人民币，注册各类企业212家，其中工业企业53家，建成了以乳业、酿酒、造纸、林产品开发、生物制药、新型建材、房地产开发、商贸物流为主的企业群体。国家西部大开发战略实施以来，招商引资和区域建设不断取得新的突破，各项主要经济指标逐年攀升，生产总值、工业增加值、商品销售总额、外贸进出口总额、财政收入等主要经济指标连续增长，区内商住、医疗、教育、交通、金融、物流等服务设施日趋完善，道路、排水、供水、供热、供电、电信等基础设施配套到位，形成了以工业为主、工贸并举、产业聚集的经济新区。

2004年合作区完成生产总值2.01亿元，增长80%；工业增加值1.01亿元，增长153.5%；工业总产值3.28亿元，增长147.1%；固定资产投资3.82亿元，增长17.4%；外贸进出口总额0.77亿美元，增长36.8%；地方财政一般预算收入4260万元，增长77%。

合作区重视招商队伍的建设和招商人才的引进，项目推介水平不断提高，安琪酵母、永昌管业、天洁纸业、老山制药、天药生物等一批疆内外知名企业落户合作区。现今，合作区已呈现出投资升温促进产业聚集，产业聚集又促进投资升温的良好态势。2004年，合作区签约合同金额达7.8亿元，到位资金3.1亿元。

在对外贸易方面，截止2004年12月，合作区注册外贸企业11家，完成进出口总额7766.58万美元。其中进口8.19万美元，出口7563.39万美元，同比增长36.76%。

在发展经济的同时，合作区加强园区软硬环境的建设。提出“环境立区”的经营理念，完善“封闭式管理，开放式经营”的运行机制，大大改善了合作区投资的软环境，加强基础设施建设，硬件配置发生根本性转变，承载能力得到增强，并通过ISO14000国际环境管理体系的认证。

在今后的发展过程中，伊宁合作区将继续本着“精细化，人性化，制度化”的服务原则，“亲商、安商、富商”的服务理念，“零障碍、低成本、高效率”的服务目标，加大招商力度，发展高新技术产业和重点企业，为伊宁市经济的发展起到推进作用。

新疆房地产业协会

新疆房地产业协会会长李建新

新疆房地产业协会副会长兼秘书长臧小军

新疆房地产业协会副会长陈代元

新疆房地产业协会成立于1985年10月，是由从事房地产管理、开发经营、物业管理、房地产交易、中介机构、房屋拆迁管理等企事业单位及相关单位自愿组成的行业协会。现有会员单位510家，设会长1名，副会长8人，秘书长1人，常务理事68名，理事86名。其中房地产开发企业占会员总数的三分之二。协会组织机构健全，内部制度完善，运作规范，团结紧密。现有工作人员14人，下设秘书处、《新疆房地产》杂志编辑部，培训部、财务部等，并成立了房地产开发、物业管理等五个专业委员会。近年来指导各地相继成立了石河子市、乌鲁木齐市、昌吉市、巴音郭楞蒙古自治州、阿克苏地区五个二级房地产业协会，同时帮助指导克拉玛依、伊犁、哈密等地州即将成立房地产业协会。

新疆房地产业协会四届三次理事扩大会议

新疆房地产业协会在自治区民政部门及建设厅的领导和支持下，积极发挥政府赋予行业协会的职能。一、抓好住房消费，促进产业发展，扩大社会影响。二、提高行业整体素质，积极组织开展业务培训和调研活动，为全体会员及政府服务。三、努力办好房地产交易展示会，积极培育房地产市场，为企业和居民双向服务。四、办好会刊，做好信息宣传和为社会服务工作。五、及时完成其它各项任务，大力提高协会自身素质。

随着房地产业的快速发展，新疆房地产业协会在为推动自治区住房制度改革、住宅建设、培育房地产市场、促进住房消费、推动经济发展，以及在做好为政府、为企业、为消费者"三个服务"方面创造性的开展工作，为新疆的房地产事业的发展做出了一定贡献，曾多次被评为自治区和建设厅先进社会团体。

实现可持续发展，新疆联通力担电信运营商

新疆联通公司领导班子

通信行业发展到今天，早已跳脱出传统技术层面的意义，它的终极价值是助力于构建和谐公平的全球信息社会，让所有人群都能平等享受沟通的快乐，从而真正消除数字鸿沟，维护通信秩序的均衡和有效。

新疆联通成立六年来励精图治、开拓创新，致力于提升公司经营规模、运行效率、盈利水平、创新能力、服务质量、核心技术等各个方面，在发展中改革、在改革中发展。

公平：新疆联通倡导移动通信服务人人可用

通信技术在全球领域的发展已经进入一个深化阶段。作为西部边陲地区，虽然新疆的移动电话普及率已经接近内地发达省区水平，但是，在建设公平的电信消费环境方面仍然有待进一步完善和提高，数字鸿沟依然存在。因此，新疆联通把“创建公平的信息社会”置于发展中的首要位置，其目标就是对乡村地区、贫穷地区、弱势群体的通信需求均衡对待，争取早日消除数字鸿沟。

作为自治区具备提供综合业务能力的基础电信运营商，新疆联通一直在为消除城市和乡村的数字鸿沟而进行不懈努力，而新疆联通公司目前的网络覆盖能力已经为实现这一目标奠定了坚实的基础。在CDMA网络建设三期二阶段工程结束后，新疆联通的GSM和CDMA两个移动通信网已全网络覆盖全区所有地州市城市、所有县城、高速公路及主要交通干道、旅游景点、发达乡镇及农村地区。

时至今日，新疆联通的GSM网络和CDMA网络，不仅可以提供稳定和高质量的语音业务，更能够提供基于CDMA1X精品网络的一系列丰富多彩的数据增值业务。

根据信息产业部及自治区通信管理局的要求和安排，自2004年起，新疆联通公司在继续深化通信服务在全区的普及工作的同时，致力于创造通信服务的“公平信息社会”，履行普遍服务义务，承担了新疆维吾尔自治区的“村通工程”的建设任务，目标为解决目前不通电话的1313个行政村的通信工作，目前已完成了喀什、和田、阿克苏、伊犁、昌吉、巴州、塔城、阿勒泰、哈密、克州、博州等11个地区155个未通村的村通目标。

经过几年的快速发展和投资，目前新疆联通的网络容量已经能够容纳更多的用户加入到通信用户群体中来，在网络覆盖和网络质量方面，联通也有实力进一步加快“村村通电话”工程的实施，为更多的用户提供服务。近年来，联通移动通信用户数量保持持续增长。

公平：新疆联通为消费者创造良好消费环境

据自治区通信行业管理部门统计，截止2004年新疆移动电话用户数量超过488.2万户，全区平均每100人中有24.9人拥有一部手机，居全国前列。但是，我区移动通信用户的总体消费能力较低，人均每月话费（ARPU）一直处于国内低水平行列。

新疆联通公司积极参加社会公益活动回报社会

"公平"责任

中国联通公司总裁尚冰来新疆分公司视察工作

这样的事实表明，一方面，语音业务仍然是相当一段时间内区内移动通信消费的主要形态；另一方面也说明，公平的消费环境，不仅是要让用户用得上移动通信服务，还要用得起移动通信服务。

创建公平的信息社会，意味着消费者只有在一个公平的市场化消费环境中，才能够享受到公平的消费服务。根据新疆联通2005年的工作部署，各地州市分公司都将坚持以市场为导向，并在两网协调发展、稳定用户以及实现数据业务差异化发展等方面积极进取，通过有力举措控制运营成本，不断提升移动通信服务水平，为用户创造更为良好的移动通信消费环境。

从2005年"3·15"开始，新疆联通在提高服务质量、提升服务形象方面推出一项重大举措：在全区范围内开展以"心系客户，倾情承诺"为主题的系列服务创优活动，向广大用户作出四项郑重承诺，即"话费误差、双倍返还；短信差错、先行赔付"、"坚决制止消费陷阱"、"服务协议公平诚信"、"电话卡余额、妥善处理"。

同时，依托于联通公司先进的多业务统一网络平台，2005年"5·17"，新疆联通还面向全区集团行业用户推出"一网联通"集团用户解决方案，只要一根光缆专线就可以为集团用户轻松实现包括：视讯会议、可视电话、宽带互联网、数据传送、VPN、193长途电话、IP电话等各类业务需求，更加显示了联通公司多业务统一网络平台的领先技术实力，以及为集团用户带来的消费便利。

公平：新疆联通积极营造可持续发展环境

"创建公平的信息社会"、消除电信应用的数字鸿沟，这些愿景的实现都需要有一个良好的、可持续发展的通信消费环境，从而形成电信运营商与消费者之间的良性互动。新疆联通正积极通过业务和运营方面的协调，携手疆内各大电信运营商和产业价值链上下游，共同为创建一个和谐的电信产业环境而努力。

为实现可持续发展，首先必须做到的是电信运营商的自律。新疆联通在实际工作中积极主动与其他运营商共同维护市场竞争秩序，通过沟通和协商的办法来解决问题。

2005年，新疆联通实现可持续发展，突出表现在两网协调方面的成就。G&C双网，既立足于语音，又远瞻于面向未来的数据增值业务前景，为联通可持续发展道路奠定了坚实的基础。世界风双模手机的推出已为联通实现双网协调发展奠定了第一步基础，伴随联通双模卡的推出，更将这种实现可持续发展的态势进一步巩固，为新疆联通公司当前及今后的发展营造了可成长的空间。

面向未来，新疆联通将坚持科学的发展观，按照"理性、务实、积极"的发展策略，坚定不移地推动公司的改革和发展，努力提高企业核心竞争力，为创建公平的信息社会、推动自治区国民经济发展、建设和谐社会贡献力量。

"3·15"公司大型咨询活动现场

新疆联通公司在"3·15"举行咨询活动

美克投资集团有限公司

新疆美克总部大厦全景

美克样品间

美克股份公司

北京美克美家丽泽店夜景

天津环球操作中心夜景

天津工业园沙发生产线

美克总部大厦阳光四季厅

美克投资集团有限公司(以下简称美克集团)是一大型现代化企业集团，主要由美克国际家具股份有限公司、美克国际家私(天津)制造有限公司、远东木业有限公司、新疆美克家私有限公司、美克美家家具装饰有限公司、新疆美克化工有限公司、上海美克资产管理有限公司等十余家公司组成，总资产约25亿元。集团总部设在新疆乌鲁木齐，目前共有员工10000余人。

美克集团生产的高档家具产品主要销往美国、加拿大、欧洲、日本、澳大利亚等国家和地区，其中对美国的出口占到亚洲在美国市场同类产品的85%。天津美克工业园位于天津市经济技术开发区，占地约1000亩，截至目前共建成6家工厂。2000年11月，美克股份在上交所成功上市。

美克集团的高速发展，首先得益于强大的开发设计能力。集团目前已跻身世界著名家具生产设计商行列，产品开发设计时间从30天缩短为6天，公司投资1.2亿元修建的美克研发大厦，进一步增强了美克的产品开发能力。美克的产品开发范围涵盖所有家居用家具，配合独创的世界领先的涂饰工艺，使美克产品色彩多样且充满文化内涵和田园风格，从而赢得用户的青睐，产品风行欧美。2002年，美克公司顺利通过ISO9001国际质量体系认证。

2001年集团引进国外先进的经营管理模式，与美国最著名的家具品牌——依森·艾伦股份有限公司达成协议，在中国国内开发连锁零售店。截止到2004年11月，美克·美家七家零售店2004年年销售总额突破一亿元，目前，“美克·美家”在天津、乌鲁木齐、上海、北京、成都、杭州、大连等地的10家家具内销连锁店已开张营业。

美克投资集团在做强做大家具产业的同时，积极响应自治区党委、政府号召，充分利用新疆石油天然气资源，发展石油天然气化工作为美克集团新产业拓展的战略重点，本着“高起点、高投入、高技术、高国际化”的原则，制定了“以天然气制乙炔和天然气制甲醇路线为基础，加工生产下游化工产品，发展精细化工产业”的发展战略，规划建设具有国际水平的、总投资近百亿元、年综合利用天然气8亿方、规划用地4300亩、年销售收入50多亿元的美克化工工业园。它的建成对加快巴州乃至新疆经济发展将产生积极带动作用。

天津工业园全貌

中国石油塔里木油田公司

克拉 2——夜景

塔里木油田公司办公大楼

〔基本概况〕2004 年是塔里木油田公司的决战之年，跨越之年，是油田发展史上具有重大影响和里程碑意义的一年。一年来，全体甲乙方干部职工牢记“稳定东部、发展西部，实现我国油气资源战略”的重任，遵照油田党工委“决战 2004，实现新跨越”的总体要求，励精图治，奋勇拼搏，各项工作取得全面胜利。

〔油气勘探〕坚持油气并重方针，以寻找大油气田为目标，自觉加压，主动出击，积极实施“勘探突破年”活动，大打勘探进攻仗，在 16 口井新获工业油气流，探井成功率达到 43.59%。在塔中、塔北、库车和塔西南等地区取得一个新突破、两个新发现、五个新进展和两个重要苗头的好成绩，油气勘探进入全面加快发展、实现大发现和大突破的关键阶段。新增三级油气储量当量 3 亿吨，实现了储量高增长。

塔里木油分公司党工委书记、总经理孙龙德在一线视察工作

〔油气开发〕西气东输全线投产供气，开创了油田天然气事业发展的新纪元。经过万余名建设者艰苦卓绝的努力，牙哈凝析气田天然气 9 月 1 日提前进入西气东输管道；12 月 1 日，中国最大的整装天然气田——克拉 2 大气田正式投产供气，西气东输工程全线贯通。

优化调整老油田，有效控制了产量递减和含水上升。加快建设新油田，产能大幅增长，产量持续攀升。持续推进勘探开发一体化，规模不断扩大，效益稳步提高。天然气产能规模强势跃升，油气产量稳定增长，油气产能突破 1000 万吨，实现了油气开发的高水平和高效益，油田进入油气并重，规模化加快发展的新阶段。

〔炼化生产〕塔西南公司炼油技改工程竣工投产，原油加工能力达到 50 万

物资吊装

克拉2–生活营地

西气东输管线建设

检查设备

吨/年。塔石化45万吨/年合成氨、80万吨/年化肥项目启动上马，工程建设前期工作按计划实施。塔里木油田上下游一体化发展格局加快形成。塔西南公司全年加工原油35万吨，生产化肥46万吨，双双超额完成任务指标：全年实现主营业务收入19.07亿元，利润8000万元，经营业绩创历史最好水平。

〔HSE管理〕认真实施生活小区美化、亮化工程，加快配套设施建设和改造，为广大职工群众营造了一流的工作生活环境。2004年，油田先后涌现出“全国五一劳动奖状(奖章)”、“全国青年文明号”、“全国青年突击队标兵”、“全国三八红旗集体(红旗手)”等全国先进集体和个人，小区获得自治区“安静小区”和“绿色社区”荣誉称号。

〔发展目标〕2004年5月，集团公司党组着眼塔里木油田加快发展的形势和国家能源战略安全的迫切需要，对塔里木油田提出了“1521”发展目标。“15”就是到2010年每年新增探明石油储量1亿吨、天然气500亿立方米；“2”就是到2010年油气产量当量超过2000万吨；“1”就是建成一流的现代化油气田，可与国际大石油公司的油田相媲美。

新疆八一钢铁

新疆八一钢铁股份有限公司成立于 2000 年 7 月 27 日，2002 年 8 月 16 日在上交所上市。公司主营业务为钢铁冶炼、轧制、加工及销售。目前，公司拥有员工 4500 人，其中大专以上学历 1009 人，具备 300 万吨的综合产钢能力，产品覆盖棒、型、带、线、管、板等。

作为自治区最大的国有上市公司，八一钢铁股份有限公司近几年依靠科技进步和技术创新，在销售收入和利润方面每年保持两位数的增长速度。2002 年实现销售收入 31.83 亿元、利润 1.86 亿元；2003 年销售收入 47.6 亿元，利润 3.87 亿元；2004 年销售收入 65.4 亿元，利润 5.35 亿元，上交税金 4.65 亿元。2003 年八一钢铁股份有限公司被中国企业改革与发展研究会评选为"2003 年度中国上市公司百强"。2004 年，"八一钢铁"被评为"2004 年度中国上市公司企业竞争力 100 强"，名列沪深股市 1314 家上市公司的第 25 位。

新疆八一钢股份有限公司立足国内外钢铁行业的发展态势，先后从意大利达涅利公司、德国德玛克公司引进了小型连续式棒材轧机生产线、高速线材轧机生产线、70 吨超高功率直流电弧炉等 90 年代先进技术设备，形成一条"电炉——炉外精练——连铸——连轧"和两条"转炉——炉

不断挖潜、不断改进、不断发展的转炉炼钢厂

新近投产的 40 吨转炉是八钢 2005 年三百万吨钢目标的重要保证

股份有限公司

外精练——连铸——连轧”四位一体超短流程生产线。同时，公司大力实施产品结构调整，由生产建材为主向板材方向转变，2003年投资10多亿元引进彩涂板生产线、镀锌板生产线、冷轧薄板生产线，2004年投资20多亿元建设电转炉炼钢生产线、热轧生产线，实现了产品结构的多元化。目前已经达到了年产300万吨钢的生产能力。

近几年，公司先后被评为“自治区名牌企业”、“全国重合同守信用企业”、“全国质量工作先进企业”、“国家首批质量免检产品”和“全国钢铁工业实物质量金杯奖”等，2003年还被搜狐网站评选为新疆最具成长力企业10强，被中国企业改革与发展研究会评选为“2003年度中国百强上市公司”。2004年被中国质量检验协会授予“全国建材行业质量可信产品”、“全国建材业质量诚信先进示范企业”。近两年公司产品在兰新铁路复线、南疆铁路、宝兰二线和黄河上游青海公伯峡大型水电站和青藏铁路线等多项国家重点工程中连续中标。2005年公司将完成二次创业的第一步，实现产钢300万吨，主营业务收入100亿元的目标。

引进世界先进技术和装备的70吨电弧炉

全套引进世界先进技术和装备的小型材轧钢厂

曾为八钢发展做出巨大贡献的线材轧钢厂仍在继续发挥着潜力

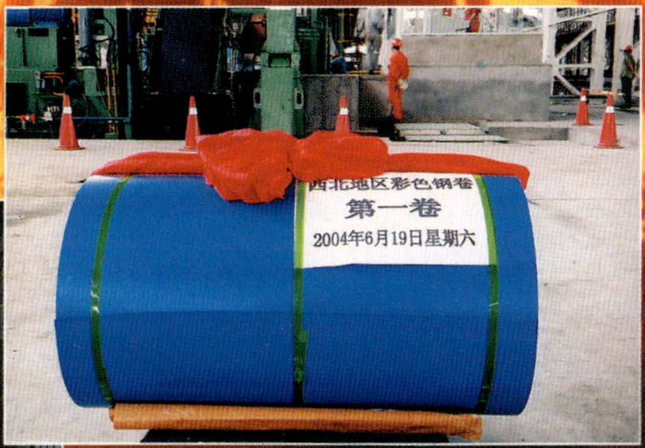

新近投产的镀锌彩涂生产线生产出西北地区第一卷彩涂卷板

通过技术进步和改造焕发新活力的中型材轧钢厂

具有国内先进水平的冷轧薄版生产线

新疆机场（集团）有限责任公司

2004年4月16日，民航总局和自治区人民政府共同签署了《机场移交书》，将原民航乌鲁木齐管理局管辖的机场移交自治区管理，由此，新疆机场（集团）有限责任公司应运而生，成为自治区一个主要经营航空地面服务和保障、航空客货运销售代理、房地产、仓储物流、商业、旅游及其他业务，拥有资产18亿元人民币的现代航空运输保障企业。这一年，新疆机场集团经历了“5·18”货包机事故血与火的洗礼；成功地承办了2004年度国家级反劫机综合演习；实现了集团公司旅客吞吐量年500万人次大关的突破；与新疆民航各单位共同创造了运输飞行安全50周年和空防安全50周年的优秀记录。

目前，新疆机场（集团）有限责任公司管理乌鲁木齐、喀什、伊宁、塔城、阿勒泰、库车、且末、富蕴（停航保管）、吐鲁番（停航保管）、阿克苏、和田、库尔勒、那拉提（在建）等13个机场，同时拥有广告公司、汽车维修服务公司、物业管理公司、地面服务公司、房地产开发公司、旅游公司、机场建设工程公司、酒店管理公司、凯亚信息网络公司等12家全资、控股、参股公司。

乌鲁木齐国际机场航站楼面积6.8万多平方米。承担着疆内13个机场的中转任务。已开通国内、国际航线96条。2004年预计完成旅客吞吐量超过390万人次、飞行起降40888架次、货邮行7.8万吨。同比增长40.7%、40%、12.3%。现有南航新疆公司、海航新疆公司两家基地航空公司，是国家民用一级机场，我国西部门户机场和国际航班备降机场。

民航运输业作为国民经济体系的先行性行业，伴随国家经济的增长，民航业又步入了一个新的发展阶段。新疆机场集团将紧紧抓住民航和自治区政治经济快速发展的机遇，坚持“安全第一”，树立和落实科学的发展观，努力把乌鲁木齐国际机场打造成为中亚区域性枢纽机场。做大做强新疆机场业，为自治区的改革开放和经济建设做出新的更大的贡献。

和田机场

乌鲁木齐机场全景

乌鲁木齐机场航站楼外景

乌鲁木齐机场贵宾厅

乌鲁木齐机场出港厅

新疆乌鲁木齐矿业(集团)有限责任公司

新疆乌鲁木齐矿业(集团)有限责任公司是一个以煤炭开采加工为主业，兼营发电、供电、城市供热、建材、机械制造、汽车运输、工程设计施工、房地产开发等产业的跨地区、跨行业的国有控股企业集团。

新矿集团拥有资产总额20亿元，员工10062人。现有主要生产矿井6对，生产能力470万吨/年，下辖二十余家多经企业，已成为一个集煤、电、建材、五金、塑料、农副产品加工等为一体的大型综合经济实体。

科技创新，强大煤炭主业。新矿集团所属矿井拥有“高产高效矿井”、“自治区现场管理先进单位”、“自治区级文明单位”、“质量标准化矿井”、“全国民族团结进步先进集体”、“全国煤炭系统思想政治工作优秀企业”等多项荣誉。

新疆乌鲁木齐矿业(集团)有限责任公司坚持弘扬“诚信为本、求实创新、负重奋进、勇争一流”的企业精神，在国家实施西部大开发的伟大战略中，有着广阔的发展前景。到2007年新矿集团将建成以乌鲁木齐本部为中心，以南疆巴州库尔勒塔什店金川煤矿、北疆昌吉硫磺沟屯宝煤矿、呼图壁宽沟煤矿、玛纳斯涝坝湾煤矿为两翼的三大煤炭基地，实现煤炭产量和销售收入两个翻番，成为新疆境内最大的煤炭供应商。拥有一家上市公司，通过融资形成煤——电/热——耗能产业链和煤——煤液化/气化——煤化工产业链，发展成为对新疆经济有较大贡献的现代控股投资集团公司。

乌鲁木齐矿业(集团)党委书记、董事长　姚　伟

乌鲁木齐矿业(集团)副董事长、总经理　胡开江

新疆维吾尔自治区图书馆

新疆维吾尔自治区图书馆始建于1930年8月，原名新疆省立图书馆，迄今已有74年的历史。1955年10月，新疆维吾尔自治区成立，定名为新疆维吾尔自治区图书馆；1999年3月18日新馆开馆之际，江泽民总书记题写了馆名。图书馆馆舍占地50余亩，总建筑面积24700平方米，设计藏书容量300万册，阅览席位2500个。人员编制86人，现任馆长张君超。有汉、维、哈、蒙、回、柯尔克孜6个民族的工作人员79人。其中少数民族职工占33%；研究馆员1人，副研究馆员8人，中级职称34人，大专以上学历占78%。现在藏书100万册(件)。

报刊阅览室

近两年来，图书馆坚持以“三个代表”重要思想为指导，坚持“读者至上，服务第一”的宗旨，坚持“求真务实”的馆训，全面落实“建章立制抓管理，提高素质抓服务，开门办馆抓规模，开发资源抓效益，求真务实讲奉献，拓宽思路求发展”的办馆思路。在工作上主要有以下几点突破：深化服务形式，开办少数民族分馆，设立二十多处图书流动站。构建科学藏书体系，逐步形成特色馆藏。面向青少年读者，开展阵地建设。2003年12月自治区图书馆少儿馆正式挂牌，同时启动了“少儿图书银行工程”。拓宽服务思路，开办电子阅览室。实施少数民族文献的数据化建设。读者队伍渐趋稳定，读者数量稳中有升。近两年年均到馆人数达20万，图书借阅册次30多万。

我们的目标是通过两至三年努力，固定读者队伍人数要达到5万人以上，馆藏图书增加到150万册(件)，全面实现管理服务计算机化，力争建成两个地方文献数据库，综合办馆条件，办馆水平达到地方一流水平。

“我爱图书馆”万人签名活动

新疆维吾尔自治区图书馆与北京市图书馆开展“手拉手”活动

铁路房产 TIELU FANGCHAN

新疆铁路

新疆铁路房地产开发总公司是具有国家二级开发资质的房产企业。创建于1993年，十年风雨历程，目前注册资金已达3144.6万元，总资产为23267万元。在继承铁路优良传统作风的同时建立了一套完善现代企业管理制度和科学系统的管理机构。2001年11月顺利通过ISO9001国家质量体系的认证。公司下属三个基层单位：铁路银桥铝合金厂（1998年被自治区建设厅评为全疆铝塑加工优秀企业）；铁深地板采暖有限公司（目前是美国泰亚集团上海深化学建材有限公司新疆总代理）；阳光物业管理股份有限公司。总公司下属六个职能部门：企划部、工程部、财务部、市场部、办公室、销售中心。以房地产开发、物业管理、地板采暖为一体的综合性企业，公司技术资金雄厚，创效能力稳定，有良好的社会声誉。

铁路房产追求高品质是其永恒的目标，营造万千温馨家园，是其执着的追求，铁路人纵横天下的气派，必将为新疆的经济繁荣做出更大的贡献。

房地产开发总公司

近两年，公司依托铁路强大优势及良好信誉，以其雄厚的经济实力适应市场经济发展及城市规划的需要，2000 年上半年在乌市黄金地段开发了“新秀小区”、“佳苑小区”，同时收购木材厂原住宅区 12.5 万平米土地进行开发，成功地推出了铁路“世纪花苑”，经专家评审，该小区被自治区列为精品小区。铁路“世纪花苑”简洁、明快、大气以其独特的设计规划赢得了诸多消费者的赞誉。

新疆铁路房地产开发总公司总经理　崔鹏林

小区一角

世纪花苑小区广场

与时俱进的新粮集团金谷房地产公司

公司董事长兼总经理　马英武

新疆金谷房地产开发有限责任公司创立于 2000 年 7 月，是隶属新疆粮油集团公司的国有独资企业，注册资本金 4000 万元，具有国家房地产开发二级资质。公司下设财务部、综合部、工程部、审核部、按揭部、销售公司 6 个职能部门及金谷物业、金谷型材、金谷广告三个子公司。员工总数 102 人，营销人员 68 人，拥有高级技术职称人员 4 人，中级 10 人，初级 15 人。

公司自创立以来，始终坚持以市场为导向、以质量为保障、以大规模经济适用房开发为主导的经营思路；恪守住户第一、信誉至上的经营理念；不断强化自身硬件建设，积极探索新时期居民住宅开发建设的创新之路。累计为社会提供了数千套高品质的住房，取得了社会效益、经济效益的双丰收。其中金谷小区 13178 平方米，144 户，当年开工，当年售罄。四季风情园小区总开发量 20 万平方米，目前已开发了 15 万平方米，总投资 1.8 亿元，共 1669 户，已售出 1500 余套，均已竣工入住。位于乌鲁木齐市黄金地段（小西门）新华北路 80 号的金谷大厦，是乌鲁木齐市 2003 年“绿色通道工程”之一。其总建筑面积 63000 平方米，总投资 2.5 亿元。由于在设计上充分融入了景观生态学设计理念，建成后已成为乌市标志性建筑之一。

由于良好的信誉带来良好的口碑，使金谷房产公司在同行业评选活动中屡获殊荣。在 2001 年“新疆首届优秀商品房小区（楼盘）”评选活动中，分别荣获“最受公众欢迎的商品房开发企业”奖、“消费者满意楼盘”奖及“消费者物业管理满意小区”奖三个奖项。2002 年四季风情园小区荣获“乌鲁木齐优秀住宅小区”和“优秀物业管理小区”两个奖项。2004 年金谷房产荣获“新疆维吾尔自治区第一届房地产开发综合实力三十强企业”之一。

前进的道路永无止境，在企业发展的道路上，金谷房产将诺守质量立业、技术兴业、信誉守业的企业信条；致力于坚持以人为本、科技先行、市场导向、质量至上、持续发展的企业方针，为社会提供更多的高品质住房，为改善社会居民的住房条件而不断努力！

董事长、总经理：马英武

电　话：0991-2811587、2304180、2308387（办）

传　真：0991-2304985

地　址：中国新疆乌鲁木齐新华北路 80 号

邮　编：830002

金谷房产

金谷房产

小区休闲场所

小区休闲廊架

小区绿化一角

新疆金成房地产开发有限公司

新疆金成房地产开发有限公司由金成集团投资开发，成立于2000年6月14日，注册资金为2000万元人民币。

金成房地产集团有限公司于2000年7月随浙江省政府经贸代表团赴疆考察洽谈，与乌鲁木齐市高新技术产业开发区签订了投资4.9亿元、占地265亩的"高新产品市场及新洲城市花园"项目协议，并于2001年7月26日动工建设。

总经理　卢连平

新疆金成房地产开发有限公司成立以来，积极响应西部开发号召，努力加强东西两地经济文化的交流与合作，引进东部先进的经营开发理念，并使其融入"高新产品市场及新洲城市花园"项目；公司的成立和项目的开发，得到了两地政府的重视。

"高新产品市场及新洲城市花园"位于乌市城北高新技术开发区内，东起鲤鱼山路、南依鲤鱼山公园、西至天津路、北临苏州路，占地265亩，总建筑面积26.5万平方米，容积率1.52，绿化率33%，建筑密度30%，总投资4.9亿元人民币。

"高新产品市场及新洲城市花园"规划设计强调以人为本，追求高尚、典雅，讲究艺术性，充分体现亲和、自然、温馨、高贵和丰富多彩，园区设计突出绿色主题，建筑形式以欧陆风格为主调，融入新疆地方民族特色，由别墅、多层、小高层等建筑组成，形成高低错落的社区空间。项目的开发建成，将把一个缩影的城市花园展现在乌市城北，成为乌市城市建设的一个亮点。

新疆金成房地产开发有限公司秉承集团公司的开发理念和宗旨，精心组织、强化管理、加强了制度建设、队伍建设、思想建设，注重企业文化建设。公司逐步成为开发理念超前、经营稳健、注重信用、开发领域不断扩大的一家以房地产开发为主业的专业公司。2003年12月22日，公司的"房地产开发"ISO9001:2000质量管理体系通过认证，组建成立了"新疆金厦物业管理有限公司"和"乌鲁木齐市江南春文体有限公司"；2003年11月12日，"新疆金成房地产开发有限公司昌吉市分公司"成立，规划建设占地430亩、以商业住宅为一体的金成·维也纳春天广场，总投资5.8亿元。

新洲城市花园由金成房地产集团·新疆金成房地产开发有限公司投资开发，小区位于乌市苏州路80号，总建设用地265亩，总建筑面积为26.5万平方米，容积率1.5，绿化率33%，建筑密度30%，预计总投资4.9亿元人民币。

一、超前的规划设计

新洲城市花园由浙江大学建筑设计研究院设计，规划设计强调以人为本，追求高尚、典雅，讲究艺术性，充分体现亲和、自然、温馨、高贵和丰富多彩，园区设计突出绿色主题，建筑形式以欧陆风格为主调，融入新疆地方民族特色，由多层、小高层等建筑组成，形成高低错落的社区空间。项目的开发建成，将把一个缩影的城市花园展现乌市城北，成为乌市城市建设的一个亮点。2004年2月5日，"新洲城市花园(一期)"以：环境较好、居住建筑单

体外观色彩造型有所突破。被评为《2003 年度城市规划行业十个优秀建设项目》。

二、独特的建筑结构

外观造型独特，采用框架剪力墙结构，标准层高为 2.9 米，局部层高为 5.6 米，抗震系数高。外墙采用 19 公分厚的新型建材保温，蘑菇石和外贴铁红色高档面砖。阳台、窗台等局部以外墙涂料点缀，独创北欧斜屋顶，坡形屋面采用进口多彩玻纤瓦。小区全部采用壁挂炉地板辐热采暖，突出保温、节能、实用、美观等特点。

三、优美的生态环境

新洲城市花园融鲤鱼山公园为一体揽景入胜，空气好无噪音，一年四季风景如画，“静”、“净”、“景”一应俱得，采用借景、对景的方式将公园景观引入社区，给小区营造绿色的、清新的生活空间，使整个社区充满健康、安静、祥和的气氛。

四、完善的社区配套

社区内部配备 5000 平方米的中央喷泉广场，3800 平方米的社区专属会所，涵盖休闲、健身、娱乐的功能，中心幼儿园能使您的孩子健康的成长、成才。11000 平方米双层地下停车场，人车分流，在保护您爱车的同时，又有效降低环境的污染，提高了社区的生活质量。

五、人性化的户型设计

新洲城市花园以“造百姓公寓、建精品楼盘”为宗旨，开发户型面积从 92.05 平方米的两居至 177.28 平方米四居不等，可供随意选择，更有豪华复式户型，彰显您的生活品质，户型方正实用、动静分区，采光良好，视野开阔，每一寸空间都物尽其用。

六、星级的物业服务

新洲城市花园由获得 ISO9001:2000 国际质量认证的新疆金厦物业管理有限公司进行物业管理，秉承“业主第一、服务至上”的原则，为业主提供房屋修缮、环境卫生、绿化、治安、消防、车辆管理等服务。严格依据政府有关部门的规定标准执行相关收费标准。

金成房地产开发有限公司开发的“新洲城市花园”得到社会和广大消费者的认可并多次荣获各种荣誉。

2003 年 5 月 18 日“新洲城市花园”被新疆(华凌)房地产交易会组委会评为“名牌楼盘”称号。

2003 年 10 月 22 日，“新洲城市花园” 作为乌鲁木齐住宅小区项目，参加了北京建设部举办的《第四届公共工程和市政基础设施博览会》；

2004 年 2 月 5 日，“新洲城市花园(一期)”以：环境较好、居住建筑单体外观色彩及造型有所突破。被评为《2003 年度城市规划行业十个优秀建设项目》；

2004 年 3 月 10 日，“新洲城市花园” 荣获由新疆经济报、都市消费晨报、航空旅游报、新疆欣文媒体投资有限公司组办的 2004 年读者评选“我最喜爱的楼盘”称号；

2004 年 5 月 20 日，“新洲城市花园”荣获“十大品牌楼盘”殊荣，并由 2004 新疆春季房地产交易展示会向社会隆重推出。

2004 年 9 月 29 日，由新疆房地产业协会组织的首届“十佳精品楼盘”的评选活动中，新洲城市花园荣获“十佳精品楼盘”称号。

新洲城市花园一期鸟瞰图

鸟瞰效果图

新疆徕远集团　徕远房产

广场效果图

新疆徕远集团成立于2001年，隶属于新疆生产建设兵团国有资产管理经营公司，主营外贸、房地产开发、汽车贸易、酒店多个行业，旗下有新疆徕远房地产开发有限责任公司、新疆博望汽车销售有限公司等一大批实力强、发展潜力巨大的子公司。

徕远房产作为新疆硕果仅存的几家大型国有房地产开发公司之一，公司长期秉承国有企业用实力说话，靠信誉发展的优良传统，不仅得到了广大消费者的长期信任，更获得了各级党委、政府的大力支持。

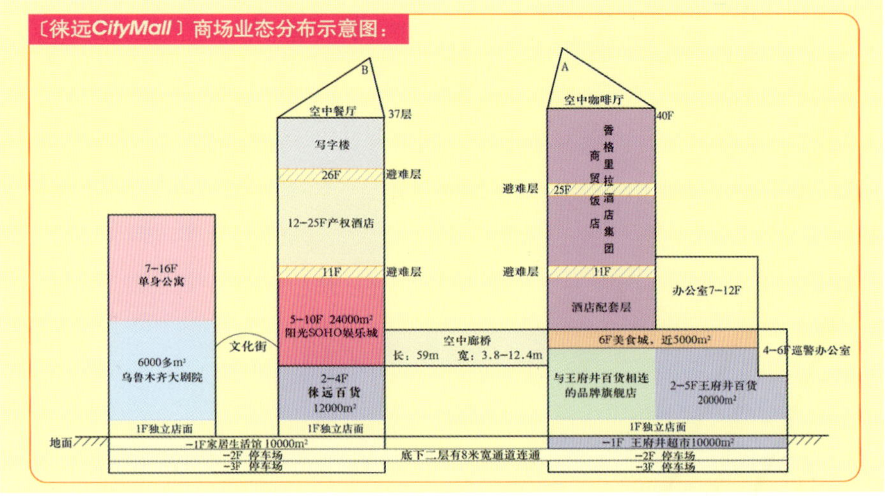

与北京王府井百货签约仪式

与香格里拉酒店签约仪式

开盘热销

徕远广场夜景效果图

此次斥资12亿打造的徕远广场 City Mall 项目通过对土地资源的合理整合及对建筑群的科学规划，在3.5万平方米的黄金地段上规划出了近30万平方米的高价值地产物业。这项被列入乌鲁木齐市2003年重点建设项目的城市标志性建筑，不仅位居城市政治经济文化中心，而且占尽天时、地利、人和之优势。徕远广场将是集购物、餐饮、娱乐、休闲、信息、办公于一体，与国际消费流行趋势全面接轨，引进更多的世界五百强企业和知名品牌如五星级酒店香格里拉，新中国第一店北京王府井百货，阳光 SOHO 娱乐城等，把徕远广场建成一个多种行业于一体的最具魅力和个性，最具规模的都市商业和商务中心，不可替代的成为全疆首座市中心真正意义上一站式城市购物中心 City Mall。

如果说西部大开发战略给乌鲁木齐"国际化商贸城"注入了新的活力，那么徕远广场将是"一座桥"，一座沟通南北，贯穿东西的商务之桥，一座集文化、商务、景观为一体的乌鲁木齐真正的标志性建筑，一条奔向新经济生活的绿色通道。徕远广场，一个乌鲁木齐的、新疆的、中国的、世界的 City Mall。

LAIYUAN PLAZA 徠遠廣場

徕远·财富天下

首府市中心30万m^2超大型CITYMALL

新疆金元房地产开发有限责任公司

总经理 朱留根

金城花园小区

金元房产

XINJIANG JINYUAN FANGDICHAN KAIFAYOUXIAN ZERENGONGSI

新疆金元房地产开有限责任公司是由国家一级企业——兵团一建为主要股东的有限责任公司。公司现有职工 15 人，其中高级工程师 1 人，工程师 5 人。公司成立于 2000 年 3 月，设有董事会、监事会，资质等级为四级，注册资金 500 万元。

新疆金元房地产开发有限责任公司所开发的经济适用房，主要面向工薪阶层，以其实惠的价格、良好的信誉备受购房者的青睐。现已成功开发的小区有市五星北路金城花园小区、市五星北路金盛花园小区。其中金城花园小区开发面积为 17332 平方米，交通方便，地处工商银行干校隔壁，一侧临近水塔山葡萄山庄度假村，文化氛围浓厚，自然环境优美，是安居乐业之首选。金盛花园小区总开发面积为 8370 平方米，地处五星北路兵团一运司院内，交通方便，经典户型设计，小区内绿树成荫，环境优雅，空气清新，不失为一处颐养天年、修身养性之佳居。

2004 年我公司在青年路开发的金鑫花园小区，投资 2240 万元，总建筑面积为 26407 平方米，该小区位于青年路 32 号，原兵团洪福工贸公司院内，离日月星光花园 100 米，离水磨沟公园葡萄山庄仅 500 米，地势比较优越。附近有兵团二中、42 中、建工中学、八一中学等学校，医院有兵团医院、建工医院、儿童医院，4 路、14 路、29 路、59 路、902 路直达小区，条件优越。周边出行、购物、就学、就医环境十分便利。此楼盘 8 月 16 日正式开盘销售，户型吸纳了各大房地产公司的精典户型，打造出了 38 种户型，从 47 平方米的单身公寓到 160 平方米复式空中花园，满足了大众百姓的购房需求，销售情况良好。

新疆金元房地产开有限责任公司成立四年来，本着“以人为本，信誉至上，开拓创新，优质取胜”的企业宗旨，积极探索房地产企业经营之道，准确的把握房地产市场的脉搏，经营机制灵活，不断发展壮大，已在新疆房地产市场中崭露头角，是新疆房地产业的一颗璀璨的新星。

金鑫花园

金盛小区一角

阿克苏新农房地产有限责任公司

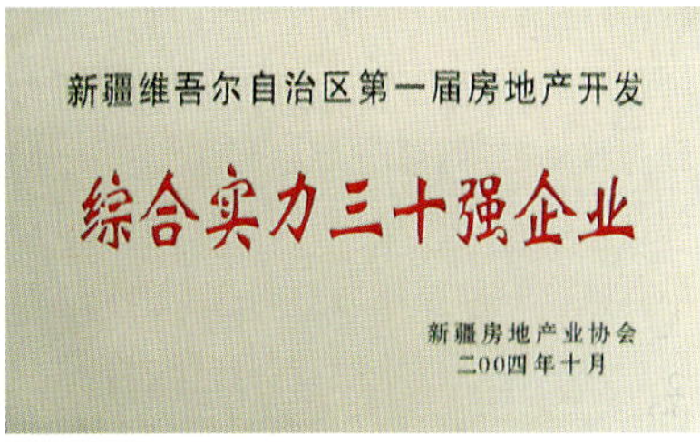

董事长　涂昭荣

阿克苏新农房地产有限责任公司前身是农一师天南房地产开发公司，于 2002 年由塔里木农业综合开发公司收购成立了阿克苏新农房地产有限责任公司。2002-2003 年开发建设项目有：①温馨花园住宅小区 88442.11 平方米，计 1075 套；②阿拉尔桃源一、二期工程 57600 平方米；③新农大厦 22600 平方米；④图木舒克市开发住宅小区 40144.39 平方米；⑤阿拉尔政府办公楼 18000 平方米；⑥阿拉尔迎宾馆 8800 平方米。开发总面积达 204725.1 平方米，2003 年竣工面积 150800 平方米。实现销售收入 11632 万元，实现利润 2600 多万元。

2004 年开发建设项目：①时代广场 34600 平方米；②城市花园住宅小区 56000 平方米；③创业新天地 43000 平方米。开发总面积 192842 平方米，竣工面积 118205 平方米。

截止 2004 年底，新农房产公司开发总面积达 32.56 万平方米。2003 年获阿克苏市十强纳税企业第二名，2004 年被阿克苏地区、农一师联合评为地区重点扶优扶强保护企业，被自治区房地产业协会评为房地产企业综合实力 30 强，被全国市场诚信建设组委会评为“质量、服务、诚信示范单位”，中国房地产市场管理委员会“百姓放心房地产开发企业”称号，国家统计局和企业信息发布中心“中国房地产领先企业”称号。

公司坚持“以人为本，人企合一”宗旨，通过合理有效地利用股东股入到公司的财产，使其创造出最佳经济效益，实现股东利益和社会利益的最大化。公司本着“敬业、和谐、诚信、务实”的企业精神，成为阿克苏、农一师、阿拉尔和新农开发新的经济增长点。

董事长：涂昭荣
总经理：王　勇
电话(传真)：0997-2150340
地　址：新疆阿克苏市南大街 1 号(新农大厦 17 楼)
网　址：www.xjxnzy.com

乌鲁木齐市公共交通总公司

公共交通总公司党委副书记、总经理　陆建春

第二公司 8 路公交车规范化展示

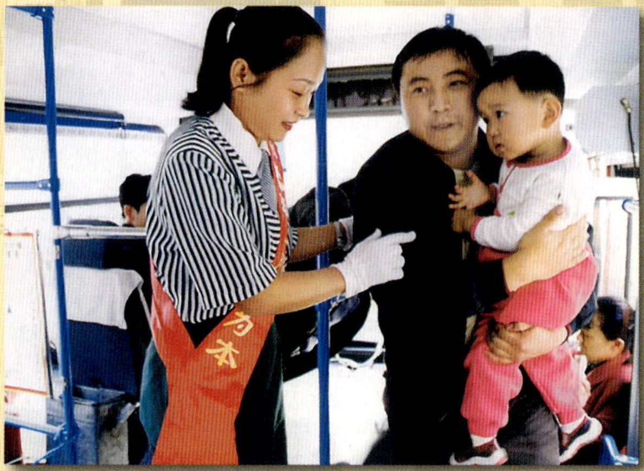

公交优质服务

第五公司车场

乌鲁木齐市公交始建于 1953 年，1965 年成立乌鲁木齐市公共汽车公司，1993 年改制为乌鲁木齐市公共交通总公司。50 多年来，公司全体员工团结奋进，艰苦创业，无私奉献，锐意进取，使企业不断发展壮大。目前，总公司从业人员 8496 人，营运线路 99 条，线路长度 1493.8 公里，线网长 526 公里，设置客站 2125 个，营运车辆 2572 辆，年总行驶公里 1.49 亿公里，年客运量 5.6 亿人次，总资产 4.52 亿元。总公司下属一、二、三、四、五、六公司、劳动服务公司、兴盛巴士公司（控股）8 个主营公司以及广告公司、物业公司、IC 卡公司、经济开发中心、房地产公司、燃料公司、技校、旅游公司、热力公司 9 个辅业公司。是首府乌鲁木齐市城市客运市场中服务功能齐全，专业技术力量雄厚的大型企业。

近年来，总公司对外坚持“服务为本，乘客至上”的宗旨，确定“服务树形象、形象创品牌、品牌出效益”的经营理念。通过创建文明诚信企业，积极向社会公开服务承诺，提出了服务投诉为“零”，安全责任事故为“零”的奋斗目标。对内坚持深化企业改革，解放思想，实事求是，积极扩大营运生产规模及经营领域，调整企业内部组织结构、经营结构和产权结构，在体制、机制、管理和经营理念上进行大胆尝试。紧紧围绕“抓管理、降成本、促服务、增效益”的总体思路，使企业取得了较好的经济效益和社会效益。

企业先后获得自治区、乌鲁木齐市企业全面整顿先进企业、自治区一级企业、自治区“天山杯”、市“红山美”杯竞赛活动先进集体、优胜单位，新疆城市交通系统优质服务竞赛优胜企业、全国职工教育先进单位、全国城市公共交通系统优质服务竞赛优胜企业、全国公交行业规范化服务优秀单位称号。

提升精强主业　开拓发展新业
全力打造新疆天宏集团经济发展航母
——新疆天宏纸业股份有限公司

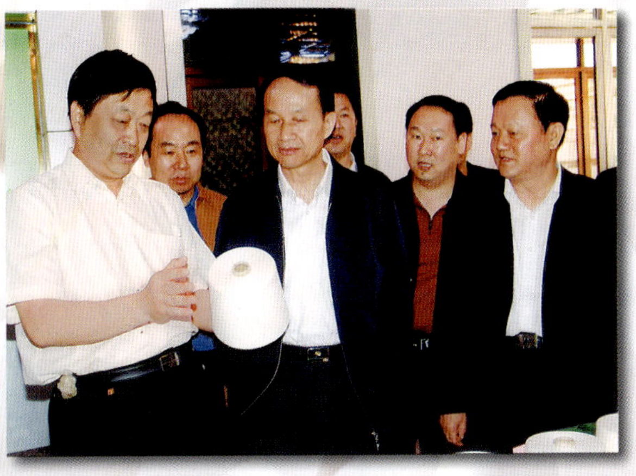

兵团司令员华士飞视察天宏新八棉

新疆天宏董事长王世超与哈萨克斯坦代表签定投资合作协约

新疆天宏纸业是目前区内拥有一定规模和经济实力的上市公司，主要生产经营：双胶纸、书写纸、胶印书刊纸、精品书写纸、静电复印纸、钢纸原纸及生活用纸等三十多个纸产品和各类高中低档棉纱等。

2005年天宏纸业继续坚持用科学的发展观总揽全局，以市场为导向，以科技为核心，以资源为纽带，以项目为带动，注重创新企业结构框架，不断优化规模效益、科技效益和品牌效益，立足企业实际，突出项目重点，精强提升主业，拓宽发展新业，加速企业技术进步和产品升级，增加经济总量，努力提高企业的核心竞争力。2005年将完成天宏新八棉10万锭棉纺生产项目。6000吨生活用纸扩建项目、年产10000吨废纸脱墨浆生产线项目、湖南常德天宏分公司年产4万吨文化用纸技改项目、哈萨克斯坦阿拉木图茂林派生纸厂6000吨卫生纸生产项目。在扩大天宏产品在国内销售市场的同时，努力开拓在中亚等国外的销售市场，力争在经济结构和战略调整、扩大生产规模上实现新突破；在创新营销策略、强化内部管理、提高企业经济运行质量上实现新突破；在加快企业自身发展、提高经济总量上实现新突破。“十一五”期间，还将充分利用新疆丰富的棉短绒资源，开发兴建3.4万吨棉浆粕、60万锭轻纺、3万吨再生新闻纸、2-5万吨绿色环保包装业项目，50万亩芨芨草生态建设等项目，力争使生产总值达到35亿元，从而实现真正意义的做大做强新疆天宏集团。

以务实、创新、诚信、卓越的企业精神，全力打造新疆天宏集团跨越式发展的经济航母。

办公地址：新疆石河子市西三路
公司法定代表人、董事长：王世超
公司总经理：赵云忠
电子信箱：fzq63@163.com
网　　址：http//www.thpaper.com
联系电话：0993-7526011
传　　真：0993-7526088
邮政编码：832009

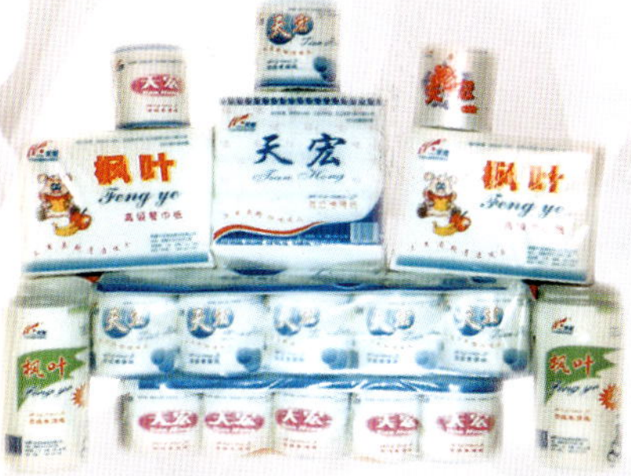

天宏纸业生活用纸

天宏新八棉生产车间

新疆送变电工程公司

国家电网公司领导来公司检查指导工作

新疆送变电工程公司是新疆电力公司的全资子公司，创建于1959年4月，现为国家送变电工程施工壹级企业。经过四十年的不断拓展，现已发展成为承建各种电压等级的送变电工程施工、火电建设；高压电网运行、检修；输变电工程调试、设计；铁塔、铁件加工及电杆制造；货物运输以及对国外承揽输变电工程等经营项目的综合性施工企业。公司现有职工644人，各类专业技术人员243人。

公司具有年施工500千伏输电线路300公里或220千伏输电线路600公里，以及同时安装500千伏和220千伏变电站的能力。具有国家乙级电气设备安装调试资质，年安装调试220千伏变电站4座或安装调试110千伏变电站8座的能力；具有110千伏及以下送变电工程设计资质；具有年生产10000根电杆的能力，具有年生产铁塔、铁件10000吨、热镀锌12000吨的能力。

公司是一支技术精湛、专业配套、能征善战的施工队伍。四十多年来，立足新疆、面向全国、艰苦创业、励精图治、累计完成送变电项目250余项，建成投资500千伏及以下高电压等级输电线路5800多公里；安装调试变电站工程250多万千伏安；建筑工程35000多平方米，工程优良品率均在97%以上。其中部分工程曾获“部优工程”和国家电力公司“达标投产输变电工程”称号。新疆送变电工程公司构筑了新疆220千伏高压输电线路主电网骨架，为国家的电力工业建设做出了应有的贡献，并于1997年9月取得了ISO9002:1994标准质量体系认证。2002年10月通过了ISO14001:1996标准环境管理体系认证和OHSAS18001:1999标准职业健康安全管理体系认证。2000年被国家电力公司和全国水电工会联合授予“安全施工生产1000天”、“楼哈输电工程安全施工生产”荣誉称号。先后荣获西北电力集团公司“思想政治工作优秀企业”；乌鲁木齐市“文明样板小区”；新疆维吾尔自治区授予的“文明单位”荣誉称号，1999年、2000年荣获新疆电力公司“先进企业”荣誉称号，2000年8月30日被国家电力公司授予“文明单位”荣誉称号。2001年被新疆电力公司评为“经营管理先进企业”和“财务管理先进企业”。2003年荣获新疆维吾尔自治区质量管理奖；乌鲁木齐市AAA级信用企业称号；中电联电力行业标准化企业；荣获新疆电力公司“安全生产先进企业”、“安全文明生产达标企业”等荣誉称号。2004年获全国“守合同　重信用”企业称号。

公司全力推进现代化管理，注重科技进步，建立了严密的质量保证体系和严谨的安全质量管理网络。全体员工将本着“奋斗、严谨、学习、创新”的企业精神，以“优质、安全、环保、高效、持续改进送变电工程产品质量、运行维护质量、职业安全卫生和环境的绩效”为宗旨，以质量信誉求生存，以经济效益求发展，为祖国的电力建设做出新的更大的贡献。

“我为党旗添光彩”演讲比赛

金纺股份
JINFANG STOCK

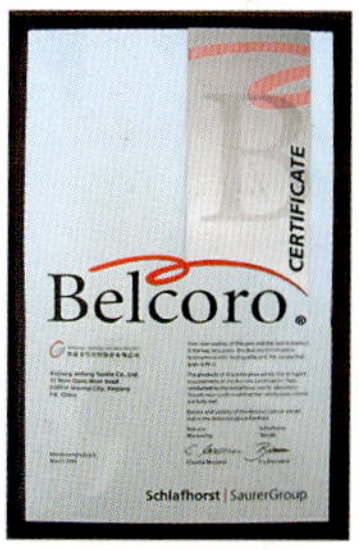

新疆金纺纺织股份有限公司

新疆金纺纺织股份有限公司成立于2002年7月1日，公司坐落于乌鲁木齐市秀美的旅游风景区水磨沟河畔，是由新疆八一钢铁集团有限责任公司、新疆维吾尔自治区供销社、新疆维吾尔自治区国有资产投资经营有限公司、新疆维吾尔自治区技术改造投资公司、新疆鼎新投资发展有限公司五家单位共同出资成立的拟上市股份公司。2003年底公司进行了增资扩股，重组整合原新疆纺织工业(集团)公司生产单位，现有职工3775人，资产总额6.105亿元，股本金3.525亿元。

公司下属有棉花加工厂、七个纺纱、织布厂及一个动力厂，具有年产皮棉7000吨的棉花加工生产线，拥有环锭纺173000锭，气流纺12192头，各类织机765台，具备年产棉纱45000吨、棉布3000万米的生产能力。公司集棉花收购、加工、纺织为一体，实现了规模化效益，是目前全疆最大的纺织企业。为适应市场变化的需求，公司积极引进国际上最先进的技术装备，已投入运行的31台德国赐来福公司产AUTOCORO288、312气流纺机，是当前国际上最先进的气流纺纱机型，以其工艺流程短、自动化程度高及利用先进的信息化技术对生产过程进行全方位全过程监控的优势，产品质量达到国际领先水平，使公司具备足够的实力参与国内、国际市场竞争。

凭借科学的管理、雄厚的技术、先进的装备，公司可生产环锭纺7^S—120^S优质纯棉精梳、普梳纱线及化纤纯纺、混纺纱线；气流纺6^S—60^S优质针织、机织、牛仔纱线，以及平纹、纱卡、府绸、防羽布、起绒布等各种高品质布匹，其中有15个品种获自治区优质产品称号，32^S纱获部优产品称号，精梳系列产品成为自治区首批名牌产品，成功试纺并批量生产的精梳120^S填补了自治区环锭高支纱的空白，试纺的彩棉系列产品荣获自治区科委颁发的新产品证书，气流纺“金巧”牌16^S—32^S等主导产品已获德国赐来福公司Belcoro品牌授权，40^S、50^S气流纺纱的生产，填补了国内高支气流纺纱产品的空白，气流纺柔软针织纱和高支机织纱具有国内外高品质先进水平。公司于2003年通过了ISO9001:2000质量管理体系论证。

物化天宝，人杰地灵。我公司坚持以“艰苦奋斗、求实奋进、开拓创新、追求卓越”的企业精神为导向，秉承“顾客至上、质量第一、用心至善、服务至诚”的质量宗旨，竭诚为广大用户服务。我们坚信，诚恳与勤奋的果实必然是美好的，我们将怀着美好的心愿和业内同仁与我们的祖国共同发展进步。

特吕茨勒高效并条机

AUTOCORO-312 气流纺纱机

FA506 细纱机

新疆煤田地质局

党组书记、队长敬益武在会议上作工作报告

新疆煤田地质局何深伟局长(左)热情寄语我队全面完成各项任务

新疆煤田地质局党组书记张旗(右三)参加勘查队五届二次职工代表大会

新疆煤田地质局综合地质勘查队隶属新疆煤田地质局,为国有事业单位。专门从事水文、地质勘查工作,是一个集基础地质、矿产地质、水文地质、工程地质、环境地质、地球物理、地球化学、测绘、遥感地质、煤层气调查、煤矿技术服务、水源勘查等勘查、研究及技术服务、成果汇交和科研为一体的研究、应用综合机构,同时开展遥感成图、矿山监测、地理信息研究、开发应用业务和铁路、公路、桥梁及城市测绘业务,城市地下管线勘测业务,供水井凿井工程施工业务,环境评价与地质灾害防治工程业务,并提供机械加工、汽修服务及卷闸门、橡胶件制品等产品。

现在拥有各类高级工程师20余人,工程师50余人,工程技术人员200余人,下辖生产科、普查分队、测量分队、物探分队、水文工程处、数字化室、制图室、劳动服务公司、新星橡胶制品厂等9个工作部门及6个职能科室。拥有国家颁发的地质勘查资质,地球物理勘查甲级资质,遥感地质乙级资质,测绘乙级资质和自治区颁发的环境评价与灾害地质防治工程乙级资质及水井凿井甲级资质。形成了门类齐全,勘探手段完善,技术力量雄厚的综合地质勘查单位。

单位目标拥有①钻探:工作以拥有1500型和KP2000型为代表的仪器设备和工作手段;②地面物探:工作以拥有光泵磁力仪、瞬变电磁仪、高密度电法仪、浅层三维地震仪、管线仪为代表的仪器设备和工作手段。地球物理拥有以数字测井仪为代表的仪器设备和工作手段;③遥感地质、测绘工作拥有以GPS全球定位仪、全站仪、经纬仪、平板仪、水准仪(电子)和手提电脑为代表的仪器设备和工作手段及优良的交通、通讯、办公设备和先进的资料管理、数字化处理及制图技术,确保了工程项目优质、高效、安全、快捷地竣工和成果提交。

在近25年来的工作实践中,综合地质勘查队始终奉行"规范管理、技术先进、质量一流"的质量方针,依靠先进技术,提供一流的地质成果,累计完成国家、地方出资的战略性、基础性、公益性、煤矿建设应用性地质勘查项目和以煤矿企业为主的各项生产地质报告等技术服务项目40余项,探明煤炭储量1.6万亿吨,所有成果,报告均达良级以上,项目合格率达100%。同时①物探有效完成了托克逊柯尔碱水源勘查(物探找水)项目,有效拓展并建立了城市管线勘查,送变电基础勘查与评价等社会项目;②测量有效完成引额河济克河测绘工作,哈密市、乌苏市

测量分队职工在"引额济克,北水南调"工程中策马出发

干部职工踊跃参加雅玛里克山绿化劳动,连年出色完成任务

综合地质勘查队

自治区有关领导亲临我队检查指导工作

新疆煤炭工业管理局、煤炭生产安全监察局党组书记杜鲁坤·托首提(右二)亲切慰问老职工

等城市测绘，乌市乌拉泊、鸿雁池水库大坝观测、乌市水上乐园整体规划地形测绘等社会项目；③环境评价及地质灾害防治工程有效完成了和田县布雅煤矿环境评价及地质灾害防治工程、乌市民族公墓绿化水井环境评价等社会项目；④钻探能顺利完成深度达1500米、口径达3米的专门钻探和工程地质勘查施工任务；⑤物探找水成功地在乌市雅山找到了绿化水源及大口径水井凿井工程等新的经济增长点。工作足迹遍布天山南北，为新疆经济建设做出巨大贡献，在承接的国家、自治区及社会市场项目中，所完成的遥感地质、测绘、物探、计算机制图等专业领域的工作和研究成果多次获上级好评和客户赞誉，树立了良好的单位形象。

融汇进我国西部大开发战略的强劲实施中，综合地质勘查队坚定实施“依法治队闯市场、科教兴队争一流”的发展战略，以更加完善的工作技能和优质的工作成果，在开发边疆建设建设边疆的宏伟大业中再展英姿、续写辉煌。

物探分队职工在托克逊柯尔碱实施电法找水作业

单位地址：乌鲁木齐西山路89号
邮　　编：830009
电　　话：0991-8772826　8771422
传　　真：0991-8771422

水文钻机为伊宁巴彦岱乡打出甘甜的地下水

304钻机在吐哈煤田进行钻探作业

新疆哈密煤业（集团）有限责任公司

哈密煤业(集团)有限责任公司

车辆穿梭的煤炭外运场景

流光异彩的露天矿生产夜景

气势恢弘的露天矿掘场

工艺先进的矿井综采工作面

新疆哈密煤业(集团)有限责任公司,是自治区直属的七个大型企业之一,位列自治区2003年30强工业企业,是新疆主要的出疆煤生产基地。集团公司的前身是始建于1958年的哈密矿务局,2001年1月18日经自治区人民政府批准改制为新疆哈密煤业(集团)有限责任公司。集团公司总部设在哈密三道岭。

依托三道岭矿区,哈密煤业(集团)公司以建立现代企业制度为目标,积极实施“以煤为主,煤与非煤共同发展”战略,构建跨地区、跨行业、跨所有制的多元化经营格局,目前拥有26家子(分)公司及一些辅助单位,主要分布在以三道岭为主的东部矿区和以昌吉市为主、辐射硫磺沟镇以及吉木萨尔县的西部矿区,员工总数9800人,资产总额18亿元,是一个以煤炭产业为主,集棉纺、电力、建材、石材、仓储、化工、金属冶炼、汽车运输、物业管理、农牧养殖等为一体的大型综合企业集团。

2004年,哈密煤业(集团)公司煤炭主业实现了大发展,通过加大对生产的投入和技术改造,总体年生产能力已经稳定在600万吨以上,比“十五”计划的发展目标提高了350万吨,为满足日益增长的市场需求奠定了基础。2004年生产煤炭420.8万吨,完成销售总量419万吨(其中铁路外运303万吨),分别比上年增长了9.94%和9.40%,实现利润1000万元以上,销售收入、工业增加值、国有资产保值增值率、职工收入等主要经济指标均比往年提高,企业经济实力和市场竞争力明显增强,实现了跨越式发展目标。

中国华融资产管理公司乌鲁木齐办事处

袁肇绩总经理在向公司杨凯生总裁汇报工作

中国华融资产管理公司（以下简称“华融公司”）于1999年10月19日在北京成立，是具有独立法人资格的国有独资非银行金融企业。公司资本金：100亿人民币。公司在全国分设了30个办事处，乌鲁木齐办事处于2000年4月26日正式挂牌成立，负责收购、管理和处置中国工商银行新疆分行的不良资产。

根据《金融资产公司条例》和有关规定，华融公司的业务范围包括：收购并经营中国工商银行等金融机构剥离的不良资产；追偿本外币债务；对所收购本外币不良贷款形成的资产进行租赁或者以其他形式转让、重组；本外币债权转股权，并对企业阶段性持股；资产管理范围内公司的上市推荐及债券、股票承销；发行金融债券，向金融机构借款；财务及法律咨询，资产及项目评估；通过市场化方式收购管理和处置境内金融机构的不良资产；运用现金资本金对所管理的政策性和商业化收购不良贷款的抵贷实物资产追加投资；接受财政部、中国人民银行、国有银行及其他金融机构、工商企业的委托，管理和处置不良资产；接受委托，从事经金融监管部门批准的金融机构关闭清算业务；中国人民银行、中国银行业监督管理委员会批准的其他业务。乌鲁木齐办事处在公司的授权下开展以上业务。

五年来，华融公司通过不断创新和专业化、市场化的成功运作，积极盘活不良资产，较好保证了资产回收的最大化，有力地推动了国有商业银行的改革发展，促进了国有企业减负脱困、转换经营机制和建立现代企业制度，并承担了国家赋予的稳定社会经济秩序的重任，成为我国金融战线的一支骁勇善战的轻骑兵。

袁肇绩总经理在签署债转股协议

办事处资产处置审查委员会在审议处置项目

办事处党委召开民主生活会

发展中的新疆科学技术出版社

新疆科学技术出版社始建于1990年10月，当时社名为新疆科技卫生出版社(K)。为适应建立和完善社会主义市场经济体制以及科技出版事业的发展，经新闻出版社总署批准，于2002年12月更名为新疆科学技术出版社。

新疆科学技术出版社是由新疆维吾尔自治区新闻出版局主管、主办的出版事业单位，是新疆惟一一家专门出版科学知识与技术的出版社。使用维吾尔、汉、哈萨克、蒙古、柯尔克孜等五种文字出版各类科技专著及科技工具书；科学基础知识和应用技术类图书；各级各类科技科普读物；交通、劳动、体育、科普等方面的政策、法规、理论著作；学生学习和职工培训教材教辅及科普读物等。全社现有10个民族组成的职工110人，其中维吾尔、哈萨克、蒙古、柯尔克孜等少数民族职工79人，占职工总数的72%；专业技术人员101人，占职工总数的93%，其中编审3人、副编审37人、编辑37人、助理编辑15人。

新闻出版总署版权司司长王自强(前排右一)、对外合作司副司长谢爱伟(前排左一)在自治区新闻出版局局长米吉提·卡德尔(左二)陪同下来新疆科学技术出版社督察。前排右二为新疆科学技术出版社党委书记、社长王跃平。

新疆科学技术出版社党委书记、社长王跃平同志(左二)在北京举办的四种文版《放飞神舟》首发式上发言。前排左起第一位是总编辑阿不都尼衣木同志

新疆科学技术出版社实行社党委领导下的社长负责制。党委书记、社长王跃平，总编辑阿不都尼衣木。

新疆科学技术出版社经过10多年的发展，已拥有一支专业水平较高的编辑出版队伍，出版规模不断壮大，经营水平不断提高，出版能力不断增强，策划出版了一批既体现新疆民族地域特色，又体现时代精神，为自治区科技发展、经济建设和文化积累服务的精品图书，形成了自己的风格和特色，已出版各文种图书3000多种。全社现年平均出版图书一般在700种左右(其中再版258种左右)；年平均销售码洋2615.65万元左右；年平均销售收入1416万元左右。

出版社在抓好重点书、精品书出版的同时，精心组织出版的中小学教辅用书，得到广大中小学校和学生的认同和喜爱，产生了品牌效应。

10多年来，新疆科学技术出版社先后有100多种图书分别荣获省部级以上图书奖，其中哈萨克文《医药志》获第三届国家图书奖；汉文《中国杀虫植物志》等2种图书获中国书奖，维吾尔文《简明农机辞典》等8种少数民族文字图书获中国民族图书奖，《中国新疆地区油气地质特征及资源评价》等16种各文种图书获新疆维吾尔自治区图书奖。1995年、1997年、1999年连续三届被新闻出版总署评为全国良好出版社。2004年被新闻出版总署授予全国服务“三农”图书出版发行工作先进单位、被自治区党委宣传部授予自治区宣传思想工作先进集体。

有一人获得中国韬奋出版奖，一个被评为全国百佳出版工作者，一人获第五届全国优秀中青年(图书)编辑奖。

新疆科技政策研究所

科技政策研究所干部职工一起讨论工作

新疆科技政策研究所代表团访问俄罗斯科学院远东研究所，双方进行学术研讨

新疆科技政策研究所是新疆唯一专门从事科学技术政策研究的机构，重点开展决策咨询服务和软科学研究工作。设有政策研究室、战略研究室、综合室和科技咨询中心。实行开放的研究机制，常年聘有兼职研究员、特约研究员，与决策和管理部门、高等学校、科研单位有着广泛的联系。主要研究领域涉及科技政策法规与科技管理、科技体制改革与对外经济技术合作、科技经济一体化与产业技术创新、科技进步评价与指标体系、科技进步与区域发展、发展与环境等，并提供科技、经济的信息咨询服务。多次承担国家、新疆以及国外资助的软科学研究项目，取得一系列重要成果。

国家软科学项目管理部门领导来我所对“中、俄、哈、蒙阿尔泰区域联合开发的研究”课题进行项目中期检查

科技政策研究所主持完成的部分研究成果

学校领导班子成员：主任院凌雷（右三），党委书记、副主任、副院长张守梅（右二）、党委副书记、纪委书记、副主任、副院长白克立·乌麻尔（右四）、副主任、副院长孟繁有（右一）、党委委员、组织人事部部长于万海（右五）

少数民族干部正在接受业务培训

教职工正在用自编、自导、自演的节目热烈庆祝教师节

新党员在烈士墓前举行宣誓仪式

伊犁师范学院

自治区党委副书记、自治区主席司马义·铁力瓦尔地在伊犁州党委书记张国梁等人的陪同下来学院视察工作

伊犁师范学院的前身是1948年成立的新疆省立伊犁专科学校。1980年5月经国务院批准成立伊犁师范学院，隶属自治区管理。2003年11月经自治区人民政府批准，原伊犁教育学院并入伊犁师范学院，新的伊犁师范学院实行区州共建，以自治区为主。

在自治区党委的领导下，学院取得了快速的发展。学院现有在编教职工1268人，其中专职教师612人，专职教师中教授、副教授及高级职称的人员197人。有全日制普通本、专科学生8145人，另有各类成人本、专科学生近7000人。校本部占地面积近600亩，另有2000亩土地的校办农场。奎屯校区占地面积1101亩，另有2500亩土地作为后备教学发展用地。

学院以普通本科教育为主，采用汉、哈、维三种语言教学，经过多年建设，我院本部现有中语系、外语系、数学系、法经系、计算机科学系、教育科学系、生物化学与环境科学系、人文学院、物理与电子信息学院、体育学院、艺术学院11个院系和成人教育学院及哈萨克文化研究所、教育科学研究所两个研究机构。奎屯校区设有文理系、工程系、应用技术系、生命与资源环境系、基础部、艺术中专部六个教学系部。共有22个本科专业和11个专科专业，覆盖了高等师范教育的绝大部分专业和部分非师范教育专业。

学院的校园绿化面积达60%以上，建筑面积27.82万平方米，校园网络已经投入使用，各类先进教学设备可满足各种教学需要。图书馆藏书近60万册。

校园一角

2004年新年音乐会

伊犁师范学院

和田师范专科学校

各族学生看书学习

自治区党委副书记努尔·白克力视察学校

校领导构建学校宏伟蓝图

优美的学习环境

和田师范专科学校是一所由新疆维吾尔自治区主管的全日制师范类专科学校，学校是以维吾尔族学生为主体共有17个民族（少数民族师生员工在全校占99%以上）组成的民族高校。

学校是自治区全额预算管理事业单位。现有教职员工500余人。学校教学设施比较完备，拥有理化、计算机等专业基础教学实验室28个，教学用计算机近400台，多媒体教室15个（共800座），语音教室41个（共200座）。编辑出版有国内外公开发行的维、汉两种文字的国家二级学术刊物《和田师范专科学校学报》。

2004年，学校13个教学单位开设有22个专科和专业方向，自2003年开始，与新疆师范大学在数学教育、生化教育和语言教育等三个专业联合招收普通本科班。2002年起，学校先后与新师大、新大联合举办了中国少数民族双语教育、思想政治教育、维吾尔语言文学教育三个专业的研究生班。

成人教育学院承办和田地区义务教育师资的培训及南疆地区少数民族职工的岗位培训和继续教育。并与新大、新师大联办覆盖我校各专业的专升本学历教育。

学校是国家汉语水平考试、国家普通高等教育成人考试、全国高校非计算机专业计算机等级水平考试、自治区现代维吾尔语正字正音水平考试等国家、自治区级考试的考点。

学校发展定位：立足南疆，面向社会，服务基层，以师范教育为主，适度扩大非师范教育，以教学为中心，科研为基础，办好普通全日制专科教育，适度推进成人教育和高等职业技术教育，创造条件发展本科教育。发展总目标：突出民族性、地域性、师范性，创造条件，进一步把和田师范专科学校建设成和田地区培养培训各类专门人才特别是中小学教师的重要基地、传播先进文化提升文化品位的有效辐身射点、意识形态领域反分裂斗争的坚强阵地。近3年具体发展思路是：以邓小平理论和“三个代表”重要思想为指导，以发展为主线，以改革为动力，紧紧围绕一个核心（以学科建设为核心），抓好三支队伍（教师队伍、管理队伍、实验技术队伍），推进五项建设（教学设施建设、公共服务体系建设、后勤保障体系建设、校园文化建设、校园环境建设），实现南疆地区的六个“一流”（一流的设施，一流的管理，一流的校园环境，一流的教师，一流的学生，一流的社会声誉）。

学校多媒体教学

校文艺队在教学主楼前排练

新疆伊斯兰教经学院

学院综合楼

自治区党委常委肖开提·依明视察我院

新疆伊斯兰教经学院是经国务院和自治区党委、人民政府批准建立的我区惟一一所宗教高等院校，同时也是全国惟一一所用本地少数民族语言（维吾尔）授课的伊斯兰教经学院。学院1983年动工筹建，1987年6月竣工开学，学校占地面积56亩，建筑面积17800平方米，总投资2100万元人民币。学院是自治区民委（宗教局）下辖的二级局事业单位，学院设有办公室、教务处、学生管理处、总务处等四个处室，教职工编制50名，办学规模160人。其中有专职教师22人。另有退休职工14名。自1995年起在校学生达到办学规模要求（即达到160人的规模）。

我院坚持党的领导，坚持社会主义方向，坚持宗教信仰自由政策，坚持独立办教的原则，通过培养教育，造就一支热爱祖国，拥护党和政府的领导，坚持走社会主义道路，积极引导宗教与社会主义相适应，维护祖国统一和民族团结，具有较高文化水平和宗教学识，并能联系广大信教群众的年轻一代宗教教职人员队伍。

学院教职工认真学习《宗教事务条例》

根据国家宗教局和自治区党委统战部、自治区民委（宗教局）的安排意见和原则，学院严格按照“三七开”的比例开设文化课和宗教课。文化课占30%，开设的课程有政治课、基础汉语、维吾尔语言文学、地理、历史和体育。宗教课占70%，开设的课程有阿拉伯语、阿拉伯语语法学、阿拉伯语修辞学、阿拉伯文学、《古兰经诵法学》、《古兰经》诵读规则学、宗教道德学、教义学、圣训学原理、教法学、教法学原理、圣训注解、《古兰经》注和伊斯兰文化等15门课程。

对于五年制本科生，学习期满成绩合格者，学院颁发大学本科毕业证书。

学生在认真上课学习

世界伊盟秘书长来学院参观

中共乌鲁木齐市水磨沟区委党校

党校领导研究工作

中共乌鲁木齐市水磨沟区委党校是中共水磨沟区委、区人民政府直属事业机构。实行校长负责制，级别为正科级。校址位于乌市温泉西路68-1号。区委党校现实有工作人员5人，其中中共党员4人，共青团员1人；高级讲师1人，中级讲师2人，初级讲师1人；大学学左4人，大专学历1人。

中共水磨沟区委党校以教学为中心，按照区委的工作部署和组织部门对干部培训工作的要求，对区属各部门、驻区各单位的各级党员干部开展多种类型的培训，充分发挥了党校“三个阵地、一个熔炉”的作用。

水磨沟区委、区政府将水区委党校和培训中心作为基地，先后由乌鲁木齐人事局批准水区党校成立“乌市水区公务员培训基地”；由乌鲁木齐市劳动和社会保障局批准认定乌市现代科技培训中心为再就业培训定点机构；由水磨沟区政府批准成立“水区科技活动中心”。近年来，水区党校开展了多层次、宽领域的培训，对区属党员干部开展培训、轮训；开展国家公务员各类培训、轮训工作；开展科学技术知识培训工作；协助乌市市委党校开展学历教育；开展南疆赴水磨沟区挂职干部的理论培训工作；开展下岗失业人员再就业培训工作；开展计算机社会化培训工作等等。

2002年水区科级干部学习十六大精神培训班在党校举行，左起党校常务副校长沈智敏；区委副主任冯新荣；区委书记高尚诚；区委党委宣传部部长刘毅勇

举办水磨沟区区直“三个代表”重要思想培训班

喀什师范学校

党委书记、副校长　何登荣

党委副书记、校长　海仁沙·瓦依提

喀什师范学校是一所集大专、中专、高中、师资培训为一体的综合类学校。是喀什地区重要的素质教育基地。学校始建于1935年，位于喀什市色满路494号，占地面积170亩，总建筑面积84526平方米。校园结构布局合理，各种教学设施齐全，办学历史悠久，师资力量雄厚，学习环境优美，校园硬化率达54%，绿化率达31%，1993年4月获自治区级文明单位称号，建校以来共培养各类毕业生3.9万余人，为我区的基础教育事业做出了卓越的贡献。学校主要面向喀什地区及农三师培养农村一线小学教师，兼开展民语言中小学校在职教师各类培训工作，从2003年起开始招收双语实验高中和普通高中。2004年在校生1330名，其中大专生632名，在职培训213名，高中生205名。学校现有维、汉、回、柯尔克孜、乌孜别克等民族的在职教职工227名，其中专任教师159名，行政后勤人员68名。2004年，学校教师在疆内外发表论文57篇，在喀什地区成功举办个人画展2次。组织41名美术专业学生参加亚洲书画协会与西安新世纪文艺研究会联合举办的“龙杯”青少年书画比赛，获金奖24名，银奖14名，铜奖3名。

喀什师范学校真诚邀请社会各界朋友光临指导，力争办社会满意、家长放心、南疆一流的学校。

一流的电教设备

优美的教学环境

乌鲁木齐职业大学

校党委书记　艾力垦·阿布都热依木

校长　陆计明

乌鲁木齐职业大学创建于1985年。办学十九年来，学校坚持以发展为第一要务，紧紧围绕“突出高等职业教育特色，提高教学质量”这个中心，依托办学体制优势，艰苦奋斗，开拓创新，取得了令人瞩目的成绩，为地方经济发展培养2万余名高级应用型人才，被中国高职研究会喻为“西北高职教育明珠，独具特色育人摇篮”，连续十二年被评为新疆维吾尔自治区级文明单位。

目前，学校校舍建筑面积13.6万平方米，馆藏图书20余万册。拥有一支理论水平较高和实践经验丰富的教师队伍，副教授以上职称教师占教师总数的38%，“双师型”教师比例达40%。先后开设39个专业和专业方向，涵盖文学、法学、经济学、教育学、工商管理学、理工、计算机、外语、艺术等学科。学校以普通大专学历教育为主，兼配其他形式，下设人文学院、工商管理学院、外国语学院、信息工程学院、旅游学院、体育系、汉教部、继续教育学院、现代教育技术中心和附属乌鲁木齐外国语实验中学等教学部门，全校各类在校生总数近10000人。

学校拥有先进的教学设施，建有34个设备先进的专业功能实验、实训室，已经建成22个校外专业实训基地。在教学过程中，突出职业特色，强化实践性教学环节和学生动手能力培养，毕业生就业率一直居新疆高校前列，得到了社会各界高度评价。

今后，我们要立足当前，着眼长远。按照创建优秀高职院校和示范性高职院校的发展思路：在培养目标上，坚持以服务为宗旨，以就业为导向，为地方经济发展培养德才兼备的高技能应用型专门人才；在专业设置上，坚持以市场需求为导向，对准市场设专业，对准岗位设课程，对准实践抓教学，不断提高教学质量；在学校定位上，坚持科学的人才培养模式，把学校办成培养多层次、多规模、高技能应用型人才的综合性高职院校；在发展方向上，坚持创新观念、创新思路、创新精神，经过几年努力，把学校创建为国家级示范性高职院校。

通讯地址：
新疆乌鲁木齐市幸福路72号
邮　　编：830002
网　　址：
http://www.uvu.edu.cn/
电　　话：
0991-8823664（党政办）
0991-8825404（招办）
0991-8823460（成人招生）
传　　真：0991-8819092

校园一角

新疆大学旅游学院职业培训中心

新疆大学旅游学院职业培训中心（原自治区接待服务技校）2001 年 11 月并入新疆大学，创建于 1983 年 11 月。二十年来，为新疆旅游服务行业输送了万余名专业技术人才，同时开办了岗前培训、在职培训、下岗职工再就业培训班，并赢得了良好的社会声誉。依托旅游学院本着资源共享，协调发展的目标，年均招生 500 余人、年均培训人数 2500 余人。毕业生"双证书"比例 95.96%，就业率达 100%以上。具有自治区旅游局定点培训单位等多个资质，主体专业有宾馆服务与管理、中式烹饪、计算机应用、导游、旅游英语、调酒师、西餐烹调、西餐服务等专业。有教学实训室 8 个，其中客房实训室 3 个，餐饮实训室 2 个、烹饪实训室 2 个，计算机教室 2 个，建立教学实训基地 30 余家。培训目标明确，坚持就业靠技能、技能靠培训的理念，在加强文化基础课的同时，突出专业课的实践技能训练。全面推行素质教育，倡导理论联系实际，重视培养学生正确的世界观、人生观、价值观。在院领导班子的大力支持下，中心领导团结奋进、改革创新、办学指导思想明确，重视内部管理体制改革。在教学方面大胆改革，不断聘请教学管理专家考核指导，保证教学督导工作顺利开展。

职业培训中心团结奋进的领导集体

中心将职业指导和就业教育渗透到整个教育过程中，教育学生树立正确的职业理想和职业观念，全面提高学生职业素质和职业能力，为学生就业、创业和升学提供了必要的帮助与指导。使学生在适应社会、融入社会的同时，得到了自我发展。

电话：0991-8588137　　传真：0991-8588133

地址：乌鲁木齐市延安路 64 号　　邮编：830047

国际合作办学与交流，瑞士国际酒店旅游管理学院马克丹·泽拉院长与旅游学院领导等在自治区对外友好交流中心合影

旅游学院毕业生供需双方见面会，我中心毕业生就业率达 100%以上

为了配合教学科研工作需要，加强学生综合素质，学院组建了多功能计算机室，能同时容纳 50 名学生上机实践，图为计算机操作课

新疆大学旅游学院参加 2005 年中国国内旅游交易会掠影

新疆移动通信公司

白志刚总经理深入基层调研

根据国家关于电信体制改革的总体部署和要求，1999 年 8 月 16 日新疆移动通信公司正式成立。2004 年 6 月，在国务院统一部署下，根据中国移动集团公司“整体上市、分步实施”的思路，新疆移动通信公司在香港、纽约成功上市，正式更名为新疆移动通信有限责任公司（以下简称新疆移动）。

新疆移动主要经营移动话音、数据、IP 电话和多媒体业务，并具有计算机互联网国际联网单位经营权和国际出入口局业务经营权。除提供基本话音业务外，还提供传真、数据、IP 电话等多种增值业务，拥有“全球通”、“神州行”、“移动梦网”、“动感地带”、“天山通”等知名品牌。公司秉承“沟通从心开始”的企业服务理念、“追求客户满意服务”的企业经营宗旨，努力为客户提供一体化的优质服务，极大地满足了客户多样化的通信需求。

新疆移动作为疆内惟一专注移动通信发展的通信运营公司，在网络建设与业务发展方面始终保持领先地位，经过不断地发展与建设，建成了质量一流、覆盖完善、技术领先、通达全国、连接世界的精品网络。移动网络规模和客户数量在疆内遥遥领先。截止 2004 年 8 月，网络已全面覆盖全疆 88 个地、州、市县，主要交通干线已实现连续覆盖，对高速公路覆盖达 95%，对乡镇团场和主要国道覆盖达 90%。网络总容量达到 320 万门，客户总数达到 270 万户。与 177 个国家和地区近 242 家移动通信运营商开通了国际漫游业务；与 69 个国家、57 个运营商开通了 GPRS 国际漫游，国际短信通达 99 个国家。

面对西部大开发的实施及自治区信息化发展提供的广阔舞台，新疆移动将继续发扬”改革创新、只争朝夕、艰苦奋斗、团队合作”的企业精神，以”创世界一流通信企业”为长远目标，坚定不移地贯彻中国移动集团公司”服务与业务领先”的战略（简称“双领先”战略），精细化实施新疆移动的三年战略规划——“市场运营水平与内部管理能力提升”的战略（简称”双提升”战略），通过持续不断地管理创新，加快建立现代企业制度，实现公司从规模型发展向规模效益型发展转变，积极推进自治区国民经济和社会信息化发展进程，努力为新疆的繁荣昌盛和稳定做出自己应有的贡献。

草原飞虹(摄影)　黄永中